ENCYCLOPEDIA OF PAINTING

ENCYCLOPEDIA of Painting

Painters and Painting of the World from Prehistoric Times to the Present Day

BERNARD S. MYERS, Editor
The City College, New York

Contributing Associates:

MILTON W. BROWN
Brooklyn College

GEORGE R. COLLINS
Columbia University

BEATRICE FARWELL
Metropolitan Museum of Art

JANE GASTON MAHLER
Columbia University

MARGARETTA SALINGER
Metropolitan Museum of Art

HUTCHINSON, LONDON.

Hutchinson & Co. (Publishers) Ltd.
178-202 Great Portland Street, London, W.1

London Melbourne Sydney Auckland
Bombay Johannesburg New York Toronto

First published in England 1956
Prepared and produced by Chanticleer Press, New York

 Text and plates printed by Smeets Lithographers, Weert, The Netherlands.

PREFACE

PREPARING a one-volume encyclopedia on any subject accentuates the usual problem of how far to go and where to stop, how to maintain a balance between the essential facts and effectiveness of presentation. Within the number of words and illustrations prescribed by the aim of producing a portable and not too costly volume we have tried to give an all-over picture of the outstanding painters, movements, styles and techniques from the most ancient times to the present day. The editor and contributing associates to this volume have attempted also to establish a just proportion between the past and the present, the purely factual and the essentially critical, the Orient and the Occident, the specifically biographical entry and the general descriptive entry or definition.

Features of special interest to both the general public and the student of art include an extensive section on the Orient (China, Japan, India and Persia), a thoroughgoing but selective section on the art of the United States, and an equally inclusive coverage of the many European and other countries contributing to the art of our own times.

We may note finally that in contrast to other available encyclopedias in English, the present volume is richly illustrated. The approximately one thousand color plates and black-and-white pictures relate in every case to the biographical or descriptive entries which they illustrate, although they are not necessarily keyed to specific descriptions in the text. All illustrations are in or near the entry which they illustrate. In addition, the color plates have been numbered and are referred to by number in the text.

The various personalities, movements, techniques and definitions are listed in the usual alphabetical fashion, with the partial exception of the Oriental material, which is specially treated because of its relative unfamiliarity to the Western reader. Here the names of the best-known and outstanding Oriental painters may be found as listings in their alphabetical places within the body of the book; these listings refer the reader to the appropriate era or dynasty within the special sections on Chinese, Japanese, Indian or Persian painters. For lesser-known Oriental names the reader may turn directly to the national entry and scan the listings under each dynasty thereof for the appropriate entry. This arrangement helps the reader find a desired name and at the same time, by grouping the entries of each Oriental culture, provides a historical survey of the painting of each country.

In alphabetizing the names of Italian painters, we have followed the prevailing practice of books on Italian art of alphabetizing such names—with a few unavoidable exceptions—

according to the painter's first or given name: e.g., Antonello da Messina, Raphael, Michelangelo.

Where the editors felt that a cross-reference to another entry was necessary, the word *see* in parenthesis was used, but the reader will find that almost all names or terms that figure prominently in any entry are themselves given a separate entry elsewhere in the book. It should also be noted that for many entries, especially of the general kind, e.g., abstract painting, pertinent illustrations will be found accompanying the entries of individual painters elsewhere in the book.

There has not been—nor indeed could there have been—any attempt to achieve completeness in a one-volume encyclopedia of this kind. It is felt, however, that the most representative and noteworthy painters in each historical era and country have been included. By the same token, it was neither possible nor desirable to list the countless representatives of the manifold art movements of our own time beyond the leading and most typical figures. To do so would have been to overweight this period to the disadvantage of other periods.

With regard to responsibility for the various contributions, this is divided as follows:

Milton W. Brown: all United States painting; Italian painters born after 1476 exclusive of living artists; the major Flemish entries; and the general article on stained glass.

George R. Collins: all Spanish painting; ancient painting; medieval painting; French painters through Impressionism; the briefer Flemish entries; and general articles on enamel, illuminated manuscripts, mosaic, Byzantine, Early Christian, Egyptian, Gothic, Greek, Roman, and Romanesque painting.

Beatrice Farwell: Italian painters born before 1476.

Jane Gaston Mahler: all Oriental painting, including China, Japan, India and Persia.

Bernard S. Myers: all British entries; all Mexican and other Latin-American entries; modern European painters from the late nineteenth century to the present day; Australian and Canadian painters; Portuguese painters; and general articles, including oil painting, prehistoric painting, Jewish painting and Expressionism.

Margaretta Salinger: Dutch and German entries exclusive of the moderns.

The considerable task of editorial supervision for the entire project was accomplished by Milton Rugoff of Chanticleer Press; the gathering of the large number of photographs in black-and-white and in color was also done under his direction.

The editors also wish to thank Alan McCulloch of Melbourne, Australia, for supplying material on Australian painters; Marilyn Lutzker of New York for research assistance; Mrs. George R. Collins for assistance in manuscript revision; Mr. Wang Chi-ch'uan for help with the choice of Chinese painters; and Mrs. Bernard Myers for research aid and for intensive work in several areas of manuscript preparation.

ACKNOWLEDGMENTS

THE acknowledgments for an illustrated work of this kind would be almost limitless if one were to enumerate all the museums, galleries, government agencies and private collectors who have made photographs in color and black-and-white available. Although individual picture credits are listed at the back of the book, particular mention must, however, be made of the generosity and assistance of the National Gallery of Art, Washington, D.C., the unfailing helpfulness of the librarians of the Art and Architecture Division of the New York Public Library, and the special acts of cooperation or kindness of the following:

Addison Gallery of American Art, Phillips Academy, Andover; Albright Art Gallery, Buffalo; Baltimore Museum of Art; Bodleian Library, Oxford University; Brooklyn Museum; Detroit Institute of Arts; M. H. de Young Memorial Museum, San Francisco; Fogg Art Museum, Harvard University, Cambridge; Frick Art Reference Library, New York; Hispanic Society of America, New York; Institute of Contemporary Art, Boston; Isabella Stewart Gardner Museum, Boston; Kress Foundation, New York; Mauritshuis, The Hague; Metropolitan Museum of Art, New York; Minneapolis Institute of Arts; Morgan Library, New York; Museum of Fine Arts, Boston; Museum of Modern Art, New York; Museum of Top Kapu, Istanbul; National Gallery of Modern Art, Rome; National Gallery of Canada, Ottawa; National Gallery, London; Philadelphia Museum of Art; Phillips Gallery, Washington, D.C.; Prado, Madrid; Smith College Museum of Art, Northampton, Mass.; Stedelijk Museum, Amsterdam; Toledo Museum of Art, Ohio; Whitney Museum of American Art, New York; Worcester Art Museum.

Also the following: Art News, New York; Babcock Galleries, New York; The Bamboo Studio, New York; Grace Borgenicht Gallery, New York; Alice Boney, New York; Carstairs Gallery, New York; Downtown Gallery, New York; Dr. Han Li-wu, Advisor to the President, Republic of China, Formosa; Sidney Janis Gallery, New York; Knoedler and Co., New York; Kootz Gallery, New York; C. T. Loo, New York; New York Graphic Society, N.Y.; H. E. Smeets, Weert, Netherlands; Wildenstein and Co., New York.

Also the following: American Fund for Israel Institutions, New York; Australian News and Information Bureau, New York; Austrian Information Service, New York; Belgian Information Center, New York; The Roy Bernard Company, New York, and Inter Nationes, Bonn, Germany; British Information Services, New York; Information Office, Canadian Consulate General, New York; Casa de Portugal, Portuguese Official Information Bureau, New York; Danish Information Office, New York; Government of India Information Services, New York; The Kosciuszko Foundation, New York; Pro Helvetia, and the Consulate General of Switzerland, New York; Swedish American News Exchange, New York.

KEY TO ABBREVIATED NAMES OF MUSEUMS

Antwerp	Musée Royal des Beaux-Arts, Antwerp
Berlin	Kaiser-Friedrich Museum, Berlin
Boston	Museum of Fine Arts, Boston
Brera	Pinacoteca di Brera, Milan
Brussels	Musee Royal des Beaux-Arts, Brussels
Chicago	Art Institute of Chicago
Cook Collection	Cook Collection, Richmond, England
Corcoran	Corcoran Gallery, Washington
Dresden	Gemäldegalerie, Dresden
Frankfort	Stadelsches Kunstinstitut, Frankfort
Freer	Freer Gallery of Art, Smithsonian Institution, Washington
Frick Collection	Frick Collection, New York
Guggenheim	Guggenheim Museum, New York
Hermitage	Hermitage Museum, Leningrad
London	National Gallery, London
Louvre	Musée du Louvre, Paris
Mauritshuis	Mauritshuis, The Hague
Metropolitan	Metropolitan Museum of Art, New York
Modern Museum	The Museum of Modern Art, New York
Munich	Bavarian State Art Gallery (Alte Pinakothek), Munich
Naples Gallery	Pinacoteca del Museo Nazionale di Napoli
Nelson	Nelson Gallery of Art, Kansas City, Missouri
Paris, Modern Museum	Musée d'art moderne, Paris
Philadelphia	Philadelphia Museum of Art
Pitti	Palazzo Pitti, Florence
Prado	Museo del Prado, Madrid
Siena	Pinacoteca Nazionale, Siena
Stedelijk	Stedelijk Museum, Amsterdam
Tate	Tate Gallery, London
Uffizi	Museo degli Uffizi, Florence
Urbino Gallery	Galleria Nazionale delle Marche, Palazzo Ducale
Vatican	Pinacoteca Vaticana (Vatican Picture Gallery), Rome
Venice Academy	Academia di Belle Arti, Venice
Vienna	Kunsthistorisches Museum, Vienna
Wallace Collection	Wallace Collection, London
Washington	National Gallery of Art, Washington
Whitney	Whitney Museum of American Art, New York

ENCYCLOPEDIA OF PAINTING

A

Aba-Novak, Vilmos (1894-1941). Hungarian oil and tempera painter interested primarily in subjects drawn from the folk life of his country. His technique is basically naturalistic and figurative.

Abbasid School (see PERSIAN PAINTERS: ABBASID SCHOOL).

Abbate, Nicolò dell' (1512-1571). Italian painter of the Maniera (see) who worked at Fontainebleau with Primaticcio. Born in Modena, he studied with his father and the sculptor Begarelli. In 1547 he went to Bologna, where he worked in the Palazzo Poggi (Bologna University) and the Palazzo Leoni. He arrived in France in 1552 and began his close collaboration with Primaticcio. It is difficult to distinguish the work of these two painters in the decorations of the palace of Fontainebleau, but Nicolò is usually credited with the galleries of Ulysses and Henry II as well as the room of Mme D'Estampes. He also designed tapestries and enamels. The overrefined and precious style of Fontainebleau influenced the decorative arts of all of Europe in the sixteenth century.

Abbey, Edwin Austin (1852-1911). American historical painter in the traditional academic manner who worked in London for many years. He first became known for black-and-white illustrations in *Harper's Magazine*. Admitted to the Royal Academy in 1898, Abbey recorded the coronation of Edward VII for the Buckingham Palace collection. He also did decorations in the Boston Public Library and the Pennsylvania State Capitol.

Abd Al-Samad (see INDIAN PAINTERS: AKBAR PERIOD).

abstract art. A term used to describe non-representational or non-naturalistic forms of expression. Although generally applied to most of the modern movements, e.g., Fauvism, Cubism, Expressionism (see separate entries), it may also be applied to such older forms as Egyptian painting, Romanesque painting, Byzantine painting and mosaics and other styles to the degree that these also "abstract" or reduce the original object to a series of non-photographic shapes, lines or colors. It is a relative rather than an absolute description, so that an object may be more or less abstract, varying from the slightly less than naturalistic to the unrecognizable.

Abu'l Hasan (see INDIAN PAINTERS: JAHANGIR PERIOD).

academic painting. A term used to denote conservative, traditional painting and often associated with the official, national academies. It implies the utilization of the styles and techniques of the past and may be applied to any outmoded style. Although a style may have been considered forward-looking at a certain point, e.g., Impressionism during the 1870's, the use of the same style a generation or so later may be considered "academic." Example: many present-day Impressionist painters.

Accademia di Belle Arti, Venice. The Academy of Fine Arts is one of the most important general repositories of Venetian painting of the Renaissance. It contains, among many other works of art, Titian's Assumption, Giorgione's Gypsy and the Soldier, Tintoretto's St. Mark Rescuing a Slave, Titian's Presentation in the Temple and the same artist's last and unfinished picture, the Pietà of 1576.

Achilles Master (mid-5th century B.C.). Greek vase painter. One of the outstanding exponents of the red-figured fine style, this master takes his name from an amphora in the Vatican representing Achilles and Briseis. More than 150 works have been attributed to him and he is considered a ranking decorator of white-ground vases. An example of the latter is the Euphorbus with Oedipus in the Louvre.

Adams, Wayman (1883-). Contemporary American painter. Born in Muncie, Ind., he studied at the John Herron Art Institute in Indianapolis and later with Chase and Henri. He painted street scenes in Spain and then in San Francisco and New Orleans, but is best known for the portrait painting to which he later turned. His portraits are bravura impressions in the tradition of Sargent and Chase.

Adler, Jankel (1891-1947). Polish-born Expressionist associated with the modern German school in which he was active in Düsseldorf until 1933 and the advent of the Nazis. He died in England. His art may be described as powerfully and individualistically primitive in feeling and form. It is clearly influenced by the arts of Africa and Oceania.

Aegean painting. Liveliest of ancient traditions of painting was that of the Aegean cultures: Crete, Mycenaean Greece and the islands of the Cyclades. It was an art of fanciful stylization, but of a strong feeling of naturalism deriving from its aesthetic of flowing lines and brilliant colors. Aegean painting stands in sharp contrast to the stable forms of Egyptian and Near Eastern painting. All three traditions were intensely decorative, but Aegean art was devoid of the stiff and pompous effects of the great land empires. Although its centers were swallowed up in history, the Aegean culture profoundly affected Mediterranean art. In its day it probably contributed to the enlivening of the New Kingdom period in Egyptian painting (see), and its colonies on the eastern littoral of the Mediterranean were apparently a source of the new vitality of Greek painting (see) during the seventh century B.C.

The original center of Aegean culture was Crete with its palaces like that of Minos at Knossos. This palace, built of timber-bonded rubble, was divided into such an intricate arrangement of rooms and courts that its form may have given rise to the myth of the Labyrinth. All important wall surfaces were, apparently, covered with painted murals. An early example is the fresco of a Boy Gathering Saffron (c.2000 B.C.). As in much Cretan decorative painting there was no emphasis on ground line; stylized flowers and rocks intrude from both top and bottom into the area of figure action. The details are in yellow and white on a red ground, with the boy's flesh painted blue. It is easy to understand how Cretan art caught the imagination of modern artists at the time of its discovery, about 1900. Aegean painting is at its best when drawing on themes of nature, as can be seen in the frescoes of Flying Fish, of Dolphins or of Lilies. The late Minoan period in Crete (end of second millenium B.C.) abounds in compositions of religious character. These include stately processional figures, paintings of crowds at shrines and a delightful fresco of acrobats and a bull. Although its aesthetic is different, Cretan painting resembles Egyptian in several respects. It showed no clear development, but existed throughout its career essentially full-blown. It was primarily decorative, linear in outline and it never developed a chiaroscuro. It also employed somewhat similar conventions in the presentation of bodies, heads, eyes, etc.

At the height of Cretan civilization there existed on the mainland of Greece a related culture called Mycenaean. Its

AEGEAN PAINTING. Minoan frieze at Knossos Woman Carrying Box. Copy by Gillieron in Metropolitan Museum of Art, New York

people were perhaps more northern in stock, but certainly Cretan in taste. It outlasted the Cretan empire, but fell to the invading Dorians about 1100 B.C. Its mural painting was Cretan in style, although inferior in execution. Among the subjects were again processional groups, rendered rather stiffly, and a Boar Hunt which retained much of the liveliness of the Cretan style. There is also a Bull fresco, which suffers badly by comparison with the Cretan example.

Aegean pottery styles are among the richest of the ancient world. The history of the craft was one of a struggle between stylized and naturalistic motifs. In its beginnings polychrome was practiced in highly abstract patterns of interlocked spirals and floral motifs. Then naturalistic elements like the standing lilies of the frescoes came into vogue. Vases with decorations in zones were also produced, but late in the culture. Marine forms were as popular on vases as in murals, but the octopus was chosen as a more suitable vase coverer than the Flying Fish or Dolphins of wall painting. Certain Mycenaean-type vases are particularly striking because of their tall attenuated forms ornamented with a stylized lily or octopus. These show a fine feeling for the artistic possibilities of broad undecorated backgrounds. (See illustration.)

aerial perspective. A painting technique designed to convey the impression received by the eye when an object is far away and difficult to see because of the blurring and dimming of its form and color. By softening the outline and lessening the color intensity, the painter conveys the feeling that a distant object is out of focus. Example: The paintings of Piero della Francesca.

Aertsen, Pieter (1508-75). Dutch painter of figures and still lifes. He was the pupil of Allart Claesz. in Amsterdam, and spent nearly eighteen years traveling throughout the Netherlands. He stayed many years in Antwerp, returning to Amsterdam about 1555. His religious pictures were mediocre, but his genre paintings forthright and strongly realistic statements of contemporary life.

African painting. Sometimes referred to as Bushman painting because its best-known examples were done by the Bushmen of the Kalahari Desert region south of the African Congo. It is an art of peoples who still live on a historically primitivistic level, nomad hunters of a type comparable with our paleolithic ancestors (see PREHISTORIC PAINTING). Their constant preoccupation with snaring and killing animals gave them a heightened sense of the reality of these creatures. On the rocks of this poor land have been found both animal and human paintings which although generalized in form show a remarkable sense of realism with regard to pose, movement, etc. These immediately bring to mind the works of earliest man in the Paleolithic age; and like those prehistoric works the Bushman paintings distinguish between man and beast, the former made more abstract than the latter. This may result from an understandable caution against a too recognizable human portrayal that, falling into enemy hands, might, through defacement, cause injury or death to the subject. Conversely a naturalistic portrayal of animals could only help in the attainment of the hunter's chief purpose in life, the successful hunt on which life itself depends. Thus this kind of painting, whether practiced by the African Bushman or other primitive peoples on a comparable cultural level, has a basically religious and functional purpose. It may be compared in that sense with any other kind of painting in which the artist is the agent who pictorializes or makes concrete an important tribal wish or urge.

Agabiti Pietro Paolo (c.1470-1540). Italian, school of the Marches. A painter, sculptor and architect best represented by the many paintings and terracotta groups preserved in the towns where he worked: Sassoferrato, Jesi and Cupramontana. His style stems from Venice and shows an affinity with that of Lorenzo Lotto. His handling is dry and often weak in anatomical details but his color is rich and splendid.

Aguirre, Ignacio (1902-). Mexican easel painter, fresco and graphic artist; co-founder of the Popular Graphic Art Workshop. He has taught in various Mexican schools and given one-man shows in the United States. His work is characterized by strong simple representational forms.

Akbar Period (see INDIAN PAINTERS: AKBAR PERIOD, 1556-1605).

Aken, Jerome van (see BOSCH).

Alba Madonna, The, by Raphael (see).

Albani, Francesco (1578-1660). Italian painter, one of the leading followers of the Carracci. Born in Bologna, he

ALBANI. Actaeon Surprising Diana. University of Arizona, Kress Collection, Tucson

studied there under the Fleming, Denys Calvaert, but c. 1595 joined the Carracci Academy, where he studied mostly with Agostino. In the 1590's he had several palace commissions in Bologna, notably the Palazzo Fava where the Carracci had worked previously, but went to Rome c. 1600, together with Guido Reni, and worked with Annibale in the Galleria Farnese. After the death of his wealthy wife he returned to Bologna in 1616 and lived the rest of his life in comparative luxury, the head of a large and very productive workshop, producing many altarpieces as well as mythological paintings. He became most famous for his paintings that involved children; they were widely imitated and influenced later French art. His output became progressively more mechanical and repetitious. Among his better works are the early landscapes done in Rome for the Aldobrandini Chapel; these may have influenced the French painter Poussin. He thought of himself as something of an esthetician and poet. (See illustration.)

Albers, Josef (1888-). German-born American contemporary painter in the non-objective geometric tradition. Born in Westphalia, he studied in Berlin, Essen and Munich. From 1923-33 he taught at the Bauhaus (see) school of design until its closing by the Nazis. He came to the United States and was made chairman of the art department at Black Mountain College (1933-50). From there he went to Yale University as head of its Department of Design. (See illustration.)

Albertina Museum, Vienna. One of the world's most important collections of graphic arts, including drawings and watercolors.

ALBERS. Homage to the Square: "Ascending"
Whitney Museum of American Art, New York

Albertinelli, Mariotto (1474-1515). Florentine painter closely associated with Fra Bartolommeo, with whom he studied under Cosimo Rosselli and with whom he had a working partnership at various times. He finished Fra Bartolommeo's Last Judgment in Santa Maria Nuova when his partner entered a monastery in 1500. Altarpieces painted independently are in the Uffizi and the Academy in Florence. His style, a weaker version of Fra Bartolommeo's, aims at a simple and dignified monumentality. (See illustration.)

Albi Museum, Albi, Fr. Located in the city where the French painter Toulouse-Lautrec was born, this museum features his work.

Albright, Ivan Le Lorraine (1897-). Contemporary American painter. Born in Chicago, he studied first at the Art Institute and later at various other institutions in the United States and France. During World War I he did surgical drawings for a medical unit. In the early 1930's his large, painstakingly meticulous renderings of reality with their moral intentions and morbid overtones achieved great notoriety. He paints the ordinary with a microscopic attention to detail, enshrouding it, however, with an aura of decay and horror. Although not an orthodox Surrealist, his works resemble the productions of that school not only in their precision of rendering but in their sense of eerie unreality.

Albright Art Gallery, Buffalo, N.Y. A general collection with increasing emphasis on contemporary European art, it includes such notable works as Gauguin's Yellow Christ, Rouault's Mr. X, and Matisse's Notre Dame.

Aldegrever, Heinrich (c.1502-before 1561). German engraver, goldsmith and painter of portraits and altarpieces. He probably began as a goldsmith and perhaps as a sculptor. Early in his career he came in contact with the art of Dürer in Nuremberg, and his own style reflects that of the Dürer circle, especially of the brothers Beham and Pencz. From about 1528 on he worked in Soest. An ardent supporter of the Reformation, he was highly regarded in his own day. His figure style is often mannered, with reflections of Italian motifs that he did not understand, and some influence from Cranach and Holbein. But he was a master of the art of ornamental design, and exerted an enormous influence on all sorts of crafts, including goldsmiths' work, and on woodcuts and engravings.

ALBERTINELLI. Madonna and Child with Infant St. John the Baptist and Angel Metropolitan Museum of Art, New York

Alexander, John White (1856-1915). One of the leading academic painters in America at the turn of the century, he is best known for his portraits and murals, the most famous of the latter being the Evolution of the Book in the Library of Congress and the Crowning of Labor in the Carnegie Institute. After achieving success as an illustrator, he studied painting in a variety of places abroad and with a number of artists—Duveneck and Whistler among them. His art is eclectic, given to broad, fluid brushwork, competent but superficial.

Alken, Henry (1785-1851). British painter of landscapes and hunting scenes depicting typical aspects of the countryside and the life and movement of the chase. Prints after his paintings are still popular.

Allegretto Nuzi (active c.1345-1373/4). Founder of the school of the Marches, he was active chiefly in Fabriano and drew his inspiration from the Florentine Bernardo Daddi and the Sienese Lorenzetti. Frescoes attributed to him in the sacristy of San Domenico and the cathedral at Fabriano reveal a dramatic and popular narrative power. His drawing is not refined but he possessed a highly developed sense of ornamentation.

Allegri, Antonio (see CORREGGIO).

Allori, Alessandro (1535-1607). An Italian Maniera (see) painter and slavish follower of Michelangelo and Bronzino (who brought him up after his father's death and whose name he adopted). His style is pompous, exaggerated and weak, but he had many commissions and decorated palaces and churches in and around Florence. He finished the decorations of Pontormo, del Sarto, and Franciabigio for the Medici Villa at Poggio a Caiano and did a copy of the Michelangelo Last Judgment for the Annunziata in Florence.

Allori, Cristofano (1577-1621). Florentine painter, son of Alessandro, who like his father took the name of Bronzino. He left his father's studio to study with Gregorio Pagani and was influenced by the coloristic reforms in Florentine painting which at the end of the sixteenth century were spearheaded by Cigoli, a pupil of Alessandro. He was a better and more famous painter than his father, a constant observer of nature, as his drawings attest, and one of the best draughtsmen and colorists of his time. Among his works are many excellent portraits.

Allston, Washington (1779-1843). The first important American Romantic painter of the nineteenth century; born in South Carolina and attended Harvard, where he did some painting as well as writing. After settling his estate in 1801, he studied in England at the Royal Academy under Benjamin West, and later in Paris among the works in the then newly formed Louvre collection. After that he spent four years in Italy, mostly in Rome, where he became intimate with Coleridge, Wordsworth, Southey and Thorwaldsen. He went back to Boston in 1809, but after his marriage left again for England in 1811 with his wife and his student, Samuel F. B. Morse. He came home for good in 1818, settling in Boston and later in Cambridgeport. During this quarter of a century he was a central figure in the intellectual life of New England,

ALLSTON. Moonlit Landscape. Museum of Fine Arts, Boston

influencing a whole generation in thought and taste. Even in college, Allston had been interested in the "Gothik," and in Europe he fell naturally for that time under the influence of the sixteenth- and seventeenth-century Italians, but especially the romanticism of Salvator Rosa, Claude Lorrain and Fuseli. Though he did many religious and historical paintings in the stilted academic mode of that age, his most important works are dramatic landscapes which range from the mysteriously foreboding to nightmares of horror, many of them recalling Hawthorne and Poe. Always a painter of mood, his early works in Rome (1805-08) were imaginative landscapes based on his journey through the Alps and the Roman countryside, characterized by a classical largeness, clarity and grace. The most dramatic paintings belong to the years (1811-18) spent in England. A mood of dreamy grace and reverie, begun then, increased after his return to the U.S. (See illustration.)

Alma-Tadema, Sir Lawrence (1836-1912). A British painter of Graeco-Roman genre subjects. Born in Frisia of Dutch parentage, he studied in Antwerp, worked in Rome, and settled in London in 1869. He specialized in reconstructions of ancient Roman life, rendering marble effects in terms of paint. He was very popular in his day, rivaling Leighton and Poynter in the treatment of these themes.

altarpiece. A decorated screen, panel or series of panels, movable or fixed, placed upon or to the rear of an altar. It was often decorated with painting or sculpture and in this usage is peculiar to the Christian Church. An early example is the enameled Pala d'Oro of S. Marco Venice (eleventh century and later). The late medieval altarpiece usually consisted of several hinged panels (triptych, polyptych); these closed and were decorated inside and out. Minor panels sometimes appeared along the predella or base. By the sixteenth century the altarpiece often consisted of a large framed canvas behind the altar, introduced into the architecture. Also architectural were the towering altarpieces (retablos) of many scenes and panels employed in Spain and England, where they often filled the entire rear of the apse and so protected the altar from view from the ambulatory behind it.

Altarpiece of the Lamb by Hubert and Jan van Eyck (see).

Altdorfer, Albrecht (c. 1480-1538). German architect, painter, engraver and woodcutter. He was trained by a miniaturist and in 1511 made a trip to Austria, where he encountered the works of Pacher. Altdorfer's pictures are often of small format, and his style shows great freedom and rich invention. A vein of poetry and illusion gives them charm, and in his later style, the grandiosity of conception and the use of Renaissance architecture and detail never dull the interest of his storytelling or decoration. (See illustration.)

Alte Pinakothek (Old Pinakothek), Munich. (See BAVARIAN STATE ART GALLERY, Munich).

Altichiero (c.1330-c.1395). Italian painter who worked in Verona for a number of years and was called to Padua about 1370, where his most important work is to be found. There he painted a series of "famous men" for Francesco Carrara, of which only a portrait of Petrarch remains (in the Palazzo del Capitano). His chief works in Padua are the frescoes in Sant' Antonio and in the Oratorio di San Giorgio. His style, influenced by Giotto's Paduan frescoes, shows more concern for painterly unity in composition than for the dramatic qualities emphasized by Giotto. In 1390 he was back in Verona where he painted frescoes in the church of St. Anastasia. Founder and greatest master of the early Verona school, he is probably the most significant painter of the fourteenth century in northern Italy.

Alva de la Canal, Ramón (1898-). Mexican easel painter and fresco artist; credited with one of the first true frescoes in the modern Mexican movement at the National Preparatory School, 1922 — the idealized and soberly colored Spaniards Planting the Cross. He also did the interior frescoes in a gigantic hollow monument to the patriot Morelos at Janitzio, Michoacán, 1935-37.

Al-Wasiti (see PERSIAN PAINTERS: ABBASID SCHOOL).

ALTDORFER. Forest with St. George
Alte Pinakothek, Munich

AMBERGER. Kaiser Karl V
Formerly State Museum, Berlin

Amalteo, Pomponio (1505-1588). Venetian painter, sculptor, architect, and engraver, pupil and son-in-law of Pordenone, who imitated his master but without the latter's power or originality. He worked almost entirely in the Friuli and in Treviso. His frescoes are superior to his easel paintings and the outstanding work of his career is the choir decoration completed in 1535 for Sta. Maria de' Battuti in S. Vito.

Amberger, Christoph (c.1500-1561). German painter. He was the pupil of Burgkmair, whom he succeeded as the most important painter in Augsburg. As a young man Amberger went, like most of his contemporaries, to study art in Italy. He was deeply influenced by Titian and the broad monumentality and classic beauty of such paintings as the altar of the Virgin in the Cathedral at Augsburg are directly traceable to the deep impression made on him by the work of the famous Venetian painter. Amberger is chiefly known for his portraits, which also reflect in their dignity and strength the Italian prototypes that he had admired. The decorative paintings with which he adorned the façades of houses in Augsburg have long since perished. (See illustration.)

Ambrogio da Predis (c.1450-c.1506). Italian painter, originally from the school of Vincenzo Foppa, he was the oldest of the Milanese followers of Leonardo da Vinci and collaborated with Leonardo during the latter's first stay in Milan. He worked on the London version of Leonardo's Madonna of the Rocks, and the lute-playing angels are considered his work. Two portraits, one in London and the other in Vienna, are his important authentic works.

American Gothic by Grant Wood (see).

American Indian (see PRE-COLUMBIAN PAINTING).

American Scene painting. An American realistic genre school of the twentieth century. As a revival of realism in the 1920's and a return to contemporary American subject matter, it has connections with the earlier Ashcan School (see), but the emphasis is shifted to smalltown and rural life. Its earliest exponents were Edward Hopper and Charles Burchfield, whose art often contains at least the implications of criticism. Toward the end of the decade a new group consisting of Thomas H. Benton, John S. Curry and Grant Wood, called Regionalists, turned to a more romantic and nostalgic portrayal of American life, and had in the 1930's a great many followers throughout the U.S.

Amiet, Cuno (1868-). Swiss painter briefly associated with the Brücke group in Dresden, one of the two major German Expressionist movements. Along with Nolde and Schmidt-Rottluff, Amiet contributed some graphics to the 1907 Brücke album. The art of Amiet, based on French Post-Impressionism, and especially on Gauguin, is interesting evidence of the relationship between French and German painting in the early years of this century. His affiliation with the Brücke owes its existence to an exhibition which he happened to have in Dresden in 1906, where the richness of his color and generally decorative approach were of interest to the group.

Amigoni, Jacopo (1675-1752). Venetian painter, a follower of Ricci and Solimena, in tbe tradition of Tiepolo, who did a great many palace decorations and Rococo portraits in Germany, England, and Spain.

Amstel, Jan van (c.1500-40). Flemish landscape painter. No certain works are known by him, but he appears frequently in documents and may be the same artist who signed his work with the monogram J A M S L in Brunswick. Thought to have been a teacher of Pieter Brueghel.

Analytical Cubism (see CUBISM).

Anatomy Lesson, The, by Rembrandt (see).

1. ANGELICO. The Madonna of Humility. National Gallery of Art, Mellon Collection, Washington, D.C.

ANDREA DI BARTOLO. Christ in Benediction
Detroit Institute of Arts

Andrea da Firenze (Andrea Bonaiuti) (active 1343-77). Florentine painter whose major work, frescoes (commissioned 1365) in the Spanish Chapel of Santa Maria Novella, is based on a religious treatise, Passavanti's *Mirror of Penitence,* and includes scenes from the life of St. Peter Martyr, a Crucifixion, and St. Thomas in Glory, as well as the allegorical Way to Salvation. His frescoes (1377) in the Campo Santo, Pisa, illustrating the life of St. Ranier, are preserved in spite of the great damage to the Campo Santo in World War II. Andrea is the most strongly Sienese of the post-Giotto generation in Florence, deriving elements from the Lorenzetti and Simone Martini. He is particularly noted for his skill in composing large areas of undivided wall space, a development of the anti-Giottesque tendency that marked his generation.

Andrea da Murano (active 1462-1507). This Venetian painter received his training under his brother Hieronymus, whose shop furnished woodcarving and painting for church use. He collaborated with Bartolommeo Vivarini and was influenced by him. His most important extant work is the high altar of Sta. Maria in Trebaseleghe, which was begun in 1484 and for which he received payment in 1507. His style is characterized by conventional draughtsmanship and a rather hard manner.

Andrea da Salerno (see SABATINI, ANDREA).

Andrea del Castagno (see CASTAGNO, ANDREA DEL).

Andrea del Sarto (see SARTO, ANDREA DEL).

Andrea di Bartolo (active by 1389, died 1428). An Italian painter from Siena, he was a close follower of his father, Bartolo di Maestro Fredi, and later came under the strong influence of Taddeo di Bartolo. His only signed paintings are an Assumption in the Whitney collection, New York, an Annunciation and Saints in SS. Pietro e Paolo, Buonconvento, and a picture owned at one time by the Wildenstein Gallery, New York. Andrea's painting is able but not original. Many works previously thought to be by Taddeo di Bartolo are now ascribed to him. (See illustration.)

Andrea di Cione (see ORCAGNA).

Andrea di Niccolo di Giacomo (c. 1440-after 1514). Sienese painter who was a pupil of Matteo di Giovanni Bartoli and collaborated with Giovanni di Paolo in 1470. He executed numerous commissions for churches and confraternities in and around Siena. His major extant work is an altarpiece of the Madonna and Child with St. Roche and St. Sebastian. His art, based on that of his teacher and on the works of Neroccio di Landi and Benvenuto di Giovanni, is distinguished by a dark and greenish tonality.

Angelico (Fra Giovanni da Fiesole) (1387-1455). Fra Angelico, as he is called, was the major Florentine exponent of the Gothic tradition which lasted beyond 1400 and formed a distinct current in Florentine art of the fifteenth century. He eventually came under the influence of the innovations of his more scientific contemporaries, Masaccio and the architect Michelozzo, so that his art partook of Renaissance formal elements while remaining essentially medieval in content. He was born Guido or Guidolino di Pietro, and took the name of Giovanni when he and his brother Benedetto entered the Dominican monastery at Fiesole in 1407. It is presumed that the years between 1407 and 1418 were spent in Cortona and Foligno, to which cities the Dominican chapter of Fiesole was forced to flee because of its political sympathies in the Great Schism. After the Council of Constance in 1418, the chapter returned to Fiesole, where it remained until 1436. It is presumed that Fra Angelico was a practicing painter when he entered the monastery but the identity of his teacher is not recorded. In style his early work is close enough to Lorenzo Monaco's to warrant the assumption of scholars that that artist was his teacher. Only five of the enormous number of his works are dated by documents, but we possess sufficient evidence to construct an outline of his career.

His life divides into three periods according to his place of work: Fiesole (1418-36), Florence (1436-45), and Rome (1445-55). Several altarpieces of the Fiesole period are extant, including the Madonna dei Linaiuoli, commissioned by the linen merchants in 1433, now in the San Marco museum,

Florence. In the same museum are the Madonna della Stella, the Coronation of the Virgin, and the Last Judgment, all from this period. Another Coronation is in Paris. These panels establish several elements of his style that are characteristic of all his work: stylization and spirituality of expression especially in faces, liberal use of gold, light and brilliant color, and skillful draughtsmanship and composition in space. In 1436 Cosimo de' Medici gave to the Fiesole Dominicans the ruined monastery of San Marco in Florence, and the chapter moved there. The building was restored by Michelozzo between 1436 and 1443, and remains a monument of Renaissance architecture and a museum of Fra Angelico. From 1436 to 1445 Angelico, with the help of several assistants, painted for the chapter many frescoes in the cloister, chapter house, corridors, and individual cells of the monks. This was the major work of his Florentine period, during which he became increasingly aware of the innovations of Florentine artists in perspective, architecture and landscape. It is assumed that he was in close contact with Michelozzo during these years, and Renaissance architectural forms replace the Gothic ones of his earlier work. Consistent linear perspective and an awareness of light and cast shadow lend a Renaissance aspect to the medieval content. The frescoes are of a particularly devotional and intimate nature, and many include figures of Dominican friars as witnesses to the events of Christ's life. He painted a Madonna and Saints for the high altar about 1440, and of this period also are the Deposition with lunette scenes by Lorenzo Monaco, and a Lamentation (all in San Marco). In the last two, recognizably Tuscan landscape appears for the first time in the backgrounds. In 1445 he was called to Rome by Eugene IV, and except for a few months in Orvieto in 1447 and about three years back in Fiesole (1449-52), he spent the rest of his life in Rome. In Orvieto he painted half of the vault of a chapel in the cathedral; one of his assistants here, Benozzo Gozzoli, took over the project when apparently Angelico abandoned it. In Rome he decorated one chapel (now destroyed) with the help of Gozzoli and others; and did another, the extant chapel of Nicholas V, with scenes from the lives of St. Stephen and St. Lawrence. Compared with the San Marco frescoes, these show considerable development along Renaissance lines, though they are still pervaded by the unworldly Gothic piety that Angelico retained. Details are more realistic, compositions more complicated, and architecture is integrated more fully into the compositions. Increased modeling with light and shadow in these works tends to obscure the clear, bright color typical of earlier works. Fra Angelico died in 1455 in the Dominican monastery of Santa Maria Sopra Minerva. His art bespeaks a life of pure faith and single-minded piety, which accounts for the name Angelico by which he is best known. Since his beatification he has also been called Il Beato Angelico. Benozzo Gozzoli and Francesco Pesellino both owe something to Angelico's art, though neither was actually his pupil. (See color plate 1.)

Angelus, The, by Jean François Millet (see).

Anguiano, Raúl (1909-). Mexican easel painter and graphic artist; member, Popular Graphic Art Workshop. He has also painted frescoes in various public buildings in Mexico City. While on a 1949 government expedition, he made color copies of Mayan frescoes at Bonampak and studies of the primitive Lacandonian Indians of Chiapas. These show penetrating characterizations and effective draughtsmanship.

Anguisciola (Anguissola), Sophonisba (1527-1623). A Cremonese painter who is most famous for her fresh and finely handled portraits. She studied with Bernardino Campi and later in Milan with Bernardino Gatti. She had five sisters, all of whom she taught to paint. In 1559 she went to Spain to serve as court portraitist for Philip II and, after marrying a wealthy Sicilian gentleman, moved to Palermo. There she died at ninety-six, having led a rich and productive life, highly regarded both intellectually and artistically by her contemporaries.

Ansano di Pietro (see SANO DI PIETRO).

Anselmi, Michelangelo (1491-1554). Born in Lucca, he studied with Sodoma in Siena and then moved to Parma (1516) where he fell completely under the spell of Correggio. He worked in many of the churches in Parma and completed the decorations of Parmigianino in the Madonna della Steccata. A mediocre follower of Correggio, his forms are harsh, his expression exaggerated, and his figures mannered.

Ansuino da Forlì. Italian painter active in Padua in the fifteenth century. His work is known only through frescoes (destroyed in World War II) depicting episodes from the life of St. Christopher (forming part of the cycle by Mantegna) in the Eremitani Church in Padua. He was of the school of Squarcione. Documents refer to other church decorations in Padua, now lost, in which he collaborated, possibly with Fra Filippo Lippi.

Antolínez, Claudio José Vicente (1635-75). Spanish painter of Madrid. He practiced a vivid Baroque style derived from the teaching of Francesco Ricci and his own study of the Venetians. Characteristic is his Immaculate Conception with Cherubs in the Prado. He was haughty in character and inclined to defend his honor by the sword.

Antolínez y Sarabia, Francisco (1644-1700). Spanish painter of history and landscape. Nephew of José Antolínez and follower of Murillo. He is best known for small paintings of biblical subjects and of the Life of the Virgin.

Antonello da Messina (c.1430-79). Although Antonello was born in Sicily and spent a good part of his active life there, his importance to fifteenth-century painting touches on north Italian art, particularly Venetian, and even displays important connections with the Flemish school. He is sometimes classed among Venetian painters, with whom his art has more in common than with any other local style. He was born Antonello di Giovanni degli Antonj at Messina, the son of a sculptor. His earliest dated works reveal that he had been in contact with the painting or at least felt the influence of the Flemish school. This influence may have come to him through Spain, or Spanish artists working in Sicily, who were much indebted to Flemish art. It is possible, but not likely, that he actually visited the Netherlands. His earliest known work, Christ Crowned with Thorns (signed and once dated 1470, now in the Metropolitan), is painted in the oil technique that had been practiced since the early fifteenth century by the van Eycks in Bruges, but which was unknown in Italy until about the 1470's. The history of this painting indicates that it was probably painted in Sicily. There is no record of Antonello's having visited Venice before 1475, where he used to be credited with having introduced the oil technique. Furthermore, Bartolommeo Vivarini was already using this technique in Venice by 1473, which would indicate that it came to Italy through various channels. Antonello is first heard of in Messina in 1457, and is known to have been there from 1460 to 1465, but from then until 1473 there is no record of his activity except for the dated painting of 1470. Works done before his trip to Venice include a signed Madonna of the Rosary, dated 1473 (Messina gallery), another Christ Crowned with Thorns of the same year (Piacenza museum), an Annunciation of c.1474 (Syracuse, Sicily, museum), and a Crucifixion of 1475 (Antwerp). In all these his style shows a sharp observation of nature, the luminous, jewel-like color obtainable only with oil glazes, and a sense of light and atmosphere surrounding the convincingly modeled forms that is closely allied with the van Eyck tradition in Flemish painting. In Venice in 1475 and 1476 he painted an altar for San Casciano, parts of which are preserved in the Vienna museum.

ANTONELLO DA MESSINA. Crucifixion
Musée Royal des Beaux-Arts, Antwerp

Although all of Antonello's extant works were painted within less than ten years, there is a marked difference between those painted before and after his stay in Venice. From the Venetians he evidently learned a softer and broader manner and greater lyricism of expression. What he gave to Venice may not have been the oil technique but certainly some of the means of exploiting it. His light and shade, used for modeling, for defining space, and for emotional expression, seem to have affected Giovanni Bellini and Alvise Vivarini. These painters are thus separated from the tradition of the elder Vivarini. Among his post-Venetian works are the St. Jerome in his Study and a second Crucifixion of 1477 (London), and a St. Sebastian (formerly in Dresden) that shows the influence of Mantegna, especially in the device of foreshortening both architecture and figures. A number of his portraits belong in the forefront of the development of portraiture in the late fifteenth century. Aside from their Flemish realism, they embody a new, more plastic and more personal approach to the rendering of a sitter, with the head in three-quarter view and the eyes looking out toward the spectator. (See illustrations, including color plate 2.)

Antoniazzo Romano (active 1461-1508). The only local artist of any importance in late fifteenth-century Rome. The Vatican at this time was heavily patronizing Florentine and Umbrian painters. A number of well-authenticated altarpieces by Antoniazzo indicate an artist of mediocre talent working under the influence of such Umbrian masters as Fiorenzo di Lorenzo, Melozzo da Forlì, and the early Perugino. His major work is the fresco decoration of the apse of Santa Croce in Gerusalemme, Rome. His art is mild and serene, and, with the exception of frescoes with figures in a landscape, he seems to have preferred the tooled gold backgrounds characteristic of a much earlier period.

Antonio da Fabriano (active 1450-85). Italian painter whose style shows a dependence on the work of Lorenzo Salimbeni and the Vivarini. A number of signed and dated works by him are in churches and galleries in Fabriano and Sassoferrato, and other works in the region have been attributed to him.

Antonio da Ferrara (Antonio di Guido Alberti) (1390/1400-1449). Born in Ferrara but must have moved at an early age to Urbino, since his art is wholly Umbrian in character and is based on the style of Gentile da Fabriano. He may have been a pupil of the painter Matteo Gennari, whose sister he married. Signed frescoes by him are preserved in a chapel near Pesaro, and an altarpiece (1439) is in the Urbino gallery. His style is characterized by a certain harshness and vigor; it influenced later Ferrarese painters, including Tura and Cossa.

Antonio Veneziano (active c.1370-88). Italian painter active in Siena, Florence and Pisa. In 1384-87 he completed the St. Ranier frescoes begun by Andrea da Firenze in the Campo Santo at Pisa. Other frescoes by him are now lost except for some ruined fragments of Passion and Marian subjects in Florence. His Venetian origin is perhaps responsible for the lively color and play of light observed in the Pisan frescoes.

Apelles (second half of 4th century B.C.). Outstanding Greek painter of the fourth century, he was born about 370 B.C. in Kolophon. He studied at Ephesos and spent twelve years at Sikyon, one of the major local schools into which Greek painting had divided in his century. Here he trained with Pamphilos who had, by rules and science, reduced the technical aspect of painting to an academic discipline. At about 340 B.C. Apelles was settled at the Macedonian court where he worked for Philip and Alexander. His work was in great demand and he traveled much throughout the Greek world. We know a good deal about him from description and anecdote in literature but the nature of his style is not clear. Vase paintings were no longer evidence for monumental painting in this era because the illusionistic tendencies of the latter diverged from the decorative tradition of ceramics. In Apelles' case our usual source, Pompeian painting and mosaic, is not revealing. It would appear that he did much to refine the use of spatial and modeling chiaroscuro, perhaps in a Rembrandtesque fashion. He used the traditional four-color palette, but employed a unique glazing which preserved the freshness of his colors and the activity of his forms. Most famous of his subjects were an Aphrodite Rising from the Sea painted for Kos and removed by Augustus to Rome, and Calumny, an allegory directed at a rival painter at the Ptolemaic court. Of his several portraits of the Macedonian monarchs, the realism of the equestrian portrait of Alexander is supposed to have caused a horse to whinny at it.

Appel, Karel (1921-). Self-taught Netherlands painter who has been living in Paris since 1950. His style is an abstract development of the figurative Expressionism widely practiced in Holland and Belgium in the 1920's and 1930's, and stands halfway between that earlier style and the Abstract Expressionism of today.

Apt, Ulrich (active by 1481-1532). German painter. He worked in Augsburg, where he repeatedly held office in the city government. His painting bears the impress of the elder Holbein and of Burgkmair, and he was also influenced by Jörg Breu, whom he assisted in 1516 on the decoration of the Town Hall. Apt's style is characterized by constricted forms and old-fashioned local color.

aquatint. A graphic or print technique developed to

give the tonal effect of a wash drawing. This eighteenth-century process consists of covering a copper plate with powdered resin in thicker or thinner deposits as required. The acid is then permitted to bite through the tiny spaces between the grains of resin to form a mass of tiny close-together depressions in the plate which when inked give the tone quality desired. This method is often used in conjunction with ordinary etching, of which it is a variant, as in Goya's Disasters of War.

arabesque. A type of animal or flower ornament, generally flowing and curving in form. The term is also used to signify most other sinuous ornaments or patterns.

Araldi, Alessandro (c. 1460-1528). Italian painter of frescoes and altarpieces who lived and worked in Parma. An extremely eclectic painter, he borrowed elements from all the well-known masters of his time, especially Pinturicchio. He made a copy of Leonardo da Vinci's Last Supper for the cloister of San Paolo at Parma.

Arcangelo di Cola da Camerino (active 1416-29). Italian painter, school of the Marches, who appears to have worked in Città di Castello, Florence and Rome. His one extant signed painting (a diptych) and other works attributed to him reveal close contact with the linear Gothic art of Gentile da Fabriano, with whom he may have worked in Rome in 1422, if not before. He also absorbed some of the more plastic elements of Florentine style.

archaism. The use of styles from the past to lend dignity, special flavor or other desired qualities to a contemporary work of art. Exemplified in the work of the so-called classical period of Picasso.

architectonic. A term describing the kind of painting in which a tightly controlled, generally geometric and often monumental arrangement is projected as an experience in spaces and forms as such rather than in the subject. The work of Cézanne and Mondrian illustrate this quality.

Arena Chapel frescoes by Giotto (see).

Arenal, Luis (1909-). Mexican easel painter, lithographer and muralist; member, Popular Graphic Workshop. He has studied and worked on murals with Siqueiros, especially those at the new University City in Mexico. He has exhibited in the United States. His frescoes, influenced by Siqueiros' dynamic realism, may be seen in Bellevue Hospital, New York, and in the Governor's Palace of Guerrero, Mexico.

Aretusi, Pellegrino (called Munari) (active 1483, died 1523). Italian painter, school of Modena. He was locally trained but about 1510 was drawn to Rome by the fame of Raphael, whose assistant he became in the decoration of the Vatican Loggie. He also worked on decorations (now lost) in various Roman churches. Back in Modena after Raphael's death (1520) he painted altarpieces. His early work is characterized by fine detail, lively color and distinctive figure types. Later his art became a weak imitation of the High Renaissance style of Raphael.

Armory Show. The first major exhibition of modern art in the U.S., held at the Sixty-ninth Regiment Armory, New York City, February 17 to March 15, 1913. Arranged under the auspices of the Association of American Painters and Sculptors, it was largely inspired and directed by Arthur B. Davies, president, and carried out by Walt Kuhn, secretary, with the help of Walter Pach. It included works from Ingres and Delacroix through the contemporary movements of Fauvism and Cubism, as well as a selected survey of contemporary American art. This mammoth display of the development of modern art had a profound effect, influencing a whole generation of American artists. In spite of public shock, press ridicule, and critical attack, the exhibition was a sensational success. It later travelled to Chicago and Boston, and in all a quarter of a million paid to see it and some three hundred works were sold.

Arnolfini Marriage, The, by Jan van Eyck (see).

Arp, Jean (1888-). Alsatian-born Surrealist painter, sculptor and theorist, influential in France, Germany, Switzerland and now the United States. Generally associated with the more abstract aspects of Surrealism (see) and known for the free-form cutouts in overlapping layers of colored wood which he began to use in 1917 under the influence of the "Improvisations" of Kandinsky. Arp's colored wooden forms, however, show a humorous spontaneity and suggestiveness that ally them to the "unexpected" and "surprising" characteristics of Surrealism with its evocations of ideas and shapes. Arp exhibited at the Second Blue Rider graphics show in 1912, worked in Paris for a while and then settled in Zurich in 1915 where he soon helped found the Dada (see) movement and participated in various Dadaist magazines, especially the famous Cabaret Voltaire. In 1919-23 he furthered Dadaism in Germany and after 1925 performed the same function in Paris, where he remained until the fall of France in 1940 drove him to Switzerland. He came to the United States in 1950 under commission from Harvard University for a large-scale mural relief. See also COLLAGE. (See illustration.)

Arpino Il Cavaliere d' (Giuseppe Cesari) (c. 1560-1640). Italian Maniera (see) painter, one of the most famous artists of his day. His retarded style stood in opposition to the newer eclecticism of the Carracci and the naturalism of Caravaggio, but he still received great commissions and was internationally respected. He worked in turn for Popes Gregory XIII, Clement VIII, Paul V, and Urban VIII, and in France for Henry IV, Louis XIII, and Cardinal Richelieu. Born either in Rome or Arpino, he studied first with his father, and as a child prodigy decorated a façade in Rome

2. ANTONELLO DA MESSINA. Madonna and Child
National Gallery of Art, Mellon Collection, Washington, D.C.

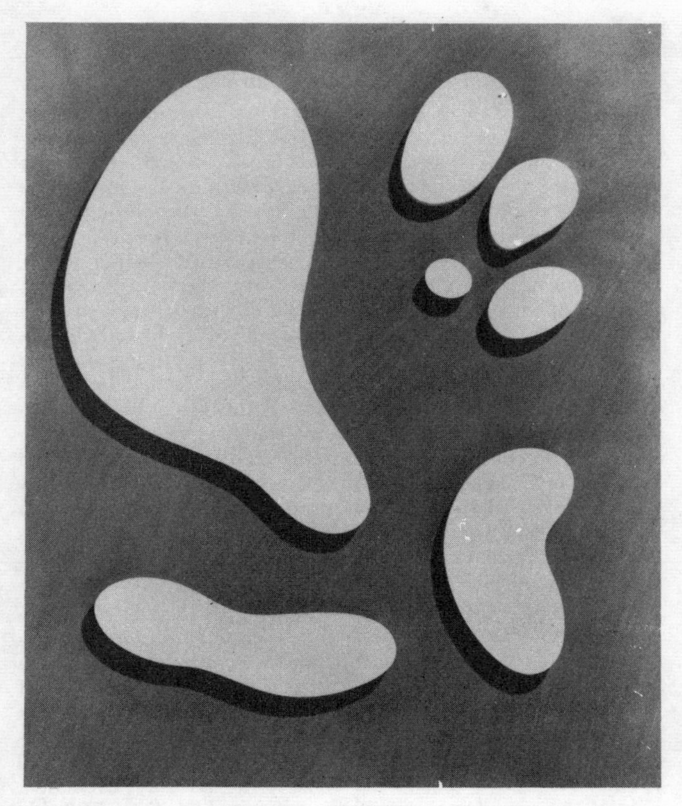

ARP. Yellow Constellation. Sidney Janis Gallery, New York

ARPINO. Perseus and Andromeda.
Metropolitan Museum of Art, New York

at the age of thirteen. From that point on he followed an unbroken road to honor and wealth, covering endless walls with mannered and complex decorations. (See illustration.)

Art for Art's sake. A term used to describe the kind of painting in which forms, colors, textures, lines and spaces are arranged and manipulated for their own sakes rather than for their religious, historical, political or moral content. As a doctrine it appeared in both painting and literature early in the nineteenth century and by the end of the century had become a major force in the arts.

Art Institute of Chicago. One of the leading general collections in the United States, it is best known for its Impressionist and Post-Impressionist paintings, and especially for works by Monet, Van Gogh, Seurat (Sunday Afternoon on La Grande Jatte), and Gauguin.

Artist's Mother by J. A. M. Whistler (see).

Art Nouveau. A type of expression characterizing the work of many European artists during the 1890's and early 1900's. In its most typical form it makes use of flowing curvilinear lines and free, loose ornament based on such organic or growing things as flowers, branches and trees. Wild roses and nasturtiums seem to have been popular in this connection because of their sinuously flowing forms. Art Nouveau (literally, new art) was not especially popular in France but found its greatest expression in Central Europe and Britain as part of the mystical spiritual revolt against the overwhelming materialism of the time. Sometimes known as Jugendstil (from the Munich magazine *Die Jugend*, or The Youth) or the *Yellow Book* style as well as Art Nouveau, it marks the paintings of Edvard Munch in Norway, the illustrations of Aubrey Beardsley and other *Yellow Book* contributors in England, the architectural ornament of Henry van de Velde in Holland and of Louis Sullivan in the United States, and the industrial art forms of the Wiener Werkstätte in Vienna. Its effect can also clearly be seen in the work of Hodler, Gauguin, Van Gogh and other painters of the period.

Ashcan School. American Realist school of city genre painters of the early twentieth century; active mostly in New York. The original group, led by Robert Henri and including George B. Luks, John Sloan, William J. Glackens and Everett Shinn, was first active in Philadelphia in the 1890's. They were then known as the Philadelphia Realists, and after migrating to New York around the turn of the century were called the New York Realists. The origin of the term Ashcan, a derogatory reference to their concern with slums and squalor, and its first use, is in question, although sometimes attributed to Art Young. They dealt with colorful and intimate aspects of city life in a romantic and sentimental manner, and painted in a gray tonality based on the art of Manet, Daumier, Gavarni, Guys and Forain. In their own day this turn toward contemporary reality at a time of esthetic gentility struck many as socially radical and led to a storm of criticism. Painting in a similar vein, but not part of the original group, were Jerome Myers and Eugene Higgins. Of the younger generation influenced by the style were George W. Bellows, Rockwell Kent, Gifford Beal, Leon Kroll, Glenn O. Coleman, Guy Pène du Bois and Edward Hopper, to name only a few. The original group formed the nucleus of the Eight and was active in the Armory Show.

Asselin, Maurice (1882-1947). French painter of intimate subjects and landscapes. He worked in the Cézanne tradition and is loosely associated with the Fauve point of view.

asymmetric. Describes a kind of informal balance. May be contrasted with the more formal or symmetrical balance involved in such an arrangement as that of a scale with equal-sized pans revolving around a central point. Asymmetry—also referred to as occult, active or informal balance—may be illustrated by a typical Dutch landscape painting of the seven-

AVERCAMP. Scene on the Ice. Mauritshuis, The Hague

teenth century, e.g., a Ruysdael in which a large element such as a tree or windmill on one side of a composition is balanced against a number of smaller elements on the other side or against a deeply inward-projecting space.

Atkins, Caven (1907-). Canadian painter trained at the Winnipeg School of Art. He has developed a brightly decorative Fauve type of painting.

Atl, Dr. (Gerardo Murillo, 1877-). Mexican easel painter, draughtsman, writer, poet, student of volcanology. Atl was a fermenting influence in the revolutionary movement in art in Mexico. He was one of the first to preach mural art and a national culture and did an important scholarly study of Mexican colonial architecture, painting and popular arts. His art is almost exclusively landscapes and some self-portraits done in a personal wax-crayon technique called Atl-color. It favors sweeping panoramas and displays an especially great feeling for mountains.

Attic. Relating to Attica or Athens in Greece and the artistic styles developed there. See GREEK PAINTING.

Auberjonois, René (1872-). Modern Swiss painter whose works are primarily figurative, highly charged with emotion, and often symbolic.

Audubon, John James (1785-1851). Said to have been born in Santo Domingo, Audubon's early life was shrouded in mystery, even giving rise to the legend that he was the lost Dauphin. He was brought up in France and came first to the U.S. in 1804. According to his *Journal* he returned in 1806 to France and spent several months in the studio of J. L. David. He came again to the U.S. in 1807, and after various unsuccessful business ventures, portrait painting, and teaching he turned to ornithology, spending many years in studying the birds of America. In 1826 he took his results to London where they were engraved and issued singly from 1827 until 1838, when they were finally collected under the title *The Birds of America* (the text, *Ornithological Biography*, was issued later). Back in the U.S. the work was reissued in smaller format editions and before his death he managed to produce with his father-in-law one volume of the projected *Viviparous Quadrupeds of North America.* Though not intended as art, his paintings of nature are imbued with a magnificent sense of design—meticulous yet monumental, displaying originality in color and brilliance in draughtsmanship. (See illustration).

Avanzi, Jacopo (active last quarter of 14th century). A Bolognese painter formerly confused with Jacopo Avanzo, a Veronese artist who worked in Padua. Little more is known of Jacopo Avanzi than that he signed an extant Crucifixion (Rome, Colonna Gallery) and painted an enamel for the town hall of Bologna in 1384.

Avanzo, Jacopo (active last quarter of 14th century).

AUDUBON. Pacific Loon
New-York Historical Society, New York

AVERY. Music Maker
Durand-Ruel Gallery, Paris

BALDUNG-GRIEN. Adoration of the Kings
Königliche Galerie, Berlin

Veronese artist formerly confused with Jacopo Avanzi da Bologna and with a Jacopo da Verona who worked in Padua. Avanzo's signature is found in the fresco decoration of the Oratory of St. George, Padua, where he collaborated with Altichiero. The impressive narrative style of the two painters, deriving from Giotto, is so similar that their hands in this large and important decoration have not been satisfactorily distinguished.

Avercamp, Hendrick (1585-1634). Dutch painter. He studied with Pieter Isaacsz. and in his early works reveals the influence of Coninxloo and Pieter Brueghel the Elder. He specialized in winter scenes, in which his sprightly, well-painted little figures combine with fresh color to create entertaining and original effects. (See illustration.)

Avery, Milton (1893-). Contemporary American painter in the tradition of Matisse and Fauvism (see). Born in Altmar, N.Y., he studied at the Connecticut League of Art Students. His art is characterized by sensitive drawing, distorting but not destroying reality, and subtle relationship of color applied thinly in large areas. (See illustration.)

Aztec painting (see PRE-COLUMBIAN PAINTING).

B

Baburen, Dirck van (c. 1590-1624). Dutch painter. He studied under Paulus Moreelse and then spent eleven years in Rome, absorbing the tradition of Caravaggio. Returning to Holland he became one of the chief masters of the *tenebroso* school, made up of followers of Caravaggio. See TENEBRIST.

Bacchiacca (Francesco d'Ubertino) (1494-1557). Florentine painter influenced by Mannerism (see) though not completely a part of the movement. He studied with Perugino, fell under the influence of his friend del Sarto, and later Michelangelo. He absorbed a great many different tendencies—Franciabigio, Albertinelli, Raphael, and Vasari, as well as Pontormo, and was apparently influenced by the engravings of Lucas van Leyden and Dürer. He was a minor painter whose best works are charming smaller pictures.

Baço, Jaime (see JACOMART).

Bacon, Francis (1910-). British painter who spent his youth in Ireland but has since worked independently in England. He has exhibited since 1932, working toward the rich and refined paint surface and the somewhat eerie figure subjects with Romantic overtones that now characterize his work. Bacon's style is highly dramatic and symbolic.

Badger, Joseph (1708-65). Born in Charlestown, Mass., he was a housepainter and glazier; between 1740 and 1760 he did naively crude portraits which are simple, direct, and, especially in the characterization of children, quite charming.

Baglione, Giovanni (1571-1644). Italian painter, part of the Maniera (see) circle in Rome working for Sixtus V, but best known as an art historian *(Lives of Painters, Sculptors and Architects*, 1642, and *The Nine Churches of Rome*, 1639). Though a violent anti-Caravaggist, he was still influenced by that master, at least in his easel paintings.

Bagnacavallo (Bartolommeo Ramenghi, the elder) (1484-1542). Bolognese painter born in Bagnacavallo, he was at first influenced by his master, Francia, later in Rome by Raphael and finally by Dosso. He was active in Bologna, decorating the Convent of S. Michele in Bosco. Although derivative, his color is good, his figures graceful and his landscape backgrounds interesting.

Bakhuysen, Ludolf (1631-1708). Dutch painter who specialized in marine scenes that are characterized by a stormy, tempestuous mood. He studied under Allart van Everdingen and Hendrick Dubbels and spent most of his life in Amsterdam.

Baldovinetti, Alesso (1425-99). Oldest of the generation of painters whose art made up the complex of later fifteenth-century style in Florence. His art was based on that of Fra Angelico and Fra Filippo Lippi, and thus partakes more of the lyrical and spiritual qualities of those painters than of the monumental and scientific tradition of Masaccio. Baldovinetti was born in Florence of a respected patrician family and his name is first registered in the painters' guild in 1448. There is no factual evidence that he was a pupil of Fra Angelico, although he worked on a project directed by Angelico for paintings on sacristy cupboard doors in SS. Annunziata. His entire documented activity was in Florence,

BALLA. Swifts: Paths of Movement and Dynamic Sequences
Museum of Modern Art, New York

where he executed a number of important fresco commissions that are now lost. We know from a journal he kept that he also made designs for stained glass windows and mosaics. The three sacristy cupboard doors preserved in the museum of San Marco reveal an affinity with Fra Angelico's style, and the influence of Domenico Veneziano, especially in the color. A Madonna and Saints and an Annunciation (c. 1455-60) in the Uffizi show close relations to both Angelico and Fra Filippo Lippi. A damaged fresco of the Nativity (1460/62) is in the cloister of SS. Annunziata and fragments of a later fresco project (1471) are in Santa Trinità. His best-preserved and finest single panel is the Madonna Adoring the Child (c. 1460) in the Louvre. This and the Nativity fresco reveal Baldovinetti as a master of realistic landscape. Late altarpieces in the Florence Academy and in Sant' Ambrogio are inferior in quality and were probably done in part by pupils. (See color plate 3.)

Balducci, Matteo (active 1509-55). Umbro-Sienese painter, born in Fontignano near Perugia and active mostly in Siena and vicinity. A provincial and eclectic painter, he was a pupil of Pacchiarotto and assistant of Sodoma for six years in Siena, and later became an assistant and follower of Pinturicchio, who had the greatest influence on him.

Baldung-Grien, Hans (c.1480-1545). German painter and draughtsman, and a designer of woodcuts and stained glass. He was a friend of Dürer's and very probably studied under him in Nuremberg in the early years of the sixteenth century. In 1509 he acquired burgher's rights in Strasbourg and settled there permanently. From 1512 to 1516, however, he worked at Freiburg-in-Breisgau, creating his masterpiece on the high altar of the cathedral there. He adorned the central panel with the Coronation of the Virgin and the wings with other scenes from her life. Baldung was an extremely gifted and imaginative artist, whose great talents were directed toward the expression of complicated mood, and sober, often tragic feeling. The delineation of the human form was his special interest and he endowed postures and silhouettes with a peculiarly personal, expressive and rhythmic grace. The popular German theme of "Death and the Maiden" gave him an opportunity to make the most of rich female forms by allowing him to contrast them with ghastly skeletons and create complex, closely interwoven designs. His drawings are especially fine and his woodcuts impressive and full of invention. The Markgraf Christof of Baden, whose portrait he painted more than once, was Baldung's special patron. (See illustration.)

Balen, Hendrik van (1575-1632). Flemish Italianate painter. Apparently studied under van Noort and in Rome, and was a teacher of van Dyck and Snyders. He was frequently assisted by other painters, among them de Momper, Snyders and Jan Brueghel. He painted many small landscapes on wood and copper with biblical or mythological scenes. He also did large religious paintings in a more monumental style.

Balla, Giacomo (1871-). Italian Futurist painter and teacher of Boccioni and Severini in Rome around 1904. He was a signer of the Futurist Manifesto of 1910 and a faithful adherent to its program through the 1920's. Later, settling in Rome, he turned to a more representational manner. Balla's Futurist work is interesting for its various solutions of the problem of kinetic motion, e.g., his Leash in Motion (or Running Dog) in the Museum of Modern Art, but not quite as interesting aesthetically as the work of other members of the group. See FUTURISM. (See illustration.)

Balthus (1908-). Shy, retiring French painter of Polish descent (real name, Balthasar Klossowski). His art is related in form to that of Courbet and Derain, both for figures and landscape painting. What differentiates him from this relatively traditional viewpoint is a strange poetic quality in his work which lends it an intensity of feeling that recalls the Neue Sachlichkeit (New Objectivity) of the modern Germans.

Bamboccio (see LAER, PIETER VAN).

bamboo symbolism. A term referring to the Chinese practice of associating bamboo with sturdy yet flexible character; a quality attributed to the ideal scholar-poet. See Su Shih in CHINESE PAINTERS: SUNG DYNASTY.

Barbari, Jacopo de' (c. 1440-before 1516). It is not certain whether this German-Italian painter and engraver received his training in his native Germany, or in Venice, where he was active until about 1500. From then until his death he worked in Germany and Flanders, mostly for royal or noble patrons. His early works are a mixture of the Venetian and German styles; his later production, especially his many engravings, is almost completely Germanic, depending on the styles of Dürer and Cranach. He was a skillful but eclectic artist, capable of adopting the styles of greater men around him but having no true personal style.

Barbiere, Domenico del (see DOMENICHINO).

Barbieri, Giovanni Francesco (see GUERCINO).

Barbizon school. A name given to the initiators of landscape painting in France in the nineteenth century. These painters were thrown together by common aims and poverty; Barbizon is the name of a village on the edge of the Forest of Fontainebleau where most of them resided at one time or another from the 1830's on. The desire of the group was to paint nature as seen, a doctrine in direct antithesis to the prevailing classical theory. This attitude stemmed from the contemporary Romantic movement, although French Romantic painting had at first expressed itself in literary rather than nature imagery. The trend toward landscape painting in France was inspired by the English, through visits of the watercolorists, exhibitions of Constable and especially through the permanent residence in Paris of Bonington. Several of the Barbizon group then turned to a study of the

3. BALDOVINETTI. The Annunciation
National Gallery of Art, Kress Collection, Washington, D.C.

BARNA DA SIENA. Crucifixion
Collegiata Collection, San Gimignano

Dutch landscape and animal painters of the seventeenth century. The greatest and most independent of the "school," Camille Corot (see), seems rather to have developed from those constant sources of French inspiration, Poussin, Claude and the Italian Journey. Nominal head of the group was Théodore Rousseau (see), a man of strong will and rebellious temperament who painted still scenes in a somewhat Dutch manner. More of a figure painter was François Millet (see), who infused peasant scenes and labor with Victorian liberal sentiment. Charles Daubigny (see) interested himself in plein-air principles and so not only anticipated Impressionism, but actually associated with members of that younger group. Others of the Barbizon painters were Dupré, Diaz de la Peña, Troyon, Harpignies, Jacque and François. Despite difficult beginnings, by mid-century most members of the group were in vogue.

Barker, Thomas (1767-1847). Commonly known as "Barker of Bath." British painter of portraits, genre and landscape; conventional in style.

Barnaba da Modena (active c.1364-c.1383). One of the few painters of any importance from Modena, he did most of his work in Genoa. His art is based on the Byzantine style from Venice that pervaded much of northern Italy until half a century later, but it reflects also the Gothic developments of the contemporary Sienese school. He is first heard of in Genoa in 1364, went to Pisa to finish frescoes begun there by Andrea da Firenze, a purpose that was not fulfilled, and is last heard of again in Genoa in 1383. His decoration of the ducal palace at Genoa is lost but signed and dated panel paintings are extant in Frankfort, Berlin, Turin, and the church of San Giovanni Battista at Alba.

Barna da Siena (active middle of the 14th century). An Italian painter from Siena who is one of the most highly respected followers of Simone Martini and Lippo Memmi, though very little is known of his life. The work on which his reputation rests is a fresco cycle on the life of Christ in the Collegiata at San Gimignano. Among the several panel paintings attributed to him are: Christ Bearing the Cross (Frick Collection), four panels of saints (Siena gallery), and the Marriage of St. Catherine (Boston). His color and his types recall Lippo Memmi and Simone, but his strong and tragic compositions in the fresco cycle show a definite affinity with Duccio's treatment of the same subjects in the Siena Majestas. (See illustration.)

Barnes Foundation, Merion, Pa. Founded by the late Dr. Albert C. Barnes as a school and private museum, this institution contains one of the best collections of modern art in the world. Especially noted for its magnificent group of Renoirs, Cézannes, Soutines and Matisses, the Foundation is potentially (it is not yet open to the public) one of the most significant art educational forces in the United States.

Barocci, Federico (1526-1612). Umbrian painter who was born in Urbino and worked there and in Pesaro, Rome, Milan, and Genoa. A follower of Correggio, he produced an art which because of its softness of forms and pastel color may seem to modern tastes oversweet and mannered, but which in its revolutionary treatment of light, movement, and space, and in its emotionalism, was extremely important to the general development of seventeenth-century Baroque art in Europe, influencing both Bernini and Rubens. He began his career under his father, Ambrogio di Federico, and studied with Battista Franco, a Venetian influenced by Michelangelo, working in the Cathedral of Urbino between 1546 and 1551. He was then sent to his uncle, Bartolommeo Genga, architect to Guidobaldo II, in Pesaro and c. 1546 went to Rome where he studied Raphael. He was working in Rome in 1560 with the Maniera (see) painter Federigo Zuccari in the Casino of Pope Pius IV when he was taken very ill. From then on he worked only sparingly and slowly, refusing all large commissions. Among his most famous and much copied works are the Madonna del Popolo (1579, Uffizi), a Deposition (Perugia Cathedral), and an Entombment (Confraternita di Santa Croce, Sinigaglia).

Baronzio, Giovanni (Giovanni da Rimini) (active middle of 14th century). Italian painter; pupil or follower of Giuliano da Rimini. Two signed works exist, a cross in the church of San Francesco at Mercatello (1344) and an altarpiece in the Urbino gallery (1345). Frescoes in the church of Santa Maria in Porto Fuori near Ravenna and others in Ravenna have been ascribed to him. Through Giuliano, his art stems from the sculptural style of Cavallini, though it retains elements of the local Byzantine manner.

Baroque. As a period this term refers to the art of the late sixteenth and the seventeenth century in western Europe. It is generally associated with the architecture, sculpture and painting of the counter-Reformation, with their dramatic compositions, dynamic and infinitely extending spatial qualities and theatrical lighting effects. Anti-classical in both form and spirit, it stressed violent emotional expression, asymmetrical rather than symmetrical arrangements and open rather than closed compositions. Although expressing itself in its most characteristic form in the Catholic and/or aristocratic art of painters like Rubens, Murillo, Caravaggio, etc., it also has its counterparts in such Protestant painters as Rembrandt or even Vermeer. The latter may be considered Baroque by virtue either of their emphasis on melodramatic lighting, as in Rembrandt, or through asymmetry and extension into infinite space, as in Vermeer.

Baroque Museum, Vienna. An important collection of seventeenth- and eighteenth-century works in various media. It is sometimes said to express the most significant period in the history of this city.

Bartholemé, Paul Albert (1848-1928). French painter, better known as a sculptor. Studied with Menn in Geneva and Gerôme in Paris. From 1879 he exhibited sentimental portraits and rustic genres in the moralizing style of Bastien-

Lepage, with an occasional touch of Manet's manner. With the death of his wife in 1886 he retired to sculpture, producing a series of funereal figures which were consolidated in 1895 into his popular Monument to the Dead (Père Lachaise).

Bartolini, Luigi (1892-). Italian painter, graphic artist and critic; belongs to the Expressionist aspect of modern Italian painting and is best known for the delicately expressed power of his etchings.

Bartolo di Maestro Fredi (c.1330-1410). A prolific and influential Italian painter who was most active in Siena but also worked in San Gimignano and Montalcino. He first shared a studio with Andrea Vanni and later collaborated with Luca di Tommé and with his son Andrea. His frescoes in the Collegiata at San Gimignano (probably 1356) are his major work, and he executed various other fresco commissions there and in Siena. Among his important panel paintings are: Coronation of the Virgin (1388, Montalcino gallery), Assumption of the Virgin (Boston), Epiphany (Siena), and Presentation (Louvre). His style derives from Lippo Memmi and Pietro Lorenzetti and is characterized by its gaiety, charm and brilliant color. (See illustration.)

Bartolommeo, Fra (1472-1517). Italian, Florentine. He was not an innovator like many of his Florentine contemporaries. Reflecting the influence of the dominating men of his time, Leonardo da Vinci, Raphael and Michelangelo, his art is dignified, monumental and rather impersonal. He was also considerably affected by the fanatic religious reformer Savonarola, whose sermons caused him in 1497 to burn all his works that were not strictly religious in content, and may have caused him to enter a monastery in 1500. Born in Florence, he entered the shop of Cosimo Rosselli in 1485 with his close friend the painter Albertinelli, and in 1492 opened a shop with Albertinelli. In 1498 he began a Last Judgment for Santa Maria Nuova, which Albertinelli took over when Bartolommeo entered the Dominican monastery at Prato in 1500. For four years he lived there in retirement and did very little painting. He was made director of the painters' workshop in San Marco, Florence, in 1505, and after a trip to Venice in 1508 resumed the partnership with Albertinelli. In 1514 he went to Rome, where he fell under the influence of Michelangelo and Raphael. The same year he contracted malaria and after some further activity in Lucca and Florence died in 1517. His most famous work is the Lamentation of 1516 in the Pitti Palace, done under Leonardo's influence. Other works are in the same gallery and in the Uffizi, in the cathedral and gallery of Lucca, and in the cathedral of Volterra.

Bartolommeo della Gatta (Piero d'Antonio Dei) (1448-1502). Italian painter of the Umbrian school. His style was influenced by Piero della Francesca and by Signorelli.

Bartolommeo Suardi (see BRAMANTINO).

Bartolommeo Veneto (see VENETO).

Basawan (see INDIAN PAINTERS: AKBAR PERIOD).

Baschenis, Evaristo (1607-77). A Bergamese painter of realistic portraits and still lifes. He is especially interesting for his many trompe-l'oeil (see) compositions of musical instruments.

Bassa, Ferrer (active 1324-48). Spanish painter of Barcelona. Considered the founder of the important Catalan school of painting of the late middle ages. Better known from documents because most of his works have disappeared, he was the favorite and court painter of Alfonso III and Pedro el Ceremonioso. Besides murals and altarpieces, there is record of his spending an entire year in illuminating a book. His only extant work is a cycle of murals executed in oil and dealing with the Life of the Virgin and the Passion of Christ in the Convent of Pedralbes, Barcelona (1346-48). These reveal him to have adopted the styles of Florence, Siena and Avignon with local flavor. His figures are Giottesque with a Sienese sense of spatiality. (See illustration.)

Bassano, Francesco (Francesco da Ponte, the Elder) (1470/75-1539/41). Italian painter, father of Jacopo, who was the most famous of a family of painters. Francesco the Elder worked in Bassano as a painter and as an explorer and mining entrepreneur. His style was wholly dependent on that of Bartolommeo Montagna (see).

Bassano, Francesco (Francesco da Ponte, the Younger) (1549-92). The eldest and favorite son of Jacopo (see) and his closest disciple, he worked together with his father and brothers. His most important work was the decoration in the Doge's Palace, for which his father made a rare trip to Venice to help him.

Bassano, Girolamo (Girolamo da Ponte) (1566-1621). Son and pupil of Jacopo (see). He began to study medicine in Padua, but returned to carry on the workshop after the death of Jacopo and Francesco.

BARTOLO DI MAESTRO FREDI. St. Anthony Abbot
National Gallery, London

BASSA. Virgin and Child with Angels
Convent of the Pedralbes, Barcelona

Bassano, Jacopo (Jacopo da Ponte) (c.1510/1515-92). A part of the great tradition of Venetian sixteenth-century painting, he avoided the monumentality and pomp of his more famous contemporaries and developed instead a style of intimate, genre translation of biblical, mythological, and historical scenes. His work is characterized by rural and anecdotal detail, rich though somber color, sharp and brilliant contrasts of light and shade, an almost Baroque treatment of movement and space, and lyrical landscapes. Jacopo probably began under his father Francesco the elder, and later in Venice c. 1535 studied with Bonifazio Veronese, and perhaps Palma Vecchio. His first works, until c. 1542, exhibit the influence of Bonifazio and Pordenone, but from that time until c. 1560 his art shows the impact of Parmigianino's Mannerism (see), learned perhaps from engravings, and possibly even some influence from northern Europe and central Italian realism. This Mannerist element was, however, transformed by Bassano, who remained always essentially Venetian in feeling. His art of this period seems to have had some effect on both El Greco and Caravaggio. In his late style, from the 1560's to his death, he discarded the Mannerist influence and developed the individual style for which he is known. However, the attribution of works still remains problematic, since at the same time he established the large workshop in which both his sons Leandro and Francesco worked with him. One undisputed painting of this period, dated 1562, is in S. Tienisto, Treviso. Typical of the period also are an altarpiece in Angarano, a Flight into Egypt (Ambrosiana, Milan), and a Last Supper (Borghese Gallery, Rome). (See illustration.)

Bassano, Leandro (Leandro da Ponte) (1557-1622). Son, collaborator, and imitator of Jacopo. He worked also in Venice and for Emperor Rudolf II. He specialized in genre painting but did portraits as well. He is essentially more mannered, weaker, and more conventional than his father.

Bastiani, Lazzaro (c.1430-1512). Most important member of a family of painters active in Venice in the fifteenth century. He worked in a style related to the Paduan and Venetian masters of the period, and especially Carpaccio, who is believed to have been his pupil. Only two dated works by him (of 1484 and 1490) are known. His talent was mediocre, and his drawing and composition rather stiff, but some of the presumably late works reveal a handling of light and perspective that ally him with Gentile Bellini.

Bastien-Lepage, Jules (1848-84). French painter of portraits, rustic genre and occasional classical subjects. A student of Cabanel before and after 1870, he first exhibited in 1873 with an allegory, Spring. The sentiment of his rural style often recalls Millet and the technique approaches at times the looseness of Manet. Well known is his Joan of Arc Listening to Voices (Metropolitan) completed a few years before his early death.

Battistello (see CARACCIOLO, GIOVANNI BATTISTA).

Bauchant, André (1873-). French painter of the so-called primitive group or Sunday painters. He takes his themes from nature or history and treats them with loving care for detail as well as a delicate sense of rhythmic pattern.

Baudin, André (1895-). Modern French artist, trained in a provincial school of decorative arts, who developed after World War I amid the friendships of the writer Max Jacob, the painter Juan Gris and others. His art combines some of the qualities of Cubist multiple vision with a decorative linearism and a poetic, even mystical mood.

Baudry, Paul Jacques Aimé (1828-86). French eclectic painter of portraits, historical subjects and mural decoration. His style, based on Italian study of Correggio and the Venetians, was in the end slightly touched by Impressionism. He assisted in the decoration of the Paris Opera House.

Bauhaus. A school founded in 1919 by the architect Walter Gropius at Weimar under the influence of such movements as de Stijl of Holland and of Constructivism (see) and Suprematism (see) from Russia. At the beginning the orientation of the Bauhaus was Expressionist and during that period from 1919 to 1926 Gropius invited Klee, Feininger and Kandinsky to the school as teachers. Even after the Bauhaus moved to Dessau in 1926 and changed to geometric, Constructivist and generally functional attitudes, these painter-teachers stayed on. During the second period, from 1926 to 1933, other painter-teachers were on the Bauhaus faculty, notably Moholy-Nagy and Schlemmer. With the advent of Hitler the Bauhaus closed. See also EXPRESSIONISM, NEO-PLASTICISM.

Baumeister, Willy (1889-). German modernist painter who studied at Stuttgart with Adolf Hölzel. Baumeister was a professor at the Frankfort Academy from 1928 to 1933, his tenure ceasing with the rise of National Socialism. Since 1946 he has been a professor at the Academy in Frankfort. His art, abstract in the international abstract Surrealist sense, is considered among the best in contemporary Germany. (See illustration.)

Bavarian State Art Gallery, Munich. This is the former Alte Pinakothek or Old Pinakothek famed for its collection of European paintings from the fourteenth to eighteenth centuries. It includes works by Botticelli, Raphael, Titian, Rogier van der Weyden, Memling, Dürer, Grünewald, Rubens, van Dyck, Rembrandt and Boucher.

Bawden, Edward (1903-). British watercolorist, decorator, designer of theatrical décor, and book illustrator. His delicate, rather sardonic paintings rely on slight linear forms and transparent color.

Bayeu y Subias, Francisco (1734-95). Spanish court painter. Fellow townsman and brother-in-law of Goya. Francisco studied with Luzán in Zaragoza and with A. González Velázquez in Madrid, and then did decorative work under Mengs. He later served as director of the Santa Barbara tapestry works and as director of the Academy of San Fernando. His output was enormous, including decorations for the royal castles and religious paintings for churches and convents. He also earned money making printed copies of Spanish masters. His official style is cold and classically academic, but his tapestry cartoons portray a new and radical interest in middle-class genre. Both tendencies affected Goya, who was under Bayeu's tutelage when first in Madrid.

Bayeu y Subias, Ramón (1746-93). Spanish painter and etcher. Brother and pupil of Francisco, whom he accompanied to Madrid. He helped Francisco and Mengs and worked with Goya in Zaragoza in 1780. His style was based on Tiepolo, as was Goya's at that time. His etchings are of two classes: original inventions and copies after paintings by Guercino, Ribera and his own brother.

Bazaine, Jean (1904-). French painter and art critic who has written for the *Nouvelle Revue Française* and other journals. In 1935, in company with such painters as Gromaire and Goerg, he founded the *Salon du Temps présent*. His style is abstract in the Expressionist vein.

Bazille, Jean Frédéric (1841-70). Pioneer Impressionist painter of France. Friend of Monet and Renoir in Gleyre's studio, member of the discussion group at the Café Guerbois, Bazille exhibited a precocious example of Impressionism (see) in his Family Group (1868). He was an early exponent of plein-air painting, developing its principles in company with Monet and Renoir. His promising career was cut short by death in the Franco-Prussian war.

Baziotes, William (1912-). Contemporary American painter of bold amoebic-form abstractions which sometimes have the appearance of symbolic or ideographic meaning. Born in Pittsburgh, he went to the National Academy of Design (1933-36), and taught and painted under the W.P.A. art project (1938-41). (See illustration.)

Bazzi, Giovanni Antonio (see SODOMA).

Beal, Gifford (1879-). Contemporary American painter of holiday and entertainment scenes. His early works, after a period of marine subjects, were vigorous, boldly painted scenes of city activities belonging with those of the young Bellows, Kent, and Kroll. Later, he turned to a more decorative and brighter manner, losing in the process a good deal of his earlier vitality. Born in New York, he studied with W. M. Chase, F. V. DuMond, and H. W. Ranger.

Beardsley, Aubrey Vincent (1872-98). British artist in black-and-white best known for his book illustrations and caricatures, the latter typical of anti-Victorian tendencies of the last decade of the nineteenth century. Trying to escape from the materialism of life around him, Beardsley developed a cynical style with a decoratively sinuous line and often applied it to morbid, erotic, or fantastic themes. The mock medievalism of his illustrations for *Morte d'Arthur* and the fascinating "decadence" of his illustrations for the *Yellow Book* magazine represent high points of his work. See ART NOUVEAU and DECADENT ART.

Beauneveu, André (active c.1360-1402). Franco-Flemish illuminator and sculptor. He executed sculpture for Charles V and others and was in the service of the Duke of

BASSANO, JACOPO. Portrait of a Gentleman
National Gallery, London

BAUMEISTER. Composition with Hand and Figure
Private Collection, Germany

BAZIOTES. Primeval Landscape. Philadelphia Museum of Art

Berri. For the latter he assisted in the illumination of a Psalter (Bibliothèque Nationale) in which he painted a series of figures in grisaille (see) that show him to have been a forceful modeler of independent style.

Beaux, Cecilia (1863-1942). American academic portrait painter in the Sargent manner. She achieved great success in her day and won many prizes. Born in Philadelphia, she studied here and abroad with many famous academicians and painted many notables, including Theodore Roosevelt, Cardinal Mercier, Clemenceau and Lord Beatty.

Beccafumi, Domenico (Domenico Mecarino, Meccherino, Mecuccio) (1486-1551). Together with Pacchia and Peruzzi, the leader of Sienese Mannerism (see). Born in delle Cortine, the son of a peasant, Beccafumi was discovered by the owner of the estate on which his father worked and was sent to Siena to study. In gratitude he took his patron's name. In 1510-12 he was in Rome studying Michelangelo and Raphael, and later in 1540 worked at the Castel Sant' Angelo with Pierino del Vaga. His early work shows the influence of Raphael and Fra Bartolommeo, and of Sodoma, with whom he worked in the Oratory of S. Bernardino in Siena. His later work is strongly influenced by the Mannerist features in Michelangelo's art, which he tended to exaggerate. He designed pavements for the Cathedral of Siena (1517-25 and 1544-46) and in his last years occupied himself almost exclusively with sculpture for the cathedral.

Beccaruzzi, Francesco (active 1520-50). A Venetian painter from Conegliano, influenced by Pordenone and Titian, he worked in the vicinity of his home city and Treviso. His art exhibits a certain beauty and warmth of color best exemplified in his masterpiece, the Stigmata of St. Francis (Venice Academy), which was originally painted for S. Francesco, Conegliano.

Beckmann, Max (1884-1950). Distinguished German Expressionist painter and graphic artist. He first studied painting at the Weimar School of Art and was influenced by the monumentality of Hans von Marées. After three years he traveled to Florence and Paris, absorbing the message of the Old Masters, particularly Piero della Francesca and the French primitives, and admiring the contemporary work of Cézanne and Van Gogh. From 1904 to 1914 in Berlin he participated in the Secession movement which showed both Impressionist and Post-Impressionist art. He soon moved from a classically conceived type of painting to a realistic and then a Realist-Impressionist approach in which emotionality plays an important part. The transition point came in the World War I years when Beckmann's experiences as a corpsman in Belgium and France were a great spiritual shock. From this point on, such paintings as The Night, The Woman Taken in Adultery, and, in 1920, The Family, move toward a cold reality in keeping with the growing New Objectivity spirit of the later war years and immediate postwar period. From 1923 to 1932 this bitterness changed to a kind of frozen dream-world quality characteristic of the second stage of the New Objectivity, when the horror of the postwar years yielded to sheer disillusionment. By this time Beckmann's art had reached its typical form, with tightly compressed space suggesting both Post-Impressionist and medieval practices, a harsh contour line from medieval sources, and a richness of color that bespeaks the color symbolism of our times. After

1932 Beckmann's art evolved the complex personal and poetic symbolism that marks him as one of the foremost masters of the modern era. This development is found in the great triptychs such as The Departure, The Actors, Blindman's Buff, as well as in individual works like the magnificent Christ in Limbo (1948) and the many significant graphics of the last period. See EXPRESSIONISM. (See illustration.)

Bedoli, Girolamo (Girolamo Mazzola) (c.1500-69). Born in San Lazzaro and active in Parma, he was an imitator of Correggio and especially of Parmigianino, with whom he worked. His style was an exaggeration and hardening of Parmigianino's, but still brilliant in color, enamel-like in finish, with a Manneristic grace in the handling of figures.

Beechey, Sir William (1753-1839). British portraitist of the Georgian period; example of a highly successful artist in an era when a portrait in oils was considered a necessity by anyone who could afford it. He was painter to Queen Charlotte and did an equestrian picture of George III that caused a sensation. His work is represented among the approximately two hundred portraits of Eton boys, which were left by custom at the Provost's Lodge of that school in lieu of the required leaving-fee; among the other artists represented there are Reynolds, Romney and Gainsborough.

Beham, Barthel (1502-1540). German painter and engraver. He studied first in his native city of Nuremberg with his brother Hans, a pupil of Dürer. About 1527 he went to Munich, where he entered the service of Duke William IV of Bavaria, and among his important works is an extensive series of portraits of members of the ducal house. Aside from a voyage to Italy near the end of his life, it is probable that Beham made a visit there about 1520, for his work, which includes many antique and allegorical subjects, reveals the influence of the Italian engraver Marc Antonio and shows an intimate knowledge of Italian art. (See illustration.)

Bell, Clive (1881-). British critic of art and literature best known for his pioneer modernist works: *Since Cézanne*, 1922, and *Landmarks in Nineteenth-Century Painting*, 1927. He was one of the first to emphasize the form elements as such in modern art. This is the theory of "significant form."

Bellechose, Henri (active c.1400-c.1444). Flemish court painter to the Dukes of Burgundy. He was born in Brabant and succeeded Jean Malouel at the Burgundian court. Between 1416 and 1425 he worked for Jean sans Peur and later for Philippe le Bon at the Chartreuse de Champmol, the Palace of Dijon and other ducal castles. The Holy Communion and Martyrdom of St. Dionysius, ordered for the Chartreuse, is now in the Louvre. This painting, perhaps started by Malouel, is a fascinating agglomeration of mystical symbolism not unlike some Avignon masterpieces in mood. Another attribution to Bellechose and Malouel is the large circular Pietà in the Louvre of about 1400-1410 which is somewhat more Parisian in appearance. His later career was eclipsed by the van Eycks.

Bellegambe, Jean (c.1470-c.1533). Flemish painter of Douai, called "le maître des couleurs" because of the richness of his color effects. In 1510 he did paintings (now lost) for Sant-André-de-Douai, in 1511 the Legend of St. Hubert for the Abbaye de Flines. In 1515 he was called to Cambrai and between 1516-20 he executed his famous polyptych for the Abbaye d'Anchin (Douai). This consists of nine panels, the

BECKMANN. The Gipsy
Stedelijk Museum, Amsterdam

BEHAM. Chancellor Leonhard von Eck
Metropolitan Museum of Art, New York

interior ones representing the Adoration of the Trinity with the Madonna and John the Baptist. His style is highly individual with its delicately elongated figures and ornamental Gothic architecture. But he also shows the influence of Flanders—the sentimentalism of Quentin Metsys—and some of the taste of the French school of Amiens. He was much renowned locally and several of his descendants were painters.

Belle Jardinière, La, by Raphael (see).

Bellini, Gentile (1429-1507). Of the two sons of the Venetian painter Jacopo Bellini (see), Gentile (the older) is the less interesting, partly because fewer of his works are preserved than of Giovanni, but also because unlike Giovanni (see) he adhered to a patriotic and historical kind of art that did not lead to new horizons. He has, however, left a valuable record of the appearance of Venice and some of its illustrious citizens, and his voyage to the Near East is a reminder of the close connections between Venice and the Orient. His first signed work is his portrait in 1465 of Beato

4. BELLINI, GENTILE. St. Jerome in the Wilderness. Toledo Museum of Art, Libbey Collection

5. BELLINI, GIOVANNI. Agony in the Garden. National Gallery, London

Lorenzo Giustiniani (Venice Academy), the Venetian patriarch. He also signed a set of painted organ shutters representing four saints (Museum of San Marco). The style of these is closer to Mantegna than anyone else. Though it is assumed that the Bellini sons received their earliest training from their father, they must also have been in close contact with Mantegna, who was their brother-in-law. In 1466 Gentile was commissioned to paint two scenes from Exodus for the Scuola Grande of San Marco. In 1469 he was knighted and made a count of the Palatinate by Emperor Frederick III. In 1474 he was charged for life with the care of paintings in the grand council chamber of the Doge's palace. With Giovanni he painted battle scenes (destroyed in a fire in 1577) in this palace. In 1479, at the request of the Sultan of Constantinople for a good portrait painter, Gentile was chosen, and soon sailed for the Near East. The only certain work preserved from his sojourn in Constantinople is a portrait of the Sultan (London). From his return in 1480 until his death in 1507 many documents attest to his activity in Venice. Besides those mentioned, the only thoroughly documented portrait is of Caterina Cornaro, Queen of Cyprus (Budapest museum), painted late in his career. A number of profile portraits of Venetian Doges are attributed to his earlier period, notably two in the Correr museum, Venice, and the Andrea Vendramin in the Frick Collection. Gentile's turn from the profile to the three-quarter-view portrait may reflect the visit of Antonello da Messina to Venice in 1475-76. Two altarpieces of the Madonna (one in Berlin and one in London) are signed by Gentile. His most interesting and perhaps most important works are four large canvases painted late in his career. Three of these (Venice Academy) represent the Miracles of the Reliquary of the Holy Cross and are dated 1496, 1500 and c.1501. The subject matter is little more than a patriotic excuse to paint the familiar places of Venice peopled with Gentile's contemporaries. Many figures are no doubt portraits and two of the compositions feature Andrea Vendramin. The pictures are somewhat rigidly and monotonously composed, but their color is rich, unified in tone, and luminous. They reveal an interest in architecture and perspective comparable to Jacopo Bellini's. The fourth canvas, the Preaching of St. Mark in Alexandria (Brera) was begun by Gentile in 1504, and completed by his brother Giovanni. In it, Gentile was able to make use of his knowledge of Oriental architecture and costumes. The brightness of color and fine effect of light in this picture make it more pleasing than the others and it has been suggested that these qualities may result from the collaboration of Giovanni. (See color plate 4.)

Bellini, Giovanni (c.1430-1516). Considered the greatest Venetian painter of the fifteenth century. His life was long, his output prodigious, and his style was decisive not only for his famous pupils Titian and Giorgione but for the direction taken by Venetian painting in the sixteenth century. He may be called the founder of the Venetian High Renaissance style. The illegitimate son of Jacopo (see), he was born about 1430, and is first heard of as a painter in 1460 and 1464, when he worked with his father and his brother Gentile (see) on decorations (now lost) in Padua and Venice. He presumably received his training from his father and must have been in close contact with his Paduan brother-in-law Mantegna in his early years. In 1471 he is recorded as maintaining a studio in Venice with his brother. He took over from Gentile the care of paintings in the Doge's palace in 1479 when Gentile went to Constantinople, and continued the cycle of battle pictures Gentile had begun there (destroyed by fire in 1577). From this time on many documents and dated works indicate that he lived continuously in Venice. At Gentile's death in 1507 he completed the picture of St. Mark Preaching which Gentile had begun for the Scuola di San Marco. In his late years he was held in great esteem, had many commissions, and was extremely influential among the younger generation of painters. In 1506 Dürer wrote from Venice that Giovanni Bellini was very old but was still the greatest of them all. The last work he dated was painted in 1515.

Bellini's work presents a clear and gradual evolution of style from the precise approach to nature of the fifteenth century to the monumental and poetic treatment of the High

BELLINI, GIOVANNI. The Feast of the Gods
National Gallery of Art, Widener Collection, Washington, D.C.

Renaissance. He is justly famous for his emphasis on and skillful handling of color and light, and for the grace, gentleness and devotional character of his figures and compositions. He changed from tempera technique to oil in mid-career, and his use of the latter medium established its predominance in Venetian art thereafter. He probably knew this technique before the visit to Venice of Antonello da Messina, the painter once credited with having introduced it in Italy. With one notable exception near the end of his life, Bellini's painting was almost exclusively of sacred subjects. His early style was closely related to that of Andrea Mantegna, but differs from it in his greater emphasis on color and light, and in his more emotional and less scientific expression in both figures and landscape. Important examples of this period (the 1470's) are the Agony in the Garden (London), the Lamentation in the Brera, Milan (the greatest of many on this theme), the Coronation of the Virgin (Ducal Palace, Pesaro), the Transfiguration (Naples), and the Resurrection (Berlin). By the 1480's he had developed a mature and completely personal style, softer and more luminous than his early work, with greater freedom of movement of figures in space. The great altarpieces of this period make use of architectural settings within which figures are bathed in light and atmosphere. Three altarpieces may be singled out: the "San Giobbe" altar (Venice Academy), painted in the mid-1480's; the altar of 1488 in San Pietro Martire, Murano, and, of the same year, the altarpiece of the church of the Frari, Venice. All of these represent the Madonna flanked by saints in architectural settings. Also of this period is the well-known allegorical panel, inspired by a religious poem, sometimes called the "Madonna of the Lake" (Uffizi). In Bellini's late works (1500 and after), his compositions become still more harmonious and monumental, with broader forms and more open space, and richer and softer handling of color. Landscape, always important, becomes a regular, idyllic touch in his work, and relates it closely to what his pupils Giorgione and Titian were doing at the same time. The Madonna and Saints in the church of San Zaccaria, Venice, of 1505, is a truly High Renaissance work, evolved out of the altarpieces of his middle period. A Baptism of Christ in Santa Corona, Vicenza, makes particularly broad use of landscape. Bellini's one great profane work, the Feast of the Gods (Washington), completed in 1514, was painted for Alfonso d'Este of Ferrara. It is an allegorical and rather reserved bacchanal, in which classical antiquity is blended with Renaissance poetry in the most characteristic Venetian manner. It is generally agreed that Titian assisted the aging master in this work; the left half of the landscape is believed to be his. A few portraits by Bellini are extant, and many more are attributed to him. The most celebrated is that of Doge Leonardo Loredano in the London National Gallery. He also painted innumerable devotional pictures of the Madonna and Child, noted for their variety and grace. Works by Bellini are to be found in museums and collections throughout the Western world. Important examples in the United States, besides the Feast of the Gods, are an early Madonna Adoring the Sleeping Child (Metropolitan), and the St. Francis in

Ecstasy (about 1480), now in the Frick Collection. (See illustrations, including color plate 5.)

Bellini, Jacopo (c.1400-c.1470). The head of an artist family that dominated Venetian painting in the late fifteenth and early sixteenth centuries. Though less known than his famous sons Gentile (see) and Giovanni (see), he doubtless transmitted certain interests and elements of style to them and to his son-in-law Andrea Mantegna. Jacopo was the son of a plumber of Venice and received his artistic training from Gentile da Fabriano. In 1436 he painted a Crucifixion (later destroyed) for a chapel in the cathedral of Verona, and in Ferrara in 1441 he painted a portrait of Lionello d'Este that the patron preferred to one done at the same time by Pisanello. The year 1443 finds him back in Venice, and in 1453 marrying his daughter Nicolosia to Mantegna. In 1460 he and his two sons signed an altarpiece (now lost) for the Gattamelata Chapel of San Antonio, Padua, and in 1466 he collaborated with them again in a decoration (lost in a fire, 1485) for the Scuola di San Marco. The only other significant evidence of his activities as a painter are the four extant paintings signed by him: a Crucifixion (Verona museum) and three half-length Madonnas (Venice Academy, the Brera, and the Tadini Gallery at Lovere). The Brera Madonna is dated 1448. The Crucifixion is considered early, paralleling in style the work of Fra Angelico (1436-65). Of the considerable group of half-length Madonnas that have been attributed to Jacopo the most important is in the Uffizi. Their most notable feature is their rich color, laid on in separate strokes suggesting miniature mosaic work. Far more important than the paintings for an understanding of Jacopo's talent are the two sketch books by him that are preserved in the Louvre and in the British Museum. Without these, Jacopo would certainly be considered a minor figure. The drawings are in pen and ink and silverpoint, one group being on paper and the other on vellum. They embrace an extraordinarily wide variety of subjects and motifs, and reveal a keen interest in secular life and classical antiquity that never would have been suspected from the paintings. Jacopo was evidently fascinated by architecture and by the problems of perspective and foreshortening. These interests, and his manner of rendering mountainous landscape, relate the drawings to the style of Mantegna. They are essentially still Gothic, however, and their dependence on Gentile da Fabriano is equally apparent. Many of the drawings appear to be well-developed compositions of traditional subjects, as though projects for paintings. In this and in their emphasis on architecture they differ from the drawings of Pisanello, which are often compared with them. (See illustration.)

BELLOWS. Lady Jean
Collection Stephen C. Clark, New York

BELLINI, JACOPO. Francis Petrarch
Knoedler Gallery, New York

Bellotto, Bernardo (called Canaletto) (1720-80). Venetian landscape painter, nephew and pupil of Canaletto, whose name he took. From 1747 onward, he lived and worked abroad, first in Dresden for Augustus III, King of Poland and Elector of Saxony, for whom he painted views of Dresden. With the outbreak of the Seven Years' War, he fled to

Vienna, where he worked for Empress Maria Theresa and Prince Liechtenstein (1759-60). Back in the employ of Augustus, he worked first in Warsaw and then again in Dresden in 1762. After a stay at the Russian court (1766-67), he returned to Poland as court painter to Stanislas Augustus. During those last years he painted not only architectural views but religious and historical subjects and equestrian portraits. (See color plate 6.)

Bellows, George Wesley (1882-1925). American painter, disciple of Henri and younger member of the Ashcan School (see). Born in Columbus, O., he attended Ohio State University, but decided on an artistic career and in 1904 came to New York. He studied with R. Henri, K. H. Miller and H. G. Maratta. He opened a studio in 1906 and in 1908 his first landscape won a prize at the National Academy of Design. In 1909, at the age of twenty-seven, he was elected an associate of the National Academy, one of the youngest in its history. In 1910, he became an instructor at the Art Students League; he also taught at the Ferrer School and the Art Institute of Chicago. He died in New York of acute appendicitis. His earliest work is in the broad, vigorous realistic style of the Ashcan School; from the beginning, however, he showed a predilection for more active and spectacular city themes and painted city life and prize-fights with broad bravura. After the Armory Show he moved out of the Ashcan School orbit. His work became technically more subtle but also, perhaps because of his interest in dynamic symmetry and set palettes, more restricted and formal, confined largely to portraiture and landscapes. The earlier gray tonality gave way to a higher pitched palette, the earthy vigor to compositional grandeur and technical virtuosity. In 1916 he took up lithography and produced many prints of great tonal subtlety. (See illustrations, including color plate 7.)

Benaglio, Francesco. Italian painter, active in Verona in the second half of the fifteenth century. One signed altarpiece (1462) by him is in San Bernardino, Verona. He was a close imitator of Mantegna. In 1475 he was sentenced to prison for making obscene wall paintings in the house of a Veronese nobleman.

Benozzo Gozzoli (see GOZZOLI, BENOZZO).

Benson, Ambrosius (died 1550). Flemish painter of Lombard origin. Active in Bruges where he continued the styles of Gerard David and Isenbrant. In 1519 we know him to have been admitted to the painters' guild of Bruges and from 1526-30 he exhibited his paintings there regularly in the January and May fairs. Two paintings of the Holy Family bear his monogram: one in Brussels with side panels and one in Nuremberg. On the basis of these, which show that he was still employing the Lombard sfumato in his shadows, can be made a number of attributions: The Deipara Virgo (Antwerp), the Polyptych of St. Anne (Prado), the Pietà (London), and the portrait of George Baron Hastings (Brussels). (See illustration.)

Benson, Frank Weston (1862-1951). American painter and etcher. Active in Boston, a member of the group known as the "Ten," he painted figure pieces, still lifes and portraits in the genteel and sentimental manner of the late nineteenth century. He also executed a series of murals for the U.S. Library of Congress—Graces and Seasons—but is perhaps best known for his sporting etchings. Born in Salem, Mass., he studied at the Boston Museum School and at the Académie Julian with Boulanger and Lefebvre.

Benton, Thomas Hart (1889-). American genre painter and muralist, leader of the regionalist American Scene painters. Born in Neosho, Mo., the son of a U.S. Senator, he

6. BELLOTTO. View of the Tiber. Detroit Institute of Arts

7. BELLOWS. Stag at Sharkey's. Cleveland Museum of Art, Hurlbut Collection

spent his youth in Washington, D.C. At an early age he began his artistic career as an illustrator for a local newspaper, then studied at the Art Institute of Chicago, and in 1908 went to Paris. On his return to the U.S. in 1913, he was influenced by Cubism and Synchromism. After a tour of duty in the U.S. Navy during World War I, he traveled through the U.S. sketching the American scene. His murals of American life for the New School of Social Research (1930) and the Whitney Museum of American Art library (1931) sparked a renascence of mural painting as well as the American scene in art. In the mid-1930's he renounced modern art and the "effete" East and returned to the mid-West and regionalism. He disavowed the social content of his earlier work and painted a romantic and nostalgic picture of American rural life. His subsequent work exaggerated his formal devices, and though his art became richer in color it became also drier and more stylized in form. Together with Grant Wood and John Steuart Curry, who were painting similar subjects, he dominated one whole phase of American genre and mural painting of the 1930's. With the revival of abstract art in the 1940's his influence in American art dwindled. (See illustration.)

Benvenuto di Giovanni (1436-c.1518). Italian painter, one of the many pupils of Vecchietta, he is first encountered painting frescoes in the Siena baptistry, doubtless as an assistant to his master. A number of signed and dated panel paintings reveal an eclecticism that drew on Florentine, Umbrian and even Venetian masters, particularly in the later works. Important works on panel are a Madonna triptych (1475) in Montepertuso, the Assumption of the Virgin (1498) in the

BENSON, AMBROSIUS. Portrait of a Man
Philadelphia Museum of Art, Johnson Collection

Metropolitan, and a Madonna altar (1509) in Sinalunga. Benvenuto's son, Girolamo, continued his father's manner well into the sixteenth century.

Bérard, Christian (1902-49). French Neo-Romantic painter whose style formed under the influence and advice of such men as Maurice Denis, Bonnard and especially Vuillard. His attitude toward painting was unusual, for he looked upon it as something very private and personal, and showed an unwillingness to exhibit or even to have his work photographed. In addition to sensitive décors for the London and Monte Carlo Ballets Russes, Bérard is best known for highly charged, inward-turning portraits which betray a certain morbidity and spiritual fatigue. He utilized a representational style which seems related to the Picasso works of the Blue Period. See NEO-ROMANTICISM. (See color plate 8.)

Berchem, Nicolas (1620-83). Dutch landscape painter noted for his effectively dramatic and picturesque compositions filled with shepherds, ruins and similar elements. He was exceedingly popular in his day, especially with collectors. A pupil of Jan van Goyen, the naturalistic landscapist, and J. B. Weenix, the picturesque landscapist, Berchem combined the virtues of both approaches. In spite of his facility and popularity, and in spite of the avariciousness of his wife, Berchem's later style was as worthwhile aesthetically as his earlier work. He went on year after year producing the picturesque pastorals which are his particular contribution to Dutch painting. The constructional methods of Claude and the recessional devices of Elsheimer became part of his technique; the way in which he had figures moving away into the composition, their backs turned to the spectator, was his own special device.

Berckheyde, Gerrit Adriaensz. (1638-98). Dutch painter of architecture and landscape. He was a native of Haarlem, where he studied painting under his older brother Job and Frans Hals. With Job he traveled in the Rhineland, visiting Heidelberg before returning to settle in Haarlem. His paintings of buildings are distinguished by a charming attention to detail and to the play of light on stone and brick that relates them to the works of van der Heyden.

Berckheyde, Job Andriaensz. (1630-93). Dutch painter of architecture, landscape and genre. The pupil of Jacob de Wet, he traveled in Germany, and on returning to Haarlem joined the guild and settled there.

Berdecio, Roberto (1910-). Bolivian-born easel painter and muralist associated with the Mexican school; member, Popular Graphic Art Workshop; Guggenheim Fellow, 1940, for perspective studies and space conceptions. His sensitive lithographic portrait heads and landscapes show a keen sense of plastic organization, surface textures and linear rhythms.

Berenson, Bernard (1865-). American-trained art historian and one of the world's outstanding writers on various phases of Italian art. Born in Lithuania, he has lived most of his life in and around Florence, with occasional trips to the United States. His publications include such works as *Drawings of the Florentine Painters*, 1903; *North Italian Painters of the Renaissance*, 1907; *Venetian Painters of the Renaissance*, 1916; *Sienese Paintings*, 1918; *Medieval Art*, 1930; *Aesthetics and History in the Visual Arts*, 1949. Berenson is important in modern criticism for his ability to combine the methods of modern scholarship with a highly intuitive but significant approach to the problems of connoisseurship.

Berettini, Pietro (see CORTONA, PIETRO DA).

Berghe, Fritz van den (1883-1939). Belgian Expressionist and theoretician of the second Laethem-Saint-Martin group. He began as an Impressionist but while spending the World War I years in Holland with his friend de Smet he came under German influence and turned toward Expressionism. His art dealt with social themes and although impregnated with a fanciful and often Surrealist quality, it displays a vital interest in the everyday world. See LAETHEM-SAINT-MARTIN. (See illustration.)

Berlinghieri, Berlinghiero. Active in Lucca, first half of the thirteenth century. One of the best known of the painters associated with the early Franciscan movement. His art stems from indigenous Italian traditions rather than from Byzantium, and it is certain that he was trained in Tuscany, though he was Milanese by birth. He was the father of Barone, Marco and Bonaventura, all of whom were painters. One signed and dated Crucifix (1228) is preserved in the

BENTON. American Life: Power. New School for Social Research, New York

gallery at Lucca, and other Crucifixes have been ascribed to him.

Berman, Eugène (1889-). Russian-born Neo-Romantic painter associated with that movement in France since 1920; has been living in the United States since World War II. His travels in Italy in 1922 were the basis for the subject matter of his work and to a certain extent the morbid, dream-world, introspective style in which they are projected. Berman's world is that of the subconscious but it is a subconscious dominated by unease and unhappiness filled with a certain oppressive quality that is peculiarly his. The backgrounds are frequently architectural and deep and the figures seen in their confines are as though asleep in a frozen world. He has distinguished himself in the realm of theatre design, where his imaginative landscapes and architectural perspectives have been particularly effective. See NEO-ROMANTICISM. (See illustration.)

Bermejo, Bartolommé (also called de Cárdenas and Rubeus) (active to after 1498). Spanish painter of Córdoba, active in Aragon and Barcelona. His artistic origins are mysterious; he displays at first Flemish and later broad Italian tendencies, suggesting travel in both those areas. Important painter and rival of Jaime Huguet, he is supposed to have introduced the oil technique into Aragon. The Flemish exactness of his early style is seen in the Santo Domingo de Silos of the retablo of Daroca (1474, Prado) with its northern architectural background and Spanish overall glitter of decoration. His later romantic chiaroscuro, recalling Giorgione, is observable in the Despla Pietà of 1490 (Barcelona Cathedral). Signed works exist in Italy, suggesting a sojourn there. He also designed stained glass. (See illustration.)

Bermúdez, Cundo (1914-). One of the leading Cuban painters, formerly a diplomat. Groups of musicans are one of his favorite subjects. His Cubist-derived forms are reduced to abstract two-dimensional patterns with intricate rhythms of line and bright vibrating colors.

Berne Museum of Art, Berne. General collection of nineteenth- and twentieth-century European art with strong concentration on Swiss artists. This museum is the most important repository of the work of the Swiss painter Ferdinand Hodler.

Berruguete, Pedro (died 1503/04). Outstanding Castilian painter of his time, working in an Italianate manner reminiscent of Ghirlandaio, Perugino or Carpaccio. Possibly

BERGHE, VAN DEN. Portrait of Edouard Anseele
Beaux-Arts Museum, Ghent, Belgium

BERMEJO. St. Domingo de Silos
Prado, Madrid

BERMAN. Paludes.
Knoedler Galleries, New York

8. BÉRARD. Portrait of René Crevel
Albright Art Gallery, Buffalo

BERTRAM, MASTER. Birth of Christ. Kunsthalle, Hamburg

Berruguete was the "Pietro Spagnolo" who collaborated with Justus of Ghent in the service of the Duke of Urbino in 1477, there learning the Italian style. We know that he worked for the Cardinal Cisneros in the Cathedral of Toledo (c.1483-97), but little survives. His best extant works were perhaps done later for Santo Tomás, Avila, and are now in the Prado. These show a lively anecdotal manner with Italian handling of perspective and anatomy. The paintings are full, however, of the flat ornamental and airless qualities of the native Spanish primitives. A good example is a Miracle of Santo Domingo, which shows the burning of the books.

Bertholle, Jean (1909-). French Surrealist painter whose art, affected by medieval manuscript painting, has moved into the area of the symbolic. His forms are simplified under the influence of modern Cubism. They are, however, charged with the visionary quality of the Surrealist fear world and of manuscripts like the famous Saint-Sévère Apocalypse. The latter also imparts a violently primitive quality to his art.

Bertram, Master (active by 1367-after 1379). German painter of altarpieces. He seems to have been employed by the city of Hamburg in 1367 and was in Lubeck eight years later when Charles IV paid a state visit to that city. His style bears certain resemblances to that of Master Theodoric of Prague. His most important work, the altarpiece of St. Peter, painted in 1379 and now in the Kunsthalle at Hamburg, shows a straightforward treatment of narrative, and a striving to model forms and give them plasticity. (See illustration.)

Besnard, Paul Albert (1849-1934). French easel and mural painter who developed in the tradition of Ingres and who was later influenced by the Pre-Raphaelite school. His mural works are typified by the paintings in the Petit Palais in Paris. Toward the end of his life he became director of the Ecole Nationale des Beaux-Arts. Besnard is one of the last representatives of the old academic tradition in France.

Best-Maugard, Adolfo (1891-). Mexican painter, writer and art educator. Early sponsor of Mexican nativism, he organized Pavlova's 1918 Mexican Ballet. Director of federal art education, 1921-23, he worked to re-establish national values in Mexican art through use of craft forms, as in his own art.

Betto, Bernardino di (see PINTURICCHIO).

Beuckelaer (Bueckelaer), Joachim (c.1530-c.1573). Flemish painter. Specialist in still lifes, kitchen interiors and didactic subjects. He was the pupil of his uncle Pieter Aertsen. He worked for Antonio Mor, filling in the draperies and other secondary details of his portraits. The Ecce Homo was his favorite religious subject.

Bianchi-Ferrari, Francesco (1457-1510). Italian painter of the school of Modena. His style is related to that of Mantegna and Ercole Roberti and is characterized by a metallic quality and hardness of contours reminiscent of intarsia-work. A chronicler names him as the teacher of Correggio, whose early works tend to confirm this statement.

Bibbiena, Ferdinando Galli (1657-1743). A painter of elaborate Baroque theatrical scenery. Born in Bologna and active in Modena, Piacenza, Barcelona, Vienna, and Parma, where for twenty-eight years he worked for the Farnese family. He studied first with Cignani and later with Paradosso, Aldovrandini, and Mannini.

Bicci di Lorenzo (1373-1452). He represents a conservative element in Florence that maintained the late fourteenth-century Gothic tradition at the same time that Masaccio and others were creating the new Renaissance style. He belonged to a family of painters, being the son of Lorenzo di Bicci and father of Neri di Bicci. His style was formed in the tradition of Agnolo Gaddi, to which he later added elements of Gentile da Fabriano's manner when that master was in Florence (1422-25). In 1433 he painted an altarpiece that is a virtual copy of Gentile's Quaratesi altar of 1425. In about 1441

9. BINGHAM. Result of the Election. National Gallery of Art, Washington, D.C.

he is listed as an assistant, along with Piero della Francesca, on the frescoes Domenico Veneziano executed in the church of Sant' Egidio, which may account for a slightly increased plasticity in his latest work. Tax records and the number of extant dated works indicate that his shop flourished. He was at best a master of mediocre talent but a sound craftsman. His preserved works are in excellent condition.

Bichitr (see INDIAN PAINTERS: JAHANGIR-SHAH JAHAN PERIOD).

Biddle, George (1885-). Contemporary American painter in the realist tradition. His portraits and genre scenes are competent, linear, and precise renderings, lacking in warmth and color. Born in Philadelphia, of a noted family, he was educated at Groton and Harvard where he received a law degree. He studied art at the Pennsylvania Academy of Fine Arts and in Munich and Paris. He was instrumental in the formation and administration of the W.P.A. art project. In addition to easel paintings Biddle has also done graphics and mural paintings, the latter represented by the frescoes in the Department of Justice Building, Washington, D.C. and in the Supreme Court, Mexico City, D.F. (See illustration.)

Bierstadt, Albert (1830-1902). One of the most popular American painters of the late nineteenth century, whose romantic glorification of the West brought between $5,000 and $35,000 a painting. He was born in Germany and in 1832 came to Massachusetts, where he spent his youth. In 1853, he returned to Germany to study in Düsseldorf with Achenbach and Lessing, and then travelled in Italy and Switzerland. He came back to the U.S. in 1857 and a year later accompanied a surveying expedition to the Rocky Mountains and Yosemite Valley where he made sketches which became the basis of his later paintings. His grandiose versions of America's natural wonders later gave way to a more sentimental rendering of Indians and wild animals. (See illustration.)

Bigordi (see GHIRLANDAIO, DOMENICO).

Bihzad (see PERSIAN PAINTERS: TIMURID PERIOD).

Bikaner School (see INDIAN PAINTERS: BIKANER SCHOOL).

Biliverti, Giovanni (1576-1644). Florentine painter, born in Maastricht, and son of a Flemish goldsmith, Giacomo Giovanni Bilivelt, who worked in Florence. He was first interested in Correggio, but then came under the influence of his teacher, Cigoli, with whom he worked in Rome c.1595.

Bingham, George Caleb (1811-1879). A popular painter of the American West, whose paintings in lithographic reproduction brought him fame and fortune. However, it is only recently that the monumental realism of his art has been recognized and his place in American art firmly established. Born in Augusta County, Va., Bingham moved in 1819 with his family to Franklin, Mo. After an early apprenticeship to a cabinetmaker and some study of law and then theology, he turned in 1830 to portrait painting. There is some evidence that he studied with Chester Harding or at least saw him paint. At any rate he was established at St. Louis as a portrait painter c.1835, and after a short period of study at the Pennsylvania Academy of Fine Arts, pursued the same profession in Washington, D.C., 1840-44, after which he returned to Missouri to do the genre pictures which eventually brought him fame. He became the expression in paint of vigorous frontier life during the era of Jacksonian Democrary. In such pictures as Fur Traders Descending the Missouri (Metropolitan), Shooting for the Beef (Brooklyn), and the Election series, he depicted at first-hand and with heroic power the everyday life of river-boatmen, hunters, and ordinary citizens. In 1856 Bingham went to Düsseldorf for three years, where the versions of life in the new West that he continued to paint grew more stilted and less immediate. (See illustrations, including color plate 9.)

Birch, Thomas (1779-1851). Born in London, he came to the U.S. with his father, a painter and engraver, in 1793.

BIDDLE. Spring in Tortilla Flat
Whitney Museum of American Art, New York

He painted portraits in Philadelphia, but is most noteworthy as one of the earliest of the marine landscapists in the U.S.

Birth of Venus, The, by Sandro Botticelli (see).

Bishandas (see INDIAN PAINTERS: JAHANGIR PERIOD).

Bishop, Isabel (1902-). Contemporary American painter. best known for Rubenesque studies of working girls done with sympathy and sensitivity. Born in Cincinnati, she began her studies in Detroit and continued them in New York under K. H. Miller.

Blackburn, Joseph (active in America 1752-1763). An English or Scotch painter, trained in the tradition of Hudson and Highmore, he painted portraits in Bermuda and New England. His art has the mannered elegance of the typical society portraitist of the period. A mediocre artist, his portraits with their conventional backgrounds are good in color but unimaginative, repetitious, and faulty in drawing.

black-figured style (see GREEK PAINTING).

Blake, William (1757-1827). British painter, engraver, poet and mystic. An imaginative genius of tremendous originality, his art was not truly accepted until almost a century after his death, when he became a strong influence. His vital energy and passion lifted his art to a new visionary plane, entirely personal in quality. The mystical paintings and sketches evoke another world; they influenced a youthful group of later followers known as The Ancients, including among others John Linnell and Samuel Palmer. Among the different kinds of work done by Blake are unique paintings and engravings that illustrate his own sensitive poetry, the works of Dante and the Bible. Often compared with that of Michelangelo in the expressiveness of physical forms, Blake's style is more clearly related in both form and spirit to the Mannerists of the mid-sixteenth century. The British painter sets his elongated forms in motion across the surface of the page or sheet, maintaining a certain two-dimensionality within which the forms twist and writhe in their somewhat artificial (i.e., mannered), yet very expressive fashion. Apprenticed to an engraver at fourteen, Blake pursued the illustrator's career while writing his own poetry and painting watercolors. He evolved a special method of color printing, producing illuminated editions of his own writings with colored drawings. A fanatically honest person, he resisted patronage and its implications, remaining obscure until 1818 when his disciple Linnell formed a group around him, buying his drawings and helping to secure such commissions as the illustrations for the *Book of Job* and the *Divine Comedy*. (See color plate 10.)

Blakelock, Ralph Albert (1847-1919). An American Romantic landscape painter whose life was marred by tragedy, he is noted for his moonlit scenes done with originality and sincere poetic feeling. Heavy with pigment, these somber landscapes of silhouetted trees against golden skies are sensitive, romantic evocations of the mystery of darkness. In its earlier phase his art is related to the Hudson River school (see), but after a trip to the West (1869-72) he introduced Indian life into his work. He later became progressively less concerned with reality and more with poetic effect. Blakelock was born in New York City, the son of a physician, and studied medicine at the City College. He turned to painting and

BIERSTADT. The Buffalo Trail, Museum of Fine Arts, Boston

attended Cooper Union Institute for a short period, but was largely self-taught. His painting did not meet with public favor, and, dogged by poverty, supporting a large family, forced to sell his paintings for next to nothing, he broke down and was committed to an asylum in 1899. Seventeen years later, after he had achieved fame and his pictures were attracting record prices, he was rediscovered and his release arranged. He was showered with honors, voted a full member of the National Academy of Design, and exploited by dealers. But none of this meant anything to him any longer, and returning to the asylum in 1918, he died the next year. His art is close to that of Albert P. Ryder, not only in appearance, since both produced heavy layers of paint by successive glazing, but also in sensitive introspection and Romantic mood. (See illustration.)

Blanch, Arnold (1896-). Contemporary American painter. His art was formerly characterized by a poetic treatment of ruin and decay but he has more recently turned to abstraction. Born in Mantorville, Minn., he studied with Henri, Sloan, and K. H. Miller.

Blanchard, Jacques (1600-38). Italianate painter called "the French Titian." He became an exponent of colorism through his studies of Titian while working for the Duke of Savoy in Italy. His style proved popular on his return to France and he was engaged in much official decoration, including the Hôtel of President Perrault. His favorite subjects were Madonnas and Holy Families.

Blanche, Jacques Emile (1861-1942). French painter and man of letters. A specialist in portraits and still lifes, he studied with Gervex and Humbert and exhibited regularly from 1882. His portraits, which include many of the foremost personalities of his time, are in a lively style based in part on the conventions of eighteenth-century English artists and on the tonal effects of Whistler. Besides individual portraits he has painted numerous groups such as that of the Thaulow Family (Luxembourg). As a writer Blanche published novels of the modern world of art such as *De Gauguin à la Revue Nègre* and contributed volumes on Cézanne and on French primitive painters of the late medieval period.

Blarenberghe, Louis Nicolas van (1716/19-1794). French painter of Netherlands origin. Noted for his works in gouache and in miniature. He learned the painting of battles from his father and from van der Meulen. His series of the naval battles of Louis XV, now in the Louvre, is a historic document. He is also known for his harbor views.

Blashfield, Edwin Howland (1848-1936). American mural painter in the academic tradition who produced a great many decorations in an eclectic manner typical of the period —pompously classical machines without inspiration. He was born in New York City and studied in Paris with Bonnat, Gérôme, and Chapu, from whom he inherited the standard academic technique and attitude. His most noted murals are in the dome of the Library of Congress, the Court House in

BLAKELOCK. Moonlight. Brooklyn Museum

BINGHAM. Shooting for the Beef. Brooklyn Museum

BLES, DE. Christ in Limbo. Detroit Institute of Arts

10. BLAKE. Queen Katherine's Dream. National Gallery of Art, Rosenwald Collection, Washington, D.C.

Baltimore and the state capitols of Minnesota, Iowa, and Wisconsin.

Blaue Reiter, Der (see EXPRESSIONISM).

Bles, Herri Met de (1480?-after 1550). Flemish painter of landscape and history. Chroniclers differ as to his origin, his travels and even his name, which appears variously as: Blesius, Civetta, Henrice da Dinant. He lived a long time in Italy. In Flanders he appeared as a friend and rival of Joachim Patinir, to whom he was possibly related. He may also have lived in Amsterdam and have taught Franz Mostaert. He produced many paintings, mostly landscapes, which he signed with an owl, the nickname of Bouvignes where he may have been born. He made little compositions of great delicacy with brightly colored figures in the landscape. He is supposed to have painted Dante's Inferno in the Doge's Palace, Venice, and the Tower of Babel (Venice Academy). (See illustration.)

Bloemaert, Abraham (1564-1651). Dutch painter who perfected a strongly Italianate style. He studied first in Utrecht and then for a period of several years in Paris. After working in Amsterdam a short time he settled in Utrecht, where he was the master of a number of excellent Dutch painters, including Jacob Cuyp and the Honthorst brothers.

Blondeel, Lancelot (1496-1561). Flemish painter, engraver and architect. Probably traveled in Italy, judging from the Italian reminiscences in his work—garlands, cupids and arabesques. He especially designed cartoons for tapestry, sculpture and goldsmith work. He and van Scorel were hired to repair the van Eyck altarpiece in Ghent. He preferred religious subjects, which he complicated with architectural motifs and paint of gold.

Bloom, Hyman (1913-). Contemporary American Expressionist painter active in Boston. Born in Latvia, he came to the U.S. in 1920 and studied at the Boston Museum School with Denman Ross and Harold Zimmerman. Influenced by Soutine, he paints in a highly emotional and richly pigmented style. His earlier works dealt with Jewish life and religious ritual; later he turned towards images of death, decay, and putrefaction; and more recently to bodies being dissected—all painted with a jewel-like opulence. (See illustration.)

Blue Boy, The, by Thomas Gainsborough (see).

Blue Rider, The (Der Blaue Reiter: see EXPRESSIONISM).

Blume, Peter (1906-). Contemporary American painter who works in a style of meticulous realism with Surrealist overtones. His earliest work was an outgrowth of Cubism (see), but in the early 1930's he turned toward Surrealism (see) and achieved recognition with South of Scranton (Metropolitan), which won first prize at the 1934 Carnegie International. In The Eternal City (1934-1937, Museum of Modern Art) he undertook a social statement of complex symbolism. His most recent work has been almost purely a minutely detailed transcription of reality. He was born in Russia, grew up in Brooklyn, and studied at the Educational Alliance, Art Students League and the Beaux-Arts. (See illustration.)

Blythe, David Gilmor (1815-1865). Born in East Liverpool, Ohio, he spent most of his life in Pittsburgh, first as an apprenticed woodcarver and later as a painter of portraits and satiric genre. During the Civil War, he followed the 13th Pennsylvania Regiment, sketching scenes of action which he later painted.

Boccaccino, Boccaccio (c.1467-1524/5). Italian, school of Ferrara. He probably learned his art in the shop of Ercole Roberti or another local painter. Later he was influenced by the Venetians Bellini, Cima and Giorgione. Before 1506 he was active in Ferrara, Venice and Cremona, and from 1506-19 he painted his major work, the frescoes in the cathedral of Cremona.

Boccioni, Umberto (1882-1916). Italian Futurist painter and sculptor who studied with Balla in Rome; a signer of the First Futurist Manifesto, Milan, 1910. He was one of the most intelligent and original of the Futurist school, outstanding as a sculptor (as in the well-known Unique Forms of Continuity in Space, Museum of Modern Art) and in the realm of aesthetic theory. He prepared the Manifesto of Futurist Sculpture, 1912, advancing the use of unconventional machine-derived materials for sculpture. The kind of fluid movement developed by Boccioni, one form flowing into another, is very effective not only in the suggestion of movement but also in the projection of his "States of Mind." See FUTURISM. (See illustration.)

BLUME. Light of the World
Whitney Museum of American Art, New York

BOCCIONI. Dynamism of a Football Player
Sidney Janis Gallery, New York

BLOOM. The Rabbi. Collection Earle Ludgin, Chicago

Böcklin, Arnold (1827-1901). Swiss easel and mural painter noted for his mysticism, symbolism and generally poetic approach. There is an emotional intensity and a vibrant physical quality in works like the famous Play of the Wave that suggest the later Lovis Corinth in Germany. Pictures like the Odysseus and Calypso are nineteenth-century equivalents for the mysticism of Munch and Hodler, while the morbid intensity of his famous Isle of the Dead appears to have had a direct effect on the artistic development of Giorgio di Chirico. To a certain extent he was influenced by the mysticism

BOHROD. Landscape near Chicago
Whitney Museum of American Art, New York

BOILLY. Portrait of a Young Man
Philadelphia Museum of Art, Johnson Collection

of Botticelli and the psychotic quality of the Flemish painter Hugo van der Goes.

bodegón (Sp.). Literally a tavern or eating-house; used in Spanish painting to describe pictures involving fruit, vegetables, game, fish and other edibles in a tavern or kitchen setting.

Boeckhorst, Johann (known as Jan Lange) (1605-68). Flemish painter of German origin. Pupil of Jacob Jordaens. In 1635 he assisted in the decorations for the entry of the Cardinal-Infant Ferdinand into Antwerp. In 1636 and 1639 he traveled in Italy. He did church paintings, history and mythological subjects in a decorative manner. His History of Apollo served as the model for a series of eight tapestries.

Bohrod, Aaron (1907-). Contemporary American painter of genre and cityscapes. Born and active in Chicago, he studied with Sloan, Robinson, and K. H. Miller. Under the W.P.A. he executed several murals in Illinois and was the recipient of Guggenheim fellowships in 1936 and 1937. More recently he has been resident artist at the University of Wisconsin. (See illustration.)

Boilly, Louis Léopold (1761-1845). French painter, engraver and lithographer. Son of a wood sculptor who was apparently his only tutor, Boilly specialized in portraits and paintings of manners and customs. His output was enormous, amounting to an estimated 5,000 portraits and 500 genres, the majority of which are still in private collections. Active in Paris from 1784, Boilly survived the Terror despite his reputation for risqué subjects and marketed paintings of social manners to all regimes down to the Restoration. From 1817 he expressed himself in the new medium of lithography. His style is one of great exactitude with a polished finish to his paintings, stemming probably from his study of the Dutch, particularly Terborch and Pieter de Hooch. Typical is the Arrival of the Stagecoach (1803, Louvre). (See illustration.)

Bol, Ferdinand (1616-80). Dutch painter of portraits and history. He studied in about 1635 in Amsterdam with Rembrandt, to whose works his own show so strong a resemblance that they have frequently been confused. Bol became exceedingly popular and was often called upon to fill important civic commissions, chiefly for large group portraits.

Boltraffio, Giovanni Antonio (1467-1516). Milanese painter, one of the group of imitators of Leonardo da Vinci that sprang up when that master worked in Milan. Boltraffio spent most of his life in his native city, but was active for short periods in Bologna (1500) and Rome (1513). Except for typical Milanese elements in his work—heavy, immobile forms and somewhat awkward compositions—he was from the start wholly dependent on Leonardo, who came to Milan in 1485. His early works are mostly half-length figures of Christian or mythological personages, drawn in a rather dry and painstaking manner and finished with a hard and glossy paint surface. Characteristic of his female types are full and rounded chins and thin hands with outspread fingers. Later he painted larger and more involved compositions, of which the best example is the Casio Madonna with Saints and Donors (1500) in the Louvre. He was outstanding in the Milanese school as a portrait painter, and has even been suggested as the author of the Belle Ferronnière (Louvre), otherwise attributed to Leonardo. (See color plate 11.)

Bombois, Camille (1883-). French primitive painter (of the self-taught group) that includes Rousseau and Vivin. Descended from country folk, Bombois has been both a day laborer on farms and a member of a wrestling troupe. In 1907 he began to study the Old Masters in the Louvre and to paint. When he returned from a distinguished service in World War I he found that his wife had succeeded in selling all of his pictures. Since 1923 his reputation has been growing and his paintings of people and landscapes, directly seen and unsophisticated, are among the most effective of their kind. (See illustration.)

Bonaiuti, Andrea (see ANDREA DA FIRENZE).

Bone, Muirhead (1876-1953). Scottish painter and etcher who began as a student of architecture. Influenced by Whistler and Meryon in etching, he did a series of scenes of his native Scotland. He is also known for his brilliant topographical landscape drawings and his magazine illustrations.

Bonfigli, Benedetto (active 1445-96). Italian painter in Perugia who, along with others, perpetuated the courtly,

BOMBOIS. Before Entering the Ring
Museum of Modern Art, New York

narrative style of the Florentine Benozzo Gozzoli after that master visited Umbria. Most of his work was executed in Perugia, where he became a renowned citizen and held public office. His chief undertaking was the fresco of a chapel in the town hall (begun in 1455 and not quite finished at his death) depicting the Crucifixion and scenes from the life of St. Louis. Many important panels on sacred subjects are in the Perugia gallery.

Bonheur, Marie Rosalie (Rosa) (1822-99). French painter of animals best known, perhaps, for her gigantic Horse Fair (Metropolitan). Trained only by her father, a landscapist, she early showed great determination in the pursuit of her career and was a quick success as an animal painter. Her paintings, which once commanded a great price, are marked by conscientious observation of movement and detail, but academic color.

Bonifazio Veronese (Bonifazio de' Pitati) (1487-1553). Venetian painter who was born in Verona and about whose identity there has been a great deal of confusion. Because of a variety in style and quality and a difference in recorded names, his works were at one time ascribed to three distinct hands. At present they are considered the works of one painter (probably a pupil of Palma Vecchio), whose best works date 1530-40. In 1531, he began decorations in the Palazzo Camerlenghi, Venice, which were finished by his pupils and others, including Tintoretto. His only signed work is an altarpiece now in the Palazzo Reale, Venice, which was originally executed (1533) for the Scuola dei Sartori. On the whole he is quieter and more refined than Palma Vecchio, and an excellent colorist, though he was lacking in temperament and his work is devoid of compositional interest. He painted with a great deal of anecdotal detail and is important for his influence on Jacopo Bassano. His style declined precipitously after 1540, either because of a protracted illness or the great number of commissions he undertook and relegated to his workshop.

Bonington, Richard Parkes (1802-28). British painter in oils and watercolor. Showed great talent at an early age with a variety of themes and techniques but became best known as an exponent of the Romantic landscape, i.e., the landscape of mood. Taken to France at an early age, he learned watercolor and lithography there. At fifteen he studied under Baron Gros in Paris, where his work began to sell, and also in London. His presence in France may be considered a direct influence on the rising school of landscapists in that country. During his short lifetime he did seascapes, Italian scenery pictures, and historical studies typical of the Romantic age—all in rich colors and strong contrasts of light and shade. After 1824 he turned to oils and under the influence of Delacroix did a number of Orientalist illustrations for the *Arabian Nights.* In his last few years the young Englishman was affected by the rising star of the great landscapist Constable. We may distinguish between the early dexterity of Bonington in watercolor and his later work in oils. The earlier style was at that time still an English novelty with its delicacy of execution, its feeling for light and a charm that is independent of the subject portrayed. From here the transition to the spontaneous emotive handling of oils characteristic of the young Romantics was but a short step. With Turner and Constable, Bonington is responsible for the pochade fashion, i.e., rapid records in oil paint of transitional and fleeting effects in nature. (See color plate 12.)

Bonnard, Pierre (1867-1947). An outstanding French painter of the Nabis (see) group and particularly of its Intimist branch; began as a law student, then went to the Beaux-Arts; from there to the Académie Julian where he met Denis, Vuillard, Sérusier and others. It was Sérusier who brought the message of Gauguin and Japanese prints to the group, and especially to Bonnard. Bonnard participated in the formation of the Nabis and shared a studio with Vuillard, Maurice Denis and the theatrical producer Lugné-Poë. He contributed to the artistic work of the periodical *La Revue Blanche,* helped with the sets and costumes for the Théâtre de l'Oeuvre and did a set of lithographs for the picture dealer-publisher Ambroise Vollard in connection with *Quelques Aspects de la Vie de Paris.* His first exhibition was in 1896 at the Durand-Ruel Gallery. He then did more illustrations for books, some quite influential in setting the tone for the modern illustrated book through the mingling of text with pictures. A good many of these very beautiful books are part of Vollard's extensive and continuing publishing program in which many artists took part. Bonnard's early style as a painter and member of the Nabis group is typical of the Intimist side of their effort and distinctly parallel to that of Vuillard, with whom he was very friendly. But basically he appears to have been drawn to the beauty of Impressionist color for its own sake, and once he had moved away from the literary and symbolic atmosphere of *La Revue Blanche,* his art became a more imaginative kind of Impressionism; he ventured into deliberate but not too disturbing dissonances of color and into minor keys that have a charming decorative effect. This decorativism, however, is abstract in the full modern sense of the word, and its structural quality was shortly after to prove of great interest to such painters as Matisse. More than this, Bonnard's feeling is for the large space in the mural sense and if his murals are not altogether traditional in their relationship to the wall, they have a powerful and still patently emotive effect that parallels the mural interests of certain members of Die Brücke in Germany. His art, however it may suggest Impressionist color, is never purely light-describing but reduces the various elements to a preconceived design of form and color, contributing to the Fauve movement of the pre-World War I period and apparently later receiving from it in turn certain clear stimuli. Bonnard's own description of his painting was that it lay somewhere between Intimism and decoration. See FAUVISM, INTIMISM, SYMBOLISM. (See illustrations, including color plate 13).

Bonnat, Leon Joseph Florentin (1834-1923). French painter and collector. Trained by Madrazo in Madrid, Cogniet in Paris, much-traveled in Italy and the Orient, Bonnat went through a series of styles. He was influenced by Caravaggio, Ribera and the Bolognese. Among his official commissions is the Martyrdom of St. Denis (Pantheon, Paris) and among his portraits, that of Victor Hugo. His private collection is now the Museum of Bayonne.

11. BOLTRAFFIO. Portrait of a Youth
National Gallery of Art, Booth Collection, Washington, D.C.

Bono da Ferrara (active mid-15th century). Ferrarese painter, a pupil of Pisanello in Verona and later in the Squarcione shop in Padua. He was among those who, with Mantegna, helped paint the frescoes (destroyed in World War II) in the Eremitani church there. He also worked for the Este of Ferrara, and one signed painting by him is known, a St. Jerome in the London National Gallery.

12. BONINGTON. Scene in Normandy
National Gallery, London

Bonsignori, Francesco (c.1445-1519). Veronese painter known as a pupil and follower of Mantegna in Mantua, but before entering that shop (c.1490) he was active in Venice and Verona, where the local styles were not without influence on his art. He became a court painter to the Gonzaga in Mantua and acquired a reputation as a portraitist. His style is Mantegnesque but he was one of the most independent of Mantegna's pupils. He excelled in facial expression, and his subdued but pleasing color shows the influence of the Veronese school at its best. (See illustration.)

Bonvicino, Alessandro (see MORETTO DA BRESCIA).

Bonvin, François (1817-87). French painter and engraver of genre. Of humble and difficult origins, Bonvin struggled, self-taught, to an important place amongst French Realistic painters. Like his contemporary, Courbet, Bonvin showed an early interest in the Dutch and Flemish paintings of the Louvre. He traveled in the Lowlands and was a supplier to the late nineteenth-century craze for domestic genre and still lifes, such as the Copper Fountain (Luxembourg).

13. BONNARD. The Tablecloth. Phillips Collection, Washington, D.C.

BONNARD. Nude. Museum of Modern Art, Brussels

BORDONE. Daphnis and Chloe. National Gallery, London

BONSIGNORI. A Venetian Senator
National Gallery, London

Bordone, Paris (1500-71). Venetian painter born in Treviso. He was a student of Titian and was influenced also by Giorgione and Palma Vecchio. Although a close follower of Titian, he was forced, because of the enmity of his former teacher, to work in other areas—throughout northern Italy, in France for Francis II and the Cardinals of Lothringen and Guise, and in Augsburg for the Fuggers. Unfortunately most of these works are now gone. He was an excellent painter in the Venetian tradition, perhaps closest to Palma Vecchio and with something of Lotto's lyricism, a fine colorist, a virtuoso of flesh painting, but with an essentially phlegmatic temperament. (See illustration.)

Borduas, Paul Emile (1905-). Canadian painter from Quebec province who grew up "between the river and the mountain orchards" of his native village. He was taught by a local painter, then at Montreal and Paris, emerging finally as a leading abstract painter.

Borgognone (Ambrogio da Fossano) (c.1450-1523). Milanese painter who worked for many years for the Sforza family in the Certosa at Pavia, where he painted frescoes and altarpieces, and designed stained glass, choir stalls and ornaments for the façade. His conservative and quiet style is based on that of Foppa, though later works reveal superficial influence from Leonardo da Vinci and certain unexplained suggestions of northern European influence. Major works by him are preserved in the Brera and in London, and an Assumption of the Virgin is in the Metropolitan.

Borrassá, Luis (active 1380-1424). Spanish painter of Barcelona. His adoption of the International Gothic style (see) led to great activity, rivaling that of his influential contemporaries the Serra family. He was much employed by Juan I of Aragon and by cathedrals and convents around Barcelona. Typical of his manner is the retablo of St. Peter (Tarrasa).

Bosch, Jerome (Hieronymus van Aeken) (active 1488-1516). Flemish painter born in Hertogenbosch (Bois-le-duc) of a family of painters originally from Aachen (Aeken, Aix-la-Chapelle). He worked all of his life in his home town, and

BOSCH. Bagpipe scene in hell (detail from Garden of Earthly Delights). Escorial, Madrid

achieved a unique international reputation, being mentioned by van Mander and even Vasari (see), collected by Philip II of Spain and Felipe de Guevara, and acting as advisor to Charles V of Spain. He painted religious pictures, devilries, allegories, and genre scenes. He treated visions as real and reality as a vision, which makes him especially popular among contemporary Surrealists, but he was essentially a deeply religious and mystic artist. He was a pessimistic moralist, mistrusting both God and man, viewing the world as an accumulation of delusive phantoms, in which the borderlines between hallucination and reality, men and devils, animate and inanimate objects, good and evil are obliterated. Earthly life to him was a phantasmagorical dream, and paradise not much different from hell. He painted in a meticulously realistic manner scenes which are absolutely fantastic in conception. His art grows out of the medieval tradition of drollery and is archaic in its composition and perspective but modern in its illusionism and reality. His art seems a sport in the general tradition of Flemish painting, yet it had a profound influence in subject and technique on subsequent painting. and especially Brueghel. He painted on the periphery of art and his attitude is the obverse of the false security and the empty dogma of serene order immortalized in the art of the High Renaissance. It is logical to assume that he was trained by his father, but the first record of his activity is as a designer of stained glass and tapestries. He is listed as a member of the Confraternity of Notre Dame of Bois-le-duc (1480-1512) and five signed works exist: St. John of Patmos (Berlin), Temptation of St. Anthony (Lisbon), Adoration of the Magi (Prado), the Altarpiece of the Hermits and the Altarpiece of St. Julia (both Doge's Palace, Venice). His early work shows some connection with Geertgen tot Sint Jans and the Master of the Virgo inter Virgines, but he had a limited repertoire which he repeated, and both attributions and dating are therefore extremely difficult. Among his attributed works are the Ecce Homo, the Haunted Garden, the Seven Deadly Sins, and the Hay Wagon (all in the Escorial), Calvary (Ghent), the Prodigal Son (Rotterdam), the Quack (Prado), the Juggler (St. Germaine-en-Laye), and the Boat of Fools (Louvre). (See illustrations, including color plate 14.)

Boscoreale paintings. One of the greatest cycles of Roman mural painting known today. These paintings were discovered in 1900 in a country house at Boscoreale near Pompeii. This villa was decorated in the Architectural Style (II) of Roman painting (see), which was popular in the first century B.C. One side room, now in the Metropolitan, was painted with urban and rural vistas, of a remarkably illusionistic type. The reception room had a series of large figures painted against a red wall, similar in effect to the Villa of the Mysteries in Pompeii. These figures, rendered in an especially dignified fashion, are remarkable for their psychological insight. Their exact identities are unknown but it is usually assumed that they were historic personages. The Metropolitan possesses a woman playing a lyre; the Naples Museum has a superb study of a philosopher. (See illustration.)

BOSCOREALE PAINTING. Woman with Lyre
From Boscoreale Villa, Pompeii
Metropolitan Museum of Art, New York

Both, Johannes (Jan) (c.1618-52). Dutch painter and engraver who studied with his father and under Bloemaert. With his brother Andries he made a trip to France and Italy. In Rome, where he stayed for some time, he came under the influence of the French painter Claude Lorrain, whose classical landscape style had a permanent effect on his painting of landscape. Returning to Utrecht he became head of the painters' guild. His landscapes occasionally show small figures illustrating biblical and mythological themes, but for the most part they are golden, romantic panoramas with rustic details in the Italian manner.

Botticelli, Sandro (1444/5-1510). One of the most important and individual figures of the late fifteenth-century Florentine school. His art was closely associated with the humanist culture and learning centered in the ruling circle of the Medici family, and especially with Lorenzo the Magnificent. With Botticelli begins the trend toward poetic and philosophical expression in art that depends on the interests of its patrons and that characterizes much of the painting of the High Renaissance after 1500. Stylistically, Botticelli is an offshoot of the lyrical, realist art of Fra Filippo Lippi, and the mystical abstraction of his later work has been called a revival of Gothic tendencies. He created a type of grace and beauty of face and figure so personal to him that it is instantly recognizable to anyone having the least acquaintance with Renaissance art. Alessandro di Mariano dei Filipepi, called Botticelli, was born in Florence sometime between March, 1444 and February, 1445, the son of a leather curer. His nickname comes from his eldest brother, who was called "il Botticello," or "little barrel." He was apprenticed first to a goldsmith, then to Fra Filippo Lippi, and it is assumed he worked later with Verrocchio, whose influence is apparent in his earliest extant works. His entire professional life seems to have been spent in Florence, except for the years 1481-82, when he worked in Rome on the Sistine Chapel wall frescoes.

His work falls into three divisions, the 1470's, the 1480's and the late style of the 1490's. He was registered in the guild of St. Luke in 1472, though some works from his hand are dated as early as 1469-70. In this early period, influence is discernible from Fra Filippo Lippi, Verrocchio, and the Pollaiuoli, but by 1480 Botticelli had developed a completely individual style. In the mid-1470's he began to be heavily patronized by the Medici, and painted frescoes (now lost) in the Palazzo Vecchio relating to their successful suppression of the Pazzi revolt. The Adoration of the Magi of c.1478 (Uffizi) contains many Medici portraits and a presumed self-portrait. There are independent portrait panels from about 1478 of Giuliano de' Medici (Berlin) who was murdered in that year, and of Simonetta Vespucci (the identification is uncertain), Giuliano's mistress who had died in 1476. The Mars and Venus of about the same time (London) is an allegory relating to these lovers. About 1478 Botticelli painted the two large panels for which he is best known, the Primavera (Spring) and the Birth of Venus (both in the Uffizi). These works represent a flowering of secular humanist spirit, and frank and open use of figures from classical mythology. Their subjects are free interpretations of classical and contemporary poetry popular in the Medici circle, and they were painted for a Medici villa at Castello. Among the most lyrical and poetic works to come out of the Renaissance, they sum up Botticelli's early development in the graceful, slightly melancholy figures in which detailed anatomy is sacrificed for smooth, linear elegance, in their unreal and tapestry-like, flower-studded setting, and in their youthful and sensuous exuberance.

The middle period, the 1480's, begins with Botticelli's part in the fresco decoration of the Sistine Chapel walls in the Vatican (1481-82). Three large compositions from the Old Testament show his powers of composition on a large scale and again include various Medici portraits and recognizable Florentine buildings. Ghirlandaio's work on the same project is similarly concerned with his Florentine patrons and their background. Several religious works of this period establish Botticelli's application of his graceful ideal to the figures of sacred legend, particularly the Madonna and angels. Four well-known paintings of this group are in the Uffizi: the Madonna and Child Enthroned, the Coronation of the Virgin, and two tondi (circular pictures), the Madonna with the Pomegranate and the Coronation of the Virgin with the Magnificat. Botticelli's late work of the 1490's reflects the unsettled state of civic affairs in Florence, and his own personal turn away from the secular and the poetic toward a religious mysticism. He was an avowed follower of the fanatic religious reformer Savonarola, who was set up as head of the republic by the French invader Charles VIII in 1494. His protector Lorenzo de' Medici had died in 1492 and the successors were forced to quit Florence. Typical paintings of this period are the Calumny of Apelles (Uffizi), the Lamention over Christ (Munich), and the highly spiritualized Nativity (London), signed and dated 1500. These works are austere and abstract, and display an excited nervousness quite at variance with the relaxed grace of his earlier work. After 1500 Botticelli appears to have painted little, and no work after this date is extant. A large group of drawings illustrating Dante's *Divine Comedy* are preserved in Berlin and in the Vatican Library. They were begun for the Medici about 1485, and left unfinished when the patrons fled the city. Botticelli's pupil Filippino Lippi carried on his lyrical and linear style, giving it a personal and rather mannered aspect. (See illustrations, including color plate 15.)

Botticini, Francesco (1446-97). A minor Florentine master who received his training in the large shop of Neri di Bicci, as did Cosimo Rosselli. His art is associated with the lyrical-realist style of Verrocchio and Botticelli. He entered Neri's shop in 1459, painted an altarpiece for the Pieve at Empoli, and was the father of Raffaello Botticini. The Empoli altar (now in fragments in the museum there) is his major authenticated work. A well-known painting of Tobias and the Archangels (Uffizi) is attributed to him.

Botticini, Raffaello (1477-after 1520). Minor Florentine painter, son and pupil of Francesco Botticini (see), he painted altarpieces based on his father's style and influenced by that of Perugino.

Bouché, Louis (1896-). Contemporary American genre painter who paints the pleasant aspects of life with a light and airy realism. He studied in Paris with Simon, Ménard and Laurens and then in New York with DuMond, Linde and Mora. For a long time he practiced mural decoration and only in 1932 did he turn to easel painting.

Boucher, François (1703-70). Popular exponent of the Rococo style of painting in France. As the de Goncourt brothers wrote, "Boucher was one of those men who indicate the taste of a century, express, personify, embody it. In him, French eighteenth century taste was manifest, in all the peculiarity of its character." Boucher stands for the academic triumph of the new intimate Rococo "realism" over the pompous "Grand Style" of the days of Louis XIV. This Rococo style stems, of course, from the fragile art of Watteau which Boucher learned in the process of engraving copies of Watteau's work. But he converted Watteau's manner into a decorative formula of larger and more precise forms, more appropriate for the walls and ceilings he was constantly commissioned to decorate. With Boucher the human form inclined toward a stereotype of doll-like, winsome proportions, of peach-colored flesh, often in situations of gay and frankly erotic abandon, as can be seen in numerous of his masterpieces in the Wallace Collection, London.

Student at first of his father, Boucher revealed his talent early in life and was placed in the studio of Le Moyne. At the same time he supported himself with designs for the engraver de Cars. He became accomplished in the art of engraving and was one of those selected by de Julienne to assist in the monumental publication of Watteau's oeuvre. Meanwhile, at the age of twenty, he won the Prix de Rome with a composition from the Bible. In 1728 he took the customary Italian trip for about three years, during which time he appears to have studied the Venetians and the late Italian Baroque painters such as Tiepolo, Albani and Baroccio. In 1731 he returned to Paris and henceforth seldom stirred from there. He became the most sought-after painter of his day, winning considerable personal fortune. He was elected to the Academy in 1734 on the basis of his Rinaldo and Armida. He rose within the Academy to director in 1765, the same year that through the influence of Mme de Pompadour he succeeded Carle van Loo as first painter to the king. He was popular in court circles, where he served as the tutor of Mme de Pompadour in painting and engraving. However, his personal life was apparently that of a good industrious bourgeois; in 1733 he had married a young beauty, and they appear to have lived in faithful domesticity, despite rumors to the contrary.

14. BOSCH. Adoration of the Magi
Philadelphia Museum of Art, Johnson Collection

Boucher worked in different media and handled a wide variety of subjects. With him drawings became a finished product, rather than the means to an end, and he was perhaps the first to exhibit publicly and to sell drawing studies. The Albertina Museum, Vienna, is rich in these. He was much employed in decorative projects. A considerable portion of his designs were for the Beauvais tapestry factory. The painting of new intimate rooms in the Rococo style was his speciality, as can be seen at Versailles and in the panels of the Frick Collection. These projects led him to explore the art of landscape, to which he was a major eighteenth-century contributor. His pursuit of the informal turned him often to rustic, barnyard genres of a gay confusion. This style contrasts strongly with the serious structure of genre by his contemporary Chardin. Boucher also brought mythological subject matter of the classical style down to the measure of his Rococo taste. The heroine of his paintings was often Venus. and the basic drama, her triangle with Mars and Vulcan (e.g., in Wallace Collection). He continued with the pastoral tradition of Watteau, as can be seen in his paintings in the Louvre, and frequently he converted it to the contemporary fad for chinoiserie. He also did portraits and is especially renowned for several he painted of Mme de Pompadour (National Gallery, Edinburgh; Versailles; Wallace Collection), who was his intimate friend and purchased many of his major canvases. (See color plate 16).

Boucicaut Master (active 1400-10). A Franco-Flemish miniaturist of the Paris School. His work in the Hours of the Maréchal de Boucicaut shows him to have been an important innovator in the areas of fluid technique, atmospheric perspective and architectural space.

15. BOTTICELLI. The Adoration of the Magi. National Gallery of Art, Mellon Collection, Washington, D.C.

BOTTICELLI. Birth of Venus. Uffizi, Florence

Boudin, Eugène (1824-98). A French marine painter noted for the atmospheric quality and charm of his pictures. A native of Le Havre, he specialized in seascapes of the coasts of Brittany, Normandy and Holland. These he painted in a misty fashion, emphasizing the foggy weather so often found in northern Europe.

Bouguereau, Adolphe William (1825-1905). Popular French academic painter of the late nineteenth century. Destined by his family for a career in business in La Rochelle, Bouguereau rebelled and joined Picot's studio in Paris. His style, a sentimental eclecticism, combined the idealism of Raphael, del Sarto and Reni with photographic exactitude of detail. His paintings included mythological scenes, genre, religious subjects and histories. Concerning his more progressive contemporaries he remarked, "I am very eclectic as you see; I accept and respect all schools of painting which have as their basis the sincere study of nature, the search for the true and the beautiful. As for the mystics, the impressionists, the pointillistes, etc., I don't see the way they see." He received many official awards and was an officer of the Légion d'Honneur. (See illustration.)

Boulogne, Jean de (see VALENTIN, LE).

BOTTICELLI. Portrait of a Youth
National Gallery of Art, Washington, D.C.

16. BOUCHER. Diana and Callisto
M. H. de Young Memorial Museum, San Francisco

BOUGUEREAU. The Two Sisters
Metropolitan Museum of Art, New York

Bourdichon, Jean (c.1457-1521). French painter and miniaturist of Tours. Painter to the French royal family from Louis XI to Francis I, Bourdichon is best known for his Hours of Anne of Brittany (Bibliothèque Nationale) illuminated for the wife of Louis XII between c.1500-07. Of his portraits and religious panels described in the royal accounts we have little evidence besides the triptych in Naples and a portrait of Anne of Brittany. Four vellum miniatures in the Masson collection represent the Stages of Society: primitive man, poor man, artisan, rich man. It is clear from the evidence of the records that Bourdichon exerted an influence on the development of the Renaissance in France far greater than his survived works attest.

Bourdon, Sébastien (1616-71). French painter and engraver. Although essentially academic and conservative, Bourdon was a harbinger of the romantic breakdown of the classical tradition which was to come. Son of a glass painter of Montpellier, Bourdon worked with Barthélemys in Paris before going to Rome in 1635. In Rome he developed two styles. Through his contact with Poussin and Claude he absorbed the classical manner as demonstrated in his Discovery of Coral (Munich), which is based on a drawing by Poussin. He also learned from Peter van Laer to paint rollicking genre of "Bambocciata" in the latter's Dutch manner, and in some cases he shows a resemblance to the Le Nain brothers. The Gypsy Camp (Louvre) is of this type. On the basis of an anecdote that he copied a Lorrain landscape and sold it as his own, Bourdon has been called a mere plagiarist, but he was quite an independent artist, according to the eclectic standards of his day. Although he was a Protestant and was imprisoned by the Roman Inquisition, Bourdon painted many religious subjects and was for a time court painter to Christina of Sweden. He had been active in the foundation of the Academy in 1648 and on his return from Sweden in 1654 he was made Rector and delivered a series of learned lectures. Bourdon was an ingratiating, if not forceful painter, rendering romantic and decorative the serious style of Poussin. He is most popular for his paintings of Dutch realistic vein and for his portraits. There is no known chronology of his two styles, which were apparently practiced simultaneously.

Bousianis, Giorgio (1887-). Contemporary Greek painter of figure compositions. Noted for his mystic intensity and the dissolved forms that in their dematerialized character lend an unearthly quality to his paintings.

Bouts, Aelbrecht (c.1460-1549). Flemish painter of Louvain. Second son of Dirk Bouts, he practiced a rather sugary style derived from his father. He worked for three years on an Assumption of the Virgin for the church of St. Pierre, probably the triptych now in Brussels. In 1518 he restored a Crucifixion in the Hôtel de Ville, originally perhaps by his father. (See illustration.)

Bouts, Dirk (Thierry, Dierik) (c.1415-75). Flemish painter born in Haarlem, whose style combines features of both van Eyck and van der Weyden. He transcribed the visual symbols of van der Weyden into the pictorial elements of van Eyck, losing the fervor of the former and never achieving the power of the latter. Although he was obviously capable of emotional intensity, he was incapable of translating it into dramatic action, and his figures in the most violent of situations remain placid and inexpressive. He was, however, an excellent painter, capable and sincere, with a fine feeling for landscape and a brilliant palette. Very little is known of his early years and nothing of his studies, though he may have been a pupil of Rogier van der Weyden. He came to Louvain c.1448, married a young girl of a wealthy family, settled there, and became town painter c.1468. His earliest dated painting, the Portrait of a Man (1462, London), is already a work of his maturity. On stylistic grounds the works showing the strongest Rogierian influence are placed in his early period (1440-57) and include the Life of the Virgin Triptych (Granada), which shows a strong Eyckian flavor, the Altar of the Virgin (Prado), the Entombment (London), the Deposition (Louvre), the Calvary (Berlin), and the St. John at Patmos (Rotterdam). His mature style (1457-75) includes the larger projects for Louvain—the Martyrdom of St. Erasmus (c.1458, St. Pierre, Louvain); the great Altar of the Last Supper (1464-67, St. Pierre, Louvain), done originally for the Collegiate Church; and the commission for the two large compositions for the Hôtel de Ville (1468). Of this project the Last Judgment no longer exists; of the second or Justice portion, he finished only two scenes of the Legend of Otho (1470-75, Brussels). His last work was the Martyrdom of St. Hyppolitus (St. Sauveur, Bruges) for which Hugo van der Goes finished the wings. (See color plate 17.)

Boyd, Arthur Merric (1920-). Australian regional painter; born in Melbourne, the eldest son of a third generation of Australian painters and potters. Probably the most thoroughly Australian of all the regionalists, Boyd is best known for his lively and imaginative paintings of the Wimmera District. His subjects are usually man's struggles against the elemental forces of nature and the denizens of the Wimmera. He employs a high-pitched blue and gold palette, generally rendered in tempera. (See illustration.)

Bramante, Donato (1444-1514). Italian, Umbrian. Known chiefly as one of the great architects of the Renaissance, rather than for the few paintings by him that have survived. Born in or near Urbino, he received his training there, probably under the architect Laurana, and his painting developed under the influence of Melozzo da Forlì. He visited Padua and Mantua, lived in Milan from 1474 to 1499, and spent the last

BOUTS, AELBRECHT. Jesus at the House of Simon the Pharisee
Musées Royaux des Beaux-Arts, Brussels

BOYD. The Mining Town. Courtesy of the Artist

17. BOUTS, DIRK. Portrait of a Man
National Gallery, London

years of his life in Rome, where his architectural masterpiece. the plan for the new St. Peter's, was conceived but never carried out. Painted works by him are in the Brera and the Castello in Milan, the Badia of Chiaravalle, and the Certosa of Pavia. Like Alberti and Mantegna, he was a student of classical antiquity, and his paintings are affected by this study and by his architecture. A close follower in Milan was Bartolommeo Suardi, called Bramantino.

Bramantino (Bartolommeo Suardi) (c.1470-1536). Originally a pupil of the Milanese Butinone and later influenced by the Umbrian architect Bramante (hence his name). He worked in Milan and Rome, and perpetuated the characteristics of fifteenth-century art although he was active mostly in the sixteenth century. After 1525 he was court painter and architect to Francesco II Sforza in Milan.

Braque, Georges (1882-). Outstanding French modern painter. In addition to the pioneering work in Analytical Cubism that he shared with Picasso, he may also be credited with the development of a thoroughly original and exciting version of Cubism (see) mingled with Fauve color effects. He was the son of a decorator and "Sunday painter" and began to study art in 1893, coming to Paris in 1900 and attending various conventional art schools there. In 1906 he began to show at the Indépendants, spent the summer with Othon Friesz and through him became for a short time part of the Fauve movement under the influences of Van Gogh and Gauguin. He exhibited with the Fauves in 1907 and sold all his pictures, and in the same year made an arrangement with the dealer Kahnweiler and met Picasso. In 1908 he fell. like Picasso, under the influence of Cézanne and was said by one critic to be reducing everything to "little cubes." His period of Analytical Cubism starts in 1910, and he soon after began to incorporate letters into his works. His Synthetic Cubism of 1912, apparently developed under the influence of his background as the son of a decorator, utilizes a new and artificial method of rebuilding the impression of the figure through the use of so-called *papiers collés* (see) or pasted papers, actual pieces of wallpaper, playing cards, etc., introduced into the picture. After his war service Braque turned to a kind of serene decorative painting, using large bold color areas but with the residuum of Cubist form still dominant. Since that time he has introduced innumerable variants of this form and color combination. Although disparate in theory, the combined styles in his hands are altogether harmonious and effective. See also FAUVISM, SIMULTANEITY. (See color plate 18.)

Bray, Jan de (c.1627-97). Dutch painter of portraits and of biblical and historical subjects. He studied with his father in his native city of Haarlem, where he lived and where most of his works are still preserved. His large group portraits are interesting in composition and in characterization, and his broad rich style is intensely personal.

Brea, Ludovico (c.1443-1523). A Piedmontese Italian painter who worked chiefly in Nice and is well represented there. He was influenced by the Franco-Flemish tradition current in the Piedmont, and by Foppa, with whom he worked on an altarpiece in Savona.

Brera Picture Gallery, Milan. A collection of outstanding paintings by the sixteenth-century Lombard pupils of Leonardo such as Boltraffio and Solario. It also contains works by Venetian painters, works by Mantegna and Correggio and the famous Marriage of the Virgin by Raphael.

Brescianino, Andrea del (Andrea de' Piccinelli) (active 1507-25). Painter active in Siena (1507-24) and then entered in the Florentine guild in 1525. His style was based on the High Renaissance manner of the Florentines and Raphael, but was also influenced by the new generation of Mannerists (see).

Bridge, The (Die Brücke) (see EXPRESSIONISM).

Bridges, Charles (active America 1735-c.1740). An English portrait painter out of the tradition of Lely and perhaps even from Kneller's studio. He was active in Virginia for about five years, painting standardized portraits of superficial elegance, after which, according to family tradition, he returned to England. Some thirty portraits are now ascribed to him.

Brill, Paul (1554-1626). Flemish painter, active in Rome. Brill occupies an important position in the international history of landscape painting. He carried the sixteenth-century Flemish traditions to Rome. There, under his influence and that of Elsheimer and contemporary Italians, was developed a romantic style of rendering the Italian scene that influenced Claude and Poussin, especially the former. Brill's first style was largely in miniature on copper with sharp divisions between the distances. Under Elsheimer's influence his compositions became larger, bolder and more leafy, and finally they became more colorful. He could also blow up his smaller compositions to fresco size and he was in demand for the decorative qualities of his picturesque vistas. (See illustration.)

British Museum, London. Famous for its magnificent library of printed books, perhaps the largest in the world. Also noted for its department of manuscripts containing such world-famous examples as the Lindisfarne Gospels, Queen Mary's Psalter, as well as the collections known as Cottonian, Harleian and Royal, the mass of Greek papyri from Egypt, and a fine print room; the latter includes one of the best collections of Chinese painting in Europe. Outside the realm of two-dimensional art, the Museum is known for its Mesopotamian, Egyptian and Greek sculptures, including the Rosetta stone from Egypt and the priceless Elgin Marbles from Greece.

18. BRAQUE. Still Life with Grapes. Phillips Collection, Washington, D.C.

BRILL. Classical Landscape. M. H. de Young Memorial Museum, San Francisco

BROEDERLAM. Panel of Diptych: The Nativity
Mayer v.d. Bergh Museum, Antwerp

BRONZINO. Portrait of a Young Man
Frick Collection, New York

Broederlam, Melchior (active 1381-1409). Flemish painter to the Dukes of Burgundy. Best-known forerunner of the van Eycks, Broederlam was born in Ypres, where he apparently spent most of his life. He worked for the Count of Flanders from 1381 until he entered the service of Philip the Bold of Burgundy in 1385. In 1392 he was commissioned to paint the shutters of an altarpiece of the Chartreuse de Champmol. In these panels, now in the Dijon Museum, Broederlam attempts to make spacious landscape for his Parisian-style figures and employs many of the devices of contemporary Sienese painting. The scenes deal with the Life of the Virgin and the lovely landscape of the Flight into Egypt anticipates the use of this subject by later Flemish artists to present natural settings. (See illustration.)

Bronzino, Agnolo (Agnolo di Cosimo di Mariano) (1503-72). Florentine Mannerist painter, pupil and assistant of Pontormo. One of the few painters who seem to have been able to get along with Pontormo, he assisted him at Certosa. and after doing his own fresco at Pesaro, returned to help him at Careggi and Castello. All of these works are now destroyed. He worked also in the court of Urbino (1530-32) and was in Rome in 1546 where he came under the influence of Michelangelo. He was most popular as a portrait painter although he did allegorical scenes in the typically involuted and intellectual manner of the period. His portraits of the Medici circle have an aristocratic sophistication and refinement which may be the result of the strict and ceremonious air which the Spanish Eleanora de Toledo brought to Florentine society when she married Cosimo I. His style is characterized by a sculptural purity, an elegant linear precision, brilliant, almost unmodified local color in refined gradation, and an enamel-like finish. See MANNERISM. (See illustrations, including color plate 19.)

Brook, Alexander (1898-). Contemporary American still-life and figure painter. Like many of his contemporaries he was influenced by Jules Pascin and took to painting studio pictures of the nude and semi-nude female figure; these are rich in pigmentation but contrived. Born in Brooklyn, he studied at the Art Students League with J. C. Johansen and K. H. Miller, and later taught there. He was one of the leading young American artists of the Whitney Studio Club. He executed a mural for the Post Office Department in Washington, D.C.

Brooklyn Museum, Brooklyn, N. Y. General collection emphasizing contemporary American and European art; also the pre-colonial art of the Latin-American countries.

Brouwer, Adriaen (1605/6-38). Greatest Flemish seventeenth-century genre painter, he had a profound effect upon both Flemish and Dutch genre painting. He is supposed to have led a life of bohemian debauchery ending in premature death. Born in Oudenaerde, he went to Antwerp (c.1620), was in Amsterdam (1625), Haarlem (1626-31), and then returned to Antwerp (1632), where he remained until his death. Although there is some question as to his having studied with Frans Hals, he was undoubtedly influenced by the Dutch master. His early works (1621-26), brightly colored peasant scenes, show the influence of Brueghel, and are archaistic in manner. After his contact with Hals he was influenced by the latter's gray tonality, and began to seek atmospheric effects, virtuosity of brushwork, and animation of expression. In the early 1630's, after his return to Antwerp, his art became much more subtle and atmospheric, his compositions more integrated. and he achieved greater narrative concentration. His last style (1632-38) is characterized by an increased proportion of figure to space, a growing fluency of movement, a greater delicacy of rendering, and an interest in facial expression. His last works achieve a true monumentality in spite of their smallness. His art as well as his life was a conscious attempt,

BROWN, FORD MADOX. Christ Washing St. Peter's Feet. Tate Gallery, London

and one of the earliest, to *épater les bourgeois*. He represented the peasant not as romantically robust or sentimentally high-spirited, but in squalor and depravity. He had many followers, none of whom could match his sensitivity of observation or execution: Quast, the Ostades, Heemskerk and Molenaer among the Dutch, and Craesbeck (his companion in madcap adventures and his devoted disciple), Ryckaert, and Teniers. (See color plate 20.)

Brown, Ford Madox (1821-93). British painter and member of the Pre-Raphaelite Brotherhood (see)—together with William Holman Hunt and Dante Gabriel Rossetti—which was a Victorian reaction against High Renaissance techniques and what they called the Grand Style. Their own method, presumably based on the pre-High Renaissance period, was inclined to mysticism and medievalism and may be considered part of the Romantic revolt against materialism. Brown was trained on the Continent and was influenced by Holbein and Fragonard. Although individualistic in his approach, he reflects Pre-Raphaelite principles in his handling of such themes as Wycliffe Preaching before John of Gaunt and Chaucer Reading to Edward III. Drama and character in his work are expressed through vitality of design, draughtsmanship and strong color. Twelve frescoes in Manchester Town Hall, 1849-64, are typical of his literal and detailed version of the school. His later works are more romantic and sensuous. (See illustration.)

Brown, John (1752-87). Scottish painter who went to Rome in 1771 and there came under the influence of a Romantic, Fuseli. He made drawings of many Sicilian ruins. After returning to Scotland, he did pencil portraits in life size and miniature. Later in London he drew Roman and Greek marbles, illustrations for Homer and similar classical works. His most interesting works, however, are figure studies of fashionable women; these are genuinely subtle caricatures with a faintly charged atmosphere that gives them an eerie, exciting unreality.

Brown, John George (1831-1913). American painter of sentimental genre; best known for his bootblack urchins. Born in England, he studied art in Edinburgh, went to London as a painter and finally (c.1854) came to New York, where he studied at the National Academy of Design.

Browne, Byron (1907-). Contemporary American semi-abstract painter. Born in Yonkers, N.Y., he studied at the National Academy of Design, but began experimenting with Cubism in 1929 and was one of the organizers of the American Abstract Artists in 1936. He exhibited with that group until 1946.

Bru, Anye (Hans Brun) (active c.1500). German painter resident in Barcelona. He has recently been recognized as the author in 1504-07 of the famous retablo of San Cugat del Vallés, once thought to have been done by Master Alfonso of Cordoba (see) in 1473. The Martyrdom of St. Cucufas from this altar is remarkable for its graphic portraiture and landscape and for the gruesome realism of the decapitated saint. It is not as precocious a work as once thought, however, and although the bloodletting fits into a Spanish tradition continuous down through El Greco, Goya and Picasso,

19. BRONZINO. Madonna and Child with St. John the Baptist
Kress Collection. New York

the technique of the paintings is part of the international Renaissance of about 1500.

Bruce, Edward (1879-1943). Contemporary American painter of simplified and stylized landscapes somewhat in the manner of Neue Sachlichkeit (see). Born in Dover Plains, N.Y., he was a lawyer and business man before he turned to painting. He was instrumental in the organization of the Public Works and was its director. He later became Secretary of the Advisory Committee on Fine Arts of the Treasury Department.

20. BROUWER. Peasants Smoking
Metropolitan Museum of Art, New York

Bruce, Patrick Henry (1880-1937). One of the first American painters to do pure abstractions. He was born in Virginia, studied with Henri, and settled in Paris in 1907. There, together with A. B. Frost, he joined the Orphist group of Delaunay, and exhibited a pure abstraction in the Salon des Indépendants as early as 1914. See ORPHISM.

Brücke, Die (see EXPRESSIONISM).

Brueghel (family). A long lineage of Flemish painters. The eldest and most important was Pieter Brueghel the Elder (c.1525/30-69) (see). He had two sons, Jan or Velvet Brueghel (1568-1625) (see) and Pieter the Younger (1564-1637/38) or Hell-fire Brueghel, so called because of his hells and scenes of conflagrations. Hell-fire had a son Pieter III (1589-1638/39). a mediocre artist. Velvet had two sons: Ambrosius (1617-75) and Jan II (1601-78) who imitated their father. Velvet's three daughters married painters: Borrekens, Kessel and David Teniers II. Jan Brueghel II in turn had five sons, all painters, but none good: Jan-Peeter (born 1628), Abraham (1631-90), Philip (born 1635), Ferdinand (born 1637) and Jan Baptist (1647-1719). It might be noted that the Kessels, the Teniers and the Abraham Brueghels continued producing artists for several generations. (See illustrations.)

Brueghel (Bruegel) the Elder, Pieter (called the Droll or Peasant) (c. 1525/30-69). Flemish painter from the small village of Brueghel. His own spelling was Bruegel. One of the great painters of Flanders, he did religious subjects, fantasies, and genre scenes of peasant life. Unique in sixteenth century art, he was still highly regarded, successful, and much admired by his contemporaries, especially by the Emperor Rudolph, who bought all of the pictures now in Vienna. According to the historian van Mander, he studied in Antwerp with Pieter Coecke van Aelst and later with Jerome Cocke (1550). He entered the Antwerp guild in 1551 and took a trip to Italy, perhaps with Martin de Vos, traveling as far as Sicily and making drawings of nature rather than the antique (1522-23). On his return he did drawings for engravings by Jerome Cocke. He eventually settled in Brussels (c.1563), married a daughter of Pieter Coecke. had two sons and lived a peaceful and successful life as a painter and part of a circle of liberal humanists—among them Ortelius, Plantin. Hogenbergh, and Goltzius. His paintings, influenced by the humanism of the circle, had a moral and philosophical significance. His art, as opposed to that of Bosch, is not pessimistic but expresses a belief in life as an all-pervading force. He saw man as dominated by the forces of nature and although the peasant may appear uncouth and vulgar he is still admirable because he is closest to nature, the symbol of natural man. His concern with nature led to some of the most magnificent and cosmic landscapes in the history of painting. His art like that of Bosch has a very definite literary basis, though the sources are different—in his case proverbs and metaphors. His art is also characterized by a satirical inversion, the *Monde Renversé*, dealing with the foolishness of man and the wiseness of fools. His religious subjects and fantasies are seen in terms of contemporary peasant life. Influenced by Dürer, sixteenth-century German draughtsmen, and probably Michelangelo, he presents the peasant as a monumental and heroic figure in all the richness of his daily life, painted in great detail, with beautiful simplicity of color and exquisite invention.

His paintings are dated 1557-68. The earliest show the influence of Bosch and this continues in certain later subjects: the Triumph of Death (1561, Prado), the Fall of Rebel Angels (1562, Brussels), Dulle Griete (1562, Antwerp, Musée Mayer van den Bergh), all of which are archaic in composition but very advanced in their realistic treatment, atmospheric effects, and technical execution. His treatment of peasant life begins with complex scenes of a metaphorical nature,

21. BRUEGHEL THE ELDER, PIETER. Landscape with the Temptation of St. Anthony Abbot
National Gallery of Art, Kress Collection, Washington, D.C.

Proverbs (1559, Berlin) and Children's Games (1560, Vienna); and then continues with the more monumental landscape conceptions of the months (c.1565, 3 in Vienna, 1 in New York, 1 in Raudnitz). It ends with the late style in which the figures become larger and dominant: Land of Cockaigne (1567, Munich), the Blind Leading the Blind (1567, Naples), Bird's Nest (1568, Vienna), Peasant Dance and Peasant Wedding (both 1568, Vienna). His religious scenes are treated as genre subjects in great landscapes with many figures: Tower of Babel (1563, Vienna), Bearing of the Cross (1564, Vienna), Adoration of the Magi (1564, London), Conversion of St. Paul (1567, Vienna). (See illustrations, including color plate 21.)

Brueghel, Jan (called Velvet Brueghel) (1568-1625). Flemish painter, son of Pieter the Elder; famous for his small pictures of botanical and zoological subjects, though he also did religious, historical, and genre pictures, all painted with meticulous detail and enamel-like color and characterized by a graceful poetic imagination. Born in Brussels, he came early to Antwerp, where he studied with Pieter Goetkind, became a member of the guild (1597), and lived all his life except for short visits to Italy (1594, 1596), Prague (1604), and Nuremberg (1616). He had two sons, eight grandsons, and four great-grandsons, all of whom were painters. He was extremely popular, became quite wealthy, received many honors and was greatly admired by Rubens, with whom he collaborated: for instance, he painted the accessories in Rubens' Madonna with Garland (Munich; Louvre), and Rubens painted the figures in his Paradise (Mauritshuis). Renowned as a painter of plants and animals he also collaborated with van Balen, Rottenhammer, Frans Franken II, de Momper, Brill, and Neef. On his return from Italy he worked for the Archduke Albert, executing fifty pictures, including many versions of "The Five Senses" and "The Four Elements," which are among his finest works. He is the first of a series of Flemish little masters. There are 54 of his paintings in Madrid, 41 in Munich, 33 in Dresden, and 29 in Milan. (See illustration.)

Brun, Hans (see BRU, ANYE).

Brunswick Monogrammist (see AMSTEL, JAN VAN).

Brusasorci, Domenico (1516-67). An Italian painter born in Verona. He was a pupil of his father, Agostino, and also of Caroto, and was influenced by the great Venetians. A protégé of Cardinal Gonzaga, he worked in Mantua, but most of his activity was in Verona. Although eclectic, he had a fine sense of color.

Brusselmans, Jan (1884-). Belgian painter and lithographer whose first inspiration came from Courbet and Jordaens. Later he moved on to Impressionism and the Neo-Impressionism of van Rysselberghe, arriving finally at his own carefully laid out and rigid "constructions." Although revealing a rigid formal restraint, these depict still life and people in a tense and strangely lighted atmosphere that creates its own mood and world.

Bruyn, Bartholomäus the Elder (1493-1555). German portraitist and religious painter. Like his son Barthel the Younger, he was active in the government of his native city of Cologne. His altarpieces are often derivative, but many of the heads in them are portraits, and it was in this field that

BRUEGHEL THE ELDER, PIETER. The Wedding Dance. Detroit Institute of Arts

BRUEGHEL, JAN. A Village Scene. Detroit Institute of Arts

Bruyn's talent lay. His likenesses are well observed, convincing, and painted with sureness.

Brygos Painter (early fifth century B.C.). Greek vase painter. It is not clear whether he was the Brygos who signed vases as potter. This painter was perhaps the outstanding master among the red-figured severe-style painters. His productions are vibrant with a new physical activity and employ innovations in modelling and polychromy. Example: the cup with the Sack of Troy (Louvre).

Buffet, Bernard (1928-). French painter who represents a sparsely colored, thin-figured, angular Expressionism. It is perhaps more convincing from a technical than from an emotional point of view.

Bugiardini, Giuliano (1475-1554). A contemporary of the creators of the High Renaissance style in Florence but himself a painter of little originality. As a pupil of Ghirlandaio he knew Michelangelo, and he assisted Albertinelli in completing certain unfinished works of Fra Bartolommeo. In his rather thin, dry style he also incorporated elements from Perugino and Leonardo da Vinci.

Buonaccorsi, Pietro (see PIERINO DEL VAGA).

Buonconsiglio, Giovanni (called Il Marescalco) (?-1535/37). Italian painter of Vicenza, active mostly in Venice where he appeared first in 1495. A follower of Bartolommeo Montagna, he was influenced also by Bellini, Vivarini, and Mantegna.

Burchfield, Charles Ephraim (1893-). American genre and landscape watercolor painter, one of the earliest exponents of the rural American scene. Born in Salem, Ohio, he worked first as an accountant; later he attended the Cleveland School of Art on a scholarship. After serving in the U.S. Army during World War I, he worked as a designer of wallpaper until 1929, when he resigned to devote himself to painting. His early work (1916-18) consisted of landscapes in a romantic mood evocative of childhood visions. After the war, he did realistic watercolors of small-town ugliness and squalor similar in attitude to the stories in Sherwood Anderson's *Winesburg, Ohio*. After that his work vacillated among scenes of romantic mystery, idealized and symbolic landscapes, and further realistic studies of small-town America, seen sympathetically and humorously, with an occasional note of grandeur. During the period of modernist experimentation after the decline of the Ashcan School, he maintained almost by himself the interest in the American scene which later developed into the regionalist movement. (See illustration.)

Burgkmair, Hans (c.1473-before 1531). German painter and engraver. His career in Augsburg covers the first three decades of the sixteenth century, when that city was a center of Renaissance learning and culture. His art, however, had its foundations in the old school of painting, for he had studied with Martin Schongauer. As a young artist he made the first of two or three voyages to Italy, and his painting therefore took a decisive turn toward simple, heavy drapery, monumental repose, and especially toward the darker, richer palette that he admired in Venetian painting. The wealthy Fugger family called on Burgkmair to decorate their palace in Augsburg, and the Emperor Maximilian also employed him. (See illustration.)

BURCHFIELD. November Evening
Metropolitan Museum of Art, New York

BURGKMAIR. Martin Schongauer
Alte Pinakothek, Munich

Burial of Count Orgaz by El Greco (see).

Burlin, Paul (1886-). Contemporary American Abstract Expressionist painter. Born in New York, he studied in England, exhibited at the Armory Show, moved to Santa Fe in 1913, and lived in Europe from 1921 to 1932. His early work was influenced by Cubism (see) and he even experimented for a short time with Futurism. Following World War II, his art showed the influence of Surrealism (see) before evolving into a kind of Abstract Expressionism characterized by heavy twisting contour lines and emotionally disturbing color dissonances. He taught at Washington University, St. Louis, and in 1954-55 at Union College. (See illustration.)

Burliuk, David (1882-). Contemporary American painter born in Russia. He began his studies in 1899 in Odessa and continued them in Munich, Paris, and Moscow. He was associated in 1911-12 with the Blaue Reiter and Der Sturm groups in Germany. Back in Moscow he founded Russian Futurism. He left Russia and spent some years in Japan before coming to the U.S. in 1922. After a period in which he painted in what he called the Radio Style he turned to a more naturalistic and pseudo-naive kind of Expressionism which has characterized his work ever since.

Burne-Jones, Edward Coley (1833-98). British painter and decorator. A Romantic and a lifelong rebel, he was associated with the later-Pre-Raphaelite movement. In 1857 he worked with Rossetti in decorating the walls of the Oxford Union with illustrations from the *Morte d'Arthur*. Under the influence of Ruskin he drew flowers and foliage and copied Tintorettos. He became interested in Greek literature and pagan mythology and while in Italy was influenced by Botticelli, Mantegna and Signorelli, developing at the same time his knowledge of medieval and Renaissance literature. A meticulous craftsman, he made painstaking preparations for his paintings: studies, figurines, sketches, outlines of various kinds, and careful underpainting. In spite of this, the lack of technical knowledge made his and other Pre-Raphaelite paintings blacken and peel. He preferred to decorate homes, churches and furniture, design tapestries and stained-glass windows. After 1863 he was closely associated with William Morris in the latter's attempt to bring back the age of handicrafts. Yet Burne-Jones was also enraptured by the past from another point of view—the spiritual—and this he tried to express in his church windows, tapestries and illustrated books. In 1881, again in association with the William Morris group, he opened the Merton Abbey factory for the production of decorative works. During the 1890's the vogue for his literary subject pieces diminished as the new Whistlerian dictum of

BURLIN. Epiphany of a Hero. Private Collection, New York

BURNE-JONES. The Golden Stairs. Tate Gallery, London

"Art for Art's sake" (see) came into favor. Burne-Jones's contribution is not in the highly detailed works for which he is generally known but rather in those pictures which, showing the greatest sense of unreality, of existence on another plane, allow the lines to flow harmoniously and musically. See PRE-RAPHAELITE BROTHERHOOD. (See illustration.)

Burra, Edward (1905-). British watercolorist of humorous genre themes, as well as more violent symbolic works which derive from his reactions to the Spanish Civil War. He has also exhibited with the Surrealists.

Burroughs, Bryson (1869-1934). American painter of mythological subjects in the academic manner. Born in Hyde Park, Mass., he studied at the Art Students League and in Paris for five years, where he was influenced by Puvis de Chavannes. He was curator of paintings at the Metropolitan Museum of Art (1909-34).

Busch-Reisinger Museum, Cambridge, Mass. Until recently known as the Germanic Museum, this collection specializes in works by German artists of all periods.

Busi, Giovanni de' (see CARIANI).

Bustos, Hermenegildo (1832-1907). Self-taught Mexican provincial painter and portraitist. After Estrada, the most important provincial painter of his time.

Buytewech, Willem (1591/92-1624). Dutch painter, draughtsman and etcher. He worked briefly in Haarlem, but mostly in Rotterdam. His charming depictions of manners and costumes mark the transition from empty Mannerism to typical Dutch painting.

Byzantine painting. The term Byzantine is employed rather loosely to describe various historical phenomena. In general it means the art of the Christian epoch in the Eastern Mediterranean, an art that came into being when the city of Byzantium, from which it derived its name, was re-named Constantinople in the early fourth century. Constantinople, then, was the focal point of Byzantine painting, but owing to losses of its monuments, our best knowledge of the art is seldom derived from examples in the city itself. The Byzantine styles of painting and mosaic not only represent one of the major artistic traditions of the medieval period; they are of particular importance for their influence upon the nascent arts of Western Europe. On walls, on portable panels, and in the pages of manuscripts, Byzantine culture produced one of the most sumptous arts of all time. Popularly thought of as rigid in form and unchanging in style, the term Byzantine actually embraces a variety of manners of painting and types of forms. In the later middle ages the art of Byzantium served both as an inspiration to the creation of iconic images in the West and as a repository and model of the Antique tradition of plastic form and liveliness.

For the period before the ninth century, it is customary to use the terms Early Byzantine and Early Christian interchangeably. Early Christian art was in many ways an extension of late Imperial Roman forms and was subject to the same regional and provincial variations that characterized that pagan tradition. Although in general the early Churches pursued similarly a transcendental symbolism, a number of distinct styles seem to have arisen in Rome, Gaul, Spain, North Africa, Egypt, Palestine, Syria, Asia Minor, and Constantinople. Categorically, we refer to the western group of styles as Early Christian (see) and the eastern group as Byzantine, assuming Constantinople to have been most representative of the latter. However, as nothing important remains of Constantinopolitan painting before the ninth century, we base our knowledge of its style on such holdings of Justinian as Ravenna in Italy, which geographically speaking is West Christian. Actually, the monuments are so few and so isolated in the Early Byzantine (and Early Christian) period that it is more rewarding to examine their innate artistic qualities than their historical interrelationships.

A certain difference in taste is to be seen in Byzantine painting before and after the Iconoclastic Controversy (over image worship), which lasted from 726-867. Throughout the entire history of Byzantine painting there is an emphasis on floating coloristic effects, flat forms, limited space, decorative highlights and detail, and neutral backgrounds in deep color or gold. However, before the eighth century these effects were less systematized than later. In Early Byzantine art there was a close identity between religious and political symbolism, echoing the important position of the Emperor in ecclesiastical affairs. Our most conclusive evidence for the character of Byzantine painting previous to the Controversy is in the rich mosaics of Ravenna and Salonika (see EARLY CHRISTIAN PAINTING, MOSAIC PAINTING). We learn little, on the other hand, from the simple ornamental mosaics that adorned Justinian's great church of Hagia Sophia when it was constructed in the sixth century. The recently uncovered figure mosaics of this building, the leading church of Byzantium, were all

22. BYZANTINE SCHOOL. Enthroned Madonna and Child 13th Century. National Gallery of Art, Mellon Collection Washington, D.C.

added later (ninth to twelfth centuries), many as special votive panels endowed by important personages. There are also frescoes from the early period in provincial areas, but as in the Greek paintings of San Saba and Santa Maria Antiqua in Rome it is difficult here to isolate Byzantine elements from local tendencies. Movable paintings are almost lacking except in books (see ILLUMINATED MANUSCRIPTS). The Dioscorides Codex, produced in Constantinople, tells more of its Hellenistic model than of the current Byzantine style; the purple codices of Rossano, Vienna, and Sinope cannot be localized but merely give us an inkling of the rich colorism of the imperial art.

With the disappearance of figurative or representational art in the doctrinal dispute over images in the eighth to ninth centuries, painting apparently turned to ornamental and landscape forms, as can be seen in the work done by Byzantine craftsmen for the Moslems in Damascus and Cordoba.

From the ninth century on, the distinct character of Byzantine painting is clearer and more easily differentiated from both Western and Asiatic art. It portrayed the official dogma of the Eastern Orthodox Church, and retained its distinctive character even when it was engulfed by the Turks (fifteenth century) and had spread to the Balkans and Russia. Following the triumph of the iconodules or pro-icon party in the ninth century, the iconography became more purely biblical and liturgical, paralleling the monkish isolation of its religion from the secular world. The carefully adjusted community of icons no longer mirrored the Justinian hierarchy, but seemed to take on a magical and strongly personal relation to the worshipper in the little domed churches of the late Byzantine periods.

The "Second Golden Age," or mid-Byzantine period (ninth to twelfth centuries), saw a revival of the classical tradition in Greek lands. This can be detected in the classical architecture of such manuscripts as Stavroniketa 43 (tenth century) and in the statuesque effect of the mosaics of Daphni (eleventh century). Although the thematic organization of manuscript and mural cycles became standardized during the Comnenian Dynasty of the eleventh and twelfth centuries, there were several different aesthetic traditions observable. Less sculptural than Daphni, but more human in an expressionistic way, were the eleventh-century mosaics of Nea Moni in Chios and St. Luke in Phocis. Another style, devoid of subtle compositional effects, is seen in the provincial frescoes of Cappadocia (tenth and eleventh centuries) or the Marginal Psalters of the same period. The latter carry their illustrations as a gloss in the margin of their pages. They represent a different tradition, probably monastic, which contrasts with "aristocratic" productions of Constantinople like the Gospels in Paris (Greek Mss. 74) of the eleventh century.

At this time some of the richest mid-Byzantine mosaics, at least from the viewpoint of expanse of gold, appeared in the West in Italian cities of the Adriatic and in Norman foundations of Sicily. In S. Marco, Venice, there are intrusions of local style owing perhaps to the employment of Italian craftsmen. The Norman kings, however, seem to have exerted themselves to rival the Byzantine Emperors and the product, for example at Monreale (twelfth to thirteenth centuries), is close to the imperial style. However, the iconographic system suffered because of its application to a long basilica instead of to a small

BYZANTINE. Mosaic of Early Christian Period. Theodora and Her Court. San Vitale, Ravenna

central church. In parts of Italy the mid-Byzantine style was reproduced in fresco in a hard schematic fashion called "maniera greca." This can be seen at S. Angelo in Formis (eleventh century).

The sack of Constantinople by the Crusaders in 1204 and the break-up of the Empire produced a hiatus in creative activity. Later under the Paleologue Emperors of the twelfth to fifteenth centuries there came another, limited revival. Again the inspiration was apparently the Antique, but not the monumental classic so much as the anecdotal, landscape tradition. This is seen in the mosaics of the Church of the Chora, Constantinople (early fourteenth century), where a more human sensibility and a concern for natural landscape effects prevails. However, Byzantium never carried these Duccio-like effects to the logical conclusion of a naturalistic art of measurable space.

Other regions — the Balkans, Russia, and Crete — practiced fresco instead of mosaic painting for reasons of economy and perhaps taste. Much of this work demonstrates the new sense of human feeling, an expressionism generally called "Macedonian," perhaps because of its provincial origins. Nerezi, Milesevo, and Gracanica in Jugoslavia and Mistra in the Greek Peloponnesos are examples of this.

Following the fall of Constantinople to the Ottoman Turks in 1453, the Orthodox painting tradition carried on elsewhere: in Russia, Mt. Athos, Crete, etc. The Byzantine style had first produced appreciable effects in Russia in twelfth-century Kiev. Vladimir and Novgorod succeeded Kiev in artistic importance in the late middle ages, giving way to Moscow during the times we call Renaissance. The church of St. Demeritos at Vladimir and the Savior Church of Nereditsa (Novgorod) are examples of early work in the "Macedonian" style. The growth of Moscow in artistic importance was owing partly to Theophanes the Greek (active c.1400), who brought an expressionistic style there from Novgorod. His follower, Andrei Roublew (see), is the best known of Russian painters.

Crete, associated with Venice from 1204, practiced a more conservative, less personalized tradition and was noted for the production of icons. Best known of these craftsmen was Andrea Rico of Candia in the sixteenth century. From Crete came the culminating artist of the Byzantine style, El Greco (see). Mt. Athos in Greece also preserved the Greek style, but in a crystallized, stereotyped fashion evident from the Painter's Guide, a rule book for painters assembled by Dionysius of Fourna on the basis of sixteenth-century practices.

Other forms of Byzantine painting included painted wooden panels, portable (miniature) mosaics on wood, and enamel work (see). These techniques were used for the standard type of icon (see). In the late Orthodox church, such icons were assembled decoratively on an iconostasis or screen separating the church from the sanctuary. This screen had originated in Justinian's times as a low barrier, but in fourteenth-century Russia the barrier grew into a tall wide screen covered with panels in set arrangement not unlike the western altarpiece (see). (See illustrations, including color plate 22.)

C

Cabanel, Alexandre (1824-89). French painter of easel- and wall-paintings. Student of Picot, he was a quick success with his history paintings, allegories and portraits. He is especially known for titillating nudes such as Venus Anadyomene (Luxembourg) for which Napoleon III paid a fortune.

Cabrera, Miguel (1695-1768). Muralist and portraitist, the best-known Mexican painter of the Spanish Colonial period. He rises above the official academic level through the sensitivity of his interpretation and structure. Most Mexican churches of the eighteenth century had pictures by him.

Cadmus, Paul (1904-). Contemporary American painter. His caustic genre paintings, executed with meticulous detail, have consistently shocked the public in their frank portrayal of sex and horror. He was born in New York and naturally gravitated toward art, since his father was a commercial lithographer and his mother an illustrator. He studied at the National Academy of Design and the Art Students League. His earliest work, before 1926, was as an etcher. He later did layouts for an advertising agency (1928-31), executed murals for the W.P.A. and the Treasury Department (1934-37), and ballet sets and costumes (1938).

Cagli, Corrado (1910-). Italian-born artist who has spent much time in the United States. While active in the 1930's in the so-called Roman school he painted in a representational and occasionally allegorical manner. He has since turned toward abstract formulations, partly under the influence of Chirico's space compositions and of the later Picasso.

Caldara, Polidoro (see POLIDORO DA CARAVAGGIO).

Caliari, Paolo (see VERONESE).

Callahan, Kenneth (1906-). Contemporary American painter of mystic visions. Born in Spokane, Wash., he studied at the University of Washington and in London, Paris, Florence, and Mexico (1926-28). His early style, in which he executed several murals in the Northwest, was representational and somewhat Expressionistic. More recently his art has turned toward Surrealism and he paints the images suggested in the forms of rocks and clouds.

Callot, Jacques (1592-1635). French draughtsman and etcher. As recorder of genre and scenes from Italian comedy Callot is important for his influence on the eighteenth-century French tradition. His life was as picaresque as the subjects of his etchings. After considerable success in Italy he returned to Lorraine in the service of the Duke. In a series of etchings, the Miseries of War, he recorded the horrors of the Lorraine campaigns. He also did religious subjects, such as St. Anthony and the Prodigal Son, that have strong genre overtones. His style is extremely lively, the figures rendered in a piquant, mannered way. The great debt that Watteau owed to him can be observed especially in the single figure studies of modes or of stock characters in the Commedia dell' Arte.

Calmady Children, The, by Thomas Lawrence (see)

Calvaert, Denis (1540-1619). Flemish painter, active in Italy. After training in Antwerp, Calvaert went to Italy for further study under Italian masters and helped Sabattini in the Sala de' Re in the Vatican. In Bologna he attracted as pupils Domenichino, Guido Reni and Francesco Albani. Meanwhile he had developed from a Flemish painter of landscape to an Italian painter of such religious subjects as the Noli me tangere (Bologna).

Camaro, Alexander (1901-). German painter (and dancer) who began his work under Otto Mueller, the Brücke painter, in Breslau. From 1928 on, Camaro was Mary Wigman's dance partner. Since the war he has been living in Berlin as a professor at the High School for Plastic Arts. He shows in his painting a Fauve delicacy—perhaps the inheritance from Mueller—mingled with an eerily refined, almost Surrealist mood.

Cambiaso, Luca (1527-85). Genoese painter born in Moneglia. He studied first with his father, and later with G. B. Castello, a Bergamesque painter from whom he absorbed the Venetian style. He studied also in Florence and Rome. His art reveals many diverse influences, including Michelangelo, Raphael, and Correggio, and more specifically Pierino del Vaga and Pordenone, who was then working in the Palazzo Doria. He was extremely precocious and at the age of fifteen

CAMBIASO. Madonna and Child between St. John the Baptist and St. Benedict
Museum of Fine Art, Kress Collection, Houston

CAMPENDONK. Seeshaupt. Private Collection, Germany

was assisting his father in the decoration of a great many façades and interiors in Genoa, work which he continued later with Castello. After Castello left Genoa for Spain in 1567, he was the leading painter in the city until he was also called to Spain in 1583 to be court painter to Philip II and to decorate the Escorial. (See illustration.)

Cameron, David Young (1865-1945). Scottish painter and etcher, associated with the Glasgow school of the 1890's. His tense linear renderings of Scottish mountain scenery have a high emotional content.

Camoin, Charles (1879-). French Fauve painter who studied at the studio of Gustave Moreau along with Marquet. In 1912 he made a trip with Marquet and Matisse to Morocco, and for a long time his work was very much under the influence of Matisse. Later he leaned more toward the style of Renoir and Bonnard.

Campagnola, Domenico (c.1482-c.1562). Italian painter born in either Padua or Venice; best known for his landscape style. Very little is known about his life and he remains a problematic figure in relation to the paintings of Titian, Giorgione, and Sebastiano del Piombo. He was a relative or pupil of Giulio Campagnola, perhaps worked with Titian on the Scuola del Carmine and the Scuola del Santo (1511), but was active mostly in Padua. He was also active in engraving and in making woodcuts, through the medium of which his many landscape themes were spread; and he was probably the first to make a profession of drawing. He left a great many drawings which have been wrongly attributed to Giorgione and Titian.

Campaña, Pedro (Peter de Kempener) (1503-80). Spanish painter of Flemish origin. Famous for his learning and proficiency in the fields of mathematics, architecture, astronomy and sculpture. Around 1529 he was active in Italy, where he studied the styles of Raphael and Michelangelo. He imported these to Spain in Mannerist versions. From 1537-62 he was active in and around Seville, where he painted his famous variations of the Descent from the Cross. By 1563 he had returned to Brussels in the service of the Duke of Alba, managing a tapestry factory. His style is a vigorous Mannerism (see) of the type popular in Spain in mid-century. His Descent has strong affinities with such followers of Michelangelo as Daniele de Volterra and Il Rosso, but retains a certain Spanish intensity and two-dimensionality.

Campendonk, Heinrich (1889-). The youngest member of the German Blue Rider group of Expressionist painters in Munich. A pupil of the mystic Thorn-Prikker at Krefeld, he was invited by Marc and Kandinsky to join them and in 1911 moved in with the group at Sindelsdorf. He contributed two paintings to the first Blue Rider exhibition of December 1911-January 1912 and after war service from 1914-16 settled down in Seeshaupt. In 1926 he was called to the Düsseldorf Academy but was discharged by the Nazis in 1933. He went to Holland and became a professor at the Royal Academy of Plastic Arts in Amsterdam, where he still lives. Campendonk's style is a combination of Delaunay's color dynamism and space penetration with the gentle primitivism of Bavaria where the Blue Rider movement was formed. He is for the most part interested is identifying himself with the simple peasants of the area, just as Marc is with animals, and Klee with children and mentally disturbed persons. He has also done a number of interesting animal paintings which add to the impression that he is trying to be at one with his natural environment. See EXPRESSIONISM. (See illustration.)

Camphuysen, Govert (c.1624-72). Dutch painter of interiors, landscapes with animals, and portraits. He may have studied first with his brother Raphael, but surely came into contact in his early years in Amsterdam with Paul Potter and perhaps also with Isaack van Ostade. From about 1652 to 1663 he worked in Sweden but the end of his life was spent in Amsterdam. Camphuysen was an able painter and his pictures are filled with interesting details.

Campi, Antonio (?-1587). Cremonese painter, second son of Galeazzo, and active mostly in Milan and other Lombard towns. A thoroughly cultured man, he was an architect, a sculptor and writer, publishing a history of Cremona illustrated by Agostino Carracci. He worked in the style of his older brother Giulio (see), but his color is drier and he is generally inferior.

Campi, Bernardino (1522-c.90). Cremonese painter, not a member of the noted Campi family of painters but a student of Giulio Campi (see). He was active in Milan and Reggio Emilia. His altarpieces were in the graceful manner of Parmigianino and Correggio and his frescoes, under the influence of Giulio Romano, were cold and academic.

Campi, Giulio (c.1502-72). The most famous member of the Campi family, he was born in Cremona, the eldest son of Galeazzo. A very prolific painter, he was active in Cremona, Milan, Mantua, Brescia, and Piacenza. He studied first with his father and then with Gatti and Il Sojaro. His art shows the influence of Mannerism (see) and of Lotto, but is essentially based on Romanino and on Pordenone, who was then at work in Cremona. His later paintings exhibit the influence of Raphael.

Campi, Vincenzo (1536-91). Cremonese painter, the son of Galeazzo and pupil and assistant of his brother, Giulio. Active in Cremona and Milan. His religious paintings are superficial and his best work was in portraiture, still life, and genre scenes.

Campigli, Massimo (1895-). Florentine-born Italian painter; lived in Paris from 1919 to 1939. His early work reveals the influence of Seurat, Picasso and Léger, and his later work such diverse sources as Egyptian, Pompeian, Etrurian, medieval, and early Renaissance material. One of the best known of the younger Italian painters (having a special gallery at the Venice Biennale, 1948), Campigli has worked very successfully in portraits and general figure compositions and is noted for the elegant archaism of his style. The stylized and cylindrical forms of Léger and Seurat, the textures of antique painting, the formal arrangements of the early Italians, all have played an important part in his evolution.

Campin, Robert (c.1378-1444). Flemish painter born in Valenciennes, who settled in Tournai (1406) and became town painter (1410). He was the teacher of a Rogelet de la Pasture and Jaquelot Daret. In 1909, Hulin de Loo identified him with the Master of Flémalle. The question remains unresolved, some scholars claiming that he was a mediocre and unimportant painter, and that Rogelet is not, as others believe, identical with Rogier van der Weyden. See MASTER OF FLEMALLE and DARET.

Canal, Antonio (see CANALETTO).

Canaletto (Antonio Canal) (1697-1768). Italian painter famous for city views and especially those of his native Venice. He studied and collaborated with his father Bernardo, a theatrical decorator. He also studied with Luca Carlevaris and went to Rome in 1719 to study perspective with G. P. Pannini, the most famous of those interested in this manner. He returned to Venice in 1722 and became the leading painter of city views, working for Count Algarotti and the English consul, Smith. The latter induced him to go to England in 1746 and again in 1751, where he painted many views of English cities and estates and was elected a member of the Royal Academy in 1763. Before that he had spent 1740-42 in Rome doing Roman scenes. He established a popular genre which had its continuation in the work of his two leading pupils, Bernardo Bellotto, his nephew and closest follower (who also used the name of Canaletto and with whose work the older man's is often confused), and Francesco Guardi. He left a prodigious number of paintings (which came out of a large workshop and are therefore of varying quality) and many etchings. His paintings are sharp and clear, simple in massing though meticulously detailed, and crisply and cleanly handled. (See color plate 23.)

Canaletto (see BELLOTTO, BERNARDO).

Candid, Peter (or de Witte; also called Pietro d'Elia Candido) (c.1548-1628). Flemish decorative painter, active in Florence. Born in Bruges, Candid went to Italy where he was associated with Vasari in work for the Grand Duke of Tuscany. He collaborated in painting the Sala Regia of the Vatican and the dome of the Cathedral of Florence. He also worked in Munich.

Cano, Alonso Referring to the rule of the Emperor Char-architect. This universal man, arrogant in his relations with others, led a stormy life. As a painter he was of great merit,

23. CANALETTO. Eton College. National Gallery, London

although less influential than as a sculptor. He was born in Granada and was trained there by his father, a sculptor. They moved to Seville in 1614 where he studied painting with Pacheco, Herrera and Juan del Castillo; and sculpture with Montañés. He then practiced a lucid, sculpturesque style not unlike that of his enemy Zurbarán, e.g., S. Inés (Berlin). In 1638, as a result of a duel, he fled to Madrid where he was introduced to the court by his fellow student, Velázquez. Here he was employed as a restorer of the royal collection of Titian and Rubens paintings. His study of these and of the van Dycks lent a strong Flemish flavor to his own style, as can be seen in his Virgin and Child (Prado) and in his three portraits of former kings (Prado). The mysterious death of his wife in 1644 brought about his arrest by the Inquisition and Cano fled to Valencia where he painted for the Chartreuse. During 1624-64 he was occupied at Granada Cathedral where, after a ten-year dispute with the clergy, he was granted an intendancy. During this period he also again received royal commissions in Madrid. His chief work in Granada, where he had finally settled, is the cycle of The Joys of Mary (in the Cathedral). His late style rises on occasion to the dreamy exuberance of Murillo. (See illustration.)

Cantarini, Simone (called Simone da Pesaro, Il Pesarese) (1612-48). Italian painter and etcher born in Oropezza. He was an imitator of Guido Reni (see) with whom he worked in Bologna. After studying Raphael in Rome he was in the service of the Duke of Mantua, but most of his activity was in Verona and the Marches.

Cantú, Federico (1908-). Mexican easel painter, muralist and engraver; assistant to Rivera in the painting of the Secretariat of Education murals. He has traveled in Europe and the United States, and his art is more European than Mexican, tending toward poetic and religious formulations.

CANO. Portrait of an Ecclesiastic
Hispanic Society of America, New York

Cappelle, Jan van de (1626-79). Dutch painter and engraver of seascapes and winter scenes. For the most part self-taught, he formed his atmospheric style by studying the works of Simon de Vlieger. He practiced the trade of dyer as well as painter and is said to have been the friend of Rembrandt and Eeckhout in Amsterdam.

Cappuccino, Il (see STROZZI, BERNARDO).

Caracciolo, Giovanni Battista (called Battistello) (c. 1570-1637). Neopolitan follower of Caravaggio. He studied with Fabrizio Santafede and Francesco Imparato, but his style is an amalgamation of the eclecticism of the Carracci and the dramatic late style of Caravaggio. After a trip to Rome in 1612-14 some influence of Raphael was apparent.

Caravaggio, Michelangelo Merisi da (c.1573-1609). One of the revolutionary geniuses of Italian art, he was not only a key figure in the development of Baroque painting, but also the fountainhead of modern Realism. Fundamentally a realist, his early style in its clear lighting shows the influence of Mannerism (see), but his mature work is characterized by a unique dramatic chiaroscuro (see). Born in Caravaggio near Milan, the son of a mason, he was sent at the age of eleven to Milan as an apprentice to Simone Peterzano. A remarkably precocious youth, he was in Rome at the age of sixteen, and studied there with d'Arpino, but had difficulty making a living because of his age. However, through the intercession of a French art dealer, he gained the patronage of the Cardinal del Monte and the Marchese Giustiniani. Among his early works, which are very difficult to date, are the Bacchus (Uffizi), the Rest on the Flight to Egypt (Galleria Doria, Rome), the Fortune-Teller (Louvre), and the Fruit Basket (Ambrosiana, Milan). In 1590-93 he received his first important public commission for the Contarelli Chapel in S. Luigi dei Francesi, for which he did the three paintings of the St. Matthew series. It took him five or six years to complete this group; the first version of St. Matthew and the Angel was rejected for its general realism and the specifically low-class characterization of the saint, but the project established his fame as an important new figure in the Roman firmament, standing opposed to the intellectual Maniera of Zuccari and the eclectic classicism of the Carracci. Though there were violent objections to his art in both ecclesiastic and artistic circles, he had just as strong adherents in both. Thus he continued to receive religious commissions, executing two paintings for the Cerasi Chapel in Sta. Maria del Popolo (c.1600); the Madonna di Loreto (c.1604, Vatican) for S. Agostino; the Madonna of the Serpent (Borghese, Rome, 1605) for Sant' Anna di Palafrenieri, which was refused; the Death of the Virgin (1607, Louvre) for Sta. Maria della Scale, which was also unacceptable; and the Madonna del Rosario (1606, Vienna).

During these years, despite his artistic reputation and the importance of his patrons, he lived a life of bohemian disorder. Police records list many arrests for brawling, and in 1606, after killing a man in a fight, he was forced to flee to Naples. Here he immediately received commissions, executing two paintings for S. Domenico Maggiore (1607). In 1608 he was in Malta, where he was made a Knight of Malta, did two pictures for S. Giovanni and painted a portrait of Olaf de Vignacourt (Louvre). However, he made enemies and had to flee to Sicily, and worked in Syracuse, Messina, and Palermo. On his return to Naples he received a pardon from Rome, but in an effort to avoid his Maltese enemies who had followed him, he embarked on a series of adventures which ended in his death from malaria in Port'Ercole. He was an intensely serious and profoundly human artist, never coarse or vulgar, even lyrically tender. He was revolu-

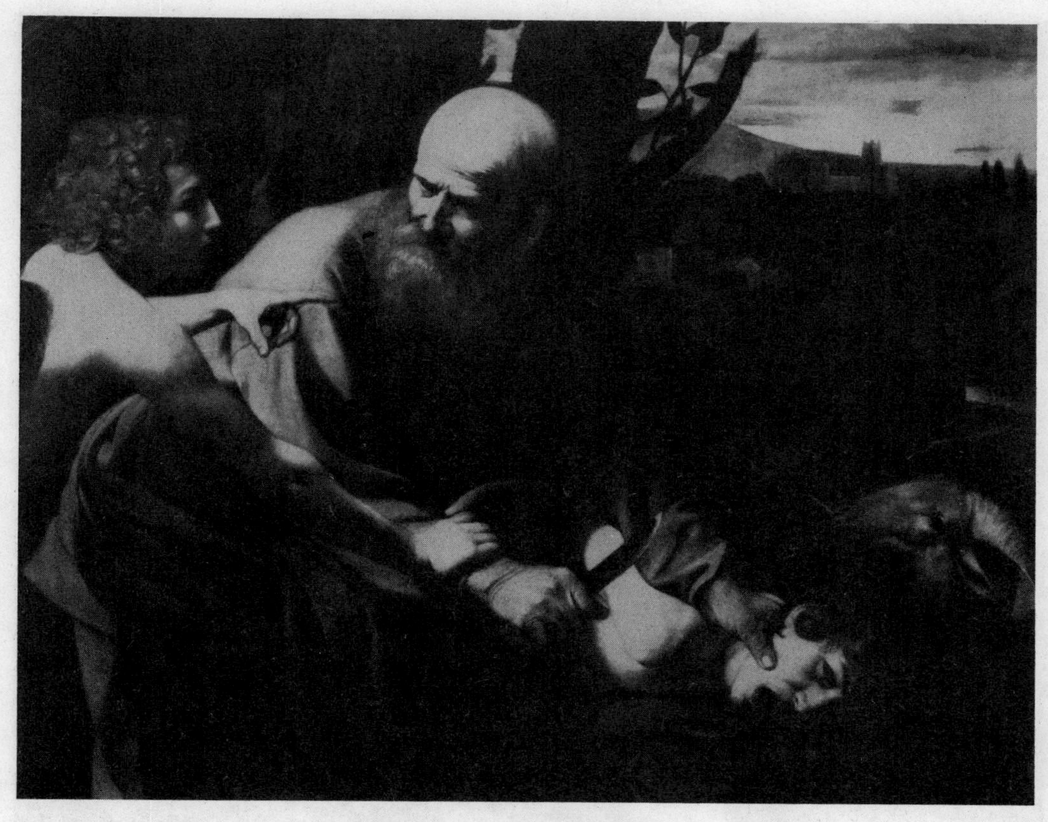

CARAVAGGIO. Sacrifice of Isaac. Uffizi, Florence

tionary in his complete rejection of the intellectual and esthetic standards of his time, and in his return to the world of physical and emotional reality. Like Giotto before him, he reinterpreted for his own age religious dogma in terms of human experience, and his effect on subsequent painting was profound and extensive. (See illustrations, including color plate 24.)

Cárdenas, de (see BERMEJO).

Card Players by Paul Cézanne (see).

Carducho, Vicente (1578-1638). Spanish painter, engraver and critic. Today renowned more for his writings on artistic theory than for his large oeuvre of mural decorations. Vicente was born in Florence and was taught by his brother Bartolomé, who had taken him to Spain at the age of eight. He assisted Bartolomé in his work as court painter in Valladolid. Upon Bartolomé's death he succeeded him as royal painter and continued the decorations for the Prado in Madrid, although not as Bartolomé had planned. Vicente was an indefatigable worker and his paintings appear in most Spanish cities of that time. Born into the Italian eclectic tradition, he did not hesitate to adopt the style of others. viz., his series of fifty-five paintings for the Charterhouse of El Paular, which is based on a special study he made of Carthusian cycles by F. Ribalta and Sánchez-Cotán. His style has a certain correctness and artificiality characteristic of later sixteenth-century Mannerists. He had many pupils, best known of whom was the adroit decorator, Francisco Ricci. As an engraver he is known only for his Death of Abel and Penitent Saint. His *Diálogo de la pintura* (Madrid, 1633) was one of the most important Spanish treatises on art. In it he succinctly introduced his Spanish readers to the accomplishments of the Italian schools and reported on many contemporary Spanish painters. At this rather late date he adhered to Mannerist principles in oppostion not only to Caravaggio but also to the new Spanish naturalism of Velázquez and Ribera. He stressed the moral purpose of art.

Cariani (Giovanni de' Busi) (c.1480-1550). A Venetian painter born near Bergamo. He was at first a follower of Giovanni Bellini and of Palma Vecchio, for whom he worked as an assistant, but later imitated the poetic mood of Giorgione and Lorenzo Lotto. His finest work is in portraiture. where his style is simple, strongly modeled and realistic.

Carles, Arthur B. (1882-). Contemporary American abstract painter born in Philadelphia. He studied at the Pennsylvania Academy of Fine Arts, shortly with Matisse in Paris, and exhibited at the Armory Show. Influenced by modern art, his style has become increasingly abstract since the 1930's.

Carlos, Frei (fl.1517-c.1553). Portuguese painter of Flemish descent; sometimes referred to as the "Portuguese Fra Angelico" because of the purity and simplicity of his religious sentiments. Between 1520 and 1540 he painted a series of pictures with Renaissance architectural backgrounds for the monastery of Espinheiro. In addition to Italianate influence he also shows the effect of the style of Quentin Metsys, especially in the proportion. pose and costume of his figures.

Carnevale, Fra (active 1451, died 1484). Dominican monk whose activity is associated by documents with Urbino. He was among the architects and engineers who worked for the ducal household there and is reported to have painted altarpieces, though none can with certainty be ascribed to him. Two panels in the Boston Museum and the Metropolitan, believed to be from the same altarpiece, are often ascribed to him. They are painted in a grave and spacious style closely related to that of Piero della Francesca.

Carolingian. Referring to the rule of the Emporer Char-

24. CARAVAGGIO. St. John the Baptist. William Rockhill Nelson Gallery, Kansas City

lemagne during the early ninth century A.D. From the Latin *Carolus* or Charles. See ILLUMINATED MANUSCRIPTS.

Carolus-Duran, Emile Auguste (or Charles Emile Auguste Durand) (1838-1917). French academic painter. Already a student of painting at the age of eight in Lille, Carolus-Duran soon turned to perusal of the Old Masters in Paris, Italy and Spain. His first success was a religious painting, Evening Prayer, and then he produced a sensation with his Assassin (Lille) which shows the influence of Courbet. Study of Velázquez led to the Lady with the Glove (Luxembourg) and to much success in the field of portraiture. In his period of greatest fame following the Franco-Prussian War he showed himself stronger in portraits than in larger compositions. He was a grand-officier of the Légion d'Honneur and a director of the Academy. (See illustration.)

Caroto, Giovanni Francesco (c.1480-1555). Italian painter of Verona; a pupil of Liberale da Verona but also worked under Mantegna in Mantua. He was later influenced by Raphael. Frescoes and other works by him are in Verona.

Carpaccio, Vittore (c.1455-1526). Italian painter of the Venetian school; of a slightly later generation than the brothers Gentile and Giovanni Bellini, who dominated Venetian painting during most of Carpaccio's lifetime. He derived stylistic elements from both of them, and developed a characteristic manner of his own, utilizing elements of color, light and animated, realistic detail common to all Venetian painting of his period and related to the art of northern Europe. His emphasis on minute detail, especially in landscape, has led to the occasional mis-attribution of some works to Andrea Mantegna, who had an early influence on his art. Characteristic of Carpaccio's personal style is the use of many figures. small in relation to the picture format, and the individualized, thin and angular or even awkward character of these figures. His skill as a draughtsman and his enamel-like, glowing paint surface have appealed to the Surrealist artists of the twentieth century, on whom his art appears to have had some influence. Whether Venice or Capodistria was Carpaccio's birthplace is in dispute, but it was more likely the former. Nothing is known of his early life, but he is assumed to have been a pupil of Lazzaro Bastiani. His first dated work (1490) is one of the scenes from the life of St. Ursula now in the Venice Academy. His services were apparently in great demand by the various *scuole* or confraternities of Venice and his most important works were narrative cycles done for such institutions. He received payments for work in the Doge's palace in 1502, and in 1507

25. CARPACCIO. A Saint Reading
National Gallery of Art, Kress Collection, Washington, D.C.

CAROLUS-DURAN. Mrs. William Astor
Metropolitan Museum of Art, New York

when he assisted Giovanni Bellini with work left unfinished by Alvise Vivarini at his death. In 1508 he was member of a commission to evaluate frescoes by Giorgione. In 1511 he wrote to Francesco Gonzaga at Mantua, offering for sale a large picture of Jerusalem, which the duke evidently bought, since it was later listed in an inventory of his collection. In the years 1516-23 he was at work at various times in Capodistria and nearby towns, but was back in Venice in 1523.

The works for which Carpaccio is best known are four narrative cycles executed for various confraternities. Earliest and most famous of these is the cycle on the life and martyrdom of St. Ursula (1490-95), painted for the Scuola di Sant' Orsola but now in the Venice Academy. Nine large canvases depict the history of the saint according to her story in the *Golden Legend* of Jacopo Voragine. Like Gentile Bellini. Carpaccio uses familiar settings of contemporary Venice peopled with citizens in rich and brilliant costume as background for the sacred legend. One scene in this series, the Dream of St. Ursula, is particularly renowned for its pervading and mysterious light, which enhances the dreamlike quality of the composition. The second major cycle is a group of nine scenes from the lives of Saints George, Tryphonius and Jerome, painted (1502-1507) for the Scuola di San Giorgio degli Schiavone, where they are still to be seen. Especially noteworthy in this group are the St. George Slaying the Dragon, with its strange and macabre details, and the St. Jerome in his Study, which, like the Dream of St. Ursula. subordinates the small figure to space and light. This series shows little or no stylistic development over the St. Ursula group. At about the same time he painted six scenes from the life of the Virgin for the Scuola degli Albanesi (now dispersed among museums in Bergamo, Milan and Venice). The fourth group consists of four scenes from the life of St. Stephen, painted about 1511-20 for the Scuola di San Stefano

CARPACCIO. Virgin and Child
National Gallery, Kress Collection, Washington, D.C.

CARR. Blunden Harbour
National Gallery of Canada, Ottawa

(also scattered, in Berlin, Paris, Milan and Stuttgart). The third and fourth series are inferior in quality to the first two, and were probably executed with extensive help from assistants. Notable among the many single paintings by Carpaccio are The Courtesans (Correr Museum, Venice), an extraordinary fragment of contemporary Venetian life (perhaps cut down from a larger composition), and a fine example in the Metropolitan, the Meditation on the Passion of Christ. Late altarpieces similar in type to those of Giovanni Bellini are in San Vitale, Venice, the Venice Academy, and the cathedral of Capodistria. (See illustrations, including color plate 25.)

Carr, M. Emily (1871-1944). Canadian painter; studied in San Francisco and England and is known as the pioneer painter of Indian subjects in British Columbia where she was born. Author: *Klee Wyck, The Book of Small, The House of All Sorts.* Only mildly affected by the primitive quality of her themes, her painting remains figurative throughout. (See illustration.)

Carrà, Carlo (1881-). Italian painter, originally one of the five Futurists of 1910 and an active protagonist of their program. By 1915 he had decided to return to Giotto and other late medieval, early Renaissance masters. From 1917 to 1921 he was a member of the *Scuola Metafisica* (metaphysical school) founded by Chirico and active in their chief publication, the well-known *Valori Plastici* (see). He used the other painter's mannequins, measuring instruments, angled floors, toys, etc., but gave his painting an atmospheric quality based on older Italian art rather than Chirico. There is a lightness and charm to Carrà's color that suggests masters like Piero della Francesca. See FUTURISM. (See illustration.)

Carracci, Agostino (1557-1602). Born in Bologna, he formed together with his cousin Ludovico and his younger brother Annibale the Bolognese Academy. Though derivative at first from Mannerism (see), the eclectic style of the Carracci was finally anti-Mannerist and pre-Baroque in character. Agostino was the most intellectual and academic (see) of the three and was more important as an engraver. However, his most famous painting, The Communion of St. Jerome (Bologna), had a great deal of influence. He studied at first with Fontana and Passerotti, and was then sent to Tibaldi to learn engraving. He may also have studied with Cornelius Cort, the Dutch engraver, and sculpture with Allesandro Minganti. After working in Venice, he went with Annibale to Parma to study Correggio, and returned to Bologna in 1582. In 1584 all three worked under the direction of Ludovico on the Fava Palace. Criticism of the decorations led to the formation of the Academy in 1585, where Agostino organized courses in perspective, architecture, and anatomy, and lectured on subject matter and composition. He worked with Annibale in the Gessi Chapel of S. Bartolommeo, in the Magnani Palace (1592) and the Sampieri Palace (1593-94). After a quarrel with Ludovico, he went to Rome to work with Annibale in the Farnese Palace, but after a dispute with him left for Parma. There he worked on the Palazzo dei Giaroini but left his work unfinished when he retired to a monastery.

Carracci, Annibale (1560-1609). Born in Bologna, the younger brother of Agostino and cousin of Ludovico; the most gifted of the three, he formed with them the Bolognese Academy. His realism, based on Venetian painting, is anti-Mannerist, but unlike that of Caravaggio it is modified by a classical strain. He is most important for the work of his Roman period in which he introduced the classical line, carried on in the seventeenth century by Domenichino, Albani, Poussin, and Sacchi. A student of Ludovico, he worked also in the studio of Tibaldi. At eighteen, his first paintings, the Crucifixion (S. Niccolò di S. Felice) and the Baptism (S.

Gregorio), were attacked for their excessive realism. In 1580 he joined Agostino in Parma, returned to Bologna in 1582 and after working with Ludovico and Agostino on the Fava Palace in 1584, combined with them in the formation of the Academy, where from 1585 to 1595 he taught technique. He collaborated with his brother in the decorations of the Gessi Chapel in S. Bartolommeo, the Magnani Palace (1592), and the Sampieri Palace (1593-94). After a dispute with Ludovico he left for Rome and was commissioned by Cardinal Odorado Farnese to decorate the Farnese Palace, his most important and influential project. The theme of this work, The Reign of Love, conceived by a learned prelate, Monsignor Agucchi, in its neo-paganism fits the classicizing tendencies of Annibale. After a quarrel with Agostino in 1600, he retired to a house on the Quirinale and seems to have gone through a period of melancholy depression. He began to paint again in 1606 but only sporadically. He was in Naples in 1609 but returned to Rome, where he died. (See illustration.)

Carracci, Ludovico (1555-1619). Bolognese painter, cousin of Annibale and Agostino, and leader of the Bolognese Academy. The oldest of the three, he is today the least regarded yet the most important for the development of the Bolognese Baroque through Guido Reni and Guercino. In his youth he showed little promise, was considered slow by his teacher, Prospero Fontana, and in Venice was discouraged by Tintoretto. He persevered, however, and went to Florence to study del Sarto, to Parma for Correggio and Parmigianino, and to Mantua for Giulio Romano and Primaticcio. Returning to Bologna in 1578, he was influenced by Bagnacavallo and Tibaldi. He soon achieved great importance in Bologna as the leader, together with his cousins, of a new school. Criticized for their excessive realism in the decoration of the Fava Palace (1584), they formed an academy based on an anti-Mannerist eclecticism. The program was motivated by the selection of what seemed to them the best features of the art of the past—classical design, Lombard color, Michelangelesque power, Titian's truth and naturalism, Correggio's purity, Raphael's symmetry, Tibaldi's discretion, Primaticcio's invention, and a little of Parmigianino's grace. Ludovico spent a short time in Rome in 1602, but most of his activity was confined to Bologna, where he continued as head of the Academy after the split with his cousins. He worked with pupils in the Cortile of S. Michele in Bosco and at the Cathedrals of Bologna and Piacenza. He died in Bologna. (See illustration.)

Carreño, Mario (1913-). Cuban painter; studied and exhibited in Havana, Mexico and Madrid. His art shows intense energy, juxtaposes brilliant complementary colors, and achieves special textural effects through the addition of pieces of cloth, rope and masses of heavy pigment to a glossy Duco surface.

Carreño de Miranda, Juan (1614-85). Spanish painter of Madrid. Student of de las Cuevas and Roman, he was one of the successors of Velázquez as court painter. His style is a composite, based upon Rubens, van Dyck and close study of his friend Velázquez. Velázquez brought him to the court and Carreno did numerous copies of his works. Carreno's early paintings were largely religious and mythological murals, as, for example, those in the Alcázar of Madrid and the

CARRA. Funeral of the Anarchist, Galli
Museum of Modern Art, New York

CARRACCI, ANNIBALE. Silenus Cathering Grapes
National Gallery, London

CARRACCI, LUDOVICO. Susannah and the Elders
National Gallery London

CARREÑO DE MIRANDA. Charles II, King of Spain
Hispanic Society of America, New York

Cathedral of Toledo. Later, because of his position, he specialized in portraiture and was a particular favorite of Charles II. Most famous are his studies of the King (e.g., Prado) and of the Queen Mother dressed as a nun (e.g., Bilbao). He enjoyed great fame, had many students and, in fact, refused several honors. (See illustration.)

Carriera, Rosalba Giovanna (1675-1757). Born in Venice, she worked first as a miniaturist, but turned to pastel portraits. Her Rococo style is characterized by a Dresden-china prettiness. Among her patrons were the most important people of Europe. Her portraits achieved international repute and she was called to work both in Paris and Vienna.

Carrière, Eugène (1849-1906). French painter known for his maternal subjects and his melancholic style. Possessor of a quite original and somewhat symbolic manner, Carrière was first drawn to painting by the influence of La Tour's pastels in Saint-Quentin. He studied with Cabanel but resisted his influence. By the 1880's he had developed his characteristic misty, monochromatic, enveloping style. His favorite subjects were domestic scenes of maternalism and feminine nudes, for which his large family constantly served as models. Because of the psychological impact of his highly personal style he was much discussed in his day. Famous are his portrait of Verlaine (Luxembourg), La Maternité and the Crucifixion (Luxembourg), and large decorative paintings in the Hôtel de Ville, Paris.

Carroll, John (1892-). Contemporary American painter of highly stylized nudes, portraits and figure-pieces. His early work was realistic, but he turned in the 1930's toward an elegant artificiality which became the hallmark of his style. Born in Kansas, he studied at the Mark Hopkins Institute, the University of California (engineering), and with Frank Duveneck in Cincinnati.

Carrucci, Jacopo (see PONTORMO).

cartoon. In the fine arts this term refers to a preliminary full-scale drawing or sketch for a painting, stained-glass window, mural, etc.

Casas Carbó, Ramón (1866-1932). Catalan painter and man of letters. Champion of the Spanish cultural movement, Modernismo, of the turn of the century. A precocious draughtsman, Casas had academic training in Barcelona before entering at the age of eighteen the Paris studio of Carolus-Duran who was then enthusiastic about Velázquez. Casas' self-portrait was at this time in the Paris Salon. On his return to Barcelona he launched with Spanish friends in the '80's and the '90's of the last century the "modernista" movement, a Spanish parallel to the tones and décor of Art Nouveau. He became the central figure of the Quatre Gats group and edited both of its magazines, *Pel y Ploma* (1899-1904) and *Forma* (1902-08). Through these associations he became a close friend of and strong influence on young Picasso, whose portrait he drew in 1901. This circle of artists and its magazines did much to "discover" El Greco, Catalan Romanesque painting and other forgotten elements of the Iberian heritage. Casas's plein-air style and bohemian tastes (Le Moulin de la Galette) did not prevent recognition by conservatives, and in 1908 he traveled through America at the expense of a millionaire industrialist and practiced his talent as a portraitist—this despite his association in that

CASAS CARBÓ. The Beggar Woman
The Hispanic Society of America, New York

period with the Catalan insurrections, commemorated in La Carga (1909, Barcelona) and Garrote vil. While his paintings of Spanish life were important, he is best known for his portraits, which appear in galleries in both hemispheres. He was engaged to paint a great many portraits, ranging from simple families to kings. (See illustration.)

Casilear, John William (1811-93). American landscape painter of the Hudson River school (see), who painted serene aspects of American scenery in New York and Vermont. Born in New York, he studied engraving with Peter Maverick and at the National Academy of Design.

Casorati, Felice (1886-). Italian painter associated with the city of Turin, where he teaches at the Albertina Academy. A studio figure painter, his works are marked by a classical reticence and a controlled arrangement mingled with a somewhat romantic and atmospheric quality. He is one of the most important Italian artists of his generation.

Cassatt, Mary (1845-1926). Generally considered America's most famous woman painter, this daughter of a wealthy Pennsylvania family lived most of her life in France and played a part in the Impressionist movement. Born in what is now part of Pittsburgh, she had early training at the Pennsylvania Academy of Fine Arts. Then in 1868, against the wishes of her father, she went to Paris to become a painter, continuing her studies in Italy, Spain, and Belgium, and being successively influenced by the art of Correggio, Velázquez, and Rubens. She exhibited at the Paris Salon in 1872 and 1874, but her works were rejected in 1875 and 1877, and she never exhibited again. At about this time she was invited by Degas to join the notorious and reviled Impressionists, and continued to exhibit with them. Although she had some contact with Manet, Renoir and Cézanne, her closest friend among the Impressionists and her artistic mentor remained Degas. Her dependence upon him is most apparent in her oils and pastels. She was a sincere and competent craftsman though more pedestrian and sentimental than Degas. Her sensitive renditions of mothers and children have brought her world fame, but her most original contribution was probably in the field of etching and the color-print; in the latter her typical subjects show the lessons she learned from Japanese prints. In 1892 she was commissioned to paint the north tympanum of the Woman's Building at the Columbian Exposition in Chicago and in 1904 was awarded the Légion d'Honneur. During her life she was instrumental in the formation of the Havemeyer Collection. By 1914 she was practically blind and could work no more. (See illustrations, including color plate 26.)

Cassinari, Bruno (1912-). Italian Expressionist painter of great force and individuality. At one time a member of the New Art Front, he now works in solitude, developing his extremely personal variant of this modern style. He shows great sympathy for the work of Modigliani and retains a distinctly figurative form.

cassone (It.). A large chest having either elaborately

26. CASSATT. The Boating Party. National Gallery of Art, Dale Collection, Washington, D.C.

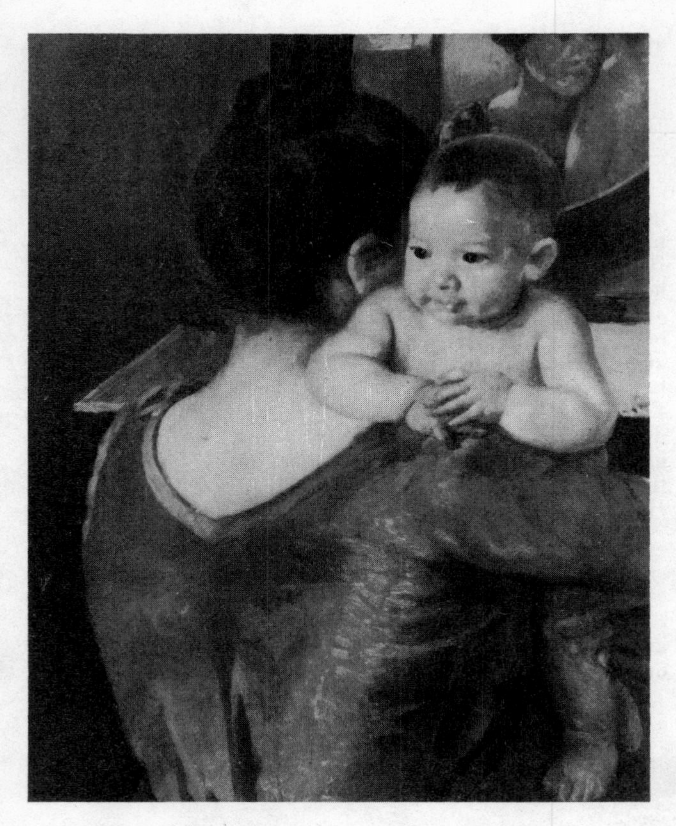

CASSATT. Mother and Child. Brooklyn Museum

carved or painted panels; one of the most characteristic types of Italian furniture.

Castagno, Andrea del (1423-57). One of the most important of the scientific group of artists active in Florence in the first half of the fifteenth century. His art is a logical development of the innovations of Masaccio and the sculptor Donatello. Andrea (or Andreino) di Bartolommeo di Simone was born of lowly parentage in Castagno in the Mugello Valley. According to Vasari, his talent was discovered by Bartolommeo de' Medici, under whose protection he was brought to Florence and trained as a painter. Whether this is true or not, his earliest recorded work (now lost) was a fresco on the Podestà façade, representing the vanquished enemies of the Medici who returned from exile in 1434. He spent a period in Venice before 1444, making cartoons for mosaics in San Marco, and painting, together with a certain Francesco da Faenza, frescoes in the chapel of San Tarasio in San Zaccaria. This decoration, signed and dated 1442, is the earliest extant work of Castagno. Of the several representations, those of the Evangelists and part of the frieze of putti are considered to be by him. In 1444 he was back in Florence and was paid for the cartoon for a stained glass window of the Deposition for the cathedral, at the same time that Uccello was paid for a similar work. Three major fresco works, done on different occasions and now gathered together in the refectory of Sant' Apollonia (now a Castagno museum) in Florence were all done probably between his return from Venice and about 1449. Most notable of these is the Last Supper, painted in the refectory, with representations in an upper course of the Crucifixion, Entombment and Resurrection. This Last Supper serves as a prototype of the subject for the rest of the fifteenth century until Leonardo's more famous treatment of it in Milan. It is among the earliest attempts to make the space in a picture continuous with the actual space of the room where it is painted, which was first attemped in Masaccio's Holy Trinity in Santa Maria Novella. Two frescoes of the Crucifixion, painted for Santa Maria degli Angeli, were moved to Sant' Apollonia. Of these only the one including the Virgin, St. John the Evangelist and Saints Benedict and Romuald is universally attributed to Castagno. The third fresco is the series of nine famous men and women, originally a decoration for the Villa Carducci in Legnaia. It includes the well-known figure of Pippo Spano and ideal portraits of Dante, Petrarch and Boccaccio. From about 1449/50 is the panel of the Assumption of the Virgin, now in Berlin. Later frescoes are the Trinity in the Carboli chapel of SS. Annunziata (1454/5), and the equestrian portrait of the military hero Niccolò da Tolentino (1456) in the cathedral of Florence, done as a pendant to Uccello's portrait of Sir John Hawkwood, which was painted twenty years earlier. A panel of the Crucifixion by Castagno is in the London National Gallery, and a portrait that has been attributed to him is in the Washington National Gallery. Castagno's earliest work reveals a somewhat coarse but vigorous style closely related to Masaccio and Donatello. His art is refined and developed in the frescoes at Sant' Apollonia into a monumental and forceful conception of the human figure in convincing space. As with Masaccio, gravity and intensity of expression are achieved more by monumental form and composition than by facial expression and gesture. Drapery is used to enhance the force of the figures and all forms are plastically modeled in light and shadow, with consistent mastery of anatomy and perspective. Decorative effects are introduced in realistic rendering of colorful marble and mosaic ornament (especially in the Last Supper). The Passion scenes reveal a relation to Domenico Veneziano, especially in their light coloration. The series of famous men is one of the earliest examples of illusionistic placing of figures in false architectural niches so that the figures seem to emerge from the wall into the room. Hands, feet and heads overlap the painted architectural frames to create this effect. Castagno was also one of the first to treat the halo as a material object, with the head reflected on its apparently polished surface. The equestrian portrait in the cathedral may be considered a parallel in painting of Donatello's Gattamelata statue in Padua, and in general Castagno's art seems closer to that of the sculptor than to any contemporary painter. (See illustrations, including color plate 27.)

Castellanos, Julio (1905-1947). Mexican painter, stage designer, fresco and graphic artist who in the late 1920's tried to stem the nativist tide in Mexican art by means of the neo-classicism of modern French and Italian art. He painted a charming fresco allegory of Heaven and Hell in a primary school at Coyoacán, 1933. His work shows highly disciplined draughtsmanship and composition as well as deep feeling for his themes. (See illustration.)

Castiglione, Giovanni Benedetto (called Il Grechetto) (1616-70). Italian painter of animals and still lifes; he also did religious and mythological subjects, which gave him an excuse to paint accessories. Born in Genoa, he studied with G. B. Paggi and G. A. De Ferrari, and was active in Rome, Naples, Venice, Bologna, and Mantua. His etchings, influenced by Rembrandt, are excellent.

Castiglione, Giuseppe (1698-1768). Italian painter of the Jesuit order; he worked first in Genoa before going to China as a missionary, where he painted in a mixture of Western and Eastern styles. Also an architect, he built the emperor a palace in Peking in the European manner. See Lang Shih-ning under CHINESE PAINTERS: CH'ING DYNASTY.

Castillo, José del (1737-93). A Spanish painter and etcher. He was a tapestry designer active for the factory of Santa Barbara in Goya's youth. He was sent to Italy to study and became an assistant to Mengs upon his return. He made tapestry cartoons under the direction of Mengs and later with Goya under Bayeu. He printed copies of the masters and illustrations for *Don Quixote*.

catacombs. The underground burial passages of ancient Rome or Alexandria associated with the earliest years of Christianity. Important for the wall and ceiling paintings found there, as well as for examples of early Christian sarcophagi.

Catena, Vincenzo di Biagio (c.1470-1531). Like many of his Venetian contemporaries, Catena was a pupil and follower of Giovanni Bellini. Though he was an able painter, his early work is harder in drawing and texture, and less profound than Bellini's. Later he came under the influence of Bellini's greater pupil, Giorgione. He painted many portraits in addition to devotional subjects. Paintings by him are in most of the principal European museums.

Caterino Veneziano (active 1362-82). Venetian painter who in 1367 collaborated with Donato di San Vitale on a cross for the church of Sant' Agnese (now lost), and again worked with Donato in 1372 on the Coronation of the Virgin in the Querini-Stampalia gallery, Venice. In 1375 he signed a Coronation now in the Venice Academy.

Catlin, George (1796-1872). Self-taught American painter of Indian life. Born in Pennsylvania, he practiced law until 1823, painted portraits in Philadelphia, Washington, Albany, and Richmond until 1830, and then in 1832 began a stay among the American Indians, living with 48 tribes and painting 310 oil portraits and 200 scenes. In 1841 he issued an illustrated account of his experiences, *Letters and Notes on the Manners, Customs, and Conditions of the North American Indian*. In 1837 he arranged a show, which included his Indian Gallery along with live Indians, and toured the U.S., England, and France until 1852, when it was overtaken by

CASTAGNO. The Youthful David. National Gallery, Widener Collection, Washington, D.C.

CASTELLANOS. The Hut. Instituto Nacional de Bellas Artes, Mexico City

27. CASTAGNO. Crucifixion. National Gallery, London

financial difficulties. He offered his collection to the Smithsonian Institution in 1846 and it was finally accepted in 1879 (about one third of it was later destroyed by fire). His last years were spent in travel and painting in South and Central America (1852-57) and in Europe (1858-70). (See illustration.)

CATLIN. Buffalo Chase
United States National Museum, Washington, D.C.

Cauchon, Robert (1914-). Canadian painter originally trained as a blacksmith and joiner. In a somewhat primitivistic style, he does simple, straightforward scenes of life around him.

Cavagna, Giovanni Paolo (1556-1627). Italian painter of religious scenes and decorations; born in Bergamo and active there and in the vicinity. He studied with Baschenis the elder, and was influenced largely by Moroni, and somewhat less by the Venetians, Titian, Veronese, and Lotto.

Cavalcanti, Emiliano di (1897-). One of the pioneers of the modern movement in Brazilian painting. He does genre and still-life themes of semi-primitivistic quality, the outlines bold, the forms angular.

Cavallini, Pietro (active c.1270-c.1334). Roman painter and mosaicist whose work stands as the earliest attempt by an Italian to break with Byzantine formulas of representation and strike out in the direction of plastic illusion and rational space. How far he antedates Giotto in this is debatable, but it is agreed that he played a considerable role in the formation of the great Florentine's style. Of the many works attributed to Cavallini by Ghiberti and Vasari, only two are extant: the well-preserved mosaics in the apse of Santa Maria in Trastevere, Rome, 1291, and fragmentary remains of an extensive fresco cycle in Santa Cecilia, Rome, which were covered with whitewash until 1900. The Vatican possesses old watercolors depicting frescoes that Cavallini executed in San Paolo fuori le Mura, and fragments are preserved inside the same church of mosaics he made on the façade. The frescoes are lost but the watercolors of them reveal three cycles, made at different times between 1270 and 1303 (according to contemporary personages referred to or

28. CÉZANNE. The Card Players. Collection Stephen C. Clark, New York

depicted). The famous mosaics in Santa Maria in Trastevere present scenes from the life of the Virgin. Cavallini's iconography in this cycle is thoroughly Byzantine, but the rendering of the figures is plastic to a degree that suggests some study of antique sculpture. The remains of the frescoes in Santa Cecilia (generally dated about 1295) indicate that the whole church was originally decorated with scenes from the Old and New Testaments. A fresco in San Giorgio in Velabro, Rome, is also attributed to Cavallini. There is a stylistic connection between Cavallini's Roman school and certain frescoes in the Upper Church of San Francisco at Assisi. Other works associated with his school are a fresco of the Madonna and Saints in Santa Maria in Aracoeli, Rome, a mosaic of the same subject in San Chrisogono, Rome, and a panel of the Nativity in the Philadelphia Museum. (See illustration.)

cave painting (see PREHISTORIC PAINTING).

Cavedone, Giacomo (1577-1660). Bolognese painter born in Sassuolo; a follower of the Carracci. He studied with Ludovico, Passarotti, and at the Baldi Academy, and in 1610 with Guido Reni in Rome. Active in Bologna, Modena, and neighboring towns, his early works (1610-20) are the best known. His excellent color indicates a Venetian influence.

Cazin, Jean Charles (1841-1901). French painter, engraver and ceramist. Of rather unstable disposition, Cazin went from landscapes to harbor studies to histories to ceramics. He practiced various techniques including that of wax, and studied variously Poussin, the Italians, Dutch and Flemish. Outstanding are his Souvenir de fête (Petit Palais, Paris) and Mortuary Chamber of Gambetta (Luxembourg).

Cedaspe, Paulo (see CÉSPEDES, PABLO DE).

Cennini, Cennino (late 14th century). A Florentine known to the history of art as the author of a book on the art of painting *(Il Libro d'Arte)* rather than as a painter. He worked twelve years with Agnolo Gaddi, on whose death (1396) he moved to Padua, where he perhaps spent the greater part of his life. No painted work of Cennino's is known today but his treatise is a valuable document on the techniques of the Giotto tradition.

Cerano, Il (see CRESPI, GIOVANNI BATTISTA).

Ceresa, Carlo (1609-79). Bergamese painter born in S. Giovanni Bianco. He studied with Daniele Crespi and perhaps Reni, and painted religious pictures, but is much better as a portraitist in the manner of Moroni.

Cerezo, Mateo (1635-85). Spanish painter of Madrid. Outstanding student of Carreno, whom he joined after instruction from his own father in Burgos. His style was a rich Baroque colorism founded upon the Venetians as well as on the Flemish. An example is the Assumption of the Virgin in the Prado. His output was enormous, and like others of his day he was renowned for the painting of bodegones (see). Only two signed examples of the latter exist today, in Mexico. Much of his career was spent on mural decoration and he contributed many examples to the contemporary taste for

CAVALLINI. Head of Christ (detail).
Convent of St. Cecilia, Rome

CÉSPEDES. The Last Supper. Provincial Museum, Seville

the Immaculate Conception. His last great work was a Christ at Emmaus for the Convent of the Augustinians, Madrid.

Cernuschi Museum, Paris. Specializes in Chinese and Japanese art.

Ceruti, Giacomo (called Il Pitocchetto) (active latter half of 18th century). Lombard painter from Milan or Brescia who did some fine portraits, but is best known for still lifes presaging in both scheme and execution modern conceptions of the subject. He also executed religious paintings in Padua and Brescia.

Cesare da Sesto (1477-1523). Italian, Lombard. One of the less important followers of Leonardo da Vinci in Milan. A Madonna by him is in the Brera.

Cesari, Giuseppe (see ARPINO, IL CAVALIERE D').

Céspedes, Pablo de (also called Paolo Cedaspe) (1538-1608). Spanish painter and critic. His style was an academic Mannerism learned from F. Zuccaro, among others, during two periods in Rome. Typical of the involved gesturing and format of this style are his Last Suppers (Museum, Seville, and Cordoba Cathedral). He studied philosophy and Oriental languages and practiced sculpture and architecture. He wrote two treatises on art. One, a prose discourse, compares the arts of the ancients and the moderns. The other, the *Poema de la Pintura,* exists today only in fragments quoted by Pacheco and Ceán Bermudez. Though little known, the beauty of his poem marks it as one of the most perceptive didactic writings of its day. (See illustration.)

Cézanne, Paul (1839-1906). Outstanding pioneer modern French painter whose influence has been evident on a great many successive French and other European schools of painting. He stands as a full stop between Impressionism (with its emphasis on transitory and descriptive light values) and the form-searching, color-exploiting, emotion-provoking art of such diverse movements as Cubism (see), Fauvism (see), and Expressionism (see). Thus Cézanne's Post-Impressionism (see) becomes the chief source of the form experience which lies at the basis of so much early and later twentieth-century art. Born at Aix-en-Provence the son of a hatmaker turned banker, he was educated in that city with Emile Zola as one of his school-friends. He worked in the Aix School of Drawing where he took a second prize in 1858; he also studied music. He took his Lycée degree in Letters in 1859 and wished to go to Paris to study art but his father insisted that he study law. After spending 1860 painting on his own in a manner suggesting Caravaggio, he was permitted to go to Paris and enrolled in the Académie Suisse. There he met Guillaumin and Pissarro; the latter was to exert a strong influence on him. Cézanne visited the Louvre and the Salon and was rejected at the Ecole des Beaux-Arts; returning home, he took a job in his father's bank but painted during the evenings and did murals at the family estate at Jas de Bouffan. In 1862-64 he made his second stay in Paris with new friends that included Bazille, Monet, Renoir, and Sisley. With Zola he visited the Salon des Refusés and reiterated his

CÉZANNE. Still Life
Stedelijk Museum, Amsterdam

CÉZANNE. The Bathers. Philadelphia Museum of Art, Wilstach Collection

admiration for Delacroix and Courbet; his Romantic manner, with its dark "lurid" tones, persisted until 1872. Returning to Aix, 1864-70, he divided his time between there and Paris, regularly sending to the Salon and regularly being refused. During the Franco-Prussian war he stayed at L'Estaque near Marseilles, living with a young model who was later to become Mme Cézanne.

In 1871 Cézanne returned to Paris and in 1872 his son Paul was born and he visited Pissarro at Pontoise. The following year he settled at Auvers-sur-Oise near his friend Dr. Gachet (later Van Gogh's physician) and painted the well-known House of the Hanged Man and other works showing the influence of Pissarro; he also met the art dealer Père Tanguy. In 1874 he participated, through Pissarro, in the First Impressionist Exhibition. His participation was opposed and his contributons were the most derided of all. Two years later he refused to join the Second Impressionist Exhibition, but entered the Third, in 1877, with seventeen pictures. By 1878 Cézanne had finshed with Impressionist practices. In 1882 Renoir visited him at L'Estaque; there were perceptible traces of influence on Renoir from this contact. From 1884 to 1888, while Cézanne was staying chiefly at Gardanne, a small hill-town near Aix, the classical, i.e., formal and architectonic, element in his painting became increasingly evident. He finally married his model Hortense Fiquet in 1886 and broke with Zola, whose novel *L'Oeuvre* contains the character of an unsuccessful artist very much like Cézanne. In that same year his father died, leaving him enough money to do what he wished.

In 1892 Cézanne produced the five versions of the Card Players, the Baigneuses series, and the Montagne Ste.-Victoire. All these exemplify the controlled, deliberately limited space which was destined to influence the entire course of modern art. They reveal his search for a closed, complete composition within this limited space, and the exploitation of all the form possibilities of a theme or motif rather than

CHAGALL. The Lovers. Stedelijk Museum, Amsterdam

29. CHAGALL. Snowing. City Art Museum, St. Louis

the narrative or emotional meaning of a subject. The gradual growth of a following became apparent at this time. In 1900 he showed at the Centennial Exhibition, the Berlin Nationalgalerie bought a picture of his, and Maurice Denis painted Hommage à Cézanne. In 1904 an entire room at the Salon d'Automne was devoted to him. Visitors began coming to Aix from everywhere. The following year he exhibited at the Salon d'Automne again and at the Indépendants; these shows had enormous impact on the nascent Fauve and Cubist movements. (See illustrations, including color plate 28.)

Chabot, Hendrik (1894-1949). Netherlands painter and one of the most important of her Expressionists. During his twenties he worked both as sculptor and painter in heavy turgid forms, but gradually freed himself and escaped into violently emotive deformations of form and color designed to evoke a sense of psychological disturbance. He worked throughout World War II, painting the German occupation of Holland, using hard, awkward and tragic forms, as in his Jewish Refugees.

Chagall, Marc (1887). Distinguished Russian-born painter of the School of Paris. Because of the natural fantasy of his style he has become known, among other things, as a pioneer in the Surrealist movement. The son of a poor Jewish fish-merchant, Chagall arrived in Paris in 1910 and settled down at The Beehive near the slaughterhouses. Between 1910 and 1914 he met among others, La Fresnaye, Delaunay and Modigliani, as well as a number of important poets. Chagall's painting during those pre-war years presents

30. CHARDIN. The Fountain. Wildenstein Gallery, New York

a combination of more or less Cubist form, the new anti-Cubist color ideas of such painters as Delaunay and La Fresnaye, and a highly developed and poetic imagination to which he was already giving free play. Thus, although he participated in the form experiments of his time and the attempt to "liberate" Cubism from its static quality and drabness of color, he added what has been called the possible-impossible component—the sense of the unexpected and the fantastic that was to appeal to the later Surrealists and make them point to Chagall as an ancestor. He was in Russia when World War I broke out and in 1917 was appointed Commissar of Fine Arts for his own province of Vitebsk. In 1919 he did a number of mural paintings for the lobby of the Jewish Theatre in Moscow, but by 1922 he had left Russia. Back in Paris, he did a series of illustrations for Gogol's *Dead Souls* in a Vollard edition of the book and moved on to his real fame. His style became broader and more decorative, always preserving the poetic and fantastic element but without the faceted forms of Cubism. For the latter he substituted one of the richest palettes in modern painting. with which he achieves not only the unpremeditated effects of the earlier works but a deeper poetry, a more universal

CHAMPAIGNE. Three Portraits of Cardinal Richelieu
National Gallery, London

CHARLOT. Mexican Kitchen
Associated American Artists Galleries, New York

CHARDIN. Self-Portrait. Louvre, Paris

quality that allies him to the figurative or representational Expressionists of our time. (See illustrations, including color plate 29).

Châlons, Simon de (also Simon de Mailly or Malhy) (active 1535-62). French painter of Avignon. Active in the workshop of Henri Guigo, Simon practiced an Italo-Flemish style. His Incredulity of St. Thomas is in the Louvre.

Champaigne, Philippe de (1602-74). French painter of Flemish origin. Born in Brussels, Champaigne worked with two little-known Flemings and a landscapist, Fouquiere, before coming permanently to Paris at the age of nineteen. Although his best paintings reveal a basic Flemish objectivity, and he was resident at the Luxembourg in the days of Marie de' Medici, Champaigne shows no traces of the style of Rubens. Rather, he tempers his Flemish exactitude with the detached abstraction of Poussin, his friend and one-time associate. Champaigne has been called "the painter of Port Royal" because of his many associations with that important lay convent. The simplicity and pious quietism of certain of his religious works has led to the comparison of his style with the Jansenist self-denial of the convent. However, this mood is to be found in other French painters of the period, and Champaigne also painted for the Jesuits and for Cardinal Richelieu (who terminated the order). Both his daughters entered Port Royal and one of Champaigne's most effective paintings of the austere type is a votive portrait of the abbess and his daughter Catherine (Louvre), celebrating Catherine's miraculous cure by the abbess. Champaigne's eclectic, decorative style can be seen in the Presentation (Brussels), which derives from Italian formulas. Perhaps his greatest merit is to be found in his portraits, which were much celebrated in his day. The van Dyck tradition is seen in this work, but Champaigne adds a personal touch of serious scutiny, e.g., his portraits of Richelieu and of Robert Arnaud. Famous among his paintings was the Vow of Louis XIII (Museum Caen), a bit of Baroque pastiche. (See illustration.)

Chao Meng-fu (see CHINESE PAINTERS: YÜAN DYNASTY).

Chardin, Jean Baptiste Siméon (1699-1779). French painter of still lifes, interiors and portraits. Chardin was representative of the new middle-class taste in art of his day. Nevertheless he interests us more now for the way in which he anticipated attitudes of later centuries in painting. The careful scrutiny in his method and the homogeneous flecking of his colors suggest the new modes of envisaging nature which occupied the attention of nineteenth-century painters. He shared this modernity with the critic Diderot, who grew enthusiastic about him, saying, "He is the great colorist... the great magician... the sublime technician... he is nature itself." His employment of still-life and even of genre scenes as vehicles of artistic arrangement looked forward to Cézanne and the modern abstractionists.

Chardin was born in Paris of a humble family. His artistic beginnings were also humble. A student of P. J. Cazes, he assisted J. B. van Loo in the restorations of frescoes at Fontainebleau, and he painted the rifle in a hunting scene by Noël Coypel. His reputation was earned with a surgeon's signboard which he decorated with a street scene. In 1728 he successfully exhibited still lifes in the open-air exhibition at the Plâce Dauphin. These included The Ray, presently in the Louvre. Having already joined the Academy of St. Luke through the influence of his craftsman-father, Chardin was enjoined to apply to the Royal Academy. He was elected in 1728 with considerable applause and with the strong support of Largillière, who was fascinated with the Flemish cast of Chardin's work and with his scientific treatment of color and light. Chardin's paintings quickly became the rage, but sold only for small sums and he apparently never lived on their income. They were frequently published as engravings, especially the genres, with little verses below, but he did not appear to realize on this business. Business-like he was, however, in his simple bourgeois manner: from 1752-55 he was treasurer of the Academy, and with his wife's aid he put its books in order, following embezzlements on the part of his predecessor. For twenty years he served as tapissier of the Louvre, which included the delicate and exacting task of hanging the pictures for the Salons, a duty for which his career of pictorial arrangement had ably equipped him.

Chardin's manner of still-life painting represents a rather sharp break with previous tradition. Still life had originated as a symbol of hospitality and good living or as an island of technical virtuosity in a painting of nobler subject. Chardin shifted the emphasis to the pictorial value of the represented objects themselves. This had been anticipated in the margins of certain late medieval paintings and in the statuesque but airless bodegones (see) of Zurbarán and Sánchez-Cotan in Spain. However, Chardin's interest was also an atmospheric one. Indeed it might be said that the palpability of atmosphere and the personality of light were his ultimate objectives. So he constructed within the compass of two unities: the abstract interplay of the solid (and planar) geometry of the objects and the cohesion of the canvas by a uniform, homogeneous color system and brushwork. All of this was arrived at by an intense, close examination of the actual objects and by the credo that anything was worthy to be painted. This latter doctrine moved him to choices of humble kitchen objects, bits of ordinary life, simple closed interiors. In genre, for instance, it led to a concentration on the immediacy of the mannequin-like forms. It excluded any feeling of extension beyond the framed vignette; there was no allusion to a continuum or world-system which had characterized most Baroque painting. That which the eye perceived was usually presented without comment except that of artistic selection and arrangement. Chardin came to genre painting in mid-career. He based it on the then popular Flemish tradition. He delighted in moralizing subjects but rendered them in statuesque rather than anecdotal manner. His portraits are characteristically sober in pose and scrutiny, but achieve a bit of Rococo spirit through the live colorism of his pigments. (See illustrations, including color plate 30.)

Charlet, Nicolas Toussaint (1792-1845). French painter and engraver. An associate of the early French Romantics, Charlet studied with Gros and traveled with Géricault. From an early age he was accomplished at drawing and quickly became a virtuoso in lithography, an art he taught to Géricault. He was a great admirer of Napoleon, opposing the Restoration, taking prominent part in the July Revolution, and by his art doing much to perpetuate the Napoleon-image that dominated so much of the thought of the time. On this theme he produced the Episode in the Retreat from Russia, the Crossing of the Rhine at Kehl by Moreau and the Convoy of Wounded.

Charlot, Jean (1898-). French-born painter prominent in the modern Mexican movement. Born in Paris of partly Mexican lineage, he came to Mexico in 1921, participated in the first mural experiments with encaustic and fresco in the National Preparatory School (1921) and there did one of the first frescoes (1922). Staff artist with a Carnegie Archaeological Expedition to Chichén-Itzá (1926-29), he received impressions of Yucatán that have since persisted in his work. Charlot's importance, however, goes far beyond his charming, decorative Mexicanist paintings and color lithographs: he has written many articles and books that set him apart as an authority on modern Mexican art. He has always been a forceful advocate of the mural as public art and has shown a strong feeling for Mexican culture itself. He has recently been teaching in the U.S.A. and Hawaii. (See illustration.)

Charonton (Quarton), Enguerrand (active 1447-61). French painter. Important documented master of the School of Avignon in the late middle ages. Charonton was born in Laon about 1410, but we know of his activity only in Provence where he worked alone and (in 1452) with Pierre Villate on a Madonna of Misericorde which shows an understanding of current Flemish and Italian innovators. In 1454 Charonton painted the great altarpiece of the Coronation of the Virgin for which we have the contract stipulating subject matter down to the smallest detail. He is one of the outstanding masters of his day and his monumental style caused at one time the attribution to him of the famous Pietà of Avignon, now considered anonymous.

CHINA. MING DYNASTY. Bird Splashing
Print from Ten Bamboo Studio
Museum of Fine Arts, Boston

Chase, William Merritt (1849-1916). American painter and teacher. Born in Indiana, he grew up in Indianapolis, where he worked in his father's shoe store before turning

CHINA. SUNG DYNASTY. Scholars Collating Chinese Texts. Museum of Fine Arts, Boston

31. CHINA. T'ANG DYNASTY
Head of a Bodhisattva from Tun-huang
Fogg Art Museum, Harvard University, Cambridge

to art. He studied in Indianapolis and later in New York, and then opened a studio in St. Louis, producing still lifes and flower-pieces. In 1872 he went to study at the Munich Academy, where he met Duveneck, Twachtman, Shirlaw, and Currier. In 1877 he visited Venice with Twachtman and Duveneck and was impressed by Tintoretto, and then Spain, where he copied Velázquez. On his return to the U.S. in the same year he began a long and distinguished career as painter and teacher. He taught first at the Art Students League, and also at the Pennsylvania Academy of Fine Arts and the Brooklyn Art School. Beginning in 1891, he held summer classes at Shinnecock, L.I., and in 1896 opened his own school in New York. From 1903 to 1913 he took classes abroad and in 1914 undertook his last teaching venture—a summer school in Carmel, Calif.. His early work was in the dark color tonality of Munich, but his contact with the work of Velázquez and Hals revolutionized his style and brought it within the orbit of Manet and of Whistler, whom he met and painted in 1885. His mature style is close to that of Sargent, broadly Impressionistic and brilliant in brushwork. He painted portraits and landscapes, but is perhaps best known for studio still lifes of bric-a-brac and dead fish, which served as vehicles for the display of his virtuosity.

Chassériau, Théodore (1819-56). French painter and etcher. Son of the French consul in Santo Domingo, Chassériau decided his career at ten and entered Ingres' studio at thirteen. Although he derived his style from Ingres and Giorgione, his mood was Romantic and he was drawn to Delacroix's colorism and Oriental subject matter. He was able to synthesize the antithetic styles of Ingres and Delacroix and became a successful decorative painter. His murals in St. Merri, St. Roch and the Cour de Comptes, although damaged, reveal him as one of the most creative decorators of his day. His career was influenced by much travel throughout southern Europe and North Africa, the latter suggesting to him some of his more sensual types.

Chávez Morado, José (1909-). Mexican painter, fresco and mosaic artist, and engraver; co-founder of the Popular Graphic Art Workshop. Although he has done mural decorations, Chávez Morado is best known for woodcuts characterized by macabre humor and for other caricatures. Former chief of the Plastic Arts Section, Secretariat of Public Education, he has also directed the Workshop for Plastic Integration, National Institute of Fine Arts. His murals are at the new University City and in the Secretariat of Communications and Public Works, Mexico City.

32. CHINA. SUNG DYNASTY. Chou Chi-ch'ang
Transfiguration of an Arhat
Museum of Fine Arts, Boston

Ch'en Jung (see CHINESE PAINTERS: SUNG DYNASTY).

chiaroscuro. The arrangement or treatment of the light and dark areas in a work of art, such as a drawing or painting, whether in monochrome or color; the art or practice of so arranging the lights and darks as to produce a harmonious effect. This term has frequently been used in a narrower sense, referring to the technique whereby certain Renaissance and modern painters have created the illusion that their subjects are surrounded by space. This latter, three-dimensional sense calls to mind such painters as Raphael, Leonardo da Vinci, Caravaggio and Rembrandt. Leonardo's mysterious haze is more properly called "sfumato" (see), from the Italian term meaning "smoked." Caravaggio's school is referred to as Tenebrist (see), an allusion to its dramatic Baroque emphasis on deep shadows.

Ch'ien Hsüan (see CHINESE PAINTERS: YÜAN DYNASTY).

China, Development of painting in

In the painted pottery of proto-historic China one may find a clue to the direction taken in later periods, for the patterns on these wares lean toward linear design and abstract motifs filled with swirling forms. In these designs, moreover, the light and dark elements tend to alternate and complement each other in balanced and asymmetrical space-areas. There is already a preference for the contrast of filled and empty, or positive and negative, areas, and for the line that may suggest movement or delineate form. There is little that can be identified with the physical world, except for a few stylized animals or ghostly-looking human beings. Even at that time the realm of the spirit was important to the Chinese painter.

Early records occasionally describe painted wall decorations and portraits of worthy men and women. But since they were painted on silk or on walls long since gone, we must base our conception of them on descriptions or on fragments of lacquer, painted pottery and bronze dating from the third century B.C. By the second century A.D. we know that line had become more important than color, character more important than physical appearance, a sense of movement more important than verisimilitude, and that brush stroke was already a key factor in the painter's act of creation. Appropriate subjects were derived from man's relationship to his fellow man according to Confucian ethics and ancient ceremonial, and from man's relationship to the world of the spirits, the shades of departed ancestors, the inhabitants of the Isles of the Immortals, and the lesser sprites of folk imagination. Confucianism and Taoism had already opened two doors; one led to good conduct and the maintaining of a harmony between heaven and earth by means of ritual and a respectful regulation of one's affairs; the other led toward the harmony with nature that might come to the pilosopher who retired from the world and trusted to intuitive perception rather than the written word for his glimpses of Universal Order. These two trends influenced painters and their work. In later eras, the lives of artists fitted into two main categories, that of scholar, poet, or public servant (and one man could be all of these), or that of hermit. The favorite subjects were figure-studies of the sages, historical personages and events (see illustration), and paragons of filial piety—all in the Confucian tradition—or of magicians, demon-quellers, Immortals, nymphs, fairies and imaginary creatures—all inspired by Taoist thought. Another main subject was landscape—the mountain-and-water picture dear to all Chinese. Obscure places as well as the sacred mountains, rivers and lakes were painted in all seasons and under all conditions. Next to the majesty of great heights, man was put in his proper, insignificant place. Parts of the panorama, such as trees (especially bamboo), rock formations, flowers and birds, were singled out as symbols of growth and life. Despite experiments in line, form and color, and changes in compositional scheme, these subjects formed the core of inspiration for the majority of Chinese artists.

When Buddhism became a powerful force in Chinese life in about the fourth century A.D. new themes were introduced. Thousands of devotees took up painting to gain merit in a future life, or became patrons of painters. Buddhist cave-temples and other sanctuaries followed plans developed in India for ritual purposes; walls and ceilings were covered with murals expressing fundamental Buddhist ideas in an iconography developed in the mother country and in Central Asia. Banners and votive offerings were painted on silk and hemp cloth for use on ceremonial occasions. The murals and banners of Tun-huang, Kansu, are as significant in Chinese art as the Sistine Chapel in European art. Because these images had to conform to Indian ideals in form, color, and proportion, there was a wave of foreign influence that reached its climax in the T'ang period in the eighth century (see color plate 31). The Buddhas, Bodhisattvas (lesser deities who were on the threshold of Enlightenment), Arhats or Lohans (holy men who belonged to monastic orders; see color plate 32), Lokapala (symbolic guardians of the Law in time and space), Vajrapani (muscular guardians armed with weapons), Apsarases and other minor deities of sky and earth, all were a part of the Buddhist hierarchy. Foreign at first in physiognomy and dress, they gradually became Chinese (see color plate 33).

One contemplative sect of Buddhist adherents, the Ch'an group, had ideas so similar to those of the Taoists that it became possible for the hermit-painters to serve both equally well. They followed no set rules but waited in meditation for an inspiration and then painted rapidly in a spontaneous burst of energy. Painted in monochrome, their pictures are masterpieces of understatement. In their hands ink alone could suggest color and form. Mu Ch'i and Liang K'ai of the Sung period, Chu Ta and Tao-chi of the Ch'ing period in China, Shubun and Sesshu of the Ashikaga period were of this "untrammeled" group.

By the Sung period painting had become a passion for some men, a pastime for others. It was an essential accomplishment for the Superior Man, a profession for the court painter, a delight for the poet, an aid in meditation for the monk, and for the collector a prize as valuable as ancient jade. The greatest of the collectors was the Emperor Hui Tsung (1082-1135 A.D.); he was a painter as well as a patron. His example was imitated by later Chinese rulers, and by Japanese, Mongol, Persian and Mughal Indian sovereigns. For the connoisseur, standards of judgment had been crystallized as early as the fifth century and set down as canons by Hsieh Ho. According to these the artist might be classed as Divine, Wonderful, Able, or Spontaneous, or in terms of one of four degrees of merit. The painter's use of his brush was as personal as his handwriting, so that painting and calligraphy were almost inseparable sister arts. Paintings were classified according to types of brush stroke. Pai Miao work was done with a fine brush in careful outline, sometimes with a touch of watercolor; Kung Pi also was a fine line drawing, often with the addition of gold and green in an archaic style; Mo-ku Hua, the boneless manner, dispensed with outlines, producing form by means of color tones in various shades and depths: P'o Mo was an ink-splash technique; Fei Pai called for a flowing, running style; Hsieh-i entered into spontaneous creation, making use of line and tonal wash in quick, rhythmic strokes.

The forms in use included murals, screens (both folding and one-panel), scrolls, and album pieces. Hanging scrolls (generally called kakemono by Westerners), consisted of a painting mounted with silk brocade borders on a fine paper backing; there were rollers at each end, and a loop of silk for hanging. When not in use the scroll was rolled, and put into a silk case and a special box made of wood or other fine material. The handscroll, or makimono, was mounted and cared for in the same way, but was meant to be unrolled and viewed flat, about a foot of the painting to be seen at one time, starting from the right and rolling to the left. Though a roll might be as long as fifty feet, each section of it was a pleasant picture in itself, and the viewer, giving careful attention to each detail, progressed in time and space. The album piece was a single painting, rectangular, round, or fan-shaped, mounted on single sheets of stiff paper, or bound together under brocade covers.

The painter sat on the floor, or on a low seat, with his paper or silk laid flat on a table. At hand were brushes of various sizes, a water-pot and ink sticks (pine soot compressed into a solid) or pigment. The artist dipped his stick into water and ground it on a special stone, the amount of ink and water depending on the effect desired. The brush was held at right angle to the wrist, the motion originating in the shoulder. The tip of the brush could be manipulated to give a fine line or a thick one, or to spread a tonal wash. Years of disciplined effort were required before the painter could hope to achieve any notable success, for there could be no erasures or overpainting, and preliminary sketches were rarely used.

A painter had several names. His family name was written first and then his *ming* or personal name; as he matured he was given a *tzu*, or courtesy name, and as he won success in his art, he took a *hao*, or literary name, which might be descriptive of his personality, his studio, or his place of origin. In time other *hao* could be added. Many painters had a classical Chinese education in literature and history that involved as many as three academic degrees, and court painters were given special titles and rewards.

All paintings other than murals were fragile in construction, and exquisitely mounted. They were to be handled reverently: a hanging scroll was to be rolled up and protected and a handscroll was to be seen by two or three congenial friends, who would study it with delight, usually while they were quietly drinking tea together. Public display in a museum was unthinkable and painting for a competition, except one sponsored by the Emperor, was unheard of. Religious paintings were done for a particular place in a temple, usually as symbols of divine power. None was intended to catch the eye of the public. Only in modern times have there been museums in China; and the treasures in them have come largely from former imperial collections. With all the upheavals in China, many scrolls and murals have been destroyed. Some of the most noted of those that survive have never been adequately photographed or published, since the owner usually regarded them as entirely personal. Certainly this was the attitude of the Sung period collectors, and the tradition held into the Yüan period. While Mongol taste was for color and action in art, the most patriotic Chinese painters went in for monochrome. Most artists retired to the country rather than collaborate with the "Barbarians." Ni Tsan and Huang Kung-wang were experimenters, but they created their clear, cool, spotless landscapes away from the "dusty world." By the Ming period painting had become so much a part of Chinese life that one cannot begin to enumerate the names of artists famous enough to be recorded. The two principal groups were the Wu led by Shen Chou, and the Chê led by Tai Chin. The first were scholars and poets—the Wen Jen revered by later generations; the second were for the most part professionals. Independent geniuses were not highly regarded by the connoisseurs, for their work was considered not refined enough to merit serious attention. Critics were outspoken in the Ming period. Past judgments were reassessed and new ones offered. Among the most famous of the many publications of the period was the "Treatise on the Paintings and Writings of the Ten Bamboo Studio" (1633), a series of sixteen volumes of color prints illustrating watercolor techniques. It reproduced flowers, fruits, birds (see illustration), and stones. It is not the oldest example of color printing in China, but it marks a time of notable achievement. In Chinese opinion a print could never rival a painting, because the process of mechanical reproduction lacked the artist's personal touch, but they had already mastered the arts of line and color printing, and of gauffrage.

The fall of the Ming dynasty brought an end to a great era in the painting arts. With the Manchu conquest of 1644, loyalists like Chu Ta and Tao-chi went into retirement, while others, like the Four Wangs, continued to work in the Ming tradition or in earlier styles. Men turned to the past, rather than to nature, for inspiration; and in portraits of ancestors or the imperial family emblems of rank became important and resemblance to the actual subject secondary.

In the twentieth century every phase of Chinese painting is still being carried on by many artists. There is a revival of woodblock printing, much of it under European and Russian influence, and there is much painting on silk, paper, and canvas. Many artists, like Hsu Pei-hung (see), have studied in Europe and the United States; others, like the the venerable Ch'i Pai-shih (see), work in the native tradition. Again there are many painters in exile; some are masters of brush and ink and the delicate line; others paint in oils and try to reconcile the past with the present, or to forget the past as they merge into an International Style.

The following are the principal stages or periods in the development of Chinese painting :

The Six Dynasties (386-581)
Sui Dynasty (581-618)
T'ang Dynasty (618-907)
The Five Dynasties (907-960)
Sung Dynasty (960-1279)
Yüan Dynasty (1279-1368)
Ming Dynasty (1368-1644)
Ch'ing Dynasty (1644-1912)
The Republic (1912-)

Chinese Painters: The Six Dynasties (386-581)

CHANG SENG-YU (fl. 6th century). A master who served in South China at the court of Liang Wu-ti. He is noted for his use of color to give the impression of "relief," building volume through pigment. This revolutionary concept of form and color originated in India and came to China via the trade route centers of Central Asia. He painted numerous temple frescoes, and two of his scrolls, The Brushing of the Elephant and The Drunken Priests, as well as the traditional Confucius Asking about the Ceremonies, are noted in histories of Chinese painting.

KU K'AI-CHIH (c.345-c.406) (courtesy name Ch'ang-k'ang). A native of what is today Wu-chin, Kiangsu; son of Yüeh-chih, assistant secretary of the Imperial Secretariat. Famous as a wit, painter and fool, he was known for his poems and eccentricities. He served Grand Marshal Huan Wen and Governor Yin Chung-k'an as aide-de-camp and was Cavalier Attendant-in-ordinary when he died. Some of his miscellaneous writings and a work called *Ch'i-meng chi (Memoirs for Enlightening the Purblind)* are still known in fragmentary form. He loved music and singing, and is said to have believed in magic. It is possible that he belonged to a Taoist cult called T'ien-shih tao that flourished in his native city. Though Ku lived in troubled times, he did not suffer exile, but seems to have remained in favor and enjoyed life. His name usually heads the list of known painters who are important as individuals in the long history of Chinese painting, not only because of his successful career, but also because of the chance preservation of three works attributed to him. Most important of these is his Admonitions of the Imperial Preceptress (British Museum). The Nymph of the Lo River (Freer) and a landscape scroll (Metropolitan) are obviously later adaptations of his work. The Admonitions scroll, illustrating Confucian tenets of the Han dynasty, is a series of episodes, each explained by notations in a vertical line of calligraphy. The silk has faded and the colors are dim: traces of red and yellow are still visible, but the blues, greens and intermediate

CHINA. T'ANG DYNASTY. CHOU FANG. Tuning the Lute and Drinking Tea. Sung copy of T'ang scroll. William Rockhill Nelson Gallery, Kansas City

hues are practically gone. It is the brushwork, the firm outline of each figure, that still delights the beholder. The flowing robes, graceful gestures, floatings scarves and charming faces suggest the refinement and subtlety already dominant in Chinese painting. Ku, indeed, has been described as a painter who could suggest character by the way he placed hairs on a chin or dotted the pupil of an eyeball.

LU T'AN-WEI (fl. 5th century). Active in Nanking and considered a master on a level with Ku K'ai-chih. He painted Buddhist subjects as well as the Confucian Meritorious Worthies of the Past, and was noted for his calligraphy in the "single-stroke" style. Lu was described as being single-minded, grave, courtly and correct.

Chinese Painters: Sui Dynasty (581-618)

CHAN TZU-CHI'EN (late 6th, early 7th century). Reckoned one of the great painters of his period. We are told that he painted in an elegant, minute style. He did palaces and temples, Buddhist images and historical themes.

WEI-CH'IH PO-CHIH-NA (fl. 6th century). Native of Khotan, Central Asia, he went to China and astonished everyone with his foreign way of painting. Like the Indian painters of the Ajanta murals, he brought out the roundness of forms by using graded tones of color to indicate volume, an entirely new concept for the Chinese. He specialized in foreign and Buddhist themes.

Chinese Painters: T'ang Dynasty (618-907)

CHANG HSUAN (fl. 8th century). A native of Ch'ang-an, where he was active under the Emperor Ming Huang. He excelled in painting the palace gardens on screens, the Emperor amusing himself at games and pastimes, members of the nobility at sports and on outings, gentlewomen and their daily occupations, saddle horses, pavilions and terraces, flowers, trees and birds.

CHANG NAN-PEN (fl. 9th century). Native of Szechuan province, he was active from 880 on as a painter of Buddhist and Taoist themes in fresco and scroll form.

CHANG TSAO (fl. 8th century). Famous literary figure and painter of pine trees, he served in high offices, and was author of the *Hua Ching (The Realm of Painting)*. He did murals, scroll paintings, and folding screens. His technical dexterity is often commented upon. Once he is said to have used two brushes simultaneously, drawing a separate branch with each, one branch alive, the other dead. He was known for his use of a stump brush, and for smearing the ink on the silk with his hand. He acknowledged no master, but took the creative processes of nature as his model.

CHOU FANG (fl. 8th century). Known also as Chung-lang, he was a native of Ch'ang-an in Shensi. He was a courtier, a painter of Buddhist murals, portraits, and genre studies of court life. Many of his scrolls were taken to Korea and are doubtless the source of Chinese influence in Korea at the time. A copy of one of his scrolls, called Ladies Amusing Themselves, is now in the Nelson Gallery. (See illustration.)

CHU CHING-HSÜAN (fl. early 9th century). A native of Suchou, a scholar in the Imperial Han-lin College, and author of the valuable book, the *T'ang Ch'ao Ming Hua Lu (Famous Painters of the T'ang Dynasty)*, written about 840.

HAN KAN (?720-780). A native of Ch'ang-an. The Emperor summoned him to serve in the palace in order to paint His Majesty's horses. He did this so successfully that he was later elevated to the "inspired" class of painter. Other masterpieces by him were the Deities (for the Triple Gate of the Pao-ying Temple), as well as the Celestial Monarch of the North (in the Western Precinct), and Bodhisattvas and a Paradise Wall (on the front of the Buddha Hall). Another set of Buddhist murals depicting twenty-four Holy Men was done for the Tzu-sheng Temple. He did some of the work in black and white, some of it in light colors. His ability to suggest volume and projection is noted by literary critics, who said that the sleeves he painted seemed about to part from the wall and that the famous horse Yao-ma seemed to come right out of the picture. His versatility was indicated by paintings still extant in the mid-ninth century which ranged in subject matter from high priests to saddle horses, and from Bodhisattvas to demon deities.

LI CHAO-TAO (8th century). A great-great-grandson of the founder of the T'ang dynasty, and son of General Li Ssu-hsun; noted as a painter and courtier. He was known as "Little Li," for he did not equal his father in strength of brush, though his paintings of seascapes, birds, beasts, figures, and buildings showed great ingenuity and intelligence. He was a court chamberlain as well as a prolific painter.

LI SSU-HSUN (fl. 651-716). A great-grandson of the founder of the T'ang dynasty, he was famous as a general and a landscape painter. He was a magistrate, a governor and an army officer. The Emperor Ming Huang summoned him to paint a wall and landscape screens in the Ta-t'ung Hall. He excelled both in calligraphy and painting; landscapes painted with a forceful brush were his specialty. He is regarded as founder of the northern school. General Li was called "Big Li" to distinguish him from his son Li Chao-tao (see above).

33. CHINA. SUNG DYNASTY. Bodhisattva
William Rockhill Nelson Gallery, Kansas City

SUN WEI (fl. after 880). Lived in Szechuan province and is the outstanding painter in Western China in this period. A predecessor of those painters who disregarded academic rules, he was "untrammeled," and could suggest movement and sound with great economy of line; his brushwork was exquisite, and his atmospheric effects were said to be beyond description. He did religious themes, dragons, birds, dogs, pines and rocks. Eighteen pictures of many types were listed in the Sung Imperial Catalogue.

TAI SUNG (fl. 8th-9th century). He was the most renowned painter of water buffaloes in his time and was much copied by later painters. His scenes of rural life were also highly prized.

WANG HSIA (d. 805). Known as Wang Mo, meaning "Ink Wang." Famous for painting landscapes by splattering ink in a way that defied conventional classification. He was therefore called "untrammeled"—and is undoubtedly a predecessor of certain followers of Ch'an Buddhism who were thought to be spontaneous, unacademic and "uncouth." He wandered through river and lake regions, comforting himself with wine. When he was ready to paint a hanging picture, he would get drunk, fling ink on the scroll while laughing and singing, rub the ink on with his hands, wave his brush around, or scrub with it. Wherever the ink fell he would follow its configurations to make mountains, rocks, clouds, or water—all without a trace of an ink blot.

WANG WEI (698-759) (courtesy name Mo-ch'i; known also by official title of Yu-ch'-eng). In the mid-eighth century, during the An-Lu-shan rebellion, he was captured by rebel forces and compelled to serve as Censor at Lo-yang. A devout Buddhist, he studied Sanskrit, and eventually gave his country villa at Wang Ch'uan for use as a monastery. The outstanding landscape painter of his era, he is regarded as founder of the southern school and leader of those who were both poets and painters. He used color as well as a firm line and graded tone to depict each rock, tree, house, etc., with maximum clarity. One of the first artists to regard the long horizontal scroll as an overall composition, the extant copies of his work indicate that he stressed rhythm of design, the harmony of parts, and the unity of nature.

WE-CH'IH I-SENG (fl. 7th century). A native of Central Asia, his sovereign sent him with a letter of recommendation to the Chinese court in 627. Described as excellent in painting frescoes, he painted in the foreign manner, i.e., using color to give a plastic roundness to forms, and thereby exerted great influence on T'ang painting.

WU TAO-TZU (fl. 8th century) (known also as Tao-hsüan). A native of Yang-ti, Honan. Orphaned when very young, he became famous at an early age and attracted the attention of the Emperor Ming Huang, who summoned him to serve in the palace some time during 713-42. He was active until after the middle of the eighth century. His is probably the greatest single name in the history of Chinese painting, and his ability has been the despair of all later artists. Wu was a mural painter of great power, a man inspired by deep study of Buddhist and Taoist lore, a keen observer with a remarkable memory, a colorist, and a calligrapher who had studied with the renowned Chang Hsü. Good copies of his work are regarded as treasures, for all authentic originals disappeared as a result of the destruction of Buddhist temples by imperial decree in 845, or natural deterioration. Wu painted some three hundred murals for the Emperor, and for Buddhist and Taoist establishments. He could paint a perfect circle with one sweeping stroke of the brush; and his portrayals of Hell were so moving that butchers and fishmongers changed their trade so that they would not be guilty of taking life and thereby breaking Buddhist Law. Some of the murals were carried out in ink alone; others were filled in with color. Some were so excellent that stone engravings were made of them, and the rubbings taken from these stone tablets still serve to give a hint of his virtuosity, though the stone can hardly capture the full sweep of his line. Thus the majesty of his art has been transmitted, however imperfectly, to us.

YEN LI-PEN (died 673). Son of painter Yen Pi of the Sui dynasty, he was born in Ch'ang-an. A man of affairs, he was a member of the Council of State and a Junior Premier with the rank of Duke. He was commanded to paint the portrait of his sovereign T'ang T'ai Tsung (627-50) and of scholars and other historical personages. His famous Thirteen Emperors (Boston) has survived the centuries.

YEN LI-TE (fl. 7th century). Elder brother of Yen Li-pen, he served at the beginning of the T'ang period as a designer of court costumes, insignia and vehicles. As a painter he excelled in portraying the foreign visitors and tribute-bearers who flocked to Ch'ang-an and in painting exotic subjects in general. Like his brother, he apparently used fine line and color for the figures, with emphasis on costume detail and marks of rank.

Chinese Painters: The Five Dynasties (907-960)

CHING HAO (fl. late 9th-early 10th century) (courtesy name Hung-ku-tzu, or Master of the Broad Valley). A native of Ho-nai. He was a man of great learning and refinement, a master of landscape painting, and reputed author of the *Hua Shan-shui Chueh (Secrets of Landscape Painting)*. In his painting he combined, to masterly effect, the firm outlines of Wu-Tao-tzu and the graded washes of Wang Hsia. Usually in the foreground of his vertical scrolls are pines with twisted branches, oaks with gnarled trunks, rocks pushed up by primeval forces, and flowing water. In the middleground, foothills with rustic houses, winding paths and waterfalls rise toward towering peaks. The distant mountain-tops push almost to the upper border of the silk, their crystalline forms clearly defined and the mountain foliage delicately suggested. Many poems were inspired by his landscapes, and two great painters were his pupils, Kuan T'ung and Fan K'uan. Among his works extant in the eleventh century were landscapes representing the four seasons, Peach-tree Spring, Mount T'ien-t'ai (the headquarters of a Buddhist sect), and Three Peaks. The record also indicates that he painted for a monastery a fresco depicting Kuan Yin on Mt. Potalaka. The Sung Imperial Catalogue lists twenty-two pictures by him, mostly landscapes.

CHU-JAN (10th century). A priest-painter, native of Chung-ling (i.e., Nanking), he is associated with Tung Yüan, who is said to have been his master. His style of landscape painting, using "moist ink" to give misty atmospheric effects and spacious views, has been much admired. The soft tonality of rock formations and the clustered dots that suggest moss, as well as the piling up of mountain masses (see illustration), served to inspire Yüan and Ming dynasty painters. He painted frescoes as well as scrolls. His ability to paint the secluded places of nature and give life to all parts of his scrolls was attributed to his training as a Buddhist priest. The Sung Imperial Catalogue lists 136 landscapes by him.

HSÜ-HSI (10th century). A native of Chung-ling (i.e., Nanking), descendant of a long line of officials in Kiangnan. An individualist who rebelled against the elegant academic court art and is ranked as one of the foremost painters of bird and flower scrolls. He also painted bamboo, animals, fish and crabs, grasses and insects, vegetable sprouts, and fruit trees. Full of creative power, vigorous and dynamic, he was a born leader. He could suggest a range of color simply by the subtle use of ink. A picture of his, Cranes and Bamboo, is described as done in dark ink with a coarse brush, the details sketchily dotted in and then smeared with blue and green—and yet it was considered as convincing as if created by Nature herself.

HUANG CH'UAN (d. 965). Native of Szechuan, he was a court painter at the age of seventeen. He became Inspector of the Royal Workshops and was granted the right to wear gold and purple. An eclectic, he drew his inspiration from the great masters of the past, and carried on courtly tradition in a fine, precise style and elegant color. He painted bamboo, birds and flowers, dragons and figure studies. The catalogue of the Emperor Hui Tsung lists 349 pictures by him.

KUAN HSIU (832-912). Born in Chekiang (family name Chiang; courtesy name Te-yin; studio name Ch'an-yüeh) and placed in a Ch'an Buddhist monastery at an early age. He was a promising student of the scriptures, and showed great talent in calligraphy, painting and poetry. His imaginary portraits of the disciples of the Buddha and of the Arhats (sages of extraordinary powers) estabished an iconographic theme of great importance in Chinese and Japanese art. In the careful outline and detailed painting of the Yen Li-pen style, he depicted those who had brought the Law of the Buddha to China. They were Hindus, Central Asiatics, and other foreigners—distinguished as such by prominent bone structure, big noses, bushy eyebrows, large eyes and unkempt beards or moustaches. He did these figures in isolated mountain settings, showing each as possessed of supernatural powers or lost in meditation. This ability to portray inner psychological states, as well as the weird and alien appearance of holy men, was a remarkable departure in Chinese art. At least nine sets of his Arhat and Disciple portraits were recorded in Chinese temples. Some were said to have been taken to Japan, where they, or later copies, are still extant.

KUAN T'UNG (fl. early 10th century). A native of Ch'ang-an, and a pupil of Ching Hao. One of the three landscape painters classed as divine. He was noted for his crystalline execution of vast rock formations, the dense luxuriance of his trees, and the antique elegance of his terraces and pavilions. Evidently Kuan was a careful student of geology, an experimenter in spatial relationships, and a master of the brush. The catalogue of the Emperor Hui Tsung lists ninety-four pictures by him, including such titles as Nightfall and a Clearing Sky, Landscapes of the Four Seasons, The Peach-Tree Spring, and Early Morning Journey.

Chinese Painters: Sung Dynasty (960-1279). Northern Sung (960-1127); Southern Sung (1127-1279).

CHAO CH'ANG (11th century) (courtesy name Ch'ang-chih). A painter from Kuang-han, Szechuan, his clear luxuriant flower paintings were much copied and admired. In 1010 he did a commission for a nobleman in K'ai-feng—studies of growing vegetables, overripe melons and fresh fruit. He made careful studies of the life-cycles of plants and flowers, noting

CHINA. THE FIVE DYNASTIES. CHÜ-JAN. Landscape
National Museums and Library, China

the appearance of bud, blossom and fruit at different hours and in different seasons. He was said to have been long unsurpassed in his handling of color. For his studies of cut flowers and branches he is said to have used preliminary sketches. He painted grasses and insects, birds and rocks, but his name ranks highest as a flower painter. Some 154 of his works were listed in the Sung Imperial Catalogue.

CHAO MENG-CHIEN (1199-1295) (courtesy name Tzu-ku; studio name I-chai). From Hai-yen in Chekiang. Descended from the Imperial Sung line, he was a poet and a painter of flowers (narcissus, plum-blossoms and orchids), bamboo, and rock formations. Refined and sensitive brushwork, great technical skill and poetic feeling have led Chinese critics to consider him one of the greatest masters of his time. His lineage, his distinction as a scholar, calligrapher, and government official, his amiable nature, and long life (he died at ninety-seven) add lustre to his name. He wrote a *Treatise on Plum Blossoms (Mei P'u)* giving directions to painters of this, his favorite subject.

CHAO PO-CHU (fl. 12th century) (courtesy name Ch'ien-li). A relative of the imperial family. Active in the Painting Academy of the Emperor Hui Tsung, he moved south to Hang-chou when the Tatars invaded K'ai-feng. He was said to have been the favorite painter of Emperor Kao Tsung, and was made Keeper of the Imperial Seal for Eastern Chekiang. Most of his paintings were of the scroll type—landscapes, Taoist figures, birds and flowers—painted in the conservative style of Li Ssu-hsün and Wang Wei, in which careful outline and rich color were important.

CH'AO PU-CHIH (1052-1110) (courtesy name Wu chiu; studio name Kuei-lai-tzu). Official as well as painter, he served in various posts and finally became Governor of Ssu-chou in Anhui. Noted as a writer, calligrapher, and painter, he was the ideal Sung official. He made a careful study of the brush style of T'ang and Sung masters and his work must have been eclectic, but contemporary comment refers to it as excellent. His most famous painting is Lao-tzu Riding on a Buffalo.

CHAO TA-NIEN (fl. 1080-1100) (courtesy name Ling-jan). Descended from the imperial line, he served as Imperial Commissioner for Defense in Kuang-chou (Honan), was a literary man, and an art tutor to the Emperor Hui Tsung as well as a noted painter of landscapes. A colorist and an experimenter in space-composition, he did bamboo, trees of all kinds, ducks and geese. Using mist and soft tones to express mood, he seems to have been the first master of landscape to achieve a lyrical, intimate approach.

CH'EN JUNG (fl. mid-13th century) (studio name Ch'en So-weng). Government official, eccentric character and poet, as well as painter, he became a magistrate in Shansi, then in Kiangsi, and finally a governor in Fukien, his native province. He is best known for his dragon painting; examples of his work are preserved in China, Japan, and the U.S.A. (Boston). His approach was the "spontaneous" one approved by the Taoist: "When he was drunk, he shouted, took off his cap, dipped it in ink, and then smeared and rubbed with it, making a rough picture that he afterwards completed with the brush." His painting of bamboo and pine trees was "as graceful as willows and as strong as iron hooks and chains." The great thirty-three-foot scroll of the Nine Dragons (Boston) portrays the mysterious symbolic creatures of sea and sky as they emerge from dashing waves, mist, and cloud, or appear behind crystalline rocks and a spate of foam. For dramatic power, rhythm, and the suggestion of primordial force, it stands alone. (See illustration.)

CHOU CHI-CH'ANG (fl. 12th century). An artist working in Ning-po in the Southern Sung period, whose signature and the date 1178 were inscribed on a set of Five Hundred Arhats. With Lin T'ing-kuei, he seems to have painted one hundred panels (silk, in full color) that were taken to Japan in the thirteenth century. Eighty-two of them are still in the Daitoku-ji in Kyoto and ten in the Museum of Fine Arts, Boston. Precious examples of authentic Sung religious painting, they inspired numerous copies in Japan. Groups of Arhats are shown descending from heaven in lordly fashion or engaged in magical practices. Exceptionallly interesting are figure studies of the holy men of various nationalities, guardians in military attire, and earthlings of all kinds, from mountain men to scholars. (See color plate 32.)

CHU JUI (fl. 12th century). A native of Hopei (Chili) who became a court painter. He was appointed *tai chao* (Painter-in-Attendance) before 1162, and was given the Golden Girdle as a mark of approval. Noted for centuries as a landscape painter, he drew inspiration from his native province, a rugged mountain country. He painted rural life of the north with grandeur and sensitivity. Among his subjects are Traveling by Mule Cart, Feeding Horses in the Snow, Bullock Carts Going up the Mountain Trail. He used the careful, detailed outlining of rock, tree, man, and animal that the court painters of the Northern Sung period admired. He painted usually in monochrome but with such sweeping power that his work stands alone in his period.

FAN AN-JEN (fl. mid-13th century) (courtesy name Fan-t'a, meaning The Otter, because of his knowledge of creatures of

CHINA. SUNG DYNASTY. CH'EN JUNG. Dragon Scroll (detail). Museum of Fine Arts, Boston

CHINA. SUNG DYNASTY. FAN K'UAN. Landscape
National Museums and Library, China

the water). He came from Ch'ien-t'ang in Chekiang, and was active in the Southern Sung period. Noted for his painting of fish, crabs and waterplants, he portrayed them in natural settings, conveying an extraordinary sense of the movement of water and the rhythm of each form of aquatic life. His line is clear, pure, and powerful, his spacing excellent.

FAN K'UAN (fl. c.990-1030). Born Fan Chung-cheng (courtesy name Chung-li) but nicknamed K'uan the Generous, by the people of his native place, Hua-yüan in Shensi. He is described in old texts as an old-fashioned man, stern about some things but careless of formality, a lover of wine and of the solitude of nature. He is considered one of the great landscape painters of his time. After studying the art of Li Ch'eng, he wandered about the countryside observing every aspect of the changing scene, finally retiring to a beautiful place in the Chun-nan Mountains. In the style that emerged, the structure of earth and crag and tree was clear and strong, revealed by a master of light and shade and of fine brush technique. (See illustration.)

HSIA KUEI (fl. c.1180-1230) (courtesy name Yü-yü). A

CHINA. SUNG DYNASTY. HSIA KUEI. Landscape
National Museums and Library, China

native of Ch'ien-T'ang in Chekiang. A court painter, he was active in the reign of the Emperor Ning Tsung, became a *tai chao* (Painter-in-Attendance) and received the Golden Girdle as a mark of esteem. He was a contemporary of Ma Yüan and ranks with him among the greatest Chinese painters. In temperament and technique the men differed, for Hsia Kuei was concerned with dramatic rendering of water, wind, and jagged rock formations. The great thirty-four-foot scroll, Ten Thousand Miles of the Yangtse River, is a masterpiece of sustained inventiveness and virtuosity of brush stroke. It begins with rushing waters near their source in mountain country, and follows them through dangerous rapids, widening bays, and finally the broad mouth of the river as it empties into the sea. He painted another scroll, twenty-eight feet long, on a similar theme, but it is not so overwhelming in scope. He skillfully combined views of wide lakes, promontories of stone topped by trees, quiet coves, villages, mountains and open sky. His brushwork was free and bold: instead of outlining each leaf he suggested a mass of foliage by tonal washes; instead of using a ruler for architectural motifs he did them quickly in freehand. Outlines of rocks were made heavy and jagged; the surface of stone was suggested by a combination of rich black ink and a light, dry brush. In human figures a few strokes were used to suggest the whole body, and even the personality and the occupation, and the power of wind and rain were conveyed by figures bent and braced, or by driven leaves. Atmosphere, whether of mist or of sunlight, was obviously of utmost importance. (See illustration.)

HSI-CHIN CHU-SHIH (fl. 13th century). A monk-painter of one of the Buddhist monasteries of the Ning-po area in the Southern Sung period. His paintings of Lohans were listed in Japanese records. Ascribed to him are a set of the Ten Kings of Hell (Metropolitan), painted in color on silk, which give an interesting insight into the thirteenth-century Chinese concept of purgatory.

HUANG CHU-TSAI (933-993) (courtesy name Po-han). Youngest son of Huang Ch'üan, the famous painter of flowers and birds in Szechuan. When the Sung dynasty was established, father and son were welcomed by the new regime, for both had great reputations in West China. Chü became first Director of the Sung Art Academy and was commissioned to search for masterpieces and make critical catalogues. Under his direction various halls on the palace grounds were decorated by specialists in bird and flower, or dragon, painting, and many scrolls were made for the imperial collection. A rapid worker, he did a fresco of water and rocks for a Taoist temple in one afternoon. The work of father and son, marked by clarity, precision, and beauty of coloring, set the standard of the Academy of Painting.

HUI TSUNG (1082-1135). The posthumous name of Chao Chi, the eleventh son of Emperor Shen Tsung. He became Emperor in 1101 and ruled until 1126; he is noted as a collector, a patron of the Northern Sung artists, and a painter in his own right. In his youth he associated with the painters Wang Shen and Chao Ta-nien. He re-activated the Academy of Painting and formed the Hsüan Ho collection of paintings, calligraphy, bronzes and other art objects, by far the most impressive Imperial Collection up to that time. The catalogue of its paintings, the *Hsüan-ho Hua P'u*, is an important source of information for the art of the twelfth century and earlier. The collection was dispersed, and many items destroyed, when the Chin Tatars sacked the capital. As patron, the Emperor took a great personal interest in the artists who formed the T'u Hua Yüan, which we call the Academy (though it was not an academy in the European sense). The members had to pass examinations in painting religious themes, in figure studies, architectural drawing, "fur and feathers" (animals and birds), flowers, bamboo, and landscape; they were also examined in literature, calligraphy, and the classics to see whether they were gentlemen with a cultured background. As members of the T'u Hua Yüan they held high rank, wore robes of purple silk and a special insignia of gold and jade. The Golden Girdle was given some of the members as a special mark of imperial favor. Though the Emperor claimed to dislike the conservatism of the Confucianists, he did approve only of such artistic expression as was to his own taste. The themes he suggested for painting competitions have a marked literary flavor and he evidently did not care for the "untrammeled," spontaneous art of the Ch'an type. His own work has been vastly admired, his knowledge described as expert and his brushwork as "divine," but it is more than likely that he put his seal on some paintings that he particularly admired but that are not really by his hand. The Five-colored Parakeet (Boston) and Dove on a Peach Branch (Inouye collection, Tokyo) are authentic, and indicate a predilection for a few branches carefully painted on silk, and a single bird placed most expertly in the linear design. Careful outlines, delicate color, a suggestion of growth within the branch and blossoms, a genuine understanding of each species of bird, and fine brushwork are characteristic. However, some of the landscape scrolls attributed to him embody innovations and a power of imagination not consistent with his personality and skill. So great was his love for art that he neglected the affairs of state; the Chin Tatars overran North China, he fled, was taken prisoner, and died in captivity. His heir was taken south by loyal courtiers and the Southern Sung capital was established in Hangchou.

KUO CHUNG-SHU (fl. 10th century) (courtesy name Shu-hsien). From Lo-yang in Honan. A genius who was a candidate in the Imperial College at the age of seven. He was rapidly advanced to the post of Great National Teacher under Emperor T'ai Tsu but his love of drinking forced him into retirement in the Hua Mountains. He was recalled by the Sung Emperor T'ai Tsung but his careless remarks and heavy drinking again caused banishment. He was famous for his architectural drawings; he used ruled lines, was interested in perspective angles, problems of proportion, etc. He is regarded as the founder of the "chieh-hua" (boundary painting) manner of fine brush rendering.

KUO HSI (fl. c.1020-90) (courtesy name Shun-fu; called Ho-yang after his birthplace in Honan province). One of the outstanding landscape painters in Chinese art, and author of the *Lin Ch'üan Kao Chih (Great Message of Forests and Streams)*, a compilation of his sayings set down by his son Kuo Jo-ssu. He was admitted to the Imperial Academy of Painting while very young, and modeled his work upon the landscapes of Li Ch'eng. He then began to develop his own style—"the older he grew, the stronger his brush became." Critics agreed that his boldness and strength were without equal—that his mountains were painted with wrinkles like clouds and were coiled like snakes, his stones were shaped like devils' faces, and his branches were like the talons of a bird of prey. He liked to paint on a large scale and the grandeur of his compositions reflects his interest in space problems; he advised that one should look at great vistas from a distance and observe shapes under changing atmospheric conditions. He also stresses the importance of studying each detail to capture the essential nature of things. Unfortunately few of his authentic paintings have survived. A scroll in the Freer Gallery, Autumn in the Yellow River Valley, is attributed to him, and gives a hint of his majestic composition, his ability to suggest the character of a beloved countryside, and to paint with poetic sensitivity.

LIANG K'AI (fl. 13th century) (courtesy name Feng-tzu, meaning Crazy Fellow). First an academician, he became a court painter about 1202-4; he received the Golden Girdle, but in later years hung it in the courtyard of the Academy as a symbol of detachment from official life and traditional painting. He then retired to a Ch'an temple in Hangchou, where Mu Ch'i lived and worked. It is not clear whether he became a monk, but his painting style and choice of subject indicate positive adherence. His early landscapes and his pictures of Sakyamuni on His Way to the Bodhi Tree are carefully executed in line and tone. Later paintings are concerned with Ch'an personalities—for example, The Sixth Patriarch Chopping Bamboo; The Sixth Patriarch Tearing a Sutra (see illustration); Pu t'ai Watching Fighting Cocks, etc.—and illustrate the principle that Buddhist revelation may come at unexpected moments of relaxation or simple labor. In style, they are splendid examples of the Ch'an ideals of simplicity, directness and the oneness of man and nature. With staccato strokes of a brush heavily laden with ink, he hastily set the images on the paper, leaving much to the imagination. This "coarseness" and "brusqueness" so different from the early, meticulous work modeled on Wu Tao-tzu's art, have offended Chinese critics of the literary school but have been treasured in Japan. Even when he painted historical figures, he chose the understatement of a few telling lines, achieving the greatest expressiveness by an economy of means, as, for example, in his portrait of the poet Li T'ai-po. His own love of wine must have made him feel a tender regard for Li, who, while tipsy, reached for the reflection of the moon in the Yellow River, and was drowned.

LI CH'ENG (d. 967) (courtesy name Hsien-hsi). Descended from the imperial clan of the T'ang Dynasty. Though his grandfather and father were noted classical scholars, his only ambition was to lead a quiet life, and he refused all honors and advancement. He, too, studied canonical books and histories, but his greatest pleasure lay in painting landscapes, and he never ceased to be inspired by the beautiful mountains of his native province. Full of trees and rocks, mist and haze, peaks and ranges, his paintings reproduce Shantung scenes, but his conceptions suggest a universality, a sense of the movement of Yang and Yin, and the idea of continuous change in nature. The life force, *ch'i*, so essential to the greatest painting by Chinese standards, was manifest in his works to a remarkable degree. Objects were done in light ink, carefully outlined, and the water, sky and open spaces were filled with white pigment, thus giving the effect both of solidity and spaciousness. His wrinkled rocks became the standard for copyists for nearly a thousand years. Fond of wine and poetry, a skilled musician, and father of a noted son, Chio, he was regarded as the liberated type of scholar-gentleman. The Sung Imperial Catalogue claimed 159 paintings for him.

LI CH'IH (late 11th-early 12th century) (courtesy name Fang-shu). A native of Yang-ti in Honan. Friend of the great poet-painter, Su Shih, and author of the important *Descriptive Catalogue of Paintings*, the *Hua P'in*, on works of the T'ang and early Sung periods.

LI KUNG-LIN (1040-1106) (courtesy name Po-shih; studio name Lung-mien or Li Lung-mien). A scholar as well as a painter, he studied Buddhism and Taoism, and was reputed to have mastered both. He had a notable collection of bronze ritual vessels, jade pieces, and treasures of all kinds, and was extraordinarily talented in many directions. In his painting he equaled the masters of the T'ang period; his Buddhist images were worthy of Wu Tao-Tzu, his horses surpassed Han Kan's, and his landscapes were like Li Ssu-hsun's. The surviving works attributed to him are marked by elegant, strong lines and splendor of design.

LIN T'ING-KUEI (fl. 12th century). One of the painters of the Five Hundred Arhats done at Ningpo in Chekiang and taken to Japan in the thirteenth century. With Chou Chi-ch'ang, he painted one hundred of the famous silk panels in full color.

LI SHAN (fl. early 13th century). A native of P'ing-yang in Shansi, he served the Chin Tatars in North China. The purity of his line, delicate tonality of his washes and fine sense of structure, evoked the admiration of other painters and caused his landscapes to be copied by later generations.

LI SHENG (fl. 10th century) (courtesy name Chin-nu). Born in Ch'eng-tu, Szechuan, a noted landscape painter particularly admired by Mi Fei. He trained himself by studying the T'ang masters and by careful observation of nature. He painted every detail of rock and tree in exceptionally fine brushwork, but with spirit and majesty. The scenic wonders of West China were his favorite subjects: the Wu-liang River, the sacred peaks and deep ravines. He also painted such classic themes as Rain on the Hsiao and Hsiang Rivers. All of these became models for later artists.

LI SUNG (1166-1243). Started life as a carpenter's boy, was adopted by the painter Li Ts'ung-hsün, and became a court painter, a Painter-in-Attendance serving under three Emperors of the Southern Sung. He painted historical narratives, seascapes, and a scroll in the Palace museum collection entitled Immortals Telling Fortunes. Though he was required to paint the glories of the past, he brought a fine sense of dramatic incident and a clear, exact style to his portrayals.

LI T'ANG (fl. c.1100-30) (courtesy name Hsi-ku). A native of Ho-yang in Honan, he moved south to Hangchou when North China was taken over by the Tatars. He was then over seventy-five years old, and had spent his life in the capital at K'ai-feng, where he had been an official in the Academy and a friend of the Emperor. He was thus one of the oldest and most influential painters in the New Academy at Hangchou, and taught the disciplined style of Northern Sung brushwork to younger men. Traditional landscapes are attributed to him, but he is better known for droll, rustic genre scenes, and for his painting of water buffaloes. They are precise in detail and fine in line, but endowed with life and personality.

LI TI (fl. c.1130-80). A native of Ho-yang in Honan, and honored member of the Painting Academy of the Emperor Hui Tsung, noted for his detailed and spirited rendering of bird and flower studies, landscapes, and water buffaloes. His meticulous line, delicate color, and fine handling of space were much admired by his imperial patron.

LIU SUNG-NIEN (fl. 1190-1230) (courtesy name Liu Ch'ing-po-men or An-men). A pupil of Chang Tun-li; also studied the work of Chao Po-chü. He became a court painter. He did hanging scrolls of land pes, fan paintings, and historical scenes in which figures are as important as setting. His large compositions are marked by a lofty spirit, harmonious design and careful brushwork; his sense of poetry is more clearly manifest in his small studies.

CHINA. SUNG DYNASTY. LIANG K'AI
Sixth Patriarch Tearing a Sutra
Private Collection, Japan

LU HSIN-CHUNG (fl. 13th century). An artist who worked in Ning-po at the end of the Southern Sung period. His signature appears on two of the set of Sixteen Arhats (fifteen are in Boston) and it may be assumed that his signature has been trimmed from the others, for they are by the same hand. They are done on vertical panels of silk and in full color and gold. Each arhat is shown in an architectural or landscape setting, painted carefully but with a touch of fantasy appropriate to men supposedly endowed with supernatural qualities. Certain modern styles may be suggested by the perspective angles and the effect of seeing all sides of an object at once.

MA FEN (or Pen) (fl. end of 11th century) First of several famous painters of the Ma family, he is less important than his followers. He was a Painter-in-Attendance in the Academy under the Emperor Hui Tsung and was said to have painted The Hundred Apes, The Hundred Horses and similar groups of other animals. Because of this the famous scroll of The Hundred Wild Geese, now in the Honolulu Academy of Arts, has been attributed to him by some authorities. See MA KUNG-HSIEN below.

MA HO-CHIH (fl. 12th century). One of the favorite painters

CHINA. STYLE OF SUNG DYNASTY. Contemplation
Daitoku-ji, Kyoto

of the Emperor Kao Tsung of the Southern Sung; rose to a high official position. He was noted for his Buddhist painting, landscapes, and illustrations of ancient poems and ballads. It was said that his pictures were used to illuminate scrolls of the Emperor's calligraphy. His style was swift and spirited; garments blown by the wind, leaves fluttering on trees, the scudding of clouds, running water and men walking hint at his interest in problems of motion.

MA KUNG-HSIEN (fl. c.1130-60). Grandson of Ma Fen, and uncle of Ma Yüan and Ma Kuei. He upheld the honor of the family as a noted court painter. A painter of landscapes, figures, birds and flowers, he is best known for the Discussion between the Ch'an Hermit Yüeh Shan and the Philosopher Li Ao. This signed painting (at the Nanzen-ji, Kyoto) portrays the two men on a high terrace beneath a towering pine tree. The Ch'an monk, with shaven head and unkempt clothes, is seated in a rustic chair; Li Ao stands before him in proper cap and flowing robe. The suggestion of inner power in the Ch'an monk and of actual conversation between the two men is as striking as the spacious setting. It is done in the monochrome style that leaves much to the imagination although it is more detailed than that of Mu Ch'i or Liang K'ai.

MA LIN (fl. c.1215-c.1225). Son of Ma Yüan, he became a Painter-in-Waiting in the Academy of Painting. His early work is careful in outline, traditional in subject matter, charming to look at. He then came under the influence of Ch'an thought and the careful outlines gave way to broad tonal washes. He also discarded narrative subjects in favor of landscapes suggested by a few quick strokes of the brush, or legendary figures associated with Ch'an Buddhism, such as Han Shan and Shih Te.

MAO I (fl. c.1170). Son of Mao Sung; a renowned court painter of animals, especially puppies and kittens. He became a *tai chao* in Hangchou during 1165-73 and may have lived to the end of the century. His works have been very much admired in both China and Japan. The charm of his intimate and humorous studies, as well as his skill in rendering animal forms, has caused his name to be associated with that of his father Mao Sung (fl. c.1150).

MA YUAN (fl. c.1190-1234) (studio name Ch'in-shan). In the fourth generation of famous painters in the Ma family, he was nephew of Ma Kung-hsien and younger brother of Ma K'uei. A noted court painter under Emperors Kuang Tsung and Ning Tsung, he was still active in the reign of Li Tsung. He was a great favorite of the imperial family and later art critics have declared that he excelled all other court painters in his landscapes, figures, flowers and birds. Most admired by critics were his strength of line, elegance of form, composition (especially the balance between unfilled areas and mountains and rivers), and fine clear color. He used burnt ink to give trees and rocks definite outlines, a diluted wash for scars on rocks, a rather dry, compressed brush for branches and leaves, and a stumpy one for picturesque old pines. For buildings he employed a foot-rule to get proper alignment and applied color to beams and balustrades. His renown caused later artists to make faithful copies of his scrolls and put his name on them, and forgeries are therefore legion. Any painting in which a lonely philosopher gazes out over a misty valley or sits inside a beautifully painted pavilion beneath a gnarled pine is usually attributed to Ma Yüan. (See illustration.) The serenity of his art, the unity of man and nature, the picturesque handling of rocks, trees and mountains, are still appreciated; and even copies of his work are imbued with a sensitive poetic charm.

MI FEI, and also Fu (1051-1107) (courtesy name Yüan-chang; studio name Nan-kung). Native of Kiangsu. Received a military appointment in Anhui and then became a court painter and official. A precocious child, at the age of six he was able to memorize one hundred poems a day. His love of the past was so great that he dressed in the fashion of the T'ang dynasty and became a renowned collector of ancient painting and calligraphy. He was eccentric, impatient and headstrong. As a connoisseur his judgment was severe and highly respected. He had copied the masters of the past with great devotion but became famous for a style that he himself developed, that of the ink-play or ink blob, in which he stressed tonal value, and the building of form by touching the tip of the brush to paper (or silk) rather than by reliance on line. Much as he admired Wu Tao-tzu and Li Lung-mien, he determined to make his own contribution to Chinese painting and calligraphy—and succeeded. He preferred monochrome but was truly a painter rather than a draughtsman, creating pulsating masses that suggest color even though they are untinted. Because he was a noted calligrapher and portraitist as well as a master of landscape, he must at times have used the old linear style. Scholar, critic and author, he wrote the *Hua Shih*, which embodies his personal opinions and aesthetic standards and is a valuable source book on the history of Chinese painting. His influence on later Chinese and Japanese painters and on later connoisseurship was enormous, and his is one of the great names in Chinese painting.

MI YU-JEN (1085-1165) (courtesy name Yuan-hui; studio name Lan-cho Lao-jen). Like his father, the famous Mi Fei, a renowned painter and government official; unlike his father he enjoyed official life. It is said that his self-esteem increased with each promotion and that he easily forgot old friends. However, as a follower of Ch'an Buddhist thought, with its emphasis on meditation and harmony with nature, wordly affairs were forgotten when he sat cross-legged like a monk. He inherited his father's independence as an artist and carried the ink-play tonal technique to perhaps greater heights. A horizontal scroll in the Freer Gallery, Clearing Autumn on the Ch'u Mountains, is attributed to him. About 92x9 inches, showing wooded hills and the autumn mist, it is notable for the beauty of composition and handling of tonal areas. Like so many Sung artists, Mi Yu-jen was interested in space for philosophic reasons. That interest, however, was expressed with perfect understanding of the formal requirements of a painting and particularly of the horizontal scroll, which is unrolled gradually, about twelve inches being viewed at one time. The movement of massed tones, the contrast of mountain and river, mist and foliage, the delicate adjustment of foreground to background, attest to his sensitive perception and technique.

MU CH'I (fl. 13th century). A monk-painter whose real name was Fa-ch'ang; came from the Shu country (Szechuan) to Chekiang. He lived first in the Ching-shan temple, then in the Liu-t'ung ssu near Hangchou, which he made into a center of Ch'an Buddhist thought and painting. He is said to have been a pupil of Wu-chun, but information about him is scant, largely because his style was so "coarse" that the literary record-keepers did not consider him fit for "refined enjoyment." However, Japanese critics and artists inspired by Zen (Ch'an) ideals appreciated his art from the first and his paintings were collected by the powerful Ashikaga Shoguns and by Japanese Zen temples. His influence in China and Japan has been a major force outside the literary tradition. Using the P'o Mo (ink-splash) technique and graded washes, he reduced forms to their components and yet endowed them with significance and spiritual power. Some of his paintings were intended for temple use, as an aid to meditation (e.g., the famous Persimmons, which consists of a few rounded, abstract ink studies) or to recall such fundamental Buddhist principles as love of mankind and the oneness of nature. Part of his personal vision, they were rendered with a subtle understanding of inner rhythm as well as outer appearance and were painted with a delicate balance of filled and empty spaces. They depict a particular locale but have a universal significance.

SHIH K'O (fl. 10th century). Native of Shu (Szechuan), this independent Westerner went East to K'ai-feng in 965 after the conquest of Shu, but disliked the formal atmosphere of the imperial court and returned to his homeland. He was witty, argumentative, imaginative, and contemptuous of the world's opinion. Ink sketches of two monks which are attributed to him are revolutionary in their freedom of brushwork, economy of line and absence of color, and in this respect anticipate the Ch'an Buddhist art of the next few hundred years. Since it is said that Shih K'o enjoyed doing figures that were outlandish and amusing, these could indeed be his. Even such a scene as the Jade Emperor Holding Audience is described as revealing his humor as well as imagination. Twenty-one of his works are recorded in Emperor Hui Tsung's collection.

SU SHIH (1036-1101) (courtesy name Tzu-chan; studio name Tung-p'o). A native of Mei-shan (Szechuan) and a son of the scholar Su Hsün. In 1060 he entered public service and thereafter held a succession of posts. When he was transferred in 1072 from Hangchou to Huangchou, he built a hut on the Tung-p'o or Eastern Slope of the Hill and thereafter used the name as his *hao* (see). He made many friends and enemies, spent much time in exile and part of the time at court. In 1086 he was recalled to the capital and filled a number of high offices but fell into disfavor and was eventually banished to Hainan Island. For such a poet, scholar and public official, this exile in the distant provinces was a bitter experience. In 1101 he was restored to honor by the Emperor Hui Tsung but died soon afterwards. He stands in the very first rank not only as a painter but also as poet and essayist. As was appropriate to a philosopher-poet-painter, he specialized in the painting of bamboo, both as a symbol of resiliency and uprightness and as a growing thing that could best be portrayed by a scholar's calligraphic brushstroke. Each painting was usually inscribed with a poem.

SU TUNG-P'O (see SU SHIH above).

TS'UI PO (fl. second half of the 11th century) (courtesy name Tzu-hsi). A native of Hao-liang in Anhwei, a man of great gifts and independent character, and an excellent naturalist. He became a court painter and was often called on to paint lotus, wild ducks and geese. He was noted also for his exquisite rendering of Buddhist and Taoist themes.

Tung Yüan (fl. 10th century) (courtesy name Shu-ta). A native of Chungling, i.e., Nanking, he served the last Li prince before the Sung dynasty was established. He was Assistant Director of the Northern Park. He did excellent paintings of landscapes, Buddhist and Taoist themes, nature studies of wild geese, water buffaloes, tigers and an imaginative work called Sporting Dragons. His style was described as being like Wang Wei's in wet ink and like Li-Ssu-hsün's in color, and he was praised for the subtle tones of his washes and his ability to handle space. The peaks and ranges in his works were said to emerge and then disappear, and clouds and mist seemed palpable, obscuring forms at one moment, revealing them at the next (see illustration). He did not manage these effects by trickery or sheer virtuosity but by a careful study of nature, an understanding of "the very truths of Heaven." The misty blue vapors, the strong thrust of tree trunks and branches, the streams rushing through rocky channels and under bridges, the shadowy islands, the fishermen's coves—all were reflections of his homeland. The Sung Imperial Catalogue lists seventy-eight of his paintings.

WEN T'UNG (fl. 11th century) (courtesy name Yu-k'o; studio names Hsiao-hsiao and Shih-shih). Local governor of Ling-yang, but far more famous as a painter. To judge by the high praise of him by his close friend, Su Shih, his bamboo paintings raised this theme to a place of major importance in Chinese art. Associated with Wen is the use of bamboo as symbol of flexible strength, that which bends before adversity but is not broken. His brushwork, and especially his technique of thickening or thinning the ink and of changing pressure on the brush to achieve subtle tonal effects, has been admired by later painters. Leaves seem to overlap and to be poised as though capable of instant change. Abandoning the careful contour lines of his predecessors, he demonstrated the beauty of a monochrome painting that was close to calligraphy.

WU YUAN-YU (fl. late 11th century) (courtesy name K'UNG Ch'i). Originally from K'ai-feng in Honan. He was a noted

CHINA. SUNG DYNASTY. TUNG YÜAN. Landscape
National Museums and Library, China

painter of birds and flowers, a pupil and friend of Ts'ui Po, and an important military man. His painting seems to have been a hobby, a way of relaxing from his duties as a general. In his birds and flower pieces he broke away from academic tradition: a greater freedom of composition, informality of approach and poetic sensitivity differentiate his work from that of the court painters. He had many pupils and it seems likely that in his later years he put his seal on their works to help satisfy the demand for his paintings. Attributions, therefore, are made with caution. The Emperor Hui Tsung's collection ascribes 187 pictures to him.

YING YU-CHIEN (fl. early 13th century). A monk of the Ch'an sect of Buddhism; served as secretary of the Ching'tzu ssu, the famous temple on the West Lake of Hangchou. He is said to have followed the priest-painter Hui-ch'ung and was apparently contemporary with Mu Ch'i. Three landscapes by Ying are in Japanese collections. They are painted with the utmost freedom in the ink-splash style, merely suggesting the forms of rock, tree or temple. Light and dark washes seem to melt into the paper and truly to be created by "sudden enlightenment." A poem is inscribed to the left of the scenes in calligraphy that is in harmony with the painting. More precise but no less spirited is his painting of a rock orchid, now also in Japan.

Chinese Painters: Yüan Dynasty (1279-1368)

CHAO MENG-FU (1254-1322) (courtesy name Tzu-ang; studio names Sung-hsüeh, Tao-jen, Shui-ching, etc.) Born at Hu-chou, Chekiang, of a family descended from the first Sung emperor, he was educated at the Imperial College in Hangchou and was a hereditary official. Upon the fall of the House of Sung, he retired into private life until he was summoned in 1286 to the Mongol court in the north. Found to be an able administrator he became an important official and a great favorite of the Emperor. This gifted aristocrat was a model of Confucian virtue, versatile calligrapher, fine scholar and one of the Six Masters who led the painters of the Mongol period. Because he collaborated with the conquering Mongols, he was criticized by patriots but others admired his ability to guide the barbarians toward a Chinese way of life. In landscape he copied the T'ang painter Wang Wei; for horses he turned to Han Kan (T'ang). He also did figure-studies and flowers, but the majority of the copies of his works show horses and landscapes. Considered the foremost Chinese painter after the Sung period, there are hundreds of later copies of his works. He painted in a precise line, sometimes using color, as in the blue-green landscape after Wang Wei now in the British Museum; at other times he let graded washes suggest color. Both his calligraphy and painting may be described as "gentle, elegant and harmonious," the art of a classicist, not an originator.

CHAO YUNG (1289-?) (courtesy name Chung-mu). Born in Wu-hsing, Chekiang, son of the illustrious Chao Meng-fu and the Lady Kuan Tao-sheng. He was taught by both his parents and became a skillful painter and calligrapher. Like his father he specialized in landscapes and horse paintings, though his work is not considered as fine as that of his parent.

CH'IEN HSUAN (fl. 13th century) (courtesy name Shun-chü; studio name Sun-feng, etc). Originally from Wu-hsing in Chekiang. Living in the declining years of Sung rule, he refused to have anything to do with the conquering Mongols. He retired to the country, practiced his painting, played on the flute and wrote poetry. Sometimes his melancholy was eased with rice wine, for he found that when he was just a little tipsy, his "mind and hand were attuned." He studied T'ang painting for inspiration and is noted for his scrolls and album pieces of birds on flowering branches (see illustration), insect life, trees, landscapes and figure-studies. He used color with line, as well as the "boneless style" of color application without line. The beauty of small things in nature stirred him deeply and the paintings attributed to him, as well as those bearing his name, are much prized for this quality.

FANG TS'UNG-I (fl. 14th century, still active in Ming Period) (courtesy name Wy-yu; studio name Fang-hu). From Kuei-hsi in Kiangsi; became a monk in the great Taoist monastery of Shang-ch'ing-kung there. His landscapes were evidently painted in true Taoist manner—as the result of sudden inspiration. His blobs and dots of ink of the "*hsiao sa,*" or light and scattering technique, recall the art of Mi Fei of the Sung period. Critics agree that he was one of the Immortals. Without clearly defined outline but with delicate washes and graded tones, he suggested movement, moisture, nature in a state of flux, solids becoming voids, and Yang and Yin interacting.

HSUEH CH'UANG (fl. 14th century) (courtesy name P'u-ming). A monk painter noted for his monochrome studies of reeds and orchids. These symbols of resiliency and refinement were painted in rhythmic strokes that suggest the vitality and grace of the fragile plants bowing before the wind. (See illustration.)

HUANG KUNG-WANG (1269-1354) (courtesy name I-feng; studio name Ta-ch'ih-tao-jen, meaning the Big Taoist Fool). Born Lu Chien and adopted by the Huang family. He was one of the Six Great Masters of the Yüan period. Born in the Wu country of Kiangsu, he lived there for a time and then in Chekiang. He was vastly admired by Ming and Ch'ing dynasty critics, who speak of him as a prodigy, a "divine boy." In his youth, Huang became expert in every branch of literary and philosophic study. He was office clerk with the visiting censor in western Chekiang, but gave this up to wander about the countryside visiting Buddhist and Taoist

CHINA. YÜAN DYNASTY. CH'IEN HSUAN. Dove and Pear Blossoms. Cincinnati Art Museum

temples. He then chose to be called the Big Taoist Fool, indicating his scorn for worldly success and his preference for a hermit's life. He had studied traditional painting in his early days but soon developed his own style. It is said that he would sit motionless for hours in a bamboo grove, that he could be lost in meditation in the midst of a raging storm, that he climbed the highest peaks to observe clouds. This lofty quest for fundamentals is reflected in his painting. He painted to express his sense of unity with nature, and the painting of his old age is marked by as much power and originality as his earlier work. He could be meticulous, as when he crowded a composition with undulating mountains covered with verdure, but he is most admired for his clear, simple, abstract studies of nature.

JEN JEN-FA (fl. 14th century) (coutesy name Tzu-ming; studio name Yüeh-shan). A government official, author of a famous treatise on water supply. In painting he is best known for his studies of horses (Horses Feeding, Victoria and Albert Museum; Horses and Grooms, Fogg Museum) and for landscape scrolls (in Chinese and Japanese collections).

JIH-KUAN (see WEN JIH-KUAN below).

KAO K'O-KUNG (fl. 13th century) (courtesy name Yen-ching; studio name Fang-shan). Born at Ta-t'ung in Shansi of a family that migrated from Central Asia. He received a classical education and entered government service under Kublai Khan. In 1275 he became an official and rose eventually to the Presidency of the Board of Justice. In later years he went south to the beautiful Hangchou area to enjoy leisure, and there studied the mountains and clouds and mist, and expressed himself in painting. He was described by Ni Tsan as "a pure and most unusual man, outshining the vulgar world." With Ni and four others, he is classed as one of the Six Great Masters of the Mongol period.

KU AN (fl. mid-14th century) (courtesy name Ting-chih). Native of Huai-yang, Kiangsu. An official who served as judge in the Yüan-t'ung era. A noted painter of bamboo, one of his studies was done with Ni Tsan and Chang Shen. One of his strong clear works is owned by the Cincinnati Museum.

KUAN TAO-SHENG (1262-1319) (courtesy name Chung-chi; studio name Yao-chi; called Wei-kuo-fu-jen). Born in Wu-hsing in Chekiang. Wife of Chao Meng-fu, she is one of the outstanding woman artists in the roster of eminent painters. Like her husband and son she did landscapes; her specialties were bamboo, flowers, birds, exotic rocks and Buddhist images. The delicacy and refinement of her brushwork are joined to a subtle sense of compositional values. She painted small handscrolls, hanging scrolls and album pieces; critics often inscribed poems and words of praise on them.

KUNG K'AI (fl. late 13th-early 14th century) (courtesy name Sheng-yü; studio name Ts'ui-yen). Described as "eight feet tall and with a beautiful beard," he was a scholar and calligrapher of note, an eminent painter who refused service with the Mongols. Though he schooled himself by studying old masters, his rich imagination and originality lend his work particular interest. The Starved Horse, done in monochrome and without any setting, is most impressive; the Demons with Chung K'uei the Demon-queller treats the supernatural humorously (see illustration); and his landscapes reflect his poetic nature. To him, animals and men are individuals rather than symbols, yet he gives them a timeless significance.

LI K'AN (1245-1320) (courtesy name Ching-pin; studio name Hsi-chai). Native of Chi-ch'iu near Peking; served under Kublai Khan and three successive Khans. He is noted for his bamboo painting and his essay on that art, the *Chu P'u* (published c.1312), a historical study and painter's manual illustrated with his own sketches. He advised that one should first have a complete mental image, then begin work rapidly and "pursue the vision as the hawk strikes down for the hare." He was a man of great culture and a member of the Privy Council under Emperor Jen Tsung.

NI TSAN (1301-74) (family name Hsiu; courtesy name Yüan-chen; studio names Yün-lin, Ching-man-min, etc.) From Wu-hsi in Kiangsu. One of the Six Great Masters of the Yüan period, he has inspired painters throughout succeeding centuries. He loved the quiet life and eventually distributed his ample means to relatives and retired into dignified poverty, far from "the dusty world." He was called Unapproachable Ni and the Spotless Scholar. Stopping frequently at Buddhist monasteries in his travels, he was at home in a monk's

CHINA. YÜAN DYNASTY. HSUEH CH'UANG
Orchids. Brooklyn Museum

CHINA. YÜAN DYNASTY. KUNG K'AI

Chung K'uei the Demon-queller on His Travels. Freer Gallery of Art, Washington, D.C.

cell. He painted as he went, giving his paintings freely to congenial people, but refusing to paint for worldlings. His landscapes reflect his love of purity, clarity and detachment. Although he had collected ancient paintings and loved the past—he even used old-fashioned calligraphy—he was an innovator in his art. He eliminated as much as possible the wrinkles in rocks and mountain formations, rich foliage and the graded washes suggesting mist and vaporous atmosphere; instead he stressed skeletal structure. His trees are often stark vertical shafts with leaves barely indicated by horizontal strokes worked out from the trunk. There was little interest in roundness of branches, texture of bark, literal suggestion of light and shade, or the movement of leaves in a breeze. Water is not a pattern of curling lines; it is blank paper with a few shadows to suggest shores, and between the shores a broad pellucid river, eternally calm and pure. In the background may be seen a diminishing headland (in a nearly European perspective) of crystalline rocks unadorned by dense growth, sketchily painted in cubistic forms. An innovator, his art is nonetheless in the great tradition based on a close observation of nature; it is never so abstract as to be divorced from the land he loved. (See illustration.)

SHENG MOU (fl. first half of the 14th century) (courtesy name Tzu-chao). Son of Sheng Hung; from Chekiang. He painted landscapes, figures, flowers and birds. He found inspiration in the Sung dynasty painters Chu-jan and Fan K'uan and in the works of his neighbor Wu Chen. Sheng was more popular than Wu during his life, but later critics gave him a lesser place.

TS'AO CHIH-PAI (d. 1355) (courtesy name Yu-yüan; studio name Yün-hsi). Served as professor in a government college during the reign of Kublai Khan but resigned to become a hermit. He devoted himself to a study of the Taoist classic, the *I Ching*, and the analysis of Sung dynasty painters, especially Li Ch'eng and Kuo Hsi. Though not so austere and subtle as Ni Tsan, he sought for clarity of composition and dealt with the fundamentals of landscape motifs.

WANG MENG (c.1320-d.1385) (courtesy name Shu-ming; studio names Huang-hao, etc.). Born in Wu-hsing in Kiangsu, nephew of Chao Meng-fu, and one of the Six Great Masters of the Yüan period. Famous for his calligraphy and poetry, he was able to write a thousand characters in a few moments. With a fine scholarly background, he became an official, first as "law-secretary" at the capital, then as a district magistrate in Shantung. His brilliant career came to a tragic ending when he died in prison, a victim of political intrigue. A busy man of affairs, he nevertheless enjoyed painting landscapes. He kept white silk stretched across one end of his study and painted for as long as three years on one vast composition. He firmly established the "*wen-jen-hua*," or literary mode of painting that was to continue for the next five hundred years; and he generally is admired by critics of the same gentleman-scholar-painter type as himself. He lived near the great Sacred Mountain, the T'ai Shan, and his most prized works depict that awe-inspiring mass of rock and earth. He was energetic, rapid in his brushwork and fond of detail, combining as many as twelve types of wrinkle or fissure in one massif in order to give an impression of "dragon's veins." He portrayed every tree, shrub, leaf, moss, lichen, waterfall, bridge, etc., so meticulously that one may profitably examine each part with a magnifying glass. Conscious of the enclosing frame, pushing his volumes upward in a dynamic spiral, he gave unity to his work by powerful rhythmic lines structurally conceived. The ease with which his art was copied indicates that it was not so much the spontaneous work of a philosopher as the complex expression of a brilliant technician. (See color plate 34.)

WEN JIH-KUAN (fl. mid-13th century). The monk Tzu-wen (better known by his studio name Jih-kuan) came from Hua-t'ing in Kiangsu and lived at the Ma-nao monastery at Hang-chou. A true follower of the Ch'an ideal, he was unconventional in appearance and manner. Both his calligraphy and the free, fluent painting of grapes for which he was noted reflect his independence of academic restraint. His grape leaves, it was said, "resembled tattered priestly garments."

WU CHEN (1280-1354) (courtesy name Chung-Kuei; studio names Mei-hua-tao-jen, etc.) From Chia-hsing in Chekiang. One of the Six Great Masters of the Yüan period, he is known especially for his landscapes, bamboo and flower painting. Poet as well as artist, the verses he inscribed on his paintings heighten their meaning and add to their decorative effect. A collection of his poems, entitled *I Mo (Ink Remains)*, was made in the seventeenth century by Ch'ien Fen. Disturbed by the unsettled time in which he lived, toward the end of Mongol rule in China, he chose the life of a hermit, disdaining fame and fortune. He studied the ancient Book of Divination (the *I Li)*, became adept at telling fortunes and thus earned enough to exist in dignified poverty. Seeking the company only of Buddhist and Taoist monks, he "hid his shadow among the reeds" and painted for pleasure. He wrote the epitaph for his own tomb: "The Pagoda of the Plum-blossom Monk." His Taoist tendencies are manifest in his painting, for he

34. CHINA. YÜAN DYNASTY. Wang Meng. A Landscape. Freer Gallery of Art, Washington, D.C.

was unconventional and his work was done on the spur of the moment as ink-plays *(hsi-mo)* intended to suggest inner meaning and not outward aspect or color. The bamboo, flowers and landscapes are simple and seem to evolve out of nebulous space. He gave away his paintings to all simple folk who liked them. Ni Tsan said of him: "When he got drunk, he swung the brush and painted the air of the mountains, the haze, the mist and the clouds flawlessly." (See illustration.)

YEN HUI (fl. 14th century) (courtesy name Ch'iu-yüeh). From Chiang-shan in Chekiang. Little is known of his life, for Chinese critics were not so pleased by his work as were Japanese. He was described as a good painter of Taoist and Buddhist subjects, with a gift for portraying the supernatural. Except for a landscape attributed to him (in the former Imperial Collection), the works bearing his name are figure-studies. In these, as in his landscapes his boldness of line is remarkable; it helps to explain why Japanese connoisseurs and artists have admired him. The hanging scrolls of Two Taoist Immortals in the Chion-ji, Kyoto, show men dominating their natural settings, not immersed in them. Both have Western faces, with eyes (of a non-Mongol type) that suggest an inner and mysterious power. One is releasing a spirit from his horny hand and looks like a sage of the Arabian Nights who can control genii. The ability to depict a psychological quality is unusual in the fourteenth century, and Yen Hui did it with great dramatic effect. His works have been copied frequently in Japan.

Chinese Painters: Ming Dynasty (1368-1644)

CHANG LU (c.1464-c.1538) (courtesy name T'ien-ch'ih; studio name P'ing-shan). One of the few painters of the Chê group who came from North China. He was born in K'ai-feng, Honan, and it is said that his fellow northerners valued his paintings like jade, whereas the southern connoisseurs considered them lacking in refinement. His figures, like those of Wu Wei, were strong and vigorous, interesting to look at "although wanting in refinement and beauty." He painted fishermen at work, and also liked Taoist subjects such as Lao-Tzu on a Water Buffalo or Two Hermits Listening to a Crane. He painted in broad tonal washes, evidently using a rather dry brush. There is a breadth, a sense of mystery and a hint of the instantaneous inspiration and quick execution that stems from the Taoist and Ch'an Buddhist ideal. It is no wonder that his art has been much admired in Japan, where Zen (Ch'an) inspiration has been so vital.

CH'EN CHI-JU (1558-1639) (courtesy name Chung-shun; studio names Mi-kung and Mei-kung). From Hua-t'ing, Kiangsu. He was a writer, editor and poet, and a friend of Tung Ch'i-ch'ang and Mo Shih-Lung. In painting he specialized in landscapes, plum blossoms and bamboo as well as "strange stones." At twenty-eight he retired from official life and devoted himself to a study of Ch'an Buddhism and the pursuits of a gentleman of means—gardening, tea-drinking,

CHINA. YÜAN DYNASTY. NI TSAN. Landscape
The Bamboo Studio, New York

CHINA. YÜAN DYNASTY. WU CHEN. Landscape
National Museums and Library, China

chess and the study of literature. He practiced calligraphy and painting in the same spirit. He was a noted art critic, his approval of a painting in the form of a colophon giving it definite prestige. In his *Shu Hua Chin T'ang* he discussed such matters as good ways of enjoying paintings, how to adorn them, and the calamities that may befall them. His other works contain miscellaneous observations on painting, calligraphy, history and aesthetics. His own paintings reflect the Ch'an ideal of relaxation and spontaneity; they are typical "ink-plays" by a gentleman-painter of the late Ming period.

CH'IU YING (fl. early 16th century) (courtesy name Shih-fu; studio name Shih-chou). From T'ai-ts'ang, Kiangsu. He became a pupil of Chou Ch'en and after briefly imitating the dashing technique of his teacher, perfected his own style of delicate brushwork. He moved to Suchou, where he was a friend of Wen Cheng-ming and other painter-connoisseurs of the Wu group, though he himself was not a scholar or poet. Although a true eclectic and a student of traditional artists, he developed a distinct personal technique based on precise drawing with the point of the brush and the addition of color. He is best known for blue-green landscapes of mountains and rivers, figure-studies of mythological and historical personages, architectural arrangements (using ruled lines). and for the daintiness and elegance typical of one phase of Ming taste.

CHOU CH'EN (fl. c.1500-35) (courtesy name Shun-ch'ing; studio name Tung-ts'un). A native of Suchou, friend of T'ang Yin, pupil of Ch'en Hsien. He followed Sung tradition, basing his work on Li T'ang and the Ma-Hsia school of landscape painting. Though he lived in the Wu country and was friendly with members of the poetry-writing group, he produced decorative pictures like the Chê artists. One of his landscapes. dated 1534, was an imitation of Tai Chin's misty mountains His figure painting displays more freedom in brushstroke than most landscapes in Sung style. There is strength, humor and realism in his character studies. In his illustrations of Ming peasant life, thatched huts, rustic walls and farm animals are not dwarfed by trees or mountains, but are done on a scale that allows for realistic details. As one critic pointed out, he did "not lend an air of remoteness and silence or an effect of distance and tranquility" to his studies of rural life, but, like most Ming painters, experimented and was not content with tradition.

CHU TUAN (fl. c.1506-21) (courtesy name K'o-ch'eng; studio name I-ch'iao). From Hai-yen, Chekiang; one of the Chê School. He was summoned to court in 1501 and became the favorite painter of Emperor Wu Tsung. True to Chê tradition and the imperial taste, he based his painting on the Sung masters, especially Ma Yüan and Kuo Hsi, achieving an effect that was decorative, refined and accomplished. Every element in his landscapes is meticulously outlined, graceful in form and harmoniously placed. Also notable is a sense of vastness, a point of view that enables one to look out over a broad expanse and yet see every detail. His manipulation of space areas is noteworthy, particularly in the shore landscapes of which he was especially fond. He stands high among Ming artists. (See illustration.)

HSIANG SHENG-MO (1597-1658) (courtesy name K'ung-chang; studio names I-an and Hsü-shan chiao). From Chia-hsing in Chekiang. Grandson of the famous collector Hsiang Yüan-pien, he had a good opportunity to study masterpieces of the past. At first he was influenced by Wen Cheng-ming and did large landscapes in a scholarly style, but later he produced informal album sketches that were closer to Sung and Yüan studies. In his painting a single branch of flowering peach will extend across the paper in a delicate and subtle line; each bud, blossom and leaf is a symbol of growth and change rather than a display of virtuosity. His paintings of bamboo, orchids, river grasses and small creatures of land and water reflect the spirit of a philosopher and poet, adept at capturing the exquisite, airy forms invisible to less sensitive men.

HSUAN TSUNG (1398-1435). Fifth Emperor of the Ming Dynasty, ruling in the Hsüan Te period, 1425-35; called Chu Chan-chi and later known as Hsüan Tsung. A well-meaning monarch, he lightened the grain tribute and established customs-houses at important centers. He fostered the art of painting at court and was himself a creative artist, painting flower and animal studies, and especially cats, monkeys and goats. He painted with a fine brush, outlining each motif clearly and placing color within the contour lines.

HSU LIN (fl. early 16th century) (courtesy name Tzu-jen; studio names Chiu-feng and K'uai-yüan-sou). Born in Suchou but moved to Nanking; one of the Chê group. He was a child prodigy, passed the district school examinations at fourteen and acquired great skill in poetry, literary composition, and calligraphy of the seal-character type. He did landscapes, flowers and grasses. In his Winter Scene, white peaks are separated from the grey sky by a surely drawn outline with little variation in its thickness. This appealed to Japanese taste and was imitated by Japanese artists for its clarity, power, and tendency toward simplification. The wrinkled, cleft rocks, and the gnarled trees with roots like dragon claws and branches like angling rods, are dramatized Sung motifs. His figures are good character studies, though they seem tiny in the overpowering landscape settings.

HSU WEI (1521-1593) (courtesy name Wen-ch'ing and Wen-ch'ang; studio names T'ien ch'ih and Ch'ing-t'eng). Native of Shan-yin, Chekiang. An unpredictable person, he was noted for both prose and poetry, for his ability as a dramatist, calligrapher and painter. In his own opinion his grass-writing style of calligraphy was his greatest work; then came his poetry, prose and, last of all, painting. Later critics reversed the order, putting his painting first. His is an untrammeled and inimitable style. Much of his independence of character is reflected in his brushwork, which was consid-

CHINA. MING DYNASTY. CHU TUAN
A Man and Boy in a Boat under Trees
Museum of Fine Arts, Boston

ered "unfinished" by connoisseurs of the precious kind of painting done by literary men.

Ku Ning-yuan (fl. 1636) (courtesy name Ch'ing-hsia). From an old Suchou family of officials. He preferred the life of a gentleman-painter and collector to serving the government, and spent his days enjoying his art treasures, reading, and playing host to great scholars. A painter of moderate talent, he is better known for the *Hua Yin,* a most interesting Ming discussion of aesthetics and painting techniques.

Lan Ying (1578-after 1660) (courtesy name T'ien-shu; studio name Chieh-sou and Shih T'ou-t'o). From Ch'ien-t'ang, Chekiang. This last representative of the Chê group was one of the most original among late Ming painters. His landscapes were based on the famous masters of the Sung and Yüan dynasties; he is also noted for figure-studies, birds, flowers (especially orchids) and stones.

Li Liu-fang (1575-1629) (courtesy name Ch'ang-heng; studio name T'an-yüan). Native of Hsieh-hsien, Anhui; lived in Chia-ting, Kiangsu. He was a scholar, poet, and prolific painter. Many of his scrolls are in famous Far Eastern collections. His landscapes were based on the work of Tung Yüan of the Sung period and Wu Chen of the Yüan period,

CHINA. MING DYNASTY. Attributed to Lin Liang
Ducks and Reeds
Metropolitan Museum of Art, New York

but were executed in a free, sketchy manner.

Lin Liang (fl. 1457-1505) (courtesy name I-shan). Came from Kuangtung province. Although he may have become a court painter earlier, he was certainly serving in the palace under the Emperor Hsiao Tsung (1488-1505), by whom he was appointed Officer in the Imperial Guard. Noted for his monochrome painting in the free tonal style, he specialized in birds, flowers, bamboo and fruits. Unlike Ming decorative painting, his nature studies reproduce the actual habitat of game birds. (See illustration.)

Li Tsai (fl. 1426-35) (courtesy name I-cheng). Came from P'u-t'ien, Fukien. He was called to court in the Hsüan Te period and worked with Tai Chin. Both painted in the manner of Sung dynasty masters, as part of the attempt of Emperor Hsüan Tsung to revive China's great tradition after its interruption by the Mongol conquest. Li Tsai was a leader in the Chê School of refined decorative painting.

Liu Chueh or Chio (1410-72) (courtesy name T'ing-mei; studio name Wan-an). From Suchou; a poet, calligrapher and official. A man of prominent social position, he served as a secretary in the Board of Punishment until the age of fifty. when he retired to a country villa and created a famous garden. Devoting his later years to poetry and painting in solitude, he was a *Shih-ta-fu* (gentleman-painter), precursor of the Wu School that followed his friend Shen Chou. He looked to the independent painters of the Yüan dynasty for inspiration, liking especially the unrestrained style of Wu Chen.

LU CHI (fl. 1488-1505) (courtesy name T'ing-chen; studio name Lo-yu). From Yin-hsien, Chekiang. Summoned to the court at Peking in the Hung Chih period, he was much admired and made an officer in the Imperial Guard. In his youth he studied the great masters of the past and came to be known for his elegant decorative paintings of birds and flowers, grasses and trees.

LU CHIH (1496-1576) (courtesy name Shu-p'ing; studio name Pao-shan). From Suchou; pupil of Wen Cheng-ming. Noted for bird and flower paintings in the Sung style of Hsü Hsi and for elegant mannered flower pieces suited to late Ming taste. He painted landscapes as well. (See color plate 35.)

MA SHOU-CHENG (fl. 1600-1620) (studio names Hsiang-lan, meaning Fragrant Orchid, and Yüeh-chiao). This noted woman painter from Nanking was a great friend of the author Wang Chi-teng, whose *Chronicle of Painting in the Wu Prefecture (Wu Chün Tan Ch'ing Chih)*, 1563, was used by many Ming painters. Although "Fragrant Orchid" was a sing-song girl on the Ch'in-huai river at Nanking, she achieved fame for her paintings of flowers and bamboo. Her style was described as "easy and free, beautiful and quiet, resonant with life."

MO SHIH-LUNG (fl. c.1567-82) (courtesy name Yün-ch'ing and also T'ing-han; studio name Ch'iu-shui). From Sung-chiang (Hua-t'ing), Kiangsu, but later lived in Shanghai. He was a renowned critic, author of the *Hua Shuo (Treatise on Painting)*, poet, calligrapher, and painter of landscapes. Considered the greatest talent of his time, his company was sought by scholars and persons of high rank. His painting is less distinguished than his critical and writing ability. With Tung Ch'i-ch'ang, who was younger, he held endless discussions of aesthetics and the proper approach to a history of Chinese painting. They clarified the division of painting into northern and southern schools, basing their ideas on theoretical principles as well as on a careful examination of past artists. This intellectual approach, and especially the emphasis on the literary school, the "*wen jen hua*," has exerted a fundamental influence on Chinese connoisseurs.

SHEN CHOU (1427-1509) (courtesy name Ch'i-nan; studio names Shih-t'ien and Po-shih-weng). From Suchou in the beautiful Wu country. Shen Chou is one of the great masters of Chinese art, a versatile and prolific painter, beloved by all, and still influential. A gentleman-painter, not attached to the court or living by his art, he came of a distinguished line of scholars, calligraphers and poets. He was virtuous by every Chinese standard, following Confucian ethics and Taoist speculation. Men of like disposition turned to him for inspiration and in this sense he is regarded as founder of the Wu School. The Wu painters were not an academy or studio, but gentlemen-poets and philosophers who used painting as a means of expression. Most of their works are inscribed with verse or have words of praise written by friends or later critics. Shen Chou's versatility is almost bewildering. Both Sung and Yüan artists inspired him; of the latter, Huang Kung-wang and Ni Tsan interested him in his middle years, but finally Wu Chen became his favorite. This led to a greater freedom and strength of brushstroke in his later art. His earliest dated picture (1464) is small, detailed and elegant in style though rustic in subject matter. Called Spring in the Mountains, it shows a group of thatched buildings nestling beneath towering peaks. Following this, many signed paintings appear, such as: Man on a Donkey, 1468, a delicately humorous work, "done as a pastime on the day of the winter solstice"; an album of 1471 in which the influence of Wang Fu may be noted; others of 1475 inspired by Ni Tsan; another in 1492 inspired by Tung Yüan and others, but all of them rendered with freedom and spontaneity. Sometimes one is especially conscious of his line; at other times, of tonal wash areas. In about 1500 he began to paint larger works and became more experimental in technique. He did a horizontal scroll some twenty feet long and numerous vertical scrolls in which he played with space areas, line and tone. His inspiration always came from nature; although some of these later paintings are quite abstract, they are usually inspired by actual locales. One is made aware also of his love of sounds and fragrances. His poems and the delight of his little men in the world around them hint at his own enjoyment. (See illustration.)

TAI CHIN (fl. c.1430-50) (courtesy name Wen-chin; studio names Ching-an and Yü-ch'üan Shan-jen). Came from Ch'ien-t'ang, Chekiang, and was founder of the Chê school, named after this province. He was summoned to court but his superior talent and independent spirit caused some jealousy. Not until after death did he receive the recognition he deserved. It was said that in his landscapes he united the merits of various masters, but copied in particular the works of Li T'ang and Ma Yüan (both Sung period). He was described as a painter of divine beings, human figures, animals, birds and flowers, whose copies of the old masters were so perfect that not even good connoisseurs could distinguish them from the originals. Neither scholar nor poet, he was not elevated to the rank of gentleman-painter. In the mid-sixteenth century Ho Liang-chün said that in his pictures of Lohans and Taoists he used the "iron-wire" stroke and also

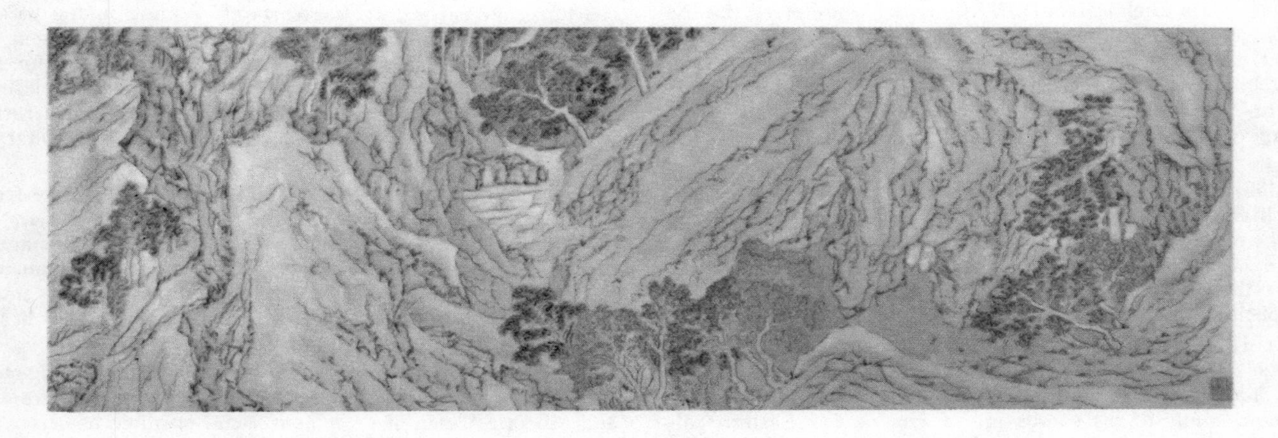

35. CHINA. MING DYNASTY. Lu Chih. Landscape. William Rockhill Nelson Gallery, Kansas City

CHINA. MING DYNASTY. SHEN CHOU. Landscape. The Bamboo Studio, New York

at times the "epidendrum leaf" (long continuous strokes as strong as iron wire and as graceful as orchid leaves), but that in his pictures of human beings he used the "silkworm head" and the "mouse-tail" stroke (abrupt rhythm, economy of line, and spontaneity). Not stemming from the literary tradition, he did not, like the men of the Wu School, place poems and comments on his paintings. In the two scrolls in the Freer Gallery, one sees fifteenth-century China through the eyes of a great independent artist. In one, Fishermen on the River in Autumn, sections suggest modern Western work, yet the busy fishermen are truly Chinese (see illustration). This is a genre art depicting the China of hard work and unceasing struggle for existence. The other scroll, Autumn Winds and Breaking Waves, has an irresistible rhythm: the wind bends trees before it and the undulating lines of waves express the power of water. Rocks are built up in broad strokes of the brush, some formed of rich black ink, others graded in softer tones. Men battle the elements of sea and sky. One recalls Hsia Kuei and his love of stormy weather, but the technique used here is much freer than that of the Sung master.

T'ANG YIN (1470-1523) (courtesy names Po-hu and Tzu-wei; studio name Liu-ju Chu-shih). From Suchou in Wu-hsien. He was a brillant and erratic painter specializing in landscapes, figure studies and flowers. He had a fine classical education and rivaled famous poets of the past in his own writing. His early education in painting was with Chou Ch'en. He soon surpassed his teacher, who is said to have then filled orders that T'ang Yin was too lazy to execute. So great was his versatility that it is difficult to establish his chronological development. He could paint in the manner of Sung and Yüan masters or in quite original ways. Some of his landscapes are tightly organized, each rock and tree portrayed with careful contour lines; in others he stressed mood and went in for stormy winds and heavy tonal mists. Of the small studies, some suggest modern Western art, for he emphasized abstract motifs (such as the pattern of a woven rush fence, house screens or fishing nets) and played with spatial relationships. He painted bamboo in an elegant calligraphic style, breaking from tradition to depict it as a welter of leaves growing from stems that are barely suggested.

CHINA. MING DYNASTY. TAI CHIN
Autumn River Landscape with Fishing Boats. Freer Gallery of Art, Washington D.C.

CHINA. MING DYNASTY. T'ANG YIN
Lady on a Banana Leaf
Metropolitan Museum of Art, New York

He loved exotic rocks with water-worn holes, and banana trees and palms. Of his figure studies, some are carefully outlined and traditional, the colored fabric patterns regular and minute, the faces of women done with great delicacy, the flower arrangements and ornaments exquisite. In contrast to this are such rapid sketches as Lady on a Leaf (see illustration). An Arhat in Meditation (Yamamoto collection), a remarkable example of his power to suggest a person deep in contemplation, is a painting of sensitivity, elegance and inner power. Literally all things seem to have been possible in his art.

TUNG CH'I-CH'ANG (1555-1636) (courtesy name Hsüan-tsai; studio names Ssu-po and Ssu-weng). From Hua-t'ing near Suchou. A great scholar and high official, a calligrapher of great renown an art critic and connoisseur of the first rank, an author and painter, he is regarded as the leading figure of Ming art in his locale. In spite of a promising beginning, he felt a distaste for public life, largely because of his study of Ch'an Buddhism, in which the meditative rather than the active life is regarded as the greatest good. He repeatedly retired from his office to his home in the Wu area but was recalled to serve in higher posts. He lived to be eighty-one and was admired for his kindness as much as for his great accomplishment. His hand was so trained by calligraphy and his mind so attuned to intellectual examination that he developed a disciplined, self-conscious approach to painting. He has been called the Cézanne of Ming artists because of a love of classic tradition combined with a wish to restate old ideas in new forms. His prestige as calligrapher and art critic are greater than his fame as a painter. With Mo Shih-lung and Ch'en Chi-ju, he discussed the fundamental principles of painting and set up categories of painters. Study of their opinions (Tung's are clearly set forth in his treatises, *Hua Yen* and *Hua Ch'an Shih Sui Pi*, edited after his death) is essential for a full understanding of later Chinese taste and art.

WANG E (fl. 1488-1521) (courtesy name T'ing-chih). A native of Feng-hua, Chekiang; court painter in the Hung Chih period (1488-1505) and officer of the Imperial Guard in the Cheng Te period (1506-21). He was called by Emperor Hsiao Tsung "the Ma Yüan of our time." One of the Chê school, he studied the Sung masters as a youth and also sketched from nature. He was so faithful to Sung compositional formulas and motifs that it has been suggested it was he who painted many accomplished works of art formerly assigned to the twelfth and thirteenth centuries.

WANG FU (1362-1416) (courtesy name Meng-tuan; studio names Yu-shih and Chiu-lung Shan-jen). From Wu-hsi, Kiangsu. This "Friend of Stones" and "Hermit of the Nine Dragon Mountain," as his studio names describe him, was a man of resolute and independent disposition, the greatest of the early Ming landscape painters. He was one of the few in his period to work in the manner of Ni Tsan and Wang Meng of the previous (Yüan) dynasty. Sometimes he would paint meticulously, sometimes with vigor and spontaneity. His respect for past tradition and his love of freedom (coupled with the inspiration of wine) may account for his two methods.

WANG MIEN (1335-1407 or c.1415) (courtesy name Yüan-chang; studio name Lao-ts'un, etc.). From K'uai-chi, Chekiang; specialized in painting plum blossoms and in poetry. A noted eccentric, his life is recorded in the *History of the Ming Dynasty* and *Biographies of Ming Painters* written in the late sixteenth century. Many anecdotes are told of his early days as a shepherd lad with a leaning toward literature. He studied military science as well as history and literature, became a school teacher, shunned official position, and in the end devoted himself to painting his favorite flower.

WEN CHENG-MING (1470-1559) (original name Pi; courtesy name Cheng-ming, later taken as his name; later courtesy name Cheng-chung; studio name Heng-shan). Born to a prominent family in Suchou, a descendant of the Duke of Hsing-kuo and other highly placed men. Scholar, calligrapher, poet and painter of the Wu school, he was regarded during his lifetime and later as a model of refinement, taste, and high ethics. In his youth he studied poetry, calligraphy and painting under great masters. Under the influence of Shen Chou, he studied the landscapes of the Northern Sung artists and the traditionalists of the Yüan period, especially Chao Meng-fu. From c.1500 through his middle period, he served in the capital as an official (a *tao-chao)* in the Han-lin Academy, writing the history of the preceding reign and explaining the classics. He was liberally rewarded and much admired, but it is thought that he became bored with official life, resigned and went back home. He spent his last thirty years mainly in his home city, where he gave full attention to painting. He gave his paintings only to scholars or good friends, refusing them even to members of the imperial family. He entertained congenial companions in his home, sipping tea or wine, burning incense, discussing literature, or examining antiquities and strangely shaped stones—the typical pleasures of the perfect gentleman of the sixteenth century. In the history of Chinese painting he is classed as one of the Immortals. Nearly a hundred of his works are still treasured in collections throughout the world. Most of them are signed, many are dated, and many of the hanging scrolls have poems inscribed on the upper section. Some of the pictures are small album pieces, sketches intended to delight the lover of fine brushwork or to remind the artist of some happy hour; othes are very large (one is about 11 x 3 feet). Like many Chinese and Japanese experts with the brush, he could paint in three styles: a quick, spontaneous manner in which tonal washes are important; a style combining "classic," precise, elegant strokes with some tonal shading; and a fine, painstaking manner in which line is more important than tone. His love of strange rocks is reflected in his painting, and his trees have an unforgettable quality of strength and life. Their roots literally seem to grasp the earth, their branches turn in abrupt angles, and the trunks are three-dimensional, rounded, and suggest the living spirit of the tree. In all his work one feels a keen mind, a sensitive perception, and an absolute control of the brush. (See illustration.)

Wu Wei (1459-1508) (courtesy names Shih-ying, Lu-fu and Tzu-weng; studio name Hsiao-hsien). From Wu-ch'ang, Hupei; a leader in the Chê school. He was a self-taught painter, a genius of eccentric habits, but honored by both Emperors Hsien Tsung and Hsiao Tsung. It is an indication of the relaxation of court standards at the end of the fifteenth century that a habitual drinker and woman-chaser, uncouth and irresponsible, could be held in high esteem. Finally, however, even the liberal Emperor Hsien Tsung and his court could no longer tolerate him, and he was expelled. With his independence of spirit, it was natural that Wu Wei liked Taoist subjects and rural types—woodchoppers, fishermen and farmers—and painted them with striking fidelity, understanding and sometimes with humor. They are individuals rather than symbols and they are in their proper settings. The artist's ability to simplify and dramatize, using strong brushstrokes, gives these pieces a decorative quality characteristic of the Chê school.

Yang Wen-ts'ung (1597-1645) (courtesy name Lung-yu). Born in Kueichou in southwest China but spent much of his life in Nanking. He was one of the Nine Friends in Painting, as well as a high official, scholar, and calligrapher of note. He was magistrate of Nanking when the Ming rulers took refuge there and he led the military defense of the city. When it fell, he fled to Fukien and led the Ming forces in a last stand, but was defeated, captured and put to death by the Manchus. His painting was based on a careful study of Sung and Yüan masters, but he was too original a genius to adhere too closely to anyone else's style. His large landscapes have more of the crowded, massive mountain-water composition, in the literary taste, than do his album pieces and fan paintings. One album, dated 1638, is full of delightful and informal scenes done in an expressionistic way. A lonely philosopher enjoying the autumn colors, a fisherman sailing home before the wind, even simple cottages on a terrace, bespeak a feeling for nature that is anything but academic. The delicacy of tone in his ink washes, the economy of line, and the harmony of each detail with more massive forms, demonstrate a sensitive perception and an extraordinary technique.

Yao Shou (1423-1495) (courtesy name Kung-shou; studio name Ku-an). From Chia-shan, Chekiang. This poet, calligrapher and painter served for a time as censor and as prefect of Yung-ning until his retirement to his native home. Freed from official duties, he journeyed about in a boat, sketching, composing poems and singing. This freedom from restraint and love of nature are reflected in his painting. He specialized in painting landscapes (in the style of Wu Chen), bamboo, birds, flowers, stones and fungi. He is one of the outstanding brush-technicians of his time.

Chinese painters: Ch'ing Dynasty (1644-1912)

Chang Feng (fl. c.1645-70) (courtesy name Ta-feng; studio name Sheng-chou Tao-shih). A native of Nanking. He entered official life by passing the *chu-sheng* examination while the Ming dynasty was in power, but on the fall of the Ming he renounced his degree and retired from public life. He then lived in abject poverty in a small hut, wrote beautiful poetry, engraved seals and painted. He was a devout Buddhist, signed himself "True Buddha Incense in the Empty World," and is often classed as a monk-painter, though there is no reference to him as a member of an order. Some of his landscapes are notable for their tonal delicacy and fine manipulation of washes; others are purely linear, abstract and calligraphic; still others use both tone and line. In all of them there is an ease of execution and a sure arrangement of spatial areas that reflect his temperament.

Cha Shih-piao (1615-1698) (courtesy name Erh-chan; studio name Mei-ho). A native of Hai-yang Anhui; one of the Four Masters of Anhui, noted for his landscape painting and writing. He passed the *chu sheng* degree in the Ming period but after the fall of the dynasty, stopped studying for examinations and gave most of his time to painting and calligraphy. He came of a well-to-do family, was a connoisseur of bronze ritual vessels and paintings of the Sung and Yüan periods, and enjoyed a quiet, leisurely life. His serene approach to life is reflected in his art. Using great economy of line, he painted in the natural, "unrestrained" manner and without apparent effort.

Chin Nung (1687-d. after 1774) (courtesy name Shou-men; studio name Tung-hsin). From Hangchou but lived for a long time in Yang-chou, Kiangsu. A critic of painting and a traveler, he did not himself learn to paint until he was fifty. He began by doing bamboo in the Sung manner, then plum blossoms, studies of horses, and finally Buddhist figures and landscapes. His remarks on painting, especially on his own work, were collected by a friend and published as the *Tung-hsin T'i Hua (Annotations of Tung-hsin)*. These imaginative and cryptic remarks gave glimpses of his personality and his interest in meditative Buddhism. Although he was not ordained as a priest, he led the life of a monk, expressing himself in few words and lines. He was the most influential of the Eight Strange Masters of Yangchou, a circle of gifted men. An experimenter in line and spatial relationships, he would doubtless have been at home in the twentieth century. Simple, direct and original, he painted with singular freedom.

CHINA. MING DYNASTY. WEN CHENG-MING
Cypress Tree and Rock
William Rockhill Nelson Gallery, Kansas City

Even his architectural motifs are brushed in according to his personal vision rather than for optical illusion. Proportion, tonal value, line—all are challenging, mysterious and delightful. Noted as a calligrapher and poet, he nonetheless painted with fewer literary overtones than the usual scholar-artist; he approached his scrolls and album pieces from the visual point of view. He was described as "an independent character who had little veneration for old masters."

CH'IN TSU-YUNG (fl. c.1850-80) (courtesy name I-fen; studio name Leng-yen Wai-shih). From Wu-hsi, Kiangsu. He painted landscapes based on the work of Wang Shih-min. A lover of the past, he was traditional in his painting. His books on the art of painting, the *T'ung Yin Lun Hua* and the *Hua Chüeh* (he also edited the *Hua Hsüeh Hsin Yin)*, are important contributions to our knowledge of Chinese painting.

CHU TA (fl. c.1630-50) (courtesy name Jen-wu; studio names Pa-ta Shan-jen, Hsüeh-ko, Ko-shan and Shan-lu). A descendant of the imperial Ming family. Born in Nanch'ang, Kiangsi, he passed one of the lesser academic district examinations while the Ming dynasty was still in power. Shortly afterward he seems to have become a Buddhist monk. Deeply affected by the fall of the royal house, he became one of the hermit-painters who sought seclusion in remote mountains, away from the splendor of the Manchu court. Known for eccentric behavior, it is said that he eventually went mad. He had a partiality for wine and took refuge from the troubled world in painting and calligraphy. Possessed of an extraordinary talent, he painted landscapes, flowers, birds, bamboos and trees. He was not bound by any rules and his brushwork was considered careless, if strong, by his contemporaries. He painted as if on the spur of the moment but with an unfailing sense of fine composition, in which the unfilled areas are especially telling. The instantaneous inspiration and rapid stroke and the liking for bare spaces express the Ch'an approach to life. The sketchiness of his work is deliberate, the kind of simplicity based upon great skill and knowledge. Among his works are large landscapes and smaller album leaves. Humor and liveliness, enjoyment of the inconsistent, the almost-human expressions of bird and animal, are as noteworthy as his powerful brushstrokes. For all of his originality, he still chose traditional subjects and consciously followed certain Yüan and Sung masters. However, he did not copy, but reinterpreted earlier works in his own free impressionistic manner. His large landscapes lack the engaging touches of humor of his album pieces, but possess a grandeur of spirit and a creative imagination which put many of his contemporaries to shame. (See illustration.)

FANG I-CHIH (fl. c.1640-71?) (courtesy name Ch'ang-Kung; studio names Lu-ch'i and Mi Chih). Native of T'ung-ch'eng, Anhui. He became a monk after the fall of the Ming dynasty in 1644 and called himself Hung-chih. Son of a distinguished family, he took his *chin shih* degree in 1640. His versatility was worthy of a man of the Italian Renaissance; he was well versed in the classics, astronomy, geography, mathematics, phonetics, philology, medicine, history, calligraphy, stone-engraving and music. He was a poet, compiled several encyclopedias, wrote learned treatises, ballads and songs, played the flute and drums, performed in theatricals, was a famous raconteur, an expert in dice-playing and other games—and became a painter after he became a monk. A friend said "there was no art which he did not master." An ardent Ming loyalist, he had been an official in the Han-lin Academy and tutor to a royal prince. His later poetry and painting are done in the Ch'an Buddhist manner, in the fewest possible words or strokes of the brush, cryptic and paradoxical, regardless of intelligibility. His few landscapes (one before he became a monk, two or three after he secluded himself) bear the mark of genius. The late works, done with swift, unpremeditated brushstrokes and in a sketchy manner, are original and strange.

HUA YEN (c.1680-1755) (courtesy name Ch'iu-yo; studio name Hsin-lo Shan-jen). A native of Fukien but lived most of his life in Yangchou and Hangchou. He was classed as one of The Eight Strange Masters of Yangchou—painters of the Ch'ien Lung period woh were not court-painters or traditionalists but followed their individual bent. Because of Hua Yen's fame, especially as a painter of animals, his life and works are well recorded. One contemporary said that he had rid himself of the bad habits of his time, did not seek for prettiness, and was like "a sound in an empty valley." He was a good poet, old-fashioned and simple. Some of his early landscapes indicate his faithful study of old masters, for they are carefully painted in the blue-green

CHINA. CH'ING DYNASTY. CHU TA
Bird on a Rock. The Bamboo Studio, New York

tradition. He then began to use the freer ink-splash form and to improvise. His figure-studies of all types reflect his interest in character and personality. Even his renowned animal paintings endow the subjects with human reactions; they are done with humor and delicacy. At a time when many were painting sterile academic pieces, he "revealed something entirely new, a truly extraordinary art ... exceedingly clever and natural"—to give a contemporary opinion.

HUNG-JEN (fl. c.1644-93) (priest-name Chiang T'ao; courtesy name originally Liu-ch'i; after he became a monk, Chien-chiang). Native of Hsieh-hsien, Anhui, he is one of the Four Masters of Anhui province. He had taken the *chu sheng* degree before the fall of the Ming dynasty, but after 1644 renounced the world and gave himself to meditation, poetry, and landscape painting. He began his study of painting by emulating the Sung masters, then devoted himself to Ni Tsan of the Yüan period. His own style is clear, distinct, and even more spare of detail than Ni Tsan's. Even in long, hanging scrolls of massive mountains, one is not overpowered by the whole but fascinated by each exquisite part. He also painted bare trees, bamboo, stones and plum blossoms, and in them his fine and structural clarity were at their best.

KAO CHI-P'EI (1672-1732) (courtesy name Wei-chih; studio names Ch'ieh-yüan, Nan-tsun and Ch'ang-po Shan-jen). A Manchu from Mukden who resided in Peking as an official,

CHINA. CH'ING DYNASTY
KAO CHI-P'EI. Man Under Umbrella
British Museum, London

36. CHINA. CH'ING DYNASTY. Tao-Chi. Landscape
Freer Gallery of Art, Washington, D.C.

and eventually as vice-president of the Board of Justice. He is noted as a finger-painter of extraordinary skill, a man of great imagination and the ability to portray the strange and grotesque. Initially he painted in a rather academic linear fashion, but his finger-painting amused and intrigued people so much that most of his late work is done in this free tonal style. He did landscapes, birds, flowers and trees, Taoists and ordinary mortals. (See illustration.)

KUNG HSIEN (fl. c.1656-98) (courtesy name Pan-ch'ien; studio name Yeh-i). Born near Suchou, Kiangsu, but lived in Nanking; known as one of the Eight Masters of Nanking. An eminent painter of landscapes, he was noted as calligrapher and poet and as author of a technical treatise on painting, the *Hua chüeh.* An album prepared for students, the *Shou T'u Hua Kao,* contains sketches of various types of stones, tree trunks and branches, leaves, etc., along with advice to the beginner. He is described as being old-fashioned, eccentric and difficult to get along with. He had a cottage af the foot of the Ch'ing-liang Hill where he cultivated a small garden of flowers and bamboo, received his friends, who were Ming loyalists, and never visited the market places of the town. Many of his paintings have been preserved, most of them landscapes painted with a firm short brush, each form clearly outlined and boldly expressed. His manner is original, trees and rocks being arranged arbitrarily and not according to natural proportion. Some of the literary men regretted that there was so little refinement in his art, so little grace or subtlety. His love of nature and his quick, sure technique reflect Taoist tendencies. His use of ink and his handling of abstract forms in a seemingly casual way sometimes seem surprisingly modern. He did scrolls, fans and album pieces, usually with an inscription in forceful calligraphy placed conspicuously against the sky.

K'UN-TS'AN (fl. c.1650-75) (courtesy names Shih-ch'i and Chieh-ch'iu; studio names Po-t'u and Ts'an Tao-jen). A native of Wu-ling, Hunan. He was a genius of the late Ming period who became a monk at forty. A true ascetic who painted in devotion to the Buddha, his influence has increased with the passing years. He was a silent solitary man, racked by lifelong illness and subsisting on tea and a few grains of rice a day. Although there is no definite information as to the Buddhist sect in which he was ordained, he is called a Ch'an monk in inscriptions and his painting indicates that he was a Ch'an follower with strong Taoist elements. One picture, assumed to be a self-portrait, portrays a monk seated in a bird's nest high in a gnarled tree, his chin resting on folded hands, his expression one of great concentration. The inscription says: "The question is how to find peace in a world of suffering. You ask me why I came hither; I cannot tell the reason ... according to my understanding, all that exists is emptiness." His paintings reflect the inner power, accumulated energy and sense of communion with the forces of nature that resulted from his way of life and his philosophy. In hanging scrolls, long hand-scrolls, and album pieces, one feels the interaction of elemental forces, the ancient upheaval of earth, the rush of waters and the growth of all living things. K'un-ts'an had studied Yüan masters and used many of their "shorthand" methods of brush application. In his work the dots, sweeping strokes and graded washes are often brought together in a very complex fashion; he was not one of the Ch'an painters who sought absolute economy of line and composition, though he did at times stress the abstract aspect of rocks, trees and architecture. Since he ignored the scholarly and official world, he is not included in their lists of great men, but even in his own day connoisseurs considered his work priceless. With Shih-tao, another monk painter of genius, he is called one of the Two Stones, for the Chinese character *shih* means stone.

LANG SHIH-NING (1688-1766). Giuseppe Castiglione, an Italian, who was born in Milan but came to Peking in 1715 and died there. He painted for the Emperors K'ang Hsi and Ch'ien Lung, who held him in high regard and made him one of the principal members of the Imperial Painting Bureau. Some fifty-six of his works, most of which have been reproduced, are listed in the Imperial Catalogue. He did many studies of flowers and animals, painted portraits and served as architect for the European-style Rococo buildings and gardens adjoining the Old Summer Palace, called the Yüan Ming Yüan. Lang Shih-ning (as the Chinese called him) tried to combine Chinese brushwork and delicate color with Italian concepts of perspective and modeling in light and shade. His work is interesting but not great by the standards of either East or West. His imperial patrons no doubt valued him because he did "realistic" portraits (such as the Ch'ien Lung Emperor receiving Kazak chieftains) and painted unusual animals. The admiration of the Chinese for "quaint" European art apparently paralleled eighteenth-century Europe's craze for Chinoiserie. Two of Castiglione's drawings of Conquests of the Emperor Chi'en Lung were engraved in Paris. Other Europeans, foreign missionaries, who painted in China during the same period include Ignatius Sichelbarth (called Ai Ch'i-meng, 1708-80) and Denis Attiret (called Wang Chih-ch'eng, 1708-68). Their work pleased the Emperor but is of little importance in the history of Chinese painting.

SEN CH'UAN (fl. c.1723-76) (courtesy name Heng-chai; studio name Nan-p'ing). From Wu-hsing in Chekiang; went to Japan on the invitation of a Japanese patron and spent three years in Nagasaki. He exerted considerable influence in southern Japan and was a prolific painter of animals, birds and flowers; these are still treasured in Japanese collections. Colorful, decorative and spirited, true to nature in each form, he pleased his patrons and was richly rewarded.

TAO CHI (fl. 1660-1710) (courtesy name Shih-t'ao; studio names Ch'ing-hsiang Lao-jen, etc.). From Honan province; descended from the prince of Ch'u of the Ming dynasty. He became a monk of the Ch'an sect and therefore held no official position, scorning wordly affairs. Noted for his independence of character, his love of nature and seclusion, he was ignored by contemporaries of more conventional tastes, but is admired today as one of the most outstanding and original Chinese painters. His favorite subjects were landscapes (both album and scroll size), bamboos and orchids. His writing and his love of literature are both notable. One of his essays, the *Hua Yü Lu*, is an important contribution to the theory and practice of painting. It shows Taoist inspiration and reveals his attitude toward the past ("the works of old masters are instruments of knowledge by which one may enter a new road"), toward technique ("the method which consists in not following any method is the perfect method"), and toward nature. He was a highly trained painter, versatile, poetic, able to grasp the essentials of a motif in a few strokes of the brush. For all his love of old masters, he produced paintings of extraordinary originality, full of unexpected touches. His Taoist leanings are demonstrated in forms that look normal but emerge from backgrounds filled with mystery, and in a juxtaposition of cliffs, trees and clouds according to an inner vision, not a visual impression. His small figures looking up toward misty heights or listening to the song of birds, are men attuned to the beauties of nature. Sometimes he painted in staccato, angular style, merely suggesting the branches of a tree or the outline of a path; at other times the ink was rich, black, rounded and swirling (as in Mountains in Mist, Sakuragi collection, Tokyo). He used blobs of the ink for contrast with such swirling lines to lead the eye toward some focal point in a painting. Misty areas were done in light washes or the faintest suggestion of color. Often a poem (his own or a famous one out of the past) or inscription heightened the mood expressed by the painting. Some albums contain paintings based on actual impressions, such as the Eight Views of the Huang Shang; others are purely imaginary. (See color plate 36.)

WANG CHIEN (1598-1677) (courtesy name Yüan-chao; studio names Hsiang-pi and Jan-hsiang An-chu). Born in T'ai-ts'ang, Kiangsu (near Shanghai). He came from a family prominent in cultural affairs and was grandson of the famous poet, collector and art historian Wang Shih-cheng. Young Chien thus had an opportunity to study a superb collection of paintings and he copied them assiduously. He is the second of the famous Four Wang Masters of this period and also one of the Nine Friends in Painting. He and his friend Wang Shih-min discussed art and were instrumental in transmitting ideals and techniques to the younger generation. He served as governor of Lien-chou (in Kwangtung) but did not like official life and eventually gave his time to painting. Like Wang Shih-min he was prolific, and many of his works have survived. The earliest, dated 1638, a landscape of verdant hills rising above water, was extravagantly praised by his contemporaries. He turned out one landscape after another, generally in Northern Sung or Yüan style, sometimes in monochrome or in ink lightly embellished with color, at other times in full color like a T'ang painting. In them the rolling mountains usually sweep away from foreground trees and rocks, directing the eye upward in a spiral. Only in album paintings did he seem to sketch places from his own memory and not in the style of some earlier master.

WANG HUI (1632-1717) (courtesy name Shih-ku; studio names Keng-yen San-jen and Ch'ing-hui Chu-jen, meaning Master of Pure Radiance). From Ch'ang-shu, Kiangsu. He is third of the famous Four Wangs and studied with Wang Chien and Wang Shih-min. The latter said: "He marks the highest perfection of art in our time," and this opinion was shared by many contemporaries. He started to paint as a boy and during his long successful life produced hundreds of pictures, most of which are recorded in Far Eastern collections. Rather than ally himself with one of the many schools of his time, he studied the old masters. An eclectic who could paint in many different styles, some of his early imitations of past masters were mounted as antiques to fool connoisseurs. There are practically no sketches done entirely in a personal style, and even in his most informal study the mountains recall one artist, the trees another, the rivers a third, etc. When published, the poems and words of praise addressed to him by noblemen and officials filled ten volumes. Though he was called a recluse *(shan-jen)* and a Taoist, he seems to have been accessible to the hundreds of people who sought him out. His energy must have been boundless, for he painted large hanging scrolls, long handscrolls, fans and sets of album pieces, working even by candlelight. Much of it is done in ink with light color, except when he was working in the manner of a colorist or of some master of monochrome. A great eclectic, versatile beyond belief, he kept alive a grand tradition.

Wang Kai (fl. c.1680) (courtesy name An-chieh; studio name Lu Ch'ai). A native of Hsui-shui, Chekiang, but lived in Nanking. He painted landscapes based on Sung and Yüan masters and imitated Kung Hsien. He compiled *Chieh-tzu Yüan Hua Chuan (The Repertory of Painting of the Mustard Seed Garden)*, named after the Mustard Seed Garden in Nanking, where amateurs gathered to discuss art. The book was a general outline of the theory and practice of Chinese painting, with woodblock illustrations taken from drawings. Since its first publication in 1679 (in five thin volumes) there have been many editions in Europe (it has been translated into French) as well as in the Far East. Wang Kai did drawings for some of the original publications; his landscapes are less interesting than the pages devoted to bamboo and plum blossoms done by another artist. It served as a copybook for later generations, who turned to it rather than to nature itself or to the old masters, and thereby fell into an academic approach to art. As a treatise on theory it still holds a high place in Chinese aesthetics, for it is systematic and complete. As a painter, however, Wang Kai was of minor importance.

Wang Shih-min (1592-1680) (courtesy name Hsün-chih; studio names Yen-k'o and Hsi-lu Lao-jen). From T'ai-ts'ang, Kiangsu. First of the famous Four Wangs and one of the Nine Friends in Painting, he is prominent in all the important treatises on Ming and Ch'ing artists. Grandson of a prime minister and son of a famous official, he inherited the *feng ch'ang* title given to those in charge of the Imperial Ancestral Temple. But he disdained public life, preferring to spend his time with ink and brush or chanting poems. When the Manchus established the Ch'ing dynasty, he "closed his door and devoted himself to the study of ancient things," to prose and poetry, calligraphic art and painting. Even as a youth he was distinguished for his excellent education, breeding, modesty, connoisseurship, and respect for the past. We are told that when he acquired a painting, he silently concentrated upon it until he had assimilated every part of it, and then he would jump up, shouting and clapping his hands. After a lifetime spent in copying Sung and Yüan masters, Wang chose Huang Kung-wang (Yüan dynasty) as his guide and transmitted Huang's style to his son. Though he did some flower studies, the majority of his many recorded paintings are landscapes. Some were monochromes, others were touched with color. He emphasized structure in some; elsewhere he played with atmospheric effects. Chinese connoisseurs particularly admire his large hanging scrolls, full of dense forests, peaks beyond peaks in boundless space, and very "literary" tone.

Wang Yuan-ch'i (1642-1715) (courtesy name Mao-ching; studio name Lu-t'ai). Born in T'ai-ts'ang, Kiangsu. Grandson of Wang Shih-min, who was his first teacher, he became the fourth of the Four Wang Masters. Official, scholar, author and specialist in landscape painting, he is one of the great men of his time. At one time or another a district magistrate, a censor, member of the Han-lin (Academy), in charge of the imperial collections of painting and calligraphy, vice-president of the Board of Revenue, and compiler of the *P'ei Wen Chai Shu Hua P'u* (an encyclopedia of calligraphy and painting), he must have been a busy man indeed, and yet he spent much time painting. The Emperor enjoyed watching him and often leaned over his table, forgetful of the passage of time. Wang insisted on the best paper and ink, used a double hair brush, and often went over his compositions many times; he remarked of one that it took him three or four years to complete. He had an analytical mind, studied the great masters of the past, and based his own art on Huang Kung-wang (Yüan dynasty). He realized that the old masters had studied nature and so sought the same inspiration, but he confessed that he tended to see in the natural forms of rocks, trees, mountains, etc., the painting methods of the past.

CHINA. THE REPUBLIC
HSU PEI-HUNG (JU PEON). Horse
Collection Alice Boney, New York

As a rule, he painted in ink with light color. His known works are numerous but it should be noted that he added his signature to the work of pupils and assistants and that "seven or eight out of every ten pictures that pass under his name are made in this way." His landscapes are so valuable that he gave one to each of his subordinates at the beginning of winter, so that "it could serve for the acquisition of a fur coat." He also wrote an important treatise, the *Yu Ch'uang Man Pi (Scattered Notes on a Rainy Window)*, and the critical notes on his paintings were collected under the title of *Lu-t'ai T'i Hua Kao*. A conscious aesthetician, he avoided all narrative in landscapes and painted them traditionally, in a rather austere style, and using only the motifs and brushstrokes necessary for significant form.

Wu Li (1632-1718) (courtesy name Yü-shan; studio name Mo-ching). From Ch'ang-shu, Kiangsu, where he grew up with Wang Hui, his friend and fellow artist. Both started painting with Wang Shih-min and both became famous. Wu Li devoted most of his leisure hours to painting, but also played the lute. He was a recluse, a lonely seeker for the Tao and the

37. CHINA. THE REPUBLIC. Ch'i Pai-shih. Flowers and Fruit
Collection Alice Boney, New York

secrets of the Immortals. His interest in philosophy and religion led him to accept Christianity, and he entered the Jesuit order in 1682 and became a priest in 1688. The interval was spent in the Portuguese monastery at Macao. Wu Li had expected to take the long journey to Rome but was persuaded by the Portuguese Jesuits to stay with them. His Christian name was Simon Xavier at baptism and he was known as Acunha after ordination. He was sent to Shanghai and Chia-ting as a missionary, lived in Chia-ting for the last thirty years of his life, and was buried in the Jesuit graveyard outside Shanghai. Throughout his life, he painted in the pure Chinese manner. His early paintings were in the Sung manner, meticulous and refined. Then he turned to the Yüan painters, finding their "freedom from dust," their pure, chill landscapes, very much to his taste. His eyes were always open to the beauties of nature, especially to the unusual in rock formations or mountains, and he saw in them deep symbolic meanings. Later landscapes are marked by delicacy of brushwork and an underlying rhythm of structure. Trees and mountains curve in vast convolutions, sometimes accented by line, at other times loaded with dots or choppy horizontal strokes. In one, The Old Snow Man on Huang Shan, of 1703, he suggests mysterious, nearly human forms in mountain peaks and crags. In his album pieces there is an intimate and loving portrayal of actual scenes. Untouched by European techniques, his painting remained traditional in subject matter, composition and brushwork; in that he was a Taoist to the end.

WU TA-CH'ENG (1835-1902) (courtesy name Cheng-k'an; studio name Ch'ing-ch'ing, etc.). Born in the Wu country of Kiangsu. He was a calligrapher of note and a prolific painter of landscapes, figures and flowers. A lifelong civil and military official, he was active against the Russians in Manchuria and the French in Tientsin, and served as governor of Kwantung and Hunan provinces. An archaeologist of note, he collected ancient bronze vessels, jade and seals, and wrote authoritatively about them. A brilliant and versatile man in the scholar-statesman tradition, he was stricken with paralysis in 1899 and died three years later.

YU CHIH-TING (1647-1705) (courtesy name Shang-chi; studio name Shen-chai). Born in Yangchou, Kiangsu. A court painter in the K'ang Hsi period, noted for his figure painting and portraits, though he did landscapes, flowers and animals as well. It is said that his fame as a portraitist was unsurpassed and that he depicted most of the famous men of his day. His greatest achievement, however, was in painting young ladies, such as a Maid Bringing a Candle to Her Mistress (British Museum, signed and dated 1684). The fine flowing line recalls the work of Ku K'ai Chih (see THE SIX DYNASTIES), and the delicate color perfectly reflects the Chinese ideal of the flower-like beauty of women. So great is the refinement of the lady portrayed that one senses the dramatic contrast of Chinese nobility and Manchu vigor that must have existed in the early Ch'ing days when the "barbarians" began to rule. The gentle melancholy, the weary graceful gestures, hint at a sensibility approaching effeteness and present the appealing frailty of the exquisite.

YUN SHOU-P'ING (1633-90) (original name Ko; courtesy name Cheng-shu; studio name Nan-t'ien, etc.). From Yang-hu, Kiangsu, of a prominent but poor family. Because his father had been a Ming loyalist, he would not accept any official position under the Manchus. Material things had no interest for him; he would not sell his paintings to uncongenial buyers but gave them gladly to friends and sympathetic admirers. His output was tremendous; his flower paintings were the greatest of his time and still rank among the best in Chinese art. But he lived simply, was of an open, pleasant and noble character, at home to scholars and poets. Sensitive, refined and modest, he was a poet in his approach to his art as well as a writer of verse. He discussed the fine points of painting with his lifelong friend Wang Hui and studied the Sung, Yüan and early Ming artists, copying many of them but always interpreting in his own way. He painted landscapes in his early years but felt inadequate when he compared his work to that of the old masters or of Wang Hui. Later he turned to bird and flower studies, looking to Sung artists for inspiration, especially Hsü Hsi and his grandson Hsü Ch'ung-ssu, who had painted in the "boneless manner" (without ink outlines but with form expressed in pure color in varying tones). One critic said of his birds, fish, flowers, etc., that they "seemed to be fluttering and moving." For all his respect for the past, he insisted that each artist should have a style of his own, and then one could "freely play with the winds and rains, spread out the verdant green, model the hills and valleys and grasp the essentials." He did not crowd his paintings as did so many contemporaries; like the Sung artists, the unfilled areas were important in his art. He painted large hanging scrolls, long handscrolls, fans and album pieces. In the smaller studies he is especially charming, his color sense superb.

Chinese Painters: The Republic (1912-)

CH'I PAI-SHI (1863-). Born in Honan; went to Peking in 1917, where he now lives. Of peasant stock, he served an apprenticeship as cabinetmaker before beginning to paint. A close study of the *Mustard Seed Garden* (see Wang Kai, CH'ING DYNASTY) led him to try drawing with the brush. Acknowledged as the Grand Old Man of twentieth-century Chinese painting, his work is in the tradition of the Ch'an painters, especially of Chu Ta (Ch'ing dynasty). It is spontaneous, free, brusque, and based on an intimate knowledge of natural forms. Like the Ch'an painters, he has been criticized for boldness and lack of refinement by those who stem from the literary tradition, but his appeal to people of all countries and backgrounds is immediate and universal. His subtlety and strength of line have been compared favorably with that of Matisse and other Europeans; and he parallels them as colorist and experimenter. He has turned out a prodigious number of pictures—landscapes, figure studies, animals, fish and flowers—all dynamic in style. (See color plate 37.)

HSÜ PEI-HUNG, called Ju Peon (1895-1953). Born in Yiksing, Kansu. He studied in China, then for four years in Paris, returning to his native land about 1930. While in Europe, he painted in oil in European style, but after taking up residence again in China, strove to achieve a twentieth-century blending of Chinese and Western techniques. He used Chinese ink but worked in problems of light and action not usual in the Chinese tradition. His dramatic combination of Chinese and European elements resulted in boldness of brushwork and a spirited rendering of form. (See illustration.)

Ch'ing Dynasty (see CHINESE PAINTERS: CH'ING DYNASTY, 1644-1912).

Ching Hao (see CHINESE PAINTERS: FIVE DYNASTIES).

chinoiserie. A type of painting, print or other art form derived from or influenced by the subject matter of Chinese art or life, often emphasizing a delicate, curving and colorful kind of ornament. It is generally associated with the Rococo art of the eighteenth century and may be exemplified by some of the paintings of Boucher.

Chirico, Giorgio de (1888-). Greek-born Italian painter; son of a construction engineer for railroads, which helps account for the trains and draughtsman's instruments in his pictures. He studied first in Greece with a number of local painters and then at the Polytechnic Institute at Athens. On the death of his father, his mother moved the family to Munich, where young Giorgio, already very much interested in following art as a career, could pursue his studies. At the Academy of Fine Arts he enlarged his already considerable technical training. The most important effect of this period however, was the strong stimulus he received from the works of the nineteenth century German-Swiss Romantic painter, Arnold Böcklin. The influence of this master, particularly evident in the earlier works of Chirico (1911-17) accounts in great

38. CHIRICO. Anguish of Departure
Albright Art Gallery, Buffalo

measure for the continuing emphasis in his art on the supernatural. Influence also came from the romantic and imaginative works of Gustav Klimt, Max Klinger and Alfred Kubin; the last-named artist's Vision of Italy is strikingly similar to Chirico's own later haunted squares with their troubling silence and symbolic statuary. In Munich Chirico also encountered the writings of Nietzsche, whose curious *Stimmung*, or mood, with its suggestions of autumn afternoons and their long shadows again parallels the effects of Chirico's painting. In Italy from 1909 to 1911 he painted in a Böcklinesque manner and then moved to Paris, where his career really began. He reached his characteristic style in 1913 and 1914 with such works as Nostalgia of the Infinite. He soon attracted the attention of a small group of artists and critics, particularly the writer Guillaume Apollinaire, who admired his talent "for depicting the fatal character of modern things."

Although Chirico's pre-World War I paintings ran counter to the general trend toward two-dimensional, space-controlled Cubism as illustrated in the work of Picasso, Braque, Gris, etc., they did conform to a general pattern of proto-Surrealist works (by such painters as Chagall and Henri Rousseau) emphasizing psychological rather than purely formal factors. Chirico projected his pictures on the basis of a far-reaching spatial environment, a bland and relatively unvaried surface texture and, most important, a lyricism of mood and a dreamlike quality that is particularly his. The frightening lighting effects and long, unnatural shadows, the mingling of Renaissance towers and modern smoke-belching chimneys, the strange Victorian statues standing menacingly quiet and accusing, gazing across the deserted squares—these are all part of the painter's way of evoking a dream world—his own recollections sublimated in what he called "memories of Italy" and "piazzas of Italy." Around 1915 he turned to the mannequin themes, faceless, voiceless and eyeless creatures with a strange evocative poetry of mood, as in The Disquieting Muses. He returned to Italy in 1915, was sent as a soldier to Ferrara and there in 1917 with Carlo Carrà launched the idea of metaphysical painting. The character of this art may be summed up in Sir Herbert Read's words (actually written about Paul Klee): "... the metaphysical painter seeks to find some plastic equivalent, not for the content of the thought, but for its felt intensity." Thus in Ferrara Chirico moved from the far-reaching and dream-evoking spaces of the Italian piazzas to the narrow rooms and their provocative still-life compositions. The actual fabric of the painting became heavier and richer than before, while the still-life objects were animated, given human roles, made to act out implausible events that, combined with the extreme naturalism of their portrayal, places Chirico in the role of godfather to the Surrealist movement of the early 1920's. After the war Chirico turned to a kind of mystical neo-classicism that is not generally as well thought of as his earlier works. The final stage in his development as an artist was his turning against the modern movement in general, a movement which he had done so much to launch. With the possible exception of Modigliani, he is the most influential and even most important Italian painter of the twentieth century and one of the really creative figures of our time. See VALORI PLASTICI. (See color plate 38.)

Ch'iu Ying (see CHINESE PAINTERS: MING DYNASTY).

Chodowiecki, Daniel Nicolas (1726-1801). Polish-born painter and engraver associated with the eighteenth-century German school. He is noted for thousands of vignettes and illustrations, many of them for such books as *Don Quixote* and *Clarissa Harlowe*. In addition, he presents in many of his engravings a picture of the German life of the time and its social and intellectual aspirations that has as much historical value as a written document. He became director of the Berlin Academy in 1797.

Chou Ch'en (see CHINESE PAINTERS: MING DYNASTY).

Chou Fang (see CHINESE PAINTERS: T'ANG DYNASTY).

Christus, Petrus (c.1415-72/73). Flemish painter usually considered an assistant to Jan van Eyck and the continuer of his workshop. He is, however, not mentioned in Bruges records until after the death of Jan. Born in Baerle, he became a citizen of Bruges (1444) and left dated pictures signed Petrus or Petr XPI. He was obviously influenced by van Eyck, but also by van der Weyden, except that authorities do not agree as to which of the influences was earlier. There also appears to be some influence from Bouts and the Haarlem landscapists. He was essentially an unimaginative though competent painter, sober and meticulous, but lacking either the sensitivity or inventiveness of van Eyck. His versions of the master's themes display a lack of atmosphere and general pictorial richness, yet he is curiously more advanced in his treatment of perspective and even invents a new portrait type—a figure in the corner of a ceilinged room. Among his signed and dated works are the Portrait of a Man (1446, London), Portrait of a Monk (1446, Metropolitan), St. Eloy as a Goldsmith (1449, Lehman collection, New York), the Berlin Diptych (1452) based on the Metropolitan van Eyck, and a Madonna and Saints (1457, Frankfort). Among the works attributed to him are the Portrait of a Young Woman (c.1446, Berlin) and Portrait of a Young Man (c.1452, London); the Madonna with the Carthusian Monk (Frick Collection) is attributed to van Eyck and Petrus Christus. The Pietà (Brussels), ascribed to him by most scholars, is a masterpiece, showing a strong influence of Flémalle, and thus posing the problem whether it is an early or a late work. (See color plate 39.)

Chromo-Luminarism (see NEO-IMPRESSIONISM).

Chü-jan (see CHINESE PAINTERS: THE FIVE DYNASTIES).

Chung K'uei the Demon Queller. A Taoist magician who is a favorite subject of Chinese painters. Grotesque in appearance, his large eyes suggest hypnotic power. See Kung K'ai in CHINESE PAINTERS: YÜAN DYNASTY.

Chu Ta (see CHINESE PAINTERS: CH'ING DYNASTY).

Chu Tuan (see CHINESE PAINTERS: MING DYNASTY).

Church, Frederick Edwin (1826-1900). A member of the second generation of Hudson River school landscapists, he achieved his greatest fame with his canvases of the Andes, the icebergs of Labrador, scenes from Jamaica, Europe, and the Near East. His meticulously handled interpretations of majestic nature brought him popular acclaim and wealth, but his career was cut short by illness in 1877.

Cifrondi, Antonio (1657-1730). Born in Clusone, he studied with Franceschini in Bologna, and was one of the best of the eighteenth-century Rococo decorators of Bergamo. He was a prolific though careless workman, active in northern Italy as well as in France.

Cignani, Carlo (1628-1719). The last important painter of the Italian Baroque, he was very highly esteemed in his own day, executed many commissions, and had a great many students. He studied with Albani and was influenced by Correggio, the Carracci, Reni and Guercino. He was active in Rome, Bologna and Parma, and Forlì, where he executed his most important work, the Dome of the Cathedral.

Cigoli, Ludovico Cardi da (1559-1613). Florentine anti-Mannerist painter; he was born at Castel Vecchio near Cigoli. He studied with Alessandro Allori and Santi di Tito, but was later influenced by Correggio and Barocci and is important for subsequent Baroque developments. His most famous work is the Deposition (Pitti), 1592-97.

Cimabue (Cenni di Pepi) (c.1240-c.1302). There is very little documentary evidence of the activity of this Florentine painter, though his fame in his own time and later is attested to by Dante's reference to him in comparison with Giotto and by the injudicious liberality with which Vasari attributes works to him. In 1272 a "Cimabove pictore de Florencia" was called as a witness in Rome. In 1301-2 Cimabue was director of mosaic work at the cathedral of Pisa. In 1302 he was commissioned to paint an altarpiece, together with "Nichulux Aparechiati," for the New Hospital at Pisa. Scholarly opinion on the attribution of works to Cimabue runs from a minimum of some hand in one mosaic at Pisa to a maximum of a long list of controversial attributions. Only four monuments are generally agreed to be by him in whole or in part: *1.* the mosaic of the Deesis in the Pisa cathedral (1302); *2.* a large panel painting of the Madonna with Angels in the Uffizi; *3.* the Madonna with Angels and St. Francis in the Lower Church of San Francesco, Assisi; *4.* certain frescoes in the apse and transepts of the Upper Church at Assisi. The Pisa mosaic represents the Lord Enthroned, flanked by the Virgin and St. John. Only the figure of St. John is considered to be Cimabue's work, though he probably supervised other parts of the execution. This mosaic is in relatively good condition. The Uffizi Madonna, also in good condition, shows that Cimabue was at home in the Byzantine tradition, but affected by the new tendencies of the late thirteenth century toward grace and naturalness of posture and facial expression. The Madonna in the Lower Church at Assisi is closely related to the Uffizi Madonna but its present surface is largely a product of the seventeenth century. Cimabue's major work at Assisi was in the Upper Church (c.1288-96). Here he is believed to have executed a considerable part of the transept and apse decoration, which is in sadly dilapidated condition. The central subjects represented are two Crucifixions, scenes of the Apocalypse, scenes from the life of the Virgin, and Acts of the Apostles. Cimabue probably planned the entire series but much of it was executed by helpers. A Madonna panel in the Louvre is closely related to the Uffizi Madonna but is generally ascribed to a follower. Cimabue appears to have been Florentine by birth, generally Tuscan in artistic background, and much affected by the Roman school which is well represented in Assisi. His influence was not great and his art was soon overshadowed by that of Giotto, but he holds an important place in the development of the dramatic narrative style that flourished in Florence after his time. (See color plate 40.)

Cima da Coneglano (Giovanni Battista Cima) (c.1459-c.1517). Venetian painter, one of the many pupils of Giovanni Bellini, on whose art his own is based. He was a native of Conegliano, but was probably in Venice by 1489. His earliest dated picture, a Madonna Enthroned with Saints, was painted in 1489, and is in the museum at Vicenza. He is recorded as a painter in Venice until 1516, when he appears to have returned to Conegliano, dying there in 1517 or 1518. His production, like that of Bellini, consisted chiefly of altarpieces representing the enthroned Madonna with saints, and of smaller devotional panels of the Madonna and Child. He does not display the originality and inventiveness of Bellini and the small Madonnas are somewhat repetitive. His drawing and figure construction remained harder and stiffer than his master's and in general his mode of expression was less profound. He became, however, a master of the representation of light and one of the best colorists in Venice. His compositions developed more and more into a vehicle for these qualities, with open landscape backgrounds replacing the traditional apse or niche for the enthroned Madonna. There are important altarpieces by him in the museums of London, Berlin and Milan, and in churches and the Academy in Venice. (See illustration.)

Cinquecento. Italian word meaning five hundred and used in art as a short way of referring to the 1500's or sixteenth century. In a general way it refers to the later Renaissance in Italy although chronologically it takes in the period of Mannerism and eclecticism as well.

Cione, Jacopo di (see JACOPO DI CIONE).

Cione, Nardo di (see NARDO DI CIONE).

City Art Museum, St. Louis, Missouri. A generalized but select grouping of objects in painting, sculpture and the decorative arts from all the major periods in the history of art.

Claude (see LORRAIN).

Clavé, Pelegrín (1810-80). Mexican painter born in Barcelona. He came to Mexico in 1847, became Director of the Academy of San Carlos, and reorganized art instruction in Mexico along the lines of traditional practice in Europe.

Cleve, Cornelis van (1520-67). Flemish painter of portraits and religious subjects. Son of Joos van Cleve. Cleve was supposed to have gone mad in London in 1554 as a result of artistic rivalry with Antonio Mor. Paintings attributed to him are similar to those of his father but with more influence of Raphael and del Sarto. His principal work is the Adoration of the Magi (Antwerp).

Cleve, Joos (Josse) van (Joos van der Beke van Cleef) (c.1485-1540). Flemish painter identified with the Master of the Death of Mary who was named after two versions of that subject in Cologne and Munich. The Cologne version has been established as commissioned from van Cleve by Nicaise Hacquenay in 1514 and completed in the following year. Obviously from Cleves, from stylistic evidence he must have studied with Jan Joest in Calcar. He is recorded in Antwerp from 1511, when he entered the guild, to 1525, when he was a senior for the first time. From then to 1535 there is a hiatus in the records which is explained by evidence that he was traveling in Italy, France, England, and Spain, after which he reappeared in Antwerp. A fine colorist and an able portraitist, his art was at first rather bourgeois in character, but probably through the influence of Metsys and later through his travels in Italy and the courts of Europe, working for Francis I and Henry VIII, became more Italianate, aristocratic, and even Mannerist (see). In his later works, perhaps as a result of his Italian travels, the influence of Leonardo became pronounced. His style, though originally derived from the indigenous style of David, later showed so many influences that his works have been variously ascribed to Dürer, Holbein, Gossaert, and van Scorel. Among the works attributed to him now are the Self-Portrait with Wife (Uffizi), formerly given to Metsys, Holy Family (Brussels), Adoration of the Magi (S. Donato in Genoa, and in Antwerp), Virgin and Child (Vienna), Annunciation (private collection, Paris), Portrait of a Man (Munich), Deposition (Louvre), and the Epiphany Altar (Naples Museum). (See color plate 41.)

Cleveland Museum of Art, Cleveland, Ohio. Representative and general collection of the arts of many different periods. It is especially noteworthy for its examples by eighteenth- and nineteenth-century American painters, e.g., Copley, Stuart, and Hesselius. There are also important examples of Italian and nineteenth-century French paintings.

Clouet, François (before 1522-1572). French court painter. Succeeded his father Jean as painter to the king and valet de chambre for the French monarchs Francis I, Henry II, Francis II and Charles IX, thus making the name "Clouet" synonymous with the best portrait painting of the century in France. His style is somewhat more certain than his father's since there exist two paintings signed "Fr. Janetii." There is also a series of outstanding portrait drawings of contemporaries which can be attributed to François for the same reason that others are credited to his father Jean (see). One of the signed paintings (Cook Collection) is of a nude woman in a bathtub with children and with domestic activity in the background. This is one of a group of such erotic portraits of the era based in idea on Titian's Venus. In this case Diane de Poitiers, mistress of Henry II, has been

CIMA. Madonna and Child. Knoedler Galleries, New York

39. CHRISTUS. St. Eloy as a Goldsmith. Collection Robert Lehman, New York

suggested as the model. The other signed work is a portrait of his neighbor, the apothecary Pierre Cutte (Louvre). This also derives from Italian sources, much resembling the format of Vasari's portraits. In general the style of François is more Italianate and polished than that of his father, although his standing portrait of Henry II (Uffizi) suggests knowledge of Holbein's Ambassadors. Among other important portraits that can be attributed to François on the basis of the above are the standing portrait of Charles IX (Vienna), bust of Charles IX (Vienna), busts of Henry II (Versailles and Florence). François was held in great esteem and was extolled by Ronsard, Pasquier, Dubillon and De Buttet. (See color plate 42.)

Clouet, Jean (called Janet) (c.1486-1541). French court painter, primarily of portraits. Father of François Clouet (see). Born in Flanders, Jean served from 1516 as court painter to Francis I at Tours and Fontainebleau, earning the title of valet de chambre. Certain portraits and religious paintings by Jean are recorded in documents, but no sure or signed work has come down to us. However, it has been possible to associate a distinctive style with him. It was customary in those days for the wealthy to collect and distribute crayon portraits of themselves, largely executed in red and black chalk and sometimes serving as models for oil paintings. Such a collection of 130 items of homogeneous style is in the Museum of Chantilly, and as they represent Francis I and other important courtly figures of the period of Jean, it is assumed that they were done by Jean as painter to the king. They reveal that he practiced an accomplished, detailed style, somewhat less elegant than that of his son or the Italianate Fontainebleau painters, but more delicate than contemporary Flemings. Several portraits in oil follow the style of these drawings and can be attributed to Jean. These include a bust of Francis I (Louvre), an equestrian portrait of Francis I (Uffizi), the dauphin Francis (Museum Antwerp), Charlotte of France (privately owned), Claude duc de Guise (Pitti), Louis Monsieur de Nevers (Museum Bergamo) and an unknown Scholar (Hampton Court, England). Jean is clearly

40. CIMABUE. Christ between St. Peter and St. James Major. National Gallery of Art, Mellon Collection, Washington, D.C.

42. CLOUET, FRANÇOIS. Diane de Poitiers
Worcester Art Museum

the point of origin of French Mannerist portraiture of the sixteenth century. (See illustration.)

Cock, Jan de (called Wellens) (died before 1529). Flemish painter of Antwerp. Father of Hieronymus and Mathys Cock. He was in 1506 a master, in 1520 dean of the painters' guild. In 1507/8 he was occupied in Nôtre Dame de

41. CLEVE, JOOS VAN. Madonna with the Carnation
William Rockhill Nelson Gallery, Kansas City

CLOUET, JEAN. Guillaume Budé
Metropolitan Museum of Art, New York

COELLO, CLAUDIO. St. Dominic. Prado, Madrid

COCK. The Annunciation
Museum Plantin Moretus, Antwerp

Noël. To him is attributed a series of Italianate prints with the monogram C.H.O.K. (See illustration.)

Codesido, Julia (1892-). Peruvian painter and graphic artist; belongs to the nationalistic nativist school along with Sabogal. She uses striking linear figures and strong contrasts of bold, flat color areas, large in scale.

codex. Used to describe handwritten books or manuscripts made up of separate leaves (like present-day printed books) and thereby distinguished from the earlier scrolls or rotuli. It came into use around 100 A.D. The first illustrated codices belong to the fourth century A.D.

Coello, Claudio (1630/35-1693). Last of the line of great native Spanish painters, Coello was noted in his day for his technical virtuosity, which was eclipsed in the last year of his life by the arrival from Naples of Luca Giordano, the famous "*fa presto.*" Son of a Portuguese artist, Coello trained with Francisco Ricci, from whom he derived his decorative facility. The paintings for San Plácido, Madrid, executed while with Ricci, already demonstrate his florid style. Through the good offices of Carreno he was invited to copy the royal collection of Titian, Rubens and van Dyck. He was the outstanding fresco painter of his day, and he had large commissions in Toledo, Zaragoza and Madrid, in some of which he was assisted by Donoso or Palomino. Most of these are lost today, but we can recognize his taste for large intricate compositions in the bravura and complications of his canvases. Charles II appointed him King's painter and in 1685 he succeeded his friend Carreno as pintor de cámara. Coello had devised elaborate street decorations and arches in honor of the King's wedding to Marie Louise of Orléans, and in 1687 he completed his masterpiece, the Adoration of the Sacred Form for the sacristy of the Escorial. This composition, an elaborate bit of Velásquen depth organization, is

COLE. Dream of Arcadia. Toledo Museum of Art

obliquely twisted à la Baroque. It represents the transfer by Charles II of a mysterious sacramental wafer to the sanctuary of the church. It recalls Raphael's Mass of Bolsena, but with seventeenth-century flourishes. (See illustration.)

Cola dall' Amatrice (Nicola di Filotesio) (c.1480/90-c.1547+). Central Italian painter and architect. Born in Amatrice, he is said by Vasari (see) to have been a student of Marco Calabrese. His early style is influenced by Crivelli, but his later by the High Renaissance manner of Michelangelo and the Umbrians. He was active in Ascoli, but after c.1530 turned to architecture.

Cole, Thomas (1801-48). This most famous member of the Hudson River school was born in Lancashire, England, and worked as a textile designer and an engraver before he migrated to the U.S. with his family in 1818. In this country he first studied wood engraving, taught drawing and painting in his sister's school, designed wallpaper, and then became an itinerant portrait painter. In 1823 he entered the Pennsylvania Academy of Fine Arts and in 1825 moved to New York where his landscapes immediately aroused the enthusiasm of Trumbull, Durand, and Dunlap. In 1826 he was established in a studio in Catskill, N.Y., and was the recognized leader of the American Romantic landscapists, painting along the Hudson River, in the White Mountains (1828), and in Europe (1829-31 and 1841-42). Cole belongs to the general tradition of early nineteenth-century Romanticism. He was a close friend of the poet William Cullen Bryant and like him tried to express the magnificence of the American primordial landscape. His early work tends toward the meticulous and rather prissy realism of the Hudson River school, but he soon developed into a broader and bolder romanticism which led to sheer fantasy and finally religious moralism. His art appears to have been influenced in its more lyrical aspects by Claude and Poussin, in its more wildly romantic moments by Salvator Rosa, and in its moments of mad grandeur by Turner. Such paintings as the five panels composing the series Course of Empire, commissioned by Luman Reed and now in the New York Historical Society, which were the products of a fanatically moralistic approach, are today again in favor for what appear to be their Surrealist qualities. (See illustration.)

COLEMAN. Downtown Street
Whitney Museum of American Art, New York

Coleman, Glenn O. (1887-1932). American genre painter in the Ashcan School (see) tradition. Born in Springfield, Ohio, he had his early training in Indianapolis and worked as a newspaper illustrator before coming to New York in 1905 to study with Chase, Henri and Shinn. While

CONINXLOO. The Parents of the Virgin
Musées Royaux des Beaux-Arts, Brussels

CONSTABLE. Sea off Brighton
National Gallery, London

working at odd jobs to stay alive, he drew and painted scenes of New York in the intimate manner of the Ashcan School. During this period he contributed drawings to the *Masses* along with Sloan and Bellows. Later, in the 1920's, he translated his early drawings into lithographs, recapturing with nostalgic charm an era that had already disappeared. However, by this time (c.1927) his painting style had begun to change. Influenced by modern art and especially by Cubism, he turned from the picturesque aspects of Greenwich Village life to depicting the impersonal masonry masses of the city's buildings in an increasingly abstract way. (See illustration.)

collage. The French word for pasting; applied to a special Dada technique of pasting together unrelated fragments of photographs, sections of newsprint, parts of old catalogues and other kinds of material. These are joined by the application of color, charcoal, pencil and similar artistic media for the purpose of creating a new relationship between basically disparate materials. The technique was invented by Max Ernst and is perhaps best illustrated by the series of Fatagaga paintings he did in collaboration with Jean Arp. Through these chance-directed, subconscious-inspired joinings the artists hoped to destroy conventional reality and create a new reality based on the accidental, the unforeseen and the often very unconventional, the latter element generally supplied by the title. Collage was of major importance in the Dada movement. See PAPIERS COLLES.

collotype. A method of reproducing paintings, drawings and other pictures in color or black and white through the use of gelatin plates.

color orchestration (see ORPHISM).

Colquhoun, Robert (1914-). British oil painter born in Scotland. He paints chiefly figure subjects whose largeness of conception and general starkness seem to reflect his study of painting in Belgium and Holland.

complementary. A color which completes, strengthens or brightens another. For example, red-green, blue-orange, yellow-violet have this mutual effect.

Conder, Charles (1868-1909). British painter and lithographer. Conder was a member of the New English Art Club with Sickert, Wilson, Steer and others. This group, set up in 1885, was formed to express the discontent of the more modern spirits with Academy practices and traditions, and it organized its own exhibitions. He studied first in Melbourne, Australia, and then in Paris where, under the influence of the poetry of Verlaine and the painting of Fragonard and Lautrec, he produced the painted fans for which he is perhaps best known. These delicate and charming pictures on silk with their Watteau-like themes, their glowing colors and the quality of the silk itself achieve a unity of effect which is unique.

Coninxloo, Cornelis van (active 1529-59). Flemish artist. The younger of two artists of this name and head of the "School of Frankenthal." He painted a tabernacle of Pasquier Borremann (1529-30). He is apparently the author of the Genealogy of Mary of 1526 (Brussels). Also attributed to him is the Magdalene altar of the Brussels Museum. (See illustration.)

Constable, John (1776-1837). British painter and one of the foremost landscapist in history. Constable represents a full step forward in the modern development of landscape art. He was a product of eastern England with its luxuriant meadows, distant horizons, picturesque villages, and above all its ever-changing sky with constantly moving cloud formations. The latter were for him "the key note, the standard of scale, and the chief organ of sentiment." Although Constable's outlook on nature was primarily naturalistic, his individuality of style and interest in "sentiment" made him part of the Romantic period in which he lived. His naturalism appears in the projection of landscapes whose elements are in constant movement under natural conditions of light; his more Romantic side emerges through the expression of nature's power and his own exultation therein. Yet his approach was not nearly so Romantic as that of Turner. Constable enjoyed clouds, sunshine, trees and fields for their own sakes, in addition to viewing them as potential vehicles for human emotions.

The son of a prosperous mill owner, Constable showed a taste for sketching at an early age, but did not become a serious art student until 1799; he entered the Royal Academy School in 1800. When he first exhibited there two years later, he wrote to a friend that there was nothing in the exhibition worth looking up to and that there was "room enough for a natural painter." From this point onward, Constable developed his own style of painting, but fame was slow to arrive. In 1824, when he was fifty, in company with some of his countrymen he showed a number of landscapes at the Paris Salon. Among these was the since famous Hay Wain, for which the painter was awarded a gold medal. In his own land, however, there were few people who appreciated what he had to offer and very little market for landscapes. In his early days he had to supplement a meager income by doing portraits, while spending as much time as possible painting landscapes. He was made an associate of the Royal Academy in 1819 and elected to full membership in 1829, but he felt that this honor had come too late in life to have much meaning.

Perhaps the most interesting thing about Constable's technique was the fact that he made quick sketches setting down his first spontaneous and emotional reactions to natural beauties; these visual impressions, even more than his finished works, are regarded as his real contribution. To accomplish his aim of rendering the living, moving quality of nature, he used broken touches of color. On a foundation of warm reddish monochrome he would build up the fresh blues and greens of nature, the individual spots of paint often laid on with a palette knife in the modern manner. The sparkles of light and color and the deliberate roughness of textures broke with the tradition of smooth painting. Besides the intrinsic merit of Constable's work, it is also historically important for the effect it had on both the Romantic and Impressionist groups. The spontaneity of such painters as Delacroix may be traced in part to Constable; and the Impressionist search for momentary effects through broken colors, complementary color relationships, and white highlights owes as much to this British painter. (See illustrations, including color plate 43.)

Constructivism. A non-objective movement having its origin in Russia under the influence of the *papiers collés* and especially the other "constructions" of Picasso, which utilized such solid materials as pieces of glass, wood, etc. for a series of relief forms. These reliefs of Picasso still adhered to naturalistic titles such as Still Life and although the early Russian makers of "constructions" followed this direction, another group, including the sculptors Gabo and Pevsner, employed the technique in making three-dimensional arrangements of a purely non-representational nature. Although Constructivism by definition is a three-dimensional art and a form of sculpture (however freed from the pedestal or the wall by means of suspension on wires), it also affected painting and the graphic arts, as in the non-objective and illusionistic three-dimensional paintings and graphics of El Lissitzky.

contrapposto. From the Italian, meaning "opposed"; it refers to the painting or carving of the human body so that the upper portion moves or twists in one direction and the lower in an opposed direction.

conversation piece. A type of English eighteenth-century painting in which family groups are shown against the background of their properties. The figures are generally shown as engaged in some simple activity such as passing each other fruit, having tea, or watching children at play.

Copley, John Singleton (1737/8-1815). The outstanding American portrait painter of the colonial period, he is believed to have been born in or near Boston, though no actual record of birth or baptism exists. His father died in the West Indies while John was still an infant and in 1748 his mother married Peter Pelham, an English engraver then living in Boston. He probably studied with his stepfather and knew the work of Smibert, but since both older men died in 1751 his training was short. He set up as a portrait painter and his earliest known paintings date from his fifteenth year. His early works (before c.1760) show an increasing control of craft and a growing realism and power, but are still dependent on the English style of Hogarth, Hudson, and Highmore, and eventually Reynolds as transmitted through Smibert, Pelham, Feke, Badger, Greenwood, Blackburn, and English engravings. By 1760, however, his personal style of realistic observation, plastic clarity, and painstaking craftsmanship were already established, and he was without peer among portraitists in America. He was in great demand and, until his departure for England in 1774, continued to paint the likenesses of leading citizens, their wives, and children—in Boston, New York,

43. CONSTABLE. The Haywain. National Gallery, London

and Philadelphia—with perception and honesty. The limitations of his environment and a vague ambition toward greater things led in 1766 to his sending abroad Boy with Squirrel, a painting of his half-brother, for submission to the Society of Artists. Though he received high praise from both Reynolds and West and encouragement to settle in England, he postponed the trip until the eve of the Revolution. After his arrival in England, he set out in 1775 to copy the Old Masters in Italy. Travelling through Europe, he returned to London to find his family among the first Tory emigrés from the Revolutionary War. On the whole the rest of his life in England was not a happy one. Through hard labor he acquired the grace of the English portraitists, attempted large-scale historical paintings like The Death of Chatham and The Death of Major Pierson, both now in the Tate Gallery, but his reputation as well as his art declined, his health failed, and he spent his last years in loneliness, regret, frustration and tragic senility. His finest works in their naive, though for the time revolutionary, realism date from his American period, e.g., Nathaniel Hurd (Cleveland Museum of Art), Mrs. Thomas Boylston (Harvard University), Governor and Mrs. Thomas Mifflin (Historical Society of Pennsylvania). Though at first in England he continued to produce more sophisticated portraits, e.g., Mrs. Ford (Wadsworth Atheneum), his art could not survive the elegant artificiality of London taste and ended in such failures as The Knatchbull Family (private collection). (See color plate 44.)

Coppo di Marcovaldo (active third quarter of 13th century). A Florentine painter recorded as having been conscripted for the battle of Monteaperto between Florence and Siena in 1260. In 1261 he signed the Madonna del Bordone in Santa Maria dei Servi, Siena. From 1265 to 1274 documents refer to his activity in Pistoia. Of works referred to, a Crucifix preserved in the cathedral there is now considered to be by his son, Salerno. Other works generally accepted as his are a Madonna in the church of the Servi at Orvieto and a Crucifix in the Muso Civico at San Gimignano. Coppo's art precedes that of Cimabue and displays a mixture of Italian Romanesque and Byzantine elements. Mutual influence passed between him and his contemporary Guido da Siena, and his influence on lesser Florentine painters of his time was considerable.

Coptic painting. Coptic Egypt produced one of the most distinctive local styles of Early Christian times. By Coptic is meant that period in Egypt between the Peace of the Church (fourth century) and the Moslem Conquest (seventh century). It refers to the sub-antique style of the Egyptian communities of the Upper Nile as opposed to the Mediterranean tradition of the thoroughly Hellenized Delta. Coptic art was basically the expressive style of the autonomous Egyptian Coptic Church, but it contained many pagan elements, both Pharaonic and Graeco-Roman. This was perhaps owing to its essentially decorative character and its consequent retention of many popular ornamental features of Antique art. This same tendency toward the decorative allowed Coptic painting to lose itself easily in the art of the conquering Moslems at a later period. The origins of Coptic painting are to be found in the extremely literal Fayum portraits (see) of the first to fourth centuries. But the Christian style abandoned this excellent modeling for the most uncompromising frontality and flat pattern, as seen in the sixth-century apse painting at Bawit. Often Coptic compositions seem to be a rigid variant of early Byzantine imperial images. This can be observed in the Madonna from Morgan Manuscript 612 (New York), whose date of 893 attests to survival of the Coptic community into Moslem times. Although hard and strongly rectangular in the late Coptic manner the ornamental interlaces and two dimensional tensions of this manuscript remind one of the painting of the Irish monasteries.

Coques, Gonzales (1614-84). Flemish painter called "the little van Dyck." Coques was a pupil of Pieter Brueghel III and of David Ryckaert the Elder, whose daughter he later married. He had a considerable reputation and in 1671 was made official painter to the count of Monterey, governor of the Low Countries. He was a fervent admirer of van Dyck and attempted to paint in his manner. He painted portraits, family groups, genre, landscapes and animals. These were very popular in England, where most of his pictures are today.

CORINTH. Still Life with Flowers and Fruits
Private Collection, Germany

COROT. Countryside. Private Collection

COROT. Genzano, near Lake Nemi. Wildenstein Gallery, New York

His portraits were small in size and elegant, painted with great delicacy. His group portraits were posed in gardens or on terraces. He painted many notables throughout northern Europe.

Corbino, Jon (1905-). Contemporary American painter born in Sicily. Arriving in the U.S. in 1913, he studied at the Ethical Culture School, the Art Students League and the Pennsylvania Academy of Fine Arts. He paints men and animals in compositions of vigorous movement in a Rubenesque manner.

Corcoran Gallery of Art, Washington, D.C. General collection of European and American modern paintings. It also contains collections of sculpture and ceramics.

Cordoba, Pedro de (active 1475). Spanish painter of the school of Cordoba. Known for a signed Annunciation in the Cathedral of that city pointing to strong influences from Italy and the North. This painting is peculiarly rich in late medieval mystical symbolism.

Corinth, Lovis (1858-1925). The most vigorous and original of the German Impressionists, Corinth is also known for his etchings, lithographs and polemical articles. He studied in various German academies, then in Paris with Bouguereau, keeping in mind the Flemish tradition of the seventeenth century and the more recent developments in French Realism down to Manet. His earliest successful paintings dealt with mythologies, sacred themes and still life, turning from there to a more contemporary type of expression and becoming part of the "advanced" Secession movement. All of his works, whether ancient or modern in subject, are touched with the powerful Rubens-Jordaens spirit embellished, in his case, with the purer, cleaner colors of modern Impressionism. One of the lustiest spirits of modern times, Corinth was a powerful swashbuckling figure, an exciting teacher and controversial writer, first on behalf of the modern movement and then, as it went beyond him, against it. (See illustration.)

Corneille de Lyon (or de la Haye) (died c.1574). French portraitist and miniaturist. Born in Holland, active in Lyon. He painted royalty although he was not resident for so long a time at the court as were his contemporaries the Clouets (see). His portraits are somewhat more simple, direct and naturalistic than the Clouet's Italianate type. They can be distinguished at times by a somewhat naive awkwardness.

Cornelisz., Cornelis (1562-1638). Dutch painter. He studied in his native Haarlem and in Antwerp. He visited France and also submitted to the influence of Italian art. As leader of the Haarlem Mannerist painters his influence, notably in his group portraits, was such that it extended even to Frans Hals.

Cornelisz. van Oostsanen, Jacob (c.1470-before Nov. 1533). Dutch painter also known as Jacob Cornelisz. of Amsterdam. He was a good draughtsman especially in elaborate decorative details. He emulated his Flemish contemporaries and was the forerunner of such admirable Dutch painters as Lucas van Leyden and Jan van Scorel.

Cornelius, Peter (1783-1867). German Romantic painter. He studied at the Academy in Düsseldorf. From 1800 to 1811 he worked in Frankfort on the Main, and then spent eight years in Rome. He thereafter directed the new Academy at Düsseldorf, and for sixteen years the Academy in Munich before he was called in 1841 to Berlin. He was one of the chief mural painters on a large scale in Germany.

Corot, Camille Jean Baptiste (1796-1875). French landscape and figure painter, important as a transition between the early nineteenth-century tradition of classical composition and the later Romantic sensibility toward nature. An influential force amongst painters of the century, Corot nevertheless remained aloof from the doctrinal disputes which made turbulent the careers of most of his contemporaries. He was the son of a successful hairdresser. Started in business, he came late to painting when a small independent income was made available to him; again in contrast to his colleagues, he was never in want but rather assisted his friends financially in various ways. He started as a painter after nature, entered the studio of Bertin and in 1825 took a trip to Italy which permanently affected his style. The paintings of this early Roman period are in our day often considered his best. The Forum (Louvre) and the View of Narni (Louvre) are examples. He studied Italian landscape through the eyes of a nineteenth-century Poussin, composing it in discrete masses and planes and in a sort of gridwork of chiaroscuro. There is an odd dichotomy between the actuality of the forms and their rough abstract surfaces; between the expansiveness of the space and the gulfs or barriers he erects to our entrance into it.

44. COPLEY. Mary Warner
Toledo Museum of Art, Libbey Collection

On his return to France in 1828, he traveled about, mostly in Normandy and in Brittany, painting characteristic scenes of local color. The Harbor at Honfleur (Louvre) is an example which reveals a new feeling of plein-air brightness, but essentially the same detachment of his Roman period. This aloofness can be seen in the View of Chartres (Louvre) painted in 1830, the year of the Revolution. Much of the intricacy and fragility which we associate with the Gothic building is here played down in favor of a strongly cubic, chalky effect. Right-angle relationships are set up in the foreground and between the steeples and clouds so that the pointed asymmetry of the building is obviated.

During the late 1830's, perhaps as a result of a second voyage to Italy, Corot embarked on large historical subjects such as Hagar in the Wilderness (Metropolitan), which is thematically in the manner of Poussin. These did not come off. Then in the 1840's and 1850's his style changed radically to the filmy atmospheric studies for which he is popularly known. To judge from their subjects, e.g., Nymphs Dancing (Louvre), it suggests a new orientation around the personality of Claude Lorrain. A romantic sentimentality, absent formerly, pervades these studies; witness the title Souvenir de Mortefontaine. His cubic structures of former times still lurk in the background but they are now screened by a film of foliage. This effect is intensified by the technique of brushing over oils while they are still wet. Thus a veil is interposed between ourselves and the intimate vignette of nature, and we are invited to reverie. The veil thickens in some cases, e.g., The Pool at Ville d'Avray, so as to obscure our vision, repel our entrance. Certain accents are contributed to the general grayish tonality by the introduction of small figures with bright hats or vests. This period in his life brought him great popular and academic success. He received a series of medals and honors, and when he served on the jury for Salons he was able to influence decisions in favor of promising young artists. In 1871 he performed a final, remarkable change in his style with the Belfry of Douai (Louvre). Here, although his static, planar elements are still present, the air is clear again and drenched in Impressionist light. The composition now is of the new clipped type in which one glances into a landscape that is not completely conditioned by pictorial relationships to the frame.

Corot is less known for his figure studies, a personal art which like Chardin's employed the human figure (in this case invariably female) as a source of pictorial experimentation. These studies follow in development the styles of his landscapes. They range from transformations of Raphael (Woman with the Pearl, Louvre) and statuesque portrait types (Agostina, Washington) to his middle style of nudes reclining in filmy landscapes. (See illustrations, including color plate 45.)

Corporation Art Galleries, Edinburgh. Collection of works of local Scottish artists.

Correggio (Antonio Allegri) (1494-1534). Italian painter of the High Renaissance whose art combined the "disegno" (see) of Michelangelo and the chiaroscuro and sfumato (see both) of Leonardo. Although he belongs to the generation of Mannerists, he is not one of them; instead, in his naturalism and illusionism he takes the first step toward the Baroque. In his fresco decorations especially he achieves, through daring perspectives, liberated movement of figures, and ecstatic emotionalism artistic concepts which are fundamental to the development of the Baroque. In his easel paintings the modeling may appear too soft, the color too sweet and the emotion vapid, at least for modern tastes, but there is no denying the power and inventiveness of his great decorations. Born in Correggio, the nephew of a painter, Lorenzo Allegri, with whom he may have studied, he was trained under Antonio Bartolotti in Correggio, and perhaps with Bianchi-Ferrari in Modena and Francia in Bologna. He visited Mantua and Parma, but as far as is known, not Rome, and yet he certainly saw works of Mantegna, Leonardo, Michelangelo, and Raphael. In 1514 he returned to Correggio, worked in the Palazzo dei Signoria and executed an altarpiece for S. Francesco (now in Dresden). His first great fresco commission was the decoration of the quarters of the Abbess Giovanna di Piacenza in the Convent of S. Paolo in Parma (1518). Here he produced a lovely, completely pagan idyll on the Diana theme, which is radical in an ecclesiastic as well as esthetic sense. After returning in 1519 to Correggio to be married, he settled in Parma and remained until the death of his wife in 1529, after which he returned again to his birthplace. In Parma he accepted a commission to decorate S. Giovanni Evangelista; the Coronation of the Virgin which he did for the choir dome here was destroyed in 1584 (a copy by Cesare Aretusi is in the new choir and

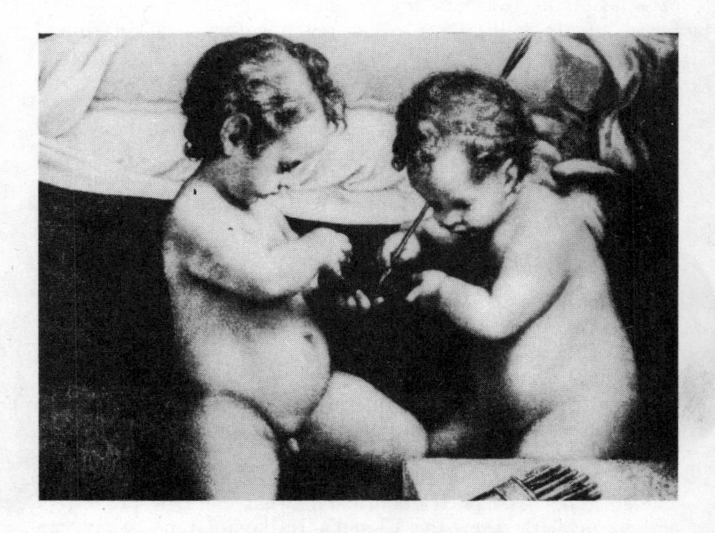

CORREGGIO. Danaë (detail of putti). Borghese Gallery, Rome

45. COROT. Gascon Blonde. Smith College Museum of Art, Northampton, Mass.

CORREGGIO. Four Saints:
Peter, Martha, Mary Magdalen and Leonard
Metropolitan Museum of Art, New York

original fragments are in the London National Gallery), but the Christ in Glory of the main dome remains in all its daring foreshortening and spirited movement, as one of the greatest monuments of Italian art. Before finishing this project he undertook in 1522 to decorate the cupola, presbytery, and apse of the Cathedral, for which he received payments in 1526 and 1530, but which he left incomplete at his death. The octagonal dome still contains, though badly damaged, his exhilarating conception of the Assumption of the Virgin, with its many tumbling figures and off-center composition, probably executed 1526-30. Among his most famous altarpieces are the Madonna and St. Jerome, called Day (c.1528, Parma Gallery), and the Nativity, called Night (c.1530, Reggio Gallery). He also did a series of erotic scenes from mythology, full of elegant and voluptuous grace, upon which so much of his fame rests. These were done for Federigo Gonzaga of Mantua and Isabelle D'Este and include the Io and Jupiter and the Ganymede (Vienna), the Danaë (Borghese, Rome), and the Leda and the Swan (Berlin). (See illustrations.)

Cortese, P. Giacomo (see COURTOIS, JACQUES).

Cortona, Pietro do (Pietro Berettini) (1596-1669). The outstanding Italian painter of the High Baroque, he was active in Florence and Rome, where he executed some of the most important commissions of the period. His flamboyant and luxurious conceptions, painted in a loose and free style, were the official embodiment of the Church Triumphant under Clement VII and Urban VIII. Born in Cortona, he studied first with the Florentine Andrea Commodi then active in Cortona. In 1612, he followed Commodi to Rome and, after the latter's departure in 1614, worked with Baccio Carpi and studied Raphael, Michelangelo, Polidoro da Caravaggio, and the antique. His first Roman period (1620-40) opened with a commission for four paintings for Marchese Marcello Sacchetti and continued with work at Sta. Bibiana for Cardinal Francesco Barberini (c.1625), S. Pietro and S. Lorenzo in Damaso (1628-32), Chiesa Nuova (1634), and the Palazzo Barberini ceiling (1633-39). The Florentine period (1640-47) opened with his refusal of Cardinal Mazarin's offer to go to France. He went instead to Florence, where he worked on the four great chamber decorations of the Palazzo Pitti. The second Roman period (1647-69) includes the Palazzo Pamfili for Innocent X (1651-54), the Palazzo Barberini (1653), and the mosaics of S. Pietro (c.1650). In 1650 he refused Velázquez's request to come to Spain and in 1653 he published with the theologian Giovanni Domenico Ottonelli the *Trattato della pittura e scultura*. He was also active as an architect.

Cosmati, The. A group of Roman mosaicists, marble-workers and architects active from the twelfth to the fourteenth century. The name Cosmati derives from Cosmas, a first name that appears in two of the several families which practiced the same decorative style. They were famous for elements of church furniture: chancels, choir stalls, pulpits, cathedras, altars, etc., as well as for pavements inlaid with a patterned mosaic of marbles cut from antique Roman materials and interspersed with cubes of colored glass. Their style developed from early medieval flat patterns to a strongly classical decoration in about 1200. They then came under the Gothic influence of the Trecento. Only in their last years did they develop a sculptural tradition comparable to that which had flourished in northern and southern Italy since Romanesque times.

Cossa, Francesco (1435-77). One of a group of fifteenth-century Ferrarese painters who were subject to the influence of the Paduan Mantegna to the north and the Umbrian Piero della Francesca to the south. He was probably a pupil of Cosimo Tura, the first important Ferrarese painter. Though his style is related to that of Tura, it is more reserved and monumental, indicating a predominance of Umbrian influence. He went to Bologna in about 1470 to decorate the Schifanoia Palace with frescoes, of which seven are still preserved. They represent scenes from the twelve months of the year, based on medieval astrological calendars but peopled with figures out of classical antiquity and the daily life at the Ferrarese court of Borso d'Este. The subjects and style are related to the secular art at the contemporary court of the Medici in Florence, especially that of Benozzo Gozzoli. Cossa's major altarpiece, representing the Madonna Enthroned with Saints and a Donor (1474) is in the gallery at Bologna. The Berlin museum possesses a well-known allegorical figure of Autumn which is frequently attributed to Cossa. He was the teacher of Lorenzo Costa. (See color plate 46.)

Costa, Lorenzo di Ottavio (c.1460-1535). Italian painter from Ferrara; a pupil of Francesco Cossa and Ercole Roberti, and strongly influenced by Venetian painting, especially by Alvise Vivarini. He was later associated with Francesco Francia in Bologna. He succeeded Mantegna as court painter to Francesco Gonzaga at Mantua on Mantegna's death in 1506. His art is representative of the transition from the fifteenth century to the High Renaissance style. One of his early works in fresco, the Madonna Enthroned with a group portrait of the Bentivoglio family (1487, San Giacomo Maggiore, Bologna), illustrates the tendency throughout Italy at this time to incorporate bourgeois portraits and everyday subject matter in religious paintings. Two works of his Bologna period, the Coronation (1501), in San Giovanni in Monte, Bologna, and the Lamentation (1504), in Berlin, show a broadening of style and a greater interest in space and landscape, indicating the influence of Venetian painting. His late work is represented by an allegorical painting, the Kingdom of Comus (1511/12) which was begun by Mantegna for the library of Isabella d'Este at Mantua. Still later is the Investiture of Federigo Gonzaga as Captain of the Church (1522), now in a Czechoslovakian private collection. These works show a greater complexity of composition than his early style and an emphasis on active figures in landscape. (See illustration.)

Cosway, Sir Richard (1740-1821). British miniaturist prominent in the fashionable world of his day; elected to the Royal Academy in 1770. At various times he was a picture-dealer, drawing master and decorator of snuff boxes. Cosway devised a miniature style suitable for working on an ivory base. His brushwork was fluent and easy, his color balanced, and his figures and their background are gracefully and charmingly blended.

Cotman, John Sell (1782-1842). British landscapist of the Norwich school (see); made his living as a drawing master; elected president of the Norwich Society of Artists in 1811. He visited France several times from 1820 to 1822 and illustrated two volumes of the *Architectural Antiquities of Normandy* for his patron, the antiquary Dawson Turner. In 1834 an appointment as drawing master at King's college, London, was secured for him by the painter Turner. Cotman was a serious painter of somewhat Wordsworthian mood who composed in masses, subduing the details in a way reminiscent of many moderns. The harmony of the various elements and the generally controlled pattern were more important to him than the effects of light and distance that interested so many other painters at that time. His preferred motifs were large shapes such as buildings and bridges, projected in quiet color schemes and with a strong, serene beauty. (See illustration.)

COSTA. St. Lucy. Metropolitan Museum of Art, New York

COTMAN. Seashore with Boats. Tate Gallery, London

Cottet, Charles (1863-1924). French painter and etcher. Lesser-known associate of the great artists of the turn of the century. After an apprenticeship with Maillard, Roll and Puvis de Chavannes, Cottet associated with the progressive artists. He joined the Impressionist opposition to the Academy and exhibited in 1897 with Art Nouveau. His own style parallels the artistic crisis of his generation, turning in about 1894 from a lively and Impressionist color scheme to a heavy, dark and melancholic technique. He profited much from travel in North Africa, the Near East, Italy, Spain and Ireland. Foremost among his works are Evening Rays, and Port du Camaret (Luxembourg), Burial in Brittany (Lille), and a symbolic triptych, In the Country of the Sea.

Coubine, Othon (1883-). Czech-born French painter related in style to the Fauves. He arrived at this stage through trying Impressionism and then Van Gogh, emerging finally with a sensitive style particularly effective in its application to landscapes and their moods.

Courbet, Gustave (1819-77). Stormy personality in the nineteenth-century French development of Realism in painting. Breaking with the long history of French painting, which had been so intensely associated with Paris and which had so continuously enunciated the importance of its own historical past, Courbet posed as a "self-taught" artist and assumed the air and accents of the provinces. Although of strongly Romantic taste at first, he cast aside the imaginative sensibilities of that movement and declared, "In particular, the art of painting can consist only in the representation of objects visible and tangible to the painter." He was born in Ornans (Franche-Comté) of peasant extraction and of revolutionary lineage, facts that he made clear in his famous Burial at Ornans (1849, Louvre). In this composition, which he called "an historical picture," history is contemporary and meaningful, not of the past. Time, it is true, is suggested by the range of ages present at the grave-side, and the range of types suggests a sociological analysis of the community. But the action, such as there is, is frozen in the present, round about the empty pit of the grave. And the allegory of "birth-to-death," which is so apparent in the popular woodcuts from which he drew his idea, is nearly lost in his meticulous recording of dull physiognomies in a humdrum landscape.

In the early development of his style Courbet relied primarily on painting from the model and on copying in the Louvre. However, he did spend time in the ateliers of Flajoulot, Steuben and Hesse. His early works are romantic or literary in sentiment, but already show his independence of tradition and his frank materialism of technique. The Lovers in the Country (1845, Lyon) or the Man with the Leather Belt (1849, Louvre) are examples of this. On the other hand, the After-Dinner at Ornans (1849, Lille) suggests a study

46. COSSA. The Crucifixion
National Gallery of Art, Kress Collection, Washington, D.C.

of the Le Nains, who were "discovered" by his circle. The presentation of a medal for this painting admitted Courbet to the Salons, set off controversy and began the running battle with the authorities and public alike which Courbet carried on throughout his lifetime. Courbet at this time won his reputation as a social revolutionary by taking part in the events of 1848 and painting such studies as the Stone Breakers (1849, Louvre). This was interpreted as social comment. In contrast to this type of subject matter, Courbet constantly painted studio nudes, such as the Bathers of 1853, about which a critic remarked, "This creature is such that a crocodile wouldn't want to eat her." Whether these were painted out of pure sensuous delight on his part, or to ridicule the academic practice of nude studies, is not quite clear. Certainly arrogance was a frequent element in his work, as evidenced by his own posturing in the Meeting with Bruyas (1854, Montpellier).

In 1855, on the occasion of the Exposition Universelle, Courbet was refused entry to the Salon, so he organized a private exhibition of his canvases in the vicinity. It was for this occasion that he prepared his famous Studio. He called this "a real allegory of seven years of my artistic life." In it he pictures himself, the artist, in action, and through this action serving as the catalyst between the common man in his manifold (and miserable) aspects and the Parisian élite. Discarded are the trappings of romantic pretensions, and several are the allusions to the naive eye and child art. At this point social implications tend to drop out of Courbet's art, and henceforth his paintings usually make only artistic allusions. He paints figure studies, landscapes, seascapes, hunting scenes. The last relate to an old royal tradition of French realism (see DESPORTES, OUDRY), but also reveal Courbet's love of the hunt and his feeling for thick pelts, thick pigment. Some of the most beautiful (and innocuous) of his works are flower pieces painted while he was imprisoned for the part he was presumed to have played in the Commune of 1871. He died in exile in Switzerland. (See illustrations, including color plate 47.)

Courtauld Institute, London. A teaching institution for special students. It owns a small but fine collection of modern paintings from Post-Impressionism on.

Courtois, Jacques (called P. Giacomo Cortese or "il Borgognone") (1621-75). French painter and etcher. A spirited painter of battles and sieges, he spent most of his life in Italy. He occasionally did landscapes and finally became a Jesuit, turning to religious pictures.

Cousin, Jean. The name of two French artists of the Fontainebleau School, father and son. Jean the Elder (c.1490-1560) was a painter and sculptor best known for his Eva Pandora (Louvre), an allegorical type based on Leonardo and Mannerist models. He published a book on perspective (1560). His son and pupil Jean (c.1522-c.1594) was a man of so many accomplishments that he was called "the French Michelangelo." His Last Judgment (Louvre) may partly account for this epithet. He illustrated books, published treatises on human proportions and on portraiture, designed sculpture and stained glass. Although he was also compared to Dürer in his day, we know little about him; in fact the distinction between father and son is not yet clear.

Coutaud, Lucien (1904-). French painter, scenic designer, tapestry designer and muralist. He is noted for a decorative semi-Surrealist style that has been very effective in terms of public display.

Couture, Thomas (1815-79). French painter of history and genre. If only for his relations with Manet, who remained several years in his studio, he is one of the most significant academic artists of the century. Couture studied with Gros, with Delaroche, and in Italy on a Prix de Rome. He is best known for his enormous Romans of the Decadence (1847, Louvre), a painting of archaeological allusion, bright colorism, tight detail, and subdued eroticism which epitomizes the vulgar academic taste of the day. His portraits are in a realistic vein and somewhat more powerful. Despite his successes in painting and his important position as a teacher, in the end he renounced his art and died embittered. He wrote *Studio Conversations.* (See illustration.)

Covarrubias, Miguel (1904-). Mexican painter of illustrative, bright, nativist picture, well known internationally as caricaturist, illustrator and writer. He has worked in Europe, Africa, the United States, and the Orient in these fields and on archaeological investigations. Recently he was Director of the Department of the Dance in the National Institute of Fine Arts. He is professor of Art History in the National School of Anthropology, Mexico.

COURBET. Young Woman with Mirror
Metropolitan Museum of Art, New York

47. COURBET. Greyhounds on the Beach. City Art Museum, St. Louis

Covert, John (1882-). Contemporary American painter. Influenced by Marcel Duchamp, he was one of the earliest exponents of complete abstraction in the U.S., but left art for business in 1923. His early work has more recently received recognition and since 1949 he has been painting again.

Cox, David (1783-1859). British landscapist. Although at first a theatrical scene painter, Cox soon developed an interest in landscape expressed in skillfully handled watercolor with subtle cloud and sky effects. Since he received little recognition during his lifetime, he was forced to make his living as a drawing teacher. In 1813-14 he produced a *Treatise on Landscape Painting* for the guidance of his pupils. This was followed by other texts. (See illustration.)

Cox, Jan (1919-). Belgian painter and graphic artist of great sensitivity and mystic imaginativeness. His forms are outlined in bold linear contours and distorted for purposes of greater expressiveness and otherworldliness.

Cox, Kenyon (1856-1919). American academic mural painter. Born in Warren, Ohio, he studied at the Pennsylvania Academy of Fine Arts and with Gérôme and Carolus-Duran at the Ecole des Beaux-Arts. An influential teacher, lecturer, and writer, he was one of the leading opponents of modern art.

Coypel, Antoine (1661-1722). French painter and engraver, son of Noël. Something of a youthful prodigy, he was early deluged with honors and positions. He studied with his father and accompanied him to Rome, where the latter was Director of the Academy. Here he was advised and influenced by Berini and Maratta. Upon his return to France at nineteen his became a career of large decorative commissions culminating in the directorship of the Academy under the Regent(1714). Characteristic of his oeuvre and representative of his inclination toward the Rubenists is his sumptuous theater decoration, Esther before Ahasuerus (Louvre).

Coypel, Charles Antoine (1694-1752). French painter and engraver, son of Antoine. As the last of the Coypel artistic dynasty, he completed the conversion of the family style from Poussin to the intimate manner of the eighteenth century. He inherited the family honors (Painter to the King, Director of the Academy), but he had a penchant for genre and treated historical subjects in the new familiar manner. His talent revealed itself early and, like his father, he was admitted to the Academy at the age of twenty. His literary interests led to the writing of several plays and the illustrating of *Don Quixote* and Molière. (See illustration.)

Coypel, Noël (1628-1707). French history painter and founder of the artistic dynasty of that name. A student under Poncet and Quillerier, he remained faithful throughout his life to the style of Poussin and to the administration of Le Brun. Most of his career was spent in official decorative work in the Louvre, the Tuileries and Versailles.

Cozens, Alexander (c.1717-86). British watercolor landscapist; born in Russia and came to England in 1742;

COUTURE. Female Head
Corcoran Gallery of Art, Washington D.C.

became a drawing teacher at Eton and from 1781 on was instructor to the sons of George III. Considered one of the most original watercolorists of his time, Cozens was preoccupied with problems of composition. His pictures are often imaginative exercises done with a brush in sepia or black ink on brownish paper. He also produced "blot drawings," using ink blots as the basis of the composition and brush or pen to complete the picture. Cozens wrote various books and treatises on landscape composition and theories of beauty. (See illustration.)

Cozens, John Robert (1752-99). British watercolor landscapist. The son of the painter Alexander Cozens, he was also a gifted artist but his career was cut short by mental trouble in 1794. The younger Cozens' work was very much admired by John Constable. It is notable for its unity of tone and breath of composition, and its feeling for the romantically expressive possibilities of nature. Color in his work was not as important as with other British watercolorists. He was an inspiration to Cotman, Girtin, De Wint and the young Turner.

Craesbeck (Craesbeke), Joos van (c.1606-1654). Flemish painter of genre and inn scenes. Until about 1651 he supported himself as a baker. He had meanwhile studied with Brouwer, frequenting taverns with his master and painting brawls in his manner. He also painted domestic interiors, painters' studios and religious subjects, the last in the manner of Rembrandt. Rembrandt's influence increases in all his later works.

Cranach the Elder, Lucas (1472-1553). German painter of portraits, religious pictures and mythological and classical subjects; also engraver and woodcutter. He probably began the study of art with his father in his birthplace, the village of Kronach in Bavaria. By 1503 he had moved to Vienna. In 1505 he was employed by the electors of Saxony at Wittenberg, and passed the rest of his life there, becoming burgomaster of the town and painting successively for Frederick the Wise, John the Steadfast, and John Frederick the Magnanimous. Their likenesses, first painted by Cranach, were repeated a great many times by members of his busy workshop, including his sons, Hans and Lucas the Younger, and by many other assistants. In 1508 Cranach made a journey to the Netherlands. He strongly embraced the German Reformation and was a close friend of Martin Luther. Cranach's witty and fertile mind devised countless original and

COX, DAVID. A Windy Day. Tate Gallery, London

COYPEL, CHARLES ANTOINE
Perseus Freeing Andromeda. Louvre, Paris

COZENS, ALEXANDER. Landscape with Firs
Tate Gallery, London

charming interpretations of classical themes and his paintings of Venus and Cupid and of the Judgment of Paris are unsurpassed in German painting. His art is a rare combination of thoroughly sound and painstaking technique, which imparts to everything he did exquisite quality and finish, and a gift for decoration that renders his figures, the details of costume, and his landscape settings unusual and delightful. Cranach was undoubtedly influenced by Dürer in his early years, but the light-hearted gayety of his paintings offers the strongest contrast to the habitual sobriety of Dürer's work. (See illustrations, including color plate 48.)

Cranach the Younger, Lucas (1515-86). German painter and designer of woodcuts. The son of the more famous Lucas Cranach the Elder (see), he appears to have entered his father's busy workshop as a boy and to have remained there all his life, becoming its director after the death of Lucas the Elder. The paintings that are entirely his lack the excellent drawing and the sparkling invention of his father's work.

Crawford, Ralston (1906-). Contemporary American painter born in St. Catherines, Ontario. He studied at the Otis Art Institute, Los Angeles, the Pennsylvania Academy of Fine Arts, and the Barnes Foundation. Influenced by Cubism, his paintings of industrial subjects have moved toward increased abstraction.

Crawhall, Joseph (1861-1913). British watercolorist noted for paintings of birds. Came to London from the North, spent some years in Paris and then went on to Glasgow during the years of the Glasgow school, a group of anti-Academy painters similar to the London New English Art Club. The bird drawings in which Crawhall specialized are remarkable for the ease with which a few touches of the brush render the effect of plumage.

Crayer, Jaspard de (1584-1669). Flemish painter. A pupil of Raphael Coxie, he became painter to the Brussels court. In Ghent with his pupil Jan van Cleef, he worked on the decorations for the entry of the Cardinal Infant (1634) and eventually became painter of the court of Madrid. He was a friend and imitator of Rubens. Among his paintings are the Madonna with Saints (Church of Alost) and an Assumption (Brussels).

Creation of Adam by Michelangelo (see).

Credi, Lorenzo di (1459-1537). Italian, Florentine. A faithful pupil of Verrocchio, he perpetuated his master's shop and style almost without noting the revolutionary changes the arts were undergoing during his lifetime. Born Lorenzo d'Andrea d'Oderigo, he came from a family of goldsmiths and by 1480 had entered Verrocchio's shop. He continued work on various projects left behind when Verrocchio went to Venice in 1481. Although Verrocchio requested in his will that Lorenzo take over the work on his unfinished Colleone monument, Lorenzo turned it over to another man. He was a respected member of the artistic community in Florence, and was frequently an arbiter in disputes and a judge of other artists' work. He was also entrusted with the restoration of works by important earlier artists (Fra Angelico, Castagno, Uccello). His extant works are numerous, but few are dated, and there is little stylistic development except a certain awareness, in what must be later works, of the formal arrangements in altarpieces by Fra Bartolommeo and Raphael. He was one of those who burned their mythological paintings in Savonarola's famous Fire of Vanities in 1497. One figure of Venus has survived (Uffizi) and its bland and heavy qualities typify Lorenzo's work in general. His many Madonnas, Adorations and other religious works perpetuate the naturalism and sweetness of Verrocchio without the vitality of that master. (See color plate 49.)

Crespi, Daniele (c.1590-1630). Milanese painter born in Busto. A pupil of G. B. Crespi and Procaccini, he was an imitator of the Carracci. He was active in Milan, where he decorated the Ducal Palace, the Certosa of Garegnano, considered his masterpiece, and the Certosa of Pavia. His Last Supper (Brera) is probably his best-known work. His style, inferior to that of his teachers, is exaggerated and Manneristic.

Crespi, Giovanni Battista (called Il Cerano) (1557-1633). Milanese painter, sculptor, and architect born in Cerano. He was the greatest of the seventeenth-century Lombard painters. His eclectic style combining the influence of Mannerism (see) and early Baroque naturalism is characterized by simple and clear composition, rich color, and great virtuosity. His earliest influence is from Gaudenzio Ferrari, but after studying in Venice and Rome he settled in Milan where he was director of the Academy and supervisor of cathedral decorations.

Crespi, Giuseppe Maria (called Lo Spagnolo) (1664-1747). Bolognese painter, admirer of Ludovico, he studied with Canuti and Cignani, and was influenced by the works of Guercino, Barocci and Correggio. He was a prolific artist whose religious works are academic though vigorous in chiaroscuro (see) and spontaneous in execution. His genre scenes, slightly humorous, anecdotal, and naturalistic, have a grace, mobility and elegance which had their influence on Piazzetta and Pietro Longhi.

Cretan painting (see AEGEAN PAINTING).

Cristoforo, Tommaso di (see MASOLINO).

CRANACH THE ELDER. Venus and Amor
German National Museum, Nuremberg

Crivelli, Carlo (c.1430-1495). One of the most curious personalities of fifteenth-century Venetian art. Coming originally from the Vivarini family tradition, to which he added elements from Paduan art (Squarcione and Mantegna), he developed a personal style based on line, sumptuous color and ornament, and a certain morbid and spidery quality that makes his work immediately recognizable. He is presumed to have been the son of a painter, Jacopo Crivelli, and to have spent some time in the shop of the Vivarini. The first and only record of him in Venice is a sentence to prison on a charge of rape and sequestration of a sailor's wife. After serving the term, he seems to have fled Venice forever, and can be traced stylistically and by the distribution of his works from Padua to many small towns in the Marches. He received two titles late in life which thereafter appear in his signature. His production is exclusively sacred in subject and consists mostly of compartmented altarpieces and small panels of the Madonna and Child. He treated the subject of the Lamentation many times in an iconographical form similar to that of the early Giovanni Bellini. Two fine examples in America are in the Gardner Museum, Boston, and the Metropolitan. An exceptional and important work is the large Annunciation of 1486 (London), in which may be seen his assimilation of the rendering of perspective and space, and forms encrusted with the usual rich ornamentation. His decorative and realistic swags of fruit, adopted from the Paduan school, became almost an obsession, and appear much enlarged and emphasized in nearly every picture. Beginning with the crisp and clear modeling and realistic detail of the Vivarini, and a sense of form possibly developed in Padua, his style undergoes a gradual transformation into the strange, personal mannerism of his late works. Three altarpieces may be singled out as typical in this evolution: a polyptych of the Madonna and Saints (1476, London), a triptych with the same subject (1482, Brera), and the Coronation (1493, Brera). (See color plate 50.)

Crivelli, Vittorio (active 1481-1501). A Venetian by birth, he did most of his work in the Marches, and especially in Fermo. He imitated the style of Carlo Crivelli (see), whom he assisted and who may have been his brother.

Crödel, Carl (1894-). French-born painter associated with the modern German school; studied archaeology and art history at the University of Jena. After World War I, he turned to painting, in which he was self-taught. As an abstract painter he was dismissed by the Nazis from his post in the Industrial Art School at Halle-Giebichenstein; he returned there after 1945 and since 1951 has been a professor at the Munich Art Academy.

Crome, John (1768-1821). British landscape painter of the Norwich School (see); known as Old Crome. An im-

48. CRANACH THE ELDER. Martin Luther and His Friends
Toledo Museum of Art

49. CREDI. Madonna and Child with the Infant St. John
William Rockhill Nelson Gallery, Kansas City

portant force in the development of British landscape in general, Crome founded in Norwich one of the few successful English provincial schools of painting. His art owes a great deal to the Dutch naturalists, particularly Hobbema, whose techniques he combined with his own knowledge of the quality of light in England, the nature of its countryside, tree forms, turf and moorland. By subordinating less important elements and concentrating on general and large areas such as field and sky, Crome achieved an effective unity of light and shade that gives his art its individual flavor. The Romantic elements that exist in his painting stem from the example of Richard Wilson. Crome first made his living as a coach and sign painter; then he established himself as a drawing master. He was over thirty when he painted his earliest known picture, The Cow Tower. At this point he began to study the Dutch and turned to the painting of English woods, meadows and downs in various moods of light, air and space. In all these works the light is a vitalized and all-pervading force. As his art developed, the emotional aspect became more important. In 1803 he founded the Norwich Society of Artists and there most of his work was shown from 1805 on. He did chiefly oils, some watercolors and many etchings, the latter mostly of architecture and antiquities. He would often make watercolors and drawings of landscapes outdoors and then return to his studio to convert these into oils. With Richard Wilson, Crome may be regarded as a transition to the more Romantic attitude of the nineteenth century. (See illustration.)

Cropsey, Jasper Francis (1823-1900). American landscape painter of the Hudson River school (see). Especially attracted by autumn scenery, he painted in the Catskills and the White Mountains.

Cross, Henri-Edmond (1856-1910). Member of the French Neo-Impressionist group along with Seurat and Signac; his real name is Henri Delacroix(i.e., of the Cross). He exhibited for the first time at the Salon in 1881, painting in a dark and realistic manner. He then turned to Impressionism and showed at the Indépendants from 1884 to 1891. He became friendly with Seurat and Signac, who turned him toward Pointillism. In 1891 he settled in the South, where

50. CRIVELLI, CARLO
Madonna and Child Enthroned with Donor
National Gallery of Art, Kress Collection, Washington, D.C.

CROME. Moonrise on the Yare. Tate Gallery, London

the light of Provence raised the tempo of his color. His studies of classical art were then joined with increasingly exuberant color; he painted a number of mythological subjects in this manner. His brilliance of color and solidity of form influenced early works of Matisse and other Fauves. See NEO-IMPRESSIONISM. (See illustration.)

crosshatching. A kind of shading produced by the intersection of two or more series of parallel lines. The degree of distance between the individual lines determines the degree of light-and-dark effect.

Cruikshank, George (1792-1878). British artist, caricaturist and illustrator known primarily for his vivid political cartoons and his many book illustrations. By natural inclination and national background he was a humorous artist in an age in which there were many other established caricaturists, including such artists as Rowlandson. Cruikshank became a skillful etcher of great technical and manipulative ability. A prolific worker, he produced innumerable satires on Tories, Whigs and Radicals alike, on public events, the wars abroad, and particularly the enemies of England. Many

CROSS. Houses on the Canal. Kröller-Müller Museum, Otterlo

of his prints were hand-colored; others were done in series or for the satirical magazines of the time. His more genial side emerges in the famous book illustrations, e.g., the Life in London series or the illustrations for Dickens' *Oliver Twist*.

Cubism. A term applied to a method of visualization developed during the early years of this century before World War I. It stemmed first from the formal approach of Cézanne, with its controlled space featuring the relationship between foreground and background and the simplification and geometricization of the individual forms. A stimulus in this same direction came to the young painters of this period from African sculpture with its sharply faceted surfaces and bare forms. Thus the early or facet period of Cubism shows the breaking up of the individual form into sharply angular planes, while the composition as a whole is dominated by the compositional ideas of Cézanne. Picasso and Braque (see) were working side by side in this phase, as they did also in the next phase. This second development, between 1909 and 1911, allows the formerly clear and sharply separated facets to slip, become transparent, and merge with the background of the painting. This represents the beginning of what is known as Analytical Cubism, in which we may imagine the painter stepping into the picture space and looking at various aspects or views of the form, which he then combines in a more or less spontaneous and kaleidoscopic fashion in a composition. The painter has here analyzed or broken down the form into its component parts or views. In the following or Synthetic Cubist phase, the artist did not even bother to imagine himself walking around the object, but built up in artificial or synthetic fashion a composition consisting of arbitrarily selected aspects which to him seemed best suited for compositional purposes. This gives us a more carefully organized but less dynamic form impression than before. From this new conception of form and space many subsequent developments and influences may be traced: e.g., Futurism, Constructivism, Orphism.

Cubist-Realism. An American twentieth-century style related to French Purism (see) and German Neue Sachlichkeit (see EXPRESSIONISM), but having a unique development in the U.S. and reaching its height in the 1920's. It is characterized by a simplification of volumes, a precise and clean rendering of surfaces and a predilection for mechanical forms. Under the influence of the Armory Show, Charles Sheeler and Charles Demuth in about 1916 were simultaneously experimenting with Cubism. Although they soon turned back to Realism they retained certain elements of Cubism. Among the artists associated with this style in one way or another were George Ault, Henry Billings, Peter Blume, Edward Bruce, Elsie Driggs, Stefan Hirsch, Louis Lozowick, Georgia O'Keeffe, Morton Schamberg, Niles Spencer and Joseph Stella. They have also been called Immaculates, Precisionists and Sterilists.

Currier and Ives prints. A series of popular colored lithographs produced during the second half of the nineteenth century by Nathaniel Currier and James M. Ives. Beginning in 1857 they turned out their thousands of prints derived from original watercolors, oil paintings and drawings that were specially made for the firm. A considerable number of specialists were employed to produce these originals, one for yachts, one for hunting scenes and one (the later famous painter Louis Maurer) for horses and horse races, and many, many others. The Currier and Ives print was the most popular art form produced in America during the nineteenth century and although the partnership had its competitors in this field, their name remains the best known today.

Curry, John Steuart (1897-1946). American painter, one of the leading figures in the regionalist movement of the 1930's, along with Thomas H. Benton and Grant Wood. Born and raised on a stock farm in Kansas, he was encouraged in drawing by his mother, studied at the Art Institute in Kansas City and the Art Institute of Chicago. After five years as an illustrator he studied in Paris for a year. In 1928, his realistic study of an American subject, Baptism in Kan-

CURRY. Baptism in Kansas. Whitney Museum of American Art, New York

51. CUYP. Horsemen and Herdsmen with Cattle. National Gallery of Art, Widener Collection, Washington, D.C.

sas (Whitney Museum of American Art), gained him national recognition and established the style of romantic genre painting which he maintained until his death. (See illustration.)

Cuyp, Aelbert (1620-91). Dutch landscape painter. He was the son and pupil of Jacob Cuyp and like him was born and worked in Dordrecht. In his broad sweeping landscapes he perfected an original style so grand and noble that he is sometimes called the "Dutch Claude Lorrain." The figures in his scenes are solid and skillfully painted. The special quality of moist air and light peculiar to countries that are, like Holland, dominated by the sea, is fully apprehended in Cuyp's pictures. (See color plate 51.)

Czernin Galerie, Vienna. Known for its collection of paintings by the Old Masters.

D

Dada. A movement in painting and the other arts initiated in 1916 by Jean Arp and others in Zürich. It sprang up at the height of World War I, against which it was in direct revolt. Through such periodicals as *Cabaret Voltaire, 391, Dada* and others, as well as through nihilistic exhibitions, these disillusioned young men and women, taking the attitude that life had played them a shabby trick, set out to demonstrate the illogical nature of the world. This they did by attacking all traditional forms of logic, art, culture, etc., and by trying to be "creative" through the fortuitous (as in the Fatagaga pictures by Arp and Ernst) rather than through ordinary aesthetic logic. Among the other ways in which they mockingly asserted the bankruptcy of traditional culture was in such objects as the notorious Mona Lisa with the Moustache or the so-called Fountain (actually a urinal) that Duchamp sent to the New York Independents show in 1917. See COLLAGE.

Daddi, Bernardo (active c.1320-50). Florentine painter who was one of the most important followers of Giotto. He matriculated in the guild of doctors and apothecaries in Florence some time before 1320 and was one of the founders of the Guild of St. Luke in 1339. In 1335 he painted a Vision of St. Bernard (now lost) for the Palazzo Vecchio, and in 1347 was paid for a Madonna for the Or San Michele which may be identified with a painting that is still there. Documents suggest that he died in 1348, possibly of the plague. Three signed paintings are extant: a Madonna of 1328 in the Uffizi, another of 1333/4 in the Academy, and a Crucifixion of 1348 in the Parry collection, Highnam Court, Gloucester. On the basis of these works many other panels have been attributed to Bernardo, as well as frescoes of the lives of St. Stephen and St. Lawrence (c.1330) in the Pulci chapel of Santa Croce. Important among the panels are a Crucifixion in the Louvre, a Coronation of the Virgin in Berlin, and a polyptych in the Uffizi. Although Bernardo's style is based on that of Giotto, many of his works display a taste for bright color and Gothic line that reveals strong Sienese influence, and particularly of Ambrogio Lorenzetti. (See illustration.)

Dagnan-Bouveret, Pascal Adolphe Jean (1852-

1929). French painter. A student of Gerôme and Corot, he was also influenced through his associations with Bastien-Lepage. He began with such genre subjects as Wedding at the Photographer's (Luxembourg), turning later to portraits. Particularly successful were his Breton religious scenes such as The Blessed Bread (Palais des Beaux Arts, Paris).

Dali, Salvador (1904-). Representing the figurative side of the modern Surrealist movement, this Spanish-born painter, illustrator and writer has single-handedly made Surrealism (see) an international commodity. From the beginning an *enfant terrible,* he has created a stir wherever he has gone: at school in Madrid; exhibiting in Madrid and Barcelona; studying in Paris, and exhibiting his very provocative works there. In 1931 he collaborated on a Surrealist film, *The Golden Age*, and in 1934 illustrated Lautréaumont's *Les Chants de Maldoror*. Since 1940 he has been living in the United States, which has embraced his somewhat sensational ideas. After a retrospective exhibition at the Museum of Modern Art in 1941 his *Secret Life of Salvador Dali* was published in 1942. The publicity surrounding this painter must be separated from his significance as an artist, especially in view of the avowed shock aims of the Surrealist school in general. The painting method of Dali may be described as a creation in paint of a far-reaching dream-world space in which move clearly and coldly painted figures. These figures arbitrarily bring together incongruous details and forms—as Bosch had done in the fifteenth century and Chagall in the early twentieth. Apart from its disconcerting effect, this method prods the imagination and the conscious mind into new avenues of thought, presumably under the influence of the subconscious or the dream world from which the images are drawn. Few people will deny that these works are stimulating and thought-provoking, but few will agree on the extent of their aesthetic purposefulness. See also FANTASTIC ART. (See illustration.)

Dalmáu, Luis (active 1428-60). Spanish painter of Barcelona. Renowned for his introduction into Spain of the formulas of the van Eycks. Aside from one painting Dalmáu is known mainly through documents. In 1428 he was in Valencia in the service of King Alfonso V. In 1431 he went to Flanders on tapestry business. His one masterpiece, the Virgin of the Chancellors, was commisioned in 1443 by the Ayuntamiento of Barcelona. Although it is an obvious pastiche of several van Eyck paintings which he could have studied either in Flanders or in Spain, it is at the same time distinctly personal and Spanish. The portraits are faithful in detail but the treatment of surfaces is much more generalized than customary in the van Eyck's circle.

Daret, Jacques (Jaquelotte) (born c.1404). Flemish painter. Of an artistic family of painters, sculptors and cabinetmakers. On April 12, 1427 he entered the atelier of Robert Campin (see) along with a Rogelet van der Weyden believed by many to be Rogier van der Weyden. By 1432 he was a master and proceeded with important commissions: decorations for the Voeu du Faisan in Lille (1454), historical and religious cartoons for the tapestry works of Arras (1441-c.1453), decorations in Bruges for the marriage of Charles the Bold (1468), religious pieces for the Abbey of St. Waast. Despite the many records, paintings have only recently been ascribed to him. Because of his relationship to Robert Campin, he has been thought to be the Master of Flémalle (see), but it is now recognized that Daret's style is distinct from the latter's, and somewhat less accomplished.

Dasburg, Andrew (1887-). Contemporary American painter. Born in Paris, he came here as a child, studied with Cox, Harrison, and Henri, but was influenced by the Armory Show (see) to experiment with Cubism. After some efforts in Synchromism (see), he returned c.1917 to a more realistic vision and a simplified, cubical treatment of nature.

Daswanth (see INDIAN PAINTERS: AKBAR PERIOD).

Daubigny, Charles François (1817-78). Most modern and perhaps most sensitive of the French Barbizon school. Notable for his direct influence on the Impressionists

52. DAUBIGNY. The Farm. National Gallery of Art, Dale Collection, Washington, D.C.

DADDI. Madonna and Child Enthroned
National Gallery of Art, Kress Collection, Washington, D.C.

DALI. Daddy-Long-Legs of the Evening - Hope!
Collection Mr. and Mrs. A. Reynolds Morse, Cleveland

through young Monet. Daubigny was taught by his father, a landscapist, and traveled in Italy. He started as an illustrator, turned to landscape etching and then to landscape painting. He alone of the Barbizon school painted out of doors, and he even constructed a special boat for composing his river scenes, such as Bords de l'Oise (Bordeaux Museum). This painting was such a success at the Salon of 1859 that Daubigny became the first accepted Barbizon painter and received decorative commissions in the Ministry of State. Toward the end of his career he, like the Impressionists, painted in Holland. (See color plate 52.)

Daumier, Honoré (1808-79). Satirical graphic artist and painter of the French Realistic movement. Daumier's reputation as a caricaturist obscured his standing as a painter during his lifetime, and it has only been posthumous study of his works that has properly related him to the development of modern French painting. His output was enormous; working under journalistic contract he produced four thousand lithographic plates alone. His development of the potentialities of that inexpensive, painterly medium is one of his major claims to fame. His career passed through several phases. Of humble origin, he showed early talent for poetry and the arts. Brought to Paris as a child, he reveled in the Louvre, but was not allowed by his parents to become a painter. Instead he worked first with a lithographer and then a publisher, becoming involved in journalism. He worked for the periodical *La Caricature*, along with Grandville and others, and for it he passed six months in prison because of a cartoon, Gargantua, an attack on Louis Philippe. Upon his release he produced a series of acid comments on the political scene, culminating in the famous Legislative Belly of 1834. In the same year appeared his Rue Transnonain, vignette of a civilian massacre in Lyon. This dramatic lithograph seems to be based on a study of Géricault, and it has artistic implications far beyond its mere message. It shows him to be a master of the Baroque devices revived by the Romantics and capable of applying them unaffectedly to contemporary events. It bears interesting comparison with another image of martyrdom, David's Death of Marat. The laws censoring the press terminated this phase of Daumier's development and turned him to more harmless satire on mores, social and cultural. Such cartoons ran for years through the pages of *Charivari* and other periodicals. They range from comment on the bourgeoisie to lawyers, artists, actors, and even to such abstractions as Classic and Romantic Theory. His style by the 1850's entered its last phase, becoming broader and more cursive; and Daumier himself associated less with journalists, more with artists such as Corot, who supported him when his sight failed from overwork in 1877. His character Ratapoil, based on Louis Napoleon, is of this period and occasionally we find him rendering such figures in a striking type of sculpture.

Daumier's satire is profoundly human, never slapstick. Some of his comments are so gentle and universal that it is difficult to draw the line between tragic and comic. This certainly accounts for his delight in the stock characters of the Italian Comedy, whom he treats with deep perception for the first time since Watteau. His illustrations for Cervantes are remarkable for the understanding with which the Spanish tragicomic hero is treated. Except for political satire, most of his characters are not so clearly recognizable as Don Quixote, but are anonymous, amorphous types swept up in a crowd, recalling Pieter Brueghel's world of men. The Crowd itself is studied as a revolutionary mob, as refugees blown before the wind or as modern city-dwellers rushing for a train. Interesting in this regard are the various drawings, paintings and lithographs which Daumier produced on the subject of railroad travel, that outstanding contribution to the habits of the industrial age. In the railroad car interiors he practices arrangments by which he can unite a group of

DAUMIER. Rue Transnonain (lithograph)

DAUMIER. The Uprising. Phillips Collection, Washington D.C.

53. DAUMIER. Sancho Panza Wringing His Hands. Collection Mrs. C. S. Payson, New York

54. DAVID, GERARD
Virgin and Child Enthroned with Two Angels
Philadelphia Museum of Art, Johnson Collection

individuals thrown together by chance and lost in their own reveries. He must have profited here from a study of Rembrandt, who is one of the few painters to deal with such psychological isolation amongst individuals physically juxtaposed. Daumier's technique in painting is a brusque one of interplay rather than congruency of mass and outlined silhouette, of dark streaking lines competing with strong color areas that are built up in glazes. Inanimate elements and patterns of his backgrounds in some compositions like the Carriages, The Uprising, and The Laundress seem to have a life or to carry a symbolism of their own. (See illustrations, including color plate 53.)

David, Gerard (c.1460-1523). Flemish painter born in Oudewater, but active mostly in Bruges, and the last great painter of the Bruges school. He may have studied with Ouwater, from whom he perhaps derived some of his Dutch qualities, along with Geertgen tot sint Jans, whom he resembles in his early work. He was later influenced by van Eyck, van der Weyden, Flémalle, van der Goes, and Memling, but added an Italianate High Renaissance monumentality. His art is characterized by a solemn symmetry, a statuesque tranquillity approaching in his late works a hieratic austerity, rich color treated with delicate luminosity and atmospheric effect, an enveloping spatial unity, and a combination of naturalism and idealization. His greatest debt is to van Eyck, from whom he learned to achieve monumentality by pictorial means, but at the expense of dramatic feeling. He came to Bruges in 1483, was admitted to the guild the next year, was its head four times, and was named town painter in 1494. In 1511-12 he travelled in Italy and in 1515 settled in Antwerp, though returning periodically to Bruges. He had an extremely active and productive life and left a great many paintings. To the first period of his activity (1480-98) belong the Nativity (Budapest), the Ador-

55. DAVID, JACQUES LOUIS. Oath of the Horatii. Toledo Museum of Art, Libbey Collection

ation of the Magi (Munich), the Crucifixion (private collection, Lugano), and Madonna Enthroned (1485-90, Louvre). The second, the period of great monumentality (1498-1511), includes the Judgment of Cambyses and the Punishment of Sisamnes (both 1498, Bruges) and the Sion Altar given by him to the Carmelite convent (1509, Rouen). During the third period, probably under Italian influence, his style became even more monumental and simplified, with an elimination of detail and a growing emphasis on the human figures (1511-15): Madonna and Child between Sts. Jerome and Benoît and the Crucifixion (both Palazzo Bianco, Genoa). The last style exhibits a loss of monumentality and intensity, perhaps the result of student collaboration (1515-23): Transfiguration (Bruges Cathedral) and the Rest on the Flight to Egypt (Lisbon Museum). (See illustrations, including color plate 54.)

David, Jacques Louis ((1748-1825). Painter and political figure of the Revolutionary and Napoleonic periods in France. David is unique perhaps in the history of art for not only reflecting the spirit of his age, but for actually shaping that "spirit" through his own exertions and activities. His taste was that of Neo-Classicism, nurtured in him by his master Vien, by his stay in Rome and by his Jacobin doctrine. However, in the execution of his paintings even his contemporaries noted that he wandered from strict Neo-Classicism in several ways that are to us indicative of his position as a modern artist. His most classic subjects, such as Oath of the Horatii (1784-85, Louvre), exhibit primitive disco-ordinated compositions that are not classic. His Directoire portraits are almost Rococo in taste. The imperial compositions which he produced for Napoleon are clearly Baroque in flavor. He is, then, an artist of distinct phases and changing tastes, at his best perhaps in his portraits of the Revolutionary period, which are more Realistic than Classical, according to modern usage of these terms.

As a youth David learned from both Boucher and Vien (see), two rather contradictory masters. The Neo-Classicism (see) that he learned from Vien eventually won out, but his competition piece of 1771, the Battle of Minerva and Mars. is an example of extremely vigorous Boucher style. It was only in Rome in the late 1770's that he was won over to the doctrine of Winckelmann and Mengs. This conversion culminated later in France in the Oath of the Horatii, stimulated by a ballet based on Corneille's *Horace*. He went back to Rome to complete it, and on exhibition it created a sensation. It was purchased by the government, although it spelled the downfall of the Ancien Régime. This painting, like the Socrates (1787, Metropolitan) and the Brutus (1789, Louvre), was fraught with a severe patriotic fervor: the masculine supremacy of civic justice over the feminine weakness of personal relationships. His paintings became a rallying cry for the Jacobins, and David was catapulted into power with the Terror. In the Convention he helped lead the Revolution; as artistic director he abolished the Academy and made designs for popular fêtes. He documented the epoch with his Oath in the Tennis Court (1790, Louvre), an expanded Oath of the Horatii which is an early instance of the painting of contemporary history. His Death of Marat (1793, Brussels) is an eighteenth-century Pietà, the religious piece of the anti-clerical forces. Such portraits of that period as his own (1794) and that of Mme Chalgrin (1793) are among his most intense and powerful works.

The Directoire represented both political and artistic decline for David, although he received numerous commissions

DAVID, GERARD. Rest on the Flight into Egypt
Metropolitan Museum of Art, New York

DAVIES. Autumn, Enchanted Salutations
Babcock Galleries, New York

during that period. He withdrew into an aestheticism that produced pretty portraits like the unfinished one of Mme Récamier (1800, Louvre). An affected studio machine like the Sabine Women (1799, Louvre) seems to allegorize the conciliatory mood of the period. The style was a success, however, and David profited from exhibiting the Sabine Women in his studio at an admission charge. He declined to accompany Napoleon the Consul to Egypt, but accepted the position of first court painter from him as Emperor. For Napoleon he painted three major canvases, the first an idealized portrait of the Emperor astride a rearing horse in the Alps. Then in the tradition of the Tennis Court Oath, he painted two superb ceremonial subjects in which he com-

DAVIS. Something on the 8-Ball
Downtown Gallery, New York

bined a careful scrutiny of detail with Baroque space and verve. The Coronation of Napoleon (in which the Emperor actually crowns Josephine) was painted 1805-08; the Distribution of the Eagles in 1810. On the side (1800-14) he painted Leonidas at Thermopylae (Louvre), a work which demonstrates how insipid and precious his classical style became when it was not related to dynamic contemporary events. The Bourbons exiled David to Brussels and to an essentially sterile existence. (See color plate 55.)

Davies, Arthur Bowen (1862-1928). American Romantic painter born in Utica, N.Y. He began to sketch in the Mohawk Valley at an early age; after his family moved to Chicago in 1878 he studied art with Roy Robertson at the Chicago Academy of Design. In 1880, he went to Mexico as a civil engineer and stayed two years. On his return, he studied at the Art Institute of Chicago, and coming to New York in 1886 attended the Gotham Art Students and the Art Students League. He settled in Congers, N.Y., where he painted and did magazine illustrations. Discovered by the dealer William Macbeth, who persuaded Benjamin Altman to finance a European trip in 1893, he came under many new influences—the Venetians, the German Romantics, the Pre-Raphaelites, Whistler, and Puvis de Chavannes. His early works, under the influence of the Venetians, are pastoral scenes in rich color and heavy impasto, but c. 1903 his style became more romantically idyllic—remote visions of dainty and enigmatic figures. After a trip to California in 1905 his style, affected by Western scenery, became more monumental and solemn, with landscape overwhelming figures. Elected president of the Association of American Painters and Sculptors, he was a key figure in the organization of the Armory Show (see) in 1913. He was himself influenced by the new movements, especially Cubism, and experimented with rhythmic geometric forms, executing murals for the home of Lillie P. Bliss, whose art advisor he was, and Dancers (Detroit In-

DECAMPS. The Critics
Metropolitan Museum of Art, New York

stitute of Arts). In the early 1920's he tried to recapture his earlier style and, under the influence of the inhalation theories of Gustav Eisen, reworked earlier paintings and drawings. He also executed many lithographs and etchings and in his later years worked on designs for Gobelin tapestries. Essentially intellectual and eclectic, his art exhibits a self-conscious search for idyllic beauty and a personal style. Through it all he retained his affinity for the Romantics, for Blake and Ryder. (See illustration.)

Davis, Stuart (1894-). Contemporary American abstract painter. Born in Philadelphia, he came to New York to study with Henri in 1910 and worked as cartoonist and illustrator for *Harper's Weekly* and the *Masses*. After his break with the *Masses* in 1916, his earlier realistic style began to show the influence of modern art—at first Impressionism and later the Expressionism of Van Gogh. In 1921 he did experiments in collage, but his major work showed a semi-Cubist stylization of reality until he began in 1927 to do more radical still-life abstractions. In Paris (1928-29) he returned to a modified abstraction, painting cityscapes in the Synthetic Cubist manner, the style which he maintained on his return to the U.S., until he again began in 1938 to paint more abstractly. His subsequent work has at times approached complete non-objectivity. He uses pure color and bold pattern, and in spite of his abstraction manages to retain the flavor of the American scene. (See illustration.)

Dawlat (see INDIAN PAINTERS: JAHANGIR PERIOD).

Death of General Wolfe by Benjamin West (see).

Death of Marat, The, by Jacques-Louis David (see).

Debucourt, Louis Philibert (1755-1832). A French painter and engraver in aquatint. A student of Vien, Debucourt rebelled against the Neo-Classical doctrine and returned to the older taste of familiar genre. From 1785 he published plates in aquatint, of which he was one of the greatest French exponents. Typical is the Bride's Minuet (1786).

decadent art. A term associated with the late nineteenth-century school of Symbolists and other painters and writers interested in unusual, artificial and sometimes neurotic themes. In literature this term usually refers to the work of such writers as Baudelaire, Verlaine and Mallarmé; in painting to such artists as Munch, Beardsley and Ensor.

Decamps, Alexandre Gabriel (1803-60). A French painter, lithographer and etcher. Trained in the tradition of Jacques Louis David, he rebelled and turned toward the picturesque genre and landscape. An early interest in Oriental subjects (1827) led him to travel in Asia Minor, thus anticipating Delacroix in the Romantic field. Although many of his paintings carry impressive academic titles, his interest lay more

DEGAS. Three Dancers. Wildenstein Gallery, New York

DEGAS. Woman with Chrysanthemums
Metropolitan Museum of Art, New York

56. DEGAS. Portrait of Mlle Hortense Valpincon. Minneapolis Institute of Arts

in technical dexterity and atmospheric play of light and color—an art for art's sake. He experimented under many influences, practicing grand landscapes in the manner of Poussin, anecdotal genres like Teniers, and a series of biblical subjects. His lithographs, begun early, deal with military campaigns, political events and caricature. Despite success in the Exposition of 1855, Decamps ended his life sick and bitter. (See illustration.)

de Diego, Julio (1900-). Contemporary American semi-abstract painter. Born in Madrid, he studied there before going to Paris in 1922. He came to the U.S. in 1924 and has done stage scenery, magazine illustration, and murals. Working with novel technical means, he has treated contemporary subjects symbolically.

Degas (Hilaire Edgar de Gas) (1834-1917). Maverick of the French Impressionist movement. Withdrawn and independent in character, Degas associated with Impressionism in its origins, but was one of the first to deviate from the principles of the group in order to practice a highly personal idiom. For instance, to him the line of the Old Masters, or of Ingres, was preferable to the formless visions of Monet, and he was by no means committed to out-of-door painting. However, in him the compositional scheme is much more fractured and clipped; human beings are often withdrawn from each other and seem to exist in their own worlds of contemplation; the "Japanese" tilt of the perspective structure gives a strong sense of two-dimensional pattern to the canvas. All these things suggest the development of painting in our century. On the other hand, his colors, like the Impressionists, are strongly Rococo in taste, and he revived the eighteenth-century art of pastel.

Degas was a man of wealth, conservative background and prejudice, lacking the sociability and co-operativeness that mark the Impressionists as a group. Destined for law, he turned to painting. He was instructed by Lamothe, a follower of Ingres at the Ecole des Beaux-Arts. He is supposed to have met Ingres and to have been told, "Draw lines, young man, many lines, either from memory or from nature; that is the way you will become a great and noble artist." His paintings prior to 1870 were rather academic: either consciously historical like the Young Spartans Provoking Each Other to Combat (1860, London) or exacting portraits like the Belleli Family (1859, Louvre). These were painted during a long Italian journey. In these years he became friendly with Manet and came to the attention of Puvis de Chavannes. Following the Franco-Prussian war he was active in the Café Guerbois discussions, and on a trip to New Orleans painted the Cotton Exchange (1873, Museum, Pau), which has most of the elements of his mature style. Its observation of unusual poses, the conflict between perspective rush to the right and figure-pattern to the left, its severed forms—all are characteristic.

During the early years of Impressionism Degas was a driving force, an important organizer of the Impressionist exhibitions. But eventually doctrinal differences (such as Line) came between him and the group and in the end his misanthropic character asserted itself. From 1886 on he lived virtually as a recluse, painting for Durand-Ruel, who sold his works directly to collectors. He worked in several media: oil, pastel, engraving, lithography and sculpture. His subjects were of several basic types. Best known of his out-of-door subjects are the scenes of the race track. In his interiors he invariably assumes an oblique point of view derived in part from Japanese prints, which had been popular since the 1850's. The coordinates of these interiors are often

57. DELACROIX. Arab Rider Attacked by Lion. Art Institute of Chicago

DELACROIX. Algerian Women. Louvre, Paris

DELACROIX. Liberty Leading the People. Louvre, Paris

DELAUNAY. Eiffel Tower
Philadelphia Museum of Art, Arensberg Collection

DELVAUX. The Crucifixion. Musée Moderne, Brussels

stated by pieces of furniture, watering cans, etc., from which the figure patterns evolve. Perhaps his favorite interior scenes were those with ballet dancers. In them the graceful ballerina is often submitted physically or compositionally to the most brutal and ugly pose, or (like a Watteau man) she balances on a pinpoint and then flares out in feathers of color. The bathing and preening of women he examined constantly from an odd "keyhole" vantage point, and as his technique became more brusque, the conventional beauty of woman was lost in an agitated color pattern. His constant scrutiny of the everyday scene led him to portray a series of occupational types in which women are caught in all the awkwardness of ironing, laundering, etc. And he shows the Impressionist preoccupation with the world of pleasure, the café and bistro, except that in such social settings the figures are surprisingly isolated by pictorial means, almost sadistically de-humanized. In his most characteristic late portraits his approach to the sitter is also oblique. (See illustrations, including color plate 56.)

Degroux, Charles (1825-70). Belgian painter of lower-class themes. He was one of the first artists in the nineteenth century to revive this age-old Belgian tradition. Influenced by the growing social consciousness of his time, Degroux often expresses in his works a sense of despair as well as a distinct feeling against contemporary social injustice.

Dehn, Adolf Arthur (1895-). Contemporary American watercolorist and lithographer. Born in Waterville, Minn., he studied at the Minneapolis School of Art and the Art Students League under Robinson. His early work, almost entirely confined to black-and-white, and under the influence of Robinson, Pascin, and Grosz, was satiric and social. His later work has been concerned with lyrical watercolor renderings of the Southwestern landscape.

Deineka, Alexander (1899-). Modern Russian painter, engraver, poster designer, illustrator and teacher. Deineka came into contact with the modern Western movement during the early years of the century and later during the 1918 celebration and exhibition commemorating the first anniversary of the October Revolution. In his capacity as a teacher in Kursk under the Commissariat of Education, Deineka tried to inculcate the principles of Cubism. During the following years he developed a semi-abstract poster style and a mildly modern illustrative style for such works as Henri Barbusse's *Under Fire* and many children's books. He has managed in a general way to accommodate Soviet illustrative requirements to his own modern, machinistic style. In this style he has rendered factories, peasants, sports scenes and the tempo of life in the socialist state.

De Kooning, Willem (1904-). Contemporary American painter born in Rotterdam, Holland. He is one of the leading Abstract Expressionists in the U.S. Apprenticed to a painting and decorating firm, he studied nights at the Rotterdam Academy of Fine Arts and was eventually influenced by Jongert's de Stijl manner. He came to the U.S. in 1926, worked as a house-painter and began to paint in an abstract manner about 1934. More recently he began to introduce recognizable figures in his paintings.

Delacroix, Ferdinand Victor Eugène (1798-1863). Leader of the French school of Romantic painting and one of the greatest names in French art. Sensitive in taste, acutely aware of the tradition of European painting, and possessed of a prodigious energy, Delacroix was perhaps the richest personality of the modern French school. He not only used other media, engraving and lithography, but during a considerable part of his life he kept his famous *Journal*. This diary is a mine of information about himself, his times, the creative process, and art in general. He was born into an important French family under rather curious circumstances which suggest that he was the son of the statesman Talleyrand, whom he resembled. After lycée he entered the studio of Guérin, a hopeless academician but, as was often the case, an excellent teacher. Delacroix was also affected by the style of Gros and by the personality of Géricault, with whom he became intimate. He followed in their steps with his Bark of Dante (Louvre) for the Salon of 1822. At this point the Romanticism of Géricault and Delacroix had not expressed itself in color. The Bark was derived from Michelangelo's Last Judgment, which Delacroix knew through reproductions. He never traveled to Italy. The advent of color is seen in the Massacre of Scio (Louvre) for the Salon of 1824, in which he lightened up the background after seeing a sketch by

Constable hung for the Salon. Delacroix pursued this study of color in England in 1825, visiting various painters and admiring the fresh colors of the English school. On his return to France he painted a subject from Byron, the Death of Sardanapalus (Louvre), for the Salon of 1827 and established himself as head of the Romantics.

His early period reached a climax in 1830. the year of the barricades and of his painting, Liberty Leading the People (Louvre). It culminated a series of Romantic compositions that had begun with Gros's Jaffa; the next revolution (1848) was treated by Courbet in less heroic vein. In 1832 Delacroix was part of a French military mission to Morocco, in the course of which he discovered: "The Greeks and Romans are here at my door, in the Arabs who wrap themselves in a white blanket." He came back with mind and notebooks crammed with new experiences and exotic subjects. Algerian Women and the Jewish Wedding in the Louvre are results of this trip. Animals and hunts, originally studied from Rubens or from the Jardin des Plantes in Paris, took on a new actuality. In Spain he saw Goya and commented, "Goya is throbbing in everything around me." From 1833 he was occasionally given large decorative mural compositions through some mysterious government influence which overlooked the fact that he was kept from the Academy (largely by Ingres) until 1857. In mural projects he was able to put into effect his reverence for the Renaissance masters, and he became the most original muralist of the century.

In Delacroix's works there are a number of special types of subject. For instance he was a literary painter, delighting in illustrating the writings of Byron, Dante and Shakespeare. He had a passion for music and his portraits of Chopin and Paganini are among his best. The latter is a beautiful interpretation of performance in another medium. Animals he painted constantly, whether from nature or from imagination, such as the Horse in the Storm (1824, Budapest). True again to tradition was his penchant for religious subjects. His versions of Christ on Lake Genezareth are among his best and employ a favorite symbol of isolation, the sea. The evolution of Delacroix's style is easy to follow, since he frequently revised old subjects. One notices an increasing knowledge of color theory, leading eventually to the Impressionists and a loosening of his brushwork in Expressionist fashion. Some of his more lurid late colorings had a strong influence on the work of Renoir. (See illustrations, including color plate 57.)

Delaroche, Hippolyte (called Paul) (1797-1856). French painter of history and portraits. His anecdotal, detailed paintings are clearly related to his generation's taste for historical novels. His subjects ranged through both French and English history, e.g., The Children of Edward IV (Louvre), The Assassination of the Duc de Guise (Wallace Collection). He also did religious works. Of an artistic family, Delaroche was a student of Wattelet and then of Gros; he was befriended by Géricault and married Horace Vernet's only daughter. Much-honored and financially successful, Delaroche was a vulgar counterpart to his great contemporary, Delacroix. The latter, ironically, was elected to the Academy only after Delaroche's death and on that occasion assumed Delaroche's chair.

Delaunay, Robert (1885-1941). Distinguished modern French painter important for the impetus he lent in the field of color to the Cubist experimenters of the pre-World War I period in both France and Germany. He was interested in Neo-Impressionism, a significant fact for Delaunay's future development of vibrant color effects. He then fell under the influence of Cézanne in 1908, as did many others, and the following year began his series of Saint Séverin paintings, his Tour Eiffel and similar works in which dynamism of form and brilliance of light are combined. In 1911 the German painter Elizabeth Epstein, a Blue Rider member, showed his work to Wassily Kandinsky, and the latter invited Delaunay to send three pictures to the Blue Rider exhibition that Kandinsky and Franz Marc were then organizing. Delaunay met August Macke, Marc and Paul Klee in Paris in 1912 and influenced them in the direction of the vibrantly coloristic Cubist formations they soon projected. In 1912 he also formulated his so-called Orphism (see), in which Frank Kupka, Macdonald Wright, Morgan Russell and others participated. In this area Delaunay was animated by his love of pure color for its own sake, renouncing the importance of objects as such and allowing the colors free and imaginative play. Looking at any of his "window compositions" of that period, we can see his great appeal to men like Kandinsky, Klee, Macke, Campendonk, Feininger and others in Germany at the time. See also CUBISM, SECTION D'OR. (See illustration.)

Dello di Niccolò Delli (c.1404-1471). Italo-Spanish painter. His life and travels are fairly well documented but almost no work by him is preserved. He went to Spain in 1433, where he spent the rest of his life except for a brief visit to Florence. His chief activity was in Salamanca. Badly repainted frescoes and an elaborate polyptych in the cathedral there may be his work. His reputation must have been considerable, for Vasari devotes an entire chapter to him.

Delvaux, Paul (1897-). Belgian Surrealist painter who has also been influenced by Impressionism and Expressionism. More specifically part of Surrealism (see) than his contemporary Magritte, his work is nevertheless filled with a high degree of imaginativeness and deliberate contradictions. His paintings deliberately include nude and dressed people, quiet streets and noisy objects, ancient backgrounds and modern accessories. Member of the *Compagnons de l'art* group. (See illustration.)

Demuth, Charles (1883-1935). One of the pioneers of modern art in America. Born in Philadelphia, he studied first at the School of Industrial Art and, beginning in 1905, at

DEMUTH. After All. Norton Art Gallery, West Palm Beach

58. DERAIN. The Fruit Bowl. Private Collection

the Pennsylvania Academy of Fine Arts with Anschutz and Chase. He went to Paris in 1907 and again in 1912, studying at the Académies Colarossi and Julian. His early work shows the influence of the Realist tradition and perhaps Steinlen. By 1915 the impact of modern art was evident in his watercolors of flowers and landscapes; these show a close relationship to Marin and, ultimately, Cézanne. His figure pieces (1915-19) include vaudevilles scenes and illustrations for such books as Emile Zola's *Nana*, Henry James's *The Turn of the Screw*, and Frank Wedekind's *Erdgeist*, in which his fragile and nervous pencil line overlaid with washes of color created a mood of tension and terror. As early as 1916, he began to experiment with Cubism, fragmenting reality into a pattern of intersecting directional lines. In 1919, he turned from watercolor to tempera and oil for the creation of larger paintings of colonial and industrial architecture. Though these mature works retained some elements of Cubism, his adherence to reality and his choice of industrial subjects were fundamental to the development of the Cubist-Realist style. In spite of the emotional tension of his earlier figure pieces, his art as a whole exhibited an intellectual aloofness and an elegant precision. (See illustration.)

Denis, Maurice (1870-1943). French painter, writer, and titular leader of the Nabis (see) group of the 1890's. Although a good deal of his practice as a painter does not conform with his preaching of Nabi doctrine, Denis put forth many important ideas, of which one in particular may be quoted: "We must never forget that any painting—before being a warhorse, a nude woman, an anecdote or whatnot—is essentially a flat surface to be covered with colors arranged in a certain order." As a painter he began his career in 1888 as a Symbolist of the Sérusier-Gauguin type. Three years later he joined the Nabis in their 1891 exhibition and began to take a leading part in their program. A stay in Italy, 1895, led him to advise painters to turn to the beauties of the primitives with their spontaneous approach to life. His belief in form as the most important element is attested by his admiration of Cézanne, whom he visited at Aix together with Roussel and Emile Bernard. His well-known painting, Hommage à Cézanne, sums up his own and many others painters' feelings about the dominance of form in modern painting. See also SYMBOLISM.

Denner, Balthasar (1685-1749). German painter of portraits, historical pictures and still lifes. He studied in Danzig and at the Berlin Academy. In London and in German court circles, where he did most of his work, his overly realistic portraits enjoyed a great popularity.

Deodato Orlandi (active 1288-1301). Italian painter from Tuscany. Two signed and dated works by Deodato are known, a Crucifix in the Gallery at Lucca (1288) and a five-part panel with half figures of the Virgin and Saints in the Pisa gallery (1301).

Derain, André (1880-1954). A leading French modernist and in the pre-World War I period one of the original group of Fauves. Like most of the Fauves, he has since turned in other directions, although not toward the charm and decorativeness that have often attracted the others. From the beginning there was a clash in him between an emotional drive (manifest in his friendship with the rough-and-ready Vlaminck) and his own intellectual background, which drew him to the essentially rational art of Matisse. Thus when Derain abandoned Fauvism (see) around 1908, he turned toward traditional art of various types: the middle ages, the monumentality of nineteenth-century figure painting, the Romantic landscape, etc. Yet in all these forms the dominant force is that of building a picture rather than projecting a violent impulse in the Fauve manner. Derain was intended for the study of engineering but at fifteen he was already painting. In 1898-99 he studied at the Académie Carrière where he met Matisse; at the same time he made friends with Vlaminck. While copying Ghirlandaio's Bearing of the Cross in the Louvre, 1900, Derain was ejected by museum attendants who resented the liberties he was taking with the original. In 1901 he introduced Vlaminck to Matisse at the Van Gogh exhibition, sharing a studio with the former at Chatou, his native village. The following year he illustrated Vlaminck's first novel.

1905 was a very important year in the life of this young

painter and his friends: all the pictures in his studio were bought by the picture dealer Vollard, who soon did the same for Vlaminck; Matisse visited their studio at Chatou and advised them to participate in the Indépendants showing; and they both joined the Fauve group at the Autumn Salon. During 1907 Derain turned to studies of form rather than color, working on sculpture, experimenting with wood engraving and concerning himself generally with problems of composition. The following year, 1908, he abandoned the pure colors of Fauvism in the face of the Cubist movement with its emphasis on form and the revived interest in Cézanne. In 1909 his woodcut illustrations for Guillaume Apollinaire's *L'Enchanteur Pourrisant* mark a high point in the history of the modern illustrated book. During the 1910-12 period he began to do the form-controlled, low-toned landscapes and monumentalized figure studies that were thenceforth to be typical of his work. The figure studies at first showed clear influences of facet Cubism and then turned toward the kind of representational, mood-filled nudes that lift his art to a high place in French painting. But these, like the low-keyed landscapes, have nothing to do with the Fauve movement. Derain has here become the typical French painter who, however much he may be attracted by the violence of a given moment in history, will tend to return to the traditional rational practices of French culture as a whole. Derain's figure pieces in this way become an extension of the great figure studies of the preceding century from Ingres to Cézanne. (See color plate 58.)

Descent from the Cross by Peter Paul Rubens (see).

de Smet, Gustave (see SMET, GUSTAVE DE).

Desportes, Alexandre François (1661-1743). French painter of the hunt. He was one of those responsible for introducing Flemish characteristics into the art of France in the late seventeenth century. As a pupil of Nicasius (a follower of Snyders) Desportes was trained in the study of animals after nature. Following a brief sojourn in Poland he became an official animal painter in Louis XIV's corps of decorators. Of great personal charm, he was called to several chateaux to work, including Anet and Chantilly; and he supplied cartoons for Gobelins tapestries. Characteristic of his ingratiating work are the "portraits" of Louis XIV's hunting dogs: Bonne, Diane and Blonde Hunting Pheasant; Tane, Dog of Louis XIV Pointing Two Partridges. He was also commissioned to record the King's rare animals.

de Stijl (see NEO-PLASTICISM).

Desvallières, Georges (1861-1950). French religious painter whose style, in its symbolic overtones, was formed under the influence first of Gustave Moreau and later of Toulouse-Lautrec. He conceived the artist's purpose as apostolic and suggested that the bishopric of Paris help run an art school for this purpose. Together with Maurice Denis he may be credited with the revival of religious art in France.

Detaille, Edouard (1848-1912). French battle and history painter in the minute style of Meissonier. His Salon debut was made in 1867 with A Corner of the Atelier of Meissonier. His popularity was great, his output tremendous. He helped decorate the Hôtel de Ville and the Pantheon in Paris.

Detroit Institute of Arts, Detroit, Michigan. A general collection of European and American works of all periods. Especially noteworthy is the fresco by Diego Rivera in the courtyard and the collection of German Expressionist pictures, perhaps the best in America.

Deutsch (see MANUEL, NICOLAS).

Devis, Arthur (1708-87). British painter of charming pictures of English family life called conversation pieces (see). These dainty pictures, carefully flavored by the artist's own outlook, are a revealing projection of the character of the English upper classes at a particular moment in history.

Dewing, Thomas Wilmer (1851-1938). American tonalist painter in the genteel tradition; born and active in Boston. A member of the Ten, he had his training with Boulanger and Lefebvre and the Ecole des Beaux-Arts.

De Young Memorial Museum, San Francisco, Cal. Named after M. H. de Young, this is the leading gallery in San Francisco for traditional painting and other works.

Diamante, Fra (1430-after 1498). Florentine painter, a Carmelite monk, who is known chiefly as a pupil and assistant of Fra Filippo Lippi. He assisted his master on the frescoes in the cathedral at Prato in 1452, and succeeded Fra Filippo as chaplain of the convent of Santa Margherita in 1466, after serving a prison term and changing from the Carmelite order to that of Vallambrosa. He also helped Fra Filippo on the frescoes at Spoleto in 1468 and finished them after his master's death in 1469. In 1472 he is recorded in the St. Luke guild in Florence and in 1481 was among those employed on the fresco wall decoration of the Sistine Chapel in Rome, though his part in this work is not certainly established. Litigation marred his later life and he is last heard of in prison in Volterra. No signed or documented

DICKINSON, PRESTON. Old Quarters, Quebec
Phillips Collection, Washington, D.C.

DIX. The Parents of the Artist
Formerly Wallraf-Richartz Museum, Cologne

DOBELL. Margaret Olley. Private Collection, Australia

paintings by him are known, and it is difficult to distinguish his hand from that of Fra Filippo.

Diaz de la Pena, Narcisse Virgile (1808-76). French Barbizon painter of Spanish extraction. He began as a porcelain decorator but rebelled against the exactitude of this work and turned to painting, in romantic mode, subjects from the Orient and the middle ages. About 1840 he embarked on landscape painting in the forest of Fontainebleau. His are among the most poetic and academic of the Barbizon paintings, owing to the use of closed-in thickets flecked with light and the introduction of ideal figures, classic nymphs or vagabonds. The latter recall Salvator Rosa. In this style is his Bohemians on a Holiday. He also produced a quantity of straight figure studies called Diana, Venus, etc. Of this type is his Fairy with Pearls (Louvre).

Díaz de León, Francisco (1897-). Mexican painter, graphic artist and typographer. A founder of the open-air school system, he has also taken a leading role in the development of Mexican graphic arts through his great technical skill. He has been Director of Publications in the Palace of Fine Arts as well as the School of the Art of the Book.

Dickinson, Edwin W. (1891-). Contemporary American painter in the academic Realist tradition. Born in Seneca Falls, N.Y., he was a student of Chase and Hawthorne. More recently, the introduction of Surrealist elements in his painting has gained him increased recognition.

Dickinson, Preston (1891-1930). American painter, one of the pioneers of modern art in this country. Born in New York City, he studied at the Art Students League and then, between 1910 and 1915, in the Louvre. Influenced by the Armory Show (see), he turned first to Japanese prints and later to Cézanne for inspiration. His translation of Cézanne was Expressionistic rather than structural, with patches of color brought violently and discordantly together. After the war his art showed a Cubist-Realist simplification of form combined with a delicate version of Oriental design. His pastel landscapes have a dainty elegance even though they deal with industrial and urban scenes. In his still lifes the pastel colors often appear too strident. He traveled a good deal in Europe and Canada and died prematurely while in Spain. (See illustration.)

Diller, Burgoyne A. (1906-). Contemporary American non-objective painter born in New York. He studied at Michigan State College, the Art Students League and with Hans Hofmann. He was influenced by the de Stijl movement (c. 1934), and continues to paint in the Mondrian manner (see).

Dillon, Gerrard (1921-). Contemporary Irish painter of primitivist and Expressionist tendencies. He is completely self-taught.

diptych. A two-paneled altarpiece on hinges, usually portable, in painting, sculpture, ivory, enamel, or metal.

disegno. First used by the Italian art chronicler Vasari (see) in the sixteenth century, this term corresponds in a general way to our word "design." It is used more specifically to apply to drawing but even then it is drawing practiced as a preparation, as the "parent," to quote Vasari, "of our three arts: Architecture, Sculpture and Painting."

distemper. One of the earliest of painting media, used by the Egyptians and Greeks; it is a mixture of powdered color and size. The term derives from the French, *détrempe*, which was applied to this mixture as well as tempera. Soluble in water, it is fluid, dries rapidly, is opaque, and useful in quick work. Today it is used in art mostly for wall decorations and poster colors, and is actually more descriptive of house paints than artists' colors.

Divisionism (see NEO-IMPRESSIONISM).

Dix, Otto (1891-). German painter and graphic artist

DOESBURG. Simultaneous Counter-Composition
Collection Dr. and Mrs. Norman Laskey, New York

DOMENICHINO, IL. St. Roch
Collection Ferdinando Rizzi, Sestri Levante, Liguria

related to the New Objectivity group (see EXPRESSIONISM) formed immediately after the First World War. Up to the time of the war Dix had been working as a student of decorative painting and industrial art but after his experiences in the war his whole outlook changed. He became an ardent anti-war propagandist in print and painting, determined to show the horrors in all their clarity and cruelty. Many of his works were unfavorably received and involved him in a variety of difficulties with police, art groups, publishers, etc. Dix's most notorious creation—from the point of view of conservative critics and authorities—was the series of etchings known as War. These can only be compared with such novels on the war as those of Barbusse, Remarque, and others—the work of a generation determined to show it had been deceived. Dix did not hesitate in these etchings to test the average citizen's capacity to stomach the horrifying. Since he is frankly concerned with shocking, it is sometimes difficult to consider the aesthetic quality of this work but there can be little question of the immediacy of its effect. The paintings he began to do after the war differ from the earlier work to the extent that the typically mournful and discouraged figures are set in a cold clear light. These are genuinely expressive of the political and social apathy of the postwar period and are part of what was called the New Objectivity. Particularly striking about these works is their combination of strong and beautiful color with depressing, even repellent subject matter. See also MAGIC REALISM. (See illustration.)

Dobell, William (1899-). Australian painter; the most widely known contemporary Australian artist, largely as a result of attacks by academic painters, who attempted unsuccessfully to prevent an award being made to him in 1943. His art, however, is not actually in the avant garde of the local movement but owes much to the study of Renoir and older masters. In 1948 he won prizes for both landscape and portraiture. (See illustration.)

Dobson, William (1610-46). Known as "the English van Dyck," since he is supposed to have worked under the Flemish painter, but his art appears to owe more to the Venetian works in Charles I's collection. His smooth, thinly painted canvases suggesting van Dyck but freer and more robust in the English manner, show fine treatment of grey and ivory tones. He became a Serjeant Painter to the King.

Doesburg, Theo van (1883-1931). Netherlands architectural painter important as the founder of de Stijl (The Style) abstract movement that included Mondrian, Oud, van der Leck, and others. Very much concerned with the relationship between the painter and the architect, he made contact

DONGEN. Nudes in Interior
Sidney Janis Gallery, New York

59. DOMENICO VENEZIANO. St. John in the Desert. National Gallery of Art, Kress Collection, Washington, D.C.

with Le Corbusier in France and Gropius in Germany. The active propaganda he carried on for his ideas resulted in their spread to other parts of Europe. See NEO-PLASTICISM. (See illustration.)

Dolci, Carlo (1616-86). Italian painter born and active in Florence. He studied with Jacopo Vignali, and was quite famous for his portraits and rather sickly-sweet religious paintings. He was the last typical example of the local Florentine style as against the newer Roman tendency led by Cigoli.

Domela-Nieuwenhuis, César (1900-). Netherlandish painter of the Constructivist school. He studied painting in Berlin and in Switzerland, showing in the former place with the November Group in 1923. Already abstract in attitude, he came to Paris in 1925 and fell under the influence of Mondrian, becoming himself a member of de Stijl group and arriving thereby at an entirely non-objective, geometric formulation. He applied many of their ideas to interior decoration and posters as well as purely aesthetic "constructions" in metal and glass.

Domenichino, Il (Domenico Zampieri) (1581-1641). Bolognese painter active mostly in Rome, he was a follower of the Carracci, especially Annibale. Born in Bologna, he and his closest friends, Reni and Albani, studied first with Denys Calvaert and later at the Carracci Academy. In 1602 he went to Rome, where he lived and worked until 1630 (except for a trip to Bologna), and during which he did most of the frescoes for which he is known. He assisted Annibale in the decoration of the Farnese Palace, absorbing from his master the Roman style which became the basis of his art. He was a rather pedestrian painter but with a gift for clarity in narrative composition which led his contemporaries to call him "Raffaello Reformato" and to contrast his style with the richness and variety of Reni's as typifying the two attitudes toward painting. He is thus the most important link in the transmission to the seventeenth century of Annibale's classicistic Baroque style in decoration and heroic landscape painting. Under the patronage of Annibale and the influential brothers Agucchi, he executed many commissions in Rome and Naples—the Abbey at Grottaferrata (1609-10), the Palazzo Costaguti (1615), the Sta. Cecilia series in S. Luigi de' Francesi (1616-17), the Palazzo Mattei (1617), the apse of

60. DOSSI, DOSSO. Circe and Her Lovers in a Landscape. National Gallery of Art, Kress Collection, Washington, D.C.

Sant' Andrea della Valle (1624-28), and the pendentives in S. Silvestro al Quirinale and S. Carlo ai Catinari (c.1629). In 1630, he went to Naples to work on the Capella del Tesoro in the Cathedral, but persecution by jealous Neapolitan painters forced him to leave in 1634. He returned to Naples in 1636. (See illustration.)

Domenico di Bartolo Ghezzi (c.1400-c.1449). A pupil of Taddeo di Bartolo, he was the first truly Renaissance painter of Siena, though by no means of the stature of his Florentine contemporary Masaccio. His reputation rests on his frescoes (completed 1440) in the Scala hospital, Siena, where he deals with themes related to the institution, grouping many figures against grandiose backgrounds of mixed Gothic and Renaissance architecture shown in violent perspective. He traveled to Perugia in 1438, and left a polyptych now in the gallery there. He exerted considerable influence on the Umbrian school, and most of all on Vecchietta in Siena.

Domenico di Michelino (1417-91). Italian, Florentine. Born Domenico di Francesco, he was a close follower and no doubt a pupil of Fra Angelico. His only extant documented work (1466), now in the cathedral in Florence, is an idealized portrait of Dante standing in a landscape that includes representations of hell, paradise and the city of Florence. A number of gentle and charming sacred works are attributed to him, some of them deriving from compositions by Fra Angelico and all in a style very close to the older master.

Domenico Veneziano (Domenico di Bartolomeo da Venezia) (active c.1438-61). A member of the scientific group

61. DOU. Portrait of a Young Woman. National Gallery, London

of Florentine artists of the fifteenth century, but one who included in his style a lyricism and sense of color that set him apart. He was probably born in Venice, and is first heard of in Perugia in a letter written by him to Piero de' Medici (1438), who appears to have been well known to him. Between 1439 and 1445 he painted frescoes (lost) for the hospital of Santa Maria Nuova, with Bicci di Lorenzo and Piero della Francesca as assistants. Only two signed works by him are known, the altarpiece of the Virgin and Saints (Uffizi), and a Virgin Enthroned with God the Father above, a fresco (London). The five predella panels of the Uffizi altarpiece, his most important work extant, are scattered among private collections and the museums of Cambridge University and Berlin. The central panel (Uffizi) is a skillful composition of solidly modeled and expertly drawn figures grouped about a central axis. Domenico introduced a sense of line into the form-conscious Florentine school and his draughtsmanship is clearly evident in this altarpiece. The figure of St. Lucy in profile at the right has been the source of much controversy; because of it, a number of feminine profile portraits have at various times been attributed to Domenico. Closely associated with Domenico and frequently ascribed to him is the fresco of Saints Francis and John the Baptist in Santa Croce, Florence, and a particularly beautiful Madonna panel is in the Berenson collection at Settignano. Domenico Veneziano incorporated perspective, space, light and landscape into a style that is essentially lyrical in expression, unlike that of his more scientific contemporaries. His light, clear and delicate color is an element in this expression and suggests his Venetian origin. One of the most gifted artists in Florence at a time when talent was widespread, it is unfortunate that so little has been preserved of his work. (See color plate 59.)

DOU. The Violin Player at the Window
State Art Gallery, Dresden

Donato di San Vitale (active 1367-before 1388). Venetian painter who collaborated with Caterino in 1367 and 1372; on the latter occasion he worked on the extant Coronation in the Querini-Stampalia gallery, Venice.

Dongen, Kees van (1877-). Netherlands-born painter who has worked in Paris since he was twenty. He exhibited with the original Fauves in 1905 under the leadership of Matisse; and in company with Derain, Dufy and others has worked toward an extension of the post-Impressionism of Van Gogh and Gauguin. The elliptical, brillant color patterns of the new "wild beast" group were very congenial to the young Dutchman, and his work has continued along those lines ever since, although tempered as he became the portraitist of the Parisian world of fashion and even of its demimonde. He is also known for his brief membership in the Brücke group of Dresden, to which he was invited as an avant-garde sympathizer. See FAUVISM. (See illustration.)

Doré, Paul Gustave Louis Christophe (1832-83). French draughtsman, lithographer, etcher, painter and sculptor of prodigious talent. Doré was engaged in lithography at the age of eleven, and at sixteen was contributing to *le Journal pour Rire*. As an illustrator he not only interpreted Rabelais and Balzac and the tragicomedy of *Don Quixote*, but also produced grotesque and harrowing drawings for the *Divine Comedy* and for Poe's writings. The biting humor of the former and the deep moody chiaroscuro of the latter made him the rage in his day. His canvases, some of them huge, were less successful and soon passed out of favor. As a sculptor he produced a monument to Alexandre Dumas père in Paris.

Dossi, Battista (Battista Luteri) (?-1548). Ferrarese painter born in Trento, younger brother of Giovanni (see), with whom he worked. The landscape frescoes which they painted at Ferrara no longer exist. He designed cartoons for tapestries and is also supposed to have painted landscape backgrounds for Raphael in Rome (1517-24). His work is often confused with his brother's, but is essentially more dependent on Roman than Venetian influences.

Dossi, Dosso (Giovanni Luteri de Lutero de Costantino) (c.1480-1542). Ferrarese painter originally from Trento (the Dosso). His closest association is with the Venetians Giorgione and Titian, whose friend he was and with whom he traveled to Mantua in 1519. He is best known for his romantic landscapes, which along with those of Titian, are unique in Italian painting of the period. He executed large fresco landscapes

DOUGHTY. River Scene
M. H. de Young Memorial Museum, San Francisco

in Ferrara for the d'Estes—Alfonso I and Ercole—none of which remains and which can be inferred only from the background landscapes of his other paintings. He was known as the Ariosto of painting; was celebrated by Ariosto, whose friend he was, in the *Orlando Furioso* and painted scenes from it. He was also greatly admired by Paolo Giovio and Lomazzo, but Vasari found his work clumsy. He worked in Venice and perhaps also in Rome, but mostly in Ferrara. His style is characterized by a vividness of fancy, a freedom and vivacity of handling, and a curious romantic distribution of light. (See color plate 60.)

Dou, Gerard (1613-75). Dutch painter of portraits and genre scenes. He studied first with his father, a glass painter, and with other artists; then for three years he was the pupil of Rembrandt in Leyden in the master's early period. Dou stayed on in Leyden, working for the founding of a painters' guild, becoming one of its first members, and establishing a great school of painting there. His style shows the most elegant delicacy of color and finish, his drawing is excellent, and he skillfully used the command of light and shadow that he had learned from Rembrandt. In his genre scenes Dou rarely attempted to analyze his material or bury allegorical allusions in it, but contented himself with representing external appearances with delightful perception and accuracy. (See illustrations, including color plate 61.)

Doughty, Thomas (1793-1856). One of the earliest pure landscapists in America, he was what might be called a charter member of the Hudson River school (see). After a successful career in the leather business, he turned to art, took a few lessons in drawing and then, almost entirely self-taught, launched into landscape painting. As early as 1820 he was listed in the Philadelphia directory as a landscape painter, probably of estate views, in 1824 he was exhibiting paintings illustrating James Fenimore Cooper's *Pioneers*, and by 1826 had his first exhibition of landscape painting (at the National Academy of Design). He seems to have commuted between Philadelphia, New York, and Boston, with two European trips included (1837, 1845). Although rather unimaginative and typical of the so-called "leaf painters," Doughty was well received and financially successful, even if at times pressed for money. (See illustration.)

Douris (active c.500 B.C.). Greek vase painter. Douris was one of the great founders of the red-figured style of vase decoration. He painted not only mythology, but also genre subjects of reveling and athletics. He was influenced in turn

DOVE. Sand Barge
Phillips Gallery, Washington, D.C.

DRYSDALE. Man Feeding His Dogs
Collection C. Vyner Hall, Australia

DUBUFFET. The Little One.
Sidney Janis Gallery, New York

by the Panaitos Master and Brygos (see). His Contest of Ajax and Odysseus in Vienna shows him to have been as accomplished as Brygos but not so expressive.

Dove, Arthur G. (1880-1946). Contemporary American painter. He was one of the earliest and most original exponents of abstraction in the U.S. Born in Canandaigua, N.Y., his early work as an illustrator was in the Realist tradition. After studying in France and Italy (1908-10), he exhibited at the "291" gallery in 1910, and began his experiments in complete abstraction c.1912. He never forsook reality entirely, even in his collages, and maintained a personal color gamut which was antithetical to the general non-objective palette. Even in his abstractions he retained a poetic feeling for nature, using a large range of naturalistic color and organic forms. (See illustration.)

Downman, John (1750-1824). English pencil and crayon portraitist; studied under Benjamin West and at the Royal Academy school; traveled in Italy, 1773-75, and made a number of fine landscape drawings. He became a prolific portraitist in England, drawing in pencil, charcoal or crayon and then tinting the result. He did a number of figures and portraits in oils as well.

drawing. A form of representation, generally with pencil or pen, but also in crayon or charcoal (or with a brush as in Oriental art). The drawing may be made for its own artistic sake or as preparation for a more elaborate and finished work; e.g., painting, sculpture, building, or industrial art object.

Dresden Picture Gallery, Dresden, East Germany. One of Germany's outstanding collections of traditional painting, containing masterpieces by Antonello da Messina (St. Sebastian), Raphael (Sistine Madonna), Giorgione (The Sleeping Venus) and many others. During the events following World War II, hundreds of works from this collection were removed to the Soviet Union. There have been occasional reports of the imminent return of these works to Dresden.

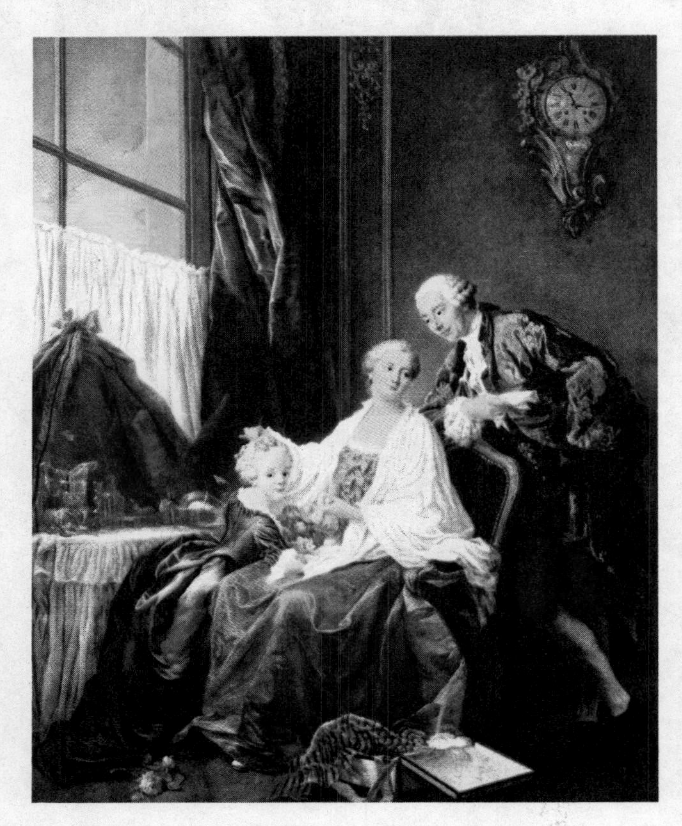

62. DROUAIS, FRANÇOIS HUBERT. Group Portrait
National Gallery of Art, Kress Collection, Washington, D.C.

Drolling, Martin (1752-1817). Flemish painter active in France. He was early in Paris where he studied the old Flemish and Dutch masters in the Louvre. He was best known for little genre scenes which came close to the manner of Greuze. A great many of his paintings were reproduced in engraving and lithograph. At one time he was engaged by the Sèvres factory to design figurines.

Drouais (family.) Eighteenth-century French painters paralleling somewhat the Coypels (see) of earlier times. Hubert (1699-1767), son of an artisan and founder of the line, practiced pastel painting and portraits, especially in miniature. His son, François Hubert (1727-75) (see) was a court portraitist and the father of Germain Jean (1763-88), a promising history painter who died young.

Drouais, François Hubert (1727-75). French portraitist. Favorite of the late court of Louis XV, Drouais was trained under Nonotte, Van Loo, Natoire and Boucher. He was the outstanding member of the Drouais family (see). He practiced a vigorous attractive style of portraiture, especially the current mythological type in which the nobility masquerades: Marie Antoinette as Hebe, Madame Du Barry as a Vestal Virgin, or several personages in a concert champêtre. He was particularly popular as a painter of women and children, and is known for the lucidity of his flesh tones and the liveliness of the color and arrangement of clothes. He epitomizes the superficial tastes of his period. (See color plate 62.)

drypoint. A type of graphic art in which the lines of the design are scratched directly on the copper plate as distinguished from the etching method in which the lines are etched or bitten into the plate by acid. The term itself may refer to the "dry" point of the needle making the scratches.

Drysdale, George Russell (1912-). A leading Australian painter born in England; came to Australia as a child. He is an interpreter of the vast loneliness of that continent's back country and is the most celebrated of its regionalists. Since World War II he has been regarded as Australia's foremost contemporary painter. Stylistically his art is said to derive from the long opposing horizontal and vertical lines of Greek classical architecture. His lean attenuated figures, prototypes of the legendary Australian of the "Never Never," conform to this pattern; and his palette is often concerned with the reds, blacks and browns of Greek painting, along with the blues and the golds of the Australian bush. Until recently he was also affected by English contemporaries like Nash and Sutherland, but this wartime influence is now disappearing. (See illustration.)

Du Bois, Guy Pène (1884-). Contemporary American painter of satiric genre subjects. Born in Brooklyn, N.Y., the son of a literary and music critic, he studied art at the Chase School with Beckwith, Chase, DuMond, Henri, and Miller, and later in Paris with Steinlen. Originally a disciple of the Ashcan School (see), he eventually was influenced by Forain (see). He also was art critic of several New York newspapers and national magazines, editor of *Arts and Decoration*, and author of monographs on Hopper, Lawson, Luks, Glackens and Sloan.

Dubuffet, Jean (1901-). French painter who went to Paris in 1918; there he met such figures as the writer Max Jacob and the painter Suzanne Valadon but never affiliated himself with any particular group. Between 1923 and 1941, when he was demobilized, Dubuffet was in and out of art and the wine business. By 1937 he was already involved, however, in the primitivist kind of painting for which he is known. He uses unconventional material, such as Spot Putty, as a background for painted reliefs, spreading it unevenly over Mason-

63. DUCCIO. The Calling of Apostles Peter and Andrew. National Gallery of Art, Kress Collection, Washington, D.C.

ite panels, then drawing a series of meandering lines along this surface with the edge of the putty knife and filling in these lines with a Japanese bamboo pen. The surface is then manipulated until a parchment-like skin is effected, and paint is added in various washes, thus creating an effect of primordial roughness and strength, a raw and deliberately uncivilized art such as might be produced by children, psychotics or visionaries. (See illustration.)

Duccio di Buoninsegna (c.1255-1319). Regarded as the founder of the Sienese school of painting of the thirteenth century and one of the greatest masters of early Italian art. His birth date and teachers are unknown, and his greatest work, the Majestas in the museum of the Siena cathedral, is the only surviving example of his art that is unquestionably by him. Duccio is first mentioned in 1278, when he was paid for painting several chests for the municipal archives. From then until 1311 he is mentioned with regularity in Siena, though as often for payment of fines and wine bills as for painting commissions. There can be little doubt that he was a spendthrift as well as active politically and in frequent trouble with the authorities. At his death his widow and family refused their inheritance, which was doubtless a liability rather than an asset. In 1285 he was commissioned to paint a Madonna for the church of Santa Maria Novella in Florence, for which the payment was 100 pounds, 50 florins, a very respectable amount. Most scholars agree that this was the famous Rucellai Madonna, now in the Uffizi, but which hung until recently in the Rucellai chapel in Santa Maria Novella. Several other documents of the 1280's and 1290's record payments to him for painting book covers. In 1302 he was paid a sizable sum for a Majestas for the chapel of the Palazzo Pubblico, but this work is unknown today. In 1308 he was commissioned to paint a Majestas for the high altar of the cathedral, with the understanding that all the work was to be done by his own hand. In November of 1310 he was requested to hasten his work, and on June 9, 1311, it was finished. It was carried in triumph from his shop to the cathedral with the clergy and nobles of the town in the procession.

The Rucellai Madonna of 1285 was ascribed by Vasari to Cimabue. It was first given to Duccio in 1898, and since then has been the subject of controversy among scholars, though all agree that it is Sienese and most agree that it is by Duccio. The great Majestas of 1311, which forms the basis for all other attributions to Duccio is still in relatively good condition. It was originally a single altarpiece on both sides, the front showing the Madonna Enthroned with saints and angels, and the back divided into many panels showing scenes from the life of Christ. Originally it stood on the high altar of the cathedral but later it was partially dismembered and moved to the cathedral museum, where it may be seen today. A few panels have been lost, and others have turned up in the London National Gallery and the Kaiser Friedrich Museum. In this work Duccio's style is based on Byzantine forms and iconography, much of which must have been available to him in manuscript illustrations. While preserving the hieratic

DUCHAMP. Nude Descending a Staircase, No. 2
Philadelphia Museum of Art, Arensberg Collection

dignity of the Byzantine style, he invested its forms with a gentle grace and humanity personal to him and paralleling in tendency the innovations of Giotto in Padua. Figures and settings are presented in convincing form and space, and the emotional expressiveness of the figures goes well beyond that of his Byzantine models, though by no means as far as Giotto's. His style is elegant and aristocratic, and emphasizes linear pattern at the expense of plasticity. Other works generally attributed to him are a Madonna adored by Franciscan monks and a polyptych of the Madonna and Saints, both in the Siena gallery, and a Madonna in the Uffizi, but all attributions to Duccio are fraught with endless dispute and conjecture. There is no record of his having made any frescoes. Duccio started a vast school, and there are many Ducciesque paintings extant as well as many names of followers, but the only two names that can be linked with particular paintings are Ugolino da Siena and Segna di Bonaventura. Out of Duccio's style came the tradition of Sienese painting that was carried on by Simone Martini, and, more remotely, by such fifteenth-century painters as Sassetta and Giovanni di Paolo. (See color plate 63.)

Duchamp, Marcel (1887-). French painter associated with Futurism and the Dada movement (see both). Brother of the sculptor Duchamp-Villon and the painter Jaques Villon, he came to the modern movement under the influence of Cézanne, joining the Cubists of the Section d'Or (see). In 1912 he painted the famous Nude Descending a Staircase, a work in which various portions of the form are repeated in Futurist fashion. This picture was shown the following year at the New York Armory Show. Duchamp became interested in the aesthetics of machinery, at the same time using some of this material for the anarchic purposes of Dadaism, which he influenced between 1916 and 1920 (as for example in The Bride Stripped Bare by Her Bachelors). In 1917 he helped found the Society of Independent Artists and in 1920 he joined Katherine Dreier in founding the Société Anonyme for the dissemination of modern art ideas in the United States. He devoted himself to chess for a long time and wrote a book on the subject. He helped edit the magazine *VVV* with the writer André Breton and Max Ernst in New York from 1942 to 1944. The collection of the Société Anonyme was presented to Yale University, Duchamp and Miss Dreier remaining the trustees. Duchamp lives and works in New York. (See illustration.)

Duck, Jacob (c.1600-c.1660). Dutch genre painter. He was probably a pupil of Duyster, and possibly also of Berchem. His pictures combine dashing costumes, abandoned mood, and a solid construction of form and space.

Ducreux, Joseph (1735-1802). French portrait and miniature painter. Son of a painter and only pupil of La Tour, he employed a realistic style with such success that he survived the Revolution and continued on into the Directoire. Most famous are a portrait of Marie Antoinette for which he was sent specially to Vienna, and of Louis XVI which he made of the monarch in prison.

Dufresne, Charles (1876-1938). French painter with Romantic tendencies, as, for example, his interests in exotic places and religious subjects; these he projects through a semi-Fauve, semi-Expressionist technique. During World War I he served in a camouflage unit commanded by Dunoyer de Segonzac.

Dufy, Raoul (1877-1953). French painter from Le Havre, the birthplace of Boudin and Monet. A member of the Fauve group of 1905, Dufy came by his love of light and movement quite naturally, having spent his childhood watching boats and the sea in their various aspects. He is ultimately perhaps the most dexterous and skillful, in a purely technical sense, of the various members of the Fauve group and by the same token perhaps the most decorative in a superficial sense. His art also divides itself into the strongly contoured and vibrant color areas of the early works and the later, less intense creations. At first he tried Cézannesque arrangements (1907-11), but these were not successful; thereafter and as a result of his friendship with Paul Poiret, the fashion designer, Dufy turned toward designs for printing on textiles. He also did ceramics and tapestry designs of various kinds, profitably using the original colorfulness of the Fauve manner. His works have become extremely fashionable; it is still possible, however, to distinguish between Dufy the commercial artist and Dufy the painter. See FAUVISM. (See color plate 64).

Dughet, Gaspard (also Gaspard-Poussin) (1615-75). French landscapist and copper engraver. Of French parentage, Dughet probably never left Italy. He became a student of Poussin, who married Dughet's sister, and he was very successful in his day in his practice of a somewhat picturesque version of Poussin's monumental landscape style. He also studied with Claude, which may account for his delight in rugged Italian mountains and in storms, in which he was a specialist. Although little known today, he had great vogue in those periods of enthusiasm for Claude such as the English eighteenth century. He painted a frescoed landscape in the Pitti Palace at the invitation of Pietro da Cortona and published a number of landscape engravings.

Dujardin, Karel (1622-78). Dutch painter and etcher. Like his master Berchem, he painted landscapes in the Romantic and picturesque Italianate style. As a young man he visited Italy and Paris. He returned to work in Amsterdam and in the Hague, where he was influenced by Paul Potter in the painting of animals. The last years of his life were spent in Italy.

Dunlap, William (1766-1839). Known as the American Vasari, author of *The History of the Rise and Progress of the Arts of Design in the United States,* he was also a painter, theatrical manager, playwright, and amateur botanist. Dunlap went to England in 1784 to study with Benjamin West and Robert Davey and returned to the U.S. to paint portraits, miniatures, historical pictures, as well as landscapes in the manner of the Hudson River school (see).

Dünwegge, Victor and **Heinrich** (active end of 15th and beginning of 16th century). German painters. Little is certain about the identity of these two painters beyond the fact that they operated together a prolific workshop, producing religious paintings of a rather pedestrian sort, related in style to the work of the Westphalian masters, and strongly influenced by Flemish art.

Dupré, Jules (1811-89). French landscape painter. Early admirer of Constable and the seventeenth-century Dutch. He was one of the first to turn French interest in the direction of nature painting. He associated with his contemporaries of Barbizon, although not situated there, was a friend of T. Rousseau and received the encouragement of Delacroix. His enthusiasm for Constable took him to England and influenced his style, as did the art of Claude and of the Dutch. He deserted his father's porcelain decorating to paint after nature and was for a time in the atelier of Diébolt, an animal painter. Characteristic landscapes are A View of Southampton (Salon of 1835) and The Great Oak (Louvre).

Durand, Asher Brown (1796-1886). American painter of the Hudson River school (see). He gave up a successful career as a commercial engraver to become a painter (c.1835). He painted portraits in Washington, D.C., until 1840 when he went abroad with Casilear, Kensett, and Rossiter. Returning to the U.S. the next year, he began to paint landscapes under the influence of Claude and Rosa. Perhaps the first American landscapist to work out of doors, the intimacy and immediacy of some of his works are related to the contemporaneous landscapes of the Barbizon school. Durand was one of the founders of the National Academy of Design and its president from 1846-62.

DUVENECK. Whistling Boy. Babcock Galleries, New York

DÜRER. Michael Wolgemut
German National Museum, Nuremberg

Durand, Charles Emile Auguste (see CAROLUS-DURAN).

Dürer, Albrecht (1471-1528). German painter, engraver, and woodcut artist. He was born in Nuremberg and began the study of art with his father, a goldsmith who had been trained in the Netherlands. When he was fifteen he was apprenticed for three years to the painter and printmaker Michael Wolgemut. Then, as was the custom with young artists of the time, he set out on a tour of the world to broaden himself by contact with the artists and monuments of other lands. He traveled for four years, visiting Colmar, Basel and Strasbourg, and after returning briefly to Nuremberg in 1494 left almost immediately for Venice. Many delightful drawings record this first journey to Italy. Back in Germany in 1495 he stayed for ten exceedingly active years in Nuremberg, producing a great quantity of paintings, as well as engravings on copper and on wood. His style in these works of his early maturity shows the influence of the German artists Martin Schongauer and the so-called Housebook Master. He reflects Mantegna too, and Jacopo de' Barbari, who had worked for a few years in Nuremberg. Dürer went to Italy a second time in 1505, and was then met with great respect and adulation, his reputation having preceded him across the Alps. In 1520 and 1521 he traveled in the Netherlands for a year, and a diary and expense account as well as a number of fine drawings help us to follow him on this journey.

Dürer must be regarded not only as the greatest German artist but as one of the great figures of the Renaissance and Reformation period. His salient characteristics were originality and intense vitality; in his work there is a vigor of

64. DUFY. Joinville. Phillips Collection, Washington, D.C.

conception and execution that often approaches rude force. A series of fascinating self-portraits bear witness, moreover, to his self-awareness and his pride. His experiences in Italy and the cultivated circle of writers and thinkers in which he moved at home led him to adopt the humanistic attitudes of the Renaissance and to assume the position of importance accorded to artists at the great courts of learning in Florence and other Italian centers. Dürer's extraordinary intellectual and artistic gifts found less expression in his paintings than in his prints. Many of his extant painted works have suffered severe damage, but it is clear from them that his color often lacks subtlety and harmony and that he indulged a tendency to overstatement. His portraits are by far his most attractive paintings, but he also produced many religious works, including the Heller altarpiece (for which he made numerous splendid drawings), the Paumgartner altar, and the panels showing the four apostles (now in the Pinakothek at Munich).

Dürer's graphic works illustrate to the full his originality and striking imagination. His famous series of woodcuts include the Apocalypse, the Large Passion, and the exquisite Life of the Virgin. Among his single engraved plates are many that have always been considered masterpieces of the art: the Dream of the Doctor; the Large Fortune; St. Eustace; St. Jerome; Knight, Death and the Devil; and the mysterious and wonderful Melencolia. (See illustrations, including color plate 65.)

Durrie, George Henry (1820-63). American popular landscape painter. Born in New Haven, he studied with Nathaniel Jocelyn and opened his own portrait studio in 1841. He soon turned to genre landscapes and became famous for his New England winter scenes reproduced by Currier and Ives.

Duveneck, Frank (1848-1919). An American painter trained in Munich, he brought to the U.S. the broad and spirited brushwork which derives from Hals, Rembrandt, and Velázquez. Born Frank Decker in Covington, Ky., he took his stepfather's name. He began his art career as a church decorator, and in 1870 went to Munich, where he studied at the Academy with Strahuber and van Dieoz and came under the influence of Leibl. After a brilliant student career, he returned to Cincinnati as a portrait painter, but after two years went back to Munich where, in 1878, he opened a school. There and in Venice he gathered around him the "Duveneck Boys," among them Twachtman, Blum and De Camp. Returning to the U.S. in 1888, he continued in Cincinnati his long and distinguished career as a teacher. From then until his death he traveled a great deal but did not paint very much. His brilliant brushwork is the hallmark of his style. Vibrant and sure at his best, he often slipped into superficial virtuosity. Unfortunately, too many of his students borrowed only the bravura of his technique without the basic vigor of his style. (See illustration.)

Duvet, Jean (1481-after 1561). French engraver and goldsmith. Formerly called the Master of the Unicorn because that animal appeared in nearly all his works. He was expert in goldwork with enamel and jewelry. He is the first well-known French copper-engraver, practicing a style so Lombard that it is suspected he traveled in northern Italy. He employed motifs from Leonardo, Raphael, Mantegna and Dürer in an overall ornamentation that recalls vividly the German master. His work is full of fantasy, especially his late engravings of the Apocalypse (1561), which vie with

66. DYCK, ANTHONY VAN. Portrait of a Lady
M. H. de Young Memorial Museum
Oakes Collection, San Francisco

65. DÜRER. The Lamentation. Alte Pinakothek, Munich

Dürer's. A curious series called the History of the Unicorn is presumed to refer to Henry II and Diane de Poitiers.

Duvillier, René (1919-). French painter and engraver who spent the years from 1940 to 1945 as a prisoner of war in Germany, Poland and Austria. His studies in the Book of Genesis on the implications of the creation of the world and his later (1950-53) researches in geomorphic shapes have resulted in non-figurative but suggestively primeval compositions that represent the sense of growth and creativity which animates all nature.

Duyckinck family. Originally from Holland, this family is associated with Colonial painting in New York. Evert I (1621-1702) came to New Amsterdam in 1638 and is listed as limner, glazier, and glass-burner. Gerret (1660-c.1710), the son of Evert, was a glassmaker and perhaps a painter. Evert III (1677-1727), the nephew of Gerret, was according to tradition the painter of six portraits in the Beekman family. Gerardus (1695-1742), the son of Gerret, has one portrait of James De Lancy attributed to him. All of them were listed as limners, and one signed painting by each is extant, but all the signatures and documents pertaining to the paintings are open to question.

Duyster, Willem Cornelisz. (1599-1635). Dutch painter

EAKINS. Home Scene. Brooklyn Museum

EARL. Miss Lucy Bradley. Detroit Institute of Arts

of portraits, interiors and guardroom scenes. He was probably the pupil of Pieter Codde. He was a careful artist, with well-observed effects of light and dark and a special skill in painting stuffs.

Dyck, Anthony van (1599-1641). Flemish Baroque painter of religious and historical scenes, but most famous as a portraitist. The favorite pupil and assistant of Rubens, his style was formed by that of his master. Born in Antwerp, he studied first with Hendrik van Balen (1609-12), was extremely precocious—his earliest dated work being a Portrait of an Old Man, 1613—and was already famous when he joined the Rubens workshop (c.1617). He executed Rubens' projects with such fidelity that it is almost impossible to distinguish his hand. His own early style up to 1620 is an exaggeration of the Rubens manner, both coarser and more refined, exhibiting a preference for muddier tones, broken color, and rougher pigment, a romantic intensity in the treatment of light, and an attitude which is at times closer to Jordaens and Caravaggio, viz., Martyrdom of St. Peter (Brussels). In 1620 he was invited to England by Charles I, spent three months there painting portraits, traveled in Italy for eight months, and then returned to Antwerp. In 1621-22 he went to Italy again and settled in Genoa, where he worked for four years doing such religious paintings as the Martyrdom of St. Lawrence (Sta. Maria dell'Orto) and some fifty-odd portraits, including the Cardinal Bentivoglio (Uffizi). The style of this period shows some influence of Raphael, but mostly the colorism of Titian and the Venetian school. Back in Antwerp in 1627 he painted many religious pictures, theatrically Baroque, oversentimental, and not among his best works, though highly thought of at the time. His portraits showed greater restraint but the color had become less warm and glowing. It was during this period that he executed the magnificent etching series of psychological portraits of contemporary artists and poets. In 1632 he went to England again as court painter to Charles I, achieved great eminence and wealth, lived lavishly, and executed with great speed and virtuosity some 350 portraits, including 38 of the king and 35 of the queen, Henrietta Maria. The Charles I in Hunting Dress (1635, Louvre) is the epitome of the aristocratic, cavalier type which he created and which became the basis of an English style throughout the seventeenth century. (See color plate 66.)

E

Eakins, Thomas (1844-1916). The outstanding American realistic genre and portrait painter of the nineteenth century. Born in Philadelphia, he copied antique casts at the Pennsylvania Academy of Fine Arts and studied anatomy at the Jefferson Medical College before going to Paris in 1866 to work at the Ecole des Beaux-Arts with Gérôme and Bonnat. Not completely satisfied with the academic style, he went to Spain to absorb the painting tradition of Ribera and Velázquez. On his return to the U.S. in 1870, he set up as a portraitist in Philadelphia, but with little success. He was an instructor of life and anatomy at the Pennsylvania Academy from 1876 to 1886, when he was forced to resign because of a scandal resulting from posing a nude male model before a mixed class. He continued to paint genre pictures and portraits, the latter mostly of his friends and family, but was without significant public recognition until his death. He continued also to teach anatomy at the National Academy of Design and won occasional prizes but after 1910, because of failing health, did little painting. Brought up in the Beaux-Arts tradition, he had had a rigid training, but he could not accept the literary subjects or the Romantic idealization of the academic school. He was a thoroughgoing realist with a passion for scientific accuracy but an equally deep feeling for the quality of paint. His earliest work, rendered in heavy impasto, very soon gave way to a series of beautifully painted outdoor scenes of sports activities, sculling, shooting, and sailing (1871-74)—Max Schmitt in a Single Scull, Pushing for Rail (both Metropolitan). Though he continued to paint outdoor scenes, such as Fairman Rogers Four-in-Hand (1879, Philadelphia Museum of Art) and The Swimming Hole (1883, Fort Worth Museum of Art), he turned toward indoor subjects and a darker tonality. The Gross Clinic (1875, Jefferson Medical College) and The Agnew Clinic (1889, University of Pennsylvania), both grand in conception and finely handled, met with disfavor because of their uncompromising realism. Rejected not only by public and patrons, but even by artists, he spent the latter part of his life in provincial neglect, painting portraits almost exclusively, except for a series of prize-fight pictures (1898-99) and a series of variations on the earlier theme of William Rush Carving his Allegorical Figure of the Schuylkill River (1908). After the turn of the century, with the rise of the Ashcan School and a new realism, he received some belated recognition and a few honors. (See illustrations, including color plate 67.)

Earl, Ralph (1751-1801). A self-taught, American itinerant artist born in Shrewsbury, Mass., he has left some striking portraits. He was apparently painting in New Haven as early as 1774, and the next year visited and painted the battlefields of Lexington and Concord. These works were engraved by Amos Doolittle and became very popular. Some time around 1780 he arrived in London, studied with West, exhibited at and became a member of the Royal Academy and took a second wife without divorcing the first. He later deserted the second wife, returned to America and resumed his occupation as itinerant portraitist in New York, Connecticut, and Massachusetts. His two finest portraits, the Roger Sherman (Yale University) and the William Carpenter (Worcester Museum), were done before his European stay. In them he shows an excellent, almost abstract, sense of design, fine and softly modeled faces, brillant color, and a simplified, stiff treatment of material. These powerful though naive portraits gave way later to more elegant, elaborate and stilted pictures. (See illustration.)

Early Christian painting. Painting of the first centuries of the Christian Church has come to us in rather fragmentary state, but sufficient to reveal its basic orientations. We depend variously upon wall paintings, mosaics and manuscripts for our present information. For instance, we must rely largely on the frescoes in the catacombs to bridge the gap between the Roman wall decorations of Pompeii and the appearance of church mosaics in the fourth century. Catacomb art, however, was exclusively sepulchral in nature, was narrowly limited in subject before the fourth century and presents very little clue to the nature of monumental painted effigy and narration of the early period. After the Peace of the Church the Christian iconography increased in richness; after catacomb burials ceased in 410 there occurred large pictorial compositions, but these latter represent the monumental church style brought under the ground. The imagery of the catacombs consisted of cryptic, if not hermetic, symbols of the salvation of the soul: orans figures, parable incidents, Old Testament parallels such as Noah in the Ark. The style was sketchy, often expressionist in detail and with a fine sense of color values. Wall panels were painted in an open, gay, decorative spirit that is best described as rococo. This non-corporeal style has been called paradisiacal and transcendental; however, it is often indistinguishable from the style of pagan catacombs and in fact pagan house decoration.

Isolated but important monuments of early mural decoration were found in the provincial town of Dura Europos on the Euphrates. Here are a pagan temple of the first century A.D. with flat provincial Roman images of priests and a Jewish synagogue of the third century A.D. with a large cycle of Old Testament narration. Our earliest Church mosaic of clearly Christian content, S. Pudenziana in Rome (c.400) retains a more volumetric quality than provincial Dura, although it is composed in strongly symbolic patterns. The tendency in imperial centers from this time on was toward increasing schematization of figures. Although largely lost today, vast expanses of the church interiors were apparently "papered" with textile-like patterns in paint or mosaic which obscured the architectonic parts and moldings that had meant so much to ancient taste. Our best evidence for this is the tiny Mausoleum of Galla Placidia, Ravenna (420-50). We are fortunate in having in Ravenna a series of churches of the Ostrogoths and the Exarchate (late fifth to seventh centuries) which must have marked the zenith in Christian mosaic painting before the Iconoclastic controversy of the eight to ninth centuries.

Fresco and mosaic of the seventh and eighth centuries, where we have evidence in the West, tended to become flatter, more angular, more isolated, e.g., San Pietro in Vincoli, Rome (c.680). Therefore it is with some difficulty that we reconcile with our sparse historical data the surprising classical feeling to be found in the paintings of S. Maria Antiqua, Rome, and in the frescoes of Castelseprio near Milan. The latter series, recently discovered, has caused a sensation in archaeological circles because of its clear comprehension of antique space, form and motion. Painted manuscripts which remain from the Early Christian period present much more varied styles than do the monumental murals. (See ILLUMINATED MANUSCRIPTS.) For instance, copies of classical scientific treatises, such as the Dioscorides Codex (Vienna) preserve as late as 512 A.D. a sense of the classical style which their models must have possessed. However, a contemporary imperial biblical manuscript, the Vienna

ECKERSBURG. Portrait of Bertel Thorvaldsen
Royal Academy of Fine Arts, Copenhagen

67. EAKINS. Between Rounds. Philadelphia Museum of Art

Genesis, shows a variety of hands, from flat to plastic, but none as classical as the Dioscorides illustrator. A contemporary liturgical manuscript on royal purple vellum, the Codex Rossanensis, comes closest, appropriately enough, to the style and composition of the Ravennate mosaics.

easel painting. Refers to a generally portable kind of painting done on an upright easel and made for relatively small wall spaces. It may be in oil, tempera or mixed media. Distinguished from the fixed or permanent large wall paintings known as murals.

Eastman, Seth (1808-75). American painter of Indian life. Born in Maine, he graduated from West Point (1829) and taught there (1833-40). He became interested in Indians while stationed on the frontier at Fort Crawford and Fort Snelling and did drawings of the Sioux and Chippewas, which he later used for paintings and illustrations. His factual rendering of Indian life and country have charm and romantic flavor, but are more important as records than as art.

Eckersburg, Christopher (1783-1853). Danish painter of portraits, historical and religious pictures, and landscapes; stems directly from the tradition of Jacques Louis David in France with its clear Neo-Classical implications. He was a good friend of the Danish Neo-Classical sculptor Thorwaldsen, whose portrait he did in the meticulous and exact style that characterizes most of his work. (See illustration.)

eclecticism. The process of choosing the best elements from a variety of styles and techniques, presumably in the interest of producing a new style with the combined virtues of all. Sometimes used specifically with reference to the academic school of the late sixteenth century in Bologna, e.g., the Carracci (see), but may be used for any painting characterized by such an approach.

Ecole des Beaux-Arts. The official French School of Fine Arts representing the traditional aims of the French Academy.

Edelfelt, Albert (1854-1905). Finnish academic painter who came under the influence of Bastien-Lepage. He may be credited with contributing to the development of the decorative arts in his country through the industrial arts workshop in Borga. (See illustration.)

Edokoro. The office of painters attached to the imperial court in Japan, to the great Buddhist temples, or in service to the military government.

Eeckhout, Gerbrand van den (1621-74). Dutch painter of portraits, biblical and genre scenes. He studied with Rembrandt in Amsterdam from 1635 to 1640 and in his scenes from the Bible followed his famous master's style. His other works show that he also felt the influence of the meticulous style of Pieter de Hooch and Terborch. Eeckhout usually employed the bright palette and rich colors that Rembrandt was using in the years before 1640. He never mastered, however, the skillful chiaroscuro and harmony of color and design that fuse all the elements in Rembrandt's work into a satisfying whole. (See illustration.)

Egyptian painting. Although this art was richly pictorial and endured for thirty centuries, it seems to have had little effect outside its own boundaries. Magnificent in its isolation, relatively unchanging in its taste, Egypt did not influence the ancient world as profoundly as did the short-lived Greek city-states. The Egyptian painters possessed a fine decorative sense, but the ultimate purpose of their art was utilitarian: to insure the survival of the deceased soul. Further, their method was one of extremely literal readability, so that the painted image vied in importance with hieroglyphic script. In spite of the gay colors and often light and lively mood, the compositional and technical strictures prescribing superimposed registers in rectangular friezes, resulted in a monotonous quality, which was perhaps intentional.

EDELFELT. Old Woman with Basket. Ateneum, Helsinki

Egyptian painting was strongly linear. Although the line itself occasionally performed gentle pleasing arabesques and so contributed a spirit of liveliness, the artist's preference was usually for style conventions that would assure monumentality. His abstract ideographic thinking, so apparent in the structure of his hieroglyphic writing, assembled artistic forms out of a series of "most obvious" parts. The spectator was isolated from the world of the painting by an insistence on profile views. Thus the iconic quality of Pharaonic sculpture was avoided and it was made clear in the painting that the mythological, ritualistic, and biographical character of the subject matter was to be sensed as a narrative: a scroll of events. Actuality was expressed in the figures, however, by presenting the eye in full-face. Shoulders also were generally frontal, in order to be explicit about the limbs and to maintain that favorite "hour-glass" shape which emphasized the symmetry of the human form. Other twists included profile feet invariably flat to the ground line, with a resultant feeling of stability.

The serious purpose, regular pattern, and symmetrical forms were somewhat relieved by gay color. Backgrounds were pale, figures and details rendered in richer and sometimes strident contrasts of a few colors. Flat effect was maintained by stress on outline and avoidance of interior modeling. An exception to the latter occurred when painting was applied to bas-relief, but even here the firm silhouettes overpowered any inner modeling. The painters demonstrated such a fine decorative sense that we regret that we have only tomb paintings left and none of the painted murals of houses and public buildings. Their compositional taste can be felt in the contrast between large-scale figures and small-scale "background" elements as well as in the interrelationships between the painted field and the rows of hieroglyphs. Egyptian painting, then, delights us for its patternistic organization and for the intricacies of its narration, but never achieves a transcendental effect, despite its total preoccupation with religious meaning.

The painting was done in tempera on various grounds, most of them so fragile that much of the art has been lost since its exposure to fresh air. As the tomb paintings were rarely finished, for one reason or another, it is easy to determine the working methods of the artists. We also have left, from the New Kingdom, a quantity of vase-fragments on which painters made preparatory drawings. Egyptian painters

EGYPTIAN. Three Girl Musicians (fresco from tomb of Nakht) Thebes

EECKHOUT. The Wine Contract National Gallery, London

EGYPTIAN. Queen Nofretari Led by the Goddess Isis Valley of the Queens, Thebes

EILSHEMIUS. Contentment
Kleemann Gallery, New York

ELSHEIMER. Tobias and the Angel
National Gallery, London

also illustrated long papyrus rolls of the *Book of the Dead,* and they ornamented coffins for burial, but our main interest lies in the freer art of the tomb-walls.

Our earliest large example, the Geese of Medum (Old Kingdom, c.2700 B.C.), shows that Egyptian painting had already developed long enough to become academic. The same general formulas govern Middle Kingdom work at Beni Hasan (c.1900 B.C.). The Golden Age of Egyptian painting appears to have been the New Kingdom. So much has survived, especially in the private funerary chapels of Theban tombs, that its development can be traced clearly. The old conventional style competed with a new realism, perhaps influenced by foreign contacts. While genre was introduced at all times, e.g., in the tomb of Menna (second half of fifteenth century B.C., Thebes), the heyday of realistic painting occurred during the reign of the heretical Akhenaten (1375-58 B.C.) and especially at his new capital of Tell-el-Amarna. An academic reaction took place after his death, and the great period of Egyptian painting closed with two centuries of ostentatious Ramassid art. While it became more conventional in the iconography of its funeral art, Ramassid painting practiced much freedom of detail and flourish of technique.

In all the stylistic changes during the long history previous to Greek conquest (333 B.C.), there was nothing to match the abrupt introduction of Graeco-Roman motifs in Ptolemaic times (see FAYUM PORTRAITS). The final phase of Coptic Christian art (see) saw a reversion to native decorative tendencies of squarish format. (See illustrations.)

Eight, The. A group of dissident twentieth-century American painters, formed as a result of the rejection of a canvas by George Luks at the National Academy in 1907. The group exhibited at the Macbeth Gallery in 1908 and included Luks, Robert Henri, John Sloan, William Glackens, Everett Shinn, Ernest Lawson, Maurice Prendergast and Arthur B. Davies. Many of these men were interested in everyday subject matter, which was anathema to the Academy; others wished to develop new and unacademic techniques—an equally unacceptable procedure. Their opponents labeled them the "Ashcan School" (see) and "Revolutionary Black Gang."

Eilshemius (Elshimius), Louis Michel (1864-1941). American painter of romantic landscapes and figure-pieces. Born in Newark, he was educated in Geneva and Dresden, returned to the U.S. in 1881, studied bookkeeping and agriculture at Cornell University, and then left to study art at the Art Students League. He was later a pupil of Bouguereau in Paris in 1886 and then traveled for twenty years in Europe, Africa, the South Seas and the U.S. He painted prolifically until 1921, but received no recognition until he was discovered by Marcel Duchamp at the Independents Show in 1917 and given his first one-man exhibition at the newly formed Société Anonyme in 1921. His earlier romantic and idyllic landscapes are among the best in American painting. His later figure-pieces of nudes in landscapes based on his memories of the South Seas show a deterioration of technique but have a clumsy and naive charm. (See illustration.)

Eisen, Charles Joseph Dominique (1720-78). French painter and master at drawing and etching. Produced *gravures galantes* in the more risqué style of the Rococo. He was at one time a favorite of Mme de Pompadour but lost her patronage, perhaps because of his own loose life. He is best known for his *Contes de la Fontaine* and for a book of decorative designs (1753).

Eitoku (see JAPANESE PAINTERS: MOMOYAMA PERIOD).

El Greco (see GRECO, EL).

El Greco Museum in the Casa del Greco, Toledo, Sp. The home of the painter, this contains twenty select works by El Greco.

Eliasz., Nicolaes (called Pickenoy) (c.1590-1654/56). Dutch painter who worked in Amsterdam, creating a style of portraiture that is distinguished for its sober characterization and painstaking presentation of the personalities of the sitters. He was one of the most gifted and considerable portrait painters before Rembrandt.

Elliott, Charles Loring (1812-68). American portrait painter born in Scipio, N.Y. He first began to draw as an assistant to his father, an architect. He came to New York to study painting with John Trumbull at the American Academy and spent several years with John Quidor. He worked at first as an itinerant portraitist in Central and Western New York State and then, in 1845, opened a portrait studio in New York City. He specialized in bust portraits and the few full-lengths that he did were inferior.

Elsheimer, Adam (1578-1610). German painter of figure subjects and landscapes. Up to about 1598 he studied with Uffenback in his native city of Frankfort on the Main. He was also a pupil of Rottenhammer in Munich and during his travels worked in Venice. From about 1600 on he was settled in Rome, and there, for the last ten years of his life, wielded great influence not only on Italian artists but all the painters from the north of Europe who flocked to Rome to study art. Elsheimer's beautiful small landscapes, with tiny figures, almost concealed in lush foliage, telling a biblical or mythological story, are noteworthy for their exquisite craftsmanship and their skillfull handling of strongly contrasted light and shadow. (See illustration.)

Embarkation for Cythera by Antoine Watteau (see).

Empire Style. The decorative style of the early nineteenth century in France in which archaeological classical details are introduced into and dominate the art of furniture-making, sculpture and even painting. Example: the painting of Jacques Louis David.

emulsion. A temporary mixture of materials with an oil and water base useful as a medium for the application of tempera paint to a surface.

enamel. A technique of the metalworker which on occasion approaches the qualities of or substitutes for painting. The process is one of applying glassy material to a metallic background, usually by fusion. Enameling seems to have been practiced in differing fashion in all ages, but it assumed especial importance in the craft work of the middle ages. As a substitute for painting, enameling is usually precious and miniature in scale, sparkling and iridescent in surface, permanently bright and contrasting in color. The origins of enameling are to be found in Egyptian, Mesopotamian, Cretan and ancient Oriental art where it was practiced for its inlay- or jewel-like qualities. It was also employed in the classical period. By medieval times various techniques were practiced. The most delicate was cloisonné, probably invented by the Persians. In cloisonné as in all fused-glass enameling, colored glasses are ground, made into a water-paste, applied to the metal and fused at high temperature. This paste is applied to a depressed area of the metal, produced in Byzantine cloisonné by beating back a portion of the thin gold plate. Divisions are achieved by erecting within the area fine flat wire fences or cloisons, sometimes soldered to their background. These cloisons function as color dividers and as drapery lines. The contrast of opaque and translucent colors, and the glint from the gold beneath the glass give a shimmer to this type of enamel like that of mosaic work. This technique reached an apogee in the ateliers of the Byzantine empire. Our earliest example from the eastern Mediterranean is the cross of Paschal I (817-824) in the Sancta Sanctorum of the Vatican. The earliest Constantinopolitan product is the Cross-reliquary of the tenth century in Limburg. The success of this technique as an exquisite substitute for painting during the mid-Byzantine period can be seen in the superb little plaques in the Metropolitan Museum.

Enameling was an important type of minor art form during the so-called Dark Ages of western Europe. Virtually all the wandering tribes, Celtic, Siberian, Nordic, seem to have practiced one or more techniques in connection with their favorite art forms: trappings and jewelry. This practice continued in the ornamentation of books, vessels and reliquaries when settled communities developed. Several techniques were employed in addition to cloisonné. They practiced "Cold" inlay in which cut pieces of colored glass or semi-precious

ENAMEL PAINTING. Louis XII (triptych). Victoria and Albert Museum, London

stone were introduced into hollowed settings, into pierced metal or behind perforated holes. The western people eventually preferred champlevé enamel in which the glass paste was placed in compartments cut into the thickness of the metal plate. This produced a more cubic, cellular effect and left the dividing metal thicker at the surface. It was employed in Romanesque ateliers with opaque colors set into thickish bronze plates whose exposed surfaces were gilded or traced with engraved lines. While an obvious imitation of Byzantine cloisonné, this champlevé achieved a strident, planar quality quite in keeping with Western taste of the time. Western output had apparently been enormous in pre-Romanesque times, with some of the best work produced in the British Isles and Ottonian Empire. By the late Romanesque period a great industry existed for enameled reliquaries, crosses and church furnishings. Best known were the centers in Limoges, the Meuse valley and the Rhineland. A number of artists are known by name, including Rugerus of Helmershausen (c.1100), Godefroy de Claire (early twelfth century), Nicolas of Verdun (1150-1225?). Many of the enameled plaques of these Western ateliers were assembled to make small chests or reliquaries in the form of buildings. Sometimes the enamel appeared in conjunction with relief work executed in repoussé or by simple attachment of cast pieces. The total effect was a sculpural, architectural one that contrasts strongly with the incorporeal, painterly quality of its contemporary, Byzantine cloisonné. Fine examples can be seen in the Morgan Collection of the Metropolitan Museum.

Italian and French enamelers of the early Renaissance perfected a new method called "painted" enamel. In this technique the colors are applied like paint to the copper sheet and are fused together without cloisons. By careful application the effect of modeling, space and atmosphere can be achieved. The product is a true painting, no longer analogous to mosaics or stained glass in appearance. Lorraine and Limoges led in this technique during the fifteenth and sixteenth centuries, producing such masters as Limousin, Raymond and the Penicauds. (See illustration.)

encaustic painting. Probably the most important method of painting of the ancients, both on walls and on panels. The pigments were mixed with a refined beeswax binder, and were applied by means of heat. The writings of the ancients suggest that there were three methods: 1) panels of wood were painted by brush and by a heated cauterium, a spoonlike instrument for spreading the wax; 2) ivory and marble were painted by incising the design with a cestrum or burin and the color was laid on in heated wax; 3) wood, linen or marble could also be painted with a brush. There is evidence that the process originated in Egypt. No classical Greek examples survive; we first hear of it as a specialty of Pausias, a fourth-century B.C. pupil of Pamphilos of Sikyon. The Fayum mummy portraits (see) were painted in encaustic, facial details rendered by cauterium, the remainder by brush. Other extant examples are the grave stelae of Pagasae (third to second century B.C.). The process was referred to by Theophrastus and Dioscorides, and was described in detail by Pliny the Elder, who termed it too painstaking for mural work. The latest traditional instance we have of its use is a set of panels from Sinai of the ninth and tenth centuries A.D. In 1845 a complete encaustic painter's kit was discovered in a tomb at St. Médard-des-Près. Modern painters such as Diego Rivera have revived the encaustic method: e.g., the latter's work in the Anfiteatro Bolívar in Mexico City, 1922.

Engelbrechtsz., Cornelis (1468-1533). Dutch painter and designer of stained glass. A native of Leyden, he directed there a busy shop in which Aertgen van Leyden and the more famous Lucas van Leyden received their training. Engelbrechtsz.'s mannerism and ornate style seem to have exerted a considerable influence on the Antwerp painters of the

ENSOR. Skeletons Fighting Over a Hanged Man. Koninklyk Museum, Antwerp

68. ENSOR. Carnival. Stedelijk Museum, Amsterdam

time. Many of his pictures were devoted to scenes from the Passion, in which he expresses a strong religious feeling with great virtuosity.

engraving. A graphic technique involving the cutting of lines on the surface of a metal plate, polishing the cut areas so as to make them parallel with the plate surface, inking the plate and printing. A cutting tool called a burin is used, the lines being made by pushing the tool along the surface of the metal. This differs from the drypoint method in that the latter involves a needle held in the hand like a pen; also in that the drypoint line is not polished down and hence, unlike the engraved line, comes out fuzzy rather than sharp.

Ensor, James (1860-1949). Belgian painter of figure subjects, genre, religious compositions, mythological themes, landscapes and still life; also engraver, etcher and lithographer. Son of an English father and Belgian mother, Ensor passed most of his childhood playtime in the family bric-a-brac shop in Ostend with its seashells, masks and souvenirs. He first painted in rather dark colors a number of naturalistic landscapes and seascapes but soon turned to mysterious, psychological (although still naturalistic) subjects such as The Lamplighter, and The Woman with the Fan, filled with silence and strangeness of mood. By 1885 his color became thinner and clearer, his subjects henceforth the skeletons representing his idea of humanity and the masked figures symbolizing its falseness. Among the best known of his satirically symbolic works is the Entry of Christ into Brussels, an extraordinary work for its time, 1888, foreshadowing on the one hand the violence of Expressionism (see) and on the other the irrational and fear-laden atmosphere of Surrealism (see). Other works of this early period suggest the Intimism of Bonnard, as in Children at Their Toilet, 1886. Along with these troubling psychological works he continued to produce realistic paintings, and often combined the two. Undoubtedly influenced by the French Impressionism of the 1870's, Ensor represents an unusually original, even brilliant adaptation and reworking of their contribution; this places him historically with the more emotive of the Post-Impressionists of the late 1880's and 1890's. He is one of the most prolific and original spirits of modern painting. See also DECADENT ART, FANTASTIC ART, SYMBOLISM. (See illustrations, including color plate 68.)

Ergotimos (mid-sixth century B.C.). Greek vase-maker. Active in Attica. The products of his workshop have been found in widely scattered sites of the Mediterranean world. Most famous of his products is the François Vase from Chiusi, which was painted by Klitias (see). Other items by Ergotimos have been found in Phrygia, Naukratis and Aegina. His son Eucheiros continued his workshop.

Erixson, Sven (1899-). Contemporary Swedish painter and textile designer. Certain aspects of his early work suggest the suburban simplicities of Henri Rousseau but he later turned to monumental effects and to compositions that lend themselves to tapestry designs.

Ernst, Jimmy (1920-). German-born contemporary American painter in an Expressionist vein. Born in Cologne, he arrived in the United States in 1938, began to study painting on his own in 1940 and had his first show in 1944. His three-dimensional compositions are dominated by clear, geometrically shaped forms that reveal a strong emotional drive.

Ernst, Max (1891-). German Surrealist painter who has been among the leading figures in that movement. He is perhaps best known for two of its outstanding techniques: the collage (see) and the frottage (see). In the first, Ernst discovered that two ideas or forms coming from entirely unrelated spheres can be brought together to create a new and unforeseen relationship. Thus he found it possible to paste together on a sheet of paper (hence the term collage or pasting) two photographic or printed fragments, join them by a touch of color or line, and produce a new reality and one more intense than that offered by either of the originals. The series of Dadaist Fatagaga pictures made by Ernst and Jean Arp in 1919 belong in this category. In a frottage or rubbing, the artist takes advantage of the suggestions of form and movement implicit in such substances as the grain of wood. By

ERNST, MAX. Descent in the Valley
Collection Mrs. Grace Borgenicht, New York

placing a sheet of paper over the area that interests him and rubbing over it with a piece of graphite, the artist is able to bring out the form-movement-emotion suggestions of the original. In 1919 Ernst helped bring the Dada (see) movement to Cologne and the following year he participated in a Dada exhibition which was closed by the police. By 1922 in Paris he was experimenting with automatic writing and in 1924 he turned to Surrealism (see), for which he produced his frottages. Since then he has produced a collage novel, frescoes, décors for the theater, and has worked on Hans Richter's famous Surrealist film, *The Dreams That Money Can Buy.* (See illustration.)

Escorial Museum (at El Escorial near Madrid). A sixteenth-century palace and monastic establishment containing a considerable number of Spanish and non-Spanish paintings, including works by Titian, Zurbarán, and others.

Espinosa, Jerónimo Jacinto (1600-80). Spanish painter of Valencia. Espinosa executed numerous commissions during the heyday of the school of that city. He was outstanding among the many followers of Francisco Ribalta, on whom his style is based. He also shows some knowledge of the school of Bologna. Among his major canvases are the Communion of the Magdalene and the Holy Family, both in Valencia.

Esquivel, Antonio Maria (1806-57). Spanish painter. Pupil of F. Gutiérrez. He learned to paint religious pictures in the manner of Murillo and to make copies of Murillo for sale. He also produced genre studies of Spanish folkways. His best work, however, was in portraiture which he practiced in a rather tight, silhouetted manner. He painted both notables and simple family groups.

Estrada, José Maria (fl. mid-19th century). Mexican painter of the provinces whose works date from around 1830 to 1860. Renowned in his own time and since for the striking lifelikeness, directness and fresh charm of his portraits.

etching. A graphic process in which the copper plate is first covered with a layer of wax or other ground and the lines are drawn through this layer by a needle. Handled like a pen, the needle cuts through the surface material and exposes the metal, which is then "bitten" by the acid into which the plate is dipped for an appropriate period. The acid attacks only those portions of the plate which have been exposed by the needle, leaving unaffected the wax-protected portion of the plate. (See illustration.)

Etruscan painting. The Etruscans were an important early Italian people who appear to have come to Italy around the eighth century B.C. and presumably from a Greek-influenced part of Asia Minor. By the sixth century B.C. this vital group of farmers, merchants, fighters and pirates had won control of the central part of Italy, the section known today as Tuscany. Within their luxurious culture they developed the art of bronze sculpture, especially in portraiture, fine ceramics and very skillfully constructed aqueducts, sewers, forts, city gates and bridges, transmitting these various skills to their Roman successors. Interested in the life after death, like many other Asiatic peoples, the Etruscans built elaborate tombs whose walls, covered with impressive paintings, give us a concrete and detailed picture of Etruscan life. The bulk of these painted tombs date from the fifth century B.C. and reflect in a very clear way the contemporary pictorial style of ancient Greece (see GREEK PAINTING). Figures are ideally proportioned and generally calm in pose and three-dimensional in bulk. Perhaps as a result of the Oriental nature of the influence they underwent in their original Asia Minor home, this art tends to be decorative in its general effect, the colors unnaturalistically bright and the flowers flatly patterned. The greatest difference between this art and that of the Greeks proper lies in the generally morbid quality of its expression. This may be owing in part to the fact that it is a tomb art, but Greek grave figures are by no means morbid, nor are those of China. It would seem, rather, that the Etruscans, like the

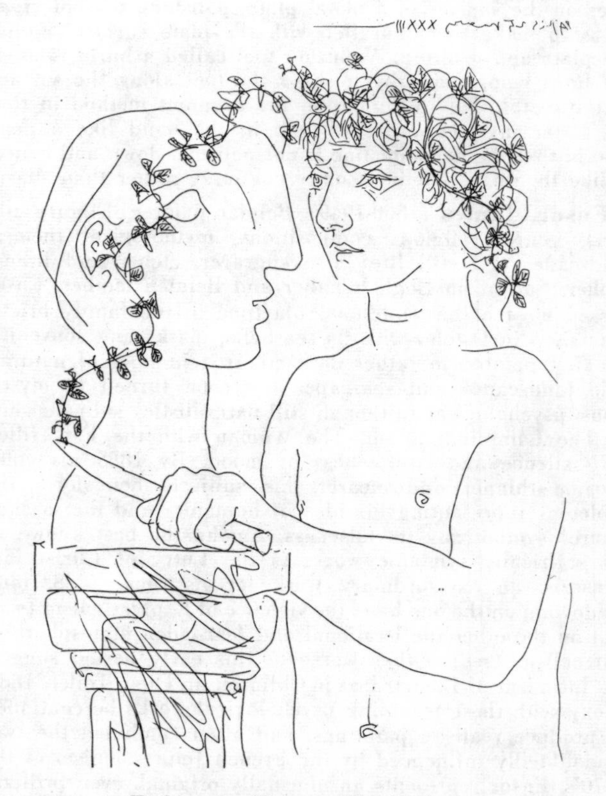

Etching by Picasso. The Sculptor
Valentin Gallery, New York

ETTY. The Bather at the Doubtful Breeze Alarmed
Tate Gallery, London

Assyrians, had something in their mental attitude that gave their pictorial art this melancholy quality. Ultimately the three-dimensional form and the seriousness of Etruscan painting appeared in the art of the Romans, who had by 280 B.C. overwhelmed Etruria. See ROMAN PAINTING.

Etty, William (1787-1849). British painter of nudes; very influential in Academy circles. He tried to express the rich warmth of flesh tones, the masses and curves of the nude form, which he called "God's most glorious work." He came to London in 1806 and was still attending the Academy life class in 1848. His home was a center for students to meet and discuss his kind of art. His conceptions were opposed by the Pre-Raphaelites, to whom his rather obvious carnality did not appeal. (See illustration.)

Euphronios (active c.500 B.C.). Greek vase painter of the late archaic period. Euphronios' workshop was important in the development of the new red-figured style of vase decoration. His broad treatment and humanization of forms can be seen in the Herakles and Antaios cup in the Louvre.

Eusebio da San Giorgio (1466/70-after 1540). Italian, Umbrian. A pupil of the Perugian Pinturicchio, he collaborated with his master and with Fiorenzo di Lorenzo. Several dated paintings by him are preserved in Perugia.

Eveleigh, Henry (1909-). Canadian painter born in Shanghai and educated in China and England; studied at Slade School, London, and Beaux-Arts, Paris. His work has a warm, mood-evoking Fauve manner suggesting the later landscapes of Derain.

Evenepoel, Henri (1872-1899). Belgian painter and printmaker born in France and brought up in Belgium. He went to Paris at twenty and after undergoing the influence of the Impressionists Lautrec and Steinlen, studied with Moreau (see). At Moreau's atelier he met the future Fauves but the mysticism of the teacher was decisive. Greatly varied in theme, Evenepoel's painting is particularly attractive in its rendition of children and adolescents, whom it handles with tenderness of mood and elegance of form. His colors are refined and subdued, tending toward grey, pink and ochre.

Everdingen, Allart van (1621-75). Dutch landscape painter. He visited Sweden while he was still a young man and this sojourn resulted in the introduction of Scandinavian scenery into Dutch painting. Many of his rugged views showing fir trees and turbulent waterfalls bear a strong resemblance to paintings by Jacob Ruisdael and have been wrongly attributed to the latter.

Evergood, Philip (1901-). Contemporary American Expressionist painter of social themes. His art is extremely varied, sometimes satirical, at others times lyrical, full of fantasy and complex social symbolism. Born in New York City, the son of a landscape painter, he was educated in England at Eton and Cambridge. He studied art at the Slade School, the Art Students League, the Educational Alliance and the Académie Julian. An extremely prolific painter, he has also been active in artists' organizations. (See illustration.)

Exekias (second half of sixth century B.C.). Greek vase painter of the black-figured style. His manner, strongly linear, shows a delicate mastery of the decorative possibilities of the vase, as well as a new attention to fullness of figure and anatomical detail. Fine examples of his compositional manner are the Dionysos cup in Munich and the Vatican vase which shows Ajax and Achilles at draughts. (See illustration.)

Expressionism. A type of painting, sculpture or graphic art (also literature, cinema and dance) in which the artist tries through suggestive distortion of form, color, space and other naturalistic qualities to destroy the external reality of a given situation and get at its "truth" or emotional essence. It is not descriptive or visual but analytical and internal, intended to penetrate the form or object so that the artist can

EVERGOOD. Lily and the Sparrows
Whitney Museum of American Art, New York

EXEKIAS. Greek vase, 6th century B.C. Dionysus Sailing over the Sea. Museum of Ancient Art, Munich

EYCK, HUBERT VAN. The Crucifixion and Last Judgment Metropolitan Museum of Art, New York

lose himself in it and thus identify with something greater or more powerful than himself. This projection may take the form of identification with the vastness of nature, a city, God, some monstrous being, a kindly animal or a simple peasant. Unlike the Impressionist with his interest in light and movement for their own sake, the Expressionist uses light for the sake of drama and to penetrate form, while movement serves to create emotional projection and a sensation of violence. Basically, then, Expressionism is emotive and soul-searching where Impressionism and Cubism are either descriptive or analytical. It is primarily a Central European movement emerging from Germany and Austria, but there are many non-Germanic Expressionists, e.g., Rouault. There are three basic types of Expressionism: the Brücke formulation stemming from Van Gogh, African sculpture and Fauvism which results in distorted but still representational and tangible forms; the Blue Rider or abstract variety, which stems more from Gauguin, Delaunay and folk art and results in a rhythmic, even musical expression in which form penetrates form and color penetrates color; and the Neue Sachlichkeit, or New Objectivity, which is representational but very intense in mood and clinical in detail. The Brücke artists include Kirchner, Nolde, Pechstein, Mueller, Schmidt-Rottluff; the Blue Rider group gives us Marc, Kandinsky, Klee, Campendonk, Jawlensky and, in certain respects, Feininger, among others; in the New Objectivity category are Otto Dix, George Grosz, the early Max Beckmann, and a number of lesser figures. Independent figurative or representational Expressionists in Germany

EYCK, HUBERT and JAN VAN. The Mystic Lamb. Cathédrale St. Bavon, Ghent

and Austria include Kokoschka, Klimt, Modersohn-Becker, and many others. Outside of this geographical area we find Rouault, Soutine, and Edvard Munch; the latter, along with Ensor and Hodler, marks the transition between Symbolism and Expressionism. Still another movement, known as Abstract Expressionism, has recently arisen in the United States; it may be described as a combination of Expressionism and Surrealism in their abstract forms with a touch of Dada. It includes Pollock, Gorky and a good many more.

ex-voto A kind of image in painting or sculpture that is designed to give thanks to God for past favors, usually of the miraculous kind, or to beg for present needs. These favors or needs often refer to illness or other calamity from which the person has been saved or wishes to be saved. Example: the retablos of Latin America.

Eyck, Hubert (Hubrecht van (c.1370-1426?). A problematic figure in Flemish painting, his existence is denied by some. Said to have been the older brother of Jan, little is known of his life except for several documents (1425-26) which list minor payments for pictures. Yet the disputed inscription on the Ghent Altar composed after his death by Jan calls him "the greatest painter in creation." The acceptance of his existence still leaves the problem of attribution, since no signed or dated works exist. The painting most commonly accepted as at least partly from his hand is the Ghent Altar in which he is believed to have painted the three large figures of the interior, the lower part of the central panel, and perhaps parts of the wings; the rest was completed after his death by Jan. He is also believed to have worked on the Turin-Milan Hours (1412-17). On the basis of the cited portions of the Ghent Altar, he would appear to be an archaic and slightly Italianizing fourteenth-century master, striving for a monumental grandeur. Other works which have been ascribed to him, though also to Jan and to Petrus Christus, are the Three Marys at the Tomb (private collection, Vierhouten), the Diptych and the "Petrus Christus" Annunciation (both Metropolitan), and the Crucifixion and the Madonna in a Church (both Berlin). He is traditionally said to have worked with Jan and with him to have invented the technique of oil painting, although the latter claim seems highly debatable. (See illustrations.)

Eyck, Jan van (c.1380/90-1441). One of the great masters of Flemish painting, he produced an art of cultured refinement, intellectual depth, and surpassing visual beauty. Developing out of the miniature tradition of the Boucicaut Master and the painting style of Broederlam, he was a realist who painted the world in all its detail and richness, who sought not the monumental, but a transfigured reality pervaded by complex and subtle symbolic meaning and expressed in pictorial terms of space and light. Born in Maaseyck, the records show that he worked as a miniaturist for the Duke of Bavaria, John of Holland (1422-25), and in 1425 began a service for the Duke of Burgundy, Philip the Good, which lasted until his death. In 1426-27 he was in Lille and in 1428 went on a mission to Portugal to paint a portrait of the Infanta Isabella, prospective wife of Philip. He settled in Bruges c. 1431 and as a cultured gentleman-painter was a highly esteemed member of the court. Efforts have been made to ascribe to him certain pages of the Turin-Milan Hours, executed (1412-17) for William IV, Duke of Bavaria, by analogy with early undated panel pictures in which the space dominates the small figures: for example, the Diptych of the Crucifixion and Last Judgment (Metropolitan), and the Crucifixion, the Madonna in the Church, and the Man with the Pink (all in Berlin). The earliest dated work, and obviously of his maturity, is the Ghent Altar, dated on completion 1432, and probably begun in 1427 on commission for Jodicus Vydt by Hubert and completed by Jan (now reassembled in St. Bavon, Ghent). In its attempt to assimilate

69. EYCK, JAN VAN. The Annunciation
National Gallery of Art, Mellon Collection, Washington, D.C.

FABRITIUS, CAREL. The Goldfinch
Mauritshuis, The Hague

the monumentality of Hubert, Flémalle, and Sluter to his own pictorialism, it marks a transition to his mature style. This altar of the Glorification of the Mystic Lamb has a grandeur of conception which may be due to Hubert. The other works of Jan's maturity are mostly signed and dated: the Tymotheos (1432), the Man with Turban (1433), and the Arnolfini portrait, 1434 (all in London); the Ince Hall Madonna (1433, Melbourne) and the Van der Paele Altar (1436, Bruges). Other works of this period not signed and dated but usually accepted are the Cardinal Niccoló Albergati (c. 1432, Viennà), the Tommaso Arnolfini (c.1434, Berlin), the Mellon Annunciation (c.1434, Washington), the Giustiniani Altar (c.1435, Dresden), the Rolin Madonna (c. 1436, Louvre), and the Madonna and St. Luke (c.1437, Frankfort). In the last years of his life his style became more austere, as in the unfinished St. Barbara (1437, Antwerp), the Madonna of the Fountain (1439, Antwerp), and his Wife Margaret (1439, Bruges). This phase is also shown in the unsigned Madonna with Carthusian, perhaps completed by Petrus Christus (c.1439, Frick Collection), and the St. Francis (Johnson Collection, Philadelphia), the Turin version of which may be a copy. His style was too subtle, intellectual and personal to achieve the popular effect and influence of van der Weyden's, and though he did have some influence he never created a school. (See illustrations, including color plate 69.)

F

Fabritius, Barent (1624-73). Dutch painter, the brother of the more gifted Carel Fabritius. He worked in Leyden and Amsterdam in his later life but passed his early years in Beemster. He was an imitator of Rembrandt and quite possibly his pupil. His style is strong but rather crude, yet many of his paintings so closely resemble Rembrandt's that they have often been ascribed to that master.

Fabritius, Carel (1622-54). Dutch painter; a pupil of Rembrandt in Amsterdam during the early 1640's. He later worked in Delft, painting exquisite works whose delicacy and finish foretells the achievement of Vermeer. The genre scenes that he is known to have painted and the decorations in elaborate perspective that he made for houses in Delft probably perished in a powder explosion along with their creator. His works are thus extremely rare today. (See illustration.)

Faes, Peter van der (see LELY).

Fairweather, Ian (1891-). Scottish-born Australian painter; a nomadic, romantic figure who first appeared on the Australian art scene in 1934 and soon became a legendary personality. Fairweather studied painting at the Slade School in London, abandoned a teaching job in Shanghai for a career in art, and has had various sensational adventures. Most of his art activities have taken place in Australia, where he is best known. The basis of his painting is Chinese calligraphy allied to a Western draughtsmanship and a sense of design derived from the art of primitive natives.

Falca, Alessandro (see LONGHI, ALESSANDRO).

Falca, Pietro (see LONGHI, PIETRO).

Falconetto, Gian Maria (c.1468-before 1540). Most prominent member of a Veronese family of painters, architects and decorators, Gian Maria worked in all these capacities. He executed frescoes in Verona (San Nazaro and the cathedral) and built several buildings and town gates in Padua. His painting style is affected by the local Veronese tradition, by Mantegna, and by his passion for the antique, especially in the representation of architecture.

Fan K'uan (see CHINESE PAINTERS: SUNG DYNASTY).

Fantastic art. A type of art in which wild, unrestrained imagination, fancy or even subconscious motivation is the projecting force of the image. It may vary from the paintings of Jerome Bosch to the works of Hans Baldung-Grien (in his late period), Hogarth, Blake, Ensor, Goya and Dali.

Fantin-Latour, Henri (1836-1904). French painter and graphic artist. Outstanding independent painter of the late nineteenth century. Constant associate of the avant garde artists of his day, Fantin-Latour stands apart from their styles. He was somewhat academic in orientation, devoting himself to strict artistic discipline and painstaking study of the Old Masters. His works are of three distinctive types. Most appreciated today, perhaps, are his still lifes and flower paintings. Typical Victorian decorative pieces, these are usually rendered with Flemish exactitude, but sometimes with a brío which recalls the contemporary work of his friend Manet. Of similar exactitude, but different in mood, are his group portraits. In tone and arrangement they suggest the influence of studio photography of the time with its sharp focus and greyish intermediate tones. Best known of these are Homage to Delacroix (1864), Studio in the Batignolles Quarter (1870) and Corner of a Table (1872). These remarkable historical documents feature important associates of Fantin-Latour and functioned as *allégories réelles*, presenting the symbolic mood of a group of mutually-dedicated intellectuals. A considerable number of Fantin-Latour's productions, largely lithographic, are allegories of mood based in a rather literary way on operatic works or musical performance. The technique here is a loose, suggestive chiaroscuro. The imagery, sometimes academic, frequently recalls the sentiment of his associates, the English Pre-Raphaelites. Characteristic of these is the Souvenir de Bayreuth, based upon his attendance at a Wagnerian cycle in 1876, and a series of bathers, nymphs and dancers. (See color plate 70.)

Faucher, Jean-Charles (1909-). Canadian painter trained at the Beaux-Arts in Montreal. He has developed a charming primitivist style utilizing everyday material.

Fauvism. Deriving from the French word *fauve* or wild beast; originally a derisive term applied to a group of painters in the first decade of this century, including Matisse, Vlaminck, Friesz, Derain, Manguin, Dufy, Marquet, Rouault and others. They were influenced by the Post-Impressionist work of Van Gogh, Gauguin, Seurat, Cézanne and Redon in the realm of rich color and architectonic form; these hues had in a measure been subdued during the 1890's by the Nabis (see) with their matte or subdued color effects on color-absorbing cardboard and their generally discreet Intimist (see) emotionality. In the early 1900's the trend begun by Post-Impressionism was taken up again: when the memorial exhibitions of Gauguin, Cézanne and other Post-Impressionists were held in those years, artists were ready for their message. Although early Fauve painting carries over some symbolic implications of the 1890's, e.g., Matisse's Joie de Vivre, it is more immediately affected by the large, bold, flat color areas of Gauguin with their decisive contour lines as well as by the color dissonances of Van Gogh. Matisse and Derain show this quite clearly in their work of 1905-06, while other members of the group and some followers, e.g., the early Braque, Vlaminck, Dufy, etc., incline more toward the fragmentative Van Gogh method. What interests all these painters, however, are the dynamic possibilities of color, its potentialities in setting the canvas into motion, but always within the compositional and formal limitations set forth by Cézanne and Seurat. It is not realism in the Impressionist sense but the essence of the form and color sensation of a given experience rendered in abstract and moving terms. Fauve work after World War I became more decorative and chic and less powerful and formal.

Fayum portraits. From the first four centuries of the Christian era we have a quantity of excellent painted mummy-portraits which were made in the Fayum, a province of Egypt settled largely by Greeks. The paintings were so vividly realistic that it is presumed that they were painted during the person's lifetime, hung on the wall of his home and later adapted to fit his mummy case. These are a continuation of the Pharaonic custom of placing idealized masks on mummy-cases, which would explain the disproportionate emphasis on the eyes as "the mirror of the soul." The fine sculptural modeling is, however, a decided break with the Egyptian tradition of painting (see). The painters represented the most unflattering of details and made readily recognizable the ethnic type of the sitter. These portraits were usually painted in encaustic (see) on wooden panels, but were sometimes painted directly on the linen shroud. (See illustration.)

Federal Art Project. Established in 1935 as part of the U.S. Works Projects Administration, this was a government program which, during the Depression, employed artists on the basis of financial need. The first attempt by the U.S. to sponsor artists on a large scale, it employed at its peak over 5,000 persons and produced more than 140,000 works of art; these were allocated to tax-supported institutions. The program allowed some artists to work on independent creative productions, but the vast majority engaged in such activities as teaching, photography, poster and graphic art projects, the preservation of national art treasures and monuments, and the execution of murals for public buildings. Among its far-reaching activities were the establishment of community centers and art galleries, and the compilation of the Index of American Design. The project was discontinued by Congress in 1939. It should not be confused with the Section of Fine Arts of the Treasury Department, which employed artists on the basis of merit.

Fei, Paolo di Giovanni (active c.1372-1410). Italian. Sienese. Pupil of Andrea Vanni and Bartolo di Fredi. Only two authentic works by this prolific master are known, a signed polyptych in the Siena gallery, and Saints Peter and Paul (1409) in the Hospital gallery, Siena. However, his characteristic style is found in a host of other panel paintings and they are attributed to him without question. Important among these are the Birth of the Virgin, Siena gallery, a Madonna in the Siena cathedral, a Madonna triptych in the Berenson collection, Settignano, and a Madonna Enthroned with Saints and Angels in the Goodhart collection, New York. His work is gay and charming, especially in color, and though a minor master he exerted considerable influence. He forms a link between the fourteenth- and fifteenth-century Sienese schools, was the master of Giovanni di Paolo, and strongly influenced Sassetta.

Feininger, Lyonel (1871-). American-born painter whose work may be generally related to the Munich Blue Rider school. Originally a brilliant violinist, he went to Germany

FAYUM PORTRAIT (EGYPT)
Graeco-Roman (2nd-2rd Century). Girl

in 1887 to study music, and there decided to become a painter. He studied both in Germany and in Paris and lived in Berlin for many years. He was associated with the magazine *Lustige Blätter* in Germany, *Le Témoin* in Paris, and the *Chicago Sunday Tribune* in the United States. In 1911, like other future Blue Rider painters, he came into contact with Delaunay's work in Paris, and in 1913 was invited by Franz Marc to show in the First German Autumn Salon. From 1919 to 1924 he taught at the famous industrial art school known as the Bauhaus (see) in Weimar, continuing with it when it moved to Dessau in 1925. In 1924 he formed, together with Jawlensky, Klee and Kandinsky, the exhibiting group known as The Blue Four. With the advent of Hitlerism, Feininger left Germany and since 1937 has been living in the United States. His relationship to the Blue Rider group may be seen in the generally lyrical character of his space penetrations; these are designed not as studies of form in the French sense but as creators of mood and as a means of breaking through surface reality toward an underlying truth. From a purely formal point of view, these paintings and watercolors may best be compared to the second or more abstract stage of Franz Marc's works; but Feininger's poetic quality, which is very high, is entirely his own. See also EXPRESSIONISM. (See color plate 71.)

Feke (Feak, Feake), Robert (c.1705-50+). Colonial American painter born in Oyster Bay, L.I. He was active in Newport, Boston, Philadelphia, and Long Island and was the leading portraitist between the death of Smibert and the emergence of Copley. According to tradition he was a sea captain who disappeared in 1750 and is supposed to have died in Barbados. Although he is said never to have had any formal training, his art shows a good deal of sophistication and elegance. His figures are stylized and dignified, his faces hard and rather empty, but he had a fine sensitivity for pigment and color, a consciousness of structure, and a notable skill in the handling of material. He left about fifty portraits, many of which are signed and dated, but some of which are still attributed to Smibert, Wollaston and John Hesselius.

Ferenczy, Charles (1862-1917). Hungarian painter and teacher; often referred to as "the Hungarian Manet." He studied abroad for many years and returned to Hungary to help found the art colony at Nagybanya. His style developed from a naturalism of the French academic type to a broader, more colorful manner under the influence of the clear and high-keyed painting of the latter part of the century.

Fernández (Hernández), Alejo (c.1470-1543). Spanish painter. Possibly of German origin, he worked first in Cordoba and then in Seville. He introduced to Seville the styles of Quentin Metsys and Giovanni Bellini, although it is not clear where he came by these influences. Much in the spirit of the time is the subject matter of his Virgin of the Conquistadors (Madrid), although its style is a bit archaic.

Fernández de Navarrete, Juan ("el Mudo") (c.1526-

70. FANTIN-LATOUR. Still Life. National Gallery of Art, Dale Collection, Washington, D.C.

71. FEININGER. Blue Coast. Gallery of Fine Arts, Columbus, Ohio

79). Spanish painter at the Escorial. Deaf from infancy on, he learned to paint in a Jeronymite monastery. He studied in Italy, apparently at the Florentine and Roman schools. Back in Spain he was hired by Philip II to work on the Escorial on the basis of his Baptism (1568). Only Spaniard to hold this honorable commission, he quickly developed an eclectic decorative style that embraced influences as remote as Michelangelo, Titian and Bosch. Nearly all the work we know today, such as his St. Jerome (1569) and the Martyrdom of St. James (1571), was done for the Escorial. Of his final project there, thirty-two large figures, he completed only eight, the rest being executed by Sánchez Coello and Carvajal.

Fernández Ledesma, Gabriel (1900-). Mexican painter, editor, stage designer and engraver. His best work is in the graphic arts. He is a connoisseur of the popular arts and edited the government art magazine *Forma.* He has done panels for the Hotel del Prado in Mexico City (1947). He has a realistic style with poetic overtones.

Ferrari, Antobello (see MELONE).

Ferrari, Defendente (active c.1510-35). A prolific Piedmontese painter born in Chivasso who worked mostly in Turin and for the Dukes of Savoy. He was possibly a pupil of Macrino d'Alba and Gian Martino Spanzotti, but his style was also influenced by the hard linearity of Gaudenzio Ferrari and by the atmospheric effects of Franco-Flemish art.

Ferrari, Gaudenzio (1471/81-1546). Provincial and popular Lombard painter of frescoes and altarpieces; born in Valduggia, trained in Vercelli under Martino Spanzotti, and active in Lombardy and Piedmont. His art shows the influence of Tuscan and Umbrian painting—Bramantino, Perugino, and even Leonardo through Luini. His anti-classical and Mannerist style is related to that of the Florentine Mannerists, but may be the result of a retarded dependence on earlier Gothic tendencies. In 1538 he settled in Milan.

Fête Champêtre by Giorgione (see).

72. FETI. Parable of the Sowing of the Tares
Worcester Art Museum

fêtes champêtres (Fr.). Rural or pastoral parties. Refers to the kind of painting in which people, often from the city, are shown against a rustic environment, sometimes with shepherds and their flocks. Such paintings are generally designed to convey a nostalgic, back-to-nature feeling. Example: Giorgione's Fête Champêtre (Louvre).

Feti (Fetti), Domenico (c.1589-1624). Italian painter born in Rome; a pupil of Cigoli, through whom he met Cardinal Ferdinand II Gonzaga, who became his patron. Before going to Mantua as court painter in 1613, he painted compositions with large figures and sharp contrasts of light and dark in the manner of Caravaggio. His second or Mantuan period exhibits a vacillation between the earlier Roman style and a new Venetian influence. Unfortunately his frescoes executed in Mantua are now destroyed. His last or Venetian period, from 1619 to his death in Venice, is under the domination of the late Venetian painters. He is most important for his small religious paintings of a genre nature, with small figures in landscapes, which he painted during this period and which were very popular at the time. In them there is a fusion of his earlier Roman naturalism with Venetian tone and color. (See color plate 72.)

FEUERBACH. Concert. National Gallery, Berlin

Feuerbach, Anselm (1829-80). German Classical Romantic painter. He studied for three years under von Schadow at the academy in Düsseldorf and then began a long series of journeys abroad. In 1850 he was a pupil of the academy in Antwerp and during the three following years worked in Paris under Couture. Then he went to Italy, and except for three years of teaching at the academy in Vienna, spent his last years in Venice. His style was one of the strongest of the nineteenth century in Germany. (See illustration.)

Fielding, Anthony Vandyke Copley (1787-1855). A British watercolorist whose landscapes were very popular during the nineteenth century.

Fiene, Ernest (1894-). Contemporary American painter born in Germany. An essentially conservative artist in the representational mode, he has tended more recently toward increased abstraction. He has done easel paintings, murals, lithographs, and etching in all genres. He studied art at the National Academy of Design and the Art Students League, and has worked abroad in France (1929) and Italy (1932).

Figari, Pedro (1861-1938). A leading Uruguayan painter; originally trained as a lawyer. He did many pictures of the life of the people, using a small format with the clear directness of folk art, vivid contrasts of color, and lush surface textures.

Fighting Téméraire, The, by Joseph Mallard William Turner (see).

Figueiredo, Cristóvão de (fl. 1515-c.1543). Portuguese painter and brother-in-law of Jean de Rouen (who founded a school of art at Coimbre in Portugal). In detail and refinement his work suggests that of the fifteenth-century French school while his sharp, almost anguished sentiment recalls the mood of the Flemish Rogier van der Weyden. He brought these qualities together in the special combination that characterizes the Mannerism (see) of that period. (See illustration.)

figurative. A term in art used to denote the degree of representational form evident in a particular work. It contrasts with non-figurative, which indicates the degree to which the work may move in a non-representational direction. Thus we may contrast the figurative quality in a Kokoschka (see) with the non-figurative quality of a Kandinsky (see).

Fiorenzo di Lorenzo (c.1440-1525). Italian painter, born in Perugia and appears to have worked there most of his life. His style, beginning in the manner of Bonfigli and Benozzo Gozzoli, forms a transition to the later decorative Umbrian style of Perugino and Pinturicchio. In mid-career he adopted some of the characteristics of Verrocchio and other Florentines. His only signed and dated painting is one of the Madonna and Saints Peter and Paul that forms the frame of a niche (1487, Perugia gallery). Associated with him or his shop (but possibly by the early Perugino or Pinturicchio) is a group of eight panels in the Perugia gallery representing scenes from the life of St. Bernardino. (See illustration.)

Fisher, Alvin (1792-1863). American portrait, genre, and landscape painter. Born in Needham, Mass., he became interested in painting while working as clerk in a country store. After some instruction, he became a portrait painter, but also did landscapes of farm and countryside. After a trip abroad, including copying at the Louvre, he settled in Boston and continued to paint portraits, genre, and the landscapes upon which his present reputation largely rests.

Flandes, Juan de (active 1496-1519). Spanish painter of Flemish origin. He served as court painter to Isabella from 1496 and worked in Palencia after her death. His pious, poetic style is seen in the miniature altar (now scattered in

FIGUEIREDO. The Holy Trinity
Soares dos Reis Museum, Oporto

private collections) he painted for her. He also painted a predella for the University of Salamanca and the high altar of Palencia Cathedral.

Flandrin, Jean Hippolyte (1809-64). French painter. Student of Magnin, Legendre-Héral and Duclaux, he developed an early enthusiasm for battle pieces. Under the influence of Ingres, however, he turned to decorative painting of history, studied in Rome and became enthusiastic about Raphael and religious subject matter. This latter interest, stimulated by contacts with the German Nazarenes, turned him to the Cinquecento and Giotto, and he developed a primitive classic style common in Ingres' circle. He also did portraits of women. He was prominent as a teacher. His religious wall paintings decorate St. Sèverin, St. Germain des Près, St. Vincent de Paul, St. Martin d'Ainay (Lyons) and St. Paul (Nîmes).

Flémal (Flémalle), Bertholet (1614-75). A Flemish painter. After training in Flanders he went to Italy (1638) and was employed by the Grand Duke of Tuscany. In Paris he did decorations for Marie de' Medici and was a member of the Academy. He was also in the employ of aristocrats in Liège and Brussels. His Mysteries of the Old and New Testament is in the Louvre. (See illustration.)

Flémalle, Master of (see Master of Flémalle).

Flinck, Govert (1615-60). Dutch painter of portraits and large historical compositions. He studied first in Leeuwarden and afterward was a pupil of Rembrandt. In the latter part of his life his works resembled those of the fashionable Van der Helst, Rembrandt's rival.

Florentine school. The longest-lived and in many ways the most influential of the Italian schools of painting. It ranges chronologically from the thirteenth through the early sixteenth century. The first stages of it take us from the Byzantine manner of the thirteenth century, exemplified by Coppo di Marcovaldo, to the more humanistic expression of Cimabue and Giotto in the early fourteenth century. The increased emotionalism and three-dimensionality of this new approach is continued by the pupils of Giotto during the latter part of the fourteenth century, e.g., Taddeo Gaddi, Bernardo Daddi and Giottino. The fifteenth-century Florentine School divided into two main groups: the monumentalists led by Masaccio, Castagno, Uccello, and other sculpturesque masters, and the lyricists led by Fra Angelico, Fra Lippo Lippi, Gozzoli and Botticelli. A more narrative and expository group includes such painters as Ghirlandaio. The sixteenth century or High Renaissance period of this school includes Leonardo da Vinci, Fra Bartolommeo, Andrea del Sarto and other painters of the serene, controlled and generalized tendency that marks this later stage.

Floris, Frans (de Vrient) (1516-70). Flemish painter and etcher. Member of an artistic dynasty of that name. Great enthusiast for Michelangelo, whose work he studied and emulated. Floris did much to spread the Italian Mannerist style in the Lowlands.

Fogg Art Museum, Cambridge, Mass. Although it was originally planned as a kind of laboratory for the Fine Arts Department of Harvard University and for the training of museum workers, the Fogg has built up an excellent col-

FIORENZO DI LORENZO. Miracle of St. Bernard
Pinacoteca Vannucci, Perugia

FONTAINEBLEAU, SCHOOL OF. The Birth of Cupid
Metropolitan Museum of Art, New York

lection of graphics, Old Master drawings and early Italian paintings.

folk art. A term used to describe the type of art produced by professionally untrained people in all parts of the world. It includes various painting media, sculpture, pottery, lacquer work, etc. In painting we find the work of the American colonial and post-colonial limner (see), the glass painters of Bavaria, the painters of retablos or miracle pictures in Mexico, and many other types. The other popular arts offer us such examples as early American carved figures on ships' prows, European wayside shrines, and American colonial pewter and brass work.

Fontainebleau, School of. The School of Fontainebleau represents at the same time the major style and the major project of French Renaissance painting in its beginnings in the sixteenth century. The origins of Renaissance painting in France, and in fact the foundation of France's modern industry of decorative arts, center in the personality and patronage of King Francis I (1515-47). In their desire to rival the cultural attainments of Italy, Francis I and his successors lavished much wealth on the Palace of Fontainebleau and through the importation of artists and works from Flanders and Italy re-activated the dormant French art of architectural decoration. The Fontainebleau style is actually not Renaissance, but Mannerist, deriving from followers of Michelangelo and Raphael who were drawn to France by attractive employment. The subjects are classical and allegorical, the forms elongated, anti-spatial and decorative in the Mannerist tradition, but with a special French elegance. Artists of the first period at Fontainebleau (c.1530-90) were mainly Italian, such as Il Rosso and Primaticcio, who successively supervised the king's projects. Among others was Niccolò dell'Abbate, an assistant. The so-called second School of Fontainebleau, beginning under King Henry IV (c.1590), featured more French artists, including Antoine Caron, Ambroise Dubois, and Toussant Dubreuil. This work is drier in quality, suggesting the influence of the Bolognese academicians and prefiguring the seventeenth-century traditions of Vouet and Poussin, both of whom had their origins in this milieu. Contemporary with the first School were famous court portraitists, usually of Flemish extraction, like the Clouets. (See illustration.)

Fontana, Prospero (1512-97). Born in Bologna, he was the most important Maniera (see) painter in Emilia. He studied with Francucci, was influenced by Raphael, Parmigianino, and Tibaldi, and worked with Pierino del Vaga in Genoa, Vasari in Florence and Rome, and Zuccari in the Villa of Pope Julius. His style is dominated by rhetorical emotion, ostentatious gestures and constricted space.

Foppa, Vincenzo (c.1427-c.1515). Born in Brescia, Foppa is regarded as the founder of the Milanese school, to which he brought elements from the art of Padua and Venice, especially of Squarcione and Jacopo Bellini. His later work was influenced by his contemporaries Andrea Mantegna and Giovanni Bellini. The soft and painterly handling in his early work gave way to a stricter and more dignified style including careful architectural and perspective rendering under the classical influence of Padua. Characteristic of his manner are morose and earnest facial expression and greyish flesh tones with neutral shadows. He worked in Milan for the Sforza family and became an honorary member of the ducal household in 1468. His earliest dated work is a Crucifixion (1456) in Bergamo, and later frescoes and an altarpiece are in the Brera. (See illustration.)

Forain, Jean Louis (1852-1931). French graphic artist and painter known for his subjects illustrating events from the legal, theatrical and political worlds. As a young man he was particularly interested in the art of Rembrandt for its handling of shadow; later he was influenced by the ideas and forms of Daumier and the drawing of Degas. The combination of these different influences give his characteristic graphics and paintings sharp light-and-dark contrast, a heaviness in forms, an emphasis on the problems of the little man and finally a lively sense of motion. Forain is at his best in the satirical etchings and lithographs on which his reputation is based. (See illustration.)

foreshortening. A technical device in drawing or painting through which the artist simulates the projection of an arm, leg or similar form out of the flat picture plane toward the spectator.

forgery. An attempt to reproduce an original work which is generally scarce or unique and consequently may have great monetary or other value. Forgery has been attempted by artists in all ages, as witness the traditional account of the attempt made by young Michelangelo to produce an ancient work of sculpture. This attempt, like many others, was based on the great desirability of the object forged. In modern times this has happened to the works of painters like Corot, which were extremely popular at the end of the nineteenth and the beginning of the twentieth century. A well-known and for a long time successful modern attempt at forgery was that made by the Hollander Van Meegeren in connection with Vermeer paintings which had been acquired by Hermann Goering, the Nazi Air Marshal. In recent years, the problem of expertizing, which has always been important, has involved modern technology, including a variety of scientific instruments and chemical tests.

Fortuny y Carbo, Mariano José María Bernardo (1838-74). Spanish painter of history and genre and etcher. Practiced an exacting type of anecdotal painting somewhat enlivened by a study of Goya. He died early but exerted great influence.

Fortuny y de Madrazo, Mariano (1871-). Spanish painter and etcher. Son of the Catalan Fortuny y Carbo (see). Self-taught through museum study, he was active in state

FOPPA. Madonna and Child
Metropolitan Museum of Art, New York

FORAIN. Sentenced for Life. Art Institute of Chicago, Winterbotham Fund

FOUQUET. Portrait of Charles VII. Louvre, Paris

FRAGONARD. Love Letters. Frick Collection, New York

scenery decoration, scenic illumination and portrait painting.

Foucquot, Jean (see FOUQUET, JEAN).

Fougeron, André (1913-). French painter, sculptor, color lithographer and decorative artist who works in a modern Baroque spirit. His style is related to the more violent recent Picasso works which in their strong linear divisions and powerful color give an impression of stained glass.

Foujita, Tsugouharu (1886-). Artist born and trained in Japan but has lived in France since 1913 and is associated with the School of Paris. His art is a synthesis of Oriental methods, which he had absorbed at the Imperial School in Tokio, and those of the Occident as represented by various contemporary European trends. His sensitive linear style is charged with an Intimist poetry of mood.

Fouquet (Foucquet), Jean (1420-1477/81). French painter to the court, active in Tours. Apparently a product of the Parisian miniature ateliers, Fouquet was in Italy between 1443-47 and is remarkable for the judicious use he made on his return of the innovations of the Italian school. In Italy his fame was such that Pope Eugenius IV commissioned a portrait from him. On his return to Tours he was employed by Charles VII, Louis XI and various court figures. He was appointed *peintre du roy* in 1475. Although there is a paucity of documentary references and indisputable works, it has been possible to assemble a group of fairly certain attributions by which to judge Fouquet's style. Best documented are the two volumes of miniatures for *Les Antiquités Judaïques* completed by Fouquet for Jacques d'Armagnac before the latter's execution in 1477. Earliest work by him is probably the Portrait of Charles VII (Louvre) in which the absence of Italianisms suggests a date before the Rome trip of the 1440's, although the epithet "*victorieux*" on the picture has suggested its connection with events of 1450-51. The works following Fouquet's return from Italy reveal a thorough understanding of Italian spatial and compositional devices as well as a delight in Roman architecture and ornament. These include a portrait of Guillaume des Ursins, a Book of Hours for Etienne Chevalier and the Diptych of Melun (now split). Both these Hours and the Diptych represent Etienne Chevalier presented by St. Stephen to the Madonna and Child. Agnes Sorel, mistress of Charles VII, is supposed to have served as model for the Madonna of the Diptych. There also exists a self-portrait in enamel (Louvre), a technique he presumably learned from his friend Filarete in Rome. (See illustration.)

Fragonard, Jean Honoré (1732-1806). Gayest and wittiest of the Rococo decorative painters of France. The ingratiating nature of his style is summed up in his signature, "Frago," a nickname. Fragonard's popularity was such in his day that when the Academic market lapsed, he was able to set up on his own and sell directly from his easel: a prototype of the emancipated artist. As a youth he was apprenticed first to Chardin and then to Boucher, developing great skill as an assistant to the latter. At the age of twenty-one he won the Rome prize with a composition called Jeroboam Sacrificing to the Idols, which was reminiscent of de Troy in style. The Rome trip proved a turning point. He learned to paint models with exactitude, but the Renaissance style struck him as gloomy, so he immersed himself in such latter-day Baroque painters as Baroccio, Pietro da Cortona, Solimena and Tiepolo. He turned out a prodigious quantity of wash and sanguine drawings of palaces, gardens, ruins and the like, rendered in a Baroque scale, peopled with Romantic genre. These studies resemble the work of Hubert Robert, in whose company many were done. These two artists were for a long time subsidized and entertained by the Abbé de Saint-Non, a wealthy amateur. For him they did many of the archaeological drawings and scenes with ruins which we associate with their styles. At this time Fragonard, already a master of many styles and a dexterous imitator, became practiced in etching.

On his return to France, Fragonard established his reputation by winning admittance to the Academy with a sensational diploma picture of the new classical type. More classical in story than in execution, the painting (the Sacrifice of Coresus) is billowy in manner and questionably erotic in intent. Purchased for the Gobelins, but not paid for, it marked his last effort as a painter of history. Fragonard turned to the amorous paintings and decorations for which he is best known. There flowed from his brush and pen a series of studies of feminine charms: lovers, kisses, clouds of cupids; beds, night gowns, pranks in the boudoir; nudes, semi-nudes, youthful Venuses—all of which make his master Boucher's love-play seem soberly Olympian. The Stolen Chemise (Louvre) and The Bathers (Louvre) are examples. The most obvious perhaps are those later done as illustrations for the *Contes* of La Fontaine. At this time he did numerous paintings and portraits in the "Spanish" style, which was being promoted by Mme de Pompadour herself. Of his decorative paintings the most famous are now in the Frick Collection, New York: Love Surprised, the Love Letter, the Crowning of Love, etc. They were first painted for Mme Du Barry's pavilion; rejected, they were taken by Fragonard to his own home in Provence. They are a perfect example of the cloudy Baroque flounces of his *fa presto* style, in which he drew tastefully upon the inventions of Murillo, Rembrandt, Boucher, Rubens and the Italians as needed. He took a second trip to Italy in 1773 in the company of his patron, the financier Bergeret (whom he had to sue to obtain payment). In that same period he married an artist and settled down to domesticity. This family life is revealed is his works. Frequent among his paintings were now a type of mawkish genre which appealed to the superficial moralism of pre-Revolutionary days. This tendency, also observed in Greuze, produced such pieces as the School Mistress (Louvre). The Revolution destroyed this world. However, protected by David, Fragonard survived as a functionary of the national museum and retired for a while to Provence. His effort to make a comeback in a market dominated by the style of David was a failure. (See illustrations, including color plate 73.)

Francesca or **Franceschi** (see PIERO DELLA FRANCESCA).

Francesco di Gentile da Frabriano (active c.1460-c.1500). Italian, school of the Marches. An eclectic painter known through eight signed paintings, he borrowed elements from Gentile da Fabriano (possibly his father and teacher) and from contemporary Venetian and Florentine masters.

Francesco di Giorgio Martini (1439-1502). Painter, sculptor and architect, one of the most important artists of the fifteenth-century Sienese school, and the only one whose reputation reached, like that of the great Florentine masters, beyond his own locality. Working as engineer and architect as well as painter, he traveled widely in Urbino, Calabria, Cortona, Naples, Milan and Pavia. In 1498 he was named directing architect of the Siena cathedral, and his most important sculptures are two bronze angels in the cathedral. The only architectural work certainly by him is the church of the Madonna del Calcinaio outside Cortona. He learned painting from Vecchietta, and had a joint workshop with his brother-in-law Neroccio di Landi until 1475, when he virtually abandoned painting for other pursuits. Two important dated altarpieces are in the Siena gallery. His painting style is charming and lyrical in the Sienese tradition, with some influence from the Florentine Antonio Pollaiuolo. (See color plate 74.)

Francheschini, Marcantonio (1648-1729). Born in Bologna, he studied first with Bibbiena and later with Cignani,

FRANCIA. Portrait of Federigo Gonzaga
Metropolitan Museum of Art, New York

FRANCIABIGIO. Portrait of a Young Man
Philbrook Art Center, Kress Collection, Tulsa

73. FRAGONARD. The Virgin with the Child in the Cradle (after "The Holy Family" by Rembrandt)
M. H. de Young Memorial Museum, San Francisco

whose most important pupil and assistant he was. He was a prolific decorator, extremely famous in his day, working for the Pope, kings, and cardinals.

Francia, Francesco (c.1450-1517). Real name Francesco di Marco di Giacomo Raibolini. An isolated artist in the relatively unproductive center of Bologna. He began his career as a goldsmith and as such was employed by the courts at Bologna and Ferrara. The earliest dated picture extant, a Madonna (London), is as late as 1492. His painting style began under the influence of Ferrarese masters, particularly Lorenzo Costa, with whom he formed a partnership in Bologna. An important early work is the Madonna with Saints and Donor (1494) in the Bologna gallery, which shows his dependence on Costa, but is softer and more sentimental in expression. After Costa left Bologna (c.1506), Francia adopted some of the characteristics of the Umbrian school (Perugino and the early Raphael), a development best seen in the Madonna in the Rose Garden in the Munich museum. He painted frescoes of the life of St. Cecilia in the oratory of that saint in Bologna in 1506. The Metropolitan owns a delicate portrait by Francia of the ten-year-old Federigo Gonzaga, painted for his mother Isabella d'Este when the child was sent to Rome as a hostage to the papal court. (See illustration.)

Franciabigio (Francesco Giudini or Giudici) (1482-1525). Florentine painter, perhaps originally from Milan. He was a pupil of Mariotto Albertinelli whom he imitated and was influenced also by Piero di Cosimo, but his style is most dependent upon his close friend, Andrea del Sarto, with whom he worked and shared a studio. They collaborated in the Chiostro dello Scalzo (before 1510), SS. Annunziata (1512), and the Medici Villa at Poggio a Caiano (1521). His fresco decorations are uninspired versions of the Florentine High Renaissance style with elements of Mannerism (see). However, his portraits of elegant, aristocratic young men are among the finest of the period. (See illustration.)

Francke, Master (active first half of 15th century). German painter. The only record of his name is in the commission given him in 1424 to paint an altarpiece for the chapel of the English pilgrims in Hamburg. On the basis of this work, now in the Kunsthalle at Hamburg, three other works have been ascribed to him: the altarpiece of St. Barbara, now in the National Museum at Helsingfors, and two paintings of the Man of Sorrows, one in the Kunsthalle at Hamburg, the other in the Museum of Leipzig. His style combines great decorative beauty with a serious interest in the representation of space. (See illustration.)

Frare (see BIANCHI-FERRARI).

Freake Master (act. 1670-80). Naive and untutored New

74. FRANCESCO DI GIORGIO MARTINI. God the Father Surrounded by Angels and Cherubim
National Gallery of Art, Kress Collection, Washington, D.C.

England painter, so-called after two portraits which he did of the Freake family (private collection on loan to Worcester Museum).

Fredenthal, David (1914-). Contemporary American painter born in Detroit. He studied at the Cranbrook Academy with Sepeshy and at the Colorado Springs Fine Art Center. He executed murals at the Detroit Naval Armory and the New York World's Fair, and served as a war correspondent for *Life*. He paints reality in a loose and fluid Impressionism.

Freer Gallery of Art, Smithsonian Institution, Washington, D.C. Devoted primarily to the arts of the Near and Far East as well as to the work of American artists. It has outstanding examples from China, Persia, Byzantium and Egypt as well as a choice selection of works by such painters as Whistler.

French, Jared (1905-). Contemporary American painter of meticulous realism with Surrealist overtones. Born in Rutherford, N.J., he studied at the Art Students League with Boardman Robinson. He executed murals under the W.P.A. and the Treasury Department.

Frenkel, Isaac (1901-). Russian-born Israeli painter who represents the figurative or representational Expressionist tradition of the Brücke school. His is a strong brooding style indicative of the sufferings he and his people have gone through in various sojourns and pilgrimages before arriving in their homeland. (See illustration.)

fresco painting. The term fresco refers to the ancient technique of "buon fresco" employed in mural painting (see), in which the painting becomes as permanent as the wall (or ceiling) on which it is executed. In fresco the pigment is mixed only with water before it is brushed onto the fresh, wet plaster of the wall. The brushing action disturbs superficially the film of lime on the plaster surface. The lime is incorporated with the pigment and, on drying, becomes the binder. The large size of mural paintings makes it necessary to paint them over periods of weeks, months, or even years, but each day's work must be completed in the three to six hours before the plaster hardens. It is difficult to match exactly one day's work with another's because of the color changes that occur during the drying stage when the plaster turns from the grey of the wet state to brilliant white. Therefore in the work of even the best artists it is often easy to pick out the day marks. If it is necessary to make a correction in any part of the dried work, the affected section must be chiseled out, replastered and painted.

The artist generally commences work at one of the top corners, then continues systematically back and forth across the wall until he finishes in one of the lower corners. This system bears no relation to the compositional or interpretative problems posed by the particular painting; these problems must be completely solved before the painting is begun. For this reason the work on the wall is usually preceded by unusually complete preliminary studies which include a full-sized cartoon (working drawing). The pigment is necessarily ap-

FRANCKE, MASTER. The Betrayal of the Shepherds
Helsingfors National Museum

plied in a thin layer, for any pigment that is not bonded with the lime will soon dust off. This limits both the darkness and the brightness of the color because some of the white lime always glows through the pigmented surface. Buon fresco as described above is particularly characteristic of Italy where it was used from the fourteenth century on as described by Cennino Cennini's *Libro dell'Arte* (written between 1396 and 1437). The history of Italian art is studded with the names of outstanding practitioners of this art form, including, among others, Giotto, Masaccio, Michelangelo and Raphael. Although it continued to be practiced during the succeeding centuries it had lost a great deal of its importance by the early nineteenth century. In our own time it has been revived in Mexico by such painters as Orozco (see) and Rivera (see).

Fresnae, Roger de La (see LA FRESNAYE, ROGER DE).

Freud, Lucien (1922-). British painter of portraits and still life. A grandson of Sigmund Freud, he came to Britain in 1932, studying later at the Central School of Arts and at Goldsmith College. During the early 1950's he was an instructor at the Slade School in London. His work, characterized by a high degree of finish, devotion to detail and extreme clarity of lighting, suggests analogies to various painters of the High Renaissance or to Dali in our own time.

Frick Collection, New York. The former residence of the industrialist Henry Clay Frick with its select masterpieces of painting and sculpture constitutes the Frick Collection. It ranges over the Italian (Titian, Giovanni Bellini), Spanish (El Greco, Goya), French (Manet, Fragonard, Boucher), English (Turner), and other important schools up to modern times. Like other collections of this type it represents the personal taste of its founder.

Frieseke, Frederick Carl (1874-1939). American Impressionist painter who spent most of his life in France. Born in Owosso, Mich., he studied in Chicago and New York, and abroad at the Académie Julian and with Whistler. His major artistic influence, however, came from Renoir.

Friesz, Othon (1879-1949). French painter and member of the Fauve group. Born at Le Havre and studied at the Lycée, where he met Raoul Dufy in 1885. The latter joined Friesz and Braque at the School of Fine Arts in Le Havre in 1895-96. Friesz won a scholarship to Paris the following year and there he met Matisse, Marquet and Rouault. He began as an Impressionist, then turned to Fauvism (see) which he practiced briefly, utilizing its color brilliance for his own artistic aims. These aims were firmly rooted in the art of the past and particularly that which allowed him to express his own robust enjoyment of life. His later works are lower in tonality but place greater emphasis on the formal structure of the composition and the three-dimensionality of the individual object. (See illustration.)

Frith, William Powell (1819-1909). British anecdotal painter who exhibited consistently at the Royal Academy, where several of his works where chosen "picture of the year." He was interested primarily in the kaleidoscopic aspect of crowds.

Froment, Nicolas (active 1450-90). French painter from Uzès in Provence. Froment, Charonton and the Master of the Avignon Pietà are the outstanding painters of the Avignon school in its heyday. Froment painted for King René of Anjou whose Italian campaigns brought the artist into the current of the Italian Renaissance. In 1461 he painted his triptych of the Raising of Lazarus. Now in the Uffizi, this painting exhibits a caricaturing realism probably derived from Flanders. Froment's other documented work is the Triptych of the Burning Bush (Aix-en-Provence) a complex and rare bit of late medieval allegory. Froment was more under Netherlands influence than were his two famous contemporaries, reflecting perhaps the taste of his patron, King René.

Fromentin (-Dupeux), Eugène Samuel Auguste (1820-76). French painter and literary figure. Best known today for his pioneering art criticism, *Masters of Past Time*, 1876, Fromentin traveled much in North Africa and painted Arab scenes, hunts and animal pictures. He also wrote novels, letters and famous descriptions of the Sahara. He sided with Delacroix against the Ingres school and in his writings extolled the virtues of Dutch and Flemish artists over the Italians. His style recalls Rubens and Delacroix, although in mid-career he reduced his colorism for a while under the influence of the tonal painting of Corot. In the Louvre are his Falcon Hunting in Algeria and Arab Women on the Banks of the Nile.

FRENKEL. The Holy Old Town of Jerusalem

FRIESZ. Landscape with Figures
Museum of Modern Art, New York

frottage. The French word for rubbing, applied to a special technique devised by Max Ernst for bringing out the suggestions of movement in such natural substances as a wooden plank or a flat rock, whose graining could be made to produce a visual effect. This is done by placing a sheet of paper on the surface of the object and running a stick of graphite over it to bring out the grain and other characteristics on the paper. This then constitutes a new artistic configuration with its own existence and reality. It can be made to suggest myriad things or be valued for itself. Frottage is important in the development of the Abstract Surrealist viewpoint.

Fry, Roger (1866-1934). British critic and painter whose great contribution lay in the introduction of Post-Impressionist art to England. From 1905 to 1910 he was Curator of Paintings at the Metropolitan. His viewpoint on the universality of artistic values is expressed in his *Last Lectures,* published in 1939. Other works include *The Arts of Painting and Sculpture,* 1932, and *Vision and Design,* 1924.

Fuhr, Xavier (1898-). German Expressionist painter not associated with any particular group. He became interested in painting after 1919, while living in Mannheim and Berlin. After World War II he settled in Regensburg; since 1946 he has been a professor at the Munich Academy. His highly individualistic art may be described as compressed and linear form filled with movement and color, showing a keen awareness of the modern methods of controlling space and using overlapping forms.

Fuller, George (1822-84). American Romantic figure painter, whose striving for poetic mood led at times to scenes of murky obscurity. This search for the sensitive nuance was characteristic of a group of American painters of the late nineteenth century, the period of Fuller's success. In the early years of this century his paintings brought record prices but his reputation has recently declined. Born in Deerfield, Mass., his early years were filled with struggle. After working in a grocery store, selling shoes, and working as a surveyor in the Mid-West, he became, together with a half-brother, an itinerant portrait painter in New York State. Later he studied with H. K. Brown, the sculptor, in Albany, the Boston Artists' Association, and the National Academy of Design. In 1859 he took a trip to Europe, where he met and was influenced by Hunt and Rossetti. He returned to Deerfield in 1860 and for the next fifteen years was a tobacco farmer, painting only in his leisure time. However, an exhibition of his paintings in Boston in 1875 was so successful that he turned again to full-time painting.

Fungai, Bernardino (1460-1516). A pupil of Giovanni di Paolo, Fungai was, like most of his Sienese contemporaries, an extremely eclectic artist. It is possible to discern in his work the influence of Pietro di Domenico and of the Umbrians Fiorenzo di Lorenzo, Signorelli and Pinturicchio. A typical early work is the Coronation in the church of the Fontegiusta,

FUSELI. The Nightmare. Goethe Museum, Frankfort

GADDI, AGNOLO. Madonna Enthroned with Saints and Angels
National Gallery of Art, Mellon Collection, Washington, D.C.

Siena; a late one, the Madonna Enthroned in the Siena gallery (1512).

Furini, Francesco (c.1600-46). Florentine painter who decorated a great many palaces and villas with nude figures in allegorical and mythological guise. His early work was under the influence of Rosselli, Allori, and Giovanni da San Giovanni; the later of Reni and the Venetians. He studied with his father, Filippo, among others, and worked with San Giovanni in Rome.

Fuseli, Henry Johann Heinrich (1741-1825). British painter and author; born in Zürich, Switzerland, but spent almost fifty years of his life in London. He became friendly with Reynolds, who encouraged him, but was most influenced by the work of William Blake. Although not a particularly original artistic personality, Fuseli had a very fanciful quality, an imagination with a macabre twist, and a strain of eroticism—all of which have made him one of the ancestral favorites of the Surrealist movement of our own times. In his own individuality he was widely influential, attracting many faithful friends and admirers, among them Mary Wollstonecraft and William Blake, who wrote a charming quatrain about him. (See illustration.)

Futurism. Dynamic machine- and war-glorifying movement in modern literature and art; launched by the poet Marinetti's Manifesto of Futurism (February 20, 1909) in the Paris *Figaro* and the following year by a manifesto of a group of young Italian painters including Boccioni, Carrà,

GADDI, TADDEO. Madonna and Child Enthroned with Saints.
Metropolitan Museum of Art, New York

Balla and Severini. This latter Manifesto of the Futurist Painters (February 11, 1910) associated itself with the rebellious ideals of the Futurist poets, i.e., against the cult of the past, for all forms of originality, and for an art that would "glorify the life of today, incessantly and tumultuously transformed by the victories of science." Thus their art was dedicated to violent movement or the simulation thereof. Through a choice of subjects derived from the hectic nightlife of their time and from their cult of speeding cars, trains, etc., they proceeded to paint elements that moved—such as wheels, legs and the like; thus the spectator received a sense of movement, as under Impressionism he received an impression of natural light. In addition, the Futurist painters fragmented their forms and with penetrating shafts of light endeavored to augment the feeling of dynamic motion. They also used color to convey the sensation of movement and this, together with the general feeling of excitement generated by their works, differentiated them from the Cubists.

Fyt, Jan (1611-61). Flemish painter. Pupil of Hans van der Berch and assistant to Frans Snyders. He is best known for his animals and still lifes done in the style of Snyders. After becoming a master in 1629/30 he traveled for some time in France and Italy. He was a busy painter and left the figures in his compositions to other artists. It is, however, now doubted that he himself ever worked with Rubens or van Dyck. He liked flecked, open painting; his compositions are more complex than Snyders', to whom he owes his color schemes. Fyt also engraved a number of prints of animals and landscapes. His paintings are in many museums. The Louvre possesses several of dogs with game.

G

Gabbiani, Antonio Domenico (1652-1726). Born in Florence, he studied in Venice with Susterman and Dandini, and in Rome with Ferri. He was an eclectic and academic painter, but very highly regarded, working in churches, monasteries, and palaces in northern Italy and in Vienna.

Gaddi, Agnolo (active c.1369-96). Italian, Florentine. Son of Taddeo Gaddi (see) and the last of the painters in the direct Giotto tradition. In 1369 he was called to Rome to paint frescoes in the Vatican, and is known to have worked in Florence and in Prato from 1394 to 1396. He died in 1396 while working at San Miniato al Monte in Florence and left unfinished in this church the only authenticated altarpiece by him. His principal work is a fresco series (c.1380) in the choir of Santa Croce, Florence, depicting the legend of the Holy Cross. His style, though dependent on Taddeo's, is an elegant, decorative and ornamental rather than a narrative one. (See illustration.)

Gaddi, Taddeo (active c.1334-66). Italian, Florentine. Probably the son of the mosaicist Gaddo Gaddi and famous as the most important personality to emerge from the school of Giotto. In 1334 he signed a small triptych of the Madonna (now in Berlin), and shortly after 1338 decorated the Baroncelli chapel of Santa Croce with frescoes of the life of the Virgin. In 1341 he painted frescoes (well authenticated but now damaged) in the crypt of San Miniato al Monte, and the following year in the choir of San Francesco, Pisa, of which only some figures in the vault remain. Between 1347 and 1353 he painted a polyptych in San Giovanni fuor Civitas, Pistoia, and in 1355 a Madonna (now in the Uffizi) for a church near Poggibonsi. Between 1359 and 1366 he was a member of the commission supervising construction of the cathedral of Florence. The most important of his works are the fresco decorations in the Baroncelli chapel of Santa Croce. Comparable to Giotto's frescoes in the Arena Chapel, Padua, they show Taddeo's interest in more complex

75. GAINSBOROUGH. The Painter's Daughters. National Gallery, London

patterns, livelier movement and more realistic detail, but less expressive and monumental interpretation than Giotto's. Taddeo was the father of the painter Agnolo Gaddi (see), and a close friend of the Umbrian mystic Fra Simone of Cascia, whose literary work parallels Taddeo's narrative painting and may have influenced it. (See illustration.)

Gainsborough, Thomas (1727-88). British portraitist and landscape painter born in Sudbury, Suffolk, the son of middle-class parents. A precocious boy, at the age of fourteen he was sent by his parents to London. There he seems to have had contact with Francis Hayman, from whom he may derive the English character of his early work—as well as his interest in having a good time. From Hubert Gravelot, the French illustrator and engraver (and friend of Hogarth), he may have derived at least in part his later Watteau-like feathery touch in landscapes. This London period resulted in little that was tangible and at the age of nineteen he was back home. Shortly afterward he married a young girl who had a private income and thereby solved his financial problems. They settled at Ipswich where Gainsborough was able to devote himself to painting portraits of the local gentry as well as landscapes for his own pleasure. In 1759 they moved on to the fashionable resort town of Bath and from this point on, portrait painting, especially of the well-to-do, became his main occupation, although landscape painting remained his real passion. In the country houses of Bath he came into direct contact, presumably for the first time, with the great portraitists of the past. It is from these masters that he learned the use of harmonious color, in particular the Rubens tradition as handed down by van Dyck in his many studies of seventeenth-century English ladies and gentlemen. He was also directly influenced by van Dyck's cool lights and silvery shadows and the silks and satins of the aristocratic sitters that artist had done so well. Gainsborough became very successful, sending many paintings to London to be exhibited and gaining a reputation there. In 1774 he returned to London, this time as a real rival to the famous Sir Joshua Reynolds, then at the height of his renown.

In London he established himself in a wing of the Schom-

GAINSBOROUGH. The Blue Boy (Master Jonathan Buttall)
Huntington Library and Art Gallery, San Marino, California

berg Palace in Pall Mall to receive his elegant clients. He soon became the favorite portraitist of the court and competed regularly with Reynolds at the Academy exhibitions, the latter becoming extremely jealous of his success and brilliant manner. From this period dates his study in blue tonalities, The Blue Boy, a portrait of Master Buttal. Gainsborough had joined the Academy as a founding member in 1768 but broke with the group in 1784 in a quarrel over the hanging of his pictures. The differences with Reynolds were only resolved at Gainsborough's death bed. Although he thought of his portrait work as so much "potboiling," the fact remains that these gracious and charming works, which tell us far more of the personality of the painter than the sitter, have a skill in handling, especially in the atmosphere and the fabrics, that places his art on a very high level. The color harmonies, here and in the landscapes, show a resolution of the problems involved and a final attractiveness that makes him part of a continuous chain leading from Rubens through Watteau and Gainsborough himself, and finally to Renoir. As for the landscapes proper, his real love, they are filled with an atmospheric warmth and poetry unique at the time, although parallel in cultural significance with the work of other landscapists of the period in England. In these works, as in his rustic genre scenes, we feel the relationship with Watteau in the fuzzy quality of the foliage and the blending of the figures with their backgrounds. Above all it is the sense of unreality with which he permeated many of these scenes, especially those done in later life, that relates him to the great French master. (See illustrations, including color plate 75.)

GALLEGOS, FERNANDO. Christ in Benediction
Prado, Madrid

Galgario, Fra (see GHISLANDI, VITTORE).

Gallegos, Fernando (c.1440-after 1507). Spanish painter. Born in Salamanca, active in the early Castilian school. He worked in oils and was strongly influenced by Dirk Bouts and van der Weyden. His earliest work which we know is the altarpiece of Saint Idelfonso in Zamora Cathedral. This shows a knowledge of the prints of Schongauer which were sold in Castilian fairs. Fernando's style was realistic and sculptural in the Flemish fashion with a frequent note of intense melodrama, viz., the Calvary (Weibel Collection. Madrid). There is also a signed triptych by him in the New Cathedral, Salamanca. Also active in Salamanca was a Francisco Gallegos who may have been a relative. (See illustration.)

Gallegos, Francisco (active c.1500). Spanish painter of Castille. Perhaps a relative of Fernando Gallegos with whom he is often confused. Executed the Altarpiece of St. Catherine in the Old Cathedral of Salamanca in 1500.

Gallén-Kallela, Akseli (1865-1931). Finnish symbolist painter who is today known primarily for his membership in the Brücke group of German Expressionists in Dresden. From 1906 to 1908 this linear and expressive painter, who was very much concerned with the mythology and spirit of his own country, was represented by graphics in the Brücke albums put out for the benefit of friends or subscribers to that organization. After this period Gallén-Kallela's art became less linear and more colorful in a half-Impressionist, half-Fauve manner. (See illustration.)

Galque, Adrián Sánchez (early 17th century). Spanish-Colonial Ecuadorian painter; first of a long line of School of Quito artists; teacher of Miguel de Santiago. His best known picture shows the first three Negroes who came to be baptized in 1598. Like other members of this group Galque's style is naturalistic and emotional.

Gambara, Lattanzio (c.1530-c.73/74). Born in Brescia, he studied there with Antonio Campi and went with him to Cremona. In 1552 he returned to Brescia, studied with Romanino and married his daughter. A prolific and skillful painter, he was active also in Parma, Asolo, Mantua, Bergamo, Salo, and Frontignano, but most of his works have been destroyed.

Gandara, Antoine de la (1862-1917). French painter. Also noted for his drawings, etchings, lithographs and pastels. De la Gandara specialized in portraits which he rendered in a tonal, modish style. He painted still lifes and views of Paris.

Garbo (see RAFFAELLINO DEL GARBO).

Garofalo, Benvenuto Tisi da (called Il Garofolo) (1481-1559). Born in Ferrara, he studied with Panetti but his early work is largely influenced by that of Boccaccino with whom he may have worked (1499). In his middle period he was a follower of Raphael, whose art he had studied in Rome. He showed an early interest in landscape and absorbed some influence from Giorgone, and in his last phase was dependent on and collaborated with Dosso Dossi.

Gaspard-Poussin (see DUGHET).

Gatch, Lee (1902-). Contemporary American painter whose art is a stylization and abstraction of reality. Born in Baltimore, he studied at the Maryland Institute and abroad with Lhote and Kisling. His early easel and mural paintings were realistic.

Gatti, Bernardino (called Il Sojaro) (c.1495-1575). Born in Pavia, he was active there as well as in Piacenza, Cremona, and Parma. He did his most important work—decorations in the Madonna della Stecatta (1560-70)—in Parma. His style is an amalgam of elements from many painters, including Raphael, Correggio and Pordenone.

Gauguin, Paul (1848-1903). French Post-Impressionist painter and graphic artist whose work was of tremendous importance in the formulation of various early twentieth-century schools: the Fauves in his own country and the Blue Rider painters of Germany. In his own time he belongs to the more intuitive side of Post-Impressionism (see), that is to the Symbolists and Nabis among others. Gauguin's father was a journalist, his mother a propagandist on the liberal side. The family left France for Peru when Louis Napoleon seized the throne in 1851, the father dying en route. Gauguin entered the merchant marine in 1865, making several trips to Rio. In 1871 he entered the stockbrokerage business and began to do very well. Two years later he married a Danish girl and also began his artistic career, painting as an amateur and starting to collect Impressionist works. In 1876 one of his pictures was accepted at the Salon. He became friendly with Pissarro in 1879 and under his influence joined the Fifth Impressionist Exhibition and the Sixth in 1881. By 1883 Gauguin who had already abandoned his family decided on painting as a career and left the stockbroker's office. The following year, visiting his wife's family in Denmark, he was unable to find exhibiting facilities or to get along with the Danes; he returned to Paris with his son Clovis in 1885, worked as a billsticker and suffered extreme privation. His first stay in Brittany (at Pont-Aven) was from June to November 1886, presumably in search of primitive and unspoiled people. In 1887 he took a trip to Panama, and the following

GALLÉN-KALLELA. Self Portrait. Finland

GAUGUIN. Self-Portrait. National Gallery, Washington, D.C.

76. GAUGUIN. Under the Pandanus. Minneapolis Institute of Art

year stayed again at Pont-Aven and began his so-called Synthetism (see) or Cloisonnism, consisting of the arbitrary rearrangement of what the artist sees into a synthetic or artificial rather than natural representation (i.e., a controlled rather than naturalistic projection). Technically this is accomplished by transforming the local color of an object into a powerful color image, in which the most characteristic color is exaggerated into a broad flat area bounded by heavy black outlines or cloisons, as in enamel work. 1888 was also the year of his first one-man show (arranged with the help of Théo van Gogh) and of a visit to Vincent at Arles which ended unhappily for both. At the World's Fair in 1889 Gauguin experienced Javanese art; he also moved away from Pont-Aven, which was becoming tourist-infested, to Le Pouldu in Brittany. Here his art took on its final and definitive form, which did not change even after his emigration to the South Seas. One of the great works of this period is the Yellow Christ with its simplification of form, its intensification of the local or immedate color of the objects shown, and the reducton of landscape to a series of related tonalities and interrelated curves moving gracefully across the surface of the canvas. By 1891 Gauguin's poverty and lack of success in Paris made him decide to leave the country and go to Tahiti where he first stayed from 1891 to 1893, painting such significant works as Ia Orana Maria and Ta Matete. But with no money coming in and ill, he returned to Paris; there a show organized at the suggestion of Degas was a financial failure although important in its effect on such painters as Bonnard, Vuillard and others of the Nabi group.

Feeling that life in France had little to offer, Gauguin returned to Tahiti in 1895 where, after a fruitful period of work but also of great suffering resulting from disease and lack of understanding on the part of the local French, he died in 1903. The example of his life in seeking out primitive, unsophisticated and unspoiled peoples, as much as his feeling for the emotional and symbolic power of color, are ultimately the chief contributions of this unusual personality and artist. Within a few years after his death, Gauguin's art was a great influence on the modern scene and his personal solution of the problems of modern civilization was a kind of escape that many tried to achieve. See also ART NOUVEAU, SYMBOLISM. (See illustrations, including color plate 76.)

Geertgen tot Sint Jans (c.1465-c.1495). Dutch painter. Geertgen, who came from Leyden and seems to have worked in Haarlem, is one of the first Netherlands painters to show strongly those characteristics of style which we customarily regard as Dutch. He is said to have been the pupil of the Haarlem painter Aelbert van Ouwater and his work shows that he was also familiar with the paintings of the Flemish artists van der Weyden and van der Goes. His landscapes are extraordinarily advanced for the age, and his religious scenes demonstrate an interest in spatial relations which make them exceptional in their time. (See illustration.)

Gelder, Aert de (1645-1727). Dutch painter from Dordrecht. He studied with Samuel van Hoogstraten. During the last decade of Rembrandt's life Aert de Gelder spent about six years as his pupil, and thus carried on into the eighteenth century the broad, freely brushed character of Rembrandt's final style. His interpretatious of subject matter were always

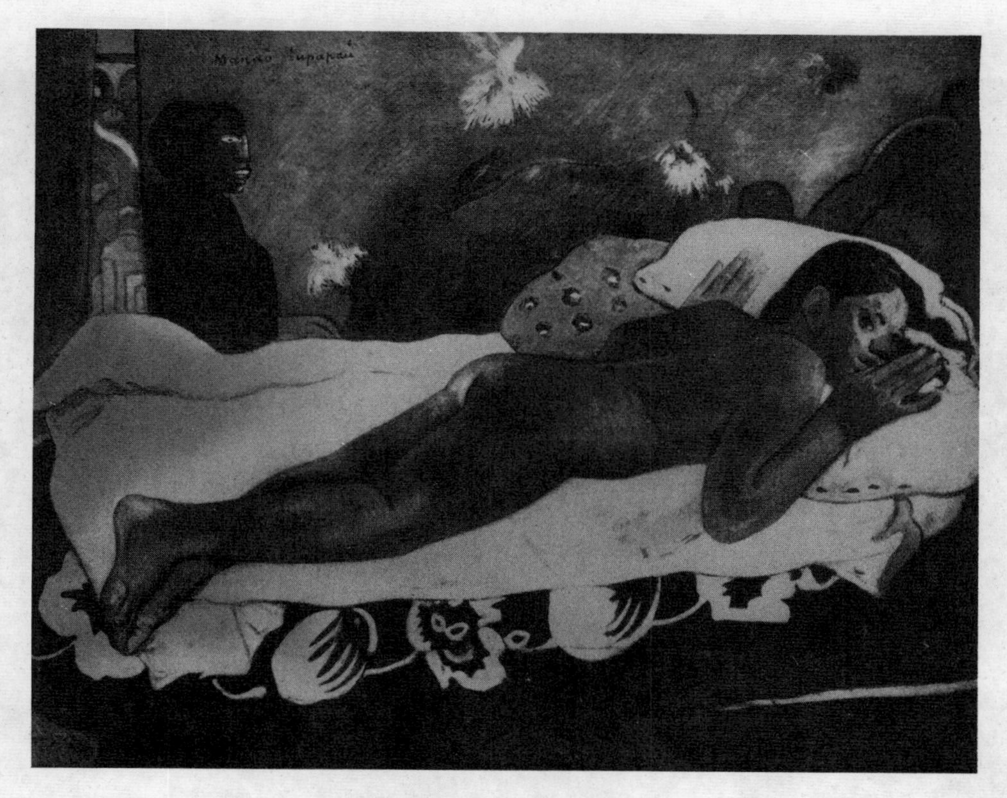

GAUGUIN. The Spirit of the Dead Watching. Collection A. Conger Goodyear, New York

vastly inferior to those of his master, lacking Rembrandt's psychological penetration and understanding of personality.

Gellée, Claude (see LORRAIN, CLAUDE).

Gennari, Benedetto II (1633-1715). Italian late Baroque painter born in Cento. He studied with his uncle, Guercino and, after going with his father to Bologna in 1649, worked in many churches and palaces. In 1672 he was in Paris as court painter to Louis XIV and in 1674 took a similar post with the Stuarts in England, following them into exile in St. Germain in 1688. He returned to Italy in 1690 and was active in Bologna, Cento, and vicinity. His early style was dependent upon the lyrical classicism of Guercino, his later closer to the more dramatic Baroque of Reni. He is equally well known for his portraits.

genre. The French word for kind or sort; it was first used in connection with painting during the eighteenth century, being applied to works with all kinds of subject matter, i.e., *de tout genre*. More specifically it refers to subjects taken from everyday life. Genre first reached its apogee in the art of seventeenth-century Holland, as in the commonplace themes of Vermeer, Hals, Steen, and many others. During the eighteenth century the works of such painters as Chardin (see) represent an extension of this kind of subject. American and other nineteenth-century examples of genre include such painters as Bingham, Mount, Daumier, and Courbet among many others. In our own century, the Ashcan School (see) of New York, and the U.S. regionalists of the 1930's (e.g., Curry, Benton and Wood) exemplify a latter-day application.

Gentile da Fabriano (c.1370-1427). Italian, Umbrian. Born in Fabriano of an old family, he was a well-established painter by the time he appeared in Venice in 1408. We know next to nothing about his earlier life and must assume that his art was learned in Fabriano, perhaps under the lingering influence of Allegretto Nuzi (died 1373/4) who brought

**GEERTGEN TOT SINT JANS. The Nativity
National Gallery, London**

78. GENTILESCHI, ARTEMISIA. Judith and Holofernes. Detroit Institute of Arts

Sienese and Florentine styles to Umbria in the mid-fourteenth century. Gentile traveled a great deal, and his cosmopolitan but still Gothic and poetic style was known to artists in many centers in the early fifteenth century. From 1408 to about 1414 he is recorded at work in Venice on frescoes for the Doge's palace. Nothing remains of this work, nor of his other fresco commissions, except for a fragment of his late work in the Orvieto cathedral. Between 1414 and 1419 he worked in Brescia, decorating a chapel for Pandolfo Malatesta. In 1419 he was called to Rome by Pope Martin V, but appears not to have stayed long, if indeed he got there at all. In 1420 he visited Fabriano, and in 1421 and 1422 was registered in the two guilds to which painters belonged in Florence. 1423 is the year of his most famous work, the Adoration of the Magi ordered by Palla Strozzi for a chapel in the church of Santa Trinità in Florence (now in the Uffizi). This painting is signed and dated, and shows in its most characteristic form the so-called International Style as it was practiced in Italy. In a crowded scene, elegantly dressed kings with their extensive retinue adore the infant Christ in the foreground, while the retinue continues into the distance which comprises wooded slopes and walled towns with a very high horizon. This setting is full of animals, birds and flowers painted in careful detail. The only other major signed and dated work by Gentile is the altarpiece of the Quaratesi family painted in 1425. The central panel of this work, representing the Madonna and Child, is in Buckingham Palace, London; the wings, with pictures of four saints, are in the Uffizi, and the predella panels representing miracles of St. Nicholas are in the Vatican gallery. Gentile was in Siena in 1424 and 1425, in Orvieto in 1425, and in 1427 died in Rome, where he was painting frescoes for San Giovanni in Laterano. This work was later finished by Pisanello but has since been destroyed. Many panel paintings are in picture galleries and private collections throughout Europe and America. Gentile's lyrical and poetic style has much in common with that of painters like Simone Martini and Lorenzo Monaco but is more richly ornamented and more naturalistic in detail. His facial types and Gothic fall of drapery even suggest a relationship with French and German manuscript illustration of the fourteenth and early fifteenth centuries. The influence of his art was felt throughout Italy; it is particularly notable in the work of Pisanello, who may have worked with him as a boy in Venice on the frescoes of the Doge's Palace. He was the teacher of Jacopo Bellini. See INTERNATIONAL GOTHIC STYLE.(See color plate 77.)

Gentileschi, Artemisia (Artemisia Lomi) (1597-after 1651). Daughter of Orazio, she was born in Rome and studied with her father and his friend, Agostino Tassi. Active in Rome, London, and Naples, she belongs to the later circle of Caravaggisti, and was Caravaggio's champion in Naples where she worked at the same time as Ribera, Domenichino, and Lanfranco. Her violent style with its brilliant rather than dark color scale, coarser than that of her father, had an important influence on Neapolitan painting. (See color plate 78.)

Gentileschi, Orazio (Orazio Lomi) (1565-1638). Born in Pisa, he studied with his brother, Aurelio, a pupil of Bronzino. At the age of seventeen he went to Rome, where he worked for the popes Sixtus V, Clement VIII, and Paul V. He was a close friend of Caravaggio and shared with him the broad and serious treatment of religious themes and the humanization of miracles and mysteries in the manner of the early Baroque. His closest connection is with the earlier lyrical style of Caravaggio and his art is characterized by clarity and simplicity, a Tuscan linear elegance, and a feeling for color and material. Nine years older than Caravaggio, he may even have influenced him. In 1620 he left Rome for Ancona and Fabriano; then went to Genoa (1621-24), where

77. GENTILE DA FABRIANO. Madonna and Child
National Gallery of Art, Kress Collection, Washington, D.C.

79. GÉRICAULT. Head of a Negro.
Albright Art Gallery, Buffalo

he met van Dyck and worked for Carlo Emanuele of Savoy; in 1625 he was in France working for Marie de Medici; and the following year he became court painter to Charles I in England and finally settled there permanently.

Gerard of Haarlem (see GEERTGEN TOT SINT JANS).

Géricault, Jeau Louis André Théodore (1791-1824). Influential young painter of early nineteenth-century France. His great promise and early death have left critics uncertain whether he should be considered the Romantic predecessor of Delacroix or a Realist anticipating Courbet. His career as a painter lasted less than fifteen years, during which he produced a remarkable quantity of work. This tremendous energy, like that of his idol Michelangelo, seldom carried through to the completed painting, but expressed itself in sketches and unfinished experiments. Horses were an obsession with Géricault (finally leading to his death) and his greatest canvases were usually of riders. Although Géricault was the first to break decisively with the school of David, he was complimented by the latter at his first Salon. He also visited the exiled David in Brussels.

Géricault studied with Carle Vernet and with Guérin, during which time he produced sculptural drawings of Michelangelesque type. So he surprised his master and the Salon of 1812 with a Baroque painting of the Officer of the Imperial Guard (Louvre) that seems to derive from a motif of Giulio Romano's. More battle paintings followed, including the Wounded Cuirassier (1814, Louvre), and, carried away by his enthusiasm, he joined the Bourbon Musketeers in support of the Restoration. In 1816, presumably because of a love-affair, Géricault went to Italy. During his three-year stay he studied and copied the Masters and antique art. The Poussinesque study of the Riderless Horse Race (Louvre) is characteristic of that phase.

Upon his return he painted his most famous single canvas, the Raft of the Medusa (1819, Louvre), and thereby associated himself with the Romantic cry for emancipation and reform. In a scandalous incident the seamen of the wrecked transport Medusa had been set adrift on a raft in the Mediterranean. Géricault was involved with the pamphlets that rocked France in protest to the government, and he carefully prepared a painted memorial to the cause. He constructed his history painting by the most exacting study: questioning survivors, drawing corpses, studying atmosphere and launching a trial raft on the sea. There followed a long series of compositional sketches in line and wash, evolving finally the rocking pyramid which he used. Amidst a stiff breeze and general excitement the hero, a Negro, climbs to the peak of a knot of human bodies and waves at a ship, small on the horizon. The colors were murky, the poses histrionic, but the effect electric. Official circles were not too pleased, however, and Géricault was persuaded to send the canvas to England where it earned him considerable money as a traveling exhibit.

It was in this connection that Géricault visited England in 1820 with Charlet (see) and initiated a new period in his life, with new enthusiasms. As a result of political events England was at this time separated from France by more than the Channel, and Géricault was slow to warm to its art. However, he slowly became absorbed in the English landscape, genre and watercolor paintings, and he abandoned his own dramatic manner for a more matter-of-fact one. Best known are his scenes of horse-races based on the English sporting print. The sculptural effect of his former style was converted into crisp silhouettes, organized in flat patterns of chiaroscuro. The whole structure became a more painterly one. The Derby at Epsom (Louvre) is a good example. He began to sketch the plight of the working man, the horrors of the slave trade, thus intensifying his own social consciousness, which he had earlier demonstrated in the Raft of the

GÉRICAULT. Raft of the Medusa. Louvre, Paris

Medusa. That his English enthusiasms were carried back to France we can see in the stolid genre character of the Limekiln (1824, Louvre). After his return he was commissioned by Dr. Georget of the Salpetrière hospital to make physiognomic studies of the insane. This project apparently fascinated him for both its realism and for its study of nonconformist personality. The paintings, e.g., the Assassin (Ghent), are among his best. On the whole, however, his last years were unhappy ones; he died in 1824 at the age of thirty-three of complications resulting from a fall from a horse. (See illustrations, including color plate 79.)

Gerini (see LORENZO DI NICCOLO GERINI and NICCOLO DI PIETRO GERINI).

Gerôme, Jean Léon (1824-1904). French painter, sculptor and engraver. He emerged as a famous academician with his Cock Fight (Salon of 1847) and perpetuated the dry style of his teachers, Delaroche and Gleyre. He traveled in the Near East and produced a series of Oriental genres and figure studies. But his main interest was in the romantic archaeological past—exemplified by his paintings of gladiators: Thumbs Down and "We who are about to die, salute you." In his period of success he was a controversial figure in the debates between progressive and conservative critics. Amongst his sculptures is an equestrian statue of Bonaparte (Luxembourg).

gesso painting. Much painting, especially in ancient and medieval times, was carried out on a ground prepared with gesso (plaster of Paris). This was particularly true of painting in the middle ages when the gesso (white chalk in glue) was applied to the surface of a carefully selected wooden panel in several smoothed coats, producing an excellent white mat surface for tempera pigments (see). A mural surface can also be prepared for painting by coating it with gesso, although the bond is not as permanent as in fresco painting (see). Gesso grounds are used on canvas, here applied in aqueous solution; however, this technique frequently leads to flaking or all-over crackling. Gesso may also be built up and modeled before being painted or gilded, as in panels of the Spanish Gothic schools.

Gestel, Leo (1881-1941). Netherlands Expressionist painter. Like many of his contemporaries, he followed a good many different styles before arriving at his own. Studies of Cubism enabled him to produce highly disciplined figures in which powerful color is subdued. Contact with the Belgian Expressionists added an emotional component to his later favorite subjects: workmen, horses and nudes. His influence in Holland has resulted in the so-called School of Bergen.

Ghirlandaio, Benedetto (1458-97). Italian, Florentine. Younger brother and collaborator of Domenico Ghirlandaio (see). He and a third brother, Davide, took part in many of the large fresco commissions of their more famous brother, and the singling out of Benedetto's hand is a controversial matter. He began as a miniature painter but gave up this activity on account of weak eyesight. He made a short trip to France in 1494, and his only signed picture (badly damaged) is in a church in the Auvergne district.

Ghirlandaio, Davide (1452-1525). Italian, Florentine. Probably an even closer collaborator of Domenico Ghirlandaio (see) than his brother Benedetto. He may have had early training from Castagno and Verrocchio, but like Benedetto he was a weaker painter than Domenico and quickly adapted himself to Domenico's style when he became a member of the shop (c.1470). Davide was also a mosaicist; a mosaic of the Madonna, signed by him, is in the Cluny Museum, Paris.

Ghirlandaio, Domenico (1449-94). One of the most prolific fresco painters of the late fifteenth century in Florence, he sums up the trend throughout the century toward realism of figures, settings, landscape and details. His art is competent and self-assured, but is somewhat pedestrian and impersonal in character when compared, for example, to that of his contemporary Botticelli. He maintained a large workshop, including his brothers and other artists (such as Mainardi) well known in their own right and his extensive fresco commissions were executed with their assistance. He was born Domenico di Tommaso Bigordi and received his training under Baldovinetti and, it is assumed, Verrocchio. The influence of both these masters is evident in his early work, especially in his first major fresco project (about 1470) in the church of Sant' Andrea at Brozzi, near Florence. Besides a few important altarpieces (in Pisa, Lucca, and the Uffizi and Santa Trinità at Florence), his entire life was taken up with fresco commissions in Florence and nearby towns, and at Rome. Their chronology, after the work at Brozzi, is as follows: 1472-3, a Madonna of Mercy and the Lamentation, Vespucci chapel, church of the Ognissanti, Florence; 1475, scenes from the life of S. Fina, Collegiata, San Gimignano; c.1475, decorations with philosophers and prophets (fragmentary), Library of Pope Sixtus IV, Vatican; c. 1476 damaged fresco of the Last Supper, Badia of Passignano, near Florence; 1477-78, lost decoration of the Tornabuoni burial chapel, Santa Maria Sopra Minerva, Rome; 1479, frescoes in the Badia at Settimo; 1480, frescoes in San Donato at Polverosa, and three famous frescoes of the Last Supper plus a figure of St. Jerome in the Ognissanti, Florence; 1481, a part in the wall decorations of the Sistine Chapel undertaken jointly by Ghirlandaio, Botticelli, Cosimo Rosselli and Perugino (Ghirlandaio's most important work here is the Calling of the First Apostles); 1482-83, the Story of St. Zenobius, Palazzo Vecchio, Florence (executed mostly by pupils); 1485, scenes from the life of St. Francis, and an altarpiece of the Adoration of the Shepherds, Sassetti Chapel, Santa Trinità, Florence;

GHIRLANDAIO, RIDOLFO. Portrait of a Young Lady
San Joaquin Pioneer Museum and Art Galleries, Kress Collection, Stockton

80. GHIRLANDAIO, DOMENICO. Saint Michael
Kress Collection, New York

and lastly, 1485-86, his largest and most impressive decoration, the frescoes in Santa Maria Novella on the lives of the Virgin and St. John the Baptist. Michelangelo, who studied under Ghirlandaio, may have been one of the many assistants on this last fresco cycle. Ghirlandaio also made designs for mosaics which were executed by his shop, and a large number of drawings by him are preserved, mostly composition and figure studies for his work in fresco. One of the most popular artists in the Florence of his day, his clientele consisted of the great mercantile and banking families of Florence, many of whose portraits appear in the fresco cycles they commissioned. It was, in fact, as a portraitist that his realism was put to its best use, and he painted a number of independent portrait panels (two of which are in the Metropolitan). His fresco compositions are grandiose and imposing, with many figures placed against elaborate architectural or landscape settings. Much in these backgrounds is recognizable, such as views of Florence and San Gimignano and typical Tuscan landscape. These decorations are of a type that continued to be done into the High Renaissance and are the precursors of the great fresco works of Michelangelo and Raphael. Ghirlandaio's expression, however, was essentially narrative and realistic in the fifteenth-century tradition, and not, like the works of the great masters of the High Renaissance, ideal. (See color plate 80.)

Ghirlandaio, Ridolfo (1483-1561). Born in Florence, the son of Domenico, he became, after his father's death, assistant to his uncle, Davide. He also studied with another uncle, Benedetto, and with Fra Bartolommeo, Piero di Cosimo, and Granacci. He had an excellent early technical development, but, steeped in the art of the fifteenth century, he could not make the transition to the sixteenth. Though he imitated Leonardo and Raphael, the results are eclectic; and in time his style deteriorated. He had, however, a large workshop with many students and assistants and was the official painter for many years of the Signoria and the Medici. (See illustration.)

Ghislandi, Vittore (called Fra Galgario or Paolotto) (1655-1743). Italian portraitist, a friar of the order of S. Francesco di Paolo in the monastery of Galgario at Bergamo where he was born. He studied with Cotta and Bianchini, and later with Bombelli in Venice and Adler in Milan. His style is transitional from Baroque to Rococo, rather dark in color but vivacious in expression.

Giacometti, Alberto (1901-). Swiss painter and sculptor; his work in the latter medium has gained the most attention. Although he began as a painter, he turned during the 1930's to the practice of Surrealist sculpture, producing his characteristic dreamlike elongations of form. During the years since World War II he has turned increasingly to painting and drawing. His pictorial works vary from highly representational figure studies and drawings to a kind of painted form—his most recent—in which the typical deformations of his sculptures are reproduced very faithfully. (See illustration.)

Giambono, Michele di Taddeo (active c.1420-62)

GIACOMETTI. Portrait of Artist's Wife
Sidney Janis Gallery, New York

81. GIORGIONE. Adoration of the Shepherds. National Gallery of Art, Kress Collection, Washington, D.C.

GILLES. Lament for the Head of Orpheus
Private Collection, Germany

One of several Venetians who perpetuated the Gothic tradition, deriving his style from Gentile da Fabriano, Pisanello and Jacobello del Fiore. Besides various painting commissions, he did a group of mosaics in the Mascoli chapel of San Marco, some of them showing stylistic development toward the more scientific approach that had become important in Venice after the middle of the century.

Giampietrino (Giovanni Pedrini, Gian Pietro Rizzi) (active c.1520-40). Lombard painter active in Milan. In its painstaking and delicate chiaroscuro, his style shows the influence of Leonardo and Flemish painting. Attempts have been made to identify him with Giovanni di Petro of Como, and Giovanni da Milano, called Pavese. An altarpiece in the Cathedral of Pavia contains the only fixed date, 1521.

Gibbs Master (act. in America 1670). Named after three paintings, dated 1670, which he did of children of the Gibbs family (private collections). A naive and untrained artist similar to the Freake Master and perhaps the same.

Gilles, Werner (1894-). German modernist; studied first at Kassel and Weimar. In the latter city he also worked from 1919-24 at the Bauhaus, where Feininger was his teacher, and afterwards spent many years in France and Italy. His style, although individualistically modern, shows an especial awareness of Picasso. (See illustration.)

Gillot, Claude (1673-1722). French painter known also for drawings and engravings. Important as a teacher and friend of Watteau. Student of J.B. Corneille, Gillot rebelled against the classical academic doctrines to paint gay genres, modes and intrigues in the spirit of Callot (see). He was employed as a scenery designer and recorded scenes of the Italian Comedy, a taste imparted by him to Watteau, his assistant from 1705-08.

Giordano, Luca (1632-1705). Born in Naples, the son and pupil of Antonio, his art was based on that of Ribera and Pietro da Cortona, with elements of Venetian color. One of the outstanding figures of the Italian Baroque and one of the most famous artists of his age, he was extremely

GIORDANO. David and Bathsheba. National Gallery, London

gifted, skillful, inventive, prolific and amazingly quick (thus Luca Fapresto meaning "Luca the Speedy"). He had great technical virtuosity, painted in all genres, and according to contemporary estimates produced some 5,000 oils. He is said to have painted the Cupola of the Tesoro di S. Martino in forty-eight hours and the high altar of S. Francesco Saverio in one day. However, he was not an essentially original artist and his chameleon efforts in various styles are almost forgeries. Widely admired in his day, he worked in Naples, Rome, Florence, Venice, Bergamo, and Genoa, and went to Spain in 1692 as court painter to Charles II. (See illustration.)

Giorgione (Giorgio, or Zorzo Barbarelli del Castelfranco) (1478-1510). One of the great painters of the Venetian High Renaissance about whom perhaps less is actually known than any artist of comparable stature. Born in Castelfranco, he probably studied, together with Titian, under Giovanni Bellini in Venice. From the records it is known that he worked with Titian on the decorations of the exterior of the Fondaco dei Tedeschi, which no longer exists except in the vague suggestions of Zanetti's eighteenth-century etchings. In the sixteenth-century record of Marcantonio Michiel's *Anonimo Moreelliano*, sixteen works by Giorgione are listed, of which four are identified and traditionally accepted—The Virgin of Castelfranco (c.1504, Castelfranco), the so-called Three Philosophers (c.1505, Vienna), the Giovanelli landscape, called Tempest (c.1505, Venice Academy), and the Sleeping Venus (c.1510, Dresden) probably finished by Titian. Among the other works that have been attributed to him, the best known are the Fête Champêtre (Louvre), the Concert (Pitti Palace), and the Judgment of Solomon (private collection, England). Characteristic of all but the Castelfranco Madonna is a problematic subject matter; in all there is a poetic, romantic, musical mood, a unity of figures and landscape, and a rich local color in warm tonality and beautiful combination. He was a creative genius whose conceptions displaced the Quattrocento style of Bellini and affected a whole generation of Venetian painters (1505-20)—Titian, Lotto, Palma Vecchio, and Sebastiano del Piombo—and subsequently spread throughout much of sixteenth-century Italian painting. (See color plate 81.)

Giottino (Giotto di Stefano). Italian, Florentine, active third quarter of the fourteenth century. Of this artist we know only that he was listed in the St. Luke Guild in 1368 and that in 1369 he was employed in the Vatican. He is presumed to be the son of Stefano Fiorentino and may have worked with him at Assisi. His personality and work are hopelessly confused with Maso di Banco (see).

Giotto di Bondone (1266?-1337). One of the greatest figures in the annals of Italian painting, Giotto was largely responsible for stylistic innovations that ushered in a new era in art history. He was born at Colle, in the Commune of Vespignano north of Florence, and lived in Florence during the greater part of his artistic career. In consequence of his renown numerous legends grew up concerning his beginnings, most of which are without foundation, but have been transmitted by the notoriously inaccurate Vasari. Tradition has it that he was the pupil of Cimabue, but there is little evidence for this. He early shows himself to be closely allied with the Roman school, and there can be little doubt that as a young man he was in contact with the art of Pietro Cavallini and the sculpture of the Pisani. Our knowledge of his life depends on a modest number of documents and a wealth of conflicting and often unverifiable statements by contemporary and later writers. In 1312 he was inscribed in the guild of doctors and apothecaries to which painters belonged in Florence. Acts of 1311, 1312, 1314, 1320, 1321, 1325 and 1326 reveal that during these years he lived in Florence in the quarter of Santa Maria Novella. There are records of his having worked in Naples for King Roberto between 1329 and 1332. In 1334 he was appointed chief architect of the cathedral of Florence, one of the greatest honors conferred upon him. Contemporary and later accounts tell us that Giotto was active in Rome, Naples, Avignon, Padua, Assisi, Rimini, Ravenna, and a number of other cities in Italy and France. He was probably at work in Rome around 1298-1300, where he is supposed to have painted a fresco in San Giovanni in Laterano, and mosaics and an altarpiece for St. Peter's (now lost). Of these, the "Navicella" mosaic now in the portico of St. Peter's is a work celebrated by tradition and universally ascribed to him, but has been so completely restored that it is of no value in determining Giotto's early style. The only other presumed early work has been a source of unending controversy: the scenes from the life of St. Francis in the Upper Church of San Francesco at Assisi. Recent scholarship is prone to deny any of these frescoes to the hand of Giotto, although there is undeniably a close relationship between them and Giotto's other acknowledged frescoes. His greatest extant monument, the fresco cycle in the Arena Chapel at Padua, was probably painted shortly after the consecration of the chapel in 1305. This work comprises thirty-eight scenes from the lives of Joachim and Anna, the Virgin and Christ, in three rows on the side walls, and a Last Judgment on the entrance wall. Below the narrative scenes are personifications of the Virtues and Vices. Incidental decorations were probably executed by assistants, but Giotto undoubtedly planned the entire scheme and personally painted the large scenes and the Virtues and Vices. The frescoes are still in excellent condition; they reveal to the full Giotto's formal and narrative powers in his rendering of three-dimensional figures in convincing and natural action, with dramatic expression, composed in monumental groups sustained by landscape or architectural backgrounds. In these works there is scarcely a trace of the conventionalized Byzantine forms that were current in Florentine art of the immediately preceding generation. The other accepted frescoes by Giotto are scenes from the life of St. Francis, and scenes from the lives of Saints John the Baptist and John the Evangelist, in the Bardi and Peruzzi chapels, respectively, in Santa Croce, Florence (after 1317). These works are so much repainted that little but the composition represents Giotto's original conception. The development they reveal in his style is toward greater monumentality. Some critics attribute to Giotto a few frescoes in the Magdalene chapel of the Lower Church of San Francisco, Assisi. Four panel paintings are generally accepted as from the hand of Giotto: a Crucifix (sacristy of the Arena Chapel, Padua); the Death of the Virgin (Berlin); the "Ognissanti" Madonna (Uffizi); and a panel of St. Stephen (Horne Collection, Florence). The Stigmatization of St. Francis in the Louvre bears his signature but is considered to be a product of the workshop. Giotto's activity as architect to the Florence cathedral late in life involved plans for the façade (not executed), and the planning and decoration of the campanile. The execution of relief decorations of the campanile, representing the creation and works of man, has been frequently attributed to Andrea Pisano, probably from designs by Giotto. Two storeys of the tower had been built when Giotto died.

GIOTTO. Enrico Scrovegni Presenting the Model of the Chapel (detail from The Last Judgment)
Arena Chapel, Padua

GIOTTO. Meeting of Joachim and Anna
Arena Chapel, Padua

Giotto's importance to art history lies in his having introduced the major pictorial problems that European painters dealt with from his time to the twentieth century. These problems are: the convincing depiction of human (or divine) figures and actions in terms of visual and psychological reality, and, for this purpose, the representation of three-dimensional form and space on a plane surface. Giotto's solutions to these problems were appropriate to and consistent with his own genius and the demands of his time. His achievement was accomplished without accurate knowledge of linear perspective and anatomy, though the possible exploitation of these resources was implicit in his work, and was taken up by later artists. With him and his generation the practice of imitating the formulas and conventions of other artists was replaced or at least supplemented by the study of nature in the form of models and actual landscape. The effect of these innovations was profound and instantaneous. Within a generation the Italian Romanesque and Byzantine styles were virtually wiped out, at least in Florence, and others centers rapidly followed suit. This artistic revolution would have taken place in any event, but Giotto happened to be its focal figure owing to his extraordinary technical and psychological gifts and to his location in Florence, the center of progressive thought

82. GIOTTO. Madonna and Child. National Gallery of Art, Kress Collection, Washington, D.C.

in his time. Giotto's art is a visual expression of the humanization and secularization of thought and life that announced the Renaissance in Europe. He invested the figures and histories of the Christian religion with human emotions and dramatic force heretofore unknown in European religious art. His figures and compositions embody qualities of dignity, humility and simple monumentality that have held their own as an artistic achievement in spite of all the developments of Renaissance and later painting. The renown Giotto enjoined during his lifetime is attested to by the tributes of Dante, Petrarch, Boccaccio and other contemporaries, and by the honors with which he was buried. His immediate following was tremendous and to a large extent anonymous, though individual hands have been singled out by connoisseurs. The two most important personalities that follow in Giotto's wake are Taddeo Gaddi and Bernardo Daddi. But the full implications of his art were not realized and carried further until they were taken up by Masaccio in the early fifteenth century. (See illustrations, including color plate 82.)

Giovanni Antonio (see PORDENONE).

Giovanni Bonsi. Italian, Florentine, active second half

83. GIOVANNI DI PAOLO
Miracle of St. Nicholas of Tolentino
Philadelphia Museum of Art, Johnson Collection

of the fourteenth century. One work by this follower of Bernardo Daddi, a polyptych signed and dated 1370, is in the Vatican gallery.

Giovanni da Fiesole (see ANGELICO, FRA).

Giovanni d'Alemagna (Zuane da Murano) (active c. 1440-50). German-Italian, school of Venice. This presumably German-born painter was a collaborator of Antonio Vivarini and was also his brother-in-law. All the known paintings on which he worked were done together with Antonio. His hand in these works may be recognized by his more precise detail and his more delicate color, characteristics that suggest a relation with the contemporary Cologne school in Germany. The major products of the collaboration are altarpieces in the church of San Zaccaria, the Cappella degli Ognissanti, and the Academy, all in Venice.

Giovanni dal Ponte (1386-1437). Italian, Florentine, real name Giovanni di Marco. Though active during the most decisive years of the early Renaissance, this reactionary follower of Spinello Aretino adhered consistently to fourteenth-century traditions. He painted altarpieces and bridal-chest panels, and some frescoes in Santa Trinità.

Giovanni da Milano (active c.1350-69). Italian, Lombard, active in Florence. This painter first appears in Florentine records in 1350. By 1366 he owned property there and became a citizen. The last record of him is in 1369, when he was called to Rome by Urban V. Two signed and dated panels are known: an altarpiece in the Prato gallery (1354) and a Lamentation in the Florence Academy (1365). Also in 1365 he decorated the Rinuccini chapel of Santa Croce with scenes from the life of the Virgin, his most important work. Stylistically allied with Orcagna and Andrea da Firenze, his art belongs to the anti-Giottesque trend toward less natural and more hieratic expression.

Giovanni da Oriolo (active 1443-1473/4). Italian painter, active in Faenza, who is known through one preserved work, a portrait of Lionello d'Este (London) painted in a north Italian style suggesting Pisanello.

Giovanni da San Giovanni (see MANNOZZI).

Giovanni da Udine (Giovanni Nanni or dei Ricamatori) (1487-1564). Venetian painter, architect, and decorator, born in Udine and active mostly in Rome, the best decorative painter of the period. Working with Raphael, he invented a style of ornamentation based on the newly discovered decorations of the Baths of Titus. He created a new art form, combining painting and stucco, small in scale, rich in color, naturalistic in form, and capricious in composition, which became the basis of sixteenth-century decoration. At the same time he devised a modern style by synthesizing the fifteenth-century decorations of Perugino and Signorelli with Roman classical forms. He studied first with Giovanni Martini da Udine and later in Venice with Giorgione (1510-11). He came to Rome, entered Raphael's workshop, and began his long career as a decorator in Rome, Florence, Cividale, Venice, and Udine. Among his countless works are the Farnesina (1516) and the Loggie of the Vatican with Raphael (1517-19), and the Hall of Pontiffs in the Vatican with Pierino del Vaga 1523+), both in Rome; and the Medici Palace (1520) in Florence.

Giovanni del Biondo del Casentino (active 1356-92). Italian, Florentine. A number of works by the same hand were brought together under the name of this painter when two signed works came to light. These are a fragmentary altarpiece in Santa Verdiana, Castelfiorentino (1360) and a Madonna in the Siena gallery (1377). Another important work is the Rinuccini Altarpiece (1379) in Santa Croce, Florence. Giovanni's manner, derived from Andrea Orcagna and Nardo di Cione, partakes of the tendency away from space representation, but is distinguished by its heavier, less refined forms.

Giovanni di Bartolommeo Cristiani (active in Pistoia, 1366-98). Italian. Two authenthic works by Giovanni are extant: an altarpiece of St. John the Evangelist in the church of San Giovanni fuor Civitas (signed and dated 1370), and ruined frescoes of the Virtues in the portico of the cathedral of Pistoia. A polyptych in the Acton collection, Florence, has been ascribed to him. His art, showing little originality, is wholly dependent on Florence, particularly on Orcagna.

Giovanni di Francesco (Master of the Carrand Triptych) (active c.1446-59). Italian, Florentine. The name of

GIRODET. Atala in the Tomb. Louvre, Paris

GIRTIN. Kirkstall Abbey, Yorkshire
Victoria and Albert Museum, London

the painter of a triptych representing the Madonna and saints in the Carrand Collection of the Bargello, Florence, depends upon his identification with the painter of a documented fresco over the entrance of the Loggia degli Innocenti, namely, Giovanni di Francesco. A number of paintings have been ascribed to this hand, revealing an eclectic personality working under the influence of Andrea del Castagno and of Baldovinetti.

Giovanni di Paolo (c.1403-82). One of the most individual Sienese painters of the time. A pupil of Paolo di Giovanni Fei, he later became a follower of Sassetta, and his colorful, decorative manner may be classed in the International Gothic Style. He was prolific and his work displays the utmost variety and imagination. Early works show the unmistakable influence of Fei but are already stamped with Giovanni's personal style. His figures are languid and graceful, with wistful or even ugly faces, and the color is clear and bright. Later his forms become heavier and his color darker, and a lifelong tendency toward bizarre distortion is more pronounced. A fine early work is the Assumption in the Collegiata, Asciano; a typical late one is the Madonna Enthroned with Saints in the Cathedral at Pienza. He is seen at his most imaginative in a now dismembered polyptych of St. John the Baptist. Several of his works are in the Metropolitan Museum. The works of an imitator, Giacomo del Pisano, have been confused with his. (See color plate 83.)

Giovenone, Girolamo (c.1490-1555). Born in Novara and active in Vercelli, he was the head of a family of painters. His art is a transition from an older provincial Piedmont tradition to the newer style under the influence of Gaudenzio Ferrara.

Girard d'Orléans (died 1361). French painter. Favorite of Jean le Bon (1350-64), he followed his monarch into captivity in London and Avignon. During imprisonment he is supposed to have painted Jean's portrait (Louvre), the first French easel picture.

Girodet de Trioson, Anne Louis (1767-1824). A French painter. Girodet is noted for having emerged from the classical atelier of David to paint, in somewhat mannered style, subjects and compositions that anticipate the later Romantic movement. Already in 1787 his sketch for a Pietà used thick pigment, Baroque structure and rich chiaroscuro to produce a mysticism out of step with his contemporaries. During the Napoleonic period he turned to old Celtic mythology and painted, in an academic technique, Ossian Receiving the Generals of Napoleon. In 1808, inspired by Chateaubriand's poem, he painted The Burial of Atala, which clearly reflects the anti-rational religious revival of the time. The Mannerism of his style is to be seen in the obscure

GIUNTA PISANO. St. Francis
Church of St. Mary of the Angels, Assisi

GLACKENS. Luxembourg Gardens. Corcoran Gallery of Art, Washington, D.C.

allegorical Danaë (Wildenstein & Co. New York). (See illustration.)

Girolamo dai Libri (1474-1555). Italian, Veronese. Girolamo was a book illustrator, from which profession he derives his name, but also painted altarpieces. His painting was influenced by Mantegna, Montagna, and Francesco Morone, and is characterized by its accurate drawing of details and its light and fresh color. A large altarpiece by him is in the Metropolitan.

Girolamo (Rizzo) de Santacroce (act. 1503-1556). Born in Santa Croce near Bergamo, he was in Venice in 1503, possibly as an apprentice and assistant to Gentile Bellini. His style, influenced by Giovanni Bellini (whose assistant he later became) and subsequently Cima, became more monumental in composition, and under the impact of Giorgione, more coloristic in handling.

Girtin, Thomas (1775-1802). British landscapist known particularly for his watercolor drawings. He spent part of his childhood apprenticed to various drawing teachers and by eighteen was an efficient topographical draughtsman, doing important work for an author about to publish a book on old monasteries and castles of England. Among his fellow students were the young Turner and John Sell Cotman. By 1796 the ill-fated Girtin had reached his own style. His use of an all-over harmony in his watercolors was undoubtedly good, but the attempt to make the watercolor as important as a painting and still give an extremely naturalistic impression was destined to cause considerable trouble during the nineteenth century. Yet he was the first to use local color in the shadows on an object, an important step in the development of the outdoor viewpoint. His palette is generally sober, unlike the sunlight and atmospheric effects of his friend Turner, but is part of the new Romantic attitude in its strength of feeling. (See illustration.)

Gischia, Léon (1904-). French decorative painter; friend of Léger and collaborator of Léger, Le Corbusier and others in various decorative works. His style combines the geometry of Léger with the color quality of Matisse.

Giudini (Giudici), Francesco (see FRANCIABIGIO).

Giunta Pisano. (known activity 1229-55). Italian, Tuscan. The name given to a painter who signed himself Juncta Capitinus pictor and is thus distinguished from other thirteenth-century Pisan painters with the name of Giunta. Two of his signed Crucifixes are in SS. Ranieri e Leonardo, Pisa, and Santa Maria degli Angeli, Assisi, both prototypes of a large number of central Italian Crucifixes inspired by the Franciscan movement. They represent Christ dead on the cross, His face bearing the evidence of great suffering, and His body rendered in a swinging S-curve. They differ from the Crucifixes of the Lucchese Berlinghieri in containing more Byzantine stylistic elements and in representing Christ dead rather than alive. (See illustration.)

Glackens, William James (1870-1938). American genre painter and illustrator, an original member of the Ashcan group and the Eight. Born in Philadelphia, Glackens worked for the *Philadelphia Press* and other papers as an illustrator, meanwhile attending the Pennsylvania Academy of Fine Arts, until 1895, when he went to Paris. It was during this period that he met Henri, Luks, Sloan, and Shinn, who were later to form the nucleus of the Ashcan School (see). After his return from Paris in 1896, he settled in New York and followed a successful career as an illustrator and cartoonist for the New York *World*, New York *Herald*, *McClure's*, *Scribner's*, and the *Saturday Evening Post*. In 1906 he visited France and Spain, after which the Impressionist influence became more apparent in his work. He spent an increasing amount of time painting and in 1925-32 lived and painted in France. In 1908 he took part in the historic exhibition of the Eight and in 1913 helped organize the Armory Show. In his later years he won many prizes and was elected a National Academician in 1933. His early style was in the dark tonality of Henri and the early Manet, but he later lightened his palette in the Impressionist manner and eventually became a confirmed disciple of Renoir. Concurrently his subject matter moved from the intimate city genre of the Ashcan School (in which however he tended to

GOES, VAN DER. Portrait of a Man
Metropolitan Museum of Art, New York

GOLDBERG. The Fascinator
National Gallery of Canada, Ottawa

be humorous and light) to landscapes of holiday mood, and, finally, to portraits and nudes in a richer and warmer range of color. (See illustration.)

Glarner, Frítz (1899-). Contemporary American non-objective painter in the Mondrian tradition. Born in Zurich, Switzerland, he studied at the Royal Institute of Fine Arts in Naples and in Paris. He came to the U.S. in 1936 and had his first one-man show in 1946.

glaze. Applies to thin layers or films of either translucent or opaque color used to build up the forms in a painting. It is the very essence of the oil painting (see) technique in which it affords an important method of control for the amount of light that is permitted to come through successive layers or glazes of paint. It is this factor that gives oil painting its special characteristics of depth and richness.

Gleaners, The, by Jean François Millet (see).

Gleizes, Albert (1881-1953). French Cubist painter and theoretician. Began as an Impressionist and in 1910 exhibited with the first Cubist group at the Indépendants and the Autumn Salon. In 1912 he showed at the Section d'Or (see) an informal grouping of progressive, mainly Cubist artists which he had helped organize. Together with Metzinger he published the first book on Cubism (see) that year, *Du Cubisme*. In 1913 he showed at Der Sturm in Berlin and at the Armory Show in New York. By 1919 he had turned toward a religious type of expression, later helping to found associations of peasants and artisans. In 1939 he retired to the south of France and a few years later returned to the Catholic faith, holding an exhibition of religious art at the Vatican in 1950. His art is a colorful version of standard Analytical Cubism.

Goerg, Edouard-Joseph (1893-). French painter, printmaker and book illustrator who was born in Australia of French parents. A pupil of Maurice Denis and influenced by Goya, Daumier and Rouault, this painter has produced a poetic and even fantastic type of engraved work and gentle, lyrical paintings of young women or pleasant ones of flower arrangements.

GONÇALVES (style of). St. Francis
Museu Nacional de Arte Antiga, Lisbon

84. GOSSAERT. Adoration. National Gallery, London

Goes, Hugo van der (c.1440-82). Flemish painter who attempted to combine divergent tendencies—the linear emotional patterns of Rogier van der Weyden, the infinitesimal realism of van Eyck, and the monumentality of his friend, Joos van Ghent. His art is, therefore, torn between grandeur and realism, pictorialism and linearity. He carries on the aristocratic refinement of Rogier, adding a personal note of melancholy introspection, perhaps a prefiguration of his own eventual madness. He was an original master at a time of slavish copyists of Rogier, creating a popular art in which lower-class types and increased individualization are introduced. Although he painted many pictures, only a few authenticated works remain, and many only in copies. Though he was a famous painter, he had no pupils, but exerted influence upon Gerard David, the Master of Virgo inter Virgines, the Master of Moulins, Schongauer, Ghirlandaio, and Lorenzo de Credi. Born in Ter Goes (Zeeland) or Ghent, he was active in the latter city from 1465 to 1475 when he retired to the monastery of Roode Kloster (Rouge Cloître) near Brussels, where he spent his remaining years haunted by intermittent fits of madness. Among his early works are the two donor portraits for the Bouts St. Hyppolitus Altar (Bruges), and the Vienna Diptych. The great pictures of his mature style are the Adoration of the Magi (Berlin) and his most famous painting, his only completely authenticated work, the Portinari Altarpiece (c.1475, Uffizi) executed for Tommaso Portinari, Medici agent in Bruges. His last works, done while at the monastery, are the intensely moving and dramatic Death of the Virgin (Bruges) and the Adoration of the Shepherds (Berlin). (See illustration.)

Goitia, Francisco (1884-). Mexican painter, draughtsman and teacher; an important progenitor of the modern Mexican movement. He traveled in Europe, 1904-12; was active in the Mexican Revolution; studied Indian life in Teotihuacán Valley and Oaxaca, from which came the inspiration for his most important works. Goitia, who sought to find "the sorrows of the race," has produced an art of great humanitarian quality and mystic feeling, as in the despairing and dramatic Tata Jesucristo, the picture of an Indian wake. His melancholy native types and tragic scenes have long influenced Mexican artists but he has only recently become known to the general public.

Goldberg, Eric (1890-). Canadian painter born in Germany; studied at Beaux-Arts, Paris, and Julian Academy, Paris, and also in Berlin under German pre-Expressionist Lovis Corinth. His warm romantic figure studies are suggestive of various European styles. (See illustration.)

Gonçalves, Nuno (fl. 1450-1471). Portuguese painter who worked as royal artist during the reign of Alfonso V; noted in fifteenth-century painting for his personal manner of handling tempera (see). Instead of the usual gesso preparation Nuno painted directly on the wooden panel, presumably to avoid future flaking. His forms are marked by great solidity, his draperies by a crisp, almost wooden modeling that suggests the effects of contemporary Flemish painters.

GOSSAERT. Portrait of a Man
Mauritshuis, The Hague

This may be a result of the stay of Jan van Eyck (see) in Portugal during 1429. (See illustration.)

González, Bartolomé (1564-1627). Spanish court painter. Pupil of the Italian Patricio Caxes, he employed the Mannerist format in a quantity of official portraits. He succeeded Pantoja de la Cruz as royal painter.

González, Gorivar (d.1671). Spanish-Colonial Ecuadorian painter; next in line of the School of Quito group after Galque and Santiago. His style is based on the Venetians, especially Tintoretto, and is marked by clear bright color.

González Camarena, Jorge (1908-). Mexican muralist and easel painter. Interested in the fusion of formal expression and poetic feeling, he has worked in a subdued but powerfully vibrating color and with strong three-dimensional forms. These are for the most part concerned with Mexicanist themes, though non-political in outlook. He has done murals in commercial buildings, in the Cuicuilco Museum (1948), the Social Security Institute of Mexico (1950), and a polychrome bas-relief for the Library of the Technological Institute of Monterrey, Mexico.

Gorky, Arshile (1904-48). A contemporary American painter, one of the earliest Abstract Expressionists. Born in Armenia, he studied at the Polytechnic Institute in Tiflis, Russia, before coming to the U.S. in 1920. He studied engineering for three years at Brown University but turned to art in 1923. His early work was semi-abstract in the Picasso manner, but he turned to free-form abstraction about 1936 and influenced many of the younger Abstract Expressionists.

Gossaert, Jan (called Mabuse) (c.1478-1533). Flemish painter, famous for the importation of Italian Renaissance style. A fully formed Netherlands artists, Gossaert traveled to Italy in the suite of the Duke of Burgundy, his major patron. Here he copied the Italian masters and learned to adapt them to his Flemish background in a somewhat Gothic way. Major religious works by him are the Epiphany (London) which employs the intricate architectural perspectives that were a favorite with northern Mannerists, and the Agony in the Garden (Berlin) which uses Lombard chiaroscuro. His Adam and Eve (Berlin) is a typical Renaissance study of the nude. Gossaert is noted for his fine direct style of portraiture, somewhat on the Italian model, as seen in his portraits of Jean Carondelet. (See illustrations, including color plate 84.)

Gothic painting, Painting of the Gothic period (thirteenth to fifteenth centuries) saw the development of spatial effects and human values in the art. The previous Romanesque style, like Byzantine painting in the East, had structured itself along two-dimensional lines with strong references to the surface and frame of the panel, wall or book-page. All implications of the forms, their placement and interrelationships, corresponded to universal, theological values, although it is quite true that a certain individual expression persisted in subsidiary areas of pictures. This last aspect grew in

GOTTLIEB. Black, White and Pink. Kootz Gallery, New York

Gothic painting to a true secularism; holy narrative took on an anecdotal quality and many types of popular and courtly genre were painted for their own sake (the Lorenzetti brothers in Siena). Painters competed in their efforts to inject human sentiment not only into narrative subjects like the Nativity but even into holy images, viz., the Nursing Madonna. New delights in Nature, as suggested by St. Francis, were marvelously interpreted by Giotto and the Sienese masters. Study of Nature in her moods (Jean Pucelle) was followed by close scrutiny of her appearances, i.e., landscape painting (the Limbourg brothers). While figures were early placed in architectural settings (Psalter of St. Louis, 1256) this was not at first deeply spatial in quality, but instead functioned in the shallow perforated sense of a Gothic triforium arcade. The International Style painters (see) around 1400 produced a truer sense of panorama with their S-curved spatial effects in landscape, although their style was at the same time very patternistic. The picture surface as an entity was finally eliminated by the French and Flemish painters of the early fifteenth century and by the discovery of true linear perspective in Florence. This new spirit, that of the Van Eycks and Masaccio, belongs to the story of Renaissance painting.

The Gothic style of painting was a widespread one and embraced several media. Panel and wall-painting, stained glass and tapestry, miniature book-art and enameling were all part of the tradition. Although all the countries of Europe were touched by the style, there were a number of main creative centers. Paris, the Lowlands and England were at one pole; the cities of Italy at the other, especially Florence and Siena. Less important but still significant were Provence, Catalonia, Valencia to the south; Germany and Austria to the east.

Gottlieb, Adolph (1903-). Contemporary American painter of pictograph abstraction. Born in New York, he studied briefly at the Art Students League, but his major influences are from Klee and Miró. His gigantic stained-

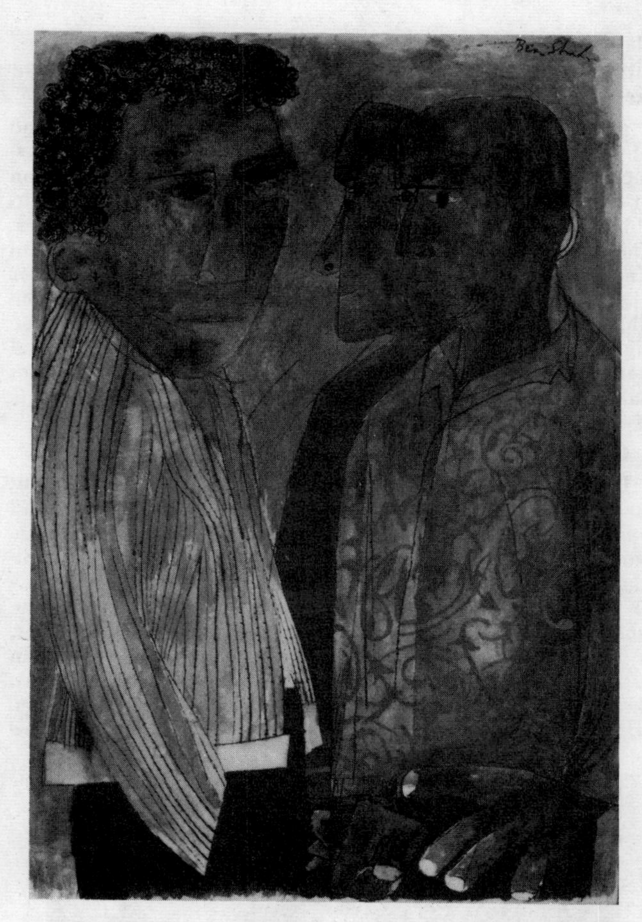

Gouache by Ben Shahn. Anger. Private Collection

GOYA. The Bullfight. Metropolitan Museum of Art, New York

glass windows in the Park Avenue Synagogue, New York City, is an example of the potential relationship among architects, designers and artists. (See illustration.)

gouache. An opaque type of watercolor painting. Instead of the brilliant and predominantly white effect of a translucent watercolor, where the paper furnishes a major portion of the effect, the gouache is more sober in quality and suitable for several other and often more dramatic purposes. The opaque effect of the gouache is caused by the mixing of zinc white (Chinese white) with the regular watercolor pigments. It was widely used during the Middle Ages for the illumination of manuscripts and was also popular during the eighteenth century, when is was often used by continental watercolorists. It is very often employed today by American painters, particularly those interested in atmospheric effects of a certain muted type. (See illustration.)

Govardhan (see INDIAN PAINTERS: JAHANGIR PERIOD).

Goya y Lucientes, Francisco José (1746-1828). Giant among Spanish painters. Goya emerged from the moribund Spanish tradition of the Ancien Régime and through his paintings and etchings profoundly affected Western art from his day to the present, especially the divergent movements of Impressionism and Expressionism. Goya was born in the small town of Fuendetodos and was first taught by his father, a master-gilder. After study in the academy of José Luxán in Zaragoza, he went to Madrid as an associate of Francisco Bayeu, a fellow townsman in the service of Raphael Mengs. Official Spanish painting of this era, in the absence of native talent of its former Golden Age, had relied on imported styles: the Baroque Italians Giordano and Tiepolo, a galaxy of French Rococo decorators and finally the Romanized Bohemian Mengs, who had imposed on Madrid a frigid Neo-Classicism. When in 1766 he was rejected by the Madrid Academy for the second time, Goya went to Italy, where he won a competition in Parma. During the 1770's he returned to Zaragoza and was engaged in fresco work. He was also employed by the royal tapestry works of Madrid through the influence of Mengs and of the Bayeus, whose sister he married. The genre scenes he designed in this capacity show him to be a Rococo decorator in the style of the Venetians.

85. GOYA. Don Manuel Garcia de la Prada
Des Moines Art Center, Coffin Memorial Collection

The following decade saw his complete conquest of the court of Carlos III; he became a court painter in 1786 and was named *pintor de cámara* by Carlos IV in 1789. In this period commenced his brilliant series of portraits, e,g., those for the Dukes of Osuna and Alba. He appears to have been stimulated in technique by the royal collection of Velázquez, which he had been commissioned to copy in etching. This was a period of personal optimism, revealed in his letters, as he enjoyed his court associations and studied the liberal ideas of the Encyclopedists then current in Spanish intellectual circles. The 1790's marked the height of his official popularity; he was chosen president of the Royal Academy in 1795, first painter to the king in 1799. But this was also the beginning of an introversion brought on by illness (1792), long convalescence (1793) and resultant deafness. This is the period of his "silvery" style of painting and of his Caprichos. In the latter a gay Italian genre form was turned into biting satire on social mores, with an almost vicious double-entendre. The frescoes of San Antonio de la Florida, Madrid, (1798) are his best big decorative commission before the Napoleonic invasion of 1808 which threw the Peninsula into years of war and confusion.

The death of his friend the Duchess of Alba (1802), of his wife (1812) and the horrors of the wars combined with his nervous affliction to embitter Goya. His dashing Rococo technique was converted into a ruthless naturalism in the drawings and etchings of his later career. A strongly expressionist manner, developed in planar chiaroscuro, gave his work a remarkably modern character. He also became at this point a stimulus to the European Romantic movement; he had turned the Rococo into Romanticism in Spain without the usual Neo-Classical intermezzo. These tendencies are realized in the Disasters of War and the Bull Fights, etchings of the period 1808-20. They have their counterpart on canvas in such works as the Executions of the Third of May (1814, Prado). His attitude in both series of etchings was that of a commentator, describing the spectacle first from one side and then from the other, allowing the images, with cryptic captions, to speak for themselves. These two purposes, that of bitter exposure of the foibles of man and that of universalizing his themes by use of popular allegory, come to their fruition in the Disparates (1819). This is a series of dream-proverb absurdities which weave the old Spanish adage, "*La vida es sueño*"—and its converse: "To die is to awaken." Goya was out of sympathy with the restoration of Fernando VII in 1814 and he retired to a house in the country, La Quinta del Sordo. Here in fresco on the walls of his own home the Disparates were translated into pigment of a most radical chiaroscuro. In a painted world of horrors summoned up by his fertile imagination, the final conversion was made from the social masquerade of his early Rococo painting to the double-edged satire of his pessimistic personal imagery. In 1824 after the collapse of the Cortes he went into voluntary exile in Bordeaux. (See illustrations,- including color plate 85.)

Goyen, Jan van (1596-1656). Dutch landscape painter. He studied with Esaias van de Velde and traveled widely in the Netherlands and abroad, recording his impressions in

86. GOZZOLI, BENOZZO. Rape of Helen. National Gallery, London

delightful sketches. He was one of Holland's most gifted painters of landscape and from him stems the great tradition of rendering nature in all her atmospheric truth. Besides painting, he speculated in real estate, tulip bulbs, and works of art.

Gozzoli, Benozzo (1420-97). The last of the Florentines to adhere to the Gothic tradition of Gentile da Fabriano and Fra Angelico. As with Filippo Lippi, his style develops under the continually growing influence of other, more architectural tendencies in Florentine art, and, like Lippi, he lived a long, active life. He was born in Florence, but nothing is known of his earliest training. In 1444 he signed a three-year contract to work as an assistant to Lorenzo and Vittorio Ghiberti, who were then busy on the reliefs for the second pair of bronze doors for the baptistry. This contact with sculpture perhaps gave his art a degree of plasticity uncommon among the Gothic painters. Between 1447 and 1449 he assisted Fra Angelico in Rome and Orvieto, and his early style reflects the art of Angelico more than that of any other master. Between 1450 and 1452 he painted frescoes in two churches at Montefalco (San Fortunato and San Francesco) and in 1453 did frescoes in Viterbo (destroyed). Between 1452 and 1458 documents indicate his presence in Rome, but he returned to Florence in 1459 and began work on his most famous decoration, the fresco cycle of the Journey of the Magi in the chapel of the Medici palace. This chapel originally displayed an altarpiece by Filippo Lippi, the Adoration of the Christ Child (now in Berlin); Benozzo's frescoes represent the approach of the Magi to this separate painted scene, and on the walls nearest the altar he painted hosts of angels in adoration. The processions advance in courtly splendor with enormous retinues through a landscape inspired by the hills around Florence and animated with much natural detail. The three kings are portraits of Lorenzo de' Medici, the Emperor of Byzantium (John Paleologus), and the Patriarch of Constantinople. These two eastern dignitaries had come to Ferrara in 1439 for a council dealing with the threat of Turkish invasion. Lorenzo's retinue includes portraits of other members of the Medici family and a self-portrait of Benozzo. The chapel is small but has a high ceiling, and Benozzo skillfully solved the problem of decorating such a confined space with large painted surfaces. After finishing this work Benozzo went to San Gimignano for four years (1463-67), where he painted frescoes of the life of St. Augustine in the church dedicated to that saint. In this cycle he dealt with more complicated problems of perspective and foreshortening than in the Medici palace works. He painted a St. Sebastian altarpiece for the same church in 1464, as protection against the plague which broke out in that year.

Benozzo's later life was taken up with a vast series of twenty-five scenes from the Old Testament for a wall of the Campo Santo in Pisa. Although in these works perspective and the use of architectural settings are highly developed, the cycle is stylistically still reminiscent of late fourteenth-century decoration in the Gothic tradition. (These frescoes were badly damaged, some of them irreparably, in World War II.) Benozzo interrupted this work for a trip to Rome in 1483, where he painted frescoes (destroyed) in Santa Maria Mag-

GRAVES. Journey. Willard Gallery, New York

giore. After a few commissions for altarpieces and tabernacles in the 1490's, he died in Pistoia in 1497. Important altarpieces by Benozzo from various periods in his career are in the Vatican gallery and the church of Santa Maria in Aracoeli, Rome, the galleries of Perugia and Terni, and the Collegiata at San Gimignano. His art was not influential for later generations, since it was somewhat old-fashioned even for his own day. In Florence, Cosimo Rosselli and Pier Francesco Fiorentino are the only major painters who display some dependence on his art. (See color plate 86.)

Granet, François Marius (1775-1849). A French painter. At one time a student of David, he is famed for his pilgrimage on foot from Aix to Paris and for his painting Choir of the Capuchin Church on the Place Barberini (Salon of 1819), which he copied sixteen times in order to satisfy the demands of his wealthy clients.

Grant, Duncan (1887-). Scottish modernist; showed great promise in the pre-World War I years. Well known as a decorative designer, Grant has also done a number of mural panels as well as more or less representational and charming landscape scenes.

graphic arts. In the broadest sense this term applies to anything that is predominantly linear in effect, e.g., a line drawing, as contrasted with the broad and pictorial effect of oil painting or watercolor. More specifically graphic arts refer to the various print processes that produce etchings, drypoints, engravings, lithographs, woodcuts, etc.

Graves, Morris (1910-). Contemporary American Surrealist painter. Most famous for his paintings of birds, he has attempted to evolve a mystic symbolism to express his subconscious. Born in Fox Valley, Ore., he spent his youth in Washington and in Texas. He later traveled in Japan and Puerto Rico, and has been greatly influenced by Chinese art. He paints in a style of involved linearity, in largely monochromatic but subtle tonality, and with an unusual element of wit. (See illustration.)

Greco, El (Doménikos Theotocopulos, Doménico Theotocopuli) (1541-1614). Most stirring of Spain's religious painters. An unusual personal genius in whom the divergent tendencies of Spanish Mannerism, Venetian colorism and late Byzantine icon-painting reach their apogee. His idiom is remarkable in that it has been described as both Mannerist and Baroque, terms that are usually antithetical. To modern taste he is both a prototype of Expressionism and a "painter's painter" who by radical fragmentation of the object-texture anticipated Impressionist brushwork. El Greco, as the Spaniards called this immigrant, was born near Candia in Crete, probably of the upper class. He was trained in the prevailing Byzantine (see) manner of painting as practiced in Crete. His Mt. Sinai of this period is in Budapest.

When about twenty-five he went to Venice, which had ruled Crete since 1204. There he was referred to as a "pupil of Titian," although his paintings of this period, e.g., the Expulsion (Minneapolis Institute), suggest rather the influence of Tintoretto. In Rome he studied Michelangelo's work and enjoyed the friendship of the miniaturist Giuli Clovio. It was to the latter that he made interesting references concerning the nature of his "inner light." By 1577 El Greco was in Toledo, the old Spanish capital, in which he passed the rest of his life and which figured in several remarkable paintings, including the View of Toledo (Metropolitan). Spain was a rallying point for Greeks against the Turks in those times and Toledo was the spiritual center of the huge Spanish Empire, remaining so long after the removal of the court to Madrid. During 1577-80 El Greco painted a retablo for Santo Domingo el Antiguo, Toledo, of which portions exist today. The Trinity (Prado) contains elements of Dürer and Michelangelo; the Assumption (Chicago) is based on Titian's. These were already rendered with less particularism than the work of his Venetian period, and by breaks with Renaissance perspective rules the Assumption gains a new expressive directness. His Espolio of the same period (Toledo Cathedral) suggests an enthusiasm for Flemings like Bosch. By 1580 his local fame led to an invitation by Philip II to paint the Martyrdom of St. Maurice for a chapel of the Escorial. His flamboyant manner did not suit the austere taste of the Spanish monarch any more than did that of Morales (see) and this was apparently his last commission for the Court.

Perhaps El Greco's most famous painting is the Burial of Count Orgaz, painted for the church of Santo Tomé, Toledo. In this apotheosis of the Spanish chivalric ideal, the good Count is seen lowered into his grave by Sts. Stephen and

GRECO, EL. Head of St. Francis
Hispanic Society of America

Augustine before an audience of friars, prelates and nobles. In a visionary composition that seems almost a satire of Raphael's Disputá, the heavens receive the Count's soul in a paroxysm of ecstasy. There is much in both mood and mechanics of this drama that recalls other Spanish mystics of the period such as Santa Teresa of Avila, San Juan de la Cruz, or St. Ignatius Loyola. By the turn of the century, El Greco's style reached its late phase, in which, at a distance, the forms of his paintings seem to be consumed by his loose brushwork and flamelike patterns. The format is often radical, overly tall or long, in keeping with his other tendencies to exaggerate in order to dematerialize. The Crucifixion (Prado), Resurrection (Prado) and late Immaculate Conception (?) (Toledo) are examples. El Greco also designed architectural settings for his altarpieces, as in Santo Domingo el Antiquo, Toledo. He was wealthy and highly successful in old Toledo; of odd habits and given to luxury, his contemporaries tell us. However, he died poor owing to the depression that hit Toledo following the expulsion of the Jews and Moriscoes, her craftsmen. Either because of their popularity or because of his own custom as an icon-painter, he was wont to duplicate his paintings and revise old themes. This was also done by his numerous assitants and followers, to the confusion of later connoisseurs. (See illustrations, including color plate 87.)

Greek painting. The outstanding contribution of the Greeks to the history of painting seems to have been the development of the medium as a three-dimensional art with naturalistic detail in the fifth and fourth centuries B.C. However, the exact way in which this came about is not quite clear because of the absolute lack of paintings of the classical Greek epoch. Instead we must rely on inadequate literary descriptions and on the evidence of the ceramic art of vase painting. There also exist many later Roman frescoes (see) which archaeologists tell us are derived from Greek originals, but their value as evidence for the latter is questionable. The history of Greek painting began in the Dark Ages that followed the Dorian invasion of about 1100 B.C. The vase painting of that period was of strongly geometric pattern, little related to the naturalistic Aegean art (see) that had preceded it. This geometric tendency, standard in the Mediterranean at the time, can best be studied in the great funeral vases from the Dipylon cemetery of Athens (eighth century B.C.). While deities were represented and funeral scenes depicted, the main purpose of the painters seems a decorative one. In the seventh and sixth centuries, all the centers of Greek vase-making showed a strong influence of the East (Orientalizing Style). This influence apparently came both from Asiatic sources and from surviving colonies of the old Aegean powers. The miniature perfume vases of Corinth ("Proto-Corinthian") and vases from the Ionic centers of Asia Minor, Rhodes and Egypt are examples. They show a delight in textile-like patterns of ornamental and animal friezes of strongly curvilinear qualities. A similar liveliness can be seen in more monumental painting of the time: the painted metopes of Thermos and the terracotta sarcophagus of Klazomenai.

GREEK. Vase painting, 6th century B.C.
Musician Playing Double Pipes
Yale University Art Gallery, New Haven

GRECO, EL. Burial of Count Orgaz
Church of St. Tomé, Toledo

Athens assumed the major role in Greek painting only in the late sixth century when her black-figured pottery dominated the Mediterranean market. An early masterpiece of this period is the François vase in the Louvre (see Klitias painter). This black-figured style presented crisply silhouetted forms on a reddish slip with incised detail, a strongly linear art. Among well-known painters who worked in this style were Nikosthenes, Amasis and Exekias (see). There exists a quantity of funerary plaques which show that the same style was used in monumental painting. During the last quarter of the sixth century painters developed a new technique of modeling figures on the red ground in a background painted black. This red-figured style soon led to a greater feeling of plasticity; its first exponents, the wall-painter Kimon, the vase painters Epiktetos and Euphronios, pioneered in the struggle with the intricacies of the human form.

Until the middle of the fifth century a series of archaic

87. GRECO, EL. Christ at Gethsemane. Toledo Museum of Art, Libbey Collection

conventions such as frontal eyes and decorative pleats were retained in what is called the "severe" red-figured style. But at that time, largely under the influence of Polygnotos of Thasos (see), Greek monumental painting became spatial, modeled and interpretive of human moods. The accompanying vase painting, the "fine" red-figured style, quickly became encumbered with foreshortening, spatial effects and polychromy that destroyed much of its ceramic character. The Achilles Master (see) decorated vases in the Fine style. He was also noted for his mastery of the contemporary fashion of painting on a white ground. This was a particularly delicate linear art, almost Chinese in flavor. Many of these vases were decorated for funeral purposes and had a fine elegiac mood about them.

From this point, when monumental and vase-painting were forced along different paths, our knowledge of the former becomes highly conjectural, based on literary sources. We have minute descriptions of the subjects of murals such as those of Polygnotus, but little evidence as to style. Linear perspective was supposed to have been invented about 460 in the painting of stage scenery. In the following century Zeuxis (see), Nikias and Apelles (see) apparently made important discoveries in realism, especially with regard to light and shade. It is also clear that in Hellenistic times a great variety of poses, a refined chiaroscuro modeling and an expanded palette were all available. Some evidence of this can be seen in the provincial painted stelae of Pagasae (third to second century B.C.) and in the Fayum portraits (see) of Egypt. (See illustrations, including color plate 88.)

Greene, Balcomb (1904-). Contemporary American abstract painter. Born in Niagara Falls, N.Y., educated at Syracuse, Columbia, and New York Universities, he is largely self-taught as a painter. He works in an architectural, geometric style.

Greene, Stephen (1917-). Contemporary American Neo-Romantic painter. Born in New York, he studied at the Art Students League, the National Academy of Design, William and Mary, and Iowa State. Influenced by Shahn, his work is morbid, introspective, and Surrealist in overtone.

Greenwood, John (1727-92). An American Colonial painter born in Boston or nearby. He also was engraver, japanned furniture, and built organs. He did some forty portraits before leaving for England at the age of twenty-five, many of which are still attributed to Smibert, Blackburn, and Badger. His figures are upright and tense, with masklike and chalky faces, and staring eyes.

Greuze, Jean Baptiste (1725-1805). Most misunderstood artist in the history of French painting. Even in his own day he was misunderstood by the critic Diderot who extolled the moral virtue of his titillating canvases and by a wife who dispensed her favors on the side. Greuze's strong point was genre, and it was in this category that he was accepted into the Academy, despite his own pretensions to history painting. This genre was directed, often in a naughty Rococo way that belied its purpose, toward the uplifting of Man through moral lesson and emphasis on family duties. It was simple and obvious in intent, detailed in presentation; as Diderot commented, "true to nature." To Greuze nature meant the rustic, and his subjects were a clear parallel to physiocratic thinking of his day, which called for a return to the simple order of the farm. And lastly his models were dewy-eyed and abandoned, calculated to provoke just that state of sentimental reaction so popular in a society whose women, bled for paleness, were given to nervous seizures and to weeping on the slightest provocation. Greuze's troubles began early when he broke with parental authority to become a painter. Perhaps this and later marital troubles lay behind his yearning to depict the virtues of a settled domestic life. We do not know with whom he studied; he was brought to the attention of the Academy by Silvestre, to whom he had shown his work. He achieved a sudden success with his painting of the Father of the Family Explaining the Bible to his Children (Salon of 1755), and he was received as an associate in the Academy. In that year he departed for Italy and to amorous adventure with a Roman princess. Disparity in station frustrated this sentimental affair, and Greuze returned to France. In Paris he married the beautiful daughter of a bookseller—at her own urging, he later testified. She served as his model, bore him children, squandered his money and developed into a shrew. In the 1780's her promiscuity became so offensive that he obtained a legal separation.

89. GREUZE. The Painter Etienne Jeaurat
M. H. de Young
Memorial Museum, Oakes Collection, San Francisco

88. GREEK. Vase painting. Attic
Museum of Fine Arts, Boston

Greuze's personality was a vain and probably difficult one. He was much incensed, for instance, at being accepted by the Academy in 1769 as a genre painter although his trial canvas dealt with history. He chose to paint a subject with the long-winded title of Emperor Severus Reproaching His Son Caracalla for Having Attempted to Assassinate Him in the Defiles of Scotland. This composition, now in the Louvre, is quite out of keeping with Greuze's usual work. However, the patriarchal theme and the austere classical setting might have been received with greater enthusiasm twenty years later when Neo-Classicism was in fashion. Greuze also anticipated Neo-Classicism in his use of bas-relief composition for his narrative canvases, such as the Paternal Malediction (Louvre). In this work certain figures are based on the antique Niobid group in Rome, an allusion perhaps to the loss of children. Lest the moral lesson of such paintings be misunderstood, Greuze was in the habit of writing detailed explanations to the public upon the appearance of his works And vitriolic letters flowed from his pen when critic or the Academy misused him on any occasion.

Some of his subjects were constructed in series; for instance the consequences of the son's actions which brought on the Paternal Malediction are related in the pendant piece, The Son Punished (Louvre). His greatest success in the line of didactic genre, however, was the Village Bride (Louvre), which caused a sensation in the Salon of 1761 and drew a long eulogy from

GREUZE. Head of a Girl. National Gallery, London

Diderot. He painted excellent, exacting portraits, but better known are his "portrait-type" allegories. These works, labeled Innocence, Grief, Dead Bird, etc., are tender studies of girls whose innocent gestures are belied by the disarray of their garments. Most famous of these is the Broken Pitcher (Louvre) which was purchased by Madame Du Barry. (See illustrations, including color plate 89.)

Grilo, Sarah (1920-). Argentine abstractionist; member of a group of advanced modern painters in Buenos Aires. Her European-influenced forms are derived from nature but adapted imaginatively in abstract unworldly shapes with fragile linear tracery and delicate use of color.

Gris, Juan (1887-1927). Pseudonym of a well-known Spanish-born painter associated with the Cubist group of Paris. He began at the School of Arts and Crafts at Madrid and by 1904 had fallen under the influence of the Jugendstil, or Youth Style, as a result of reading German magazines. He moved to Paris in 1906 and there met Picasso and the various avant-garde critics. In 1912 he exhibited for the first time at the Indépendants and did his first papiers collés in emulation of Braque. He exhibited with the Cubists at the Section d'Or (see) show that same year in a kind of acknowledgment of their debt to Cézanne. His paintings of that period have a wonderfully transparent quality as one plane intersects another within the deliberately narrow space of the canvas. It is an original formulation and quite different from anything done by the other Cubists. This architectonic element was reinforced around 1916 by the addition of vivid color quality, and in 1920 he joined in the last Cubist show. Gris's rather poetic manner of looking at things, from this point on, made him useful as a painter of sets for Diaghilev's Ballet Russe in 1923-24. He is outstanding among those painters in the modern school who are intensely aware of the formal structure of a canvas. (See illustrations, including color plate 90.)

grisaille. From the French "gris" or grey; refers to monochromatic, or one-colored painting, generally in grey. Used both for easel painting and for stained glass. Example: Odalisque by Ingres (Metropolitan).

Gromaire, Marcel (1892-). A French Expressionist whose work is related in quality to that of many modern Flemish painters such as Permeke. Considering Gromaire's mixed French-Flemish parentage, this is not surprising, especially in view of his pre-war travel in Belgium, Holland and Germany. Since 1920 he has produced the characteristic monumental, darkly colored studies of peasant and working-class life that are his specialty and are so unusual in the modern French school. Besides contemporary Flemish influences, we may also note those of medieval art, French and Flemish primitive painting, Brueghel, Rembrandt, and finally the modern form-consciousness of Cézanne and of Seurat. (See illustration.)

Gropper, William (1897-). Contemporary American social realist painter and cartoonist. Born in New York City, he studied at the National Academy of Design, the New York School of Fine and Applied Arts, and the Ferrer School with Henri and Bellows. Although he achieved fame through his vigorous and inventive black-and-whites as a cartoonist for newspapers and magazines, most of them left-wing, he has also executed murals and continues to paint easel pictures on social themes. His style stems from Brueghel and Daumier, and is characterized by incisive drawing and a loose expressionistic handling of paint. (See illustration.)

Gros, Baron Antoine Jean (1771-1835). Forerunner of French Romantic painting. Delacroix commented, "Gros has elevated modern subjects to the level of the ideal... he has seen his heroes through the lens of his enthusiasm." Gros

GRIS. Jars and Glass
Kröller-Müller Collection, Otterlo

was a history painter, but he painted current history as had his master David before him in The Oath in the Tennis Court. As with David's Imperial spectacles, Gros energized his histories by Baroque methods. However, to the Davidian's chagrin, he employed a new brilliant coloring and impressionistic background instead of the traditional sculptural effects of Neo-Classisism.

Both Gros's parents were artists. At fifteen he was entered in the studio of David. During the Revolution he was in Italy, studying Rubens and van Dyck. Through the good offices of Josephine he was introduced to Napoleon in 1796, and he was put on the project of confiscating Italian art for the French Musée Centrale. He lived in close association with the Consul and so was able to paint battle pictures of an authenticity hitherto unknown. At this time he sketched the stirring portrait of Napoleon on the Bridge of Arcole (Louvre) carrying the tricolor of the new Republic. This was earlier than David's canvases of hero-worship and it set a pattern for the adulation of Napoleon by soldiers and civilians of the early nineteenth century. It is a more powerful image than David's equestrian portrait of the Emperor. Back in France, Gros created a Salon sensation in 1804 with his Pest House of Jaffa (Louvre and Boston). This picture commemorated the dramatic entry of Napoleon into his army hospital during the plague. He is represented as standing among a group of his officers and touching one of the many infected soldiers and Arabs by whom he was surrounded. This incident Gros had not witnessed and he felt free to draw upon his imagination and on certain Baroque traditions that he had apparently learned from plague pictures in the Italian collections. We can follow his thinking in a series of studies which culminate in the final image of Napoleon reaching

GROMAIRE. Portrait of Mlle S. S. Detroit Institute of Arts

GROPPER. Isolationist
Associated American Artists Galleries, New York

out with the healing gesture of St. Roch or St. Carlo Borromeo. It has been suggested that there was a tradition in France of the divine healing power of a monarch. The painting also reflected the new taste for exotic Oriental settings that was brought in by Napoleon's campaigns. The miraculous powers of the Leader were further emphasized in the painting, Napoleon at the Battle of Eylau. Against a dreary impressionistic landscape of snow and shellbursts, Napoleon sits on a horse, surrounded by officers, captives and the wounded. A Lithuanian presses forward to kiss his boots, his dying soldiers salute him as they emit their last breath. A new mood of heroism, suffering and color had invaded the formulas of David's school. More impetuous a battlepiece was the Battle of Aboukir (1806), for which he did studies in a very loose technique.

True to the doctrine of David, if not to his style, Gros was picked to continue the school after his master's exile. His success continued under the Restoration in portraits of Louis XVIII and Charles X and in mediocre paintings of French history with genuine medieval detail. He continued to exhibit at the Salons until his death in 1835, but his last years were troubled ones. With no battles to paint, he turned back to the pages of history and tried classical subjects. The students and public preferred his modern manner, but David, whose own style withered in Brussels, urged him towards the old Grand Style. The tensions eventually led to Gros's death by suicide. His importance, then, is a significant, but fleeting one, associated with his early works for Napoleon. In them he represented a clearer reaction to David than did Prud'hon. He affected posterity largely through his influence on Géricault and Delacroix in their formative years. (See illustration.)

Grosz, George (1893-). German-born American painter and graphic artist originally associated with the Dada and New Objectivity schools in Germany in the last years of World War I and immediately afterward. He began as an illustrator in a typically critical vein, turning to Futurism in painting for a while as a means of injecting some of the turbulent spirit of modern times into his work. When the anarchistic and destructive Dada movement appeared in 1917, he adopted its viewpoint and participated in many of its activities along with many other disillusioned soldiers. From here he moved on to what was to be his signature as an artist: a kind of nervous, twisting pen-and-ink line that contained all the bitterness and hatred he could muster against the bourgeoisie, the militarists, the clergy and other

90. GRIS. The Coffee Mill. Saidenberg Gallery, New York

groups which in his Germany represented the "reactionary" side of existence. These drawings are among the great contributions of modern German art. During the middle 1920's he passed on to the mournful, clearly lit, detailed and photographically painted forms of the New Objectivity style of that time, but did not cease his attacks on the things that seemed to him wrong. When Hitler came to power in 1933, Grosz left Germany and went to the United States. There he has made a new reputation for himself, concentrating on romantic landscapes and sensuous nudes, both done in a characteristically fuzzy technique. That Grosz had not entirely forgotten his past social interests is attested by the series of symbolic war pictures and related subjects done during World War II. See EXPRESSIONISM, MAGIC REALISM. (See illustration.)

Grüber, Francis (1912-). French Fauve painter whose work reaches a higher pitch of emotional intensity than most of the members of that group by virtue of its "cruelty" of form and color. Distinctly melancholy in tone and subject matter, he delights in showing dejected people, desolate landscapes and scenes of war.

Grünewald, Matthias (1475/80?-1528). German painter, architect and engineer. The date of his birth is not certain and the name of his teacher is unknown, but his wonderful and awe-inspiring Isenheim altarpiece is perhaps the foremost monument of German art. Grünewald is mentioned in the archives of Aschaffenburg in 1501. From 1508-14 he was official painter to the Archbishop of Mainz, and after 1514 court painter of Albrecht of Brandenburg, Elector of Mainz. The Isenheim altarpiece, now in the Museum at Colmar, was finished before 1511. It consists of two pair of mighty wings enclosing a carved shrine; on the inner wings are pictured scenes from the life of St. Anthony, the Annunciation and the Resurrection, and a Virgin and Child attended by music-making angels. When the wings are closed, the exterior discloses a Crucifixion against an ominously dark sky. It is a representation of incomparable expressiveness, in

GROS. Horseman Mounting His Horse. Galerie Charpentier, Paris

91. GUARDI. View on the Cannaregio, Venice. National Gallery of Art, Kress Collection, Washington, D.C.

which the emotion and the mystical significance are enhanced by agitated drawing and clangorous color. Excitement and animation pervade every detail of the work and are as evident in the architecture and the gnarled trunks of trees as in the forms of the actors in the sacred drama. The pictures that Grünewald painted in later life reflect his growing awareness of the Renaissance in Italy, where he may have visited, but they seem lifeless and tame in comparison with his masterwork. (See illustration.)

Guardi, Francesco (1712-93). Venetian painter; most famous for his views of Venice, he also did marines, figure pieces, portraits, and landscapes with ruins. Though he grows out of the topographic school of Canaletto, he was much more interested, in an impressionistic way, in the shimmer of changing light and color, painting with a vivacious and light touch the pageantry of Venetian life. Born in Venice, the son of a decorative painter, Domenico, he studied first with his brother, Antonio, who painted Rococo altarpieces. He later worked under Canaletto and knew the paintings of Tiepolo, who was his brother-in-law. He was mainly influenced, however, by Longhi, Ricci, and Magnasco, and inherited the latter's taste for fantasy. Little is known of his actual life and most of his known works date after 1760. He was not highly regarded by his contemporaries and was considered simply a follower of Canaletto. Most of his patrons were English living in Venice. Many of the paintings attributed to him are probably by his brother Niccolò, and his son Giacomo. Seen today as a forerunner of Impressionism, his sparkling landscapes with their loaded highlights are valued far above those of his contemporaries. (See color plate 91.)

Guariento (active 1338-c.1370). One of the first painters of importance in Padua after Giotto. Various records refer to him between 1338 and 1365. From 1365 to 1368 he painted the Coronation of the Virgin in the Hall of the Grand Council in the Doge's palace, Venice (painted over by Tintoretto, and

GROSZ. No Let-up. Museum of Modern Art, New York

GRUNEWALD. The Expectant Virgin
Detail from altarpiece in Colmar, France

GUARIENTO. Jesus Christ on the Cross
Civic Museum, Bassano

later destroyed by fire). In September of 1370 he is referred to as deceased. According to early accounts, he decorated the Cappella Maggiore of the Eremitani church (partially preserved despite damage to the church in World War II) and the palace of the Capitano del Popolo, both at Padua. A signed Crucifix is in the museum at Bassano, and frescoes have been attributed to him in the same town. His Gothic style was eventually influenced by the Giotto frescoes of the Arena Chapel. (See illustration.)

Guercino (Giovanni Francesco Barbieri) (1591-1666). One of the leading painters of the Italian Baroque. Highly thought of in his day, though less so now, his best works are in a lyrical rather than dramatic vein. His version of Baroque is based on a synthesis of Correggesque sfumato (see) and Venetian color rather than a union of Caravaggio and Bolognese art. He was extremely active in Emilia, producing all types of painting and decoration. Born in Cento near Ferrara, blind in one eye (thus Guercino, squinter), he studied with Bertozzi, Gennari, and Zagoni, and absorbed the Emilian style of Bonone, Schedone, and Ludovico Carracci. His earliest works were decorations for houses and churches in Cento and his first important commission was the Madonna in Glory in S. Agostino (1616). In 1617 he was in Bologna, working for Archbishop Ludovisi and others; the next year in Venice, where he was influenced by Titian; and in 1621 he went to Rome to do the portrait of Pope Gregory XV. Here among his many commissions was the decoration of the Casino Ludovisi in which his Aurora, with its lyrical, poetic, coloristic, and painterly handling established his style and importance. Though his reputation in Rome was high he returned to Cento in 1623 and spent the rest of his life in a kind of artistic isolation in Emilia, continuing his own manner but with a consistent deterioration through stylization and idealization. His major pupils were Crespi, Preti, and Mola. (See illustration.)

Guérin, Pierre Narcisse (1774-1833). French painter and lithographer. Student of Regnault, Guérin perpetuated the Neo-Classic tradition of David with subjects drawn from Roman history and French classical drama. He is famous as the teacher from whose atelier emerged Géricault, Delacroix, Scheffer and Cogniet. His Phedra Accusing Hippolytus before Theseus (Louvre) was a sensation in the Salon of 1802.

Guernica by Pablo Picasso (see).

Guerrero, Xavier (1896-). Mexican painter. Together with Siqueiros and Rivera he founded the revolutionary paper *El Machete*, 1922. He collaborated on early frescoes with Rivera and experimented in techniques of mural painting. He is widely traveled. He did murals in Escuela México in Chillán, Chile, 1941, while Siqueiros was at work there. His basic belief is in realism "as a universal human language fulfilling a social function."

Guerrero Galván, Jesús (1910-). Mexican easel painter, stage designer, mural and graphic artist influenced by the French moderns of the neo-classical 1920's. His art shows solidly proportioned, sculpturesque figures filled with poetic mood and arranged decoratively; earth colors predominate. He did a mural in the National Electrical Commission Building, Mexico City, in 1952.

Guggenheim Museum New York. A collection devoted primarily to works of non-objective art (see) by such masters as Kandinsky (the most significant part of the collection), Xceron, Moholy-Nagy and others, as well as somewhat more representational Cubist or Purist-derived works by Gleizes, Wadsworth, Léger, Delaunay, etc. There are in addition interesting examples of the work of such painters as Chagall and Seurat. Although organized originally to show only the

GUERCINO. Christ and the Woman of Samaria
Detroit Institute of Arts

GUTTUSO. Melon Eaters. Museum of Modern Art, New York

non-objective, the museum has been reoriented to present every worthwhile aspect of the modern tradition.

Guglielmi, O. Louis (1906-). Contemporary American painter; employs meticulous realism to express social symbolism. More recently his art has tended toward abstraction. Born in Cairo of Italian parents, he came to the U.S. in 1914 and had his art training at the National Academy of Design.

Guidi, Virgilio (1892-). Italian painter, son of a sculptor and grandson of an architect; worked as decorator and restorer, copying many paintings by Old Masters. Although associated with the conservative Novecento movement, his representational painting suggests the simplifications of form found in Oskar Schlemmer.

Guidini (see FRANCIABIGIO).

Guido, Alfredo (1892-). Argentine easel painter, muralist, ceramist and graphic artist; he leads the more modern group. He rebelled against the standard Argentine Impressionist manner; uses large, simply blocked-out forms. He decorated the Argentine Pavilion, N.Y. World's Fair, 1939.

Guido da Siena (active c.1250-1275). Italian, Sienese. The date given of a Madonna of his in the Palazzo Pubblico in Siena is 1221 but on stylistic evidence cannot be earlier than 1270. A dossal (altar back) of the Madonna and Saints in the Siena gallery is dated 1270 and is generally attributed to Guido or a close follower. While related to other Tuscan works of the thirteenth century, his art was especially influential in the founding of the Sienese style as exemplified by Duccio.

Guilano di Arrigo (see PESELLO).

Guillaumin, Jean Baptiste Armand (1841-1927). A French Impressionist painter and etcher. Lesser known member of the group (see IMPRESSIONISM), Guillaumin exhibited in both the Salon des Refusés of 1863 and the first group show at Nadar's studio in 1874. Although he began with Parisian street scenes, he is better known for rural landscapes. He was a close associate of Pissarro, whom he portrayed in his Pissarro Painting.

Guston, Philip (1912-). Contemporary American painter born in Montreal, Canada. His earlier genre subjects were broadly realistic though somewhat stylized. It was in this manner that he made a reputation as a mural painter. However, more recently he has turned toward complete abstraction. He studied at the Otis Art Institute in Los Angeles.

Gutiérrez, José (1902-). Mexican easel painter and muralist, widely known for his work in development of synthetic paints, especially vinylite and pyroxylin; has developed an ethyl silicate compound for use in outdoor mural painting. His art has recently been concerned with perspective illusions and dynamic movement. He is Director of Chemical Research for Plastics in the National Polytechnical Institute, Mexico City.

Guttuso, Renato (1912-). Italian painter who began with the anti-classical "Roman School" of the 1930's (see SCIPIONE and MAFAI) together with Cagli and others. Around 1939 he became involved in the progressive *Corrente* movement in Milan, a local variation that broke up during the war. A member of the anti-German Resistance movement, Guttuso published *Gott mit Uns*, a book of bitterly anti-Nazi drawings. After the war he was active in various vanguard groups culminating in the New Art Front. In spite of the left-wing convictions of many of its members, it is to Expressionism and the abstractions of Guernica that they turn for inspiration in their socially minded works: e.g., Guttuso's The Maffia, 1948, Museum of Modern Art, N.Y. (See illustration.)

Guy, Francis (1760-1820). American landscape painter born in England. Apprenticed to a tailor, he had a varied career as tailor and dyer. He was self-taught as a painter, literal and naive, and his landscapes are the result of first-hand observation and meticulous rendering.

Guys, Constantin (1802-92). French painter and caricaturist best known for his wash drawings of Parisian demimondaines. The son of a naval commissary, Guys was in Greece with Byron, became an officer in the French army and later an illustrator for the *Illustrated London News*. In this capacity he covered the Crimean War. Until 1856 London was his center of activity; after that he returned to Paris and began to produce his witty and delicate drawings. These are not critical or uncritical, but merely observations of the life of his time, set down with an everpresent charm and grace, an amazingly skillfull way of summing up a particular character or situation.

Guzmán de Rojas, Cecilio (1900-). The best-known Bolivian nativist painter. His themes deal with the Indians and the land; he portrays people in brilliantly colored dress. The figures are more flat-patterned than three-dimensional.

Gwathmey, Robert (1903-). Contemporary American painter born in Richmond, Va., he treats the life of the Southern Negro. He received his art training at the Mary-

92. HALS. Officer. Wildenstein Gallery, New York

land Institute of Design and the Pennsylvania Academy of Fine Arts, and later taught at Beaver College and the Carnegie Institute. He had his first one-man show in 1941. His paintings of Southern life are imbued with a deep sense of social justice and executed with a refined feeling for pattern and color. His style, though realistic in intent, is dependent on abstraction and his use of flat, rich color separated by black lines conveys the impression almost of stained glass. (See illustration.)

H

Haitian painting. A contemporary manifestation devoted to naive or primitive painting. To the extent that the islanders practicing this spontaneous kind of painting are less in contact with the tradition of professional art than other primitives of the modern French or American type their work is more genuinely primitive in spirit, more unlearned in quality. Apparently the only art forms known to them are the commercial colored religious lithographs imported from Cuba or on magazine covers. High-keyed in color, flat and linear in form, two-dimensional in space and brilliantly decorative in its final effect, this art would seem to be a genuine reflection of Haitian culture, with biblical themes, voodoo subjects and genre details brought together casually but effectively. The artists are supported by the state, which sells their product at modest prices through its National Art Center. See PREHISTORIC PAINTING.

Hall, Peter Adolphus (1739-93). Swedish-born miniature-painter associated with the French school of the eighteenth century. A talented musician and dancer in addition to being a skilled painter, Hall gained admittance to the highest social levels. He is considered to have been among the best miniaturists of the time.

Halpert, Samuel (1884-1930). American painter born in Russia but came to the U.S. as a boy. He was one of the earliest Americans to be influenced by the modern movement, especially Cézanne; his art resembles that of Marquet (see) in its broad and vigorous handling of color, its solidity of modeling, and its treatment of light. He studied first at the National Academy of Design and then in Paris with Léon Bonnat at the Ecole des Beaux-Arts. He worked, exhibited, and traveled in Europe until 1911 and then returned to the U.S. He eventually settled in Detroit and taught painting at the Society of Arts and Crafts.

GWATHMEY. Sowing
Whitney Museum of American Art, New York

93. HARNETT. Music and Literature
Albright Art Gallery, Buffalo

Hals, Dirck (1591-1656). Dutch painter of genre scenes and portraits. He was the younger brother of Frans Hals and possibly his pupil. It is thought that he traveled in Italy; he also shows the influence of the Haarlem painter Hendrick Pot. He was one of the first Dutch painters to develop the elegant interior scenes or "conversation pieces" which were to become important in Dutch painting. His style is marked by fine color and tone, and by skillful composition.

Hals, Frans (1580/81-1666). Dutch painter of portraits and genre scenes, who holds, along with Rembrandt, a place of prime importance among Holland's painters. Born in Antwerp, Hals went as a youth to Haarlem and spent a very full and productive life there. He was the pupil of Karel van Mander, who is better known for biographies of Dutch and Flemish artists than for his painting. The impression of exuberance and health conveyed by the art of Hals contrasts strangely with a personal life that seems to have been far from happy. Although he was apparently a very popular and prolific artist, heading the painter's guild in Haarlem, it appears that he never achieved even a reasonably steady income and during his last years was dependent on civic assistance.

His most important works, a long series of group portraits done throughout his career, have remained in Haarlem and it is only there that his work can be thoroughly known and studied. Although Rembrandt painted three imposing and masterly group portraits, it may be asserted that it was Hals who made the major contribution to the development of this special kind of composition. The earliest of these guild portraits was made in 1616 and shows the officers of the company of St. George in a rather showy self-conscious arrangement around a banquet table laden with still life. Heavy draperies, a brilliant diagonal banner and a good deal of bright color animate the scene. In the next two corporation pieces, painted about 1623/24 and in 1627, the space becomes more compressed, the color more subdued, with a marked increase in tensions and more interest in the psychological differentiation of types. Others followed in 1633 and 1639, and in them a stylistic progression may be traced toward the two very great paintings made almost at the end of his life, the male and female regents of the hospital for old men in Haarlem. In these pictures, which he painted in 1664, the color, which has been gradually reduced to a prevailing harmony

HALS. The Bohemian. Louvre, Paris

of tones, has now become nearly monotone. The artist has restricted his palette to various subtly differentiated shades of steely grey. These great late paintings are marvels of characterization, sombre strength and dignity. The two most striking aspects of Hals's art are its abundant vitality, which is especially evident in the works of his earlier and middle life, such as Laughing Cavalier, and the brilliant virtuosity with which he used his brush. This dexterity of brushwork, which lends a purely pictorial beauty to each of his pictures, becomes in the latest ones, where there is no longer the distraction of a varied palette, impressionistic and incomparably effective. In these it has become a thing of beauty in its own right. All of Hals's portraits exhibit his extraordinary power to seize upon personality less through painstaking analysis than flashes of insight. (See illustrations, including color plate 92).

Hals Museum, Haarlem, Neth. Richest repository of works by Frans Hals; located in his native city.

Han Kan (see CHINESE PAINTERS: T'ANG DYNASTY).

Han-lin. The imperial academy to which outstanding Chinese painters were appointed. The members were held in high regard, and those who attained the *tai chao* degree (Painter-in-Waiting) had access to the Emperor's private rooms as courtiers holding royal favor.

hao. In China the literary, familiar, or studio name used by authors and painters. There may be several, each indicating a change of residence, a special event, or a characteristic quality.

Harding, Chester (1792-1866). A competent though not remarkable American portrait painter, who had a varied career as drummer-boy in the War of 1812, cabinet maker, peddler, tavern keeper, and sign painter before he became an itinerant portraitist in Kentucky, Ohio, and Missouri. After some study at the Pennsylvania Academy of Fine Arts, he settled down to portrait painting in Washington, D.C., Boston, and Northampton: In his last years he painted such notables as Webster, Calhoun, Marshall and Sherman.

Harnett, William Michael (1848-92). The most popular late nineteenth-century American painter of trompe-l'oeil (see) still lifes. He was born in Ireland but was brought to Philadelphia as a child. He worked first as an engraver and studied at the Pennsylvania Academy of Fine Arts and in New York. In 1878, he painted and exhibited in London and Paris, and later spent four years in Munich. In the 1880's he settled in New York and painted still lifes which commanded prices as high as $10,000 each. However, his

HART. The Bahamas. Whitney Museum of American Art, New York

work found no place within the genteel tradition of American art and he fell into complete obscurity; he was rediscovered only recently, perhaps because of the superficial resemblance of his art to Surrealism. His still lifes are characterized by a boldness of design and a remarkably meticulous though broad handling. His subject matter consisted of commonplace objects—guns, musical instruments, books, pipes, etc.—and he had a special predilection for compositions with objects hanging from wooden doors, including, especially, paper, envelopes, and printed material, all of which he rendered with great fidelity and rich color. (See color plate 93.)

Harpignies, Henri Joseph (1819-1916). French painter and graphic artist. Watercolorist and landscape painter of the Barbizon type. He turned from business to study painting with Achard. He was at first much drawn to Italy where he traveled and lived. There emerged from his study of the Italian masters his Vue de Capri (Salon of 1853). Throughout his career he was also much affected by the various styles of Corot. They shared the poetic style with which Harpignies interpreted many regions of France. He exhibited with the New Water Colour Society of London and his aquarelles have been much sought after.

Hart, George Overbury "Pop" (1868-1933). American watercolorist who was noted for his spirited genre paintings of scenes from many parts of the world. Born in Illinois, he worked first in his father's glue factory and later spent a life wandering and painting. He visited many countries, had many kinds of jobs, and studied in many schools. He maintained through it all a personal and colorful though somewhat naive style, characterized by a spirited Impressionistic handling of color and movement. He studied at the Chicago Art Institute and Académie Julian among others. He worked as an itinerant sign painter down the Mississippi to New Orleans. Later he painted billboards and amusement park signs in New York and New Jersey and movie sets during the summers, traveling to warmer climates in the winter, where he did his watercolors. He also did etchings and lithographs. (See illustration.)

Hartley, Marsden (1877-1943). One of the pioneers of modern art in America. Born in Lewiston, Me., he moved to Cleveland as a boy, worked as an office boy and studied art with John Semon and later on a scholarship with Cullen Yates and Nina Waldeck at the Cleveland School of Art. In 1900 he came to New York and attended the Chase School and the National Academy of Design, but the following year abandoned his studies and moved to Maine, where he painted Impressionistic mountain landscapes until 1908. In 1909 he had his first one-man show, at Stieglitz' "291" Gallery, where his Black Landscapes, showing the influence of Ryder, were not well received. In 1912 with the aid of A. B. Davies and Stieglitz he went aboad, painted abstract compositions and exhibited with the Blaue Reiter group in Munich and Berlin. He was again abroad in England, France, and Germany from 1914 to 1916. In Berlin he continued painting large Expressionist abstractions in bold color. After 1919, he renounced abstraction for a personal, Fauvelike Expressionism. In 1919-20 he was in the Southwest, painting high-keyed Expressionist landscapes, a style which he continued in Europe after a successful auction of all his works. In Provence (1924-26) he painted landscapes under the severe discipline of Cézanne's art. After his return to the U.S. in 1930, he traveled widely, doing landscapes, marines, still lifes, and genre pictures in a bold, rich, and harsh-colored Expressionistic style. He also wrote poetry and art criticism. (See illustration.)

Hartung, Hans (1904-). German-born painter of the modern French school. In his youth Hartung was interested in astronomy and optics, but he has also been drawing and painting since the age of thirteen. During the 1920's he was influenced successively by Rembrandt, the German Impres-

HARTLEY. Fox Island, Maine. Addison Gallery of American Art, Phillips Academy, Andover

HASSAM. A Back Road. Brooklyn Museum

sionists Slevogt and Corinth, then Kokoschka, Nolde and Marc among the Expressionists. By 1922 his style had become fully abstract, though his family tried to force him into a representational type of painting. His first exhibition was held in 1931 and a few years later he left Nazi Germany for France, where he served in the French Foreign Legion during World War II and gained French citizenship. His art may be considered an abstract improvisatory style halfway between the formulation of Kandinsky and that of Masson.

Harunobu (see JAPANESE PAINTERS: TOKUGAWA PERIOD).

Hassam, (Frederick) Childe (1859-1935). American Impressionist painter, etcher, and lithographer, member of the Ten. Born in Dorchester, Mass., he studied at the Boston Art School, was apprenticed to an engraver, and then became an illustrator. In 1883 he went to Paris where he studied with Boulanger and Lefebvre at the Ecole des Beaux-Arts, but he was affected by Impressionism and thereafter painted in that manner. On his return to the U.S., he settled in New York and painted its bustling life with a sparkling palette. Although this remained his favorite subject he also did landscapes of rural New York and New England. During his lifetime he received a host of medals and awards and was elected a member of the National Academy in 1906. In 1915 he began to do etchings and lithographs and, though well along in life, he executed over 350 plates, seeking to achieve the effects of sunlight even in black-and-white. (See illustration.)

hatching. The arrangement of groups of intersecting or parallel lines so close together as to form areas of shading and thus of light-and-dark effects. Its clearest application is in the area of black-and-white drawings, etchings, woodcuts, etc., but it is also to be found in the field of painting, as in the works of Delacroix.

Hay Wain, The, by John Constable (see).

Haydon, Benjamin Robert (1786-1846). British historical painter and diarist who painted in the grand manner but whose craftsmanship was not quite equal to the manner. He was the teacher of Sir Edwin Landseer, the animal painter.

Haye, de la (see CORNEILLE DE LYON).

Hayman, Francis (1708-76). British designer and portraitist who did conversation pieces (see), interesting people and scenes of the day, decorations (for Vauxhall Gardens, where he copied Hogarth's Four Times of Day for the boxes), elegant costumes, theatrical scenery, etc. A drawing-master, he seems to have taught Gainsborough for a while and to have initiated him into the delights of the big city. One of the original members of the Royal Academy, he was on terms of friendship with all of London's artists.

Hebert, Antoine Auguste Ernest (1817-1908). French painter of history, genre, portraits and religious works. He studied with David d'Angers and Delaroche and spent time in Italy, where he was Director of the French Academy (1867-73). He specialized in melancholic studies of sickly female types, but made his greatest success with an Italian anecdote, Malaria (Salon of 1850).

Heckel, Erich (1883-). German painter, graphic artist and an original member of Die Brücke in Dresden, 1905. In 1901 he got to know the painter Schmidt-Rottluff in Chemnitz, and in 1904, while studying architecture at the Technical High School, made the acquaintance of Kirchner and Bleyl. With the three others he formed the Brücke association in 1905. From 1907 on, Heckel devoted himself exclusively to painting and graphic work. Along with the others he moved on to Berlin in 1911, doing the Brücke portfolio for that year, and the following year he and Kirchner did wall and ceiling decorations at the Sonderbund show in Cologne. During the war he was a medical orderly in Belgium, and produced his Madonna of Ostend. Heckel's style crystallized into a mystical, poetic version of the Expressionist search for identification with something larger than self; it said, in effect, man is

HECKEL. Frau Heckel. Detroit Institute of Arts

very tiny and the world very large. In 1937 he was stigmatized as "degenerate" by the Nazis and in 1944 his studio was destroyed in a bombardment. In 1949 he was made a professor at the Academie in Karlsruhe. See EXPRESSIONISM. (See illustration.)

Heda, Willem Claesz. (1594-1680/82). Dutch painter of still life. He was born and spent his life in Haarlem, where he was a member of the painters' guild. Like his son Gerrit, whom he trained, he did work of exquisite delicacy and finish.

Heem, Jan Davidsz. de (1606-83/84). Dutch painter of still life. He was born in Utrecht, and worked there and at Leyden, where he came under the influence of the young Rembrandt. In 1636 he settled for some years in Antwerp. His skillful combinations of flowers and edibles with silver and crystal were very important in the formation of the tradition of still-life painting.

Heemskerck, Maerten van (1498-1574). Dutch painter of portraits and religious subjects. He studied with Jan van Scorel in Haarlem and spent his working life there. During a three-year sojourn in Italy, he was profoundly affected by works of Michelangelo and Raphael that he saw in Rome. It is there that his art acquired the breadth and monumentality by which it is distinguished.

Heian Period (see JAPANESE PAINTERS: HEIAN PERIOD, 794-1185).

Hélion, Jean (1904-). French painter, critic and editor who began as a student of engineering and architecture and was drawn in 1926 to the work of the Cubists and Mondrian. He also met Van Doesburg in 1930 and helped edit *L'Art Concret* that year; later he was active in the *Abstraction-Création* group in Paris. His style is geometric in a three-dimensional Constructivist sense with the forms arranged for their own sakes and without reference to any reality but their own. He was in the U.S. from 1932 to 1940 and again during the later part of World War II, after escaping from a German prison camp.

HENRI. Mary
Addison Gallery of American Art, Phillips Academy, Andover

HEMESSEN. Portrait of a Lady. National Gallery, London

Hellenic. A term applied to a period of ancient Greece ranging from about the eighth century B.C. to the end of the fourth century B.C. It includes the early archaic style, the classic idealizations of the Golden Age in the fifth century B.C. and the beginnings of emotional projection in the fourth century.

Hellenistic. A term applied to Greek civilization from the time of Alexander the Great at the end of the fourth century B.C. down to Roman times. It includes all those areas which were influenced by the Greek viewpoint during that period: Egypt, Asia Minor, Syria, etc. Stylistically it signified a change from the still controlled emotions and idealized forms of the fourth century to a new intensified naturalism and emotional expression.

Helst, Bartholomeus van der (1613-70). A Dutch painter of individual and large group portraits. He probably studied under Nicolaes Eliasz. in Amsterdam. He was Rembrandt's chief rival, his smoothly painted, handsomely composed portraits evidently proving more attractive than Rembrandt's to patrons who sought only a good likeness and a well-executed picture.

Hemessen, Jan Sanders van (c.1504-before 1566). A Flemish painter of Antwerp. Student of H. van Cleef, but in style strongly under the influence of Metsys and Gossaert. Of his life little is known except that he was Dean of the painters' guild in 1548. Recently Hemessen has been identified with the Brunswick Monogramist, who was previously thought to be Jan van Amstel (see). If this is the case, Hemessen was a close link to Pieter Brueghel, because the Brunswick Feeding of the Five Thousand swarms with small pre-Brueghelian figures. Otherwise Hemessen painted Mannerist compositions of large figures, especially religious works

HERRERA THE YOUNGER.
Apotheosis of St. Hermengilous. Prado, Madrid

cast in genre settings, such as the Prodigal Son amongst the Harlots (Brussels). He also painted genres of a bawdy nature and such famous horrors as the Operation for the Stone (Prado). (See illustration.)

Henner, Jean Jacques (1829-1905). French painter from Alsace. German-trained, he passed from an enthusiasm for Holbein to Correggio and Prud'hon as a result of study in Italy. Although he painted history and portraits he is best known for his prostrate nudes in dreamy landscapes rendered in murky chiaroscuro. Popular was a profile head, Fabiola, which he did in several versions.

Henri, Robert (1865-1929). American portrait and landscape painter, and influential teacher. Born in Cincinnati, he studied at the Pennsylvania Academy of Fine Arts and then in Paris at the Ecole des Beaux-Arts as well as the Académie Julian with Bouguereau and Fleury. Unsatisfied by the narrow academic tradition, he traveled in Europe and absorbed the art of Hals, Velázquez, Manet, Courbet, and Whistler. Out of this realist tradition emerged his style, a broad and vigorous handling of the appearance of reality. In 1891 he began his career as painter and teacher in Philadelphia, where he met Luks, Sloan, Glackens, and Shinn, and inspired them to paint contemporary American life in the manner of Manet, Goya, Daumier, and Guys. He later taught in New York at various schools, was a member of the Eight, helped organize the Independents' Exhibition in 1910, the Armory Show in 1913, the MacDowell Group shows and finally the Independents' Show of 1917. He fought all the battles of freedom in art and for juryless and prizeless exhibitions. He imbued all his students with a concern for life and adventure in art. His own work was largely confined to portraits, with an occasionally spirited landscape in the manner of Manet, but with a virtuosity of brushwork which was closer to Sargent. Early in the century he turned from commissioned portraits and full-length pictures of women to studies of racial and national types, which he called "My People." He traveled extensively, painting fluent and vibrant studies of Irish peasants, Spanish gypsies, New England Yankees, American Indians and Negroes, and especially many appealing pictures of children. (See illustration.)

Henry, Edward Lamson (1841-1919). American anecdotal genre and historical painter. Born in South Carolina, he studied briefly in New York and Philadelphia and later in Paris with Gleyre. He achieved an early and popular success.

Henry VIII by Hans Holbein the Younger (see).

Herlin, Friedrich (active 1459-after 1488). German painter. He was active in Nördlingen, where most of his works are preserved. The various altarpieces he painted during a period of nearly thirty years make it clear that he was trained by a Netherlandish painter, perhaps actually in the Low Countries, and later in life renewed his contacts with the art of Flanders. The style of Rogier van der Weyden seems to have exerted a profound influence on him and is clearly reflected in the Presentation in the Temple painted for the high altarpiece of the church of St. George and now in the Town Hall at Nördlingen.

Hermitage Museum, Leningrad. The most important museum in the Soviet Union for traditional painting as well as for medieval ivories and gold ornaments of Scythian, Siberian and similar origin. It is particularly well known for its collection of Rembrandt paintings, the high point in a representative group of traditional works. Since it owns a great many works nationalized by the Soviet government after the Revolution, the Hermitage has an unusually large number of art objects in its vaults. Its collections have recently been enriched by a group of modern paintings from the disbanded New Museum of Modern Western Art of Moscow (see).

Hernández, Alejo (see FERNÁNDEZ, ALEJO).

Herrán, Saturnino (1887-1918). Mexican painter who represents a transition from the late nineteenth-century European style of pre-Revolutionary painting to the present national viewpoint. His themes are regional and his drawing and coloring academic.

Herrera the Elder, Francisco (1576?-1656). Spanish painter, etcher and medalist. One of the founders of the school of Seville. As an early exponent of the tenebrist style (see), he painted in a stolid and heavy fashion that marked a departure from the Mannerist formulas then in vogue in Andalusia. He studied with Luis Fernández and was briefly, perhaps, the master of Velázquez. However, he had such a sharp temper that his career was marred by unpleasant incidents with colleagues and even with his own children. He appears to have caught the attention of Philip IV in 1624 with an Apotheosis of San Hermengildo, a subject also painted by his son. This, with a series of paintings of St. Basil, marks his early mature style. His color was freshened and his naturalism deepened by working together with Zurbarán on the series of the Life of St. Bonaventura in the church of that name in Seville. The quality of Spanish reticence in his three paintings of that series is one of the strengths of Herrera's style. After 1640 his manner grew softer under the influence of the Venetians. Most of these later works were done in Madrid where he went toward the end of his life. Herrera had little following, partly because his students could not endure his bad disposition. His enemies were numerous and they accused him, at one time, of employing his knowledge of metal-engraving to produce counterfeit money.

Herrera the Younger, Francisco (1622-85). Span-

HIGHMORE. Portrait of a Girl. Detroit Institute of Arts

ish painter and architect. Son and pupil of Francisco Herrera the Elder (see). He fled to Rome in part because of his father's temper. In Italy he was famous as a still-life painter and was called "lo Spagnuolo degli pesci" for his specialty of fish painting. After his father's death he returned to Seville, where he painted a St. Francis and a Triumph of the Sacrament for the Cathedral. He was elected an official of the Seville Academy, but left for Madrid where he was attached to the court and did fresco decorations for a number of churches. His style was weaker than that of his father, but with a certain excellence of color. (See illustration.)

Hesdin, Jacquemart de (active 1384-1410/11). Franco-Flemish miniaturist. Painter to the Duke of Berri, for whom his shop did four extant Books of Hours. Best-documented are Les Grandes Heures du Duc de Berri (Bibliothèque Nationale) and Les Très Belles Heures de Jehan de France, Duc de Berri (Brussels). These, especially the Brussels Hours, show Jacquemart's atelier to have been an important transmitter of Italian style to the North.

Hesselius, Gustavus (1682-1755). Born in Sweden, he came to America in 1712. He worked in Delaware, Maryland, and Pennsylvania, painting portraits which are honest but awkward, timidly drawn, and chalky in color. His most important works are two unusual portraits of Indian chiefs, Lapowinsa and Tishcohan (Historical Society of Pennsylvania), and a Last Supper (private collection, on loan to the Philadelphia Museum) which he painted for a church in Maryland and which was the first publicly commissioned large religious picture in America.

Hesselius, John (1728-78). Colonial American portrait painter, son of Gustavus Hesselius (see). He was brought to Philadelphia by his family in 1735, was trained by his father, but later came under the influence of the English painter, Wollaston. In 1763 he married a wealthy widow and lived the rest of his life near Annapolis. He was a competent painter, an imaginative colorist, and one of the first to introduce an American note in portraits, especially in settings.

HIRSCH, JOSEPH. Portrait of an Old Man
Museum of Fine Arts, Boston

HIRSCH, STEFAN. Pic of Orizaba
Whitney Museum of American Art, New York

Heward, Prudence (1896-). Canadian painter who has worked in Montreal and in Paris at the Colarossi Academy and under Guérin. He paints in an effective Magic-Realist style.

Hicks, Edward (1780-1849). An American amateur painter, self-taught. He is famous for his naive and charming

94. HICKS. The Peaceable Kingdom. Brooklyn Museum Collection

rendering of The Peaceable Kingdom, of which he made at least twenty-five versions. Based on Isaiah 11 : 6-9, it depicts the animals lying down with each other, and sometimes in the background William Penn making his treaty with the Indians. Born in Attleboro, Pa., he was apprenticed to a coachmaker, became a coach- and house-painter, but after 1810 was an itinerant Quaker preacher in many states of the Union. (See color plate 94.)

hieratic. Consecrated to sacred or priestly use; has its primary meaning in connection with matters solemn and religious. Example: Byzantine mosaics.

Higgins, Eugene (1874-). American genre painter whose art falls within the Realist tradition. Born in Kansas City, he lived in cheap boarding houses with his father, a stonecutter. He was early impressed by Millet's illustrations for children and the novels of Victor Hugo. He attended art school in St. Louis (1890-91) and worked on grandiose schemes by himself. In 1897 he went abroad and studied with Laurens, Constant and Gérôme at the Académie Julian. He won prizes and gained recognition for his drawings and paintings of the poor in Paris before his return to the U.S. in 1904. His sympathetic studies of poverty and suffering were described as visual equivalents of Hugo and Gorky. His dependence upon the art of Millet finally led to a more generalized and heroic treatment of the hard life of peasants and to a much more academic manner.

highlight. A spot of bright light or high value on a particular object, generally the illusion of a reflection cast by a light source; it is usually achieved by the addition of a dab or touch of white or other brightening hue.

Highmore, Joseph (1692-1780). British painter and pupil of Godfrey Kneller. He is best known for his illustrations for Richardson's novel, *Pamela;* these were twelve oil paintings of indifferent quality but expressing the dominating sentimentality of the time. He did a series of portrait drawings for the Installation of the Knights of the Bath in 1725 and then a long series of portraits of eighteenth-century personalities. (See illustration.)

High Renaissance. A term referring to the later development of the Renaissance (see) and generally applied to the first thirty years of the sixteenth century, i.e., from 1500 to 1530. It takes in the careers of such artists as Michelangelo. Raphael, Leonardo, Titian, Giorgione, Fra Bartolommeo, Il Sodoma and Andrea del Sarto among many others.

Hill, Carl Frederick (1849-1911). Swedish pioneer modernist who began with Impressionism and developed a personal style that almost anticipates the emotionally violent effects of Van Gogh. Like the latter, he suffered from a severe mental illness which forced him into retirement in a little provincial town in Sweden; there he produced a series of highly imaginative, dreamlike drawings of an exciting and entirely personal kind.

Hindu painting (See INDIA, DEVELOPMENT OF PAINTING IN.)

Hiroshige (see JAPANESE PAINTERS: TOKUGAWA PERIOD).

95. HOBBEMA. Landscape with Water Mill. Minneapolis Institute of Arts

96. HOFER. Still Life with Grapefruit. Detroit Institute of Arts

HODLER. Portrait of a Woman. Detroit Institute of Arts

Hirsch, Joseph (1910-). Contemporary American painter of social genre. Born in Philadelphia, he studied at the Pennsylvania Museum School of Industrial Art and with George Luks. He was in Europe and the Orient on a Wooley Fellowship and in 1939 his Two Men won the popularity vote at the World's Fair "American Art Today" exhibition. He treats common subjects dramatically, creating forceful images in a rich impasto. A war artist during World War II, he has spent several years in Paris since that time. (See illustration.)

Hirsch, Stefan (1899-). Contemporary American painter born of American parents in Nuremberg, Germany. He painted without instruction in European museums and studied later in this country with Hamilton Field. Influenced by Cubism, his cityscapes are reduced to essential volumes. (See illustration.)

Hispanic Museum, New York. This collection of the Hispanic Society of America comprises paintings, sculptures and other arts produced in Spain from the early middle ages to the early twentieth century. Among its most valuable possessions are paintings by El Greco, Velázquez, Goya and, among more modern painters, Sorolla.

Hobbema, Meindert (1638-1709). Dutch painter of landscapes and city views. Hobbema studied in Amsterdam with Jacob van Ruisdael, the most famous landscape painter of the day, and he himself achieved an importance in this field second only to that of his master. From the first, however, a personal character distinguishes his works from those by Ruisdael; where the latter infused his scenes with stormy passion, organizing the elements into sweeping Baroque compositions on a heroic plane, Hobbema persisted in a truthful presentation and rendered his scenes pleasantly human by the inclusion of houses, canals and watermills. He painted few pictures in the second half of his life, when he held the more lucrative and secure post of customs inspector. (See color plate 95.)

Hodgkins, Frances (1870-1947). Self-taught New Zealand painter of landscapes and still life noted for the poetic quality of her works and their fluid color. She taught at the Académie Colarossi in Paris.

Hodler, Ferdinand (1853-1918). Outstanding Swiss painter. Brought up in conditions of extreme poverty, he lost both parents and worked with his stepfather to help support a large family. His early works, realistic in spirit and precise in draughtsmanship, derived their inspiration from Millet and Holbein. He studied for a while in Madrid and Paris. During the 1870's he had been torn between art and science; in the 1880's the conflict was between art and religion, as with Van Gogh, and was resolved by Hodler's turning to an art of ideas rather than of form for form's sake. In his figure compositions we get such works as the mystical and poetic Night, first of a long series of similar pictures, including Disillusioned Souls, The World-Weary, Eurythmy, and Glance into Infinity. In a way they parallel in meaning the more or less contemporaneous works of the Symbolists in France, although without any apparent influence. In his landscapes during the same period Hodler evolved what he called "parallelism," in which the various parts of a picture (such as mountains, lakes and clouds) are all parallel to each other and parallel to the picture plane as well. This makes for a formality and control of the pictorial elements that suggests once more the contemporary Post-Impressionists, particularly Cézanne, Seurat and Van Gogh. The final point of interest to be noted is the often curvilinear nature of Hodler's drawing, a fact that tends to relate him in a general way to the Art Nouveau (see) of the entire European continent. Toward the end of his life he broke away from these formal principles. See also DECADENT ART, EXPRESSIONISM, SURREALISM. (See illustration.)

Hofer, Karl (1878-1955). German Expressionist painter and muralist. Until 1901 he studied in the Academy of his

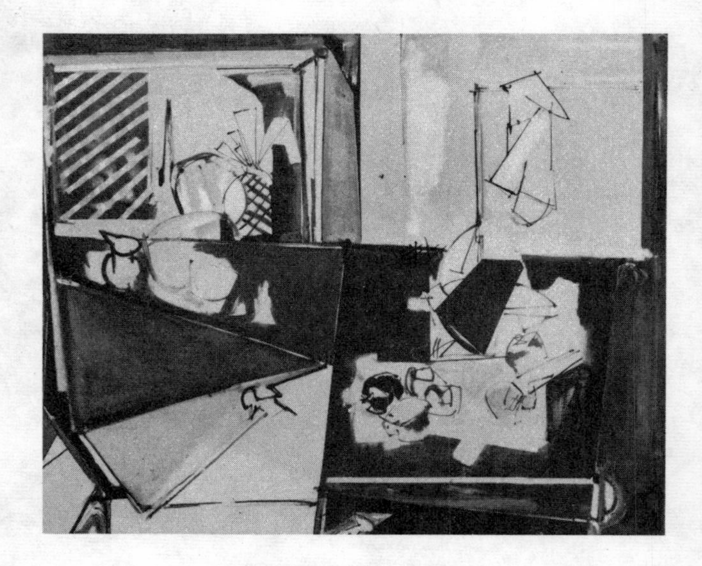

HOFMANN. Magenta and Blue
Whitney Museum of American Art, New York

HOGARTH. The Rake's Progress, III. Sloane Museum, London

native Karlsruhe and was impressed by the "Romantic Classicism" of Hans Thoma and Arnold Böcklin. Marées, with his moody monumentality, also figured in this early development. Hofer's evolution has always shown these parallel qualities: an interest in powerful sculpturesque forms—Buddhist sculpture, Thoma, Marées and finally Cézanne—and, side by side with this, a typically German desire to infuse the formal quality with strong emotional content. Thus his Swiss mountain landscapes suggest the Cézanne analogies, but the significant difference is that Hofer's have a Romantic quality as well; similarly, the Card Players derives from the same source and is touched with the German artist's excitement. During the post-World War I period he produced a number of stark and disillusioned works typical of that time, turning later to charming figure and still life compositions. Hofer suffered the loss of his studio in World War II and bravely set to work to repaint the lost pictures. See EXPRESSIONISM. (See color plate 96.)

Hofmann, Hans (1880-). Contemporary American Abstract Expressionist. He is extremely influential as a teacher, maintaining schools in New York and Provincetown. He studied in Munich, spent ten years in Paris (1904-14), returned to Munich where he had a school until he left for the U.S. in 1932. After 1939 his work became increasingly abstract, bold in color and calligraphic in pattern. (See illustration.)

Hogarth, William (1697-1764). British painter of satirical moralities who showed considerable originality in his approach but apparently gave first consideration to the moral effectiveness of his work. Born in London, he became an apprentice to a master from whom he learned copper engraving and the making of bookplates, showcards and book illustrations. In 1720 he became independent and began to study painting with Sir James Thornhill, whose daughter he married. Hogarth began his own career as a portraitist working in the conversation piece (see), but found himself temperamentally unsuited for this work. His real fame began with the six pictures known as A Harlot's Progress, 1731, which he engraved the following year with great success. This series was soon followed by others: A Rake's Progress, The Four Times of the Day, etc., as well as individual subjects all dealing with the life of the time, as in The Shrimp Girl. We can see Hogarth's art at this point as part of the same social development that was producing the novels of Henry Field-

HOGARTH. Calais Gate. Tate Gallery, London

97. HOLBEIN THE YOUNGER. Sir Henry Guildford. Detroit Institute of Arts

ing and others. Cutting himself off from the Renaissance tradition and "grand manner" generally, Hogarth projected a new pictorial epic. With his phenomenal memory for faces he was able to people his works with a vast, teeming gallery of psychological and physical types. In these paintings and the engravings made from them he showed the evils of high life and the pitfalls of low life. Always filled with detailed symbols and allusions, these paintings undoubtedly had more exact meaning for his contemporaries than for the casual viewer today but they are still clearly social documents of unparalleled importance. His historical paintings and portraits were not nearly so successful as his satires, and Hogarth carried on a lifelong feud with the rich dilettante art collectors and so-called connoisseurs. In spite of their unpopularity, his portraits are important works—straightforward, unaffected, sincere and powerfully delineating their sitters in a way that was rare at that time. (See illustrations.)

Hogue, Alexandre (1898-). Contemporary American painter who portrays in a hard, realistic manner the desolation caused by land erosion in the West. Born in Memphis, Mo., he was raised in Texas, and studied at the Minneapolis Institute of Arts.

Hoitsu (see JAPANESE PAINTERS: TOKUGAWA PERIOD).

Hokusai (see JAPANESE PAINTERS: TOKUGAWA PERIOD.)

Holbein the Elder, Hans (c.1465-1524). A German painter important to the history of art not only because he was the father and probably the first teacher of the more famous Hans Holbein the Younger (see) but as an artist in his own right. He was a strongly individual painter, working at the moment of transition from the old style to the newer art of the Renaissance. It is not known who taught him to paint and there is too little left of the early art of Augsburg to determine what influences shaped him. He headed a shop in Augsburg that produced altarpieces and, though also called to nearby Ulm and to Isenheim, worked principally in that city. Between 1490 and 1493 he traveled to the Low Countries

98. HOMER. The Gulf Stream. Metropolitan Museum of Art, New York

and on this and possible subsequent journeys westward absorbed those impressions of Flemish art which make themselves felt in all his painting. In 1501 he went to Frankfort on the Main and about this time new elements began to appear in his painting; it is possible that these are the result of contact with Grünewald, and the influence, to a lesser degree, of Hugo van der Goes. He never went to Italy, but his late works are replete with richly ornamented architecture and other motifs that must be ascribed to the influence of the Italian Renaissance transmitted to him through prints and the works of other German painters. He never, however, really assimilated Italian ideals of form and modeling, remaining always in his exaggeration and intensity an early German artist. (See illustration.)

Holbein the Younger, Hans (1497/98-1543). German painter of religious subjects and especially of portraits; also designer for stained glass and woodcuts. He probably received his original training in art from his father, the Augsburg painter Hans Holbein the Elder (see). He was no doubt also influenced at an early age by Burgkmair. As a boy Holbein went to live in Basel, a German Swiss city which was a center of humanistic learning and had a large population of prosperous bourgeois tradesmen. Before he was twenty Holbein went to Lucerne to decorate the mansion of Jacob van Hertenstein. On his return to Basel he became a member of the painters' guild and acquired Swiss citizenship. Up to 1526 he was constantly employed in Basel, filling commissions for paintings and furnishing designs for glass and for woodcuts.

Holbein's relations with the philosopher and writer Erasmus had begun as early as 1515 when he took part in the illustrating of Erasmus's *The Praise of Folly*. From this time on the friendship and patronage which the scholar profferred the artist exerted a steady influence on his career. It was owing to Erasmus that Holbein in 1526 made his first trip to England, remaining there for two years and executing the first of many works for Henry VIII—decorations for a celebration at Greenwich. He also established himself as a portraitist, beginning a group portrait of the family of Sir Henry More. Though this large painting appears not to have been completed, the many drawings he made of the individual members of the family are exquisite records of his draughtsmanship and his masterly ability to characterize his subjects.

HOLBEIN THE YOUNGER. Mrs. Pemberton
Victoria and Albert Museum, London

From 1528 to 1532 Holbein worked again in Basel. He

HOLBEIN THE ELDER. Ecce Homo. Alte Pinakothek, Munich

made splendid portraits of Erasmus and decorated the Town Hall and the Haus zum Tanz. Though these mural decorations have perished, the drawings for them reveal his skill as a draughtsman and his elegance as a decorator. The last eleven years of his life were spent in England. His services were sought by the entire English court and by ambassadors and numerous resident foreigners. He painted so many of the important people of the time that his portraits nearly constitute an illustrated history of the reign of Henry VIII. His likenesses are always dignified, cool and detached, and done with a tireless attention to detail that reconstructs for us the

HOLZEL. Before Sundown. National Gallery, Berlin

living image of a personality. His crayon drawings for these painted portraits are remarkable in their finesse and subtlety. (See illustrations, including color plate 97.)

Hölzel, Adolf (1853-1934). Outstanding German painter, muralist, stained-glass designer and teacher. From 1906 to his death he was associated with the Stuttgart Academy, where many pre-World War I Expressionist students received a unique stimulus from this teacher. His own profoundly mystical and symbolic painting with its large color areas and enamel-like effects suggests the heritage of the middle ages. Its application in the fields of mural painting and stained glass are almost inevitable. One must classify him as a proto-Expressionist who had a great deal of influence on the nascent Expressionist movement through his teaching as well as his example as a painter. (See illustration.)

Homer, Winslow (1836-1910). With Eakins the leading Realist genre painter of the nineteenth century in America. Born in Boston, he had no formal art training before being apprenticed to a lithographer. From 1857 to 1875 he did illustrations for *Ballou's Pictorial* and *Harper's Weekly*. He moved to New York in 1859, where he attended evening classes at the National Academy of Design and studied painting with an obscure French painter, Frederic Rondel, in 1861. The next year he covered the Civil War for *Harper's* and did his first oil. He achieved his earliest recognition as a painter in 1866 with Prisoners from the Front (Metropolitan), and the same year turned to painting his characteristic naturalistic genre scenes—The Morning Bell (private collection) and the Croquet Scene (Chicago)—before sailing for France. On his return to the U.S. in 1867, he began his many scenes of farm life and children in New York and New England, continued active as an illustrator of books and magazines, and from 1875 to 1879 painted Negro subjects. In 1881 and 1882 he was in England doing watercolors and drawings at Tynemouth, the basis for some of his later oils and etchings of rescues at sea. He settled at Prout's Neck, Maine, in 1883 and undertook a long series of paintings of fishermen on the Grand Banks, and in Nassau the following year began his many watercolors of the West Indies.

Thereafter he traveled and painted in the Adirondacks, Maine, and Canada, and, during almost every winter after 1898, in the West Indies or Florida. His earliest work dealt almost entirely with farm life, children, and women, and was executed in a naturalistic style similar to, but unconnected with, that of the early Monet and of Boudin. The bright and sunny quality of this period gave way after his English

HOMER. The Hunter. Philadelphia Museum of Art, Elkins Collection

experience to dramatic scenes of the sea done in larger scale, seen heroically and painted with somber power, as in Eight Bells, 1886 (Addison Gallery of American Art). Eventually the struggle of man against the forces of nature was transformed, as in Coast in Winter, 1892 (Worcester Art Museum), into a purer symbol of natural violence. In his later years, under the influence of the English watercolor style, his earlier tight watercolor manner became brilliantly loose and pure, especially in his sun-drenched impressionistic studies of the West Indies. Though he won recognition during his lifetime as one of America's leading painters and enjoyed popular esteem, he was not especially successful financially. The homely charm of his early work and the masculine vigor of his later work did not fit into the general framework of academic painting and his maturity was spent as something of a recluse both personally and artistically. (See illustrations, including color plate 98.)

Honthorst, Gerard van (1590-1656). Dutch painter and engraver of historical scenes, genre, and especially of portraits. He was the pupil of Abraham Bloemaert in his native city of Utrecht, but the determining influence upon his style came during the many years he spent in Italy. There he came to know the works of Caravaggio, and his early pictures show the strongly contrasted artificial lighting that he learned from them. The latter part of his life he devoted entirely to the painting of portraits, which were much sought after, and for a number of years he was painter to the court at The Hague.

Hooch, Pieter de (1629-after 1688). Dutch painter of domestic interiors and scenes from daily life. He was a pupil of Berchem in Haarlem and then entered the service of a wealthy merchant as "painter and footman." In this capacity he lived in Delft, where he inevitably felt the influence of Carel Fabritius and Jan Vermeer. De Hooch's paintings of the Delft period are his best. They are mostly pleasant scenes of middle-class people, mothers, housewives and comfortable burghers engaged in ordinary tasks or enjoying simple pleasures. He had a gift for painting the glow of sunlight in cozy rooms and his interiors are attractively serene. He dealt with space at this time in an interesting manner, suggesting the limitations and relations of space areas to each other. In his later pictures he seems to have come in contact with the work of Hoogstraten; under this and other influences his style changed as he moved in 1667 from Delft to Amsterdam. In the larger metropolis both his own ambitions and popular demand drew him away from his former unpretentious subject matter to scenes of high life and elegance. He was much less well adapted by temperament and artistic gifts to this kind of painting, and the pictures that he made at the end of his life, showing fashionably garbed ladies and gentlemen strolling in formal gardens or disporting themselves in noble halls, are indisputably inferior to his earlier ones. (See color plate 99.)

Hoogstraten, Samuel van (1627-78). Dutch painter of still life and interiors. He studied with Rembrandt about 1642 in Amsterdam but most of his working life was spent in his native city of Dordrecht. He traveled widely, visiting England and Italy, and spent some time in The Hague. His early works show the very strong influence of Rembrandt, but later he reflects also the styles of Metsu, Pieter de Hooch, and Jan Steen. He was the author of a pedagogical work about the art of painting, and was also the master of Houbraken, one of the foremost biographers of Dutch artists. He painted many religious pictures, composing them in Rembrandt's manner, and freely using chiaroscuro. (See color plate 100.)

Hopper, Edward (1882-). Contemporary American realistic painter and etcher of genre subjects. Born in Nyack, N.Y., he attended the Chase School (1900-05), where he studied with Chase, Miller, and Henri, and became a disciple of the Ashcan School (see). His earlier dark manner was lightened by the influence of Impressionism during his stay in Paris in 1906-07. On his return to the U.S., he continued to paint in oil and watercolor, and began to do etchings which won him some recognition. He sold his first painting, an oil, from the Armory Show in 1913, but had to wait almost ten years for the next sale, a watercolor. In the meantime he worked as an illustrator and did etchings. With the success

99. HOOCH, PIETER DE. Interior. Toledo Museum of Art, Libbey Collection

of his watercolor show in 1924, he gave up illustration and soon moved into the forefront of American realistic painting. Together with Burchfield, he paints small-town America, its people and architecture, but unlike the latter, he derives from the Ashcan tradition and paints city genre as well. Like the Impressionists, he sees the world in terms of light, but he has never used their technical devices. He employs a harsh, sharp light, natural or artificial, to emphasize the material existence of the world he knows—a small-town street, a Gothic mansion, a cafeteria, a theater. There is an overtone of criticism in the harsh reality of his vision, in the reproduction of the emptiness of small-town life and the cold impersonality of city existence. He transformed the sentiment of the Ashcan painters into something more objective, just as he transformed their Impressionistic brushwork into something more solid. (See illustration.)

Hoppner, John (1758-1810). British society portraitist educated at the Royal Academy by George III and elected a member in 1791. A rival of Lawrence, he devoted himself to Whig ladies while the latter specialized in Tory dames. Hoppner also did members of the royal family and in 1793 was appointed portraitist to the Prince of Wales. Usually he imitated Reynolds although occasional touches of Gainsborough are also visible. (See illustration.)

Hovenden, Thomas (1840-95). Born in Ireland, he came to New York in 1863, studied at the National Academy of Design at night, and later for six years in Paris with Cabanel. After painting Brittany scenes, he turned to American genre compositions of the sentimental literary type which were so popular at the time. The most famous of these is probably Breaking Home Ties (Philadelphia Museum of Art).

Hsia Kuei (see CHINESE PAINTERS: SUNG DYNASTY).

Hsieh Ho (c.500 A.D.). Chinese author of the treatise *Ku Hua P'in Lu*, which gives the famous Six Canons, principles formulated as a basis for the appreciation of Chinese painting. These are still regarded as the foundation of Chinese art criticism.

Hsü Hsi (see CHINESE PAINTERS: THE FIVE DYNASTIES).

Hsü Lin (see CHINESE PAINTERS: MING DYNASTY).

Huang Kung-wang (see CHINESE PAINTERS: YÜAN DYNASTY).

Huber, Wolf (c.1485-1553). German painter, wood engraver and draughtsman. He settled in his early life in Passau, where he became official painter to the court of bishops. His style was formed by that of Pacher and Altdorfer, and he also submitted to the pervasive influence of Albrecht Dürer. Italian Renaissance art had also spread north of the Alps by the time of Huber, and his later elaborate compositions show his awareness of it.

Hudson River school. American Romantic landscape school of the nineteenth century (from about 1825 to 1870). Though not at any time an organization, a good many of the artists knew each other and painted the scenery of the Catskill Mountains along the Hudson River, but did not limit themselves to that area. Their attitudes toward nature varied from the fanciful and sublime to the intimate and lyrical; their subjects from the Eastern Appalachians to the Western Sierras, but in almost all cases treated with meticulous detail. The early group included Thomas Cole, Thomas Doughty, Asher B. Durand, Samuel F. B. Morse, Alvin Fisher, and Henry Inman; the next generation, John W. Casilear, John F. Kensett, Worthington Whittredge, Jasper F. Cropsey, Frederick E. Church and Albert Bierstadt.

hue. Term referring to actual name of a particular color: red, green, yellow, etc., and to the place it occupies in the color spectrum or wheel. It is more generally known as the color and represents the most elementary way we have of describing this condition of an object or form. The hue or color may be accurately characterized by its value, which is the amount of light and dark it contains; is may also be described in terms of its intensity, i.e., the amount of grey with which it is saturated.

Huet, Jean Baptiste Marie (1745-1811). French painter and etcher. Member of a considerable family of artists, including his sons Nicolas (born 1770), François (1772-1813) and Jean-Baptiste (born 1772). The elder Huet is best known for his animal paintings, an art which he developed from study with Dagomer, Renou, Leprince, Boucher and Lépicié.

100. HOOGSTRATEN, SAMUEL VAN
Peep Box: Dutch Interior
Detroit Institute of Arts

HOPPER. Dawn in Pennsylvania. Frank Rehn Gallery, New York

HOPPNER. The Ladies Bligh. Frick Collection, New York

Success came quickly, he was much represented in the Salons and he was hired by Gobelins. His animal studies are noted for their accurate observation of detail and action. He also produced landscapes, classical subjects and watercolors. He was engaged in many graphic publications including *sujets galants* of a risqué kind and Rococo ornamental types.

Huguet, Jaime (c.1415-92). Spanish painter of retablos. Manager of a large and successful atelier and perhaps the outstanding personality of Catalan Gothic painting. He was born in Barcelona and learned from his uncle Pedro Huguet and from his neighbor, the master Bernardo Martorell. During 1435-44 he was in Zaragoza where it is presumed he painted his triptych of St. George (Barcelona and Berlin). During 1446-47 he was in Tarragona. It is now thought that to this period belongs the panel of Madonna, Child and Angels formerly associated with a "Master of Pedralbes." By 1449 Huguet was established in Barcelona, where he married, served as an official of the guild and took part in the political events of 1464-72. From 1454-57 he worked on the retablo of San Antonio Abad, perhaps completed by others. By 1460 he had finished his masterpiece, the retablo of San Abdón and San Sennén (Santa Maria Tarrasa). In 1465 he painted that of the Constable of Portugal for the Royal Chapel of Barcelona. His last period is represented by the enormous retablo of San Augustín (1464-86) of which he apparently did only the central Consecration scene, the rest being painted by his most important assistant, Rafael Vergos. Huguet not only associated with the Vergos family, but also used many collaborators, among them his brother Antonio, Miguel Nadal, Pedro Ramírez and Pedro Alemany. While acquainted with the Flemish innovations affecting Spanish painting in his day, Huguet tended to reject them and to continue with a native brand of crisp realism painted against backgrounds of decorative gilt and marquetry.

Hui Tsung (see CHINESE PAINTERS: SUNG DYNASTY).

humanism. Today generally used in connection with any form of expression concerned with the importance of the human being. In the past it more often referred to so-called humanistic studies, i.e., classical literature and philosophy. In the history of painting it is associated with the increased interest in human beings, their activities and the world in which they function, a notable characteristic of the Italian Renaissance of the fourteenth to sixteenth centuries. It is paralleled by somewhat similar, although differently expressed, interests in the art of fifteenth-century Flanders. This general change in the north and south of Europe stands in sharp contrast to the medieval interest in spiritual things and the anonymous condition of man in that culture.

Humayun Period (see INDIAN PAINTERS: HUMAYUN PERIOD, 1530-56).

Hunt, William Holman (1827-1910). A British Pre-Raphaelite (see) painter endowed with a reforming spirit that prescribed the stern discipline of the Italian primitives for what he felt was ailing art at the time. Hunt rendered detail with a kind of microscopic vision. The curious lack of a distinction in his paintings between near and far objects

HUNT, WILLIAM HOLMAN. Claudio and Isabella. Tate Gallery, London

gives them a certain hard unreality. At the same time he painted directly on a wet white underpaint that gives a brilliant tone to the surface colors superposed on it and aids in creating an almost clinical clarity. Hunt's later work was mostly religious and used an almost private set of mystic symbols, but the approach was still didactic and detailed. He visited Palestine in search of accurate background material. He published his memoirs, *Pre-Raphaelitism and the Pre-Raphaelite Brotherhood*, in 1905. (See illustration.)

Hunt, William Morris (1824-79). An American Romantic painter, he was influential in Boston society where he proselytized for the Barbizon school (see) and especially Millet. Born in Vermont, the son of a Congressman and brother of Richard M., the architect, he first studied painting with Gambadella, an Italian artist who was a friend of his family, attended Harvard, and then went to Europe for his health. He studied sculpture in Rome and Paris, and after a taste of the Düsseldorf Academy, he worked with Couture in Paris from 1847 to 1852. Later he met Millet, lived in Barbizon and bought many Barbizon pictures. He returned to the U.S. in 1855 and in 1862 settled in Boston, where he became an intellectual and cultural leader. Working very slowly and spasmodically he painted sensitive and poetic pictures in the Barbizon tradition. His inherent lack of strength and faulty technical training led to an art which, although full of charm and promise, remains essentially incomplete.

Hurd, Peter (1904-). Contemporary American painter and illustrator of Western life. Born in New Mexico, he had a military education, studied art with N. C. Wyeth and at the Pennsylvania Academy of Fine Arts, and then returned to New Mexico. There he raises polo ponies and does murals and illustrations in a realistic but stylized manner.

Huysum, Jan van (1682-1749). Dutch painter of flowers who studied with his father. With the strongly Baroque compositions that were much admired in his day he carried the tradition of Dutch flower painting into the eighteenth century.

I

icon. An image or representation. More especially a religious image painted or sculptured to a fixed or conventional representation or symbolism. The term is of particular meaning to Byzantine culture which in early Christian times applied "icon" to every depiction of Christ, the Virgin, saint or incident of the Holy writ whether carved or painted, movable or monumental. The modern Orthodox Church defines icon as a representation of sacred subject on a portable plaque of wood, stone or metal whether executed in paint, enamel or mosaic. According to the second council of Nicaea (787) icons may be honored by relative worship (kissing, offerings) but not with the supreme worship due to God alone. The preciseness of definition and the clear account of the magic reality and miraculous powers of icons found in Orthodox theology resulted from the bitter Iconoclastic Controversy of the eighth and ninth centuries in Byzantium.

iconoclast. An image destroyer; referring originally to a Byzantine sect that opposed representations of God and the Saints and during a certain period was influential enough to cause the destruction of many images. By extension of meaning it has come to signify anyone who destroys an idol whether artistic or ideological. See BYZANTINE PAINTING.

iconography. The art of representation by pictures or images; the description or study of portraiture or representation. With the expansion of art-historical study during the past century the latter meaning has gained in importance. The description or analysis of subject matter or meaning in art and the research into the origins of artistic signs and symbols is a modern historical science. A fruitful study is that of pagan motifs which were applicable in a meaningful way in early Christian imagery. The elaboration of symbolism in the cult of the Virgin in the later middle ages is in accordance with the changing of artistic styles. Minor iconographic details, such as the presence or absence of a beard on an image of Christ, can sometimes reveal the provenance of a painting as assuredly as a signature.

iconostasis (see BYZANTINE PAINTING).

Illuminated Manuscripts. Manuscripts have apparently functioned as a significant art form since earliest historical times. Although ordinarily considered a "minor" art, even in periods of most sumptuous output, in certain epochs the fragile manuscript was almost the major medium of artistic expression. Such was frequently the case in the medieval period in the Western world when the Book was an object of ritual and veneration, the Word magical and revelatory, the scribe an instrument of the Holy Spirit (cf. St. Matthew of Munich Gospels, c.1000). The artistry of manuscripts assumes various forms. The writing itself and the composition of the text are an art, although not generally studied as such in the West. Playful enlargement of the initial letters and of opening phrases is "illumination" in its most precise sense, and it has been a specialty of certain eras and regions, notably amongst the Irish medieval foundations. Illustration is the other type of decoration: either as a gloss of isolated fragments scattered throughout text and margins or as well-defined "picture" panels up to full-page in size. Either illumination or illustration can produce independent "frontispiece" pages, the former decorative, the latter perhaps portraying an author or a dedicatory scene.

Manuscript materials range (in historical order) from papyrus and skins, parchment (invented in Pergamum *(sic)* in the second century B.C.), and paper (introduced to the West in the eighth century A.D.). Books were of roll form until Roman Imperial times when, c.100 A.D., the codex, or book of folded pages as we now know it, was invented. Our knowledge of the format and illustrations of rolls we get from the Egyptian Books of the Dead and from later Hellenistic scientific treatises, both perfunctorily decorated; or by inference from Roman triumphal columns, Homeric cups and late manuscript copies. Ancient codices are also rare, no deco-

ILLUMINATED MANUSCRIPT. Samuel: Detail of Head from Paris Psalter. Bibliothèque Nationale, Paris

101. ILLUMINATED MANUSCRIPT. The Windmill Psalter. British, 14th Century. Morgan Library, New York

rated ones surviving from before the fourth century A.D. Our best "classical" illustrations are already post-pagan in date; the Ambrosian Iliad of the fourth century (Florence) already employs an expressionistic shorthand, and the Codex Romanus of the fifth (?) century (Vatican) is composed in the fashion of early medieval times. The Early Christian period in the Mediterranean provides us with several classes of decorated books. The Bible is represented by the Vienna Genesis in Greek on royal purple vellum (generally dated the sixth century) and by the Rabula Gospels in Syriac of about 586. Another book on purple vellum, the Codex Rossanensis (generally dated the sixth century) was apparently for liturgical use. Scientific treatises continued to be copied in the old classical centers of learning, viz., the Vienna manuscript of Dioscorides (Constantinople c.512). This last is the only Constantinopolitan painting known before the Iconoclastic Controversy of 726-843 which cut off the pictorial tradition in the eastern Mediterranean as effectively as the contemporary barbarian inroads did in West Roman lands. An artistic resurgence came in ninth- and tenth-century Byzantium, especially in the court of Constantine Porphyrogenitos (905-959) whose enthusiasm for classical learning apparently produced the Paris Psalter (Bibliothèque Nationale) and Joshua Roll (Vatican Library). This movement matured in the exquisitely constructed compositions of the following century, e.g., the Menologium of Basil II (Vatican Library). The pages of this second Golden Age, a period of tremendous output of books, are classically monumental like the church mosaic cycles of the time. During the last centuries of Byzantium, ornamentation became increasingly lavish and then manuscript arts gave way to icon painting in popularity.

In the scriptoria of western Europe illuminators were applying their Northern aesthetic of dynamic, involved linear patterning to the book. A rich, non-figurative, ornamental tradition arose which, at times, allied itself with the narrative, anthropomorphic tendencies of Mediterranean culture. Irish monasteries, insular and continental, evolved the richest, most dynamic and intricate of these knotted, interlaced styles, as can be seen in the Book of Durrow (before 700?), the Lindisfarne Gospels (c.700?) and the Book of Kells (c.800?). Meanwhile in France Merovingian bookcraft was enriched, as a result of Charlemagne's encouragement, by infusions of this insular type of art and the late classical style of the Mediterranean. This Carolingian Renaissance, so involved with written learning, saw the invention of our modern script, the minuscule, by Alcuin of York (735-804) along with an enthusiastic copying of ancient books. Alcuin's scriptorium was at Tours, which with the so-called "Ada" School produced the most exacting, monumental patterns and effigies, e.g., the Ada Gospels (early ninth century) and the Bibles for Charles the Bald (mid-ninth century). Less architectonic, but more calligraphic and expressionistic was the so-called "Reims" or "Palace" tradition which expressed itself equally well in intense and agitated line (Utrecht Psalter, early ninth century) and in intelligent handling of antique illusionism (Aachen Gospels, c.800).

With the collapse of the Carolingian dynasty this art withered locally but spread to the east and west. England, where the involved linear pattern was endemic, under "Reims" influence produced the Winchester and Canterbury schools of the Anglo-Saxon period. The Benedictional of Aethelwold (c.980) is effusively and transcendentally linear in this respect. Meanwhile, the Ottonian emperors of Germany, heirs to the Carolingian empire, grafted onto that artistic inheritance the powerful plasticity of the mid-Byzantine style from the East. There resulted a peculiar intensity of expression, tremendous theocratic images of the rulers and a fine sense of classical forms (the last derived from imperial rummaging in Italian libraries). The Codex Egberti (c.985) and the Munich Gospels (c.1000) of the Schools of Trier and Reichenau exemplify this. In Spain the Mozarabic community of that shrunken Christian state produced one of the most isolated, yet original of medieval styles, especially inventive in abstract pattern and flat strident color: vehemently anti-classical. Especially popular with these peninsular illuminators were books of Beatus' Commentary on the Apocalypse. These were to exert tremendous influence on Romanesque iconography of The Last Judgment. See MSS. No. 644 (ninth or tenth century), Morgan Library.

These three traditions and others played a role in forming the Romanesque manuscript style, which was new mainly in its structuring of the page. All forms were now possessed of firm outlines, and the areas thus designated were consolidated and welded together into an abstract geometrical unity. Iconography was enriched and in their wealth of systematically ordered meanings the miniatures compare with sculptured façades. The figure took on a new mass and form which held a sense of organic life, not through anatomical articulation but by linear pattern. This can be seen in the great bibles such as the Stavelot Bible (British Museum, 1093-97).

The Gothic manuscript style, like its sculpture, resulted from a humanizing of types and an inner drive to intricacy. Alcuin's clear minuscule became the angular, buttressed black Gothic script. During the twelfth and thirteenth centuries illumination spread in vegetative bars from the initials to frame whole portions of the text; scenes moved into the initials which in turn expanded in a shallow spatial fashion to accommodate the action; and Romance and *drôlerie* invaded the margins as they did in the cathedral sculpture. In full-page scenes, also, new spatial arrangements competed with older patternistic compositions. During the fourteenth century the pages pulsated with the secular activity of the margins which were given up to extending bars and vines, as in Jean Pucelle's Belleville Breviary. Not only did the illuminators assume a personality themselves, but in the initials dramatic scenes were now enacted in cathedral architecture before checkered backgrounds. The last step is to be seen in the International Gothic Style (see) of the turn of 1400 when painting in the north literally lifted itself out of the pages of the manuscript onto the easel. This process can be followed in the successive careers of the Boucicaut Master (see), the Limbourg Brothers (see), the van Eycks (see) and Jean Fouquet (see) in France and Flanders. In Italy this transformation took a somewhat different direction when, in the fifteenth century, panel painting may be said to have invaded the domain of the manuscript in a celebrated succession of illuminators such as Crivelli, Attavanti, Girolamo da Cremona and Liberale da Verona. In both North and South the new perspective vision replaced shallow Gothic space, and in the south there was an increased use of classical ornament. This finally turned up in Fouquet's Hours of Etienne Chevalier (1452-60) in France. The invention of printing in the fifteenth century terminated hand illumination of books, but of course substituted for it the rich resources of the graphic arts. See also PERSIAN PAINTERS. (See illustrations, including color plate 101.)

illusionism. In its broad sense this involves every type of art designed to create an illusion of the actuality of nature and its detailed forms, light, etc. A more limited meaning refers to the art of late antiquity, e.g., Roman painting and relief sculpture, in which this was the guiding aim.

Imola, Innocenzo Francucci da (1490/94-1547/50). Bolognese painter born in Imola, he was a pupil of Francia in Bologna and Albertinelli in Florence, through both of whom he absorbed the influence of Raphael. His style is an eclectic mixture of Florentine and Bolognese elements, stiffly monumental in composition and harsh and unpleasant in color. He was at first active in Imola, but came to Bologna to work for Count G. B. Bentivogli c.1517, remaining there the rest of his life, except for a period in Faenza (1525-30). Among his works are the fresco decorations in S. Michele in Bosco (1517+) and a Marriage of St. Catherine (1539, S. Giacomo Maggiore). His leading pupils were Primaticcio and Fontana.

impasto. From the Italian word meaning paste; a term applied to the physical substance of a painting, often, though not neccessarily, implying that it is thick and heavy and stands out in relief. It has come to mean the thickness of paint applied to the surface.

Impressionism. The term impressionism, or impressionist painting, describes a kind of painting which is flecked and somewhat formless, as opposed to that which is linear and clearly silhouetted. It is applicable to many epochs. The term Impressionism, however, applies to a particular late nineteenth-century style centering in Paris. There are several examples of pre-nineteenth-century impressionism, in most of which the loose brushwork is exhibited only in certain details or areas and does not become a universal fabric of the painting, e.g., Roman wall painting, the portraits of Hals or Velázquez. In each of these, as in Claude's sketches, a sense of classical structure is also present, and in the impressionism of Sung painting there is a nature-calligraphy which may well remind one of Van Gogh. In Watteau and Chardin, where pigment texture is more assertive, the forms are strongly structured and these artists also differ in subject matter or sensuousness from impressionism.

The name of the nineteenth-century movement, although appropriate, was accidentally (and maliciously) derived from one of Monet's paintings, Sunrise: an Impression, in the first group exhibition of 1874. The movement is most accurately defined in terms of its time-span: Impressionism was a style popular in varying degree among a group of Parisian artists of different nationality from the late 1860's to the early 1880's. By the 1880's a change had occurred in the style of most of these artists which is most simply described by the awkward term "Post-Impressionism" (see). In the late nineteenth century Impressionism spread throughout the world, and the work of most "founders" of modern art had its origins in some phase of it.

Although subject matter is generally less important than mode of execution in Impressionism it can be said that the Impressionists invented a new genre of the big (Haussmannized) city and of Sunday in the country or on the beach. It is a distinctly middle-class and urban landscape. These starving artists, confident in the validity of the material world, gave poetic form to the Good Life and to the Leisure Hour, thought to be within the reach of all: e.g., Renoir, the Boating Party (1881); Manet, at Père Lathuile's (1879). In composition, the Impressionists stressed the transitory, the instantaneous relation of parts and brushstrokes as though echoing the meaningless bustle of urban life: random molecular contacts among human beings, as in Pissarro, Avenue de l'Opera (1898) or Degas, Viscount Lepic and His Daughters (1873). The heroes of the drama became light and atmosphere, revealing themselves in color sensation as recorded by the artist in pigments. These artists exhibited a pseudoscientific interest in light and color phenomena, paralleling but not exploiting the contemporary researches of Helmholtz and others. Their attitude was more empirical and lyrical than theoretical. The Impressionists popularized the habit of painting out-of-doors (called plein-airism), although the result was that the canvases looked less like the scene they confronted than did many works done inside Dutch studios of the seventeenth century: e.g., Renoir, Monet Painting (1873). The play of light so dissolved the forms that frequently reflections (which they liked) seemed as authentic as the objects reflected, or the canvas seemed as convincing when inverted, like Caillebotte's Seine at Argenteuil (1874). Colors were chosen in a revolutionary new way, used purely, brightly and in separate strokes. The result was that the modeling effect of the Old Masters disappeared in a general brightness of rainbow palette. On the other hand, no color expressed itself largely or dramatically as in Rubens; there was a general low key with bright spots small and dispersed, as in Watteau or Corot. Painting thus became a mode of vision, a method of applying pigment, a sheer sensuous delight: Degas, Dancer (1874); Manet, Apples and Grapes.

The major artists associated in the Impressionist movement were Monet, Renoir, Pissarro, Sisley, Bazille and Morisot (see entries). Manet and Degas (see both) worked with the group. Among the younger generation which built directly upon Impressionism were Cézanne, Gauguin, Van Gogh, Seurat, Signac (see each). The roots of the movement were in the Salon des Refusés of 1863 in which were exhibited works by Manet, Pissarro, Jongkind, Guillaumin, Whistler, Fantin-Latour and Cézanne. Manet became the leader of these dissidents and others at the Café Guerbois. Meanwhile Monet, Renoir, Bazille and Sisley left Gleyre's studio (1864) to paint out-of-doors near Fontainebleau. The dominant style at that time was flat and tonal, with the influence of Courbet, Corot and Daubigny predominant. The Franco-Prussian war scattered and decimated the group, some wandering to England and new influences. The web or crusty technique of discontinuous brushstrokes was being worked out in those years, especially by Monet and Renoir. From 1874-86 most of the group entered the special Impressionist exhibitions which were set up in competition with the Salons. The late 1870's were years of public ridicule and bitter poverty for most of them. By the mid-1880's the plight of most had improved but the movement was in crisis. Participation in their exhibitions fell off and several of the group struck out in new directions in search of expressive or structural form. This was stimulated, of course, by the impact of the younger members: Cézanne, Seurat, Van Gogh and Gauguin. Monet, long the leader, showed less change than others perhaps, and Sisley was quite untouched by the crisis.

Inayat (see INDIAN PAINTERS: JAHANGIR-SHAH JAHAN PERIOD).

India, Development of Painting in. The earliest extant paintings of importance are in the Ajanta cave-temples of Western India. Dating from about the third century B.C to the end of the Gupta period (about 700 A.D), the vast chapels and monastic halls were decorated with murals of Buddhist deities. Forgotten for centuries, damaged and neglected, they have come to the attention of the modern world and are recognized as among the greatest works of art ever, produced. (See color plate 102.)

Around the walls, long processionals of men and elephants. courtiers and beggars, seem almost to move in horizontal progression, while fruits, flowers, birds, and cloud goddesses are part of a carefully ordered ceiling decoration. The unity of man and nature is suggested by the happy combination of human, animal, and floral forms. There are no cast shadows; volume is suggested by graded tone; rock formations and buildings seem to thrust outward from the wall in a perspective convention peculiar to India and other Asiatic countries. In time the influence of the religious centers at Ajanta, Bagh, Badami, and Ellora spread to Ceylon, to Afghanistan, and thence across Central Asia to China (see color plate 31) and Japan.

In the post-Gupta years up to the seventeenth century the most interesting examples of painting are the illuminated texts of the Jain religion, though wall painting and decorative work on cotton cloth were always a part of folk art. Made of palm leaves (until paper was introduced from Persia in the fifteenth century), the Jain scriptures were illustrated with small paintings of gods and heroes done in vigorous line and bold masses of color in intricate flat patterns. Figures were stylized, angular, symbolic, with large eyes and hands deliberately distorted for maximum expressiveness. These serve as a link to the important Hindu schools of Rajput painting; for strong line, intense color, and exaggerated gesture are characteristic of the indigenous art that flourished for a number of centuries in local schools under Hindu patronage.

Rajputana is the name of an administrative district in Northwest India but the term Rajput painting may be applied to the art of an area including the Punjab Himalayas of the North, Bundelkhand in the East, part of the Deccan in the South, and part of Gujerat in the Southwest. The subdivisions of Pahari and Rajasthani refer respectively to the Hill States and the cities of the plains; within these there were centers of activity, or qalams, where painters worked in groups for their patrons, often with distinguishable local styles. The patrons were Rajput princes who kept Hindu civilization alive during the long periods of Moslem domination from 1000 A.D. through the nineteenth century. Patriarchal, essentially feudal in character, the princes maintained poets and painters in their households. The most important phase of their painting lasted for about three centuries (c.1500-c.1800 A.D.). In the foothills of the Himalayas the principal centers were at Basholi, Chamba, and Kangra, while Rajasthani work of outstanding quality was produced at Jaipur, Jodhpur and Jammu.

With the rise of a vernacular literature in the fifteenth century, the stories of Rama and Sita, Krishna and Radha, and other lovers and heroes were brought closer to the people by new versions of traditional epics and love poems. Love was the principal theme; every phase of emotion was systematized and presented in a particular situation. A Situation (see illustration) is typical of the Basholi School in its monumentality of design, clarity of line, and intensity of feeling expressed by gesture and the use of color—gold and bright red against cooler tones of olive green, blue, and chalk white.

INDIA. BASHOLI SCHOOL. A Situation
Victoria and Albert Museum, London

INDIA. JAIPUR SCHOOL. Head of Krishna
Metropolitan Museum of Art, New York

INDIA. KANGRA SCHOOL. The Lady and the Mirror
Victoria and Albert Museum, London

INDIA. KANGRA SCHOOL. The Gathering Storm
Victoria and Albert Museum, London

102. INDIA. Details from Ajanta. Recipient of a Prince's Generosity (Cave XVII, late 5th century A. D.), and A Queen (Cave I, 6th century A. D.)

In Rajputana a unique development was the form called the Ragmala, a painting of an ideal hero (Raga) or heroine (Ragini) related in mood to a musical theme and to a poem, all three expressing a phase of love associated with seasonal change or an emotion felt during certain hours of the day or night. Thus the Todi Ragini (see color plate 103) portrays a lovelorn lady seeking to charm the hearts of deer and peacocks with her melancholy music. Even after Persian influence had become strong in the Mughal court and subsequently spread out to the Rajput qalams, the painting of Ragmalas continued, though the somewhat primitive directness of the early ones gave way to increasing delicacy of line and more subtle use of tonal shading, as in Gathering Storm (see illustration). Portraits produced at Jaipur reflect the same trend. Grace and elegance took the place of vigor; even so Hindu a subject as Krishna (see Head of Krishna) was done primarily as a line drawing with small areas of subdued shading that scarcely suggest the blue skin tone and flashing jewels usual in Hindu iconography.

The merging of the Rajput and Mughal traditions (see Lady with Mirror; also The Kite) resulted in Kangra painting of the eighteenth century, with its soft coloring and playful mood. Since the names of Rajput painters were seldom recorded unless they worked for the Mughal court, they remain shadowy presences. After the conquest of North India by the Mughal Babur and his descendants during the sixteenth century, a basically Persian culture was introduced (see Four Horses). Both Babur and his son Humayun visited Iran, and while the latter was in exile from 1539 to 1555, he visited his cousin Shah Tahmasp and induced two outstanding painters, Mir Sayyid Ali and Abd al-Samad, to enter his service when he returned to India. From about 1550 to 1650 painters were brought from all parts of India to serve with Persians and Central Asiatics under royal Mughal patronage.

Among the other influences in painting at this time was book illustration. The large illustrations on cotton cloth for the *Hamza-nama* were the first of a long series of book illustrations produced in the ateliers of Akbar, Jahangir and Shah Jahan. Added to the Persian and Rajput styles was a current of European influence introduced by Jesuit missionaries, Portuguese traders, and English diplomats. A close study of the Bible illustrated by Flemish artists and of oil paintings of Christian themes painted in Italy opened new avenues to the court painters. They began to experiment with perspective angles, open vistas, changes in scale and modeling in light and shade. Sometimes they copied the European work exactly; at other times they attempted to achieve a realistic effect while retaining the vigorous outline and intense color of their native style.

During the reign of Jahangir, 1605-28, this interest in realism was responsible for careful nature studies of flowers and birds, or such unsparing portraits as that of Inayat Kahn—a courtier addicted to opium—made by order of the Emperor just before Inayat died (see illustration). Night scenes, inspired perhaps by paintings of the Nativity, became important in Asiatic art for the first time. Gradually, moreover, the Mughal artists achieved a balance and clarity that had previously been lacking.

Under Shah Jahan, 1628-58, the true Mughal style was firmly established. Pure in line, cool in color, serene in mood, it turned away completely from Persian complexity of composition and from Hindu preoccupation with emotion. The great subject was portraits, subtle in rendering features realistically, conventional in pose, handled with poise and precision. But when Aurangzeb took the power from his father in 1658 he broke up the royal atelier and the painters went to Kangra and Amber in the hills, or across the plains to Bikaner or the Deccan.

After a lapse of nearly a century and a half there is now a great renaissance of painting in India. Modern artists, trained in local schools or in the studios of Europe and United States, have revived traditional styles or have run the gamut of the major experimental phases of European art in the astonishingly brief span of fifteen to twenty years.

The following are the principal periods or stages in the development of Indian painting:

Mughal
- Humayun Period (1530-56)
- Akbar Period (1556-1605)
- Jahangir Period (1605-27)
- Jahangir-Shah Jahan Period (early 17th century)
- Shah Jahan Period (1627-58)

Hindu
- Bikaner School (17th-early 18th century)
- Rajasthani-Pahari-Deccani Styles
- Modern Period.

Indian Painters: Humayun Period (1530-56)

MIR SAYYID ALI (fl. c.1540-1575). A Moslem from Tabriz who was named Nadie al-Mulk (Marvel of the Realm) in 1544 by the Emperor Humayun. He was the son of the great Persian master Mir Mansur. He met Humayun when the latter was in exile, joined him at Kabul in 1549, and went to live at his court in 1555. Here he was placed in charge of the fifty painters set to work on the huge *Romance of Amir-Hamza,* which was to contain 1375 miniatures. After his retirement his position was taken by Abd al-Samad (see AKBAR PERIOD). He is also known as the famous poet Juda'i. The *Amir-Hamza,* begun in 1550, is the first Indian manuscript we have, and is done in a Safawid style that is the link between the Persian and the Indian schools.

Indian Painters: Akbar Period (1556-1605)

ABD AL-SAMAD (Abdus Samad, Sayyid, or Khwajah Abdul Samal) (fl. c.1525-1600). A Mohammedan, native of Shiraz, he went to India to serve under Emperor Humayun (1530-1556) who called him "Sweet-pen." He took over supervision

103. INDIA. RAJPUT, 17TH CENTURY. Todi Ragini
Museum of Fine Arts, Boston

INDIA. KANGRA SCHOOL. The Kite
British Museum, London

of the *Amir-Hamza* from Mir Sayyid Ali (see HUMAYUN PERIOD). In 1577 Akbar appointed him Master of the Mint and in 1587 Revenue Commissioner. He gave Akbar lessons in drawing when the emperor was a boy and remained his confidant and advisor. Besides being influential in Akbar's court, he was an expert calligrapher and designed the beautiful coins the Emperor issued around 1577. He was famous for teaching Akbar, but he is perhaps most celebrated as the instructor of the Hindu painter Daswanth. It is said that he excelled in portraiture, notably in delineating the features and expression of the Emperor. Besides the *Amir-Hamza,* we have a copy he made of a painting by the Persian artist Bihzad (c.1500) (see), whose works were greatly valued in India at this time, and an illustration from the 1593 *Khamsa.* As a teacher he had the responsibility of training the more than one hundred Hindu and Moslem artists who collaborated on the great *Hamza-nama,* the romance of a Moslem hero, Amir Hamza, who was related to Muhammad. Nearly 2,000 very large illustrations (22x28½ inches) painted on cotton were turned out by painters recruited for the task from every section of India. With a group from such different backgrounds, it was natural that the final result should reflect a certain amount of confusion. The compositions were elaborate, with many of them full of action. The costumes, weapons, trees and strong color were of indigenous inspiration; architectural ornament, most of the conventions of perspective, and the love of detail stemmed from Persia; and European influence is obvious in the use of shading to suggest volume and depth, and in some figure groups copied from Biblical illustrations. In later years these three strong currents would be blended in paintings of greater clarity and in true Mughal taste; this was the first rather awkward and ambitious step in that direction.

AMAL (Amal-i-Muhammad 'Ali) (fl. c.1600). A Mohammedan painter in the court of Akbar. The magnificent Poet in a Garden, generally attributed to him (although this has been questioned) reflects Persian style in many respects but uses the large, true flowers that delighted the Mughals. It thus represents a singularly successful blend of Persian and Indian modes. (See color plate 104.)

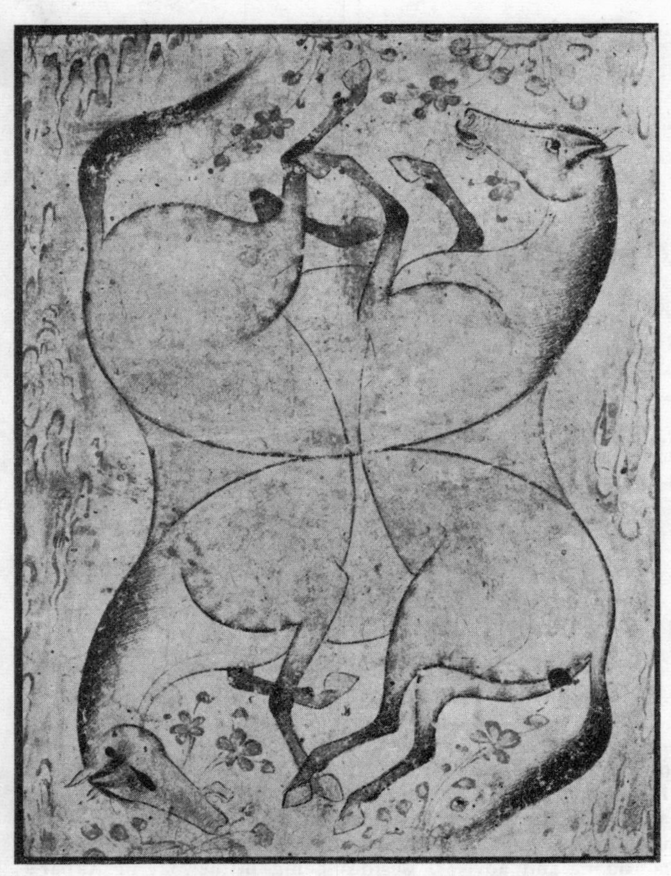

INDIA. AKBAR PERIOD. Four Horses
Museum of Fine Arts, Boston

BASAWAN (fl. c.1590). One of the three best Hindu painters in the court of Akbar; he had been a pupil of Abd al-Samad (see) but shows no Persian influence. He was said to be unsurpassed in original sketching, portraiture, and color blending, as well as in fine background painting. He was under European influence in making these backgrounds, in draughtsmanship and in representation of volume. In the 1570 *Darabnama* his work shows little individuality, but in the 1590 *Baharistan* there is typical Indian sensibility with less emphasis on outline than usual and harmonious subdued colors. He collaborated on at least twenty-nine of the illustrations for the 1598 *Razmnama.* He liked to include architectural interiors in the Italian Renaissance style, although the ornamentation was in the Mughal manner. The forced perspective angles and cramped relationship between figure and setting are disconcerting but the expressiveness of each face and the splendid animals and birds give great charm to his justly famous art.

DASWANTH (fl. 16th century). A Hindu who rose from the Kahar (palanquin-bearer caste) to be regarded as the ablest painter of his time. Early in life he began to draw and paint figures, working even on walls. By chance Akbar noticed his work, summoned him to court, and placed him under the tutelage of his own drawing master, the famous Persian Abd al-Samad (see). He soon outstripped the other painters and was called the First Master of the Age. His talents were dimmed by madness; subject to deep melancholia, he took his life in 1584. No work solely from his hand survives. He collaborated with others, as was the custom, on the great projects of Akbar's atelier, including the *Jaipur Razmnama* and the *Bankipur Timurnama.*

KESU (Kesava Das, Kesu-dasa, Kaisu, Kesu Khurd, Kesu Kahar) (fl c.1590). A Hindu from Gujarati who became a painter in the court of Akbar. The name Kesu Kahar refers to his lowly caste, the palanquin bearers. He was interested in European pictures, and in 1588 did an entire album of

INDIA. JAHANGIR PERIOD. Inayat Khan Dying
Museum of Fine Arts, Boston

INDIA. AKBAR PERIOD. KESU
Receiving the News of the Birth of Prince Salim
Victoria and Albert Museum, London

copies, including the St. Martin by Maerten van Heemskerck brought to India by a Jesuit. He also worked in Indian styles: one study of pheasants, done with his friend Kanka, is typical, showing the early flat style in which color rather than graded tone was used. He also drew the outlines for an illustration for the *Akbarnama,* Receiving the News of the Birth of Salim (see illustration).

LAL (fl. c.1600). One of the three leading Hindu painters at the court of Akbar. Besides collaborating on twenty-nine miniatures in the 1598 *Razmnama,* an illustration in the 1590 *Baharistan,* and one in the 1593 *Khamsa,* he contributed to the 1605 *Akbarnama.* To judge by the few paintings for which he alone was responsible, he painted in a vivacious manner, using bright color and animated figures. Typical is the abrupt transition from the foreground plane (usually occupied by a number of courtiers, equestrians, etc.) to distant hills; except for graded tones that accent convolutions, this represents the Persian tradition. Nearby, however, there are likely to be castles and walled cities inspired by northern European painting; and another portion of the scene may suggest a fairytale land copied from a Book of Hours. He was an experimenter, ready to repeat a detail from one spot to another. The result is naive and beguiling.

MADHO (Madhu, Madu, Madho Khanazad or Madhu Khanahzad, Madhava, Madhu Kalan) (fl. c.1600). Hindu painter. Confusing as are the records of this name, perhaps Madhu Kalan (the elder) can be distinguished from Madhu Khurd (the younger). This Madhu worked in the service of Abd-ur-Rahim, commander-in-chief under Akbar. His first dated work is the illustration in the 1585 *Timurnama,* and three years later in the *Iyar i-Danish.* With other leading painters in Akbar's school he worked on the *Baharistan* of 1590 and the *Akbarnama* of 1605, for which he painted eight portraits. Following the Persian tradition, his work is always delicate and conscious of surface patterns. In the 1610 *Anvar-i Suhaili* he shows himself an accomplished bird painter. His compositions, typical of the early phase of Mughal painting are too complex for true beauty.

MISKIN (Miskina) (fl. c.1600). A Moslem court painter whose work appears in most of the illuminated manuscripts from 1570 through 1605. His early style shows little individuality, but by the *Baharistan* of 1590 his illustrations are notable for grace and fluidity of line. Many of his preliminary sketches have been preserved. One of his paintings, now in the Bodleian Library (see illustration), is typical of early Mughal composition and figure study.

PADARATH (Pidarath) (fl. c.1600-1625). A Hindu who contributed a large picture to the 1605 *Akbarnama,* showing an interest in surface design that carries the eye upward through the composition. In a collection that belonged to Jahangir and Shah Jahan, he is represented by a painting of the clear, realistic kind much preferred by Jahangir; it shows a long-haired sheep done with emphasis on the mass woolliness of the animal as seen against a soft rose background. He is also represented in the 1610 *Anvar-i Suhaili.*

SANWLAH (Sanwal Das, Sanwalsh) (fl. c.1585). A Hindu

INDIA. AKBAR PERIOD. MISKIN. Camp Scene
Bodleian Library, Oxford

104. INDIA. EARLY MUGHAL. Poet in a Garden. Museum of Fine Arts, Boston

painter in the court of Akbar. In 1573 he accompanied the Emperor on a forced march in order to paint a military campaign. His works appear in the *Darabnama* and the *Baburnama* of 1570. He also contributed to the 1588 *Iyar i-Danish* and the 1605 *Akbarnama,* and painted Princess Humay playing polo. He used a considerable variety of styles; at times he experimented with the kind of atmospheric effect he saw in the European paintings he copied; other studies reflect the strength and intensity of the true Rajput manner. This tendency to experiment is characteristic of the Akbar era.

Indian Painters: Jahangir Period (1605-27).

ABU'L HASAN ('Abd al Hamid Musavrir) (fl. c.1589-1630). A Mohammedan, he was the favorite portrait painter of Jahangir, who gave him the title of Nadir az Zaman (Wonder of the Age). Though born a Khanazad (i.e., in the palace of the Emperor), he was the son of the Persian painter from Herat, Aqa Riza. He first worked for Jahangir's father Akbar, but the son had patronized him as a prince and felt responsible for his career. Jahangir tells in his famous Memoirs (the *Jahangir-nama)* how this artist of Persian descent received endless praise and encouragement. Abu'l Hasan was extremely proficient and interested in drawing, as shown by his accurate, shaded copy of the Dürer engraving of St. John. His skill in portraiture is evidenced by the likeness he made of Jahangir, surrounded by symbols in a varied *Album of Painting,* and by the delicately drawn and colored illustration of The King and the Brahman, frontispiece of the *Anvar-i Suhaili,* done in 1610. One of his most beautiful paintings, Bullock Chariot, was drawn from the life that he saw in villages on expeditions with Jahangir. A red cart, drawn by a pair of oxen, executed in exquisite line and tonal shading, is set on a tilted ground-plane painted somewhat in the Persian tradition, with tufts of grass and leaves spaced carefully about a sand-colored hill. One driver wears a red coat; the other, blue. At the top is a benediction written in Persian, framed in horizontal panels. Cooler in color than Rajput painting, less detailed than Persian, using calligraphic line in the Chinese manner, it is a most successful blending of all three. Attributed to him is another masterpiece, the Chenar Tree. In this, also, there is a subtle combination of Persian, Chinese, and indigenous tradition. Flaming spring colors have turned the leaves of a plane tree into a tapestry of delicate design against a golden sky. Mauve and beige rocks form a jagged horizon line, while flocks graze on green grass in the middle ground and lavender flowers echo the rocks. The realistic grey of the tree trunk emphasizes the russet of a huntsman's dress and the fur of frisking squirrels. It is both real and unreal, partly of the imagination and partly of the visible world.

BISHANDAS (Bishan Das, Bishndas) (fl. c.1615). A Hindu, one of the chief portrait painters of Jahangir, who had previously worked in the court of Akbar. In 1617 Jahangir sent Bishan Das and an ambassador, Khan Alam, to Persia to do portraits of the Shah and his court. On his return from this mission, the painter was duly rewarded with an elephant. In his *Memoirs* Jahangir says of Bishan Das that "he was unequalled in his eye for taking likenesses." Almost a dozen examples of his work are known. An early picture of Babur laying out the plans for his garden was done with Nanha (who painted the faces); it is minute in detail, still very Persian in many respects. Later paintings have a breath of vision, clarity and serenity that mark the peak of the seventeenth-century Mughal style. In another, The House of Sheikh Ful, a "mad devotee who lives in Agra," the rather complex setting of houses and trees is presented in line and graded tone; it is a series of abstractions in which the finely-drawn portraits of the Sheikh and his companions take their place in a unified scheme full of mystic atmosphere.

DAWLAT (Daulat) (fl. c.1625). A Hindu who worked in the courts of Akbar, Jahangir and Shah Jahan. One of Akbar's finest painters, his portrait (showing a bearded, intense-looking man) appears on the frontispiece of the 1605 *Khamsa.* His work is in the 1588 *Iyar i-Danish* and the 1605 *Akbarnama;* although there is a great deal of detail, each small figure is expressive. The colors used are the reds and yellows of the Rajput tradition.

FARRUKH BEG (fl. c.1580-1620). A Moslem from the Kalmak tribe of central Asia. He began his career under Akbar's brother Hakim, but on this patron's death in 1585 he entered the Emperor Akbar's service. He continued in the royal atelier under Jahangir and when Abd al-Samad and Mir Sayyid Ali died, became head of the school. One painting attributed to him is an album piece depicting a page boy, done in the Persian tradition. His works show the open spacing of the Persian tradition rather than the confusion of the Indian style of this period and also a stylized rather than a realistic approach to figure representation. He included minute architectural ornamentation and typical Persian rock formations and floral motifs. An effort to achieve individuality in each face indicates a development toward a later Mughal style of portraiture. He is an admirable transitional artist.

GOVARDHAN (Govardan) (fl. c.1600-1625). A Hindu, son of the painter Bhawani Das, he was one of Jahangir's chief portrait painters and, before that, had worked for Akbar. His painting integrated Indian, Persian, and European styles into a true Mughal approach. Many works are attributed to him, doubtless not all his, but the best are clear, with interesting, expressive faces. One of the best known, and typical, is the record of a court function presided over by Jahangir, in which the ceremony of the Sprinkling of Rose-water (commemorating an old Persian festival) took place. The Emperor, the center of attention, is dressed in court robes, with the usual golden halo about the head to indicate his importance. Courtiers, lady musicians, the bearer of the scented water, and a scribe, are arranged in a series of verticals on each side of the imperial throne. A flowered carpet runs straight up the page in the old Persian fashion, but architecture and sky betray European influence. Each face is an exquisite portrait, the mood calm, the color generally subdued. The old vitality of India is there, but the intensity of Rajput style has given way to a more serene approach, an ordered elegance.

MANOHAR (fl. c.1575-1650). A Hindu painter who entered the atelier of Akbar, worked mostly for Jahangir and then for the enlightened Prince Dara Shikoh during the reign of Shah Jahan. He was known as one of Jahangir's chief portrait and animal painters. His work always shows much Indian tradition. In group scenes he seems more interested in making each face a portrait than in effective composition. One such painting, a processional with two black elephants at the center and equestrians pacing behind banner-bearers and musicians, is awkward in perspective and foreshortening but gives an excellent idea of the men and women in Jahangir's court. It is less confused than the large scenes in paintings of the Akbar period, but it lacks the clarity of most work from the period of Shah Jahan.

MANSUR (Ustad Mansur, Mansur Naqqash, Nadir-ul-Asar). (fl. c.1595-1630). A Moslem; one of the chief painters of the reign of Jahangir. Of the work he had done for Akbar, several small botanical drawings appear in the *Baburnama* of c.1600. The greater part of his work, however, was undertaken as a record of the beauty of the visible world for Jahangir, who liked "the living present." Master of drawing, a keen observer of birds, animals, and flowers, he painted with objectivity and clarity. He went to Kashmir with his sovereign and made studies of more than one hundred flowers in the fabulous gardens there, a work he started about 1620. The Red Lilies doubtless was painted then: against a sand-colored background the red blossoms and green leaves are shown as a botanical specimen, not as a plant bent by the wind as in a Chinese painting. A dragonfly and a butterfly exquisite in color, but motionless, seem to be suspended above the flowers. Everything is precise; this may be the result of his training as a designer, for the "Naqqash" of his signature implies that he was one of a group who worked out patterns to be used in fabrics, leather, or architectural inlay, such as the floral motifs in semi-precious stones in the Taj-Mahall. Impeccable craftsmanship, rather than rhythm or poetic suggestion was therefore essential. Two drawings of musicians indicate his skill in figure studies, and a delicate painting of a chameleon on a bough hints at his fine sensibility in capturing the shy, tentative character of that rather unlovely creature. Indian cranes, a splendid cock, and other bird subjects place him in the forefront of specialists in nature studies. (See illustration.)

INDIA. JAHANGIR-SHAH JAHAN PERIOD. INAYAT
A Group of Ascetics. British Museum, London

INDIA. JAHANGIR PERIOD. MANSUR. Pair of Cranes
Victoria and Albert Museum, London

MUHAMMAD NADIR (fl. c.1620). A Moslem from Samarkand who was one of the chief portrait painters in the court of Jahangir and also worked for Shah Jahan. He and Muhammad Murad developed portrait painting with the black outline. His portraits—and we have many of them—are very expressive: one man looks vapid, another tragic, and a third spiritual. Typical is the three-quarter-length study of the seated figure of Sher Muhammad Nawab (British Museum): the body is sketched in with a few clear lines and a little hatched shading in the stripes of the robe, and the face beneath a round turban is most exquisitely modeled. A dark beard, moustache and dark eyebrows call attention to the wonderfully animated eyes and mouth. The left hand is raised to punctuate some

INDIA. SHAH JAHAN PERIOD. BAL CHAND
Three Sons of Shah Jahan
Victoria and Albert Museum, London

fine point in the conversation. There is no indication of background, no other object competes with the man himself in this little masterpiece.

Indian Painters: Jahangir-Shah Jahan Period (early 17th century).

BICHITR (fl. c.1630). A painter under both Jahangir and Shah Jahan, but principally under the latter. He painted telling portraits of Jahangir, Shah Jahan and their nobles as well as garden scenes in which his vital interest in character delineation is always apparent. A drawing in gold, showing Prince Murad on an elephant, is an early work; later, he did a number of "apotheosis" portraits very much influenced by European painting, with singing cherubs and symbols of kingship surrounding the Emperor. One of the most striking portraits is that of Shah Daulat, a celebrated Muhammedan saint credited with magical powers. The holy man in white robe and turban is placed against a black background. A nimbus in fine gold lines extends out from a circle of darkness that surrounds the profile view of the head. As is usual in early seventeenth-century portraiture, the body is turned to a three-quarter view. There is no ground-plane, no setting—only inky blackness in the rectangle around the standing man. A border of gold arabesques on a rose-colored ground separates this black area from margins adorned with flowering plants painted in the "botanical study" manner that marked this period.

HASHIN (Mir Hashin, Mir Muhammad Hashim) (fl. c.1630). A Moslem who was one of the foremost painters in the court of Shah Jahan and had before that worked under Jahangir. He was a portrait painter who sometimes reached the heights of naturalism, as in the picture of a nobleman with a bulbous nose or that of a crafty courtier of Jahangir. His portraits of both Emperors are in a more official manner and make the men look stern and regal. His painting of Timur, Babur and Humayum in a garden (done in the Shah Jahan style) is an interesting mixture of Indio-Persian and Rajput styles combined in a purely Indian and individual manner.

INAYAT (Inayat Ullah Sayyid) fl. c.1631). A Moslem painter who worked under Jahangir and Shah Jahan. He appears once in the 1605 *Akbarnama* with a painting in which there is the usual confusion of figures. His later work, however, is in the mature Mughal style, clear, serene, and with the open space that came in during the seventeenth-century. European influence may have been responsible for this; it surely was the inspiration for his firelit study of ascetics in a darkened landscape. Torchlight or firelight in darkness, mark a new interest in light-dark problems such as one seldom sees in any other Asiatic art. Nativity scenes and northern European painting brought this to the attention of Mughal artists. His Group of Ascetics (see illustration) is completely Indian in theme; the oneness of nature is brought out in the similarity between the roots of the banyan tree and the lean arms and legs of the ascetics. Each one of these men is portrayed as an individual. The overall color tone is beige and golden brown except for a few dark green notes in clothing and background plants, and the same color is repeated in the massive foliage of the tree.

Indian Painters: Shah Jahan Period (1627-58)

BAL CHAND (Balchand, Balchand awal) (fl. c.1625). A Hindu court painter whose work first appeared in the *Akbarnama* and then in the albums of Jahangir and Shah Jahan. The portraits he did in his later years were done in the clear outlines and soft colors of the mature Mughal style. (See illustration.)

KEHARDAS (fl. 1650-1675). With the painter Shamdas he fled in the train of the prince Solaiman Shekuh from persecutions of the Emperor Aurangzeb to the hill town of Srinagar. Both fathered a line of painters who belong to the local Rajput school of painting rather than the Mughal of their fathers. None of the paintings of Kehardas is known.

MUHAMMAD FAKHIRULLAH KHAN (Muhammad Khan) (fl. c.1640). A Moslem who was the leading artist under Shah Jahan. In a portrait album done for the Emperor he appears as a middle-aged, handsome, serious and serene man. He inherited and carried on definite Rajasthani traditions—so much so that he has been called a Mussulman painter working in Jaipur.

Indian Painters: Bikaner School (17th-early 18th century).

RUKN AL-DIN (fl. c.1690). Moslem painter who worked for the Maharaja of Bikaner. In 1690 he did a portrait of the Maharaja, Anup Singh. Painted in an old-fashioned Mughal court style typical of the period of Shah Jahan, when the single equestrian study was popular, the Maharaja is portrayed as a military man riding a prancing horse. The head of the ruler is in profile, the torso in a three-quarter view, while the horse is so slightly modeled as to suggest a silhouette. The orange coat of the Maharaja, a black circular shield, strings of white pearls, and golden turban, belt, jodhpurs and slippers are the dominant color notes, for the sky is grey and the ground a light green. Depth is suggested by the walls and domes of a distant town; a few puffy clouds are outlined in the sky, and a curious group of ghostly riders, perhaps on a dim mountain top or in the sky itself, are almost lost in a haze.

USTAD MUHAMMAD RAFIK (fl. c.1700). Painter of the School of Bikaner. In about 1700 he did a portrait of Raja Kesri Singh, brother of Anup Singh, showing him attacked by a lioness. Painted in a modified Mughal style, the subject is shown in profile, astride a dappled horse, as he pierces the lioness with his lance. The theme might have come from ancient Persian art, but the soft grey-green tones are part of seventeenth-century Mughal tradition, and the heavy rain

INDIA. CONTEMPORARY. ROY. Madonna with St. John. Information Service of India

clouds beyond a distant hill recall the indigenous Ragmala art of the Rajputs. Realism is still present, since it is the portrait of an individual, and the blood flowing from the wounded lioness looks natural. A simplification of forms makes one aware of contour lines, especially of the beauty of the line in the bodies of the animals.

Indian Painters: Pahari Style

MANAKU (fl. c.1830). Worked under the patronage of Sudarshan Shah (d.1859) in the Pahari country of the Himalaya foothills. His work reflects in fine detail the beauty of mountain scenery. One of his best paintings is Blind Man's Buff, in which Krishna and his friends and flocks of cattle are portrayed among flowering trees at dusk. A full moon rides in a sky scattered with stars, but the darkness does not dim the color of costumes or flowers. The human figures are set in lively action, and the cows are especially notable for the fineness with which they are drawn and the mood of contentment they convey. Thus a Hindu subject, a Persian delicacy in the flowering branches, and a bit of European realism in the handling of space and the night sky, are blended into a painting of universal appeal.

MOLA RAM (Mola Rama) (1760-1833). From Garhwal; a direct descendant of the painter Kehardas (see above). He became court painter to Ludarshan Shah, whom the British had put on the throne of Garhwal when they expelled the Nepalese in 1815. An infant prodigy, he was known as a painter by the time he was fifteen. He in turn fathered a line of painters, including his son Jvala Rama, grandson Atma Rama, and great-grandson Balak Rama Sah. He is the only Pahari painter we know by name, and the lateness of his work reflects the mid-eighteenth-century Mughal style as well as late Garhwal work.

Indian Painters: Modern Period

BENDRE, N. S. (1910-). Born in Indore, he studied at the Indore School of Art and later in New York; he is now

INDIA. CONTEMPORARY. SHER-GIL
The Old Storyteller. Information Service of India

105. INGRES. Mme Moitessier. National Gallery of Art, Kress Collection, Washington, D.C.

Professor of Painting, University of Baroda. Clarity of design and color, a strong, interesting line, and the ability to suggest an inner vitality in simplified design mark his work.

HEBBAR, K. K. (1912-). Born in South India; he had his art training in Bombay and later in Paris. He is an experimenter, trying various forms of expression. A recent trend is toward archaistic simplicity in color and design, used to portray the contemporary scene.

MOOKHERJEE (MUKERJEA), SAILOZ. A Bengali who studied at the Government School of Art, Calcutta, and visited England and the Continent before World War II. He has been an experimenter in techniques, doing landscape and figure studies with true poetic vision. He has had exhibitions in the important art centers of India.

RAVAL, RASIK. A Bombay painter who has achieved a considerable reputation in recent years. Although some of his work suggests the beauty of traditional frescoes, the forms are handled with suavity and sophistication that is entirely of the twentieth century.

ROY, JAMINI (1887-). Born in Bankura, West Bengal. A popular and prolific painter, his style is based on a folk-art tradition, full of color, rhythm and a joy in everyday things.

Clear outlines, flat color tones, and traditional themes handled in a seemingly naive manner result in pictures that have instantaneous appeal. He lives in Calcutta and exerts wide influence. (See illustration.)

SHER-GIL, AMRITA (1912-1941). A Sikh girl who went to Paris to study, and returned in the mid-1930's to India, where she drew inspiration from the traditional arts of her native land in formulating a twentieth-century mode of expression. Neglected in her lifetime, she became an acknowledged leader after her untimely death at the age of twenty-nine. She has been called the greatest painter of modern India. (See illustration.)

TAGORE, ABANINDRANATH (1871-1951). A native of Bengal, brother of Rabindranath, he is the founder of the modern Indian school of painting. He began to paint in the 1890's, but his most characteristic work dates from the early years of the twentieth century. He was an experimenter, but in all his pieces there is a delicacy of line and color, and a lyrical, almost radiant effect. His pictures are usually small in size, refined and exquisite. He made a thorough study of ancient Hindu theories of painting and helped to arouse interest in them. He was an accomplished writer of Bengali prose and was president of Rabindranath's International University at Santiniketan.

TAGORE, GAGANENDRANATH (1867-1938). A native of Bengal, the elder brother of Abanindranath; considered one of the greatest painters of modern India. A versatile, bold and brilliant man, bound to no particular school, he was always interested in new effects. Though he sought new means of expressing himself in line, color, and atmospheric experiments, his art is peculiarly Hindu in its emphasis on emotional responses. He was noted for satire and caricature as well as landscapes, portraits and genre.

Ingres, Jean Auguste Dominique (1780-1867). Led the conservative forces in French painting of the early nineteenth century. A product of the classicism of David, Ingres fought tenaciously against the succeeding movements of Romanticism and Realism and succeeded, for instance, in keeping Delacroix out of the Academy until 1857. He was not actually a Neo-Classicist, and is more properly described as academic. Despite his opposition to the later movements, his own art was penetrated by them both, giving rise to strong contradictions within it. For instance he delighted in the sensuous, even sensual implications of standard Romantic subjects such as odalisques and harems, e.g., the Turkish Bath (1863, Louvre). His drawings are full of corrections, not sketchiness but an effort to arrive at a successful compromise between his ideal concept and his observation of the model. This produced strange anatomical silhouettes at times, as in the neck of Thetis in Jupiter and Thetis (1811) or in the body of the large Odalisque (1814, Louvre).

His art is the archetype of "Art for Art's sake;" the linear patterns and arabesques that fascinated him are to be enjoyed for their own sake, viz., the fragment of Virgil Reciting the Aeneid (Brussels) which served later for the abstract speculations of Picasso. The origin of this artificial theory of aesthetics is, of course, to be found in his classical training. "To wish to dispense with the study of the ancients and the classics is either folly or laziness." he said. His early work reveals this clearly: Oedipus and the Sphinx (1808, Louvre) is constructed according to principles of classical bas-relief composition. He turned in his study of the antique, however, to the same primitivism that characterized the Barbus (i.e., bearded ones) group. These artists, impressed by the flat linearism of Greek vases and archaic sculpture, studied the styles of Botticelli and the Cinquecentists, thus sowing the seeds of Pre-Raphaelitism. This archaism produced in turn other conflicting tendencies within Ingres' complex style. He was long called "Gothic," and only in

106. INNESS. The Lackawanna Valley. National Gallery of Art, Gift of Mrs. Huttleston Rogers, Washington, D.C.

INGRES. Odalisque. Metropolitan Museum of Art, New York

mid-career did he establish himself at the head of the classical forces of the Academy. The epithet arose because of the Eyckian detail of canvases like Roger and Angelica (1819, Louvre) and from the "Troubadour" type of painting, i.e., subjects dealing with the establishment of the French monarchy (popular during the Restoration). A famous example was the Vow of Louis XIII for the Salon of 1824.

Ingres' father was a sculptor and a musician; Ingres often supported himself with his violin. He worked with Vien, Vigan and Briard before entering David's atelier in 1797. He left in 1798 after a dispute about his own archaistic tendencies. He won the Prix de Rome in 1801 but could not afford the Italian trip until 1806. In the interim he studied Renaissance artists and then in Rome developed an adulation for Raphael that is apparent in such works as the Virgin of the Host (c.1840). He spent fourteen years in Rome and four in Florence, returning to Paris in 1824 with a quantity of "Troubadour" paintings. These were well received by the young Romantics and Ingres became a popular teacher. Ten years later he succeeded Horace Vernet as Director of the School of Rome. He returned again to France in 1841 amidst official enthusiasm, and he held a great retrospective exhibition of his painting in the Exposition Universelle of 1855. He died in 1867 after a life of official honors and international renown.

The basis of his art was line: a line with its own apparently inevitable unrolling form. To Delacroix he said, "line is probity itself," and Delacroix once described him as "a Chinese or a Japanese artist who has strayed into Greece." His sources were many, his motives complex. A favorite subject was the female nude, which he handled with a delicacy absent in the stock academic paintings of the era. His career is punctuated by them: that of 1808 (Louvre), the Odalisque of 1814 (Louvre) and the Source of 1856 (Louvre). In contrast to these idealized constructions stand his grimly exact portraits. Some are as sharp and precise as a Clouet or Holbein, viz., M. Bertin (1832, Louvre). There is also a large group of delicate portrait drawings, especially family groups, many done as "potboilers" during his first stay in Italy. (See illustrations, including color plate 105.)

Inman, Henry (1801-46). American portrait painter and miniaturist, he also did charming genre scenes, but preferred landscapes. These he did in the Romantic manner of the Hudson River school, although in a more intimate and lyrical style. He was born in Utica, N.Y., of English parents who moved to New York City in 1813. The next year he entered the studio of J. W. Jarvis and eventually became his assistant, traveling with him for seven years and painting backgrounds and accessories in his portraits. In 1823 he opened his own portrait studio in New York and was for a time successful. He helped form the National Academy of Design and was elected vice-president. In the 1830's he was in Philadelphia as director of the Pennsylvania Academy of Fine Arts, but after the failure of investments and a serious decline in health he moved back to New York. In 1844 some friends arranged for a trip abroad to paint portraits of Wordsworth and Macaulay. Although he left competent portraits of some famous personages, among them Marshall, Van Buren, Seward, Clinton, and Hawthorne, he is best remembered for his sweetly sentimental genre pictures and his poetic landscapes.

Inness, George (1825-94). American Romantic landscape painter. Born in Newburgh, N.Y., he moved to Newark, N.J., as a boy, worked in a grocery store and for a map-making firm in New York. Practically self-taught, he did his first painting in 1841. He exhibited at the National Academy of Design in 1844, and went abroad in 1847 and several times subsequently. In the U.S. he lived and painted in various parts of New York and Massachusetts and traveled in Yosemite and California. He was elected to the National Academy in 1868, but did not achieve real financial security until 1875 when Thomas B. Clarke became his major patron. His early work was in the tradition of the Hudson River school (see), grandiose compositions handled with minute detail, but as early as 1854 some influence of the Barbizon school (see) became evident. The lyrically poetic mood did not achieve its full dominance until c.1860; the wildness gave way to calm, the grandeur to intimacy, detail to broadness. In the last years of his life, the silvery tonalities and mystical mood of Corot had its influence and at the very end the evanescent nuances are close to Whistler. (See color plate 106)

intarsia. A type of veneer decoration in which designs are cut out in a variety of materials, including wood, mother-of-pearl, ivory, metal, etc., with all pieces of the same thickness, joined together as one continuous flat piece, and then applied as such to a second surface, usually wood. Another type of intarsia, widely practiced in the Italy of various epochs, uses a variety of colored and differently grained marbles cut into thin slabs, joined together and attached to a flat wall surface. See MOSAIC PAINTING, COSMATI.

International Gothic style. A particularly elegant style of painting which flourished in all countries of Europe around the year 1400. This style employed many of the latest researches of painters in space, light, atmosphere and modeling, but retained a late Gothic taste for the intricately organized and flamboyantly decorated surface. S-curve linear patterns, gilded surfaces, coloristic detail, enamel-like technique are hallmarks of the style. Although painting before and after this epoch is strongly regional, there are many anonymous panels executed during it that cannot be localized geographically. The style is also in a way the swansong of the miniaturist, as exemplified in the pages of the Boucicaut Master, the Limbourg Brothers and the Rohan Master. Representative panel painters in this tradition were Master Francke (Germany), Gentile da Fabriano (Italy), and the Vergos Family of Spain (see each).

Intimism. A kind of late nineteenth-century painting associated with the Nabis (see), a Paris group of symbolically inclined artists that included Roussel, Vallotton, Sérusier, the sculptor Maillol, Bonnard and Vuillard. The latter two represent the Intimist branch of this "movement." Most of the Nabis tended toward simplification of the literary content that had marked Symbolist painting in the period immediately preceding them; for the elaborate subject matter of those earlier works they substituted a simple genre content of rural settings, street scenes, etc. Bonnard and Vuillard represent an indoor version of this approach, closing off their people from the world outside and providing the warmth and restful atmosphere of the home, symbolically as well as actually. These simple interiors are charged with a palpable sense of being away from the world, sheltered and immune.

Isaac Master (active late 13th century). A name given to the anonymous Italian master who painted scenes from the life of Isaac in the Upper Church of San Francesco, Assisi, in a style resembling that of the Roman Cavallini.

Isenbrandt (Ysenbrant), Adriaen (died 1551). Flemish painter, also known as the Master of the Seven Griefs of Mary. Follower and possible pupil of Gérard David, but we know little of his life. He was in Bruges and a master of the painters' guild in 1510. There has been attributed to him a group of paintings centered about the Seven Griefs of Mary in the Church of Our Lady, Bruges. In this painting the Virgin sits pensively on a throne flanked by seven panels depicting her griefs. The style is that of Gérard David but rather softer. It has also been suggested that Isenbrandt assisted in the Marriage at Cana (Louvre) by David. Other attributions include the Adoration of the Magi (Lübeck), a triptych of Nativity, Epiphany and Flight into Egypt (Metropolitan) and The Presentation (Bruges). (See illustration.)

Isenheim Altarpiece by Matthias Grünewald (see).

Islamic art (see PERSIA and INDIA).

ISENBRANDT. The Gold Weigher
Metropolitan Museum of Art, New York

Israels, Jozef (1824-1911). Dutch painter of historical and romantic subjects, and of realistic genre. He studied first at the Academy in Groningen and afterward in the Hague; he was also a pupil of Picot in Paris. Israels spent some time living among the Dutch fishermen, whose simple but difficult lives provided his favorite subject matter. He evolved a style and palette well adapted to the expression of the homely sentiments that he favored.

Izquierdo, Maria (1906-). Mexican painter; a student of Tamayo and the outstanding woman of the modern Mexican group. Her work is related both to Surrealism and to the popular arts. She shows interest in textures and brilliant color, and her painting is generally vigorous and earthy.

J

Jacobello del Fiore (c.1370-1439). Earliest of the many Venetians strongly influenced by Gentile da Fabriano. Important works by him are in the Doge's palace and the Venice Academy.

Jacob of Amsterdam (see CORNELIS VAN OSTSANEN).

Jacomart (Jaime Baço) (c.1413-61). Spanish painter from Valencia. Of great fame, according to many documents,

107. JAPAN. HEIAN PERIOD. Benten Playing Biwa
William Rockhill Nelson Gallery, Kansas City

but we have only one extant work and a meagre knowledge of his style. He was a favorite of Alfonso V, whom he joined in his Italian campaigns at Naples in 1442 after considerable urging. Jacomart's activity in Valencia was several times interrupted by calls to Italy to do costumes, banners, altars and paintings, now lost. The only documented work by him is the altarpiece in the church at Cati (1460). So late as to suggest the work of his assistants, it nevertheless indicates that his style was Eyckian and thus foreign to the Italian taste of his patron Alfonso V. Others contend that his Italian trips instilled in him a taste for the Italian Renaissance which he brought back to Valencia.

Jacopo, Giovanni Battista di (see ROSSO, IL).

Jacopo da Valenza (active 1485-1509). Venetian school. A pupil and follower of Bartolommeo Vivarini, and a painter of minor stature whose manner in several signed and dated works is a hard and metallic version of his master's.

Jacopo del Casentino (active soon after 1300, died 1358). One of four councilors who signed the regulations of the painters' corporation of Florence organized in 1339. One signed painting is known, a triptych of the Madonna, Saints and the Crucifixion (Don Guido Cagnola collection, Milan). Among other works attributed to him, the most important are a Madonna tabernacle on the Palazzo dell'Arte della Lana, Florence, an altarpiece of St. Bartholomew in the Uffizi, another of St. Miniatus in San Miniato al Monte, Florence, and a triptych (center panel in Berlin and wings at University of Göttingen). Jacopo was a fairly important and independent member of the following of Giotto. His types and proportions are particularly close to those of the Saint Cecilia Master.

Jacopo di Cione (active 1369-94). Florentine painter; brother of Nardo di Cione and Andrea Orcagna, and least noteworthy of the three. Only two documented works by him are known, both collaborations. In 1368 he was charged with finishing the St. Matthew panel begun by Orcagna (Uffizi), and in 1373 he painted, with Niccolo di Pietro Gerini, a Coronation of the Virgin (Uffizi). Among other works attributed to him is a Coronation and Saints (London). Attributions to him are based on their rejection from the oeuvre of Nardo or Orcagna. The style of all three stems from the Giotto tradition but reacts against it in reaffirming the extensive use of flat gold backgrounds and suppressing the definition of space. (See illustration.)

Jacquemart-André Museum, Paris. A distinguished private collection turned into a public museum under the Institut de France. It contains outstanding examples of all the schools of painting and sculpture from antiquity through the eighteenth century.

Jahangir Period (see INDIAN PAINTERS: JAHANGIR PERIOD, 1605-27).

Janet (see CLOUET, JEAN).

JACOPO DI CIONE. St. Peter Freed from Prison
Philadelphia Museum of Art, Johnson Collection

JAPAN. NARA PERIOD. 8TH CENTURY. Detail of
Kako Genzai Inga-kyo scripture. Jobon Rendai-ji, Kyoto

108. JAPAN. KAMAKURA PERIOD. Burning of the Sanjo Palace (detail). Museum of Fine Arts, Boston

Janssens, Pieter (c.1640-before 1700). Dutch painter of genre. His art is clearly connected with that of Pieter de Hooch, and he may have come in contact with Hoogstraten. He was interested in the representation of space.

Japan, Development of Painting in. Following the introduction of Buddhism in Japan in the sixth century A.D., new arts and crafts came in from the continent of Asia. By the eighth century a firm foundation had been laid for the development of a great painting tradition. Local artists, under the tutelage of monks, copied kakemono (hanging scrolls of silk or paper) of Buddhist deities; in iconography the images stemmed from India, but in style and technique the great source of inspiration was China. Thus the folding screen, the sliding door or single-unit screen, the hanging scroll and the makimono handscroll became an integral part of Japanese art, as did mural painting to a lesser degree. The famous frescoes of the Golden Hall of the Horyu-ji temple of Nara have no worthy successors.

Early handscrolls, such as the Kako Genzai Inga-kyo (see illustration), an illustrated scripture of the life of the Buddha in which text and picture could be seen at a glance, were used as models by Japanese students. Thus Chinese architecture, furniture, dress, and landscape motifs were accepted as part of Japanese art, as were space and perspective conventions, pigments, brushes, and paper. Each figure was painted in a firm black outline within which clear, bright color was placed. There were no cast shadows, no focussing on a central point. A bird's-eye view, or view from a high angle, was usual; one looked down upon a roof, but at the same time one could see inside the house. Figures might be abruptly cut off because the spectator should supply the missing portion in his imagination. From this study of the art of the T'ang period of China a true Japanese form evolved in which there was a lively inventiveness of expression. "Yamato-e," or painting in the indigenous manner based on cultural traits distinctly Japanese, emerged in the Heian period (794-1185). The new capital city of Heian-kyo (modern Kyoto) was a center of court life, a place where elegance, luxury, intellectual sensibility and artistic refinement characterized the aristocrats who served the emperor (see color plate 107).

A secular art came to rival the more traditional religious art. Themes were drawn from the new vernacular literature, such as the *Tales of Genji*, or from the turbulent political scene, or from the constant friction between church and state, even between sect and sect, as each group struggled for a position of influence. Highborn courtiers in stiff brocade robes and black hats were portrayed with stylized, expressionless faces, but the people of the streets were caricatured; misshapen forms and grimacing countenances heightened the drama as brawls and battles were depicted in the e-makimono (picture scrolls). Satire was used as a weapon against a rather effete, formal court, and a sometimes pompous church hierarchy; beneath the suave exterior there lay pent-up passion or laughter that found an outlet in art. The caricatures attributed to Toba Sojo, and the Ban Dainagon by Mitsunaga

**109. JAPAN. TOKUGAWA PERIOD. Hokusai
Mt. Fuji and Great Waves. Museum of Fine Arts, Boston**

JAPAN. KAMAKURA PERIOD
Fugen on an Elephant. Museum of Fine Arts, Boston

were produced in late Heian times. The painful side of life, such as the diseases and infirmities of man, or the potential punishments of Hell, were painted in the same era, and done with a violence and relish for suffering unique in Oriental art. Japanese artists chose a path leading away from the Chinese ideal of moderation and harmony and blazed a trail marked by drama, brusqueness, extraordinary delicacy, and clarity of form.

At the beginning of the Kamakura period (1185-1333) a military leader took the reins of government from the imperial house; Minamoto no Yoritomo, whose portrait was painted by Takanobu (see HEIAN PERIOD), was appointed Shogun and instituted a rule that was to last for some five hundred years. Kyoto remained a ceremonial city with the emperor in residence there, but troubled times lay ahead for the feudal lords. Civil war is vividly portrayed by artists at the peak of the Yamato style; the Burning of the Sanjo Palace (see color plate 108) and the Kitano Tenjin Enjin by Nobuzane are among the masterpieces of thirteenth century art. Religious paintings also reflect the dynamic character of the era. Soft colors of the previous period were replaced by deeper tonalities; gold leaf was used for jewels, garments, and haloes. Rich mountings in brocade and gold were popular. Even the portrayal of a loving saviour became splendid and remote; Fugen coming down from Heaven to welcome the soul of a devotee is an image of majesty high above the earth (see Fugen on an Elephant).

In a less sumptuous style other Buddhist painting veered toward realism, as in the portrait of the Priest Myo-e. Line, not color, was the medium of expression, a line so charged with energy that it sweeps upward like smoke. The serene detachment of the meditating monk seated in a forest is typical of the followers of Zen Buddhism. Members of this sect, called Ch'an in China, believed in retirement from the world, or even from large monasteries and elaborate ritual, to seek the Buddha-principle in solitude. Much of the painting of the Muromachi, or Ashikaga, period (1333-1568) is inspired by Zen ideals of austere simplicity, understatement, and absence of ornament. Following the lead of Chinese masters, a great group of Suiboku (water-and-ink) artists began to paint landscapes, birds and flowers, priests, sages and eccentrics. By means of the brushstroke alone, a personal expression of each artist's inner vision was given tangible form. Distant views of Chinese mountains were painted by Shubun and his followers (see MUROMACHI PERIOD), while Sesshu led all of the rest in his incomparable nature studies.

The Yamato tradition was kept alive by the Tosa school of artists serving at the court. Toward the end of the Muromachi period a new school was founded by Kano Masanobu and his son Motonobu. The best elements of the colorful Tosa style and the subtle ink painting of the Zen men were combined to produce most of the outstanding contributions of the next period, the Momoyama (1568-1615). In the latter half of the sixteenth century the Ashikaga shoguns were replaced by warlords who ushered in a period of peaceful prosperity. These military men became the chief patrons of the arts; they liked luxury and splendor, and Kano artists supplied them with screens of dazzling color on gold foil and silver backgrounds. What might have been vulgar display was held in check by the innate Japanese love of clarity, purity of form, and a fondness for nature; the gold ground served to isolate each bird or flower (see color plate 109). Tohaku and Niten were almost alone in their continuation of the Suiboku taste for simplicity and subtlety.

Early in the seventeenth century the shogunate government again changed hands. Tokugawa leaders chose Edo (modern Tokyo) as their military capital and a long period of peace (from 1615 to 1867) ensued. Farmers and merchants enjoyed a new wealth and they flocked to Tokyo to see the sights. A real genre art, the Ukiyo-e ("Pictures of the Fleeting World") came into being to fill their need for souvenirs of the big city with its popular theater, courtesans, street festivals, and famous views. Woodblock printing, first learned from China and used primarily for book illustration, became the chief medium of expression and actor prints, teahouse advertisements, and landscapes were turned out in great number. Some painters such as Itcho Hanabusa (1652-1724) worked in the Ukiyo-e style (see A Folk Dance) although it was considered beneath the dignity of the Kano school to fill orders for plebeians.

Tosa men still confined themselves to the classical Yamato-e subjects and style, while Korin, Kenzan, and Hoitsu interpreted old themes with boldness and skill. A new school, the Nanga, was started by Chinese literati who had a large following among poets and other individualists. Western painting was introduced in the southern port cities by the Dutch; realism began to alter Japanese art as painters like Okyo and Watanabe Kazan experimented with shading and perspective and went about with sketchbooks.

In recent times (Showa era, since 1926) the interest in

JAPAN. HEIAN PERIOD. Attributed to Mitsunaga. Detail from Ban Dainagon Ekotoba. Sakai Collection, Tokyo

European trends has increased. There is an active group of Surrealists, and almost all of contemporary Japanese painting reflects the influence of the abstractionists. These new developments will no doubt become a part of Japanese idiom, for ancient Buddhist tradition led to a production of mystical, non-representational themes, and the even more ancient Shinto led to an emphasis on cleanliness that is responsible for the immaculate clarity already noted in the history of Japanese art.

The following are the principal periods or stages in the development of Japanese painting:

Heian Period (794-1185)
Kamakura Period (1185-1333)
Muromachi Period (1333-1573)
Momoyama Period (1573-1614)
Tokugawa Period (1614-1868)
Meiji Period (1868-1911)
Showa Period (1926-)

JAPAN. TOKUGAWA PERIOD. Itcho Hanabusa. A Folk Dance. Collection Kinju Kanda, Tokyo

JAPAN. HEIAN PERIOD. Attributed to Takanobu Minamoto-no-Yoritomo. Jingo-ji, Kyoto

Japanese Painters: Heian Period (794-1185)

MITSUNAGA (fl. 12th century). A court painter (family name Tokiwa, probably of Minamoto clan) who worked at the Imperial Palace in 1173. Attributed to him are the three scrolls (collection of Count Sakai) of Ban Dainagon E Kotoba, anecdotes about a court official and a fire that took place at the Otenmon Gate of the Imperial Palace in the ninth century (see illustration). This is a masterly painting of narrative, full of dramatic incident and vivid genre scenes; it makes skillful use of horizontal composition, color, and firm contour lines in black ink. Also attributed to him are: Kibi Daijin (Boston), the story of the envoy Kibi on a mission to China, and scrolls depicting the Buddhist themes of the Hungry Demons, Hell and Diseases. Mitsunaga was noted for fine character studies, delightful touches of humor and dramatic presentation.

TAKANOBU (1142-1205). Fujiwara no Takanobu was a noted poet and a master of painting. A courtier, he lived in Kyoto and is mentioned by other court nobles in their personal notes and diaries. His most authentic and typical works are five portraits in the Jingo-ji temple of Takao (Kyoto). The best-known of these is the portrait of Minamoto no Yoritomo (see illustration), first Shogun of the Kamakura period, who established the strong military governmental control that was to influence Japanese life for the next seven hundred years. In spite of the deliberate simplification, the implacable and proud character of Minamoto is made admirably clear.

TAKAYOSHI (fl. mid-12th century). Son of the court noble Fujiwara no Kiyotsuna. He was chief artist at the Imperial Palace and is credited with decorative paintings on doors of temples and shrines, as well as a portrait of ex-emperor Toba. The most famous work attributed to him is a scroll-set illustrating *Tales of Genji*, a novel by Murasaki Shikibu. His work is an outstanding example of the Yamato-e style. Each scene is composed as an individual tableau, with no effort to suggest the full narrative scope. The basic line work (both freehand sections and those features, principally architectural, drawn with rulers) is secondary to the color. Pigment thickened with glue is placed within these confining lines. In general, decorative elements, such as costume, architecture, musical instruments and flowers, predominate. Faces are expressionless, but mood and deeper emotion are suggested through color and design. Abstract forms (as in the simplification of large areas occupied by figures hidden in voluminous court robes) result from a subtle, entirely Japanese concept of space. The effect is of a refined and exquisite art.

TOBA SOJO (1053-1140). (Buddhist name, Kakuyu) Son of a noble descended from the imperial line. Born at Uji, he was sent to the Onjo-ji temple to study under abbot Kakuyen. At the age of thirty he was made abbot of Shitenno-ji, where he served twelve years. He then retired to the Onjo-ji on Lake Biwa near Kyoto, and spent thirty-two years in seclusion. A scholar of the Tendai doctrine, he was made abbot of the Shokongoin, on the palace grounds at Toba, and in 1132 given the rank of Sojo. Attributed to him are the Kowadera Engi, Shigisan Engi, and Choju Giga (the Kozan-ji scrolls). In addition, the Fudo of the Daigo-ji bears an inscription naming him as author. There are no authentic records of his work; a little over a hundred years after his death, the above attributions were made and his fame as a painter of humorous and satirical sketches was established. His work is characterized by extraordinary skill in brush technique, with color of secondary importance. Some of the animals of the Kozan-ji scrolls are straight nature studies, but the majority of the frogs, hares, monkeys, etc., are given human qualities and portrayed with wit and irony (see illustration). Keen observation of man and nature mark the Shigisan-Engi scrolls, with the narrative power of the artist balancing that of the text.

TSUNETAKA (fl. latter part of 12th century). Grandson of Takayoshi, painter of Genji scrolls, Fujiwara no Tsunetaka was a court painter and vice-governor of the province of Tosa. It is claimed that he adopted the name of this province, which became the name of the school established in the early sixteenth century; the Tosa style, courtly, traditional and literary, does indeed continue the kind of painting for which he was famous. The school kept alive the Yamato-e style, cherishing the classic Japanese literary and poetic themes, portrayed in an aristocratic manner and handed down from father to son. The Saigyo Monogatari, as well as the Yukimi Goko, are attributed to Tsunetaka, but without historical foundation. Both show a poetic approach to art, a love of nature, and a refined style. Another famous thirteenth-century scroll, the Taima Mandara Engi, also by an unknown painter, is in this poetic tradition. Buddhist in import, it differs radically from the dramatic, brusque narratives based on political history.

Japanese Painters: Kamakura Period (1185-1333)

EN-I (fl. 13th century). A priest-painter about whom nothing is known except his signature as painter of the famous Ippen Shonin E-Den (the pictorial biography of Priest Ippen), dated 1299. This scroll, in color on silk, and about twenty-five feet long, portrays the life of a priest of the Buddhist Nembutsu sect. Although devoted to his religious activities and travels, this masterpiece is famous for its full landscape background and realistic figure study. The skillful working together of the many parts, the poetic rendering of atmospheric change in soft tones of green, blue and grey, and the suggestion of panoramic sweep, make it notable.

KEION (fl. 13th century). Named in Yamato Nishiki (nineteenth century official list of painters of Yamato-e) as painter of the famous scrolls of the Heiji Wars, but the attribution is not accepted. The Heiji Monogatari Emaki, three scrolls (one in Boston), color on paper, are among the most famous of thirteenth-century paintings dealing with historical incident. There is a sensitive balance of effect between the overall composition and the individual character study. Against the light background of the paper the clearly outlined figures—

in armor, court robes and religious habit—are placed as part of milling crowds, or in isolated nervousness. Red and yellow enrich their gowns, red drips from wounds, and red and yellow flames whirl upward in billowing black smoke. Blue and green pine needles serve as a foil for the more dramatic colors. Faces are individualized and reflect the emotion of the person involved in the drama. Roof lines cut across the paper in bold diagonals seen from above, but many of the figures are drawn as though seen from below or full front. As another touch of realism, the speed of a moving cart is indicated by the blur of whirling spokes. The painter appears to have had an overall plan for all three scrolls.

MOKU-AN REI-EN (d. c.1348). A Zen priest who is regarded as the pioneer in Chinese ink monochromes (the Suiboko school). Little is known of his life except that he went to China about 1326 and died there. He is sometimes called the second Mu Ch'i and has caused considerable confusion by his close following of the Sung master, though he is not nearly so great an artist.

NAGATAKA (fl. latter half of 13th century). Fujiwara Nagataka (name after he became a Buddhist priest, Kaishin or Kaikan) lived in Kyoto, was a pupil of his father, Iyenobu, and worked in the Yamato style. Two scrolls, dated 1293, illustrating Mongol invasions of 1274 and 1281 (Moko Shurai E Kotoba), are ascribed to him. Valuable as a historical document, faithful in rendering armor, weapons, horses and individual episodes, it nevertheless lacks the full dramatic power of the Heiji Wars series.

NOBUZANE (1176-c.1268). Fujiwara no Nobuzane (professionally called Jakusai) was the son of Fujiwara no Takanobu and was, like him, a courtier, poet and painter of Kyoto. He is known for his portraits (painted 1221) of Emperor Go-Toba, the poet Teika, and a concert and poetry party held in the Imperial Palace. Four important scroll works are attributed to him; the "Thirty-six Poets," the Kitano Tenjin Engi, the Murasaki Shikibu Nikki, and the Kegon Engi, but is is doubtful that the latter two are his. The Zuijin (Imperial Guards), studies of nine equestrians, is sometimes assigned to him. The Kitano Tenjin Engi, a set of nine scrolls, color on paper, each about twenty-two feet long, illustrates the story of Sugawara-no-Michizane, a scholar and statesman (845-903) accused of intrigue and banished to the island of Kyushu. After his death in exile, the charges were repudiated and Michizane was consecrated as deity of the Kitano Tenjin, the shrine that now owns the scrolls (another copy is in the Metropolitan). Some of the compositions are not well organized and certain figures are out of proportion, but these scrolls reveal remarkable imagination and freedom of expression as well as beauty of color.

TAKAKANE (fl. early 14th century). Takashina Takakane, Chief Painter of the Edokoro, lived in Kyoto. He is claimed by the Tosa school as one of their line, but there is no evidence that he used the name of Tosa. He painted an image of the Buddhist deity Sarasvati for Emperor Go-Fushimi (ruled 1299-1301) and in 1330 he made a copy of a scroll of the Kamo festival painted by Fujiwara no Tamenobu. His most famous work is the twenty-roll set of the Kasuga Gongen Ken Ki (records of the miraculous virtue of the Kasuga incarnation), dated 1309. Painted on silk, with selected pigments and gold and silver, kept originally in a sacred Shinto shrine, the Kasuga Jinja at Nara, where it is rarely on display, this set of makimono is in splendid condition. All of the earlier efforts of Yamato-e painters may be said to reach a culmination in this nearly faultless work of art. Another of his works is the History of Hosso Buddhism.

Japanese Painters: Muromachi Period (1333-1573)

BOMPO (1344-c.1420). Gyokukei Bompo (courtesy name Gyokuen, professionally called Shorin) was a noted painter of orchids in the Chinese style. He lived in Kamakura, and then became head priest first of temples in Bungo and later in Kyoto. An understanding of the potential beauty of Chinese ink, the suggestion of life in leaf and blossom, and a subtle use of empty spaces are characteristic of the art of the Zen sect in which he was a leader.

BUNSEI (fl. mid-15th century). Priest-painter of the Suiboku group and a follower of Shubun. He was a Zen monk, resident in the Daitoku-ji, Kyoto. Though little is known of his life, his fame as a portrait painter makes him outstanding among the monochrome specialists who worked in the literary Chinese manner. In 1452 he painted excellent likenesses of two priests, Yoso So-i and Yoki, and the supposed portrait of Yuima Koji (the Indian Vimalakirti, disciple of Sakyamuni), dated 1457. In the latter he has given great intensity of expression to the bearded face with its wrinkled brow and prominent nose; it is an entirely Japanese face, whereas robe and cap are more in the Chinese style. There is no background, no rich fabric, only the challenging, troubled face and a half-length figure covered by a voluminous robe; calligraphy occupies nearly half of the space in this hanging scroll.

DASOKU (fl. late 15th century). Soga Dasoku (family name Soyo) was contemporary with Sesshu, and a painter of Suiboku studies. He was founder of the Soga school. Born in Echizen, he lived in Kyoto, where he painted sliding screen panels in landscapes and birds and flowers for the Shinjuan monastery. In both his landscape and figure studies strong line and heavy shadows of dark tone are contrasted with delicately shaded areas. Dasoku is still a controversial figure among the painters of this period; some critics doubt the attributions made to him.

GEI-AMI (1431-85). Shingei (professionally called Gakuso) lived in Kyoto where he studied with his father No-ami and later served the Ashikaga Shoguns. Though he was trained in the Shubun tradition of Chinese monochrome painting, his style indicates a boldness and clarity that make his work unmistakably Japanese in feeling. One of his most famous works is Viewing the Waterfall. Another is his portrayal of Jittoku, a Zen character who "swept away the cobwebs of ignorance with his broom" and was a gay child of nature, content to wander in solitude or in the company of the equally happy Kanzan. (See illustration.) His second son So-ami carried on the family tradition as painter and connoisseur.

JOSETSU (fl. early 15th century). Priest painter who lived in the Shokoju-ji Temple, Kyoto, and was an early leader in the development of the Suiboku (Chinese monochrome) landscape school. His most famous painting, Catching a Catfish in a Gourd portrays an unkempt fisherman holding a small gourd beside a stream where a large catfish idles

JAPAN. HEIAN PERIOD. TOBA SOJO
Caricature of Judo Wrestling. Kôzan-ji, Kyoto

JAPAN. MUROMACHI PERIOD. GEI-AMI
Jittoku Laughing at the Moon. Museum of Fine Arts, Boston

among the reeds, perhaps symbolizing everyman's vanity in trying something beyond his powers—a Zen thought. The choice of a countryman rather than a scholar, nobleman or warrior, as hero, the lyrical beauty of the tonal landscape and the subtlety of brushwork reflect the direct influence of China's Sung period. The foreground stream, the delicate bamboo and the distant mountain are in true Sung tradition. Close relationship between painting and calligraphy is as characteristic of the early Suiboku work in Japan as of the literary painting of China.

MASANOBU (1434-1530). Kano Masanobu (familiarly called Shirojiro, professionally called Yusei), the son of Kagenobu, lived in Kyoto and founded the Kano school there. He was appointed official governmental artist of the Ashikaga Shogunate and was noted for paintings of landscape, portraits and various Buddhist themes. Unlike most of his artist contemporaries, he was not one of the Zen group. He was a professional painter and the school he founded carried on the ideals of the professional throughout the next few centuries. Like the Zen priests, he turned to Chinese painters for inspiration, but his interpretation of favorite Chinese and Buddhist subjects was Japanese in feeling. Thanks to him and his son Motonobu a happy adjustment of Chinese and Japanese methods was made. The color, boldness of design and clarity of the Yamato style were joined to the subtle painting in ink tones that had come from China. His two authentic extant paintings are Hotei under a Hill and Shu Moshuku Viewing Lotus Flowers. Following him are his sons, Motonobu and Yukinobu. Three sons of Motonobu carried on the Kano School: Yusetsu (1514-62), Hideyori (d. 1557), Sho-ei (1519-92); and Eitoku, son of Sho-ei, was the outstanding Kano painter of the Momoyama era.

MINCHO (1352-1431). Real name Kitsuzan (professionally called Hasoai and, as Warden of the Tofuku-ji monastery in Kyoto, Cho Densu); he was an outstanding Zen priest-painter. He followed Chinese models in doing a series of the Five Hundred Arhats or Buddhist sages, and also copied the Taoist Immortals, or men of magical powers, by Yen Hui. These were not exact reproductions and the Japanese character of the painting may be clearly discerned; his line is more dramatic, his space areas are clear rather than tonal, and he tends toward patterns of hair and garment. In line and color, his work is of professional excellence. One of the most appealing paintings that bears his signature is a portrait of the priest Sho-itsu Kokushi, shown as an old man seated in a great thronelike chair.

MITSUNOBU (1434-1525). Tosa Mitsunobu, son of Tosa Mitsuhiro, reputedly grandson of Tosa Yukihiro. He became chief painter in 1469, and after Tosa Hirochika died, chief of Shogunate governmental artists. He was given the highest honors possible for an artist, and more works have been attributed to him than to any other Tosa artist. In scroll painting, his Kiyomizudera Engi of 1517 is outstanding, and his version of the Kitano Tenjin Engi by Nobuzane is noted as an authentic example of Yamato tradition in the sixteenth century. The Seiko-ji Engi and Seisui-ji Engi (histories of monasteries) indicate that he enjoyed the strong patronage of the great Buddhist foundations of the Muromachi period. His art is notable for its elegance, liveliness and grace of form. He painted birds and animals, trees and grasses, not as symbols, but rather as living creatures. At this time Tosa painters of lesser stature were regarded as men of a fading tradition, too conventional to compete successfully with the dominant Zen masters of monochrome. A social change had also taken place and the nobility and the monasteries were no longer able to patronize artists of this type. Thus the rise of the Kano school, with its professional outlook, and its wish to decorate walls with more daring and splendid patterns, is a sign of the times. Mitsunobu's daughter was married to Kano Motonobu, thus joining literally as well as artistically the Tosa fortunes with the Kano. The old Yamato tradition and the fresh influence from China blended to produce the vital painting of the Momoyama period.

MOTONOBU (1476-1559). Kano Monotobu, (professionally called Eisen and Gyokusen) lived in Kyoto, where he studied under his father, Masanobu, and strengthened the Kano school. For religious instruction he went to the priest Sokyu, founder of a Zen monastery, the Reiun-in, and there painted numerous sliding-door panels (since remounted as scrolls). In the Daisen-in and Tokai-in, he painted wall decorations on panels and screens (still extant) of such subjects suitable for monasteries as trees and flowers (symbol of changing seasons, birds (symbol of virtues as well as seasonal change), and mountains and rivers. Inspired by Chinese painting, he also included the sages of old, Buddhist deities and their attributes. To the monochrome of the pure Zen style he added color. Like other gifted Chinese and Japanese monks, he could paint in three ways: with bold outlines, graded washes, or a combination of both. Unlike the monk-painters, though, was the brushwork, dramatic sense of color, and gold-leaf background. When he painted a traditional literary subject, he used ruled lines for architecture, plaeed figures in Japanese dress against the abstract patterns formed by line and color, and stressed the angular aspect of forms. Even when he did Chinese subjects, he manifested the flair

JAPAN. MUROMACHI PERIOD. SESSHU. Spring and Summer
Freer Gallery of Art, Washington, D.C.

of the decorator, designing compositions effective from a distance. He improved the technique of the Kano school, and made it a dominant force in Japanese painting. His wife was daughter of Tosa Mitsunobu.

NO-AMI (1397-1471). Real name Nakao Shinno (professionally called O-sai and Shun-o-sai); he lived in Kyoto where he served the Ashigaka government under three successive Shoguns. His official duty was to appraise Chinese paintings and calligraphy, but he was also a noted painter, landscape gardener, and poet, as well as an adept at tea-ceremony. He was a pupil of Shubun and, like his teacher, specialized in Chinese monochrome. Although he is known as a landscape painter, his most famous extant works are two images of Kwannon, the Bodhisattva of Mercy (one in the Asano collection, the other in the Mizoguchi collection). He was the first of the Ami family of painters, father of Gei-ami, grandfather of So-ami.

SESSHU (1420-1506). (Buddhist name, To-yo; also called Bikeisai and Biyo). Came of a peasant family in Bitchu province, and was enrolled in a Zen Buddhist temple c.1430. About 1440 he went to Kyoto and lived until c.1460 in the courtly splendor of the ancient capital, though his residence was in the Shokoku-ji, a center of Zen thought and culture. The Zen priests were excellent linguists, handled many works of art in the trade between China and Japan, and used paintings in their temples to aid in meditation. Sesshu became a pupil of the monk Shubun, who was an artist of outstanding merit as well as an overseer of buildings and grounds. Monk-painters often did not sign their works, and in his period of study under Shubun, Sesshu's painting is unsigned. In his thirties Sesshu was appointed "Host to Visitors" to the temple. About 1460 he was invited to become abbot of a smaller temple near Yamaguchi, seat of the Ouchi family. As exporters of paintings and lacquer ware, importers of Chinese and Korean art, they valued his advice in foreign trade. In 1467 he set sail for China, and visited various Chinese art centers before going north to Peking and the imperial court, where honors were heaped upon him. On his return to Japan, his reputation was increased tenfold, for he had seen the favorite lakes and mountains of Sung painters, visited the renowned gardens of China, and talked to Ming artists; he returned with sketches and paintings of mainland scenes. After discharging his duties to the Ouchi, he opened a studio in Bungo which he called the Heaven-Created Painting Pavilion. Students and pilgrims flocked to his door and he then did several of his most famous paintings inspired by his visit to China. A few years later he set out again, this time journeying around Kyushu Island, where he enjoyed the grandeur of gorges and streams, created gardens, encouraged other artists, and continued to paint well into the 1480's. His most favored pupil was Shugetsu. During his later years he concentrated on Zen themes and the Zen technique of suggesting much with a few brushstrokes or ink splashes. For another favored pupil, the priest Soen, he painted one of his greatest landscapes in this style in 1495, his seventy-sixth year. He continued to paint for the next ten years, active until the end. Like the Chinese masters who inspired him, he could work in several types of brush technique, notably in a meticulous rendering of detail, or a combination of careful outline and graded washes, or the running style of ink splashes made with rapid strokes of a saturated brush. Hsia Kuei was his favorite Chinese model; his bold conceptions of rock and tree, his liking for turbulence in nature, and his great technical facility inspired Sesshu to magnificent achievement in his own idiom. Purity and clarity are characteristic of his work, as are dramatically jagged lines, dots that seem to dance in space, and subtle tonalities that suggest volumes. His long makimono (such as the fifty-foot Mori scroll), screens, album pieces, and studies of the seasons, of birds and flowers (see illustration) are considered the greatest in Japanese art.

SESSON (1504-89). Born Satake (professionally called Shukyosai, Shukei and Kakusen-rojin) at Ota, he lived at Hetari in northeast Japan and later in Iwashira. He followed the great Sesshu as a Suiboku artist, painting monochrome

JAPAN. MUROMACHI PERIOD. SESSON. Wind and Waves
Nomura Collection, Kyoto

JAPAN. MUROMACHI PERIOD
Attributed to Shubun. Landscape (lower half of scroll)
Museum of Fine Arts, Boston

landscapes and bird and flower studies. He is noted for his dynamic brushstroke, and the freedom and energy of his line and composition. A pair of panels, portraying Hawks on Pine Trees (ink on paper, in the National Museum, Tokyo), are among his best works. The famous Wind and Waves (see illustration), with its storm-tossed boat blown close to shore, is a memorable painting of the forces of nature. The delicate tonal study of an Egret in the Moonlight reflects the poetic feeling of the painter and demonstrates his ability to use graded washes.

SHO-EI (1519-92). Kano Naonobu (called Genshichiro, Tadanobu and Oinosuke) took the name of Sho-ei on becoming a priest. He studied with his father Kano Motonobu in Kyoto and worked for the Ashikaga Shogun. He was the inheritor of Kano family tradition and served as teacher to his famous son Eitoku.

SHOKEI or KEI SHOKEI. (fl. c.1490-1510) (familiarly called Sekkei; professionally called Hinrakusai). A painter of the Suikobu monochrome school and a Zen priest in Kamakura. He studied painting with Gei-ami in Kyoto from 1478-81 but developed a distinctive style of his own. He followed Hsia Kuei of the Sung dynasty in China, but there is a Japanese love of contrast and clarity in his landscapes. He did Zen subjects, both figures and landscapes. His most famous album is the Shosho Hakkei, the Eight Scenic Views of the Confluence of the Hsiao and Hsiang Rivers (in Honan Province, China); this, of course, was a traditional landscape theme, not one that he had actually seen, but his portrayal of moonlight on the sandy beach, or of fishing boats putting into a bay, or of the night rain on the river, reflect the love of an island man for shore and water, and clear vistas into infinity.

SHUBUN (fl. early 15th century). Tensho Shubun, a priest of the Zen monastery, Shokoku-ji, Kyoto, was famous as a painter, sculptor and the first chief of the Edokoro (Office of Painters) organized by the military government in imitation of the Imperial Edokoro. The Shogun Yoshimochi sent him to Korea in 1423 to obtain Buddhist texts; thereafter he was appointed first painter to the Shogunate. From 1430-50 he was a leader in the Suiboku monochrome style of painting based on Chinese models of the Sung and Yüan periods; his landscapes, though small in scale, were vast vistas of mountain and water with a lone hermit's cottage or secluded pavilion. His subtle use of tonal washes was in the Chinese tradition, for unlike later Japanese artists he did not stress decorative value through the dramatic contrast of light-dark areas. Among his intimate studies are the Shoshu Sojin (Farewell to a Friend in Autumn) and Choshoken (Listening to the Wind in the Pines). Several large landscape screens attributed to him are significant because they were not monastic in spirit but intended for the pleasure of lay patrons; the taste of the latter for monochrome created a demand for Suiboku that temporarily eclipsed the indigenous Yamato-e. (See illustration.)

SHUGETSU (d. c.1510). Tokan (familiarly called Takashiro Gonnokami; professionally called Shugetsu) was a pupil of Sesshu in the Suiboku School. He traveled in China and there must have become acquainted with the Ming artists who influenced his art. He returned to Japan and lived in Yamaguchi in Suo. Birds and flowers as well as landscapes were his specialty. He painted in the Ming manner, with fine control of line, graded tone and delicate color. He lacked the boldness and genius of Sesshu, but his scrolls are skillfully done, poetic and sensitive in feeling.

SO-AMI (1472-1525). Shin-so (familiarly called So-ami) lived in Kyoto and carried on the tradition of Chinese monochrome (called Suiboku) transmitted to him by his father Gei-ami and his grandfather No-ami. He completes the group of three members of the Ami family who served the Ashikaga Shogunate as painters, landscape gardeners and experts in purchasing art objects. He is famous also as author of the *Kundaikan Sa-uchoki*, the oldest book on art collecting and appraisal in Japan, in which he set down the family secrets of connoisseurship. He, too, like Shugetsu, was a specialist in landscape painting on scrolls and screeens. The delicacy of graded washes used to portray mist and mountain were as characteristic of his refinement as of Zen philosophy and taste.

SOEN (fl. c.1500). Josui Soen was a pupil of Sesshu, a follower of the Suiboku tradition of the Zen monk-painter. He lived in the Enkaku-ji Temple in Kamakura and specialized in monochrome landscape painting.

Japanese Painters: Momoyama Period (1573-1614)

EITOKU (1543-90). Kano Kuninobu (called Genshiro as a boy; professionally called Eitoku) was the grandson of Kano

JAPAN. MOMOYAMA PERIOD. EITOKU. Whose Sleeves?
Metropolitan Museum of Art, New York

Motonobu and studied with his father Shoei. He is regarded as the most distinguished of the Kano line, as well as the foremost painter of the Momoyama period. He lived in Kyoto, but must have left his native city from time to time to execute commissions for the two military leaders Oda Nobunaga and Toyotomi Hideyoshi. This was a period of magnificence and living on a grand scale. The dominant generals and war-lords constructed castles and villas of spacious dimensions. For the decoration of walls they chose screens rather than frescoes or tapestries, and their favorite decorators were the Kano group led by Eitoku. On sliding door panels and folding screens Eitoku painted bold designs against backgrounds of gold leaf. Thus, the taste of their patrons, the problem of covering large areas, and the natural emergence of the Japanese genius after a period dominated by the Chinese monochrome style, led to the flowering of a dramatic and splendid art. Most of the castles have been destroyed and with them the screens by Eitoku but some have survived in temples and art collections. In the Juko-in (Buddhist monastery), Kyoto, a set of sixteen screens is still extant, painted when he was about twenty-four years old. On one set of four sliding doors he painted a single plum tree whose trunk and branches twist in dynamic curves and thrust out in strong diagonals. There is still a recollection of Chinese influence in the choice of bamboo, mandarin ducks and delicate grasses as minor notes in the composition, but the clarity of form hints at a maturity of Kano ideals. Another screen of Kara-shishi (fabulous lion-like beasts) is now in the imperial collection. Set against a green mountain almost hidden by the gold of cloud and water, the muscular animals suggest tremendous power. Muscles and mane are purposely exaggerated; color is as important as line. Also attributed to him are several screens ornamented with folded kimonos hanging on racks (see illustration). There is no story, no symbolism; only the enjoyment of abstract pattern.

HIDEYORI (d.1557). Kano Hideyori (also called Joshin) lived and worked in Kyoto, where he studied with his illustrious father Motonobu. One of his screens, Maple-Viewers at Takao (Tokyo National Museum), is considered important because it is the oldest known example of its kind, a genre painting. People from all walks of life had been included in the great narrative scrolls of the Heian and Kamakura periods, but plebeians had not been thought worthy subjects in themselves; they were only part of the whole spectacle of life. In the Maple-Viewers there are no heroes—neither princes nor generals in armor— only city-folk, relaxed and happy in a pleasant setting of maples and pines, beneath a sky where the geese honk as they head southward. Some are dancing, others drink tea, a mother nurses her baby as she chats with friends. Their kimonos hang in easy folds, their hair straggles a bit about the face, and there is a friendly animation of expression as they gossip. Here is a moment halfway between the first flowering of the Yamato style of Heian times and the art of the printmakers, the Uikyo-e masters of later periods.

KOETSU (1558-1637) (professionally called Taikyoan, Jitokusai, Kuchuan and Tokuyusai). Descended on his mother's side from the distinguished Hon-ami family. He lived in Kyoto all of his life, refusing to take up residence in Tokyo to be near the Shogun. In 1615, settling on land near Kyoto given him by the Shogun he transformed a bandit-ridden wasteland into an artist's colony and established his famous teahouse (now the site of the Koetsu-ji, a temple erected in his honor). A devout Buddhist, loyal supporter of the imperial line, renowned calligrapher, landscape gardener and woodcarver, master of Raku-ware tea utensils, connoisseur of swords (the family business before his time), innovator in lacquer techniques, accomplished musician, a scholar versed in Chinese and Japanese letters, a painter of note (even though he painted as a hobby), he is one of the most remarkable figures in Japanese art. Though eligible by birth and attainment to be a courtier, he preferred living austerely, giving himself to the pursuit of art. He was sought after by other connoisseurs and he encouraged other artists. He collaborated with Sotatsu on a series of scrolls from 1606 to about 1625. His love of simplicity is reflected in his painting. Using flowers and grasses as a theme, he made interesting patterns of color against gold and silver backgrounds. In his lacquer work, he is credited with being the innovator of the lead inlay combined with gold and black. He would have been at home with his contemporaries, the scholar-painters of the late Ming period in China, or with the versatile artists of the Renaissance in Italy; but his art is completely Japanese. Painter of screens, fans, scrolls and album pieces of extraordinary beauty, it is nevertheless his calligraphy that collectors prize most of all his work.

KO-I (d.1636). Kano Ko-i (courtesy name Churi) was a pupil of Mitsonobu. He served Lord Tokugawa at Kii, educating Takanobu's three famous sons, Tanyu, Naonobu and Yasunobu. Ko-i is said to have been deeply influenced in his later years by the Chinese painter Mu Ch'i and the monochromes of Sesshu. Both of these Zen monk-painters were masters of the brush, and it was doubtless his admiration for them that led Ko-i to stress the use of ink on the part of his three distinguished pupils. Certainly, these Edo Kano

JAPAN. MOMOYAMA PERIOD. NITEN. Shrike
Nagao Museum, Kanagawa

leaders used less gold leaf and more tonal effects than the Kyoto Kano painters.

KYUHAKU (1577-1654). Kano Naganobu (familiarly called Genshichiro) was the son of Kano Shoei, with whom he worked. He carried on the Kano tradition, serving under the Tokugawa Shoguns. He lived in Suruga. A minor painter of the Kano school, he was a younger brother of the famous Eitoku. The scroll of the Taima Mandara Engi (history of the Taima Mandara) and the gay screens called Kaka Yuraku (Merriment under the Cherry Blossoms) bear his signature. The latter, a genre painting of a picnic, is a forerunner of Ukiyo-e, though it is worth noting that the participants in the picnic are aristocrats, not plebeians.

MITSUNOBU (1565-1608). Kano Mitsunobu (familiarly called Ukyonoshin) was eldest son of Kano Eitoku, with whom he studied and carried on the tradition of the family in Kyoto. He is credited with considerable work on the vast projects undertaken by the Kano group. In 1600 he did the sliding doors in the Kangaku-in monastery, ornamenting them with trees, birds and flowers.

NITEN (1584-1645). Miyamoto Musashi (professional name Niten) was born in Harima, son of Shimmen Munisai; he came of a samurai family that served Kato Kiyomasa. He excelled as a swordsman and painter. In his paintings he chose the Suiboku monochrome, not perhaps because of any religious association or philosophic theory, but rather because his training with the sword had given him incredible speed, force and accuracy. He could direct the brush to paper, making a line sweep upward like a rapier thrust, so full of intensity that there was no need to adorn it further. With just such a line he did the branch in his famous painting of a tiny shrike (see illustration). In simplicity of composition and economy of line he is close to some of the great Chinese painters, but the spirit of his work is Japanese in its vigor and keenness.

SANRAKU (1559-1635). Kano Mitsuori (familiarly called Heizo and Shuri; professionally called Sanraku), the son of Kimura Nagamitsu, was born in Omi and lived in Kyoto, where he joined the Kano group as pupil of Eitoku and served Toyotomi Hideyoshi. With the members of his adopted family he worked on the decorative panels designed for use in palaces and monasteries. The sliding doors of the Daigaku-ji and Tenkyu-in monasteries of Kyoto are ascribed to him, and it is known that he collaborated with Kano Naganobu on the Taima Mandara Engi scrolls. When Kano Mitsunobu left Kyoto, Sanraku stayed in the old imperial city and kept the family tradition alive as head of the Kyo Kano line. Like Eitoku before him, he designed bold compositions. Against gold-leaf backgrounds his plum trees, peonies, birds and other nature studies were magnificent in color and dynamic power. Not as spontaneous as Eitoku's work, there is already a hint of hardness of outline and of being dominated by conventions in the flowers and leaves of the Sanraku panels. The colors are kept within inked outlines; although there is variety in the brush stroke, there is not the vitality or inventiveness Tanyu is noted for. Sumptuousness was his gift, and the great Buddhist halls of Kyoto are still sought out by lovers of the grand Momoyama style; the "Peony Hall" of the Daigaku-ji is so named because of the decorated sliding doors ascribed to Sanraku.

SANSETSU (1590-1651). Kano Heishiro (familiarly called Nui-no-suke; professionally called Dasokuken, etc.) He was a pupil and son-in-law of his adoptive father Sanraku. He was born in Hizen, lived in Kyoto and worked with the Kyo Kano group. Eventually he became head of that famous studio and directed its activities in the old Imperial City. In the typical Kano style he did bird and flower studies on sliding door panels, painted against gold-foil backgrounds. Combining a love of nature, the ability to isolate small, exquisite ferns and blossoms, and the decorator's knowledge of effective design, he proved worthy of his predecessors. One of his helpers, Kano Sadanobu (1579-1623), and other Kano artists, are credited with having done the paintings on the sliding doors of the reception hall in Nagoya Castle in 1614. These were removed for safekeeping in World War II and survived the destruction of the fortress.

TAKANOBU (1571-1618). Kano Takanobu (familiarly called Ukonshogen) was a follower of his father Eitoku and took part in the numerous activitites of the Kano group in Kyoto. His wife was daughter of Sasa Narimasa, a distinguished warrior of the late sixteenth century. Their sons Tanyu, Naonobu and Yasunobu carried on the family tradition in Tokyo. In the service of the imperial court at Kyoto, Takanobu painted a portrait of Emperor Goyozei in the Sen-yu-ji monastery. For a Kano painter to be appointed official artist of the court, taking the position given usually to a Tosa man. was an indication of the way in which the professional decorators eclipsed the traditionalists even in social prestige.

TOHAKU (1539-1610). Hasegawa Tohaku (familiar name Kyuroku; professionally called Nobuharu and Tohaku) founded the Hasagawa school based on his own distinctive style. He was born in Nanao, and then went to

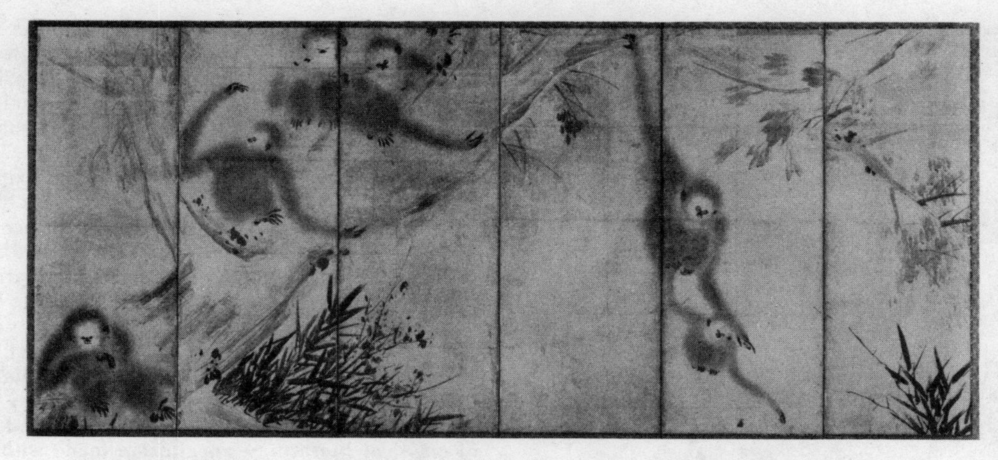

JAPAN. MOMOYAMA PERIOD. TOHAKU. Monkeys. Museum of Fine Arts, Boston

Kyoto, where he studied painting. He was greatly influenced by Mu Ch'i, the Chinese painter of the Sung period whose works were imported to Japan, and by Sesshu, who was the undisputed leader of the Suiboku monochrome painters of the Muromachi period. Other artists of the Momoyama period produced decorative, colorful screens for military leaders, but Tohaku, alone in an era of sumptuousness, painted screens entirely in ink, or ink on a delicate background of powdered gold. The Kano men generally used gold foil cut in squares, whereas Tohaku scattered tiny particles on the paper surface of each screen, and then used graded tones ranging from grey to black to carry out his design. He was a master of the Chinese method of brushstroke. He specialized in monkeys (see illustration), trees, and flowers.

YUSHO (1533-1615). Kaiho Shoeki (courtesy name Yusho) studied the Kano technique with Kano Motonobu; he then founded the Kaiho School based on the work of Liang K'ai, famous Zen painter of the Sung dynasty in China. He was born in Omi. While still a youth, he became a service boy in the Tofuku-ji monastery. In later life, while living in Kyoto, he frequently associated with samurai who served the great military lords, and it is said that he had the character of a samurai rather than an aesthete. Noted as a painter of screens, he specialized in Chinese ink monochromes and brightly colored decoration. His sliding panels in the Kennin-ji, Kyoto, are bold in design but sober in black and white tonal values; they depict dragons, pine trees, birds and flowers. For the Myoshin-ji monastery he painted screens using color and rich black pigment. The Tokyo National Museum owns a set of his six-fold landscape screens dated 1602; these are dramatically decorated with mountains, pine trees and misty valleys. His forceful line, like that of Niten, suggests the swordman's skill in handling the brush.

Japanese Painters: Tokugawa (Edo) Period (1614-1868)

AOKI MOKUBEI (1767-1833). Renowned potter and painter who lived in Kyoto. He is regarded as one of the greatest of the Bunjin-ga (the literati or non-professional group) who specialized in excellence of brushstroke and landscape motifs. His ability to simplify a composition and use line to the greatest advantage makes him outstanding in his period.

BUNCHO (1725-94). Ippitsusai Buncho (family name Kishi Uemon; professionally called Soyoan and Hajintei) was a printmaker of Ukiyo-e who studied in the Kano school. He specialized in actor prints of the great Kabuki performers ir male and female roles, and did a series of famous courtesans of the Yoshiwara, each with her name and address on a folded love-letter. His actor prints are graceful, subtle in line and color, sometimes amusing, but rarely charged with power. He seems to have admired the slenderness and delicacy of men playing women's roles, for he stresses tiny hands, elongated figures, and the circling hem of the kimono. In fact, the upper body hidden by sash and wide sleeve is separated from the sweeping border of the robe by an unnatural slimness from hip to ankle. The mannered elegance of women (both of the dream-world of the theater and the professional charmers) is displayed in settings made intricate by the inclusion of striking architectural detail, lanterns, flower-arrangements, curtains and furniture, or a landscape of intimate proportions. In 1770 he collaborated with Shunsho on a three-volume picture book, *Butai Ogi.*

BUSON (1716-83). Taniguchi In (also called Shinsho; professionally called Yosa Buson, Choko, Shunsei, etc.) was a leader in the Nanga school. He was born in Settsu but went to live in Tokyo while a youth. There he began to write *haikai*, or short poems, for which he became famous. He painted in Chinese style; small sketches reflected the mood of his poems, while screens and scrolls were bolder in design.

CHOKI (fl. c.1789-95). Eishosai Choki is a controversial figure among the Ukiyo-e artists of Tokyo of his time. A few prints of great delicacy and beauty bear his name, but they are limited to a period between 1789-95; it has been proposed that he is the same as Shiko, a book illustrator, but their styles are so different that it is hard to believe that a mediocre illustrator and a great painter can be the same. Portraits of geisha girls, full length and half length, were depicted with singular grace and sympathy, and beauty of composition. His children have a beguiling naturalness, and one print, of a child chasing fireflies in the dusk of a summer evening, is unique among Ukiyo-e works.

DENZEN (1748-1822). Nagata Zenkichi (professional name Aodo Denzen) was born in Iwashira. He experimented with oil pigment and copper-block printing. He was influenced by European painting, and Western ideas of space and mass are manifest in his work, though the themes-such as his View of Mt. Asama—are Japanese.

EISHI (1756-1829). Chobunsai Eishi came of a family of high social and military standing; he was a direct retainer of the Shogunate. His early training was in the Kano school, but he did his best work in Ukiyo-e between 1780 and 1800. From 1799 on, he devoted himself to painting. His skill with the brush is evident in both his paintings and prints. The spirit of his work is more aristocratic than is usual in the art for the masses, and his figures are marked by grace and nobility. In general, his work is less vigorous and colorful than that of some of his contemporaries. Among his most distinguished pupils were Eiri, Gokyo and Eisin.

JAPAN. TOKUGAWA PERIOD. HARUNOBU
Girls Playing Cat's Cradle
Metropolitan Museum of Art, New York

FUKKO YAMATO-E, or "Restored Yamato-e," refers to a school of artists of the late eighteenth and early nineteenth centuries who hoped to revive the glory of Japan's indigenous style of the Heian period. Active in the group were Tanaka Totsugen (1768-1823), Reizei Tamechika (1823-1864), Ukita Ikkei (1795-1859), Watanabe Kiyoshi (1778-1861) and others. The growth of this movement came at a time of rising nationalism, when royalists were working toward a restoration of actual rule to the imperial court and scholars were interested in classical literature. The Restoration School hoped to bring new life to traditional themes, revive the splendor of the past and free painting from the mannerism resulting from too close adherence to twelfth-century style.

GOSHUN (1752-1811). Matsumara Toyoaki (courtesy name Hakubo; familiarly called Bunzo and Kaemon; professionally called Yuho, Katen, Gekkei and Goshun) was born in Owari and lived in Settsu and Kyoto. He studied under Onishi Suigetsu and Buson. The latter, a noted poet and painter, influenced him in the direction of elegance and lyrical beauty, but later he became acquainted with Okyo and strove for a more realistic approach. Although he learned from Okyo to experiment with perspective and the realistic portrayal of solid form, his painting continued to reflect his poetic approach to nature. He founded the Shijo school, based on qualities from both Buson and Okyo. He specialized in misty landscapes, figure studies, and in birds, flowers, animals and fish. He was noted also as a calligrapher and writer of the short poems known as *haikai.*

GYOKUDO (1744-1820). Uragami Gyokudo painted in the tradition of the literati who regarded their landscape screens and scrolls as a hobby, not as a professional art. An original talent, he painted with vigor and complexity, giving a fresh power to traditional themes.

HARUNOBU (1725-70). Suzuki Harunobu (familiarly called Jihe; professionally called Choeiken), one of the great masters of Ukiyo-e prints, lived and worked in Tokyo. A pupil of Shigenaga, he was influenced in his early years by Toyonobu. By 1764, when he perfected the "brocade print" (a process that made it possible to print in more than ten colors, including intermediate tones or half-tones in purple and grey), he stood alone as the great master of Ukiyo-e work. In the six years before his death in 1770, he produced a large number of designs that are far superior, in poetic quality and elegance, to any similar work up to that time. Unlike the Torii men who specialized in actor prints, or the artists who did street scenes and women of the Yoshiwara, he turned to the Japanese home for inspiration. Young girls of good family became his central theme. He delighted in showing them as they went about their daily tasks or walked out with a chaperone or suitor. He captured their adolescent moods, their enchantment with the beauties of the world, their vanities and small triumphs. Sometimes there is a gentle satire as a modest maiden plays the role of an august sage of classical literature—an allusion made with the utmost delicacy. The figures are small in scale, placed in house or garden, or buffeted by wind and rain that emphasize their physical frailty. Often there are bands of cloud in the upper section of the print, or streams flowing through gardens recalling a beauty of natural setting first manifest in the Yamato-e. The heads nod on slender throats, the hands are unbelievably small, and the elegant, simple kimonos modestly cover the rest of the body, except for the dainty feet. Not only did he use more colors than had been possible before, but he also went in for relief printing, or gauffrage, that gave a subtle surface modulation. Some six to seven hundred prints of his are recorded. (See illustration.)

HIROSHIGE (1797-1858). Ando Hiroshige (familiarly called Tokube and Juemon; professionally called Utagawa Hiroshige, Ichiyusai, Ryusai, etc.) was the son of a man who was adopted into the Ando family and was a minor official in the Tokyo fire-police brigade. The son was named Tokutaro Ando and was given his father's post when he became an orphan in 1809. When fifteen years old, he joined the studio of Utagawa Toyohiro; in 1812 he won a diploma and was given his first professional name. Two sons-in-law who were lesser artists have used his name, which accounts for the uneven workmanship and garish color of some Hiroshige prints. He lived in Tokyo except for frequent journeys about the countryside. He sketched wherever he went, working in a brush style akin to the Chinese. The sketches are highly regarded, as are the prints that were developed from them. He was a prolific artist who turned out thousands of landscapes, some actor prints, advertisements, poetry cards, guide-books, and other illustrated books before he was stricken with cholera in his sixty-second year. He saw his native land with a poet's eyes and he portrayed it swept by the wind, buried beneath drifts of snow, touched by moonlight, drenched by rain, clouded in mist, or warmed by the autumn sun. It was a fascinating panorama that inspired him, not landscape as a setting for figures, though people were often a part of the panorama, but the vast reaches of land, sea and sky. Less inclined to stress detail than Hokusai, he relied on tonal shading as much as on line to suggest space and mood. Of his many famous prints there are several series: in 1848 he published the Fifty-three Views along the Tokaido (the three-hundred-mile road between Kyoto and Tokyo), and supplemented the original issue in 1851, 1856 and 1858. During 1850-67 he turned out ten small guide-books, the Souvenirs of Edo, and in 1857 the One Hundred Views of Mt. Fuji. There were also Famous Views of Kyoto, Eight Views of Lake Biwa, Eight Views of Edo, a series of Bridges, and several delightful bird and flower prints on which his poems were inscribed. Some of the prints suggest gaiety and splendor, and others are printed in subtle greys and greens; some capture the hushed stillness of a night when spirits walk abroad, and others are lashed by storm. Even the suggestion of sound is achieved—water lapping on a shoal, or the creaking gear of men pushing up a mountain path, or the high honking of wild geese in flight.

HOGAI (1828-88). Kano Enshin (professionally called Hogai) was a pupil of Kano Shosen-in. He lived in Tokyo, where he was one of the most distinguished of the nineteenth-century Edo Kano Kobikicho group (see NAONOBU). He specialized in landscape and figure painting.

HOITSU (1761-1828). Sakai Tadamoto (courtesy name Kishin; professionally called Oson, Keikyodojin, Nison-an, Uka-an, Hoitsu) was born in Edo, the second son of Lord Sakai of the Himeji castle. He later went to Kyoto and became a priest in 1793. In 1810 he returned to Tokyo, where he published *Korin Hyakuzu (One Hundred Masterpieces of Korin)*, Kenzan's works etc. He was a distinguished poet, musican and calligrapher, a noted master of tea-ceremony, skillful in archery and horsemanship, and known as a connoisseur of swords. His house near Tokyo was a gathering place for literati and virtuosi. He studied the technique of the Kano and Ukiyo-e schools, was influenced by Chinese painting, but above all admired the work of Korin and brought about a revival of the Korin school. Eventually he developed his own style, one that was somewhat more realistic than seventeenth-century art and thus appropriate to the period in which he lived. He is noted for screen paintings, especially Summer and Autumn Grasses, for hand-scrolls, such as Flowers of the Four Seasons, delicate panels, quite literary and poetic, and a book of color prints, *Bancho Sokugoshi*, 1817, now a collector's item. All of his work reveals sensitivity and aristocratic taste.

HOKUSAI (1760-1849). Nakajima Tamekazu, (familiarly called Tokitaro and Tetsuzo; professionally called Katsukawa Shunro, Soshunro, Gumbatei, etc.). Born in the artisan class (his father made metal mirrors for the Shogun) he left home in his early teens to become an engraver, but at eighteen decided to study in Tokyo in Shunsho's school. Too unruly for that disciplined life and art, he was expelled, but had learned much during his eight years there. At twenty-six he earned a partial living by illustrating his own texts, usually comic, and sold almanacs and red peppers in the street. In 1804 he painted a colossal figure in the courtyard of a temple, working on paper eighteen yards long by eleven yards wide, using brooms, tubs of water and ink, to the amazement of a crowd of onlookers. On other occasions he made microscopic pictures on grains of rice or wheat. In 1807 his association with the novelist Bakin began, with Hokusai illustrating Bakin's stories. In 1817 he went to Nagoya; in 1818 to Osaka and Kyoto. When nearly seventy years old, he produced three sets of large color prints—sets of Waterfalls, Bridges, and the Thirty-Six Views of Mt. Fuji (see color plate 109). He had returned to Tokyo but left in 1834 and lived in Uraga. In two years he tried the big city again, but a terrible famine led to a dead art market, and he was poverty-stricken; in 1837 his house burned, and only his brushes were saved. He kept on painting—truly a "man mad with painting," as he described himself—until his death in his ninetieth year. He had studied everything that came before his eyes—nothing was too trivial to merit attention, nothing too sublime for him to try to capture it. He loved Japan—the cultivated fields, the villages and cities, mountains, rivers and sea-girt shores, the people at work and play, the birds, flowers and insects, the very winds that swept down the hillsides and across the rice paddies, and he has recorded all of it. Original, versatile, sometimes poetic—but sometimes too much inclined to include distracting detail—always working with enormous vitality, he gave his life to his art. Some one hundred and sixty publications were illustrated by him—novels, plays and stories, book of legendary subjects—as well as color prints for festive occasions, sketch books, Views of Edo, stopping-places along the Tokaido (the road from Kyoto to Tokyo), and the Views of Fuji. Some were printed in graded tones of one color, others were done in many colors. He was an artist of the people and he depicted their restless energy in his vision of a changing world.

JAPAN. TOKUGAWA PERIOD. KAZAN
Portrait of Ichikawa Beian
Collection Goro Katakura, Tokyo

IPPO (1798-1871). Mori Takayuki (courtesy name Shiko; familiarly called Bumpei; professionally called Ippo) was born and lived in Osaka and studied under his adoptive father, Mori Tetsuzan. He specialized in animals, birds and flowers, using brushstroke and color to bring out the inherent character of each. He painted the sliding doors of the Imperial Palace in the Ansei era.

ITCHO (1652-1724). Taga Shinko (familiarly called Sukenoshin; professionally called Hanabusa Itcho, Choko, etc.) was born in Osaka. He studied under Kano Yasunobu and founded the Hanabusa school. He was a part of the gay and fashionable world of Tokyo and is noted for his cartoons and paintings of the "Fleeting World," or Ukiyo-e. His genre painting is done with the cartoonist's eye for character and is executed in a rapid brushstroke. People interested him

JAPAN. TOKUGAWA PERIOD. KENZAN
Flower Baskets
Collection Tomitaro Hara, Yokohama

more than street scenes; he often painted figures against a plain background to give full value to sweeping contour line and bold pattern. (See illustration under JAPAN, DEVELOPMENT OF PAINTING IN.)

JAKUCHU (1713-1800). Ito Shunkyo (professionally called Tobei-an and Jakuchu) was born in Kyoto, studied in the Kano school and then turned to Chinese painting of the Yüan and Ming dynasties. A decorative painter who loved sumptuous color, he spent thirteen years creating a set of thirty hanging scrolls of animals, birds, plants, fish, etc. (now in the Imperial Household Collection).

KAIGETSUDO (c.1714). It is not known who this painter was; it has been suggested that he was someone who used several personal names, or that he represents a group using one surname. The latter interpretation is preferred in Japan. There are twenty-two surviving designs for prints of this group; of them, twelve are signed Kaigetsudo Dohan or Norishige, seven are signed by Kaigetsudo Anchi (or Yasutomo), and three are signed by Kaigetsudo Doshin (or Noritatsu). There was also a painter Kaigetsudo Ando (or Yasunori) who was not, apparently, associated with these prints. Each print shows a woman, usually displaying a gorgeous costume. These are the ladies of the Yoshiwara, courtesans who dazzled the countryfolk who flocked to Tokyo to see the sights and visit the women of the Green Houses. The obi (sash) tied in front, and the splendor of their gowns indicate their profession. They seem to be calendar prints, for the designs on their garments are symbols of the seasons.

KAZAN, WATANABE (1793-1841). Watanabe Sadayasu (courtesy name, Shian Hakuto; familiarly called Nobori; professionally called Kazan, Gukaido, etc.), was born in Tokyo of the samurai class, serving Lord Miyake of the Tawara clan. A pupil of Buncho, he studied both European and Nanga styles of painting. He combined the Chinese use of line and command of brush with the realism, especially of modeling in light and shade, he had learned from European painting. He did bird, flower and insect studies and was a noted portrait painter. The most famous of his portraits is that of his teacher Ichikawa Beian (see illustration); he had made a preliminary sketch, noting the bone structure, wrinkled skin, and other realistic details but in the final painting in color on silk he simplified the surface treatment. It is a subtle, masterly work, as dramatically simple as earlier Japanese portraits, as sensitive as a Chinese portrait, and a faithful likeness in the Western sense. He dared to criticize the Tokugawa regime for its isolationist policy; as punishment, he was confined to his native town in Tawara, and there committed suicide.

KENZAN (1663-1743). Ogata Shinsei (courtesy name I-in; familiarly called Kenzan; professionally called Shoko, Toin, etc.) studied under his elder brother Korin. He lived most of his life in the Kyoto area but moved to Tokyo toward the end of his life. He was a noted calligrapher and potter, as well as a painter. His painting, like his writing, is quick, dramatic and tends toward abstraction. Famous works: Hollyhocks; Flower Baskets (see illustration); Iris; Crow on a Rock.

KIYOHIRO (fl. c.1751-65). Torii Kiyohiro, pupil of Kiyomasu II, is noted for his actor prints, most of them little masterpieces of two-color (rose and green) printing. Line, color and richness of fabric design are held in balance. He was fond of depicting two actors beneath cherry or willow trees, with the downward sweep of delicate branches in harmony with the flowing lines of the costumes. The hands tend to be too small for the rest of the body, but heads and feet are in scale; and the faces suggest masks, recalling the aristocratic "Noh" drama where masks are worn and pantomine must suggest mood and narrative. After 1765, when Harunobu became famous for his more complex printing techniques, Kiyohiro withdrew from the field of print design.

KIYOMASU I, II, and III (1694?-1716). Torii Kiyomasa I was related to Torii Kiyonobu I; it is believed that he was the eldest son. An unusually gifted youth, he died at the age of twenty-two. Shortly after, someone else (perhaps a younger brother) began to issue prints under the name of Kiyomasu, continuing to do so until the death of Kiyonobu I in 1729, when this second Kiyomasu assumed the name of Torii Kiyonobu II. At this time it is possible that another member of the family (Kiyomasu III) began to use the signature; he is sometimes designated as Kiyomasu II (1706-63). All of these sons of Kiyonobu specialized in actor prints. In the work attributed to Kiyomasu I, there is greater majesty and serenity than in the prints of Kiyonobu I and faces are portrayed with greater delicacy and sympathy. Hands, faces, and feet are unnaturally small as they are seen emerging from the billowing volumes of kimonos. These figures are more like fashion-plates than actors in dramatic roles.

KIYOMITSU (1735-85). Torii Kiyomitsu, the third of the Torii line, was a pupil of his father Kiyomasu II and a contemporary of Kiyohiro. He was a prolific artist who lived and worked in Tokyo. He is known especially for his three-color actor prints, though it is said that he collaborated with Harunobu when the latter successfully launched his "brocade prints." His prints are not large (they average 12½x5¾ inches) but the actors are more dashing than in the relaxed, gentle scenes of Kiyohiro. They move or carry some object —a basket of ferns, a bow and arrow, a pair of bird cages swinging from a shoulder-pole, a musical instrument, etc. The fabric patterns are not in themselves as complex as in certain other prints, but the overall compositions, plus the writing that fills the space around the figure, gives an impression of dense and dynamic design. Perhaps because he produced so many prints, the quality is rather uneven.

KIYONAGA (1752-1815). Seki Shinsuke (familiarly called Shirakoya Ichibe; professionally called Torii Kiyonaga) is an outstanding Ukiyo-e artist. Born in Uraga, he went to Tokyo and became a pupil of Kiyomitsu. After the death of his master, he was adopted by the family, inherited the estate of Torii, and carried on the great tradition of theater prints. Many critics consider him the greatest print artist, one who carried the development of this popular art to its classic peak. There is poise, grandeur and a controlled complexity of design in his work. He liked diptychs and triptychs printed on separate sheets of paper. The set called A Picture Gallery of Beautiful Girls of the Licensed Quarters displays these beauties and their admirers in both exterior and interior settings. The women are taller than those of the early Ukiyo-e series, more relaxed than the theater people, and often quite informal in pose, suggesting the heat of the Edo summer. Other series of Sayonara (Farewell) groups include boats and boatmen, views of the Sumida River, and a distant glimpse of the city. In a different spirit he designed the Princesses, or Court Ladies, in the formal, elegant brocaded gowns of the tenth and eleventh centuries. This was a rare intrusion in an art designed for a plebeian public and indicates the people's appreciation of their stately heritage. There is a striking range of color in his prints, though he preferred mauve, rose, moss-green, pale yellow, and shades of grey and blue. The large figures are set against the diagonal lines of porches, roofs, etc., or in landscapes that suggest vast distance. Household utensils, mosquito nets, rolled screens, etc.—all the accessories of genre art—are included, as are birds, flowers and other touches of nature and the out-of-doors.

KIYONOBU I (1664-1729). Torii Kiyonobu, a leader in the early Ukiyo-e school, was born in Tokyo and spent his life there. He is founder of a distinguished line of printmakers whose main interest lay in the theater. He was a pupil of his father Kiyomoto, a painter of theatrical signboards. Like his contemporary Moronobu, he first began to work as early as 1687 as a book illustrator. By 1695 he had made enough outstanding actor prints to attract public attention. These prints are large (some about 23x12½ inches), and since they are sometimes hand-colored with "tan" (actually a red-orange) and pale yellow, are called tan-e. Bold designs, influenced no doubt by his apprenticeship under his father as a theater signpainter, suggest the dramatic power of the individual actors in their most famous roles. Men played feminine parts, practiced graceful gait and gestures, and wore women's kimonos. These costumes consisted of several layers of robe, each of a different color. If the actor was famous enough the outer kimono would be embroidered or imprinted with his insignia set among bold designs of symbolic flowers, birds, clouds, fans, plaids, checks, etc. (See illustration.) The contour lines vary in width and are drawn in sweeping curves and angles. A hint of the setting—a spray of cherry blossoms, a tree, or a shrine in the background—is sometimes given but the single figure occupies most of the print area. His signature and seal help to balance the composition. Though he is best known for these large theater prints he is also known for the erotic prints which he (like many contemporaries) issued in album form.

KIYONOBU II (see KIYOMASU I).

KIYOTADA (fl. c.1710-40). Torii Kiyotada, a printmaker of Ukiyo-e, studied with Kiyonobu in Tokyo, where he lived and worked. Not many of his prints have survived, but he seems to have been a master of abstraction who would have felt at home in the twentieth century. One outstanding print (about 11x6 inches, hand-colored in orange and yellow) shows an actor of the Ichikawa clan performing a violent dance. The costume is adorned with the "box within a box" crest of the Ichikawa, balanced by rows of parallel black lines printed in heavy ink. Only the head and one hand are visible; the rest of the body is hidden by the stiffened robe. The contours of sleeves and trousers crackle like lightning and weapons swing out to create a dynamic design, the center of energy being in the torso. There is no modeling in tone, no clear indication of body structure, but thanks to the vibrant outline, the hand thrust outward with fingers separated, the expression of emotion on the face, and the clever use of pattern, it is one of the most interesting of early eighteenth-century prints.

KORIN (1658-1716). Ogata Koretomi (familiarly called Kariganeya Tojuro; professionally called Hoshuku, Korin,

JAPAN. TOKUGAWA PERIOD. KIYONOBU I. Actor
Brooklyn Museum

etc.). One of Japan's foremost painters, expert also in calligraphy and designs for lacquer, ink-stone boxes and tea-ceremony utensils. Born in Kyoto, son of Ogata Soken, a rich merchant, he was distantly related to Koetsu. He studied under his father, an amateur of some note, and then with the Kano masters, Tsunenobu and Yasunobu. He was much influenced by Sotatsu and Koetsu. His sketchbooks indicate a careful study of nature (see illustration), but his finished paintings are simplified, stressing decorative quality and dramatic use of color. This is especially true of his painting on screens, such as the Iris, the Cranes, the Waves (one in Boston, another in the Metropolitan), Plum Blossoms, and Deer. Inspired by his copies of Sotatsu's work and by his study of Chinese painting, he experimented with a tonal, calligraphic kind of brushwork unlike the striking abstractions and deliberate distortions of his screen painting. A watercolor painting, Azaleas, was made without contour lines; colors were applied, one over the other, while the initial work was still moist. The technique is akin to that of Chinese masters of the Sung and Yüan periods. The effect is poetic, exquisite—closer indeed to literary standards than the dramatic arts. He was a poet, using the *Hokku* form of delicate allusion expressed with the greatest possible economy, and accompanied his poems with appropriate paintings. Though he is most famous as a painter of birds and flowers, he also depicted gods, immortals, genre subjects, and did three portraits. In the Korin school his influence continued beyond his lifetime. Watanabe Shiko (1683-1755) worked in his studio, and Sakai Hoitsu (1761-1828) carried on his great tradition.

KORYUSAI (active c.1766-88). Isoda Masakatsu (familiarly called Shobe; professionally called Koryusai) was a pupil of Shigenaga of the Ukiyo-e group of Tokyo. He came of a family of somewhat higher standing than that of other print designers. In 1780 he won recognition for his painting and thenceforward devoted himself to the art of the brush rather than the printing-block. Among his prints are some unusually large ones (reminding us that, as a painter, he was accustomed to working on a grander scale than those who did book-illustration and small prints). He is noted for his pillar-prints (average size, about 11x5 inches), his designs for folding-fan papers (an arc about twenty inches long), and his series of fashion-plates (about 11x5 inches), One of these is called Fresh-dyed Designs of Teahouse Beauties, another The Flowers of the Twelve Months, and still another Fashion Plates: New Designs as Fresh as Young Leaves. The papers designed to be mounted on folding fans and the series of famous courtesans give names and addresses for the benefit of potential patrons. With his interest in fashion, it was quite natural that he should make much use of sumptuous robes, elaborate coiffures and intricate fabric patterns. Sometimes he places his Tokyo beauties within an urban setting; at other times there is only a tinted background. His colors are lyrical—deep rose, mauve, dark blue, orange, yellow, grey, and moss-green. Though much of the print production was frankly commercial, his bird and flower pieces and the bits of verse sometimes inscribed on the fans suggest that he had a more poetic side.

KUNISADA (1786-1864). Tsunoda Kunisada (familiar name Shozo; professionally called Utagawa, Toyokuni III, Ichiyusai, etc.). He was born at Katsushika in Musashi and lived in Tokyo, where he studied with Toyokuni I, starting at the age of fifteen. Later he studied with Ikkei. He illustrated story-books, and turned out actors prints and landscapes. He is known especially for the subtle tonal values of his landscapes; some areas were printed without contour lines in a technique that resembles the watercolors of Sotatsu, though his skill as a printmaker in no way matched that of earlier artists.

KUNIYOSHI (1797-1861). Igusa Kuniyoshi (familiarly called Magosaburo and Taroemon; professionally called Utagawa Kuniyoshi, Ichiyusai and Cho-oro) lived in Tokyo, where he became a pupil of Toyokuni. He studied the work of the Tosa, Kano and Maruyama schools and evolved his own style of print-designing. His prints were numerous; the landscapes have a less universal appeal than those of Hokusai and Hiroshige, but reveal his interest in the views near Edo, and in problems of space and atmosphere that could be resolved by the use of graded tone. His most popular works, however, were figure studies of actors and samurai.

MASANOBU (1686-1764). Okumura Masanobu (familiarly called Genroku and Genhachi; professionally called Hogetsudo, Tancho-sai, etc.). He was a master of early Ukiyo-e, perhaps a pupil of Torii Kiyonobu, but he worked independently of the Torii line. He was a leader in the production of hand-colored prints, prints enriched with black lacquer, and the Benizuri-e (two-color pictures usually printed in pink and green). On some of his prints he gives his name as his own publisher, and the address of his shop, The Red Gourd. He produced erotic prints (Hill of Dyed Color Specimens of Bedrooms), single figures on page-size sheets of paper (about 12x6 inches), and pillar prints on long narrow strips (about 28x6 inches). The latter were designed to be tacked up on the vertical supports in the average home. His style, refined, sensitive, poetic and serene, differed from the theatrical poster-like work of his Torii rivals. The line is not so heavy as the Torii line, nor used to suggest so much volume; it is flowing, without much variety in width. The patterns on kimonos are intricate; in his pink-and-green prints some areas are printed without black contour lines. Though he portrayed people of all walks of life, he gave them a dignity that recalled the nobler subjects of the past, with literary overtones, bits of poetry adorning the page, or the suggestion of mood and seasonal change.

MITSUOKI (1617-91). Tosa Mitsuoki (Buddhist name, Josho; professionally called Shunkaken) was a distinguished painter of the Tosa school, the last of the line of any real importance. With the decline of the nobility, the Tosa men under their patronage shared their eclipse. They had also lost prestige with the increasing popularity of the Kano school. There was a temporary revival of Tosa fame and fortune when Mitsuoki went to Kyoto to be chief painter of the Edokoro. Later he became a priest. He is remembered for bird and flower paintings done in a painstaking, accurate, fine brush technique.

MORONOBU (1625-c.1694). Hishikawa Moronobu (familiarly called Kichibe; professionally called Yuchiku) was a leader in Ukiyo-e. He first studied design with his father, an embroiderer and maker of textile patterns. He was born in Awa, then moved to the Tokugawa capital, Tokyo. He worked at painting, mainly in the Tosa style, till he became interested in printing. Before his time, printing was generally confined to devotional woodcuts given out at temples; he realized the possibility of adapting the indigenous painting tradition to the print technique, opening the way to a major phase of Japanese artistic expression in the next two hundred years. Between 1657, when his first dated book came out, and his retirement to the priesthood in his later years, he illustrated many volumes and issued several series of printed pictures in folding albums without a text. Confined at first to small-scale designs, the breadth and power of his work gradually increased, and at the same time the technical skill of cutters and printers improved. By 1670 it became evident that these advances would allow a true print art; instead of thinking in terms of brushwork and color as a painter used them, he and his contemporaries in the Ukiyo-e gave their major effort to prints. Aside from his book illustrations, Moronobu issued prints depicting the life of Tokyo, genuine genre scenes of people in the streets or at their daily tasks. Two of the series, Flower-viewing at Ueno and Views of the Yoshiwara, are printed on sheets of paper (about 6x16 inches) in black and white; the enrichment of color was to come later. There is no shading for atmospheric effect or

JAPAN. EARLY TOKUGAWA PERIOD. KORIN. The Wave
Metropolitan Museum of Art, New York

modeling; all forms are linear, based on design-formulas that had been developing since the Heian period.

NANGA SCHOOL. The Nanga or Nanso-ga group, who followed the southern style, were Japanese of the Tokugawa period whose art was modeled on that of the literary painters of China. The rise of Neo-Confucianism under the Tokugawa Shogunate, who encouraged a revival of Chinese classical learning, was accompanied by renewed interest in Chinese painting. Whereas the Suiboku school of the fifteenth and sixteenth centuries had turned for inspiration to the Sung period in China, the Nanga followers looked to the poet-philosopher-painters of the Ming and Ch'ing dynasties. Like them, many of the Nanga painters were amateurs, men of many accomplishments for whom painting was a hobby. A number of Chinese priests had settled in Japan, bringing scrolls and albums of Ming art with them; some of these were painters in the southern style who encouraged their Japanese students to take up the same pursuit. In 1720 Nagasaki was visited by I Fu-chiu, a Chinese merchant who painted landscapes, and in 1734 by Fei Han-yüan. More Chinese books, scrolls, albums, and treatises on art were imported, and the influence of China became widespread. The Japanese pioneers of this movement were Nankai (1677-1751) and Nankaku (1683-1759); the former was a physician serving the lord of Kii province, and both were authors and poets. Next in importance was Sakai Hyakusen (1697-1752), who was born in Nagoya, studied painting in the Kano school, and then began to paint in the Chinese manner. The real leaders of the poet-painters were Buson and Taiga (see both). In the eighteenth century Osaka became a center of the Nanga school. Among its followers there were Kimura Kokyo (1736-1802), Fukuhara Gogaku (1730-1799), Totoki Baigai (1749-1804), Okada Beisanjin (1744-1820) and his son Okada Hanko (1782-1846), and Hamada Kyodo (1766-1814). The painters of Kyoto who then became leaders in the field included Rai San-yo (1780-1832), Aoki Mokubei, distinguished potter and painter (1767-1833), Nakabayashi Chikudo (1778-1853), Urakami Gyokudo the gifted eccentric (1745-1820), and Tanomura Chikuden (1777-1835). The Southern Chinese style became popular in Tokyo in the late eighteenth and early nineteenth centuries. Tani Buncho (1763-1840) and his leading pupil Watanabe Kazan (see) painted in the late Ming manner. In Kyushu, Kushiro Unzen (1759-1811) is notable, while in Kii province the leader was Kuwayama Gyokushu (1746-1799). Each artist strove for subjective expression, using brush and ink for inscriptions and poetry as well as for the landscape, bird or flower study, or the portrait. Thus the linear, tonal monochrome art had its adherents while the gay genre Ukiyo-e stressed pattern, color, and constant change within an urban world.

NAONOBU (1607-50). Kano Naonobu (familiarly called Shume; professionally called Jitekisai), formerly Kazunobu or Iyenobu, was second son of Kano Takanobu. He studied under Koi, his father, and his elder brother Tanyu. Like his elder brother, he moved to Tokyo and worked for the Tokugawa Shogunate. He was given a house at Kobikicho; his assistants are called the Kobikicho Family of the Edo Kano. Perhaps because Naonobu's teacher Koi was said to have made a serious study of Chinese painting, this influence is apparent in Naonobu's work. Under the Tokugawa Shoguns there was a policy of promoting peace by means of a renewed study of Confucian ethics. This is reflected in numerous screens and panel paintings made for the Shoguns that portrayed the Chinese sages, Paragons of Filial Piety, Great Emperors of the Past, etc. Thus in the work of Naonobu, Chinese inspiration is manifest both in subject matter and technique. A pair of six-fold screens in Boston portrays Chinese sages who stand for the highest Corfucian concepts. Technically, the screens, done at the height of Naonobu's power, are masterly. Using rich black ink in powerful strokes, he suggests, with the greatest economy, the body beneath drapery. For the setting, tonal washes are used in a subtle gradation. Such a combination of boldness and sensitivity explains much of Naonobu's fame and why so few of his followers could attain comparable heights.

OKYO (1733-95). Maruyama Masataka (courtesy name Chusen; familiarly called Iwajiro and Mondo; professionally called Sensai, Issho, etc.) was born in Tamba and lived in Kyoto; he was the pupil of Ishida Yutei but also studied Dutch etchings and learned the technique of European perspective. Later he studied the style of Shen Nan-p'in, a Chinese painter living in Nagasaki, who painted in the new, realistic manner. Okyo applied the new ideas of perspective shading to traditional subjects. He founded the Maruyama school, was considered the most advanced painter of his day in the Western style, was praised by the court, and painted many masterpices for Buddhist monasteries and other patrons. He made hundreds of sketches from life and noted down all kinds of facts in his search for objective truth. Though he did not neglect rhythm and the suggestion of inner life in his animals, flowers, trees and birds, he tried to see with the scientific detachment of a European and paint them as they actually appeared. Thus, rounded form, texture, the play of light and shade entered into his art. Thanks to his perceptivity and great technical skill, the imported ideas and the native style are happily blended. His influence was great. Goshun studied with him, as did Nagasawa Rosetsu (1755-99), Komai Genki (1747-97), and Yamaguchi Soken (1759-1818). Other realists who followed his lead were Mori Sosen (1759-1821), Shirai Naokata (c.1810) and Ganka (1756-1838).

SHARAKU (fl. 1794-95). The identity of Toshusai Sharaku (familiarly known as Saito Jurobe) remains a mystery. He is said to have been an actor in the aristocratic Noh drama in the service of Lord Awa, but he is known to the world as the designer of Ukiyo-e prints of singular power. Sharaku (whose name means "one who likes to draw what he sees") seems to have produced the 138 known prints by him in a period of only ten months. They are studies of actors in the plebeian Kabuki theater, full-length figures and half-length, in pairs and singly, usually of actors dressed for their favorite roles. The men's faces are made up as simpering women or savage heroes, and Sharaku's treatment of face and dress points up the inherent drama in each figure. Their conceit, stupidity and overplaying, the strutting upon the stage, the mincing gait of the men who traditionally played the parts of women, and the grimacing countenances of the Ichikawas in ferocious dramas—all are recorded with merciless sharpness by one who apparently had no formal training as a print designer. Against backgrounds of flat tone, sometimes sprinkled with mica to catch the light, the bold forms are made to stand out. Strong lines and effective color schemes here create the most theatrical of theater prints.

SHIBA KOKAN (1737-1828). Shiba Shun (professionally called Fugendoin, Shumparo, etc.) was one of a prominent group of painters profoundly influenced by "Dutch learning," especially in the manipulation of light and shade. His views of Mt. Fuji, in color on hemp cloth, and his copper-block prints reflect his eclectic style.

SHIGEMASA (1738-1820). Kitao Shigemasa (familiar name Kyugoro; professionally called Kosuisai, Karan, Tairei, etc.) lived in Tokyo, where he was an Ukiyo-e master and founder of the Kitao school. During his long life (he was a contemporary of Harunobu in his young manhood, and of Hokusai and Hiroshige in his later days), he designed prints and illustrated books. He studied with Shigenaga and from him learned to design three-color prints. With Harunobu's success in polychrome printing, he also became adept in that technique. He was properly proud of his drawing and his skill in unusual fabric designs. Balance of line and color, maturity of form, and a psychological awareness of the individual enable him to achieve a serene beauty that contrasts with the exaggerations of the theater-print artists. He did a number of prints in a landscape setting but is best known for his two-figure studies. Among the latter is one set, Beautiful Women of All Four Directions, done about 1777, and another, Popular Beauties Compared to the Eight Views, of about 1779-80.

SHIGENAGA (1697-1756). Nishimura Shigenaga (familiarly called Magosaburo and Magojiro; professionally called Senkado) was one of the early leaders in Ukiyo-e print work. He was influenced by Kiyonobu and Masanobu and is said to have been the teacher of Harunobu. His female figure studies were made in the era of hand-coloring and the enrichment of surface with black lacquer and gold dust.

SHUNCHO (fl. c.1780-95). Katsukawa Shuncho (familiarly called Kichizaemon; professionally called Yubundo, Toshien, etc.) lived in Tokyo. He was a pupil of Shunsho and a contemporary of Kiyonaga; the latter exerted some influence on his style, but Shuncho's women are less grand than Kiyonaga's, with a softer, more gently feminine grace. The technical excellence of the printing of his designs indicates that he gave particular attention to that phase of Ukiyo-e art.

SHUNEI, or SHUNYEI (1762-1819). Isoda (familiarly called Kyujiro; professionally called Katsukawa Shunei and Kyutokusai) lived in Tokyo, where he first studied under Shunsho, and then began to work independently on actor prints. Most of these are small, some showing full-length figures in dramatic settings, others half-length against a background of flat tone. Like Sharaku, he was interested in the personality of the actor rather than the role, but there is a more sympathetic portrayal in his work. Distinctive grace and rather subdued color are characteristic. Some of his portraits seem to be in the old Yamato tradition; understatement, fine manipulation of abstract forms, and a certain aloofness are unusual in the actor prints as a whole, and in these Shunei recalls the aristocratic past.

SHUNMAN (1757-1820). Kubo Shunman lived in Tokyo, where he studied with Nahiko and Shigemasa in the Ukiyo-e school. A contemporary of Kiyonaga, he was nearly overshadowed by that master, but emerged about 1790 as a remarkable designer and one of great originality. During 1785-89 he produced prints touched by a poetic lyricism unusual in the Ukiyo-e school. Many of them were three-part and six-part panels. By about 1791 he stopped producing prints of the usual type and devoted himself to book illustration and writing satirically humorous poems. In his prints, the subdued color and silvery tonalities are in keeping with graceful line and refined gesture. He is more like a literary painter than other Ukiyo-e masters.

SHUNSHO (1726-93). Katsukawa Shunsho (familiarly called Yusuke; professionally called Jugasei, Ririn, etc.), pupil of Shunsui, was a master of Ukiyo-e. He lived in Tokyo, where he specialized in actor prints and conducted a school in which several famous men learned their art. He was a distinguished painter as well as print designer. He seems to have given most of his attention to prints because older men of the Torii line either went into retirement or tried to emulate Harunobu's work. The popular demand for prints of the Kabuki theater actors was so great that Shunsho made them his specialty and founded the Katsukawa school of theatrical print artists. Most of his famous prints were made during 1769-81; they average about 12 x 6 inches in size. The male actors, in both masculine and feminine roles, are portrayed in a strikingly dramatic fashion. In the Kabuki theater tradition their faces were made up in heavy weblike lines of brown, maroon or black placed so as to stress the power and terror inherent in the part, with the rest of the face painted chalk-white; this make-up and the customary elaborate costume were particularly effective in Shunsho's prints. Full settings, such as snow scenes, spring gardens, rain storms, etc., were used. Though his prints are not as large as the poster-advertisements of an earlier period, nor his lines as heavy, he achieves remarkable effects by using distortion, caricature, and contrast, together with the beauty of a subtle coloring unknown to the pioneer actor print designers. One is conscious of the weight of the body in his figures, of a great thrust downward, or of a pushing upward (for male roles), and a deliberate feminine wavering when women were his subject. Warriors, priests, ghosts, and courtiers are suggested with equal fidelity. The fabrics are sometimes complex in design, sometimes consciously simplified in broad areas of color bound by subtle lines. He was a master of color, line and space composition.

SOSEN (1749-1821). Mori Shusho (courtesy name Shukugai; familiarly called Hanaya Hachibe; professionally called Sosen, Jokansai, etc.) was a pupil of Okyo and learned to combine Japanese and European methods under that master. He was born in Nagasaki and lived in Osaka. His animal studies are of particular interest.

SOTATSU (fl. early 17th century). Nonomura Sotatsu (professionally called Taiseiken or Tawaraya) was a distinguished painter who lived in the late Momoyama and early Tokugawa (Edo) periods. He founded his own school, based on a revival of traditional Yamato-e subjects and ideals portrayed in the vigorous manner characteristic of his time. He lived in Kyoto and was associated with the Daigo-ji temple. His love of the past inspired a renaissance of indigenous themes and styles of painting, but he brought original genius to his interpretations, especially in boldness of design. Sometimes humorous (such as his famous Gods of Wind and Thunder, painted on two-fold screens with gold-leaf backgrounds), his painting could at other times be philosophical and poetic. He used full color or monochrome, experimenting in the latter with the "wet brush" used so effectively by Mu Ch'i and other thirteenth-century Chinese. These experiments suggest the artist's interest in technical expression, rather than the dedicated monk's adherence to Zen tradition represented by Sesshu and other Suiboku masters. For all of his economy of line, his art is not as austere as some examples of pure Suiboku work. He was a friend of Koetsu's and together they created most exquisite poem scrolls. Sotatsu usually painted the background, using gold, silver, or delicate colors to portray grasses, flowers, vines, butterflies, etc., in irregular patterns. Over this Koetsu wrote the poems in his famous calligraphy, spacing them perfectly to harmonize with the decorations made by his friend. Though this collaboration would seem to lend itself to a small composition, one of their masterpieces, Vines and Flowers, painted in gold and silver (Hatakeyama collection, Tokyo), is more than twenty-seven feet long. Versatile painter of screens (see color plate 110), fans and album pieces, he kept alive the literary and historical heritage of the medieval period, and served as inspiration to Korin and his group.

SUGIMURA (fl. c.1680-98). Sugimura Jihei Masataka was contemporary with Moronobu. Very little is known about him except that he made at least one painting and a few prints for books and albums. Some of the prints formerly assigned to Moronobu, including a series of erotic prints and single-figure studies, must now be attributed to him because his name has been discovered woven into fabric design. Like Moronobu, he depends on clarity of outline and interesting textile pattern to achieve striking designs.

TAIGA (1723-76). Ikeno Arina (courtesy name Taisei; familiarly called Shuhei; professionally called Taiga, Kasho, etc.) was a distinguished painter of the Nanga school. He was born in Kyoto, where he came under the influence of Gion Nankai, who aroused his interest in the Chinese painting of Ming and Ch'ing times. His work reflects his learning, his understanding of Zen precepts in its spareness and purity, and hints at a humorous turn of mind. He painted door panels, screens, and album pieces, all of them bearing the mark of his originality.

TAN-YU (1602-74). Kano Morinobu (familiarly called Shirojiro and Uneme; professionally called Tanyu, Byakurenshi. etc.) was born in Kyoto, eldest son of Takanobu. He studied under Koi and went to Tokyo in about 1614 to serve the Tokugawa feudal government. Nominated chief official artist of the Shogunate government in 1621, he founded a "school," or "family," called the Edo Kano Kajibashi, and monopolized all official work. A prosperous and diligent association of professional artists, its fame spread far and wide. Feudal lords followed the lead of the Shogun and employed Kano school painters outside of Edo. Examples of the early work of Tanyu are in Kyoto (sliding screen panels in the Nijo castle) and, before they were destroyed in World War II, in Nagoya Joraku-den. It is evident that he copied many Chinese paintings; and the records tell us that he had a famous collection of copies of Chinese and earlier Japanese art. He painted with less boldness than Eitoku; there is strength and beauty of line, but his space-concepts are nearer the Chinese ideal. Master that he was, he set the tone for all later Edo Kano artists.

TOYOKUNI I (1769-1825). Utagawa Toyokuni (familiarly called Kumakichi; professionally called Ichiyosai; and generally known as Toyokuni I because others used the same name) was a Tokyo artist, a printmaker of portraits, actors, landscapes, and scenes of the passing world. His work is of uneven quality. Some of it is of singular beauty, ranking almost with that of the old masters, but in trying to meet popular demand in his later years he produced designs that were mediocre. To add to the confusion concerning his work, many imitators and followers have used his name. Most of his best works were done before 1800; they are expert in line and color, and delicate in tone. A series of standing actors belongs to this group. His later phase, marked by crude color and uninspired composition, is contemporary with the rise of Hiroshige.

TOYOKUNI II (1777-1835). Utagawa Toyokuni (familiarly called Genzo; professionally called Kunishige, Toyoshige, and Toyokuni II, for he was a pupil of Toyokuni I) lived in Tokyo, at Hongo, as a pottery dealer, an illustrator of storybooks and a designer of color prints. His studies of women are among his most successful works.

TOYONOBU (1711-85). Ishikawa Toyonobu (familiar name Nukaya Shichibei; professionally called Meijodo Shuha, Nishimura Magosoburo, or Shigenobu, in his early period, and, after about 1742, Ishikawa Toyonobu) was one of the most famous of the early Ukiyo-e school. He specialized in figure studies, most of them hand-colored. He did Beauties of Three Cities—personifications of cities as lovely women—as well as actors in famous roles and sundry city types. He designed pillar-prints that were 25x6 inches in size, and even in this narrow vertical space, he omitted a quarter of the body, allowing an unfilled area to balance the richly decorated portion. He designed several triptychs of actors dressed as women. In this he was a forerunner of Kiyonaga, though the latter preferred more complex designs. Grace and sensitivity marked his work. His actors stand serenely, often glancing downward, and suggest a gentle melancholy. The fabric patterns of their kimonos are sometimes so variegated that they would be disturbing if handled by an artist of less skill. A poem written in cursive script indicates his fondness for literature and delicate allusion. It is hard to believe that this was an art intended for plebeians and looked down upon by aristocrats.

TSUNENOBU (1636-1713). Kano Tsunenobu (familiar name Ukon; professionally called Yoboku, Seihukusai, etc.) was a pupil of his father Naonobu. He lived in Edo, where he led the Edo Kano Kobikicho group after his father retired. In 1709 he painted panels of sliding doors in the imperial court, and was attached to the Sento Palace as a painter. Like the other great professional decorators of his group, he did both Chinese and Japanese subjects with a dignity worthy of their places in the homes of the great in Tokyo. Though he lacked the dramatic flair of his great-grandfather Eitoku, and the strong brush technique of his father Naonobu, he is considered an outstanding painter of his time.

UTAMARO (1753-1806). Toriyama Shimbi (courtesy name Toyoaki; familiarly called Yusuke; professionally called Kitagawa Utamaro) lived in Tokyo. He was a pupil of Sekien and was influenced by Kiyonaga in his early days, but he soon developed an individual style and is recognized as one of the great masters among the printmakers. He opened a school of his own, and from 1780 to the close of the century he produced a succession of brilliant prints. He experimented with various techniques to bring his figures out in bold relief, painting the background in flat colors, such as yellow, pink, or pale blue, and sprinkling them with powdered mica to give them sparkle. Sometimes the figure was printed without contour lines; at other times the line was so fine as to be almost invisible. He and his printer achieved incredibly fine over-printing to give gauzy effects. Best known for his handsome figure studies of the beauties of the Yoshiwara district, he called himself Priest of the Green Houses. Half-length studies of the reigning belles of the late eighteenth century, with their elaborate coiffures, rosebud mouths and languid gestures, or full-length figures of the beauties in casual poses were among his repertory. He did several series of women of all ages, and of girls and women of various social levels in their daily occupations. There is greater range and variety in his work than in that of Kiyonaga or Sharaku. He designed landscapes, and bird and flower studies with the same sense of poetry, beauty of line, and mastery of space and composition as in his better-known genre scenes. For some critics his work is too exquisite; for others it is the culmination of Ukiyo-e.

YASUNOBU (1613-85). Kano Yasunobu (familiarly called Shidojiro and Genshiro; professionally called Eishin, Bokushinsai, etc.) studied with Ko-i and with his elder brother

110. JAPAN. TOKUGAWA PERIOD. Sotatsu. Poppy Screen. Museum of Fine Arts, Boston

Tanyu. The youngest son of Kano Takanobu, he followed his elder brother to Tokyo, where he worked for the Tokugawa Shogunate. He was given a house at Nakabashi, where he brought together a group of painters known as the Edo Kano Nakabashi family. With the other Edo Kano families, he set a standard of excellence in craftsmanship that was the envy of all rivals. Bold brushwork and a fine sense of design (essential to the large screens painted for the Shogunate and other patrons) marked the style of Edo Kano of which he was a part. Chinese subjects, birds and flowers, nature studies, etc., were a part of their repertory.

ZESHIN (1807-91). Shibata Junzo (professionally called Zeshin and Tairyukyo) lived in Tokyo. He was a pupil of Suzuki Nanrei and Okamoto Toyohiko. Noted for his studies of flowers, birds and animals, he is especially well known for his use of lacquer as a painting medium. Whether he made a small album or a scroll, he captured the beauty of the fragile, exquisite growing things that he saw. Fern fronds, butterflies, insects, etc., took on a jewel-like clarity when he painted them. There is a hint of humor and compassion in his attitude; it is not objectively realistic but recalls the feeling for nature of the ancient Buddhists. His prints have the same clarity, humor and exquisiteness that he gave to his lacquer painting.

Japanese Painters: Meiji Period (1868-1911)

GAHO (1835-1908). Hashimoto Masakuni (professionally called Gaho and Shoen) was a Kano painter who studied under Shosen-in. He lived in Tokyo, where he was a professor at the Tokyo Art School and a member of the Imperial Art Committee. He specialized in landscape and figure painting.

KOGYO (1866-1919). Terasaki Kogyo (professionally called Sozan and Tenrai Sanjin) was among the prominent Tokyo painters of the Inten school who exhibited in the Ueno Exhibition of 1907. He traveled repeatedly in China and was strongly influenced by Chinese art. His mastery of brush technique, coupled with a fine decorative feeling, gives a unique character to his landscapes and figure studies. He was a professor at the Tokyo Art School and member of the Imperial Art Committee.

Japanese Painters: Showa Period (1926-)

SEIHO (1864-1942). Takeuchi Tsunekichi was born in Kyoto, son of a restaurant owner; he was instructed by Tsuchida Eirin, a follower of the Goshun school. He then entered the studio of Kono Bairei (1844-95) in 1881 and progressed rapidly in his painting; before his death, Bairei bestowed the professional name of Seiho (Living Phoenix) upon his most distinguished pupil. In 1900 he went to Europe and fell under the spell of romantic European painting and the challenge of realistic portrayal of forms in space. On his return to Japan, he sought to combine Oriental monochrome with European modeling in light and shade; using an eclectic style he specialized in doing wild animals, bamboo, dragons and landscapes. In 1910 he received a commission to do murals for the great Buddhist monastery in Kyoto, the Higashi Hongan-ji; and some of this work was done as late as 1934. He was a pioneer among Japanese painters who looked to Europe for instruction, a trend that has increased enormously in the twentieth century.

TAIKAN (1868-). Yokoyama Taikan exhibited in the Ueno Show of 1907 in Tokyo as one of the prominent painters of his time. He had his early training in the Kano school, under Hogai and Gaho. Like so many artists of the early twentieth century, he experimented with European techniques, evolving an eclectic style of outstanding vigor and intensity. His landscapes reveal an understanding of structural form, which he painted with graded tones and crisp contours, and an unusual ability to suggest atmospheric change. Even when he painted a specific place, such as Mt. Fuji in its natural setting, he conveyed a sense of the universal, timeless quality of earth, water and sky.

Jarvis, John Wesley (1780-1839). American portrait painter born in England, nephew of the founder of Methodism, after whom he is named and with whom he lived as a child. He came to Philadelphia, where his father had settled, in 1785. As a boy he ran errands for the Philadelphia sign painters and later was apprenticed to David Savage, engraver. He set up a partnership with Joseph Wood in New York, doing profiles and miniatures. Almost entirely self-taught, he became a popular portrait painter in New York City but worked as far south as New Orleans, making a great deal of money and spending it rapidly. He was convivial and rather bohemian. His portraits, though competent, suffer from shallowness of thought and hastiness of execution. Both Thomas Sully and Henry Inman worked as his assistants. (See illustration.)

Jawlensky, Alexi von (1864-1941). Russian-born member of the German Expressionist school; began his art

JARVIS. Reverend James Everett
Detroit Institute of Arts

training at the Academy in St. Petersburg in 1889 where he was influenced by the realist Ilya Repin. In 1896 he moved to Munich, where he met another Russian painter, Wassily Kandinsky. He also became interested in Matisse and Hodler, both of whom ultimately influenced him considerably, Matisse in the boldness of large color areas, and Hodler in the use of a powerful contour line and a curvilinear quality. In 1905 he painted in Brittany in the wake of Gauguin and in 1909 became one of the founders of the New Society of Artists in Munich. His art at this point began to show flaming color applied to large areas, bold contours, and the general intensity of mood that characterizes Expressionism (see). In 1912 Jawlensky was included in a Blue Rider exhibition put on in Berlin at Der Sturm galleries. Together with his two-dimensional and rhythmic designs, and the symbolic nature of his color, this enables us to relate him to the Munich side of the Expressionist movement, known as The Blue Rider. In 1924, along with Feininger, Kandinsky and Paul Klee, he helped form the so-called Blue Four group which was shown in Berlin and in America. His last work, from 1929 on, shows an increasingly abstract quality, as though influenced by Cubism, and presents a formal severity that for some suggests the Russian icons of the painter's youth. These sharply edged heads show him moving in the same abstract direction as many of his Blue Rider associates. (See illustration.)

Jeanneret-Gris, C. E. (see LE CORBUSIER).

Jellett, Mainie (1897-1944). Contemporary Irish modernist painter who studied in London under Walter Sickert and in Paris with André Lhote and Albert Gleizes. The acknowledged leader of the modern group in Ireland, she illustrates the value of joining School of Paris techniques with Irish temperament. As a non-representational painter she realized instinctively the affinity between that kind of painting and the medieval manuscript and jewelry tradition of Ireland. These elements were joined with the native color quality of the Irish landscape for a new kind of religious art. In 1943 Miss Jellett organized the annual exhibition known as Irish Living Art.

Jennys, J. William (18th-19th century). One of a family of three American portrait painters who worked in the seaboard states from Boston to Charleston. Although their family relationship is unknown their styles are related. His portraits are rendered with clarity and sharp definition.

Jeu de Paume Museum, Paris. Famous for its collection of nineteenth-century French Impressionist paintings, of which it has historic examples.

Jewett, William (1795-1874). American portrait painter born in Haddam, Conn. Apprenticed first to a coachmaker, he met Waldo in Connecticut (1813) and returned with him to New York, becoming his student and then partner. This collaboration was the longest and most consistent in American painting and produced portraits that were solid and competent but without great distinction. He is often confused with William Smith Jewett (1812-73), a portrait painter born in South Dover, N.Y., and active in California.

Jewish painting. Although it is generally believed that the Jews have been forbidden by the Second Commandment ("Thou shalt make no graven image") to create pictorial art, the facts do not bear out this belief. Assuming, as many scholars do, that this injunction refers to idolatry rather than to the making of paintings and other art forms, and taking into account the fact that the Talmud (i.e., the Law) and similar writings contain no prohibition against art, we must examine the facts. These would indicate that remains of Jewish art from the pre-Roman period are very meagre because of the many attacks on Jerusalem and its ultimate destruction by the Emperor Hadrian. On the other hand there are remains of about forty synagogues dating from Roman and early Christian times; these are found in places as far apart as North Africa, Malta, Delos, Aegina and Miletos in Greece, the cities of Priene and Dura-Europos in Asia Minor and in Rome itself. In centers such as Alexandria, Rome and Dura-Europos we find a flourishing Jewish community during those early centuries of the Christian era and in the latter two cities there are still evidences in their catacombs of a typical

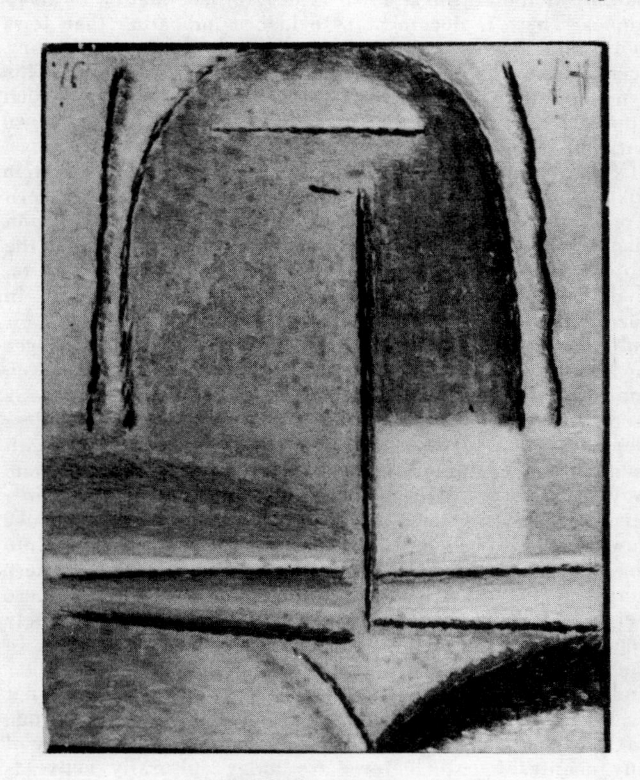

JAWLENSKY. Abstract: Head
Private Collection, Germany

JOHNSON, EASTMAN. Corn Husking at Nantucket. Metropolitan Museum of Art, New York

funerary art related in certain melancholy overtones to that of the early Christians. Instead of the Christian symbols, however, we find Jewish cult objects such as seven-branched candelabra, the Ark containing the Torah scrolls, and certain symbolic birds and animals. Again during the time of the Moslem occupation of Spain there are evidences of Jewish artistic activity. The handsomely decorated synagogues of Toledo and other centers show activity in architecture, and a series of thirteenth- to fifteenth-century manuscripts attest their activity in that field. Although Jewish painters were apparently active in Spain they do not appear to have developed their own style in either subject matter or techniques. There is documentary evidence indicating that Jews worked for Christian patrons as well as Jewish, even painting scenes from the Christian cycle of religious subjects. This sense of integration in the Christian community, which apparently prevented the Jews from developing their own national style, disappeared when during the Reconquest of Spain from the Moors, the Jews were finally driven from that country. In such countries as Germany and northern France they were segregated in ghettos and forced in upon themselves. This together with the high development of the popular arts in Germany enabled the Jews to strike out on their own. Their most important activity henceforth was in the field of manuscript and later book illumination. Their subject matter stemmed from their own national experiences in both the religious and the secular sphere, extending even into representations of the persecutions to which the Jews were subjected in their new homelands. This more or less popular Jewish art tradition began as early as the thirteenth century and continued down into the modern period in one way or another. With the Emancipation in the early nineteenth century this local tradition or series of traditions broke down and the body of Jewish artistic life was absorbed into the fabric of European civilization. Only in the Eastern outposts of Europe, such as Poland and Russia, did there persist a folk tradition of Jewish art in the form of uniquely constructed wooden houses with brightly painted ceilings. In the West, however, many names of Jewish writers, musicians and finally painters begin to appear—not as Jews, but rather as Frenchmen, Germans and Americans. To what extent one can say that there is a distinctly Jewish flavor to the art of any country in which Jews are today culturally active is problematical.

Joest, Jan (d.1519). Dutch painter from Haarlem whose chief work is the altar of the St. Nicholas church in Kalkar, done between 1505 and 1508. He was a follower of Geertgen tot Sint Jans, a relationship evident in Jan's lighting effects and angularities of form. One also notes touches of influence from Rogier van der Weyden but inasmuch as Jan belongs to the end of the fifteenth and beginning of the sixteenth centuries he develops a certain almost Italianate breadth of style.

John, Augustus (1878-). British painter and draughtsman. Born in Wales, John came to the Slade School in London in 1894. His career has shown a carefree, even gypsy quality; he has traveled a good deal in Europe and America, painted scenes of gypsy life and vivid characterizations of everyday types. A lifelong associate of Sir William Orpen, John was elected to the Royal Academy in 1928, resigned, and was re-elected in 1940. He gained the Order of Merit in 1942. John is very much interested in solidly drawn traditional forms with an overlay of vivid color, the whole integrated by a rhythmic design and careful draughtsmanship. He is well known for his portraits of famous persons, e.g., Bernard Shaw, James Joyce and Gustav Stresemann. (See color plate 111.)

Johnson, (Jonathan) Eastman (1824-1906). American portrait and genre painter; born in Maine and apprenticed to a lithographer at the age of fifteen. He began painting portraits before 1846 in Washington, D.C., and later in Boston. In 1849 he left for Düsseldorf, where he shared a studio with Leutze. went on to Paris and London, and settled in The Hague for five years, making a distinguished reputation. He returned to the U.S. in 1855, painted Indian and frontier life in Wisconsin (1856-57), portraits in Cincinnati and Washington (1857-59), and then settled in New York and began to paint genre pictures. During the Civil War he did sketches of the Union Army in the field. After 1885 he returned almost exclusively to portraits again. His portraits are strong and realistic, combining the detail of the Düsseldorf manner with elements of the traditional Dutch style. In their precision of handling and literary subject his genre pictures are derived also from Düsseldorf, but are American in theme and at their best stronger and simpler in statement. It is, however, on his later landscapes, done at Nantucket and in the Catskill Mountains, that his reputation will probably rest. These are broad, spirited, and impressionistic in an original way, without specific connection with the Impressionist movement. (See illustration.)

Johnson, Henrietta (active America 1708/10-28). A

JONGKIND. Moonlight. Stedelijk Museum, Amsterdam

pastel portraitist. Said to have been born in Surrey, England, she worked mostly in Charleston, S.C., where she was married to the rector of St. Philip's. Her portraits are not very well drawn, but fresh, delicate, and luminous in color.

Johnston, David Claypoole (1799-1865). American genre painter and caricaturist, called the American Cruikshank. Born in Philadelphia, he was apprenticed to Francis Kearney (1815) and began to do caricatures (1819) which were too strong to print. He turned to acting, finally settling in Boston and resuming satirical drawing and genre painting.

Jones, David (1895-). British watercolorist and wood engraver of animal, landscape and various romantic themes. He has been influenced by Celtic literature and by the writings of Jacques Maritain and has studied under the sculptor Eric Gill.

Jones, Joe (Joseph J.) (1909-). Contemporary American painter. In his early work, under the influence of Benton and Gropper, he was a Social Realist; he then became a regionalist, and more recently a realist in a lighter vein. Born in St. Louis, he worked as a house painter and had his beginnings as an artist on the Federal Art Project.

Jongkind, Johan (1819-91). Dutch painter and etcher who occupied an important role in the development of Impressionism. Educated in Holland, he was by 1846 in France. He joined the Barbizon painters, but is noted more for seascapes painted in the vicinity of Le Havre than for landscapes. Here in watercolor and oil he developed a transparent, luminous technique of recording transitory effects of light which had much influence on Sisley, Pissarro and Monet, and especially the last. Jongkind was undoubtedly the greatest Dutch painter since the seventeenth century, but he passed his life in poverty (as did most of the Impressionists) in spite of the fact that his work was seized upon and popularized by the de Goncourt brothers. Although he spent part of every year in Holland, the Louvre is richer than his homeland in his works. (See illustration.)

JOUVENET. Descent from the Cross. Louvre, Paris

111. JOHN. Portrait of Dr. Gustav Stresemann
Albright Art Gallery, Buffalo

Joos van Ghent (see JUSTUS OF GHENT).

Jordaens, Jacob (1593-1678). After Rubens the outstanding Baroque painter of Flanders. Coarser, more commonplace, less universal than Rubens, he is, at his best, robust and powerful, expressing an earthy exuberance that has become synonomous with the Flemish character. He painted for a lower class than did Rubens and van Dyck, and his art both in subject and manner reflects this connection. His early style shows remnants of Mannerism (see), but is most dependent on Caravaggio—especially in the crowded compositions with large figures in strong chiaroscuro and bold foreshortening pervaded by a vulgar realism. He was, however, early influenced by Rubens and, like him, became even looser in style during the late 1620's. In the 1650's the impact of van Dyck made itself felt and his style increased in fluency, his color became more delicate and his composition even classical. In his late years he seems to have become feeble-minded and his art deteriorated. Born in Antwerp, he entered the studio of van Noort, stayed with him eight years, and married his daughter in 1616, the year he was admitted to the guild as a watercolor painter. He then executed large decorations and designs for tapestries. By 1621 he was head of the guild and had a great workshop, with many students undertaking large decorative projects. He did not receive important commissions until after the death of Rubens, but then executed works (later destroyed) for Charles I of England and the King of Spain, among others. He also did many religious paintings, but is best known for his riotous and joyous genre and banquet scenes, of which the most famous are the various illustrations of the proverbs The Rite of the Bean or Epiphany Feast, The King Drinks, and As the Old Sing, So Pipe the Young.

Jorge Inglés (active c.1455). Spanish painter and miniaturist of Castille. Worked for the Marqués de Santillana, a poet. It is not clear whether his name means that he was of foreign origin, but he was clearly among the first to introduce the Flemish style into Spain. For his patron in 1455 he painted a retablo of Angels for the Hospital of Buitrago, which is still in the collection of the Santillana family. Besides containing verses by Santillana, this altarpiece is remarkable for the portraits of him and his wife that appear in two of the panels. Jorge also is supposed to have done illumination for the Marqués' historical and religious writings.

Josephson, Ernest (1851-1906). Swedish painter and graphic artist who in the 1880's became the spearhead of the movement against academicism of younger Swedish artists. Under the dual influence of Titian and Rembrandt, he turned to a rich kind of realism modernized through the clean colors of Manet. During a severe illness Josephson began to do drawings of an often mystical type deriving their inspiration from the Bible, Shakespeare and such other sources as the legends of his own country. These drawings show an exciting purity and tension of line.

JUANES, JUAN DE. The Last Supper. Prado, Madrid

112. KANDINSKY. Light Picture, No. 188. Guggenheim Museum, New York

Jouvenet, Jean (1644-1717). French painter. Most important member of a large Norman family of artists of possible Italian origin. Jouvenet painted for years under the influence of Le Brun, who taught him how to compose the decorative "machine" compositions in vogue at the time. He was admitted to the Academy in 1681 with his Esther before Ahasuerus. It was only after the death of Le Brun that Jouvenet revealed himself as an outstanding Rubenist, and during the remainder of his career he was an exponent of the Lowland style. Typical of this late phase is his dramatic Descent from the Cross (Louvre) which is based on Rubens' painting of the same subject. His High Altar of Notre Dame is similar to the vast spatial interiors popular among Dutch painters. (See illustration.)

Juan de Flandes (see FLANDES, JUAN DE).

Juanes, Juan de (Juan Vicente Masip) (c.1523-79). Spanish painter, Valencian school. Son and pupil of Juan Vicente Masip the Elder, whose name he bore. He based his style on Raphael, Leonardo, Michelangelo and other Italian masters, and developed an intensely dramatic Mannerism. This intensity, repeated again and again in devotional pictures, was a popular quality and led to the veneration of his pictures as holy objects: for instance, the Last Supper in the Prado in which Christ elevates the wafer. He is noted also for small paintings in miniature technique such as the little retablo of San Nicolás in Valencia. His adeptness at portraiture is seen in the character of his religious canvases and in the likeness of such notables as Don Louis Castellá de Villanova (Prado). (See illustration.)

Juárez Juan Rodríguez (1675-1728). Spanish-Colonial Mexican painter whose painting varied from a brilliant, clearly colored form to a dramatic and sombre style. A prolific artist, he became one of the best-known Mexican painters of his time.

Jugendstil (see ART NOUVEAU).

JUSTUS OF GHENT. The Calvary. Cathédrale St. Bavon, Ghent

Jules, Mervin (1912-). Contemporary American painter of social genre in a satirical vein. Born in Baltimore, he attended Baltimore City College and Maryland Institute, and studied with Benton at the Art Students League. Lately his work has become less satirical and more abstract.

Junaid (see PERSIAN PAINTERS: TIMURID PERIOD).

Justus of Ghent (Joos van Wassenhove) active 1460-80). Flemish painter who emigrated to Italy. Justus was the outstanding painter of Ghent after the van Eycks and was an important influence in Flanders before entering the service of the Duke of Urbino in 1472. Of his pre-Italian works, most important are an Adoration of the Magi (Metropolitan) and a large Calvary in St. Bavo's, Ghent. These show him to have borrowed freely from his predecessors, van der Weyden, van Eyck, Dirk Bouts and the Master of Flémalle, but at the same time to have evolved an unusually broad style for the Lowlands. It may have been this which attracted the Italians to him. In Urbino, where he collaborated with Pedro Berruguete, he painted a Last Supper and a series of portraits of humanists. (See illustration.)

K

Kahlo, Frida (1910-54). Mexican painter and wife of Diego Rivera. A sensitive realist, she combined Surrealist and New-Objectivity elements, depicting many autobiographical episodes in her own dream language.

Kaiser-Friedrich Museum, Berlin. One of the most important of pre-World War II German museums, the building now lies in ruins in East Berlin and the remains of its collection of paintings is in the Collecting Point at Wiesbaden. The paintings of this great museum, like so many others, were dispersed to various parts of Germany before and during the war. Many of the Berlin objects were kept in that city until late in the war; a number were then removed to mines in Middle Germany. At the time of the occupation of Berlin one of the storage towers fell into the hands of the Russians; another was broken into and set on fire, and 411 important pictures were thus lost. In addition the Russians confiscated about 330 paintings together with all kinds of other art forms. The remaining works from the Kaiser-Friedrich include such important works as Rembrandt's Man in a Golden Helmet and Lotto's Portrait of a Man in a Biretta.

KANE. Liberty Bridge, Pittsburgh
Addison Gallery of American Art, Phillips Academy, Andover

kakemono. In Japanese painting a hanging scroll; it is mounted on paper, faced with silk damask or brocade, with rollers at each end. When not in use it is generally rolled up, placed in a silk case, and kept in a nest of boxes. The kakemono is put on display in the tokonoma, an alcove reserved in the average Japanese home for a painting and a flower arrangement. Both should be appropriate to the occasion and the season of the year; they are not part of the permanent decoration of the room. Religious kakemono were used as altarpieces.

Kalf, Willem, (1619-93). Dutch painter of strong but extremely refined still life. He studied with Hendrick Pot and came under the influence of Rembrandt. He also passed about five years in Paris and may have visited Italy. He is generally considered the outstanding still-life painter of Holland.

Kamakura Period (see JAPANESE PAINTERS: KAMAKURA PERIOD, 1185-1333).

Kandinsky, Wassily (1866-1944). Outstanding painter, teacher and theorist of non-objective art (see), associated with the abstract side of German Expressionism (see) known as The Blue Rider. The Russian-born Kandinsky was first interested in law and ethnology, turning to painting in 1896 by going to Munich to study. He was in touch with the developments in the modern French school, contributing to the Paris Autumn Salon in 1904, 1906 and 1907. In 1909 together with Jawlensky he set up the New Artists Federation and in the following year did his first completely non-objective works. In 1910 he wrote and in 1912 published *Concerning the Spiritual in Art,* which has become one of the most influential of all books on art. Late in 1911 he and Marc opened the first Blue Rider exhibition, the two also working on the famous Blue Rider Album. With World War I Kandinsky returned to Russia and played a leading role in art educational circles. After the war he returned to Germany as part of the Bauhaus (see) teaching staff at Weimar. In 1924 with Jawlensky, Klee and Feininger, he formed the Blue Four group. His *Point and Line to Plane* became one of the Bauhaus textbooks in 1926. The first one-man exhibition of Kandinsky's art in Paris was in 1929. In 1933 he left Germany for Neuilly-sur-Seine near Paris, where he became an important force in the modern French school although he did not settle in France until World War II. In reviewing Kandinsky's style, we may think first of the lyrical, improvisatory early works beginning around 1913 and designed to create a gentle, almost musical and not too precise mood. A second important phase is the geometric, which resulted from his contact with Constructivism (see) and other Russian schools. Here the accent was still on spontaneous movement and lyrical color but the forms had by then crystallized into spheres, rectangles, etc. Most contemporary non-objective painters have felt the impact of Kandinsky's work or his general outlook. (See color plate 112.)

Kane, John (1860-1934). American painter born of Irish parents in Scotland. A so-called primitive or amateur painter, he was a coal miner at nine, and in Pittsburgh worked as a mill-hand, street paver and house painter. The most famous of the many twentieth-century amateur artists in America, he painted Pittsburgh cityscapes and landscapes in his spare time. He received his first recognition in 1927 at the age of sixty-seven, when the Carnegie International hung his Scene from the Scottish Hills. (See illustration.)

Kantor, Morris (1896-). A contemporary American painter born in Russia. In his early days in the U.S. he earned money doing cartoons; later he received art training from Homer Boss and at the Independent School, and for many years painted in his spare time. In 1927 he went to Paris, and was influenced by Cubism, but in the 1930's returned to a more realistic rendering of the American scene. In more recent years his art has again exhibited a tendency toward abstraction.

Kao K'o-kung (see CHINESE PAINTERS: YÜAN DYNASTY).

Karfiol, Bernard (1886-1952). A contemporary American painter born in Hungary of American parents. He studied at the National Academy of Design in New York and the Académie Julian in Paris and exhibited at the Salon. A realistic painter of studio nudes and interiors with figures, he was influenced to some extent by the Armory Show. Later he turned to Cézanne and especially Renoir for inspiration, executing opulent nude studies. His subsequent work became progressively drier and more formal.

Kauffmann, Angelica (1741-1807). A Neo-Classical German painter very popular in her day. She was influenced to a great extent by the theories of Wincklemann, who turned her to painting insipid classical allegories. She is perhaps more interesting to the student of eighteenth-century life, especially in her involvement with a footman who posed as a count.

Kaulbach, Wilhelm von (1805-74). German illustrator and painter of portraits and historical subjects. After studying with his father he entered the Academy at Düsseldorf. In 1826 he went to Munich and in 1849 became the director of the Academy of Painting there. He made several trips to Italy, which reinforced his tendency toward a serene and balanced monumental style. His mural paintings and classical compositions, as well as his numerous book illustrations, were greatly admired by his contemporaries.

Kaus, Max (1891-). German painter and engraver who shows the influence of the Brücke school. He began as a pupil of Erich Heckel, whose romantic spirit is often reflected in Kaus's work. In graphics the influence seems to be rather that of Kirchner. Kaus's strong individuality is often tempered by the somewhat mannered primitivism that stems from the Brücke group, but at its best his art expresses a strong sense of the loneliness of modern man.

Keene, Charles Samuel (1823-91). British artist who worked in black-and-white, doing genre subjects drawn from contemporary life; influenced Walter Sickert. He is best known for magazine caricatures of the foibles of the time as well as his illustrations for *Robinson Crusoe, The Cloister and the Hearth,* etc.

Kemp, Roger (1910-). Australian painter born in Melbourne and trained at the Melbourne Gallery school. Kemp has pursued a solitary course among his contemporaries. His painting has an architectonic basis involving a complex arrangement of opposing lines, tones and color paralleling musical composition.

Kempener, Peter de (see CAMPANA, PEDRO).

Kensett, John Frederick (1818-72). American landscape painter in the second generation of the Hudson River school. He achieved in his later pictures a vision and a mood very close to the French Impressionists but without the use of broken color. Born in Connecticut, he studied with his father and was apprenticed to his uncle, both engravers. He painted in his leisure time and went abroad from 1840 to 1848, painting and sending pictures home for exhibition. Although he took a Western trip in 1866, he preferred the more intimate landscape of the East. His earlier work was in the romantic and precisely detailed manner of the Hudson River school, but he developed toward a much broader and more realistic handling of nature.

Kent, Rockwell (1882-). A contemporary American painter, engraver, lithographer, and illustrator, as well as writer, lecturer and explorer. He studied first with Chase, then with Abbot H. Thayer, who had the greatest influence upon him, and later with Miller and Henri. After several years at the Columbia School of Architecture, he turned to painting. A vigorous painter of the grandeur of nature, he has combined his art with travel from the Arctic to the Antarctic. His earlier paintings of wild and distant landscapes later gave away to the decorative wood engravings and illustrations which have brought him his greatest fame. (See illustration.)

KENT. Adirondacks. Corcoran Gallery of Art, Washington, D.C.

Kenzan (see JAPANESE PAINTERS: TOKUGAWA PERIOD).

Kerkovius, Ida (1879-). Distinguished modern German painter and tapestry designer. A pupil of Adolf Hölzel in Stuttgart, Kerkovius derived from that source a sense of rhythmically applied color and line as well as an almost mystical mood. In her work she represents a symbolic Fauvism, two-dimensional and decorative in such a way that the transition from the painted to the woven image is almost automatic. The style in the latter medium and its very existence in one sense is due to the work that Kerkovius did with Kandinsky and Klee at the Bauhaus from 1920 to 1923.

Kernstock, Karoly (1873-). Hungarian Post-Impressionist who founded a group (known as The Eight) in Hungary for the furtherance of Post-Impressionist ideals. He specializes in powerful figures of young men and of horses in two-dimensional vertical compositions.

Kessel, Jan van (1626-79). Flemish painter. Pupil of his uncle Jan Brueghel II. He painted landscapes, birds, flowers and insects in the latter's style. He was a master in the guild and a captain of the civic guard in Antwerp.

Kessel, Jan van (1641/42-80). Dutch painter of landscapes and city views. His pictures show that he was influenced by the three great contemporary specialists in landscape: Jacob van Ruisdael, Hobbema and Philips Koninck.

Ketel, Cornelis (1548-1616). Dutch painter of allegories and portraits. He studied with Blocklandt, worked briefly at Fontainebleau, and spent eight successful years in London. His penetrating characterizations and skillful compositions helped to lay the foundation for the great school of seventeenth-century Dutch painting.

Keyser, Thomas de (1596/97-1667). Dutch painter of portraits and historical pictures; also an architect. His portraits are lively and expressive; he exerted some influence on Rembrandt and in turn received impressions from him. The last years of his life were occupied with civic building in Amsterdam.

Kirchner, Ernst Ludwig (1880-1938). German paint-

113. KIRCHNER. Seated Woman (Franzi)
Minneapolis Institute of Arts

er, graphic artist and ideological leader of the Brücke group organized in Dresden in 1905. His first real contact with art occurred during a study trip to Nuremberg when he came into contact with traditional German engravings. In 1901 he began to attend architectural school while painting on the side. He started to etch and derived a good deal from the work of Rembrandt. By 1904 he was trying to break away from naturalism under the influence of Pointillism, Japanese art and primitive African sculpture. With his friend Erich Heckel he tried to assimilate this material, and the following year, the two of them along with Karl Schmidt-Rottluff and Fritz Bleyl formed the group now known as Die Brücke (The Bridge). That same year he received his architectural degree and also did his first lithographs. In 1907 he met the Swiss Cuno Amiet, the Finn Axel Gallén and the Germans Emil Nolde and Max Pechstein. Thus enlarged, the group had its first two exhibitions in 1906, and during the next few years worked together summer and winter, sharing their quarters, models, materials, etc. Otto Mueller joined them in 1910 and in the following year the group moved to Berlin where there was greater scope. By 1912 Kirchner's philosophical Expressionism (see) had formed; harshly contoured, often masked figures move singly or in groups through a world of distorted space and color that expresses the lonesomeness and isolation of modern man. The chief influences, besides those already mentioned, were Edvard Munch and Vincent Van Gogh. Kirchner served in the army and was invalided out, going to Switzerland where he spent the rest of his life. His new Swiss style was grandiose and equally effective; and a small group of painters gathered about him. Under Hitler, over six hundred of his works were confiscated as "degenerate" in 1937. This and his worsening health caused him to commit suicide in 1938. (See color plate 113.)

Kisling, Moïse (1891-1953). Polish-born painter associated with the School of Paris, to which he was drawn in 1910 from his native Cracow. In France he became interested in the abstract painters Picasso, Braque and Gris but his style was still basically under the influence of Cézanne until the time of World War I, when his service in the Foreign Legion won him French citizenship. After the war he liberated himself from the influence of Cézanne and moved, like Derain, toward a monumentality of form and freedom of color, although with a more precise form and contour, and a cooler, more individual kind of coloring.

Kiyohiro (see JAPANESE PAINTERS: TOKUGAWA PERIOD.)

Kiyonaga (see JAPANESE PAINTERS: TOKUGAWA PERIOD.)

Kiyonobu (see JAPANESE PAINTERS: TOKUGAWA PERIOD.)

Klee, Paul (1879-1940). Born in Switzerland to a German father and a Swiss mother, Klee is associated with the Munich Blue Rider wing of German Expressionism (see). He came to Munich at nineteen to study art and after a trip to Italy produced a series of grotesque and cleverly satirical allegories in etching, quite representational in form but already characteristic of his later half-concealed irony. By 1908 he had undergone the influence of Cézanne, Van Gogh and especially the fantastic work of Ensor. In 1910 he got to know the poetic and highly imaginative art of Alfred Kubin. The following year he met members of the New Artists Federation and those who were soon to form the Blue Rider group, and participated in the second Blue Rider Exhibition in 1912. Klee's style at this point was still entirely representational, although increasingly grotesque and fanciful as well as more indirect and oblique in spirit than the earlier etchings. His visit to Paris in 1912 and his contacts with Delaunay, Le Fauconnier and Picasso gave his work a new Cubist bent in terms of his own already highly developed fantasy. Although the effects of Cubism remain apparent in Klee's art well into the 1930's, the basic quality of his painting is draughtsmanship of a very special and personal kind, a line with a life and a tone of its own, guided and directed by the artist into all sorts of fantastic paths espressive of his not always immediately apparent meaning. He shares with other members and sympathizers of the Blue Rider viewpoint the desire to identify himself with other creatures, in his case the mind of the child or of the mentally disturbed. Klee's fantasy and free-form quality has, like the poetry by Kandinsky's painting, been especially influential on the Abstract Expressionists of the 1950's. See also BAUHAUS. (See illustrations, including color plate 114.)

Klimt, Gustav (1862-1918). Distinguished Austrian painter, designer and illustrator. He is associated with the Symbolist movement of the end of the nineteenth century and also with the Art Nouveau (see) or Jugendstil movement in the last decade of that century and the first decade of the twentieth. His work in the industrial art field of that day, with its swinging linear rhythms and organic plantlike forms, is typical of the Viennese movement as a whole, in which Klimt took a leading part. He is also looked upon as an influence on the painting of Oskar Kokoschka. See EXPRESSIONISM, SYMBOLISM.

Klinger, Max (1857-1920). German painter, sculptor and engraver. Although his paintings appear to be chiefly con-

KLEE. Child Consecrated to Suffering. Albright Gallery, Buffalo

114. KLEE. Gay Repast. Collection Mrs. Gabriel Hauge, Washington, D.C.

cerned with mythology and allegory, the engravings have a new and more personal style that brings him within the compass of the Symbolist movement of the latter part of the century. His book, *Painting and Drawing* (1891), was an important influence in its time. (See illustration.)

Klitias (first half of 6th century B.C.). Greek vase painter. He painted the François vase (Florence), greatest masterpiece of the early Attic black-figured style. This large krater, or wide-mouthed vase, is decorated with four friezes rich in mythology and a fifth of orientalizing motifs. It exhibits the characteristic tight, precise, engraved style of Attica. Klitias is known to have painted a number of extant vases, most of them made by Ergotimos (see).

Knaths, (Otto) Karl (1891-). Contemporary American painter born in Wisconsin. As a student at the Art Institute of Chicago, he was impressed by the Armory Show, but continued to paint Impressionistically. By 1930 his art had turned toward abstraction; it has become increasingly abstract but without ever losing completely the elements of reality.

Kneller, Sir Godfrey (1646/9-1723). British portraitist who was born in Germany, studied in Italy and came to London around 1675, where he was so successful as a portrait painter as to succeed the old favorite, Peter Lely. He became Portrait Painter in Ordinary to the Crown and worked under five different kings and queens of Britain. He painted in the van Dyck manner, although with far less subtlety, and mass-produced society portraits: court beauties, Admirals, Whig members of the Kit Kat Club, and others.

Knight, Laura Johnson (1877-). Contemporary British painter known for circus and ballet pictures. These are characterized by well-balanced strong designs as well as experiments with various types of natural and artificial illumination. (See illustration.)

Koch, Pyke (1901-). Netherlands painter of the Magic Realism school, a self-taught artist who has spent a great deal of time studying the techniques of the Old Masters. His work concerns itself with the differences between our ideals and the way we actually live. Painted in light and dark with

KLINGER. Dead Mother. Düsseldorf Museum

KNIGHT. Spring in Cornwall. Tate Gallery, London

subdued colors, there is a sense of bitterness and tragedy in such works as the Bertha of Antwerp, and in its clinical clarity it suggests the New Objectivity painters of Germany.

Koerner, Henry (1915-). Contemporary American painter born in Vienna. He studied at the Vienna Academy of Applied Arts and came to the U.S. in 1939 after a year in Italy. His meticulously rendered genre scenes have a Neo-Romantic flavor and an almost Surrealist symbolism.

Koetsu (see JAPANESE PAINTERS: MOMOYAMA PERIOD).

Kokoschka, Oskar (1886-). Austrian painter, graphic artist, dramatist, sculptor and a leading member of the Expressionist group of Central Europe. While still a student, Kokoschka was very much impressed by the art of the South Seas and Africa shown in the Vienna museums. From 1904 to 1908 he was student at the Vienna School of Arts and Crafts. His first paintings and poems date from 1907; the following year he exhibited for the first time at the Viennese Kunstschau, creating something of a scandal. His illustrations for *The Dreaming Children* of that year show traces of the influence of Gustav Klimt and the Jugendstil manner in their sensitive yet decorative linear effects. In 1909 a second Kunstschau exhibition and the performance of two of his plays, *Murder—Woman's Hope* and *Sphinx and Straw Man*, made Vienna unsafe for this dissident artist and he went to Switzerland. Later in Berlin he contributed to *Der Sturm* review and did his first penetratingly psychological portraits at this time. On his 1911 show in Vienna, the Austrian Crown Prince expressed the opinion that he deserved to have "every bone in his body broken." From Kokoschka's friendship with Alma Mahler came the marvelous The Tempest and other works. Seriously wounded in the war, he was invalided out with a slight mental imbalance. Appointed to a professorship at Dresden in 1919, he suddenly gave up this job in 1924 and began the years of wandering. The rise of the Nazis drove him from Berlin to Vienna, to Prague and finally to London, where he spent World War II. Long before, however, his contribution was adready clear, especially in its stimulus to the Brücke group in Berlin; it led the way toward distortions of form, color and space for the sake of greater expressiveness and of penetration beneath the surface of everyday reality.

KOKOSCHKA. Arnold Schönberg. Collection Knize, New York

His analyses of all sorts of people (many of them the leaders of European culture), using a dematerializing technique that lays bare their souls, are among his leading contributions. See EXPRESSIONISM. (See illustrations, including color plate 115.)

Kollwitz, Käthe (1867-1945). One of Germany's most distinguished graphic artists and sculptors. Although she painted very little, her contributions in the fields of etching, lithography and woodcut were sufficiently important to earn for her a high place in the art of the late nineteenth and early twentieth century. The wife of a physican who devoted himself to the poor in Berlin and the sister of a militantly progressive newspaperman, Käthe Kollwitz naturally became the protagonist of the underdog, the poor and oppressed of the Kaiser Wilhelm period and the sufferers of the period between the two World Wars. Among her more important prints are: illustrations for Gerhardt Hauptmann's *The Weavers,* known as The Weavers' Revolt; for Zola's *Germinal;* The Peasants War series (1902-08)) and an anti-militarist series climaxed in the great poster No More War! (See illustration.)

Konijnenburg, Willem van (1868-1943). Netherlands painter associated with the modern Symbolist movement at the end of the nineteenth century. He went through a period of Barbizon imitations and from there into Impressionism. By the end of the century, like many of his contemporaries, he arrived at a linear kind of symbolic representation that idealized his subject matter.

Koninck, Philips (1619-1688). Dutch painter of wide panoramic landscapes, grand in their scope and lighting and with fine effects of clouds and sky. He studied with his brother Jacob in Rotterdam and early in the 1640's with Rembrandt in Amsterdam, where he settled. He had an extremely individual style, preferring views of flat country and composing them with great subtlety.

KUBIN. Illustration. Private Collection, Germany

KOLLWITZ. Portrait of a Woman Worker with Blue Shawl Private Collection, Germany

Konrad of Soest (active first quarter of 15th century). German painter. A large altarpiece in the church at Wildungen is dated 1404 and names this artist as its author. His style, graceful and still medieval, has been identified in several other paintings. He appears to have worked in Dortmund.

Kopman, Benjamin (1887). Contemporary American Expressionist painter and lithographer. Born in Russia, he came to the U.S. in 1904 and studied at the National Academy of Design. His early work was related to German Expressionism and the fantasy of Chagall; his later is closer to the French Expressionism of Rouault.

Korin (see JAPANESE PAINTERS: TOKUGAWA PERIOD).

Koryusai (see JAPANESE PAINTERS: TOKUGAWA PERIOD).

Krimmel, John Lewis (1787-1821). American portrait painter and miniaturist born in Germany. He came to Philadelphia in 1810 and produced genre pictures in the satirical vein of Hogarth and Wilkie, but with little financial success.

Krohg, Per (1889-). Norwegian easel and mural painter best known in his native land for his many murals in public buildings. One of a large group of Scandinavian painters who left their respective countries for Paris in the early 1900's, he studied with Matisse and for a long time showed clear traces of that influence in large flat decorative areas of color. During the 1930's he returned to Norway and developed a more national style, although the influences of Van Gogh and Matisse are still evident in his later works. A romantic and eclectic talent, he moves easily from style to style but now clearly reflects the forms and colors of his country's landscape.

115. KOKOSCHKA. The Harbor of Marseilles. City Art Museum, St. Louis

Kroll, Leon (1884-). Contemporary American painter. Born in New York City, he studied with Twachtman at the Art Students League, at the National Academy of Design, and with J. P. Laurens in Paris. He has been a teacher, muralist and winner of top prizes in academic exhibitions for many years. His early work belongs to the vigorous brush tradition of Bellows. His later works, influenced somewhat by Cézanne and Renoir, are largely formal studio products in the academic manner.

Kröller-Müller Museum, Otterlo, Neth. A nationalized private collection of modern paintings featuring among others the works of Van Gogh.

Kruyder, Herman (1881-1935). Netherlands painter who began as a house painter, studied for a while at an art school and then turned to doing stained glass. He began paintings as a romantic realist and then, under the influence of Henri Rousseau and the Belgian Expressionist Constant Permeke, moved in the direction of an ornamental mystical painting in which fear, horror and amazement at the world dominate.

Kubin, Alfred (1877-). Distinguished Austrian painter, graphic artist, illustrator and writer. He is associated with the earlier stages of the Blue Rider movement, participating through the 1912 exhibition put on by Herwarth Walden at Der Sturm galleries in Berlin. Beginning under the influence of Max Klinger, the nineteenth-century mystic, Kubin has been affected by Redon, Ensor and Munch. Since 1906 he has been living at an inherited castle near Wernstein in upper Austria. His style is predominantly that of the graphic artist, filled with the kind of elongations that affected young

KUHN, WALT. Blue Clown
Whitney Museum of American Art, New York

Paul Klee and immersed in the fairytale world whose fables become Kubin's commentary on our existence. See EXPRESSIONISM. (See illustration.)

Kühn (Ketclin, Kitchin, Kyhn), Justus Engelhardt (active in America c.1708-17). A German portrait painter who was active in Maryland. He painted awkward and stiff portraits, especially of children, with fanciful Baroque backgrounds, great attention to detail, and naive charm.

Kuhn, Walt (1880-1949). American painter of portraits and still life. Born in New York, he began his career as a cartoonist in San Francisco in 1899, contributing also to many eastern publications. He studied painting abroad, though not formally, and taught at the New York School of Art (1908-09) and the Art Students League (1926-27). For many years he was art advisor to the well-known collectors John Quinn and (after the death of the painter A. B. Davies) Miss Lillie P. Bliss. In 1912 he was elected Secretary of the Association of American Painters and Sculptors and together with Davies, its president, organized the famous Armory Show. His early works were in the Ashcan tradition, but after the Armory Show he was obviously influenced by the modernists, especially Matisse and Picasso. In the 1920's his style reached maturity. His vigorous and at times brash realism found its best expression in the portraits of circus and vaudeville performers, whom he represented as proud and sensitive individuals incongruously dressed in the blatant finery of their craft. (See illustration.)

Ku K'ai-chih (see CHINESE PAINTERS: THE SIX DYNASTIES).

Kulmbach, Hans Suess von (c.1480-1522). German painter; the pupil and assistant of Dürer. He was also strongly influenced by Jacopo de' Barbari, with whom he may have studied. His altarpiece (1513) in the church of St. Sebald, Nuremberg, was based on drawings provided by Dürer. It shows Kulmbach, especially in his use of harmonious color, as a true interpreter of the much admired Venetian style. In the middle of his career, about 1515, he spent a few years in Cracow, and the fairytale mood of the pictures painted at this time suggest that he came in contact with the work of Altdorfer. On his return to Nuremberg his style resumed its former dependence on the Dürer formulas (see). (See illustration.)

KULMBACH. Girl Making a Garland
Metropolitan Museum of Art, New York

KUNIYOSHI. Amazing Juggler. The Downtown Gallery, New York

Kung Hsien (see CHINESE PAINTERS: CH'ING DYNASTY).

Kung K'ai (see CHINESE PAINTERS: YÜAN DYNASTY).

Kuniyoshi, Yasuo (1893-1953). American painter born in Japan. He came to the U.S. in 1906, studied in the Los Angeles School of Art and Design, with K. H. Miller at the Art Students League, at the National Academy of Design, and elsewhere. He was in Europe in 1925 and 1928, and in Japan and Mexico in 1935. He was the first president of Artists Equity. His early work, full of fantasy and a sly humor, and executed with delicate precision, was dependent upon that of Campendonk and Chagall. In the 1930's he turned to studio arrangements of nudes and still lifes that were, somewhat like Pascin's, sensitively drawn and painted in delicate nuances of grey. His compositions eventually took on Surrealist overtones and in his last years, perhaps

LAERMANS. The Drunkard
Musées Royaux des Beaux-Arts, Brussels

under the influence of Ben Shahn, his palette became more strident and high-keyed. (See illustration.)

Kunsthalle, Bremen. Outstanding for its collection of German Expressionist art. Before the war it was also important as a repository of the works of the Masters. Many of these, e.g., Renoir, Cranach, Masaccio and the famous Dürer watercolors, were lost; however, others (e.g., Rembrandt and Liebermann) have been acquired since the war.

Kunsthalle, Hamburg. A general collection outstanding for its nineteenth- and twentieth-century Germans, e.g., Nolde, Marc, Heckel, Friedrich, and Schmidt-Rottluff. The magnificent group of French moderns it possessed before the last war was removed from the walls by the Nazis and sold out of the country. Some of these are today to be found in the United States in public and private collections.

Kunsthaus, Zurich. A collection of paintings, sculpture and graphic arts.

Kunsthistorisches Museum, Vienna. Contains the old imperial collections of Old Master paintings, particularly the works of Rembrandt, Rubens, Hals, Brueghel and Delacroix.

Kunstmuseum, Basel. One of Europe's outstanding collections of modern art, unusual in that it includes works from every part of the Continent, with strong representation from Germany, Belgium, France and Holland.

Kuo Hsi (see CHINESE PAINTERS: SUNG DYNASTY).

LA FARGE. Maua, Our Boatman
Addison Gallery of American Art, Phillips Academy, Andover

Kupka, Frank (1871-). Czech painter, engraver, draughtsman and book illustrator; associated with the development of Synchromism, or color orchestration. His and other painters' attempts to "free color from form" resulted around 1912 in a whole series of works filled with color movement, such as his own Fugue in Two Colors or certain works by Kandinsky. See ORPHISM.

L

Ladbrooke, Robert (1770-1842). British landscapist and intimate friend of Old Crome, with whom he founded the Norwich school (see). His work is characterized by precision and great detail serving to express his personal warmth and love of nature.

Laer, Pieter van (before 1595-before 1660). A Dutch

LA FRESNAYE. Mappemond. Phillips Collection, Washington, D.C.

LANDSEER. Alexander and Diogenes. Tate Gallery, London

painter (known in Italy as "Bamboccio") who invented a picturesque genre. He probably studied painting in the academy in Haarlem, but before 1610 he went to Rome and became a pupil of Elsheimer; he subsequently joined the circle of Poussin and Claude. His lively scenes of Italian peasants and soldiers were very successful in Italy. About 1639 he returned to Holland and exerted a considerable influence on Dutch painting.

Laermans, Eugene (1864-1940). Belgian painter moved by the spectacle of human misery. Like Degroux he was affected by the lessons of the past (i.e., in the work of Brueghel, Bosch, etc.) but probably had even greater effect on those who followed him. His somewhat symbolist and rhythmical compositions may be looked upon as foreshadowing Flemish Expressionism. (See illustration.)

Laethem-Saint-Martin, School of A group of modern Flemish painters associated with this little village in Belgium during the early years of the twentieth century. Generally in revolt against the representationalism of the Impressionist movement, they were Symbolists in the so-called first Laethem group, e.g., de Saedeleer and van de Woestijne, and Expressionists in the so-called second Laethem group, including de Smet, Permeke and van den Berghe.

La Farge, John (1835-1910). American painter and stained-glass designer. He was an extremely sensitive and in many ways original artist whose incompleteness of training and inherent weakness kept him from achieving the fullness of his promise. Influenced by the aestheticism of the Pre-Raphaelite movement (see), he had a profound effect on American taste through writing, lecturing, and teaching. Born in New York City, of a French family, he first studied with his grandfather, Binsse de St. Victor, a miniaturist. In 1856 he went to Paris, worked with Couture, and met Gautier, Puvis de Chavannes, Rossetti and Millais. He studied the Old Masters in Munich, Dresden and London. Returning to the U.S., he worked with Hunt in Newport and was strongly influenced by him. In 1876 he was invited by Richardson to do murals in Trinity Church, Boston, and the next year executed a series (destroyed by fire) for St. Thomas', New York. His most famous mural, the Ascension in the Church of the Ascension, New York, is eruditely academic and uninspired. His similarly academic stained-glass windows are less important as art than as an influence in the revival of the technique. In 1886 he traveled in Japan, Samoa, and the South Seas, and absorbed Oriental impressions which influenced the character of his art. (See illustration.)

LARGILLIÈRE. Portrait of Princess Rakoczi
National Gallery, London

LaFosse, Charles de (1636-1716). French painter of history. Pupil of Le Brun, he took prominent part in the large decorative commissions of the time both in France and England.

La Fresnaye, Roger de (1885-1925). French painter associated with the early development of Cubism (see). Up to 1908-09 his painting was very much under the influence of Maurice Denis. Between 1910 and 1913 he was interested in Picasso and Braque. He was part of the group that met regularly at Jacques Villon's studio for the Section d'Or (see) association. After leaving the army in 1917, he did a whole series of Cubist watercolors and drawings. These are quite different in spirit from either Picasso or Braque in that they emphasize joyousness of color and a straightforward rhythmical relationship of forms rather than the kaleidoscopic effects of Analytical Cubism. The figures vibrate in their limited space and their planes do penetrate the space in which they are set, but they are seldom as fragmented and as deliberately contrived as in the orthodox Cubists. (See illustration.)

La Hire, Laurent de (1606-56). French painter and etcher. Product of the School of Fontainebleau, La Hire became an eclectic decorative painter in the tradition of Vouet. His sources range from Raphael to Caravaggio to his contemporary, Poussin. He designed for Richelieu (the Palais Royal) and for the royal tapestry works. Late in life he painted mainly landscapes.

Lam, Wilfredo (1902-). One of the best known of modern Cuban painters, Lam has been closely associated with Picasso and with the writer André Breton, author of the first Manifesto of Surrealism. His painting often suggests some of the Africanist mannerism of Picasso and the humorously frightening effects of Surrealism combined with the magical and ritualistic symbolism of his own Afro-Cuban background.

116. LANCRET. La Camargo Dancing. National Gallery of Art, Mellon Collection, Washington, D.C.

Lancret, Nicolas (1690-1743). French painter of fêtes galantes. With Pater, Lancret is the outstanding follower of Watteau and at times practiced a style almost indistinguishable from Watteau's. Like Watteau he was a student of Gillot and from that time on painted in the new informal style "after Nature." The individuality of his best works reveals itself in a more anecdotal or descriptive genre than Watteau's. It is a less sublimated style. As was popular in England, Lancret painted series-subjects such as the Four Ages and the Four Seasons (for Louis XV). He illustrated the amorous *Contes de la Fontaine,* and it can be observed that the love-play of his fêtes is usually more obvious, more pointed than in the works of his master. (See color plate 116.)

landscape. A painting, print or drawing of a given scene in nature, this kind of art is revealing of the attitude of the artist toward the world at a given moment in history. Landscape painting as an art in itself and not as mere background is, with the possible exception of certain Roman painting, a relatively new thing, emerging as late as the seventeenth century of our era. Although some of the first landscapists were Italians, the full flowering of this art is to be found in seventeenth-century Holland, where such painters as Ruysdael, Hobbema and others exemplify the category. During the Rococo eighteenth century, landscape was not as widely practiced except in England, where Wilson, Crome and Gainsborough brought into being the naturalistic-Romantic landscape. During the nineteenth century the Romantics, particularly Turner, Constable, Bonington and others in England and the Barbizon painters in France (e.g., Rousseau, Daubigny, Corot) showed a new manner of treating nature. It is still a widely practiced form of painting in the twentieth century, appearing in all the modern schools.

Landseer, Sir Edwin (1802-73). British painter of animals who enjoyed great popularity during the Victorian era mainly because of the sentimental and human qualities with which he endowed his animals. A youthful prodigy who could draw with both hands, he was trained by his father, an engraver, and by Benjamin Haydon, who made him dissect animals and copy the Elgin Marbles. Landseer exhibited at the Royal Academy when only thirteen years of age, developing in the direction of saccharine studies of "human" animals, e.g., Dignity and Impudence. At the age of seventy he modeled the lions at the base of the Nelson Monument in Trafalgar Square, London. (See illustration.)

Lanfranco, Giovanni (1582-1647). Born in Parma, at first a student of Agostino and later of Annibale Carracci, he collaborated with the latter and Domenichino in the Galleria Farnese, Rome (after 1600). He worked also in Parma, Piacenza, and Naples. His style, deriving from Correggio and the conservative classicism of the Carracci, finally leads to the full illusionistic Baroque, e.g., the decorations of the Villa Borghese (1618) and the Palazzo Costaguti (c.1620), the dome of S. Andrea della Valle (1625-28) and the choir of S. Carlo ai Catinari (1646-47), all in Rome, and the ceiling of the Certosa di S. Martino, Naples (1633+).

Lange, Jań (see BOECKHORST, JOHANN).

Largillière, Nicolas de (1654-1746). French painter, primarily of portraits. Born in Paris, brought up in Antwerp, learned his trade as an assistant to Lely in London. He is one

117. LATOUR. Young Smoker. Wildenstein Gallery, New York

of several transitional figures between the Poussinist tradition and the colorism of the eighteenth century; he supported Chardin's entry into the Academy. In France, Largillière was befriended by van der Meulen and was elected to the Academy for his portrait of Le Brun. As a portraitist he prided himself on his patronage among the wealthy middle class with whom he did a thriving business, painting individuals and families in a flurry of rich silks and satins. The informality of pose, the landscape settings and feeling of atmospheric space make his portraits a clear bridge to Rococo taste. (See illustration.)

Larianov, Michel (1881-). Russian abstract painter who in 1909 developed a type of painting known as Rayonnism, a dynamic form of space penetration consisting of rays of light and suggesting in some ways the work of the Futurists. He has lived in Paris for many years.

Laroon, Captain Marcellus (1679-1773). British genre painter, musician, and adventurer who served for twenty-five years in the British army. His sketches from contemporary life, painted with a light touch, an almost French quality of daintiness, are his best work.

Lascaux caves (see PREHISTORIC PAINTING).

Lastman, Pieter Pietersz. (1583-1633). Dutch historical painter. He studied in Amsterdam with Gerrit Pietersz. In 1603 he went to Italy and spent some years in Rome, coming under the influence of Elsheimer and Caravaggio. Returning to Amsterdam he established himself as an important painter and teacher, becoming the master of Jan Lievens and Rembrandt. Lastman's own style was somewhat crude, but from his heavy-handed pictures the young Rembrandt studied and borrowed, adapting to his own uses the reflections of Italian art which he found in them.

Last Supper, The, by Leonardo da Vinci (see).

Latour, Georges de (1593-1652). A French tenebrist painter of Lorraine. The nature of Latour's art has become apparent only recently. A contemporary of Poussin, his name was lost to posterity until 1863 when a book of a documentary nature was published by Alexandre Joly, archivist of Nancy. No paintings were associated with this name, however, until Hermann Voss began in 1915 to indentify a number of works as Latour's which had been variously ascribed to Le Nain, Vermeer, Spaniards and certain Caravaggesque painters. Other attributions and publications followed, and Latour's compositions have become increasingly popular, eclipsing the Le Nains in the exposition of Peintres de la Realité in 1934-35. Of his life little is yet known except that he was of rather humble origin, rose to become painter to the king, but was mainly active in the service of the Duke of Lorraine. Lorraine was then subject to plague (1631) and war (1632), which affected his career. Against the plague Latour painted several versions of the protector St. Sebastian for the King, the Duke and others. These reveal his "night" style, a severely archaic tenebrism derived perhaps from the Dutchman Honthorst rather than Caravaggio himself. Especially favored was the device of light dramatically cast from a shielded candle as in the Education of the Virgin (Frick Collection). His sharply-defined shapes have a structure rivaling Poussin's and a simple piety similar to Le Nain's. His subjects are almost exclusively religious, although among his signed "daylight" scenes is a Card Sharp composition, and some genres are attributed to him. (See color plate 117.)

LAURENCIN. Mother and Child. Detroit Institute of Arts

LA TOUR, MAURICE Q. DE
Portrait of Mme de Pompadour. Louvre, Paris

La Tour, Maurice Quentin de (1704-88). A French portraitist, especially in pastels. His careful, almost clinical study of the face in portraits, to the exclusion of literary attributes, marks him as one of the great eighteenth-century naturalistic painters. His studies are simple, sincere and nearly always ingratiating because of smiles and other fleeting expressions. His life was full of incidents caused, even with royalty, by his strictness in sittings. His adoption of the new pastel technique and its consequent vogue led to considerable resistance among the academic oil painters. He was much sought after and was lodged in the Louvre as painter to the king. In 1755 he exhibited a famous full-size portrait of Mme de Pompadour in pastels. Also famous are his many self-portraits. (See illustration.)

Laughing Cavalier by Frans Hals (see).

Laurencin, Marie (1885-). French painter and graphic artist who began to show her pictures at the Indépendants exhibition in 1907. Some of her early work, especially the woodcuts, shows traces of primitive influence owing perhaps to her friendship with Picasso, who had made considerable use of this material. There is also a Near Eastern quality in her paintings such as is found in the work of Matisse, but from the beginning this influence and that of Fauvism are generally diluted in a charmingly Rococo, even trivial manner suitable to the purposes of theatrical and decorative work. (See illustration.)

Lautrec (see TOULOUSE-LAUTREC).

Lawrence, Jacob (1917-). A contemporary American semi-abstract Expressionist painter. Born in Atlantic City, N.J., he studied at the Harlem Art Workshop under the W.P.A. and at the American Artists School (1937-8), worked for the Federal Art Project (1939-40), traveled in the South (1941-42), and served in the U.S. Coast Guard (1943-45). He utilizes strident color and powerful design to depict the social problems and aspirations of Negroes in Harlem and the South. (See illustration.)

Lawrence, Thomas (1769-1830). An outstanding British portraitist, Lawrence, one of sixteen children of an innkeeper, showed great talent from childhood on and by 1780 was the mainstay of the family. He sold small oval pastel portrait drawings of the nobility, of well-known local military figures etc. Coming to London in 1786 he began to paint in oils, entered the Academy and undertook to emulate the social manners of Reynolds. Lawrence had a very successful career and in 1792 succeeded Reynolds as painter to the king. He was elected to the Royal Academy two years later. An accomplished draughtsman and designer, a charming person, he became the foremost portraitist of his day, painting European monarchs, heroes of the Napoleonic wars and others. Qualitatively he lacks the dignity and power of Reynolds and the subtle charm of Gainsborough. The external attractiveness of his style is illustrated by The Calmady Children, 1824 (Metropolitan).

Lawson, Ernest (1873-1939). American Impressionist landscape painter, a member of the Eight. Born in San Francisco, he studied first in Kansas City and then in New York with Weir and Twachtman, both Impressionists. Although a member of the National Academy he allied himself with the more radical elements in the art world. After the Armory Show his art reflected the influence of Cézanne.

Lazo, Agustín (1900-). A Mexican painter and stage designer. Widely traveled, he has done much for the development of the new Mexican theatre movement. His art shows a poetic kind of Magic Realism with Surrealist overtones.

LAWRENCE, JACOB. Tombstones
Whitney Museum of American Art, New York

LEBRUN, RICO. Vertical Composition
Collection Mr. and Mrs. George Dangerfield, N.Y.

Leal, Fernando (1900-). Mexican easel painter, muralist and engraver; worked in fresco and encaustic in the National Preparatory School in 1922 and in the Anfiteatro Bolívar from 1931 to 1933. His later work has moved toward religious subjects.

Le Brocquy, Louis (1916-). A contemporary Irish painter; known as a portrayer of the Irish scene but has run the gamut of modern painting from Manet and Goya through the Impressionists, Post-Impressionists and a Cubist-derived style which he has used to project his folk ideas. The individualistic, thin, elegant, almost Oriental contour line that describes his figures is probably the result of his long-time interest in the Orient.

Lebrun (see VIGÉE-LEBRUN).

Le Brun, Charles (1619-90). French decorative painter. His organization of the French Academy and his association with its early years far outweigh the importance of his own work as a painter. During the ascendancy of Colbert as King's Minister, Le Brun ruled French painters with an iron hand, promoting the cause of his Poussinists against the in-

118. LÉGER. Sisters. Saidenberg Gallery, New York

his colors to the three primaries together with grey and black-and-white backgrounds. In this way he tries to "purify" his painting and give it universal meaning.

Le Clerc, Jean (1587/88-1633). A French painter and copper-engraver of Lorraine. Like his friend Callot, active in Italy. He painted in the Doge's Palace, Venice. He engraved religious works after his Italian master, Carlo Saraceni.

Le Corbusier (Charles Edouard Jenneret) (1887-). Distinguished Swiss architect, painter, writer and theoretician; his influence has been exerted through his (and Ozenfant's) Purism (see) of the 1920's as well as through his manifold experiments and projects in architecture. In painting, his work and Ozenfant's are not easily distinguishable; they generally stand for purification of the loose and improvisatory methods of both Analytical and Synthetic Cubism. Finely machined parts and characteristically mechanical sections such as spheres, cylinders, etc., become the forms to which reality is reduced. For joint publications, see OZENFANT.

Lee, Doris Emrick (1905-). Contemporary American painter of humorous genre scenes. Born in Illinois, she studied at the Kansas City Art Institute, with Lhote in Paris and with Arnold Blanch.

Le Fauconnier, Henri (1881-1946). A French pioneer Cubist who apparently did not receive the recognition he deserved for his work. Exhibiting with Delaunay at the In-

surgent Rubenists. In the *conférences* which he delivered before the Academy he contributed important chapters to the academic theory of painting. A pupil of Vouet, Le Brun became *peintre du roi* at the precocious age of nineteen. He abandoned Vouet for the latter's rival Poussin, with whom he went to Rome. After three years of copying the masters, he returned to France, where he received much employment, and led in the organization of the Academy in 1648. Although he had worked at Vaux-le-Vicomte for Fouquet, his allegiance was to the rival faction of Mazarin, who introduced him to Court in 1660. Colbert then employed Le Brun and the Academy as important cogs in the totalitarian machine of state which he and Louis XIV were fabricating. Le Brun was appointed director of the royal tapestry and furniture works founded in 1667. His major decorative projects in this period were the Petite Galerie of the Louvre, the Stairway of the Ambassadors and Galerie des Glaces at Versailles, and Colbert's château of Scéaux. Typical of his style are the Alexander series dedicated to Louis XIV and the Portrait of the Jabach Family, a work that testifies to the importance of the wealthy bourgeoisie in Louis' plans. With the fall of Colbert in 1683, Le Brun was replaced in all capacities by Mignard, a Rubenist. He retired from public life and devoted himself to religious paintings of the type of the Entry into Jerusalem (Louvre).

Lebrun, Rico (Federico) (1900-). Contemporary American painter born in Naples, Italy, where he received his earliest training. In 1924 he came to the U.S. to establish a stained-glass factory in Illinois, and remained. His earlier work, inspired by the art of the Italian Renaissance, showed imaginative power and a remarkable technique. In recent years his art has become more abstract. (See illustration.)

Leck, Bart van der (1876-). Netherlands painter and member of de Stijl group yet very much concerned with art as a social force. Unlike other members of the group (e.g., Mondrian), he does not altogether abandon the physical world but sets up a series of severe relief-like figures, reducing

LÉGER. Profile on a Vase. Musée des Beaux-Arts, Liège

119. LE NAIN, LOUIS. Landscape with Peasants. National Gallery of Art, Kress Collection, Washington, D.C.

dependants show of 1911, he helped organize Room XLI in which were grouped the most advanced Cubists of that moment. During World War I, which he spent in Holland, he became affiliated with the Expressionists, forming a bond between the movement in the Netherlands and Belgium and that emerging in France in such painters as Gromaire.

Lefebvre, Jules Joseph (1836-1912). French painter in the academic formula. Student of Cogniet. Typical of his cold precise style is Truth, of which he did several versions.

Léger, Fernand (1881-). Outstanding French painter and designer of fabrics, mosaics, ballet décor and other media. He is generally associated with the pre-World War I development known as "machine art." This is Léger's own variant of the Cubist fragmentation of form, which he has evolved since 1909. At first (from 1897 to 1902) Léger was interested in architecture; after that he worked at the Beaux-Arts for a while and then moved to The Beehive settlement in Montparnasse, where he came into contact with vanguard groups. He progressed through Impressionism and Neo-Impressionism (chiefly as represented by Signac), and then underwent the influence of Matisse and the Fauves. In 1910 through the dealer Kahnweiler he met Picasso and Braque, and produced his own brand of faceted and broken Cubist forms in that year. During the following few years he adopted a more dynamic and colorful type of Cubism (see), exhibiting at the Berlin gallery of Der Sturm and in New York at the Armory Show. His experiences in the transport corps in the army and the drawings he made of the large armored machines, then emerging as part of the new tools of war, apparently had considerable effect on him. When he was invalided out, he began a period in which objects, people and whole cities are reduced in his works to dynamic machine-like forms distributed within a shallow canvas space that restricts their back-and-forth movements. In the 1920's he made contact with de Stijl group in Holland and the Purists in France. His travels in the United States confirmed him in attitudes he had already formed. Léger has done décors for many ballets, designed fabrics and mosaics and created one film, *Ballet Mécanique*. See also SECTION D'OR. (See illustrations, including color plate 118.)

Legros, Alphonse (1837-1911). French painter, etcher, lithographer and sculptor. Unusual among French graphic artists for his melancholic fantasy. As a painter he was influenced by Millet and Courbet. Through Whistler, with whom he exhibited at the first Salon des Refusés, he was invited to England, where he spent the rest of his life.

Leighton, Frederic (Lord Leighton of Stretton) (1830-1896). British painter of classical subjects in the most traditional manner. Brought up abroad, Leighton became well known by the age of twenty-five and settling down in London in 1860 fell into the routine Academy pattern. He was the president of the Royal Academy from 1878 to 1896, when that institution was in its heyday as a social institution, training center and cultural influence. The progressive painters of the following generation were to react very strongly against these very qualities. Leighton's own work is eclectic, marked by scholarly drawing revealing great knowledge, if not absorption, of the masters of the past, pleasant color schemes, and skilled but traditional designs.

Lely, Peter (Pieter van der Faes) (1618-80). British portraitist of the Restoration period; born in The Hague, studied portrait painting in the van Dyck tradition but could shift, when necessary, to a more straightforward approach. He arrived in England in 1641 and soon became popular. Lely painted for Charles I, continued to do portraits all through the Commonwealth period and became court painter at the time of the Restoration—a remarkable instance of flexibility and adaptability. To increase production in his studio and to meet a great demand for copies of all kinds, he employed many assistants. Although Lely used the methods of van Dyck, he was far less talented; but he was famous for his handsome women of the Restoration type and the lovely flesh tones, sensuous colors and luxurious charm with which he invested them. He was a good draughtsman with a sense of decorative design and he left a tradition of good workmanship behind him. (See illustration.)

Le Moyne (Le Moine), François (1688-1737). French genre and history painter. A student of Galloche at the age of thirteen, Le Moyne became a brilliant academician and first painter to the king, only to die a suicide. His decorative style was based on the Venetians; he was an admirer of Michelangelo and Pietro da Cortona. He painted the Salon d'Hercule at Versailles.

Le Nain (the brothers). Family of French genre painters of the mid-seventeenth century. They were Antoine, called "the Elder" (c.1588-1648), Louis, called "the Roman" (c.1593-1648) and Mathieu (1607-77). They are noted for their stolid, matter-of-fact, primitive realism. Although renowned in their day, they went out of fashion until the French realistic movement of the past century when they were "discovered" by Champfleury. Since that time they have been subjected to considerable scholarship. Their popularity in our day may owe something to the "magic realism" of their tonal landscape backgrounds. Both Antoine and Louis were elected to the Academy the year they died; Mathieu was later knighted. Old records are at variance, but it is clear that they collaborated closely. Of their individual styles one can say little that is certain. To Antoine are attributed the small group paintings on copper and wood such as The Procession (Louvre). These are the most primitive—it was said he could not render hands well. The figures have a dumpy relation to the frame, although the effect is not without charm. Louis seems to have painted in a broader manner, with more grasp of the contemporary work of Italy, Holland and even Spain. The Wagon (Louvre) is characteristic of his outdoor scenes. The Supper (Louvre) has such pious dignity that it may be a realistic version of the Eucharist. Mathieu, the youngest, liked scenes of soldiers and of gambling, which he painted with the flourish of Terborch and the younger Dutchmen, e.g., The Guard (Berckheim collection, Paris). The brothers were famous for portraits, but few have survived. (See color plate 119.)

LELY. Portrait of Frans van Helmont. National Gallery, London

Lenbach, Franz von (1836-1904). German painter of genre and portraits, he is especially known for his likenesses of many of the great men of the nineteenth century.

Leonardo da Vinci (1452-1519). The renown of the Florentine painter Leonardo throughout the history of art is paralleled only by that of Michelangelo and Raphael. He is thought of as the type of the Renaissance man, active and distinguished in several branches of art and science. He was possessed by the kind of curiosity about the physical world that ushered in the modern era of empirical enquiry and that led him to a knowledge of the structure of living things and the forces of nature unsurpassed by any man of his time. He was a painter, sculptor and musician, an engineer and inventor, a mathematical theorist, and a draughtsman of the highest order. His style of painting was based on this fund of knowledge and on his keen powers of observation.

Leonardo was born in 1452 in the town of Vinci, near Empoli, the illegitimate son of the notary Piero da Vinci and a peasant girl named Caterina. He was brought up in the well-to-do home of his father's parents. At an early age he went to Florence and entered the shop of Verrocchio, where he remained until 1472. In that year he was first listed in the painters' guild, and was also brought before the court on a charge of sodomy. He was busy with independent commissions in Florence until 1482, after which he went to Milan for a stay of seventeen years. Attached to the court of Lodovico Sforza of Milan, he applied his genius to music, engineering, decorating, planning of pageants and festivals, and probably writing his *Treatise on Painting.* He had been called to Milan to design and execute a bronze equestrian monument to Francesco Sforza, but this was never completed. While there he did paint the celebrated Madonna of the Rocks (Louvre), and he and his pupil Ambrogio da Predis did a second version of the same composition (now in London). Even more celebrated is the mural painting of the Last Supper (1495-98) in the refectory of Santa Maria delle Grazie in Milan. In 1500 Leonardo was in Venice as a military engineer. In the same year he returned to Florence and stayed until 1506, with the exception of a short period (1502-03) during which he studied provincial fortifications and engineering projects in the service of Cesare Borgia. During

LEONARDO DA VINCI. Last Supper. Santa Maria delle Grazie, Milan

this Florentine sojourn he painted the portrait of the wife of Francesco del Giocondo, or "Mona Lisa" (1503-7, Louvre); he also started on frescoes of the Battle of Anghiari for the Palazzo Vecchio but never completed these and they are now lost except for contemporary copies, drawings and an engraving. He also worked on theoretical mathematical problems, dissected cadavers in a local hospital, and began the Madonna and Child with St. Anne (Louvre) but did not finish it for several years. In 1506-07 he went again to Milan for another ill-fated sculpture project, the monument to Gian Giacomo Trivulzio, which was not finished and is known only through drawings. At this time he established a relation with the French court through Charles d'Amboise, the French governor of Milan. After another short stay in Florence (1507-8), he returned to Milan and remained there until 1513, busying himself with hydraulics and aeronautics, and continuing his anatomical studies. From 1513-16 he worked in Rome under Leo X, doing various jobs in the Vatican, making measurements on St. Peter's, and painting various works (now lost). In 1516 he went to France and lived in the castle of St. Cloud near Amboise until his death on May 2, 1519. He was buried in the cloister of a church that has since been destroyed.

Leonardo's painting is known to us through a mere handful of works, some of them unfinished and others partly executed by pupils. The earliest work from his hand is an angel appearing in Verrocchio's Baptism of Christ (Uffizi), done c.1470, when Leonardo was still a pupil. Relatviely early is the Adoration of the Magi (1480-82, Uffizi), an unfinished work which shows Leonardo's independence of his teacher's shop and a certain relation to other more realistic fifteenth-century masters, especially Pollaiuolo and the sculptor Donatello. The Madonna of the Rocks, begun in 1483, is the first completed painting that establishes the style for which Leonardo is best known. In a pyramidal composition alive with realistic detail, unity is attained by a pervading light which defines the figures in the dark grotto by gently modeling them and by the breathable atmosphere which surrounds them. Here also is the beginning of the characteristic smiling female face which Leonardo's followers imitated, frequently without grasping the more fundamental elements of his art. The Last Supper in Milan, in very poor condition owing to Leonardo's technical experimentation, is nevertheless impressive testimony to his mastery of anatomy and perspective and his concern with the psychological and iconographical content of religious art. This work miraculously survived the almost complete destruction of the refectory during World War II. The Mona Lisa, also in poor condition, was renowned in Leonardo's time for its realism, and later for the suggestion of mysterious femininity it seems to express. It affords a good example of aerial perspective in the panoramic landscape background, achieved by diminution of color and value contrasts toward the far distance. Leonardo speaks of this observable phenomenon in his writings and was one of the first to apply it to painting. For most of his painted works there are many preliminary drawings extant. Leonardo's painting is only a portion of his contribution to art and science in the western world. His *Treatise on Painting* and the *Notebooks* are of the utmost importance for an understanding of his genius. He left a large group of followers in Milan, among whom the ablest was his direct pupil and collaborator, Ambrogio da Predis. (See illustrations, including color plate 120.)

Lépicié, Michel Nicolas Bernard (1735-84). French genre painter. Pupil of Van Loo and of his own father, who had engraved many of Chardin's paintings. After early failures in the historical manner of Van Loo, Lépicié turned to familiar genre in the styles of Chardin and Greuze. An example is A Mother Feeding her Child (Wallace Collection).

Le Prince, Jean Baptiste (1734-81). French painter and copper-engraver. Much traveled, versatile and prolific artist who practiced history, portrait, genre and landscape painting. His style, a pleasant one, derived from his master Boucher and from the Dutch.

Lessing, Karl Friedrich (1808-80). German painter; great-nephew of the famous writer. He studied at the Berlin Academy and in Düsseldorf. In 1858 he was called to Karlsruhe to become director of the gallery and spent the rest of his life in that city. His narrative paintings, though freely executed, abound in detail that tends to weaken the dramatic effects he sought.

Le Sueur, Eustache (1617-55). French painter noted for his sincere religious style. Le Sueur began in company with Le Brun as a student of Vouet, but both turned from their master to the style of Poussin. First a book-decorator, he became one of the twelve founders of the Royal Academy in 1648, and received a number of decorative commissions for *hôtels* and for the Gobelins. Although influenced by Raphael, Le Sueur seems much more individual, less derived, than many of his contemporaries. His religious works are almost saccharine sweet but the best, a series on the Life of St. Bruno is of an impressively pious quietism. The abstract simplicity of this series calls to mind the teachings of Port Royal and

120. LEONARDO DA VINCI. Virgin of the Rocks. National Gallery, London

resembles the best Carthusian paintings of Spain by Zurbaran, Ribalta and Sánchez-Cotán.

Leutze, Emanuel (1816-68). American historical and genre painter born in Germany. He is most noted for the popular painting, George Washington Crossing the Delaware (Metropolitan). Brought to Virginia as a child, he did not begin to paint until he was twenty-two. In 1841, after having saved enough money he went to Düsseldorf, where he studied under K. F. Lessing and lived for the next twenty years. The Washington as well as other historical pictures were painted there. He returned and settled in the U.S. in 1859. In 1860 he was commissioned to decorate the stairway of the Capitol and painted the noted Course of Empire mural. His style was painstakingly exact in research and execution, his art more concerned with the creation of tableaux rather than pictures.

Levi, Julian E. (1900-). A contemporary American painter in the Neo-Romantic tradition. Born in New York City, brought up in Philadelphia, trained at the Pennsylvania Academy of Fine Arts, he paints scenes of the sea shore with Surrealist overtones.

Levine, Jack (1915-). Contemporary American painter of social themes. Born in Boston and trained at the Boston Museum Art School under Denman Ross, his style is Expressionistic and related to that of Soutine and El Greco. His major paintings are allegorical in form and satirical in intent. He came to recognition first for his striking social satires, such as The Feast of Pure Reason (Museum of Modern Art), done under the W.P.A. He did a series of sensitive biblical studies in the early 1940's. Since his service in the U.S. Army he has been painting large pictures of satirical comment on contemporary American life expressed with painterly virtuosity and richness.

Levitsky, Dmitri (1735-1822). A Russian portraitist of the eighteenth century who worked in the French manner of that day and was influenced by a wide variety of painters from France, including Perronneau, Greuze and La Tour.

Lévy, Rudolph (1875-1944). German Fauve painter who belongs to a small group that fell under the influence of Matisse. Lévy was the center of the group, which met at the Café du Dôme in Paris and included such men as Moll and Purrmann. All of them shared the desire to augment the intensity and symbolic quality of color that had finally been liberated from Naturalism and could be devoted to the purposes of expressiveness. He is believed to have died in the Auschwitz concentration camp in 1944.

Lewis, Wyndham (1884-). British painter, writer, originator of Vorticism (see) and its short-lived periodical *Blast*. Owing a good deal to Cubist and especially Futurist influences, he became a violent partisan of international modernism, believing that the machine age had made nationalism in art obsolete. More important, he was among the first (1919) to point to a new relationship between painter and the architect-engineer.

Leyden, Lucas van (1489?-1533). Dutch painter, engraver, and woodcut artist. He began his studies with his father and continued them under Cornelis Engelbrechtsz. In 1521 he appears to have been in Antwerp, for Dürer on his Netherlands voyage made a silverpoint portrait of him in that year. His prints betray the influence of Dürer. He was a great master of decorative and ornamental composition and his engravings are among the best in the sixteenth century. His drawings are always sensitive in feeling as well as technique. (See illustration.)

Leyster, Judith (1609-60). Dutch painter of animals, still life, genre and portraits; wife of the painter Jan Miense Molenaer. She lived near Utrecht where she came under the influence of Terbrugghen. Subsequently she became a pupil of Frans Hals in Haarlem and closely imitated his work, painting many pictures that have been attributed to him. She was highly regarded by her contemporaries.

Lhermitte, Leon Augustin (1844-1925). French painter and etcher. He painted open, airy rural scenes in a technique that was tighter and more exacting than that of the Impressionists. He worked in the spirit of Millet.

Lhote, André (1885-). French Cubist painter, teacher and theoretician who has written with understanding about the art of geometricized forms. Always a great admirer of classical art and its formal implications, he was attracted to Picasso and Braque and sought to produce a more colorful and less static version of the Cubist method. But because of his tendency toward precision and dryness of form, he does not always succeed in giving his pictures the kind of flexibility he hoped for. Lhote may be classified with Delaunay, Gleizes and La Fresnaye as part of the movement to give Cubism (see) a more colorful quality. See also SECTION D'OR.

Liang K'ai (see CHINESE PAINTERS: SUNG DYNASTY).

Liberale da Verona (1451-c.1535). The most dramatic of several minor Veronese painters dependent on Mantegna and the Vivarini, he began as a miniaturist in Verona. He later worked in Siena, Florence and Venice.

Liberty Leading the People by Eugène Delacroix (see).

Li Ch'eng (see CHINESE PAINTERS: SUNG DYNASTY).

Licinio, Bernardino (c.1489-before 1565). A Venetian portrait painter born perhaps at Poscante near Bergamo. A pupil of Pordenone, he was influenced by his master as well as by Palma Vecchio, Giorgione, Bonifazio, and Cariani.

Lie, Jonas (1880-1940). American academic landscape painter. Born in Norway, his art training began very early there and in Paris. After his arrival in the U.S. in 1893 he studied at the National Academy of Design, the Art Students League and Cooper Union while working as a textile designer. In 1906, during a trip abroad, he was influenced by Monet, and returned to do conservatively Impressionistic landscapes, city and construction scenes in New England, Utah, and Panama. His Panama Canal paintings, now at West Point, brought him his first recognition. He was president of the National Academy of Design from 1934 to 1939.

Liebermann, Max (1847-1934). Leader of the German Impressionist movement and also known as an exciting etcher and draughtsman. He began as an academic artist, but turned gradually to the realism of Millet and Courbet in France and that of Menzel and Leibl in Germany. Around 1884 his style became more vigorous and naturalistic and from 1890 on he moved toward French Impressionism. In 1899 he became president of the New Berlin Secession movement which represented for some time the bolder spirits in the art of that country. His style, like that of other German Impressionists (such as Corinth and Slevogt) and unlike the Frenchmen who presumably influenced him, is tempered by an interest in emotional and symbolic problems. He treats such themes as the working-class, the grandeur of nature and the loneliness of man. (See illustration.)

Liechtenstein Galerie, Vienna. A collection known for its Renaissance and Baroque works.

Lievens, Jan (1607-74). Dutch painter and engraver of historical subjects, portraits, and landscapes. Lievens studied first in Leyden and then in Amsterdam with Lastman, Rembrandt's master. He spent some years in London and Antwerp. His decorative pictures were highly prized in Holland.

Ligozzi, Jacopo (c.1547-1626). Venetian painter and miniaturist born in Verona. He worked in Florence for the Grand Dukes Francesco I, Ferdinand I, Cosimo II, and Ferdinand II, becoming court painter and director of the gallery. He was a painter of religious and mythological scenes in a classical Baroque style but was also noted for his treatment of animals, fruit, flowers and other nature subjects.

Li Kung-lin (or Li Lung-mien) see CHINESE PAINTERS: SUNG DYNASTY).

LEYDEN, VAN. Temptation of St. Anthony. Musées Royaux des Beaux-Arts, Brussels

LIEBERMANN. Rider on the Beach. State Gallery, Munich

Limbourg brothers (Pol, Herman, and Jehanequin Malouel) (active before 1399 to before 1439). Franco-Flemish book illuminators. Nephews of Malouel (see). Born in the Netherlands, trained by a Parisian goldsmith, active for the Dukes of Burgundy and for the Duke of Berri, these brothers are the most famous miniature painters of all time. They show a complete grasp of the innovations of the Boucicaut Master of Paris and of Jacquemart de Hesdin whom they succeeded in the service of the Duke of Berri. Pol had painted the Breviary of Jean sans Peur while in Burgundian service. For Berri they executed the Heures d'Ailly (1406-14) and their great masterpiece the Très Riches Heures du Duc de Berri (Musée Condé, Chantilly) which was painted 1413-16 and finished posthumously. The well-known Calendar landscapes of this manuscript are a monument in the development of landscape painting. (See illustration.)

limner. Literally one who draws, paints, portrays or delineates. More specifically a type of folk painter during the colonial and early Republican period in America. Generally anonymous, these painters present an unsophisticated and even untaught viewpoint, a detailed two-dimensional kind of painting. In many ways dependent on the late Elizabethan tradition of England, this art shows a keen sense of decorative values, an intuitive feeling for color and a directness and simplicity far removed from the aristocratic portrait tradition of seventeenth- and eighteenth-century Europe. In spite of what are clearly technical insufficiencies the limner of the colonial period, interested primarily in achieving a likeness for his patron, has left us a considerable number of arresting psychological studies. (See illustration.)

linear. Referring to the kind of painting that emphasizes contours and outlines rather than three-dimensional masses of form or light-and-dark effects.

linear perspective. The means used for simulating the third dimension on a two-dimensional surface, involving the use of lines that converge as they move away from the spectator and create the illusion of distance.

Lin Liang (see CHINESE PAINTERS: MING DYNASTY).

Linnell, John (1792-1882). British landscapist; follower and patron of William Blake. He painted large pictures of English scenery with striking sky effects but generally conservative approach. He also did portraits, miniatures, and illustrations for the Scriptures.

Lintott, Edward Barnard (1875-1951). Contemporary British painter; trained in Paris in a conservative manner. He had diplomatic assignments around World War I and later moved to the United States. His portraits of notables in England and the United States show harmonious color, well-planned designs and good qualities of likeness, but limited psychological insight.

Lippi, Filippino (c.1457-1504). Last exponent of the lyrical Florentine tradition that passed from Fra Angelico through Fra Filippo and Botticelli. The illegitimate son of Fra Filippo Lippo and the nun Lucrezia Buti, he was born in Prato, where his father was employed, and had his earliest training from Fra Filippo and his assistant, Fra Diamante. In 1472 he was registered in the Florentine painters' guild as an associate of Botticelli and this connection was to have a decisive influence on his art. He may even have assisted Botticelli on the Sistine Chapel wall frescoes in Rome. Back in Florence he received various commissions in the 1480's, including the completion of frescoes left unfinished by Masaccio in Santa Maria del Carmine (1484). It is fairly easy to distinguish his hand in these works by the graceful elongation of his figures, although he adapted his personal style to the dignified monumentality of Masaccio.

LIMBOURG, POL DE. October
(from "Très Riches Heures du Duc de Berri")
Musée Condé, Chantilly

LIMNER, UNKNOWN AMERICAN. De Peyster Boy with Deer
New-York Historical Society, New York

In 1489-90 he decorated a Cardinal's chapel in Santa Maria Sopra Minerva in Rome, where his developed personal style is first fully apparent. His elaborate compositions, nervously agitated figures, bright color and detailed architectural settings are characteristic, and are developed and extended in his final great fresco decoration, the Strozzi chapel in Santa Maria Novella, Florence (1500-02). Among his altarpieces the best known is the Adoration of the Magi of 1496 (Uffizi). Several later altarpieces exhibit the same mannered and nervous style as the late frescoes. (See illustration.)

Lippi, Fra Fillippo (c.1406-69). He stands at the head of a group of early Renaissance Florentines who took into account the formal and technical innovations of Masaccio and the other scientific painters, but who also retained elements of the lyrical, Gothic style of Fra Angelico and his antecedents. Other painters of this group were Francesco Pesellino and Benozzo Gozzoli. Fra Filippo was born in Florence, the son of a butcher, and in 1421 took his vows in the Carmelite order. He is recorded as a member of the Florentine chapter of the order until 1431, but not until 1430 as a painter. After 1431 it is assumed he lived as an independent artist outside the convent. His early works reveal independent handling of various stylistic elements drawn from Masaccio, Masolino and Gentile da Fabriano and his entire output shows a more than general affinity with Fra Angelico. Any parallel drawn with Angelico, however, must begin and end with stylistic considerations, since Fra Filippo's life was the very antithesis of that of the saintly monk from Fiesole.

Fra Filippo was convicted of forgery, was sued for breach of contract, was notoriously tardy at finishing commissions, and, perhaps his most publicized escapade, abducted from a convent of which he was chaplain a nun who ultimately bore him two children, one being the painter Filippino Lippi. Despite these actions, he continued to receive ecclesiastical posts and important commissions. He had powerful friends in the Medici family and was highly respected for his art, the quality of which none could question. He was at work in Padua in 1434 on frescoes in San Antonio (now lost), but his earliest dated work is from 1437, a Madonna in the gallery of Corneto Tarquinia. In 1442 he was appointed by Pope Eugene IV as rector of the church of San Quirico Legnaia and in 1450 became chaplain of a convent in Florence. He was removed from these offices after the forgery conviction, but in 1456 was made chaplain of the convent of Santa Margherita in Prato, where the episode with the nun Lucrezia Buti took place. In 1452 along with Fra Diamante he was already at work on the frescoes in the choir of the cathedral in Prato. But he also undertook numerous outside commissions and only after threats from the Bishop of Prato did he finally finish his work in the choir (1464). The frescoes represent scenes from the lives of St. John the Baptist and St. Stephen, with the four Evangelists represented in the vault. From 1468 to his death in 1469 he worked on frescoes in the vault and apse of the cathedral at Spoleto, representing the Coronation of the Virgin and other scenes from her life and that of Christ. In these Fra Diamante did most of the execution from Fra Filippo's designs. Fra Filippo was buried in Spoleto at the request of local authorities who, according to Vasari, pointed out the great number of illustrious men buried in Florence and the few in Spoleto.

Fra Filippo painted a great many works on panel and the chronology of these is not certain. It is generally believed that works exhibiting the influence of Fra Angelico are relatively early and those of a more architectonic character later. One of his most appealing early works is the Madonna

LIPPI, FILIPPINO. Tobias and the Angel
National Gallery of Art, Kress Collection, Washington, D.C.

121. LIPPI, FRA FILIPPO. Madonna and Child
National Gallery of Art, Kress Collection, Washington, D.C.

Adoring the Sleeping Child (Berlin). From the 1440's is the Coronation of the Virgin in the Uffizi; and in the same collection is the well-known Madonna in profile with angels, a painting that influenced many later artists. Along with Fra Angelico, Fra Filippo instituted the type of the lovely and lyrical Madonna and Child that is unalterably associated with the Florentine Renaissance. His influence was felt throughout the second half of the fifteenth century by many great masters including Botticelli, Ghirlandaio, and even Leonardo da Vinci. (See illustrations, including color plate 121.)

Lippo Memmi (see MEMMI, LIPPO).

Lippo Vanni (see VANNI, LIPPO).

Lissitzky, El (1890-1941). A Russian painter, architect, editor and theoretician. Well known for his work as a Constructivist after World War I. Influenced by the Suprematism (see) of Malevich in 1919, Lissitzky turned increasingly to geometric abstractions in the years that followed, working with van Doesburg and the architect Miës van der Rohe in Holland and Germany. In 1925 he designed the gallery for abstract art in the Hanover Museum, Germany. See CONSTRUCTIVISM, NON-OBJECTIVE ART.

Li Ssu-hsün (see CHINESE PAINTERS: T'ANG DYNASTY).

lithography. Invented in the late eighteenth century, this is a graphic arts technique that simulates the effect of a pencil or crayon drawing. The artist draws with a grease pencil or crayon on a stone surface which is then wet down with water in preparation for printing. When the ink (also greasy) is applied to the stone, it sticks only to the grease-penciled areas and is rejected by the water on the rest of the block. Present-day lithography is also done on specially prepared metal plates, although artists still prefer stone. Example: Daumier prints.

Llanos, Fernando de (to after 1525). Spanish painter. Collaborated with Yanez de la Almedina on twelve panels for the doors of the high altar of Valencia Cathedral (1507-09). As the influence of Leonardo da Vinci is strong here, either of the two may be the "Fernando espagnolo" who assisted Leonardo on the Battle of Anghiari cartoon. De Llanos spent the rest of his career in Murcia.

Lochner, Stephan (active before 1442; d.1451). One of the most charming and gifted of the early painters of Cologne; he came from the Upper Rhine, bought a house in Cologne in 1442 and held office in the city council there. In 1520 Dürer stopped in Cologne and to his careful notation about paying to see Lochner's altarpiece we owe our knowledge of this artist's name. His early style, as shown in the Last Judgment in the Wallraf-Richartz Museum, Cologne, is rather Gothic, with much detail and thin, overgraceful figures, and he may have followed a Netherlands prototype in this painting. His great Adoration of the Magi, chief treasure of the cathedral in Cologne, shows considerable advance in pictorial skill, with an attention to masses, weight of figures, and space, that suggests the influence of Konrad Witz. The Presentation in the Temple (1447, Darmstadt Museum) achieves a notable harmony in the relation between figures. Lochner's style is closely tied to the old tradition of painting in Cologne and was perhaps also influenced by Lucas Moser.

LIPPI, FILIPPO. Madonna and Child
National Gallery, Kress Collection, Washington, D.C.

LOCHNER. Three Saints. National Gallery, London

Though his love for light fresh color, and the sweetness of the faces imbue his work with an appealing religious quality, its strength, especially in the later works, and his interest in purely pictorial problems secure for him a place among the most important early German painters. (See illustration.)

Lomazzo, Giovanni Paolo (1538-1600). Milanese painter, much more famous for his writings on art than for his painting. He studied with his uncle, Gaudenzio Ferrari and later with G. B. della Cerva and is said to have introduced Mannerism (see) to his native city, but he left few works because of an early blindness. In 1584, he published his treatise on painting, sculpture and architecture.

Lombard, Lambert (1506-66). Flemish painter and architect. Traveled in Germany, and studied in Rome, where he knew Vasari. Through his many pupils he did much to popularize the Italian style in Flanders.

Lomi, Artemisia (see GENTILESCHI, ARTEMISIA).

Lomi, Orazio (see GENTILESCHI, ORAZIO).

Longhi (Falca), Alessandro (1733-1813). Born in Venice, son of Pietro, he was a pupil of Nogari and continued in the genre manner of his father, but also did portraits. In his art the Venetian Rococo begins to show evidence of a neo-classicism. He achieved some fame as a writer with his book on the lives of Venetian painters, published in 1762.

Longhi (Falca), Pietro (1702-85). A Venetian genre painter whose scenes of provincial bourgeois society, rendered in a clear and cheerful palette and with vivacity and humor, are charming commentaries on contemporary life. Unlike Hogarth, he was not moralistic, but treated social decadence with an air of pleasant raillery similar to that of the Venetian writer Carlo Goldoni, with whom he was often compared. The son of a goldsmith, he worked with his father, but later turned to painting, studying first with Antonio Balestra in Venice and later with G. M. Crespi in Bologna. His early works under the influence of Balestra are religious, eclectic and somber, but the teachings of Crespi changed his palette and directed him toward genre painting. In 1734 he decorated the Palazzo Sagredo in Venice with The Fall of Giants. With the growth in popularity of genre painting in Venice, he became its leading exponent. The problem of attribution of his work is far from being resolved. (See color plate 122.)

López y Portaña, Vicente (1772-1850). Spanish painter and designer for copper engravings. Successor to Goya as Madrid's fashionable painter and portraitist. In style he practiced the academic principles of Mengs, with a certain Baroque flair.

Lorenzetti, Ambrogio (active 1319-48). Sienese painter, a brother of Pietro Lorenzetti (see) and possibly his pupil. First mentioned in 1324, though a Madonna panel at Vico l'Abate now universally attributed to him is dated 1319. Probably in 1331 he painted frescoes of St. Louis Received by Boniface VIII and the Martyrdom of Franciscan Monks at Tana in the church of San Francesco in Siena. In 1332 he worked in Florence and in 1334 matriculated in the guild of doctors and apothecaries there. He received a commission for work at Cortona in 1335, of which nothing remains. The same year he is again at Siena and apparently settled there. The works for which he is best known, the Allegories of Good and Evil Government in the Siena Palazzo Pubblico, were painted from 1337 to 1339. It is presumed that he and his brother Pietro both died in the plague of 1348. Among Ambrogio's important but undated works are a polyptych of the Madonna and Saints in the Siena gallery and a Majestas in the gallery of Massa Marittima. The commission for the famous "government" frescoes was apparently the attempt of a corrupt government to justify and glorify itself. Ambrogio seized the opportunity to express himself in landscape, genre and classical forms very forward-looking for the time. His style is dependent on that of his brother Pietro, who in turn was indebted to Duccio. Both Lorenzetti infused the Ducciesque forms with a sculptural vigor derived from the sculptor Giovanni Pisano, and advanced the pictorial conception of rational space in Sienese painting. Their art was Gothic in

122. LONGHI, PIETRO. Fortune-Teller
National Gallery, London

LORENZETTI, AMBROGIO. Madonna and Child
National Gallery of Art, Kress Collection, Washington, D.C.

its narrative and emotional expression. Of the two, Ambrogio was the more refined and lyrical in style. His presence for a time in Florence may account for some of the Sienese influence discernible in the art of the Florentine Bernardo Daddi and other Giotto followers. Both Ambrogio and Pietro were exceedingly popular in their day and profoundly influenced later Sienese painting. (See illustration.)

Lorenzetti, Pietro (active 1305-48). Sienese painter, a brother of Ambrogio Lorenzetti (see), possibly his teacher and generally believed to have been the older of the two. Little is recorded of Pietro's activity up to 1320, when he was commissioned to paint a large polyptych for the bishop of Arezzo (now in the Pieve di S. Maria there). In 1326 he was paid for a Madonna and Saints for the Opera del Duomo, Siena, and he signed the Madonna in Sant' Ansano, Dofana, in 1328. Probably in the late 1320's he and his pupils executed a fresco cycle including scenes from the Passion in the Lower Church of San Francesco at Assisi. Documents of 1329-35 show him at work in Siena; in 1340 he signed a Madonna now in the Uffizi, and 1342 is the year of his last dated work, the Birth of the Virgin now in the Opera del Duomo, Siena. He probably died during the plague of 1348. Undated frescoes by him are in the Servi Church at Siena. Pietro's art owes much to Duccio in its early phase, though the evidence is insufficient to say that he was Duccio's pupil. The voluminous nature of his forms allies his art with that of the sculptor Giovanni Pisano, while in technique he is related to Simone Martini. He shares with Simone the Gothic tendency toward emotional exaggeration, but his execution is rougher and more hasty, and his forms much heavier and less lyrical. (See illustration.)

Lorenzo da Viterbo (c.1437-after 1476). Italian. The most important local artist of the fifteenth century in Viterbo, he executed his chief work, a fresco cycle on the Life of the Virgin in Sta. Maria della Verità (now a museum) in Viterbo. The major influences on his style came from Florence and the Umbro-Florentines.

Lorenzo di Credi (see CREDI, LORENZO DI).

Lorenzo di Niccolò Gerini (active 1392-1411). Florentine painter; a follower of his father Niccolò di Pietro and also influenced by Spinello Aretino and by Lorenzo Monaco. He assisted his father at Prato, and between 1399 and 1401 he executed with his father and Spinello an altarpiece of the Coronation of the Virgin (now in the Florence Academy). He signed a panel of St. Bartholomew (1401) in the gallery of San Gimignano. In 1402 he painted an altarpiece for San Marco (now in San Domenico, Cortona) and a Madonna triptych in the church of Terenzano. Lorenzo was a skilled draughtsman and colorist. His compositions were sober and monumental until he adopted the decorative Gothic manner of Lorenzo Monaco. (See illustration.)

Lorenzo di Pietro (see VECCHIETTA).

LORENZETTI, PIETRO. St. Catherine
Metropolitan Museum of Art, New York

LORENZO DI NICCOLO GERINI
Madonna and Child Enthroned with Four Saints
Oratorio di Santa Maria delle Grazie, Stia

Lorenzo Monaco (c.1370-1425). Florentine painter. Before he became a Camaldolite monk in 1391, his lay name was Piero di Giovanni. It is believed he came to Florence from Siena, where he may have been trained by Bartolo di Fredi. In 1392 he was sub-deacon in the Convento degli Angeli in Florence. He painted panels, frescoes and book illuminations. His earliest known work is a damaged fresco of the Lamentation (c.1395) in the cloister of the Oblati, Florence, and his most important work in fresco is the cycle of scenes from the life of the Virgin in Santa Trinità, executed 1420-24. His two best known altarpieces are the Coronation of the Virgin (1413) and the Adoration of the Magi (1420-22), both in the Uffizi. He did many book illuminations between 1409 and 1413, examples of which are preserved in Florence. His art belongs to the late fourteenth-century Gothic tradition of Siena and Florence, which is transmitted by him to the fifteenth century and comes to flower in his presumed pupil Fra Angelico. His elongated figures are animated by the decorative sway of drapery common to the Gothic style, but they are grouped and articulated in rigidly horizontal compositions with receding architectural or landscape backgrounds. His color is luminous and decorative. (See illustrations, including color plate 123.)

Lorenzo Veneziano (active 1356-79). Venetian painter, possibly a pupil of Master Paolo; chiefly known through several signed and dated panel paintings in Venice, Padua and Vicenza. He belongs to the beginning of the Venetian movement away from Byzantine style.

Lorjou, Bernard (1908-). Self-taught French Expressionist. The solidity of his forms suggests the tradition of Courbet but the singing violence of color brings to mind the influence of Van Gogh. The peasant-like awkwardness and power of his style recall similar effects in the work of Gromaire.

Lorrain, Claude (Claude Gellée) (1600-82). Founder of the romantic or picturesque tradition in French landscape painting. In fact the work "picturesque" was coined by the English to describe effects in nature similar to those observed in impressionistic paintings of the type of Claude's. Claude was a worshipper of classical antiquity, and he associated with Poussin in Italy as they pursued that ideal together. At the same time he anticipated several aspects of nineteenth-century Impressionism. Sandrart tells us that "Claude lay before daylight and into the night in the fields so that he learned to depict the morning and the evening glow with great naturalness." He apparently sketched and in some cases may have painted before nature. He studied nature with

LORENZO MONACO. Madonna and Child with Angels
Metropolitan Museum of Art, New York

123. LORENZO MONACO. Coronation of the Virgin (center panel)
National Gallery, London

reference to color, atmosphere and changing light conditions and transferred these effects to his canvases by a shimmering technique that approximated Impressionism while still retaining the solidity of forms. His drawings, especially in wash, are constructed of veils of chiaroscuro patterned like those of Chinese landscape painters; and they come even closer to Impressionist dissolution of form than do his paintings.

In contrast to his learned friend Poussin, Claude was virtually illiterate, and as such resembled the "naive eye" with which the later nineteenth century approached nature. Born in Lorraine, he was an orphan at twelve years. He assisted his brother, a wood engraver, and was brought to Rome by a merchant. Moving to Naples he there learned painting from the German Wols. Back in Rome he was apprenticed to Agostino Tossi, a painter of harbor scenes whose style reflects the influence of his friend Paul Brill. In 1625 Claude worked for a while in Venice and returned to Lorraine. After two years' vicissitudes he came back permanently to Rome. His earliest known paintings are two battles (Louvre) of about 1631. There followed a series of etchings based on studies of the Roman Campagna. Of the two landscape styles forming in Italy, Claude was influenced more by the northern tradition of Brill and Elsheimer than by the constructions of the Italian Carracci (which influenced Poussin.) This can be clearly seen in his early etchings. These presented exciting romantic incidents such as the Storm (1630), or Elsheimer types such as the Flight into Egypt. Many of his paintings can be dated by means of his *Liber Veritatis*, a collection of about two hundred drawings made by Claude after his finished pictures. It was once thought that the publication was to prevent counterfeiting of his landscapes (which started early) but it is now assumed that he did this to preserve for himself the motifs of paintings sold abroad. The book was begun by Claude in the 1640's when he was painting on commission for the King of Spain. It was obtained (in part) by the Duke of Devonshire and engraved in 1770.

The style of Claude's painting shows little development except for a certain broadening with maturity, under the influence of Poussin. Unlike the complex pictorial structure of Poussin, Claude organized simply and by stereotyped formulas. The space of his paintings seems to be constructed as a huge box, marked in its recession by a series of planar elements parallel to the canvas. A classical sense of measure can be felt in the firm foreground platform and the stagelike elements which intrude at intervals from the sides. Where possible he employed light-dark alternations receding on grass or on water, as in the Embarcation of St. Ursula (London). Many of his designs are based on crossed diagonals drawn from the corners, as in the Embarcation of the Queen of Sheba (London) or on such a system doubled in reference to a central object, as in Landscape with Apollo Temple (Rome). He delighted in painting into the sun, thus disembodying the solid forms of nature and turning trees into a filmy radiance, e.g., Hagar's Banishment (Munich). His reliance on light and atmosphere as vehicles of expression is demonstrated by the series-paintings he did showing several times of day. Examples of this are the Morning and Evening (Hermitage), which also have religious titles. Figure painting did not interest Claude, and he practiced the Flemish system of delegating that portion of his canvas to assistants. Among those he so employed were Filippo Lauri, Jan Meil, Jacques Courtois and Francesco Allegri. (See illustrations, including color plate 124.)

Lo Spagnolo (see CRESPI, GIUSEPPE MARIA).

Lotto, Lorenzo (1480-1556). Italian painter born in Venice of a Bergamese family, he traveled a great deal and was active in many places—Venice, Treviso, Recanati, Rome, Bergamo, and Ancona. He belongs to the great tradition of Venetian High Renaissance painting, developing in his later works into the realistic proto-Baroque. He was highly regarded by Titian and attracted the young Caravaggio. He was a pupil of Alvise Vivarini and his earlier works (1500-08) exhibit the influence of his master as well as of Bellini and

LORRAIN, CLAUDE. Embarkation of the Queen of Sheba
National Gallery, London

124. LORRAIN, CLAUDE. Landscape with Nymphs and Satyrs Dancing. Toledo Museum of Art, Libbey Collection

Antonello da Messina. The paintings of his Roman period (1509-13) reflect the impact of Raphael's art. Then, back in Venice and Bergamo (1513-25) he produced many great altars which show a new dependence upon Correggio. In Treviso (1525-48) he developed his ripe style under the influence of Titian, Giorgione, and Palma Vecchio, a dramatic monumental manner moving from the classical richness of the High Renaissance to the broad freedom of the early Baroque. It was during this period that he also painted his great portraits, with their profound psychological insight and beautiful pigmentation. In the last years of his life in Ancona (1549-56), his art exhibited a growing religiosity and a turn to an austere monochromatic scale. He died in a monastery at Loreto. (See illustration.)

Louvre Museum, Paris. One of the greatest art collections in the world, containing works from all periods in almost every medium: outstanding examples of Egyptian, Mesopotamian, Greek (the Venus of Milo, the Victory of Samothrace), Roman, medieval, and Renaissance (Mona Lisa and the Madonna of the Rocks by Leonardo, Concert in the Open Air by Giorgione, Titian's Allegory of Alfonso d'Avalos, Raphael's La Belle Jardinière, Cimabue's Virgin Enthroned; and equally significant works from the Dutch, Flemish (Ruben's series on the Life of Marie de Médicis), French, Spanish, and German. There are also magnificent examples from the nineteenth century and up to the threshold of modern times.

Luco di Tommé di Nute (active 1355-89). Listed in the painters' guild in Siena in 1355, and served the republican government as a councillor in 1373, 1375 and 1379. He signed and dated three extant works: a Crucifixion in the Pisa gallery (1366), a polyptych in the Siena gallery (1367), and another in the gallery at Rieti (1370). Another polyptych is in the Siena gallery; and of other works attributed to him the most important is an Assumption at Yale University. His style, stemming from that of Lippo Memmi, also owes a great deal to the Lorenzetti and to Simone Martini. Hard drawing, angular and wooden figures, and the rejection of rational space in composition characterize his work.

Lucas y Padilla, Eugenio (1824-70). Spanish romantic painter. Imitator of Goya and Velázquez, but not without merit of his own. Lucas took lessons at the Academy, but was mostly self-taught in the Prado. His colorful genre scenes went unnoticed or were attributed to the masters he imitated until long after his death when collectors "discovered" him.

Luce, Maximilien (1858-1941). French painter, engraver and journalist of the Left. He came into the modern movement via Neo-Impressionism and through Pissarro and Signac. Luce was well known in French art circles of the late nineteenth century for his anarchist sympathies and during the 1894 bombings in Paris he was imprisoned, following the famous "Trial of the Thirty." After his visit to the Van Gogh

LOTTO. Portrait of a Man
Isaac Delgado Museum of Art, Kress Collection, New Orleans

LUKS. The Spielers
Addison Gallery of American Art, Phillips Academy, Andover

Borinage region in 1896 he turned to industrial themes, dropped the Divisionist technique and utilized broad simple planes of color.

Luciani, Sebastiano (see SEBASTIANO DEL PIOMBO).

Luini Bernardino (c.1475-1531/2). The most important and most gifted of the group that sprang up around Leonardo da Vinci during his activity in Milan. Luini's art shows traces of the older Milanese tradition of Borgognone and a similarity to his conservative contemporary, Bramantino. But close contact with Leonardo is reflected in his neutral coloration, soft and carefully graded modeling, compositional use of gesture, and the well-known, mannered smile common in the painting of all Leonardo followers. An early fresco decoration for a private villa, with many scenes from classical mythology, is in the Brera. Later frescoes, for the most part less involved than those of Leonardo, are in Santa Maria dei Miracoli at Saronno (c.1525), Santa Maria degli Angeli at Lugano (1529), and San Maurizio in Milan (1529-30). An altarpiece of the Entombment of St. Catherine is in the Brera. (See color plate 125.)

Luks, George Benjamin (1867-1933). American genre painter, a member of the original Ashcan School (see). Born in Williamsport, Pa., the son of a doctor and a mother who had some talent as a painter, he studied at the Pennsylvania Academy of Fine Arts, and in Düsseldorf, Paris, and London. On his return to the U.S., he became a newspaper illustrator in Philadelphia where he met Henri, Glackens, Sloan, and Shinn, who were later to form the nucleus of the Ashcan School and the Eight. After his adventures in Cuba (1895-96), where he was sent by the Philadelphia *Bulletin* to cover an insurrection and where he was condemned to death, he came to New York and worked for the *Herald* and the *World*. His paintings of life in the coal mines and on New York's East Side were not well received and, in 1907, when one of his pictures was rejected by the National Academy of Design it led to the exhibition of the Eight. He was active in many progresive art movements and organizations, including the Association of American Painters and Sculptors; taught at the Art Students League, and, after a dispute, founded his own school. His early paintings show the influence of Munich and Duveneck rather than Düsseldorf, and, under the influence of Henri, his style tended toward the grey tonalities of Manet and Hals. With the other realists of the period, he painted the drama of city life with vigor and a kind of breathless excitement. The lustiness of his style is best expressed in such works as The Spielers (see illustration) and The Wrestlers (Boston), both done in 1905. His later works became more high-keyed, muscular, superficial and uneven. In these later years he did, besides many hurried portraits, a few fine character studies, such as his Otis Skinner (Phillips Collection).

lunette. A curved or rounded window or wall space.

Lurçat, Jean (1892-). French painter and tapestry designer of note who came into the modern movement via Cézanne; after World War I he turned to a kind of decorative Fauve expression and later found this eminently suitable for tapestry design. During the course of his travels in Spain and the Sahara in the 1920's, he arrived at a conception of broad arid landscapes with a poetry and mood of their own; these have also been incorporated into the modern form of tapestry which Lurçat has been projecting since 1915. (See illustration.)

Lu T'an-wei (see CHINESE PAINTERS: THE SIX DYNASTIES).

Luteri (see DOSSI).

Luxembourg Museum, Paris. At one time the museum of modern art for Paris, the number of works of art it contains have been reduced since the French Senate moved into the building. The more modern paintings have been taken to the Musée d'art moderne, and only the more conservative nineteenth-century works remain.

M

Mabuse, Jan (see GOSSAERT).

McCulloch, Alan McLeod (1907-). A leading Australian art critic, draughtsman, painter and writer. Born in Melbourne, he spent eighteen years working in a bank, studying at Melbourne art schools at night. He subsequently traveled extensively in Europe and America. As art critic for the Melbourne *Herald*, a foremost sponsor of art, he holds perhaps the most influential critical position in Australia. His best-known paintings are Expressionistic interpretations of Italian subjects.

Macdonald-Wright, Stanton (1890-). Contemporary American painter born in Charlottsville, Va. Trained at the Ecole des Beaux-Arts, the Académie Julian and the Sorbonne, he developed in 1912 along with Morgan Russell the abstract style of Synchromism. About 1920, he returned to a more representational art influenced by Chinese painting and philosophy. For many years he has been teaching at the University of California at Los Angeles.

Mc Evoy, Ambrose (1878-1927). British portraitist, specializing in elegant women. As in Gainsborough, whom McEvoy greatly admired, his sitters have an air of inherited refinement. He used the former's supposed method of a recognizable face with a superimposed sensitive expression. The fluidity of his style made him particularly effective as a watercolorist.

McFee, Henry Lee (1886-1953). American still-life painter born in Missouri. He studied at the School of Fine Arts in St. Louis, later in Pittsburgh, and then with Birge Harrison at Woodstock, N.Y., where he settled. His early work, under the influence of Andrew Dasburg, was Cubist in character; his later work became more conservative.

McGuiness, Nora (1905-). Contemporary Irish painter who delights in rendering the *fauve* richness of her native Donegal country. Her art is primarily coloristic and atmospheric and distinctly representational in approach. In recent years she has become well known for paintings of the people and streets of Dublin, delighting especially in the faded charm of old Georgian houses in that city.

Machiavelli, Zanobi (1418-after 1476). A few signed works by this little-known Florentine painter reveal him to have been a follower, perhaps a pupil, of Pesellino, and later to have been influenced by Benozzo Gozzoli. His style is within the lyrical trend of Florentine Renaissance art stemming from Fra Angelico. Signed works by him are in museums in Berlin, London, Dublin and Dijon.

Mac Iver, Loren (1909-). A contemporary American painter of poetic city genre in the Neo-Romantic vein. Born in New York City, she studied at the National Academy of Design and the Art Students League, and later worked on the W.P.A. She has done illustration and designing and painted several murals for steamships. Her earlier subjects were largely perceptive transformations of fragments of reality, but since about 1949 her scope has widened to include large-scale romantic cityscapes.

Macke, August (1887-1914). Member of the German Blue Rider group formed in Munich in 1911. Macke began as a student of traditional and industrial art, made a first trip to Paris and then went to study with Lovis Corinth, the German Impressionist, in Berlin. A second Parisian trip followed in 1908; in 1909-10 while staying at the Tegernsee he met Marc, Kandinsky and Jawlensky, future members of the Blue Rider circle. Macke and Marc became very close friends, going to Paris together in 1912, where the impact of Delaunay's art became crucial for the group. In 1914 Macke made a trip with Paul Klee to Kairouan in North Africa; he joined the army soon after and was killed almost immediately. With his gentle, dreamy women and children going about their daily tasks, his simply abstracted forms, colorfully presented and semi-Cubist in character, suggesting again the influence of Delaunay. Macke is the poet of the Blue Rider group. See EXPRESSIONISM. (See illustration.)

LURÇAT. Bather. Collection T. Catesby Jones

Madonna of the Rocks by Leonardo da Vinci (see).

MACKE. Girl Reading on a Blue Sofa
Private Collection, Germany

125. LUINI. Portrait of a Lady
National Gallery of Art, Mellon Collection, Washington, D.C.

Madrazo y Agudo, José de (1781-1859). Spanish engraver and painter; pupil of David in France, Madrazo practiced a cold Neo-Classical style as seen in his Death of Viriatus (Prado). He was director of the Academy and of the National Museum.

Maeck, Philippe (1927-). Belgian-born artist who emigrated to Brazil seeking a new outlook. His designs are Cubist-derived and reminiscent of Klee; the abstract patterns are overlaid with vivid tropical colors and have the added element of mood.

Maella, Mariano Salvador de (1739-1819). Spanish academic painter of history, landscape and portrait. Studied at the Madrid Academy and in Rome, and on his return worked under Mengs. He survived as court painter throughout the political changes of the reigns of Charles II, Charles IV, Joseph Bonaparte and Ferdinand VII. His portraits of Charles II and IV are in the National Museum, Mexico.

Maes, Nicolas (1634-93). Dutch painter of portraits and genre. He was a pupil of Rembrandt in Amsterdam and under that influence developed a strong style and painted excellent pictures related to those his master made in the late 1640's. The last decades of his life, however, were devoted to the production in quantity of fashionable portraits, mannered and superficial in comparison with his earlier work.

Mafai, Mario (1902-). Italian painter and member with Scipione of the Roman school; also reacted against the dry classicism of the Novecento art of the 1920's—in his case with a delicate and sensitive treatment of flower subjects as well as themes taken from demolition scenes in the streets of Rome.

Magdalen Master (active second half of 13th century). Florentine painter. A number of panels exhibiting the characteristics of one hand have been grouped under this name, which stems from an altar frontal representing S. Mary Magdalen (Florence Academy).

Maggiotto (Domenico Fedeli) (1713-94). Venetian painter of mythological and religious pictures, he also did moralizing genre studies. Born in Venice, he was a pupil and follower of Piazzetta, with whose works his are often confused.

Magic Realism. A naturalistic or photographic kind of twentieth-century painting in which the artist is at great pains to reproduce the elements of nature as carefully as possible but in which he also creates an emotional tension and a sense of suspense. It may be exemplified by the valori plastici (see) painters of Italy, the New Objectivity painters of Germany, such as George Grosz and Otto Dix, a good many of the modern Netherlands painters, and some of the social painters of the United States during the depression of the 1930's. In each country the components vary to some extent but it is important to note that the movement has an international flavor.

Magnasco, Alessandro (called Lissandrino) (677-1749). Italian genre painter born in Genoa. He painted scenes of popular life, soldiers, courtesans, street-singers, alchemists, mountebanks, and monks—all with a wild romantic fantasy. Continuing in the tradition of Salvator Rosa and influenced by the picaresque world of Callot, his wild and sinister landscapes are peopled by caricatured figures in violent action. His art seems to express the morbid fervor of the Counter Reformation, to depict men as the victims of a storm-tossed world. His style is a transition from the serious and sober Baroque to the fantasy and vivacity of the Rococo. His original, exaggerated manner of *al tocco* (free brushstroke) rendering influenced Guardi. The son of a painter, Stefano, he studied in Milan with Filippo Abbiati, but was influenced first by Morazzone, Tintoretto, and Bassano. He worked for Gian Gastone, the last Medici duke, in Florence (1703-10). and in Milan (1711-31) and Genoa (1731-49). He is said also to have been a portrait painter but no portraits of his have been identified. (See color plate 126).

Magritte, René (1898-). Belgian Surrealist painter. He participated in the French Surrealist movement during 1928-30 but has remained entirely personal in his interpretation of the spiritual meaning of this art form. Instead of "following" any of the leaders of Surrealism, he has evolved an entirely fresh kind of symbolism that brings his art within the general area. (See illustration.)

Maids of Honor (Las Meninas) by Diego Velázquez (see).

Mailly, Simon de (see CHALONS, SIMON DE).

Mainardi, Sebastiano (active by 1482; d.1513). A little-

MAGRITTE. The Eye. Museum of Modern Art, New York

126. MAGNASCO. The Baptism of Christ. National Gallery of Art, Kress Collection, Washington, D.C.

documented but prolific Florentine painter known chiefly as a close follower and shop assistant of Domenico Ghirlandaio (see), whose sister he married. His earliest works, especially the dated Annunciation (1482) in the Collegiata, San Gimignano, show a strong influence of Verrocchio and in later works that of Ghirlandaio. He painted many charming and wistful Madonnas and Nativities, especially in the tondo (circular) form, and in his production appropriated some of the characteristics of Filippino Lippi's style. (See illustration.)

Maino (Mayno), Fray Juan Bautista (before 1586-1649). Lombard painter active in Spain. Originally Caravaggesque, in Spain he studied with El Greco and was a friend of Velázquez. There resulted a style heavy in form but light in atmospheric qualities, owing mostly to Velázquez. His Reconquest of Bahía del Salvador (Prado) is in subject matter an excellent example of the spirit of the conquistadors.

makimono. A horizontal scroll painting that is intended to be seen while sitting at a low table. It should be unrolled slowly from right to left, about a foot at a time. For mounting and care, see CHINA, DEVELOPMENT OF PAINTING IN.

Malbone, Edward Greene (1777-1807). America's outstanding miniaturist. An excellent draughtsman and original composer, he painted with simplicity and directness, in fresh, delicate color harmonies. Born in Rhode Island, he died prematurely in Georgia. His earliest training was with Samuel King in Boston, and he began his independent career in Providence at the age of seventeen. He worked in Boston, New York, Philadelphia, and Charleston before going to England with Allston to study at the Royal Academy. He returned to continue his career in the U.S. in 1801.

Malevich, Kasimir (1878-1935). Russian painter and theoretician who began as a Fauve painter in Moscow in 1908-10. He went on to Cubism in the next few years, and founded the Suprematist movement in Russia in 1913. Suprematism (see) was a non-objective (see) formulation dominated by pure geometric forms. Since it was original with Malevich, he occupies an important historical position. He remained in Russia throughout his life. (See illustration.)

Malouel, Jean (d.1419). Flemish painter. He was in Paris as painter to Isabeau de Bavière, and in 1397 succeeded Jean de Beaumetz as court painter to the Dukes of Burgundy, Philippe le Hardi and Jean sans Peur. In 1398 he was commissioned to paint five altarpieces for the Chartreuse de Champmol. One of these, finished by Henri Bellechose (see) is apparently the Holy Communion and the Martyrdom of St. Dionysius now in the Louvre. Malouel may also have started the large circular Pietà in the Louvre. He is known to have painted the statues of the Well of Moses and to have executed a portrait of Jean sans Peur for the King of Portugal. He is thus one of the oldest panel painters in northern Europe. (See illustration.)

Malraux, André (1895-). Distinguished French novelist and critic originally trained in Oriental languages and archaeology. Active in the Chinese revolution in the 1920's,

MAINARDI. Portrait of a Girl. National Gallery, London

MALEVICH. Suprematist Composition
Museum of Modern Art, New York

MALOUEL and BELLECHOSE. Martyrdom of St. Denis
Louvre, Paris

the Spanish Civil War in the 1930's and World War II, Malraux has also found time for a number of highly esteemed novels as well as two searching works in the criticism of art: the *Psychologie de l'art* (published in English in 1949 as two volumes, *Museum Without Walls* and *The Creative Act)*, and *The Voices of Silence,* 1953.

Mander, Karel van (1548-1606). Dutch painter, poet, and biographer of artists. He studied with Lukas de Heere in Ghent and then with Pieter Vlerick. In 1573 he went to Italy, pursuing his studies in Rome. He returned to the Low Countries about 1577. His style is based on the Flemish and Italian versions of Mannerism (see), with a clear influence from the school of Fontainebleau, but he marks a transition in his later works to the trend toward realism. His biographies of Dutch and Flemish artists constitute one of our best sources for studying the painting of the Netherlands.

Manessier, Alfred (1911-). French painter and decorator who, under the dual influence of Cubism and Expressionism, has produced an art of deliberately religious meaning dedicated to the inner spirit rather than the appearance of man.

Manet, Edouard (1832-83). Precursor of French Impressionism (see). Manet's constant exploration of new modes of vision brought the first clear break with the Renaissance manner of presenting nature. His re-examination of the Old Masters made possible the advent of Impressionism, with which he associated himself intellectually. Of wealthy conservative background, a student for six years of the academician Couture, Manet seemed to be constantly seeking respectability for his painting, but instead he figured in some of the most sensational incidents of the nineteenth-century salons.

It was after considerable vacillation that this sophisticate entered Couture's studio. He was constantly at odds with his teacher because of his loose technique of painting, but from Couture he gained his exquisite handling of tones. This was augmented by study of the Venetians, Velázquez and the Dutch school, both in the Louvre and abroad. In 1859, however, his Absinthe Drinker was refused by the Salon and a private showing provoked much criticism. Apparently a public conditioned to Ingres' classically-derived style could not endure the stiff self-conscious poses and the sober, flatly silhouetted forms of Manet's art, and the concentration on painterly structure at the cost of story ran against recent Romantic tendencies. Even Courbet's canvases seemed narrative in comparison with this new art. His Spanish subjects of 1861, the

MANET. Luncheon on the Grass. Louvre, Paris

Guitar Player, etc., were a success, but at the Salon des Refusés of 1863 he exhibited his Déjeuner sur l'herbe (Luncheon on the Grass) and in 1865 his Olympia. Both provoked such scandal that in 1865 Manet retired to Spain in confusion.

Both these paintings had been studiously based on Renaissance prototypes. The Déjeuner in both form and mood was suggested to him while he was copying Giorgione's Concert in the Louvre. He worked on it for a year. The noncommital confrontation of nude women and clothed gentlemen in a park was too much for contemporary mores. And the concentration of the artist on the mode of painting to the point that the still life of discarded clothes competed in importance with the figures: this was unintelligible to public and critics. Then in the Olympia the hard profile of the nude body and the insinuating form of the black cat came as a shock to Western art. Such papery forms, solid color areas and courtesan themes were familiar however in Japanese prints. These were just in vogue and Manet was to use them in 1868 in his portrait of Zola, who had come to his defense.

Manet became the rallying point for a group of artists at the Café Guerbois, out of which grew the Impressionist movement. He staged a one-man show at the Exposition of 1867, but with little success. The Franco-Prussian war intervened and then in 1873 he scored a triumph with the Bon Bock (Philadelphia), a Halsian picture. However, his style was already changing toward the fresh palette of the Impressionists. He never deserted the Salons to take part in their group exhibitions, nor did he accept fully the open-air painting, but such canvases as In the Boat (1874, Metropolitan) and Argenteuil (1875) used the new palette. At this time his work also shows the clipped composition of the Impressionists that seems to snatch a fragment out of real life. However, his forms remained fairly tactile, and in subject and treatment he owed more to Degas perhaps than to the other Impressionists. Scenes in restaurants and bistros culminated in the great masterpiece of his career, The Bar at the Folies Bergères (London), exhibited the year before his death. In this he retreated somewhat from his Impressionism to the earlier pursuit of the delectable in painting. Our minds are muddled, our senses titillated by the curious perspective world that confronts us on the canvas. That it, and all art, is to be *enjoyed* and not understood, Manet tells us by sionists that seems to snatch a fragment out of real life. a vintage. (See illustrations, including color plate 127.)

Manetti, Ruttilio (1571-1639). Born in Siena, a pupil of Vanni and influenced by Salembeni, he became later (after 1615) a follower of Caravaggio. His early works are superficial, but he developed into the best, next to Gentileschi, of the Tuscan Baroque painters of the seventeenth century. His paintings are vigorous, with crude but lively color and violent chiaroscuro.

MANET. Guitar Player. Metropolitan Museum of Art, New York

Manfredi, Bartolommeo (c.1580-1620). Born in Ustiano near Mantua, he studied with Roncalli-Pomarancio, and came to Rome between 1610 and 1619. His art developed out of the second period of Caravaggio's style, and is characterized by strong modeling, bright colors, and an emphasis on genre. He used religious scenes as an excuse for genre painting and had a great influence on Honthorst and the Utrecht school. He left no signed works and attributions to him are difficult.

Mani (see Persian Painters: Sassanian Period).

Maniera. An Italian late sixteenth-century style of painting derived from Mannerism (see). It was a transformation of the spiritual and intellectual attitude of the latter into a decorative and aesthetic formula, utilizing its exaggerations and distortions for purely formal ends. It had its origins in Rome among the followers of the Mannerists and spread from there north via Fontainebleau. Among its major exponents were Primaticcio, Nicolò dell' Abbate, the Zuccari, the Cavaliere d'Arpino and Pomarancio. It was especially against this style that the Early Baroque of Caravaggio and the classicism of the Carracci was a revolt.

Mannerism. An early sixteenth-century style originally described as a perversion of the art of the Italian High Renaissance under the impact of the North. It is now identified as an important and conscious revolt against classicism. It is characterized by a return to spirituality and emotionalism, sometimes even Gothic in feeling, a revolt against the ordered

127. MANET. In a Boat
Metropolitan Museum of Art, New York

rationality, normalcy and naturalness of the High Renaissance. This result was an elegant and complex intellectuality, a sinuous linearity, an ambiguity of space, a distortion and exaggeration of proportion and movement, and a pronounced aestheticism for its own sake. The movement had its first expression in Florence about 1520 with Pontormo and Rosso, and developed in Rome, where the latter met Parmigianino in 1524. After the Sack of Rome in 1527 and the dispersal of artists, Parmigianino spread the style in northern Italy and Rosso brought it to Fontainebleau in France. Its origins are varied and its germs are discernible among many High Renaissance artists but its major sources were Michelangelo and Dürer. The leading members of the second generation of Mannerism included Bronzino, Vasari and Salviati. It influenced many artists, among them Tintoretto, El Greco, and a great many in northern Europe. Translated into a decorative style, it became known as the Maniera (see).

Mannozzi, Giovanni (called Giovanni da San Giovanni) (1592-1636). Florentine painter born in San Giovanni Valdarno, he studied with Matteo Rosselli and was active in Florence and Rome. A popular painter in the academic tradition, he was influenced by Caravaggio and may have in turn influenced Cortona.

Mansueti, Giovanni (c.1470-1530). Venetian adherent of Gentile Bellini, he marks a transition between Bellini and Carpaccio.His chief works, representing Miracles of the Reliquary of the Holy Cross, are in the Venice Academy.

Mansur (see INDIAN PAINTERS: JAHANGIR PERIOD).

Mantegna, Andrea (1431-1506). Most important north Italian painter outside Venice in the fifteenth century. His skill in perspective and draughtsmanship, and his eager study of classical antiquity ally him with the most progressive tendencies in Italian painting of his day. His style is thoroughly north Italian, but contains Florentine elements transmitted to Padua by the visits of Fra Filippo Lippi, Uccello and the sculptor Donatello. He was a friend of the Florentine architect Leon Battista Alberti. At the same time Venetian influence is not lacking in his work, particularly that of Jacopo Bellini, whose daughter he married.

Mantegna was born in Isola di Carturo between Vicenza and Padua. As a small child he was adopted by Francesco Squarcione, the head of a painting workshop who is known to have introduced many painters to the works of classical antiquity. The famous frescoes of the Eremitani church at Padua were executed during 1449-54. In 1454 he married Nicolosia, Jacopo Bellini's daughter, and in 1456 dissolved a contract that had bound him to Squarcione. This disagreement was possibly precipitated by a commission of that year to paint the well-known altarpiece for San Zeno Maggiore in Verona, which was finished in 1459. The major triptych sections representing the Madonna and Saints are still in San Zeno, and the predella panels are in the Louvre and the museum at Tours. From 1458 on, Mantegna was in the service of Lodovico Gonzaga, whose ducal court was at Mantua, and earned a title of nobility. In the next decade he became known as a humanist and scholar of antique art. He was a frequent guest at the court, became a friend of Alberti, who designed the church of Sant' Andrea in Mantua in 1472, and was sought out by collectors of antiquities for his opinions. Of the many fresco decorations he undertook for the Gonzaga only one remains, the bridal chamber of the Castello di Corte at Mantua (1468-74). Plans for the decoration of the theater in the same palace were not carried out, but the cartoons for them, nine scenes of the Triumph of Julius Caesar, are preserved in the British royal collection at Hampton Court. This work (1482-92) was interrupted by a trip to Rome at the request of Pope Innocent VIII to decorate a chapel (since destroyed) in 1488-90. Contact with antiquities in Rome affected Mantegna's art, and the results are apparent in the Triumph scenes done after his return to Mantua. Cardinal Sigismondo Gonzaga had given Mantegna

128. MANTEGNA. St. Jerome in the Wilderness. Museu de Arte, São Paulo

a family chapel in Sant' Andrea, and in 1504 the painter made a testament in which he left funds for the decoration of this chapel; part of this plan he actually carried out himself (the Holy Family). He was buried in the chapel.

Mantegna's most important works are the two great fresco decorations in Padua and Mantua. In World War II the entire apse containing Mantegna's frescoes in the Paduan church of the Eremitani was destroyed, one of the greatest art losses suffered in Italy. Two sections that had been removed to Venice are preserved, the Martyrdom of St. Christopher (already in a damaged condition), and the Assumption, which was probably painted mostly by Niccolò Pizzolo, a joint contractor with Mantegna in this decoration. The frescoes represented scenes from the lives of St. James and St. Christopher. In these key works of his early style Mantegna carried out elaborate perspective schemes unifying the view of several sections on one wall. Perspective and foreshortening of figures created dramatic effects, and a knowledge of classical architecture, ornament and costume was used to advantage. An important and related early altarpiece (c.1464) is the Agony in the Garden (London). Characteristic of Mantegna's mature style are the family pictures of the Gonzaga in the bridal chamber of the Castello di Corte in Mantua. Considered extremely important is the illusionistic painted cupola of the ceiling there, on which Mantegna concentrated all his knowledge of perspective to create an imaginary balustrade with cupids and women, all foreshortened, and beyond them an open sky. This was the starting point of a tradition of illusionistic ceiling decoraton that passed through Correggio and into High Renaissance and Baroque art. Related to this work is the canvas of the Lamentation (Brera), in which Christ's body is seen from the feet, completely and convincingly foreshortened. His other important late works (in the 1490's) are the Parnassus and the Triumph of Virtue over Vice (Louvre), painted for the study of Isabella d'Este in the Castello at Mantua. These classical subjects parallel Botticelli's mytho-

MANTEGNA. St. James Led to Execution
Detail from Life of St. James, Eremitani Chapel, Padua

logical works, but differ from them considerably in form. Color, movement, space and atmosphere are emphasized. Also representative of Mantegna's broad and colorful late style is the Madonna of Victory (Louvre), painted in 1495-96 after a Gonzaga victory over the French. Mantegna was one of the few fifteenth-century artists to work in the new medium of copper engraving, and his prints of mythological and religious subjects form a parallel with this art as practiced in Florence by Antonio Pollaiuolo. Mantegna's influence was felt throughout north Italy. He had assistants in both Padua and Mantua, and many young artists who came to learn at the Squarcione shop in Padua learned more from Mantegna. (See illustrations, including color plate 128.)

Maratta (Maratti), Carlo (1625-1713). Roman painter born in Camerano, mostly famous for his late Baroque (see) decorations, though he also did portraits. He came to Rome in 1636, where he was a pupil of Andrea Sacchi and for a long time his assistant. His style was imitative of Guido Reni and also influenced by Correggio.

Marc, Franz (1880-1916). German painter and a leading member of the Blue Rider side of the Expressionist movement. Originally a student of philology and theology, Marc turned to art in 1900 and traveled to Italy and France. In 1904 he came abreast of the Impressionist movement and became interested in Japanese woodcuts. The following year he was attracted first by animal painting and then by the Jugendstil or Art Nouveau with its emphasis on organically curving lines and two-dimensional decorative design. In 1907 in Paris he came upon the art of Van Gogh and Gauguin and soon after began his continuing series on the theme of horses. By 1910, as a result of experimenting with pointillist color, his paintings were freed of naturalistic color. The animal themes, with their billowing outlines and large bold areas of Synthetist rather than true-to-life color, took on a majestic and symbolic meaning. In 1911 he worked very closely with Kandinsky on the preparation of the Blue Rider Album and the first Blue Rider Exhibition. The contact with Delaunay in 1912 and admiration for the Futurists turned his art in a new dynamic direction. Through intersecting planes of color, his animals became part of the background on which they were placed—the background elements fusing with the foreground. His sense of identification with the animals, who symbolized a purer type of humanity, never ceased. He was in the trenches in 1914 and did a Field Sketch Book, 1916, whose forms are almost completely non-objective, yet filled with the most disturbing feeling of a world returned to the primordial—doubtless as a result of his experiences at that moment. He was killed at Verdun, March 4, 1916. See EXPRESSIONISM, SYNTHETISM. (See illustration.)

MARC. Tower of the Blue Horses
Formerly National Gallery, Berlin

Marchand, André (1907-). French painter, scenic and tapestry designer who has produced a striking figurative art. In his work accentuated contour lines of an angular type are combined with large strongly contrasting color areas in a distinctly Expressionist manner.

Marco d'Oggiono (c.1475-1530). Lombard painter born in Oggiono, active in Milan, and a student and follower of Leonardo. Especially in his early work (1490-1512) is the influence of Leonardo strong. He copied the latter's paintings and used his drawings as the basis for his own work, and his Salvator Mundi (Borghese, Rome) has often been attributed to the older master.

Marcoussis, Louis (1883-1941). Polish-born painter and engraver of the French Cubist school who came into the modern movement through Impressionism and was then drawn toward Cubism through his friendship with La Fresnaye. He

MARÉES, VON. The Oarsmen
National Gallery, Berlin

did a good deal of painting on glass and engraving. See SECTION D'OR.

Marées, Hans von (1837-1887). German painter who was very influential among his contemporaries and many subsequent artists through the monumentality of his forms and compositions. Painters as diverse as the Swiss Arnold Böcklin and the German Max Beckmann owe to Marées some of their sense of the philosophic meaning of art and its possibility of expression through monumental arrangements of figures. Thus he may have represented what Puvis de Chavannes did for many Frenchmen; and, to the more modern Germans he can be considered the equivalent of Cézanne. (See illustration.)

Marescalco, Il (see BUONCONSIGLIO, GIOVANNI).

Margaritone d'Arezzo (active second half of 13th century). A native of Arezzo, he was thought by Vasari to have lived from 1236 to 1316. His works include a Madonna with lateral scenes (London) and an altarpiece in the sanctuary della Vertighe near Monte San Savino. He also seems to have specialized in filling the demand for portraits of St. Francis; several such signed works have survived, all patterned after one prototype. His style is conservative, and Italian Romanesque rather than Byzantine. (See illustration.)

Mariano, Agnolo di Cosimo di (see BRONZINO, AGNOLO).

Marin, John (1870-1953). American painter of Expressionistic landscape watercolors. Born in Rutherford, N.J., he was raised by a grandmother and two aunts, studied engineering at Stevens Institute and worked as a draughtsman in an architect's office. In 1899 he entered the Pennsylvania Academy of Fine Arts, where he studied with Anschutz and Breckenridge, and then studied with DuMond at the Art Students League (1901-03). He went to Paris in 1905 and. except for a few trips back, remained there until 1911, traveling, painting, and etching. In 1909, he met Stieglitz (see) through Steichen (later famous as a photographer) and had his first showing at "291," the Stieglitz gallery. On his return he became a member of the Stieglitz group, and settled down to almost uninterrupted painting of the Maine coast. Recognized finally as one of the outstanding American contemporary artists, a pioneer modernist and our greatest watercolorist, he was practically unknown on his return to the U.S. in 1911. Before that date his paintings were in the general

MARGARITONE D'AREZZO. St. Francis of Assisi
Church of S. Francesco, Castiglion Fiorentino

129. MARIN. Singer Building
Philadelphia Museum of Art

tradition of Impressionism and his etchings dependent upon Whistler. Though his Tyrol watercolors of 1910 showed some Fauve influence, it was only after his return to the U.S. that the influence of modern art became evident. His earliest scenes of New York exhibit a violent disintegration of form, but after he went to Maine in 1915, his landscapes achieved a sense of equilibrium between Cubist order and Expressionist emotion. Essentially an Expressionist, his art always retained its Cubist elements, especially strong in the 1920's, and even at times approached complete abstraction. His color, however, always remained naturalistic and lyrical. Later in life he returned to oil painting and even did circus scenes, but he is best remembered for his watercolor landscapes. (See color plate 129.)

Marinus (Claeszon) van Roymerswaele (c.1493-after 1567). Flemish painter known for his representation of bankers, tax collectors, business men. Marinus' paintings have frequently passed for works of Quentin Metsys, whom he copied without, perhaps, being his student. He was also affected by contemporary German painting. He was well known in his day in both Italy and Spain. Typical of his work is the Banker and His Wife (Louvre). (See illustration.)

Mariotto di Nardo (active 1394-1424). Florentine contemporary of Lorenzo Monaco, he was trained probably in the workshop of Lorenzo di Niccolò Gerini. No signed paintings by him are known, and knowledge of his style depends on the identification of certain extant works with those referred to in documents. Two works in this category are the Madonna and Saints (1394) in San Donnino at Villamagna near Florence, and a Virgin and Child in the Bigallo, Florence. Other attributed works are grouped around these, and the total picture is of a painter who first worked in the style of his master and later came under the influence of his greater contemporary, Lorenzo Monaco. (See illustration.)

Maris, Jacob (1837-99). Dutch landscape painter. He studied at the academies of painting in The Hague and in Antwerp, and also worked in Paris. He traveled extensively. Returning to Holland he became the leader of the "Hague School," translating the Dutch countryside into painting with wonderful accuracy of color and atmospheric tone.

Marmion, Simon (d.1489). Franco-Flemish illuminator and panel painter. Active in Amiens, Valenciennes, Tournai and for the Duke of Burgundy. Known as the "prince d'enluminure," this artist of Picardy seems to have been an important influence in the Franco-Flemish area during his lifetime. Attributed to him are several panels and a large number of miniatures. His chief work, now lost, was an altarpiece of twelve panels of the Life of St. Bertin finished in 1459 for the Abbey of St. Omer. Two panels apparently from this are in Berlin and show him to have been an artist of great refinement, delicate technique and a fondness for fantastic architectural settings. Also attributed to him is a St. Jerome and Donor (Philadelphia). (See illustration.)

Marquet, Albert (1875-1947). French painter and member of the Fauve group. He and Matisse shared hard times during the early years and became lifelong friends. A man of strong social convictions, he was also an artist of great sensitivity and ability as a draughtsman. Although a genuine member of the Fauve movement, his participation therein consisted more of a dynamism of movement than an explosiveness of color. His later work, like that of the majority of his colleagues, was less directly exciting. See FAUVISM.

Marsh, Reginald (1898-1954). Contemporary American painter of city genre. He studied first with his parents, both painters, and, after receiving his education at Yale, worked as an illustrator and cartoonist on the New York *Daily News, Vanity Fair,* and *The New Yorker*. He studied painting later with K. H. Miller as well as Luks and Sloan at the Art Students League. He found his subject matter in the teeming excitement of city life, its crowds at work and play, and he preferred scenes with a great many figures in a complex interplay of movement and anatomical display. He did exuberant paintings and etchings of New York City life—the Bowery, Coney Island, burlesque houses, etc. The best of these capture the flavor of the city; others in their exaggeration of types and movement tend to become superficial caricatures. He also did a good deal of book illustration. (See illustration.)

Martin, Fletcher (1904-). Contemporary American genre painter and illustrator. After a varied career as a harvest hand and lumberjack, and in the U.S. Navy, he worked for many years in a printing business while painting in his spare time. He finally turned entirely to painting under the W.P.A. in 1935, and achieved recognition for his stylized treatment of typically American subjects. He has more recently done a great deal of commercial art and illustration,

MARINUS VAN ROYMERSWAELE. St. Jerome
Musée Royal des Beaux-Arts, Antwerp

and his paintings have shown a tendency toward abstraction.

Martin, Henri Jean Guillaume (1860-1943). French painter. Academic convert to Pointillism (see), Martin studied under Laurens but was drawn to a clear type of statuesque open-air painting after a trip to Italy (1885) and a study of Giotto and the primitives. His decorative painting, e.g., Hôtel de Ville in Paris owes something to Puvis de Chavannes. He was from the start an official succes.

Martin, Homer Dodge (1836-97). An American landscape painter. He was one of the generation which finally broke with the literal manner of the Hudson River school (see) and turned to the broader treatment and more intimate romanticism of the Barbizon school (see). He was influenced by Whistler, after meeting him in 1876, and by the Barbizon painters while working in Honfleur in Normandy (1881-86). Returning to the U.S., he continued to paint his memories of Normandy, viz., View on the Seine (Metropolitan), until failing eyesight forced him to retire. Born in Albany, N.Y., the son of a carpenter, he studied for a while with J. M. Hart at the National Academy of Design, but was essentially self-

MARIOTTO DI NARDO. The Virgin and Child with St. Philip and St. John the Baptist Galleria dell' Accademia, Florence

MARMION. Choir of Angels National Gallery, London

MARSH. Why Not Use the El?
Whitney Museum of American Art, New York

taught. He was painting and trying to sell landscapes at the age of sixteen and in 1862 had a studio in New York. (See illustration.)

Martínez de Hoyos, Ricardo (1918-). A Mexican painter and theatrical designer. He did sets and costumes for a Hanya Holm ballet to the music of Carlos Chávez. In painting, his Indianism is expressed through nude forms and landscapes rather than costume effects: his arrangements are severely geometric and effective, the colors subdued but emotionally meaningful.

Martino di Bartolommeo (active by 1389, died c.1434). Sienese painter who was a pupil and close imitator of Taddeo di Bartolo. From 1396 to 1405 he was in Pisa, painting among other works the still extant frescoes in San Giovanni of Cascina. Later he decorated chapels in the Siena cathedral. Important panel paintings are two polyptychs in the Pisa gallery, and a polyptych and a triptych in the Siena gallery. Martino was a minor painter whose work is confused with that of Taddeo di Bartolo and that of Andrea di Bartolo in the latter's mature period.

Martorell, Bernardo (died c.1452). Spanish painter, miniaturist and stained-glass designer of Barcelona. His hand is now recognized in the important Catalan paintings once ascribed to a Master of St. George. He has two phases: early International Gothic, as in the Altarpiece of St. George (Chicago and the Louvre); later a broader, more spatial manner, as in the Altar of Transfiguration (Barcelona Cathedral).

Marzal de Sax, André (active 1394-1410). Spanish painter of Valencia and founder of a large school there. Probably from Saxony, he practiced a German version of the Gothic International Style. He collaborated frequently with Pedro Nicoláu, as in the Doubting Thomas (formerly in Valencia Cathedral).

Marziale, Marco (active c.1492-c.1507). Venetian painter who continued Gentile Bellini's narrative decorative style in a somewhat provincial manner. He worked in Cremona and Venice and was employed for a time on decorations for the Doge's palace. There are altarpieces by him in Venice, London and Berlin.

Masaccio (Tommaso di Giovanni di Simone Guidi) (1401-c.1428). The most important Florentine painter of the first generation in the fifteenth century. It is frequently said of him that he took up the art of painting where Giotto left it, and carried forward in fifteenth-century terms the monumental use of form and space the older master had introduced. Considering the shortness of his life, his achievements are almost incredible. He was born in Castello di San Giovanni Valdarno and Vasari says he was a pupil of Masolino, with whom he collaborated on the famous frescoes in Santa Maria del Carmine and possibly on other works. In 1422 and 1424 he was registered in the two painters' guilds in Florence. He appears to have been twice in Rome and he died there c.1428. In 1426 he was in Pisa and executed an altarpiece for the

MARTIN, HOMER DODGE. Normandy Coast. Babcock Galleries, New York

MASACCIO. Musical Angel. Detail from Madonna and Child. National Gallery, London

Carmine church there (partly preserved in various collections). We know, too, that he was in contact with the sculptor Donatello and had Andrea di Giusto as an assistant.

With few documents, and Masaccio's short life-span, it is almost impossible to speak of "early" and "late" works. A painting generally accepted as one of his first, variously dated from 1416 to 1425, is the Madonna and Child and St. Anne in the Uffizi, which may have been produced in the shop of Masolino. About 1425 he may have assisted Masolino in Rome with frescoes in the church of San Clemente. The Pisa altarpiece of 1426 was lost in the eighteenth century, but parts of it have since been recovered. The center panel representing the Madonna and Child is in London, and lateral saints and predella panels are in Pisa, Vienna, and Berlin. Masaccio's most important work was his part in the decoration of the Brancacci chapel in Santa Maria del Carmine, Florence. It is generally agreed that he and Masolino painted this cycle together, but the parts assigned to each have been a source of controversy. Modern scholarship gives to Masaccio St. Peter Healing the Maimed with His Shadow, St. Peter Baptizing, The Tribute Money, The Expulsion from the Garden, and parts of The Distribution of Alms and the Resurrection of the King's Son. This last composition was left unfinished by both collaborators, and was completed two generations later by Filippino Lippi. Considered one of Masaccio's last works is the majestic fresco (unfortunately badly preserved) of the Trinity in the church of Santa Maria Novella in Florence. This work includes one of the earliest representations of purely Renaissance architecture, the design of which has sometimes been attributed to Brunelleschi. A panel of the Crucifixion, also considered "late," is in the Naples Museum.

Although Masaccio doubtless received his training from Masolino, his genius led him to reach back beyond the Gothic style of the late fourteenth century and to take up the formal and expressive problems Giotto dealt with in the frescoes of Santa Croce and the Arena Chapel. To that monumental style Masaccio added the element of light, including a consistent light source and cast shadows, and the projection of space by means of mathematical perspective implying a single viewpoint for the beholder. His compositions are distinguished from those of Masolino in the Brancacci chapel by their stark simplicity and avoidance of all unnecessary detail, as well as by the solidity and impersonal quality of the figures. It seems probable that he studied works of classical antiquity, although no specific reference is made to them in his paintings. With these characteristics Masaccio joined Donatello and Brunelleschi in sculpture and architecture, forming the triumvirate that created the Renaissance style of Florence. Artistic aims established at this time were to remain basically unchallenged until the end of the nineteenth century. Masaccio's profound influence was felt in his own and the following generations by Uccello, Castagno, Filippo Lippi and Benozzo Gozzoli. His art was honored by such men as Botticelli, Leonardo da Vinci, Michelangelo and Raphael. (See illustrations, including color plate 130.)

Masanobu, Kano (see JAPANESE PAINTERS: MUROMACHI PERIOD).

MASO DI BANCO (attributed to) St. Anthony of Padua Metropolitan Museum of Art, New York

130. MASACCIO. Profile Portrait of a Young Man
National Gallery of Art, Mellon Collection, Washington, D.C.

Masanobu, Okumura (see JAPANESE PAINTERS: TOKUGAWA PERIOD).

Masip (or Macip) the Elder, Juan Vicente (c.1490-1550). Spanish painter of Valencia. Father of Juan de Juanes (see) with whom he collaborated and with whose works his own were once confused. He painted in the style of Raphael but also showed influences of the local styles of Llanos and Yanez. He founded the Masip atelier. Most certain of his works is the retablo in Segorbe Cathedral.

Masip the Younger, Juan Vicente (see JUANES, JUAN DE).

Maso di Banco. (active second quarter of 14th century). The life and works of this Florentine painter are only sketchily reconstructed from documents and from later references which tend to confuse him with Giottino. Some writers therefore bring together all the works associated with Maso and Giottino under the name of Giottino. Of the many works Maso must have painted according to early accounts, those extant that may be ascribed to him are the frescoes of the life of St. Sylvester in the Bardi chapel, Santa Croce, Florence, the Lamentation of San Remigio in the Uffizi, and fragments illustrating the legends of Saints Stephen and Bartholomew in the Cavone chapel of the Badia. He may also have painted a fresco (now fragmentary) of the Expulsion of the Duke of Athens from Florence (recorded in 1343) in the palace of the Podestà. As seen by some critics, Maso holds a stylistic position between Stefano Fiorentino and Giottino, who may have been his pupil. He painted in the tradition of Giotto, in whose school he doubtless learned his art. His refined forms and his compositions are less dramatic than Giotto's, and exhibit a Sienese tendency in emphasizing decorative rather than narrative qualities. (See illustration.)

Masolino di Panicale (Tommaso di Cristofano di Fino) (c.1384-1447). Florentine painter whose art constitutes a link between Florentine Gothic painting of the late fourteenth century and the new Renaissance style of Masaccio in the fifteenth. He was born at Panicale between 1383 and 1384, learned his art from Starnina, and painted frescoes in several buildings at Castiglione d'Olona between 1425 and 1435. Probably between 1424 and 1427 he executed his share of the Brancacci chapel frescoes in Santa Maria del Carmine, Florence, in which his pupil Masaccio collaborated to his everlasting renown. The sections thought to be by Masolino are the Fall of Man, the Preaching of St. Peter, most of the Raising of Tabitha, and parts of the Healing of the Cripple. The decoration of the vaults and lunettes (destroyed) was probably also done by Masolino. Frescoes in San Clemente, Rome, are assumed to have been executed by him with Masaccio's help around 1425. Other works by Masolino are at Bremen (Madonna, dated 1423) and Empoli (frescoes, 1424), and parts of a lost altarpiece are in the museums of Naples and Philadelphia. His style is gentle and lyrical, and though it takes into account the new tendency toward solidity of modeling and projection of space, it never accomplishes the integration of these factors or achieves the monumentality that characterizes Masaccio's style. (See color plate 131.)

131. MASOLINO. The Annunciation
National Gallery of Art, Mellon Collection, Washington, D.C.

Mason Master (active America c.1670). Named after his portraits of the Mason family children, he was a naive and untrained craftsman who worked in New England.

Massacre of Scio by Eugène Delacroix (see).

Masson, André (1896-). Well-known French abstract Surrealist noted for the poetic imagination and rich color of his fanciful treatments of dreams, erotica and what he calls metamorphoses. He joined the Surrealists in 1924 and exhibited with them, working under the joint literary and artistic influence of such figures as William Blake, the Marquis de Sade, Chinese literature, Franz Kafka and Nietzsche. The work of painters like Masson has had wide influence, especially in the United States where the contemporary so-called Abstract Expressionists may trace at least one line of development back to him. See SURREALISM. (See illustration.)

Masson, Henri (1907-). Canadian painter born in Belgium, he began his art in Brussels and has continued since 1922 in Canada. He paints the people and things he knows and sees about him every day, using a pleasant semi-Impressionist manner that is almost a reaction against the bleakness and coldness of the landscape. (See illustration.)

Massys (see METSYS).

Mastelletta (Giovanni Andrea Donducci) (1575-1655). Bolognese painter of small lyrical landscapes derived from Dossi, dell' Abbate and the Venetians. A product of the Carracci Academy, his early work follows Parmigianino.

Master Alfonso (active c.1465-73). Spanish painter of Cordoba. A documented artist, he was once thought to have been the genius of his time. In 1473 he contracted to paint a retablo for San Cugat del Vallés which, if it had been painted at that date as formerly thought, would mark him as a great innovator in Renaissance technique and realism. It has recently been discovered that the altarpiece was painted later in the following century by Anye Bru (see). No works are presently known by Alfonso.

Master of the Bambino Vispo (active early in 15th century). Florentine painter. A number of works by the same hand from the school of Lorenzo Monaco are grouped under this descriptive name (Master of the Lively Infant).

Master of the Carrand Triptych (see GIOVANNI DI FRANCESCO).

Master of the Castello Nativity (active second half of 15th century). Florentine painter. A group of altarpieces and devotional panels have been attributed to the anonymous painter of a Nativity panel in the royal villa of Castello near Florence; hence his name. His style contains a combination of plastic and lyrical elements derived from Baldovinetti, Fra Angelico and Fra Filippo Lippi.

Master of Flémalle (1375-1444). A Flemish painter; identified by Hulin de Loo in 1909 as Robert Campin (see) although this designation is disputed. He was earlier called the Master of the Mousetrap from a detail in the Mérode Altar, the Triptych of the Annunciation. He was also known as the Master of Mérode after the owner of this triptych, and the Master of Flémalle after the Belgian town from which the Städelsches Museum (Frankfort) pictures are supposed to have originated. The triptych, now consisting of the middle panel of the Virgin in an interior and a left wing of St. Joseph as a carpenter making a mousetrap, is in the Mérode Collection, Brussels. A Veronica and a Madonna and Child with a Trinity in grisaille on the reverse are in the Städelsches Museum, Frankfort. Based on these, other works have been attributed to the master. Among his early works, along with the Mérode Altar, are listed the Nativity (c.1420-25, Dijon), the Somzée Madonna (London), a Madonna and Child (Leningrad; other versions Richmond, Brussels), and a Virgin in Glory (Aix). Among his attributed later works, along with the other Frankfort pictures, are the Good Thief (c.1430, Frankfort), a fragment of a Descent from the Cross of which the central panel exists in a copy in Liverpool, and the Werl Altar (1439, Prado). All this still remains problematic, and some scholars insist that the works attributed to Flèmalle are actually early works of Rogier van der Weyden (see). Whatever the truth, these paintings exhibit a fanatical striving for dramatic emotion and a great monumentality, together with an almost feverish interest in detail. His art seems an outgrowth of the miniature work of Malouel and Bellechose, influenced by the monumentality of the sculpture of Sluter and the Tournai School. In the Mérode Altar he seems torn between the grand and the commonplace, between fervor and facts, between Gothic formalism and contemporary realism. The Annunciation may have affected van Eyck's Annunciation in the Ghent Altar, but his major influence was upon Rogier van der Weyden, though his late works are definitely influenced in turn by Rogier, especially in the Werl Altar, which would make it easy to see here simply a development in Rogier's art. Yet it must be said that Flémalle's art, so powerful and almost uncouth, so earthy and commonplace, so stridently emotional, is incompatible with the subtle elegance and emotional complexity of Rogier's personality. (See illustration.)

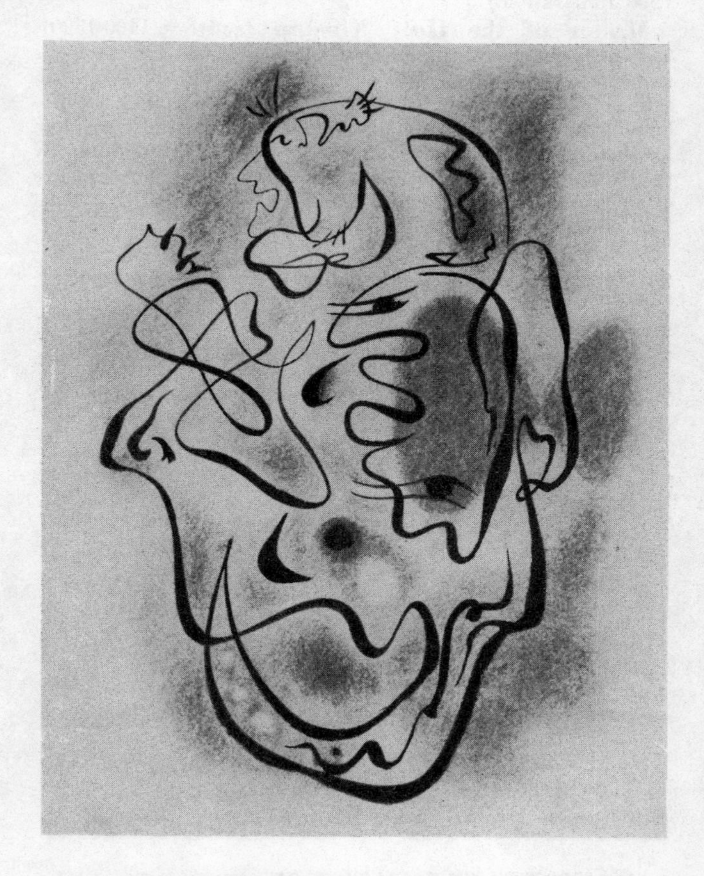

MASSON, ANDRÉ. The Cat. Valentin Gallery, New York

MASSON, HENRI. Choir Boys
Courtesy of the Artist, Canada

Master of the Holy Blood (early 16th century). An anonymous Flemish master of Bruges. He is named for his work in the chapel of the Confrérie du Saint Sang in Bruges, of which he was a member. Here he painted an altarpiece of the Deposition from the Cross which shows that he was a follower of Quentin Metsys. He also painted an altarpiece of the Deipara Virgo in the Church of St. Jacques, Bruges. (See illustration.)

Master of the Holy Kinship (active c.1480-1520). German painter and designer of stained glass. He takes his name from the altarpiece showing the Holy Family with saints (now in Wallraf-Richartz Museum, Cologne). A Cologne painter, he was influenced in his early works by Stephan Lochner and the Master of the Life of Mary, and later by the Netherlanders, especially Rogier van der Weyden. He often achieves a monumental and decorative effect that links him with the artists of the Renaissance.

MASTER OF FLÉMALLE. The Annunciation
Musées Royaux des Beaux-Arts, Brussels

MASTER OF THE HOLY BLOOD. Deipara Virgo
Église St. Jacques, Brussels

Master of the Legend of St. Lucy (late 15th century). Anonymous Flemish painter also known as the "Master of Bruges of 1480." His chief work was the three-paneled altarpiece representing the Legend of St. Lucy in Bruges. This painting shows the influence of Rogier van der Weyden and Memling. A Madonna and Child with Angels in Brussels is also by him.

Master of the Legend of St. Ursula (active 1480-90). Anonymous Flemish painter of Bruges. This artist, probably a miniaturist, is named from the diptych of the Legend of St. Ursula painted for the Convent of the Black Sisters, Bruges. This painting of eight episodes was completed somewhat earlier than Memling's famous Shrine of St. Ursula (1489). The artist was influenced by Memling and Rogier van der Weyden. (See illustration.)

Master of Liesborn (active 1460/70). German painter. He takes his name from the five altarpieces that he made before 1465 for the monastery church at Liesborn, near Münster. His charming, late medieval style, deriving from the school of Cologne, had a wide influence on other German painters.

Master of the Life of Mary (active c.1463-80). German painter and designer of stained glass. He takes his name from the eight panels showing scenes from the life of the Virgin (in Munich), that came from the church of St. Ursula in Cologne. This Cologne painter reflects so vividly the works of Rogier van der Weyden and Dirk Bouts that a training in a Netherlands workshop must be assumed for him. (See illustration.)

Master of Messkirch (c.1500-43?). German painter. His chief work, the Adoration of the Magi painted as the high altarpiece of the church at Messkirch, indicates that the style of this remarkable anonymous colorist was formed by the art of Dürer and Burgkmair.

Master of Moulins (active 1480-1500). French painter in the Bourbon Court. This artist, who has sometimes been wrongly identified with Jean Perréal (see), has left us a number of pictures of definite style, although he himself remains anonymous. His most important work is the triptych of the Cathedral of Moulins in Boulbonnais (c.1490), which shows the Madonna and Angels flanked by donors Pierre of Bourbon and Anne of France. The colors are brilliant, the pigment pellucid in a Flemish way although the facial types are uniquely his. A Nativity at Autun (c.1480) draws on van der Goes. Other attributions include a Madonna (Brussels), Mary Magdalene (Louvre) and portraits of the Bourbon family. This artist had a fine sense of Renaissance amplitude of composition, vying with Fouquet. (See illustration.)

Master Nicolás Francés (d.1468). Spanish painter of Castille. Probably of French origin, this exponent of the International style executed the high altar of the Cathedral of Léon c.1434.

Master of Pedralbes (see HUGUET).

Master of the St. Bartholomew Altarpiece (c.1450-c.1510). German painter named for his chief work, the altarpiece of St. Bartholomew (c.1505/10), once in the church of St. Columba, Cologne, now in Munich. This painter of the Cologne school apparently worked as a young man in the Netherlands, possibly in Utrecht. He shows the influence of the painters of the north Netherlands, and of Rogier van der Weyden, whose Columba Altarpiece he must have known in Cologne. His art is exquisitely finished, beautiful in color, and so mannered and stylized that he has been called "the Crivelli of the North."

Master of St. George (see MARTORELL).

Master of St. Severin (active end of 15th, early 16th century). German painter and designer of stained glass. This Cologne painter is named for the two panels, each showing a pair of saints, in the sacristy of the church of St. Severin in Cologne. His style is awkward, old-fashioned and linear, and shows a strong influence from the Low Countries, especially from the north Netherlands, transmitted to him presumably by the Master of the Legend of St. Ursula.

Master of the Seven Griefs of Mary (see ISENBRANDT).

Master of the Unicorn (see DUVET).

Master of the Upper Rhine (active c. 1400). The identity of the German painter who fashioned a delightful Virgin and Child with saints and angels in a garden of flowers (Frankfort) is unknown. The picture shows French influence and many characteristics of the Gothic International Style but is animated chiefly by a mysticism and winsome charm that are typically German.

Master of the Virgo inter Virgines (fl. c.1450-c.1475). Dutch painter whose name derives from the Mary with Women Saints in Amsterdam; he appears on the Netherlandish scene after the middle of the fifteenth century. He is generally related in style to the painters of the southern Netherlands (i.e., Flanders) in compositional effects and richness of costume details but the frequent stark effects, wealth of imagination and almost deliberate awkwardness bring him within the orbit of the northern or Dutch Netherlands.

Matisse, Henri (1869-1954). An "Old Master" of the modern French school A remarkable painter, seulptor, lithographer and designer of stained glass, he was influential in the formulation of the modern anti-representational and form-expressive idea. The titular leader of the Fauve group of 1905, his influence has ranged all over the world. Matisse's style changed perceptibly with the years in a rich presentation of the possibilities of color expression for its own sake without the representational, narrative or philosophical "impedimenta" of traditional art. His purpose, like that of other artists of our time, was to present to the spectator the sum of his own visual and emotional experience of a given section of nature and to do so in terms of new and formally organized patterns of colors, forms, textures, etc.

The son of a grain merchant, Matisse was intended for the study of law. During the course of a convalescence he became interested in painting and in 1892 he studied in Paris under Bouguereau. In 1893 he met a number of his

MASTER OF THE LEGEND OF ST. URSULA
Diptych of Virgin and Child: Donors
Musée Royal des Beaux-Arts, Antwerp

MASTER OF THE LIFE OF MARY
Visitation of Mary. Alte Pinakothek, Munich

MASTER OF MOULINS (with Assistants)
Meeting of Joachim and Anna. National Gallery, London

132. MATISSE. White Plumes. Minneapolis Institute of Arts

future collaborators in Gustave Moreau's class at the Beaux-Arts school. Through 1896 his colors were dark in the traditional Old Master sense. At this time he discovered Daumier, Degas, Lautrec and the Japanese print and turned to the Seine for inspiration, sharing a studio with Marquet on the quais. In 1897, as he got to know Pissarro, Matisse caught up with Impressionism. The next few years find him following the Pointillist discipline, a useful experience for the later Fauve ideals of setting the canvas in motion. Although the Pointillist tendencies remain, there are evidences around the turn of the century of the mood of the Intimists and an awareness also of the structural methods of Cézanne. During this early period, color in his work is still far from arbitrary in the later sense of the so-called expressive distortions of Fauvism; it is used rather for the purpose of form-sensation in the Cézanne sense. Matisse's interest in form for form's own sake is also attested by the first sculptures of the period 1899-1904, but the influence of the Pointillists—particularly Signac, with whom he was friendly—markedly influenced his outlook. In 1903 he had joined the newly founded Autumn Salon (Salon d'Automne). By the end of 1904 he had turned (perhaps under the influence of the Gauguin memorial exhibition put on by the Autumn Salon) toward the kind of broad flat areas of contoured color that was to distinguish his contributions to French painting for the next few years.

The 1905 exhibition of the Autumn Salon marked the emergence of the Fauves as a group. In 1906 Matisse opened his academy and students came to him from everywhere. He met Picasso at Gertrude Stein's house. In 1909 there are signs of the influence of Near Eastern, i.e., Persian art, as in the Red Fish. In 1911-13 he made two trips to Morocco, where the bare and precisely laid out landscape helped bring forth some of his finest works. By this time the last vestiges of direct emotionalism that were evident in the pure Fauve works of 1905 had disappeared. He evolved successive new methods of rendering form experience through color relationships. Characteristically, these were bold, decorative and plastically creative, i.e., having their own reality as art or painting. The period 1913-17 was one of "austerity and architectonics" owing in some measure to World War I and the influence of Cubism. From 1917 to approximately 1929 Matisse was in the south of France experimenting in a variety of ways, moving inevitably toward his avowed ideal of an art of relaxation and pleasure, an art which pleases the eye, then the mind, and only remotely the soul. In the 1930-39 period he was busy planning and executing a mural commission for the Barnes Foundation (see); he also worked on illustrations for an edition of Mallarmé's poems, illustrations for Joyce's *Ulysses,* designs for tapestry and glass and finally the backdrop and costumes for the Ballet Russe production of *Rouge et Noir* in 1939. During World War II as in World War I Matisse was in Nice. A notable accomplishment of this period was the decorations in the chapel at Vence. Giant retrospective exhibitions of his art during 1948-50 in Philadelphia, Paris, Nice and Lucerne were a measure of his critical position in the postwar artistic world. See also FAUVISM. (See illustrations, including color plate 132.)

MATISSE. Odalisque
Baltimore Museum of Art, Cone Collection

Matsys (see METSYS).

Matta Echaurren, Roberto (1911-). Chilean abstract Surrealist painter and architect deriving both arts from the School of Paris. He has had considerable influence in his native country and in the United States. His art shows a rich coloristic imagination with softly flowing and merging space elements; it has a fearful yet playful Surrealist quality. Although abstract, the forms are distinctly evocative and suggestive, often with erotic motivations. See SURREALISM. (See illustration.)

Matteo da Gualdo (c.1435-1507). Umbrian painter most strongly influenced by the Venetian Carlo Crivelli. His style is stiff and provincial and given to affected gestures and elongation of anatomical forms.

Matteo da Viterbo (active 1343-66). One of the Sienese painters working in the school of Simone Martini (see) at Avignon. Matteo and his assistants painted the frescoes in the Palace of the Popes there. These frescoes attempt but do not achieve the grace and spirituality of Simone's decorative Gothic style.

Matteo di Giovanni di Bartolo (Matteo da Siena) (c.1430-95). Sienese painter whose three extant dated works (1470, 1477 and 1487), being all from a late period, make his chronology problematical. He was influenced by Domenico di Bartolo and Vecchietta. Later he displays an affinity with Florentine painting (Antonio Pollaiuolo) and with the Umbrian Piero della Francesca. He painted in several styles, producing elegant and harmonious devotional pictures, scenes of violent action with classical architectural settings, and late works characterized by heaviness of form and dullness of color in marked contrast to the rest of his prolific output.

Mattson, Henry Elis (1887-).Contemporary American seascape painter born in Sweden. He came to the U.S. in 1906, worked in Worcester, Mass., as a mechanic and studied at the museum school there. In 1916, he studied briefly with John Carlson in Woodstock, N.Y., where he settled. He has continued to produce variations on the single theme of the sea—romantic, rich and luminous in color. (See illustration.)

Maurer, Alfred Henry (1868-1932). American painter born in New York, the son of Louis Maurer, a Currier and Ives artist. He studied at the National Academy of Design and with Chase, and in 1901 capped his brilliant early career by winning a first prize at the Carnegie International with a portrait in the Whistler manner. In Paris he was influenced by the Fauves and changed his style. One of the pioneers of

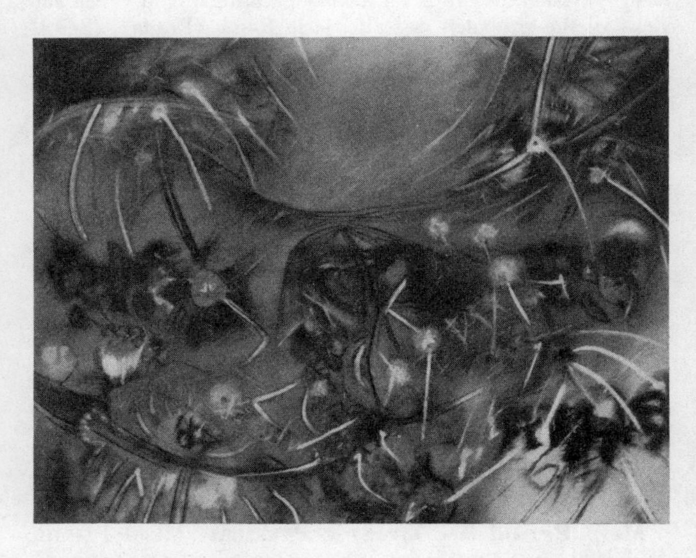

MATTA. Summer Seed. Sidney Janis Gallery, New York

MATTSON. Wings of the Morning
Metropolitan Museum of Art, New York

modern art in America, his work was exhibited by Stieglitz in 1909 at the gallery "291" and was harshly criticized, but he continued until the time of his suicide to paint Fauve-like females and Cubist still lifes. (See illustration.)

Mauritshuis, The Hague, Neth. Well-known collection of traditional Dutch paintings.

Mayan painting (see PRE-COLUMBIAN).

Mayer, Marie Françoise Constance (La Martinière) (1775-1821). French painter in oil, pastel and miniature. Student of Suvée and Greuze. She was influenced by David and by Prud'hon, with whom she lived in the Sorbonne, and because of whom she committed suicide.

Ma Yüan (see CHINESE PAINTERS: SUNG DYNASTY).

Mazo, Juan Bautista Martínez del (1612-67). Spanish painter of Madrid; a faithful disciple of Velázquez, with whom his works are frequently confused. He entered Velázquez' studio as a youth, married his daughter Francisca and collaborated with the great painter on several works including the View of Zaragoza (Prado). He made copies after Velázquez and the Italian masters and adapted Las Meninas to a curious portrait of his own family (Vienna). He succeeded Velázquez as first court painter in 1661 and painted many fine portraits of the court, e.g., Infanta Margarita (Prado). His reputation also rests on history paintings, landscapes and views of the city such as Calle de la Reina (Prado). (See illustration.)

Mazzola, Filippo (c.1460-1505). This north Italian provincial painter, school of Parma, was subject to pervading influences from Venice, especially Giovanni Bellini and Antonello da Messina.

Mazzola, Francesco (see PARMIGIANINO).

Mazzolino (Mazzoli), Ludovico (c.1480-1528). Italian painter born and active in Ferrara, a follower of Lorenzo Costa and Ercole de' Roberti. He painted small and precise pictures in a clumsy though brightly colored manner.

Mecarino, Domenico (see BECCAFUMI, DOMENICO).

Mechau, Frank (1904-46). American painter of Western life, horses, and frontier scenes. Born in Denver, he studied at Denver University, Denver Academy, the Art Institute of Chicago, and in Paris (1929-30). He also executed murals for post offices in Washington, D.C., and Fort Worth, Tex. His art has a dry, spare quality and is highly stylized in terms of rhythmic pattern.

Meiji Period (see JAPANESE PAINTERS: MEIJI PERIOD, 1868-1911).

Meissonier, Ernest (1815-90). French painter and illustrator. He worked in a traditional manner influenced by Dutch seventeenth-century painting, devoting himself to military subjects, battle scenes and everyday scenes from the life of his time. Detailed and meticulous in his approach, he lacks the sense of formal compositional relationships that marks the work of the Dutch "little masters" whom he apparently emulated. Among the books he illustrated are *Paul and Virginia* and *The Vicar of Wakefield.*

Meistermann, Georg (1911-). German modernist painter and stained-glass designer. He studied at the Düsseldorf Academy. Although he has been active for years as a stained-glass painter, he has also done a good deal of conventional painting in the period since the war. His cultivated feeling for strong line is combined with a boldly arranged series of color areas in a pleasing and effective kind of abstract Surrealism. (See illustration.)

Melcarth, Edward (1914-). Contemporary American Neo-Romantic painter who has more recently turned to social themes. Born in Louisville, Ky., he studied at the Chelsea Art School, London, the Académie Ranson, Paris, and with Karl Zerbe in Boston.

Melchers, Gari (1860-1932). American Impressionist painter of religious and genre subjects. Born in Detroit, the son of a sculptor, he studied with Von Gebhart in Düsseldorf and later at the Ecole des Beaux-Arts with Boulanger and Lefebvre. He maintained one studio in Paris and another at Egmond in Holland. Among his many murals are one for the

MAURER. Twin Heads
Whitney Museum of American Art, New York

MAZO. A Duel in the Prado. National Gallery, London

Columbian Exposition (now in University of Michigan Library), Library of Congress, Detroit Public Library, and the State Capitol, Jefferson City. From 1909 to 1914 he taught painting at the State Academy of Art in Weimar. He was a regular winner of prizes and awards both here and abroad. (See illustration.)

Meldolla, Andrea (see SCHIAVONE).

Meléndez (Menéndez), Luis Eugenio (1716-80). A Spanish court painter, born in Naples and studied in Madrid, Naples and Rome. He became a court painter to Charles III and in 1773 achieved renown with his Holy Family painted for the portable oratory of the Princess of Asturias. He is best known for his miniatures and still lifes.

Meliore Toscano (active 13th century). Tuscan painter known by a signed and dated polyptych representing the Saviour and Saints (1271), in the Parma gallery. Three Madonnas attributed to him are in San Leolino, Panzano, the museum at Fiesole, and the Turin gallery. These works display a blend of Byzantine style with the indigenous Tuscan Romanesque.

Meloni Altobello (active c.1497-1517). Born in Cremona, he worked with Boccaccini. His early style is derivative from Costa and Mazzolino, but he later comes under the influence of Romanino who was then at work in the Cathedral of Cremona, where he himself executed scenes from the life of Christ (in 1517) in the Venetian High Renaissance style.

Meloni da Carpi, Marco (active 1504-37). Italian painter who may have been a pupil of Francia. His art, influenced by that of Perugino and Cima, is sweet and slightly naive.

Melozzo da Forlì (1438-94). One of the most important Umbrian artists to develop out of the immediate circle of Piero della Francesca. Though there is no documentarv evidence that he was a pupil of Piero or assisted in the frescoes in Arezzo, he was decisively influenced by him. Melozzo was born in Forlì, was at Rome in the early 1470's, and worked at the court of Urbino about 1473-76, when the

MEISTERMANN. David before Saul
Private Collection, Germany

MELCHERS. Mother and Child
Art Institute of Chicago, Deering Collection

MEMLING. Portrait of a Man. Mauritshuis, The Hague

Fleming Joos van Ghent was there in the service of Federigo da Montefeltro. Melozzo probably designed the portraits of famous men and the seven liberal arts panels that were executed by several artists for the ducal palace (now dispersed among European museums). In about 1476 he returned to Rome, and probably remained there. His major works in Rome are a group portrait of Sixtus IV and papal court dignitaries (Vatican), and a fresco of the Ascension in the church of Santi Apostoli that includes the music-making angels for which he is famous. His ability to make figures of this latter kind appear to be swaying directly overhead is important in the development of the illusionistic "open ceiling" of the type done during the fifteenth century by Mantegna and later by Correggio and the painters of the Baroque.

Memling (Memlinc), Hans (c.1435-94). Flemish painter of German origin, born near Mainz, in Selingenstadt or Mömling. He may have studied with Stefan Lochner in Cologne and was perhaps in Brussels working with Rogier van der Weyden c.1460, before finally settling in Bruges in 1466. He is the most charming of the great Flemish masters and his art is appealing in its sweet simplicity, tender mysticism, unaffected grace, serenity, and childlike faith. He was neither original nor profound, adapting compositions and emotional symbols borrowed from van der Weyden to the pictorial richness of van Eyck. Yet he achieved in his own meticulous and delicate miniature manner, perhaps because of the very calmness of his temperament, a spacious symmetry which approaches the monumentality of the High Renaissance. His first period, dating to 1475, is characterized by a dependence upon the late style of Rogier van der Weyden though without the latter's intensity or power of expression. A reconstructed early polyptych (scattered in London, Madrid and Vienna) is based on the Columba Altar of Rogier. Other works of this period are the Sir John Donne Triptych (1468, Chatsworth), the Portinari Passion (c.1470, Turin), the Last Judgment Altar (c.1473, Notre Dame, Danzig), and the Madonna and Child (1472, Liechtenstein), which is the model for his many subsequent versions of the same theme. The work of his maturity covers the period of his activity as town painter of Bruges (1475-87) and includes some of his most beautiful paintings: the Granada Diptych (c.1475), under the influence of Hugo van der Goes; the Deposition Triptych (c.1480); the St. Catherine Altar (1479), recapitulating the Donne Triptych; and the Adoration of the Magi Altar (1479, all in the Hôpital St.-Jean, Bruges); the monumental Madonna and Child (1485, Louvre); and his masterpiece, the St. Christopher Triptych (c.1485, Bruges), commissioned in 1484 by William Moreel, burgomaster of Bruges.

Major works of his last years include the Martin Nieuwenhove Diptych (1487) and the great Shrine of St. Ursula (1489, both in the Hôpital St.-Jean, Bruges) the latter decorated with eight panels on the sides and six medallions in the roof (probably by students), fairy-tale gems in bright, fresh color, miniature masterpieces; and the Triptych of the Passion (1491, Lübeck). He was a born portraitist, and the more than twenty-five portraits that have come down to us are among the masterpieces of Flemish art. Minutely realistic, psychologically reflective, they compose a gallery of wealthy local as well as foreign merchants and their wives. Among the best of these are Tomasso Portinari and Wife (1474, Metropolitan), Barbe van Vlaedenbergh (c.1478, Brussels), Sybella Sambetha (1480, Hôpital St.-Jean, Bruges), and William Moreel and Wife (1484, Brussels). Except for a passing influence on Gerard David, he had little influence and few followers. (See illustrations, including color plate 133.)

Memmi, Lippo (active by 1317, died 1356). Sienese painter who was undoubtedly a pupil of his father Memmo di

133. MEMLING. Madonna and Child with Angels. National Gallery of Art, Mellon Collection, Washington, D.C.

Filipuccio of San Gimignano but early came under the strong influence of his brother-in-law Simone Martini. Lippo is first found collaborating with his father in a frescoed Majestas in the Palazzo Pubblico of San Gimignano in 1317 that is closely related to Simone's Majestas of 1315 in Siena. In 1333 Lippo signed with Simone the Sant' Ansano Annunciation (Uffizi), but the extent of his collaboration in this work is debated. In 1341 he was employed on the construction of the Torre della Mangia in Siena, making architectural models. A signed Madonna for the church of St. Francis in Avignon is dated 1347, but it is not certain that Lippo joined Simone in that city. Four signed Madonnas are in Orvieto, Siena, Berlin and Altenburg. (See illustration.)

Memmi, Simone (see SIMONE MARTINI).

Mendelson, Marc (1915-). Belgian painter of a semi-abstract Surrealist type. Within the framework of his always legible forms, he maintains a magical quality, especially for the character of inanimate things.

Méndez, Leopoldo (1903-). Mexican painter and graphic artist known especially for woodcuts and caricatures; a founder and guiding spirit of the Popular Graphic Art Workshop. Having developed under the influence of Posada and Orozco, he is interested primarily in the idea of social justice. He did a fresco in the government Graphic Workshops (with Zalce), 1936, and one in a Maternity Clinic, Mexico City (with O'Higgins), 1946-47. He is noted for dynamic intensity of movement and feeling, a linear expressiveness of forms, and a powerful chiaroscuro. (See illustration.)

Mengs, Anton Raphael (1728-79). German painter. As a young boy he was taken to Rome, where he studied painting. Between 1745 and 1751 he was court painter in Dresden but the remainder of his life was divided between Italy and Spain. In 1761 he became the first painter to Charles III at Madrid. Though he was capable of excellent characterization and created some splendid portraits, many of his official commissions resulted in an empty and superficial repetition of the eighteenth-century Rococo formula. He was an important force in the development of the Neo-Classical ideal. (See illustration.)

Menzel, Adolf von (1815-1905). German realist painter of genre and historical scenes. He studied briefly at the Berlin Academy but for the most part was self-taught. Except for short trips to Paris and Italy, he remained in Berlin, where he was the most important painter of his time. His style is almost Impressionist, personal, and identifiably German in its emotional overtones. His interest in the way objects are revealed under light, traceable to the influence of Constable, reached a level in which light became a mood-evoking instrument. (See illustration.)

Meo da Siena (first half 14th century). Painter active in Perugia. A signed polyptych and other works ascribed to him are in the Perugia gallery. Deriving from the school of Duccio, he had a profound influence on the development of Umbrian painting.

Mercier, Philippe (1689-1760). French portrait and genre painter and copper engraver. Imitator of Watteau and Teniers.

MEMMI, LIPPO. Madonna and Child with Donor
National Gallery of Art, Mellon Collection, Washington, D.C.

MÉNDEZ. Print from the Mexican Revolution Series

MENGS. Youthful Self-Portrait
Kupferstich Kabinet, Dresden

Born in Germany he traveled all over western Europe, finally settling in England. There his fêtes champêtres were a great success and were much copied by English engravers. His Les Conjurés (Louvre) has been taken for a Watteau.

Mérida, Carlos (1893-). Guatemalan painter in the Mexican school since 1919; he has done easel pictures, murals, stage designs, graphics. One of the few abstract painters in Mexico, he has combined the techniques of modern art, especially abstract Surrealism, with the folklore themes of the modern Mexican movement. This is expressed in characteristically bright decorative color and form arrangements whose interplay sometimes suggests the humorous and evocative quality of Klee.

Merson, Luc Olivier (1846-1920). French painter ot history. Son of the critic Charles Olivier Merson, he studied with Chassevant and Pils and won the Rome prize of 1869. As his diploma picture he painted Leucothoë et Anaxandre. He was a defender of the nineteenth-century Beaux-Arts tradition, and renounced his post as Professor of the Ecole in 1894 because of encroachment of the doctrines of modern art. He took part in the decoration of the Palais de Justice. During five years' travel in Italy he came strongly under the spell of the primitives, as witnessed by his Saint Edmond Martyr, King of England, a legend of the sixteenth century.

Metropolitan Museum of Art, New York. One of the world's outstanding collections, ranging through all periods in the history of art and including all media. Extremely well-balanced, it contains outstanding sections on Egyptian, medieval, Colonial American, nineteenth-century French, Far-Eastern and other art. It has recently established a special department for the development of the art of the United States. Its services are far-ranging and valuable.

METSU. Musicale. Mauritshuis, The Hague

Metsu, Gabriel (1629-67). Dutch painter of genre. The son of an obscure Flemish artist, he probably began the study of painting in his native city of Leyden under Gerard Dou. The solid draughtsmanship and meticulous finish he learned under this artist are the foundation of his development. He worked at Leyden and was one of the first members of the newly formed painters guild. In 1654 or soon after he transferred to Amsterdam where the pervasive influence of Rembrandt's style brought into his work a new interest in light and shadow. Jan Steen and Vermeer also exerted a certain influence on him. He must be counted among the foremost Dutch painters of interiors and genre and his contribution to this kind of painting is distinctly personal. Somewhat more wholesome and less elegantly fashionable than Terborch's, and less absorbed than Vermeer's with abstract pictorial problems of density and space, Metsu's paintings of everyday life are always cheerful and gracious. The family pictures in Berlin and in the Metropolitan show parents, children, and servants enjoying a comfortable and pleasant home and are probably faithful transcriptions of the domestic life of many Dutch bourgeois. (See illustration.)

Metsys (Matsys, Massys), Cornelius (before 1508-c. 1580). Flemish painter and copper engraver. Son of Quentin Metsys, he was a master in Antwerp by 1531 and went to Italy about 1562, where he made copies after Raphael. He was less accomplished as a figure painter than his brother Jan and found his strength in landscape, of which he did both paintings and prints.

Metsys (Matsys, Massys), Jan (1509-75). A Flemish painter of Antwerp. Son of Quentin and brother of Cornelis Metsys. Master in 1531, he was banished as a Protestant and apparently spent his exile in France and Italy. His most certain works date after his return about 1550. They include Lot and His Daughters, Susanna and a Holy Family in Brussels and many in other European museums. (See illustration.)

METSYS, JAN. Susanna and the Elders. Musées Royaux des Beaux-Arts, Brussels

134. METSYS, QUENTIN. Flight into Egypt
Worcester Art Museum

135. MICHELANGELO. The Holy Family. Uffizi, Florence

Metsys (Matsys, Massys), Quentin (1466-1530). Flemish painter whose art formed the transition from the spirituality of the fifteenth century to the secularism of the sixteenth. First important painter of the Antwerp school, he arrived in 1491 and became a master of the guild in 1493. He came to prominence at the time of great commercial prosperity in Antwerp and had a profound influence on subsequent Flemish painting. His art is a synthesis of the Flemish Gothic heritage and the newer Italian Renaissance ideas, and curiously parallels the early Mannerist developments in Italy. A man of humanist culture, the friend of Erasmus and More (both of whose portraits he painted), he exhibited in his art a largeness of vision, a great range and subtlety of color, a refined chiaroscuro, and an interest in common people and in character delineation. Born in Louvain, he was first influenced by the great master of that school, Dirk Bouts, whose pupil he may have been. He absorbed the styles of van Eyck and van der Weyden through the art of Bouts and Gerard David as is evident in his earliest works, such as the paintings of the Madonna and Child in Berlin and Brussels. His earliest dated work, the Triptych of the Legend of St. Anne (1507-09, Brussels), executed for the Confraternity of St. Anne in Louvain, shows the first evidence of Renaissance ideas in Flemish art. In his masterpiece, the Triptych of the Lamentation of Christ (1508-11, Antwerp), ordered by the carpenters guild for the Antwerp Cathedral, he exhibits an even greater realism and an increased dependence upon Italian art, especially Leonardo. His realism, his interest in individual types and even caricature has its most complete expression in such genre pictures as the Money Changer and His Wife (1514, Louvre) which influenced a whole generation of Flemish artists—his sons Cornelis and Jan, Joos van Cleve, Marinus van Roymerswaele, Jan van Hemessen, Peeter Huys and Pieter Aertsen. (See color plate 134.)

Metzinger, Jean (1883-). French Cubist painter and theoretician. His early scientific education first drew him to the exact coloristic laws of Neo-Impressionism; then he came under the influence of Picasso and Braque. His own contribution is summed up in a book he wrote with Gleizes, *Du Cubisme*, 1912. See CUBISM, SECTION D'OR.

Meulen, Adam van der (1632-90). Flemish battle, genre and landscape painter. Active in France, where he followed Louis XIV on his campaigns and faithfully depicted his activities in tapestry cartoons for the Gobelins and in large decorative compositions for châteaux.

Meunier, Constantin (1831-1905). Belgian painter of genre, landscapes and portraits, but better known as a sculptor. Influenced by Charles Degroux toward a realistic viewpoint and for a long time interested also in monastic scenes, he turned finally to the glorifications of workers that characterize his art both as painter and sculptor of massive and grandiose figures.

Meza, Guillermo (1917-). Among the leading younger artists in Mexico, Meza has exhibited in the United States and is known for his poetic landscapes filled with fanciful figures, his soft cool colors and fine draughtmanship.

mezzotint. A graphic arts process or print technique in which a metal plate is given an all-over burr or light plowing by means of a metal roller equipped with teeth. From this more or less uniformly stippled background the required design is then scraped and polished out. It was devised in the eighteenth century principally to reproduce portraits. See also ENGRAVING.

Michel, Georges (1763-1843). French landscape painter. One of the first to abandon the monumental style of eighteenth-century landscape for intimate studies drawn from nature. He was an isolated forerunner of the Barbizon school. He painted thickly in a Rembrandtesque manner and did many panoramas of the windmills of Montmartre. His life was apparently an unhappy one, domestically and financially.

Michelangelo Buonarroti (1475-1564). Florentine sculptor, painter and architect. With Leonardo da Vinci, Raphael and Titian, he was one of the greatest and most influential masters of the Italian High Renaissance. Though he was primarily a sculptor, he practiced the arts of painting and architecture with magnificent skill and also wrote poetry. His greatest works, commissions for extensive painting and sculptural decorations, are awesome and overpowering. They were inspired by the theology and philosophy of the greatest men of his day, yet are almost completely aesthetic expressions through the medium of the human body. He drew on the visual traditions of the great plastic masters of the early Florentine Renaissance, Giotto, Masaccio, Donatello and Signorelli, and their contributions tell in the austere monumentality of his art. His life coincided with the greatest temporal power of the papacy, and his work was subject to the vicissitudes of politics and warfare no less than to his own passionate and individual outlook on the world.

Michelagniolo di Lodovico di Lionardo di Buonarroti Simone was born in 1475 in Caprese, Casentino, the son of a respected civil official, and was placed at an early age in a Latin school. In 1488 he entered the painting shop of Domenico and Davide Ghirlandaio, and in 1489 an academy of sculpture conducted by Giovanni Bertoldo, who had been a pupil of Donatello and was custodian of Lorenzo de' Medici's collection of classical sculpture. The gifted pupil was soon noticed by Lorenzo and between 1490 and 1492 was a guest in the Medici household. There he formed a part of the circle of scholars and writers with whom the Medici surrounded themselves and was introduced to a Neo-Platonic and Christian philosophy that affected his thought for the rest of his life. In 1495 he is supposed to have forged an ancient Roman sculpture which was sold to Cardinal Raffael Riario in Rome; when the hoax was discovered, the cardinal was so impressed with the young sculptor's work that he arranged to have the youth invited to Rome. Thus Michelangelo first visited Rome from 1496 to 1501. Two well-known pieces of sculpture of this period are the Bacchus (Bargello, Florence), and the Lamentation (St. Peter's, Rome). In Florence, between 1501 and 1505, he made the famous marble David (now in the Florence Academy but formerly in front of the Palazzo Vecchio, where a replica now stands). He also undertook to paint in the Palazzo Vecchio a fresco of a battle scene, but this project was cut short at the cartoon stage by a call to Rome from Pope Julius II, and the composition is known only through replicas of the lost cartoons. The only accepted easel painting by Michelangelo was painted in this period, the Holy Family in the Uffizi (c.1503). In Rome in 1505 Michelangelo signed the first contract for the Tomb of Pope Julius, an ill-fated project which was completed only in 1545 in much reduced form and after five different contracts. Originally planned for St. Peter's, it now stands in the church of San Pietro in Vincoli and includes the renowned figure of Moses, completed in 1516; the famous "slaves" in the Louvre and the Florence Academy were originally intended for this tomb. In 1506 the tomb project was dropped by the Pope in favor of his plan for the decoration of the Sistine Chapel ceiling and resumed only after his death by contract with his heirs. A break with Michelangelo over this change in plan was followed by reconciliation and the artist's contract to paint the ceiling, which he did single-handed between 1508 and 1512.

Michelangelo's reputation as a painter rests on this enormous and awe-inspiring work, the interpretation of which is still today a source of controversy and new publications among scholars. It represents scenes of the Creation and the story of Noah, surrounded by architectural motifs peopled with decorative figures and interspersed with monumental prophets and sibyls. The artist's application of sculptural thought to painted decoration is everywhere apparent here. His next great commission (1520) was for the Medici tomb chapel in San Lorenzo, Florence, executed between 1524 and 1534, again with many changes and interruptions. The chapel, or new sacristy, was designed by Michelangelo, and the sculptures include a Madonna and Child, idealized portraits of the Medici princes Lorenzo of Urbino and Giuliano of Nemours, and the four famous decorative figures of Night, Day, Morning and Evening. The years 1527-30 saw the invasion of Italy by Austrian and Spanish troops. Michelangelo was made governor general of fortifications in Florence, fled the city when it was besieged, and returned after its fall in 1530.

In 1533 or 34 Michelangelo received a commission from the Medici Pope Clement VII to paint the Last Judgment on the altar wall of the Sistine Chapel, a task completed in 1541. In this as in many other instances, Michelangelo treated a traditional subject in a completely new way. The undivided wall is a mass of figures, composed into a unity and made intensely expressive by their individual movement. Under the moral and anti-classical impact of the Counter Reformation, the many nude figures were clothed with painted loincloths by Daniele da Volterra later in the sixteenth century. On completion of this work, Michelangelo undertook his last painting commission, the decoration of the chapel of Pope Paul III in the Vatican, with scenes of the Conversion

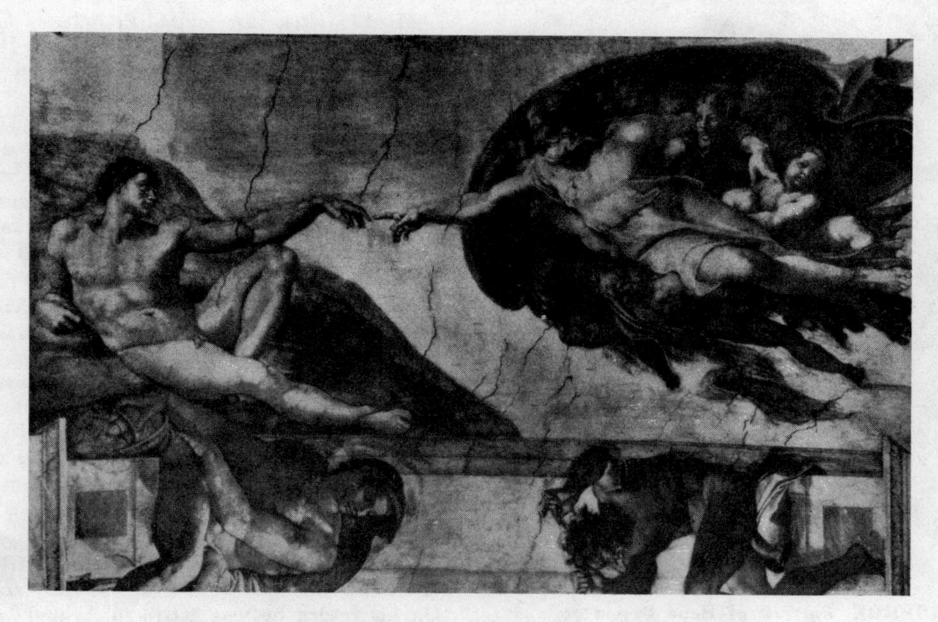

MICHELANGELO. Creation of Man. Sistine Chapel, Rome

MICHELANGELO. Women with Children
Detail from The Deluge. Sistine Chapel, Rome

MIGNARD, PIERRE. Portrait of René Descartes
National Gallery, London

of St. Paul and the Crucifixion of St. Peter (1541-50). From 1546 on he was retained as architect by Pope Paul, and directed the plans for the renovation of St. Peter's which occupied him, along with other architectural activity in Rome, for the rest of his life. Important sculptures of the late period are two groups of the Lamentation, in the cathedral of Florence and in Milan (the "Rondanini" Pietà). The artist died in Rome in 1564 and was buried there, but his body was secretly removed to Florence, where it was again buried with full honors in Santa Croce. Michelangelo's influence on subsequent art is incalculable. Sixteenth-century painting and sculpture of the succeeding generation is saturated with readily recognizable elements of his style, though none of the Mannerist artists achieved his stature. Every later artist attempting heroic expression through the human body has had to take him into account, and his influence was still strong in the nineteenth century in the painting of Delacroix and Daumier and the sculpture of Rodin. (See illustrations, including color plate 135.)

Michele da Verona (c.1470-1536/44). Venetian painter probably born in Verona and active there from 1515 to 1531. He was a pupil of Domenico Morone and later was influenced by the Quattrocento Venetian manner of Jacopo Bellini and Carpaccio.

Michele di Matteo (active 1416-48). Bolognese painter influenced, like many others of his generation, by Gentile da Fabriano. He has been confused with a still less consequential painter of the same name who came to Bologna from Modena later in the century.

Michelino, Domenico (see Domenico).

Michelino da Besozzo (active 1394-1442). Prominent member of the early school of Milan, but his authentic extant works are few. He is recorded as having worked on frescoes, miniatures and stained glass. One small altarpiece (Siena Gallery) seems to be his and a damaged fresco in the Borromeo palace, Milan, is ascribed to him. These works are in a late Gothic, courtly style parallel to the other contemporary north Italian schools and to similar work in France and Germany.

Micon (active after 472 B.C.). Greek sculptor and painter of the circle of Polygnotos. Famous for his depiction of horses and action, Micon painted murals in the Theseum of Athens which were described by Pausanias.

Miel (Milo), Jan (called Petit Jean) (1599-1663). Flemish painter and etcher active mainly in Italy. He executed religious decorations and is also known to have painted figures in Claude Lorrain's landscapes.

Miereveld, Michiel Jansz. van (1567-1641). A Dutch painter and engraver of portraits. He studied with Willem Willemsz. and with Blocklandt of Utrecht. He lived in Delft, but was very popular in The Hague and a favorite painter of the princes of Orange. His own works were much copied by his numerous pupils but they failed in their versions to reproduce the high quality of his composition and execution.

Mieris the Elder, Frans van (1635-81). Dutch painter of portraits, history and genre. He was the pupil of the glass painter Torrenvliet, and also of Gerard Dou and Abraham van den Tempel. He worked at Leyden, held offices in the guild there and trained many painters. In their homely ease and fine rendering of light on stuffs his best works are comparable to those of his more famous contemporaries.

Mi Fei (see CHINESE PAINTERS: SUNG DYNASTY).

Mignard, Nicolas (1606-68). French painter and etcher. Called "Mignard d'Avignon" to distinguish him from his younger brother Pierre. Schooled in the style of Fontainebleau (see), Nicolas spent two years in Italy copying the Carracci. On his return he was active in Avignon and at the court of Louis XIV, especially in connection with the decoration of

MILLAIS. Ophelia. Tate Gallery, London

the Tuileries. He painted portraits, including that of Louis XIV.

Mignard, Pierre (1610-95). French portrait and history painter. Trained in Fontainebleau and the school of Vouet, Mignard went to Rome for twenty years, earning himself the sobriquet "Mignard le Romain." His type of Madonna, based on the Italians, provoked the term "Mignardise" (sugar-sweet). He is famous for the political position he took at the side of Vouet in the Academy of St. Luke and against Le Brun and the Royal Academy. Upon the death of Colbert (1683), Mignard as head of the Rubenists replaced Le Brun in all his capacities, thus heralding the revolutionary change of taste from that of the Poussinists toward colorism. His strong point was portraiture, viz., that of his friend Molière. He also attempted decoration, as in the dome of the Val de Grâce. (See illustration.)

Millais, John Everett (1829-96). British Pre-Raphaelite painter; a child prodigy who easily developed skill as a craftsman, producing effective naturalistic pictures. He was a founding member in 1848 of the Pre-Raphaelite Brotherhood (see). He was influenced by Hunt toward close observation and conscientious detail in furtherance of his own technical proficiency, but he lacked creative imagination. His later work degenerated in quality although it was still tremendously popular. He was elected president of the Royal Academy in 1896. (See illustration.)

Miller, Alfred Jacob (1810-1874). American portrait painter. Born in Baltimore, he studied with Sully and in Paris, and worked in his home city and Washington, D.C. He is best known for a series of paintings of American Indian life, which were the result of a trip to the Far West with the Scottish traveler, Sir William Drummond Stewart, who commissioned them. The pictures are now in Scotland.

Miller, Kenneth Hayes (1876-1952). American painter and teacher. Born in Oneida Community in central New York, he studied with H. S. Mowbray and Kenyon Cox at the Art Students League and with Chase at the Chase school. A European trip brought him under the influence of the Renaissance masters. His earlier work was in the poetic tradition of Ryder, but he later gave up his mythological subject matter for contemporary city genre and his idealizing style for realism. He was one of the most influential art teachers, first at the New York School of Art and after 1911 at the Art Students League. (See illustration.)

Millet (Milet, Milé, Millé), Jean François (called Francisque) (1642-79). French landscape painter and etcher. Born in Antwerp where he studied with Francken. He copied Poussin and painted classical landscapes in the manner of Dughet.

MILLER, KENNETH HAYES. The Shopper
Whitney Museum of American Art, New York

MILLET. The Sower. Louvre, Paris

136. MIRÓ. Woman, Bird and Stars. Private Collection

Millet, Jean François (1814-75). French genre painter and graphic artist. Calling himself the "peasant of peasants," Millet in his mature period painted the simple religious and family life of the farm worker. His life was a difficult one. A precocious youth, he went from his native farm village to the Parisian studio of Delaroche. He did not fit in, and so left to teach himself in the Louvre and support himself by hack work. For a number of years he struggled to survive with portraits, biblical pieces, eighteenth-century nudes and signboards. In 1847 he was admitted to the Academy with his Oedipus; the following year he retired to the village of Barbizon (see), where he became a leading figure in the school of that name. Success was long in coming, however, and only in the 1860's did his paintings begin to sell. He was not a landscapist like his colleagues in Barbizon, but concentrated on figure studies of individuals and groups at work. His technique shows some of the impasto of Rembrandt and the brusqueness of Daumier. His postures are those of Michelangelo applied to ignoble subjects. His colors are tonal and rather muddy, the total style academic in the nineteenth-century sense. The subject matter, e.g., the Sower, the Angelus, the Gleaners, was revolutionary, but in a sentimental, Victorian way. He was called radical, but we can see today that his approach was most dignified and traditionalist. His featureless human beings lack the sharp comment, for instance, of Daumier. (See illustrations.)

Minden, Meister Bertram von (see MEISTER BERTRAM).

Ming Dynasty (see CHINESE PAINTERS: MING DYNASTY, 1368-1644).

miniature. A term used to describe the various types of painting in minature. At first it was applied to the vermilion-colored (Lat. *minium)* decorations on the borders and initials of illuminated manuscripts (see) in the middle ages. The term was ultimately transferred to all small-size paintings and in particular the small portrait medallions of the period from the seventeenth to the nineteenth century in Europe. In

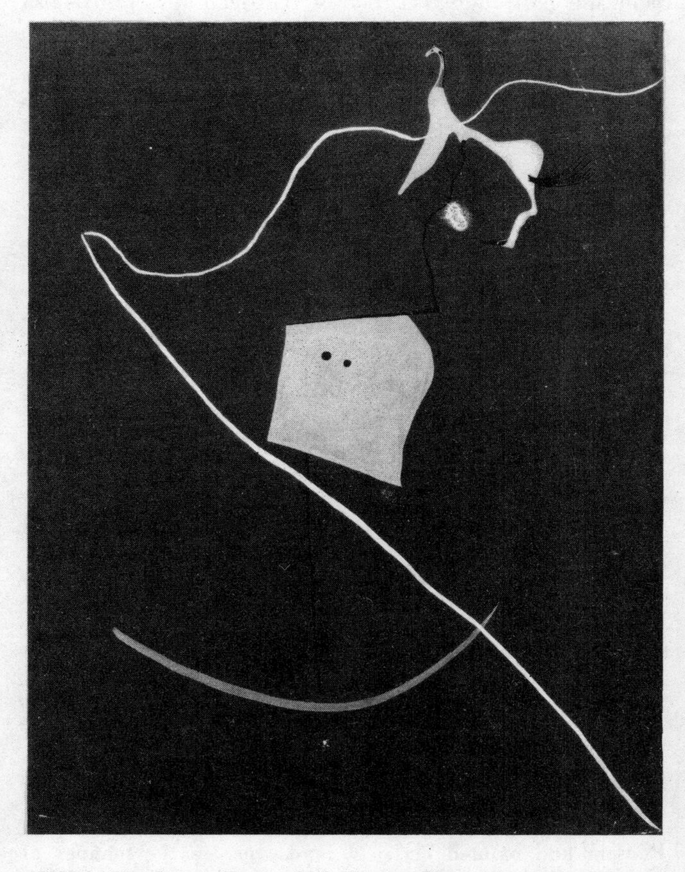

MIRO. The Circus. Formerly Collection Chester Dale, New York

Pepys' time they were known as "paintings in little" and "limnings" and for a time the miniature painter was even spoken of as a limner (see), a term which in American usage came to be applied to the itinerant portrait painters of the colonial period. In Europe the small-size portrait was done by specialists as well as by such well-known painters as Lancret, Prud'hon, Largillière, and others; it was also practiced in the United States. Miniature paintings either as portraits or as book illustrations occur in the Near and Far East and especially in Persia and India (see separate entries).

Minoan painting (see AEGEAN PAINTING).

Mirbel, Lisinka Aimée Zoé de (born Rüe) (1796-1849). French painter of portraits in miniature. She got her start during the Restoration in France with a portrait of Louis XVIII and continued after 1830 with the members of the Orléans family.

Miró, Joan (1893-). Outstanding and influential Spanish-born abstract Surrealist of the School of Paris. Miró emerged into the modern school while still in Spain, undergoing there the influence of Van Gogh and the Fauves, an important element in his bold and decorative color effects. He first visited Paris in 1919 and for a while came under the influence of Cubism, an influence evident in a later tendency to show simultaneous and disparate views of the same object. In 1925 he participated in the first Surrealist exhibition at the Galerie Pierre in Paris. His 1929 trip to Holland made him especially admiring of Vermeer, although from a different point of view than that of such an derivative artist as Dali. In 1930 he showed a group of collages in Paris, then went on to do décors for the Ballets Russes de Monte Carlo, two large murals including the well-known example in the Terrace Plaza Hotel in Cincinnati, sculpture and ceramic decorations. Miró's style is dominantly two-dimensional, Fauve-colorful and graphic in the same sense as that of Klee, who is suggested in the later work of the Spaniard. His most characteristic pictures, such as Dog Barking at the Moon, show a tendency to exaggerate one particular part of a body—animal or human—and to project it along an extended neck, leg or torso to another part of the brilliantly colored canvas, where it is brought into somewhat startling contact with its counterpart there. Thus he isolates and at the same time makes important the outstanding details in his work. Miró's works of the 1920's and '30's are all characterized by a wonderfully humorous imagination together with one of the most extraordinary feelings for color in modern painting; later works sometimes take on a more sombre quality. We may classify his work as halfway between the representational and non-representational aspects of Surrealism. (See illustrations, including color plate 136.)

137. MODIGLIANI. Head of a Woman
Collection Julian and Joachim J. Aberbach, New York

Mir Sayyid Ali (see INDIAN PAINTERS: HUMAYUN PERIOD).

Mir y Trinxet, Joaquín (1873-1940). Spanish landscape painter known for his poetic sensibility and bright coloring. A product of Impressionism, Mir rebelled against the academic teachings of Caba and Graner with whom he studied. Although Catalan and a colleague of Nonell, he is parallel to, rather than part of, the official Modernista group of Barcelona. His ingratiating luminous landscapes won prizes from 1897 on, and his charcoal sketches of the life of Barcelona were also popular. In the manner of the Impressionists Mir went to special locations to produce his interpretive landscapes. He was particularly fond of Mallorca, the campo de Tarragona and la Cardana. Typical of these landscapes are L'hort de l'ermita and L'alzina i la vaca (Museum of Modern Art, Madrid). (See illustration.)

MIR Y TRINXET. The Lantern. The Cathedral, Tarragona

Mitsunaga (see JAPANESE PAINTERS: HEIAN PERIOD).

Mitsunobu (see JAPANESE PAINTERS: MUROMACHI PERIOD).

Mme Récamier by Jacques Louis David (see).

modeling. The attempt to give a third dimension to a particular form through the use of light-and-dark effects, cross-hatching, or special color relationship.

Moderne Galerie, Vienna. Part of the Belvedere Museum; it contains late nineteenth-century and early twentieth-century masters such as Hodler and Klimt.

Modersohn-Becker, Paula (1876-1907). German painter whose work represents an instance of Germany's coming abreast of the modern movement, that is, of Cézanne, Gauguin and Van Gogh. She is identified with early Expressionism (see) although entirely independent of group affiliation, arriving at her formulation of the contemporary artist's problem by herself. She attended art school in Berlin, 1896, but, dissatisfied, moved on to the artists' colony at Worpswede, near Bremen, where she painted peasants and poor people. But the naturalistic genre painting of this group seemed insufficient for her. The unsuccessful results of a solo exhibition in Berlin, 1899, sent her to Paris in 1900 and, after her marriage to Otto Modersohn, again in 1901. The influence of Cézanne was already very strong; she also spoke in her letters of Vuillard, Denis, and Bonnard. Since her work and that of her husband moved toward different ends, she left him by 1906 and went to Paris, where she was very much affected by the Gauguin Memorial Exhibition that year. Her already Cézannesque forms were there given a brilliant decorative coloristic impulse. To this combination is added that great sympathy for the poor and for humanity in general that gives German art during this period part of its special quality. Her husband joined her in Paris and they returned in 1907 to Worpswede, where a few weeks after the birth of her daughter, the painter died suddenly at the age of thirty-one. (See illustration.)

Modigliani, Amedeo (1884-1920). Distinguished Italian-born painter and sculptor associated with the School of Paris. Son of poor Jewish parents, he was born in the Leghorn

MODERSOHN-BECKER. Self Portrait
Basel Museum, Switzerland

MODIGLIANI. Nude. Koninklijk Museum, Antwerp

ghetto, suffering serious illnesses during his boyhood. After casual art training at Capri and Venice, he arrived in Paris, 1906, with money inherited from a rich uncle. For a few years he lived what he thought was an Aubrey Beardsley-Oscar Wilde kind of life, taking his work very casually in spite of his considerable gifts—or perhaps because of them—and falling into habits of dissipation. He became a café character and alcoholic, often without his own lodgings, taking drugs and moving from one affair to another. Attracted by the African Negro sculpture that had interested Picasso and others in the Parisian group, Modigliani took the smooth long oval forms as the basis of his painted faces, repeating the pointed chins, oval-shaped eyes, flaring nostrils, etc. A sensitive draughtsman, he achieved a delicate and pure line that gives both his painting and the sculpture an abstractness of form and restrained emotive tension. There is a gentle melancholy quality in many of his works that suggests the influence of Botticelli. Within the admittedly narrow range of his subject matter—faces and figure painting—he manages to achieve a considerable variety of emphasis and expression, although the differences are subtle. It is possible, as some have felt, that Modigliani's sculpture is more powerful than his painting, but the fact remains that certain categories of the latter art, particularly the sensuously attractive and effective nude studies, are among the most exciting works in modern painting. See PRIMITIVISM. (See illustrations, including color plate 137.)

Mohammedan painting (see INDIAN PAINTERS and PERSIAN PAINTERS).

Moholy-Nagy, Laszlo (1895-1946). Hungarian-born painter, designer, typographer and theoretician associated with the Bauhaus (see) school in Germany. His painting, which is non-objective (see), stems from the tradition of three-dimensional constructions in space or on a flat surface (articulated by Constructivists such as Malevich) and is, like the Purism (see) of the 1920's, entirely machinistic in approach. Moholy is also responsible for considerable pioneer work in photography and introduced its study to the Bauhaus; like his important work in typography and poster design, this was turned to the uses of industrial design ,for which the Bauhaus was ultimately very significant. Moholy edited the school's series of books between 1925 and 1930. In 1937 he came to America, where he founded the Institute of Design in Chicago to carry on Bauhaus traditions. (See illustration.)

Mola, Pier Francesco (1612-66). Born in Coldrerio near Como, he was largely active in Rome. He absorbed a great many influences—the Maniera (see), the Carracci, and the Venetians—and did some large commissions in the Baroque manner, but is most important for his charming romantic landscapes with small figures. The son of an architect who moved to Rome in 1616, he studied with Orsi and d'Arpino, and later in Bologna with Albani. (See color plate 138.)

Molenaer, Jan Miense (c.1610-68). Dutch painter and engraver of portraits, genre, and biblical subjects. In his early works, he shows so strong an influence from Frans Hals that it is probable that he, like his wife Judith Leyster (see), studied under that master. Later in Amsterdam he betrays the pervasive influence of Rembrandt, but his pictures of this time are somewhat careless in execution.

Moll, Oskar (1875-1947). German Fauve painter who during his 1907-08 stay in Paris became friendly with Matisse, from whom this influence was directly derived. In 1918 he was called to the Breslau Academy, and was its director from 1926 to 1931. From 1934 to his death he lived in Berlin. Moll is typical of the German Fauve movement, which also included Levy and Purrmann.

MOHOLY-NAGY. Great Aluminum Picture
Collection Sibyl Moholy-Nagy, New York

MONET. The Seine at Argenteuil. Wildenstein Gallery, New York

138. MOLA. Rest on the Flight into Egypt
William Rockhill Nelson Gallery, Kansas City

Momoyama Period (see JAPANESE PAINTERS: MOMOYAMA PERIOD, 1573-1614).

Momper, Josse (or Jodocus) (1564-1635). Flemish landscape painter. Member of a large family of artists whose works are frequently confused. A transitional decorative artist between Brueghel and the later Dutch landscapists.

Monaco, Lorenzo (see LORENZO MONACO).

Mona Lisa by Leonardo da Vinci (see).

Mondrian, Piet (1872-1944). Netherlands painter. His early work was influenced by traditional Dutch painting. He was in Paris during 1910-11 and there fell under the influenc f Picasso and Cubism, after which he went through (1914-17) his "plus-and-minus" period, a phase in which small vertical and horizontal lines were set in loose opposition to each other. Mondrian led in the formation of de Stijl group, 1917, turning at the same time to his first purely abstract paintings. In 1920 he founded Neo-Plasticism (see) with its development of the non-objective (see) idea. In 1932 he was with the Abstraction-Création group in Paris but left it for London in 1938 and New York in 1940. There at the age or sixty-eight he was very well received, finding stimulation and excitement in the American scene. He died in New York, his last and unfinished work the Victory Boogie Woogie. (See color plate 139.)

139. MONDRIAN. Composition. Albright Art Gallery, Buffalo

Monet, Claude (1840-1926). Outstanding French Impressionist landscape painter. An artistic prodigy, Monet began his landscape study at his home, Le Havre, where he painted with the plein-air painter of weather, Boudin, and the Dutchman Jongkind, an atmospheric interpreter of exquisite touch. In Paris Monet found the studio of Gleyre stifling and, with Bazille, Sisley and Renoir, he abandoned it for the Forest of Fontainebleau. These painters were at the time affected by Corot, Daubigny and Courbet. By the mid-1860's Monet was employing the clear, flat colors of his early maturity and was actively associated with the radical Café Guerbois group, in which Manet figured so prominently. During the Franco-Prussian war he was in London with Sisley and Pissarro, and there he met the dealer Durand-Ruel. Following the war Monet worked closely with Renoir and together they developed the characteristic broken-color technique of middle-Impressionist painting. Monet is notable for applying this method in clinical fashion to "series" paintings of the same subject, such as the Gare St. Lazare under changing light conditions. The result is, perhaps, more subjective than scientifically convincing, especially in the later series of Rouen Cathedral and the Thames, which are imbued with poetical fancy and a highly personal color sense. These latter paintings with their modern symbolic overtones reveal the crisis that Impressionism passed through in the 1880's when its outstanding members changed from objective to subjective modes of vision. Monet was simple in character and did not show that flair for theorizing and writing that marked several of his contemporaries. See IMPRESSIONISM. (See illustrations, including color plate 140.)

Mongol Period (see PERSIAN PAINTERS: MONGOL PERIOD, 1256-1353).

monochromatic. Featuring one hue or a color scheme based on the various tints of that one hue or color. Thus a painting may be made up of different but harmonizing shades: e.g., blue, as in The Blue Boy by Gainsborough.

Montagna, Bartolommeo (c.1450-1523). The principal master of the provincial school of Vicenza, he worked there and in Venice. His sober and rigid early style, deriving from Mantegna, was later modified toward more mellow light and color by contact with the contemporary Venetian masters Carpaccio and Giovanni Bellini. An impressive altarpiece by him is in the Basilica di Monte Berico near Vicenza.

Montagne Ste-Victoire by Paul Cézanne (see).

Montenegro, Roberto (1885-). Mexican easel painter, muralist, editor, illustrator, stage designer and engraver; he organized the Museum of Popular Arts in Mexico City. A versatile and prolific producer, he has done various frescoes in his characteristically decorative and elegant line.

Monticelli, Adolphe Joseph Thomas (1824-86). French painter. An interesting personality who threw off an early classical education to produce a personal, highly poetic style which was little appreciated during his lifetime but is now much sought after. His vague little figures, reminiscent of Watteau and rendered in a flecked, crusted mosaic technique, had a strong influence on Van Gogh. The mood is colorful but mystic and dreamy. (See illustration.)

Moore, Henry (1898-). Distinguished British sculptor and draughtsman who has been influenced by primitive sculpture, the sculpturesque paintings of Masaccio and the expressiveness of Picasso. The primordial quality of his sculptures with their impression of half-human, half-plant organisms is also reflected in the series of drawings done during World War II in Moore's capacity as a war artist. These papers dealing with the life of London's air-raid shelters are among the most fluid in form and emotionally stirring of our time. (See illustration.)

Mor, Anthonis (1519?-76). Dutch painter of portraits and history. He was born in Utrecht, where he studied painting with Jan van Scorel. Mor's career was international. In 1550 he was in Rome and in the same year traveled to Lisbon at the command of Charles V to paint the royal family of Portugal. He worked in England, painting the portrait of Mary Tudor and painted for the court of Philip II in Madrid. In his later years he was active in Utrecht, Brussels and Ant-

140. MONET. Paris from Princess Gardens (detail). Oberlin College, Oberlin

MONTICELLI. Flowers in a Blue Vase
Paul Rosenberg and Company, New York

werp. His portraits have always been highly esteemed for their penetration into personality and technical excellence. (See illustration.)

Morales, Luis de (called el Divino) (d. 1586). Spanish devotional painter of Estremadura. His artistic origins are obscure. He demonstates many of the progressive accomplishments of his day, from northern realism to Leonardesque sfumato, learned perhaps from nearby Portugal. But these are employed in old-fashioned, almost medieval stereotypes of sacred images that had little appeal to the courtly taste of his age. His career was long and prolific, but he was poverty-stricken and isolated in a province that had produced more soldiers than artists. With such popular success that he was called "Divine," Morales concentrated on a few favorite subjects: the Pietà, the Virgin and Child, Christ Bearing the Cross, the Ecce Homo. His style of execution was Mannerist, a Michelangelesque Mannerism like Juan de Juanes', but with more tender sentiment. When he was invited to submit a trial painting of Christ Bearing the Cross to the competition for work at the Escorial, it was refused by Philip II, who preferred more classicizing styles. Morales' popular appeal carried weight, however, and in 1581 the king extended him a pension. To the end he produced his pious devotional paintings of emaciated figures, and he had many imitators who continued after his death. His earliest work, dated 1546, is a Madonna in Badajoz. In the 1560's he painted a number of retablos in rather Germanic style. His Italian manner manifests itself more in the later works in Salamanca. His most dramatic, and repetitive, period comes at the end of his career. (See color plate 141.)

Moran, Thomas (1837-1926). American landscapist who was born in Bolton, England. He was one of the latter-day Hudson River painters; his earlier more intimate landscapes

MOORE. Study for Northampton Madonna and Child, Number 1. Valentin Gallery, New York

MOR. Portrait of a Nobleman. Art Institute of Chicago

held promise, but his later huge canvases, the result of a trip with a government exploration party to Yellowstone, the Grand Canyon, and Yosemite, achieved, like those of Bierstadt, a monumental dullness. His work was, however, very popular.

Morandi, Giorgio (1890-). A leading Italian painter whose reputation is based not only on his early twentieth-century works but also on later efforts. Many Italians consider him their greatest living painter. He began with Cézanne as his ideal and set out to do extensive form research within a very narrow subject range: still life and some landscape. He has been compared with Mondrian in the formal ordering of the various parts of his compositions, their constantly and delicately achieved sense of balance and the continuous variations within the range of his bottles and bowls. Yet Morandi is representational in outlook and distinctly poetic in his approach to a highly personal type of color. Thus, while Purist in formal approach, his works also possess a high lyrical quality. See PURISM, VALORI PLASTICI. (See illustration.)

Morazzone, Il (Pier Francesco Mazzucchelli) (1571-1626). Lombard painter born at Morazzone near Varese, he studied in Milan, Rome, and Venice. Influenced by Procaccini, he is the most dramatic painter of the Milanese school, crude, realistic, and intense.

Moreau, Gustave (1826-98). French symbolist painter. Trained by Chassériau, he employed a style that was an amalgam of Ingres and Delacroix. He delighted in complex exotic subjects based on the Bible and classical mythology, which he painted with original chiaroscuro effects, e.g., Salomé, 1876. He is most important, perhaps, for his teaching of the younger artists, including Matisse and Rouault of the Fauve movement.

Moreau, Luc-Albert (1882-1948). A French painter, draughtsman and lithographer best known for his paintings of World War I, in which he took a very active part. He lived through the Fauve and Cubist movements, although the bulk of his work is not markedly affected by either of these movements and remains direct and representational in quality.

Moretto da Brescia (Alessandro Bonvicino) (c.1498-1554). Prolific Italian painter born in Brescia and active there as well as in Venice, Bergamo, Milan, Verona, Trento and Rome. He has been mistakenly described as a pupil of Titian. His first recorded work (1516-18) was as assistant to Fioravante Ferramola in the decoration of the organ shutters in the Cathedral of Brescia. His art was influenced by the Venetians and by the earlier Brescian painter, Romanino. His many religious paintings in their broad and simple classicism, enriched by Venetian naturalism and color, are important for the Carracci and the anti-Mannerrist (see) movements of Bologna and Milan. His art is characterized by a unique grey-green tonality and in his portraits he seems to have been influenced by his pupil Moroni. (See illustration.)

Morisot, Berthe (1841-95). A feminine member of the French Impressionist movement. She practiced etching and lithography in addition to painting. Daughter of a cultivated artistic family, she received assistance from Corot and from Edouard Manet, whose brother Eugène she married. At first primarily a portraitist, she began in 1873 to paint out of doors, as in Woman Seated on a Bench Sewing (Pau, Museum). See IMPRESSIONISM. (See color plate 142.)

Morland, George (1763-1804). British painter of picturesque genre compositions seen against romantic backgrounds of nature. His scenes of English village life descend from such Dutch popular genre artists of the seventeenth century as Ostade. Morland's works are distinctly sentimental in character, painted in an appealing manner with a touch of old-fashioned morality as in Hogarth. His paintings and the engravings from them were popular at the beginning

MORANDI. Still Life. Museum of Modern Art, New York

MORETTO DA BRESCIA
Portrait of Conte Sciarra Martinengo Cesaresco
National Gallery, London

141. MORALES. Virgin and Child. National Gallery, London

142. MORISOT. In the Dining Room
National Gallery of Art, Dale Collection, Washington, D.C.

143. MORONI. Titian's Schoolmaster
National Gallery of Art, Widener Collection, Washington, D.C.

of the nineteenth century because of the pervasiveness of the Rousseau viewpoint in France and England. His contented farmers had a certain nostalgic appeal later in the nineteenth century. (See illustration.)

Moro da Verona, Il (see TORBIDO, FRANCESCO).

Morone, Domenico (c.1442-c.1518). Veronese painter known through a few signed and dated paintings and some badly damaged frescoes. Certain Paduan elements in his colorful style recall Mantegna, whose classical draughtsmanship possibly came to him through his teacher Benaglio. His son Francesco was also a painter.

Moroni, Giovanni Battista (c.1525-78). Born in Albino near Bergamo, he was a student of Moretto da Brescia. He is noted as a portraitist rather than as a religious painter. His portraits, broadly handled, elegant, and coolly objective, were much influenced by Venetian painting, especially Titian and Lotto. Moroni's earlier work is characterized by a subtle silvery tonality which later tends to become grey and dull. One of the great portraitists of the sixteenth century, he was admired even by Titian. He not only renders the material fact with rich simplicity but is capable of profound psychological insight. (See color plate 143.)

Moronobu (see JAPANESE PAINTERS: TOKUGAWA PERIOD).

Morris, George L. K. (1905-). Contemporary American abstract painter in a geometric manner. Born in New York City, he went to Yale and studied art at the Art Students League and with Léger in Paris.

Morris, William (1834-96). British painter-poet; founder of the Arts and Crafts Movement, which tried to revive handicrafts in an increasingly mechanized age. He was brought into the later Pre-Raphaelite movement (see) by Rossetti and was also a close friend of Burne-Jones with whom he had studied at Oxford. Morris, whose original training had been in architecture, was interested in painting in the course of his friendship with Rossetti and, after his own marriage, turned to decorating as a career. His firm, founded in 1862, did church decoration, stained-glass windows, fabric and furniture design, etc. It is in his attempts to spiritualize decoration and reform book design and typography that his artistic importance lies rather than in his painting. His painting is that of a conventional Victorian sentimentalist; it lacks the vigor and psychological penetration that makes his poetry his true monument.

Morse, Samuel Finley Breese (1791-1872). American portrait and landscape painter, he is, however, much more famous as the inventor of the telegraph. Born in Charlestown, Mass., the son of a noted geographer, he went to Yale and studied with Allston. In 1811 he went abroad with Allston and met and became friendly with Turner, Lawrence, Coleridge and Wordsworth. In 1815 he returned to the U.S. and did portraits in New York, Washington, D.C., and Charleston but with only moderate success. He helped found the National Academy of Design and in 1826 was elected its first president. In 1829 he went to Europe again and painted Romantic landscapes which are among his most interesting works. He returned in 1832 and in 1836 gave up painting to concentrate on invention. (See illustration.)

mosaic painting. Mosaic is, like buon fresco (see FRESCO PAINTING), one of the most permanent ways of making a flat design adhere to a wall, ceiling or floor surface. In this case bits (tesserae) of colored material are embedded in plaster or other adhesives to make up the design or to form the figures. The tesserae may be of a standard size and cubic shape (opus tessellatum) or may be irregular in size and shape. The Romans designed ornamental stone mosaic floors in which identically cubic tesserae were laid in regular grid rows, producing the design (usually geometrical) by variation of color only. Mosaic floors also exist in which the tesserae were merely pebbles of rounded shape. Mosaics representing figures or scenes usually employ tesserae of varying size, the dimensions and the arrangement of the little cubic bits being a function of the modeling (opus vermiculatum). Mother-of-pearl and semi-precious stones were sometimes used as mosaic material by both Mediterranean and Central American cultures. An exceptional type of inlay related to mosaic is opus sectile, a stone intarsia in which the pattern is produced not by many small bits but by fewer, large plaques of stone cut to the pattern and fitted together like a "jig-saw" puzzle. When used decoratively as at S. Vitale, Ravenna (c.526-47) this is sometimes called the Incrustation style; it can also be used to make figure scenes as in the Junius Bassus mosaic (fourth century), where the pieces are intricately irregular in shape. The Mughals used this technique in India.

Although in its origins in Sumeria mosaic was used to decorate vertical surfaces by means of conical plugs of baked clay imbedded in the surface, throughout ancient times mosaic was generally restricted to the decoration of floors. Such pavements were necessarily made of stone tesserae and the colors, after exposure, would be dull unless wetted. This art reached its height in Roman times when throughout the entire Mediterranean world it was the practice to decorate pavements of courts, dining rooms and important halls of all sorts with pictorial scenes set into a variety of geometrical panels, interlaces and diaper backgrounds. In Early Christian times mosaic decoration was transferred to the wall and vault surfaces (*opus musivum*), where it had not been so commonly applied before. This was accompanied by an almost universal use of fragile glass tesserae. The translucent quality of these glass bits, whether pale or deeply colored, combined with the reflective power of gold leaf often used on the rear surface of the cube, lent a glistening richness and shimmer to the mosaic surfaces unmatched in other techniques. This was intensified by the intentional irregularity of the pieces and by setting the cubes obliquely in the wall or vault. An iridescence was set up which made the inner building surface elusive in appearance, rather than precise as in classical architecture, or mat as in Roman mosaic pavement. Add to this the sensuous and symbolic powers of the gold, which was used unadulterated over vast areas in some mid-Byzantine churches, and one can understand why the technique of mosaic painting became a potent method of dematerializing and transcendentalizing. It has been pointed out that the arrangement of the figures on the vaults, niches and pendentives amidst the flickering light of the tesserae tended to make the statuesque mid-Byzantine figures hover in front of their pictorial surfaces. This increased the magical reality of their being, as in the Annunciation at Daphni (c.1100) or the Madonna at Torcello (c.1100).

MORLAND. Stable Interior. Tate Gallery, London

MORSE. Self Portrait
Addison Gallery of American Art, Phillips Academy, Andover

MOSER. Magdalen at the Feast of the Pharisees. Panel from Magdalene Altar, Pfarrkirche, Tiefenbronn

The medieval period was certainly the golden age of expressive mosaic decoration. We observe the abandonment of Roman illusionistic mosaic, which still lingered on in S. Pudenziana (Rome, c.400), but was replaced by decorative panels of symbolic imagery in the Tomb of Galla Placidia (Ravenna, 420-50), and then finally by a fusion of ecclesiastical and imperial imagery in the gorgeous panoply of S. Vitale (Ravenna, c.526-47). This process was interrupted by the Iconoclastic Controversy (726-843) from which we have only decorative landscapes of a secular nature (mosque at Damascus, 706). The West had, in part for economic reasons, abandoned mosaic for fresco (however, see COSMATI) when Byzantine artists were sheathing the walls of Greek, Sicilian and Italian churches with gold glass during the eleventh and twelfth centuries. This neutral gold background was turned into spatial vistas in late Byzantine mosaics (see) of the thirteenth to the fifteenth century. See BYZANTINE PAINTING. (See illustration.)

Moser, Lucas (before 1390, after 1433). German painter, designer and maker of stained glass. Documents in Ulm

MOSES. McDonel Farm. Phillips Collection, Washington, D.C.

reveal little about the artist of this name who worked there in the first half of the fifteenth century. But it is probably the same Lucas Moser who signed and dated (1431) the extraordinarily advanced and skillfully painted altarpiece of the Magdalen in Tiefenbronn. (See illustration.)

Moses, Anna Mary Robertson (called "Grandma" Moses) (1860-). Contemporary American naive painter whose art, reproduced commercially in fabrics, ceramics, Christmas cards, etc., has become a national byword. Born in upstate New York, she began at seventy-six to paint genre scenes remembered from her childhood. She was discovered in 1938 and three of her paintings were shown at the Museum of Modern Art. The following year she had her first one-man show. She has produced in the neighborhood of 2,000 paintings. (See illustration.)

Mostaert, Jan (c.1475 to 1555/56). Dutch painter of religious pictures and portraits. Mostaert spent most of his life in Haarlem, but may have worked for a time at the court of Margaret of Austria in Flanders. His well-composed and firmly executed portraits betray the psychological influence of Geertgen tot Sint Jans.

Motherwell, Robert (1915-). Contemporary American abstract painter in an Expressionist vein. Born in Washington, he graduated from Stanford, and studied philosophy at Harvard and architecture at Columbia. He studied etching and engraving with Kurt Seligmann and S. W. Hayter, but is largely self-taught as a painter. He has been a very active critic, lecturer and editor, and is one of the leading theoreticians of American abstract art. (See illustration.)

motif. The theme or dominant feature of a painting. This may vary from an elaborate anecdotal motif to a religious one such as the Madonna and Child, or to the more mechanical motifs used by many modern painters, such as still-life compositions or arrangements.

Motonubu (see JAPANESE PAINTERS: MUROMACHI PERIOD).

Moulin Rouge by Henri de Toulouse-Lautrec (see).

Mount, William Sidney (1807-68). One of the earliest and most popular American genre painters, his works were reproduced by Currier and Ives in the U.S. and Goupil in Europe. His specialty was the sentimental and anecdotal depiction of rural life in Long Island, where he was born. He was early apprenticed to his brother, Henry, a sign and portrait painter in New York City; studied at the National Academy of Design, and then opened his own studio in 1829. In 1836, he returned to Long Island because of ill health and painted there the rest of his life. Though his pictures tend toward sentimentality, they are sometimes redeemed by such qualities as sensitivity and realism, viz., Eel-spearing at Setauket (private collection) and Long Island Farmhouses (Metropolitan).

Moya, Pedro de (1610-74). Spanish painter of Granada. As a soldier in Flanders he became acquainted with the Rubens style and practiced it in Spain, doing so in the manner of van Dyck, with whom he studied in London.

Mu Ch'i (see CHINESE PAINTERS: SUNG DYNASTY).

Müelich (or Mielich), Hans (1516-73). German miniature painter and maker of woodcuts. He spent his entire life in Munich, where he was a member of the painters' guild and was much employed by the court. In 1541 he traveled to Rome. His style shows the influence of Albrecht Altdorfer, and bears witness to his wide culture and his knowledge of Renaissance painting.

Mueller, Otto (1874-1930). German painter and graphic artist; a member of Die Brücke. He studied lithography at Görlitz from 1890 to 1895 and attended the Academy of Art at Dresden from 1896 to 1898. After a year of work in solitude in the Riesengebirge he came to Berlin in 1907, and a few years later joined Die Brücke, remaining in it from 1910 until its dissolution in 1913. Mueller's ancestry may have been touched with gypsy blood; he spent a good deal of time in Hungary around gypsy settlements, absorbing this distinctly primitivistic culture in a fashion reminiscent of Gauguin, whose art affected him in other ways as well. There is a slight flavor of the decadent in Mueller's art as a result of this preoccupation, but his color combinations are always decorative and bland in the Gauguin sense rather than dissonant in the Van Gogh manner. Much of his work is taken up with themes derived from gypsy life. See EXPRESSIONISM. (See illustration.)

Muenter, Gabriele (1877-). German painter and member of the Blue Rider Munich group. Student of Kandinsky in 1901, she made trips with him, particularly to North

MOTHERWELL. The Voyage
Museum of Modern Art, Rio de Janeiro

MUELLER. The Bathers. Detroit Institute of Arts

144. MUNCH. The Bridge. Stadtmuseum, Cologne

Africa. She settled in Murnau near Munich in 1909. Her style is like that of the early Kandinsky—linear, decorative and symbolically colored, but altogether figurative in character. See EXPRESSIONISM.

Multscher, Hans (c.1400-67). German sculptor and painter. He headed a workshop in Ulm that produced altarpieces combining wood carvings and painted wings. The two great works from this shop reveal him as a strong and realistic artist who must have had some familiarity with the contemporary Flemish style. Only the painted wings of the Wurzach altarpiece (Deutsches Museum, Berlin) have been preserved; the carved figures and painted wings that composed the altar of the Virgin, made for the church in Sterzing between 1456 and 1458, are now in various churches and collections.

Munch, Edvard (1863-1944). Distinguished Norwegian painter and graphic artist and important progenitor of Expressionism (see) in Germany. Raised in an environment of family misfortune wherein he lost his mother and two sisters and having witnessed the poverty of the slums of Oslo in which his father practiced medicine, Munch grew up with a sense of the futility and misery of existence. In 1886 he joined the Christiania Bohemians group and painted some distinctly "advanced" pictures dealing with human misery and loneliness, treating them in a symbolic fashion. A government grant in 1888 enabled him to go to Paris where he encountered the art of the Pointillists, Pissarro, Lautrec, Van Gogh and Gauguin. He soon turned to a style of painting that combined the free-flowing curves of Art Nouveau (see) with the large color areas of Gauguin. But it was the unique philosophical and poetic approach that made his art so important for Germans of the following generation. They were to see in him a kindred sense of isolation of the individual human being and the powerful abstract forces—love, hate, fear, etc.—that tend to swallow that being. In 1892 he was invited to exhibit at the Berlin Artists Association, but a controversy over his work caused the exhibition to close down and the ensuing scandal made his name a byword in Germany. In Paris in 1896 Munch did sets for Ibsen's *Peer Gynt* for the Théâtre de l'Oeuvre; and he exhibited at the Art Nouveau Gallery, but with little success. His art was not for the form-interested French but rather for the spiritually harassed Germans of that period. Munch's people suffer from fear, jealousy and hatreds of all kinds, but particularly from lonesomeness. His conception of nature may be stated in his own words: "I hear the scream in nature." These ideas he transmitted to central Europe. See also DECADENT ART, SYMBOLISM. (See illustrations, including color plate 144.)

Munich school. A group of late nineteenth-century American painters influenced by their training at the Munich Academy, where they studied under the German painters Leibl, Kaulbach, Strahuber, Diez, Loefftz, Trübner, Wagner and Piloty. The style is characterized by dark, warm, brown colors and broad, dashing brushwork, and was based on the older realism of Rembrandt, Hals and Velázquez. The outstanding American exponent of this manner was Duveneck, but it also included Neal, Rosenthal, Shirlaw, Chase, Vinton, Alexander, Bacher, Marr, Currier, Fitz, Muhrman and Dielman.

Munkacsy, Mihaly (1844-1909). Hungarian painter of religious, historical and narrative subjects in a semi-Realist, semi-academic technique very well suited to the needs of illustration. He is known primarily for the Milton Dictating to His Daughters (New York Public Library).

Mur, Ramón de (d. after 1435). Spanish painter of Tarragona. Painted the retablo of Guimerá (1402-12) in Vich, formerly ascribed to a "Master of Guimerá." He shares with Borrassá the credit for introducing the International

Style, although he was a much more conservative artist than Borrassá. He was associated with Bernardo Martorell, who finished his retablo of St. Peter in Vinaixa, begun in 1420.

mural painting. The decoration of walls and ceilings, obtained by a variety of techniques, shares much with the painting of movable panels and canvases, but is also governed by considerations arising out of the relationship of the decorated surface to the architecture as a whole. The painted surface must be absolutely permanent and sufficiently mat in finish to avoid glare and reflections. The design must be laid out in relationship to the spectator's position, fixed or moving, and it must relate harmoniously to the architectural effect of the room. Most permanent, perhaps, of the techniques of painting murals is that of buon fresco (see FRESCO PAINTING) in which the pigment becomes an integral part of the dry surface. A few other methods exist: encaustic (see), tempera (see) or oil (see). The oil (or varnish) paint may be applied directly to the wall or to canvas which is then attached by adhesive; both methods risk the effect of dampness and chemical change interfering with the painted surface. Modern chemistry has contributed two new methods, using liquid silicates or fired porcelain enamel, the latter appropriate for outdoor use. Throughout history the style of mural painting has closely followed that of movable paintings. Previous to the Greeks and Romans, flat effects were prized, giving way in classical times to illusionistic vistas and scenes with natural details. Medieval murals again became somewhat non-spatial, although bodies often were solidly modeled. The West, but not the Orient, broke with this tradition in the Renaissance, obtaining in the Baroque period such radical illusionistic effects as to dissolve the wall almost totally. Contemporary mural painting began with the representational and conventional wall treatments offered by the professional decorators of the late nineteenth and early twentieth centuries. During the 1920's in Mexico mural painting enjoyed a strong revival which ranged from the two-dimensional and decorative effects of Rivera, through the more three-dimensional and dramatic effects of Orozco to the multi-viewed and dynamic outdoor experiments of Siqueiros.

145. MURILLO. The Little Conception
William Rockhill Nelson Gallery, St. Louis

MUNCH. The Cry. Oslo Municipal Collections

Murillo, Bartolomé Esteban (1616-82). Most characteristic painter of the sentimental Spanish Baroque style. At one time known as the "Spanish Raphael," his style is in eclipse in our time. His forms were rendered in a brilliance of color resembling van Dyck's and were bathed in a sfumato not unlike Correggio's. He was in particular demand as a producer of religious images such as Madonnas and Immaculate Conceptions and operated almost exclusively in the service of the convents. Like his Spanish contemporaries, moreover, he alternated his religious works with genres. The saccharine quality of the ragamuffins which inhabit the latter may be owing to the urbane Spanish taste of his day and also to his association with the Franciscans. The degree to which he sublimated the down-to-earth art of his predecessors can be seen by comparing his St. Francis Embracing Christ on the Cross (Seville) with the version of the subject by Ribalta in Valencia.

Orphaned at the age of ten, Murillo was enrolled by an uncle in the studio of Juan del Castillo of Seville, where he was occupied with decorative projects. His knowledge of European painting he gained in Seville, except for three years of study in the collections of Madrid. In local collections he studied original paintings by Rubens, van Dyck, Raphael and Correggio as well as engravings of the Italians and Flemings. In 1645-46 he carried out his first important commission for the Franciscan convent in Seville. He painted scenes from the history of the Order (now scattered throughout the collections of Europe). These paintings, of a rather hard, explicit style, gained him great popularity. In 1648 he married Doña Beatriz de Cabrera y Sotomayor, who is reputed to have served as model for his Virgins. By 1654 he was undisputed head of the school of Seville and was operating a busy workshop. His manner became noticeably freer in the work of the late 1650's and 1660's, such as the canvases for San Agustín, Seville, the St. Anthony of Seville Cathedral, and the work for the monastery of the Capuchins of Seville. This last, carried out at two different times, shows an appreciable change toward his later technique of soft transitional tones. From 1670 Murillo worked, along with Valdés-Leal, in the Hospital of the Charity in Seville. This was a foundation of Don Miguel de Mañara, whose tomb there is inscribed, "Here lie the ashes of the worst man the world has known." After a career of a Don Juan, Don Miguel was turned to religion by his bride; he dressed himself in rags and worked for the hospice. Amongst canvases by Murillo in the Hospice is that of St. Isabel, Queen of Hungary, Curing the Sick. He employed a similar composition for his work in the Hospital of the Venerables (1680) in Seville. He died in a fall from the scaffolding while painting a large Betrothal of St. Catherine for the Capuchin convent in Cádiz.

Murillo's style in its mature phase is full of that operatic fantasy and hyperbole that marks the dreamy constructions and auto-sacramentals of the writer Calderón. The sense of color, light and flowery symbolism is shared by both. Murillo profited from the wave of popular enthusiasm for the doctrine of the Immaculate Conception in his century. His earliest Purísima of the Franciscans (c.1656-60, Seville) is in the statuesque tradition of Velázquez or Montanes; that of Aranjuez (c.1665, Prado) is already more rapturous; but the slender Purísima of the Capuchins (1674-76, Seville) is truly an apotheosis of scattered forms and Baroque diagonals. (See illustrations, including color plate 145.)

Muromachi Period (see JAPANESE PAINTERS: MUROMACHI PERIOD, 1333-1573).

Musée d'art moderne, Paris. This Museum of Modern Art was established during the 1930's to contain examples of modern French art from the Post-Impressionist period to the present day. It is particularly strong in works of the Fauve school.

Musée des Beaux-Arts de la Ville de Paris, Paris. This museum is housed in the Petit Palais and contains a select group of nineteenth-century French works. Particularly important is the comprehensive display of the works of Courbet.

MURILLO. Girl and Her Duenna. National Gallery of Art, Widener Collection, Washington, D.C.

Musée Guimet, Paris. Famous for its collections of Asiatic art.

Musée Royal des Beaux-Arts, Antwerp. A Belgian collection of Old Masters with emphasis on Flemish art.

Musée Royal des Beaux-Arts, Brussels. This Belgian collection is noted for its older French, Flemish (Rubens, van Dyck, Jordaens, etc.), Dutch (Rembrandt, van Goyen, Hals, Steen, etc.) and other European schools. The section devoted to modern art emphasizes the modern Belgians.

Museo Nazionale, Naples. This National Museum is primarily known for its sculptural remains from Pompeii and Herculaneum, but is also the most significant repository of paintings from those cities overwhelmed by the eruption of Vesuvius in 79 A.D.

Museum of Fine Arts, Boston. A general collection outstanding for its examples of nineteenth-century European and American painting, e.g., Sargent and Millet, as well as for its unusual examples of Chinese and Japanese painting.

Museum of Modern Art, New York. A unique institution not only by virtue of collections ranging from Post-Impressionism to the present in painting, sculpture, graphic arts, photography and films but also in its manifold educational activities. The latter include a children's school, slide and film strip production, publications, traveling exhibitions, and contact between art and industry through special exhibits, forums, etc. It has become the chief interpreter of the modern movement in this country as well as the leading representative of the American movement in foreign countries

Museums, Austria. See MODERNE GALERIE, LIECHTENSTEIN GALERIE, RATHAUS MUSEUM, KUNSTHISTORISCHES MUSEUM, ALBERTINA MUSEUM, BAROQUE MUSEUM, CZERNIN GALERIE—all in Vienna.

Museums, Belgium. See MUSEE ROYAL DES BEAUX-ARTS, Brussels, and MUSEE ROYAL DES BEAUX-ARTS, Antwerp.

Museums, Denmark. See NATIONAL MUSEUM OF DENMARK and ROYAL ACADEMY OF ARTS—both Copenhagen.

Museums, France. See ALBI MUSEUM; BESANCON MUSEUM; and the large group of Paris museums including: CERNUSCHI, MUSEE GUIMET, JEU DE PAUME, JACQUEMART-ANDRE, LUXEMBOURG, MUSEE D'ART MODERNE, LOUVRE, MUSEE DES BEAUX-ARTS DE LA VILLE DE PARIS, VERSAILLES.

Museums, Germany. See KAISER-FRIEDRICH MUSEUM and NATIONAL GALLERY—both Berlin; WALLRAF-RICHARTZ MUSEUM, Cologne; STUTTGART PICTURE GALLERY; STADELSCHES MUSEUM, Frankfort; KUNSTHALLE, Bremen; KUNSTHALLE, Hamburg, DRESDEN PICTURE GALLERY, Dresden.

N.B. The various German museums known to the visitor of the pre-World War II period are not always the museums one finds today. Because of both the war damage and looting by the Nazis during the purge of modern art from German museums, those institutions in many instances no longer have important works for which they were hitherto famous. The museums listed above are from Western Germany; no up-to-date information is available on most museums in Eastern Germany. Among museums without separate entries but of interest to the student of German art are: Düsseldorf, Kunsthalle; Mannheim, Kunsthalle; Hannover, Landesmuseum; and Krefeld, Kaiser Wilhelm Museum.

Museums, Great Britain. For Scotland, see NATIONAL GALLERY OF SCOTLAND and CORPORATION ART GALLERIES—both in Edinburgh; for England, see NATIONAL GALLERY, TATE GALLERY, COURTAULD INSTITUTE, BRITISH MUSEUM, VICTORIA AND ALBERT MUSEUM, and WALLACE COLLECTION—all in London.

Museums, Italy. See PITTI GALLERY and UFFIZI GAL-

LERY—both Florence; VATICAN PICTURE GALLERY, PALAZZO FARNESE and PALAZZO BORGHESE—all Rome; ACCADEMIA DI BELLE ARTI and SCUOLA DE SAN ROCCO—both Venice; MUSEO NAZIONALE, Naples; PALAZZO BIANCO, Genoa; BRERA PICTURE GALLERY, Milan.

Museums, Netherlands. See RIJKSMUSEUM and STEDELIJK—both Amsterdam; MAURITSHUIS, The Hague; HALS MUSEUM, Haarlem; and KROLLER-MULLER MUSEUM, Otterlo.

Museums, Spain. See PRADO, Madrid; ESCORIAL MUSEUM; and EL GRECO MUSEUM, Toledo.

Museums, Sweden. See NATIONAL MUSEUM OF SWEDEN, Stockholm.

Museums, Switzerland. See SWISS NATIONAL MUSEUM and KUNSTHAUS—both Zurich; KUNSTMUSEUM, Basel; and BERNE MUSEUM OF ART.

Museums, United States. See METROPOLITAN MUSEUM OF ART, MUSEUM OF MODERN ART, BROOKLYN MUSEUM, WHITNEY MUSEUM OF AMERICAN ART, HISPANIC MUSEUM, FRICK COLLECTION, GUGGENHEIM MUSEUM—all in New York City; ART INSTITUTE OF CHICAGO; MUSEUM OF FINE ARTS, Boston; NATIONAL GALLERY OF ART, CORCORAN GALLERY OF ART, PHILLIPS GALLERY—all in Washington, D.C.; DETROIT INSTITUTE OF ARTS; PHILADELPHIA MUSEUM OF ART; TOLEDO MUSEUM OF ART; FOGG ART MUSEUM and BUSCH-REISINGER MUSEUM—both in Cambridge; NELSON GALLERY OF ART, Kansas City, Mo.; CITY ART MUSEUM, St. Louis; SMITH COLLEGE MUSEUM, Northampton, Mass.; UNIVERSITY OF NEBRASKA ART GALLERIES, Lincoln; BARNES FOUNDATION, Merion, Pa; M. H. DE YOUNG MEMORIAL MUSEUM, SAN FRANCISCO, MUSEUM OF THE LEGION OF HONOR, SAN FRANCISCO MUSEUM OF ART—all in San Francisco; ALBRIGHT ART GALLERY, Buffalo; CLEVELAND MUSEUM OF ART; RINGLING MUSEUM OF ART, Sarasota, Fla.

Museums, U.S.S.R. See HERMITAGE, Leningrad; NEW MUSEUM OF MODERN WESTERN ART and TRETIAKOFF GALLERY—both Moscow.

Mustard Seed Garden Album. Chinese manual for painters, published in woodcuts in several volumes; a comprehensive survey of techniques to be used in depicting flowers, bamboo, rocks, trees, mountains, human figures in various situations, and animal studies. See Wang Kai in CHINESE PAINTERS: CH'ING DYNASTY.

Mycenaean painting (see AEGEAN PAINTING).

Myers, Jerome (1867-1940). American city genre painter. Not of the Ashcan group but falls within the framework of that style. He painted with naive charm and lyrical fantasy the life of New York's slums. Born in Petersburg, Va., he had a poverty-stricken and unsettled youth. After arriving in New York in 1886, he worked at designing and painting theatrical scenery and even acting in stock. He studied at Cooper Union and the Art Students League. He was discovered by a dealer and given his first one-man show in 1899 but never achieved great success.

Mytens, Daniel (c.1590-before 1648). Dutch painter of portraits. Possibly a pupil of Miereveld, he was a member of the guild in The Hague. For about twenty years he worked in England under James I and Charles I and was there one of the foremost painters of portraits before the arrival of van Dyck. He returned to The Hague about 1635. His work was influenced by both Rubens and van Dyck.

N

Nabis. A late nineteenth-century French group deriving its name from the Hebrew word for prophet and having as its ideological leader Maurice Denis, the painter. It included such artists as Ker Xavier Roussel, Felix Vallotton, Edouard Vuillard, Pierre Bonnard, Aristide Maillol the sculptor, as well as Paul Sérusier, who had been the leader of the Symbolists. Denis led discussions in the usual modern French style of a café or restaurant group and these artists also came together at the offices of the important literary periodical run by the Natanson brothers, *La Revue Blanche*. But the Nabi movement was not literary in the sense that the Symbolist movement had been; in fact, it revolted against such literary titles as The Cup of Coffee, Old Lady with Her Hens, Rural Scene, The Red Bedroom, etc. Using the palette of the Impressionists and expanding the search for proper techniques and media that marks the development of modern painting, they infused their simple genre subjects with a new kind of meaning, an emotive and even symbolic quality. Thus a typical Nabi painting is not merely a description of the light falling on a set of objects; it is rather a reserved, very personal and mood-charged representation in which the universal meaning of the given representation is projected. Some of the practitioners of this method, especially Bonnard and Vuillard, are known as Intimists. See also INTIMISM.

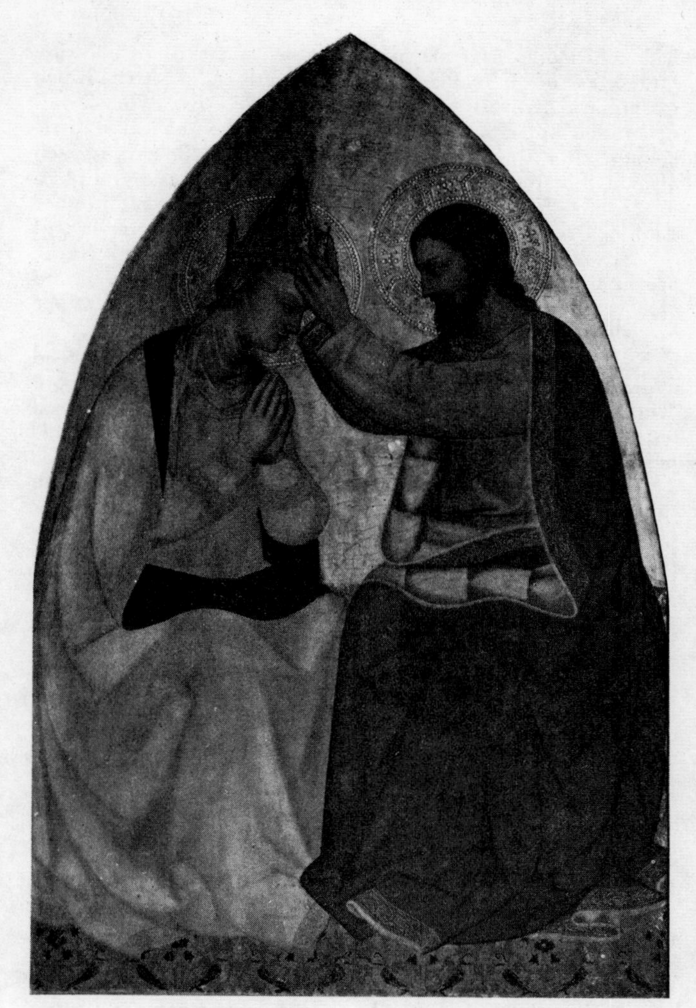

NARDO DI CIONE. Coronation of the Virgin
Victoria and Albert Museum, London

Nardo di Cione (active 1343-66). Florentine painter. brother of Andrea Orcagna and Jacopo di Cione. In 1363 he received a contract for frescoes (now lost) in the Bigallo. His chief work is the fresco decoration of the Strozzi chapel in Santa Maria Novella, painted possibly around 1355. This cycle represents a Last Judgment (including a portrait of Dante), Paradise, and Hell, the last being an illustration of Dante's *Inferno*. In these Nardo reveals considerable anatomical knowledge in rendering the nude, and skill in covering large areas of undivided wall surface with compositions which maintain a decorative unity. This anti-narrative style of wall decoration appears to have been part of the general stylistic change after the Black Death plague of 1348, and is seen also in the frescoes painted in the same church by Andrea da Firenze. Nardo's style is dependent on that of his brother Andrea Orcagna, whose hand is detected by some in part of the Strozzi chapel work. Other frescoes ascribed to Nardo are in the Badia of Florence (damaged) and in the second cloister of Santa Maria Novella. A number of panel paintings are also attributed to him. (See illustration.)

Nash, Paul (1889-1946). British painter, designer, wood engraver and industrial artist. Official war artist in both World Wars, he began as a naturalistic painter and moved on to a more symbolic and linear style around 1910. At this point the great Post-Impressionist exhibition in London made a deep impression on many of the younger men and Nash turned to a more abstract style as World War I gave his work more of an emotionally charged quality. He grew increasingly in the direction of a formal quality influenced by the Cubism of Picasso and Braque into which he injected his own brand of clarity of light and bleakness of mood. A long period of experiments showed Nash dipping liberally into the School of Paris bowl, emerging with Fauve works as well as others combining abstraction and fantasy. In 1933 he took a leading part in the formation of Unit One, a group dedicated to the modern movement in England. Nash's later works are characterized by a high-keyed color and broad spaciousness in their perspective effects, although always within the representational orbit. (See illustration.)

Nasmyth, Patrick (1787-1831). Scottish landscapist and son of a landscape painter. Known as "the British Hobbema," he is one of the best minor masters of his time.

National Gallery of Art, Washington, D.C. A national repository of traditional art formed on the basis of a number of outstanding private collections willed to the nation, such as those of Mellon, Kress, Widener and Chester Dale. In addition, the gallery has been enabled through the further generosity of Mr. Samuel Kress to acquire many Italian Renaissance paintings and sculptures from both the Henry Goldman and Clarence Mackay collections, some fine early Italian works and the Piero della Francesca from the Philip Lehman collection, early paintings and sculpture from the Otto Kahn collection and numerous others. Within a relatively short time the National Gallery has become in this way one of the most selectively chosen museums in the world. It is only permitted to show the work of artists who have been dead for more than twenty years.

National Gallery, Berlin. A collection of paintings ranging from the end of the eighteenth century to the present. This collection, like the others in Berlin, was removed from the city during the heavy Allied bombings and was hidden underground. Many of its modern works, particularly those by abstract or Expressionist painters, had been removed by the Nazis during the artistic purges of the 1937 period and sold at auction in Switzerland or disposed of otherwise.

National Gallery, London. Outstanding British collection of traditional European paintings, especially noted for Italian, Dutch and English painting. Works by Duccio, Masaccio, Piero della Francesca (an outstanding group), Leonardo's Madonna of the Rocks, Michelangelo's Entombment, Raphael's Ansidei Madonna, together with works by Correggio, Mantegna, Giovanni Bellini, Titian, Tintoretto, are representative of the Italian collection. Jan van Eyck's The Arnolfini Marriage highlights the early Flemish. There is a brilliant group of English paintings and the collection is also rich in Dutch, Spanish and other works.

National Gallery of Scotland, Edinburgh. Known for a great collection of the works of Henry Raeburn and other Scottish painters.

National Museum of Denmark, Copenhagen. One of the best national museums in the world, featuring a complete record of modern Danish art from the end of the eighteenth century to the present day. It has an outstanding collection of engravings.

National Museum of Sweden, Stockholm. A general collection.

NASH. Landscape from a Dream. Tate Gallery, London

Natoire, Charles Joseph (1700-77). French painter and etcher. Son of an architect and sculptor, Natoire studied with Le Moyne. He achieved considerable success in Rome, where he eventually became director of the School. His style was derived from Boucher and featured gay decorations of an allegorical type for *hôtels* of the day. His Three Graces is in the Louvre.

Nattier, Jean Marc (1685-1766). French painter of history and portraits. He is famous for the creation of an eighteenth-century type of young feminine beauty, generally rendered in blue tones. He led the current vogue for mythological portraits, e.g., Mme Henriette as Flora (Uffizi), that are characteristic of Rococo masquerade. He was the pupil of his father, Marc Nattier the Elder. He was a prodigy, winning the Academy's first prize at fifteen years of age. Nattier was engaged to draw the Rubens series of the Luxembourg for engravers and refused a position in the Academy at Rome. During a visit to Amsterdam he met the Czar and made a considerable reputation with his portraits and history painting for the Russian royal family. He was admitted to the Academy in 1718, took part in the Exposition de la Jeunesse in 1725 and as a regular Salon exhibitor he became spectacularly successful. Like Watteau he lost his fortune in the speculations of the Scotchman John Law, but as leading court portraitist of Louis XV he recouped in time. Nattier's paintings are a royal gallery of the times. He painted the princesses frequently and in changing guises: Mme Adelaide as Ariadne (Pitti), Duchess Elisabeth as Hebe (Stockholm), Mme Victoire as Diana (Versailles). The last-mentioned portrait has the sitter in a grotto beside the opening, recalling a device of Rembrandt and looking forward to Romantic landscape painting. (See color plate 146.)

naturalism. A term used to describe the act of reproducing in a precise manner the appearance of objects in nature. Example: The work of Vermeer. This may be contrasted with realism, in which the effect of the painting may be very convincing and "real," although the individual details are not naturalistic. Example: The work of Daumier.

Nauen, Heinrich (1880-1940). German Expressionist painter with a mystical religious bent. From 1902 to 1905 he worked in Belgium at Laethem-Saint-Martin with symbolist painters of that group; he returned to Belgium for a second visit in 1911. His art is characterized by elongated mannered figures expressive of a particular kind of religious ecstasy not unusual in Expressionist circles.

Nay, Ernst Wilhelm (1902-). German modernist painter and graphic artist who studied at the Academy in Berlin under Karl Hofer from 1925 to 1927, concentrating for a long time on graphics. Since the war his style has shown a unique kind of abstract Expressionism.

Nazarenes. A group of late eighteenth and early nineteenth century German writers and painters who tried to revive the religious spirit of the past. The movement, part of the beginnings of Romanticism, was touched off by Wackenroder's book *Effusions of a Convert to the Arts;* he urged an approach to religion through the arts of the past, the great cathedrals, the paintings and engravings of Dürer and others. The review *Athenaeum*, which Wackenroder founded in 1800, tried to draw the people's attention to the German primitive painters of long ago. It was there proposed that the art of the modern German should also be faithful, innocent, sensitive and thoughtful and that the artist live a pure and noble existence, all very medieval in thought and feeling. If this was not a particularly modern ideal which the Nazarenes proposed, it was in its way a protest against certain materialistic and repugnant aspects of modern life. Example: Friedrich Overbeck.

Neagle, John (1796-1865). A minor American portrait painter born in Boston and active in Philadelphia. He also painted landscapes, but is remembered for his portrait, Pat Lyon at the Forge (1826, Boston).

146. NATTIER. Percy O'Brien
Wildenstein Gallery, New York

Neapolitan school. A group of seventeenth-century Baroque masters working in the tradition of Caravaggio and including such painters as Luca Giordano, the Spaniard Jusepe de Ribera and the dramatic landscapist Salvatore Rosa.

Neer, Aert van der (1603/04-77). Dutch landscape painter. The first works of van der Neer, who began to paint late in his life, show the influence of the Camphuysen brothers and of Avercamp. The works of his later period are original and beautifully atmospheric snow scenes, or landscapes with strange effects of moonlight, dawn, and dusk.

Neer, Eglon Hendrick van der (c.1635-1703). Dutch painter of genre, landscapes and portraits. He studied with his father Aert van der Neer, traveled in France and spent the end of his life in Düsseldorf. His style is related in theme and composition to that of Metsu and Terborch.

Negreti, Jacopo (see PALMA VECCHIO).

Nelli, Ottaviano (active 1400-44). The most important Umbrian representative of the Gothic International Style of the early fifteenth century. His major activity was in Gubbio, where he painted frescoes in the church of Sant' Agostino. He also worked in Urbino, and decorated a chapel in the palace of the Trinci at Foligno (1424). Damaged secular frescoes in the Trinci palace resemble his work and are sometimes ascribed to him.

Nelson Gallery of Art, Kansas City, Mo. The William Rockhill Nelson Gallery of Art and Atkins Museum of Fine Arts has a relatively small but select group of paintings sculptures and objects of decorative art from all periods. It is especially interesting for its Near Eastern and Far Eastern collections.

Neo-Classical painting. A neo-classical style of paint-

NERI DI BICCI. Tobias with the Archangel
Detroit Institute of Arts

ing is, in a general sense, any period style which consciously or unconsciously resembles the ancient classical (Graeco-Roman) manner of painting or of executing bas-relief sculpture. Most frequent characteristics would be emphasis on literary subject matter, the human form, crisp geometric or frieze structure, and intelligible space organized in planar fashion. Such neo-classical principles can be observed in varying degrees in Carolingian, mid-Byzantine and other medieval periods, but are most explicit in that revival of antiquity which we call the Italian Renaissance. In its narrow, particular meaning, however, Neo-Classical painting is the style of the years before and after 1800 when, in France, the doctrine of antique revival satisfied the political and aesthetic aspirations of *ancien régime*, Jacobin revolution, Napoleonic imperialism and Academic conservatism in turn. France, owing to the personality and influence of David (see), was the center of Neo-Classical painting, although the American Benjamin West produced a precocious example of it, The Prodigal Son, in England in 1771. This was painted under the influence of the German archaeologist Winckelmann, who also sent Raphael Mengs off in that direction. Official French policy had promoted ancient themes since 1747, but not until the work of David's master, Vien, were archaeological effects popular in painting, and it remained for David to inject the movement with expressive power. Even David's vigor tended to pale into archaeological quotation or sheer aestheticism, tendencies which mark Neo-Classical painting throughout the rest of the nineteenth century. The primitives involved it with archaic and Oriental arabesques of line and Ingres made it the vehicle of romantic imagery.

Neo-Impressionism. A Post-Impressionist movement in modern painting associated with the middle '80's of the past century and also known as Divisionism, Chromo-Luminarism and Pointillism. The chief practitioners include Seurat, Signac (the group theoretician), Cross and Van Rysselberghe. The New or Neo-Impressionists grew out of Impressionism with its awareness of the complementary relationships of colors and the need for dividing colors into their components so that the eye would be able, even forced, to bring them together into a more or less pure light; this new group actually based its art on the science of optics as it was then known. They advocated an exact relationship between complementaries, e.g., red and green, rather than the inexact approximation which had been the Impressionist practice, so that a precise shade of red would be placed next to a precise and related shade of green with an infinitesimal section of the canvas between. Moreover, they promulgated specific types of compositions for different occasions: diagonally upward for joyous, diagonally downward for sad, horizontal for calm, and so on. Finally, they were interested in a permanent inner glow to be achieved by a maximum intensity of natural light, the latter in turn to be accomplished by the exact scientific relationships of the various colors. Permanence was also involved in the kind of classical, i.e., stable, compositions arranged as in Cézanne rather than the sloping, spontaneous and deliberately improvised effects of the Impressionists. Neo-Impressionist work must be considered part of the reaction against the relatively loose methods of the former movement and part of the classicism of the 1880's. It represents a phase of the form-searching that is integral in the larger movement of Post-Impressionism (see).

Neolithic painting (see PREHISTORIC PAINTING).

Neo-Plasticism. The name of a 1920 manifesto published in Paris by the group of Dutch artists known as de Stijl, one of the most significant and influential groups in the modern art world. De Stijl was organized in Holland in 1917 and marked a significant advance over previous periods in that it offered and effectuated cooperation between painters and sculptors on the one hand and architects and industrial designers on the other. Among its leaders were the brilliant Theo van Doesburg, as versatile an artist as our century has produced, the very talented painter Piet Mondrian, and the able architect J. J. P. Oud. Two elements in the de Stijl credo are immediately noteworthy: the basic form was the rectangle; the basic colors were the primaries, blue, red and yellow. This simplification was applied to all the arts with which they dealt: painting, sculpture, architecture, furniture, poster design and typography, Van Doesburg at Weimar exerted a strong influence on Gropius and the Bauhaus school generally, as well as on Miës van der Rohe's building designs,

NICCOLÒ DI PIETRO GERINI. Baptism of Christ
National Gallery, London

and a few years later on those of Le Corbusier as well. De Stijl also affected in a very substantial way the various industrial arts and the experimental film.

Neo-Romanticism. A movement in painting that began at the end of the 1920's and includes Berman, Bérard and Tchelitchew among others—painters who represent a psychological escapism analogous to that of the beginning of the Romantic movement a century earlier. The Neo-Romantics are influenced in technique by the Blue Period of Picasso, that is, by its mournful intensity, dreamlike quality and sense of pathos. These elements they used to express postwar poignancy and unashamed, but often touching, sentimentality. Their typical themes are people asleep and deserted landscapes and streets.

Neri di Bicci (1419-after 1491). The son and pupil of Bicci di Lorenzo, he was a mediocre but prolific Florentine painter. His father worked in the manner of Lorenzo Monaco, and Neri's style is also related to the Gothic holdover into fifteenth century Florentine art, with superficial additions of plastic elements from major artists of his own generation. Several of his chief altarpieces are in the Florence Academy and many devotional panels are in collections throughout the western world. (See illustration.)

Neroccio di Bartolommeo Landi (1447-1500). Sienese painter and sculptor; a pupil of Vecchietta. He conducted a workshop with his brother-in-law Francesco di Giorgio from 1468 to 1475 but his style has little in common with that of the other master. His painting was essentially conservative and devotional, and belongs to the typically lyrical Sienese tradition stemming from Simone Martini. He is well represented by the following signed and dated altarpieces: a triptych of the Madonna with Saints Michael and Bernardino (1476) and a Madonna with Six Saints (1496) in the choir of SS. Annunziata in Montisi. His later works are more complex and monumental and exhibit a certain hardening of line and of modeling.

Netscher, Caspar (1639-84). Dutch painter and engraver of portraits and genre pictures. Born in Germany he transferred while young to Holland and studied painting with

NICHOLSON. Trendrine, Cornwall
Phillips Collection, Washington, D.C.

NOLAN. Flight into Egypt. Courtesy of the Artist, Australia

Terborch. He made a trip to France in 1659 but settled in The Hague, joining the painters' guild and training many artists. His portraits of women exhibit a search for physical appeal and a superficial attractiveness that relates them more to French painting than to Dutch.

Neue Sachlichkeit, Die (The New Objectivity; see EXPRESSIONISM).

Nevinson, C.R.W. (1889-1946). British painter who was among the first to introduce Futurist ideas into England after the London Futurist exhibition of 1912. These ideas were applied to his experiences in World War I to show the destructive effect of the machine on human beings. After the war Nevinson turned to subjects from factory life, where he utilized the same austere machine forms to emphasize what he felt was the spiritual emptiness of that life. See FUTURISM.

New Museum of Modern Western Art, Moscow. Established by the Soviet government through the nationalization of two important private collections of modern art, those of Tschoukine and Morosov. Thus this institution was particularly rich in examples of work by Matisse (La Danse, La Musique, etc.) and also had good examples by Picasso, Marquet, Van Gogh, Cézanne and many other masters from Post-Impressionism onward. Recently this museum has been broken up, part of its collection going to the Hermitage in Leningrad (see) and part remaining in a new collection known as the Pushkin Museum.

New Objectivity (see EXPRESSIONISM).

Niccolò da Foligno (see Niccolò di Liberatore).

Niccolò di Liberatore (also called Niccolò da Foligno and, erroneously, Niccolò Alunno) (c.1425/30-1502). One of the most interesting minor painters of the Umbrian school, Niccolò was influenced early by Benozzo Gozzoli. His later work indicates contact with the Venetians Carlo Crivelli and the Vivarini. He was a gifted painter who easily mastered perspective and anatomy, and animated his colorful and decorative compositions with graceful movement and highly expressive faces. Had he spent his life in one of the major artistic centers he might have become an outstanding master.

Niccolò di Pietro (active 1394-1430). The first Venetian painter who was more or less free from Byzantine formulas. Three dated works are extant (1394, 1404 and 1409), of which the 1394 Madonna (Venice Academy) is most important.

Niccolò di Pietro Gerini (active 1368-1415). Florentine painter instrumental in prolonging the Giottesque tradition

147. NOLDE. The Two Goldsmiths
Collection Mr. and Mrs. Hugo Feigl, New York

into the fifteenth century. He was very prolific and trained many assistants and pupils. Important extant works are frescoes in the sacristy of Santa Croce, Florence, in the San Francesco monastery at Pisa (damaged), and in San Francesco at Prato. An Entombment panel is in the Florence Academy. (See illustration.)

Niccolò di Tommaso (active third quarter 14th century). A signed altarpiece, dated 1371, in the church of San Antonio, Naples, is the only known work of this Florentine master, who was a follower of Nardo di Cione.

Nicholson, Ben (1894-). British abstract painter who has taken the leadership in this phase of modern art in Great Britain. Beginning as an Impressionist, he became more and more preoccupied with primarily formal problems until all contact with so-called reality finally disappeared from his works. At one point, even color was dropped out of his pictures, leaving only a subtle series of variations between white and grey as his palette. Works of this extreme type are really painted reliefs (in white and grey) with recessive planes of space indicated by superposed boxlike areas. Since that phase, however, Nicholson has worked his way through a variety of Cubist and Post-Cubist experiments, echoing in his own fashion such styles as de Stijl (see) with its solid color areas and geometric compositions. Nicholson's own contribution lies in the infinite tact and delicacy that characterize his version of abstract painting. (See illustration.)

Night Watch, The, by Rembrandt (see).

Niten (see JAPANESE PAINTERS: MOMOYAMA PERIOD).

Ni Tsan (see CHINESE PAINTERS: YÜAN DYNASTY).

No-ami (see JAPANESE PAINTERS: MUROMACHI PERIOD).

Nobuzane (see JAPANESE PAINTERS: KAMAKURA PERIOD).

Nolan, Sidney (1917-). Australian painter, born in Melbourne, who has gained the reputation of being the foremost painter of Australiana. His work has a lyrical quality concerned principally with the isolation of figures in space. The theme is very important, as in his series on the life of the bushranger Ned Kelly, which is treated broadly and with the deliberate naiveté of folk art. (See illustration.)

Nolde, Emil (1867-). One of the foremost German Expressionist painters and graphic artists; associated for a time with the Brücke group of Dresden. Original name Hansen, he was born of old peasant stock in Nolde on the Danish frontier. He studied wood-carving, applied arts, furniture and other forms, and taught at the Trade and Industry School in St. Gall, Switzerland, 1892. In 1896, his first large picture, The Mountain Giants, was rejected. He took to drawing picture postcards of Swiss mountains as humans in grotesque forms, and these were successful enough to enable him to paint. He studied for a while under the mystic Adolf Hölzel at Dachau, then went on to Paris in 1900, where he was attracted by Daumier, Rodin, Degas, Delacroix, Manet and Millet. Turning to Impressionism (see) by 1904-05, he produced an Impressionism of his own, expressing the most powerful and violent impulses; he was in fact invited to join Die Brücke because of "the storm" of his color. By 1907 he quit the group and after a brief interval began in 1909 his tremendously important series of religious pictures with the Last Supper, the Pentecost, Triptych of St. Mary of Egypt and others. These show a turgid violence of feeling, a demonic and frightening mood far removed from the usual Christian interpretation but entirely appropriate to the mystique of "blood and soil" which Nolde has expressed throughout his life. His religious sincerity is unquestioned, for he feels quite deeply and identifies himself profoundly with what he depicts; it is rather the inherent cruelty of the approach that is fear-inspiring. In 1913 he took part in an expedition that crossed Russia, China and Japan on its way to the South Seas. The first volume of his autobiography, *My Own Life*, appeared in 1931; the second volume, *Years of Struggle*, with its dubious social and political overtones, was published in 1934. Despite this, in 1937 along with other modernists he suffered Nazi confiscation of his pictures, and in 1941 was forbidden to paint. After the war he was given a professorship. (See color plate 147.)

Nonell y Monturiol, Isidro (1873-1911). A Spanish painter, important in the Catalan revival of the turn of the century. Student of Graner and of Martínez Altés, he first exhibited (1893) Impressionist landscapes. He then turned to a sensational realism and "fried" colors—working with young Picasso. He spent time in Paris, where he was friendly with Vollard, and back in Barcelona he became leader of the "IV Gats" group which published *Pel y Ploma*. His studies of gypsies, scrawny abandoned women, and madmen shocked the public and are said to have influenced Picasso's early styles. His first successful show was in 1910, at which time he had become interested in the sober and solid rendering of still lifes. He unfortunately died young, just after his first triumph.

Nonnotte, Donat (1708-85). French history and portrait painter. Favorite pupil of Le Moyne, with whom he collaborated in important decorative works at St. Sulpice and Versailles. Portraits by him are in the Louvre.

non-objective art. A type of expression in which there are no recognizable objects and forms as such but in which forms, lines, colors and textures are manipulated for their own sakes. Generally applied to such styles as Abstract Expressionism (e.g., Pollock and Gorky), pure geometric expression such as that of the Constructivists (e.g., El Lissitzky) and de Stijl (e.g., Mondrian). The first entirely non-objective painting is supposed to have been done by Kandinsky in 1910 in Munich as part of the Expressionist desire to destroy reality in order to arrive at the underlying truth of existence. It was followed by the many Russian variants of this expression (Purism, Constructivism, etc.) during the pre-World War I years and then by the de Stijl painters during the 1920's. In America, where the Synchromism (see Orphism) of the pre-1920 generation had had its brief popularity, the period of 1930-1950 was marked by a tremendous surge of interest in this form of art. It still remains a worldwide force in the world of art.

Noort, Adam van (1562-1641). Flemish painter of portraits and historical subjects. Little is known of this mediocre and conservative painter and his chief importance lies in the distinction of the pupils he trained, a company that includes Vrancx, van Balen, Jordaens and Rubens.

Northcote, James (1746-1831). British painter, poet and art critic. Pupil and biographer of Sir Joshua Reynolds, Northcote lived in Reynolds' home for years, envying him constantly. In 1787 he was elected to the Royal Academy. He is noted for historical paintings in which he tried for a fresh treatment, showing genuine skill in drawing and color.

Norwich school. A group of popular nineteenth-century landscapists organized in 1803 by "Old Crome" (see CROME) as the Norwich Society of Artists. The organization consisted of local painters, mostly drawing teachers, who showed annually in the Society's exhibitions. It included Stark, Ladbrooke and Cotman among others, the founders showing greater talent than most of the succeeding artists.

Nude Descending the Staircase by Marcel Duchamp (see).

Nunez, Juan (active 1480-1525). Spanish painter of Seville. He worked in the Netherlands manner, as can be seen in his Pietà with Saints Michael and Vincent in the Cathedral of Seville.

O

Oath of the Horatii by Jacques Louis David (see).

occult balance (see ASYMMETRIC).

Ochtervelt, Jacob (1634/35-1708/09). Dutch painter of genre pictures and portraits. He is supposed to have studied with Berchem. He headed the guild in his native city of Rotterdam but spent the latter part of his life in Amsterdam. Terborch and Metsu clearly influenced his genre scenes, but he never matched their harmony and elegance.

Odalisque by J. A. D. Ingres (see).

Oderisi, Roberto (active c.1350-82). Italian painter who did frescoes in Naples in a style based on the Roman school (see CAVALLINI), with additional influence from Giotto and Simone Martini.

O'Gorman, Juan (1905-). Mexican easel painter, muralist and architect. He first distinguished himself as an architect of schools in 1932 and has since done other buildings, all in a modern idiom of which he was the pioneer in Mexico. He did frescoes in the Central Airport, Mexico City, 1937-38 (since destroyed), and in the Bocanegra Library, Patzcuaro, 1941-42. His mural technique shows a hard precise drawing with small areas of clean bright color. This technique is also used in easel paintings which have a fine Magic Realist mood. His mosaic murals appear on the Library Building of the new University of Mexico and on the Secretariat of Communications and Public Works. (See illustration.)

O'Higgins, Pablo (or **Paul)** (1904-). Born in the United States but has been part of the Mexican school as muralist and graphic artist since 1924; he worked with Rivera, 1925-27. He was a founding member of the Popular

O'GORMAN. Baptism of the Indians
Detail from fresco in the Bocanegra Library, Patzcuaro

Graphic Art Workshop, co-editor of a monograph on Posada. He paints the people of Mexico City, the industrial workers, and modern life in general. Mural (with Méndez) in a maternity clinic, Mexico City, 1946-47.

oil painting. A technique which employs an oil base as the vehicle for its pigments. This technique has varied greatly from one period to another, unlike other painting media such as fresco, tempera, encaustic and watercolor, whose usage and effect have been relatively constant. The great range and variety of oil painting through the centuries has encompassed the lush brilliance of a Titian, the dark richness of a Rembrandt and the fresh, high-keyed quality of a Manet. The oils which carry pigment are quick-drying substances that harden into a permanent crust when exposed to the air. Linseed oil is one of the commonest bases used. Often these oils are combined with a diluting medium to make them flow more freely. A varnish may be utilized in the painting mixture or by itself afterward, but in either case as a protective coating for the paint. In traditional oil painting, one of the most important factors is the priming or groundwork, as for example in Rembrandt's dark underpainting, Boucher's pink-toned bases, etc. As time elapses after the finishing of a picture, its color generally tends toward that of the groundwork, which becomes more and more the final determinant of the painting's quality. Thus Poussin's brown priming has finally triumphed over the original color of many of his pictures. Similarly Reynolds' works, often begun in grisaille or grey with glazes or layers superimposed, have suffered from the evaporation of the outside layers and have reverted to the greyish tonality of the ground. The safest method employed by older masters was to incorporate all the palette colors in the groundwork, gradually working from this stage, glaze by glaze, to the required final color harmony.

Historically, by the first half of the fifteenth century the Flemish painters who had previously used a standard tempera (see) technique had begun to use a clear quick-drying, varnish-mixed oil in final glazes over a tempera base, as with the van Eycks and their contemporaries. This addition gave greater flexibility, depth and durability to their work. After a short time, fifteenth-century Italians followed suit. Both in northern and southern Europe wooden panels still continued to be used, although less in Italy than in the north. During the sixteenth century, however, canvas became the surface predominantly utilized for oil painting. The canvas was not sized or prepared with gesso as in tempera painting, since that substance absorbed oil, but rather with other materials containing whiting, china clay, etc., which avoided this difficulty and also kept the canvas flexible and non-cracking. The chief advantage of the new oil medium was its wider range of tones—i.e., the range from light to dark within each color. Second, a larger number of actual hues or colors could be employed because the new oils and varnishes protected pigments. To this must be added the fact that, unlike other media, oil could be worked over and even corrected for a long time; the idea of a painting might be developed as the artist went along and need not be predetermined. During the centuries between the Renaissance and the 1800's, two general approaches prevailed in oil technique. One group of painters began their work on a light ground, while another began on a dark ground; the Florentines represent the first tendency and the Venetians the second. Yet painting methods, by and large, were the same throughout this long period and could even be reduced to a kind of formula. The historian W. G. Constable points out, for example, that painters in England and the United States in the eighteenth century were in the habit of first applying the background for the halftones. Over this they worked in the lights, shadows and local colors with a thin glaze, a scumble, or even a solid area of paint. Finally the highlights were put in, often with a heavy impasto. Individuals would necessarily vary this procedure in one way or another. Rubens, for instance, kept the shadows transparent; lighter portions were more heavily loaded. In the main, however, with Rubens as with other oil painters from the time of Titian on, the picture was built up in varying thicknesses of paint so that the penetration of light could be controlled by the artist.

With the nineteenth century, traditional studio practices and workshop conventions appear to have broken down (the Industrial Revolution and the emergence of Romantic individualism may have played a part here), and painting in oil changed radically. In general, the practice of using a series of glazes or layers along with scumbles gave way to so-called direct painting. Now the ground no longer played a vital role in the finished result; actually, the final color was already stated in the preliminary lay-in. By Reynolds' time many artists had lost the secret of Venetian oil painting, Goya being the last to use the Old Master methods of ground color and successive glazes. In the nineteenth century from Constable to the Impressionists the desire to show effects of natural light led to the development of broken tones of color, free brushing for sparkling effects, and flecks of white paint added with the palette knife. Thus a new phase was begun in the evolution of the oil medium, illustrating once more that flexibility of conception and variety in textures, colors and values which set it apart from all other painting techniques.

O'KEEFFE. Goat's Horn with Blue
Downtown Gallery, New York

O'Keeffe, Georgia (1887-). Contemporary American painter, noted for her flower pieces, still lifes, and landscapes of the Southwest in the Cubist-Realist style. Born in Wisconsin, she studied at the Art Institute of Chicago (1904), the Art Students League with Chase, Mora, and Cox (1905), the University of Virginia with Bement (1912-14), and elsewhere. She worked in advertising art in Chicago (1908-09), was supervisor of public school art in Amarillo, Tex., (1916-17), and head of the art department of West Texas Normal College. She had her first show at the gallery "291" in 1916 and married its director, Alfred Stieglitz, in 1918. Her first exhibited work was abstract but in the 1920's she turned back toward reality, painting still lifes, flower pieces, and skyscrapers in the immaculate style of the Cubist-Realists. Her later work in the Southwest introduced new subject matter: skulls, and mountain and desert landscape. (See illustration.)

Ollivier, Michel Barthélemy (1712-84). Fashionable French painter of the eighteenth century. He was a member

ORCAGNA. The Dead Christ with Madonna, Saint John, and Donor
Denver Art Museum, Kress Collection

of the Academy and was appointed a *peintre du roi* (painter to the king). For many years he lived in Spain, later becoming court painter to the Princesse Conti, for whom he did the charming, minutely detailed society scenes in the style of Watteau and Lancret for which he is now known.

Olympia by Edouard Manet (see).

O'Neill, Daniel (1920-). Contemporary Irish painter who has exhibited all over the world, although self-taught. For many years he worked in a garage at night so that he might spend his daylight time painting. There is a wonderfully quiet but strong poetry in O'Neill's Fauve-influenced figure subjects.

Onesimos (early 5th century B.C.). Greek vase painter. Onesimos, who signed a vase now in the Louvre, apparently was a member of Euphronios' workshop. He painted in the style of Brygos.

Opie, John (1761-1807). British portrait painter; also known for his historical subjects and genre scenes. As a portraitist he worked in the Reynolds tradition and achieved some popularity during the 1780's. During that decade he was elected to the Royal Academy and had a certain success with his Assassination of James I of Scotland and a number of sentimental pictures with "classical" themes. In his portraits, e.g., William Siddons the Actor; Self-Portrait; and David Rizzio, he was able to communicate a marked sense of patterning in the arrangement of the forms and a convincing intensity of expression.

Orban, Desiderius (1884-). Australian painter born in Hungary. Paris-trained and originally an associate of Picasso, Orban came to Australia in 1939. His low-toned canvases reflect his Hungarian background in the relationship of rich harmonies. He has had an effect on Australian art, textile and industrial design, and art education.

Orcagna (Andrea di Cione) (c.1320-c.1368). One of the most renowned Florentine artists of the fourteenth century and certainly the greatest of the second half of the century. He inaugurated a style associated with the religious reform after the bubonic plague (1348) that decimated the population of Florence and Siena. This style has been described as "anti-Giottesque," and constitutes a return to flatter and less spacious representation, while retaining the strong modeling of individual figures that Giotto inaugurated. Orcagna was the greatest of three artist brothers (see NARDO and JACOPO DI CIONE), and was active as a painter, sculptor and architect. His first major documented commission was for the altarpiece of the Strozzi chapel in Santa Maria Novella, Florence. This work, painted in 1354-57 and still preserved there, is considered by many to be the only painted work extant from his hand, except for fragments of a frescoed Triumph of Death (c.1350) in Santa Croce. It represents Christ Enthroned, extending the book of doctrine to St. Thomas Aquinas and the keys of heaven to St. Peter. These kneeling figures are recommended to the Deity by the Virgin and St. John the Baptist, and four saints flank the central group in pairs. Orcagna was in charge of the work on the stone tabernacle of Or San Michele in 1356-57 and was active in the building of the Florence cathedral. Around 1358/60 he worked on the façade mosaics and perhaps other parts of the cathedral of Orvieto. Early sources indicate he did frescoes in a few Florentine churches, but the fragment mentioned above is all that is left of them. He began a panel of St. Matthew in 1367 which was completed after his death by his brother Nardo and is now in the Uffizi. His sculpture,

ORLEY. Virgin and Child with Angels
Metropolitan Museum of Art, New York

148. OROZCO. Mexican Pueblo. Detroit Institute of Arts

exemplified by the tabernacle in Or San Michele, displays the same stylistic break with the Giotto tradition as his painting. (See illustration.)

Orchardson, Sir William Ouiller (1832-1910). Scottish portraitist and history painter. His lightness of touch suggests Gainsborough but it is used merely as a method of painting. Known for his Shakespearean themes and for scenes from the lives of Napoleon and Voltaire.

Orley, Bernard (Bernaert, Barend) **van** (c.1488?-1541). Flemish painter of religious subjects and portraits, decorator, and designer of tapestries and stained glass. His art resembles Italian Mannerism in many ways and is related to that of the so-called Antwerp Mannerists (1515-20). His style borrows from many sources: Gerard David and Provost, Antwerp and Haarlem, as well as Michelangelo and Raphael. Whether he was actually in Italy in 1514 and 1526 is debatable; he may have been influenced by Italian art through Raphael's cartoons for tapestries, which were woven in Brussels in the studio of Pieter van Aelst, and later through contact with Italian artists in the court. His style, a major break from the older Brussels tradition of Rogier van der Weyden, is characterized by an exuberant decorative fantasy, profusion of ornament, careful drawing, supple and elegant figures in animated movement, and efforts to render spatial extension through tricky foreshortening of figures and architectural structures; but it retains the indigenous Flemish predilection for saturated color. Born in Brussels of a family of Luxembourg painters, he studied with his father, Valentin. In 1518 he succeeded Jacopo de Barbari as court painter to Margaret of Austria and after her death to Mary of Hungary (1532). His most famous altars are the Trials of Job Triptych (1521, Brussels) and the Last Judgment Triptych (1525, Antwerp). He also painted many versions of the Madonna and Child and many court portraits. Of the latter the most notable still extant are the Young Charles V (Budapest), Margaret of Austria (Brussels), and Dr. Georges Zelle (Brussels). In his last years he designed a magnificent series of stained-glass windows for St. Gudule in Brussels and a great many cartoons for tapestries, the most famous of which is the Hunt of Maximilian series (Louvre). (See illustration.)

Orozco, José Clemente (1883-1949). Foremost Mexican muralist, easel painter and graphic artist; he began as a student of agriculture and architectural drawing, turning to painting in 1909. During 1910-17 he did scenes of sordid genre and Mexican Revolutionary content, and from 1922 to 1927 frescoes in the National Preparatory School, the House of Tiles (now Sanborn's) and the Industrial School at Orizaba. This early work shows generalized Renaissance forms, to which is added an increasingly emotional element through Revolutionary material used in the impressive symbolic sense that characterizes his work from then onward. His style developed monumentality, strength and, later, Expressionistic force. Color at first was subdued, structure and compositional arrangements rigidly controlled; later he would become more fluid and dynamic. From 1927 to 1932 he was in the United States, doing frescoes at Pomona College, California, the New School, New York, and Dartmouth College, New Hampshire. For the most part, these show a new quality, a looser drawing and a higher degree of symbolic and emotive content with a growing Expressionistic intensity, but they are still basically three-dimensional and figurative in form.

In 1934 begins the period of his great murals in the Palace of Fine Arts, Mexico City, and the Governor's Palace, the University, and the Orphanage, Guadalajara. Orozco now emerges as the pre-eminent painter of the Mexican mural movement, his influence extending also into the graphic arts. His works of this period show a new, flaming symbolism, often with powerful diagonal thrusts, and a looser, more graphic style; his Expressionist manner becomes fully developed. Dark contours, white highlights and dramatic reds combine with a swirling movement of figures in dynamic groups in which individual shapes are distorted. We are frequently struck by Orozco's distinction between the anonymous and even dangerous mass of people and the idealistically conceived individual. Orozco's art at this point is visualized in

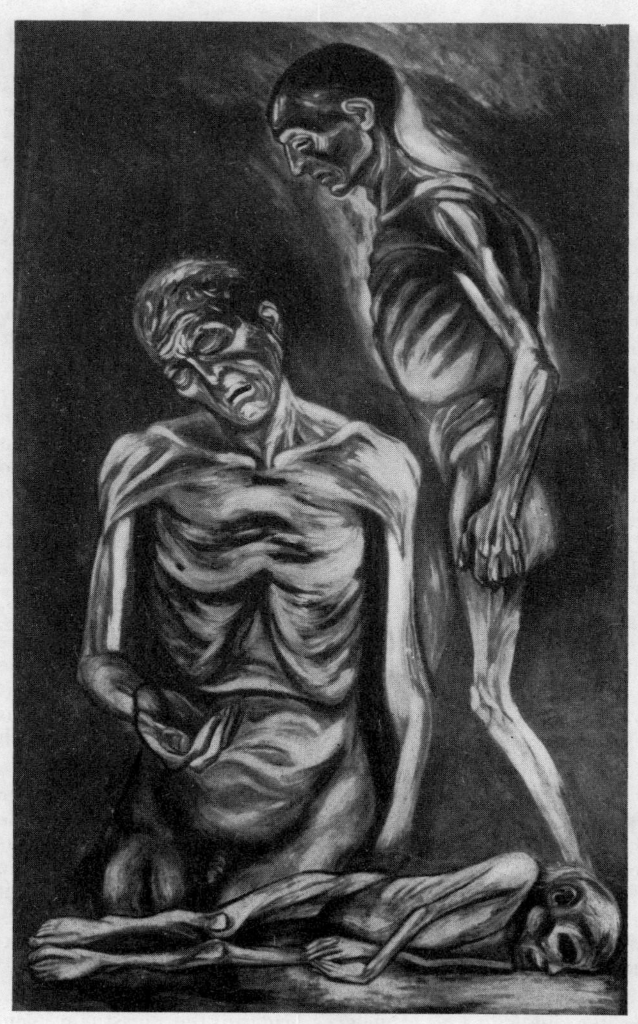

OROZCO. The Victims
Detail from fresco in the University of Guadalajara, Mexico

historical and didactic terms, yet working toward a humanistic idea, a compassion for mankind.

In 1940 he did frescoes in the Library at Jiquilpan with gigantic black-and-white drawings on the side walls and a colored painting at the far end. In the same year, the portable Dive Bomber mural for the Museum of Modern Art, New York, shows signs of the development of mechanical symbols; i.e., man crushed by the machine and the aggression of the machine in war. The murals in the Mexican Supreme Court (1941) symbolize Mexico's natural resources and the moral power of justice. His unfinished murals in the Church of Jesús Nazareno, Mexico City (1942), with their visionary and apocalyptic subject matter, reveal Orozco as a prophet of our anguished times. He makes use here of abstract explosive forms. His open-air mural in the amphitheatre of the National School for Teachers (1947) is an abstract summing up in machinistic terms of the history of Mexico. This was one of the most positive indications of a new direction for the painter; but he died two years later without fulfilling it. In 1948 he did a mural in the National Historical Museum, Chapultepec Castle, showing Juárez and the Reform, and another in the Chamber of Deputies, Guadalajara. Between 1940 and 1949 Orozco's easel painting grew in a restless Expressionist style comparable to his murals. In 1946 he received the National Award of Arts and Sciences and the following year was honored by a retrospective exhibition in the Palace of Fine Arts. His death in 1949 was a day of national mourning for Mexico. (See illustrations, including color plate 148.)

Orozco-Romero, Carlos (1898-). Mexican painter and former newspaper caricaturist. Influenced by European modern art, his work is Surrealist in its humor and fantasy, with deep spaces and vivid color.

Orpen, Sir William (1878-1931). Irish-born British portraitist and close friend of Augustus John, Orpen was the recorder of World War I and the years following. Born in Dublin, he came to the Slade School in London in 1895 and revealed early talent. His famous Homage to Manet, showing a group of art lovers before a large Manet painting, was an eighteenth-century conversation piece in modern dress. It also indicated his position in the art world; i.e., a modernism that went as far as Impressionism. During 1914-18 he did sketches in paint of scenes of war and destruction for the Imperial War Museum. These were followed by portraits of military figures, statesmen and many self-portraits. In the tradition of Hals, Goya and Manet, he showed an ability to create a form in paint without preliminary drawing. (See illustration.)

Orphism. A movement in modern French painting associated with the names of Robert Delaunay, the Czech Frank Kupka and the Americans Morgan Russell, S. Macdonald Wright and Sonia Terk. Although starting from the premises of Analytical Cubism, the Orphists felt first that Cubism at that moment lacked color and second that it was too closely

ORPEN. A Woman in Gray. Art Institute of Chicago

OSTADE, ADRIAEN VAN. The Fiddler. Mauritshuis, The Hague

tied to the object. They proceeded, therefore, to "liberate" Cubism from these difficulties, producing such works as the almost completely abstract Simultaneous Windows by Delaunay (1911) and his Homage to Blériot (1914). This point of view was especially fruitful among the Blue Rider Abstract Expressionists of Germany at the time. Delaunay's type of painting is sometimes referred to as Color Orchestration and as Synchromism.

Orrente, Pedro (c.1570-1644). Spanish painter of Murcia. Active in Valencia, Toledo and Andalusia. He was a friend of El Greco's son, but his style derived more from Bassano, whom he may have known through local tenebrists (see). He was famous for pastoral subjects which were then much in vogue in literature. He also painted religious works such as San Sebastiano (Valencia Cathedral).

Orsi, Lelio da Novellara (1511-87). Born in Novellara, his art stems from the school of Parma and especially Correggio. He worked for the Gonzaga family and was active in Novellara, Reggio, Rome, and Parma. His style is curiously related to northern Mannerism (see) and sometimes even seems influenced by German art.

Ostade, Adriaen van (1610-84). Dutch painter and en graver of portraits, rustic scenes and still life. He lived all his life in Haarlem, studying painting in the studio of Frans Hals. His fellow pupil there, Adriaen Brouwer (see), exerted a strong influence on his early style and subject matter, which consisted for the most part of tavern scenes of smoking and drinking. In his broader, middle period under Rembrandt's influence he made greater use of chiaroscuro. The pictures that Ostade painted at the end of his life are extremely refined in finish, and delicate in color and atmosphere. He influenced Jan Steen. (See illustration.)

Ostade, Isaack van (1621-49). Dutch painter of landscapes and rustic interiors. He was the pupil of his elder brother Adriaen, and like him always worked in Haarlem. The extreme similarity in their way of painting has led to a confusion between their works. Isaack's exquisite landscapes, however, and his charming little figures possess a quality peculiarly his own. (See illustration.)

Otis, Bass (1784-1861). American portrait painter, miniaturist, and engraver. Born in Massachusetts, he was active first in New York and then in Philadelphia, where he became president of the Pennsylvania Academy of Fine Arts. He also introduced lithography to the U.S. in 1819.

Oudry, Jean Baptiste (1686-1755). French painter, illustrator and etcher. Noted for his hunting scenes and paintings of animals. From Largillière he learned portrait painting, and painted Peter the Great of Russia. His strong point, however, was painting animals for his huntsman-patron Louis XV. He did much upholstery and tapestry design, heading both the Gobelins and Beauvais tapestry works.

Ouwater, Albert van (fl. c.1430-1460). Dutch painter presumably from Ouwater near Haarlem in the northern Netherlands—the Holland of today. According to one tradition he was a contemporary of Jan van Eyck; according to another he was the master of the Dutch painter, Geertgen tot sint Jans, who belongs to the last decade of the century. One of the two works that can be definitely associated with this painter is the noble and impressive Raising of Lazarus (Berlin); the other is the half-length Madonna (Metropolitan). From these two works we can deduce an artistic personality that accords with the more romantic and intense Dutch Netherlands tradition of that time. This can also be inferred from his broad manner of painting, the subdued but very effective atmosphere, the delicately nuanced handling of flesh tones that replaces the bolder polychromy of the Flemish tradition. (See illustration.)

Overbeck, Friedrich (1789-1869). German painter of the Nazarene school whose Catholic-oriented medieval attitude heralded the advent of Romanticism in Germany. He was converted to Catholicism and lived in a monastery on the Pincio in Rome, where with little emphasis on technique but much on naive feeling, he produced a number of Perugino- and Raphael-inspired pictures of the weakest sort. See NAZARENES.

Ozenfant, Amédée (1886-). Modern French painter, writer and, with Le Corbusier, a leader of the Purist movement in France. From 1906 to 1913 he studied both architecture and painting in Paris, exhibited later at the Beaux-Arts, traveled widely, worked in the propaganda section during the war and finally edited an avant garde review, *L'Elan*, from 1915 to 1917. With Le Corbusier he brought out the first Purist manifesto, called After Cubism, and shared with him

OSTADE, ISAACK VAN. Winter Landscape
Mauritshuis, The Hague

OUWATER. Head of a Donor
Metropolitan Museum of Art, New York

the first exhibition of Purist art. From 1920 to 1925 he and Le Corbusier edited *The New Spirit* and in 1925 published their *Modern Painting*. Since 1938 Ozenfant has been in the United States, lecturing and teaching. In Purism he tried to put forth the idea of a reformed or purified Cubism where, instead of irregular impressions of form, there would be hard precise machine-like parts that really represent "the modern spirit." Forms in this art would also assume the universally understood shapes that the machine produces in every culture: circles, ovals, cylinders, etc. See PURISM.

P

Pacchiarotto, Giacomo (1474-1540). Sienese painter. A pupil of Matteo di Giovanni, he later fell under the influence of Pinturicchio. Documents prove him to have lived a turbulent political and civil life, but in spite of this he was accorded many commissions by the community. One of the most skillful Sienese painters of his day, he made the transition between fifteenth-century realistic and High Renaissance idealistic style. His figures are suave and graceful and his compositions not without grandeur.

Pach, Walter (1883-). Contemporary American painter born in New York City. He is more famous as a writer on art and for his role in the organization of the Armory Show. He studied with Chase and Henri, but was later influenced by modern art.

Pacheco, Francisco (1564-1654). Spanish painter, critic and poet. He is best known today for his activities as a chronicler of the arts and as a teacher of his son-in-law, Velázquez. He was raised by his uncle, a man of letters who nurtured his nephew's literary tastes. He learned painting in Seville from Luis Fernández, under whom he copied Luis de Vargas and Pedro Campaña. He continued throughout his career a taste for Roman Mannerism learned from drawings and engravings. In 1611 he visited El Greco in Toledo, but was shocked by the latter's style. In the same decade he made the friendship of Vicente Carducho (see) in Madrid, opened an influential academy of painting there, and was named censor of painting for the Inquisition. He did religious paintings and classical themes, including an Icarus for the Duke of Alcalá in 1603. Among his portraits is an excellent one of a Knight of Santiago (Cook Collection), and a compendium collection of famous portraits in crayon. His *Arte de la Pintura (Art of Painting)*, published in 1649, occupies an important position in the history of art criticism. His rather puritanical outlook reflects his official churchly position. Otherwise he was, perhaps under Velázquez' influence, favorably inclined toward naturalism. He delighted in bodegones (see), rejected Manneristic contrivances and took a mystical position regarding naturalism: that painting should lead man away from vices and toward the veneration of God. Naturalism, then, he saw as a didactic implement in the service of spirituality.

Pacher, Michael (active by 1467, died 1498). German painter who worked at Bruneck in Pustertal, Brixen in the Tirol, and St. Wolfgang near Salzburg. His early style shows such close relations to the art of North Italy and to Mantegna in particular that it must be assumed he learned painting either directly or indirectly from that master. The spatial arrangement, deep perspective and clinging, form-defining draperies are directly traceable to Mantegna. The altarpiece of the Church Fathers, painted for the church at Brixen, and now in Munich, was finished in 1491 and undoubtedly constitutes his masterpiece. The dignified and sculptural forms, wonderfully plastic and placed in deep surrouding air and space, are very unlike those in contemporary German works, and seem more closely associated with Italian painting.

Padovanino (Alessandro Varotari) (1588-1648). Venetian painter born in Padua, the son of Dario, il Vecchio. As a child he began to paint with his father, was then greatly influenced by Titian, whom he copied, and later by Veronese. He fought a losing battle to maintain the Venetian High Renaissance beyond its time. His best works are small mythological, allegorical, and biblical paintings.

Paduan school. This side of Italian painting begins in the fourteenth century under the influence of the visiting Giotto (Arena Chapel frescoes) and continues under the impact of the later Donatello (Gattemelata equestrian monument and S. Anthony baptismal font). During the fifteenth century this university town was dominated artistically both

PALMA, JACOPO. Christ and the Woman Taken in Adultery, Palazzo Bianco, Genoa

149. PALMA VECCHIO. A Poet. National Gallery, London

by the effects of Donatello's sculpture and the painting of the Veronese masters Altichiero and Avanzo. The two most important Paduan painters of this period are Squarcione and Andrea Mantegna who both show sculpturesque and metallic qualities that betray their affinity for Donatello. The annexation of Padua to Venice ends the autonomy of that center, whose influence, especially that of Mantegna, will be seen among such Venetian masters as Giovanni Bellini, who was Mantegna's brother-in-law.

Pahari Style (see INDIAN PAINTERS: PAHARI STYLE).

Palamedesz., Anthonie (called Stevers) (1600/01-73). Dutch painter of portraits and interiors; he lived and worked in Delft, having probably studied with Miereveld. Later he was influenced by Frans Hals. His work is of very unequal quality.

Palazzo Bianco, Genoa. The gallery in this palazzo, containing a general collection of all the arts, especially Netherlands and Flemish painting, has been modernized so that its installations are unrivaled in Italy.

Palazzo Borghese, Rome. In addition to its outstanding collection of the sculptures of Bernini, this palazzo contains a considerable number of important paintings, including Baroque works of the seventeenth century, Mannerist works of the sixteenth century, and outstanding examples by Correggio, Titian, Botticelli, and Raphael, among others. There are also works by non-Italian artists.

Palazzo Farnese, Rome. A sixteenth-century building begun by Antonio da Sangallo and completed by Michelangelo. In painting it features the wall and ceiling decorations of the eclectic Annibale Carracci and his group.

Paleolithic painting (see PREHISTORIC PAINTING).

palette. Literally, the wooden board on which the painter mixes his pigments. A derived meaning is the scheme of color relationship found in a particular work of a particular artist.

palette knife. The thin flexible instrument used by painters for mixing the colors on the palette or in some instances for applying pigments to the canvas surface, e.g., Van Gogh.

Palma, Antonio (1510/15-75+). Venetian painter born in Serina, nephew of Palma Vecchio, whose name he assumed, and father of Palma Giovane. He came to Venice after the death of his uncle and studied with one of the older man's students, Bonifazio Veronese. He is sometimes confused with the latter, since he himself was called Bonifazio Veneziano. He married Bonifazio's niece and continued his workshop after the latter's death in 1553. His art is dependent upon that of his master though he later moved beyond him into the orbit of Tintoretto.

Palma, Jacopo (called il Giovane) (1544-1628). Born in Venice, the son of Antonio and grand nephew of Palma Vecchio, he studied under various masters and was influenced by many others. He was the leading painter in Venice after the death of Titian and Veronese, carrying out many decorations in the city. Formed largely on the art of Titian, his style shows influences from Tintoretto and Salviati and at one period Michelangelo and Mannerism. (See illustration.)

Palma Vecchio (Jacopo Negreti) (c.1480-1528). Venetian painter of the High Renaissance; born in Serinalta near Bergamo. He came early to Venice and may have studied under Bellini together with Giorgione and Titian, though there is no direct evidence of this. His style is close to that of his two great contemporaries but distinctive in its bright and provincial color, ample modeling, and opulent figures. He is especially noted for the robust blonde female type which he created and which may have influenced Titian. It is, however, difficult to define his position in relation to the others or to decide who influenced whom. He shares with Giorgione, Titian, and Lotto the Venetian feeling for color and richness, as well as the contemplative, poetic, musical mood. He had very few students, but had a great influence through his many followers, especially among the Brescians like Moretto and Romanino. His earliest training was probably with the Bergamesque painter Francesco da Santacroce and his early works are provincial in character—Madonna and Four Saints (1505, Zerman), and the St. Peter Altar (1508, Venice Academy). His middle period shows a close relation to Giorgione—Adam and Eve (1510, Braunschweig), and Three Sisters (1518, Dresden). His last period, covering the 1520's, indicates a reliance upon the great compositions of Titian—Barbara Triptych (Sta. Maria Formosa) and the Sacra Conversazione (Venice Academy). (See color plate 149.)

Palmer, Samuel (1805-81). British watercolor landscapist influenced by Turner and the poetry of Milton. He studied with Linnell and became a friend of Blake, his own

PALMEZZANO. Christ Carrying the Cross
Philadelphia Museum of Art, Johnson Collection

deeply imaginative quality reinforced by the latter. Palmer was a visionary painter; his series of moonlit sepia landscapes shows a unique intensity but his later work no longer had this power and vision.

Palmezzano, Marco (c.1456-after 1543). An Umbrian painter born at Forlì, he was a pupil, assistant and compatriot of Melozzo da Forlì, with whom he worked at Loreto and in his native town. In these fresco projects he executed decorations from Melozzo's designs for the Treasury of Santa Maria of Loreto, and the Feo chapel in San Biagio, Forlì. In the latter church he painted independently a lunette and the Martyrdom of San Giacomo. His style is close to Melozzo's but more conventional and heavy-handed. Altarpieces and devotional paintings by him are in Forlì, Milan, Florence, Bologna, Faenza and Munich. A self-portrait at the age of eighty is in the gallery at Forlì. (See illustration.)

panel painting. Almost any painting existing on its own free support or background, as distinguished from paintings, such as murals, incorporated in the surface of a wall. Panel painting includes primarily pictures on canvas or wood, although it may include other "free" forms.

Pannini, Giovanni Paolo (1691/92-1764/65). Architectural painter born in Piacenza, he did buildings and ruins, pageants and ceremonies. He may have studied perspective with Fernandino Galli Bibbiena, and c.1717 was a pupil of Benedetto Luti in Rome, where he was influenced by Locatelli, Rosa, and Ghisolfi. His earlier work, up to 1735, is dependent, in its sharp light and shade, upon Ghisolfi. After that date the influence of Piranesi in architecture and Rosa in figures becomes evident. The clear blue-green tonality of these paintings finally gives way in 1760 to a luminous mist.

Pantoja de la Cruz, Juan (1551-1609). Spanish court painter of Madrid. Faithful student of Sánchez Coello, he perpetuated that tight Mannerist style of portraiture into the reign of Philip III. He shows influence of Titian and Mor, whose works he copied on commission from the court. So exacting was his style that Lope de Vega attributed to him a version of the Apelles legend—to wit, that an eagle attacked Pantoja's painting of another eagle. Most of his decorative works in residences have been destroyed by fire. Among his portraits are two of Philip II as first a young man (Prado) and then aged (Escorial). For Philip III he produced the sketch employed by Giovanni da Bologna in an equestrian statue of the monarch. (See illustration.)

Paolo Veneziano (Maestro Paolo) (active c.1333, died c.1362). Maestro Paolo is the first distinct personality of the Venetian school as it emerged from its medieval Byzantine matrix. His documented works, including a Coronation of the Virgin (Frick Collection), show a tendency toward a refinement and softening of the Byzantine style, with some iconographical changes as well.

papiers collés. From the French words meaning "pasted papers," it refers to the Cubist technique of pasting bits of paper, cardboard, newspaper, playing cards and other non-painted materials into a pictorial design. Examples: the work of Braque and Picasso. See also COLLAGE.

Paret y Alcázar, Luis (1746-99). Spanish painter, etcher and architect. He studied with A. González Velázquez and learned the style of Boucher from C. F. de la Traverse. He painted the activities of the Spanish court and made a series of paintings of Spanish forts and seacoasts. As an engraver he made illustrations for the works of Cervantes and Quevedo.

Paris, Jean de (see PERREAL).

Paris Bordone (see BORDONE, PARIS).

Paris, School of (see SCHOOL OF PARIS).

Parmigianino or **Parmeggianino** (Francesco Mazzola) (1503-40). One of the three leading early Italian Mannerist painters. He lacked the inventive genius of Pontormo or the radicalism of Rosso, but he was perhaps the most famous because the engravings made after his drawings had a profound influence upon Florentine, Venetian, and later French (Fontainebleau) art. His refined, aristocratic style is characterized by a subtle linearity, grace, and elegance. Born in Parma of a family of painters, he studied first with his uncles, Michele and Pier Ilario, since his father, Filippo, died when he was only two. However, their style had little effect on him. He was essentially a follower of Correggio, who was at work in Parma in 1518. He went to Rome in 1523, where he worked for the Medici pope, Clement VII, and where he came in contact with the new Mannerist style through Rosso, who arrived in 1524. He may also have seen the Pontormos

PANTOJA DE LA CRUZ
Margarita of Austria, Queen of Spain
Museum of Fine Arts of Houston, Kress Collection

PARMIGIANINO. The Circumcision
Detroit Institute of Arts

in Florence. After the Sack of Rome in 1527 he fled to Bologna where he stayed until the coronation of Charles V in 1531, when he returned to Parma. The great commission of his last years was the fresco decoration of the Stecatta, which he never finished, since he was forced to leave because of a dispute about the contract. (See illustration.)

Parrhasios (late 5th century B.C.). Greek painter from Ephesos. According to Pliny he sought symmetry and vivacity in painting. To judge from ancient writings he may have introduced chiaroscuro modeling to replace the linearity of the Greek style. He led an eccentric and boastful life, calling himself "the friend of pleasure." Of the twenty-four subjects he is known to have painted, most deal with emotional themes requiring psychological insight.

Parri Spinelli (1387-1453). Son of Spinello Aretino of Florence, but spent most of his life in Arezzo after assisting his father with frescoes in Siena. His style is influenced chiefly by Lorenzo Monaco (see), whose Gothic tendencies he perpetuated and developed into a personal, calligraphic manner. Drawings by him are preserved in the Uffizi.

Parrocel, Charles (1688-1752). French painter of history, especially battles. He learned his style from his father, Joseph, and from LaFosse. In Rome he studied the works of Giulio Romano and Tempesta. He was an excellent horseman, served in a cavalry regiment and is especially noted for his portrayal of horses in his paintings, such as the Combat between the Infantry and the Cavalry.

Parrocel, Joseph Francois (1646-1704). French history painter and etcher. Called "Parrocel des Batailles" because of his specialty of battle pictures. He belonged to a large family of several generations of artists from Montbrison, and he trained with his brother Louis before joining J. Courtois in Rome and studying Salvator Rosa. His style derived from the latter two painters of battle-pictures. On his return to Paris (1675) he was elected to the Academy on the basis of his Siège de Maastricht. He was in considerable demand, Le Brun trying to hold him to painting, Louvois hiring him to design for the Gobelins. For the latter he did the Conquests of Louis XIV to be hung in the Invalides. He did considerable work for Versailles and for Marly, but was a victim of the professional jealousy of Mansard.

Pascin, Jules (1885-1930). Bulgarian-born painter of the School of Paris who began as an illustrator in Austria and Germany for such publications as *Lustige Blaetter* and *Simplizissimus*. He came to Paris in 1905, continuing magazine illustration until the summer of 1914, when the war caught him outside France. After travels in the United States and Cuba he returned to Paris in 1920, where he set up his studio and began his public works with large-scale, carefully drawn and representational biblical and mythological subjects and portraits. From there he went on to the delicately nuanced though bitter and ironic studies of women, often prostitutes: these relate him in a general way to Lautrec but have a certain personal grace and tenderness that clearly belong to Pascin and bespeak his sense of identification with these defeated creatures. He committed suicide in 1930 on the opening day of an important one-man show. (See illustration.)

Passarotti, Bartolommeo (1529-92). Born in Bologna, he was a realistic painter of lower-class subjects, fish-markets, butcher-shops, etc. He went to Rome in the 1550's and studied with Vignola and Zuccari, and was influenced by Correggio

PASCIN. Figure of a Young Girl
Detroit Institute of Arts

Pastel by Watteau. Young Woman Seated
Knoedler Gallery, New York

and Parmigianino. Under the impact of Venetian art and Tibaldi, however, he became not only the leader in a revolt against the Mannerism brought to Bologna by Vasari and Salviati, but the fountainhead of Bolognese realism. There in the 1560's he had a large atelier with many students, among them Agostino Carracci.

Passmore, John Richard (1904-). Leading Australian painter, born in Sydney and trained at the Julian Ashton School of Art. He spent seven years wandering and studying in Europe and returned to Australia in 1950. His painting is preoccupied with building form by means of color, the broken hues (transparent apricots and blues) being governed by a draughtsmanship that shows the influence of Rembrandt.

pastel painting. Painting by means of a chalk or crayon of pure powder color. This is the simplest of all methods of applying color to a flat surface and is not complicated by color changes due to the drying process, but the pigment flakes so easily that colors are almost fugitive, although it can be preserved by a type of fixative. Its origins were in crayon studies of the late Renaissance, but the great popularizer of the technique was Rosalba Carriera of Venice, 1675-1757 (see). Pastel reached a height of popularity in Rococo France where Quentin de La Tour was its virtuoso, and Watteau and Chardin adapted it to their different ends. It was revived in the Impressionist period by Degas and has proved to be a popular modern vehicle. (See illustration.)

pastiche.A work of art in which many different and even divergent styles are combined. In general the term is not meant to be favorable.

Pasture, Rogier de la (see WEYDEN, ROGIER VAN DER).

Patel, Pierre (called le bon Patel) (1605?-76). French landscape painter. Pupil of Vouet. Patel painted in the style of Claude Lorrain and worked with Romanelli on various royal decorative projects.

Patel, Pierre Antoine (1648-1707). French painter and copper engraver. Son and pupil of Pierre Patel (le bon), with whom he is frequently confused. He did decorative paintings in the Louvre, including four of the Months

Pater, Jean Baptiste Francois (1695-1736). French painter. Fellow townsman and faithful pupil of Watteau, he is known for fêtes galantes in the manner of his master. Friction developed between the two artists, but they were reconciled in Watteau's last weeks of life. And during that short time Pater learned much from Watteau. His works are close in style to Watteau; in fact he often copied him. Personally he was inclined, like Lancret, to be more specific in detail than Watteau and to depict more obvious amorous intrigue. His paintings suffer from hasty execution caused by his fear of poverty and his desire to sell. Conversation in the Park (Louvre) is among his best works. (See illustration.)

Patinir (Patenier), Joachim (c.1485-1524). Flemish landscape painter. Patinir developed an almost pure landscape tradition out of the background style of Gerard David. He was an admirer of Bosch and of Quentin Metsys, with whom he collaborated. He was also a particular friend of Dürer, who exchanged materials and ideas with him. He worked with several artists who executed figures while he did backgrounds: Metsys, Joos van Cleve, Isenbrandt. His landscapes are quaint and complex, of panoramic view, anticipating Brueghel's. He favored a blue-green tonality and an almost miniaturist technique of great delicacy. His favorite subject was the Rest on the Flight into Egypt, a religious motive which he could develop into a study of nature and atmosphere. A St. Jerome by him is in the Metropolitan. (See illustration.)

patrons. Those who sponsor or pay for works of art. They may be an institution (such as the medieval church), a Renaissance nobleman or king, the modern man of business or business house or anyone who has the wherewithal to pay for, and the inclination to order, a work of art. During the Renaissance period we find the names of famous royal patrons such as Francis I of France, Philip II of Spain, and Charles V of the Holy Roman Empire. At the same time important families such as the Medici of Florence (with its great Lorenzo the Magnificent), the Fuggers of Augsburg and others show the increasing importance of the middle class. In our own era patrons of this type are paralleled by the Mellons, the Kresses, the Lehmans and similar individuals or family groups

PATER. Procession of Italian Comedians
Frick Colleetion, New York

PATINIR. Penitence of St. Jerome
Metropolitan Museum of Art, New York

whose sponsorship of art is directed more to the purchase of finished works rather than to the ordering of paintings from the artist directly. In modern times the traditional type of patronage is confined to those individuals who have a building problem (which may or may not be solved by painting and sculpture), civic organizations with memorials in mind, and democratic and other governments wishing to glorify an individual or idea. A final development characteristic of twentieth-century patronage involves the corporation which may commission art to advertise a product or as a means of creating good will.

Peach-Tree Spring. A Chinese romantic poem by T'ao Ch'ien (365-427 A.D.) describing the chance discovery of an earthly paradise. It is a frequent subject of landscape painters in China.

Peale (family). Three generations of American painters brought to prominence by Charles Willson Peale (1741-1827), the son of a Maryland schoolteacher who had left England after being pardoned from a death sentence for embezzlement and forgery. He taught painting in succession to his brother, James (1749-1831), and his children, some of whom he named after famous artists—Raphaelle, Rembrandt, Titian Ramsay, Rubens and Angelica Kaufmann. Of these only two, Raphaelle (1774-1825) and Rembrandt (1778-1860), practiced art. James had four children who were artists: Anna Claypoole (1791-1878), James, Jr. (1794- 1831), Margaretta Angelica (1795-1882), and Sarah Miriam (1800-85). Rubens had a daughter who was a painter, Mary Jane (1826-1902).

Peale, Charles Willson (1741-1827). American painter and naturalist, he was in his time a saddler, coachmaker, watchmaker, silversmith, dentist, taxidermist, museum director, curator and docent as well as soldier, patriot and politician. One of the most interesting figures of the Revolutionary period he played an important part in the political and cultural life of his time. Apprenticed first to a saddler, he learned to paint as he did many things by observation and experiment, and by reading a book entitled *Handmaid of the Arts*. In 1765 he went to Boston where he watched Copley at work, and from 1766 to 1769 he was in England studying with Benjamin West. Returning to Annapolis he set up as a portrait painter. At the outbreak of hostilities he moved to Philadelphia, was elected a member of the General Assembly, and was an officer under Washington in the Revolutionary Army. As a contemporary said of him, "He fit and painted and painted and fit"; he produced a great many sketches of military figures who later made up part of his gallery of American heroes. He continued to paint after the war, but eventually retired from the field in favor of his sons, as he had earlier left miniature painting to his brother James. In his later years he was more concerned with science and his museum of natural history and arts. As a painter he was straightforward and competent; at his best he continued in the tradition of Copley with a homely sincerity which captures something of the nature of the era in which he lived. His work was extremely uneven, too often hurried and superficial, as if he had too many other things to do, but his *Staircase Group* (Philadelphia), a portrait of his two sons, is still one of the finest portraits ever painted by an American. (See illustration.)

Peale, James (1749-1831). American miniaturist, pupil of his older brother, Charles Willson (see). Active in Philadelphia, he also painted still life, landscape, genre, conversation pieces, and history scenes.

Peale, Raphaelle (1774-1825). American painter, eldest

PEALE, CHARLES WILLSON. Portrait of Colonel George Washington. Brooklyn Museum

son of Charles Willson (see). He painted charming still life which were the best of the period. He studied with his father, had a varied career in art and science, but drank too much and died in his middle years. (See illustration.)

Peale, Rembrandt (1778-1860). American painter, second son of Charles Willson (see). He studied with his father, with Benjamin West in London, and also in Paris. A mediocre painter, he is best known for his portraits of Washington.

Peasant Wedding by Pieter Brueghel the Elder (see).

Pechstein, Max (1881-). German Expressionist painter, graphic artist, draughtsman and illustrator. Member of Die Brücke group. Interested in art from his early youth, in 1900 he went to the School for Decorative Arts in Dresden and in 1903 to its Academy of Fine Arts. In 1906 he joined Die Brücke but was expelled in 1912. He traveled widely on the Continent and in 1914 visited India, China and the Pelew Islands in the South Pacific, where he was taken prisoner by the Japanese. Although part of the Expressionist movement, Pechstein is, properly speaking, a kind of German Fauve and only in occasional works does he rise to the emotive level demanded by his native school. The association with the art of the South Pacific also tends to identify him with Die Brücke and its demonic vein, but Pechstein apparently never fully assimilated the spirit of primitive art. See EXPRESSIONISM. (See illustration.)

Pecori, Domenico (c.1480-1527). Italian painter active in Arezzo. A pupil of della Gatta, he absorbed through him the hard linear style of Signorelli, which was later softened through the influence of Perugino.

Peeters (family). This was the name of a large family of artists that stemmed from Antwerp. Its most important members were Bonaventura (1614-52), a marine painter and engraver; Clara (c.1589-after 1617), who specialized in still life; Gillis I (1612-53) and Jan I (1624-before 1680), both brothers of Bonaventura, specializing respectively in landscape and marines.

Pellegrini, Alfredo (1881-). Swiss painter formed under the influence of the symbolist Adolf Hölzel in Stuttgart. He is one of the outstanding Swiss masters of decorative and mural painting. In his easel paintings he shows a lyrical quality in which softness of color is combined with poetically suggestive forms.

PEALE, RAPHAELLE. Still Life with Cake
Brooklyn Museum

PECHSTEIN. Mongolian Lady
Private Collection, Germany

Pellegrino di San Daniele (Martino da Udine) (c.1467-1547). Italian painter and sculptor who spent most of his life in Udine, with occasional trips to Venice, Ferrara, Assisi, and a journey to Rome. In a style based on that of Bartolommeo Montagna, with elements from Carpaccio, he painted frescoes and altarpieces for churches in and around Udine.

Penni, Giovanni Francesco (called Il Fattore) (1448?-c.1528). Florentine painter who, along with Giulio Romano, was Raphael's leading pupil and assistant. He collaborated with his master in decorating the Loggie of the Vatican and the Farnesina. In 1525 he did a Coronation of the Virgin after a design by Raphael for the Convent of Sta. Maria di Monteluce near Perugia. After assisting Giulio Romano in the decoration of the Palazzo del Te in Mantua, he went to Naples and remained there. His style was dry and uninspired, slavishly dependent upon that of Raphael.

Pequin, Charles (1879-). A French painter from the provinces who worked at the Beaux-Arts Academy in Paris and later exhibited at the first two shows of the Salon d'Automne. From 1908 on he showed regularly at the Salon des Indépendants. His straightforward representational style appears in many landscapes, portraits and still lifes done in a kind of modified Impressionism.

Pereira, Irene Rice (1907-). Contemporary American non-objective painter in a geometric vein. Born in Boston, she studied at the Art Students League and abroad. She worked under the W.P.A. and taught at the Design Laboratory and at Pratt Institute. She lived in England in 1950 and after her return the next year taught at Ball State Teachers College, Muncie, Ind. She is best known for her experiments with various materials, glass, metal and parchment used together with more traditional paint and treated

PEREIRA. Green Depth. Metropolitan Museum of Art, New York

as superimposed opaque and transparent layers. (See illustration.)

Perlin, Bernard (1918-). Contemporary American Neo-Romantic painter. Born in Richmond, Va., he studied at the National Academy of Design and the Art Students League, worked in Poland (1939), and served as war correspondent for *Life* and *Fortune*. Influenced by Shahn, his style is romantically morbid and delicate.

Permeke, Constant (1886-1954). Belgian Expressionist and member of the "second Laethem-Saint-Martin group" (see). A turbulent and passionate artist, he was drawn to proletarian figures—workers, farmers, sailors—whom he represented with a sombre, heavy outline and a thick handling of paint. His work is filled with great emotional power as he forces deliberately awkward forms into the limitations of the framed canvas. A high point of Belgian Expressionism, he is perhaps its most original representative.

Perréal, Jean (called Jean de Paris) (c.1455-1530). A French court painter, miniaturist and architect. This artist, one of the greatest of his day, is well documented but entirely lacking in authenticated works today. For this reason he was at one time identified with the Master of Moulins (see), but the latter's paintings do not correspond to the life-span of Perréal. Perréal was extremely active in the Bourbon court, organizing fêtes and illuminating books. He traveled in Italy and was twice sent to England to paint royalty. Current attributions to Perréal include the portrait of his intimate friend Pierre Sala in a volume of the latter's verse (London), a portrait of Louis XII (Windsor) and two portraits at Chantilly.

Perroneau, Jean Baptiste (1715-83). French portraitist. Contemporary and chief rival of Quentin de la Tour, Perroneau also did much in the new pastel technique. He drew more on the middle class for his trade and produced more stolid, matter-of-fact physiognomies, although just as vibrant in color as de la Tour. Characteristic of his informality is Little Girl with a Cat (Louvre).

Persia, The Development of Painting in. With the coming of Islam to Persia in the seventh century A.D., the Moslem reverence for the Koran and other books gave rise to the arts of calligraphy, illumination and fine bindings. Under the Abbasid caliphs in the thirteenth century the first phase of manuscript illumination on a large scale began; not yet truly Persian, it is usually described as belonging to the Mesopotamian or Baghdad school. Arabic manuscripts based on the fables of the Hindu poet Bidpai, or Greek treatises on plants, animals, physics and medicine (such as Dioscorides' *Materia Medica*, copied by Abd Allah ibn al Fazl), were illustrated by painters who fitted their rather naive pictures into whatever space had been left on the page by the calligrapher.

Influenced by Egyptian, Syrian, Nestorian Christian and Manichaean work, the early style was colorful and vivacious. The tradition of Mani (c.215-273) and his followers no doubt helped to set the course of true Iranian art in the use of brilliant color and flat pattern. The lively narrative of the adventures of Abu Zaid in Hariri's *Maqamat* were recorded in little scenes as decorative as textile design, but full of humor and picturesque detail (see Mecca Pilgrims). The greatest of the *Maqamat* illustrators was Al Wasiti; in his copy of 1237 the conventions of Persian painting, such as the close grouping of figures, lack of regard for realistic proportion, exaggeration of fabric pattern and fine handling of color, already had a strong exponent.

After the conquest of Iran and Mesopotamia by the Mongols, completed in 1258, the Il-Khans made Baghdad their winter residence and artists were brought from China and the conquered provinces to serve the descendants of Ghengis Khan in Bagdad, Tabriz and other court cities. Chinese brush technique, with its emphasis on line rather than color and the Chinese love of unfilled space and asymmetric composition came as a challenge to Near Eastern artists. The cone-shaped mountains, as in Death of Paladins in the Snowy Mountains (see illustration), wisps of cloud in the Chinese manner, tonal shading, Mongol plate armor, exotic rocks and trees, were accepted as conventions by illuminators of thirteenth- and fourteenth-century manuscripts. Favorite texts were the *Shah-nama*, or Book of Kings, the great epic of

PERSIA. BAGHDAD SCHOOL, 13TH CENTURY
Mecca Pilgrims. Bodleian Library, Oxford

Persia by Firdausi (tenth century), animal fables and treatises (see color plate 150), and books of history prepared especially for the nomadic Mongols. Rashid al Din, who wrote a history of the world which was copied and illustrated in the early fourteenth century, developed a suburb of Tabriz to house 60,000 volumes in various languages, and there the artists gathered to paint and write. Old and New Testament stories were recorded, as were facts about the people of Asia. Linear, elongated figures and more spacious backgrounds reflect Chinese influence; color was for a brief period subordinated.

Gradually two styles merged: Chinese dragons (see Rustam Fighting a Dragon), twisted trees, wave motifs (see Moses Discovered by Pharaoh's Daughters), shaded rocks, and greater interest in space, were combined with vived colors. The fury of battle inspired some spirited drawing, whether of cavalry clashes or of the "iron-horses" of Sikandar (Alexander the Great) defeating the King of India (see illustration). A romantic episode of single combat, when Prince Humay wounded his beloved Humayun who was disguised as a man,

PERSIA. 14th century. Rustam Fighting a Dragon
Fogg Museum of Art, Sachs Collection, Harvard University, Cambridge

PERSIA. Death of Paladins in the Snowy Mountains. From Firdausi's Shah-nama of 1330
Topkapu Sarayi Museum, Istanbul

PERSIA. Moses Discovered by Pharaoh's Daughters. From Rashid al Din's History of the World
About 1400. University of Edinburgh Library

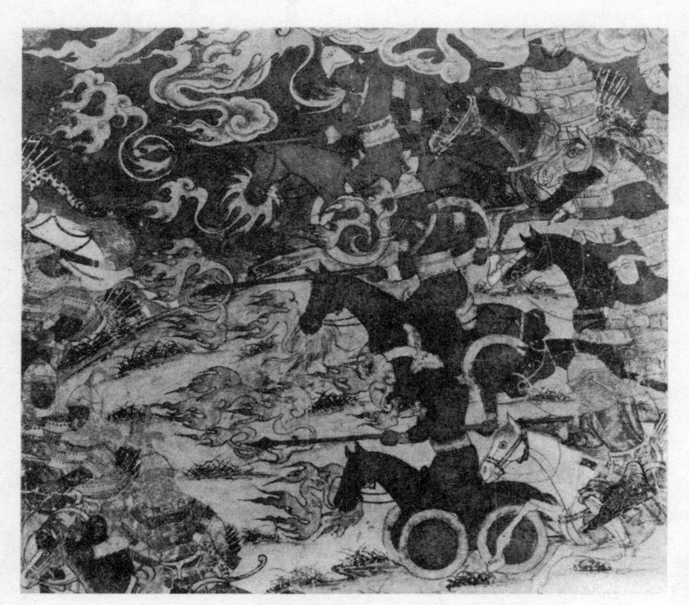

PERSIA. Sikandar Defeats the King of India
From Firdausi's Shah-nama. 14th century
Fogg Art Museum, Harvard University, Cambridge

was painted by Junaid at the end of the fourteenth century (see PERSIAN PAINTERS: TIMURID PERIOD). This is the earliest full-page illustration in which Persian and Chinese elements are joined to form the fanciful landscape that expressed the Iranian love of exquisitely designed flowers and trees. The figures are flat but there is an indication of space in the tilted ground-plane and the flight of birds in the sky.

Timur, or Tamerlane, conquered Tabriz in 1386 and Baghdad in 1404; after pillaging the cities of Persia, he returned to his native Samarkand in Central Asia. His son, Shah Rukh, chose the eastern city of Herat as his residence, and a staff of forty painters, illuminators, calligraphers and binders under the direction of Ja'far Baisunkuri was assembled there to produce books for his famous library. The developed Timurid style, subtle in composition, brilliant in color, romantic in mood, is the result of this royal patronage in the fifteenth century.

The greatest of all Persian painters, Bihzad (see PERSIAN PAINTERS: TIMURID PERIOD) lived in Herat until 1510. One of the treasures of the British Museum, the *Zafar-nama* (Book of Victories of Timur) was completed in 1467 with a series of illustrations in vibrant color and glittering gold. His skill in composition is evident in Majnun at the Battle of the Clans (see illustration), a page from Nizami's *Khamsa*.

A branch of the Timurid school was established in Shiraz

PERSIA. BIHZAD. Majnun at the Battle of the Clans
From Nizami's Khamsa, 1493.
British Museum, London

PERSIA. SHIRAZ SCHOOL, 15TH CENTURY
Rustam Rescues Bezhan from a Well
British Museum, London

by Shah Rukh's son, Ibrahim Sultan. One of the manuscripts illuminated there celebrates Rustam's exploits such as his rescue of Bezhan from a well (see illustration). The fifteenth-century use of conventional gesture, such as the finger touching the mouth in astonishment, the row of heads placed behind the tilted ground-plane to suggest distance, the full view of the opening and the bottom of the well to permit the spectator to follow the narrative, and the use of a deep blue sky sprinkled with stars to indicate night—all of these unrealistic features were characteristic of the period. Marvels of all kinds inspired the painter. When Alexander the Great was warned to turn back from his conquest of India, it is said that the Waq-Waq tree issued the warning; a Shiraz artist visualized this in Alexander and the Talking Tree (see illustration.)

The glory of the Timurid period ended when the Safawid dynasty was established in 1502. Bihzad and his pupils moved west to Tabriz, where the new royal patrons proved to be as generous as the former Shahs. The exquisite clear style gradually gave way to a bolder, more dynamic composition. Under the patronage of Shah Tahmasp some of the most sumptuous manuscript illuminations ever made were painted in Tabriz by Sultan Muhammad.

In the full sixteenth-century style trees burst out of the frame of the picture (see, for example, Khusrau Discovers Shirin Bathing), the multitudinous small plants of a century before are replaced by a few large flowers and the figures are fitted into a more undulating terrain. The old excitement and adventure begin to mellow into a philosophic, even mystical interpretation of experience. When Bahram Gur visits the Princess (see color plate 151), his journey is a symbol of the

150. PERSIA. MONGOL PERIOD. Ibex Jumping from Cliff From Manafi Al-Hayawan. Morgan Library, New York

151. PERSIA. SCHOOL OF SHIRAZ
Bahram Gur Visits the Princess. From the Khamsa of Nizami Freer Gallery of Art, Washington, D.C.

152. PERSIA. SAFAWID PERIOD.
Ustad Muhammadi Huntsmen in Landscape. Metropolitan Museum of Art, New York

search of a soul for union with its ideal. Instead of a clash of arms, there is the horn of the hunter, or a nobleman resting in a forest (see color plate 152). The mood of relaxation might be induced by wine, though orthodox Moslems were supposed to refrain from drinking (see Young Prince at Drinking Party).

Finally, as Persian prestige began to wane, it was no longer possible for one patron to keep an atelier of artists to produce fully illuminated manuscripts. A single page, or even a single figure was painted as an album piece. Without a text of history or poetry to follow, narratives were neglected, drama gave way to a melancholy resignation. Line again became important as mineral colors became too expensive for ordinary work. In the seventeenth century painters such as Riza-i-Abbasi (see color plate 154) were masters of the sweeping brushstroke and the pale shadow.

European influence brought new ideas, but they were so alien to Persian genius that they proved to be the undoing of a great tradition. Native brilliance was masked in dark tonalities as the late painters tried to work in light and shade and in the perspective conventions of the Western world.

The following are the principal periods or stages in the development of Persian painting:

Sassanian Period (226-652 A.D).
Abbasid School (12th and 13th centuries)
Mongol Period (1256-1353)
Timurid Period (1370-1500)
Safawid Period (1502-1736)
Contemporary.

Persian Painters: Sassanian Period (226-652 A.D.)

MANI (c.215-273). Descendant of a high-placed Persian family. Best known as the founder of Manichaeism, which combined the teachings of Christianity, Zoroastrianism, Buddhism and Gnosticism. Mani was a zealous supporter of the arts and was himself a painter of such renown that his enemies, the Mohammedan Arabs and Persians, remembered him less as a founder of a religion than as the prototype of a great artist. His manuscripts, written in the best ink on the best white paper and beautifully illuminated, infuriated both Christians and Mohammedans. He recorded his doctrines in a script (a variation of the Syrian script of simple, clear characters) said by his critics to be a secret invention of his own. He is supposed to have adorned his temples with mural paintings. Dust Mohammed wrote in 1544 of Mani that he used paintings to enforce his teachings and when men would ask him to perform a miracle he would take a piece of silk, retire to a sealed cave for a year, and emerge with the silk covered with wonderful pictures of men, beasts, and trees.

PERSIA. SHIRAZ SCHOOL
Alexander and the Talking Tree. Shah-nama, c.1425
Bodleian Library, Oxford

PERSIA. Khusrau Discovers Shirin Bathing
From Nizami's Khamsa. 16th century
British Museum, London

His is the first known manuscript illumination in Persia. During the reign of Bahram he was seized by the Zoroastrians as a heretic and crucified.

Persian Painters: Abbasid School (12th and 13th centuries).

ABD ALLAH IBN AL FAZL (Abdullah ben el Fadhl, Abdullah ibn al-Fadl) (fl. 1223). Mesopotamian painter who illustrated the *Materia Medica* of Dioscorides in a narrative style that followed Sassanian and East Christian traditions. Vigorous colors and gold enhance the decorative effect of the figures, who sit in European fashion or stand beside large botanical specimens of herb and tree. The original purpose of Greek and Syrian illuminators had been to describe each plant accurately, but the Mesopotamian fondness for lively narrative caused the artist to emphasize gesture and expressive faces. There is no interest in the volumes of bodies, nor in the placement of solid forms in space. The strong contour lines, enlarged fabric patterns and stylized human, animal and floral motifs reflect an interest in surface decoration that was to become constant in later Persian painting. In this early stage of manuscript illumination the calligrapher left only a cramped space for the painter to fill.

AL WASITI (Y Ahya ibn Mahmud ibn Abul Hasan ibn Kuwerrihad Wasiti, Yahya ibn Mahmud of Wasit) (fl. c.1237). Painter in Babylonia, the son of Mahmud and a descendant of Kuwwariha. He copied the *Maqamat*, or *Assemblies*, of Hariri, and illuminated it with ninety-six miniatures; these are important for our knowledge of Arab life and art during the Caliphate. He creates a rich, decorative effect, following schemes evolved by the thirteenth-century Baghdad school, and marks the beginning of many of the Iranian conventions in painting of the Mongol and Timurid periods. In his work a strip of grass indicates the foreground; there is no attempt to suggest distance, or atmospheric effect. His figures are humorous, vivacious and colorful, and dominate the scene. Architecture is part of a flat pattern, water a series of colored motifs. To the Western eye the lack of normal proportion may be disconcerting, but the beauty of color and narrative interest compensate for these minor defects of a major work of art.

JEMAL (fl. c.1184). A painter at Isfahan (later of the Mesopotamian school) under the last Saljuk ruler Tughril. The earliest well-known painter in Iran, he is mentioned in the *History of the Saljuk Rulers* of Abu Bekr Mohammed ibn Ali el Rawandi. He is said to have illuminated a collection of poetry owned by Tughril by painting a portrait of each poet represented in the collection.

Persian Painters: Mongol Period (1256-1353).

MUHAMMAD BIN-I MAHMUH EL BAGHDADI (fl. c.1350-1380). A miniaturist of the Mongol school who illustrated the *Jami at Tawarikh*, or *History of the World*, by Rashid al Din. The first part of the text, the "History of the Mongols" (now in the Bibliothèque Nationale) seems to date from the late fourteenth century. Chinese elements were incorporated in the rendering of distant hills and foaming water. This first phase of Chinese influence was of major importance to the whole development of Persian book arts; at this time line dominates, the human figure is enlarged, and setting begins to assume some significance; color is tonal and subdued.

Persian Painters: Timurid Period (1370-1500).

ABDULLAH OF BAGHDAD (fl. early 15th century). A portrait and fresco painter. Probably the most renowned painter of portraits of great conquerors, generals and statesmen, and of the battles and victories of Timur.

AMIR KHALIL (fl. early 15th century). A painter at the court of Shah Rukh at Herat, he was reputed to be one of the four marvels of the age by his contemporaries and second only to Mani. Tentatively attributed to him (by Binyon) is

PERSIA. 16th century. Attributed to Ustad Muhammadi
Young Prince at a Drinking Party
India Office Library, London

the beautiful *Kalila wa Dimna* in Teheran. Painted in full fifteenth-century style, its delicate lines, brilliant color, exquisite detail, and rather crowded effect mark the advance from earlier, more naive illustrations of these fables.

BIHZAD (Kemal ed din, Kamal ed Din) (c.1440-1527). A painter and calligrapher. The greatest Persian artist, he served as court painter for Sultan Husein Mirza in Herat. In 1510 he went with the court of Shah Isma'il to Tabriz, and after the death of Isma'il he probably did some work at the court of Tahmasp. To explain the small number of authentic Bihzad paintings it has been suggested that he was really a fresco painter and illustrated books only on occasion. Among the works he illustrated are the *Zafar Nama*, 1467; the *Khamsa* of Nizami, 1478; the *Khamsa* of Amir Khusrau, 1485; the *Bustan* of Sa'di, 1487; Nizami manuscript (British Museum), 1493; Amir Khusrau manuscript, 1496; *Layla and Majnun*, end of fifteenth century; Nizami manuscript, 1522 and 1527; and *Shah-nama*, 1537. Among his portrait drawings are the Sultan Husein Mizra, 1506, and Dervish from Baghdad, about 1490. From the School of Bihzad is a portrait of an artist in the manner of Gentile Bellini (see color plate 153.)

Master of color and design, his keen observation and grasp of individual character is reflected in his miniatures. There had been a tendency to avoid expression of deep emotion, to stereotype men, animals and flowers in an exquisite court art, but Bihzad brought a dramatic flair, a warmth and vitality to his painting that opened up new vistas for his followers. Design is still tightly held within the border of the page, the sky is a flat gold or blue or grey, the ground-plane is tilted like a tray of flowers and exotic rocks, and color of unequaled brilliance is placed knowingly in the compositional scheme to set up vibrations that underscore the dramatic theme. The unnatural proportions may be disturbing until one remembers that this is an art not bound to realism but dedicated to a true illumination, a heightening of an effect in which the tale or poem is the starting point.

GHIYATH AD DIN (Kwadje Ghiyath ad Din) (fl. c.1419). Originally from Khorasan, he was a court painter who worked at the library of Shah Rukh's son Baisunkur. He was sent to the Emperor of China in 1419 with Shah Rukh's embassy; no doubt he returned with fresh ideas from the Ming dynasty artists of the Far East and shared them with the forty or so painters, illuminators, calligraphers and binders who composed the staff of the library and academy.

JA'FAR BAISUNKURI (Mawlana Ja'far, Hakim Ja'far) (fl. early 15th century). Miniaturist and calligrapher; director of the academy of painting in Herat. He supervised book production in the library established by Baisunkur, employing forty artists to copy manuscripts. Among his works are a *Gulistan* (Beatty Collection, London), and a *Shah-nama* (1429-30, Gulistan Museum, Teheran), the peak of achievement of the Herat school. The lyrical poems of Sa'di, the *Gulistan (Rose Garden)* and *Bustan (Fruit Garden)*, inspired the Timurid painters to express themselves in delicately rendered landscapes filled with small figures and exquisite flowers. The colors are vivid and harmonious.

JUNAID NAQQASH SULTANI (fl. c.1396). Living in Baghdad, he served Ahmad the Jalairid as painter. He is credited with the illustration of the *Kwadju Kirmani*, poems by Kwaju of Kirman (1281-1352)); this is the first masterly painting of the Timurid period and presages the highest development of Persian miniature style. In full-page scale, he did flower-strewn landscapes in which hero and heroine appear almost as arabesque designs. In one of them Prince Humay has wounded his beloved Princess Humayun in combat before he discovers that she has come into the forest disguised in armor; in this world of make-believe there is no bloodshed, no shadows to hide the figures of the protagonists and their horses. On a pale lavender ground-plane scattered with flowering plants, the drama takes place; lavender and coral pink rocks adapted from Chinese mountain motifs enclose the scene, and green cypress trees push upward toward a pale pink sky in which a flock of birds are seen in isolation. A blue stream flows between mossy banks where red lilies grow, and the red is repeated delicately in banners, costumes and more distant flowers. It is a breathless, enchanted vision.

SHAH MOZHAFFER (Moshaffer Ali, Muzaffar Ali) (fl. c.1500-40). A painter and calligrapher from Khorasan or Transoxania. He is said to have designed and painted a part of the pictures in the Royal Assembly Hall of the Chihil Sutun. He is known to have worked in the Shah Tahmasp's library and painted some of the miniatures in the *Shah-nama* of 1537.

Persian Painters: Safawid Period (1502-1736).

ABD AL SAMAD. See INDIAN PAINTERS: AKBAR PERIOD.

AGHA (Aga Mirak) (fl. mid-16th century). A painter in Tabriz or Isfahan who was outstanding in calligraphy, illumination, engraving and ivory work. Probably began work at the end of the fifteenth century. Founder of the Bukhara school of painting, he is thought to have been a pupil and rival of Bihzad's. He worked in Shah Tahmasp's court library with Sultan Muhammad and is said to have painted ornamental inscriptions on many buildings in Herat. Among the works he illustrated are the *Khamsa* of Nizami, 1539-42; the complete works of Mir 'Ali Shir Neva'i, 1524; and five miniatures in the 1524 *Khamsa* of Nizami. With Sultan Muhammad he is regarded as one of the leading painters of his day, though he is less daring than his colleague. A grandeur of composition, an awareness of open space, was part of the sixteenth-century style; in this, Mirak is a conservative. Beauty of line and color, as well as elegance and sumptuousness and sophistication, are characteristic of his work.

AKA (Aqa Riza, Ali Riza) (d.1547). He came from Isfahan and was a pupil of Mir Ali of Herat. He worked in the style of Bihzad and copied pictures by Sultan Muhammad. Iskander Munahi (1616) refers to his fame as a portrait painter who had a very delicate touch. He enjoyed royal favor. His figure studies are marked by great finesse, clear design, and a sensitive calligraphic line, especially in drawing turbans and waistbands. Among the few portraits known to be his are those of a young prince, c.1570, a horse from the stable of the Shah, a copy of a portrait by Sultan Muhammad, a sitting dervish, a girl with a fan, and a girl holding a necklace.

AQA RIZA (surnamed Murid; Agha Riza) (fl. c.1600). There is much confusion concerning the identity of this painter, as well as about other Persian artists of the same name. He was apparently a Persian from Herat or Merv who went to India, where he was patronized by Jahangir. He is the father of Abu'l Hasan, who was born in 1589, by whick time Aqa Riza must have been in the service of the Mughals. In 1560 he did portraits of Shah Abbas in the new Persian style, and between 1590 and 1600 he did an Indian portrait of Jahangir as a prince. In the *Anvar-i Suhaili* two of his paintings are dated 1604; one shows European influence in the handling of background, and the other has Persian charm but little sense of action.

KASIM ALI (late 15th-early 16th century). A pupil and close collaborator of Bihzad's, he was celebrated as a painter of faces and was considered to be almost Bihzad's equal. Most of the twenty-two miniatures in a *Khamsa* of Nizami in the British Museum are believed to be his rather than Bihzad's, but could be the work of both. Manuscripts by Mir 'Ali Shir Nawai (dated 1485) in the Bodleian Library contain two miniatures signed by Kasim; these show less diversity of design than is characteristic of Bihzad, but are obviously by an outstanding painter who could endow figures and faces with life.

KEMAL OF TABRIZ (fl. 16th century). A student of Mirza Ali of Tabriz, he was a designer and painter of arabesques (called *Tarah)*, of which he is sometimes said to be the originator. Among his works are Lady with a Blue Cloth, Duel between Two Princes, Portrait of a Young Man (a drawing), and another of a stout man (also a drawing). Notable in his work is the emergence of line as an expressive medium —a characteristic of late Persian painting.

KHWAJA 'ABD AL-AZIZ (Khwaja, Kaka, Khwaja Abdul Asiz Khaka of Isfahan) (fl. c.16th century). A painter from Isfahan at the court of Shah Tahmasp. His work is characterized by sumptuous design and color in the courtly tradition.

MAWLANA MUZAFFAR ALI (fl. c.1570, died shortly after 1628). Said to have been a pupil of Bihzad and to have painted some of the pictures in the assembly hall and palace of the Chihil Sutun at Isfahan. A miniature in the Nizami *Haft Paikar* of Shah Tahmasp, dated 1539-42, depicting Bahram Gur transfixing the foot and ear of a wild ass with a single arrow, is attributed to him. It is a romantic and traditional work.

MAWLANA SHAYK MUHAMMED SHIRAZI (fl. early 16th century). Worked under Shah Abbas and took part in the building of the new palace at Kazwin. He imitated European paintings and created a vogue for them. Later he joined the royal library staff of Shah Ismael Mirza. His style, that of the school of Herat, is elegant, fine and colorful. Portrait of a Prince (formerly in Koechlin collection, Paris) is a notable example of his work.

MIR SAYYID 'ALI (fl. 16th century). First a painter under Shah Tahmasp he later worked under the Mughal Emperor Humayun. See entry under INDIAN PAINTERS: AKBAR PERIOD.

MIRZA ALI (fl. early 16th century). A painter at Tabriz who worked at the court of Shah Tahmasp and was a pupil of Bihzad and Mirak; said to have been the outstanding designer of arabesque golden ornaments of his day. He probably executed the fine ornaments and buildings in the miniature paintings of his masters. Among his works are miniatures in the *Khamsa* of Nizami and the *Shah-nama* written for Tahmasp, c.1539-43, among the most splendid manuscripts ever produced. Refinement of detail, and beauty of line and color reflect the taste of the royal patron and the extraordinary talent of his painters.

MUHAMMED AGA SADIQ (fl. mid-18th century). Known for the drawing and lacquer painting he did under Kerim Khan, who died in 1779. He did the frescoes in the Chihil Sutun, or Hall of Forty Pillars, in Isfahan in a style influenced by Riza-i-Abbasi and European painting.

MUHAMMAD RIZA OF MESHED (fl. early 17th century). A student of Mir Sejid Ahmed; he painted during the reigns of Shah Abbas and Shah Safi. As compared with fifteenth-century style his work, characteristic of the period, shows a relaxation of line and less brilliant coloring.

153. PERSIA. TIMURID PERIOD. Portrait of a Painter Freer Gallery of Art, Washington, D.C.

154. PERSIA. SAFAWID PERIOD. Riza-i-Abbasi. Lovers Metropolitan Museum of Art, New York

MUHAMMAD YUSEF EL HUSEINI (fl. c.1654). Worked in Bukhara. He was influenced by the painting of Mirak and then began to experiment with European techniques; he used light and shade to suggest modeling of the face, and dressed his figures in European costume.

MUHAMMAD ZAMAN BIN-I HAJI YUSEF (fl. 17th century). Did miniature and lacquer painting under Abbas II and later under Shah Jahan in Kashmir. Son of Haji Yusef, he was a converted Persian who was sent to Rome under Shah Abbas and returned as a Christian under the name of Paolo Zaman. Obliged to leave Persia, he went to India under Shah Jahan's protection. Among his works are two miniatures in the British Museum, Elizabeth Visits the Virgin, and The Flight into Egypt. His style reflects a training based on Italian painting. Traditional Christian themes, Italianate composition, and modeling in light and shade became a part of his eclectic style. (See illustration.)

MU'IN MUSAVVIR (fl. c.1630-1707). A student of Riza-i-Abbasi. Among his many paintings and portrait drawings the most important is one inscribed "Portrait of the late Riza-i-Abbasi, made by his pupil Mu'in in the year 1084 A.H." His drawings show his dependence upon Riza's calligraphic style which draws its inspiration from the Chinese.

MULLAH MUHAMMED RIZA (fl. c.1582-1628). A contemporary of Mir Imad, he was active at Tabriz as a calligrapher and painter. He was called to Constantinople in 1585 to work in the Imperial Arsenal and was praised by the Turks

PERSIA. SAFAWID PERIOD. MUHAMMAD ZAMAN
Iskandar's Fight with the Dragon
British Museum, London

as a great master with a delicate touch. He returned to Tabriz laden with gifts and money. Among his works is a painting of a seated dervish (formerly Goloubeff collection, Paris).

RIZA-I-ABBASI (c.1598-1643). Lived at Isfahan as painter and calligrapher in the court of Shah Abbas and later of Sufi. He did many drawings of genre scenes and portraits in a calligraphic style reminiscent of Ali Riza (Aqa Riza) His work has often been imitated and forged. A *Shah-nama* in the Metropolitan Museum containing eighty-five miniatures is thought to be his, as were fifty sketches, dated 1638-1643, in the Sarre collection (Berlin). Numerous drawings signed by him and his son were formerly in the Demotte collection, Paris. The separate portrait became more popular than manuscript illumination in the late sixteenth and early seventeenth centuries; there was no longer the clash of arms or romantic love which the painter might portray in glowing colors. Line, and delicate tints, or a limited palette, came into vogue as patronage, economic conditions, and the spirit of the times changed. (See color plate 154.)

SADIQI BEG AFSHAR (fl. c.1574). An Afshar Turk active up to the time of Shah Abbas; a pupil of Mawlana Muzaffar Ali; also a dervish, soldier and poet. He was noted for the fineness of his drawing and his skill as a portraitist. Among the few remaining of his thousands of "marvelous" portraits is an elegant drawing of a very modish court lady.

SHAH KULI NAQQASH (fl. mid-16th century). A pupil of Mirak at Tabriz. He went to Turkey and became the foremost painter at the court of Sulaiman the Magnificent. Known as a painter of the large, curving leaves called *saz*, he was famous for boldness of design and the decorative color characteristic of late Persian style.

SHAH TAHMASP I. Successor to Shah Ismael, he ruled from 1524 to 1576, and founded the Safawid school at Tabriz. Calligrapher and painter, as well as sovereign, he was taught the arts by Sultan Muhammad, and organized a library (workshop) in his court in which he employed the finest artists and craftsmen. The shop produced some of the most sumptuous manuscripts in a style characterized by great elegance of design, decorative richness and refinement of technique. Developed probably by Mirak and Sultan Muhammad under the supervision of Bihzad, all their miniatures have many features in common.

SHAIKH-ZADA MAHMUD MUZAHIB (c.1499-1537). A native of Khorasan, he became a pupil of Bihzad. A *Diwan* of the great poet Hafiz, for which he and Sultan Muhammad did the illustrations, is one of the most important early sixteenth-century manuscripts, for it shows the continuance of the Bihzad style, with its brilliance and elegant detail, into the Safawid period.

SIYAWUSH THE GEORGIAN (fl. mid-16th century). Teacher of Sultan Ibraham Mirza and Ustad Wali Jan; he was at first a gilder of manuscripts and later a painter. His drawing in the Marteau collection (Louvre), depicting a cavalier attacking a dragon, is complex in composition and shows Chinese influence.

SULTAN MUHAMMAD (Haji Muhammed Naqqash or Mir Naqqash, Mir Musavvir of Sultanie, Ustad Sultan Mohammed) (d.1555). A contemporary of Mirak, he worked in Tabriz and was a pupil of Bihzad. He was the chief painter and teacher of Shah Tahmasp and Abbas I. He was proficient in many phases of the decorative arts, including bookbinding

PERSIA. SAFAWID PERIOD. SULTAN MUHAMMAD
Ascension of the Prophet to the Seventh Heaven
British Museum, London

PERSIA. SAFAWID PERIOD. USTAD MUHAMMADI
Young Dervish with a Spear
India Office Library, London

and the manufacture of porcelains in the Chinese manner. He undoubtedly contributed some miniatures to the elaborate *Shah-nama* produced by Tahmasp's library and he illustrated a *Khamsa* of Nizami made in 1539-42 (now in the British Museum) as well as a *Diwan* of Hafiz. He also did numerous drawings and portrait miniatures of elegant youths, court ladies and princes, including an equestrian of a prince accompanied by a servant, one of the great paintings of the period. A decorative richness is manifest in his work, coupled with a daring spirit of experimentation in spatial relationships and an opening up of the tight compositional scheme that marked his predecessors. Romantic love, refinement of form, and traditional regard for rock and flower motifs are a part of his heritage but there is a new grandeur in his work that points to the future. The Ascension of the Prophet to the Seventh Heaven (see illustration) is typical. On the human-headed horse Buraq, he rides high above the earth accompanied by singing angels. The sun glows in the midst of clouds still painted in the Chinese manner, and a veil shields him from a vision too brilliant for human eyes.

USTAD MUHAMMADI HEREWI (fl. c.1580). A student and probably son of Sultan Muhammad, he also studied under Mihrab of Baghdad. He was a master of line drawing with an original lightness of style and a touch of humor. He is said to have painted lacquered bindings of the kind just coming into vogue at that time. Among his works are a landscape drawing in the Louvre, signed and dated 1578, and a landscape painting and two tinted drawings in the Metropolitan Museum. The Huntsmen in a Landscape (see color plate 153), with its large figures, open composition and elaborate border of drawings in Chinese style is as typical of the period as is the absence of strong narrative interest. Delicacy of color and grace of gesture have taken the place of the vibrant tones and elaborate detail of the previous period.

USTAD WALI JAN (fl. 16th century). A painter who worked in Tabriz, studied painting with Siyawush, and then went to Istanbul in 1573. Although his work won him high praise, his pride and vanity prevented him from acquiring real mastery in his art.

Persian Painters: Contemporary

HAJI MUSAVIR EL MULK. Working in the ancient miniature tradition of isolated flowers and trees, a tilted ground-plane and exotic rock formations, he uses modeling in light and shade for faces, and paints recognizable portraits.

perspective. The art of simulating the appearance of depth or three-dimensionality on a two-dimensional surface. See AERIAL PERSPECTIVE and LINEAR PERSPECTIVE.

Perugino (Pietro di Cristoforo Vannucci) (c.1450-1523). The most important painter produced by the Umbrian school after Piero della Francesca. He is also important as a teacher of Raphael and a major influence on that master's style. His artistic origins are obscure. He may have had early contact with Piero della Francesca, and may have worked in the shop of Fiorenzo di Lorenzo, whose style his early works resemble. He was in Florence as a young man, and registered in the painters' guild there in 1472. Much of his life was spent going back and forth between Florence, Perugia and Rome.

PESELLINO. The Trinity. National Gallery, London

155. PERUGINO. Saint Bartholomew
Kress Collection, New York

He worked in Rome several times, most importantly in 1479-82 on the Sistine Chapel frescoes (among his best works) and on a project in St. Peter's (now destroyed), and again in 1508 when he decorated the ceiling of one of Raphael's famous "Stanze." He died of the plague in 1523.

His greatest works were done from 1480 to 1500, when he was regarded as one of the foremost artists in Italy. His later work was overshadowed by High Renaissance developments with which he was unable to compete. Of the remaining Sistine Chapel frescoes (some were destroyed to make way for Michelangelo's Last Judgment), the most impressive is that of Christ Giving the Keys to St. Peter. Other important frescoes are those of Santa Maddalena dei Pazzi in Florence (1493-96), and of the Cambio (Exchange) in Perugia (1499-1507). He made his best altarpieces in this period (examples in the Uffizi and Pitti galleries). One of his most celebrated works is of c.1504, the Marriage of the Virgin (museum of Caen), which was apparently the basis for the young Raphael's treatment of the same subject in the same year (Brera). Perugino's art at its best has a serene and simple—even sentimental—quality in which emphasis on line, on clear, light color and attractive landscape takes precedence over monumentality. Although his late work is on the whole decorative and repetitive, and less interesting than the new monumental style being developed in Florence and Rome, his contribution in the realm of space composition, i.e.., the strategic placing of objects farther and farther back in the composition and the effect of this method on Raphael leave him a historically high position. (See color plate 155.)

Peruzzi, Baldassare Tommasso (1481-1536). Sienese architect, sculptor, and painter. A pupil of Bramante as an architect, he was influenced by Raphael in painting. In 1511 he built the Farnesina, perhaps with Raphael, and helped decorate the interior, especially the ceiling of the Sala di Galatea, in the manner of Pinturicchio. He developed from a Quattrocento manner into a High Renaissance phase, finally culminating in Mannerism (see). He founded a school of classical decoration similar to that of Giovanni da Udine.

Pesellino, Francesco (c.1422-59). Florentine painter whose art combines elements from the styles of his more imposing predecessors and contemporaries, Masaccio, Fra Angelico, Filippo Lippi and Uccello. He was born into a family of painters, was probably first trained by his grandfather and later probably worked with Fra Filippo Lippi. He appears to have spent his entire life in Florence, and was a painter of panels and altarpieces rather than frescoes. He painted predella scenes for an altarpiece of Filippo Lippi's, and the latter completed a work that Pesellino left unfinished at his death (altarpiece of the Holy Trinity, London). Pesellino also collaborated with Uccello on the Battle Scenes for the Medici palace. Like other painters of the time, he painted a number of secular scenes on cassone (bridal chests). Several of these are in the Gardner Museum, Boston, and a fine panel of the Madonna and Saints is in the Metropolitan. His style is delicate and devotional in spirit, while at the same time embodying the strong modeling and clarity of composition that relate it to the work of Massaccio. (See illustration.)

Peterzano, Simone (c.1540-1600). Provincial Lombard painter born in Bergamo and active in Milan (1573-92). He was Caravaggio's master (1584-8). Though he called himself a pupil of Titian his Mannerist art shows the influence of the Campis and Leonardo rather than the Venetians.

Petitot, Jean (1607-91). French painter of miniatures in enamel. He was active in England for Charles I and there obtained knowledge of certain rare purple colors. The Revolution led him to leave for Paris where he secured the patronage of the court. As a Calvinist he was later a refugee in Switzerland. We know much of him from his *Journal*.

Peto, John Frederick (1854-1907). American trompe-l'oeil (see) still-life painter. Born in Philadelphia, he was

PETO. Still Life with Lanterns. Brooklyn Museum

largely self-taught though he was enrolled at the Pennsylvania Academy of Fine Arts in 1878. He was a friend of Harnett and although many of his pictures with forged signatures have passed as Harnett's, his style is softer, the subjects more common, and the quality not as high. He never achieved much success. (See illustration.)

Pettoruti, Emilio (1895-). Argentine painter of the modern group. He has studied in Europe and has been influenced by the Synthetic Cubism of Picasso and Braque. He is Director of the Museum of Fine Arts, La Plata.

Peyronnet, Dominique-Paul (1872-). French painter of the self-taught or primitive group. His style is comparable to that of Rousseau, Vivin, Bombois, etc.

Philadelphia Museum of Art, Philadelphia, Pa. An outstanding general collection which has been enriched by the addition of nineteenth- and twentieth-century works from the Chester Dale Collection (the latter's seventeenth- and eighteenth-century pictures went to the National Gallery in Washington), twentieth-century works from the Arensberg Collection, and a great series of Old Masters from the John G. Johnson Collection, including The Virgin and St. John by van der Weyden, Bosch's Christ Mocked, Brueghel's Faithless Shepherd, two Rembrandts and other outstanding Dutch works, many fine Italian paintings, and a notable Oriental collection.

Phillips Gallery, Washington, D.C. General collection of European and American works of the nineteenth and twentieth centuries.

Philoxenos (active c.300 B.C.). Greek painter of Eretria. According to Pliny, he painted a battle of Alexander and Darius. It is assumed that the Alexander Mosaic from Pompeii is a copy of it.

156. PIAZZETTA. Virgin and Child with Adoring Figure
Detroit Institute of Arts

Piazzetta, Giovanni Battista (1682-1754). Venetian painter whose style is a synthesis of Caravaggist chiaroscuro and Venetian color. He was influenced by the Bolognese Caravaggists—Lys, Strozzi, Feti, and Ricci—as well as Guercino. Born in Pietrarossa, he worked first with his father, Giacomo, a woodcarver, and studied painting with Jacopo di Pedorola and Antonio Molinari before going to Bologna, where he became Crespi's most distinguished pupil. He returned to Venice and established himself as a painter of monumental altarpieces, but also did genre paintings. His most important work, the ceiling decoration of the Chapel of S. Domenico in SS. Giovanni e Paolo (1727), which had a profound influence on Tiepolo and eighteenth-century Venetian painting, is Rococo in style, with a nervous linearity, light, rich, and luminous color, and daring perspective. In his later work he abandoned violent effects of light and shade and shocking color for a darker tonality. He died in Venice in straitened circumstances. (See color plate 156.)

PICABIA. Three Seated Nudes
Stedelijk Museum, Regnault Collection, Amsterdam

Picabia, Francis (1878-). French abstract painter who began in the modern movement as a Sisley type of Impressionist, moving on in 1909 to Cubism (see) and becoming one of the Section d'Or group that met at Jacques Villon's studio. From 1912 to 1913 he went through a period of Orphism (see) or Color Orchestration, a deviation from orthodox Cubism, exhibiting in 1913 at the Armory Show in New York and at Stieglitz's "291" gallery. Picabia's version of Cubism consists of a series of non-objective but faceted forms whose movement is designed to suggest a particular idea such as fear, a procession, a city, etc. Later he was associated with the Dada movement (see) in New York, Lausanne and Paris. He wrote and illustrated a Dada book and helped produce a Dada magazine, *391.* (See illustration.)

Picasso, Pablo (1881-). Probably the most influential

PICASSO. Mother and Child. Valentin Gallery, New York

artist of the twentieth century; leader of the Cubist and other wings of modern French painting. One of the most talented and original creators of our times in painting, graphics, pottery, sculpture and almost every other medium, Picasso is a truly protean figure. Born in Malaga, Spain, the son of an art teacher, he made his first drawings at the age of ten. In 1895 the family moved to Barcelona, where Picasso soon had his own studio and at the age of sixteen his first exhibition. He made his first visit to Paris in 1900 and sold a few sketches to Berthe Weill. In 1901 he launched a review called *Arte Joven (Young Art)* and went on a second trip to Paris, where he studied Impressionism. This marks the beginning of his mystical Blue Period paintings with their intensity of mood and color, and their heavy-contoured, flat forms. Back in Spain, he was influenced by the Manneristic elongations and distortions of El Greco. He settled in Paris from 1904 to 1909, met Apollinaire the critic, became interested in circus folk and their romantic sadness, and in 1905 launched his Rose Period. At this time he began to sell to the rich Russian merchant Tschoukine.

In 1906 he met Matisse, was presented to Gertrude Stein and did a portrait of her showing the first influence of primitivistic sculpture—Picasso maintains it was Iberian rather than African Negro sculpture. He also began work on one of his first important compositions, Les Demoiselles d'Avignon, and finished it in 1907. The African quality of this work is very strong; it helps set the canvas in motion and gives a strength and simplicity to forms so that they all vibrate in a narrow range between the picture line and the background. That year he also made a contract with Kahnweiler, the dealer, for all his work. In 1908, inclining toward primitivism (see), Picasso held his famous banquet for the Douanier Rousseau and fell under the formal influence of Cézanne. In 1909 he spent the summer in Spain at Horta del Ebro, moving from the sharply angled forms he had been doing under the stimulus of Cézanne's geometry to an even greater degree of simplification. Now he tried to give an impression of the form of an object somewhat as the earlier Impressionists had tried to render an impression of light falling on it. This period of Analytical Cubism began in 1909 and was practiced through 1911 in company with Braque. In 1912 they went into Synthetic Cubism, a somewhat more artificial and deliberate version of their earlier fragmentation of form and simultaneity (see) of vision of various aspects of that form. From then until 1923 Picasso practiced a variety of Cubism (see), although here and there one finds naturalistic bypaths, some with intense emotional and dreamy overtones, such as the 1917 sets for Diaghilev's production of the ballet *Parade*.

In 1920 Picasso turned to his next important phase, the so-called Classical Period. In this there are clear echoes of ancient Greece and Rome, but treated in an unstilted, completely individualistic fashion, with a unique feeling for the romantic projection of self into the past. Large nude figures, gigantic heads of various kinds, mark this development. There is a touch of Surrealist dream projection which soon gives us Picasso's actual Surrealist experiments (1925 to 1927), wherein tortured forms with twisted limbs create a fear-evoking atmosphere. In 1929 he began to do the primevally-shaped and suggestive Metamorphoses, which look as though they grow out of prehistoric soil (and seemingly anticipate the late work of Henry Moore). His 1931 illustrations for the *Metamorphoses* of Ovid, on the other hand, are the purest classicism and one of the great triumphs of book illustration in our day. With the outbreak of the Spanish Civil War in 1936, Picasso took an active role in repudiation of German

PICASSO. Still Life with Guitar
Valentin Gallery, New York

and Italian armed intervention. In 1937 he engraved Dreams and Lie of Franco and painted the famous Guernica, a Surrealist-Cubist projection of the horrors inflicted on this town by the fascist bombers.

By 1938 Picasso had moved in an Expressionist direction with his double-faced heads. He spent the World War II years in France unmolested by the occupation forces; afterward he announced his adherence to Communism but continued to paint in an abstract manner that was out of keeping with the orthodox Communist approach. Since 1945 he has done a good deal in the fields of ceramics and graphic arts as well as occasional pieces of sculpture of breath-taking grandeur. There is perhaps no style in modern art that Picasso has not tried, often more effectively than those who first developed it. But his works always bear his own personal stamp, the authority of a great and genuine creativeness and originality. (See illustrations, including color plate 157.)

Pickens, Alton (1917-). Contemporary American Realist painter of symbolic social genre with Surrealist overtones. Born in Seattle, he traveled widely as a child, studied art at the Seattle Art Institute, the Portland Museum Art School, and Reed College, before coming to New York in 1939. He now teaches at Indiana University.

Picket, Joseph (1848-1918). American naive painter. Born in New Hope, Pennsylvania, his ambition was to record the life of the town. A carpenter, boat-builder, storekeeper, and carnival pitchman, he began to paint late in life and was self-taught.

picturesque. Literally, "like a picture." In painting this term refers to the specifically charming element in a given scene or story arrangement, such as its pleasantly interesting or unusual features, exotic qualities, and often its irregularity of form or wildness of aspect. In the late seventeenth century, as, e.g., in Salvator Rosa, it was associated with sublimity of feeling, and in the early nineteenth it reappears in many Romantic landscapists.

Pier Francesco Fiorentino (1444/5-after 1497). The son of a minor Florentine painter, active chiefly around San Gimignano. His prolific and repetitive output of altarpieces and devotional Madonna panels shows him influenced chiefly by Benozzo Gozzoli and Fra Filippo Lippi.

Pierino (Perino) del Vaga (Pietro Buonaccorsi) (1501-47). Florentine painter who studied first with Andrea de' Ceri and Ridolfo Ghirlandaio, but later became a pupil and assistant of Raphael in Rome. He executed decorations in the Loggie of the Vatican from drawings by Raphael—The Crossing of the Jordan, The Taking of Jericho, and Joshua Stopping the Sun. He also did ornaments in the manner of Giovanni da Udine with whom he had worked earlier. In 1523, he left Rome for Florence, Siena, and Genoa, where he worked on the Palazzo Doria after 1528. On his return to Rome he was employed by the Farnese pope, Paul III, and did decorations in the Castel Sant' Angelo and the Palazzo Massimi delle Colonne. He was essentially a decorator with a delicately involved style tending towards Mannerism (see). (See illustration.)

Piero della Francesca (Piero di Benedetto de' Franceschi) (1416?-1492). One of the towering figures of the Italian Renaissance, he was born in the Umbrian town of Borgo San Sepolcro between 1410 and 1420—probably in 1416. The earliest document referring to him (1439) finds him in Florence working with Domenico Veneziano on frescoes in Santa Maria Nuova. Prior to this he may have been in contact with the Sienese painters Domenico di Bartolo and Sassetta in Umbria. When he returned to Borgo, shortly after 1441, he was in complete possession of his own style, which incorporates elements of form, modeling, geometry and perspective that he could have learned only in Florence. It is probable that while there he was in contact with the architects

PIERINO DEL VAGA. Repose in Egypt
Pinacoteca Collection, Chiari

Brunelleschi and Alberti and the sculptor Donatello, who were the promoters of the new theory of perspective that Piero had mastered by the time he returned to Borgo. Masaccio's frescoes in Santa Maria del Carmine, Florence, were also a profound influence. He was made a councilor of the people in Borgo in 1442. In 1445 he was commissioned to paint the Madonna della Misericordia (now in the Palazzo Communale, Borgo); it was finished many years later, with a predella and smaller panels probably executed by assistants. He visited Ferrara to paint some decorations in the Este palace (now lost), and exerted some influence on the Ferrarese school. In 1451 he painted the fresco of Sigismondo Malatesta with his patron saint in the Tempio Malatestina at Rimini. Alberti also worked for both of these patrons and Piero's friendship with Alberti lasted until the latter's death in 1472, and influenced Piero profoundly.

During the period 1452-66 he painted his chief work, the magnificent frescoes of the Legend of the True Cross, in the choir of San Francesco at Arezzo. This series, drawn from several literary sources, especially the *Golden Legend* of Jacopo Voragine, has been called one of the greatest achievements of fifteenth-century Italian art. Piero's art here comes nearer than any contemporary work to the quality of ancient Greek classical style, yet without any specific reference to antique art in figures or accessories. According to Vasari he was called to Rome to decorate papal apartments by Nicholas V, but the work is lost and there is no other evidence of this trip except for a much damaged fresco in Santa Maria Maggiore thought to be by Piero. In the early 1460's he painted the profile portraits of Federigo da Montefeltro of Urbino and his wife, Battista Sforza. Between 1454 and 1469 he worked sporadically on an altarpiece for the church of Sant' Agostino in Borgo, of which four panels are extant in Lisbon,

157. PICASSO. Girl Before a Mirror. Museum of Modern Art, Mew York

London, the Frick Collection, and the Brera. About 1472 he painted the Madonna and Child with Saints and the kneeling Federigo da Montefeltro (Brera) commemorating the birth of the Duke's son and the death of his wife. During the 1470's he was close to the ducal court at Urbino and held civic offices in Borgo. About 1478 he ceased painting and until his death occupied himself with a treatise on perspective, another on the "five regular bodies," and a small book on arithmetic and geometry. In the treatises he sets forth how the visible world might be reduced to mathematical order.

Of undocumented major works by Piero the outstanding are the Baptism and the Nativity (London), the Flagellation

159. PIERO DI COSIMO. The Discovery of Honey. Worcester Art Museum

(Urbino, gallery), the Madonna del Parto (Monterchi, cemetery chapel), and the Resurrection (Borgo, Palazzo Communale). Piero's style was austere, impersonal and monumental. Once formed, it changed very little, which accounts for the difficulty in dating many of his important works. His color is cool and light, with frequent combinations of blue, grey and pink. Several paintings include extensive landscape backgrounds which reproduce faithfully the hills and valleys of his native Umbria. His influence was felt throughout Umbria and Tuscany (especially Siena), and is found in Melozzo da Forlì and Signorelli, and ultimately in Perugino and even the early Raphael. (See illustrations, including color plate 158.)

Piero di Cosimo (1462-1521). Florentine painter of singular originality who absorbed many elements from the styles of others but made them an integral part of his own. Tales of his eccentric personality stem from Vasari and may be pure fantasy but they are not inconsistent with some of his more bizarre works. His name was Piero di Lorenzo, but he derives his more familiar name from his teacher, Cosimo Rosselli, whose shop he entered in 1480. The next year he went to Rome with Rosselli to assist him on the frescoes of the Sistine Chapel walls. His hand in these may be distinguished from that of Rosselli by his closer observation of nature and his more luminous color. He was associated with the literary circle around Lorenzo de' Medici in the early 1490's, a connection that is reflected in a number of allegorical panels for private patrons. One of Mars and Venus (Berlin) is closely related to Botticelli; others deal with the early life of man on earth in a series recently analyzed by Erwin Panofsky as representing man's progress toward civilization as the result of the arts of Vulcan. Other groups deal with the contributions of Bacchus and of Prometheus to man's comfort. It is noteworthy that these were all produced at the time when the influence of the religious fanatic Savonarola was at its height and many artists destroyed their mythological pictures. Altarpieces by Piero are in the Ospedale degli Innocenti, Florence, and the Louvre. He also painted portraits, of which the most famous is that representing Simonetta Vespucci as Cleopatra (Condé Museum, Chantilly). Piero's art reflects the influence not only of his teacher and of Botticelli, but also of Verrocchio, Signorelli, Filippino Lippi and Leonardo da Vinci. His inventiveness was such that he remained independent and cannot be classed as an imitator of any of them. (See color plate 159.)

158. PIERO DELLA FRANCESCA. St. Apollonia
National Gallery of Art, Kress Collection, Washington, D.C.

pietà (It.) Literally, pity. In painting, the scene or subject

PIERO DELLA FRANCESCA. Resurrection
Palazzo Communale, Borgo San Sepolcro

showing the dead Christ resting on the knees or lap of the Virgin just after the Crucifixion.

Pietro da Cortona (see CORTONA, PIETRO DA).

Pietro di Domenico (1457-1506). Sienese painter whose style was derived from Francesco di Giorgio and Matteo di Giovanni. His later works exhibit Umbrian influence, chiefly that of Perugino. He was an eclectic, provincial and on the whole uninspired artist.

Pietro di Domenico da Montepulciano (formerly called da Recanati) (active early fifteenth century). Working in the Marches under the influence of local painters and especially Gentile da Fabriano, this provincial artist also felt the influence of Sienese and Florentine painting.

pigment. The actual coloring matter which is mixed with or suspended in a given medium such as oil, water, egg, etc., for the purposes of painting. (See OIL PAINTING, TEMPERA, GOUACHE, WATERCOLOR, FRESCO.)

Pignon, Edouard (1905-). French painter under the double influence of the strong colorism of Matisse and the form tendencies of Cubism, but who has produced an individual art of great emotional power. Many of these works suggest the coloristic dignity and strength of stained-glass windows.

Pillement, Jean (1727-1808). French decorative painter and etcher. His subjects ranged from landscape, marines and genre to flower paintings. The last he drew mainly for execution on silk in the new fad of chinoiserie. He was much traveled, working in Poland, Vienna, England and Portugal. Many of his works were reproduced by English engravers.

Pinacoteca Nazionale, Siena. Outstanding collection of Sienese paintings including works by Duccio, Simone Martini, Pietro and Ambrogio Lorenzetti, Lippo Memmi, Sodoma and many others.

Pinturicchio (Bernardino di Betto) (1454-1513). An Umbrian whose nickname refers to his small stature. He was primarily a painter of large narrative fresco decorations, the most important being those in the Vatican apartments and the Siena cathedral library. His beginnings were in Perugia, where he may have been a co-pupil with Perugino in the shop of Fiorenzo di Lorenzo. He accompanied Perugino to Rome in 1480 as an assistant on the Sistine Chapel wall decorations, and certain sections of these are attributed to Pinturicchio. In 1481 he was registered as an independent painter in Perugia and in 1484 he was back in Rome to paint frescoes of the life of San Bernardino in the church of Santa Maria in Aracoeli. These are close to Perugino in style and typically Umbrian in their subordination of figures to landscape and space. After another sojourn in Perugia he was called to Rome again by Pope Innocent VIII, and most of his later activity was in the service of the popes there. The decoration of the Borgia apartments was done for Alexander VI between 1492 and 1495, and consists of three cycles: the Hall of Mysteries, the Hall of Saints, and the Hall of the Seven Liberal Arts. They were executed with the help of assistants, and show some influence from Filippino Lippi. In 1502 Cardinal Francesco Piccolomini gave him the important task of decorating the Siena cathedral library with scenes from the life of a famous ancestor, Pope Pius II. These were done in 1503-08, within which time his patron was made Pope Pius III, an event celebrated in another fresco over the library entrance. These frescoes are noted for their monumentality, spaciousness and brilliant color. He had as a pupil Eusebio da San Giorgio, but was not particularly influential on the succeeding generation. (See color plate 160.)

Piombo (see SEBASTIANO DEL PIOMBO).

Piper, John (1903-). British painter of architecture and landscapes, and a writer on art. He has painted in two styles: an earlier imaginative and poetic manner showing south-of-England coast scenes and a more specifically abstract manner stemming from his interest in Braque, Arp, Hélion and other modern artists. Under the influence of early nineteenth-century English art, he has recently returned to the picturesque and dramatic earlier style. He is known for his paintings of bombed-out areas, having invested them with this personal

PIPER. Reclining Nude. Valentin Gallery, New York

PIPPIN. The Holy Mountain, Number 2. Collection Edward A. Brageline

PISANELLO. Vision of St. Eustace. National Gallery, London

poetic quality, the sense of sadness and decay. (See illustration.)

Pippin, Horace (1888-1946). American Negro amateur painter born in Chester, Pa. He had the desire to paint from youth but had no training. He worked on a farm, in a coal yard, a feed store and as a porter, served in World War I and was badly wounded. He began to paint his memories of war in 1930, had his first exhibition at the Westchester Community Center in 1937, and had three paintings in the Master of Popular Painting exhibition at the Museum of Modern Art in 1938, and several one-man shows in Philalephia and New York in 1940 and 1941. (See illustration.)

Piranesi, Giovanni Battista (1720-1788). An Italian engraver, architect and archaeologist who specialized in the engraving of ancient Roman architectural scenes, including broken arches, fragments of columns and similar details. What distinguished his work from that of the eighteenth-century painters of this material, e.g., Hubert Robert, is his wonderfully dramatic sense of light and dark contrasts, and the Romantic and far-reaching sense of interior space that he imparted to his structures. These qualities are seen most effectively in his famous series, I Carceri (The Prisons) in

161. PISSARRO. Spring at Louveciennes. National Gallery, London

160. PINTURICCHIO. Portrait of a Youth
National Gallery of Art, Kress Collection, Washington, D.C.

which an almost entirely imaginary architecture with supernaturally large stairways, arches and empty spaces is peopled with strange nightmarish creatures. The dreamlike quality of these works may have influenced some twentieth-century Surrealists. Piranesi seems to have had some training as a theatrical designer, studied the excavations at Pompeii and Herculaneum, and worked for a while with the painter Tiepolo.

Pisanello (Antonio Pisano) (c.1397-1455). A Veronese painter whose art forms a north Italian parallel to the Gothic International Style represented in Florence and Umbria by Fra Angelico, Benozzo Gozzoli and Gentile da Fabriano. Of these artists, he is most closely related to Gentile. He was born in Padua, the son of a Pisan clothmaker (hence his name), and received his early training in Verona in the tradition of Altichiero. He was in Venice in 1415, and between 1420 and 1424 executed a fresco (destroyed) in the Doge's palace, where Gentile had also worked shortly before. Pisanello was a portrait medalist as well as a painter, and both activities took him to many cultural centers in Italy, including Mantua (1425, 1439), Ferrara (1435, 1438/9), Milan (1440), Rimini (1447), and Naples (1448). To his medals we owe our knowledge of the likenesses of many princes of the time. He went to Rome in 1431-32 and there completed the frescoes (now lost) in San Giovanni in Laterano left unfinished by Gentile at his death. He worked for such renowned families as the Gonzaga and the Este, did a portrait medal of the Byzantine Emperor John Paleologus, and worked for King Alfonso at Naples. His important extant frescoes are in Verona (San Fermo and Sant' Anastasia), and his panel paintings are in various museums. The Louvre owns an extraordinary number of drawings by Pisanello; they reveal great vitality and a keen and detailed observation of nature. His art is in general elegant and courtly, and his style is essentially Gothic. Its relation to French production places him within the International Style. As a painter he had little influence, but as a medalist he founded a school. (See illustration.)

Pisis, Filippo de (1896-). An Italian painter with a literary background. He has been associated, at least as a writer, with Chirico, Carrà and others in the *scuola metafisica* movement in Ferrara. His own painting belongs to the Impressionist and Post-Impressionist traditions.

162. POLLAIUOLO, ANTONIO. Portrait of a Man. National Gallery of Art, Mellon Collection, Washington, D.C.

Pissarro, Camille (1831-1903). Important as the theorist and teacher of the French Impressionist movement. Eldest of the group, he was born in St. Thomas, W.I., and began at first with the Barbizon school, where he was influenced by Millet and Corot. He entered the Salon des Refusés (1863) and became a member of the Café Guerbois group. He was especially close to Monet and was the master and friend of Cézanne and Van Gogh. Already patriarch of the movement, he learned anew from Seurat in the 1880's and for some time practiced Pointillism. This association and that with Cézanne caused his paintings to have more solid structure than that of other Impressionists, as can be seen in his Orchard in Pontoise. Eye trouble finally drove him indoors and to the painting of city scenes. See IMPRESSIONISM. (See color plate 161.)

Pissarro, Lucien (1863-1944). French painter of landscape, designer of woodcuts and lithographs. Son of Camille (see), whose style he approximated. Lucien was much employed as a book illustrator in England where he settled.

Pitate, Bonifazio de' (see BONIFAZIO VERONESE).

Pitti Gallery, Florence. Located in the Pitti Palace and containing outstanding examples of Italian painting, such as

Raphael's Madonna of the Chair, and other works dating through the seventeenth century. It also has such paintings from other countries as those of Rembrandt, Rubens, and Dürer, among others.

Pittoni, Giovanni Battista (il Giovane) (1687-1767). Born in Venice, he studied with his uncle, Francesco Pittoni, was influenced by Ricci and Piazzetta, and worked in the style of Tiepolo, whom he succeeded in 1758 as president of the Venetian Academy. He painted both religious and secular subjects in a facile and spontaneous Rococo manner. He was widely recognized and popular, working in Spain, France, Poland, and Russia as well as Italy.

Pizzinato, Armando (1910-). Italian painter who was part of the Resistance against the German occupation; he was imprisoned by the fascists and liberated in 1945 to resume his work. He became part of the New Art Front with Guttuso, Santomaso and other younger painters. He expresses his class sympathies partly in Futurist terms and partly in an Expressionism of the Picasso variety.

Pizzole, Niccolò (1421-53). Paduan painter. A product of the Squarcione school, he collaborated with Mantegna on the frescoes (destroyed in World War II) of the Eremitani church in Padua. He may also have assisted the Florentine sculptor Donatello when he was working in Padua.

plane. Refers to each successive stage of depth within a painting. For example, one may speak of forms as being in the foreground plane or of objects being in a plane parallel with the front line of the painting.

Plattner, Karl (1918-). Italian-born painter who in 1952 emigrated to Brazil and has become part of the new cosmopolitan art of that country. He earns his living doing murals for homes and hotels. His work has a sophisticated, international flavor with semi-abstracted forms and a subtle harmony of tones.

plein-air painting. Literally open-air painting. This refers to the practice of the Impressionists of the 1870's in which landscape was painted for the first time in outdoor circumstances. Traditionally landscape had been done indoors, even when preparatory sketches had been made in the presence of nature. The great interest in landscape painting during the nineteenth century, first developed by the Romantics and the Barbizon painters—most of whom painted in the studio—reached its true climax in the work of such painters as Monet, Renoir and Pissarro. They went directly to the motif and painted in its presence, doing trees, fields, lakes, rivers, haystacks and other outdoor phenomena in a direct and spontaneous way. See IMPRESSIONISM.

Poccetti (Barbatelli), Bernardino (1548-1612). Born in Florence, he studied with Michele Ghirlandaio and then was active as a façade painter and fresco decorator. After a trip to Rome, where he was influenced by Raphael, he broke from Florentine Mannerism, returning to the older style of del Sarto.

Poelenburgh, Cornelis van (c.1586-1667). A Dutch painter of religious pictures and mythological landscapes. He studied under Bloemaert and spent most of his working life in Utrecht. His art was formed, however, by a long stay in Italy. In Rome, he came under the influence of Elsheimer and studied the works of such classical masters as Raphael and Albani. Charles I invited him to England and Rubens bought pictures by him. His finest works are Italianate landscapes, peopled with monumental, well-constructed nudes. These pictures were popular among Dutch and foreign collectors and he produced them in great quantity. He also headed a large school at Utrecht.

Pointillism (see NEO-IMPRESSIONISM).

Pol de Limbourg (see LIMBOURG BROTHERS).

POLLAIUOLO, ANTONIO. Hercules Overcoming the Hydra
Uffizi, Florence

Poleo, Héctor (1917-). A leading Venezuelan artist. Son of a furniture maker, he began to paint at the age of five, studied in Caracas and Mexico City and has won many prizes in his own country. His figures are characterized by calm, simplified outlines and broad color areas in bright tonalities.

Polidoro da Caravaggio (Polidoro Caldara) (1490/1500-1543). Lombard painter born in Caravaggio, a follower and pupil of Raphael; his work is sometimes confused with Michelangelo da Caravaggio's. One of the most famous painters of his day, he was highly regarded for his chiaroscuro, his knowledge of antiquity, and his decorations of façades in Rome. His drawings were widely copied and collected. He was active also in Naples and Messina, and died a violent death in the latter city.

Pollaiuolo, Antonio (1433-98). His work is a logical and vivid outgrowth of the research into nature begun by the first generation of fifteenth-century Florentines. He was a goldsmith, sculptor, painter, engraver and designer of textiles. Certain portions of his work were done in collaboration with his younger brother Piero, but Antonio is the dominating personality and his work is the more original and influential. In Christian and pagan subjects, and in all the media of which he was master, Antonio sought to examine the anatomy and movement of the human body and to exploit his findings for compositions full of action and force. Earlier artists who contributed to his style were Castagno and the sculptor Donatello. He began as a goldsmith and may have been associated with Lorenzo and Vittorio Ghiberti in the making of the later bronze doors of the Baptistry. He had a prosperous shop with many associates and pupils, and by the time he was forty owned a good deal of property. In 1484 he went to Rome with his brother Piero to undertake the making of a bronze tomb for Pope Sixtus IV and spent the rest of his life in Rome, receiving various commissions of which the last and most important is the tomb of Pope Innocent VIII. Both of these tombs are in St. Peter's. Among Antonio's easel paintings, the most celebrated is the Martyrdom of St. Sebastian (1475, London). Quite formal in composition, it is highly animated by the movement of the figures and by the detailed, panoramic view of the Arno valley in the background. Other smaller but well-known works are the Apollo and Daphne in the same gallery, the Rape of Deianira (Yale University), and the two panels of Hercules Killing the Hydra and Slaying Antaeus (Uffizi). There is also a bronze sculpture by Pollaiuolo of this last subject in the Bargello, Florence. Fragments of a fresco decoration representing dancing nude figures are still visible in the Villa della Gallina at Arcetri, near Florence. Many drawings by Antonio are extant, and textiles embroidered from his designs are preserved in Florence and Assisi. One signed engraving, the Battle of Nude Men, is celebrated as a highly effective example of his style and as an important early graphic work. Antonio's influence spread as far as France and Germany, and such masters as Signorelli and even Michelangelo owe something to him. (See illustrations, including color plate 162.)

Pollaiuolo, Piero (1443-96). The younger brother of Antonio Pollaiuolo (see); although he maintained a separate studio in Florence, he often collaborated with or assisted Antonio. He worked as a goldsmith, sculptor and painter, and had numerous commissions, some independent and some with Antonio. His chief and only clearly authenticated extant work is the Coronation of the Virgin (signed and dated 1483) in the Collegiata at San Gimignano. The tall proportions of the figures and the lack of vitality in drawing and expression are in marked contrast with the art of Antonio. Several other painted works are attributed to Piero, among which the best known are the figures of the enthroned Virtues in the Uffizi.

Pollock, Jackson (1912-). A contemporary American Abstract Expressionist. His manner of dripping paint on canvas brought him a great deal of publicity, but he has more recently begun to introduce representational forms in his art. Born in Wyoming, he studied with Thomas Benton at the Art Students League and then worked on the W.P.A. His abstract manner began c.1940.

polychrome. A term meaning many-colored.

Polygnotos (active in mid-5th century B.C.) A Greek painter. Son and pupil of Aglaophon of Thasos, he was active in Athens following the Persian wars and was thoroughly Attic in style. We know something of the character of his paintings from numerous ancient descriptions and from copies, especially on vases. It is clear that he possessed a nobleness of conception, or *ethos,* which corresponded to the idealism of the sculptors. He composed large narrative scenes, abandoning the frieze method for one of interconnected groups at different levels, symmetrically arranged against a high horizon. Along with this spatial innovation went shaded modeling and complicated poses and foreshortening. This was carried out with sober, sculptural dignity in the four-color system of his day. These tendencies, described by Pausanias at Delphi, have come down to us in such vases as the Orvieto Krater (Louvre).

polyptych. A many-paneled altarpiece (see), usually portable, either painted or sculptured, in which the separate sections fold on hinges. From the Greek polyptychon (that which has many folds).

Pomarancio (Niccolò Circignani) (c.1517-96+). An Italian painter of fresco decorations and altarpieces, born in Pomerance near Volterra and a follower of Zuccari and the Roman Maniera (see). He was active in Rome, Orvieto, and many smaller places—Mongiovani, Citerna, Città della Pieve, Cascia.

Pomarancio, Cristoforo (Cristoforo Roncalli) (1552-1626). Italian decorative painter, born in Pomerance, he studied with his namesake, Niccolò, and worked with him in Rome on the Loggie of the Vatican for Gregory VIII, and by himself in the Quirinal Palace (1583-85) and St. Peter's (1599-1606). A good draughtsman and a solid technician, his color is hard and cold, and his style continues belatedly to hover between Mannerism (see) and the Baroque (see).

Pompeian painting (see ROMAN PAINTING).

Ponce de León, Fidelio (1895-). Cuban painter of the modern school who represents the tendency to combine native Negro and Spanish elements with contemporary Mexican and European trends. He uses a pale palette of white and neutral color and a heavy impasto. He does mostly figures and portraits, frequently with an ironic touch.

Ponte, da (family name) (see BASSANO).

Pontormo (Jacopo Carrucci) (1494-1557). Outstanding painter in the style of Florentine Mannerism (see). His earlier High Renaissance style was greatly admired and he was the most famous painter in Florence after the death of Andrea del Sarto. However, under the influence of Michelangelo and Dürer he later developed a more spiritual and abstract anticlassical manner. A solitary and neurotic personality, he was an original genius capable of the subtlest intuition and emotional intensity. Born in Pontormo, near Florence, he may have studied with Leonardo and Piero di Cosimo, but his real master was Andrea del Sarto, with whom he worked after 1512 and who was most influential in his early style. His commissions came largely from the Medici family but unfortunately many of his important works have been destroyed. He worked with Franciabigio and del Sarto at Poggio a Caiano where he did a lunette, remarkably advanced for its time (c.1521). In 1522-24 he executed five scenes from the Passion

PORTINARI. Brazilian Peasants and Cattle
Detroit Institute of Arts

163. PONTORMO. Joseph in Egypt. National Gallery, London

(with the assistance of Bronzino) for the Certosa di Val d'Ema, which are now badly damaged. Dependent upon Dürer, they are even more Gothic in feeling and much more elegant in conception. His masterpiece, The Deposition, for Sta. Felicità, done in 1525, is completely Mannerist—asymmetrical, full of spatial ambiguity and complex linear rhythms. After 1530, contact with Michelangelo transformed his style and in some ways overwhelmed it. In 1536-38 he was commissioned to do two Medici villas, one at Carreggi and the other at Castello (both now destroyed). His last work, in the choir of S. Lorenzo (1545-46), was so advanced for its time that it was painted over in 1742. Among his few panel paintings still extant are a Madonna and Child with St. John (Uffizi), a Visitation (Carmignano), a Supper at Emmaus (Accademia, Florence), a Martyrdom of St. Maurice (Pitti), and a Venus and Cupid (Uffizi). (See color plate 163.)

Poor, Henry Varnum (1888-). A contemporary American painter, ceramist, and designer. Born in Kansas, he studied first at Stanford University, in England at the Slade School with Walter Sickert, and in Paris at the Académie Julian. His paintings have a pronounced decorative quality, with subtle and subdued color, and heavy impasto.

Pordenone (Giovanni Antonio di Sacchi) (c.1484-1539). Born in Pordenone and active in Venice, Lombardy, and Emilia, he executed a great many frescoes which in their proto-Baroque movement are important for the later development of the Baroque in North Italy. He began his career in Ferrara as an apprentice to Martino da Udine and in 1508 was employed by the Este family. In Rome in 1515 he fell under the influence of followers of Michelangelo—Sebastiano del Piombo and Daniele da Volterra—and later added the Venetian colorism of Bellini, Giorgione, and Titian.

Portinari, Candido (1903-). Leading Brazilian easel painter, muralist and graphic artist; he has won distinction in various parts of the world. He has done frescoes for the Ministry of Education, 1938; murals in the Brazilian Pavilion, New York World's Fair, 1939; the Library of Congress, Washington, D. C., 1941-42; and elsewhere. Like most of his contemporaries in Latin America, he is a nationalist or nativist devoting himself to themes drawn from the life of his country. His European experience and direct studies under the modern French-Japanese painter and graphic artist Foujita have given his work an abstract delicacy of form and color that brings his work within the compass of the modern art world. It is primitive and romantic at the same time. (See illustration.)

Portuense, Vieira (1765-1805). A Portuguese painter known as one of those responsible for the revival of art in that country after a long period of decline. Born in Porto, she studied in Italy and then went to England, where she became the friend and collaborator of the mezzotint engraver Bartolozzi. Her art, which is a mixture of contemporary Italian and English elements, is marked by a charming and gracious, if rather overwhelming, sentimentality, reflecting a combination of the Baroque and Rococo styles.

Post-Impressionism. A general term referring to a period in the development of modern painting—rather than an actual movement—between Impressionism and the beginnings of Fauvism and Cubism in the early twentieth century. It may be said to start in the middle 1880's with a turning away from the Impressionist naturalism of Monet, Pissarro, Sisley, Renoir, Degas, etc., which had emphasized the external effect of light or movement. The new conception of painting stressed other values: in Cézanne and Seurat we see an emphasis on form and controlled space arrangement, on permanence of effect rather than the spontaneous and the transitory; in Van Gogh and Gauguin we see the turning toward emotional and spiritual content within the framework of controlled form, as opposed to the Impressionist emphasis on purely visual effects. We may say then that Post-Impressionism is a natural reaction against Impressionism as well as a step toward the developments of the next century. The Cézanne-Seurat wing leads to the form experiments of the Cubists and other geometrically inclined artists; and the Van Gogh-Gauguin wing points toward the more intuitive and emotive art of the Fauves and Expressionists.

Pot, Hendrick Gerritsz. (c.1585-1657). Dutch painter of history, genre and portraits. He studied in Haarlem with Karel van Mander and was strongly influenced by Frans Hals. In 1632 he visited the court of Charles I in London and painted a portrait of the king. He spent the end of his life in Amsterdam, where he was the master of Willem Kalf. He was a technically able painter whose works have often been ascribed to other artists.

POURBUS, PIETER
Portrait of the Family Jan van Gindertaelen
Musée Royal des Beaux-Arts, Antwerp

164. POUSSIN. Et in Arcadia Ego
Collection Chatsworth Estates Co.

Potter, Paulus (1625-54). Dutch painter and engraver of animal pictures and landscapes. He studied with his father and with Jacob de Wet. The most famous of Dutch animal painters, he divided his brief activity between Amsterdam, Delft and The Hague. For so short a career he left a large number of pictures, fine in drawing and true to nature.

Pourbus the Elder, Frans (1545-81). Flemish history and portrait painter. His style was so close to that of his master Frans Floris that they are frequently confused. He finished work left by Floris at his death and married his niece. He was the son of Pieter Pourbus and the father of Frans Pourbus II. His marriage picture of Joris Hoefnagel is in the Brussels Museum.

Pourbus, Pieter Jansz (1510-84). A Flemish history and portrait painter. Father of Frans Pourbus the Elder and pupil of Lancelot Blondeel, whose daughter he married. He was a prominent citizen of Bruges, where he was employed by the municipality. He was acquainted with Michelangelo's Last Judgment, and he retouched the painting of that subject by Jean Proovost. He painted portraits of Charles V and Philip II. (See illustration.)

Pourbus the Younger, Frans (1569/70-1622) Flemish portraitist. Son of Frans Pourbus the Elder, he achieved great success in Flanders, Italy and France. In Paris he painted Henry IV alive and on his deathbed, and did much to perpetuate the tight Flemish style in France.

Poussin, Nicolas (1594-1665). The father of French painting and, after Raphael, probably the greatest painter in the classical tradition. Although he spent almost all his life outside of France (in Italy), he produced an art characteristically French. He was the dominant force in French painting of his century and has exerted tremendous influence on French painters ever since. Painting as an art had been re-

POUSSIN. Landscape with St. Matthew and Angel
Kaiser-Friedrich Museum, Berlin

established in modern France by Vouet (see), Poussin's predecessor, and Paris had been a crucial school in the development of late Gothic painting (c.1400), but the supremacy of French painting in recent centuries goes back directly to Poussin.

Poussin was an intellectual painter; his subjects were literary, his forms deliberate. "My nature constrains me to seek and to love well-ordered things, and to flee confusion, which is as much my antithesis and my enemy as light is to dark," he wrote to his friend Chantelou. He felt no compunction in drawing on the works of others, provided the borrowed element was transformed to fit its new employment. He quoted alike from classical mythology, the Holy Writ and the paintings of the ancients and the moderns. His was the Grand Manner, stemming from the dignity and decorum of Raphael's Roman period, but made more ample and usually more spatial by his own devices. The Grand Manner entails subjects which are elevated, not merely didactic. Beauty is Measure; color in ample areas, space traversable, forms in Greek proportion, detail generalized, sequences rhythmical and structure geometrically stable. This is exemplified in the Rape of the Sabines (Metropolitan).

Poussin was born in Normandy of a middle-class family. He studied locally with a certain Varin until eighteen. He then went to Paris where he worked with minor painters and studied the Royal collection and a collection of Italian engravings. The Bacchus and Erigone (Stockholm) is possibly of this period since it shows the hard elongated forms of the School of Fontainebleau. Despite several attempts, it was not until 1624 that Poussin got to Rome, the interim being spent in numerous commissions in French chateaux. He became a friend of Philippe de Champaigne and finally of G.B. Marino, an Italian poet who expedited his trip to Rome and introduced him to Cardinal Barberini. Although poor at first, Poussin became a favorite of the Barberini circle and especially of Cassiano del Pozzo, a wealthy collector who commissioned him to draw antique monuments.

The chronology of Poussin's paintings is difficult to determine. Although there was a general development, he was accustomed to vary his composition and style according to the subject, so that contemporary paintings of different types of subjects sometimes seem disparate in date. During his early years in Rome his style leans strongly on the Renaissance masters Raphael and Titian and on his contemporary Domenichino. For instance, the Death of Germanicus (Rome), painted about 1630 for Cardinal Barberini, is based spatially on Raphael. The Triumph of David (Dulwich Gallery) seems to draw upon Domenichino's severe architectural forms. To Titian, Poussin owed not only forms and motifs, but indeed the elegiac mood of classicism that pervades so much of his work. Before 1635 many paintings, such as Echo and Narcissus (Louvre), employ Titian's impressionistic light, color and foliage.

In 1640, after considerable royal urging, Poussin went to Paris and supplanted Vouet as first painter to the king. He was given much honor, a large salary and many decorative projects. The fact that he was by nature a careful composer of moderate-size canvases, combined with the intrigues of the established artists, made the stay an unhappy one. Within two years he was back in Rome where he had wisely left his wife and properties. There followed his great years, revered like Bernini throughout Europe, painting on commission for the leading figures of Italy and France. It was then that he executed the most powerful of his stoical and religious subjects, such as the second Sacrament series. His great landscapes also date from late in life when there was a visible interrelation between his art and that of Claude Lorrain. Fine examples are the series of the Four Seasons (Louvre) painted for Richelieu about 1664. (See illustrations, including color plate 164.)

Poussinists (see RUBENISTS).

Poynter, Sir Edward (1836-1919). A British historical painter. As a youth he worked in Rome with Leighton. In 1869, he became first head of the Slade School and in 1896 President of the Royal Academy. He wrote scholarly works reconstructing life in ancient times, e.g., Israel, thereby raising the level of public understanding of the past.

Pozzo, Fra Andrea (1642-1709). An Italian painter, architect, and writer born in Trento. Nothing is known of his

POZZO, FRA ANDREA. America
Detail from Church of St. Ignazio, Rome

Pre-Columbian painting. Nazca pottery, c.600
M. H. de Young Memorial Museum, San Francisco

early training in Trento and Como, but after a year in Milan, he joined the Jesuit order for which he became a sort of official and peripatetic decorator. He was a prolific painter of frescoes and altarpieces, a master of Baroque trompe-l'oeil decoration (especially in the creation of spatial illusions), active all over Italy and, after 1702, in Vienna. His art is especially important for the spread of the late-Baroque to Austria and south Germany. (See illustration.)

Prado Museum, Madrid. Most important repository of the works of the great Spanish painters: El Greco, Velázquez and Goya, as well as others, including Murillo and Zurbarán. In addition there are significant works of the Flemish school of the fifteenth to seventeenth century and important Italian paintings especially of the Venetian school.

Pratt, Matthew (1734-1805). American painter, son of a goldsmith, he studied first with his uncle, James Claypoole, and later with Benjamin West in London (1764-67). He practiced portraiture in Philadelphia with moderate success, and painted signs which were said to have been the finest of their kind. He is remembered most for his charming, early painting, The American Academy (Metropolitan), depicting West and four pupils in the former's London studio.

Preboste, Francisco (1554-1607). Spanish painter of Toledo. Of Italian origin, he functioned until the time of his death as an assistant to El Greco.

pre-colonial art (see PRE-COLUMBIAN).

pre-Columbian painting. Ancient art of the Americas before the arrival of the Spanish and other settlers; it also includes the art of the North American Indians (see below). In these areas, it should be noted, painting is not a major art nor are there many examples of it. In Spanish America this art, primarily abstract, is closely associated with local Indian religious beliefs and ceremonies involving nature gods. It is characterized by great vigor, even grandeur, in all its phases, ranging from the primitive to the sophisticated.

The Mayas of Guatemala, Honduras and Yucatan, Mexico, represent the greatest cultural flowering in pre-Columbian civilization. Already developed by 317 A.D, their art shows a mastery of composition in mural painting, incisive use of line and a clear, powerful sense of two-dimensional design. Their somewhat more representational pottery painting includes decorative motifs and narrative compositions in bold outlines and warm earth colors; there are also miniatures in their codices (sing., codex) which were historical records painted on deer hide or paper made from the maguey plant. Another Mexican culture is the Teotihuacán, a great civilization in the Valley of Mexico lasting from before the Christian era to around 1100 A.D., excelling in fresco painting, including imaginative scenes of the afterlife. The last Mexican culture before the coming of the Spaniards is the Aztec. This people produced a predominantly religious art, although some painted codices show aspects of everyday life, such as ball games. Sculpture, however, was more important in Aztec art.

North-American Indian painting is primarily that of the Pueblos of southwest United States, the most highly developed group, and reached its peak between 950 and 1300 A.D. Their underground ceremonial room or Kiva sometimes had painted walls with conventionalized figures and costumes, a linear, angular art influenced by flat textile designs.

In South America, pre-Columbian art is chiefly Peruvian from about the first to sixth centuries A.D. Within this area there were various local cultures, e.g., Early Chimu or Mochica, that produced pottery jars with realistic pictures of human beings and animals; the finest of these are portrait heads of warriors. All show the adaptation of subject to the shape of the jar. The Nazca art of Peru is less realistic and has more geometrical designs, and stylized and fanciful forms. The last Peruvian culture before the arrival of the Spanish was the Inca Empire. This nation, however, abandoned mural painting and used sheets of beaten gold for temple decoration. (See illustration.)

predella. Literally, in Italian, a footstool, it is the narrow step or platform at the back of the altar upon which the altarpiece rests. Usually a series of small painted panels related in iconography to the altarpiece itself.

Predis, Ambrogio da (see AMBROGIO DA PREDIS).

prehistoric painting. The period covered in this category includes roughly the thousands of years of human history before the invention of writing. It encompasses the approximately 200,000 years of the Old Stone Age, the Middle or Transitional Stone Age, and the New Stone Age, which carries us to around 3,000 B.C. Already in the first of these periods there is evidence of man's effort to decorate his tools and weapons, first with color alone and then with simple drawings. By the end of the Old Stone Age there begin to appear throw-sticks and similar objects decorated with simple lines and patterns and then with animal forms. Already at this early point in human history one finds abstracted but very realistic animal forms realized in very few lines and conveying to the spectator the sense of urgency which brought them into being. These exist both as engravings on the weapons of this primarily hunting civilization as well as on the walls of its caves. The latter have been found in greatest number in southern France (e.g., the Lascaux caves) and in northern Spain (e.g., the Altamira caves), two contiguous areas offering the richest sources for the study of prehistoric painting. In the almost absolute darkness of these caves, working by the light of a primitive stone lamp and using rough lumps of yellow and red ochre ground into powder and suspended in

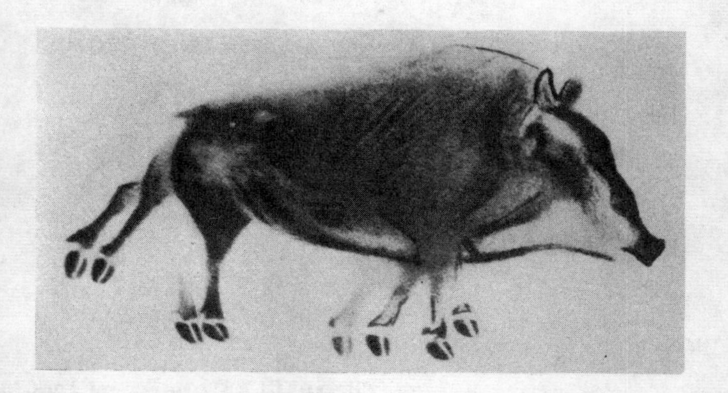

Prehistoric painting. Boar from the caves of Altamira

some form of grease, the prehistoric painter set down his half-religious, half-artistic impulses.

None of the paintings found in these caves can be described as photographic in character, yet they have a very real and immediate quality because of the artist's phenomenal ability to seize the essentials of each form and set it down in a kind of graceful artistic shorthand. It is as though this ability were related to the artist's—or his tribe's ability to seize the animal itself—a creature on which they depended for food, clothing and even light.

The tremendous importance of these animals—reindeer, bison and the like—from the point of view of their supporting life, was so great that the hunter-artist made it his business to know all about them. Is was as though the ability to give a convincing rendition of the desired animal was in direct proportion to the success of the hunt on which life itself depended. Conversely the little stick-figures of human beings we encounter in these caves of paleolithic (Old Stone Age) times are shown in a highly schematic and unnaturalistic form as though it were dangerous to set down a recognizable form lest the enemy pierce it with arrow or spear and thus bring it down. Analogies to the practices of these Old Stone Age hunters can be found in the work of such recent cultures as the African Bushman (see AFRICAN PAINTING) which, although far removed in time from that period, still represent in some ways a comparable outlook on life.

The Middle Stone Age is less rich in representational art, but the Neolithic or New Stone Age ushers in a new era. This period is associated with the development of a settled society rather than one of nomadic hunters. Here man became a householder, tiller of the soil and maker of useful objects. In these operations and the tools required for them the artist was no longer concerned with the magical practices of the Old Stone Age which helped to ensure success in the hunt. In this more stable existence man was no longer at the mercy of the unknown. Noting that things happened regularly and not altogether by chance he turned from magic to religion. He now attributed special powers to certain essences, gods, or spirits that were responsible for the regular reappearance of crops, etc. In this formative stage of human history simple decorative practices developed in the embellishment of pottery and textiles. These represent a more abstract and in many ways a more rational procedure in that man understood for the first time that there was a spiritual force or series of forces behind everyday appearances. The earlier hunter had concerned himself exclusively with such appearances in his frantic search for protection against forces he did not understand. It is at this stage of human history that ancient art in the historical sense, i.e., Egyptian, Sumerian and Oriental, began to develop. That they all took the form of a compromise between the realism of the Old Stone Age viewpoint and the abstraction of the New Stone Age ideal is not to be wondered at. (See illustration.)

Prendergast, Maurice Brazil (1859-1924). American Impressionist landscape painter, member of the Eight. Born in St. Johns, Newfoundland, his family moved to Boston where he worked at painting showcards and sketched during his weekends. In 1886 he went abroad with his brother Charles and studied in Paris at the Académie Julian with Laurens, Rossi, and Blanc, and at the Académie Colarossi. On their return they settled at Winchester, Mass., and did frame-carving. Again in 1898, he went abroad under the patronage of Mrs. Montgomery Sears and painted in Venice and St. Malo. He was again in Italy about 1910 and 1912, and, after a last trip abroad in 1914, settled with Charles in New York. Toward the end of his life, when he could no longer work outdoors, he turned from watercolors to oils. A reticent individual, he worked in almost complete isolation and yet was closer to Post-Impressionist painting than any of his American contemporaries. From the starting point of Impressionism he developed a style of bright yet delicate patches of broad color which compose into a decorative tapestry of light and movement. It was only a year before his death that he achieved some recognition when he won a $2,000 prize at the Corcoran Biennial. (See illustration.)

Pre-Raphaelite Brotherhood. A group of artists organized in 1848 by Rossetti, Hunt and Millais, and later joined by Ford Madox Brown, Burne-Jones and John Ruskin. The basis of the movement lay in the ambiguous situation of the arts and culture generally in mid-nineteenth-century Britain when the transition from the age of craftsmanship to the machine age had finally begun. The fine arts had become isolated and artificial and it was the purpose of the Brotherhood to improve on the bad taste and cultural sterility of the times. The study of nature, the revival of sound craftsman-

PRENDERGAST. In Central Park. Addison Gallery of American Art, Phillips Academy, Andover

ship were basic ideas with them. In the fine arts proper it aimed at return to a simpler pre-Raphael (i.e., pre-High Renaissance) type of expression, e.g., the simple decorativeness of Benozzo Gozzoli; in the applied arts it resulted in the Morris and Burne-Jones attempt to make fine things for the home: fabrics, furniture, etc., that would represent real craftsmanship rather than a machine-made product.

Prestopino, Gregorio (1907-). A contemporary American Realist painter of social genre. Born in New York, he studied at the National Academy of Design (1923-29) and traveled and studied in Europe (1936). His art has more recently shown elements of abstraction and the influence of Shahn.

Preti, Mattia (called Cavaliere Calabrese) (1613-69). Neapolitan follower of Caravaggio. Born of a noble family at Taverna, he studied in Naples and Rome, worked in various places, including Malta, where he died. He developed out of the Roman Baroque of Lanfranco, Domenichino, and Cortona into the realism of Caravaggio, and to this added his own feeling for Venetian color.

Previtali, Andrea (called Cordeliaghi) (c.1470-1528). Born in Bergamo, he was probably a student of Bellini. He painted portraits and small pictures with charming landscapes; these point to an influence from Palma Vecchio and Lotto. He was active in Venice and, after 1511, in Bergamo.

Prevost, Jan (see PROVOST, JAN).

Priamo della Quercia (active 1438-67). A Sienese painter, brother of the sculptor Jacopo della Quercia, and a pupil and collaborator of Domenico di Bartolo. He painted one scene of the series Domenico was commissioned to execute in the Scala hospital, Siena, in which he closely imitated his master. Part of his life was spent in Volterra, where a triptych in the oratory of St. Anthony is attributed to him. Left to his own devices in a provincial center, this mediocre artist reverted to the late Sienese Gothic style of Taddeo di Bartolo.

primary hues or colors. Generally refers to red, yellow and blue in the practice of painting. This will vary somewhat in commercial color printing or in laboratory mixing of colored light.

Primaticcio, Francesco (1504-70). An Italian painter sculptor, and architect, most famous for his work at Fontainebleau. A great organizer-decorator, he was most influential in establishing the Italian Maniera (see) in France—the so-called Fontainebleau style (see). Born in Bologna, he studied first with Francucci and Bagnacavallo, and later with Giulio Romano, and worked with the latter on the Palazzo del Te in Mantua (1526-32). Called by Francis I to help decorate Fontainebleau, he found Rosso and Pellegrini already there, but after the death of the former, assumed direction of the project in 1542. He was later assisted by Nicolò del Abbate. He continued active as organizer and designer for Francis and Henry II, and in 1559, when Catherine de Medici named him chief decorator, moved to Paris. There he established a large atelier, working at the same time on projects for the Guise family. He returned to Bologna for a short time in 1563, but was soon back in Paris and remained there until his death. His style left an indelible mark upon the art of France and northern Europe.

Primavera (Spring) by Botticelli (see).

priming. Refers to the covering of a given surface, particularly wood or canvas, with a ground color which prevents that surface from absorbing the paint applied to it. This process is similar to the sizing of a plaster wall for painting.

primitive painting (see PRIMITIVISM, AFRICAN PAINTING, LIMNER, FOLK ART, PREHISTORIC PAINTING).

primitivism. An element or interest in modern painting, sculpture, prints, etc., derived from the art of so-called primitive peoples in Africa, Oceania, Australia and other areas in which the level of civilization is well below that of the European, Asiatic or American. This primitive or "unspoiled" quality, which may also be found in the unlearned and unsophisticated works of peasants in such areas as Germany or Mexico, is cherished both for its psychological and philosophical implications of uncivilizing the too-civilized and for its formal and technical possibilities. In the latter sense it lends to modern art a kind of vigor and freshness as well as a simplicity of form that has interested such diverse artists as Picasso, Modigliani and Kirchner among many others.

printmaking (see LITHOGRAPHY, ENGRAVING, ETCHING, DRYPOINT, MEZZOTINT, WOODCUT).

Prix de Rome. Literally, the Rome prize. Awarded to the winner of the yearly competition at the Ecole des Beaux-Arts in Paris, entitling the artist to a period of study at the French Academy in Rome.

Procaccini, Camillo (c.1550-1629). Born in Bologna, the eldest son of Ercole, il Vecchio, he was active in Lombardy, Reggio, and Piacenza. Derivative of Correggio, Parmigianino, and Barocci, he was bound by the Mannerist (see) tradition of his father.

Procaccini, Giulio Cesare (c.1570-1625). Born in Bologna, the younger brother of Camillo, he came with the family to Milan where as both painter and sculptor he had a great influence. His style is dependent upon Correggio and Parmigianino, whose art he absorbed through the Carracci rather than through the Mannerism (see) of his father and brother, and is therefore more robust and Baroque.

Procaccini il Vecchio, Ercole (1515-95). Head of a family of Italian Mannerist (see) painters, the father of Camillo, Giulio Cesare and Carlantonio. Born in Bologna, a pupil of Fontana, influenced by Parmigianino and Correggio, he was active in Bologna until c.1585, when he moved with his family to Milan.

PROVOST. Wings of a triptych
Philadelphia Museum of Art, Johnson Collection

proletarian art. A term generally associated with the Marxist viewpoint in Soviet Russia; it indicates the kind of pictorial expression which is dedicated to the welfare of the proletariat or which expresses the aims and aspirations of that group. It may also be found among those artists in non-Communist countries who sympathize with that point of view. Among orthodox Leftists in recent years there has been a tendency to exclude from the proletarian category the kind of art which is too formalistic, i.e., abstract in character, even when it might be otherwise acceptable in terms of its subject matter.

Protogenes (active c.300 B.C.). A Greek painter and sculptor of Rhodes. A contemporary of Apelles, who admired his work, Protogenes rose from humble origins as a ship's painter at Rhodes to carry out important commissions in the Propylaea at Athens. He was noted for the elaborate care which he lavished upon his works. Among his paintings were a Satyr Playing the Flute and a painting of Ialysos on which he worked seven years.

Provost (Prevost), Jan (1465-1529). Flemish painter. We first hear of him in 1491 when he married the widow of Simon Marmion. Although he became a Master in Antwerp, he was mainly active in Bruges. In 1520 he worked on the decorations for the entry of Charles V into Bruges. In 1524 he painted a panel for an altarpiece in St. Donatien, probably the painting now in the Leningrad Hermitage. In 1524/25 he executed the Last Judgment (Bruges Museum) which is his most certain work and that on which all attributions hang. He enjoyed a reputation as a facile decorative artist. He was influenced by Gerard David and by the diabolism of Bosch. What he lacked of the seriousness of David he made up in liveliness and color. The different aspects of his style are represented by the Karlsruhe Madonna (his elegance of form) and the Detroit Last Judgment (his imaginativeness). (See illustration.)

Prud'hon, Pierre Paul (1758-1823). A French painter called "the French Correggio." Although befriended by David, Prud'hon inclined toward the Italian artists of the Renaissance and Baroque periods. He had studied them in Italy, where he was a friend of Canova. He was indebted particularly to Leonardo and Correggio for his soft, pervading chiaroscuro and sensuous treatment of bodies. He lacked David's revolutionary taste and continued, as it were, the elegance of the Rococo into the nineteenth century. His works were at first playful genres, but then he turned to classical myths and allegory. Vengeance and Justice Pursuing Crime is his best known work in his late serious style. He also did religious subjects such as the Assumption (1816). His domestic life was unfortunate and affected him strongly both through his unhappy marriage and the dramatic death of his mistress, Constance Mayer (see). (See illustration.)

Psalter. A type of medieval manuscript or book with illuminated pages or parts of pages in which the text is that of The Book of Psalms, i.e., the Psalms of David. Examples: the Utrecht Psalter of the University of Utrecht Library, the Paris Psalter of the Bibliothèque Nationale in Paris.

Public Works of Art Project. Established in December 1933 with money allocated by the Civil Works Administration to the Treasury Department, which administered the program under the direction of Edward Bruce. Selected on a merit basis, and paid a craftmen's wages, 3,600 artists produced more than 16,000 works of art before the project was discontinued in June, 1934. This should not be confused with the W.P.A. (See FEDERAL ART PROJECT.)

Puccio di Simone (active middle 14th century). Registered in the two painters' guilds of Florence from 1343. Two signed works by him are known: a Madonna polyptych in the Florence Academy, and a Madonna panel once in the Artaud de Montor collection. The chief influence on his art is that of Bernardo Daddi.

Pucelle, Jean (active c.1320). French book illuminator. Under the general stimulus of the Italian Trecento, Pucelle revived the School of Paris and began the conversion of the Gothic book page into a spatial art. This can be observed in the Hours of Jeanne d'Evreux (1325-28). The Belleville Breviary (1323-26) shows how he extended the northern ornamental tendencies into pages bursting with bar traceries and foliage and peopled with all sorts of life, including his signature, the dragonfly. His landscape vignettes sometimes indicate the season by weather changes, a tradition that is to reach down to Pieter Brueghel. Pucelle's influence lasted in his workshop until the mid-fourteenth century when an intrusion of Flemish artists gave rise to what is called "Franco-Flemish" art.

Pueyrredón, Prilidiano (1823-70). Argentine painter of portraits and genre scenes. He was trained in the Neo-Classical manner of the eighteenth-century Academy of San Fernando in Madrid and returned to Buenos Aires to achieve a reputation as a painter of leading personalities. In addition to these well-characterized studies he also did many genre scenes, especially of the life of the Argentine gaucho. Here he shows an animation and excitement, a skillfully related series of dark and light effects that place him in a high position in this field.

Pujol, Antonio (1914-). Mexican painter and graphic artist. He has done a fresco in Rodríguez Market, 1934, and a mural in the Electrical Workers' Union (with Siqueiros and Arenal), 1939, Mexico City.

Pulzone, Scipione (called il Gaetano) (before 1550-1598). Italian Mannerist painter born in Gaeta. He studied with Jacopino del Conte and was early under the influence of Girolamo da Sermoneta. He continued into the second

PRUD'HON. Portrait of the Empress Josephine
Louvre, Paris

PUVIS DE CHAVANNES. The Sacred Grove. Art Institute of Chicago, Potter Palmer Collection

half of the century the manner of Pontormo and Bronzino with additional features of Northern Mannerism, especially in his miniature-like technique. His portraits are finer than his religious works.

Purism. A movement in modern painting and sculpture associated with the names of Ozenfant, Le Corbusier and Brancusi. It was launched by the manifesto publication in 1918 of *Après le Cubisme* by the first two of these artists. As the title implies, they felt that Cubism had come to a dead end—in their words, it had degenerated into a decorative formula—and that is was necessary for it to be "purified" of this failing. What they proposed, therefore, was a more modern and less studio type of expression, one wherein the painter would refine his forms into universally understood mechanical elements symbolic of the era in which we live. At the same time the virtues of Cubism, its simultaneity and its latent dynamism, would be preserved; thus the average Purist painting resembles its original source in the overlapping of planes and simultaneous views of different aspects of one object, but these are now seen in the new mechanical form. This later influenced industrial design.

Purrmann, Hans (1880-). German Fauve painter who, after a period of study in Germany, spent the years 1906 to 1914 in Paris with Matisse. In 1935 he became director of the Villa Romana in Florence and during most of the succeeding years has lived outside of Germany. His style is directly derived from that of Matisse.

putto (pl., *putti).* In Italian art, a nude child figure; also a cherub.

Puvis de Chavannes, Pierre Cécile (1824-98). French painter, noted for his murals. Puvis was one of the most influential of the conservative artists of the nineteenth century. He based his style on the Renaissance but remained in contact with the young innovators of his time. He came of a very distinguished French family and started to follow his father's career of engineering. Abandoning this, he entered the studio of Henri Scheffer and went to Italy to study Pre-Raphaelite frescoes. On his return he came to know Couture and Delacroix. He exhibited a Pietà at the Salon of 1850 but was refused for a number of years afterwards. Later as a Jury member he antagonized his colleagues by his independent and progressive judgements. His first decorative project was the Museum of Picardy in Amiens, which led to a vast number of mural commissions. These ranged from rather obvious allegorical symbolism to works with a fine sense of classical quietism, such as in the Sacred Wood (Sorbonne) and Massilia the Greek Colony (Marseilles). For the Pantheon he did a part of the story of St. Genevieve, and he did a series of allegorical figures for the great staircase of the Library in Boston. Puvis' insistence on a linear, patternistic formula in the face of the prevailing realism of his day was not entirely reactionary, but set the stage for Gauguin, Seurat and Lautrec, who later studied his work. Like Ingres, his abstractions go back to such earlier masters as Fra Filippo Lippi. (See illustration.)

Puy, Jean (1876-). French painter associated with Fauvism (see). He came to Paris from Lyon, worked at the Académie Julian with Laurens and then studied with Carrière. From 1900 on he showed at the Independants as his style changed from an early Impressionism to a mild kind of Fauvism, and this remained his standard form of expression. He showed with the Fauves at the Salon d'Automne in 1905 and underwent the same abuse as they. His brilliant but by no means "wild" color gives the various nudes, landscapes and portraits he has done a joyous, spirited and decorative quality.

Pynacker, Adam (1622-73). Dutch landscape painter

RAFFAELLI. Place de la Trinité, Paris
Art Institute of Chicago, Potter Palmer Collection

165. RAEBURN. Miss Eleanor Urquhart
National Gallery of Art, Mellon Collection, Washington, D.C.

and engraver. He spent several years in Italy, where he was strongly influenced by Jan Both. Based on his impressions of Italian art he constructed great decorations for Dutch houses, which enjoyed an enormous vogue.

Pynas, Jan Simonsz. (1580-1631). A Dutch painter of religious subjects. He studied under Elsheimer in Italy; returning to Holland he established a studio in Amsterdam, where Rembrandt came as a pupil after he left Lastman. From Pynas' moving and dignified interpretation of Bible stories Rembrandt took much of the essential part of his noble spiritual conceptions.

Q

Quarton, Enguerrand (see CHARONTON, ENGUERRAND).

quattrocento (It.) Literally, four hundred. Refers to the 1400's in Italy, i.e., the fifteenth century.

Quidor, John (1801-81). An unusual American genre painter. Unique among his contemporaries, he painted scenes based on the Romantic writings of Cooper and Irving with a sense of eerie fantasy, drama, and satire. He studied for a short time with Jarvis, had an unsuccessful career as a portraitist, and was reduced to painting signs, coaches, and fire-engines to support himself.

Quirizio da Murano (active 1461-78). Venetian painter; a minor pupil of Antonio Vivarini about whom there is very little documentary evidence. Three signed paintings exist, one in the gallery at Rovigo (dated 1462), and two in the Venice Academy. His simple but highly decorative style appears to have received some influence from Giovanni Bellini.

Quirt, Walter (1902-). A contemporary American Abstract Expressionist. Born in Iron River, Mich., he attended the Layton School of Art in Milwaukee, but is largely self-taught. His earliest work was based on social themes but he later went through a Surrealist phase.

R

Raeburn, Henry (1756-1823). Scottish portraitist of individual character and unusual power who stood out successfully against the great influence of Reynolds. His simple, straightforward but incisive style is marked by honesty of characterization and an absence of the sentimentality prevalent at the time. He was skillful at recording the air and expression of a particular sitter and thereby summing up the personality. This he did with two generations of eminent Scottish men and women. He was a product of the significant intellectual movement in late eighteenth- early nineteenth-century Edinburgh with its essayists, historians, novelists and painters, and its deep-rooted consciousness of Scottish individuality. Raeburn studied in Rome during 1785-87 and returned home to become the foremost painter of Scotland. In 1815 he became a member of the Royal Academy and in 1822 a knight and His Majesty's Limner for Scotland. His male portraits are virile; his women interesting and alive. He used few coats of pigment and few brushstrokes; the thin, direct painting shows broad surfaces relieved occasionally by sharply defined shadows. There appear to have been no preliminary chalk drawings or compass measurements. Everything was studied with the eye and transmitted directly to the canvas—a revolutionary idea at the time, although a century later it would be practiced by Sargent and many others. (See color plate 165.)

Raffaelli, Jean François (1850-1924). French painter, etcher, lithographer. Renowned for his illustrations of the life and types, especially poor types, of his day. He studied briefly with Gerôme, but was essentially an Impressionist, painting directly from nature out-of-doors under Monet's influence. His paintings were constructed from elementary colors but the palette was greyish in general effect. His landscapes show many characteristic bits of the Parisian scene: La plaine St. Denis, Coin des fortifications, Sur la zône. Among portraits he did Edmond de Goncourt and Clemenceau. He collaborated with Forain in the illustrations

RAFFAELLINO DEL GARBO. The Resurrection
Galleria Antica e Moderna, Florence

166. RAPHAEL. St. George and the Dragon. National Gallery of Art, Mellon Collection, Washington, D.C.

for Huysman's *Croquis parisiennes*. He was also active as a sculptor. (See illustration.)

Raffaellino del Garbo (c.1470-1524/26). A Florentine painter of the High Renaissance; he worked in a style close to that of Filippino Lippi, who was probably his teacher. In his later works he exhibits some Umbrian characteristics probably derived from Perugino, whose work was available to him in Florence. He signed himself in several ways and his style was various enough to inspire the hypothesis that two or more painters executed the works usually ascribed to him. His matriculation in the corporation of painters in 1499 is under the name "Raphael Bartolommei Nicola Capponi pictor nel Garbo," but he is also sometimes called Raffaellino dei Carli. He is reputed to have assisted Filippino Lippi on the latter's frescoes in Santa Maria Sopra Minerva in Rome (1489-93). He is referred to in civil documents of 1513 and 1515, and is not heard of again. Vasari states that he died in 1524, but a picture presumed to be by him is dated 1526. As an artist he was insufficiently independent to avoid being swayed by the styles of others. The influence of Filippino seems to take effect only after a lag of a few years, so that in 1500 Raffaellino paints an altarpiece (Uffizi) in Filippino's style of before 1490. Several important works by him are in the Uffizi and San Spirito, Florence, and others are in the museums of London, Berlin and Munich. (See illustration.)

Raffet, Denis Auguste Marie (1804-60). French graphic artist, popularizer of military France of the early nineteenth century. Pupil of Charlet and of Gros, who trained him as a recorder of military anecdote. After a trip to Asia, he produced pictures of the Napoleonic campaigns, as usual without having witnessed the event. He worked in lithograph, etching, woodcut and copper-engraving.

Raft of the Medusa by Géricault (see).

Raibolini, Francesco (see FRANCIA).

Ramage, John (c.1746/50-1802). Irish miniaturist, one of the most successful and best of the period, active in New York (1777-94). Born in Dublin, he came to Halifax with the Royal Irish Volunteers c.1770. During the Revolutionary War he arrived with British troops in New York; later he returned to Montreal. His style is characterized by long, fine brushstrokes which give his miniatures the quality of enamels.

Ramberg, Johann Heinrich (1763-1840). A German painter and engraver. Before he was twenty a group of drawings brought him to the attention of George III of England; under this King's protection he studied for seven years in London as the pupil of Benjamin West. A lively imagination and humor distinguish his very unequal output.

Ramos Martínez, Alfredo (1881-1946). A Mexican painter with European artistic background, active in the early part of this century at the beginning of the modern Mexican movement. He brought Impressionism to Mexico and founded the very influential opên-air schools that encouraged art among the Mexican people. He lived in the United States from 1929 on. His own art is charming and decorative.

RAPHAEL. Galatea. Farnesina Gallery, Rome

RAPHAEL. Sistine Madonna. Gemäldegalerie, Dresden

Ramsay, Allan (1713-84). Scottish portraitist who studied in Italy and became Principal Painter to the King in 1761. As part of his job he had to execute ninety full-length portraits, most of which were carried out by his pupils. His finest pictures, especially those of women, show an elegance, a fine color sense and convincing character interpretation. An intellectual, he wrote on political and other subjects and was a friend of Walpole, Rousseau and Dr. Johnson.

Raoux, Jean (1677-1734). French painter of history and portraits, in the tradition of Nattier. He studied in Italy and painted for a while in England, where he befriended Watteau. He practiced the allegorical portrait in vogue at the time and introduced elements of Rembrandt's style, a tendency derived apparently from Nattier. Typical is his Mlle Prévost as a Bacchante (Tours Museum).

Raphael (Raffaello Santi or Sanzio) (1483-1520). Italian painter who most completely typifies the classical art of the High Renaissance in its ordered equilibrium, idealized naturalness, and standardized types of characters. His art exemulifies the political and philosophical strivings of the papacy under Julius II and especially Leo X for a glory to match that of ancient Rome. He was born in Perugia, the son of a painter, Giovanni Santi, with whom he probably began his training. After his father's death in 1494 he may have studied with Evangelista di Meleto and Timoteo Viti, and perhaps with Perugino in Urbino (1493-99). He may also have been Perugino's assistant in the decoration of the Cambio in Perugia (1499-1503). He was active in Florence from 1505 to 1508 and then went to Rome. There he worked the rest of his life as painter, architect, designer, and director of antiquities, and was the center of a group of artists and intellectuals at the papal court. The increasing number of commissions for portraits, altarpieces, and decorative schemes led to an ever increasing number of assistants and students in his studio.

His career divides itself logically into three periods—Perugia (1500-04), Florence (1505-08) and Rome (1508-20). His earliest style is obviously dominated by the sweet and sentimental style of Perugino and shows a marked resemblance to that of Timoteo Viti. His first major commission was the St. Nicholas of Tolentino Altar in Sant' Agostino Città di Castello (1500-01, fragments in Brescia and Naples). The first signed work is the Crucifixion in S. Domenico, Città di Castello (1503, London); it was followed by the Coronation of the Virgin (1503, Vatican), and the masterpiece of this period, the Sposalizio, or Marriage of the Virgin (1504, Brera). The Morgan Altar (Metropolitan, predella panels in London and Gardner Collection, Boston) shows a transition from the Peruginesque to the Florentine style. His activity in Florence seems limited by a lack of important commissions and he spent a great deal of time studying and making drawings after Donatello, Pollaiuolo, Leonardo, and Michelangelo. His style during this period was based on Leonardo and was very close in many ways to Fra Bartolommeo. It was then that he did his many intimate and poetic early half-length Madonnas: Duca di Terranuova (Berlin), Granduca (Pitti), Cowper (Washington), Goldfinch (Uffizi), and La Belle Jardinière (Louvre). Paintings of a more monumental character belonging to this period are the Madonna del Baldacchino (c.1508, Pitti), and the Entombment (Borghese, Rome, predella in Vatican). His two most important portraits of the time are of Angelo Doni and his wife Maddalena Strozzi (1505-07, Pitti).

His last or Roman period is dominated by the great decorations for Julius and Leo in the Vatican, and is characterized by a new and classical monumentality under the influence of Michelangelo but transformed by his own sense of calm grandeur. He began his great cycle of decorations in the Vatican with the Stanza della Segnatura (1509-11), comprising the Disputà, School of Athens, Parnassus, and Jurisprudence; continued it with the Stanza d'Eliodoro (1511-14); the Stanza dell' Incendio (1514-17), carried out mostly by students; and the Sala di Constantino, executed by his pupils after his death. The magnificent tapestry series which ranks second only to his Stanza decorations was done for Leo X and depicts the Acts of the Apostles. They were executed in Brussels by Pieter van Aelst from cartoons done in 1515-16 (seven of the original ten in Victoria and Albert, London). Of smaller compass yet important for its lyrical classicism is his Triumph of Galatea (1514), part of the decoration of the Farnesina Palace; the loggia, decorated with scenes from the story of Psyche and Amor, was carried out by his assistants (1518). The same group with the addition of Pierino del Vaga executed the Loggie of the Vatican (1517-19). The great altars of this period include the Madonna del Foligno (1512, S. Francesco, Foligno), the most famous Sistine Madonna (c.1512-14, Dresden), and the magnificent Transfiguration (c.1519, Vatican). Of the smaller altarpieces there are the Alba Madonna (1508-10, Washington), Madonna with the Veil (c.1510, Louvre), Madonna of the Chair (c.1516, Pitti), and Madonna of the Curtain (c.1516, Munich). Among his brilliant portraits are Julius II (1511-12, Uffizi), Baldassare Castiglione (1515-16, Louvre), and Leo X (1517-19, Pitti). He was the culmination of the Roman High Renaissance and its end, but he had a profound influence upon subsequent European painting, first upon his students, especially Giulio Romano, then upon later sixteenth-century painting through the Caracci, and lastly upon all of later academic art in the West. (See illustrations, including color plate 166.)

Raphaelino (Raffaello) del Colle (c.1490-1566). An Umbrian painter born in Colle near San Sepolcro. A follower of Raphael, he assisted Giulio Romano in the Vatican and in Milan, Bronzino in the Signoria in Florence, and helped spread the Raphael style in Umbria. His most important work was the decoration of the Villa Imperiale in Pesaro for Francesco Maria I della Rovere.

Rattner, Abraham (1895-). Contemporary American semi-abstract Expressionist influenced by Cubism and Rouault. His brilliantly colored canvases are a search for spiritual and psychological values. Born in Poughkeepsie, N. Y., he studied at the Corcoran School of Art, the Pennsylvania Academy of Fine Arts, the Ecole des Beaux-Arts, and other schools. He lived in Paris from 1920 to 1940. (See illustration.)

RATTNER. The Emperor
Whitney Museum of American Art, New York

Ravesteyn, Jan Anthonisz. van (c.1572-1657). Dutch painter of portraits. His style was influenced by Van Miereveld and Jacob Delff the Elder. He lived at The Hague, where he helped to form the new painters' guild, and copiously produced excellently-conceived and well-executed portraits and corporation or group pictures.

Ravilious, Eric (1908-1942). A British watercolorist, decorator and engraver whose paintings are characterised by a precise linear style and clear cool color. He did book illustrations, designs for pottery and glass and was an official war artist.

Ray, Man (1890-). Contemporary American painter and photographer. Born in Philadelphia, he studied architecture and engineering before turning to painting. He attended the National Academy of Design, but his art became abstract after the Armory Show. Under the influence of Duchamp and Picabia, he became interested in Dada and, after 1921 in Paris, was a member of both the Dada and Surrealist groups. He gave up painting for photography and films. On his return to the U.S. in 1940 he again took up painting, working in an abstract Surrealist manner.

Read, Herbert (1893-). British poet and critic of art whose best-known works include *Art Now*, first published in 1933, *Art and Society*, 1937, and *Art and Industry*, 1954 (most recent edition). He is important in Britain for his championing of modern art since before World War I and

167. REDON. White Lilacs. Albright Art Gallery, Buffalo

for having encouraged the younger British painters to follow this bent.

Realism. A type of expression in which the artist tries to give a real or convincing portrayal of a given form or scene without the minute details that one associates with the photograph. Thus a scene by Daumier or Courbet may have all the necessary form to convey to the spectator the essential reality of that situation, as may an even less detailed sculpture from the early middle ages whose emotional projection is very convincing. This is in contrast to the method called naturalism, in which the artist moves toward a detailed and photographic rendition of the scene as it occurs in nature. Thus a painting by Vermeer or Chardin may be considered naturalistic rather than realistic.

Rebull, Santiago (1829-1902). A Mexican painter of Spanish parents who emigrated to Mexico. A pupil of Pelegrín Clavé, he won the Prix de Rome in 1852. He was made director of the San Carlos Academy by President Benito Juárez in 1861 and given the order of Guadalupe by Emperor Maximilian. Like most of the painters of his time and school he represents a conventional even academic style—in his case on a relatively high level.

receding color. The kind of color that appears to be farther away from the spectator than it actually is. Example: Cool colors such as blue, blue-violet, violet, green and blue-green generally give the impression of moving away form us.

red-figured style (see GREEK PAINTING).

Redon, Odilon (1840-1916). French Symbolist painter and graphic artist. Contemporary of Monet and other Impressionists but entirely different in the direction of his thinking, Redon was not interested in what seemed to him mere representation but rather in the processes of thought as applied to art. For him thought meant a kind of imaginativeness and poetic feeling, and these give his art its special effect. A friend of the writers Mallarmé, Valéry and Francis Jammes, Redon did a good deal of writing himself, but whether writing or painting he moved in the direction of "clothing the idea with form" in the approved Symbolist sense, trying to open "magic casements" into the unseen world. He is of great interest to contemporary artists because of his ability to allow his subconscious free play toward the end of putting himself into contact with the fabulous aspects of existence. There is a rich quality to his color, a softness to his forms and an indefinable ability to give shape to ideas and fancies beyond the normal grasp. His art is at once tender and humorous, poetic and frightening, always exploring the same almost childish dream-world that was his peculiar province. See also SYMBOLISM. (See color plate 167.)

Refregier, Anton (1905-). Contemporary American painter of social themes, best known for his mural decorations. Born in Moscow, Russia, he studied in Paris and with Hans Hofmann in Munich before coming to the U.S. in 1921. In the U.S. he studied at the Rhode Island School of Design. Among his many murals the Rincon Post Office in San Francisco is the most famous. They have been attacked and even theatened with destruction because of their allegedly radical symbolism, but the artist has been defended by most of the important art organizations in the U.S.

regionalism. Name used to describe a movement in American painting of the 1930's, identified with particular sections such as Iowa, Missouri, etc., and purporting to spring more from the soil of those regions (or from America in general) than from foreign lands. May be identified with nationalism in culture generally. Examples: Grant Wood, Thomas Hart Benton, John Steuart Curry.

Regnault, Alexandre Georges Henri(1843-71). French painter of history and genre. His brilliant career was cut

168. REMBRANDT. Self Portrait.
Toledo Museum of Art, Libbey Collection

169. REMBRANDT. Woman Bathing. National Gallery, London

short by death in the Franco-Prussian war. He studied in Italy and Madrid and is famous for views of Morocco.

Regnault, Jean Baptiste (1754-1829). French painter and etcher. Contemporary and rival of David. He lived long in Rome and specialized in antique subject matter such as Diogenes Visited by Alexander (1776).

Regoyos y Valdés, Darío de (1857-1913). Spanish Impressionist painter. Regoyos studied under Haes, Pissarro and Monet and became the only Spanish member of the French Impressionist group. He was for a long time active in Paris and in Brussels, forming part of the group called "Les Vingt" in the latter city. His landscapes are closest to Pissarro and he occasionally used Pointillism.

Reinhardt, Ad (Adolph D. F.) (1913-). American abstract painter in the geometric style. Born in Buffalo, he studied at the National Academy of Design and attended Columbia and New York Universities. He was an easel painter on the Federal Art Project (1936-39), a cartoonist and illustrator, and a photographer for the N.S. Navy. His paintings are all-over patterns of subtly related patches of color His cartoon descriptions are witty and critical jibes at his contemporaries, and have led to much heated controversy and hard feelings.

Rembrandt Harmensz. van Rijn (1606-69). Dutch painter and engraver of history, landscapes, portraits and and genre. He was not only the greatest Dutch painter, but ranks as one of the greatest artists of all time. During his life and long after his death few Dutch artists resisted his influence, and it may indeed be said to have affected the entire course of European painting. He was born in Leyden of very simple parents, who, however, ambitiously enrolled their son in the Latin school there. Young Rembrandt soon abandoned book learning as such and entered on a painter's apprenticeship with Jacob van Swanenburch. About 1623 he went to Amsterdam, where he spent six months in the studio of Pieter Lastman, and the influence of this artist is strongly reflected in Rembrandt's early works. It was no doubt at this time that he was also influenced by Jan Pynas (see), with whom he is thought to have studied. Returning to Leyden, he set up his own shop and worked there until 1631, when he moved permanently to Amsterdam. His early years in Amsterdam were extremely successful. His works were much sought after and he married a young heiress named Saskia van Uylenborch, who gave him one son, the handsome little Titus, whose growth and development his father recorded in a number of well-known and appealing portraits. Saskia died while still a young woman, and a country girl, Hendrickje Stoffels, came into Rembrandt's service as housekeeper and nurse. The painter never married her because by a provision

REMBRANDT. Night Watch. Rijksmuseum, Amsterdam

of Saskia's will he would have had to forfeit a considerable estate in doing so, but Hendrickje remained all her life with the painter, who depended upon her affection and intelligence while he was being buffeted by the severe misfortunes of his later life. His taste for luxurious surroundings and the acquisition of works of art led him into debts that resulted in lawsuits and bankruptcy, but he painted constantly, developing through many markedly different phases his matchless art.

Rembrandt's output was enormous, even without counting those works that bear his signature but were produced in his studio, on his designs, by the various good painters that he trained. His early pictures are clearly drawn and vigorously painted, with a variety in coloring that decreases steadily as his famous light and shadow develops. The Anatomy Lesson of Dr. Tulp, dated 1632 (Mauritshuis), is the most important work of his first years in Amsterdam. A series of religious paintings treating the Passion of Christ also dates from this time. The famous picture in the Rijksmuseum in Amsterdam, long known as "The Night Watch," was painted ten years later and demonstrates his progression toward a more closely fused and darker style. Colors are no longer separate and independent but emerge from darkness in a mysterious golden harmony. The surfaces of his paint change during the 1640's and '50's, as he obtains richness and dramatic effect with alternations of smooth and rough passages. In the superb painting called The Jewish Bride (Rijksmuseum), made at the end of his life, he achieved a magical shimmering with light touches of thick paint marvelously applied. His devotion to nature and his unfailingly accurate observation combine with his command of light to make his landscapes objects of rare beauty. All during the years when he was producing great paintings he was also practicing etching and copper engraving, bringing to bear a technical skill equal to the majesty of his invention.

Throughout his life Rembrandt was preoccupied with character and motivation. In all his portraits as well as his religious pictures this intense probing into the essence of humanity reveals itself. He began as a very young artist to search his own face to record his appearance at various ages and in different states of mind and soul, so that we have from him a long series of remarkable self portraits, ending with one painted in the year of his death. (See illustrations, including color plates 168 and 169.)

Remington, Frederic (1861-1909). An American painter and sculptor of the Far West. Born in Canton, N.Y., he attended the Yale Art School and the Art Students League, but went West as a cowboy and later became a rancher. He then turned to writing and illustrating the life of the frontier, branched out as a painter and sculptor of life on the plains and Indian warfare, and achieved great popularity in the 1890's. His paintings are full of violent and romantic action, academically realistic, and rendered in great detail.

Renaissance. A period in the history of art that included the fourteenth- and fifteenth centuries. It represented the climax of Gothic town life in Italy with its consequent emphasis on the importance of the individual and the world in which he lived. With this stress on the dignity and humanity of the individual came an interest in the structure of the human body and the physical appearance of the environment in which that body moved. From these interests the artists of the fourteenth and fifteenth centuries developed anatomy, linear and aerial perspective (see), projective geometry and other devices that would enable them to accomplish their aim of showing the new man in the new world. In Italy especially, since it was the original site of ancient Rome, there developed a great interest in the classics of literature, the plastic arts and architecture. For those interested in these studies, the so-called Humanists, this classical orientation symbolized an affinity with a period that had been both secular and individualistic. Artistically the Renaissance period was experimental as it tried to develop and perfect the various techniques listed above and thus may be contrasted with the High Renaissance of the early sixteenth century (see). The most important schools of painting of the fourteenth-fifteenth century period include the Florentine, Sienese, Umbrian, Umbro-Florentine, Paduan, Venetian and Roman (see separate entries).

Reni, Guido (1575-1642). Bolognese painter born in Calvenzano, he was one of the leading followers of the Carracci, especially Annibale. Though not highly regarded by modern critics, who consider his art oversweet and commonplace, he was greatly admired by his contemporaries, who regarded his art as the personification of the seventeenth-century ideal of *grazia,* i.e., grace, and as a return to Renaissance ideals in the unification of Raphael and the antique. He was also an important innovator in the depiction of dogma. He did his first work with Denys Calvaert, along with Domenichino and Albani, but in 1595 joined the Carracci Academy as a kind of foreman. He came to Rome about 1600 and remained there as part of the anti-Caravaggist circle of the Cavaliere d'Arpino. Influenced during this period by Annibale, he followed the Carracci line, though he was more Baroque than his master or his other followers. In Rome he executed a series of paintings for Cardinal Borghese, decorating his apartments

REMBRANDT. Syndics. Rijksmuseum, Amsterdam

RENI. Head of the Crucified Christ
Detroit Institute of Arts

and the Borghese Chapel, Sta. Maria Maggiore, and painting the famous Aurora for the ceiling of the Villa Rospigliosi (1609). He also worked in the Palazzo Quirinale (1610). In 1614 he returned to Bologna and, after the death of Ludovico in 1619, took over direction of the Bolognese Academy. In 1629 he was invited to head the Accademia di San Lucca in Rome, but declined in order to remain in Bologna. In the 1620's his style became extremely operatic, utilizing large figures in frozen poses. His late style, after 1632, exhibits a turn to the High Baroque, a complete change to a silvery-grey tonality which unifies the picture as a whole. (See illustration.)

Renoir, Pierre Auguste (1841-1919). "Old Master" among the French Impressionist painters. As rebellious a member of the group as any, Renoir throughout his life nevertheless remained faithful to the long tradition of French art and frequently drew inspiration from the great colorists of European painting. Watteau, Chardin, Boucher and Fragonard all seemed to contribute to a new monumental art that drew its scale in part from Rubens and Veronese.

Son of a tailor of Limoges, he passed his apprenticeship painting porcelain, then turned to painting blinds and fans. He saved sufficient money to enter Gleyre's studio in Paris. With his fellow students, Monet, Bazille and Sisley he retired to Chailly near Fontainebleau. Here he met Diaz, followed Courbet and Corot. Such paintings of this period as Diana the Huntress (1867, Washington) show this. Lise (Essen), of the same period, indicates the influence of the newer style of Manet. Then we see a throwback to Delacroix in Woman of Algiers (1870, Washington) in which Renoir went off once again on his frequent tangent of richly inlaid colors. While working with Monet before and after the Franco-Prussian War, Renoir shared in developing the broken color technique that characterizes mature Impressionism (see). A comparison of La Grenouillère by the two artists in 1869 and the Duck Pond which they both did in 1873 shows clearly how the technique grew from large flat patches to a uniform crust. Although the two artists seem remarkably alike in each pair of paintings, in both comparisons Renoir reveals himself as more interested in rich color effects and solidity of form than was Monet. Likewise during the heyday of Impressionism in the 1870's, Renoir preferred figure painting to panorama. He represented the sociable aspect of Impressionism; he delighted in rendering gay groups in surroundings rich with sensuous appeal, e.g., The Loge (1874, Courtauld), Moulin de la Galette (1876, Louvre). In contrast to the Japanese qualities brought into Impressionism by Manet and Degas, Renoir revived the Rococo. The elegance of Watteau and Fragonard stimulated him as it did the poetic sensibilities of the de Goncourt brothers.

While exhibiting in Impressionist shows, Renoir also submitted to the official Salons. And during the dark days of the middle 1870's, his figure painting paid off by bringing him a series of portrait commissions, centered about that of Mme Charpentier and Her Children (Metropolitan), a great success at the Salon of 1879. The following year he went to Italy where he declared himself intoxicated with the works of Raphael(!) and developed a great admiration for Pompeian wall painting. About 1883 he declared, "I had wrung Impressionism dry and I finally came to the conclusion that I knew neither how to paint nor how to draw." He began to copy Ingres and Renaissance bas-reliefs. From this exercise came the great series of Bathers, beginning with the highly linear one of 1885-87 in Philadelphia. These monumental tendencies were also stimulated by periods spent with Cézanne; his return to traditional values can be seen in subject matter. He painted classical themes in later life and experimented with sculpture. From the time of his marriage in 1881 he developed a domestic genre similar

RENOIR. Girl with a Watering Can
National Gallery of Art, Chester Dale Collection, Washington, D.C.

170. RENOIR. Girls Playing Battledore and Shuttlecock. Minneapolis Institute of Arts

to that of late Fragonard. He painted canvas after canvas of his wife and her cherubic babies, in modern emulation of the Madonna theme. The joie de vivre of his late works belies the physical misery of their painter. He suffered badly from arthritis and about 1900 he settled at Cagnes in the south in order to relieve it. Here he reveled in the Mediterranean atmosphere and colors. Unable to render detail because of the stiffness of his fingers, he had the brushes tied to his hands and in broad strokes he turned out Olympian goddesses in hot,

RENOIR. Moulin de la Galette. Louvre, Paris

garish colors. "I want a red to be sonorous," he said, "to sound like a bell; if it doesn't turn out that way I put on more reds or other colors till I get it." (See illustrations, including color plate 170.)

Repin, Ilya (1844-1930). Best known of the Russian realists of the nineteenth century and painter of the famous pictures of Ivan the Terrible and His Son, and of the Cossacks Replying to Mahomet IV.

representational. A term used to describe the kind of art in which the painter or sculptor tries to reproduce to an appreciable extent the physical appearance of the object or person shown. It may be constrasted with non-representational art in which physical appearance is of little or no moment.

reredos. An ornamental screen of stone or wood behind or facing a church altar, frequently decorated with paintings or statuary. In small churches it is usually replaced by a dossal (dorsal), or hanging, behind the altar.

restoring. The process of bringing a work of art back to its original condition. In painting this may mean the replacement of fragments of paint that have disappeared, mending of the canvas, restretching the canvas on its frame, cleaning the pigment's surface to restore the original brightness, and so forth. In cleaning a painting of the accumulated grime of centuries there sometimes emerges something unexpectedly bright and exciting, as in the spectacular instance of the famous Night Watch by Rembrandt of the Rijksmuseum in Amsterdam.

Restout, Jean (1692-1768). French painter of history and portraits. Pupil of his uncle Jouvenet. He won the Rome prize with Venus Requesting from Vulcan Arms for Aeneas, but did not go to Rome. He rose in the Academy and received many commissions, largely for churches. His painting of Christ Healing the Paralytic (Louvre) shows his special lighting effects. He belonged to a family of several generations of artists.

retable (also Spanish retablo). This refers to an architectural framework or structure set up behind an altar and facing the congregation. Within this frame or screen is generally found one or a series of paintings, sculpture, carvings or other art forms. Retables are generally associated with Spanish art of the fifteenth and sixteenth centuries. A special variant of the retable or retablo is found in Latin America.

retablo. See RETABLE.

Rexach (Reixach), Juan (active 1443-84). A Spanish painter of Valencia. Disciple and follower of Jacomart. The altarpiece of St. Ursula for the church of Cubells (Barcelona Museum) is dated 1468 and signed by him.

Reynolds, Joshua (1723-1792). One of the outstanding British portraitists and an important influence on his contemporaries. Born in Devon, the son of a Fellow of Balliol College, Oxford, at seventeen Reynolds was apprenticed to the portrait painter Thomas Hudson. By the age of twenty he had set himself up as a portraitist among the local gentry in Devon and the naval officers at Plymouth. Taken to the Mediterranean on a ship commanded by a friend, he reached Rome in 1749 and stayed there three years. While studying, he eked out his finances by occasional copying of Old Masters, doing portraits of English visitors and the caricature portrait groups then in style. He returned to London via Paris and within a short time had achieved a considerable success. In 1755, for example, he did 120 portraits. Reynolds bought a large house with studios and exhibition gallery as well as facilities for his many students and assistants. He lived in high style and collected Old Master paintings as part of the role of being successful and fashionable, and also because his viewpoint as an artist made such collecting inevitable. Although his prices increased constantly, commissions kept pace: portraits, group pictures and historical themes. His sitters included the socially prominent people of the time and when the Royal Academy was founded in 1768, he naturally became its first president; he was also knighted. This success was the product of his exceptionally strong will and determination to succeed. An urbane and discreet opportunist, he moved in the highest aristocratic circles as well as an exclusive literary and theatrical group that included Goldsmith, Dr. Johnson, Richard Brinsley Sheridan and other celebrities. In 1784 he became principal painter to the king and employed various assistants to do the many royal portraits expected of him. At the same time he acted as agent and dealer for noblemen interested in collecting Old Masters.

Reynold's point of view as a painter was just as "safe" as his social outlook; he believed that by analysis of the Old Masters he could build a composite style of great art. He made careful studies of Rembrandt, Titian, Correggio and various French painters in the furtherance of this aim, but these eclectic procedures do not represent his best work. He did have a personal creative power and variety of pictorial invention when he chose to let himself go and to forget that he was a great man. We find many paintings with a life and a grandeur beyond the many borrowed elements. His portraits —the honest ones—are effective because their expression is related to the type of sitter, e.g., Dr. Johnson, Admiral Keppel and many others. His colors are difficult to judge today because they were not scientifically applied, so that many

171. REYNOLDS. Captain Bligh. Worcester Art Museum

REYNOLDS. The Tragic Muse (Mrs. Sarah Siddons) Huntington Library and Art Gallery, San Marino, California

RIBALTA, FRANCISCO. Christ Bearing His Cross
National Gallery, London

paintings have cracked and faded, but the form, design and pictorial rhythm are often quite impressive. Many of his portraits are originally composed in decorative pattern and organized in light and space arrangements. Although such works are distinguished by graceful and controlled movement as well as dignity, he is far less successful in his privately painted coy nudes, sentimentalized children, and such trite and inanely erotic pictures as The Snake in the Grass or Love Unbinding the Zone of Beauty. Yet Reynolds was a great force in his time and contemporaries borrowed freely the various elements of his art, particularly his self-assured manner. For twenty years he was the most prominent artist of his day, even in the face of the rising Gainsborough. He pettishly referred to his rival as "the first landscape painter of Europe," ignoring Gainsborough's portraiture, which ultimately stemmed from the same source as his—the tradition of van Dyck. (See illustrations, including color plate 171.)

Ribalta, Francisco (1555-1628). Spanish painter. As the culminating figure of the school of Valencia and harbinger of the new seventeenth-century style, Ribalta is of immense importance to the history of Spanish painting. He introduced a tenebrist (see) style in Spain; however, it is not clear whether he derived it from observation of Caravaggio's paintings in Italy, from copies of Caravaggio in Spain or from his own known enthusiasm for Raphael, Correggio and Sebastiano del Piombo. However obtained, his style is quite distinct from Caravaggio's, viz., St. Francis Embracing Christ on the Cross (Valencia), and it had great influence on Spanish naturalism of the succeeding century.

The Last Supper (Valencia Museum) is considered his masterpiece. He was the master of Ribera; and Lope de Vega praised him in verse. One of his last works, done with the assistance of his son Juan, was the retablo of the Cartuja de Porta Coeli, Valencia. (See illustration.)

Ribalta, Juan (1596-1628). A Spanish painter and poet. Son and pupil of his father Francisco (see), with whom he frequently collaborated in religious works. He also painted portraits, among them a series of nearly thirty illustrious figures of Spain, now partly in the Valencia Museum. His tenebrism, viz., The Nailing to the Cross (Valencia), seems more certainly based on Caravaggio than does that of his father.

Ribera, Jusepe da ("Lo Spagnoletto") (1590-1652). Spanish tenebrist (see) painter and engraver, active in the vice-royalty of Naples. Noted for the realistic veracity and Baroque emotionalism of his religious subjects. Born in Játiba of humble origins, Ribera was trained in the Valencian manner, probably by Francisco Ribalta. This naturalistic, heavy style he carried to Italy as a youth where he apparently studied the Venetians, the Carracci and Correggio in the north, and Caravaggio in Rome. He settled permanently in Naples in 1616. Here he gained an international reputation as one of the most individual followers of Caravaggio. As a successful artist and member of Neapolitan society he was visited by José Martinez (1625) and by Velázquez (1629, 1649) with important commissions for the Spanish court, to which he constantly exported paintings. In 1626 he was elected to the Academy of St. Luke in Rome; in 1646, he was decorated by the Pope. The study of Ribera's works is complicated by his use of assistants and by the existence of many followers. A radically realistic attitude in both painting and drawing is the keynote of his early period (to c.1630), whether he was rendering religious works such as the Martyrdom of St. Bartholomew (Madrid) or subjects inspired by the antique such as the Drunken Silenus (Naples). During the late 1630's he entered a "classical" and more gracious phase, one that was rather less Caravaggesque. Examples of this are the Ecstasy of Mary Magdalene (Madrid) or the Mater Dolorosa (Kassel). In his last years, a period marked by sorrow and ill health, he returned to his more sombre manner, viz., St. Mary of Egypt (Naples) or St. Paul the Hermit (Ragusa). (See color plate 172.)

Ribot, Theodule Augustin (1823-91). French etcher. He began his artistic career late, after many years in the building trades and as a commercial designer. He studied under Gleize and made a living by copying Watteaus for the American trade. His style was academic with influences from Ribera, Le Nain and Chardin—in fact, he was called the "French Ribera." He did history subjects, genre, portraits and still lifes. He exhibited with "les Refusés" in 1859 and was only recognized by the Salon in 1861 with his Cuisiniers. In 1870 his studio was burned in his absence and he retired to Colombes until his death. Among his pictures in the Luxembourg are Jesus and the Doctors, St. Sebastian, and The Good Samaritan.

Ricard, Louis Gustave (1823-72). An eclectic French painter and imitator of the Old Masters. After studying with Aubert and Cogniet, he copied Correggio, Titian, van Dyck and Rembrandt in the Louvre. In London he studied the English masters. He painted in a sparkling chiaroscuro derived from those old masters and was popular as a portraitist. He painted d'Heilbuth (Louvre) and created a sensation with his Madame Sabatier.

Ricci (Rizi), Francisco (1608-85). Spanish painter of Madrid. Son of the Bolognese painter Antonio, brother of Fray Juan and pupil of Carducho. He developed a rapid Baroque style of decoration and was much employed by Carlos II, who named him Painter to the King. He was renowned for his mastery of architectural perspective. He frescoed the vaults of the Cathedral of Toledo.

Ricci (Rizi), Fray Juan Andrés (1600-81). Spanish painter and writer. Son of the Bolognese painter Antonio Ricci, brother of Francisco and pupil of Maino. His religious fervor led to the writing of a treatise on the Immaculate Conception and to his entering the Benedictine Order. He painted mainly for the great monasteries, his best-known cycle being that at San Millán de la Cogolla. His style is reminiscent of several contemporaries besides Maino: Zurbarán, Espinosa and Velázquez. In addition to religious works he executed portraits, among them Don Tiburcio de Redín (Prado). He wrote and illustrated a treatise on painting, *Pintura Sabia,* which contains drawings of nudes, a rare subject in Spanish art.

Ricci, Marco (1676-1729). Venetian landscape and marine painter, nephew, student, and collaborator of Sebastiano, for whom he painted landscapes. Born in Belluno, he was active mostly in Venice but also in England with his uncle (1708-16). His art, which is the basis for eighteenth-century Venetian landscape painting, shows the influence of Rosa, Magnasco, and the Flemings.

Ricci, Sebastiano (1659-1734). Venetian painter born in Belluno, his art forms the link between the great Venetian decorators of the High Renaissance and Tiepolo, from the dark manner of the Baroque to the light of the Rococo. He helped spread the Venetian Baroque to Bologna, Florence, Rome, Emilia, and Lombardy, and at the height of his fame was called to work in Germany, Flanders, France, and England, helping to establish the Venetian over the French as the dominant decorative style. His early training was with Mazzoni and Cervelli in Venice, with dal Sole in Bologna, and he met and was influenced by Magnasco in Milan. He was the uncle and teacher of Marco Ricci.

Ricciarelli, Daniele (see VOLTERRA, DANIELE DA).

Richter, Ludwig (1823-1884). A German painter and engraver with Romantic leanings. He expressed himself best in sensitive landscapes of the area round Dresden, fresh and colorful projections of his native land. He also illustrated children's books.

Rigaud, Hyacinthe (1659-1743). French portrait painter whose work carries us from the elegance of the period of Louis XIV to the Rococo (see) of Louis XV. He won the favor of Charles Le Brun, artistic dictator under Louis XIV, and was awarded the Prix de Rome in 1685. But he stayed on in Paris, becoming one of the leading portrait painters of the upper classes and intellectuals. His portrait of Louis XIV as an old man combines a sense of psychological values with a feeling for the dignity and importance of the sitter. Rigaud has also left us a gallery of the artists and writers of the time: La Fontaine, Boileau, Racine, Bossuet, and many others—all done with admirable penetration and a feeling for the richness of clothes and other accessories.

Rijksmuseum, Amsterdam. The world's richest repository of Dutch art. Among its treasures is the famous Night Watch of Rembrandt.

Rincón, Fernande del (d. after 1517). Spanish painter

RIVERA. Scavenger. Earlham College, Richmond, Indiana

of Guadalajara. Apparently the artist who, referred to as "Antonio," was described by early chroniclers as having first embraced the Renaissance style in Spain.

Ringling Museum of Art, Sarasota, Fla. The John and Mabel Ringling Museum, although one of the newer institutions in the United States, is already among the more select collections of traditional painting in the country. It contains works by Rembrandt, Rubens, van Dyck, Hals, El Greco, Gainsborough, Murillo, Tintoretto, Velázquez and others.

Rippi-Ronai, Josef (1861-1927). Leading Hungarian modernist who was friendly with the outstanding artists of the end of the nineteenth century in Paris: Bonnard, Vuillard, Cézanne, Denis and Gauguin. Through these contacts he developed a flat, decorative and colorful style consistent with the Post-Impressionism of that day. On his return to Hungary he found his art too "advanced" and turned to a simple narrative realism and a semi-philosophical tone.

Rivera, Diego (1886-). A leading Mexican easel painter, muralist and graphic artist. His artistic background was, first, the Academy of San Carlos and the exciting graphics of Posada. He traveled widely in Europe, 1907-21, and was associated in Paris with Derain, Braque, Klee, Picasso and Gris; as a result, his early work was Cubist. He returned to Mexico in 1922 to participate in the growing artistic revolution. Between 1922 and 1930 he did encaustic murals in the National Preparatory School and frescoes in the Ministry of Education, in the Chapel at Chapingo and in the Governor's Palace, Cuernavaca. In the United States, 1930-34, he did frescoes in San Francisco, Detroit and New York (the last, in Rockefeller Center, destroyed through disagreement with the sponsors). His later murals are in the Palace of Fine Arts in Mexico, the National Palace, Hotel del Prado, Institute of Cardiology, Lerma Waterworks, new University and Social Security Hospital, Mexico City. In 1949 an exhibition of fifty

172. RIBERA. St. Bartholomew. Kress Collection, New York

years of his work was held in the National Museum of Plastic Arts.

Rivera has been involved in Mexican and left-wing world politics throughout his career; he is also influential as a painter with many direct followers. The decorative simplicity of his large-scaled forms and the bold, clear color areas lend themselves to imitation as well as to a characteristic didactic and expository style. His mood in general is lyrical rather than emotional, with the accent on narrative facility and factual detail. Far from naive, he is an extremely sophisticated personality and an active political radical. His easel paintings show a similar linear quality, while the portraits tend toward the fashionable and superficial. One of the "Big Four" (Rivera, Orozco, Siqueiros and Tamayo), Rivera remains an outstanding force in Mexico's artistic revolution. His best work is perhaps the Chapingo mural. (See illustrations, including color plate 173.)

Riza-i-Abbasi (see PERSIAN PAINTERS: SAFAWID PERIOD).

Rizi (see RICCI).

Rizzi, Gian Pietro (see GIAMPIETRINO).

Robert, Hubert (1733-1808). French painter and architect. Called "Robert des Ruines," he not only painted genre subjects in ruined settings, but also supervised the construction of picturesque gardens in the romantic vein. His career started in Rome in the company of Fragonard (see) and the Abbé de Saint Non. Together they drew, etched and painted classical ruins generally Baroque in scale, romantic in conception, showing sundry peasants and beggars subsisting in the ruins of past imperial grandeur. Upon his return to Paris in 1765, Robert was an immediate success. He painted many decorative panels of ruined landscapes based on his Italian studies. In the 1770's he began to base his landscapes on French gardens, e.g., Marly and Versailles, and on the Roman ruins of Provence, viz., the Temple of Diana at Nîmes. At this time he was lodged in the Louvre and had been named designer of the King's gardens. In this capacity he could actually create in three dimensions that which he had long projected in his paintings. His drawings for the modification of the Louvre for public display of paintings are accompanied by renderings of the gallery in a ruined state. He was imprisoned during the Revolution, and we have amusing sketches of his life in prison; he was later restored to his official position. His output was enormous and included paintings of current events such as conflagrations. (See illustration.)

Robert, Leopold Louis (1794-1835). French painter, etcher, lithographer. Almost forgotten today, he was once famous for his paintings of Italian peasantry, such as The Return of the Pilgrimage to the Madonna dell' Arco (Louvre) in the Salon of 1827. He was a student of David and of Gros and went to Italy when David was exiled to Brussels. He was much imitated.

Robert-Fleury, Joseph Nicolas (1797-1890). French painter and lithographer. Member of a large artistic family and student of H. Vernet, Girodet and Gros. He specialized in subjects from French history painted in a romantic vein similar to that of popular novels of the day. His pictures tend to be fine documents, e.g., Christopher Columbus Received by Ferdinand and Isabella the Catholic (Louvre).

Roberti, Ercole (c.1450-96). One of the lesser members of the Ferrarese school, he was a pupil of Cosimo Tura and was further influenced by the important Paduan master Mantegna and the Venetian Bellini. He was active in Bologna from the mid-1470's to 1486, completing works left unfinished by Cossa at his death. The later years of his life were spent in Ferrara in the service of the Este family, acting as a travel escort as well as painter. His most important work is an altarpiece of the Madonna and Saints (1480-81) in the Brera. Only a handful of other works are undisputably by him. Stylistic elements in his art include linear modeling, some anatomical distortion, realism of detail, and the use of light for realistic purposes. (See illustration.)

Robinson, Boardman (1876-1952). American painter, illustrator, and cartoonist. Though he finally turned entirely to painting and achieved some reputation as a muralist, it is in his early work as a cartoonist that he best expressed himself. Born in Nova Scotia, he attended the Massachusetts Normal Art School before going abroad to study at the

ROBERT, HUBERT. The Fountains. Art Institute of Chicago

173. RIVERA. Making a Motor (detail). Detroit Institute of Arts

Ecole des Beaux-Arts and the Académie Colarossi. Influenced by the art of Michelangelo, Forain, and Daumier, he worked in San Francisco and New York as an illustrator and then as a cartoonist in New York for the *Morning Telegraph* and the *Tribune*. In 1914 he went abroad with John Reed for the *Metropolitan Magazine*, and later did cartoons for the *Masses* and *Liberator* as well as illustrations for *Harper's Weekly*. From 1922 on he confined himself to illustration, painting, and teaching. In 1929 he executed a mural series, The History of Commerce, for the Kaufman Department Store, Pittsburgh, and later Man and His Toys for the R. C. A. building, New York. He was an important figure in the development of political cartooning and his style of bold realistic drawing and heroic form set a new standard and had many followers. His paintings and murals tend to formalization and are rather dry and uninspired. (See illustration.)

Robinson, Theodore (1852-96). American Impressionist landscape painter. Born in Vermont, he studied in Paris with Carolus-Duran and Gérôme (1876-78), traveled in Italy (1878-79), and from 1884 to 1892 lived largely in France. In 1888 at Giverny he met and became friendly with Monet which led to his practice and espousal of Impressionism.

rococo painting. A style referring to eighteenth-century France; it ultimately spread to all parts of Europe. It is characterized by charming, colorful costumes, animated surfaces and gracious movements; it deals generally with the lighter aspects of court life, which it ornaments with delicate gestures, highly detailed ornaments, artifical manners and a general sense of makebelieve. One of its chief preoccupations is with love. This rococo expression ranges from the sensitive and poetic imagery, the light theatricalism of Watteau at the very beginning of the century through the somewhat vulgarized and fleshy nudes of Boucher toward the middle of the century and finally to the sentimentalized, partly aristocratic, partly middle-class renditions of Fragonard during the third quarter of the same century.

ROBERTI. A Concert. National Gallery, London

Rodchenko, Alexander (1891-). Russian constructivist painter and industrial designer. He made his first non-objective (see) works in 1914 with the aid of a compass and a ruler. During the years 1915 to 1920 he was a leader in the Russian side of the non-objective movement, moving on to Constructivism (see) in the years 1917-22. Thereafter he turned to various kinds of "useful" art activities such as typography furniture design, posters, theater design. Essentially his kind of non-objective art is closely related to the Constructivist approach in which geometrical forms, both round and angular, are overlaid in a limited three-dimensional fashion.

Rodin, Auguste (1840-1917). Perhaps the outstanding French sculptor of the nineteenth century and an important predecessor of many later movements in sculpture, he also left a number of sensitive tinted drawings, many of them for an unrealized project, the so-called Porte de l'Enfer (The Gate of Hell). These drawings show an abstraction of form that may well be compared with that of many artists in our time, a feeling for light and dark values and an almost supernally delicate handling of line.

Rodrigo de Osona (active 1476-1513). The name of two Spanish painters of Valencia, father and son. Theirs was the busiest and most important workshop of Valencia in their day. Their style is a local blend of Flemish and Italian Renaissance, as can be seen in the fragments of the altarpiece of St. Dionysius (ascribed to the son), painted for the Cathedral of Valencia.

Rodríguez Lozano, Manuel (1896-). A Mexican painter of cosmopolitan background. Influenced by the classical phase of Picasso's painting in the 1920's, he specializes in sharply delineated, cleanly colored forms generally mystical in spirit. He has published monographs on Tarascan culture and colonial imagery.

Rohlfs, Cristian (1849-1938). German Expressionist painter and graphic artist. Son of a poor farmer, young Rohlfs broke his leg at the age of fifteen and during a long convalescence began to draw. His physician sent some of these drawings to the poet Theodor Storm and on the latter's advice Rohlfs began to study art seriously; he studied first in Berlin and then in Weimar, where he spent almost thirty years. He began as a Romantic landscapist but turned soon after to the Impressionism that was to affect German painting so greatly. In 1901 he was called to the Drawing School of the Folkwang Museum at Hagen; there he underwent the influence of the Pointillists and Van Gogh. From 1905 to 1906 he did his mystical, space-piercing Soest pictures. His art then turned to the angular forms, large color areas and grotesque themes for which he was thenceforth known. He began to use tempera and then watercolor for the transparent effects he wished to achieve. In 1949 he was posthumously named an "honorary citizen" of Hagen, and Barlach's sculpture, Christ Teaching, was put on his grave. (See illustration.)

Romanelli, Giovanni Francesco (c.1610-62). Italian decorative painter in the Roman classical phase of the Baroque. He was born and active in Viterbo, and in Rome in the circle of Sacchi. He studied with Domenichino and Cortona and worked with the latter. He was encouraged to break from him by Bernini, through whose influence he received many important commissions. He did tapestry cartoons for the Vatican (1637-41), in the manner of Raphael, and decorated the gallery of Cardinal Mazarin's palace (1646-48) and Anne of Austria's summer residence (1655-57), both in Paris.

Romanesque painting. The eleventh and twelfth centuries in Europe witnessed an efflorescence of monumental wall painting in addition to an increased output of illuminated books (see ILLUMINATED MANUSCRIPTS). The concentration on mural painting parallels the development of large stone churches and the emergence of figure sculpture in that period. This painting is, like other arts of the period, noted for the distinctive regional types that exist together within the generally recognizable style of "Romanesque."

The origins of the style were several. Church interiors had been continously painted throughout Christian times, although few examples exist from the two centuries following the establishment of the barbarian kingdoms in the sixth century. Our knowledge of that period is dependent almost exclusively on manuscripts of Saxon, Carolingian, Ottonian and other kingdoms. These localized traditions began to interact upon each other and to be influenced by Byzantine art of the

ROBINSON, BOARDMAN. The Club
Whitney Museum of American Art, New York

ROHLFS. Two Heads. Detroit Institute of Arts

East during the tenth to twelfth centuries. The establishment of Western control of sea and land routes contributed to this as did the cultural interrelationships which resulted from pilgrimage routes and Crusades. But most potent force was the Cluniac reform of the far-flung Benedictine order with its emphasis on pictorial teaching aids and monumental images. These elements tended to internationalize the church's didactic art, but styles varied markedly from region to region. Italian painting of the Romanesque period was strongly Byzantine in character, as seen in the lower church of S. Clemente, Rome. In Germany the tradition of the Ottonian Emperors (see ILLUMINATED MANUSCRIPTS), which had produced much fresco work, continued into the mature Romanesque period. It followed the Ottonian tendencies toward strong Northern expressionism or toward rigid Byzantine ensembles like Schwarzrheindorf. France produced a variety of styles in painting as in architecture, the best known being that of the vaults of Saint-Savin. England has lost most of her murals of this epoch, and surviving works suggest that the Normans were not impressive painters. The best English frescoes are late and already somewhat Gothic in form.

Spain is our richest source of Romanesque frescoes, although most of the extant work was probably provincial. In the Catalan school alone we detect Byzantine, Benedictine and south French influences. These influences, however, added up to a coherent style, quite representative of Romanesque thinking. We can compare, for instance, the Romanesque apse painting of San Clemente de Tahull with the contemporary Byzantine apse mosaic of Cefalù in Sicily. Both represent Christ as Pantokrator appearing in majesty above rows of saints. The Master of Tahull cared nothing for shimmering effects of gold and preciosity. His apse is firmly banded and bonded by stripes of color, architectural arcading and strong linear outlines. The banded background, however, competes in a playful way with the architectonic effect of the various inner forms. Linear play of draperies and bizarrely patterned faces eliminate any human feeling in the figures. The whole is a tense interplay of artistic elements, which enlivens the forms in a supraphysical way. Here is an ecstatic mood quite unlike the quiet dignity of the Byzantine images.

Romanino (Romani), Girolamo (1484/87-c.1562). Born in Brescia, he probably studied with Stefano Rizzi or Ferramola. His earlier style in the Lombard tradition was transformed by contact with the Venetians—Bellini, Titian, Giorgione, Lotto, and Pordenone. He had many students and assistants and was active in Brescia and its vicinity as well as Padua, Cremona, and Trento (1540). Together with Moretto and Savoldo he completes the triumvirate of Brescian painting of the early sixteenth century—forerunners of the Baroque.

Romano, Giulio (Giulio Pippi) (1499-1546). Born in Rome, he was the favorite pupil and assistant of Raphael and was influenced by Michelangelo. His style combines the Roman manner with Venetian color, which he probably absorbed from the Venetian painters then in Rome—Sebastiano del Piombo, Giovanni da Udine, and Battista Dossi. He assisted Raphael in the Stanze d'Eliodoro and dell' Incendio and possibly executed the Sala di Constantino from Raphael's designs after the latter's death. In Rome he also decorated the Villa Lante and built and decorated the Villa Madama. In 1524 he was called by Baldassare Castiglione to work for Federigo Gonzaga in Mantua, where as superintendent of buildings and decorations he transformed Mantua. He rebuilt and decorated the former stables into the Palazzo del Te with its illusionistic Sala dei Giganti (1526-34) and decorated the Palazzo Ducale (La Reggia) with scenes from the *Iliad* (1532-38). As a continuation of the classical stream of Raphael, his interest in antiquity and mythological landscape make him a forerunner of seventeenth-century classicism. An extremely popular artist in the sixteenth and seventeenth centuries, he is mentioned in Shakespeare's *Winter's Tale* (See illustration.)

Roman painting. Through discoveries of it made from time to time Roman painting has exerted considerable influence on later art. To begin with, it paralleled and contributed to Early Christian painting. Surviving examples must have influenced medieval artists occasionally by motif if not by spirit. Accidental discoveries during the Renaissance thrilled such antiquarians as Raphael and Poussin. The opening of Pompeii and Herculaneum (c.1750) contributed largely to the fad of Neo-Classicism in the late eighteenth century. Renoir appreciated the charm of Pompeian painting in the

ROMANO. The Infancy of Jupiter. National Gallery, London

ROMAN PAINTING, POMPEIIAN SCHOOL
Game of the Astragali. National Museum, Naples

late nineteenth century, but on the whole the subject has suffered during the past century from the narrow interests of iconographers and archaeologists. Its variety of expressive means is, however, bringing Roman painting back into popularity again today.

The Romans painted murals in tombs, temples and houses. Of temples we have nothing but literary information, such as the fact one Fabius Pictor, a Roman patrician, decorated the Temple of Salus in the late fourth century B.C. With tomb painting we are better provided, although we find the subject matter limited as in the Christian catacombs. It was in the mural decoration of private houses that the Romans provided the greatest display of styles and subjects, of such a variety as to enchant and puzzle us today. Many of these themes were translated into mosaic pavements, and new subjects were invented for that medium such as the Unswept Floor of Table Litter described by Pliny. The Roman was perhaps the greatest producer of stone mosaic (see). Book (codex) illustration appears to have been invented by Rome. Also several Italian cities continued the Greek manner of vase painting.

Of the early period in Italy we have only tomb paintings. Although not a Roman people, the Etruscans tell us most about early Italian taste. Their tombs at Corneto, for instance. stretch from the sixth to the second century B.C. At first they show increasing Greek influence, culminating in the fifth century when tomb interiors were adorned with Greek vases. These early tombs showed scenes of daily life; hunting, banquets and games, but from the late fifth Century, perhaps owing to the infuence of Orphic rites, Etruscan painting (see) depicted the horrors of the underworld. In the years of Etruscan decline, Italian painting style can be traced in the tombs of other tribes in South Italy. The Ruvo tomb of the fifth century B.C. shows a distinctly Greek linear style and the Lucanian tombs of Paestum (late fourth century) show more advanced modeling. The Romans also appear to have relied heavily on Greek artists; virtually the only names recorded are Greek. It would appear that when the local Roman style developed its unique character in the early Imperial period, it was the custom for Roman painters to work anonymously.

Our main evidence for Roman secular painting comes from the towns of Campania—Pompeii, Herculaneum and Stabiae, which were buried by the eruption of Vesuvius in 79 A.D. This catastrophe preserved their paintings, unlike those in Rome, where few house murals have been recovered by excavation. In Rome, however, there exists the vast material of the catacombs and other underground tombs. (See EARLY CHRISTIAN PAINTING.) We discover from the evidence of Campania and Rome that Roman mural painting went through a series of distinct styles. In the second century B.C. it was customary to decorate walls in the Greek manner of a stucco bas-relief which imitated masonry by simulated blocks of various colors and occasional painted columns (Masonry Style: I). During the first century B.C. the flat masonry wall gave way to a stately architectural illusion with landscape or figure action introduced (Architectural Style: II); examples of this are the Odyssey Landscapes (Rome) or the Villa of the Mysteries (Pompeii). During the Augustan period the painted architecture became frail and was ornamented with Egyptian elements. The wall effect flattened in some cases to delicate geometrical panels (Ornate Style: III). An example is the house of M. Lucretius Fronte, Pompeii. By the mid-first century A.D. the walls opened again in extreme Baroque illusionism and inserted landscape panels took on a comparable fantastic, airy quality with impressionistic detail (Intricate Style: IV). This can be observed in the stucco work of the Stabian Baths or in the panel of the Trojan Horse (Pompeii). Subsequent development is not clear because remains are so fragmentary, even in Rome. Perhaps there was a cyclical alternation of Styles III and IV; but there is much to suggest that different styles were practiced concurrently in Italy. There seems to have been an ever-present dichotomy of statuesque Greek and popular impressionistic Roman styles. This can also be observed later in Early Christian and Carolingian times.

The technique employed by Roman painters is not clearly understood today. Fresco, tempera and encaustic were all practiced, sometimes in combination. Subjects ranged widely, including themes from the epics, from ritual, from the theater and from everyday life. Landscapes, portraits, still lifes and

ROMAN PAINTING, POMPEIIAN SCHOOL
Detail from the House of the Vetii. Pompeii

decorative garden scenes are all to be found upon the walls of Campania. (See illustrations.)

Roman school. An Italian pictorial tradition beginning in the thirteenth century with the Byzantine conservatism of Jacopo Torriti and moving on to the solid forms and more overt emotions of Pietro Cavallini in the early fourteenth century. During the fifteenth century the Roman school was circumscribed by the efforts of the Papacy to end the Great Schism. The only painter of importance then was Antoniazzo Romano, whose style is sentimentally Umbrian. Roman painting reaches its height during the early sixteenth century under papal stimulation and patronage with the work of the great masters Raphael and Michelangelo; in them the idealizing and monumentalizing tendencies of the Roman school achieve their greatest effects.

Romanticism. A type of expression in art that emphasizes the personal and rebellious, the rejection of one's environment in favor of something far away in time or space. It may be expressed through the projection of a scene in nature in which the artist uses landscape as a vehicle for his own emotions, e.g., those of Théodore Rousseau and J. M. W. Turner, or through a scene in which the artist tries to evoke the sympathy of the audience for the suffering of his characters or of the artist himself, as in Géricault. It may also deal with so-called escapist material in which the artist seeks out a narrative from a remote era or from some far-off place such as the Near East, as Delacroix often did. Finally, it may have the protest element which involves the artist in a violent revolt against authority or a condemnation of oppression, as in Géricault's Raft of the Medusa, Delacroix's Massacre at Scio or Daumier's Uprising. In both art and literature the Romantic movement is associated with the early nineteenth century, although its origins are to be found in the late eighteenth-century culture of Germany and England whence it moved to France. Made famous by French painters, writers and musicians as well as by those from Britain and Germany, the movement gradually appears elsewhere. In the United States it occurs in the painting of the Hudson River school (see). Later in the nineteenth century it reappears in a new phase in the historical plays of Rostand. Its twentieth-century form is best illustrated in the work of the painters associated with Neo-Romanticism (see).

Rombouts, Theodor (1597-1637). Flemish painter and engraver. Originally a follower and perhaps a pupil of Abraham Janssens, he went in 1616 to Italy and returned as a Caravaggesque painter, as can be seen in the Card Players (Antwerp). By 1630 he was under the influence of Rubens, whom he believed he excelled. He was a prolific painter and had many pupils.

Romero de Torres, Julio (1880-1930). Modern Spanish figure and portrait painter. At first an Impressionist, he turned under Pre-Raphaelite influence to interpreting the spirit of his native Cordoba by means of a suave melancholic chiaroscuro. He became notorious for his sensual studies of women in this style. He was a success from the Salon of 1907, and the "gitana" (gypsy) became a stereotype with him.

Romney, George (1734-1802). British portraitist who imitated Reynold's pictorial effects, became popular in his own right and was financially very successful. After his Italian sojourn, 1773-75, he reached as high a level of social patronage as had Reynolds and Gainsborough. He often painted Lady Hamilton and used her as a model for the semi-classical subjects so popular at the time. Like Gainsborough, Romney idealized his sitters while trying to retain a likeness; and he very often represented his ladies in allegorical pictures, e.g., as Beauty, Truth, Virtue, etc., in the fashion set by Reynolds. (See color plate 174.)

Roos, Johann Heinrich (1631-85). German painter of

174. ROMNEY. Portrait of the Willett Children
Philadelphia Museum of Art, Elkins Collection

portraits, landscapes and animal pictures. He studied in Amsterdam with Dujardin. In 1664 he became court painter to Ludwig of the Palatinate in Heidelberg and worked also at the courts in Mainz and Cassel. He is known for his landscapes of the admired Italian type, showing flocks and classical ruins, touched with romantic golden light.

Rops, Félicien (1833-1898). Belgian painter and printmaker. In 1856 he founded the satirical journal *Uylenspiegel* to which he contributed his incisive political and satirical drawings. He moved to Paris in 1874 to become one of its leading illustrators. He painted in both a linear anecdotal style and in the Impressionism of his day, the former more significant in its revelation of the neurosis of his epoch, since it was used for his more critical works.

Rosa, Salvator (1615-73). Neapolitan painter, engraver, poet, musician, and actor. He expressed his flamboyant romantic temperament in dramatic landscapes and battle scenes, establishing a wild picaresque mode with its own vocabulary of unkempt natural settings peopled by saints and banditti, as opposed to the idylic classicism of Claude and Poussin; he had an abiding effect upon the development of romanticism even into the twentieth century. Born in Arenella near Naples, he studied first with an uncle, A. D. Greco, and a brother-in-law, F. Francanzano. He may have also studied with Ribera, whose influence he shows; but he very soon turned to landscape painting (in which he was self-taught), doing scenes around Naples. In 1635 he came to Rome for the first time, and after returning briefly to Naples, he was back in Rome in 1639, and there achieved a reputation as poet and actor. He found Florence more congenial during the next decade, and from 1640 to 1649 his house in Florence, the Accademia dei Percossi, was a literary and artistic center. He returned to Rome in 1649 and spent the rest of his life there. (See illustration.)

Rosai, Ottone (1895-). Italian painter active in the Futurist movement before World War I; later active in the magazine *L'Universale* while moving toward a more figurative

ROSA. Soldiers in a Ravine
Isaac Delgado Museum of Art, Kress Collection, New Orleans

style. He is concerned with the problems of the poor of Florence, rendering them with humorous warmth and a somewhat Impressionist color.

Rose, Herman (1909-). Contemporary American realist painter, mostly of landscapes. Influenced by Impressionism but especially Vuillard, he paints lyrical scenes of Brooklyn streets and Manhattan roofs and walls. Born in Brooklyn, he studied at the National Academy of Design (1926-29).

Rosenthal, Doris. Contemporary American genre painter, best known for her colorful and sympathetic studies of Mexico. Born in California, she studied at Columbia University and at the Art Students League with Bellows and Sloan.

Roslin, Alexandre Charles (1718-93). Swedish portrait painter active in France in the time of Louis XVI. After travel in Germany and Italy he first came to France in 1747 or 1748, where he was a popular painter of ladies. After the death of his French wife, also a painter, he returned to Sweden. Later he worked in Russia and then returned to live the rest of his life in Paris.

Rosselli, Cosimo (1439-1507). A somewhat eclectic Florentine painter of narrative frescoes and altarpieces; he was trained in the shop of Neri di Bicci. His early work is related to Castagno, and more closely to Benozzo Gozzoli. He executed a number of fresco and altar commissions which are now lost, and his first extant dated work (1471) is a Madonna and Child with St. Anne (Berlin). In 1481 he contracted, along with Perugino, Ghirlandaio and Botticelli to paint part of the wall decoration of the Sistine Chapel and did three sections with the help of his pupil Piero di Cosimo: the Sermon on the Mount, the Story of Moses, and the Last Supper. The influence of the colleagues he worked with in Rome is seen in the fresco of the Miracle of the Sacrament (1485-86) in Sant' Ambrogio, Florence, as well as in other late works. Besides Piero di Cosimo he had Fra Bartolommeo as a pupil. (See illustration.)

Rosselli, Matteo (1578-1650). Florentine painter but more important as a teacher. He studied with Gregorio Pagani in Florence and with Passignano in Rome. His retarded style was a carry-over into the middle of the century of the transition from Mannerism (see) and the early Baroque (see). Among his many students were Lorenzo Lippi, Vignali, Furini, Manozzi, and Franceschini.

Rossetti, Dante Gabriel (1828-1882). British painter and founding member of the Pre-Raphaelite Brotherhood (see). At first he was preoccupied with two-dimensional patterns and glowing color effects. He produced a series of watercolors of symbolic intent but medievalistic affectation in the Romantic manner. Here and in many canvases he offers such themes as Arthur's Tomb, How They Met Themselves, The Blessed Beatrice, Dante's Dream and other Pre-Raphaelite favorites. In 1857-58 with the assistance of Burne-Jones and others, he decorated the Library of the Oxford Union, a disastrous failure because of unsound technical methods. His paintings and drawings were much imitated but without any permanent or meaningful result. He is the author of The Blessed Damozel and other famous poems, many of them inspired by medieval themes and forms. (See illustration.)

Rossi, Francesco di' (see SALVIATI, FRANCESCO).

Rosso, Il (Giovanni Battista di Jacopo, Giovanni Battista dei Rossi, called also Rosso Fiorentino) (1494-1540). Florentine Mannerist (see) painter. His early work was dominated by the High Renaissance style of his teacher, Andrea del Sarto, and of Fra Bartolommeo, but the influence of Michelangelo led him to the development of a violent anti-classical manner. He was more radical, extravagant, and powerful than Pontormo and much more influential in the spread of Mannerism. His compositions are marked by confusion and spatial

ROSSELLI, COSIMO. Madonna and Child with Angels
Metropolitan Museum of Art, New York

ROSSETTI. Fazio's Mistress. Tate Gallery, London

ambiguity, his figures exaggerated, his color dissonant, iridescent, and at times oversweet. In his hands the grandeur of Michelangelo is transformed into brutal distortion. He was active in Florence until 1523 except for a visit to Volterra to paint a Descent from the Cross. He then moved to Rome, where he worked until the sack of the city in 1527 and where his style was influenced by Roman decorative art. After that he was active in Umbria, at Città di Castello and Arezzo, and in Venice. In 1530 he was called to France by Francis I to decorate Fontainebleau and was joined there a few years later by Primaticcio. There in the Salle François I he established Italian Mannerism as the basis of the so-called Fontainebleau style, the beginning of Northern Mannerism. He continued to work in France until the time of his violent death in Paris. Typical of his work are the Daughters of Jethro (Uffizi), which was done during the Roman period and is one of his most radical paintings, and the Pietà (Louvre), which was done in the late 1530's for the Constable of Montmorency and is more restrained and deeper in feeling.

Rothenstein, William (1872-1945). A British portraitist. He studied at the Slade School and in Paris. In 1917 he became Professor of Civic Art at the University of Sheffield and from 1920-35 was Principal, Royal College of Art. For a brief period of revolt Rothenstein, like many other late nineteenth-century figures, thought of himself as carrying on the Whistler tradition, e.g., in his The Doll's House of 1899, but he soon found his level as a portrait painter of such personalities as Bernard Berenson and Sir Rabindranath Tagore. These are notable for their precise and effective draughtsmanship. His son is the noted critic Sir John Rothenstein, the director of the Tate Gallery since 1938.

Rothko, Mark (1903-). Contemporary American non-objective painter. He creates canvases of large horizontal bands of thinned pigment. Born in Russia, he came to the U.S. in 1913, spent his youth in Portland, Ore., attended Yale, studied with Max Weber at the Art Students League, and worked on the W.P.A. His earlier work was Expressionist, but he turned to abstraction about 1939.

Rottenhammer the Elder, Hans (1564-1625). A German painter. The early part of his life was spent in long sojourns in Italy, at first in Rome, where he came in contact with the international circle of painters, including Jan Brueghel and Paul Brill, and afterward in Venice. Returning to Augsburg he made many wall and ceiling decorations. His mythological paintings show an elegant classicism reminiscent of the Italian artists of the early Baroque.

rotulus. A handwritten scroll, either with or without illustrations, and presumably the earliest form of book. It may be constrasted with the later codex which is similar in arrangement to the modern book.

Rouault, Georges (1871-). Distinguished French painter and graphic artist, an original member of the Fauve group (see) and perhaps the outstanding Expressionist of his country. Born in Paris, Rouault was apprenticed to a maker of stained glass in 1885, studying evenings at the School for Decorative Arts. In Gustave Moreau's class at the Beaux-Arts he won a prize with a series of religious subjects; there also he met Matisse. Moreau died in 1898 and Rouault was appointed curator of the Moreau Museum at a tiny salary. He then went through a spiritual crisis and was drawn, in one way, toward those artists who became the Fauves, while at the same time his spiritual background drew him equally to the poor and miserable. He exhibited in the first Autumn Salon in 1903 and with the Fauves in 1905. By 1911 his social subjects emerge: working people, farmers, family groups, always in the somber tonalities and the distorted forms that are the measure of his own anguish.

While the earlier paintings are marked by a sketchy Expressionism (see) like that of many contemporary Germans and Austrians (e.g., Kokoschka), Rouault soon turned toward a kind of grandiosely expressive and heavy form akin to the works of the middle ages, by whose spirit many of his works seem to be inspired. On the one hand, the textures suggest

ROUAULT. Nazareth. Museum of Fine Art, Ghent

175. ROUALT. Wounded Clown. Collection Mr. and Mrs. Keith Warner, Norwich, Vermont

enamel work; on the other hand, the contours of heavy black lines suggest the stained glass of the painter's early youth. The forms themselves have a rugged primitivistic quality recalling Romanesque sculpture. But over all there hovers a genuinely sympathetic and humane spirit, the spirit of a painter who in Expressionist fashion identifies himself with the sufferings of mankind. (See illustrations, including color plate 175.)

Roublew (Rublev, Rubljoff), Andrei (c.1365-c.1429). Russian icon and fresco painter. He was famous for establishing a new manner of modeling and linear silhouette. His style was comparable to the Paleologan fashion of contemporary Byzantium, while still retaining the charm of Russian stylization. His artistic origins are uncertain. He was active mainly in Moscow, where his surviving masterpiece, the Trinity of c.1425, is still to be found in the national museum.

Rouen Cathedral by Claude Monet (see).

Rousseau, Henri (1844-1910). Best known of the French primitives or untaught painters. In 1868 he served in the expedition to keep Maximilian on the throne of Mexico, the following year becoming a minor customs official, whence his ninckname Le Douanier, i.e., the customs officer. His first signed pictures come from 1880, and a few years later he was copying the Old Masters in the Louvre. In 1886 he began to show in the Indèpendants, a practice he followed until his death; and in this year he also resigned from the customs service. Rousseau soon met Gauguin, Redon, Seurat and Picasso and by 1891 was using exotic jungle backgrounds in his pictures, his style of that period summed up in his Sleeping Gypsy of 1897. Here he takes us into a fear-laden dream world where one is powerless to stop what is happening. As in a dream, things are seen with pitiless clarity, but the artist—no matter how much preoccupied with "the vivid trancelike immobility" of this world—paints a picture which he organizes, perhaps instinctively, into the limited space, rhythmic linear forms and bold color areas characteristic of the period. In 1906 Rousseau met Delaunay, Vlaminck, Picasso and such writers and critics as Max Jacob, Maurice Raynal, André Salmon and Guillaume Apollinaire. These men were all fond of him and able to appreciate the naturalness and spontaneity of his contribution. A high point of this relationship was the famous banquet given in his honor by Picasso in 1908. (See color plate 176.)

176. ROUSSEAU, HENRI
Liberty Inviting Artists to Take Part in the 22nd Exhibition of Independent Artists, 1906. Sidney Janis Gallery, New York

Rousseau, Théodore (1812-67). Leading painter of the French Barbizon school (see). He made his Salon debut in 1831 with a Landscape of Auvergne. He became interested in painting after nature in the manner of Constable and Bonington, to whom he was attracted in 1832. At about this time he became acquainted with Fontainebleau forest, on the outskirts of which, in Barbizon, he lived with others of his "school." For a period of twelve years he was so consistently rejected at Salons that he was known as "le grand Refusé." But by mid-century he was a success, and his group, which had done so much to popularize English and Dutch landscape, was laying the foundations of the Impressionist movement. His style is sincere and painstaking and marked by great exactitude of natural detail. (See illustration.)

Roussel, Ker Xavier (1867-1944). French painter and member of the Nabis (see) group who utilized small Impressionist strokes of clear unmixed paint for the purpose of emotionalizing and giving more poetic meaning to landscape. He used the mat, or low-keyed finish favored by the Nabis in the interests of decorative effects. He was a brother-in-law of Vuillard and friend of Denis, with whom he made a pilgrimage to Aix in 1906 to visit Cézanne. See also INTIMISM, SYMBOLISM.

Rowlandson, Thomas (1756-1827). One of the greatest British caricature-commentators; he was born in London and studied in Paris. He is noted for a prolific production of prints and drawings caricaturing the various abuses of his time and his many humorous comments on social life. He attracted attention with his Vauxhall Gardens, an elaborate composition showing numerous celebrities strolling through that famous place, and exhibited at the Academy in 1784. His types became more distorted as time went on, with certain recognizable characters soon emerging as constant factors. Rowlandson traveled all over Europe making sketches

ROUSSEAU, THEODORE. Outskirts of a Village
Philadelphia Museum of Art, Johnson Collection

ROWLANDSON. Gaming Table at Devonshire House
Metropolitan Museum of Art, New York

of what he saw. Sometimes he drew rural scenes showing luxuriant landscapes with figures of great vitality. In whatever he did there was a delicacy of pen drawing and a charming watercolor wash quality, but in his most original and least popular works he turned these talents to a gross, nightmarish conception of mankind, showing people with bestial expressions—his ultimate comment on his times. (See illustration.)

Roy, Pierre (1880-1950). French painter recognized as one of the pioneers and ancestors of Surrealism (see). Although without the alleged humor and/or cruelty frequently found among the figurative exponents of this mode, Roy is very much concerned with the subconscious, the projection into times past, and the association of objects from different levels that by their unexpected contrast give each other fresh meaning.

Royal Academy of Arts, Copenhagen. A general collection.

Rubenists. French painters of the seventeenth and eighteenth centuries who in opposition to the official Academy strictures against exuberant color allowed themselves to be influenced by the bold, warm color effects of Rubens. The latter's series dealing with the life of Marie de Médicis (done for her Luxembourg Palace) constituted a kind of unofficial academy for many later painters, e.g., Largillière, Rigaud, Watteau. Their opponents, who adhered to the strict line laid down by Poussin and the Academy in which form rather than color was glorified, are best represented by the official painter Le Brun. The latter are known as Poussinists.

Rubens, Peter Paul (1577-1640). A Flemish painter whose art is the epitome of the Baroque. His dramatic and courtly style dominates our conception of the seventeenth century, powerful, exuberant, sensuous and theatrical. He transformed men into gods, life into gorgeous pageantry, infusing all of matter with a transfigured animal vitality. He is at the same time the most complete exponent of the Jesuit Counter Reformation, the international painter of the Catholic courts of Europe. His art was so popular and his services so much in demand that he was forced to maintain a large studio and employ many assistants and collaborators including van Dyck, Velvet Brueghel, Snyders, De Vos, Wildens, and Lucas van Uden.

It is impossible in a limited space to encompass the life and prolific activity of this highly cultured, complex, and creative personality who expressed so profoundly certain aspects of his age and left such a mark on its culture. Born in Siegen, Westphalia, the son of a lawyer and official in exile, he lived in Cologne until he returned to Antwerp in 1589 after the death of his father. Here he received a classical education, served as page to a lady, and then in succession studied art with Tobias Verhaecht, Adam van Noort, and Otto van Veen. In 1598 he became a member of the Antwerp guild and in 1600 left for Italy where (except for a visit to Spain c.1603-05) he remained until 1608, traveling, studying, and working for Vincenzo Gonzaga, Duke of Mantua. On his return to Antwerp he became painter to Archduke Albert and to Isabella, established a large studio and married Isabella Brandt. After the death of his first wife in 1626 he served as a diplomat, undertaking several important missions to Spain and England. He married Helena Fourment in 1630, and died in his castle at Steen near Brussels.

The first period (1600-08) in Italy was one of study, an eclectic accumulation of influences from the antique and the older Italian masters—Michelangelo and Raphael, the Venetians, Correggio and Barocci—and his own contemporaries—the Carracci, Caravaggio and Cigoli. Of the works of this period the most important are the Triptych of Sta. Croce in Gerusalemme, Rome (1602, Chapel of Hospital, Grasse), the series of the Twelve Apostles (1603, Prado), and the Altarpiece of Sta. Trinità, Mantua (1605, now scattered). The second period (1609-14) covers the establishment of his studio and a turn from his earlier eclecticism to the development of an individual style; this style was characterized by a striving for unity in narrative action, simplicity and clarity of subject and figure, the establishment of an idealized and intensified classical figure type, and the bold, almost Caravaggesque handling of plasticity and light. The masterpieces of this period are the Erection of the Cross (1610) and especially the Descent from the Cross (1611-14), both in the Antwerp Cathedral. His mature third style (1614-22) exhibits a growing self-confidence, an increased integration and fluidity,

RUBENS. Helene Fourment. Mauritshuis, The Hague

RUBENS. Rape of Daughters of Leucippus
Alte Pinakothek, Munich

greater action and movement ending in a climax of twisting garlands of bodies. It is during this period that he executed many battle, hunt, and abduction scenes: Abduction of the Daughters of Leucippus (1615, Munich), Boreas and Orythia (1619-20, Vienna), Battle of the Amazons (1617, Munich), Lion Hunt (1617-18, Munich); as well as the Last Judgment (1616, Munich), and Fall of the Damned (1618-20, Munich). At the same time he undertook the first of his large decorative projects: the tapestry cycle of Deens Mus (1616-17, Liechtenstein Gallery, Vienna), the decoration of his own house (1616-20) and the thirty-nine paintings of the Church of the Jesuits, Antwerp (1620, burned in 1719, copies by De Wit).

His fourth period (1622-32), largely taken up with great international commissions, witnessed a profound change in style from plasticity to pictorialism. He produced the great cycle of the History of Marie de Médicis for the Luxembourg Palace (1622-24, Louvre), consisting of twenty-one gigantic compositions; the Constantine Tapestries for Louis XIII (1622-23); the Eucharist Tapestries for Archduchess Isabella (before 1628); the Henri IV cycle (1630, Uffizi); the Achilles Tapestries (after 1630); and the ceiling of Whitehall (1630-34, now ruined). His last years (1632-40) were spent in semi-retirement, but he continued to work on smaller, more intimate, and more personal projects. These last works show no decrease in his powers. Based on his copies of Titian in Spain (1628-29) and suffused by his love for the golden beauty of his young wife, his style became more coloristic, light, fluent, and richer than ever before. His production includes many love scenes, some thirty landscapes, and many portraits of his wife, himself, and family. Notable are the "Het Plesken" (Vienna), Venus Festival (Vienna), Garden of Love (1632-34, Dresden), the Flemish Kermess (1636, Louvre), and the Castle Steen (1635-40, London). (See illustrations, including color plate 177.)

Rubeus (see BERMEJO).

Ruelas (Ruela, Roelas, Roela), Juan de (1558/60-1625). Spanish painter of the school of Seville. He was important for introducing a painterly naturalism into his region, which had previously practiced a rather cold type of Roman Mannerism; as a result he is considered to be the founder of the Sevillian Baroque style. Born in Seville of Flemish extraction, he is supposed to have studied with the Titian school in Venice. Early works (1603), done in Olivares where he was a priest, deal with the Life of the Virgin. In 1616 in Madrid he was refused the vacant post of royal court painter. In 1619 he was working in the Cathedral of Seville, engaged in several paintings there. His late and most Baroque style is seen in the Martyrdom of St. Andrew (Seville).

Ruisdael, Jacob Isaacksz. van (1629-82). Dutch landscape painter and engraver. He was born in Haarlem, the son of a frame-maker and painter, and began to study painting under his uncle, the landscapist Salomon van Ruysdael. When he was about twenty-six he moved to Amsterdam, where he acquired citizenship and is also listed as a physician. He worked there for about thirty years, returning to Haarlem at the very end of his life, sick and impoverished. Cornelis Vroom and Jan van Goyen influenced his early pictures, which are for the most part views of the dunes and coastal waters. Shortly before he transferred to Amsterdam he made a journey into the eastern part of Holland, and began to incorporate the woods and higher country thereabouts in romantic landscapes full of surging rhythms and a passionate feeling for the wilder aspects of nature. The landscapes by Ruisdael that show pine woods and waterfalls were probably painted under the influence of Allart van Everdingen, who had traveled in Sweden and brought back in his pictures these Scandinavian elements. The small figures in Ruisdael's paintings

RUNGE. We Three (detail). Private Collection, Germany

177. RUBENS. Briseis Returned to Achilles. Detroit Institute of Arts

were supplied for him by such artists as Berchem, Adriaen van Ostade, Wouwermans and Lingelbach; the popular portrait painter Van der Helst also collaborated with him. Ruisdael trained Hobbema and these two, with de Koninck, are the most important representatives of the Dutch school of landscape painting in the seventeenth century. (See color plate 178.)

Runge, Philipp Otto (1777-1810). A German painter and theoretician who was very much concerned with the theory of color. His art was dominated for a long time by the Neo-Classical attitude of that day, but he later turned toward a more naturalistic viewpoint. (See illustration.)

RUSIÑOL Y PRATS. Calvario at Sagunto
Hispanic Society of America, New York

Rusiñol y Prats, Santiago (1861-1931). A Catalan painter, poet and critic. Wealthy, talented and of colorful personality, Rusinol was an associate and inspiration of the avant garde Spanish movements of 1890-1910. His paintings, Impressionist in technique, are primarily of Spanish gardens treated in a nostalgic, symbolic fashion typical of the writers of "'98." e.g., Jardín de Mallorca. In his villa "Lo Cau Ferrat" he collected the works of his contemporaries and he was one of the first to purchase El Grecos. He was a founder of the Catalan group of "IV Gats," and he frequently contributed his artistic impressions in essays to the periodical *La Vanguardia*. Much of his writing was satiric; he also produced plays of a colorful, comic character. (See illustration.)

Ruskin, John (1819-1900). A British author and critic best known for the many-volumed work *Modern Painters,* 1843-60. This project, which began as a defense of Turner's painting, broadened out to include the idea that all art is the expression of national integrity and morality. With the publication of his *Seven Lamps of Architecture* in 1849 it was clear that in Ruskin England had a major critical force, a dictatorial authority whose power was now exerted in behalf of the Pre-Raphaelite (see) painters. His 1857 work, *The Political Economy* of Art, and a number of subsequent books were directed against the pervasive mercantile spirit of the times. A positive answer to this spirit was offered in his *Sesame and Lilies,* 1865. In 1870 he became the first university professor of art. His mental breakdown in 1878 removed him from the critical scene.

178. RUISDAEL, JACOB VAN. The Cemetery. Detroit Institute of Arts

Russell, John (1745-1806). British pastel painter who studied at the Royal Academy and became an R.A. in 1788. He was portrait painter to George III and the Prince of Wales. He did miniatures and crayon and oil portraits, many of which were engraved.

Russell, Morgan (1886-1953). American abstract painter who, together with Stanton Macdonald-Wright originated Synchromism (see). Born in the Mid-West, he studied with Henri in New York and went to Paris in 1906. His first efforts at Synchromism took place in 1912 and the first Synchromist painting was exhibited in the Salon des Indépendants in 1913. He and Macdonald-Wright exhibited the same year in Munich in June and in Paris in November, when his first completely non-objective painting was shown. He was included in the Armory Show. He returned to representational painting in 1919; he continued to work in France until 1946, when he returned to Broomall, Pa. (See illustration.)

Russian icon painting. The icon in Russia was a religious panel painting of peculiar importance (see icon). Orthodox painters had to present their subjects in the manner prescribed by the Church, and as compositional design was invariable, their only fields for interpretive expression were mood, line and color. The precise nature of the icon was well established in the Greek Orthodox Church long before Russia was christianized. Russian icons date after the conversion of Vladimir in 988, at which time he presumably brought to Kiev a number of Byzantine examples. The earliest such import still surviving is Our Lady of Vladimir (Trejiakoff Gallery, Moscow), which had a strong influence on Russian painting after its arrival in Kiev from Constantinople in the twelfth century. Pre-Mongol icons of Kiev seem to have been intended for processional use as well as for church decoration; some examples copy the set Byzantine types, others are freer and more vernacular in character. Novgorod, between the thirteenth and sixteenth centuries, produced a

179. RYDER. Toilers of the Sea.
Addison Gallery of American Art, Andover

RUSSELL, MORGAN. Four Part Synchromy, Number 7
Whitney Museum of American Art, New York

wealth of icons. The manner was a strongly stylized one of much expressive power, as seen in the St. Elias of the fourteenth century. Towards the end of this century Novgorod expanded the iconostasis (see BYZANTINE PAINTING) from its low chancel size of Justinian's time to the high elaborate screen of the modern Orthodox church, on which icons of set subjects were arranged in standard patterns. At the same time appeared Theophanes the Greek, first of a succession of three great Russian icon painters. He carried the Novgorod tradition to Moscow (in 1395). He was followed by Andrei Roublew (see) and Dionysius (active c.1500). The latter reflected the late Byzantine manner. In the Muscovite period Western influences complicated the style of icons. Outstanding traditions were those of the Palace of Arms workshops (from c.1550), the Stroganov workshop (c.1580-c.1620) and Ssemjon Ushakov (1626-86).

Russolo, Luigi (1885-). Italian painter and original member of the group that followed Futurism (see) in 1910. He supported the movement both as painter and musician. For the latter purpose he invented a sound-machine with which the operator could produce a series of scratching, thumping and clanking noises representing the machine-like cacophony that his group deemed desirable. His painting is typical of the movement with its interpenetration of planes, lines of force and its general sense of dynamic movement.

Ruysdael, Jacob (see RUISDAEL).

Ruysdael, Salomon van (c.1602-70). Dutch painter of landscapes, marine scenes and still life. The name of his teacher is not known but Jan van Goyen and Esaias van de Velde certainly exerted an influence on his style. As a young man he was already established in Haarlem and was a highly respected member of the community and one of the heads of the school of landscape painting that flourished there. Salomon van Ruysdael seems to have traveled extensively through Holland and his views are always full of interest and appeal. They exhibit more variety in color and composition than those of van Goyen and at the same time are not so grandiose and ambitious as those by his more famous nephew, Jacob van Ruisdael, who was also his pupil. (See illustration.)

Ryckaert, David (c.1612-61). Flemish genre painter. Pupil of his father who bore the same name and painted landscapes. Ryckaert started out as a landscape painter, too, but turned increasingly to genre, which he rendered in the popular manners of Jordaens, Teniers and Brouwer. In later life he changed from the Dutch type to the warmer tones and colorism of the Flemish. (See illustration.)

Ryder, Albert Pinkham (1847-1917). American Romantic painter. An eccentric and recluse who lived in a debris-littered room in a New York tenement, he produced in his lifetime some 150 small paintings—poetic revelations of a mystical vision. He worked on his paintings for long periods of time, revising, repainting until they were heavy with enamel-like color, so that many of them are today in extremely bad condition. His subjects are mainly divided between free interpretations of romantic literary themes and moonlit seascapes (such as Toilers of the Sea) and landscapes. He is most famous for the rich and luminous quality of his pigment, the simple grandeur of his design, and the aura of romantic mystery which envelops his symbolic statements of man's lonely struggle against the forces of nature. Though he is the most original and individualistic of the nineteenth-century American Romantics, he belongs to the general poetic tonalist movement of the time. Born in New Bedford, Mass., he evinced an early interest in art and when his family moved to New York City (c.1868) he studied briefly with William E. Marshall and at the National Academy of Design. He was abroad several times but for brief periods. Though he worked almost entirely in seclusion, his art was not unknown or unappreciated. After his death, the rarity of his works led to growing market values and eventually to the production of fakes, and the problem of authentication. (See color plate 179.)

Rysselberghe, Théo van (1862-1926). Belgian painter who introduced French Neo-Impressionism (see) into Belgium. He went to Paris with his friend, the poet Emile Verhaeren, and there fell under the influence of Seurat. He was one of the few Belgians who gave himself wholeheartedly to the new Pointillist technique but with the significant differ-

RUYSDAEL, SALOMON. Dutch River with Church
Mauritshuis, the Hague

RYCKAERT THE YOUNGER, DAVID. In Wartime
Musée Royal des Beaux-Arts, Antwerp

ence that he injected psychological qualities into his work, e.g., The Poetry Reading, 1903. He was also interested in the revival of the decorative arts in Belgium and designed furniture, jewelry, posters and books in the Art Nouveau style (see) led by Henri Vandevelde. (See illustration.)

S

Sabatini, Andrea (called Andrea da Salerno) (c.1484-1530). Neapolitan painter born in Salerno. Information concerning his training is lacking, but his early style is dependent upon Cesare da Sesto and his later manner is based on Raphael. He was the most important and influential painter in southern Italy of that period.

Sabogal, José (1888-). Leading Peruvian painter and graphic artist of the "indigenist" or nativist school; his works are a direct expression of the life of the Indians. His earlier figures are commanding in scale, filling the space impressively and giving an impression of repose and dignity. The later paintings are more abstract in form and show tighter, more controlled space relationships. He is Director, National School of Fine Arts, Lima.

Sacchi, Andrea (1599-1661). Painter of the classicistic Baroque, born in Nettuno and active mostly in Rome. Not as famous or important as Cortona, his art like that of Poussin represents in its simplicity and severity a return to Raphael and Annibale Carracci. He was a pupil of Albani in Bologna and of d'Arpino in Rome. After 1627 he was in the service of Pope Urban VIII and his nephew Cardinal Antonio Barberini as altar, cabinet, and fresco painter. A slow and thoughtful worker, his influence was spread largely through his major pupil Carlo Maratta.

Sacchi, Giovanni Antonio di (see PORDENONE).

Sacchi, Piero Francesco (16th century). A Lombard painter from Pavia, active in Genoa from dating on pictures (1512-27) and guild membership (1520). He studied in Genoa with Berlingeri and was a follower of the Lombard style of Foppa, but with Flemish influences added.

Sacred and Profane Love by Titian (see).

Saedeleer, Valerius de (1867-1941). Belgian painter of the "first Laethem-Saint-Martin group" of symbolists; interested primarily in landscapes. He had a precise, linear, almost Oriental style.

Saenredam, Pieter Jansz. (1597-1665). Dutch painter of churches. He studied under Frans Pietersz. de Grebber at Haarlem and lived in that city most of his life. His paintings of church interiors and exteriors differ from those of his contemporaries in a poetry and charm resulting from his delicate use of pale cream and rosy colors, his tender attention to detail, and a fascinating treatment of the surfaces of stone.

Safawid Period (see PERSIAN PAINTERS: SAFAWID PERIOD, 1502-1736).

Saftleven, Cornelis (1607-81). Dutch painter and engraver of landscapes, animals and rustic interiors. His style derives from Brouwer and Teniers, and certain of his landscapes are reminiscent of Aelbert Cuyp.

Saint Cecilia Master (active late 13th, early 14th centuries). A number of works have been attributed to the same hand that executed an altarpiece representing St. Cecilia and scenes from her legend (whence the name), now in the Uffizi. Other panel paintings attributed to him are in churches in and around Florence, (one is at Oxford), and certain frescoes of the St. Francis cycle in the Upper Church of St. Francis at Assisi are also attributed to him. This master was a contemporary follower and possibly an assistant of Giotto. His style is known for its plasticity and for its architectural settings for figures. He has been identified by some as the well-known painter Buffalmacco, who figures very entertainingly in Boccaccio's *Decameron.*

Saliba, Antonello da (c.1466-1535). A Sicilian painter who studied with his cousin, Jacobello di Antonio, and perhaps for a short time in Venice. He was influenced by Antonello da Messina and Giovanni Bellini and his masterpiece is a signed and dated (1497) altarpiece, a Madonna and Child, in the Catania museum; it is refined in its color harmonies, simple and idealized in conception.

Salimbeni da San Severino, Lorenzo and **Jacopo** (active first quarter of 15th century). Little is known of these collaborating brothers in the school of the Marches except that they painted a fresco cycle on the life of St. John the Baptist in the church of San Giovanni at Urbino in 1416 and another (damaged) cycle in San Severino. These are in an animated Gothic style which is related to that of Gentile da Fabriano.

Salmon, Robert (active 1820-40). A painter of marine scenes in Boston. Born in Scotland and trained in the English marine tradition, he worked in Liverpool, Greenwich, and North Shields before coming to the U.S. in 1828. He painted some five hundred harbor views and ships from his studio on the Boston wharf.

salon. In the broadest sense this refers to all public exhibitions of art in France but it has come to mean exhibitions under the sponsorship of the Académie des Beaux-Arts or other official groups.

RYSSELBERGHE. The Painter Dorio of Regoyos
Beaux-Arts Museum, Ghent

SALVIATI. Portrait of a Boy. National Gallery, London

Salon des Indépendants A non-official "independent" salon (see) organized by a group of painters in France who in 1884 were refused by the official salon group. Its later counterpart in the United States is the now defunct Society of Independent Artists. The first French Indépendants exhibition included works by Seurat, Redon, Signac, Cross, Guillaumin and others.

Salon des Refusés. Literally, salon of the refused ones. This was set up by Napoleon III in 1863 as a result of the scandal following the refusal at the official salon of a large number of works by such artists as Manet.

Salvi, Giovanni Battista (called Sassoferrato) (1609-85). Born in Sassoferrato, he studied first with his father, Tarquinio, and then in Naples with Domenichino. In Rome he was influenced by the Carracci and Raphael. A prolific and clever copyist, he is most famous as a painter of over-sweet Madonnas in the manner of Raphael. His style is retarded and during the eighteenth century it was even thought that he was a sixteenth-century artist.

Salviati, Francesco (Francesco di' Rossi, Cecchino Salviati) (1510-63). Florentine Mannerist fresco painter, perhaps the best of the second generation. He began his career as a goldsmith's apprentice, but then studied painting with Bugiardini, Bandinelli, Piccinelli and, finally, del Sarto. His style was transformed by the influence of Michelangelo and Raphael and later by Mannerism (see). In 1530 he entered the service of Cardinal Salviati, whose name he took. He was active in Florence and Rome in the decoration of a great many palaces and churches. (See illustration.)

Sánchez Coello, Alonso (1531/32-1588). A Spanish court painter to Philip II, who referred to the artist as his "son." Sánchez Coello was of Portuguese extraction, educated in Flanders and Lisbon, cosmopolitan in outlook. He was much honored by princes, foreign courts and popes; Lope de Vega wrote of his fame. In Flanders he gained the acquaintance of Antonio Mor, through whom perhaps he came to the Spanish court of Charles V. Here he prospered. Under Philip II he took the departed Mor's place as *pintor de cámara.* He had first visited the court in Valladolid in 1552 to paint a portrait of the Infanta Doña Juana. Five years later she sent him to Lisbon to paint the king, her son. By 1557 he was permanently at the Spanish court. Sánchez Coello was a Mannerist painter, best at portraiture, which he rendered in the hard, tight style of Mor. He learned a good deal about color and brilliance of technique from Titian, whose works

SÁNCHEZ COELLO. Portrait of Infanta Isabel
Metropolitan Museum of Art, New York

180. SARGENT. El Jaleo. Gardner Museum, Boston

he had copied officially for the court. This brilliance, however, never interfered with the stolid *sosiego* or reserve of his poses, as can be seen in the dignified portraits of Alejandro Farnese (Beruete Collection) and Anne of Austria (Vienna). These are in standard Mannerist format of three-quarters or full-length figure with the painted surface enlivened by decorative detail. He was occupied in the official projects of his day, such as the decoration of the Escorial. His religious paintings are, however, generally considered inferior to his portraits; among the former are the main altar of Espinar (1574-77) and the St. Catherine for the Escorial (1578). (See illustration.)

Sánchez-Cotán, Fray Juan (1561-1624). A Spanish painter best known for his bodegones (still lifes). He was a Carthusian monk and a pupil of Blas de Prado in Toledo. His most famous still life, Bodegón del cardo (Granada) shows his crisp treatment, which was much imitated. He also did religious paintings for monasteries in Andalusia, outstanding among them the four of St. Bruno in the Carthusian monastery of Granada.

Sánchez de Castro, Juan (active 1454-84). Spanish painter. He founded the school of Seville with his brother Antón. He did numerous paintings for the Cathedral and the Alcázar in Seville.

Sandrart, Joachim van (1606-88). German painter, collector and chonicler of artists. He studied in Frankfort, Prag, and Nuremberg, and in Utrecht with Honthorst. He traveled widely, especially in Italy, and resided for about five years in Amsterdam. After a stay in Nuremberg, where his most important work, a large group portrait, is preserved in the Rathaus, he went to Vienna and painted portraits of the Emperor Ferdinand III and the Archduke, later the Emperor Leopold. In his own time his work was highly prized, but he is chiefly remembered today for his biographies of artists.

San Francisco Museum of Art, San Francisco, Calif.

181. SARTO, ANDREA DEL
Madonna and Child with St. Elizabeth
National Gallery, London

SCHIAVONE, ANDREA. David with Goliath's Head
Philbrook Art Center, Kress Collection, Tulsa

A small but very select collection of modern paintings and graphics distinguishes this institution. It also serves as the modern center in its area for many traveling exhibitions.

San Francisco Museum of the Legion of Honor, San Francisco, Calif. A good general collection of traditional works of art. It has recently been strengthened by a gift of fine Old Masters from the Samuel H. Kress Foundation.

Sano di Pietro (1406-81). Pupil of Sassetta, he was a prolific if backward-looking master who spent his life around Siena. In 1428 he was enrolled in the painters' guild; in 1439 he helped Vecchietta; and in 1447 he was paid for work done with Giovanni di Paolo. His art is a direct reflection of Sassetta's and displays some influence from Vecchietta as well. As opposed to the subtle mysticism characteristic of the school, his religious qualities are somewhat obvious, but his work is in general charming, well-executed, and opulent in its use of gold and bright color. A fresco of the Coronation of the Virgin in the Palazzo Pubblico, begun by Domenico di Bartolo, was completed by Sano in 1445. Of his innumerable panel paintings the Siena gallery owns no less than forty-two. A major altarpiece (1471) is in the church at Badia a Isola. His style reached an early maturity and his enormous output is rather repetitive.

Sanraku (see JAPANESE PAINTERS: MOMOYAMA PERIOD).

Santi, Giovanni (active by 1481; d. 1494). An Umbrian painter famous chiefly as the father of Raphael. He lived in Urbino, where Raphael was born in 1483, and was probably in contact with the court of the Montefeltri there. Flemish characteristics in his paintings were probably derived from Joos van Ghent, who worked for the duke of Urbino in the 1470's. His style has little to do with that of his famous son, who probably received his major training from Perugino.

Santiago, Miguel de (c.1620-1680). Spanish-Colonial Ecuadorian painter; best known master of the school of Quito. He was influenced by the Spanish Baroque painters of the period, producing naturalistic and very emotional, darkly colored canvases. See GALQUE and GONZALEZ.

Santi di Tito (1536-1603). Florentine Mannerist painter born in Borgo San Sepolcro. He studied in Florence with Sebastiano da Montecarlo and perhaps also with Bandinelli and Bronzino, by whom he was obviously influenced. He went to Rome in 1558, worked with Cellini, and was influenced by Salviati and the Zuccari. His style stands in opposition to that of Vasari and the followers of Michelangelo in Florence, and is a return to an earlier simplicity, clarity and academic correctness. His color is clear, his chiaroscuro especially refined, and his drawing precise.

Santomaso, Giuseppe (1907-). Venetian-born Italian painter influenced by Braque and Morandi. A member of the New Art Front with its strongly political inclinations, he remains a painter of color and tone in the tradition of his birthplace.

Santvoort, Dirck Dircksz. (1610-80). Dutch painter of portraits. He may have studied with Rembrandt, whose influence is evident in his penetratingly characterized and excellently painted portraits.

Sarabia, José de (1608?-1669). Spanish painter. Pupil of Zurbarán, whose style he followed closely. He was active in Seville and Cordoba, where he did such religious works as the Adoration (Cordoba).

Saraceni, Carlo (called Carlo Veneziano) (1585-1620). Venetian follower of Caravaggio. He studied in Rome with Camillo Mariani and then entered the circle of Caravaggio, whom he so admired that he even copied his dress and mannerism. He was also connected with the Elsheimer-Gentileschi group, and his works are sometimes confused with those of Elsheimer and Caravaggio. Active in Rome and, after 1619, in Venice (where he died of typhus), he combined Venetian color with Caravaggesque chiaroscuro.

Sargent, John Singer (1856-1925). American society portraitist of international reputation. He painted the wealthy of Europe and America, representing them with great elegance and consummate virtuosity. Born in Florence of American parents, he was early directed toward painting by his mother. He studied with Carolus-Duran (1874-76) and, after visiting the U.S., Spain (where he was greatly impressed by Velázquez), and North Africa (where he did brilliant watercolors), he opened a studio in Paris (1881). His fame grew rapidly, but put out by criticism of his work, he moved to London in 1884 and made it his headquarters to the end of his life. In the latter part of his career, he executed murals for both the Boston Library and Museum. After 1910, he turned from portraiture to watercolor again, working in the Tyrol and Venice. Although the taste for Sargent has declined and there is a tendency to regard his watercolors and oil sketches as his best work, his most important works are still those superficial yet brilliant portraits of the bluebloods of international finance. (See color plate 180.)

Sarto, Andrea del (Andrea Vanucci) (1486-1531). A Florentine painter of the High Renaissance, combining the style of Leonardo and Michelangelo. Endowed with a prodigious technical facility, he lacked temperament and inventive genius. He was an excellent colorist, though at times too brilliant; his chiaroscuro was too smooth, his composition uninspired, and his types too sweet. However, as part of a sophisticated intellectual circle in Florence, he had a strong effect on the new generation of Mannerists—Pontormo, Rosso, Bacchiaca, and Franciabigio. Born in Florence, the son of a tailor, he was apprenticed first to a goldsmith, then studied painting with Giovanni Barile and Piero di Cosimo, but was influenced most strongly by Leonardo and Michelangelo as well as Fra Bartolommeo, Albertinelli, and even Dürer. He met Sansovino, Rosso, and Franciabigio and shared a studio and collaborated with the latter. He was patronized by the Servi, who preferred young painters, and worked for them in Florence. His first commission was a cycle in SS. Annunziata with Franciabigio, and from 1512 to 1524 he worked on chiaroscuro frescoes in the Scalzo. He decorated the Medici Villa at Poggio a Caiano together with Franciabigio and Pontormo (c.1521), worked in S. Piero at Luco during the plague (1524), with Bugiardini on cartoons for the Signoria (1525), on a variety of decorations and panels for the Servi, including the Madonna del Sacco (1525-26), and the Last Supper for the refectory of the Convent of S. Salvi (1526-27). He lived in Florence but made trips to Rome, Venice and, in 1519, France. (See color plate 181.)

Sassanian Period (see PERSIAN PAINTERS: SASSANIAN PERIOD, 256-652 A.D.).

Sassetta (Stefano di Giovanni) (1392-1450). One of the most inportant Sienese painters of the early fifteenth century, although his art was still wholly medieval in spirit at a time when Renaissance characteristics were becoming dominant in Florence. He was a pupil of Paolo di Giovanni Fei, whose gay color, courtliness and charm he adopted, bringing him within the ranks of the fifteenth-century phase of the Gothic International Style. In addition he was a true Sienese mystic in the tradition of Simone Martini and Duccio, as well as a subtle master of line and composition. He partook of the advanced knowledge of modeling, anatomy and perspective common in fifteenth-century painting, but applied it to medieval purposes. His works are scattered throughout Europe and America. An important early work, reminiscent of his teacher Fei, is the Birth of the Virgin (1430) in the Collegiata at Asciano. His masterpiece is a now dismembered polyptych, the Apotheosis of St. Francis (1437-44), of which the three central panels are in the Berenson collection at Settignano. Of the subordinate panels, the best known is the Marriage of St. Francis and Poverty (Condé museum, Chantilly). Sassetta had many pupils, Sano di Pietro being the most important, but his spirit was more fully though less directly grasped by Vecchietta. (See color plate 182.)

Sassoferrato (see Salvi).

Savoldo, Giovanni Girolamo (c.1480-1548). Italian painter born in Brescia, trained prabably in Venice under the influence of Bellini, Titian, and Palma Vecchio, and with some connection with Lotto, he was active in Brescia, Florence, Venice, Milan and Treviso. Little is known of his career—he was inscribed in the Florentine guild (1508), married a Flemish woman, and is said to have painted very little and not to have been highly regarded. However, his naturalistic yet lyrical style had great influence on Caravaggio and Elsheimer. His earliest style, which shows the impact of Lombardy and Florence, was later softened by a Giorgionesque phase. Finally he developed an original severe style, characterized by remarkable dignity and repose, a fine feeling for material, and romantic landscapes in extraordinary light.

Schedoni, Bartolommeo (c.1570-1615). Italian painter born in Formigine and active in Rome, Modena, Reggio Emilia, and Parma, where he became court painter (1597). His early Mannerist (see) style was transformed by the Parmesan influence of Correggio and the Carracci. In his last years, after 1608, the impact of Caravaggio is strongly evident.

Scheffer, Ary (1795-1858). French painter, sculptor and graphic artist. Son of a German painter, he was already exhibiting at the age of twelve. While studying in Guérin's studio he met the young Romantics with whom he later associated. Despite his considerable talent at history, genre and portrait, he was never a great success. He practiced both lithography and etching.

Schiavo, Paolo (Paolo di Stefano Badaloni) (1397-1478). Born in Florence and registered as a painter there in 1429, but spent his later life in Pisa. Probably a pupil of Masolino, he was an eclectic master and was much influenced by the important Florentines of his time (Masaccio, Uccello, Domenico Veneziano and the sculptor Donatello). Many works in fresco and on panel are preserved in Florence and other Tuscan towns.

Schiavone (Andrea Meldolla) (c.1515-63). From his name obviously a Slav, he is said to have been born in Zara, but the facts concerning his life are confusing. He was active in Venice, yet from his style seems first to have been trained under Parmigianino. He could have studied with him or been his assistant in Parma, or he could have copied his drawings and engravings. In his middle period the influence of Titian and Venetian color becomes paramount but is modified in his late style by the more Mannerist conceptions of Tintoretto. (See illustration.)

Schiavone, Giorgio (1436/37-1504). Paduan painter originally from Dalmatia (real name Giorgio Chiulinovic), he became in 1456 a pupil of the Paduan Squarcione. He returned to Sebenico in Dalmatia and, except for another sojourn in Padua in 1476, spent the remainder of his life there. He appears to have become a merchant there and done little painting, though an altarpiece (lost) was commissioned in 1489 for San Giacomo in Sebenico. Paintings by him are in museums in London, Paris, Berlin and several north Italian towns, but none is dated. They are in typical Squarcionesque style, with crisp modeling and backgrounds full of classical detail.

Schlemmer, Oskar (1888-1943). German painter, sculptor and scenic designer; taught at the Bauhaus (see) school (1920-29), Breslau Academy (1929-32), Berlin (1932-33). He painted geometrically shaped human forms with generalized anonymous features. He is concerned with the emotional tensions created by the robot-like movements of figures in deep enclosed spaces. Author of *Die Bühne am Bauhaus.* (See illustration.)

Schmidt-Rottluff, Karl (1884-). German painter, graphic artist and a founding member of Die Brücke, the Expressionist group formed in Dresden in 1905. In 1901 he met and worked with Erich Heckel, another group member, in Chemnitz, and in 1905 he moved to Dresden where he met Kirchner and collaborated in the formation of the Brücke, named by him. He also taught the group the technique of

SCHLEMMER. Two Heads. Private Collection, Germany

182. SASSETTA. The Meeting of St. Anthony and St. Paul. National Gallery of Art, Kress Collection, Washington, D.C.

lithography. In 1906 he stayed on the island of Alsen, met Nolde there, and participated in the two Brücke exhibitions of that year. In 1909 he was responsible for the annual Brücke album. Like the other members of the group, he moved to Berlin in 1911, where his art took on a certain largeness of form and an abstract quality; both of these changes were the result in some measure of his pronounced feeling for African sculpture. Thus he turns from a distinctly Fauve kind of

183. SCHMIDT-ROTTLUFF. Rain Clouds. Detroit Institute of Arts

formulation, clearly evident in his earlier works, to this new kind of nature mysticism in which humanity is isolated behind its primitive masks and shielded from the world at large. In the typical fashion of Expressionism (see) the painter identifies himself with the primitivistic creatures he has projected. During his period of war service he did a famous series of religious woodcuts. With the rise of the Nazi movement, he was dismissed from the Academy in 1933; and in 1937 a large number (609) of his pictures were condemned as "degenerate," a term used by the Nazis to characterize all forms of modern art. In 1941 he was actually forbidden to paint and a Gestapo policeman set at his door to make sure he did not. After the war he was appointed to a professorship at the Institute of Plastic Arts in Berlin. (See color plate 183.)

Scholz, Werner (1898-). German Expressionist painter of the second generation. He studied at the Academy in Berlin and lived in that city until 1938. Within the Expressionist movement Scholz shows the same figurative tendency as the Brücke painters and seems, moreover, to have derived some direct influence from them.

Schongauer, Martin (c.1430-91). German engraver and painter, active in Colmar. Like so many artists of his time he received his earliest training as a goldsmith's apprentice, which accounts for some of the richness and delicacy of his style. His art was strongly influenced by a familiarity with Flemish painting, especially the works of Rogier van der Weyden. His Madonna in the Rosegarden (Colmar) is one of his most famous works, but he is renowned especially for his masterful engravings, which surpass those of his predecessors in grandeur of conception and power of execution. His drawings have been often copied. (See illustration.)

School of Athens, The, by Raphael (see).

School of Paris. A term referring to the internationalist group of painters, sculptors and graphic artists who came from all countries to late nineteenth- and early twentieth-century Paris. Their art generally is "advanced" rather than conservative, taking in such movements as Post-Impressionism, Neo-Impressionism, Fauvism, Cubism, etc. The name cannot, therefore, be taken to indicate any one style but rather an aspect of the cultural, social and political internationalism of the pre-World War I period; it was cut short by the outbreak of war. The term also refers to a school of painters, mostly illuminators, active in Paris in the late middle ages, especially the fourteenth century.

Schrimpf, Georg (1889-1942). German painter of the New Objectivity school (see EXPRESSIONISM) of the middle 1920's. He represents the pure, i.e., non-political side of that movement and differs markedly from such men as Otto Dix. Schrimpf's style is full-bodied, clear and precise, his figures sitting or standing in open spaces or empty rooms, looking away toward something they cannot have, but not with violence. The whole attitude is one of gentle, even poetic melancholy, the form classicistic. (See illustration.)

SCHONGAUER. Flight into Egypt
Metropolitan Museum of Art, New York

Schüchlin, Hans (d.1505). German painter, active in Ulm, where he was the leading painter at the end of the fifteenth century. He was prominent in the guild and civic activities, but details of his training are lacking. His style shows a knowledge of Netherlands painting and the influence of his Nuremberg contemporaries. His most important work is the signed and dated altarpiece at Tiefenbronn (1469).

Schut, Cornelis (1597-1655). Flemish painter and etcher. Known primarily as a pupil and imitator of Rubens. He was employed in 1635 on the decorations for the entry of the Cardinal Infant into Ghent and worked in Spain for Philip IV. Among his masterpieces were the Assumption of the Virgin (1647) in Antwerp and the Martyrdom of St. Gereon (about 1655) in Cologne, where he was frequently employed.

Schwind, Moritz von (1804-71). Austrian painter and engraver of mythological and literary subjects; he also did fresco decorations and book illustrations. His illustrations for Goethe's works, *Robinson Crusoe* and other books account for a good deal of his surviving popularity. In general, his painting represents the rising spirit of cultural nationalism in central Europe.

Scipione (Gino Bonichi) (1904-33). Italian painter and founder of so-called Roman school, a reaction against the formalism of the conservative, backward-looking Novecento movement. Instead of Neo-Classicism he proposed a new Romanticism based on strong emotion and direct experience. His vivid Expressionist color, derived from Chaim Soutine, has been influential in Italy.

Scorel, Jan van (1495-1562). Dutch painter of portraits and religious subjects. He studied with Cornelis Buys the Elder in his native city of Alkmaar and perhaps also with Jan Gossaert in Utrecht. Between 1519 and 1521 he journeyed through Germany and Venice to the Holy Land. The following three years he spent in Italy, where he succeeded Raphael as keeper of the treasures of the Vatican. He then returned to Utrecht, carrying back with him a lively understanding of monumental Italian forms and conceptions, which enriched his own art and that of his Netherlands contemporaries. The excellence of his portraiture is best illustrated in the many likenesses he made of Dutch pilgrims to Jerusalem (Museum of Utrecht). (See illustration.)

Scott, Samuel (c.1702-72). British painter and one of the earliest topographical draughtsmen to paint in watercolors. He did many views of London as well as marine subjects. Scott was a friend of William Hogarth. In 1732 he was one of the painters who worked on a group of large pictures for the East India Company showing its principal ports and settlements.

Scott, William (1913-). Scottish abstract geometric painter who was brought up in Ireland and there studied at the Belfast College of Art and at the Royal Academy schools. He traveled in Italy and France during the 1930's and exhibited at the Salon d'Automne in 1939. Scott served in the Royal Engineers during World War II and later published his *Poems of War* illustrated with his own lithographs. He teaches at the Bath Academy of Art. His style shows rough, blunt rectangles, squares and ovals of highly

SCHRIMPF. Girl with Tulips. Gemälde Gallery, Dessau

charged pigment arranged in flat restricted designs. (See illustration.)

scumble. The covering of a given painted area with an overlayer of a second opaque or partly opaque color that will blend with the first. In actual appearance this portion of the canvas is likely to be somewhat irregular in texture and to rise above the picture surface itself.

Scuola di San Rocco, Venice. This is the house of the confraternity of St. Roch, famous for its magnificent series of Tintoretto wall paintings, 1560-88.

Sebastiano del Piombo (Sebastiano Luciani) (1485-1547). Venetian painter active in Rome, whose art combined the Roman and Venetian High Renaissance styles. Influenced first by Cima da Conegliano and Bellini, he soon moved into the orbit of Giorgione, and some critics have even claimed the Fête Champêtre (Louvre) is by him rather than Giorgione. He was called to Rome in 1509 by the Sienese banker Chigi to work on the Villa Farnesina, where he joined the Raphael circle. He then gravitated to Michelangelo, with whom he established a very close relationship. He used Michelangelo's drawings for his own compositions and some of his drawings have been confused with Michelangelo's. He had an important influence on Roman art, introducing the looser Venetian treatment of shadow and color as well as lyrical sentiment into the monumental *disegno* of Michelangelo and Raphael. He produced some powerful religious compositions as well as very fine portraits, but worked little in his later years after being made keeper of the Pope's seal *(piombo)* in 1531. (See illustration.)

SCOTT, WILLIAM. A Memory of Corot
Toledo Museum of Art, Ohio

SCOREL. Adam and Eve. Metropolitan Museum of Art, New York

secondary hues or colors. Within the range of colors used by traditional artists this refers to orange, green and violet. Secondary colors are differentiated from primary colors which include red, yellow and blue—again if we are speaking of the colors or pigments used by the painter. In the mixing of light or in the use of inks for color printing, different hues are employed for both secondary and primary purposes.

Section d'Or, la. (Fr.) According to the artists in the group known as la Section d'Or, the "golden section" refers to the ideal proportion between the side and diagonal of a square, a proportion present in many natural as well as man-made forms and therefore of interest to the Cubist painters participating in the Section d'Or exhibition of 1912. These included Gleizes, Metzinger, Léger, Marcoussis, Delaunay, Lhote, Duchamp, Gris, Picabia, La Fresnaye, Villon and others. The importance of this exhibition—and the short-lived magazine of the same name—lay in the fact that it was the largest grouping of Cubist artists to show together up to that date and that the show itself was in the nature of a tribute to Cézanne and a demonstration of the great influence he had exercised on the Cubist movement.

Segantini, Giovanni (1858-99). Swiss open-air painter who was brought up in Italy and spent part of his childhood as a swineherd, his first drawings being those of animals he tended. He studied at the Academy in Milan and began his career as a Romantic painter, changing after a while to a clean color palette of the kind then being developed in France, although without any apparent knowledge of the methods of other artists. He settled in a mountain village in Switzerland and painted there in a mixed naturalistic-mystical style. (See illustration.)

Seghers, Gerard (1591-1651). Flemish painter. He first

SEBASTIANO DEL PIOMBO. Cardinal Bandinello Sauli, His Secretary and Two Geographers. Kress Collection, New York

SEGANTINI. Ave Maria. Segantini Museum, St. Moritz

painted in a tenebrist manner (see) learned during a long trip through Italy and Spain. Soon he became a follower of Rubens and achieved great success.

Seghers, Hercules (1589/90-c.1640). Dutch painter and etcher of landscape. He was a pupil of Gillis van Coninxloo in Amsterdam. In 1612 he became a free master in the painters' guild of Haarlem and also worked in Utrecht, The Hague and Amsterdam. His etchings are much better known than his paintings, of which only a small number have been preserved. The landscape style he perfected is highly original and completely adapted to the expression of his awe and wonder at the sublimity of nature. His painted scenes are low in key, with a very few bright notes of color, which only intensify their hushed mood. Rembrandt admired Seghers' works, owned some, and was considerably influenced by them.

Segna di Bonaventura (active 1298-1326). Sienese painter who came out of Duccio's workshop, worked in Siena, Arezzo and Lecceta, and is known through two extant signed paintings in the Siena gallery and the Collegiata at Castiglione Fiorentino. An unsigned but well-documented Majestas is in the cathedral of Massa Marittima. His style, though imitative of Duccio's (see), is quite distinct from the mass of anonymous Ducciesque painting. It is characterized by high quality of execution, fine sense of decoration both in color and line, and certain personal traits such as fluffy hair and soft, diffused modeling. Niccolo di Segna, his son, was also a painter.

Segonzac, André Dunoyer de (1884-). French painter and graphic artist who began his studies under conservative influences, took a degree at the School of Oriental Languages and turned thereafter to the modern manner in the wake of Cézanne and his Fauve followers. Although the influence of Courbet and Corot has been seen in his figure studies, Segonzac, like Derain, was attracted to the traditional values of form inherent in this material, which he always treats personally. His landscapes also show the studious formal

184. SEGONZAC. Village on the Marne
Albright Art Gallery, Buffalo

185. SEURAT. Le Chahut. Albright Art Gallery, Buffalo

approach, and here again in the modern vein of the Fauves, whom he has admired. Although not part of their group—he is younger than most of them—he may well be classified with the movement as a whole. (See color plate 184.)

seicento (It.) Literally, six hundred. Refers to the 1600's (or the seventeenth century) in Italy.

Sellaio, Jacopo del (1441/42-93). Originally trained by Fra Filippo Lippi (according to Vasari) he was a minor imitator of Botticelli and Filippino Lippi. He was registered as a painter in Florence between 1460 and 1473, and in 1480 maintained a workshop there with Filippo di Giuliano. An altarpiece commissioned in 1483, representing the Lamentation with Saints (Berlin) is his major work. Two Annunciations of 1472 and 1473 are preserved, as well as various small devotional altars and panels for bridal chests. (See illustration.)

Séraphine (1864-1934). The first name of the French painter Séraphine Louis, a self-taught artist. She was discovered and launched by the German critic Wilhelm Uhde, who was very much interested in the so-called naive painters such as Bombois, Vivin and Henri Rousseau. She had lived the greater part of her life as a housekeeper in Senlis before her accidental discovery by Uhde, to whose house she came as a day worker in 1912 and who bought all of her paintings then and there. A painter of flower pieces of extraordinary clarity and brightness, projected solely from her imagination, Séraphine could not cope with the everyday world of reality and spent the last part of her life in a home for the aged.

Serra family. The Serra family were the foremost painters in the Sienese tradition in Catalonia in the late fourteenth century. There were four, of which Jaime (active 1360-75) and his brother Pedro (active 1363-99) were the most important. They carried on the anecdotal Sienese manner introduced by Ferrer Bassa and produced innumerable gigantic, storied retablos in a standard workshop technique. Jaime directed the workshop and he certainly painted the altarpiece for the tomb of Fray Martín de Alpartil (Zaragoza). Pedro who at first collaborated with his brother, painted the altarpiece of the Holy Spirit in Manresa Cathedral (1393-94). So many works are associated with the workshop that there must have been many assistants, and the brothers themselves perhaps changed in style. The repetitious nature of the retablos is offset by their bright color and genre incident. (See illustration.)

Sert y Badia, José Maria (1876-1945). Modern Spanish muralist. His style, a pompous modern Baroque based on many prototypes including Piranesi, was famous and lucrative during his lifetime. He was patronized by Spanish religious circles. He spent many years redecorating the Cathedral of Vich with large canvas murals of the Militant and Triumphant Life of the Church. In his youth he was associated with Art Nouveau and the Catalan avant garde, but he became conservative with success, as can be seen in his decorations at the League of Nations and in American cocktail lounges. Other important commissions were the Noble Palace (London), Rockefeller Center (New York), the Ayuntamiento (Barcelona), the Palacio de Lira (Madrid). His son José Luis Sert (1902-) is an outstanding architect and townplanner.

Sérusier, Paul (1863-1927). French Symbolist painter and expositor of that movement. He was closely associated with Paul Gauguin, Maurice Denis, Bonnard, Vuillard and others connected with either Symbolism (see) or the Nabis (see).

Sesshu (see JAPANESE PAINTERS: MUROMACHI PERIOD).

Seurat, Georges (1859-91). Ontstanding French practitioner of Pointillism (see), a form of painting also known as Neo-Impressionism (see), Divisionism and Chromo-Luminarism. This style was essentially an extension and a more scientific application of the clean and divided tones of the preceding Impressionist movement. In the museums Seurat studied and copied Holbein, Poussin, Raphael and Ingres; in addition, he was influenced by Chevreuil's scientific treatise on *Harmony and Simultaneous Contrast of Colors* and by Delacroix's color methods. Together with Redon, Cross, Signac and others he founded in 1884 the Society of Independent Artists. The following year his Sunday Afternoon on La Grande Jatte (Chicago) became the manifesto of the new Pointillist movement, its thirty-eight painted studies and twenty-three preparatory drawings evidence of the formal care and permanent

SELLAIO, JACOPO DEL. David
Philadelphia Museum of Art, Johnson Collection

aims of this art. A number of these sketches were sent to the last Impressionist show in 1886 and aroused the hostility of almost all of the so-called advanced artists and critics except Félix Fénéon. La Grande Jatte was shown that same year in New York by the art dealer Durand-Ruel and again at the second exhibition of the Independents. In 1887 Seurat exhibited with the group known as Les XX in Brussels and began to exert an influence on Belgian painting.

Although his methods stemmed from those of the Impressionists, Seurat's purposes were different; he strove for permanence of effect even in the glowing colors he used, for completeness and a closed quality of composition rather than unconventionally viewed segments of nature, and for control over all the means used so that the spectator moves from one point to another as the painter wills. While he claimed that he painted by his method alone and without any other consideration, there is often a moving, even mystic quality about his work, especially in the black-and-white drawings that attracted the Symbolists of the period and influenced such men as Bonnard and Vuillard. In the generation following, his geometrical outlook is reflected in the painting of Léger and in the work of the Purists of the 1920's (See color plate 185.)

Severini, Gino (1883-). Italian painter and a signer of the original manifesto of Futurism (see). He was particularly interested in cabaret and night-life subjects, to which he turned after he settled in Paris. He was influenced by the Neo-Impressionism of Seurat, which accounts for the fact that Severini's color is generally brighter than that of his colleagues. After the war he turned to the neo-classicism of the 1920's. As part of his considerable literary activity, he has published an autobiography. (See illustration.)

sfumato (It.) Literally, smoke or vapor. Used to describe the smoky shadows that soften the cheeks, throat, etc., of a given subject. These shadows are shot through with little pinpoints of light, as in the painting of Leonardo da Vinci or Giorgione.

shading. Arrangement of different degrees or tones of light and dark so as to give a three-dimensional quality to a given form or depth to a given space.

Shah Jahan Period (see INDIAN PAINTERS: SHAH JAHAN PERIOD, 1627-58).

Shahn, Ben (1898-). Contemporary American painter of social themes. Though realistic in intention and dependent on photography, his paintings, executed in flat harsh color and incisive line, show the influence of modern art in their elements of abstraction and Neo-Romantic flavor. His art has ranged from propaganda posters for the Office of War Information (1942-43) and the Congress of Industrial Organizations (1942-43, 1945-46) to more recondite symbolic and abstract easel paintings. Born in Lithuania, he came to the U. S. as a child and lived with his family in Brooklyn. He was apprenticed to a lithographer (1913-17) and until 1930 was a commercial lithographer. He studied botany at New York Uni-

SERRA, PEDRO. Altarpiece of the Holy Spirit
Manresa Cathedral, Barcelona

SEVERINI. Still Life with Guitar
Stedelijk Museum, Amsterdam

versity and City College but left in 1922 to study art at the National Academy of Design, and later in Paris at the Grande Chaumière, traveling and studying in France, Italy, Spain, and North Africa. It was during this period that the influence of the School of Paris, especially of Rouault, became evident in his work. He returned to the U.S. in 1929 and in 1931 turned to the narrative treatment of social protest, producing several series, Dreyfus (1931), Sacco and Vanzetti (1932), Tom Mooney (1923-33), and Prohibition (1933-34), He worked with Diego Rivera on the Radio City Murals (1933), on the Public Works of Art Project (1933-34), and for the Farm Security Administration as artist, designer, and photographer (1935-38). His major murals are in the Federal housing project at Roosevelt, N.J. (1937-38), the Bronx Central Annex Post Office, executed with his wife, Bernarda Bryson (1938-39), the Jamaica, Long Island, Post Office (1939), and the Federal Security Building (1940-42). His most recent work has exhibited a more cryptic symbolism, a strange fantastic quality, and a greater concern with purely formal problems. (See illustration.)

Sharaku (see JAPANESE PAINTERS: TOKUGAWA PERIOD).

Sheeler, Charles (1883-). Contemporary American painter of industrial scenes, one of the originators of Cubist-Realism. Born in Philadelphia, he studied applied design at the School of Industrial Art, and then under Chase at the Pennsylvania Academy of Fine Arts (1903-06); he twice accompanied Chase abroad. After a trip to Europe in 1909, he worked in Philadelphia as a photographer and painted only in his spare time until he moved to New York in 1919. His paintings exhibited at the Armory Show already show the influence of Post-Impressionism and Cézanne; and as early as 1916 the impact of Cubism is evident, culminating in such paintings as Church Street "El" (private collection). By 1923 in his crayon still lifes there was a conscious return to a precise study of nature and, finally, toward the end of the 1920's a compromise between Cubism and realism, as in the immaculate surfaces of Upper Deck (Fogg Museum). Beginning with the industrial scenes based on photographs of the River Rouge Plant done for Ford, his work became photographically realistic, but with the 1940's it exhibited a return to abstraction of reality. (See illustration.)

Shen Chou (see CHINESE PAINTERS: MING DYNASTY).

Shih-ch'i (see K'UN-TS'AN in CHINESE PAINTERS CH'ING DYNASTY).

Shih-t'ao (see TAO CHI in CHINESE PAINTERS: CH'ING DYNASTY).

Shinn, Everett (1876-1953). American painter, member of the Ashcan School (see) and the Eight. Born in Woodstown, N.J., he was interested in mechanics and attended Spring Garden Institute in Philadelphia and worked as a draughtsman before studying at the Pennsylvania Academy of Fine Arts. He worked for five Philadelphia newspapers as an illustrator and met Henri, Luks, Glackens, and Sloan. In New York after about 1900 he worked for the *World* and *Harper's Bazaar* and painted, but then turned to theatrical decoration, portraiture and writing. In 1911 he executed a unique mural in the realist tradition for the City Hall of Trenton, N.J. Later in life he returned to painting and his earlier subjects—ballet dancers and entertainers. Shinn was only for a short time within the Ashcan orbit. Influenced by Degas, he turned to theatrical genre before abandoning it for theatrical decorations in the Rococo manner.

SHAHN. The Passion of Sacco and Vanzetti
Whitney Museum of American Art, New York

SHEELER. New England Irrelevancy
Downtown Gallery, New York

Shirlaw, Walter (1838-1909). American painter of sentimental figure-pieces in the Munich manner made familiar by Duveneck. Born in Paisley, Scotland, of American parents, he worked first as an engraver, studied art at the National Academy of Design and then went to Munich, where he worked under Wagner and von Kaulbach. He taught at the Art Students League and was the first president of the Society of American Artists.

Showa Period (see JAPANESE PAINTERS: SHOWA PERIOD, 1926-).

Shrimp Girl, The, by William Hogarth (see).

Shunsho (see JAPANESE PAINTERS: TOKUGAWA PERIOD).

Sickert, Walter Richard (1860-1942). British painter and outstanding Impressionist. He studied under Whistler, was a friend of Degas, and helped found the Camden Town Group in 1911 to "advance" British art. Not only was he (with Wilson Steer) the leading British Impressionist, but he utilized this technique for the treatment of dark and shadowy interiors as well as for the less appetizing portions of early twentieth-century London. In this regard he suggests some American painters of the same period.

Sienese school. An important Italian tradition stretching from the thirteenth to the early sixteenth century. As in Florence we note a shift from the stark medievalism of the thirteenth century style (e.g., Guido da Siena) to the increasing warmth and decorative linear quality of the fourteenth century as represented by Duccio and Simone Martini and their followers during the latter part of that period. The followers include Lippo Memmi, Pietro and Ambrogio Lorenzetti, Francesco Traini and others. Among the most influential

SIGNAC. Quay at Clichy. Baltimore Museum of Art

Sienese of the fifteenth century were Sassetta, Giovanni di Paolo, Domenico di Bartolo, Vecchietta, Francesco di Giorgio. This group continues the decorative trends of the previous period, adding relatively little. By the sixteenth century Siena had come to the end of its effectiveness as an art center. Sodoma with his sentimentalism characterizes this stage of Sienese development.

Sigalon, Alexandre François Xavier (1787-1837). French painter. Worked in the style of the Italian masters and made a famous copy of Michelangelo's Last Judgment for the French government. His Young Courtesan is in the Louvre.

Signac, Paul (1863-1935). French Neo-Impressionist painter and theorist. He began as an Impressionist and showed at the Salon des Indépendants in 1884, but gave up Impressionism after meeting Cross and Seurat there. It was in his studio that the Neo-Impressionists held their meetings. In 1888 he was invited to show with Les XX in Brussels, and the following year he visited Van Gogh at Arles, the latter having been interested in the technique of Neo-Impressionism (see). In 1892 Signac increased his interest in the sea, cruising up and down the French coasts from Brittany to the Mediterranean; he also began to paint in what was to become his typical manner, a variation of the technique he stoutly advocated: the substitution of a square mosaic-like spot of color for the more or less irregularly shaped dot that Seurat and others used. This, however, left his painting in a somewhat ambiguous state, the constant glow that Seurat obtained being rather difficult for Signac to achieve since the color squares were very obtrusive. His watercolors, on the other hand, retained a simple and fresh quality. In 1899 he published his famous book *From Eugène Delacroix to Neo-Impressionism,* in which the basic tenets of the movement are set forth. He remained president of the Indépendants until his death in 1935. (See illustration.)

Signorelli, Luca (c.1441-1523). One of the several Umbrian artists (such as Piero della Francesca, Melozzo da Forlì) who became so involved with fifteenth-century stylistic developments in Florence that they are sometimes referred to as "Umbro-Florentines." He was born in Cortona, but probably received his artistic training under Piero at Arezzo, and may have assisted in the great frescoes there by that master. By 1475 he was in Florence, where he came under the influence of Verrocchio and the Pollaiuoli, deriving an interest in strong modeling, anatomy and movement. Back in Cortona in 1479, he took an active part in public affairs and later (1512) served as ambassador from Cortona to Florence. In addition to projects in Florence and other cities, he went to Rome in 1482-83, where he finished a fresco by Perugino in the Sistine Chapel and painted two of his own (one since destroyed). His crowning achievement is the fresco decoration of the Brizio chapel in the cathedral of Orvieto. Here he treated scenes of the Last Judgment in an unorthodox way, with a seething mass of skillfully drawn and modeled figures, revealing his mastery of the current stylistic approach of the Florentines to anatomy, movement, light and space, and monumental decorative composition. Their brilliant and sometimes bizarre coloration are also noteworthy. Drawings for this project are preserved in the Uffizi, the Louvre and the British Museum. His later work shows little or no development, and the last part of his life was spent supervising a large shop in Cortona that produced altarpieces from his designs. During this period he went twice to Rome in fruitless attempts to obtain the patronage of the papal court. His best panel paintings were produced during his second Florentine period (1490-95), and he is noted for his influence on Piero di Cosimo and Michelangelo. (See color plate 186.)

silhouette. Portrayal of a given object in outline, with the body of the representation filled in solidly in black. It also refers to the placing of an outline or profile of a given form against another form. The term is also applied to a portrait cutout which is generally attached to a lighter background for contrast. This art form, which dates from the end of the eighteenth century, is supposed by some to have been influenced by the shadow plays of the Far East, e.g., Java. As practiced in France and Germany these shadowy outline pictures replaced miniature painting for a time but by the beginning of the nineteenth century their popularity was challenged and finally destroyed by the daguerreotype.

186. SIGNORELLI. Eunostos of Tanagra
National Gallery of Art, Kress Collection, Washington, D.C.

silk screen. A method of color reproduction which may be used either for the multiplication of replicas of an already finished painting or for an original design, as in woodcut, color woodcut, color lithography, etc. It is also used commercially for the reproduction of posters and other forms of "art work." The method involves breaking up the object to be reproduced into its chief colors, for which the silk screener then prepares a series of silk frames, each representing a different color and the areas which it is to cover in the final result. Each color frame is then covered with a substance impermeable to paint except in those areas where the paint is meant to be squeezed through onto the surface of the paper. These frames are known as silk screens, and consist of wooden frames on which silk has been stretched. The final print is also called a silk screen.

silverpoint. A type of drawing made with a thin, silver-

SIMONE MARTINI. Saint John the Baptist
National Gallery of Art, Kress Collection, Washington, D.C.

pointed instrument on specially prepared paper; the resulting impression is rather delicate. Generally used by late medieval and Renaissance artists, e.g., Leonardo da Vinci.

Silvestre the Younger, Louis (1675-1760). French painter and member of a large family of artists. Academic decorator trained by Le Brun and others. He was active in Italy, Germany and eastern Europe and illustrates the universal demand for French talent in the eighteenth century.

Simon, Lucien (1861-1945). French portraitist and painter of genre. Student of Didrier and Tony Robert-Fleury, Simon painted in the manner of Hals, mainly depicting subjects from Brittany. He also indulged in the painting of bathing girls. His best known works include The Procession (Luxembourg), Mass in Brittany (Chicago), Evening Conversation (Stockholm), Tea in the Studio (Pittsburgh).

Simone da Pesaro (see CANTARINI, SIMONE).

Simone dei Crocifissi (active 1355-99). Several documents in Bologna refer to this painter and a considerable number of signed panel paintings are extant, one of which is dated (a Crucifix in the church of San Giacomo Maggiore, 1370). In 1366 he undertook fresco decorations for the church of Mezzaratta outside the city but nothing remains of these. A polyptych and other signed panels are in the Bologna gallery.

Simone Martini (1284?-1344). One of the most original and influential painters of the fourteenth-century Sienese school. His art owes most to Duccio though there is no evidence that he was Duccio's pupil. He may have been a pupil of Memmo di Filipuccio, whose daughter he married, thus becoming a brother-in-law of Lippo Memmi. In 1315 he signed and dated the fresco of the Majestas in the Siena Palazzo Pubblico, one of his most important works and the earliest known; it has been extensively repainted, once by Simone himself, and is in deplorable condition. Soon after this work he probably went to Naples, and his picture of St. Louis of Toulouse Crowning Robert of Anjou (c.1317) is in the gallery there. His influence on local fresco painters in Naples attests to his presence in the area. In 1320 he painted a polyptych for the church of St. Catherine at Pisa (a major part of it is preserved in the Municipal Gallery and the Seminario) and a Madonna and Saints for the cathedral of Orvieto (now in the Opera del Duomo). Works of Simone's school are found in both Pisa and Orvieto. In 1321 he was back in Siena and painted a Madonna (now lost) for the Chapel of the Nine, and the next year was at work in the Palazzo Pubblico of his home city.

A considerable time between 1320 and 1325 was probably spent in Assisi, where he executed a fresco cycle on the life of St. Martin in the Lower Church of San Francesco. In this work he first manifests a close relation with French Gothic painting, examples of which he could have seen at Assisi. In 1325 he was again in Siena, painting for the palace of the Capitano del Popolo, and in 1326 he was employed by the Commune as an architect. In 1328 he painted in fresco the important equestrian portrait of Guidoriccio dei Fogliani da Reggio, Sienese captain general and hero, in the Palazzo Pubblico. In 1333 he signed, together with Lippo Memmi, the famous Sant' Ansano Annunciation (painted for the Siena cathedral and now in the Uffizi) a work which had tremendous influence all over central Italy. In 1339 he left for the papal court at Avignon and was destined never to return to Italy. His patron at Avignon was Cardinal Jacopo Stefaneschi. He painted frescoes in the cathedral, became a friend of Petrarch's and is known to have painted a portrait of Petrarch's Laura (now lost). Assisted by Matteo da Viterbo and a host of other painters from both Italy and France, he established a flourishing school in Avignon. There is practically nothing left of his work there, but an example from this period is the signed panel (1342) of Christ Returning from the Temple, now in the Liverpool gallery. A signed but dismembered polyptych with scenes from the live of Christ (preserved in Antwerp, Berlin and the Louvre) dates from this late period. These two works reveal his late style as marked by Gothic flamboyance and extreme emotional exaggeration, in contrast to the delicate lyricism of his earlier periods. The influence of his late work on northern European painting was tremendous. Simone was a master of technique and evidenced the Sienese love of precious material preciously used. He introduced the fresco technique into the Sienese school, but his own frescoes have suffered from the fact that he painted or retouched many portions *a secco* (i.e., on a dry surface) instead of in true fresco on wet plaster. His style is characterized by its seriousness, aloofness, aristocracy and spirituality. The linear quality of the tradition of Duccio achieves its highest expression in his work. (See illustration.)

simultaneity. A method developed by twentieth-century painters to show different aspects of the same form at once, i.e., the front, sides, top and bottom in one representation, as in the Analytical Cubist works of Picasso and Braque.

Siporin, Mitchell (1910-). Contemporary American painter of social themes in symbolic terms. Born in New York City, he was brought up in Chicago, where he studied with Geller at the Art Institute. He executed murals under the W.P.A. in Chicago and for Post Offices in Decatur, Ill., and St. Louis, Mo. (See illustration.)

Siqueiros, David Alfaro (1898-). Outstanding Mexican muralist, easel painter, graphic artist and theoretician. He is the promulgator of "dynamic realism," through which a genuinely social art would be presented to the greatest number of people (generally through outdoor murals), with the constant movement suitable to the dynamic age in which we live. Siqueiros fought in the Mexican Revolution in his teens; sent to Europe to study (1921-22), he conceived there the idea of a new heroic art based on native American traditions, thus helping launch the Mexican mural movement. His first murals, done in 1922 for the National Preparatory School, already show dynamic movement, architectonic forms and Revolutionary content. He organized the Syndicate of Technical Workers, Painters and Sculptors, focal point of Mexican mural activity up to 1925. A political activist, 1926-39, more concerned with trade union work than with art, he was often imprisoned by the authorities; in his 1931 Taxco confinement he did paintings and woodcuts. Here his art already shows the clear absorption of Aztec influence.

In 1932 he did murals in Los Angeles, Calif., using teams of assistants to apply spray-gun methods and industrial paints (Duco)—on outdoor walls wherever possible. In 1933 he did pyroxylin murals in Uruguay and Argentina. He renewed his political activity in 1934-5. During 1936 in New York he organized an Experimental Workshop for modern materials in painting. From 1936-39 he was a Lieutenant Colonel in the Spanish Republican Army. Returning to painting in 1939 he carried out an important neo-Realist (i.e., dynamic and social) mural in the Electrical Workers Union, Mexico City; in 1942, a brilliant mural in the Escuela México, Chillán, Chile, developed his theories further. Other mural works are in the Palace of Fine Arts, Mexico City (1945 and 1951); the new University City buildings, Mexico (1952-55); the Social Security Hospital and Polytechnical Institute, both in Mexico City (1952); and a square mural in the University of Morelia (1953). Siqueiros' work shows an increasing dynamism of figures and composition—heroic forms erupting into space through new simultaneous perspectives which enable the spectator to view the themes effectively from all approaches. He won second prize at the Venice Biennale in 1950, and a monograph on his work was published by the National Institute of Fine Arts, Mexico, during that same year. See SOCIAL REALISM. (See illustration.)

SIPORIN. Dream of the Good Life
Downtown Gallery, New York

SIQUEIROS. Dawn of Mexico
Collection International Business Machines, New York

Sironi, Mario (1885-). Italian painter originally part of Futurist and metaphysical movements later turned by pressures of the Fascist regime toward Novecento traditionalism. In his case this attempt to turn back the artistic clock took the form of a post-Baroque romanticism that could readily be identified with the past. He carried out a number of commissions in fresco and mosaic later in his career.

Sisley, Alfred (1839-99). English member of the Impressionist painters, also active as an etcher and lithographer. One of the more charming, if weaker, members of the movement. Sisley was English, although born in Paris of French ancestry. He left a career of business for painting, joining with Monet, Renoir and Bazille in Gleyre's studio, and, in 1864, accompanying them to Chailly. He called himself a pupil of Corot when he first appeared in the Salon of 1866. His style became more vivid until, at the peak of Impressionism (see) it was almost indistinguishable from Monet's. His weakness was revealed in the 1880's when the more creative Impressionists turned to new modes of expression and he alone kept on at the old style without too much vigor. His life was financially unsuccessful and rather sad. (See color plate 187.)

Sistine Chapel (see VATICAN PICTURE GALLERY and MICHELANGELO).

Sistine Madonna, The, by Raphael (see).

187. SISLEY. Le Loing à Moret. Wildenstein Gallery, New York

Sleeping Gypsy, The, by Henri Rousseau (see).

Sleeping Venus by Giorgione (see).

Slevogt, Max (1868-1932). Well-known German Impressionist painter, etcher, illustrator, muralist and scenic designer. One of the most important influences on his characteristically sketchy style is that of Rembrandt. Slevogt painted in Egypt and at the front during World War I. He taught afterward at the Academy in Berlin, did scenic designs for the Dresden Opera and a whole series of murals in different cities during the years 1924-32. His style is light and airy, often humorous, filled with a sense of movement and spontaneity that comes from his draughtsmanship rather than from ordinary Impressionist color effects. Yet its sense of continuous movement, its air of the unexpected, leads one to include it in the Impressionist category. (See illustration.)

Sloan, John (1871-1951). American painter of city genre, member of the Ashcan School (see) and the Eight. Born in Lock Haven, Pa., he attended the Spring Garden Institute in Philadelphia before studying at the Pennsylvania Academy of Fine Arts with Anschutz. He worked as an illustrator for Philadelphia newspapers and met Henri, Luks, Glackens, and Shinn. He came to New York in 1905 and subsequently worked for *Everybody's, Colliers's, Harper's Weekly,* and the *Century* as well as the *Masses,* of which he was art editor. Along with other members of the Ashcan School, he fought for progressive art movements and was active in the organization of the Armory Show and the Independents (of which he was elected president in 1918). He was an instructor at the Art Students League (1914-30, 1935-38) and its president (1931). His early illustrations and posters were in the style of Beardsley and Art Nouveau (see), but this soon gave way to the simpler illustrative style of the *Punch* draughtsmen, Keene and Leech. Henri introduced him to the art of Daumier and Gavarni and their artistic descendants, Toulouse-Lautrec, Steinlen, and Forain. From about 1900 to 1912 he produced his most perceptive and sympathetic studies of city genre in the grey tonalities and spirited brushwork of the Ashcan tradition. After the Armory Show, his summer activities at Gloucester and Santa Fé resulted in more varied subject matter and a higher-keyed palette, but in a loss of intimacy. In the 1920's, painting in the same high key, he attempted to recapture the earlier Ashcan themes and in the 1930's became involved in problems of form which resulted in a series of cross-hatched and glazed nude studies. (See illustrations, including color plate 188.)

Sluyters, Jan (1881-). Netherlands painter of Expressionist persuasion. After winning the Prix de Rome in 1904 he traveled. He rejected traditionalism and Impressionism both; instead he combined the Cézanne search for form with Fauve color effects to arrive at his own type of violent and yet arranged Expressionist treatment of peasant life and religious subjects. After World War I he turned to the painting of large smooth nudes in which the flesh seems to burn against a controlled background of drapery. Since that time he has tried to achieve an even greater simplicity of form and naturalness of expression.

188. SLOAN. McSorley's Bar. Detroit Institute of Arts

Smet, Gustave de (1877-1943). Belgian Expressionist of the second "Laethem-Saint-Martin group" (see); he began as a sign painter for inns. He came into contact with German Expressionism during his stay in Holland, 1914-18, where he also met Le Fauconnier. He is considered among the outstanding Belgian Expressionists, painting in a rigid schematized fashion that suggests primitive peasant forms. (See illustration.)

Smibert (Smybert), John (1688-1751). The first English painter of any training to arrive in America. Born in Edinburgh, he was apprenticed to a house painter, went to London, where he worked as a coach painter, copied paintings for dealers, and studied at Sir James Thornhill's London Academy. After several years in Italy copying the Old Masters, he returned to London and probably set up as a portrait painter. In 1728, he accepted Bishop Berkeley's offer to join the faculty of his proposed college for Indians in Bermuda. They arrived in Newport, R.I., the following year and when the plan failed, Smibert moved on to Boston, where he opened his studio and art shop and became the leading portrait painter. His style is in the Kneller tradition, competent and uninspired, searching for elegance rather than character. He produced a great many repetitious portraits à-la-mode. His women especially are stereotyped, with an exaggerated doll-like delicacy. His art seemed to deteriorate, although

SLOAN. Backyards, Greenwich Village
Whitney Museum of American Art, New York

SLEVOGT. The Actor d'Andrade. National Gallery, Berlin

who carried the tradition to the French court. Snayers was in great demand by the rulers of Flanders and his paintings are in many European collections. He was noted not only for accuracy of detail but also for grandness of composition and vivacity of color.

Snyders, Frans (1579-1657). Flemish painter of animals and still life. Pupil of Pieter Brueghel the Younger and of van Balen. He vies with Rubens and Velvet Brueghel for the credit for popularizing animal painting in Flanders. After returning from study in Italy in 1609, Snyders married into the de Vos family and became, with van Dyck, the outstanding assistant to Rubens. While frequently a collaborator of Rubens and Jordaens, he is without equal in his own specialty of still life and the hunt. One of the largest projects on which he worked with Rubens was the series of eighteen paintings for the Palace of La Torre de la Parada near Madrid. Among his best known works are the Stag Hunt (The Hague), Fox Hunting (Vienna), Bear Hunt (Berlin). (See illustration.)

So-ami (see JAPANESE PAINTERS: MUROMACHI PERIOD).

Social Realism. A contemporary movement in American painting, realistic in manner and critical of social, economic, and political abuses. It emerged out of the renewed realism of the 1920's but reached its height in the 1930's during the Depression. A great many American painters (and a number elsewhere, especially Mexico), stirred by the human suffering engendered by the crisis and influenced by radical political thought, turned to an artistic consideration of human relationships in modern society. Commonly identified with Socialism and Communism, it had its theoretical roots in those movements, but included a great many artists who simply expressed a critical attitude toward modern society. Historically we find its precursors in such nineteenth-century artists as Daumier. It is not to be confused with Socialist

it must be recognized that many inferior paintings are attributed to him incorrectly.

Smith, Matthew (1879-). British pioneer modernist who began slowly, arriving around 1910 at the Fauve style after having been in direct contact with Matisse for a brief period. While the latter went on to a more decorative formulation, Smith's violent drawing and vivid coloring have preserved for a long period the literal and original meaning of the *fauve* or "wild beast" style.

Smith, Thomas (active c.1650-90). An identifiable American colonial painter, but his personality is still problematic. There are several references to him in records. A so-called Self-Portrait (American Antiquarian Society, Worcester), broad and boldly modeled for its time, is the key work upon which other attributions have been made.

Smith College Museum of Art, Northampton, Mass. A relatively small but constantly growing selection of paintings, prints, drawings, sculpture and decorative arts from various periods.

Smits, Jakob (1856-1928). Belgian painter and etcher of religious scenes, genre, portraits and landscapes. Of a wandering temperament, he traveled through Europe, settling first in Amsterdam and finally in the Kempen in northern Belgium. There he produced his moody, strong pictures in which figures are often generalized in a thick dark-colored paint. But the general effect is always decorative in keeping with the artist's family background of industrial decoration and his own experience as a teacher of industrial design in Holland.

Snayers, Pieter (1512-67). Flemish painter of battles, hunts and landscapes. He was the teacher of van der Meulen,

SMET, DE. Young Girl in Blue. Musée Moderne, Brussels

SNYDERS. The Bear Hunt. Detroit Institute of Arts

Realism, the theoretical designation of art in the Soviet Union, socialist in content and realist in form. Since this presupposes a Socialist society, the American version is properly speaking critical realism. In its earlier phases, when it was being discussed in the John Reed Club, the *New Masses*, and at symposia, it was called Proletarian Art, and by people of an opposite persuasion, Propaganda Art. Since the term itself has been the center of long controversy, it is difficult to set its limits or to name its adherents, for some would deny the designation. In the 1930's when it was an influential movement in American art, it stood against all forms of Art-for-Art's-sake (see), against the romantic aspects of American Scene (see) and Regionalist (see) painting, and for a sympathetic treatment of the economic, political and social aspirations of the working-class or at least the lower-class.

Sodoma (Giovanni Antonio Bazzi) (1477-1549). Lombard painter born in Vercelli and active largely in Siena. He studied first with Martino Spanzotti in Vercelli (1490-97) and perhaps with Macrino d'Alba. In 1498 he went to Milan, where he fell under the influence of Leonardo, and then to Siena in 1501, where he came in contact with the art of Pinturicchio, then at work in the Cathedral library. In 1503 he was commissioned to decorate the Convent of Sta. Anna in Caprena and then worked in the Monastery of Monte Oliveto Maggiore (1505-08), finishing a cycle on S. Bernardino begun by Signorelli. In 1508 he came to Rome under the patronage of Agostino Chigi and began the decorations of the Segnatura of the Vatican, later entrusted to Raphael, and of the Villa Farnesina. His style was, however, not highly regarded in Rome and he returned to Siena where he had no competition. He remained extremely active though eventually declining in popularity, working in Mantua, Florence, Volterra, and Pisa. In 1518, together with Girołamo del Pacchia and Domenico Beccafumi, he decorated the Oratory of S. Bernardino and in 1525-26 executed in the Chapel of Sta. Caterina in S. Domenico what is perhaps his most famous work. He also painted a Last Supper for the Convent of Monte Oliveto near Florence (c.1527), and back in Siena did a series for the Palazzo Pubblico (1529-33), the Piccolomini altar in Sant' Agostino (c.1530), and decorated the Spanish Chapel of S. Spirito (1530+). He was active later (1540-42) in Pisa, painting for the Duomo as well as Sta. Maria della Spina. The only High Renaissance artist active in Siena, he combined the Quattrocento elements of Leonardo and the Umbrians, Signorelli and Pinturricchio, with the High Renaissance manner of Raphael. (See illustration.)

SODOMA. Saint Jerome. National Gallery, London

Sogliani, Giovanni Antonio (1492-1544). Born and active in Florence, his art spanned the transition from the fifteenth to the sixteenth century. From his beginnings with Lorenzo de Credi, he moved through the High Renaissance style of del Sarto, Franciabigio, and Mariotto Albertinelli to

Mannerism (see). His most important work is the S. Domenico for the Refectory of S. Marco (1536).

Solana, José Gutiérrez (1886-1945). Painter and writer of the deeply introspective Spanish cultural revival of the early twentieth century. His youth, devoted to painting, bears the imprint of abnormal loneliness and a lineage of fallen aristocracy. His manner is brusque, heavy, pervaded with a stolid melancholy of black accents. He based his style on the Spanish masters, especially Goya, and on Pieter Brueghel the Elder. Scenes of grief and *danses macabres* vie with backstage vignettes and café scenes—an inner expressionism of his generation. He first exhibited in 1907 and won medals in 1922, 1929, 1942, becoming by his death perhaps the most famous painter in Spain, although little known abroad. His circle of intellectual intimates is well portrayed in the gloomy Reunion at the Café Pombo, 1920. He wrote in a similar vein. (See illustration.)

Solario, Andrea (c.1465-c.1522). Although Milanese, he derived his style chiefly from Alvise Vivarini and Antonello da Messina as a result of his early activity in Venice. Returning to Milan, he developed the realistic Venetian characteristics under the further influence of Leonardo da Vinci, bringing his art into line with the High Renaissance innovations of ideal form and composition.

Solario, Antonio (called Il Zingaro) (active c.1502-14). Venetian painter active in Naples and the Marches. A follower of Bellini and Carpaccio, he was also influenced by Umbrian art. His most important work is the fresco decoration illustrating the life of S. Benedict in SS. Severino and Sosio in Naples. He has also produced some fine, meticulously handled portraits. His style combined the luminous color of the Venetians with the sweetness of Perugino.

Solimena, Francesco (called l'Abate Ciccio) (1657-1743). Neapolitan Baroque painter and architect born in Nocera dei Pagani. He studied with Francesco Guarino and Francesco de Maria, but was then influenced by Mattia Preti and Luca Giordano.

Solman, Joseph (1909-). Contemporary American painter of intimate genre and still life. Born in Russia, he came to the U.S. in 1912. He studied at the National Academy of Design and Columbia University.

Somer, Paulus van (1576-1621). Flemish portraitist. Most of his career was spent in England painting portraits for the court in a style so similar to Geeraerts' that they are frequently confused.

Sorolla y Bastida, Joaquín (1863-1923). A Spanish painter. Of humble origin and an orphan at two years, he quickly showed himself a prodigy and was admitted to the Academy at fifteen. His manner was a personal, conservative variant of Impressionism, a plein-air style drenched in sun and rendered with bright color, but retaining the solidity of the old Spanish masters. He was influenced only a little during trips to Italy and France. His specialties were anecdotal and landscape genre and portraiture. He showed a particular bent for scenes on the beach, which offered the silhouette effects always dear to Spanish art. He found watercolor particularly suitable to the lyrical mood of his painting. He exhibited throughout Europe and America and is represented in museums all over the world. (See illustration.)

Sotatsu (see JAPANESE PAINTERS: TOKUGAWA PERIOD).

Soulages, Pierre (1919-). French painter who has exhibited in various parts of the world. His style, increasingly international in character, is a so-called Abstract Expressionism which in his case and others like him is characterized by the criss-cross effect of very thick black lines on an almost neutral background.

Soutine, Chaim (1894-1943). Lithuanian-born painter associated with the Expressionist group in Paris. The son of a poor Jewish tailor in a tiny village, Soutine ran away from home at an early age and enrolled in the Vilna art school

SOLANA. The Visit of the Bishop. Museum of Modern Art, Madrid

in 1910, meanwhile working as a photographer's assistant. In 1911 he reached Paris and found a room in The Beehive, a crowded lodging in the slaughterhouse district. Here he borrowed from his slaughterer friends the joints of meat that figure as still life in his paintings. But things were very difficult and Soutine actually tried to commit suicide. Fortunately he met the art dealer Zborowski through Modigliani and sold his first pictures. In 1923 he had the further good luck to sell about a hundred paintings to the American Dr. Barnes, who was then forming his collection. The morbidity and passionate Expressionism (see) of the earlier works—comparable only to the violence and twisted form of Kokoschka—yielded to a more decorative and glowing conception in the period between 1925 and his death. (See illustrations, including color plate 189.)

Soutman, Pieter Claesz. (active by 1619; d. 1657). Dutch engraver and painter of portraits and figures. He was trained in Antwerp, possibly by Rubens, whose helper he became. From about 1624-28 he was in the service of the King of Poland and then returned to Haarlem. The influence of Frans Hals is apparent in his many portraits and in the picture he contributed to the series of decorations in the royal palace of the Huis ten Bosch, near The Hague.

Soyer, Moses (1899-). Contemporary American painter of city genre, of working people, and especially dancers. Born in Russia, twin brother of Raphael, he arrived in the U.S. with his family in 1912, and studied art at night at the National Academy of Design and at the Educational Alliance.

SOROLLA Y BASTIDA. The Two Sisters, Valencia
Art Institute of Chicago, William S. North Memorial Collection

189. SOUTINE. Page Boy. Albright Art Gallery, Buffalo

Soyer, Raphael (1899-). A contemporary American painter of intimate city genre. Twin brother of Moses, he was born in Russia, and came to the U.S. with his family in 1912. Working at odd jobs, he attended Cooper Union, the National Academy of Design, and the Art Students League, where he studied with Guy Pène Du Bois.

Spada, Lionello (1576-1622). Bolognese painter active in Emilia and at Parma, where he worked for Ranuccio and Odoardo Farnese. Born in Bologna, he was at first a Carracci pupil, specializing in architectural perspectives. Around 1597 in Rome he became a friend and close follower of Caravaggio, who used him as a model. Returning to Bologna, his imitation of Caravaggio in dress and manner led to his

SOUTINE. Portrait of a Young Woman
Stedelijk Museum, Amsterdam

being called "ape of Caravaggio." However, his art is really closer to the academicism of the Bolognese Academy.

Spagna, Lo (Giovanni di Pietro) (c.1450-1528). Spanish painter; worked in Italy in the Umbrian school. Lo Spagna, so called because of his Spanish origin, was a contemporary and a gifted pupil of Perugino. He is first referred to in 1470 as an independent master and as a Spaniard living in Perugia. An Adoration painted before 1503 (Louvre) reveals his debt to Perugino's style in its serene, decorative composition and broad landscape. Dated works show that by 1516 the influence of Raphael began to predominate. He settled in Spoleto, where an important fresco of the Coronation of the Virgin (1526) is preserved in the church of San Giacomo.

Spagnoletto, Lo (see RIBERA).

Spagnuolo, Lo (see CRESPI, GIUSEPPE MARIA).

Speicher, Eugene (1883-). Contemporary American portrait painter. Born in Buffalo, N.Y., he attended the Buffalo Fine Arts Academy and later the Art Students League in New York, where he studied with Chase and DuMond. Through Henri, in 1909, he met Bellows and the other younger disciples of the Ashcan School. Influenced at first by the Realist tradition, he eventually turned to a more conservative style. He was elected a member of the National Academy in 1927. (See illustration.)

Spencer, Niles (1893-1952). American painter of industrial landscapes in the Cubist-Realist style. Born in Pawtucket, R.I., he studied at the Rhode Island School of Design and at the Art Students League with Henri and Bellows. He became interested in Cubism about 1920 and his art showed a renewed emphasis on abstraction about 1943. (See illustration.)

Spencer, Stanley (1892-). British painter of poetic and religious themes; also of landscapes and a few portraits. He was interested at first in religious subjects, which he approached with a fervor reminiscent of the English Pre-Raphaelites of the nineteenth century and with a largeness of compositional form suggesting the early Italian masters. He has continued in this vein, adding also ideas of love and marriage. Spencer's style shows a precise and ordered arrangement and an extreme clarity of form that, although academic in ultimate derivation, is given a special character by the intensity of emotional expression.

Spinello Aretino (Spinello di Luca Spinelli) (c.1346-

SPEICHER. Marianna
Whitney Museum of American Art, New York

SPENCER, NILES. Erie Underpass
Metropolitan Museum of Art, New York

SPINELLO. Saint Mary Magdalen with a Crucifix
Metropolitan Museum of Art, New York

1410). Born in Arezzo but probably trained in the shop of Agnolo Gaddi in Florence. Extant frescoes by him are in San Miniato al Monte, Florence (c.1387), in Santa Caterina in Antella (c.1387), the Palazzo Pubblico, Siena (1408), San Francesco in Arezzo, and the Campo Santo in Pisa (1391-92). Signed panels are an altar for Monte Oliveti (1384-5), now scattered, and a triptych in the Florence Academy. Noted for its skillful and individual draughtsmanship, his style is in the dramatic narrative tradition of Giotto, though in panel paintings the flatter and more decorative influence of Orcagna and Nardo di Cione may be seen. (See illustration.)

Spruce, Everett Franklin (1907-). Contemporary American regional painter. His landscapes and still lifes are simplified stylizations of nature which balance the needs of the theme with his own adaptation of the modern viewpoint. Born near Conway, Ark., he studied art with Olin Travis in Dallas, became assistant director of the museum there, and now teaches at the University of Texas.

Squarcione, Francesco (1394-1474). A Paduan painter but more important as the director of a large workshop that transmitted to many north Italian painters an interest in classical antiquity and humanism, and the influence of the Florentines who had worked in Padua (Uccello, Fra Filippo Lippi and the sculptor Donatello). Greatest among the artists trained in his shop was Mantegna, but many of the major Venetians (Bartolommeo Vivarini, Crivelli, the Bellini, were also affected by his teaching. The chief work from Squarcione's hand is a polyptych representing five saints (1449-52) in the Padua museum.

Städelsches Museum, Frankfort, Germany. A collection rich in examples of modern German painting., e.g., Kirchner, Nolde, Beckmann, Macke.

Staël, Nicolas de (1914-). A Russian-born French painter who has created his own version of Abstract Impressionism by the use of heavy slabs of paint.

stained glass. Generally connected with the great colored glass windows of Gothic cathedrals, one of the glories of art in the middle ages, it is a kind of painting in light. More prosaically, it is glass which has been colored by the fusion of metallic oxides, the burning of pigment into its surface, or the joining of colored and white pieces. Its historic origin is obscure, but the technique probably originates in the colored glass of the Near East and not before the ninth century. This knowledge spread naturally to Italy, possibly first to Venice, which may have been a center of stained glassmaking in the tenth century. The earliest documentary reference to stained glass used pictorially is in a manuscript (969-88) referring to the rebuilding of Reims Cathedral; and the earliest reference to leading occurs in the "Miracles of St. Benoit" in which the fear is expressed that the leads would melt when the tenth-century church of Fleury-sur-Loire was set on fire It is not known which are the earliest extant pictorial windows, but evidence seems to point to the prophets in Augsburg Cathedral which may date from the mid-eleventh century. The stained glass window of the middle ages is actually a translucent mosaic held together with leads, which play an important part in the design. Finer details were painted on. The increase of window space and the practical elimination of walls in Gothic cathedrals naturally led to the decorative role of stained glass. The earliest windows had only single figures but by the mid-twelfth century medallions with pictorial scenes were already introduced. The resulting smallness of scale called for a more detailed and varied use of color and produced the jewel-like quality so evident in the thirteenth century. In the latter thirteenth and

STAINED GLASS. French, 13th century. Two Apostles (detail)
Cathedral of Sens

early fourteenth centuries grisaille painting on glass became common, transforming the mosaic quality of the window into a painting quality. There is a similarity of stained glass throughout Europe during the thirteenth century but after about 1350 national styles develop in England, France, Germany, and Austria.

In the fourteenth century the decline in technique resulting from the disastrous effects of the Black Death, together with the Cistercian ban on pictorial windows, managed to destroy the art of stained glassmaking. Taste also was for linear designs on clear glass and in the fourteenth century subject matter expanded to include contemporary life. The inevitable result was that stained glass like mosaics became attempted reproductions of paintings. More recent efforts to revive the art of stained glass have been partially successful in duplicating the quality of glass, but have unfortunately foundered on the rock of revivalism. The great centuries of stained glass were the twelfth and thirteenth. During the twelfth the designs were simple, the colors brilliant and the glass clear, the total effect breathtaking in its symphonic grandeur. The windows of St. Denis, magnificent of this period, had their effect upon those of Chartres, Bourges, Le Mans and York. Though the thirteenth century lost some of the brilliance of the earlier glass and showed too avid a predilection for lavender, it improved the design of the iron scaffolding and increased detail. The greatest example of this period is probably the windows of Chartres (1210), which influenced those of Sens, Rouen, the Ste. Chapelle, Lincoln and Canterbury. (See illustrations.)

190. STEEN. Merrymakers. National Gallery, London

STAINED GLASS. English, c.1400
Winchester College Window. Winchester

Stanfield, William Clarkson (1793-1867). British marine painter and friend of Turner. He was popular in his time for seascapes and lake scenes in oil and watercolor.

Stanzione, Massimo (called Cavaliere Massimo) (1585-1656). Neapolitan Baroque (see) painter, rival of Ribera. Born in Orta di Atella, he studied in Naples with Caracciolo, and was influenced by Artemisia Gentileschi and Ribera, and then in Rome by Annibale Carracci and Guido Reni.

Stark, Arthur James (1794-1859). British landscapist and member of the Norwich school (see). A pupil and imitator of Old Crome, Stark's landscapes show technical proficiency and a simplicity of approach.

Starnina, Gherardo (active 1387-c.1413). Florentine painter. Between 1398 and 1401 he worked in Spain (but no work of this period is known), and in 1404 he completed an important fresco cycle in Santa Maria del Carmine in Florence (now fragmentary). Frescoes of the Castellani chapel of Santa Croce were probably painted chiefly by him under the direction of his teacher, Agnolo Gaddi. Starnina forms an important link between the fourteenth and fifteenth centuries. He inherited the dramatic narrative fresco tradition of Giotto, but in panel paintings attributed to him a decorative Gothic tendency in design and drapery make him a pioneer of the style of Lorenzo Monaco and Masolino.

Stedelijk Museum, Amsterdam. Municipal Museum specializing in art of the last one hundred years with sections devoted to Van Gogh and his French contemporaries, modern Belgian masters, the late nineteenth-century School of Amsterdam, The Hague and Bergen, and contemporary Netherlandish art in general.

Steen, Jan (1626-79). Dutch painter of genre, history and portraits. He studied at the University of Leyden and afterward was the pupil of Jan van Goyen, whose daughter he married. Steen was one of the earliest members of the newly founded painters' guild at Leyden, but worked also at The Hague, Delft and Haarlem. He was Holland's foremost master of humorous genre, delighting in scenes of abandoned merriment and disorder but painting them, paradoxically, in a style distinguished by the greatest suavity and brilliance. The delicacy and freshness of his color further enhances his lively themes. (See illustrations, including color plate 190.)

Steer, Philip Wilson (1860-1942). British Impressionist painter who worked in Paris under Bouguereau and at the Beaux-Arts under Cabanel. As a landscapist in the line of Gainsborough, Constable and Turner, he must be considered, like Sickert, in the Impressionist group of moderns. (See illustration.)

Stefano (Maestro Stefano, or Stefano Fiorentino). (active first half 14th century). No authenticated work of this Florentine pupil of Giotto remains, though he was famous in his day. Frescoes have been attributed to him in the church of San Francesco, Assisi.

Stefano da Zevio (c.1375-c.1450). He represents the transition from Gothic fourteenth-century style to the early Renaissance in Verona. Continuing some elements of the earlier tradition of Altichiero, he adds a new sense of form and naturalistic expression to a style that is essentially lyrical and not unrelated to contemporary north European miniature painting.

Stefano di Giovanni (see SASSETTA).

STEEN. Pulling a Tooth. Mauritshuis, The Hague

STEER. Beach at Walberswick. Tate Gallery, London

STELLA, JOSEPH. Brooklyn Bridge: Variation on an Old Theme
Whitney Museum of American Art, New York

Stella, Jacques (1596-1657). French painter and etcher. Friend of Poussin in Rome. Stella was the pupil of his father, going at twenty years of age to Florence in the employ of Duke Cosimo. On his return to France in 1634 he was made painter to the king and was employed at decorating churches, especially for the orders of the Assumption and the Carmelites.

Stella, Joseph (1880-1946). American painter born in Italy. After two years studying medicine, he turned to painting and came to the U.S. in 1900, where he continued his studies at the New York School of Art. His earliest work as an illustrator was in the Realist tradition, but his return to Europe in 1909 brought him in contact with the Italian Futurist movement. His Futurist manner, first exhibited here at the Armory Show, continued with modification in his interpretations of industrial scenes—Brooklyn Bridge, (Yale Museum), New York Interpreted (Newark Museum) etc. His later work showed a tendency toward romantic fantasy. (See illustration.)

Sterne, Maurice (1878-). Contemporary American painter and sculptor, born in Russia. After an early youth spent in Moscow, he came to the U.S. in 1889. He studied at the National Academy of Design, where he exhibited great promise and was awarded a traveling fellowship. He spent the next decade abroad, living in Paris, Italy, Greece, Egypt, India, Burma, Java, and for several years, Bali. Influenced by modern art, the Italian Renaissance and Greek sculpture, his early work is most dependent upon Cézanne. His later paintings of Italian peasant life done at Anticoli-Corrado are more conservative and formal. He has also done murals in Washington, D.C. (See illustration.)

Steumpfig, Walter (1914-). Contemporary American Neo-Romantic painter. Born in Germantown, Pa., he studied at the Pennsylvania Academy of Fine Arts and abroad on a traveling fellowship. Although he paints recognizable genre subjects with meticulous detail, he imbues his scenes with overtones of brooding mystery and even foreboding. (See illustration.)

Stevens, Alfred (1817-75). British painter, sculptor and decorator. He made drawings and sculptures in imitation of Michelangelo, but in his own work used a rather unsuccessful still-life approach for the painting of figure pieces. He taught design, did commercial art and decorated private homes.

Stieglitz, Alfred (1864-1946). American photographer who played a leading role in the introduction of modern art to the U.S. and in the support of modern American artists. Beginning in 1905 at the Photo Secession Gallery, 291 Fifth Avenue, called "291," he first exhibited many of the leading European modernists as well as such American pioneers in the movement as Marin, Maurer and Hartley in 1909, Dove and Weber in 1910, Walkowitz in 1912, Nadelman in 1915, O'Keeffe in 1916, and Macdonald-Wright in 1917. In 1917 he was forced to close "291," but in the same year opened the "Intimate Gallery"; the latter gave way in 1929 to "An American Place," which he maintained until the time of his death. Although he exhibited the work of many American

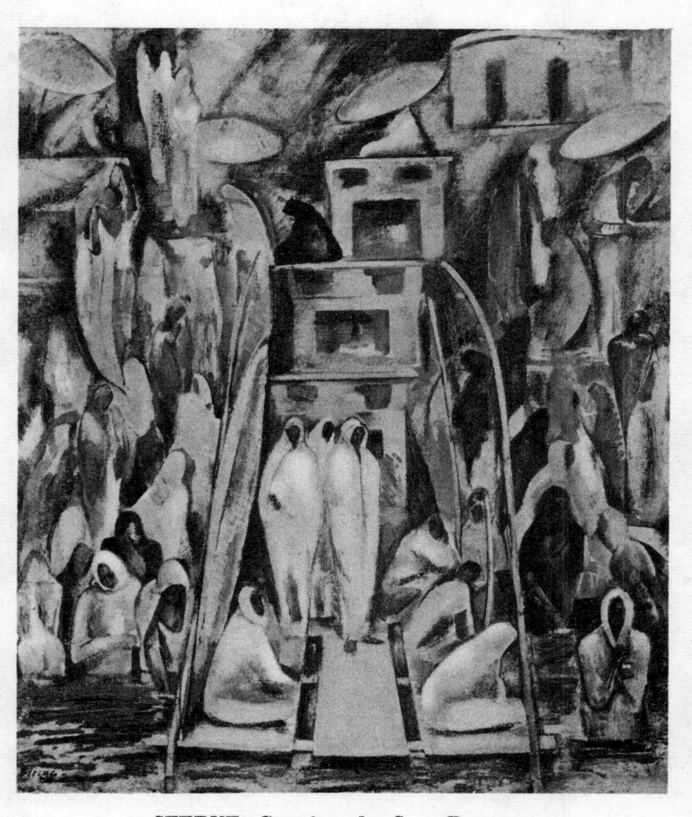

STERNE. Greeting the Sun, Benares
Babcock Galleries, New York

STEUMPFIG. Two Houses
Corcoran Gallery of Art, Washington, D.C.

artists, he was most intimately connected with Marin, Dove, Demuth, Hartley, and his wife, Georgia O'Keeffe. Born in Hoboken, N.J., he studied engineering at the City College of New York and after 1881 at the Berlin Polytechnic, where he became interested in photography. He returned to the U.S. in 1890 and founded the Camera Club. In 1902 he organized the Photo Secessionists, opened "291," and published "Camera Work" (1903-17), the outstanding magazine of art and photography of the period.

still life. A kind of painting whose subject matter is a group of inanimate forms such as fruit, vegetables, dead game or any other miscellaneous objects the painter may bring together as a theme. Still-life objects were part of the background of many types of painting from the Roman period to the seventeenth century. At that point, especially in Holland, Flanders and Spain, the still life emerged as an independent art form. During the following century it was treated very effectively by Chardin in France, who raised the still life to the status of a major art form. This tendency was reinforced in the magnificent still-life pictures of Cézanne in the late nineteenth century as well as in the somewhat earlier works of many Impressionists. The difference between the works in this field produced by traditional artists and by the masters of the late nineteenth and twentieth centuries lies in the assumption of the earlier painters that the sille life was characterized by some kind of narrative or psychological quality. In our own time the tendency is to use the still life as a pretext for painting rather than as a subject with distinctly emotional or anecdotal overtones Thus it has changed from a theme to a motif, from something charged with everyday human meaning to an aesthetic combination of forms, colors and textures.

Stimmer, Tobias (1539-83). Swiss painter known for his fresco decorations in the House of the Knight at Schaffhausen on the Rhine and for a number of excellently characterized portraits. The latter include a fine pair showing Jacob Schwytzer and his wife Elsbeth (1564, Basel) in which the monumentality of the Italian High Renaissance is combined with a detail and warmth of feeling from Germanic sources. (See illustration.)

Strozzi, Bernardo (called Il Cappuccino) (1581-1644). Genoese painter and engraver, a member of the Capuchin order. He studied in Genoa with the Sienese Mannerist, Pietro Sorri, but in the 1620's broke with Mannerism (see) and turned to the early Baroque (see). He has some connections with Caravaggio through Saraceni, but his study of Veronese, during his last years in Venice (after 1630), led to the lightening of color that is characteristic of his mature style. (See illustration.)

Stuart, Gilbert (1755-1828). The most famous American portrait painter of the Federal period. Born in Rhode Island, the son of a snuff-grinder, he is said to have studied with Samuel King. He was already painting on commission at the

STIMMER. Portrait of Elsbeth Lochmann,
Wife of Jacob Schwytzer. Kunstmuseum, Basel

191. STUART. George Washington
Museum of Fine Arts, Boston

age of fourteen. In 1770 he studied with Cosmo Alexander, a Scotch painter, and returned with him to Scotland. After the death of Alexander in 1772 he returned to the U.S., but in 1775 sailed for England, where he studied with and assisted Benjamin West. In 1783 he opened his own portrait studio in London and was immediately successful. Caught up in the glamour of London society he lived beyond his means and was soon irretrievably in debt. He left England to avoid debtors' prison and worked in Ireland from 1787 to 1793, when he returned to the U.S. It was in Philadelphia that he painted his first portrait of George Washington, known as the Vaughan type. The second effort was a full-length, known as the Landsdowne; the third, the most famous portrait of the president and the one which identifies him to posterity, was the Athenaeum, which he never finished but kept as a model from which he made over seventy copies. In 1803, he moved to Philadelphia and after 1805 lived in Boston. He was without doubt the most brilliant painter in the U.S. during that period, the official portraitist of the new republican society. He had a fluent impressionistic technique, in the manner of his English contemporaries, Romney, Raeburn, and Lawrence. His virtuosity was limited to face-painting and his efforts at anything more ambitious were failures, but in his best portraits he combines psychological probity and technical brilliance. (See color plate 191.)

Stubbs, George (1724-1806). British painter of horses. He made intensive studies of animal anatomy and in 1760-66 published a work on the anatomy of the horse, illustrated with his own engravings. This was a great success and added to his reputation as a painter. He produced some panels in enamel on earthenware which were fired by Wedgwood. In addition to scientific knowledge, Stubbs shows a feeling for form and dignified design. He is also known for his genre paintings of English rural life. (See illustration.)

Stuttgart Picture Gallery, Stuttgart, Germany. A general collection stressing the moderns, especially those of Germany and France.

Subleyras, Pierre (1699-1749). A French painter and etcher. He passed most of his life in Italy, where he was much in demand for religious commissions. Several of his compositions were converted into mosaics. The Swoon of Emperor Valens While Assisting at a Mass Celebrated by St. Basil was so commissioned. A great number of his works were done for the Pope.

Suiboku, Japanese painting in the Chinese monochrome style; it was very popular in the Muromachi period (1333-1573) in Japan.

Sui Dynasty (see CHINESE PAINTERS: SUI DYNASTY, 581-618).

Sully, Thomas (1783-1872). A successful and prolific American painter who left some 2,000 portraits and miniatures and some 500 subject pictures. His style is light and graceful, but lacking in either strength or penetration. After a poverty-ridden youth he finally achieved intermittent financial success, working mostly in Philadelphia. Born into an acting family in England, he came as a child to Charleston, S.C. His first efforts in art were with his brother-in-law, Belfons, a French émigré miniaturist. He later worked with his brother Lawrence, also a miniaturist in Richmond and Norfolk. In financial straits but intent on improving his technique he studied by observation successively with Bembridge, Trumbull, Jarvis, and Stuart. In 1809 he became an American citizen and with his own savings and the help of several patrons went to England and there studied with C.

STROZZI. Portrait of a Connoisseur. National Gallery, London

B. King and West. Here he copied the Old Masters from West's collection to pay back his supporters. His style now more polished and showing the influence of Lawrence, he returned to Philadelphia and portrait painting in 1810. In the following years he achieved fame and financial success, although not consistently. In 1837 he went to England to paint the portrait of Queen Victoria for the St. George Society of Philadelphia, his most famous though not his best portrait, a tour de force of pretty but empty elegance. (See illustration.)

Sultan Muhammad (see PERSIAN PAINTERS: SAFAWID PERIOD).

Sunday Afternoon on La Grande Jatte by Georges Seurat (see).

Sunflowers by Vincent Van Gogh (see).

Sung Dynasty (see CHINESE PAINTERS: SUNG DYNASTY, 960-1279).

Sung Imperial Catalogue. The *Hsüan-ho Hua P'u*, a catalogue of paintings in the Chinese Imperial collections of the Northern Sung period; composed of twenty parts arranged first by subject matter and then chronologically. The preface, dated 1120 by cyclical characters in the Hsüan-ho era, ends with the statement that it was composed by the reigning Emperor Hui Tsung. Scholars have weighed its authenticity as a twelfth-century work and some have ascribed it to a much later period, but it seems entirely possible that it was written by anonymous court officials at the command of the Emperor. See HUI TSUNG in CHINESE PAINTERS: SUNG DYNASTY.

Suprematism. A movement founded in Moscow by the Russian painter Kasimir Malevich in 1913 and characterized by the non-objective form of its technique and by the purely geometrical orientation of Malevich and those influenced by him. Although Kandinsky had already produced a spontaneous and amorphous or free-form kind of non-objectivity in the years immediately preceding 1913, it was Malevich who first called attention to the purely geometric and architectonic possibilities of non-objective painting, i.e., the supremacy of pure perception of form and the absence of reference to the visible world. Its logical conclusion may be found in that painter's famous picture White on White.

Surrealism. A movement in modern painting and sculpture. Its aim is to create a new or super-reality through fresh associations and relationships established by ordinarily unrelated themes and their projection. It moves a step beyond the anarchic and automatic-writing responses of the Dadaists in which the unfettered subconscious rather than the creative imagination was given full rein; instead of trying to indicate the imminent destruction of art and culture, it seeks a positive and constructive level. The Surrealist asserts that all our actions are dominated by the subconscious and that the impulses stemming from that direction can be channelized into concrete aesthetic form. Although it often claims to be directed by this subconscious apparatus and maintains that the painting or other work is done entirely under its domination, the results seem far too consciously precise and logical to be the product of a dream alone. We may distinguish two types of Surrealist work: One is the representational type exemplified by Dali and Tanguy, marked by deep perspectives indicating the movement of time and creating a dream atmosphere, clear color and highly naturalistic forms. The other, and less representational side of Surrealism, is represented by Masson, Arp and others and shows a playful combination of forms that may be half frightening, half amusing but always suggests fresh ideas and associations.

STUBBS. Gentleman Holding His Horse. Tate Gallery, London

192. SUTHERLAND. Thorn Trees
Albright Art Gallery, Buffalo

Su Shih (or Su T'ung-p'o) (see CHINESE PAINTERS: SUNG DYNASTY).

Sutherland, Graham (1903-). British painter of poetically imaginative landscapes. His art, formed under the influence of the mystical William Blake and Blake's disciple Samuel Palmer, may be described as Surrealist in its fantasy and slightly menacing quality. Sutherland conceives nature as something mysterious, even ominous, and the objects therein as symbols of human beings and their character. His mature style, developed in the late 1930's, now expresses these characteristics through a typical use of thorns and thorn bushes, apparently under the impact of his own work on the Crucifixion of the Church of St. Matthew in Northampton. More recently he has also become known for a number of expressive portraits of such celebrated personalities as Somerset Maugham, Lord Beaverbrook and Sir Winston Churchill. (See color plate 192.)

Suttermans (Sustermans) Justus (1597-1681). Flemish painter. Pupil of Willem de Vos in Antwerp, he spent most of his career in Italy, where he married three times and worked mainly in the service of the Dukes of Tuscany. His speciality was portraiture and he painted many Italian notables of the day in a style that was influenced by both van Dyck and Frans Pourbus the Younger.

SULLY. Dr. Edward Hudson. Detroit Institute of Art

Swabach-Desfontains, Jacques François Joseph (1767-1823). French painter, porcelain designer, etcher and lithographer. He has left us a graphic record of the French Revolution and the battles of the Consulate and Empire.

Swan, John Macallan (1847-1910). A British animal painter and sculptor. He did intensive anatomical research in London hospitals and zoological gardens, and his work shows an assured rendering of animal movements, body structure and general appearance.

Swiss National Museum, Zurich. A large collection of Swiss art and cultural monuments: paintings, sculpture, paneling, porcelain, ivory carvings, weapons, costumes, etc.

Symbolism. A movement in modern painting that emerged during the Post-Impressionist period and was first clearly defined by the critic Albert Aurier in the *Mercure de France* in 1891. According to this writer, the purpose of Symbolism was "to clothe the idea in a form perceptible to the senses" or, in other words, to represent abstract and general ideas such as love, hate, fear, God, in a form that could be apprehended by the senses. Gauguin was declared the leader of this movement in such paintings as The Yellow Christ, Jacob Struggling with the Angel, etc., which typified the concept that life was to be observed through the many paths of the dream world. In addition, it stipulated the use of all kinds of primitive, archaic and exotic or strange art forms that could be symbolically understood or treated. It was said, in short, that the work of art should be "ideational, symbolic, synthetic, subjective and decorative." One of its chief advocates as well as its theoretician was Paul Sérusier. The first exhibition of this group, held in 1891, included such names as Gauguin, Sérusier and many others; some, like Bonnard, Vuillard, Denis, Roussel, etc., later belonged to the Nabis; some, like Zuloaga, to the Impressionists; and finally Lautrec, who may perhaps also be included with the Nabis. Symbolism itself is a Europe-wide phenomenon encompassing Ensor in Belgium, Hodler in Switzerland and Munch in Norway, and paralleling a similar movement in European, and especially French, literature.

TADDEO DI BARTOLO
St. Thomas Aquinas Submitting His Office to the Pope
Philadelphia Museum of Art, Johnson Collection

Synchromism (see ORPHISM).

Synthetic Cubism (see CUBISM).

Synthetism. Refers to the painting methods of Gauguin and his followers in the camps of symbolists, or Nabis (see both); in it the normal appearance of nature gave way to an artifical or synthetic appearance that enabled the artist to control the various elements and have them represent an abstract or intangible idea. This was accomplished by flattening the space in true Post-Impressionist fashion, reducing the volume of the particular object to a two-dimensional or flat form, and bounding this form with a heavy curvilinear outline that suggested the flowing movement of foliage or nature in general. Color was also exaggerated, heightened, and made increasingly expressive in order to convey the feeling of the object rather than its actual appearance. The heavy boundary lines resemble those used in enamel work or stained-glass painting; hence this kind of painting is also known as cloisonnism i.e., like the cloisons or settings in enamel.

Szinyei-Merse, Paul (1845-1920). Hungarian Impressionist trained under Böcklin and under the influence of Courbet. Without having been in contact with French Impressionism, he is said to have evolved a version of this technique that paralleled the work of Edouard Manet.

T

Tacconi, Francesco (active 1458-1500). A native of Cremona, Francesco was also active in Venice, where he became an imitator of Giovanni Bellini. His brother Filippo, also a painter, collaborated with him on frescoes (now lost) in Cremona (1464). Francesco's only known work, a Madonna (London), is a virtual copy of one by Bellini.

tactile. Referring to the sense of touch. In painting, the kind of representation that gives the feeling or suggests the way in which a represented object would actually feel if touched.

Taddeo di Bartolo (1360/65-1422). The last important figure of the thirteenth century in Siena, his art brought to a close the medieval phase of Sienese painting. He was the son of Bartolo, a barber, not Bartolo di Fredi, though his art is related to that of this contemporary master. But the chief influence on his work was that of Simone Martini. He was a prolific artist and traveled widely. In 1386 he was working for the cathedral in Siena, though still a minor, and in 1393 dated his frescoes in the Collegiata at San Gimignano. In 1395 and 1397 he visited Pisa, in 1401 Montepulciano, and in 1403 Perugia, where he did two panels now in the Pinacoteca Vannucci and made his influence felt throughout Umbria. The period 1406-08 finds him in Siena painting a cycle of frescoes in the Palazzo Pubblico, and in 1411 he visited Volterra, where an important polyptych by him is preserved. His last dated painting now extant is a Madonna, 1418, in the Fogg Museum, Harvard University. Taddeo's forms and types, the occasional facial beauty and softness of expression of his figures, and his refined execution and love of decorative detail all stem remotely but directly from the art of Simone Martini (see). His art, however, lacks the spirituality and mysticism of Simone, and his figures and brushwork tend to become heavy and somewhat coarse, especially in late works. Among followers and pupils may be listed Andrea di Bartolo, Martino di Bartolommeo, and Gregorio di Cecco, Taddeo's adopted son. His greatest immediate successor was Sassetta. (See illustration.)

Tagore, Abanindranath (see INDIAN PAINTERS: MODERN PERIOD).

Tai Chin (see CHINESE PAINTERS: MING DYNASTY).

Taikan (see JAPANESE PAINTERS: SHOWA PERIOD).

Takanobu (see JAPANESE PAINTERS: HEIAN PERIOD).

Tal Coat, Pierre (1905-). French painter who began as a student of sculpture and designer of pottery models to be used in industry. Tal Coat's art has moved through Post-Impressionism to Fauvism and currently fits into the Abstract Expressionist category.

TANGUY. Time and Again...Never
Pierre Matisse Gallery, New York

Tamagna, Vincenzo (1492-1530+). Umbro-Florentine painter born in San Gimignano. He was an eclectic whose art had a long circular development from Ghirlandaio to Sodoma to Raphael to Ridolfo Ghirlandaio. He studied in Florence probably with Mainardi and Ghirlandaio, worked with Sodoma at Monte Oliveto (1505) and with Giovanni da Spoleto at Arrone (1516), and was active in Rome and Tuscany.

TAMAYO. New York from a Terrace. Pierre Matisse Gallery, New York

193. TAMAYO. Women of Tehuantepec. Albright Art Gallery, Buffalo

194. TERBORCH. Gentleman in Black
M. H. de Young Memorial Museum, San Francisco

Tamayo, Rufino (1899-). Mexican easel painter and muralist; a leading Mexican exponent of international modern styles. Tamayo has been influenced both by local artistic factors (pre-Columbian forms, native popular arts) and by modern European abstract techniques, e.g., Picasso and Braque. His warm resonant color is distinctly personal and Mexican in flavor. He lived for a long time in New York, where his contact with the modern movement first occurred. He is primarily an easel painter and opposed to the social character of the modern Mexican mural movement, having done relatively little in that field himself. His best-known murals are those at Smith College, Northampton, Mass., (1943), and the recent works (1952-53) in the Palace of Fine Arts, Mexico, where he finally joins the other Mexican "greats," Rivera, Orozco and Siqueiros, in what is now known as the "Big Four." These later works combine the narrative content of Mexican nationalist subject matter with the painter's own dynamically abstract forms and resonant glowing color. (See illustrations, including color plate 193.)

T'ang Dynasty (see CHINESE PAINTERS: T'ANG DYNASTY, 618-907).

Tanguy, Yves (1900-55). French-born painter associated with the figurative side of Surrealism (see). Tanguy came to art through an accidental view of a painting by Chirico in the window of an art gallery in Paris, and without previous training began to paint. He joined the Surrealists in 1925 and contributed to many of their group shows. He arrived in the United States in 1939 and later became an American citizen. He is more genuinely imaginative than many other Surrealists of his type, peopling his pictures with organic, amoebic creatures that exist nowhere except in his own mind. At times they also suggest the creatures that might float among the miniature mountain ranges and cold light of an imagined ocean. (See illustration.)

T'ang Yin (see CHINESE PAINTERS: MING DYNASTY).

Tao Chi (see CHINESE PAINTERS: CH'ING DYNASTY).

Tarbell, Edmund Charles (1862-1938). An American portrait and genre painter whose genteel art reflects the serene and ordered manner of Boston life. Born in West Groton, Mass., he studied at the Boston Museum School and at the Ecole des Beaux-Arts with Boulanger and Lefebvre. He was senior

195. TIBET. C. 17TH CENTURY. Principal Events in the Life of the Buddha. Collection Antoinette K. Gordon, New York

instructor at the Boston Museum School, head of the Corcoran School of Art, and a member of the Ten.

Tate Gallery, London. Also known as the National Gallery, Millbank. This collection concerns itself with more recent works than the National Gallery proper and is especially noteworthy for its great assemblage of works by J. M. W. Turner. Modern Continental masters in nineteenth- and twentieth-century examples are also well represented.

Taubes, Frederic (1900-). Contemporary American painter born in Lemberg, Austria. The son of a banker, he studied with various Viennese artists, then at Munich with Max Doerner, and at the Bauhaus in Weimar. He has a special interest in painting techniques and has written on the subject. He paints with great emphasis on cubical structure, with rich color and heavy impasto.

Tchelitchew, Pavel (1898-). Russian-born painter of the School of Paris. He is identified with the Neo-Romantic group of the 1930's, younger painters interested in achieving a kind of poetic and mournful intensity in which the pathetic and poignant are the base of operations. Bérard and Berman,

TCHELITCHEW. The Whirlwind
Metropolitan Museum of Art, New York

as well as Tchelitchew, are among the principal artists in this group. Tchelitchew expresses himself through a series of distorted and elongated forms seen from close up, so that the lower extremities are emotionally exaggerated. His later work brings him closer to the subconscious motivations of the orthodox Surrealists and is characterized by a probing into the physical interior of the brain and the body that is in many ways more disturbing than a dream world. See NEO-ROMANTICISM. (See illustration.)

Tempel, Abraham van den (1622/23-1672). Dutch painter of historical pictures and portraits. He studied with Joris van Schooten in Leyden and later was influenced by the fashionable van der Helst in Amsterdam. His portraits are sensitive, well drawn, and pleasant in color.

tempera. One of the earliest painting media, used in Egypt, Mesopotamia, and Crete, a mixture of ground pigment and an albuminous, gelatinous or colloidal medium, most often egg, either yolk and white or only yolk. Though soluble in water, it is a comparatively permanent medium which presents certain limitations—it is opaque and dries rapidly. It was used throughout the medieval period as well as the Renaissance for paintings executed on wooden panels and treated with gesso (see).

Ten, the. A group of leading American academic painters who held their first joint exhibition, "Ten American Painters," in 1898 and continued to show together. The group consisted of Frank W. Benson, Joseph R. De Camp, Thomas W. Dewing, Childe Hassam, Willard L. Metcalf, Robert Reid, Edward Simmons, Edmund C. Tarbell, John H. Twachtman and J. Alden Weir. After the death of Twachtman in 1902, William M. Chase became a member.

Ten Bamboo Studio Studies. A notable edition of Chinese color prints of the Ming period.

tenebrist. A type of painter following the dramatic light-and-dark manner of Caravaggio and found in great profusion among seventeenth-century Baroque masters, e.g., Georges de La Tour, Ribera, Zurbarán, etc.

Teniers the Elder, David (1582-1649). Flemish painter and engraver. Father of David Teniers the Younger. Pupil of his brother Juliaen and then, in Italy, of Elsheimer and Rubens. He was primarily a religious painter; the genre and landscapes once attributed to him are now known to be by his son or Elsheimer. Paintings by him exist in the church of Dendermonde and St. Paul's of Antwerp.

Teniers the Younger, David (1610-90). The leading Flemish genre painter after Brouwer. He was born in Antwerp, studied with his father, David the Elder, became a member of the guild in 1632, and in 1637 married Anne Brueghel, the daughter of Jan the Elder. In 1651 he settled in Brussels, became court painter and curator to Archduke Leopold-William, and later to Don Juan of Austria. He also founded the Academy of Fine Arts in Antwerp. Influenced by Bosch and Brueghel, but mostly by Rubens and Brouwer, from whom he inherited a light and fluent transparency, he added his own unique silvery tonality. Although he did religious (especially Temptations of St. Anthony) and mythological subjects, he is best known for his genre scenes of taverns and kermesse, alchemists and hermits. His earlier work was brighter and heavier, and his quality is uneven because of the assistance of his many students, but he repeated his popular themes in countless numbers, producing over 2,000 pictures. He had great influence and was especially popular in the eighteenth century, when he was considered the greatest of the genre painters. Among his most famous works are the Money Changer and His Wife (London), the Five Senses (Brussels), the Dentist (Cassel), the Smoker (Louvre), the Great Kitchen (The Hague), the Prodigal Son (Louvre), and the Kermess (Louvre). (See illustration.)

Terborch, Gerard (1617-81). Dutch painter and engraver of portraits and genre scenes. He was born in Zwolle and studied there with his father. Afterward he was a pupil of Pieter Molijn in Haarlem and felt the influence of Hals. He traveled to England and Münster, where in 1648 he painted a picture of the famous peace conference (London). Terborch visited Spain, painting Philip IV, and observing the work of Velázquez, whose influence was evident from then on in his own portraits. Returning to Holland he spent the rest of his life working in Deventer. Terborch's technique is exquisitely finished and his interpretations of society and manners elegant and sophisticated. (See color plate 194.)

Terbrugghen, Hendrick (1588-1629). Dutch painter of

TENIERS THE YOUNGER. The Village Doctor
Musées Royaux des Beaux-Arts, Brussels

religious pictures. He studied with Bloemaert in Holland before going to spend ten years in Italy, where he absorbed the art of Caravaggio and may have known the Italian master. Returning to Utrecht he became the foremost of the Dutch followers of Caravaggio.

Testa, Pietro (1611-50). Born in Lucca, he was trained in Rome under Pietro Paoli and Domenichino, and studied the antique as well as the façades of Polidoro da Caravaggio. He painted mythological subjects with poetic feeling and rich fantasy under the influence of Domenichino, Cortona, and Poussin. He is more famous as an etcher and was one of the finest of the seventeenth century.

Thayer, Abbot Handerson (1849-1921). An American painter of the genteel tradition. Trained in the Ecole des Beaux-Arts, he used his solidly grounded technique to glorify womanhood, creating an image of ideal beauty which had no connection with contemporary life.

Theotocopuli, Jorge Manuel (1578-1631). Spanish painter, sculptor and architect. Son of El Greco, whom he assisted and copied. He was actually more accomplished as an architect, viz., the Ayuntamiento of Toledo.

Theotocopulos, Doménikos (see GRECO, EL).

Thoma, Hans (1839-1924).Outstanding German Realist painter of the nineteenth century and follower of Courbet, with whom he studied. The monumentality of his forms, the seriousness of his mood, the general realistic concentration on sculpturesque form and the balancing of detail with general effect, all raise him well above the level of many of his contemporaries. From 1899 on he was director of the Karlsruhe Museum and a professor at its Academy.

Thornhill, James (1676-1734). A British decorative painter in the Italian Baroque tradition. He was court painter to Queen Anne and later Serjeant Painter to George I. He painted the cupola of St. Paul's Cathedral, altarpieces for several Oxford colleges, and ceilings at Greenwich Hospital and Blenheim Palace. He also did portraits of Handel and Newton. Hogarth studied in a school which Thornhill married Thornhill's daughter and assisted the older man in several decorative commissions.

Thorn Prikker, Johann (1868-1932). Netherlands muralist, stained glass designer, textile designer and sculptor. Like many others at the end of the nineteenth century he turned toward a linear, symbolic expression which for him was best represented through the industrial arts. He was influential in Germany, where he taught for some time.

Thulden, Theodore van (1606-69). Flemish painter and copper-engraver of Dutch origin. An outstanding pupil and assistant of Rubens, many of whose works he copied in engravings.

Tiarini, Alessandro (1577-1668). Born and active in Bologna, he painted in the Bolognese "grand manner." He studied with Prospero Fontana, Bartolommeo Cesi, and at the Baldi Academy, and worked in Florence with Passignano and in Pescia. Back in Bologna, he came more strongly under the influence of Ludovico Carracci and Guido Reni.

Tibaldi, Pellegrino (called il Pellegrini) (1527-96). Painter, sculptor, and architect born in Puria in Valsolda and active in Bologna, Rome, the Marches, and Spain. He is noted for his perspective decorations, and his style is a Mannerist adaptation of Michelangelo, through Vasari and Volterra.

Tibetan painting. Buddhist in theme, Chinese in format (the hanging scroll or banner, mounted on cloth and faced with silk), traditional in iconography, Tibetan painting is in a class by itself. No painters' names are known, for the monks who painted did so as an act of devotion rather than to achieve fame. The most important aspect of the art lies in its perfect adherence to established modes of portraying events in the life of the Buddha (see color plate 195), some other deity, or a church dignitary. The monk-painters used transfer patterns for the main figures, thus preserving tradition; only in such details as flowers, clouds and small episodes were they allowed to draw freehand. Colors were prescribed by law, for each color has its symbolic meaning. Influenced by Nepal, India, and China, there is an interesting fusion of borrowed motif with a native dynamic power. The contrast between serene figures in meditation and violent guardians of the Law is more striking in Tibetan painting than in any other art of the Buddhist world. (See color plate 195.)

TIEPOLO. Perseus and Andromeda. Frick Collection, New York

Tiepolo, Giovanni Battista (1696-1770). The greatest of the Rococo decorative painters, he was born in Venice and active in Venice, Bergamo, Vicenza, Milan, Verona, Padua, Udine, Würzburg, and Spain, where he died. His art, though rhetorical in subject, was superbly theatrical; dazzling, flamboyant, and extravagant; utilizing drastic spatial conceptions, involved linear grace, light and airy color, and an effortlessly graceful technique. He decorated an endless array of churches and palaces with brilliant virtuosity. He is the culmination of a great line of Italian decorative painters from Veronese and Cortona through Sebastiano Ricci and Piazzetta. He studied first with Gregorio Lazzarini, but his early work, until about 1720, was under the influence of Caravaggio and Crespi. Then, contact with the art of Piazzetta, the leading Venetian painter of the period, and Ricci, who had just returned to Venice, transformed his style into something light, gay, and fantastic. His rediscovery of Veronese about 1725 led finally to the art of his maturity. His subsequent works, too numerous to mention, may be divided into the following periods: Lombardy and Venice (1730-40), Great Decorations (1741-50), Würzburg (1751-53), Venice (1754-62), and Spain (1762-70). (See illustrations, including color plate 196.)

196. TIEPOLO. Apelles Painting Campaspe
Museum of Fine Arts, Montreal

Tiepolo, Giovanni Domenico (1727-1804). Born in Venice, the son of Giovanna Battista Tiepolo (see), whose chief assistant he was from the age of thirteen. He was dominated by his father and his style is imitative. After his father's death in Spain, he returned to Venice and worked also in Genoa and Padua. Later in life he did satiric and grotesque scenes of Venetian life which are more original and interesting.

Timurid Period (see PERSIAN PAINTERS: TIMURID PERIOD, 1370-1500).

Tintoretto (Jacopo Robusti) (1518-94). One of the great painters of the Venetian Renaissance. Not as brilliant or consistent as Titian, he was a more dramatic and inventive composer and more emotionally expressive; and although his art also leads to the Baroque in its violent movement, it is much more tied to Mannerism. The inscription which is said to have adorned the entrance to his studio—*disegno di Michelangelo e colori di Tiziano* (Michelangelo's drawing and Titian's color)—expresses the essential synthesis in his art of the Florentine-Roman and the Venetian traditions. Born in Venice, the son of a dyer (thus Tintoretto, "little dyer"), he studied for a short time under Titian, with whom he could not get on, and was influenced by Bonifazio, Veronese and Andrea Schiavone, with whom he worked. He made many drawings after Michelangelo casts which he studied under artificial lighting and from strange angles of vision, producing studies in dramatic light and shade and with exaggerated foreshortening. He seems to have painted very boldly, *alla prima* (directly), and in a sketchy manner, often leaving works apparently unfinished.

His very early works are lost, but among the paintings which seem to date before his first famous dated work, the Miracle of St. Mark (1548, Venice Academy), are the Christ Washing the Feet of the Apostles (Escorial), under the older Venetian tradition of Carpaccio and Bonifazio; the Last Supper (S. Marcuola, Venice), also retarded, but showing the influence of Parmigianino; the Birth of St. John the Baptist (S. Zaccaria, Venice), and the Miracle of Loaves and Fishes (Metropolitan). The Miracle of St. Mark, painted for the Scuola Grande di S. Marco, exhibits a new dramatic feeling as well as foreshortening. Characteristic of his style of the early 1550's are the three paintings for the Scuola della Trinità (Venice Academy): Cain and Abel, Adam and Eve, and the Creation of Animals, all definitely Mannerist in attitude; and of the late 1550's five decorative paintings in the Prado: Susanna and the Elders, Joseph and Potiphar's Wife, Judith and Holofernes, Solomon and the Queen of Sheba, and Esther and Ahasuerus. The development of a more dramatic sense of space and movement becomes apparent in the Presentation of the Virgin (1556, Sta. Maria dell' Orto, Venice) and the Marriage at Cana (1561, Sta. Maria della Salute). He continued his decorations for the Scuola Grande di S. Marco in the middle 1560's and produced two large works for Sta. Maria dell' Orto: the Worship of the Golden Calf and the Last Judgment. In 1565 he began his extensive and protracted decorations of the Scuola di S. Rocco with the decoration of the Albergo, and continued in 1577 with the large upper

TINTORETTO. Christ at the Sea of Galilee. National Gallery of Art, Kress Collection, Washington, D.C.

197. TINTORETTO. Portrait of Gabriel Emo. Kress Collection, New York

room which contains some of his most stirring conceptions. He also undertook in 1578 decorations glorifying Venice in the Doge's Palace, and in the same year two large cycles for the Duke of Mantua, but executed with the help of his studio.

Tintoretto's late style is characterized by an intense lyricism and a fantastic transformation of reality. Typical of that period are the decorations of the lower room of the Scuola di S. Rocco (1585-90), grandiose in conception, overwhelming in their psychological intensity, and stunning in their aesthetic daring. Of the same period is the series of Miracles of St. Catherine for Sta. Caterina, Venice (1580's). The culmination of his career are his last works in S. Giorgio Maggiore, Venice (1591-94), climaxed by the unearthly vision of the Last Supper, in all its fantastic space, movement and light. Though essentially a dramatic religious painter, he was capable of sensious Venetian lyricism, as, for instance, the Danaë (Lyons), Susanna and the Elders (Vienna), or Arsinoë and Ganymede (Dresden). He was also a fine portraitist; although he was not as interested in individuality and material reality as was Titian, his almost starkly simple portraits are imbued with an inner fire and vitality which was his own: Doge Mocenigo (Venice Academy), Antonio Capello(Venice Academy) and his Self-Portrait (Louvre). He had a great influence upon the Baroque, but especially on the art of El Greco. (See illustrations, including color plate 197.)

Tissot, James (1836-1902). French painter and etcher. Known for his historical and religious compositions of almost archaeological exactitude. Following the Franco-Prussian war, in which he served, he retired to a London suburb and was a great success there. He suddenly began to do only biblical subjects and spent ten years in Palestine, a result of which was the two-volume *Bible of James Tissot.*.

TINTORETTO. Bacchus and Ariadne
Ducal Palace, Venice

Titian (Tiziano Vecelli) (1477/87-1576). One of the great painters of the Venetian Renaissance and its most complete embodiment. His long, prolific and successful career covers a development from the High Renaissance, through Mannerism, to the Baroque for which his art was a major source. A magnificent painter, just as painter, with a magical sense of color, he has had a more consistent influence upon subsequent painting than any other single artist. He was born in Pieve di Cadore, came early to Venice, and is said to have studied with Sebastiano Zucatti and, along with Giorgione, under Giovanni Bellini. His first recorded activity was the decoration of the Fondaco de' Tedeschi (1507-08, now destroyed) with Giorgione. He was also active in Padua (1510-11), executing frescoes in the Scuola del Carmine and the Scuola del Santo with Campagnola. His first style (before c.1513) is dominated by Bellini and especially the romantic lyricism of Giorgione, and is characterized by a youthful vigor, realism and freedom, and a striving for beauty in material things. To this early period belong the problematic Giorgionesque paintings: the Concert (Pitti), sometimes ascribed to Girgione or both; and the Fête Champêtre (Louvre), attributed to Giorgione or Sebastiano del Piombo. The famous Sacred and Profane Love (Borghese, Rome), whose dating is difficult, is completely Giorgionesque in its poetic beauty and mood. Other works of this period are the St. Peter with Jacopo Pesaro (c.1505-10), once dated 1503; and the St. Mark Enthroned (1510, Sta. Maria della Salute, Venice) which exhibits a new dependence upon the Florentine High Renaissance.

During his second period (c.1513-30), after the death of Bellini in 1516, Titian was the city's official painter with a sinecure, but worked also for Alfonso d'Este in Ferrara and Federigo II Gonzaga in Mantua. His style shows in a more pronounced way his interest in High Renaissance monumentality, a growing sense of the dramatic and grand, and a turn to rich and simple color. After about 1520 the influence of Giorgione fades. The first of the great altars of this period is the Assumption of the Virgin (1516-18, Venice Academy), followed by the Pesaro Madonna (1519-26, St. Maria dei Frari), the Resurrection Altar (1522, SS. Nazarro e Celso), all of which show the influence of Michelangelo and Giulio Romano, but with an added Venetian sense of color and proto-Baroque movement. During the third period (1530-45) he was intimate with Aretino and Sansovino, and worked for the courts of Urbino, Mantua, and after 1532 for Charles V. His style became calmer and more restrained, more painterly and broader in execution, and developed toward unifying grey harmonies in color. The outstanding altarpiece of this period is the majestic Presentation of the Virgin (1534-38, Venice Academy). To the same period belong the many decorations of Venetian confraternities; mythological nudes such as the Venus of Urbino (1538, Uffizi); some of his greatest portraits: La Bella (1536, Pitti), the Young Englishman or Ippolito Riminaldi (1540-45, Pitti), and Paul III and his Nephews (c.1545, Naples).

The next period of his activity (1545-60) was one of universal fame. He traveled a great deal—Rome (1545-46), where he lived at the Vatican and met Michelangelo and the humanist Cardinal Bembo; Augsburg (1548-49), at the invitation of Charles V; and Ferrara and Mantua (1550). His style became more powerful than ever, deeply emotional, yet executed with great breath and ease, of paramount importance for the Baroque. During this time he painted with material opulence many variations of reclining nudes and mythological subjects, and executed religious and classical themes for the Pope, Emperor, and Philip II of Spain. Among the religious masterpieces of the period are the Holy Trinity (1554, Prado) and the Entombment (1559, Prado); and his portraits include Philip II (Prado), his daughter Lavinia (Berlin), and a Self-Portrait (Berlin). His great old-age style recaptures an earlier lyricism, but now expressed entirely in terms of color applied broadly and in broken strokes, a style which has had so profound an effect on subsequent painting. He painted slowly and intermittently, and with the help of many students and assistants. The authenticity of many of his paintings was then and is now questioned, and it is difficult to know whether some are sketches or intended as finished pictures. The great Crowning with Thorns (1570, Munich) and the magnificent Pietà (1573-76, Venice Academy), perhaps his last painting, finished by Palma Giovane, are the outstanding works of the period. In these last years he worked a great deal for Philip II, executing many religious paintings: the Last Supper, the Crucifixion, and St. Jerome (all in the Escorial), and the Adoration of the Magi and the Agony in the Garden (both in the Prado). His gallery of portraits is capped by the late Self-Portrait (1565, Prado). (See illustrations, including color plate 198.)

TITIAN. The Rape of Europa
Isabella Stewart Gardner Museum, Boston

Toba Sojo (see JAPANESE PAINTERS: HEIAN PERIOD).

Tobey, Mark (1890-). Contemporary American abstract painter of intricately involved and complex patterns. Born in Centerville Wisc., he is self-taught and has been active mainly on the West Coast. He has traveled in Europe, the Near East, and in China, where he studied calligraphy.

Tocqué, Louis (1696-1772). French portrait painter. His portraits of the court notables and prominent bourgeois of the mid-eighteenth century are in a style characteristic of the circle in which he was active: Chardin, Boucher, Quentin de La Tour and Le Moyne. He was the son-in-law of Nattier and was sent to St. Petersburg and to Copenhagen on royal commissions. Typical are his portraits of the Dauphin.

Tohaku (see JAPANESE PAINTERS: MOMOYAMA PERIOD).

Toilers of the Sea by Albert Pinkham Ryder (see).

Tokugawa Period (see JAPANESE PAINTERS: TOKUGAWA PERIOD, 1614-1868).

Toledo Museum of Art, Toledo, Ohio. General but excellent collection of paintings from the thirteenth century to the present day, including both European and American examples.

Tolsa, Manuel (1757-1816). Mexican painter born in Valencia, Spain, who became a leading architect and painter

TITIAN. Crowning with Thorns. Alte Pinakothek, Münich

in the New World. He interpreted the academic classical style with an individual grace.

Tomlin. Bradley Walker (1899-1953). Contemporary American abstract painter. Born in Syracuse, he attended Syracuse University and studied abroad for several years. His work began to show Cubist influence c.1934 and he turned toward a calligraphic abstraction c.1946.

Tommaso da Modena (1325/26-1379). The first outstanding figure to come out of Modena. Important frescoes by him are representations of founders and members of the Dominican order in the chapter room attached to San Niccolò, Treviso (1352), where he was active for several years. He probably went to Karlstein, Bohemia, where he painted panel decorations for the castle of the imperial court. His realistic style and genre details in the Treviso frescoes are probably evidence of influence from Padua and Verona. These works are unique for the time in representing isolated figures and differentiated postures as though belonging to the narrative compositions of Giotto and Altichiero (see) in Padua.

Tommé, Luca (see LUCA DI TOMME).

tonality. The general character of a painting as produced by its color scheme. This character will in effect result from the predominance of one hue or color, or from the arrangement of a group of closely related color values.

Toorop, Charley (1890-). Netherlands painter and daughter of the artist Jan Toorop. She has been influenced more by the general thought and feeling of her father's time than by his forms. Thus her art takes on a universal and poetic quality, as in her Woman in Front of a Ruin, through the largeness of the form, its stark presentation and the sense of magic tension that pervades the work.

Toorop, Jan (1858-1928). Netherlands painter who adopted the "linear idealism" or linear symbolism of the 1890's and 1900's. Toorop was born in the Dutch East Indies, which gave his opposition to Impressionism the kind of exotic flavor characteristic of the symbolic approach of Dutch artists associated with the East Indies. He was very much concerned with the re-establishment of a unity between painter and architect. He did frescoes for the Amsterdam Exchange.

Torbido, Francesco (called Il Moro da Verona) (c.1482-1562). Veronese painter of altarpieces and portraits. He studied with Liberale da Verona but was influenced by Giulio Romano, Titian, and Giorgione.

Torres-García, Joaquín (1874-1949). Uruguayan abstractionist painter. In Europe he came under the influence of Mondrian, Klee and Ozenfant. On his return to Uruguay he developed a highly personal Klee-like style suggestive of hieroglyphics.

Torriti, Jacopo (late 13th century). Roman painter and mosaicist. He signed major mosaic decorations in San Giovanni in Laterano and Santa Maria Maggiore, both in Rome. His style stems from the strong resurgence of the Byzantine style in Rome in the early thirteenth century, which coincided with a revival of the taste for mosaic.

Tosi, Arturo (1871-). Dean of living Italian painters, he was associated at one time with the reactionary Novecento group of the 1920's which tried to turn the clock back to a pre-modern viewpoint. At one extreme this group represented a fascist-inspired neo-classicism; at the other the quiet Impressionism, even intimism in the Bonnard sense, of painters like Tosi.

Toulouse-Lautrec, Henri de (1864-1901). A French painter, graphic artist and poster designer. A descendant of the counts of Toulouse, he was born at Albi (site of the present Lautrec Museum) and educated in Paris. As a boy he broke both thighs and, unable to live a normal life as a result of these crippling accidents, he turned to painting. His first studies were with Princeteau, a painter of sporting scenes, then with a succession of academic artists ending with Cormon. During 1884-85 Lautrec, who had already shown a taste for contemporary subjects and a flair for drawing, came under the influence of the caricaturists Willette and Forain as well as the Impressionist group, especially Manet, Berthe Morisot and Degas. During 1886-88 he began to frequent the cabarets of Montmartre, where he found a kind of visual excitement and movement that his crippled and dwarfed condition would never have permitted him to participate in directly and a type of society that accepted him on his own terms without regard to his ugliness.

In 1889 he began to show at the Indépendants and a few years later at the Goupil Gallery run by Van Gogh's brother Theo. Lautrec had begun to do posters in 1891 in the brilliant flat, linear and decorative style that was so uniquely his, and soon thereafter plunged into a series of illustrations for various satirical journals. In 1895 during a visit to London he met Oscar Wilde, Aubrey Beardsley, Arthur Symons and other figures of the literary-artistic world revolving about the Art Nouveau *Yellow Book*, whose viewpoint was close to that of Lautrec himself. In 1897 he became friendly with the Natansons, publishers of *La Revue Blanche*, and at this time turned from posters to color lithography. He had been doing paintings of cabaret performers, dancers, acrobats, etc., and now broadened his scope to include brothel scenes, circus subjects (as in the series called Le Cirque), nudes, medical

198. TITIAN. Venus and Adonis. National Gallery of Art, Widener Collection, Washington, D.C.

themes and even portraits. By 1899 his heavy drinking and other forms of dissipation had so weakened him that he had to be sent to a sanatorium. But the habits of many years were not to be overcome and in 1901 he began drinking heavily again, suffered a stroke and ended his hectic life at the age of thirty-seven.

Although Lautrec emerged from the Impressionist milieu in his Japanese-derived compositions and his everyday subjects, his preoccupation with sinuously flowing line related him to the Art Nouveau tradition (see), while his general attitude toward the thematic material of his paintings and lithographs is essentially that of Symbolism (see), expressing the mournfulness of a given situation (as in the Moulin Rouge) by depressing browns and greens and by the psychological isolation of the figures. Thus we may see certain general parallels between Lautrec and his contemporaries Munch and Hodler as well as between Lautrec and Nabis (see) like Bonnard and Vuillard, who relied on technique alone for the expression of their viewpoint. (See illustrations, including color plate 199.)

Tournier, Robert (1604-70). French painter. Assumed to be a pupil of Valentin, he practiced a French version of the Caravaggio manner and is often confused with Valentin. An example is The Concert (Bourges).

Towne, Francis (1740-1816). Minor British landscapist, primarily in watercolor; apparently an amateur whose work is rarely found. He is interesting for his experimental attitude in seeking to give new life to the picturesque landscape tradition through intensive study of structure. Towne tried to express both the geological and architectural structure of the mountains of Wales, Italy and Switzerland. Some of his drawings, deliberately symbolical and geometric, foreshadow certain aspects of twentieth-century painting.

Traini, Francesco (active 1321-after 1345). The most important master of the Pisan school of the mid-fourteenth century. Decorative and plastic Sienese elements in his style stem from Simone Martini and the Lorenzetti. His chief authenticated work is the signed altarpiece of St. Dominic (1344/5), the panels of which are now in the museum and the seminary of Pisa. He is associated with frescoes painted after 1350, in the Campo Santo of Pisa, the best known of which is the Triumph of Death (destroyed in World War II). The authorship of these is disputed, but owing to the local importance of Traini and the technically high quality of the frescoes, they are ascribed to him by many scholars. Their macabre and monastic content is in keeping with the new morality engendered by the great plague of 1348. (See illustration.)

trecento (It.) Literally, "three hundred." Refers to the thirteen hundreds, or fourteenth century, in Italy.

Tretiakoff Gallery, Moscow. A museum of traditional Russian art featuring nineteenth-century masters such as Repin, Verestchagin, etc., as well as the late medieval icon makers.

Tribute Money, The, by Masaccio (see).

triptych. A three-paneled altarpiece (see) on hinges, usually portable, in painting, sculpture, ivory, enamel or metal,

199. TOULOUSE-LAUTREC. Moulin Rouge : La Goulue

TOULOUSE-LAUTREC. Original etching for Artists' Journal
Metropolitan Museum of Art, New York

in which the central panel can be covered by folding the two side panels.

Tristán de Escamilla, Luis (1586?-1624). A Spanish follower of El Greco and known as his outstanding pupil. In the first decade of the seventeenth century he was associated with El Greco and their styles are so close that Tristán's Holy Trinity in Seville was long taken for an El Greco. He veers, however, toward a tigher technique and a more naturalistic point of view, which has caused him to be called a "tenebrist" (see). Whether he traveled to Italy and associated with Ribera is not clear; certainly he shows affinities with the styles of Ribalta and Ribera. He is a link between El Greco and Velázquez, who admired his painting. Tristán worked extensively in the area of Toledo, executing such major commissions as the altarpiece of the Monastery of Yepes (1616). (See illustration.)

trompe l'oeil (Fr.) Literally, "deceive the eye." The kind of painting in which the artist sets out deliberately to simulate the actual reality of a given object so faithfully as to deceive the spectator. Example: the work of the American Harnett.

Troy, Jean François de (1679-1752). French painter and etcher. Member of a family of artists, he was the pupil of his father Jean François. After winning the Prix de Rome he spent six years in Italy, returning only under pressure from the French Minister. Wealthy, successful and somewhat libertine, he painted history, genre and portraits as well as decorations in hôtels and churches of Paris. He led in the abandonment of the Grand Manner, turning to fêtes, conversation pieces and erotic subjects from history such as his Bathsheba. He drew heavily on Rubens and Veronese for spatial ideas and for Baroque architectural backgrounds. Among his more ambitious projects were two cartoon series, the History of Esther and the History of Jason, the latter on commission for the Gobelins tapestry works.

Troyon, Constant (1810-65). French landscape painter of the Barbizon school (see), he tended to specialize in livestock themes, as had such Dutch masters as Cuyp, on whose works he based his style. He is one of the best examples of the enthusiasm of the new French landscapists for the old Dutch school, although his paintings have a characteristic nineteenth-century liveliness of color and atmosphere.

Trumbull, John (1756-1843). American portrait and history painter. An artist of promise and a man of great ambition, he conceived of himself as the chronicler of the American Revolution. Unfortunately none of his projects was ever fully achieved and he lived a life of frustration. He was competent, but his portraits as well as his finished historical pictures are pedestrian. His finest things are his small battle sketches and landscapes, where he achieves spirited dramatic action and in which he reveals himself as one of America's first Romantic painters. Born in Connecticut, the son of the governor of that state, he was graduated from Harvard in 1773 and returned home to teach school. He joined the Continental Army in 1775 and was for a short period aide-de-camp of Washington, but resigned his commission in a fit of pique in 1777. His early artistic training was based on Hogarth's *Analysis of Beauty*, the *Handbook of Perspective*, and some advice from Copley. In 1780, he went to study in London but was arrested in reprisal for the hanging of Major André. He returned to England in 1784 and studied with West and at the Royal Academy, where he began his national series. Later, he was influenced in Paris by the historical paintings of David. Back in the U.S. in 1789, he projected many historical paintings, but without success, and was forced to paint portraits. In 1816 he was finally commissioned to paint panels at $8,000 each for the Rotunda of the Capitol—Declaration of Independence, Surrender of Cornwallis, Surrender of Burgoyne, and Washington Resigning—which he completed in 1824 after earlier sketches. He taught at the American Academy of Design and was its first president. In 1831 he gave his collection to Yale University in return for an annuity. (See illustration.)

Tschacbasov, Nahum (1899-). Contemporary American eclectic Expressionist painter. Born in Baku, he came to the U.S. in 1907, and began to paint only in 1930 after

TRAINI. St. Thomas Aquinas. Church of St. Catherine, Pisa

some study abroad. He paints with a rich palette, and his style varies from the naive to the Surrealist.

Tucker, Albert (1914-). Australian painter born in Melbourne. A rebel of the Melbourne art schools, he became president of the Contemporary Art Society. Beginning with a highly intelligent and eclectic facility, he produced a series of psychological portraits unique in Australian art. While in Japan as an official artist with the Australian army, he was for a time associated with the Japanese Foujita. He has lived in Paris and Rome since 1948 and has exhibited in Amsterdam, Paris and Rome.

Tung Ch'i-ch'ang (see CHINESE PAINTERS: MING DYNASTY).

Tung Yüan (see CHINESE PAINTERS: SUNG DYNASTY).

Tunnard, John (1900-). British painter of abstract compositions, generally in the free-form manner. He began as a textile designer. His style shows a subtle understanding of the backward and forward moving planes of space. (See illustration.)

Tura, Cosimo (c.1430-95). The first important painter of the school of Ferrara, he brought to that center the new developments in perspective anatomy and draughtmanship of the Squarcione shop in Padua, where he was probably trained. After 1451 he is recorded in Ferrara, where he worked as painter to the ducal court of Borso and Ercole I d'Este. His work is related to Mantegna, whom he must have known in Padua, but he developed a personal style noted for its crisp, linear modeling and its nervous and dramatic expression. Important works are preserved in London, Paris, Berlin and

TRISTAN DE ESCAMILLA. Portrait of a Magistrate
Prado, Madrid

TRUMBULL. John Trumbull, the Poet
Detroit Institute of Arts

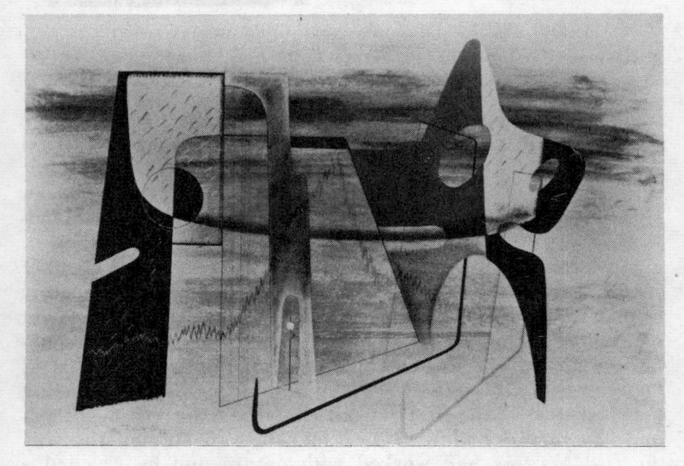

TUNNARD. Construction. Tate Gallery, London

Venice. His influence was felt by the lesser Ferrarese painters Cossa and Ercole Roberti. (See color plate 200.)

Turner, Joseph Mallord William (1775-1851). Outstanding British landscapist; a great influence on his contemporaries and later on the Impressionist painters of France. Born in London, the son of a barber, Turner showed a precocious talent for drawing. In his teens he earned considerable money by coloring prints for an engraver. He took drawing lessons, made copies in Reynolds' studio and was admitted to the Academy schools. From the age of fifteen on he exhibited at the Royal Academy; by eighteen he had his own studio. He toured the country with Thomas Girtin, sketching picturesque views, ruins and scenes of shipping. Before Turner was twenty printsellers were buying his drawings for reproduction. Artistically he advanced rapidly. His 1799 draw-

200. TURA. Madonna and Child in a Garden
National Gallery of Art, Kress Collection, Washington, D.C.

ing of Norham Castle, which he considered the beginning of his artistic career, made him an Associate of the Royal Academy. He worked in both watercolors and oils and his reputation began to rival that of the Dutch sea painters. He also gained a reputation for picturesque classical landscapes (i.e., irregularly shaped scenes of nature strewn with ancient ruins) with figures. In 1802 he became a full member of the Royal Academy and made his first foreign tour, visiting France and Switzerland. In 1807 he was appointed Professor of Perspective at the Academy. He took a house with studio-gallery to exhibit his own pictures, of which he now sold many, especially marines. Turner did much traveling, making many sketches and studying all the while the effects of sea and sky in every kind of weather. He also studied the way the Old Masters had worked with nature and he reached a deep appreciation of their methods, especially those of Claude and Watteau. He rivaled the former and derived great benefit from the fuzzy delicate manner of the latter.

Turner became increasingly successful, with profitable agreements between himself and various publishers for the reproduction of his works. Some collectors, e.g., Ruskin's father, even specialized in his watercolors. Not only did he ask high prices for the oils, but he now refused to sell the more important ones, saving them for his own collection. From about 1834 on he entered his splendid final phase in which he projected a completely personal and original expression of his experience; but the Academicians and recognized critics were unable to appreciate this development, Ruskin being his only articulate champion. The new development reached its climax around 1840 with such works as The Slave Ship (Boston), in which he moves further along the path of abstracting the forces of nature into a powerful moving symbol. Rather than the literary and more specifically Romantic symbols of earlier works, such as The Falls of the Rhine at Schaffhausen or The Fighting Téméraire, the painter now transforms his canvas into a dynamically moving symbol of a force without form, a force such as the power of the sea, the movement of rain, the dynamism of a train, the enveloping character of a fog. It is to the "inner meaning of a given idea" that works such as the Rain, Steam and Speed, Slave Ship, Whale Ship, Snow Storm, etc., are dedicated. Very prolific as well as successful during his lifetime. Turner left a large estate. His greatest contribution was the symbolic landscape, but he had also performed magnificently in the field of classical and Romantic landscapes and seascapes. His sense of movement and atmosphere mark a full step forward in the development of open-air painting and consequently toward the Impressionism of the 1860's and '70's. See also ROMANTICISM. (See illustrations, including color plate 201.)

Twachtman, John Henry (1853-1902). One of America's first Impressionist painters, he was an original member of the Ten. His landscapes became progressively lighter in key until they almost disappeared in a haze of white paint. Born in Cincinnati, he began with his father as a painter of floral designs on windows shades, studying at the Mechanical Institute and later at the Cincinnati School of Design with Duveneck. In 1876 he went to Munich with Duveneck and there was a student of Ludwig Loefftz. He was with Duveneck and Chase in Venice in 1879 and traveled in England, Holland and Germany in 1881. He then settled in Paris where from 1883 to 1885 he studied at the Académie Julian with Boulanger and Lefebvre. Returning to the U.S., he had difficulty finding work and was forced to resort to the painting of a cyclorama of the Battle of Gettysburg in Chicago. In 1890 he purchased a farm in Greenwich, Conn., and settled down to painting and teaching at Cooper Union and the Art Students League during the winter and at Newport during the summer. His earlier work was influenced by the dark tonality of the Munich school, but after his Paris stay, when he was influenced by Impressionism, he changed his

TURNER. Burial at Sea. Tate Gallery, London

201. TURNER. Rain, Steam and Speed. National Gallery, London

color gamut completely, preferred quiet lyrical scenes, and delighted especially in the painting of snow.

Tytgat, Edgar (1879-). Belgian painter and printmaker, He spent some years in England as an illustrator and returned to become one of his country's leading artists of fantasy. He treats themes of the café, theater, etc., with charm and lightness, humor and imagination; although different in character from the heavier, more brutal expression of many of his contemporaries, these are still among the most important in modern Belgium. (See illustration.)

U

Ubertino, Francesco d' (see BACCHIACCA).

Uccello, Paolo di Dono (c.1396/7-1475). One of the Florentine painters of the first generation of the fifteenth century that formulated the Renaissance style in that city. His mastery of perspective is the salient feature of his work. He was in the sculptor Lorenzo Ghiberti's workshop from 1407 to 1414, registered in the guild of doctors and apothecaries in 1415, and in the St. Luke guild in 1424. Shortly after 1425 he went to Venice, where he is said to have done a mosaic of St. Peter (now lost) on the façade of San Marco. Documents from late in his life indicate that he was in reduced circumstances. His major extant works in fresco are the equestrian figure of Sir John Hawkwood (1436) in the cathedral, Florence, and a fresco cycle on Old Testament subjects in the Chiostro Verde of Santa Maria Novella, painted with the help of several assistants. The scenes generally accepted as by Uccello are the Deluge, Noah's Sacrifice, and the Drunkenness of Noah. Perhaps his best known works are the three battle scenes (Uffizi, Louvre, and London) painted before 1457 for the Medici palace, commemorating the Florentine victory over the Milanese at San

TYTGAT. Mietje Roelants. Musée Moderne, Brussels

UDEN. The Water Mill. Musée Royal des Beaux-Arts, Antwerp

Romano. A few other small panels are ascribed to him, including the Hunting Scene in the Ashmolean Museum at Oxford. Perspective, one of Uccello's primary concerns, is heavily exploited in the Chiostro Verde frescoes, where space is extended into the far distance. In the battle scenes the space is shallower, but perspective devices are in evidence, such as the lances pointed at right angles to the picture plane. In addition to their science, these pictures have a particularly pleasing, tapestry-like decorative quality that is peculiar to Uccello. (See color plate 202.)

Uden, Lucas van (1595-1672/73). Flemish landscape painter. Son and pupil of Artus van Uden. He was mainly known as a collaborator with Rubens, for whom he executed the backgrounds and landscapes of paintings. He also did some etchings—originals, and copies of paintings by himself, Titian and Rubens. He worked with Teniers, viz., the Landscape (Brussels), the Landscape with Hermits Anthony and Paul (Dresden). (See illustration.)

Uffizi Gallery, Florence. One of the most important collections in the world, this gallery was founded by the Medici family. It is richest in examples of the masterpieces of Italian painting from the fourteenth through the sixteenth centuries; it also has a fine group of tapestries.

Ugolino di Neri da Siena (active late 13th and early 14th centuries). One of the few pupils of Duccio whose name is connected with a specific work. An altarpiece (now dismembered) which once bore his signature was painted for the church of Santa Croce, Florence, in about 1294 when the church was founded. Parts of this work are preserved in the Berlin and London museums and in private collections. His art, while very close to the humanized and Italianized Byzantine style of Duccio, is distinguished from it in being less tender and graceful, less animated in movement, and lacking the easy flowing line and harmonious grouping of the greater master. (See illustration.)

Uhde, Fritz von (1848-1911). German painter noted for the strange but exciting combination he effected between late nineteenth-century Realism and stories from sacred history. These latter he presented in contemporary dress and gave a kind of reality seldom found in religious art. His work may be regarded as a sympathetic treatment of the problem of the average man, in whom he was very much interested. (See illustration.)

Umbrian school. A movement that was centered in and around Perugia in central Italy and is characterized by an adherence to traditional Gothic linealism and sentimentality rather than the new monumentalism developed in other areas of Italy. Is was more interested in devotional ideas than in the study of techniques and methods of appraising reality. During the fifteenth and sixteenth centuries it included such painters as Fiorenzo di Lorenzo, Perugino and Pinturicchio.

Umbro-Florentine school. This group involves men who came from Umbria in central Italy but whose artistic quality was tied up with the various aspects of Florentine development, and particularly its monumentality and its striving for expressive forms. The three important painters associated with this school are: Piero della Francesca, Melozzo da Forlì and Luca Signorelli. They cover the period from the early fifteenth through the early sixteenth century.

underpainting. The preliminary coating or ground color on which the subsequent glazes or layers are placed.

University of Nebraska Art Galleries, Lincoln, Neb. One of the nation's outstanding collections of the contemporary art of Europe and America. Aided by the income from a substantial endowment, this museum has been able to make constant purchases of valuable works by Marini, Barlach, Kirchner, Calder and many others, especially United States painters and sculptors.

Ustad Muhammadi (see PERSIAN PAINTERS: SAFAWID PERIOD).

Utamaro (see JAPANESE PAINTERS: TOKUGAWA PERIOD).

Utrillo, Maurice (1883-). French painter of the moods of suburban Paris streets and buildings. Son of a little-known

UGOLINO. A Prophet. National Gallery, London

UHDE, VON. Three Models. State Gallery, Stuttgart

French painter and a professional model, Suzanne Valadon (see), who was also a painter in her own right. One of the authentic café characters of Paris and an early victim of alcoholism, he nevertheless developed an interesting painting style. Later he was institutionalized but emerged in the mid-1930's and continued his development as a painter. The famous Paris perspectives which Utrillo had been doing up to this point date back to the period 1902-08, when he worked in a suburb of Paris. These first delicately colored works, in a technique that was still Impressionist, are part of his "Montagny period." The next phase, 1909-14, the "white period," features a kind of color in which the artist sometimes applies paint like plaster, using his palette knife like a trowel to simulate the surfaces of buildings. During this period he also developed a personal and simple variant of the early Cubist manner of Picasso and Braque. His most characteristic works, done in isolation and with the aid of colored postcards, show a mingling of moody, almost Fauve coloring and a carefully laid out linear structure. (See illustrations, including color plate 203.)

V

Vaenius, Octavius (see VEEN, OTTO VAN).

Valadon, Suzanne (1867-1938). A French painter who began her Parisian existence as a wrestler and then became a model for such distinguished painters as Renoir and Puvis de Chavannes. In 1883 she had a son, Maurice Utrillo, who was to become an important painter during the early years of this century. Valadon exhibited with the very end of the Impressionist movement, then with the Symbolists, whose cloisonné line persisted in her work for a long time. Her art during the 1920's still showed this quality but tempered by the broader coloristic effects of the Fauves; and this remained her typical style.

Valckenborch, Lucas van (before 1535-1597). Member of a large family of Flemish painters that included his brother Martin (1535-1612) and his son Frederick (c.1570-1623). His specialty was landscape and genre in the manner of Patinir and Brueghel. He worked mostly outside of Flanders as a political and religious refugee.

Valdés-Leal, Juan de (1622-90). A Spanish Baroque painter of religion and allegory. He was also a sculptor, architect and etcher. Of Portuguese extraction, he studied in Cordoba with Antonio del Castillo, and was influenced by the Herrera family in Seville, where he passed most of his career. He was possessed of a brilliant technique, more striking in many ways than that of his rival, Murillo. He spent most of his life in a prodigious activity of church decoration. His biographer speaks of his irascible, unstable temperament, which is reflected perhaps in the uneven quality of his work. His first big project was a series of canvases for the Convent of Santa Clara in Carmona (1650-53). In these he showed the influence of Murillo as well as some of his own striking chiaroscuro effects. In Seville he rose to an eminent position among painters, being named *mayordomo* of the new Academy of St. Luke. One of his earliest commissions there was for the Convent of St. Jerome. Two of these canvases, the Temptation and the Scourging of St. Jerome, show him at his best. In them the directness of the Spanish Baroque has been tempered by an extreme colorism and a loose slashing brushwork that render parts of the canvas strongly expressionist. Contrary to this, of course, is the tighter technique of the allegories, Finis Gloriae Mundi and In Ictu Oculi, painted for the Charity Hospital of Seville, where Murillo (see) was also at work. These pictorial horrors exemplify the bizarre side of Valdés-Leal and illustrate the latent medievalism of Spanish taste. Of his works they are the most revered by the moderns. (See illustration.)

Valencian school. An aspect of Spanish painting encompassing the fifteenth to seventeenth centuries. It is believed that the Italian painter Starnina visited Valencia at the end of the fourteenth century and that the great Flemish master, Jan van Eyck, stopped there in 1428 during his Spanish jouney. The Valencian school of the fifteenth century, therefore, appears to be influenced by both Italian and Flemish strains as evidenced in the work of Jacomart (Jaime Baço), who spent some years in Italy. By the sixteenth century Valencian dependence on the Italians becomes more firmly rooted in the work of such painters as Yanez and Juan de Juanes. The culminating figure of Valencian painting was Ribalta.

UTRILLO. Behind the House of Mimi Pinson
Musée Moderne, Brussels

202. UCCELLO. Rout of San Romano. National Gallery, London

Valentin, le (Jean de Boulogne) (1594-1632). French Caravaggesque painter. He was early in Italy; there he studied with Vouet but was more influenced by Manfredi, Ribera and Caravaggio; he adopted Caravaggio's style in a somewhat less broad, more coloristic fashion than the master's. He was a friend of Poussin, belonged to the Barberini circle and was patronized by Pope Urban VIII. He is the most famous and closest French follower of Caravaggio, although less original than Georges de Latour and the Le Nain brothers. He painted genre and biblical subjects, and combinations of the two. Some of the genres, such as the Fortune-Teller (Louvre) seem curiously poetic and symbolic. Late in life he painted for St. Peter's the Martyrdom of Sts. Processus and Martianus. (See illustration.)

Vallotton, Félix (1865-1925). Swiss-born painter; as a member of the Nabis group (see) in Paris he produced paintings in the spirit of Intimism (see), decorative art, poster work and lithography. There are two distinct sides to his painting: one in which he shows a joyous charming color and spontaneity that prefigures a good deal of later Fauve work and even elements of the German Die Brücke; another in which his forms become hard and precise, almost clinical in the fashion of later Magic Realists or New Objectivity painters. (See illustration.)

valori plastici (It.) Literally "plastic values"; also the name of a review that appeared from 1918-21 under the aegis of Chirico and the group around him in Rome. The painters of the group include Carrà and Morandi besides Chirico and are generally referred to as the *scuola metafisica*, or metaphysical school. It began from the premise of reviving traditional art, particularly the early Italian painters from Giotto to Piero della Francesca; this meant a break with the fragmented and otherwise abstract movements of the previous decade. With the new formal orientation, the members of the metaphysical group projected a clear, emotionally intense kind of Magic Realism (see) that may be compared with similar movements of the 1920's in other countries, notably in France and in the New Objectivity of Germany.

Van or **van.** *Note:* For names beginning thus, but not listed here, look up the last part of the name; e.g., for Hugo van der Goes see GOES.

Vanderlyn, John (1775-1852). American painter of history, landscapes, and portraits; like his contemporaries, Trumbull and Allston, he lived a life of artistic frustration in an environment which had not yet found a place for his kind of painting. The first American painter to be trained in Paris rather than London, his solid and serious style derives from the art of Jacques-Louis David. He was born in Kings on, N.Y., the grandson of the colonial painter, Pieter, received some instruction from Stuart in Philadelphia, and with the help of Aaron Burr went to Paris to study with Vincent in 1796. He was back in Europe in 1803 and stayed on until 1815, painting and exhibiting, first in London and Paris, and then with Allston in Rome. His Marius won a medal at the Paris Salon of 1808 and his Ariadne was exhibited there in 1812. On his return to New York his serious historical studies found little response and he painted too slowly to be a successful portraitist. He received permission to build the Rotunda in City Hall Park, New York, to house his panoramas, but this venture failed and was taken over by the city in 1830. Also embittered by the fact that Trumbull was awarded the Capitol commissions, he retired in that year to Kingston, where he painted an occasional portrait. Belatedly, in 1842 Congress commissioned him to paint a panel for the Capitol for $1,200. Vanderlyn went to Paris to carry out the project, but inactivity had robbed him of his powers and the Landing of Columbus was actually executed by a French assistant. He died in want. (See illustration.)

Vanderlyn, Pieter (c.1687-1778). Born in Holland, supposedly a surgeon in the Dutch Navy, he appeared in New York records in 1718 and was according to family tradition a limner. Some forty provincial, crudely powerful portraits done in the Hudson Valley have been attributed to him. These attributions are questioned and one whole group given to a so-called Aetatis Suae Master.

Van Gogh, Vincent (1853-90). Dutch-born master of the Post-Impressionist period in France, representing the more emotional and intuitive side of that art. He influenced the

203. UTRILLO. Snow on Montmartre. Private Collection

early twentieth-century painting of the Fauves in France and the Expressionists of the Brücke group in Germany. Born at Groot-Zundert in Holland, he was the son of a minister and the nephew of a group of art dealers. This group was associated with the firm of Goupil et Cie., where Vincent was employed in 1869, first in The Hague and then in Brussels. He read a good deal and visited the museums in those cities. In 1873 he transferred to the London branch of the firm; and the following year he suffered his first serious disappointment in love. In 1875 he was shifted to the headquarters of the Goupil firm in Paris but did not get along with the staff, quarreled with clients, and became preoccupied with religion. The following year he lost his job, returned to England, taught for a while, and then went home to his parents. In 1877 he went to Amsterdam to prepare himself for admission to a theological school. A year later, failing to pass the examination, he came home again, tried an evangelical training course in Brussels and was finally sent as a lay preacher to the miserable miners of the Borinage in Belgium. By 1879 he had progressed to the post of temporary pastor in the heart of that black land, but his unorthodox zeal caused him to lose the job.

Out of his despair and complete destitution came the vision of turning to art. His brother Theo, then working for Goupil, began the lifelong financial and psychological help that marked their relationship. In 1880 Van Gogh did drawings of miners in the style of Millet. In 1882-83, he had a Dostoyevskian relationship with the prostitute Sien and did his first

VALDÉS-LEAL. Via Crucis
Hispanic Society of America, New York

VALENTIN, LE. Card Sharps. Dresden Museum

VALLOTTON. The Sands on the Banks of the Loire
Kunsthaus, Zurich

paintings in a thick, dark, heavy manner, and watercolors and lithographs of peasants, fishermen and nature. He was back home with his parents from 1883-85, set up a studio, worked hard and read a good deal, e.g., Carlyle, Dickens, Harriet Beecher Stowe. The climax of this early art came in The Potato Eaters (1885) where he tried to communicate the feeling of people eating the food they have dug from the earth with their own hands. In Antwerp in 1885-86 he discovered Rubens and Japanese prints, entered the Academy and tried to study seriously. The years 1886-88 mark the Paris period during which he was enthusiastically welcomed by brother Theo and met Lautrec, Pissarro, Degas, Seurat, Signac and Gauguin. He adopted the Divisionist or Neo-Impressionist technique for a short time, soon varying it to meet his own emotional needs.

The years 1888-89 find him in Arles, settled in a "yellow house with a tiny studio." There he painted with terrific enthusiasm and coloristic warmth pictures like The Sunflowers, elongating the fairly regular spots of color used by the Neo-Impressionists into his own increasingly characteristic wrigglers of paint that twist and turn their separate and group ways across the canvas surface, conveying his intensity of feeling, his restlessness, and often the tragic nature of his emotions. A short visit from Gauguin ended with Van Gogh showing signs of mental unbalance, trying first to kill the other man and then cutting off his own ear. He was hospitalized for two weeks then and again in March of the following year for the violence of his hallucinations. Yet this is artistically the most fruitful and rewarding part of his life; approximately two hundred paintings resulted from these fifteen months at Arles. At one extreme we find explosive works like The Sunflowers; at the other a series of tensely linear and symbolic pictures like The Woman of Arles. In May 1889 he asked to be admitted to the asylum at Saint Rémy and there had comparatively long periods of lucidity. In 1890 the first article on Van Gogh's work appeared in the *Mercure de France* and he made his first and only sale of a picture (for four hundred francs, at the Brussels show of Les XX). He did many copies after Delacroix, Daumier, Rembrandt and Millet in this period, pictures dealing with human and emotional problems. In May, 1890, he arrived at Auvers, became a friend and patient of Dr. Gachet, and committed suicide in July, at the age of thirty-seven.

From the beginning he had been interested in people and their problems: in this sense his career is far more consistent and far less eccentric and individualistic than the constantly reiterated biographical incidents would indicate. Van Gogh is in many ways typical of young intellectuals at the end of the nineteenth and beginning of the twentieth century, with their increasing awareness of the misery of the world. See also ART NOUVEAU, POST-IMPRESSIONISM. (See illustrations, including color plate 204.)

Van Loo, Carle (Charles André) (1705-65). A French painter and engraver. Brother and pupil of Jean Baptiste (see). He was much honored in both France and Italy. He did many decorative projects including work at Fontainebleau. His Pause in the Hunt (Louvre) represents the heavy academic handling of an eighteenth-century *fête galante.*

Van Loo, Charles Amédée Philippe (1719-95). French painter of history, genre and portraits. Son and pupil of Jean Baptiste (see). Like others of his family, an honored academician. He was first painter to the King of Prussia.

Van Loo, Jean Baptiste (1684-1745). French painter of history, genre and portraits. Student of his father Louis and member of a long lineage of French painters stemming from Flanders. He is renowned for portraits of royalty, especially a painting of Louis XV done from memory. He was a considerable success in England. (See illustration.)

Van Loo, Jules César Denis (1743-1821). French landscape painter. Specialist in snow scenes such as Snow Scene in the Louvre. He was the son and pupil of Carle.

Vanni, Andrea (c.1332-c.1414). Sienese painter whose art stems from that of Simone Martini and Lippo Memmi, and who may have been a pupil of the latter. He shared a workshop in 1353 with Bartolo di Fredi, was politically active and made diplomatic missions to Rome, Naples and Avignon. He was a close friend of St. Catherine of Siena and painted her portrait. Among important works by him are a polyptych of the Madonna and Saints in Santo Stefano alla Lizza, Siena,

VANDERLYN, JOHN. John A. Sidell
Metropolitan Museum of Art, New York

VAN GOGH. Boats at Saintes-Maries
Stedelijk Museum, Amsterdam

VAN GOGH. Café at Night
Kröller-Müller Collection, Otterlo

an Annunciation in the Fogg Museum, Harvard University, a Crucifixion triptych (signed) in the Corcoran Gallery, and the fresco of St. Catherine in the church of San Domenico, Siena. While drawing its inspiration from the delicate and flowing linear style of Simone Martini, his art tends toward a rigid, angular and sober form of expression progressing toward unpleasant hardness in his latest work. (See color plate 205.)

Vanni, Lippo (active 1341-75). Sienese painter mentioned as a miniaturist from 1341 to 1345. Miniatures of the latter date in the cathedral library at Siena reveal a strong influence of the Lorenzetti in their forthright, plastic and humanized renderings of sacred subjects. Two other dated works are known: a polyptych (1358) in Santi Domenico e Sisto, Rome, and fragmentary remains of an Annunciation in fresco in the Seminary, Siena. Among other works attributed to him are a fresco of the Madonna and Saints in San Francesco, Siena, a Madonna in the museum of Le Mans, and a battle fresco in the Palazzo Pubblico, Siena. Lippo appears to have begun under the influence of the Lorenzetti and to have come under Simone Martini's more mystical, linear and Gothic influence in his later style.

Vanucci, Andrea (see SARTO, ANDREA DEL).

Vargas, Luis de (1502-68). Spanish painter of Seville. Famous for popularizing in that school the style and fresco technique of the Roman Renaissance. He spent twenty-eight years in Italy and derived his style from the followers of Raphael and Michelangelo. His retablo of the Genealogy of the Virgin (Seville) takes its composition from Vasari. His later works are more Spanish, viz., the Pietà (Seville).

Varley, John (1778-1842). British topographical watercolor draughtsman and friend of William Blake. A teacher of drawing, his pupils included Linnell, Palmer, Fielding, Hunt, de Wint and Cox. His own work shows careful, often minute drawing and subdued coloring.

Varotari, Allessandro (see PADOVANINO).

Varotari, Dario (il Vecchio) (1539-96). Born in Verona, of a family originally from Strassburg (probably called Weirotter), he settled in Verona and was active there and in Praglia and Venice. He was the father of Padovanino, studied with Veronese, and was later influenced by Tintoretto.

Vasari, Giorgio (1511-74). An Italian architect, painter and writer famous for his *Lives of the Most Excellent Italian Architects, Painters and Sculptors*, 1550, generally known as

VAN LOO, JEAN BAPTISTE. Diana and Endymion
Louvre, Paris

204. VAN GOGH, VINCENT. Woman Rocking Cradle, Museum of Fine Arts, Boston

Lives of the Painters. In this pioneer work he traced the origins and development of Italian art in a way unique in his day, laying the foundations—in spite of many errors of fact and exaggerations—for future writers in that field. As an artist he belongs to the Mannerist school; among his most important artistic achievements is the design for the Uffizi Palace in Florence. (See illustration.)

Vasnetsoff, Victor (1848-1926). Russian painter, muralist and mosaicist who attempted to revive the tradition of Byzantine Russian icon paintings in many of his works. He is best known for his historical and folktale paintings.

Vatican Picture Gallery, Rome. A relatively small but select group of paintings are kept here, including some fine Raphaels, pictures of the Venetian school, and works of the seventeenth century, of which the Caravaggios are outstanding, as well as a number of non-Italian works. Apart from the Picture Gallery proper, the Vatican contains a number of world-famous paintings such as the Michelangelo ceiling painting in the Sistine Chapel, the Raphael wall paintings in the Papal Apartments, the work of Raphael and his pupils in the Papal Loggias and the so-called Raphael Tapestries executed in Flanders from that painter's designs.

Vázquez, Gregorio (1638-1711). Spanish-Colonial painter of Bogotá, Colombia. He was influenced by the art of Seville and distinguished for his strong draughtsmanship, rich colors, and the great dignity of his portraits.

205. VANNI, ANDREA. The Crucifixion. Gardner Museum, Boston

Vecchietta (Lorenzo di Pietro) (c.1412-80). An important painter, sculptor and architect of the Sienese school. He combined the styles of Sassetta, his teacher, especially in his pure, pale color and religious sentiment, and of Domenico di Bartolo, from whom he derived classical and architectural Renaissance characteristics. He painted frescoes in the Scala Hospital (1441 and 1448), the Siena Baptistery (1450-53, now badly repainted), and the Palazzo Pubblico (1461). Among many dated panel paintings the most important are a Madonna and Saints in the Uffizi (1457) and the Assumption in the cathedral of Pienza, which is deemed his finest work. His influence was felt in Siena through his many pupils.

Vedder, Elihu (1836-1923). American painter, illustrator, and mural decorator. Born in New York, he studied in Paris with F. E. Picot and lived in Rome and Capri after 1867, visiting and exhibiting in the U.S. His illustrations for the Rubaiyat and murals for the Library of Congress are his best-known works. He strove in his art for a universal statement based on the Old Masters and produced a completely synthetic, intellectual academicism.

Veen, Otto van (called Octavius Vaenius) (1556-1629). Dutch-born Flemish painter. Forced to flee the Dutch Protestants with his father, van Veen was active in Rome, Vienna, and Brussels. He is best known as one of the teachers of Rubens. He was a learned painter, perhaps owing to years spent with Federigo Zuccaro in Italy, which also made of him a confirmed Romanist. (See illustration.)

Velasco, José Maria (1840-1912). Leading Mexican landscapist of the nineteenth century; one of the directors and teachers at the official Academy of San Carlos. His art represents the monumentalism of classic Mexican painting in a series of lyrical forms, realistically conceived, rich in color and poetic feeling. He is the great poet and celebrant of the Valley of Mexico.

Velázquez, Diego Rodríguez de Silva y (1599-1660). Court painter to Philip IV of Spain. A major Baroque painter and one of the most profound interpreters of the artistic experience of the eye. Born in Seville of Portuguese extraction, he may have studied with Francisco Herrera the Elder, but spent six years in Seville with Pacheco, whose daughter he married. From this point on his career falls into several distinct phases. His painting in Seville reveals the teaching of Pacheco and strong influence of Caravaggio (accounting, for instance, for the quantity of bodegones (see) he painted at that time). He used thick smooth pigment, hard sharp contrasts and plastically separate bodies: a style essentially tactile like Zubarán's. Examples of this early Baroque stolidity are an Immaculate Conception for the Carmelites, an Adoration (Prado) and Christ in the House of Martha (London). By 1623 he was in Madrid where, introduced by Pacheco, he became painter to the king in the service of Olivares. His painting, mainly portraits, began to show the influence of Venetian and Flemish works in the royal collection. Typical are the portraits of Philip IV and of the Infante Carlos in the Prado. The work of this period culminated in the Topers (Prado). Curiously this painting shows no specific influence of Rubens, at that time in residence at

VASARI. The Magdalen
Museum of Fine Art of Houston, Kress Collection

the Spanish court. However, it is definitely more light and lucid than his early tenebrist (see) work and shows the growing two-dimensional, silhouetted character of his impressions. Iconographically it is a mixture of myth and bodegón, a down-to-earth classical study.

Velázquez' research into perception was twice punctuated by trips to Italy where he was able to measure his eye against the ancients. In 1629 he traveled in the suite of the Marquis of Spinola and visited Venice, Rome, Genoa, Bologna and Naples, becoming a friend of Ribera's in the latter city. He copied Renaissance paintings and, in Rome, painted the Forge of Vulcan (Prado) which he shipped home. In this painting he started with a Venetian composition and rendered it in fluid colors and silver tones, getting a more homogeneous atmospheric effect than before. On his return to Spain he was kept busy with countless portraits and decorative projects, mainly for the king. His equestrian portraits of the King, Prince Carlos and Olivares date from this period, as do such famous studies as the dwarfs, buffoons and the characters to whom he gave classical names. In 1635 for the Palace of Buen Retiro he painted the Surrender of Breda, commemorating the victory of the Marquis of Spinola over the Dutch. By this time he had abandoned classical pretensions and was painting in a plein-air style (although in the studio) that was not equaled until Impressionism.

In 1649 Velázquez again traveled in Italy, purchasing old masters to satisfy the King's appetite for paintings. On this occasion he painted the portrait of Pope Innocent X (Rome), based on El Greco's Cardinal Guevara. He also did his remarkable landscape studies of the Medici Gardens (Madrid). After his return in 1651, his official duties as superintendent of the Palace cut seriously into his painting. However, the works of this time are a fitting culmination to the career of the Knight of Santiago. The Maids of Honor (Prado), the Tapestry Workers (Prado) and the Rokeby Venus (London) are masterpieces of his dramatic constructional system. In each case space is created and measured not only by perspective, but also by the interpolation of sheets of light which emphasize the elements of planar recession. This light and the many competing centers of optical interest (including the pictorial image at the rear of the pictures) contradict the sense of centrality and classical composure to be felt in the main figure group. Here, focusing is done impressionistically: that which is more crucial or more central is in sharper detail. The dynamic interrelation of all these elements lends the paintings a dramatic quality not implicit in their subjects. Velázquez died in 1660 as a result of illness brought on by the strain of his courtly duties. (See illustrations, including color plate 206.)

Velde, Adriaen van de (1636-72). Dutch painter and engraver of landscapes with animals and figures. He studied with his father Willem van de Velde the Elder, and also with Wynants and Wouwermans. His landscapes are of the Italian type, animated with pleasing figures and well-painted animals. He often supplied the figures for paintings by other artists.

Velde the Elder, Willem van de (c.1611-93). Dutch painter of marine scenes. The father of Willem the Younger and of Adriaen van de Velde, this meticulously exact painter worked in Amsterdam, and then about 1672 went to England, where he painted for King Charles II.

VEEN, VAN. Vocation of St. Thomas
Musée Royal des Beaux-Arts, Antwerp

VELÁZQUEZ. The Surrender of Breda. Prado, Madrid

VELÁZQUEZ. Don Baltasar Carlos in the Riding School Wallace Collection, London

Velde, Esaias van de (c.1590-1630). Dutch painter and engraver of landscape and genre. The brother of Willem van de Velde the Elder, he was probably the pupil of Gillis van Coninxloo. He worked for the Princes Maurits and Frederik Hendrik in the Hague. His little scenes, animated with lively figures, are quaint and pleasing.

Velde the Younger, Willem van de (1633-1707). Dutch painter of marine scenes. He studied with Simon de Vlieger and sometimes collaborated with his brother Adriaen. He spent much of his life in England. His seascapes are effectively composed and transmit his sensitive response to the changing moods of nature.

Venetian school. Although this school begins as early as the fourteenth century with the Byzantine two-dimensionality and starkness of such masters as Maestro Paolo it is not until the fifteenth century that it achieves any importance. Here a kind of Gothic linealism becomes evident in the work of Jacobello del Fiore, Giovanni d'Alemagna and his two brothers-in-law Antonio and Bartolommeo Vivarini. An even more important aspect of Venetian painting takes us into the late fifteenth and early sixteenth century through the Bellini family, especially the poetic and tender Giovanni. His pupils, Giorgione and Titian, constitute in many ways the high point of the Renaissance in Venice. During the latter part of the sixteenth century the nervousness and tensions of Mannerism (see) appear, as in Tintoretto. The last great Venetian school belongs to the eighteenth century and includes the magnificent panoramas of Canaletto Guardi.

Veneto, Bartolommeo (act. 1502-35). Venetian painter under the influence of the Venetian and Lombard schools, with indications of a connection with northern art, especially Dürer and Lucas van Leyden. He was a pupil of Bellini and his early work is closely related to that of his master and

VERESTCHAGIN. Monks at Door of Mosque, Turkestan Museum of Fine Arts, Boston

206. VELÁZQUEZ. Pope Innocent X. National Gallery of Art, Mellon Collection, Washington, D.C.

Cima. His earliest dated work (1502) is a Madonna and Child (private collection, Venice). He produced many half-figure Madonnas in this style. In 1506-08 he was working in Ferrara for Lucrezia Borgia; he was later active in Bergamo and then in Milan. In Milan he came under the influence of Leonardo's style, developing a manner very close to that of Solario, with whose work his has sometimes been confused. A fine portraitist somewhat in the Flemish manner, his most famous work in this genre is the Ludovico Martinengo, 1530 (London). (See color plate 207.)

Veneziano, Carlo (see SARACENI, CARLO).

Veneziano, Domenico (see DOMENICO VENEZIANO).

Venusti, Marcello (1512/1515-79). Born in Como, he studied in Florence with Pierino del Vaga and was influenced by the art of Romanino and Bernardino Campi. However, his contact with Michelangelo overwhelmed the Venetian elements in his painting. He did a copy of Michelangelo's Last Judgment in its original state.

Verestchagin, V.V. (1824-1904). Outstanding representative of the Russian academic Realist movement of the nineteenth century. As a participant in several military campaigns, he was in a position to comment on the imperialistic policy of his country in the Balkans and Central Asia in such paintings as the Apotheosis of War (a pyramid of white skulls), They Triumph, etc. (See illustration.)

Vergós (family). Painters active in Barcelona in the fifteenth century. Jaime Vergós I (active 1434-60) founded the workshop which was continued by his son Jaime II (active 1460-1503) and grandsons Pablo (d.1495) and Rafael. Pablo, considered the best, was influenced by Bermejo. Rafael worked with Jaime Huguet, and painted most of the latter's retablo for the Augustinians (Barcelona Museum).

207. VENETO. Portrait of a Gentleman. National Gallery of Art, Washington, D.C.

VERMEER. View of City of Delft. Mauritshuis, The Hague

Verism. An exact, horrifyingly real kind of treatment; a meticulously precise and disturbingly clinical technique associated with the German painters of the 1920's of the so-called New Objectivity school. See EXPRESSIONISM.

Vermeer, Johannes (Vermeer of Delft) (1632-75). Dutch painter of household genre, portraits and city views. Vermeer was born and worked in Delft, where he was probably the pupil of Carel Fabritius. Although he was an important member of the guild and received high prices for his paintings, he died a very poor man. During the eighteenth century his name and reputation were unaccountably forgotten. In 1866 the art critic Thoré Bürger, after searching many years for works by Vermeer, published an essay about him, listing sixty-six pictures. Modern criticism accepts about half of this number as authentic. In these few paintings, which count among the rarest treasures of the history of art, his style is marked by a pervading serenity and order. This is the result of his extraordinary skill in representing space and the technical perfection with which he illuminated the objects enclosed in it. Animate and inanimate, they are so accurately observed and represented that they appear to exist in permanence and timelessness. Exact balance and harmony prevail. Vermeer's mastery of color and brushwork is never displayed as virtuosity, but always employed in the enhancement of the whole. (See illustrations, including color plate 208.)

Vermeyen, Jan Cornelisz. (c.1500-59). Dutch painter of portraits and religious subjects. He probably studied with Gossaert in Utrecht and was influenced by Scorel, whose friend he is said to have been. He worked among many other gifted painters at the court of Margaret of Austria in Malines, accompanied her to Cambrai and painted for her in Augsburg and Innsbruck. He also spent some time in Spain. His work is characterized by strongly contrasted light and shadow, and by pronounced modeling.

Vernet, Antoine Charles (called Carle) (1758-1836). French painter and lithographer. Specialist in horses and battle scenes. He was the son of Joseph and the father of Horace Vernet. Carle emerged as an important artist in the Empire when his Morning of Austerlitz and his Napoleon before Madrid made his reputation as a painter of contemporary events. He also did caricatures of a malicious type, such as the Incroyables and the Merveilleuses.

Vernet, Claude Josephe (1714-89). One of the few French landscape painters of the eighteenth century. Son of a decorative painter and father of Carle Vernet, Joseph is the first important French landscape painter after Poussin and Claude, and his work prepared the way for the Romantic interest in landscape. He was also an expert in the painting of marine scenes. Vernet spent most of his life in Italy. He is supposed to have strapped himself to the ship's mast during a storm on his way there in order to study the natural effects of the tempest. His marines are largely of shipwrecks and storms in the manner of Salvator Rosa, except for a series of French port views commissioned by the King. His landscapes are modernized Claudes with bits of ruin and genre activity tucked in here and there or are descriptive paintings such as the Ponte Rotto. (See illustration.)

Vernet, Emile Jean Horace (1789-1863). French military painter and lithographer. Son of Carle Vernet. His documentary battle pictures developed from the influence of his father and from the part he himself played in the defense of Paris in 1814: for example, The Defense of the Barrière de Clichy. Like his father he did caricatures in drawing and lithograph. He was a friend of Géricault. (See illustration.)

Veronese (Paolo Caliari) (1528-88). One of the great painters of the Venetian Renaissance, he lacked the powerful inventive genius of Tintoretto and the magnificent universality of Titian, but his art remains the ultimate expression of Venetian opulence. His completely secular, contemporary, and realistic interpretations of religious dogma even led eventually to difficulties with the Inquisition. His color is cool, clear and luminous, and his feeling for texture superb. He disposed hundreds of figures with magnificent ease in scenes of unparalleled pageantry. He was born in Verona and studied sculpture first with his father, Gabriele, and painting later with Antonio Badile whose daughter he married. Among his

VERNET, HORACE. Marchesa Misciatelli, Son and Nurse University of Arizona, Kress Collection, Tucson

VERNET, CLAUDE JOSEPH. A Mediterranean Seaport
National Gallery, London

early works under the influence of the Venetian-Veronese tradition are the Bevilacqua Altarpiece (1548, Verona), decorations of the Sacristy of S. Liberale, Castelfranco (1551), and for the Villa Emo, Fanzolo (1553). His first important decorative commission after settling in Venice was for S. Sebastiano (c.1555-60). After the fires of 1574 and 1577, he was called to redecorate the Doge's Palace, executed the Sala del Collegio, including the Venice Enthroned with Justice and Peace (c.1575), and the Sala del Gran Consiglio, including the splendid Triumph of Venice for the ceiling (1578-85). Among his most famous feast scenes are the earlier Supper at Emmaus and Wedding at Cana (both c.1560, Dresden), the later versions of the same subjects (both 1562-63, Louvre), and the most advanced, the Supper in the House of Levi (1570, Louvre). Although extremely active as a decorator of villas in the vicinty of Venice, only one cycle now remains, the Villa Giacomelli at Maser built by Palladio in 1560. He continued throughout his life to produce large altarpieces in the High Renaissance manner, but is remembered more for such lush mythological and allegorical paintings as the Venus and Mars (Metropolitan), Wisdom and Strength (Frick), and Vice and Virtue (Frick). His decorative style later became the basis for eighteenth-century Venetian decoration culminating in Tiepolo. (See color plate 209.)

Verrocchio, Andrea del (1435-88). A Florentine sculptor and goldsmith whose importance to the history of painting was his influence over his painter-pupils, Leonardo da Vinci and Lorenzo di Credi. He belonged to the same tradition of shop craftsmanship embracing several arts as the Pollaiuolo brothers. His real name was Andrea di Michele di Francesco Cione, and he probably served his apprenticeship with the renowned goldsmith Giuliano dei Verrocchi. Various works of architecture, sculpture and decorative minor art are recorded in his early years, the most important of which are the bronze group of Christ and the Doubting Thomas (1465) on the Or San Michele and the bronze David (1476) in the Bargello, Florence. His greatest work is the monumental equestrian bronze statue of Bartolommeo Colleoni in Venice (begun in 1479 and cast after his death), which follows the tradition of Donatello's Gattamelata in Padua and the painted equestrian portraits by Uccello and Castagno in the cathedral of Florence. It is a dramatic work, large in conception, but retaining the fine detail of the goldsmith. Verrocchio's only universally accepted painting is the Baptism of Christ in the Uffizi; it was started in the 1470's but was left unfinished and was ultimately completed by Leonardo da Vinci, who painted the angel farthest to the left and a part of the landscape. Verrocchio here displays an interest in detailed anatomy and the action of the human body parallel to that of Antonio Pollaiuolo. A number of Verrocchio's drawings that have been preserved also show a feeling for carefully graded modeling and sweetness of expression; these found their way into the art of the succeeding generation, especially in the work of Leonardo. Of other paintings attributed to Verrocchio the most convincing is a Madonna in the Berlin museum. The influence of his art was felt not only by his own pupils, but by many others, notably Botticelli and Piero di Cosimo (See illustration.)

Versailles Museum, Versailles, Fr. Paintings and other objects relating primarily to the history of France and the French monarchy.

Victoria and Albert Museum, London. Established to illustrate the development of the history of art in terms of industrial and craft forms: ceramics, engravings, illustration, design, book production, paintings, textiles, etc. It is especially noteworthy for its collection of Oriental ceramics and paintings, and its library and photograph collection.

Vieira da Silva, Maria Helena (1908-). Portuguese-born Brazilian painter; also an engraver. She went to Paris in 1928 to study with the sculptors Bourdelle and Despiau and the painters Friesz and Léger. She also studied engraving with Hayter. She settled in Rio de Janeiro in 1939. Her style is non-figurative in the abstract Surrealist vein.

Vien, Maria Joseph (1716-1809). French history painter and etcher. One of the first Neo-Classical painters. Pupil of Natoire, he reacted against his style and developed a classicistic, moralizing art that was much praised by Diderot. The Love Merchants, adapted from an ancient painting and

VERROCCHIO. Madonna and Child
National Gallery of Art, Kress Collection, Washington, D.C.

208. VERMEER. Young Girl with a Flute. National Gallery of Art, Widener Collection, Washington, D.C.

his Ladies of Corinth Decorating a Vase of Flowers are typical. He communicated this Rococo-classical taste to his pupil David, who employed it more heroically.

View of Toledo by El Greco (see).

Vigée-Lebrun, Elizabeth (1755-1842). A French eighteenth-century society painter who belongs to the period before the French Revolution although she lived half-way through the following century. Taught by her father, a portrait painter, Elizabeth began her professional career at fifteen. Shortly afterwards she married the painter Lebrun (he was also a critic and picture dealer) and was thereafter guided by him as well as by his friends Greuze and Joseph Vernet. She became the favorite portrait painter of Maria Antoinette and painted at least twenty versions of the Queen and her children during the last day of the monarchy. The sentimental and somewhat English character of her style made her a great favorite at the French court and, after the Revolution, at other courts in Europe. Vigée-Lebrun's style is pleasing rather than penetrative; decorative and colorful rather than sensitive in either color or form. For many her work represents a conventional and even artificial tradition. (See illustration.)

Vignon, Claude (1593-1670). French painter and etcher to Louis XIII and Richelieu. He spent many years in Italy, where he was a student of Caravaggio's. He was, apparently, also a friend of young Rembrandt, who had one of his engravings. He also studied in Spain, as can be seen from his Christ Washing the Feet of the Apostles, which has reminiscences of Murillo.

Villon, Jacques (1875-). A pseudonym of Gaston Duchamp, brother of the well-known sculptor Duchamp-Villon and the painter Marcel Duchamp. Painter and graphic artist, Villon has also developed a special technique for the reproduction of original paintings, a color etching method published by Bernheim Jeune. For a while he did newspaper drawings, then was affiliated with the Autumn Salon from 1904 to 1911 and became interested in Cubism (see). It was in his studio that a group of artists including Léger, Picabia, La Fresnaye, Gleizes and Metzinger met and formed the very influential Section d'Or (see) association. Villon's version of Cubism has a soft poetic quality considerably removed from the more formal versions practiced by others. (See illustration.)

Vitale da Bologna (active c.1330 to after 1359). The first painter of any importance in Bologna. Records tell us that he decorated two chapels in the city; of extant signed panels two are dated: a Madonna (1345) in the Bologna gallery, and a polyptych (1353) in San Salvatore, Bologna. His style, containing iconographic elements of Byzantine painting and decorative elements from the Sienese, exhibits a certain crudeness of execution characteristic of the Bolognese school. His influence appears in the work of Simone dei Crocifissi.

Viti, Timoteo (1467-1523). Born in Ferrara, he worked for a time with Francesco Francia in Bologna, and settled in Urbino by 1501. He worked for both Guidobaldo da Montefeltro and Cesare Borgia. He is a late representative of the decorative and manneristic Umbrian style, and a similarity has been noted between his art and some of the earliest works of Raphael, whom he may have known and perhaps even taught.

Vivarini, Alvise (c.1446-1503). Venetian painter who represents the second generation of the Vivarini family from Murano, and though his style was probably formed in the shop of his uncle Bartolommeo, he subsequently came under the influence of Giovanni Bellini and Antonello da Messina. He was the son of Antonio Vivarini, and works by him are known dating from 1475 to his death. By 1480 his work begins to display the soft and luminous color and more flexible composition of figures derived from Giovanni Bellini and Antonello. In later works he assimilates the light, the pyramidal composition and the architectural settings that are characteristic of the late fifteenth-century Venetian style. Important altarpieces are in Berlin, the Venice Academy, and the Frari church in Venice.

Vivarini, Antonio (c.1415-c.1470). Venetian painter, the oldest of a family of artists who came from Padua and settled in Murano. His style was based on that of Gentile da Fabriano (see), Pisanello and Jacobello del Fiore, and he worked in partnership with his brother-in-law Giovanni d'Alemagna until the latter's death in about 1450. After that he was influenced by his more important and much younger brother Bartolommeo (see). The most important work of the partnership with Giovanni is the Madonna Enthroned (Venice Academy). Most of the works associated with Antonio Vivarini are polyptychs with extremely ornate, compartmented Gothic frames, a form stemming from earlier Venetian altarpiece types.

209. VERONESE. Finding of Moses
National Gallery of Art, Mellon Collection, Washington, D.C.

VIGÉE-LEBRUN. Self Portrait. Uffizi Gallery, Florence

Vivarini, Bartolommeo (c.1432-c.1491). A Venetian painter. The younger brother of Antonio Vivarini, he developed his brother's Gothic style into a solider, more three-dimensional form of expression that shows a certain relation to the early work of Mantegna and other products of the Squarcione school in Padua. He was presumably born in Murano, and his prolific output indicates continuous activity from about 1448 to 1491. His earliest works were done in collaboration with Antonio, with whom he signed an important polyptych of the Madonna and Saints (1450) in the Bologna gallery; his hand may be detected in the more vigorously modeled figures. He worked independently from about 1459, when the influence of Mantegna on his style becomes more manifest. Two important works of this period are the Madonna and Four Saints polyptych (1464) in the Venice Academy, and the Madonna and Saints (1465) in Naples. In the second of these the Gothic frame and compartments are discarded in favor of a single unified space in which the symmetrical composition is richly ornamented with garlands and brocade. In later works Bartolommeo attempts more monumental figures in settings that have assimilated the Renaissance ornament of Mantegna. His manner of drawing remains tight and dry, with emphasis on linear detail, while his color is sumptuous and decorative. Bartolommeo was an almost exact contemporary of Carlo Crivelli, and the latter's art, though very individual, bears a distinct relationship to Bartolommeo's. (See illustration.)

Vivin, Louis (1861-1935). French primitive or self-taught painter who, after forty years of service in the French post-

VILLON. Soldiers on the March. Louis Carré Gallery, Paris

office department, retired at sixty-two to engage in painting. His work was perhaps the most specifically detailed among the Sunday painters, yet he was in some ways the most dreamlike.

Vlaminck, Maurice de (1876-). French painter and writer; a member of the Fauve group. Of peasant background, Vlaminck has lived in and around country areas most of his life and is a rather rugged, picturesque type; he has from time to time been a musician and cyclist as well as a painter. His feeling for nature is constant and strong, expressing itself very appropriately in the intense colors of the early Fauve movement of which he was a part. Around 1900 he shared a studio on the island of Chatou with Derain, in whose company he experienced the Van Gogh exhibition of 1901, which fired them both with the greatest enthusiasm. Vlaminck met Matisse through Derain and began to show the Indépendants. In 1901-02 he wrote the first of his three novels, *Seeds in the Wind*, illustrated with sketches by Derain. He joined the other Fauves at the Autumn Salon of 1905 in their "wild beast cage," and the following year the far-sighted dealer Vollard bought all the canvases in his studio. In 1908 he abandoned his early, Van Gogh style with its broken, impetuous and brilliant coloristic manner for the dark, romantic, even somber one which (under the influence of Cézanne's controlled space) has since characterized his work. See FAUVISM. (See color plate 210.)

Vollard, Ambroise (1865-1939). Distinguished French picture dealer and publisher of fine books, many of them illustrated by the leading figures in the Parisian art world. Vollard's greatest importance lies is his having promoted a number of subsequently outstanding artists; typical is Cézanne, whom he showed as early as 1895 in a large-scale exhibition of one hundred and fifty canvases. For the next forty or more years Vollard's shop was perhaps the most important art center in Paris. Picasso and Matisse were given their first one-man shows in his gallery in 1901 and 1904 respectively. In 1906 he bought out Vlaminck's studio. Among the many artists whom he commissioned to illustrate books for his publication program were: Maurice Denis, Bonnard, Degas, Picasso, Redon, Rouault, Chagall and Renoir. Finally, Vollard is important as the publisher of bronzes by Renoir, Maillol, Rodin and Picasso. More than any other figure he sums up the important role of the European art dealer in the conscious encouragement of artists.

Vollon, Antoine (1833-1900). French painter and etcher. Pupil of Ribot, he painted mainly still lifes, genres and portraits. He was famous as the Chardin of his time. He won medals with his Portrait of a Fisherman (1868) and After the Ball (1869). His Corner of the Market-Hall is in the Luxembourg. He was known for his technical dexterity.

Volpi, Alfredo (1895-). A Brazilian painter who was brought from Italy as a baby; a self-taught artist. He uses flat, unmodulated color patterns and extremely simplified forms; one of his works received a prize at the 1953 biennial exhibition in São Paulo, Brazil.

Volterra, Daniele da (Daniele Ricciarelli) (1509-66). Italian painter, sculptor, and architect, follower of Michelangelo. Born in Volterra, he was first influenced by the Sienese painters—Sodoma and Peruzzi. Later, in Rome (c.1540), he worked with Pierino del Vaga, through whom he came in contact with the style of Raphael. But it was his intimate connection with Michelangelo, with whom he worked closely, which had the most profound effect on his subsequent art. His most important work, and one of the most highly regarded in the sixteenth century, was his Descent from the Cross executed for the Orsini Chapel in Sta. Trinità de'

VIVARINI, BARTOLOMMEO. Adoration of the Magi
Frick Collection, New York

VOLTERRA. Elia. Collection Count Pannocchieschi d'Elci, Siena

Monti (1541). This, as well as the Ascension of the Virgin in the Capella Rovere in the same church, shows the strong influence or perhaps even assistance of Michelangelo. Some time during the 1540's he decorated the Palazzo Massimi delle Colonne. In 1558 he was called on to repaint the Michelangelo Last Judgment in conformity with the newer puritan taste of the Counter Reformation under Pope Paul VIII. He was the greatest of the Michelangelo followers, powerful and intense but troubled and uneven. (See illustration.)

Vorticism. A modern British school of painting parallel in form and meaning to that of the Cubist-Futurists on the Continent; however, the leader of the British group, Wyndham Lewis, believed his movement to be unique. Sculptors Jacob Epstein and Henri Gaudier-Brzeska, painters Wyndham Lewis and Edward Wadsworth, writers Ezra Pound, Rebecca West and other contributors to the Vorticist periodical *Blast* introduced this dynamically fragmented conception of form to Britain, shattering at the same time many of the entrenched artistic attitudes of the past. The movement lasted from 1912 to 1915 but its influence carried on beyond this point, although to conservative artists both the technique and the politics of some members of the Vorticist group, especially Lewis himself, were equally distasteful.

Vos, Cornelis de (1584?-1651). Flemish portrait and history painter. Brother of Paul, brother-in-law of Frans Snyders. He was influenced strongly by Rubens and van Dyck; in fact, his works have been mistaken for the latter's. His great strength lay in portraiture and many of his commissions came to him through Rubens. He also assisted Rubens in large projects. (See illustration.)

Vos, Marten de (1532-1603). Flemish painter. He left the Romanist painter Floris for Venice and became pupil and assistant of Tintoretto. He met with great success on his return to Antwerp, especially in the field of religious paintings and portraits. He is one of the most characteristic Flemish Mannerist painters. An example of his work is the Tribute Money (Antwerp). (See illustration.)

Vos, Paul de (c.1596-1678). Flemish painter of animals and still lifes. Brother of Cornelis. Closely associated with Rubens and Snyders, his brother-in-law. Although he remained in Antwerp, his paintings were frequently exported.

Vouet, Simon (1590-1649). Founder of the great French tradition of decorative painting. He revived the stagnant Fontainebleau school by an injection of various Italian Baroque styles which he had learned during extensive traveling. In 1627 he was called home to France by Louis XIII to head the old Maîtrisse and to supervise royal works. His eclectic formula became, with slight stylistic variations, the French academic standard for centuries. Vouet was at first, in Italy, strongly Caravaggesque but then turned to the vapid allegories, religious compositions and tapestry cartoons for which his school is famous. His administrative control was finally broken in 1648 by the political reorganization of French painting into the Royal Academy by Colbert and Le Brun (see). His drawings are much freer and more inventive than his pantings.

VOS, CORNELIS DE. Portrait of a Little Boy
Museum Mayer v.d. Bergh, Antwerp

VOS, MARTEN DE. St. Paul at Ephesus
Musées Royaux des Beaux-Arts, Brussels

Vrelant, Willem (active 1454, d.1481/82). Dutch painter of illuminations. He came from Utrecht, but after 1454 was active in Bruges, where he was a friend of Memling. The

210. VLAMINCK. Street in St. Jean. Private Collection

sixty miniatures which he contributed to the illumination of the *Chronicle of Hennegau,* and many other decorations in prayer books, show him as a skillful painter with a special gift for landscape.

Vroom, Hendrik Cornelisz. (1566-1640). Dutch painter of marine scenes. After beginning, like his father, as a painter of faience, he traveled through the whole of Europe, eventually settling in Haarlem, where he became a founder of the Dutch tradition of seascapes.

VUILLARD. Lady in Black. Musée de Luxembourg, Paris

Vuillard, Edouard (1868-1940). French painter and one of the most important of the Nabis group (see), which was influenced technically by the clean colors of Impressionism and the carefully planned geometry of Japanese prints. Spiritually, however, Vuillard like most of his fellow artists was interested in achieving a new kind of reality that went beyond mere surface appearances. His art is best described as a kind of Intimism (see) in which simple everyday things are painted with a rich brooding color and isolated, as it were, from the world at large. He was associated, like many of his group, with Lugné-Poë's Théâtre de l'Oeuvre, acting as general adviser, helping to stage such plays as Ibsen's *Rosmersholm.* He was very friendly also with the Natansons, publishers of *La Revue Blanche.* Later in life he turned to society portraits. (See illustration.)

Vytlacil, Vaclav (1892-). A contemporary American Abstract Expressionist. Born in New York, he studied at the Art Institute of Chicago, the Art Students League, and in Munich with Hans Hofmann. He has also had an extensive career as a teacher.

W

Wadsworth, Edward (1889-1949). British painter best known for his glossy, finely finished, abstract Surrealist paintings of the sea. One of the original Vorticists of the 1912-15 period, Wadsworth contributed drawings to their periodical *Blast.* The Vorticist preference for an art of the machine is reflected in Wadsworth's most typical works,

211. WATTEAU. Italian Comedians. National Gallery, Kress Collection, Washington, D.C.

which combine this mechanized quality with the clear dream-like lighting effects and perspectives of Surrealism.

Waldmüller, Ferdinand (1793-1865). Austrian academic painter who developed under the influence of Dutch painting of the seventeenth century, although his landscapes are somewhat fresher and more modern in color.

Waldo, Samuel Lovett (1783-1861). American portrait painter active with his former student and partner William Jewett in Connecticut, New York, and South Carolina. Born in Windham, Conn., he studied in London for three years with West and Copley. The collaboration between him and Jewett (see) was the longest in American art and their joint signature appeared on a great number of paintings.

Walker, Frederick (1840-75). British landscapist and genre painter; he specialized in paintings of peasant life with a Romantic approach and poetic moods. His studies of antique statuary in the British Museum lend a classical grace to his figures. He published many drawings and did illustrations for stories.

Walker, Horatio (1858-1938). American painter born in Lisfowel, Ontario. Deeply influenced by the Barbizon school and especially Millet and Troyon, he painted similar scenes based on farm life around Quebec. He had the same interest in nature and the same sentimental attitude toward the farmers, animals, and the land.

Walkowitz, Abraham (1880-). Contemporary American painter. One of the pioneers of modern art in America and best known for his studies of Isadora Duncan. Born in Russia, he came to the U.S. as a child, studied at the National Academy of Design with Ward, Maynard, and Jones, and at the Académie Julian in Paris with Laurens. He was one of the earliest experimenters in abstraction and exhibited at the gallery "291."

Wallace Collection, London. Noted especially for its unique collection of eighteenth-century French art acquired by the fourth Marquess of Hertford and Sir Richard Wallace, both long-time residents of Paris during the nineteenth century. There are also good selections of paintings from other European countries.

Wallraf-Richartz Museum, Cologne. One of the finest museums in Germany, it was recently enriched by the outstanding Haubrich collection, which constitutes its modern and most important section. Its paintings and sculptures include examples from the late nineteenth century to the present day, including post-World War II artists, thus making up for the losses incurred during the Nazi confiscation of modern works in 1937.

Wang Chien (see CHINESE PAINTERS: CH'ING DYNASTY).

Wang Hui (see CHINESE PAINTERS: CH'ING DYNASTY).

Wang Meng (see CHINESE PAINTERS: YÜAN DYNASTY).

Wang Shih-min (see CHINESE PAINTERS: CH'ING DYNASTY).

Wang Wei (see CHINESE PAINTERS: T'ANG DYNASTY).

Wang Yüan-ch'i (see CHINESE PAINTERS: CH'ING DYNASTY).

WATKINS. The Fire Eater. Philadelphia Museum of Art

Ward, James (1769-1859). British animal painter admired by Géricault on that painter's London visit in 1820. He is also known for rural, genre and anecdotal pictures under the influence of Morland. Some of his works were engraved as popular prints. Many of his paintings and engravings show animals in combat, although he specialized in studies of prize cattle painted for their proud owners. An able craftsman, he drew with intensity, giving an air of solidity to his figures by a heavy impasto. In 1794 he was appointed "painter and mezzotinter" to the Prince of Wales. His later work was influenced by Rubens.

Waroquier, Henry de (1881-). Contemporary French painter who began under the influence of Impressionism and then overlaid it with various Oriental effects, especially Japanese. Affected by Italian painting, he went through a so-called "white period," after which he turned to imaginative landscapes. His most recent works show a kind of figurative Expressionism.

wash. Generally refers to a thin layer or film of paint used in the watercolor method.

Washington Crossing the Delaware by Emanuel Leutze (see).

Washington, George by Gilbert Stuart (see).

Wassenhove, Joos van (see JUSTUS OF GHENT).

watercolor. A painting medium made of ground pigment mixed with water and a binding material, usually gum arabic, and applied to paper or silk. Pure watercolor is translucent; gouache (see) is an opaque watercolor made by the addition of some filler, usually zinc white. In a sense, both fresco and tempera are forms of watercolor, but in its pure form it was largely ignored in the West until the eighteenth century, when it had a renaissance among English painters—Cozens, Blake, Girtin, and Turner—and later among such American painters as Homer and Marin. Utilized originally for its capacity in rendering minute detail, it has become characterized by a broad and fluid handling.

Watkins, Franklin Chenault (1894-). Contemporary American painter born in New York and active in Philadelphia. Trained at the Pennsylvania Academy of Fine Arts and abroad, he worked as a commercial artist and portraitist, did mural decorations for the Rodin Museum, and finally achieved public recognition in 1931 with Suicide in Costume at the Carnegie International. (See illustration.)

Watteau, Jean Antoine (1684-1721). Most notable for the dreamlike quality of his painting, Watteau turned the course of French art from the pompous classicism of Louis XIV to the delightfully sensuous colorism of the Rococo. This transformation he affected in a brief career of twenty years marred by poverty and illness. He is the archetype of the gay, witty side of French art, just as his predecessor Poussin exemplified its formal, rationalistic aspect. So Watteau seems basic to the French aesthetic, although argument

WATTEAU. The Judgment of Paris. Louvre, Paris

might be made for him as a Fleming. He was born in Valenciennes, which had been French only six years, and his revision of French painting stemmed largely from his enthusiasm for Flemish art, especially that of Rubens.

Watteau came to Paris at eighteen and for several years was engaged in hack work, copying for art dealers and painting devotional images. From 1705-08 he worked with Gillot (see), a painter of scenery and of incidents of Italian Comedy. This made a permanent impression on Watteau, as did his work (1708) for Claude Audran, who was employed at the Luxembourg Palace. Both the Rubens paintings of the Medici gallery in the palace and the park and gardens outside had their effect. In 1709 he tried unsuccessfully for the Prix de Rome and, embittered, returned to Valenciennes. Some of his paintings of soldiers may have been inspired by troops in the vicinity of Valenciennes at that time. He had a number of excellent friends among the aristocracy and wealthy bourgeoisie of Paris: de Caylus, de Julienne, Gersaint and Crozat. Crozat had a large collection of Flemish and Venetian paintings and drawings: a new taste, running counter to the dominant classicism of the previous century. Watteau lived with Crozat, studied his collection and there met LaFosse, who nominated him as an associate of the Academy in 1712.

Watteau was nominated to the Academy in a new category: *Fêtes galantes*. Five years later he painted his diploma picture, the Embarkation for Cythera (Louvre version), which illustrates this category. Such paintings by Watteau reflected the social ideal of the century. Courtly life was a dream world of gay amorous relations between couples. Conversation was a combination of pleasantry and intrigue; existence, an inextricable mixture of real and make-believe. The garden served as a retreat from the pretentious halls of their inherited architecture. Nature was Reality—leafy picturesque nature inhabited by statues of nymphs and Venuses more real in substance than tne flounces of courtly dress. The carefully observed details of costume and setting in painting were sublimated by a web of fine, colored brushstrokes that dissolved the forms and transformed the materialism of all objects. Small and intimate in format and figure-scale, these canvases reduced Rubens' Garden of Love to Cupid-size. It was a woman's world, this petite Arcadia. Men are posed in pointed pirouettes as they entice their voluminous mates from the garden and usher them toward boats departing to the distant misty island of Love.

It all smacks of the theater, on which Watteau grounded his art, and primarily the Italian Comedy with its stock plots and characters. This popular dramatic form had been banned during the late years of Louis XIV but survived surreptitiously and was the rage of the Regency period. Watteau's treatment of Italian comedy ranged from full scenes, such as Love in the Theatre (Berlin), to exquisite portrait studies, such as the Mezzetin (Metropolitan) and Gilles (Louvre). His art then was essentially genre painting, viz., Fête in a Park (Wallace Collection) in which the same figures appear again and again, drawn from the repository of his own drawings. Most interesting perhaps of his straight genre subjects is the Signboard of Gersaint (Berlin), painted for his friend's shop in his last year. By 1720 his illness (apparently consumption) had so worsened that he went to England to consult Queen Anne's physician. Nothing could be done, so he returned to Paris, lived with Gersaint and with Vleughels and then retired to a country house where he died in 1721. In his last weeks he was reunited with his townsman and pupil Pater after long enmity. As most of his paintings had gone directly into private collections, his work was long known mainly through the copies engraved for de Julienne by Boucher and others. (See illustrations, including color plate 211.)

Watts, George Frederick (1817-1904). A British allegorical painter with an imaginative, humanitarian approach. His artistic background, apparently not entirely assimilated, features Titian and the Elgin marbles. He is known for large canvases similar to the symbolic concepts of Blake but not nearly as effective in composition; the color is interesting but the drawing loose and indecisive. Watts lived through the years in which British democracy established itself with all the attendant strains. Moved by the sufferings of the poor, he tried to paint this side of life. He may be looked upon as a reaction from Victorian materialism, first expressed realistically and them symbolically.

WEBER. Whither Now. Collection of the Artist

Weber, Max (1881-). Contemporary American painter, one of the pioneers of modern art in the U.S. Born in Russia, he arrived in the U.S. in 1891, studied with A. W. Dow at Pratt Institute (1897-1900), and taught briefly at several colleges. In 1905 he went to Paris, studied with Laurens at the Académie Julian and attended the Académie Colarossi and the Grande Chaumière. He met some of the leaders of the modern movement and in 1907 worked with Matisse. On his return to the U.S. in 1909 he had his first one-man show at the Haas Gallery and in 1911 at the gallery "291," both of which were severely criticized. His early work, 1909-11, was predominantly Fauve with an increasing emphasis on Cubist elements. From 1912 to 1916 he painted abstractions and semi-abstractions, many based on New York

212. WEST. Colonel Guy Johnson. National Gallery, Mellon Collection, Washington, D.C.

scenes, largely Cubist but with influences of Futurism. A return to realism is evident in the semi-abstractions of 1917-19 and in 1918 he did colored woodcuts in a primitivist style. In 1919 there is a clear and fundamental return to a representational style and poetic and religious subjects. Through the 1920's and early 1930's he painted predominantly idyllic figure pieces, landscapes, and still lifes under the renewed influence of Cézanne. The opulently colored and plastically powerful paintings of the late 1930's gave way in the 1940's to an art of greater abstraction and an Expressionistic emphasis on linear pattern and intensification of color. (See illustration.)

Weenix, Jan (1640-1719). Dutch painter of still life, portraits and landscapes. He studied with his father Jan Baptist Weenix and probably with Hondecoeter. For ten years he was employed near Düsseldorf by the Elector Johann Wilhelm of the Palatinate. Like his father he is especially known for his skillful compositions of dead game and fowl.

Weenix, Jan Baptist (1621-60?). Dutch painter of still life, landscapes and portraits. He studied with Bloemaert in Utrecht and with Moeyaert. He spent four years in Italy, where he worked for Pope Innocent X. In his still-life painting he was influenced by such Flemish artists as Snyders. He was the father of the painter Jan Weenix (see).

Weir, J. Alden (1852-1919). American painter, son of Robert W. who taught art at the U.S. Military Academy. One

213. WEYDEN, ROGIER VAN DER. St. Jerome in the Desert. Detroit Institute of Arts

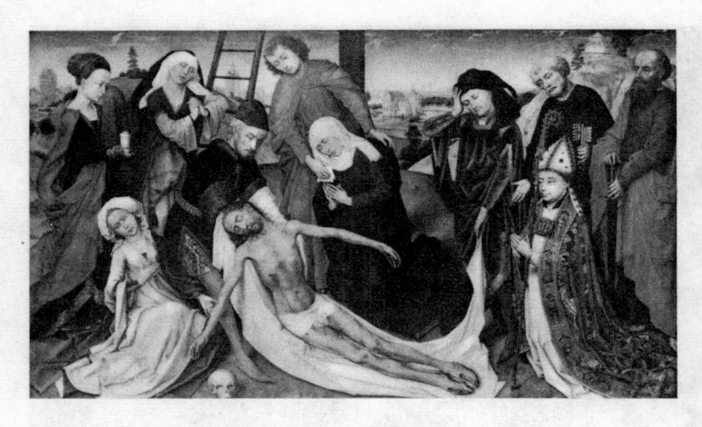

WEYDEN, VAN DER. Descent from the Cross
Mauritshuis, The Hague

of the founders of the Ten, he studied at the Ecole des Beaux-Arts with Gérôme and was influenced by Lepage, but eventually turned toward Impressionism.

Wellens (see COCK, JAN DE).

Wen Cheng-ming (see CHINESE PAINTERS: MING DYNASTY).

Werff, Adriaen van der (1659-1722). Dutch painter and engraver of portraits, history and genre: he was also an architect. He studied with Picolet and van der Neer. He made several trips to Germany in his capacity of court painter to the Elector Palatine Johann Wilhelm. His exquisitely finished pictures were much admired by his contemporaries.

Werner, Theodor (1886-). German international modernist; studied at the Stuttgart Academy. From 1909 to 1914 he was in Paris; he returned to Stuttgart from 1919 to 1929 but was again in Paris during 1930-35 and developed friendships with Braque and Miro. His painting is typical of the postwar abstract adaptations of German painters attempting to overcome the gaps of the Nazi years. It has little connection with the native Expressionist tradition and may perhaps best be classified as Constructivist in spirit.

West, Benjamin (1738-1820). American painter of portraits and historical subjects active most of his life in England. Born in what is now Swarthmore, Pa., the son of an innkeeper, he began his career as an artist by copying woodcuts and engravings as a child, painted landscapes at the age of eleven, and soon was doing commissioned portraits. In 1755-56 he was in Philadelphia, where he received his first formal education. He attended a classical school, studied painting with William Williams, and read Fresnoy and Richardson on art. With the aid of his patrons he left for Italy in 1760. In Rome he was highly regarded, moved in the highest intellectual circles, was patronized by Mengs, and copied Raphael, Correggio, and Titian. In 1763 he settled in England and worked there for the rest of his life. He met George III through the Archbishop of York, became his close friend, and was commissioned by him to do many historical paintings. He was appointed court painter in 1772, elected president of the Royal Academy in 1792; he left about 3,000 paintings and helped to train three generations of American students, including, Peale, Stuart, Sully, Allston, Trumbull, and Morse. Though a mediocre artist, he played an important part in the development of late-eighteenth-century art in Europe. He was in historical succession one of the first Classicists, Realists, and Romantics. With his American portraits behind him, he absorbed the academic tradition and took part in the classic revival. In his painting Death of General Wolfe (1772, Ottawa Museum), he helped establish the principle of realistic and contemporary historical painting. And at the height of his international reputation as a classical painter, he produced a prelude to the Romantic movement in Death on a Pale Horse, the first version of which was executed and exhibited in 1802 (Philadelphia). (See color plate 212.)

Weyden, Rogier van der (Rogier de la Pasture) (1399/1400-1464). After Jan van Eyck, the greatest of the Flemish primitives. A master of tragic pathos, he dominates a major current in Flemish art which stands opposed to the pictorialism of van Eyck. His genius is characterized by a profound psychological and aesthetic sensitivity, a tender poetic reserve, a strong feeling for rhythmic equilibrium, and most of all a fertility in the invention of emotional symbols that became the basic vocabulary of Flemish painting. He has been, and still is by some scholars, identified with the Master of Flémalle (see), but his style is less vigorous, more subtle and refined, nobler, more logically consistent, and of greater clarity. He was born in Tournai and probably trained at first as a sculptor under his father, Henry. Although a Rogier de la Pasture was honored by the town of Tournai in 1426, a Rogelet de la Pasture was inscribed in the following year as an apprentice to Robert Campin (see), and made a member of the guild of painters only in 1432. In 1435 he settled in Brussels and became town painter the following year. In 1450 he journeyed to Rome for the Jubilee of St. Anne and on his return to Brussels stopped at Ferrara to work for Lionello d'Este.

If one assumes that Rogier van der Weyden is not identical with the Master of Flémalle, then his earliest masterpiece, and one which made him immediately famous, is the Descent from the Cross (c.1432-33, Prado), devised as a painted imitation of a wood-carved relief and exhibiting his gift for transforming emotion into aesthetic symbols. Unfortunately none of his works are either signed or documented, and their relative chronology is disputed, but among the other paintings usually ascribed to this period of maturity (1430-45) are the Diptych of the Virgin and St. Catherine (Vienna), still strongly under Flémalle's influence, and the Triptych of the Annunciation (Louvre, wings in Turin), both probably before 1435. Also put in this period are the Dream of Pope Sergius (private collection, New York), the Exhumation of St. Hubert (London), and St. Luke and the Virgin (Boston), based on the van Eyck Rolin Madonna, all probably after 1435; the Triptych of the Crucifixion (Vienna) and the Altar of the Virgin (Pietà and Nativity in Granada, Christ Appearing to the Virgin in the Metropolitan), of which the so-called Miraflores Altar (Berlin) is probably a copy, both c.1440; the Crucifixion Diptych (c.1445, Philadelphia), based on the earlier Escorial version; and, finally, the Rolin Altar of the Last Judgment (1443-46, Beaune).

His late style (from 1445 to 1464) was characterized by a general softening of Gothic linearity and a final achievement of noble serenity, perhaps under thte influence of his Italian experiences. Works predating that trip are the Bracque-Brabant Triptych (Louvre), the St. John Triptych (Berlin), and the Seven Sacraments Triptych (Antwerp). The Italian influence is first seen in the Deposition (Uffizi), perhaps even painted in Florence, and is continued in the paintings of his late years: the Bladelin Altar (c.1452, Berlin) and the Columba Triptych (c.1460, Munich), showing the impact of Gentile da Fabriano. His few portraits are profound examples of psychological penetration, from the early Lady (1435, Berlin) to the Lionello d'Este (c.1450, Metropolitan), the late Laurent Froimont (c.1560, Brussels) and the Philippe de Croy (c.1560, Antwerp). His influence was extensive, perhaps because his "diagrams of emotions" were so easily assimilable, having its effect not only on Flemish art through Christus, Bouts and Memling, but also on painters in the northern Netherlands, Germany, Spain, and even Italy. (See illustrations, including color plate 213.)

Whistler, James Abbott McNeill (1834-1903). American expatriate painter and etcher. Born in Lowell, Mass. and active mostly in England, he was one of the most important figures in the development of modern art. Although he never fulfilled his brilliant promise, and his art was uneven and incomplete, his consistent championship of "Art-for-Art's-sake" (see), his incipient tendency toward abstraction (reflected in his non-descriptive titles—nocturnes, arrangements, symphonies), as well as his writing, had a profound effect upon subsequent developments in painting. Part of his youth was spent in Petrograd (1843-48), where his father was building the Petrograd-Moscow railroad and where he studied at the Academy of Fine Arts. After his father's death, he returned to the U.S. with his mother in 1849, attended school in Connecticut, and entered West Point in 1851. He was dismissed for failure in chemistry in 1854 and worked for a short time for the U.S. Coast and Geodetic Service. In 1855 he left for Paris and a career in art, studied in a desultory fashion with Gleyre, and met Courbet, Manet, Monet, Degas, and Fantin-Latour, the latter becoming a close friend. Such early works as Wapping on Thames (1861, private collection, New York), were in the Realistic tradition of Courbet.

Whistler became part of the Impressionist movement in its early phases and his White Girl, Symphony in White No. 1 (1862, Washington), hung in the Salon des Refusés of 1863, was as advanced as those of any of his French contemporaries. Unaccountably, at this historic moment he left the scene of destiny for the inhospitable environment of London, and settled in Chelsea, where he lived most of the rest of his life. He met the Rossettis, Swinburne, Moore, and Wilde, became a brilliant fixture of the Pre-Raphaelite circle, and soon achieved a reputation for advanced art and caustic wit. The impact of Japanese art had diverted him from the realistic aspects of Impressionism to a search for the subtle nuance and precious aestheticism: The Artist in the Studio (1864, Chicago) and Battersea Bridge, Nocturne, Blue and Gold (c.1865, Tate). His portraits of this period, though lacking in strength and sureness of drawing, are sensitive and subtle arrangements: the famous Artist's Mother, Arrangement in Grey and Black No. 1 (1871, Louvre) and the Thomas Carlyle, Arrangement in Grey and Black No. 2 (1872, Glasgow).

In 1876 the commission to decorate the dining room of F. R. Leyland's home resulted in the Japanese-influenced Peacock Room (Freer Gallery) and a violent dispute. The following year a series of nocturnes, including the brilliantly Impressionistic Falling Rocket, Nocturne in Black and Gold (c.1874, Detroit), brought on the famous critical attack by Ruskin and the subsequent suit for libel won by Whistler. Though he defended "Art-for-Art's-sake" with courage and wit, he lost much of his popularity and in 1879 went into bankruptcy and was forced to sell the contents of his studio. However, largely through the success of his superb etchings, he slowly regained his reputation and, although he painted little in his later years, produced such fine portraits as the Théodore Duret, Arrangement in Flesh Color and Black (1883, Metropolitan) and the Mme Camille d'Avouille (1895, Addison Gallery of American Art, Andover) and his fame increased again. (See color plate 214.)

white-ground vase painting (see GREEK PAINTING).

Whitney Museum of American Art, New York. The pioneer museum for American painting and sculpture; it specializes in the twentieth-century aspects of art without regard to so-called "schools." It is now located in mid-Manhattan where its activities can be carried on in an informal association with the Museum of Modern Art.

Whittredge, Worthington (1820-1910). An American landscape painter of the Hudson River school. Born on an Ohio farm, he came to Cincinnati and worked as a painter of houses and signs and a portraitist before turning to landscape. From 1849 to 1859 he was in Europe, studying with Leutze in Düsseldorf and traveling in France, Italy and Switzerland. After his return to the U.S., he made a trip to Colorado and New Mexico with General Pope (1865) out of which grew his later studies of Far-Western landscapes with Indians. Under the influence of Doughty, his earlier Eastern landscapes were characterized by a lyrical romanticism.

Wildens, Jan (1586-1653). Flemish landscape painter. Largely employed as an assistant to other masters, Wildens painted landscape backgrounds for Rubens, Paul de Vos, Boeckhorst, Snyders and others. Of his own works, excellent nature studies. the Winter Hunt is in Dresden, and the Landscape with Dancing Farmers is in Antwerp. His style is based on Rubens, by whom he was mainly employed.

Wilhelm, Master (Wilhelm von Herle) (active 1358, d. before 1378). German painter. He was one of the chief artists of the Cologne school and is listed in archives in the city from 1358 to 1372.

Wilkie, David (1785-1841). A Scottish painter of anecdotal pictures who began to draw at an early age and under the influence of Morland and Rowlandson produced a number of interesting picturesque genre scenes. He came to London in 1805 and entered the Royal Academy School, and then did a long series of subjects from Scottish domestic life that shows the effect of such Dutchmen as Ostade and Teniers. He studied Velázquez and Murillo in Spain and after 1828 under the influence of these painters broadened his own style and did historical subjects. He was made Painter-in-Ordinary to George IV, and continued to hold the office under William IV and Queen Victoria. His paintings of social history appealed to the growing middle class of art lovers. His sense of color and skill in detail made him a leader in the genre field, but the desire to please kept his art from further growth until it was too late.

Willink, Albert Carel (1900-). Netherlands representative of Magic Realism, of which he was the pioneer in his country. Influenced by the Italian Futurists Carrà and Severini and by Chirico, his art has a poetic and exciting quality that individualizes it. It is filled with clarity, tension and sometimes an extraordinary sense of suspense.

Wilson, Richard (1714-82). Often referred to as "the father of English landscape," this son of a Welsh minister worked in London as a portraitist and landscape painter. At thirty-five he went to Italy where he came under the influence of Vernet and Zuccarelli, both representatives of the picturesque-classical tradition in landscape. When he returned to England many years later to sell his work, he had only moderate success, but he did become a founding member of the Royal Academy in 1768. Temperamentally unable to struggle against the highly competitive artistic groups in eighteenth-century Britain, Wilson never had more than a few patrons; he lived out most of his life in poverty and died unnoticed. His lack of social grace, unwillingness to compromise with his own beliefs and the fact that he was not one of the then fashionable foreigners, all stood in the way of success. Chiefly, however, his highly personal form of pictorial expression repelled the buying public. Although influenced by the picturesque-classical tradition of Poussin and Claude with their inclination to ancient ruins strewn about a landscape, Wilson was more interested in the naturalness of the Dutch, whose almost still-life treatment of nature he followed. Later he turned more and more to the expression of emotions, thus foreshadowing the Realistic-Romantic effects of the English school of the late eighteenth and early nineteenth centuries. Cotman, Crome, Constable and Turner all in their several ways owe something to him. (See color plate 215.)

Wilson, Ronald York (1907-). Contemporary Canadian painter. Born in Toronto and largely self-taught, he has

214. WHISTLER. The White Girl
National Gallery of Art, Whittemore Collection
Washington, D.C.

worked as a commercial artist and illustrator. Since World War II he has become a member of the Academy and has painted with an official documentary mission, "Operation Muskox," at Fort Churchill (1946) and on the Alaska Highway (1947-48). These works reveal a representational and matter-of-fact style utilized in a fresh, warmly-colored and always pleasant manner.

Wimar, Charles (Karl Ferdinand) (1828-62). American painter of the Indian frontier; born in Germany. He came to St. Louis at the age of fifteen and studied with the ornamental painter Leon de Pomarede and later with Fay and Leutze in Düsseldorf (1852-56). Inspired by his contact with the Indians, he traveled and painted the life of the frontier.

Wint, Peter de (1784-1849). British watercolor landscapist, very popular in the nineteenth century; he studied drawing under John Varley and was influenced by Thomas Girtin. He is noted for the development of a greater freedom in handling the watercolor medium, using broad washes for the general structure of the design and becoming thereby an influence on modern watercolor technique.

Winter, Fritz (1905-). German painter related to the international abstract movement. After a period as a workingman, he studied for a number of years at the Bauhaus in Dessau under Kandinsky, Klee and Schlemmer. He remained in Germany during the Nazi and war years, finishing that period as a soldier and remaining a Russian prisoner of war until 1949. His art may be classified as abstract Surrealist under the influence of Kandinsky and Klee.

Winterhalter, Franz (1806-73). Famous German society portraitist of the French Second Empire period. He is noted for his portrait of the Empress Eugenie and her Ladies.

Wit, Jacob de (1695-1754). Dutch painter and engraver of decorative compositions and portraits. He studied with Albert van Spiers in Amsterdam and then went to Antwerp, where he worked under Jacob van Hal, became a member of the guild and copied the ceiling paintings by Rubens in the church of the Jesuits. Back in Amsterdam he was soon busily occupied with the ceilings, over-doors and other decorations for which he is famous. De Wit specialized in grisailles (see) simulating bas-relief.

Witte, Emanuel de (c.1617-92). Dutch painter of church interiors, domestic interiors, fish and vegetable markets, and portraits. Probably born at Alkmaar, he studied in Delft with Evert van Aelst and was influenced there by Houckgeest and van Vliet. Later in Amsterdam he came under the spell of Rembrandt. At Rotterdam he must have come in contact with other painters of church interiors, de Lorme and Van Vucht, but he surpassed all his contemporaries in his mastery of this specialty. His fine renderings of ecclesiastical architecture include not only buildings in towns in which he lived but also cathedrals in more distant places, suggesting that he traveled extensively in the southern as well as northern Netherlands.

Witte, Gaspar de (1624-81). Flemish landscape painter. Traveled in Italy and France. On his return to Antwerp he became a popular painter of landscapes and Italian views with ruins.

Witz, Konrad (1400/1410-c.1445). German painter born in Rottweil but moved to Basel probably at the opening of the great church council there. In 1434 he was admitted to a guild and the next year became a citizen. His art is based on that of Jan van Eyck (see), but shows a harsher strength than is found in Netherlanders. Witz had an extraordinary talent for landscape; his St. Christopher, with its Alpine background, is remarkably advanced for his time, displaying his understanding of refracted images in water. The picture with Christ and St. Peter (1444) in Geneva is an achievement in distant perspective unequaled by any of his European contemporaries. (See illustration.)

Woestijne, Gustave van de (1881-1947). Belgian symbolist painter of the "first Laethem group" centered about

215. WILSON, RICHARD. Landscape
Albright Art Gallery, Buffalo

WITZ. Annunciation. German National Museum, Nuremberg

WOOD, CHRISTOPHER. Church at Tréboul. Tate Gallery, London

Laethem-Saint-Martin (see). Violently anti-Impressionist, this religious mystic, ridden by tortured visions, produced a hard, almost metallic painting whose starkness suggests the later Expressionists.

Wolgemut, Michael (1434-1519). German painter and woodcutter. He must have been highly regarded in Nuremberg, for the gifted young Albrecht Dürer was apprenticed to him. Wolgemut traveled in his youth, perhaps to Flanders, and, marrying the widow of Hans Pleydenwurff, took over that master's shop. The *Weltchronik* for which he provided the woodcuts is one of the most richly illustrated German books of the fifteenth century.

Wollaston, John (active 1736-67). Born in England, he was active in America (1749-67), painting portraits from New York to South Carolina. His fashionable portraits with their conventional arrangements, artificial landscapes, and skillful rendering of material are out of the studio of Kneller.

Woman of Arles, The (L'Arlésienne) by Vincent Van Gogh (see).

Wood, Christopher (1901-30). Untaught British painter whose talent was discovered by Augustus John. With his simple approach, typically naive manner and undeveloped craft skill he did attractive flower pieces, nudes, landscapes and happy studies of London life. (See illustration.)

Wood, Grant (1892-1942). American regionalist painter, usually connected with the American Scene painters, Thomas H. Benton and John Steuart Curry. Born near Anamosa, Iowa, he worked as a metal craftsman, studied at the Art Institute of Chicago and the Académie Julian. Influenced by German Neue Sachlichkeit (see EXPRESSIONISM), the hard realism of American Gothic brought him overnight fame in 1930. (See illustration.)

Wood, Thomas Waterman (1823-1903). American portrait and genre painter best known for his scenes of New England life. Born in Montpelier, Vt., he studied with Harding in Boston and painted portraits in Canada, Washington, and Baltimore, before opening a studio in Paris in 1858. He returned to the U.S. in 1860 and painted portraits in Louisville, Ky., and Nashville, Tenn., and in 1866 settled permanently in New York, where he became president of the National Academy of Design in 1891. His genre scenes were based on annual visits to his home town.

woodcut. Graphic arts technique in which the required design is first drawn on the surface of a wooden block. After

WOOD, GRANT. American Gothic. Art Institute of Chicago

WOUTERS. Self Portrait. Musée Royal des Beaux-Arts, Antwerp

this, all the surrounding areas apart from the design itself are cut away. This leaves the design lines standing upright in a thickness sufficient to print but yet not so great as to alter their function as lines. The printed result, i.e., the sheet of paper with its design, is also known as a woodcut.

Woodville, Richard Caton (1825-55). American painter of popular genre. Born in Baltimore and trained in Düsseldorf, he settled there and continued to send his precisely detailed scenes of American life back to this country.

Wouters, Rik (1882-1916). Belgian painter, sculptor and etcher. Although considered part of the Fauve movement, there is more direct human interest in his brilliant and warmly colored canvases than in the works of such painters as Matisse. (See illustration.)

Wouwermans, Philips (1619-68). A Dutch painter of landscapes and horses. He studied with his father, with Frans Hals and Jan Wynants in Haarlem, and with Decker in Hamburg. He was especially influenced by Pieter van Laer. He painted charming figures in his landscapes and frequently provided them for landscapes by other painters. His color is fresh and his compositions are well constructed.

W.P.A. painting (see FEDERAL ART PROJECT).

Wright, Joseph (1756-93). American painter, sculptor, and engraver, the first official engraver and die-sinker of the U.S. Mint. Born in New Jersey, the son of Patience Wright, the earliest woman sculptor in the U.S., he went with his mother to England in 1772. There after studying with West and Hoppner, his brother-in-law, he became a London portraitist. After a trip to France in 1782, where he painted Benjamin Franklin, he returned to the U.S. in 1783 and followed the national Capitol from New York to Philadelphia. He painted portraits of George and Martha Washington and it is said that Washington preferred the Wright portrait of himself to all the other versions.

Wtewael, Joachim Antonisz. (c.1566-1638). A Dutch painter of mythology, religious pictures, and portraits. He spent his early years helping his father, a glass painter, and then studied for a few years under Joost de Beer. He spent two years in Padua and two more in France, before settling permanently in Utrecht. His late Mannerist style of painting reveals the influence of the Bassani, which he experienced in Italy, and perhaps also that of the school of Fontainebleau.

Wü Chen (see CHINESE PAINTERS: YÜAN DYNASTY).

Wu Tao-Tzu (see CHINESE PAINTERS: T'ANG DYNASTY).

Wyant, Alexander Helwig (1836-92). American landscape painter. His earlier work is in the Hudson River (see) tradition, but his later paintings show the influence of the Barbizon school (see) and an increasing interest in atmospheric effects. After studying in Karlsruhe with Hans Gude, a painter in the Düsseldorf tradition, he traveled in Ireland and England and came under the influence of Turner and Constable. He returned to New York and there made a reputation as a landscapist. In 1873 he accompanied an expedition to New Mexico and Arizona, could not take the rigors of the campaign, and was stricken with paralysis of the right side. He had to learn to paint with his left hand and after 1880 painted in the Catskills.

Wyeth, Andrew Newell (1917-). A contemporary American meticulous realist painter of genre subjects. Born in Pennsylvania, the son of N. C. Wyeth, illustrator, he received his training under his father.

Y

Yañez de la Almedina, Fernando (active to c.1536). Spanish painter. Collaborated with Fernando de Lanos (see) on various commissions at the Cathedral of Valencia. Following work there in the manner of Leonardo, Yañez painted in the Cathedral of Cuenca (c.1526), where his work exhibits a knowledge of Giorgione and the Venetians. His elegant style, e.g., the Resurrection (Valencia), marks him as an interesting forerunner of Spanish Mannerism.

Yeats, Jack B. (1871-). The dean of contemporary Irish painters whose reputation has become worldwide. Although he began to paint many years ago, it was during the years of the Irish struggle for independence that he began to mature as a painter and to acquire his real fame. Son of the Anglo-Irish painter John B. Yeats and brother of William Butler Yeats, the distinguished poet and founder of the Abbey Theatre, young Jack returned to Ireland to help bring about a new Irish art. He had been influenced in his youth by Impressionism, but then turned to an almost Expressionist formulation suitable to the intensity of mood experienced in this later period. His henceforth characteristic style shows a looseness of form and a brightness of color which stand halfway between the two art movements.

Yellow Christ by Paul Gauguin (see).

Yen Hui (see CHINESE PAINTERS: YÜAN DYNASTY).

Yen Li-pen (see CHINESE PAINTERS: T'ANG DYNASTY).

Young Ladies of Avignon (Les Demoiselles d'Avignon) by Pablo Picasso (see).

Ysenbrant, Adriaen (see ISENBRANDT).

Yüan Dynasty (see CHINESE PAINTERS: YÜAN DYNASTY 1279-1368).

Yün Shou-p'ing (see CHINESE PAINTERS: CH'ING DYNASTY).

Yusho (see JAPANESE PAINTERS: MOMOYAMA PERIOD).

Z

Zalce, Alfredo (1908-). Mexican easel painter, muralist and lithographer noted for the primitive strength and directness of his work; he has murals in several schools. He is a member of the Popular Graphic Art Workshop and author of the *Estampas de Yucatán*, 1945, a portfolio of eight lithographs which are unusually effective studies of Indian life. (See illustration.)

Zampieri, Domenico (see DOMENICHINO).

Zanobi, Macchiavelli (see MACCHIAVELLI ZANOBI).

Zeitblom, Bartholomaeus (1455/60-1518/22). A German painter. He may have received his earliest training in Nördlingen, but transferred to Ulm, where he was the chief painter at the end of the fifteenth century. Though he subsequently came to know the new style of Dürer and his contemporaries, he remained a medieval artist.

Zenale, Bernardino (1436-1526). Originally from Treviglio, this painter and architect was a pupil of the Milanese Foppa, and was influenced by the Umbrian painter-architect Bramante. His art contains elements of typical north Italian realism; his types are bland and rounded, and he uses architectural detail lavishly.

Zerbe, Karl (1903-). Contemporary American painter in the Neo-Romantic vein. Born in Berlin, he studied at the Munich Academy and in Italy. He came to the U.S. in 1934, worked under the W.P.A. in Massachusets, and since 1937 has taught in the Boston Museum School.

Zeshin (see JAPANESE PAINTERS: TOKUGAWA PERIOD).

Zeuxis (late 5th century B.C.). Greek painter of vases and murals. He was renowned for his introduction of realistic tricks and genre subjects into a field formerly dominated by lofty themes. His painting of the nude Helen also broke with certain previous conventions about the female model. We know his work only through ancient description. The closest we have to his painting today is probably the Herakles Strangling the Serpents (in Pompeii).

Ziem, Felix (1821-1911). French painter of architecture and marines. After voyages in Italy and the Orient, Ziem made his debut in the Salon of 1849 with Vue de Bosphore and Grand Canal de Venise. He was a friend of Gautier and Chopin and much esteemed by the former. At first he painted like Corot, but later introduced more color after the example of the Venetians.

ZALCE. The Hammock
Instituto Nacional de Bellas Artes, Mexico

ZORN. Midsummernight's Dance. National Museum, Sweden

Zoffany, Johann (1733-1810). British painter born in Germany; he came to England at twenty-five and took up the conversation piece (see) or group portrait as practiced by Hogarth and Devis. Whatever virtues these latter may have possessed, Zoffany used the form mechanically to portray the luxurious life of his patrons, carefully showing their rich clothes and most valued possessions. He recorded faces with little regard for character or expression.

Zoppo, Marco (1433-78). Painter of the Venetian school. He began his artistic career as a pupil and assistant in the shop of Squarcione in Padua, which he entered at the rather late age of twenty-one. The classicizing of Squarcione and the linear style of Cosimo Tura influenced his early work, but after moving to Venice (c.1455) he entered the circle of Bartolommeo Vivarini and Giovanni Bellini whose more colorful style he emulated. A large signed polyptych is in the church of San Clemente, Bologna.

Zorn, Anders (1860-1920). Swedish painter, etcher and sculptor; of mixed German-Swedish ancestry. He became a skillful woodcarver at eight. Later at school his pencil drawings secured him admission to the Stockholm Academy. His career as an artist began with a group of rather sentimental watercolors; he went on to success as a society portraitist in England and at home. These portraits showed a strength and freshness that are impressive and original although by no means in the modern idiom of the 1880's. Zorn was interested also in various kinds of genre subjects and handled these with the same freshness and eye for detail and changes of light. His favorite themes, however, involved the brawny peasant women of his own country, shown standing or playing nude in the water. These he did over and over again with great charm and with feeling for textural values within the

216. ZURBARAN. St. Francis. Wildenstein Gallery, New York

somewhat limited range of his artistic interests. Yet he was extremely popular in many different circles, his home at Mora in Sweden being considered an important cultural center. His contribution to the art of etching is perhaps more significant than his work in oil painting, although he considered etching a form of relaxation. (See illustration.)

Zsissly (Malvin Marr Albright) (1897-). Contemporary American painter, twin brother of Ivan Le Lorraine Albright. Born in Chicago, he was trained in Chicago, Philadelphia, and New York as a sculptor, but took up painting c.1930. His meticulous realism is close to that of his brother.

Zuccarelli, Francesco (1702-88). Venetian landscape painter born in Pitigliano in Tuscany. He studied in Florence with Paolo Anesi and in Rome with Gian Maria Morandi, and was later active in Venice, Florence, Rome, and England, where he was a founding member of the Royal Academy. A direct follower of Marco Ricci, influenced by Claude and Poussin, he produced pastoral and Arcadian landscapes containing pretty little figures painted with elegant touch and delicate color.

Zuccari (Zuccheri), Frederigo (1542-1609). One of the most famous of the Italian Maniera (see) painters. Born in Sant'Angelo in Vado, he studied and worked with his older brother Taddeo (see), was active mostly in Florence, Rome, and Venice, and traveled also to Flanders, England and Spain, where he worked at the Escorial for Philip II. He also wrote on aesthetics and founded an academy of drawing.

Zuccari (Zuccheri), Taddeo (1529-66). Italian Maniera (see) painter born in Sant'Angelo in Vado. He was the older brother and teacher of Federigo and the creator of the style for which they are noted. He studied first with his father, Ottaviano, and with Morganti in Fano, and later in Rome with sant'Agnolo, G. P. Calabrese, and Bertucci. He worked with Daniele de Porri in Vito and with Fontana in the Villa of Pope Julius (1551). His greatest influence, however, came from Raphael through Pierino del Vaga, and Correggio and Parmigianino through Porri. He was active mostly in Rome, but also in Urbino, Verona, and Venice. His two most important decorative projects were the Farnese Palace in Caprarola and the Sala Regia in the Vatican. He was the outstanding figure of the Roman Maniera and had a tremendous influence on Italian and Flemish art.

Zuloaga y Zabaleta, Ignacio (1870-1945). A Spanish painter of Basque origin, trained in his family's ceramic factory and by his own study in museums. He was an ardent student of the old Spanish masters—in particular El Greco, Velázquez and Goya. He moved from the academic atmosphere of Rome to a bohemian existence in Montmartre in the Paris of 1900 and there became acquainted with creative personalities in all fields. Upon settling in Segovia he produced a series of vigorous paintings of local folkways and portrait types. These demonstrate his powerful draughtsmanship and the alliance of modern techniques with the Spanish tradition. The mood and character of his portraits, viz., My Uncle Daniel and His Family (Hispanic Society, New York), remind one of the contemporary writings of Azorín, whom he painted. (See illustration.)

ZULOAGA. The Actress Consuelo. Art Institute of Chicago

Zurbarán, Francisco (1598-1664). An ascetic Spanish painter of religious images. His simple sculptural forms possess a dignity and quietism that reflect the early, sober phase of Spanish Baroque art. Highly personal, however, is his compositional manner, which frequently isolates each figure in individual reverie. By this device he induces contemplation in the spectator, as did the old Provencal painters and his contemporaries, the French Le Nains. Zurbarán was a native of Estremadura, to which he retired on occasion from his life as a successful painter in Seville. His artistic origins are various. But it is clear that he learned much from the work of Ribalta, Herrera, Ribera and Ruelas. He was a contemporary and friend of Velázquez, whose early style resembles his in certain respects. In 1629 when he was named *pintor de la Ciudad* in Seville, he painted, with Herrera, a series of the Life of St. Bonaventura. His fame as a painter of monkish life led to his selection in 1638 as *pintor del rey*. He performed magnificent commissions in this vein for the monastery of Guadalupe and for the Cartuja of Jeréz. Although his last years were marked by personal sorrows and lack of commissions, Zurbarán's style never faltered. In fact it showed remarkably little change throughout. Perhaps the major deviation was, in late career, a touch of the vaporous style of his younger contemporary, Murillo. Aside from the devotional aspects and visionary power of his subjects. Zurbarán is famous for his monumental treatment of still lifes, both as accessories to his figure paintings and as studies in themselves. The latter (bodegones) rank with the penetrating visions of Chardin and Cézanne. (See color plate 216.)

PHOTOGRAPHIC CREDITS

All photographs were supplied by the owner or collection credited under each illustration, except for those listed below. The number refers to the page. Where there are more than one on a page they are labelled A, B or C, reading down the left column and then the right.

14A and B. Inter Nationes
24. Frick Art Reference Library
26. Photo Mas
27B. Inter Nationes
28. Kootz Gallery
41. Babcock Galleries
46B. N.Y. Graphic Society
53B. Australian Official Photo
55B. N.Y. Graphic Society
61B. Inter Nationes
66B. Inter Nationes
74B. Canadian Information Bureau
79B. Photo Mas
80A. Alinari
84A. Alinari
122A. Inter Nationes
132. Inter Nationes
147. Downtown Gallery
148. N.Y. Graphic Society
149B. Inter Nationes
150A. Australian Official Photo
150B. Sidney Janis Gallery
151A. Frick Art Reference Library
154A. Alinari
155B. Australian Official Photo
158B. Inter Nationes
160. Three Lions
161A. N.Y. Graphic Society
163. Danish Information Office
164B. Finnish National Travel Office
169. N.Y. Graphic Society
170B. Curt Valentin Gallery
177A. N.Y. Graphic Society
178. Inter Nationes
179B. Alinari
187A. American Fund for Israeli Institutions
191A. Finnish National Travel Office
199B. Inter Nationes
206C. Casa de Portugal
209A. Downtown Gallery
213A. Photo Mas
219B. Museum of Modern Art
220A. Inter Nationes
220B. Alinari
236A and B. Inter Nationes
246. N.Y. Graphic Society
258C, 261A, 262A, 265B, 268. National Gallery, Washington
279B. Inter Nationes
282B. Photo Mas
289A. Inter Nationes
309A. Frick Art Reference Library
313B. Inter Nationes
318. N.Y. Graphic Society
320B. Inter Nationes
321A. Inter Nationes
321B. Frick Art Reference Library
323B. Alinari
325B. Alinari
327B. Canadian Information Bureau
329B. Inter Nationes
333B. Inter Nationes
336C. Inter Nationes
337C. Inter Nationes
338B. Peter Adelberg
342A. N.Y. Graphic Society
352A. Inter Nationes
353A. Kootz Gallery
355. N.Y. Graphic Society
361B. Australian Official Photo
366. N.Y. Graphic Society
369B. Frick Art Reference Library
375B. Inter Nationes
389. Frick Art Reference Library
393A. Downtown Gallery
396. Alinari
400B. Alinari
406B. Alinari
422A and B. Alinari
429. Inter Nationes
437. Inter Nationes
440B. Inter Nationes
444B. Photo Mas
454. Photo Mas
456C. Downtown Gallery
457B. de Young Memorial Museum
471B. Anderson
476B. Alinari
481A. Inter Nationes
483A. N.Y. Graphic Society
495. W. F. Mansell
497A. Alinari
498A. N.Y. Graphic Society
501. Paul Rosenberg & Co.
507A. Inter Nationes
509B. American Swedish News Exchange